BURMESE

Student Dictionary

English-Burmese / Burmese-English

Compiled by

Kyaw Swar Aung

Hippocrene Books, Inc.
New York

Hippocrene Books, Inc. edition, 2022.

ISBN: 978-0-7818-1429-4

For information, address:
HIPPOCRENE BOOKS, INC.
171 Madison Avenue
New York, NY 10016
www.hippocrenebooks.com

Published by arrangement with
Star Foreign Language Books, a unit of ibs Books (UK)
56, Langland Crescent, Stanmore HA7 1NG, U.K.

Printed at Everest Press, New Delhi-110 020 (India)

Introduction to the Burmese Language

Burmese is a Sino-Tibetan language spoken in Myanmar, where it is an official language. It is spoken by over 40 million people worldwide. The government of Myanmar designates it as the Myanmar language, but most English speakers continue to refer to the language as Burmese, after Burma, the former name of Myanmar. The Burmese alphabet is derived from the Brahmic scripts of South Indian languages.

This comprehensive bilingual Burmese (Myanmar) dictionary includes over 28,000 Word-for-Word dictionary entries and is approved for ESL/ELL students to use for standardized testing.

English - Burmese

A

a *(art.)* **တစ်ခု၊ တစ်ယောက်** Ta-Khu, Ta-Yauk

aback *(adv.)* **အံ့အားသင့်သွားသည်** ant-arr-tint-twar-the

abactor *(n.)* **ကျွဲနွားတိရိစ္ဆာန်ခိုးယူခြင်း** kywe-nwar-ta-yeik-san-kho-yu-chin

abacus *(n.)* **ကျွဲနွားတိရိစ္ဆာန်ခိုးယူသူ** kywe-nwar-ta-yeik-san-kho-yu-thu

abandon *(v.)* **စွန့်လွှတ်သည်** sont-lut-the

abandoned *(adj.)* **နစ်နာစေသည်** nit-nar-say-the

abase *(v.)* **နစ်နာစေခြင်း** nit-nar-say-chin

abashed *(adj.)* **အနေခက်စေသည်** a-nay-khat-say-the

abate *(v.)* **လျော့သည်၊ စဲသည်** shot-the, sal-the

abatement *(n.)* **လျော့ခြင်း၊ စဲခြင်း** shot-chin, sal-chin

abbey *(n.)* **ကျောင်းတိုက်** kyaung-tite

abbot *(n.)* **ကျောင်းတိုက်ဆရာတော်** *kyaung-tite-sa-ya-taw*

abbreviate *(v.)* **အတိုချုံးသည်** a-to-chone-the

abbreviation *(n.)* **အတိုချုံးခြင်း** a-to-chone-chin

abdicate *(v.)* **ဥပေက္ခာပြုသည်** oo-phyit-khar-phyu-the

abdication *(n.)* **ဥပေက္ခာပြုခြင်း** oo-phyit-khar-phyu-chin

abdomen *(n.)* **ဝမ်းဗိုက်** one-bike

abdominal *(adj.)* **ဝမ်းဗိုက်နှင့် ဆိုင်သော** one-bike-nint-saing-taw

abduct *(v.)* **ပြန်ပေးဆွဲသည်** pyan-pay-swal-the

abductee *(n.)* **ပြန်ပေးဆွဲခံရသူ** pyan-pay-swal-thu

abduction *(n.)* **ပြန်ပေးဆွဲခြင်း** pyan-pay-swal-chin

abductor *(n.)* **ပြန်ပေးဆွဲသူ** *pyan-pay-swal-thu*

aberrant *(adj.)* **အိပ်ရာထဲတွင်** aik-yar-htal-twin

aberration *(n.)* **ဖောက်ပြန်ခြင်း၊ မှုမမှန်ခြင်း** phaut-pyan-chin, mu-ma-man-chin

abet *(v.)* **အားပေးကူညီသည်** ar-pay-khu-nyi-the

abettor *(n.)* **အားပေးကူညီခြင်း** ar-pay-khu-nyi-chin

abeyance *(n.)* **ဆိုင်းငံ့ထားခြင်း** saing-ngan-htar-chin

abhor *(v.)* **စက်ဆုပ်သည်** *sat-sote-the*

abhorrent *(adj.)* **စက်ဆုပ်သော** *sat-sote-taw*

abide *(v.)* **သည်းခံသည်** *the-khan-the*

abiding *(adj.)* **ခိုင်မာသော** *khaing-mar-taw*

ability *(n.)* **စွမ်းရည်** *swan-yee*

abiotic *(adj.)* **သက်ရှိကင်းမဲ့သော** *thet-shi-kin-mae-taw*

abject *(adj.)* **ဆိုးရွားသော** *soe-ywar-taw*

abjure *(v.)* **စွန့်ပယ်သည်** *sunt-pal-the*

abjurer *(n.)* **စွန့်ပယ်သူ** *sunt-pal-thu*

ablactate *(v.)* **နို့ဖြတ်သည်** *noe-phat-the*

ablactation *(n.)* **နို့ဖြတ်ခြင်း** *noe-phat-chin*

ablate *(v.)* **ဖယ်ထုတ်သည်** *phal-htoke-the*

ablation *(n.)* **ဖယ်ထုတ်ခြင်း** *phal-htoke-chin*

ablative *(adj.)* **ဖယ်ထုတ်ထားသော** *phal-htoke-htar-taw*

ablaze *(adv.)* **တောက်လောင်သော** *taut-laung-taw*

able *(adj.)* ပိုင်နိုင်သော *paing-naing-taw*

abled *(adj.)* တတ်နိုင်သော *tat-naing-taw*

ablution *(n.)* ကိုယ်လက်သန့်စင်ခန်း *ko-lat-thant-sin-khan*

ably *(adv.)* ပိုင်နိုင်စွာ *paing-naing-swar*

abnegate *(v.)* ဖယ်ကြဉ်သည် *phal-kyin-the*

abnegation *(n.)* ဖယ်ကြဉ်ခြင်း *phal-kyin-chin*

abnormal *(adj.)* ပုံမှန်မဟုတ်သော *pone-man-ma-hote-taw*

abnormality *(n.)* ပုံမှန်မဟုတ်ခြင်း *pone-man-ma-hote-chin*

abnormally *(adv.)* ထူးထူးကဲကဲ *htoo-htoo-kae-kae*

aboard *(adv.)* ပေါ်သို့ *paw-tho*

abode *(n.)* နေအိမ် *nay-ain*

abolish *(v.)* ဖျက်သိမ်းသည် *phat-thein-the*

abolition *(n.)* ဖျက်သိမ်းခြင်း *phat-thein-ching*

abominable *(adj.)* စက်ဆုပ်ဖွယ် *sat-sote-phwal*

abominate *(v.)* စက်ဆုပ်ရွံရှာသည် *sat-sote-yun-shar-the*

abomination *(n.)* စက်ဆုပ်ရွံရှာခြင်း *sat-sote-yun-shar-chin*

aboriginal *(adj.)* ဌာနေတိုင်းရင်းသားတို့၏ *htar-nay-thaing-yin-thar-doe-ei*

aborigine *(n.)* ဌာနေတိုင်းရင်းသား *htar-nay-thaing-yin-thar*

abort *(v.)* ကိုယ်ဝန်ဖျက်သည် *ko-win-phat-the*

abortion *(n.)* ကိုယ်ဝန်ဖျက်ခြင်း *ko-win-phat-chin*

abortionist *(n.)* ကိုယ်ဝန်ဖျက်ချသူ *ko-win-phat-cha-thu*

abortive *(adv.)* မအောင်မြင်သော *ma-aung-myin-taw*

abound *(v.& prep.)* ပေါကြွယ်သည် *paw-kywe-the*

about-turn *(n.)* နောက်လှည့် *naut-hlae*

above *(prep. & adv.)* အပေါ်သို့ a-paw-tho

abrasion *(n.)* ပွန်းပဲ့ဒဏ်ရာ *pun-pae-dan-yar*

abrasive *(adj.)* ပွန်းရှတတ်သော *pun-sha-tat-taw*

abreast *(adv.)* ရင်ပေါင်တန်း yin-baung-tan

abridge *(v.)* အကျဉ်းချုံးသည် *a-kyin-chone-the*

abridgement *(n.)* အကျဉ်းချုပ် *a-kyin-chote*

abroad *(adv.)* နိုင်ငံရပ်ခြား *naing-ngan-yat-char*

abrogate *(v.)* ပယ်ဖျက်သည် *pal-phat-the*

abrogation *(n.)* ပယ်ဖျက်ခြင်း *pal-phat-chin*

abrupt *(adj.)* ရုတ်တရက်ဖြစ်သော *yote-ta-yat-phit-taw*

abruptly *(adv.)* ရုတ်တရက် *yote-ta-yat*

abscess *(n.)* ပြည်တည်နာ *pyi-tae-nar*

abscond *(v.)* တိမ်းရှောင်သည် *tain-shaung-the*

abseil *(v.)* ခြေစုံကန်လျှောဆင်းသည် *chay-sone-shaw-sin-the*

absence *(n.)* ပျက်ကွက်ခြင်း *pyat-kwat-chin*

absent *(adj.)* ပျက်ကွက်သည် pyat-kwat-the

absentee *(n.)* ပျက်ကွက်သူ pyat-kwat-thu

absolute *(adj.)* အကြွင်းမဲ့ဖြစ်သော a-kywin-mae-phit-taw

absolutely *(adv.)* အကြွင်းမဲ့ *a-kywin-mae*

absolution *(n.)* အပြစ်ဖြေပေးခြင်း *a-phit-phyay-pay-chin*

absolutism *(n.)* အကြွင်းမဲ့ အာဏာပိုင်စိုးခြင်း *a-kywin-mae-ar-nar-paing-soe-chin*

absolve *(v.)* **လွတ်ငြိမ်းခွင့်ပြုသည်** *lut-nyein-kwint-pyu-the*
absorb *(v.)* **စုပ်ယူသည်** *sote-yu-the*
absorbable *(adj.)* **စုပ်ယူနိုင်သော** sote-yu-naing-taw
absorbent *(adj.)* **အရည်စုပ်ယူသော** *a-yay-sote-yu-taw*
absorption *(n.)* **စုပ်ယူခြင်း** *sote-yu-chin*
abstain *(v.)* **ရှောင်ကြဉ်သည်** *shaung-kyin-the*
abstinence *(n.)* **ရှောင်ကြဉ်ခြင်း** *shaung-kyin-chin*
abstract *(adj.)* **စိတ်ကူးသက်သက်** *seik-ku-thet-thet*
abstraction *(n.)* **စိတ်ကူးစိတ်သန်း** *seik-ku-seik-than*
abstruse *(adj.)* **နက်နဲ့သော** *nat-nae-taw*
absurd *(adj.)* **ဖြစ်နိုင်ခြေမရှိသော** *phit-naing-chay-ma-shi-taw*
absurdity *(n.)* **ရယ်ဖွယ်ကောင်းမှု** *yal-phwal-kaung-mu*
absurdly *(adv.)* **မတော်မတရား** *ma-taw-ma-tayar*
abundance *(n.)* **အများအပြား** a-myar-a-pyar
abundant *(adj.)* **များပြားသော** myar-pyar-taw
abundantly *(adv.)* **များပြားစွာ** *myar-pyar-swar*
abuse *(v.)* **အလွဲသုံးစားပြုသည်** *a-lwe-tone-sar-pyu-the*
abusive *(adj.)* **ရင့်သီးသော** *yint-thee-taw*
abusively *(adv.)* **ရင့်သီးစွာ** *yint-thee-swar*
abut *(v.)* **ထိစပ်သည်** *hti-sat-the*
abyss *(n.)* **အသူတစ်ရာနက်သောချောက်** *a-thu-tayar-nat-taw-chauk*
acacia *(n.)* **အကေရှားပင်** *a-kay-shar-pin*
academia *(n.)* **တက္ကသိုလ်** *tat-ka-do*
academic *(adj.)* **ပညာရေးနှင့်ဆိုင်သော** *pyin-nyar-yay-nint-saing-taw*
academically *(adv.)* **ပညာရှင်ဆန်ဆန်** *pyin-nyar-shin-san-san*
academician *(n.)* **ပညာရှင်** *pyin-nyar-shin*
academy *(n.)* **အထူးပညာသင်ကျောင်း** *a-htoo-pyin-nyar-tin-kyaung*
acausal *(adj.)* **ငါးကျိုးဆက်နွယ်မှုမရှိသော** *kyaung-kyo-sat-new-mu-ma-shi-taw*
accede *(v.)* **နန်းတက်သည်** *nan-tat-the*
accelerate *(v.)* **အရှိန်မြှင့်သည်** a-shain-myint-the
acceleration *(n.)* **အရှိန်မြှင့်ခြင်း** a-shain-hmyint-chin
accelerator *(n.)* **အရှိန်မြှင့်ကိရိယာ** *a-shain-hmyint-ka-yi-yar*
accend *(v.)* **ထွန်းညှိသည်** *tun-hnyi-the*
accent *(n.)* **ဝဲသံ** *wal-than*
accentor *(n.)* **အစန်တာငှက်** a-san-tar-nyat
accentuate *(v.)* **ထင်းနေစေသည်** htin-nay-say-the
accept *(v.)* **လက်ခံသည်** *lat-khan-the*
acceptability *(n.)* **လက်ခံနိုင်စွမ်း** *lat-khan-naing-swan*
acceptable *(adj.)* **လက်ခံနိုင်သော** *lat-khan-naing-taw*
acceptant *(adj.)* **လက်ခံသော** *lat-khan-taw*
accepted *(adj.)* **လက်ခံထားသော** *lat-khan-htar-taw*
access *(n.)* **ဝင်လမ်း** *win-lan*
accessibility *(n.)* **ဝင်သုံးခွင့်ရခြင်း** *win-tone-kwint-ya-chin*
accessible *(adj.)* **ဝင်သုံးခွင့်ရသော** *win-tone-kwint-ya-taw*
accession *(n.)* **ထီးနန်းတက်** *htee-nan-tat*

accessory *(n.)* တွက်ဖက်ပစ္စည်း *twe-phat-pyit-see*
accidence *(n.)* မတော်တဆမှု *ma-taw-ta-sa-mu*
accident *(n.)* မတော်တဆမှု *ma-taw-ta-sa-mu*
accidental *(adj.)* မတော်တဆဖြစ်သော *ma-taw-ta-sa-mu-phit-taw*
accidentally *(adv.)* မတော်တဆ *ma-taw-ta-sa*
acclaim *(v.)* ချီးကျူးဂုဏ်ပြုသည် *chee-kyu-gon-phyu-the*
acclamation *(n.)* ချီးကျူးဂုဏ်ပြုခြင်း *chee-kyu-gon-phyu-chin*
acclimatise *(v.)* နေသားကျသည် *nay-tar-kya-the*
accolade *(n.)* ချီးကျူးဂုဏ်ပြုခြင်း chee-kyu-gon-phyu-ching
accommodate *(v.)* ထည့်သွင်းစဉ်းစားသည် htae-twin-sin-sar-the
accommodating *(adj.)* လိုက်လျောသော *lite-lyaw-taw*
accommodation *(n.)* နေထိုင်စရာအခန်း *nay-htaing-sa-yar-a-khan*
accompaniment *(n.)* အတွဲအဖက် a-twe-a-phat
accompanist *(n.)* လိုက်ပေးသူ lite-pay-thu
accompany *(v.)* လိုက်ပါသည် *lite-par-the*
accomplice *(n.)* ကြံရာပါ *kyan-yar-par*
accomplish *(v.)* ပြီးမြောက်အောင်မြင်သည် pi-myauk-aung-myin-the
accomplished *(adj.)* ပြောင်မြောက်သော pyaung-myauk-taw
accomplishment *(n.)* အောင်မြင်မှု aung-myin-mu
accord *(v.)* ညီညွတ်သည် *nyu-nyut-the*
accordance *(n.)* ကိုက်ညီခြင်း kite-nyi-chin
according *(adv.)* အရ *a-ya*
accordingly *(adv.)* လျော်ညီစွာ *lyaw-nyi-swar*
accost *(v.)* ချဉ်းကပ်မြူဆွယ်သည် *chee-kat-myu-swal-the*
accouchement *(n.)* ကလေးဖွားခြင်း *ka-lay-phwar-chin*
accoucheur *(n.)* အမျိုးသား သားဖွား *a-myo-tar-tar-phwar*
account *(n.)* ငွေစာရင်း *nwyay-sa-yin*
accountability *(n.)* တာဝန်ခံခြင်း *tar-win-khan-chin*
accountable *(adj.)* တာဝန်ခံသော *tar-win-khan-taw*
accountancy *(n.)* စာရင်းကိုင်ပညာ *sar-yin-kaing-pyin-nyar*
accountant *(n.)* စာရင်းကိုင် *sar-yin-kaing*
accounting *(n.)* ငွေစာရင်းလုပ်ငန်းစဉ် *ngwe-sar-yin-lote-ngan-sin*
accoutre *(v.)* တပ်ဆင်သည် *tat-sin-the*
accoutrement *(n.)* အဆောင်အယောင် *a-saung-a-yaung*
accredited *(adj.)* အသိအမှတ်ပြုသော a-thi-a-mat-pyu-taw
accrete *(v.)* တွယ်ကပ်သည် thwe-kat-the
accretion *(n.)* တစ်စတစ်စကြီးပွားလာမှု *ta-sa-ta-sa-kyi-pwar-lar-mu*
accrue *(v.)* တိုးပွားလာသည် *toe-pwar-lar-the*
accumulate *(v.)* စုဆောင်းမိသည် *su-saung-mi-the*
accumulation *(n.)* စုဆောင်းမိခြင်း *su-saung-mi-chin*
accumulator *(n.)* စုဆောင်းသူ *su-saung-thu*
accuracy *(n.)* တိကျမှု *ti-kya-mu*
accurate *(adj.)* တိကျသော *ti-kya-taw*

accurately *(adv.)* **တိကျစွာ** *ti-kya-swar*

accusal *(n.)* **စွပ်စွဲချက်** sut-swal-chat

accusation *(n.)* **စွပ်စွဲချက်** sut-swal-chat

accusative *(n.)* **စွပ်စွဲသော** *sut-swal-taw*

accuse *(v.)* **စွပ်စွဲသည်** *sut-swal-the*

accused *(n.)* **တရားခံ** *ta-yar-khan*

accuser *(n.)* **စွပ်စွဲသူ** *sut-swal-thu*

accusing *(adj.)* **စွပ်စွဲသော** *sut-swal-taw*

accustom *(v.)* **ကျင့်သားရသည်** *kyint-tar-ya-the*

ace *(n.)* **တစ်ပွင့်** *ta-pwint*

acellular *(adj.)* **ဆဲလ်မပါသော** *sal-ma-par-taw*

acene *(n.)* **သက်ရှိနှင့်ဆိုင်သော ပ်ပေါင်းတစ်မျိုး** *thet-shi-nint-saing-taw-drat-paung-ta-myo*

acentric *(adj.)* **စန်ထရိုမဲမပါသော** *san-hta-yo-mal-ma-par-taw*

acer *(n.)* **အက်ဆာပန်း** *at-sar-pan*

acerbic *(adj.)* **မာရေကျောရည်နိုင်သော** *mar-yay-kyaw-yay-naing-taw*

acetate *(n.)* **အက်ဆီတိတ် တုဒြပ်ပေါင်း** *at-se-tate-dar-du-drat-paung*

acetic *(adj.)* **ရှလကာရည်ဆန်သော** *sha-la-kar-yay-san-taw*

acetic acid *(n.)* **အက်ဆစ်တစ် က်ဆစ်** *at-cit-tit-at-cit*

acetone *(n.)* **အက်ဆီတုန်း ဒြပ်ပေါင်း** *at-se-tone-drat-paung*

acetylene *(n.)* **အက်ဆီတိုင်လင်း ဓာတ်ငွေ့** *at-se-ti-lin-drat-ngwe*

ache *(v.)* **ကိုက်ခဲသည်** *keik-khae-the*

achieve *(v.)* **အောင်မြင်သည်** aung-myin-the

achievement *(n.)* **အောင်မြင်မှု** aung-myin-mu

achiever *(n.)* **အောင်မြင်သူ** *aung-myin-thu*

achromat *(n.)* **အရောင်မဲ့ မှန်ဘီလူး** a-yaung-mae-man-bi-lu

achromatic *(adj.)* **အရောင်မဲ့သော** *a-yaung-mae-taw*

acid *(n.)* **အက်ဆစ်** *at-cit*

acid rain *(n.)* **အက်ဆစ်မိုး** *at-cit-moe*

acid test *(n.)* **အက်ဆစ် စမ်းသပ်ချက်** *at-cit-san-tat-chat*

acidic *(adj.)* **အက်ဆစ်ဓာတ်များသော** *at-cit-dat-myar-taw*

acknowledge *(v.)* **အသိအမှတ်ပြုသည်** *a-thi-a-mat-pyu-the*

acknowledgement *(n.)* **အသိအမှတ်ပြုခြင်း** *a-thi-a-mat-pyu-chin*

acme *(n.)* **အထွတ်အထိပ်** *a-htut-a-hteik*

acne *(n.)* **ဝက်ခြံ** *wat-chan*

acolyte *(n.)* **တပည့်ရင်း** *ta-pae-ying*

acorn *(n.)* **ဝက်သစ်ချသီး** *wat-thit-cha-thee*

acoustic *(adj.)* **အသံနှင့်ဆိုင်သော** *a-tan-nint-saing-taw*

acoustics *(n.)* **အသံပညာ** *a-tan-pyin-nyar*

acquaint *(v.)* **အသိပေးသည်** *a-thi-pay-the*

acquaintance *(n.)* **အသိအကျွမ်း** *a-thi-a-kywan*

acquest *(n.)* **မျိုးရိုးထက် တောင်းဆိုမှုကြောင့်ရသော ပိုင်ဆိုင်မှု** *myo-yoe-htet-taung-so-mu-kyaunt-ya-taw-paing-saing-mu*

acquiesce *(v.)* **လိုက်လျောသည်** *lite-lyaw-the*

acquire *(v.)* **ကျင့်ယူသည်** *kyint-yu-the*

acquisition *(n.)* **ရှာမှီးရရှိသော ဥစ္စာ** *shar-mi-ya-shi-taw-oat-sar*

acquisitive *(adj.)* **လိုချင်ဆန္ဒကြီးသော** *lo-chin-san-da-kyi-taw*

acquit *(v.)* **တရားသေလွှတ်သည်** *ta-yar-tay-hlut-the*

acquittal *(n.)* **အပြစ်မရှိကြောင်း စီရင်ချက်** *a-pyit-ma-shi-kyaung-si-yin-chat*
acratic *(adj.)* **ကိုယ်ကျင့်တရားမဲ့သော** *ko-kyint-ta-yar-mae-taw*
acre *(n.)* **ဧက** a-ca
acreage *(n.)* **ဧကပမာဏ** *a-ca-pa-mar-na*
acrid *(adj.)* **ညှော်သော** *nyaw-taw*
acrimonious *(adj.)* **မပြေမလည်ဖြစ်သော** *ma-pyay-ma-lal-phit-taw*
acrimony *(n.)* **မပြေလည်မှု** *ma-pyay-lal-mu*
acritical *(adj.)* **အရေးကြီးမဟုတ်သော** *a-yay-ma-kyi-ma-hote-taw*
acrobat *(n.)* **ကျွမ်းဘားပြစားသူ** *kywan-bar-pya-sar-thu*
acrobatic *(adj.)* **ကျွမ်းဘားနှင့်ဆိုင်သော** *kywan-bar-nint-saing-taw*
acrobatics *(n.)* **ကျွမ်းဘားကစားခြင်း** *kywan-bar-ka-sar-chin*
acronym *(n.)* **အတိုကောက်** *a-to-kaut-*
acrophobia *(n.)* **အမြင့်ကြောက်သော** *a-myint-kyauk-taw*
acropolis *(n.)* **ရှေးဟောင်းဂရိမြို့၏ ရဲတိုက်** *shay-haung-ga-yeh-myo-ei-yae-tite*
across *(prep.)* **ဖြတ်လျက်** *phat-lyat*
acrostic *(n.)* **ကဗျာစာပိုဒ်** *ka-byar-sar-baik*
acrylate *(n.)* **အက်ခရိုင်လိတ်ဒြပ်ပေါင်း** *at-kha-ri-late-drat-paung*
acrylic *(adj.)* **အခရိုင်လစ်ပန်းချီဆေး** *a-kha-ri-lit-pa-chi-say*
act *(v.)* **လုပ်ဆောင်သည်** *lote-saung-the*
acting *(n.)* **သရုပ်ဆောင်ခြင်း** *ta-yoke-saung-chin*
action *(n.)* **လုပ်ဆောင်ချက်** *lote-saung-chat*
actionable *(adj.)* **ဥပဒေနှင့် ငြိစွန်းသော** *au-pa-day-nint-nyi-sune-taw*
activate *(v.)* **အသက်ဝင်သည်** *a-thet-win-the*
activation *(n.)* **အသက်ဝင်ခြင်း** *a-thet-win-chin*
active *(adj.)* **တက်ကြွသော** *tat-kwa-taw*
actively *(adv.)* **တက်ကြွစွာ** *tat-kwa-swar*
activist *(n.)* **တက်ကြွလှုပ်ရှားသူ** *tat-kwa-lote-shar-thu*
activity *(n.)* **လုပ်ဆောင်မှု** *lote-saung-mu*
actor *(n.)* **မင်းသား** *min-thar*
actress *(n.)* **မင်းသမီး** *min-tha-mee*
actual *(adj.)* **အမှန်တကယ်ဖြစ်သော** a-man-ta-kal-phit-taw
actually *(adv.)* **အမှန်တကယ်အားဖြင့်** *a-man-ta-kal-arr-phit*
acumen *(n.)* **အမြင်ထက်မြက်မှု** *a-myin-htet-myat-mu*
acupressure *(n.)* **ဖိအားပေးအမှတ်** phi-arr-pay-a-mat
acupuncture *(n.)* **အပ်စိုက်ကုထုံး** *at-seik-ku-htone*
acupuncturist *(n.)* **တရုတ်အပ်စိုက်ဆရာ** *ta-yoke-at-seik-sa-yar*
acute *(adj.)* **ရုတ်တရက်ချက်ခြင်းဖြစ်သော** yote-ta-yat-chat-chin-phit-taw
ad hoc *(adj.)* **ကျပန်း** *kya-pan*
adage *(n.)* **ဆိုရိုးစကား** so-yoe-sa-kar
adamant *(adj.)* **တွင်တွင်ငြင်းသော** twin-twin-nyin-taw
adapt *(v.)* **လိုက်ဖက်အောင် ပြင်ဆင်သည်** lite-phat-aung-pyin-sin-the
adaptable *(adj.)* **မီးစဥ်ကြည့်ကတတ်သော** *mi-sin-kyi-ka-tat-taw*
adaptation *(n.)* **ဆီလျော်အောင် ပြုပြင်ခြင်း** *si-lyaw-aung-pyu-pyin-chin*
adaptor *(n.)* **ကြားဆက်ကိရိယာ** *kyar-set-ka-yi-yar*
add *(v.)* **ပေါင်းထည့်သည်** *paung-htae-the*

addendum *(n.)* ဖြည့်စွက်ချက် *phyae-swat-chat*
adder *(n.)* အက်ဒါမြွေပွေး *at-dar-mway-pway*
addict *(n.)* ဆေး၊ အရက် စွဲနေသူ say-a-yat-swal-nay-thu
addicted *(adj.)* ဆေးစွဲနေသော *say-swal-nay-taw*
addiction *(n.)* ဆေးစွဲခြင်း *say-swal-chin*
addictive *(adj.)* စွဲစေတတ်သော *swal-say-tat-taw*
add-in *(n.)* ပေါင်းထည့်ဆော့ဝဲလ် သို့မဟုတ် ပစ္စည်း *paung-htae-soft-ware-tho-ma-hote-pyit-see*
addition *(n.)* ပေါင်းထည့်ခြင်း *paung-htae-chin*
additional *(adj.)* နောက်ထပ် naut-htet
additive *(n.)* အဖြည့်ပစ္စည်း a-phyae-pyit-see
addled *(adj.)* ကြောင်တောင်တောင်ဖြစ်နေသော *kyaung-taung-taung-phit-nay-taw*
address *(n.)* လိပ်စာ *leik-sar*
addressee *(n.)* လိပ်စာရှင် *leik-sar-shin*
addresser *(n.)* မိန့်ခွန်းပြောသူ *maint-khun-pyaw-thu*
adduce *(v.)* သက်သေပြသည် *thet-tay-pya-the*
adept *(n.)* ကျွမ်းကျင်မှု *kywan-kyin-mu*
adequacy *(n.)* ပြည့်ဝမှု *pyae-wa-mu*
adequate *(adj.)* လုံလောက်သော *lone-laut-taw*
adequately *(adv.)* လုံလောက်စွာ *lone-laut-swar*
adhere *(v.)* ကပ်သည် kat-the
adherence *(n.)* စွဲမြဲခြင်း swal-myae-chin
adherent *(n.)* နောက်လိုက် *naut-lite*
adhesion *(n.)* ကပ်ခြင်း *kat-chin*
adhesive *(n.)* ကပ်သော *kat-taw*
adieu *(exclam.)* နှုတ်ဆက်ပါသည် *note-set-par-the*
adipose *(adj.)* အဆီနှင့်ဆိုင်သော *a-se-nint-saing-taw*
adjacent *(adj.)* ကပ်လျက် *kat-lyat*
adjective *(n.)* နာမဝိသေသန *nar-ma-wi-tay-ta-na*
adjoin *(v.)* ကပ်လျက် တည်ရှိသည် *kat-kyat-the-shi-the*
adjourn *(v.)* ရွှေ့ဆိုင်းသည် *shway-saing-the*
adjournment *(n.)* ရွှေ့ဆိုင်းခြင်း *shway-saing-chin*
adjudge *(v.)* စီရင်ဆုံးဖြတ်သည် *si-yin-sone-phat-the*
adjudicate *(v.)* စစ်ဆေးဆုံးဖြတ်သည် *sit-say-sone-phat-the*
adjunct *(n.)* အဖြည့် *a-phyae*
adjuration *(n.)* အလေးအနက်တိုက်တွန်းခြင်း *a-lay-a-net-tite-tune-chin*
adjure *(v.)* အမိန့်ပေးသည် *a-maint-pay-the*
adjust *(v.)* အလိုက်သင့် ပြုမူနေထိုင်သည် a-lite-tint-pyu-mu-nay-htaing-the
adjustment *(n.)* အလိုက်သင့် ပြုမူနေထိုင်ခြင်း a-lite-tint-pyu-mu-nay-htaing-chin
administer *(v.)* စီမံသည် si-man-the
administrate *(v.)* စီမံသည် si-man-the
administration *(n.)* အုပ်ချုပ်ရေး oat-choke-yay
administrative *(adj.)* အုပ်ချုပ်မှုဆိုင်ရာ oat-choke-mu-saing-yar
administrator *(n.)* အုပ်ချုပ်သူ oat-choke-thu

admirable *(adj.)* နှစ်သက်ဖွယ်ဖြစ်သော *nit-thet-phwal-phit-taw*
admiral *(n.)* ရေတပ်ဗိုလ်ချုပ်ကြီး *yay-tat-bo-gyoke-gyi*
admiralty *(n.)* ရေတပ်မတော်ဆိုင်ရာဦးစီးဌာန yay-tat-ma-taw=saing-yar-au-see-htar-na
admiration *(n.)* လေးစားမှု lay-sar-mu
admire *(v.)* လေးစားသည် *lay-sar-the*
admissible *(adj.)* လက်ခံနိုင်သော *lat-khan-naing-taw*
admission *(n.)* ဝင်ခွင့် *win-khwint*
admit *(v.)* ဝန်ခံသည် *win-khan-the*
admittance *(n.)* ဝင်ခွင့် *win-khwint*
admittedly *(adv.)* ဝန်ခံရမည်မှာ *win-khan-ya-me-mar*
admonish *(v.)* သတိပေးသည် tha-di-pay-the
admonition *(n.)* သတိပေးချက် *tha-di-pay-chat*
ado *(n.)* ချက်ခြင်းလက်ငင်း *chat-chin-lat-ngin*
adobe *(n.)* နေကျက်ရွှံ့ *nay-kyat-hswont*
adolescence *(n.)* ကြီးကောင်ဝင်ချိန် *kyi-kaung-win-chein*
adolescent *(adj.)* ဆယ်ကျော်သက် *sal-kyaw-thet*
adopt *(v.)* မွေးစားသည် *mway-sar-the*
adoption *(n.)* မွေးစားခြင်း *mway-sar-chin*
adoptive *(adj.)* မွေးစား *mway-sar*
adorable *(adj.)* ချစ်စရာကောင်းသော *chit-sa-yar-kaung-taw*
adoration *(n.)* ကြင်နာမြတ်နိုးမှု *kyin-nar-myat-noe-mu*
adore *(v.)* မြတ်နိုးသည် *myat-noe-the*
adorn *(v.)* ဆင်မြန်းသည် sin-myan-the
adrenal *(adj.)* အဒရီနယ် *a-da-ree-nal*
adrift *(adj.)* ရေစုန်မျောနေသော *yay-sone-myaw-nay-taw*
adroit *(adj.)* ကျွမ်းကျင်လိမ္မာသော *kywan-kyin-lain-mar-taw*
adscititious *(adj.)* နောက်ထပ် naut-htet
adscript *(adj.)* စာလုံးနောက်တစ်လုံး sar-lone-naut-ta-lone
adsorb *(n.)* စုပ်ယူသည် sote-yu-the
adulate *(v.)* လွန်ကဲစွာ မြှောက်စားသည် lun-kae-swar-hmyaut-sar-the
adulation *(n.)* လွန်ကဲစွာ မြှောက်စားခြင်း lun-kae-swar-hmyaut-sar-chin
adult *(n.)* အရွယ်ရောက်သူ a-ywal-yaut-thu
adulterate *(v.)* ရောသည် *yaw-the*
adulteration *(n.)* ရောခြင်း yaw-chin
adulterer *(n.)* မယားခိုးမှု ကျူးလွန်သူ ma-yar-khoe-mu-kyu-lun-thu
adultery *(n.)* အိမ်ထောင်ရေးဖောက်ပြန်ခြင်း *ain-htaung-yay-phaut-pyan-chin*
advance *(v.)* ရှေ့တိုးသည် *shay-toe-the*
advanced *(adj.)* ရှေ့ရောက်နှင့်နေသော *shay-yaut-nint-nay-taw*
advantage *(n.)* အကျိုး a-kyo
advantageous *(adj.)* အကျိုးကျေးဇူးပြုသော a-kyo-kyay-zu-pyu-taw
advent *(n.)* ပေါ်ထွန်းမှု paw-htun-mu
adventure *(n.)* စွန့်စားခန်း *sunt-sar-khan*
adventurous *(adj.)* စွန့်စားသော *sunt-sar-taw*
adverb *(n.)* ကြိယာဝိသေသန kri-yar-wi-tay-ta-na
adverbial *(adj.)* ကြိယာဝိသေသနပါသော *kri-yar-wi-tay-ta-na-par-taw*
adversary *(n.)* ပြိုင်ဘက် *pyaing-bat*
adverse *(adj.)* ဆန့်ကျင်သော *sant-kyin-taw*

adversity *(n.)* အခက်အခဲ *a-khat-a-khae*

advertise *(v.)* ကြော်ငြာသည် *kyaw-nyar-the*

advertisement *(n.)* ကြော်ငြာ *kyaw-nyar*

advice *(n.)* အကြံဉာဏ် *a-kyan-nyan*

advisability *(n.)* သင့်တော်ခြင်း *tint-taw-chin*

advisable *(adj.)* သင့်တော်သော *tint-taw-taw*

advise *(v.)* အကြံပြုသည် *a-kyan-pyu-the*

advisory *(adj.)* အကြံပေးသော *a-kyan-pay-taw*

advocacy *(n.)* ထောက်ခံမှု။ *htaut-khan-mu*

aegis *(n.)* ကမကထပြုခြင်း *ka-ma-ka-hta-pyu-chin*

aeon *(n.)* ကပ်ကမ္ဘာ *kat-ka-bar*

aerate *(v.)* လေသလပ်ပေးသည် *lay-tha-lat-pay-the*

aerial *(n.)* ကောင်းကင်ကြိုး *kaung-kin-kyoe*

aerobatics *(n.)* လေယာဉ်ကို ခက်ခဲစွာ အလှပြပျံသန်းခြင်း *lay-yin-ko-khat-khae-swar-a-hla-pya-pyan-tan-chin*

aerobics *(n.)* အေရိုးဗစ်အားကစား *a-yoe-bit-arr-ka-sar*

aerodrome *(n.)* ပုဂ္ဂလိက လေယာဉ်သုံး လေယာဉ်ကွင်း *poke-ga-li-ka-lay-yin-tone-lay-yin-kwin*

aerodynamics *(n.)*အေရိုဒိုင်းနမစ်ပညာ *a-ro-dy-na-mic-pyin-nyar*

aerofoil *(n)* ပျံသန်းရန် လေကို ထိန်းနိုင်သော လေယာဉ်တောင်ပံကဲ့သို့ အထူးဒီဇိုင်း *pyan-tan-yan-lay-ko-htain-naing-taw-lay-yin-taung-pan-kae-tho-a-htoo-de-zine*

aeronautics *(n.)* လေယာဉ်ပညာ *lay-yin-pyin-nyar*

aeroplane *(n.)* လေယာဉ် *lay-yin*

aerosol *(n.)* လေဖိအားသုံး လေမှုတ်ဘူး *lay-phi-arr-tone-lay-mote-bu*

aerospace *(n.)* လေကြောင်း၊ လေထုဆိုင်ရာ နည်းပညာ *lay-kyaung, lay-htu-saing-yar-nee-pyin-nyar*

aerostatics *(n.)* လေထုဆိုင်ရာ စတက်တစ်ပညာခွဲ *lay-htu-saing-yar-sa-tat-tic-pyin-nyar-khwal*

aesthete *(n.)* အလှရသခံစားတတ်သူ *a-hla-ya-th-khan-sar-tat-thu*

aesthetic *(adj.)* အဆင်းလှသော *a-sin-hla-taw*

afar *(adv.)* အဝေး *a-way*

affable *(adj.)* ဖော်ရွေသော *phaw-yway-taw*

affair *(n.)* ကိစ္စ *kait-sa*

affect *(v.)* ထိခိုက်သည် *hti-khaik-the*

affectation *(n.)* ဟန်ဆောင်မှု *han-saung-mu*

affected *(adj.)* ဟိတ်ဟန်များသော *heik-han-myar-taw*

affection *(n.)* ချစ်ခင်မှု *chit-khin-mu*

affectionate *(adj.)* ကြင်နာသော *kyin-nar-taw*

affidavit *(n.)* ကျမ်းကျိန်လွှာ *kyan-kyein-hlwar*

affiliate *(v.)* ပေါင်းစည်းသည် *paung-see-the*

affiliation *(n.)* မိတ်ဖက်အဖွဲ့ *meik-phat-a-phwe*

affinity *(n.)* စွဲလန်းမှု *swal-lan-mu*

affirm *(v.)* အခိုင်အမာပြောသည် *a-khaing-a-mar-pyaw-the*

affirmation *(n.)* အတည်ပြုချက် *a-the-pyu-chat*

affirmative *(adj.)* ဟုတ်မှန်ကြောင်း ပြသသည့် *hote-man-kyaung-pya-tha-the*

affix *(v.)* **ကပ်သည်** kat-the

afflict *(v.)* **ဖိစီးသည်** phi-see-the

affliction *(n.)* **ဝေဒနာ** *way-da-nar*

affluence *(n.)* **ကြွယ်ဝခြင်း** *kywe-wa-chin*

affluent *(adj.)* **ကြွယ်ဝသော** *kywe-wa-taw*

affluential *(n.)* **ကြွယ်ဝ၍ လွှမ်းမိုးနိုင်သူ** *kywe-wa-ywe-hlwan-moe-naing-thu*

afford *(v.)* **တတ်နိုင်သည်** *tat-naing-the*

affordability *(n.)* **ဈေးမကြီးခြင်း** *zay-ma-kyi-chin*

afforest *(v.)* **သစ်တောပျိုးထောင်သည်** *tit-taw-pyo-htaung-the*

affray *(n.)* **သတ်ပုတ်နှောင့်ယှက်မှု** *tat-poke-naunt-shat-mu*

affront *(n.)* **စော်ကားမှု** *saw-kar-mu*

afield *(adv.)* **ဝေးဝေး** *way-way*

aflame *(adv.)* **တောက်လောင်သော** *taut-laung-taw*

afloat *(adv.)* **ပေါလောပေါ်သော** *paw-law-paw-taw*

afoot *(adv.)* **ဟန်ပြင်လျက်ရှိသော** *han-pyin-lyat-shi-taw*

afore *(prep.)* **ကြိုတင်** *kyo-tin*

aforementioned *(adj.)* **ကြိုတင်ဖော်ပြထားသော** *kyo-tin-phaw-pya-htar-taw*

afraid *(adj.)* **ကြောက်ရွံ့သော** *kyauk-yunt-taw*

afresh *(adv.)* **အသစ်တစ်ဖန်** *a-thit-ta-hpan*

aft *(n.)* **ပဲ့ပိုင်း** *pae-paing*

after *(prep.)* **ပြီးနောက်** *pe-naut*

afterbirth *(n.)* **အချင်း** *a-chin*

aftercare *(n.)* **နောက်ဆက်တွဲစောင့်ရှောက်မှု** *naut-set-twe-saunt-shaut-mu*

after-effect *(n.)* **နောက်ဆက်တွဲအကျိုးသက်ရောက်မှု** *naut-set-twe-a-kyo-thet-yaut-mu*

aftermath *(n.)* **ဘေးဒဏ်၏ နောက်ဆက်တွဲ** *bay-dan-ei-naut-set-twe*

afternoon *(n.)* **မွန်းလွဲပိုင်း** *mun-lwe-paing*

after-party *(n.)* **နောက်ဆက်တွဲပါတီ** *naut-set-twe-par-ty*

aftersales *(adj.)* **ရောင်းပြီးနောက် ဖြစ်သော** *yaung-pi-naut-phit-taw*

aftershave *(n.)* **မုတ်ဆိတ်ရိတ်ပယ်ပြီး သုံးသောရေမွှေး** *mote-sate-yeik-pal-pi-tone-taw-yay-hmwe*

afterthought *(n.)* **နောက်ဆက်တွဲအတွေး** *naut-set-twe-a-thway*

afterwards *(adv.)* **နောက်မှ** naut-hma

again *(adv.)* **တစ်ဖန်** ta-hpan

against *(prep.)* **ဆန့်ကျင်လျက်** *sant-kyin-lyat*

agar *(n.)* **ရေညှိမှ ထုတ်သော ကျောက်ကျောပုံအဆီအနှစ်** *yay-nyi-hma-htoke-taw-kyauk-kyaw-pone-a-si-a-hnit*

agate *(n.)* **သဘော်မဟူရာ** *thin-baw-ma-hu-yar*

agaze *(adj.)* **ငေးမောနေမိသော** *ngay-maw-nay-mi-taw*

age *(n.)* **အသက်** *a-thet-*

aged *(adj.)* **အသက်အရွယ်ရှိသော** *a-thet-a-ywal-shi-taw*

ageing *(n.)* **ဇရာ** *za-yar*

ageism *(n.)* **အိုပယ်ဝါဒီ** *o-pal-war-di*

ageless *(adj.)* **ထာဝရ** htar-wa-ra

agency *(n.)* **အေဂျင်စီ** a-gen-cy

agenda *(n.)* **အစည်းအဝေးအစီအစဉ်** *a-see-a-way-a-si-a-sin*

agent *(n.)* **အေးဂျင့်** *a-gent*

agglomerate *(n.)* အလုံးဖြစ်အောင်လုံးခြင်း *a-lone-phit-aung-lone-chin*
aggradation *(n.)* ရေတိုက်စားခြင်း *yay-tite-sar-chin*
aggrandize *(v.)* သြဇာဖြန့်ကျက်သည် *aw-zar-phant-kyat-the*
aggravate *(v.)* ပိုမိုဆိုးရွားစေသည် *po-mo-soe-ywar-say-the*
aggravation *(n.)* ပိုမိုဆိုးရွားစေခြင်း *po-mo-soe-ywar-say-chin*
aggregate *(v.)* စုပေါင်းသည် *su-aung-the*
aggression *(n.)* ရန်လိုမှု *yan-lo-mu*
aggressive *(adj.)* ရန်လိုသော *yan-lo-taw*
aggressor *(n.)* ကျူးကျော်သူ *kyu-kyaw-thu*
aggrieve *(v.)* စိတ်ထိခိုက်သည် *seik-hti-keik-the*
aghast *(adj.)* မှင်တက်မိလျက် hmin-thet-mi-lyat
agile *(adj.)* ပေါ့ပါးဖျတ်လတ်သော *pot-par-phat-lat-taw*
agility *(n.)* ပေါ့ပါးဖျတ်လတ်နိုင်စွမ်း *pot-par-phat-lat-naing-swan*
agitate *(v.)* စိတ်တုန်လှုပ်စေသည် *seik-tone-hlote-say-the*
agitation *(n.)* စိတ်လှုပ်ရှားမှု seik-hlote-shar-mu
aglare *(adj.)* စူးရှတောက်ပသော *su-sha-taut-pa-taw*
aglow *(adv.)* တောက်ပစွာ *taut-pa-swar*
agnostic *(n.)* ဘုရားရှိမှုကို သံသရရှိသူ *pha-yar-shi-mu-ko-tan-ta-ya-shi-thu*
agnosticsm *(n.)* ဘုရားရှိမှုကို သံသရရှိသော ဝါဒ *pha-yar-shi-mu-ko-tan-ta-ya-shi-taw-wa-da*
ago *(adv.)* အခါက *a-kha-ka*
agog *(adj.)* ရိုးတိုးရွတဖြစ်သော *yoe-toe-ywa-ta-phit-taw*
agonize *(v.)* မချိတရိပူပန်သည် *ma-chi-ta-yi-pu-pan-the*
agony *(n.)* မချိတင်ကဲဝေဒနာ *ma-chi-tin-kae-way-da-nar*
agoraphobia *(n.)* ဟင်းလင်းပြင်အကြောက်လွန်ခြင်း *hin-lin-pyin-a-kyauk-lun-chin*
agrarian *(adj.)* လယ်ယာဥယျာဉ်ခြံမြေဆိုင်ရာ *lal-yar-au-yin-chan-myay-saing-yar*
agree *(v.)* သဘောတူသည် *ta-baw-thu-the*
agreeable *(adj.)* သဘောတူသော *ta-baw-thu-taw*
agreement *(n.)* သဘောတူညီချက် *ta-baw-thu-nyi-chat*
agricultural *(adj.)* စိုက်ပျိုးရေးနှင့်ဆိုင်သော *seik-pyo-yay-nint-saing-taw*
agriculture *(n.)* စိုက်ပျိုးရေး *seik-pyo-yay*
agriculturist *(n.)* စိုက်ပျိုးရေးလုပ်သူ *seik-pyo-yay-lote-thu*
agriproduct *(n.)* စိုက်ပျိုးထုတ်ကုန် *seik-pyo-htoke-kone*
agro *(adj.)* စိုက်ပျိုးရေးနှင့်ဆိုင်သော *seik-pyo-yay-nint-saing-taw*
agrochemical *(n.)* စိုက်ပျိုးရေးဓာတုဗေဒနှင့်ဆိုင်သော *seik-pyo-yay-dar-du-bay-da-nint-saing-taw*
agro-industry *(n.)* စိုက်ပျိုးရေးလုပ်ငန်း *seik-pyo-yay-lote-ngan*
agrology *(n.)* သီးနှံစိုက်ပျိုးမြေနှင့်ဆိုင်သော စိုက်ပျိုးရေးပညာခွဲ *thee-nan-seik-pyo-myay-nint-saing-taw-seik-pyo-yay-pyin-nyar-kwe*
agronomy *(n.)* သီးနှံစိုက်ပျိုးရေးပညာ *thee-nan-seik-pyo-yay-pyin-nyar*
ague *(n.)* တုန်ခြင်း *tone-chin*
ahead *(adv.)* ရှေ့သို့ *shay-thoe*

ahoy *(interj.)* **ဟေး** *hey*

aid *(n.& v.)* **အကူအညီ။ ကူညီသည်** *a-khu-a-nyi, khu-nyi-the*

aide *(n.)* **လက်ထောက်** *lat-htauk*

AIDS *(n.)* **ကိုယ်ခံအားကျ ကူးစက်ရောဂါ** *koe-khan-arr-kya-khu-set-yaw-gar*

ail *(v.)* **ဝေဒနာခံစားနေရသည်** *way-da-nar-khan-sar-nay-ya-the*

ailing *(adj.)* **ဖျားနာသော** *phyar-nar-taw*

ailment *(n.)* **ဖျားနာခြင်း** phyar-nar-chin

aim *(v.)* **ရည်ရွယ်သည်** *yee-ywal-the*

aimless *(adj.)* **ရည်ရွယ်ချက်မဲ့သော** *yee-ywal-chat-mae-taw*

air *(n.)* **လေ** lay

air conditioning *(n.)* **လေအေးပေးခြင်း** *lay-aye-pay-chin*

air freight *(n.)* **လေကြောင်းဖြင့်ပို့သော ကုန်ပစ္စည်း** *lay-kyaung-phit-po-taw-kone-pyit-see*

air freshner *(n.)* **လေသန့်စက်** *lay-thant-set*

air hostess *(n.)* **လေယာဉ်မယ်** lay-yin-mal

airbag *(n.)* **လုံခြုံရေးလေအိတ်** *lone-chone-yay-lay-aik*

airband *(n.)* **ရေဒီယိုလှိုင်းနှုန်း** *yay-di-yo-line-hnone*

airbase *(n.)* **လေတပ်စခန်း** *lay-tat-sa-khan*

airbed *(n.)* **လေအိတ်မွေ့ရာ** *lay-aik-mway-yar*

airborne *(n.)* **လေမှတစ်ဆင့်ကူးစက်သော** *lay-ma-ta-sint-ku-set-taw*

airbrake *(n.)* **လေဖိအားသုံးဘရိတ်** *lay-phi-arr-tone-lay-ba-rake*

airbus *(n.)* **ခရီးသည်တင်လေယာဉ်ကြီး** *kha-yee-the-tin-lay-yin-kyi*

aircraft *(n.)* **လေယာဉ်** *lay-yin*

aircrew *(n.)* **လေယာဉ်မောင်မယ်** *lay-yin-maung-mal*

airdrop *(n.)* **လေယာဉ်မှချသော ပစ္စည်းများ** *lay-yin-hma-cha-taw-pyit-see-myar*

airfare *(n.)* **လေယာဉ်ခ** *lay-yin-kha*

airfield *(n.)* **လေယာဉ်ကွင်း** *lay-yin-kwin*

airgun *(n.)* **လေသေနတ်** *lay-tha-nat*

airlift *(n.)* **လေယာဉ်ဖြင့်သယ်ပို့ခြင်း** *lay-yin-phyit-tal-poe-chin*

airy *(adj.)* **လေကောင်းလေသန့်ရပြီး ကျယ်ဝန်းသော** *lay-kaung-lay-thant-ya-pi-kyal-wun-taw*

aisle *(n.)* **မင်းလမ်းမကြီး** *min-lan-ma-kyi*

ajar *(adv.)* **ဟလျက်ရှိသော** *ha-lyat-shi-taw*

akin *(adj.)* **ဆင်ဆင်တူသော** sin-sin-tu-taw

akinesia *(n.)* **ထိန်းချုပ်ရသောကြွက်သားစွမ်းရည် ပျက်စီးခြင်း** htein-choke-ya-taw-kywat-tar-swan-yay-pyat-see-chin

alabaster *(n.)* **ကျောက်ဖြူနု** kyauk-phyu-nu

alacrious *(adj.)* **လုံးဝ** lone-wa

alacrity *(n.)* **ပြာပြာသလဲဖြစ်ခြင်း** *pyar-pyar-tha-lae-phit-chin*

alarm *(n.)* **သတိပေးချက်၊ တပ်လှန့်ခြင်း** *tha-di-pay-chat, tat-hlant-chin*

alarming *(adj.)* **စိုးရိမ်ဖွယ်ရာ** *soe-yein-phwal-yar*

alarmist *(n.)* **ခြောက်လှန့်ရေးသမား** chyaut-hlant-yay-tha-mar

alas *(interj.)* **အလိုလေး** a-lo-lay

albatross *(n.)* **ပင်လယ်စင်ရော်ကြီး** pin-lal-zin-yar-gyi

albeit *(conj.)* **သို့သော်ငြားလည်း** thoe-taw-nyar-lal

albino *(n.)* မွေးရာပါ အသား၊ ဆံပင်ဖြူပြီးမျက်ဆန်ပန်းရောင်ရှိသော လူ၊ တိရစ္ဆာန် mway-yar-par-a-tar-sin-pin-phyu-pee-myat-san-pan-yaung-shi-taw-lu-ta-yeik-san

album *(n.)* အယ်လဘန် *al-ban*

albumen *(n.)* ကြက်ဥအကာ kyat-au-a-karr

alchemist *(n.)* အဂ္ဂိရတ်ဆရာ at-gi-yat-sa-yar

alchemy *(n.)* အဂ္ဂိရတ် at-gi-yat

alcohol *(n.)* အရက် a-yat

alcoholic *(n.)* အရက်ပါဝင်သော a-yat-par-win-taw

alcoholism *(n.)* အရက်စွဲခြင်း a-yat-swal-chin

alcove *(n.)* နံရံတွင်း လိုဏ်ကဲ့သို့ အခန်းငယ် nan-yan-twin-hlaing-kae-tho-a-khan-nge

alder *(n.)* ဆောင်းရွက်ကြွေပင် *saung-ywat-kyway-pin*

ale *(n.)* ဘီယာ၊ ဗျစ်။ *beer, byit*

alegar *(n.)* ဗျစ်ဖြင့် လုပ်သော ရှာလကာရည် *byit-phit-lote-taw-sha-la-kar-yay*

alert *(adj.)* နိုးကြားသော *noe-kyar-taw*

alertness *(n.)* နိုးကြားခြင်း *noe-kyar-chin*

alfa *(n.)* အယ်လဖာ *al-far*

algae *(n.)* ရေညှိ yay-hnyi

algebra *(n.)* အက္ခရာသင်္ချာ at-kha-yar-thin-char

algorithm *(n.)* ပြဿနာဖြေရှင်းနည်းစနစ် pyat-tha-nar-hpyay-shin-nee-sa-nit

alias *(adv.)* နာမည်တု nan-mal-thu

alibi *(n.)* ဆင်ခြေ *sin-chay*

alien *(adj.)* ဂြိုလ်သား *gyo-tar*

alienate *(v.)* ကင်းကွာသည် *kin-kwar-the*

aliferous *(adj.)* တောင်ပံရှိသော *taung-pan-shi-taw*

alight *(v.)* ဆင်းသက်သည် *sin-thet-the*

align *(v.)* တန်းညှိသည် *tan-hnyi-the*

alignment *(n.)* တန်းညှိခြင်း *tan-hnyi-chin*

alike *(adj.)* ဆင်သော *sin-taw*

aliment *(n.)* အစားအစာ၊ အာဟာရ *a-sar-a-sar, a-har-ya*

alimony *(n.)* မယားစရိတ် *ma-yar-sa-yeik*

alive *(adj.)* အသက်ရှင်သော *a-thet-shin-taw*

alkali *(n.)* အယ်လ်ကာလီ *al-kar-li*

alkaline *(adj.)* အယ်လကာလီသဘာဝရှိသော *al-kar-li-tha-bar-wa-shi-taw*

all *(adj.)* အားလုံး *arr-lone*

allay *(v.)* ဖြေသိမ့်ပေးသည် *Hpay-theint-pay-the*

allegation *(n.)* စွပ်စွဲချက် *sut-swal-chat*

allege *(v.)* စွပ်စွဲသည် *sut-swal-the*

allegiance *(n.)* သစ္စာခံခြင်း *thit-sar-khan-chin*

allegory *(n.)* ရူပက အလင်္ကာတွဲ *yu-pa-ka-a-link-kar-twe*

allergic *(adj.)* ဓာတ်မတည့်သော *dat-ma-tae-taw*

allergy *(n.)* ဓာတ်မတည့်ခြင်း *dat-ma-tae-chin*

alleviate *(v.)* သက်သာစေသည် *thet-tar-say-the*

alleviation *(n.)* သက်သာခြင်း *thet-tar-chin*

alley *(n.)* လူသွားလမ်း *lu-twar-lan*

alliance *(n.)* မဟာမိတ်ပြုခြင်း *ma-har-meik-pyu-chin*

allied *(adj.)* မဟာမိတ်ဖြစ်သော *ma-har-meik-phit-taw*

alligator *(n.)* မိကျောင်းခေါင်းတို *mi-kyaung-khaung-to*

alliterate *(v.)* **အစစာလုံး အသံတူအောင်ပြု၍ ရေးသည်** *a-sa-sar-lone-a-tan-thu-aung-pyu-ywe-yay-the*

alliteration *(n.)* **အစစာလုံး အသံတူအောင်ပြု၍ ရေးခြင်း** *a-sa-sar-lone-a-tan-thu-aung-pyu-ywe-yay-chin*

allocate *(v.)* **ခွဲတမ်းချသည်** *khwe-tan-cha-the*

allocation *(n.)* **ခွဲတမ်းချခြင်း** *khwe-tan-cha-chin*

allot *(v.)* **ခွဲဝေပေးသည်** khwe-way-pay-the

allotment *(n.)* **ဝေစု** way-su

allow *(v.)* **ခွင့်ပြုသည်** khwint-pyu-the

allowance *(n.)* **ခွင့်ပြုငွေ** khwint-pyu-ngwe

alloy *(n.)* **သတ္တုစပ်** *tat-thu-sat*

allude *(v.)* **သွယ်ဝိုက်ပြောသည်** *twal-wite-pyaw-so-the*

allure *(v.)* **ညို့ဓာတ်** *hnyo-dat*

alluring *(adj.)* **ညို့ဓာတ်ရှိသော** *hnyo-dat-shi-taw*

allusion *(n.)* **အရိပ်အမြွက်** *a-yeik-a-mywat*

allusive *(adj.)* **မထိခလုတ် ထိခလုတ်** ma-hti-kha-lote-hti-kha-lote

ally *(n.)* **မဟာမိတ်ဖွဲ့သည်** *ma-har-meik-phwe-the*

almanac *(n.)* **နှစ်ချုပ်စာအုပ်** *nit-choke-sar-oak*

almighty *(adj.)***ဘုန်းတော်ကြီးမြတ်သော** *bhone-taw-kyi-myat-taw*

almirah *(n.)* **ဗီရို** bi-yo

almond *(n.)* **အယ်လမွန်သီး** *al-mon-thee*

almost *(adv.)* **လုနီးပါး** lu-ni-par

alms *(n.)* **နွမ်းပါးသူကို စွန့်ကြဲသည့် ငွေ၊ အဝတ်၊ စားဖွယ်** nwan-par-thu-ko-sunt-kyae-the-ngwe-a-wit-sar-phwal

aloe *(n.)* **ရှားစောင်းလက်ပတ်** shar-saung-lat-pat

aloft *(adv.)* **လက်ထဲတွင်** *lat-htae-twin*

alone *(adj.)* **တစ်ဦးတည်း** *the-oo-the*

along *(prep. &adv.)* **တစ်လျှောက်** *ta-shaut*

alongside *(prep.)* **ယှဉ်လျက်** shin-lyat

aloof *(adv.)* **တသီးတခြားနေသော** *a-thee-ta-char-nay-taw*

aloud *(adv.)* **အသံထွက်၍** *a-than-htwat-ywe*

alp *(n.)* **မြင့်မားသော တောင်** myint-mar-taw-taung

alpha *(n.)* **အယ်လဖာ** *al-pha*

alphabet *(n.)* **အက္ခရာ** *at-kha-yar-*

alphabetical *(adj.)* **အက္ခရာအစဉ်အတိုင်းဖြစ်သော** *at-kha-yar-a-sin-a-taing-phit-taw*

alpine *(adj.)* **မြင့်မားသော တောင်ပေါ်ဒေသရှိ** *myint-mar-taw-taung-paw-day-ta-shi*

already *(adv.)* **ပြီးနှင့်ပြီ** *pyi-nint-pyi*

also *(adv.)* **လည်းပဲ** *lal-pal*

altar *(n.)* **ယဇ်ပလ္လင်** *yit-pa-ling*

alteration *(n.)* **ပြောင်းလဲခြင်းဖြစ်စဉ်** *pyaung-lal-chin-phit-sin*

altercation *(n.)* **အော်ဟစ် ငြင်းခုံခြင်း** *aw-hit-nyin-khone-chin*

alternate *(v.)* **တစ်လှည့်စီဖြစ်သည်** *ta-lae-si-phit-the*

alternative *(adj.)* **တမားရိုးကျမဟုတ်သော** *tha-ma-yoe-kya-ma-hote-taw*

alternatively *(adv.)* **တစ်နည်းအားဖြင့်** *tha-nee-ar-phint*

although *(conj.)* **သော်လည်း** *taw-lal*

altimeter *(n.)* **အမြင့်ပြကိရိယာ** *a-myint-pya-ka-yi-yar*

altitude *(n.)* ပင်လယ်ရေမျက်နှာပြင်အထက် အမြင့် *pin-la-yay-myat-nar-pyin-a-htet-a-myint*
alto *(n.)* အမြင့်ဆုံး ယောကျ်ားသီချင်းဆိုသံ *a-myint-sone-yauk-kyar-tha-chin-so-than*
altogether *(adv.)* အတူတကွ *a-thu-ta-kwa*
altruism *(n.)* ပရဟိတဝါဒ pa-ya-hi-ta-wa-da
altruist *(n.)* ပရဟိတဝါဒီ pa-ya-hi-ta-wa-di
altruistic *(adj.)* ကိုယ်ကျိုးမငဲ့သော *ko-kyo-ma-nge-taw*
aluminate *(v.)* အလင်းပေးသည် *a-lin-pay-the*
aluminium *(n.)* အလျူမီနီယံ *a-lyu-mi-ni-yan*
always *(adv.)* အမြဲတမ်း *a-mye-tan*
Alzheimer's disease *(n.)* အယ်ဇိုင်းမားရောဂါ *al-zaing-mar-yaw-gar*
am *(abbr.)* ဖြစ်သည်၊ ရှိသည် *phit-the, shi-the*
amalgam *(n.)* ရောစပ်မှု *yaw-set-mu*
amalgamate *(v.)* ပေါင်းသည် *paung-the*
amalgamation *(n.)* ပေါင်းခြင်း *paung-chin*
amass *(v.)* စုဆောင်းသည် *su-saung-the*
amateur *(n.)* အပျော်တမ်း *a-pyaw-tan*
amatory *(adj.)* လိင်စိတ်ချစ်ခြင်းနှင့် ဆိုင်သော *lain-seik-chit-chin-nint-thet-saing-taw*
amaze *(v.)* အံ့အားသင့်စေသည် *ant-arr-tint-say-the*
amazement *(n.)* အံ့အားသင့်စေခြင်း *ant-arr-tint-say-chin*
ambassador *(n.)* သံအမတ် *tan-a-mat*
amber *(n.)* ပယင်း *pa-yin*
amberite *(n.)* အမ်းဘာရိုက်အမှုန့် *am-bar-yite-a-hmont*
ambidexter *(n.)* နှစ်ဖက်သန်သူ *na-phat-tan-thu*
ambience *(n.)* ဝန်းကျင်ဓလေ့စရိုက် *win-kyin-da-lay-sa-yite*
ambient *(adj.)* ဝန်းကျင် *win-kyin*
ambiguity *(n.)* အနက်ထွေပြားခြင်း *a-nat-htway-pyar-chin*
ambiguous *(adj.)* အနက်မပြတ်သားခြင်း *a-nat-ma-phat-tar-chin*
ambit *(n.)* ပိုင်နက် *paing-nat*
ambition *(n.)* ရည်မှန်းချက် yee-man-chat
ambitious *(adj.)* ရည်မှန်းချက်ကြီးသော *yee-man-chat-kyi-taw*
ambivalence *(n.)* စိတ်နှစ်ခွဖြစ်ခြင်း *seik-na-kwa-phit-chin*
ambivalent *(adj.)* စိတ်နှစ်ခွဖြစ်သော *seik-na-kwa-phit-taw*
amble *(v.)* စိမ်ပြေနပြေသွားသည် sein-pyay-na-pyay-twa-the
ambulance *(n.)* လူနာတင်ကား *lu-nar-tin-car*
ambulant *(adj.)* တစ်နေရာမှ တစ်နေရာ ရွေ့နေသော *ta-nay-yar-ma-ta-nay-yar-yway-nay-taw*
ambush *(n.)* ချုံခိုတိုက်ခြင်း chone-kho-tite-chin
ameliorate *(v.)* ပိုမိုကောင်းမွန်စေသည် *po-mo-kaung-mon-say-the*
amelioration *(n.)* ပိုမိုကောင်းမွန်စေခြင်း *po-mo-kaung-mon-say-chin*
amen *(interj.)* အာမင် arr-min
amenable *(adj.)* လိုလိုလားလားလက်ခံတတ်သော *lo-lo-lar-lar-lat-khan-tat-taw*
amend *(v.)* ပြင်ဆင်သည် pyin-sin-the
amendment *(n.)* ပြင်ဆင်ချက် pyin-sin-chat

amenity *(n.)* **သာယာအဆင်ပြေခြင်း** *tar-yar-a-sin-pyay-chin*
amiability *(n.)* **ဖော်ရွေနိုင်စွမ်း** *hpaw-yway-naing-swan*
amiable *(adj.)* **ဖော်ရွေသော** *hpaw-yway-taw*
amicable *(adj.)* **ချစ်ကြည်သော** chit-kyi-taw
amid *(prep.)* **အလယ်တွင်** a-lal-twin
amiss *(adj.)* **မှားသော** hmar-taw
amity *(n.)* **ချစ်ကြည်မှု** *chit-kyi-mu*
ammonia *(n.)* **အမိုးနီးယားဓာတ်ငွေ့** *a-moe-ni-yar-dat-ngwe*
ammunition *(n.)* **ကျည်** *kyi*
amnesia *(n.)* **အတိတ်မေ့ရောဂါ** a-tate-may-yaw-gar
amnesty *(n.)* **လွတ်ငြိမ်းချမ်းသာခွင့်** lut-nyein-chan-tar-khwint
among *(prep.)* **အကြားတွင်** a-kyar-twin
amongst *(prep.)* **အကြားတွင်** a-kyar-twin
amoral *(adj.)* **ကိုယ်ကျင့်တရားမဲ့သော** *ko-kyint-ta-yar-mae-taw*
amorous *(adj.)* **ရမ္မက်လျှမ်းသော** *ya-mat-hlyan-taw*
amorphous *(adj.)* **ပုံဆောင်မဲ့** *pone-saung-mae*
amount *(n.)* **ပမာဏ** *pa-mar-na*
amour *(n.)* **အချစ်ကိစ္စ** *a-chit-keik-sa*
ampere *(n.)* **အမ်ပီယာ** am-pi-yar
amphibian *(n.)* **ကုန်းရေနေသတ္တဝါ** kone-yay-nay-tat-ta-war
amphibious *(adj.)* **ကုန်းရေနေဖြစ်သော** kone-yay-nay-phit-taw
amphitheatre *(n.)* **အမိုးမဲ့ပွဲကြည့်စင်** a-moe-mae-pwe-kyi-sin
ample *(adj.)* **လုံလောက်သော** lone-laut-taw
amplification *(n.)* **ချဲ့ခြင်း** chae-chin
amplifier *(n.)* **အသံချဲ့စက်** a-tan-chae-set
amplify *(v.)* **ချဲ့သည်** *chae-the*
amplitude *(n.)* **ကြီးမားမှု** kyi-mar-mu
amputate *(v.)* **ဖြတ်တောက်ကုသသည်** *phat-taut-ku-ta-the*
amputation *(n.)* **ဖြတ်တောက်ကုသခြင်း** *phat-taut-ku-ta-chin*
amputee *(n.)* **ဖြတ်တောက်ခံရသူ** *phat-taut-khan-ya-thu*
amuck *(adv.)* **ဒေါသတကြီး** *daw-tha-da-kyi*
amulet *(n.)* **အဆောင်** a-saung
amuse *(v.)* **သဘောကျသည်** *ta-baw-kya-the*
amusement *(n.)* **ဖျော်ဖြေမှု** *phyaw-phyay-mu*
an *(art.)* **တစ်ခု၊ တစ်ယောက်** *ta-khu, ta-yauk*
anabolic *(n.)* **စုဖွဲ့ခြင်းနှင့်ဆိုင်သော** su-phwe-chin-nint-saing-taw
anachronism *(n.)* **ခေတ်တလွဲဖော်ပြချက်** *khit-ta-lwal-phaw-pya-chat*
anaemia *(n.)* **သွေးအားနည်း** *thwe-arr-nae*
anaesthesia *(n.)* **မေ့ဆေး** *mae-say*
anaesthetic *(n.)* **မေ့ဆေး** *mae-say*
anal *(adj.)* **စအို** *sa-o*
analgestic *(n.)* **အကိုက်အခဲပျောက်ဆေး** *a-kite-a-khae-pyauk-say*
analogous *(adj.)* **အလားတူသော** *a-lar-thu-taw*
analogy *(n.)* **တူညီချက်** *thu-nyi-chat*
analyse *(v.)* **စိတ်ဖြာသုံးသပ်သည်** *seik-phyar-tone-tat-the*
analysis *(n.)* **စိတ်ဖြာသုံးသပ်ခြင်း** *seik-phyar-tone-tat-chin*
analyst *(n.)* **စိတ်ဖြာသုံးသပ်သူ** *seik-phyar-tone-tat-thu*
analytical *(adj.)* **စိတ်ဖြာသုံးသပ်သော** *seik-phyar-tone-tat-thaw*

anamnesis *(n.)* အတိတ်ကို ပြန်ဖော်နိုင်ခြင်း *a-tate-ko-pyan-phaw-naing-chin*
anamorphosis *(adj.)* သတ္တဝါအခြားတစ်မျိုးမှ နောက်တစ်မျိုးသို့ ဆင့်ကဲပေါ်ထွန်းလာခြင်း *tat-ta-war-ta-myo-hma-naut-ta-myo-tho-sint-kae-pay-htun-chin*
anarchism *(n.)* မင်းမဲ့ဝါဒ *min-mae-wa-da*
anarchist *(n.)* မင်းမဲ့ဝါဒီ *min-mae-wa-di*
anarchy *(n.)* မင်းမဲ့စိုးရိုက် min-mae-sa-yite
anatomy *(n.)* ခန္ဓာဗေဒ *khan-dar-bay-da*
ancestor *(n.)* ဘိုးဘေးဘီဘင် boe-bay-bi-bing
ancestral *(adj.)* ဘိုးဘွားပိုင် boe-bwar-paing
ancestry *(n.)* မျိုးရိုး myo-yoe
anchor *(n.)* ကျောက်ဆူး kyauk-sue
anchorage *(n.)* ကျောက်ချရပ်နားရာ *kyauk-cha-yat-nar-yar*
ancient *(adj.)* ရှေးဟောင်း *shay-haung*
ancillary *(adj.)* အထောက်အကူ *a-htauk-a-khu*
and *(conj.)* နှင့် *nint*
android *(n.)* အန်းဒရိုက် *an-da-yite*
anecdote *(n.)* စိတ်ချရသော သက်သေမဟုတ်သည့် တစ်ဦးချင်းစီအမြင် *seik-cha-ya-taw-thet-tay-ma-hote-the-ta-oo-chin-si-a-myin*
anemometer *(n.)* လေအရှိန်၊ ဦးတည်ချက်၊ ရေရွေ့လျားမှုတိုင်း ကိရိယာ *lay-a-shein-oo-the-chat-yay-shwe-lyar-mu-taing-ka-yi-yar*
anew *(adv.)* အသစ်တစ်ဖန် *a-thit-tha-phan*
angel *(n.)* နတ် *nat*
anger *(n.)* ဒေါသ *daw-ta*
angina *(n.)* ရင်ဘတ်အောင့်ခြင်း *yin-bat-aung-chin*
angiogram *(n.)* သွေးကြောဓာတ်မှန် *tway-kyaw-dat-man*
angle *(n.)* ထောင့် *htaung*
angry *(adj.)* ဒေါသထွက်သော *daw-ta-htwat-taw*
angst *(n.)* လောကကို စိတ်ပျက်မှု *law-ka-ko-seik-pyat-mu*
anguish *(n.)* မချိတင်ကဲဝေဒနာ *ma-chi-tin-kae-way-da-nar*
angular *(adj.)* အရိုးငေါငေါနှင့် ဖြစ်သော *a-yoe-ngaw-ngaw-nint-phit-taw*
animal *(n.)* တိရစ္ဆာန် *ta-yeik-san*
animal husbandry *(n.)* တိရစ္ဆာန်မွေးမြူရေး *ta-yeik-san-mway-myu-yay*
animate *(v.)* သက်ဝင်လှုပ်ရှားသည် *thet-win-lote-shar-the*
animation *(n.)* သက်ဝင်လှုပ်ရှားနည်းပညာ *thet-win-lote-shar-nee-pyin-nyar*
animosity *(n.)* မုန်းတီးမှု *hmone-tee-mu*
animus *(n.)* မလိုမုန်းထားမှု *ma-lo-hmone-htar-mu*
aniseed *(n.)* စမုန်စပါး *sa-hmone-sa-par*
ankle *(n.)* ခြေချင်းဝတ် *chay-chin-wut*
anklet *(n.)* ခြေချင်း *chay-chin*
annalist *(n.)* နှစ်အလိုက်သမိုင်းပြုစုသူ *nit-a-lite-tha-mine-pyu-su-thu*
annals *(n.pl.)* နှစ်အလိုက်သမိုင်း *nit-a-lite-tha-mine*
annex *(v.)* တိုက်ခိုက်သိမ်းယူသည် *tite-kheik-thein-yu-the*
annexation *(n.)* တိုက်ခိုက်သိမ်းယူခြင်း *tite-kheik-thein-yu-chin*
annihilate *(v.)* အမြစ်ဖြတ်သည် *a-myit-phat-the*

annihilation *(n.)* **အမြစ်ဖြတ်ခြင်း** *a-myit-phat-chin*
anniversary *(n.)* **နှစ်ပတ်လည်** nit-pat-lal
annotate *(v.)* **မှတ်ချက်ပြုသည်** *mat-chat-pyu-the*
announce *(v.)* **ကြေညာသည်** *kyaw-nyar-the*
announcement *(n.)* **ကြေညာချက်** *kyaw-nyar-chat*
announcer *(n.)* **ကြေညာသူ** kyaw-nyar-thu
annoy *(v.)* **နှောင့်ယှက်သည်** *naut-shat-the*
annoyance *(n.)* **အနှောင့်အယှက်** *a-naut-a-shat*
annoying *(adj.)* **စိတ်တိုစရာကောင်းသော** *seik-toe-sa-yar-kaung-taw*
annual *(adj.)* **နှစ်စဉ်** *nit-sin*
annuity *(n.)* **နှစ်စဉ်ထုတ်ပေးငွေ** *nit-sin-htoke-pay-ngwe*
annul *(v.)* **ပယ်ဖျက်သည်** *pal-phat-the*
annulment *(n.)* **ပယ်ဖျက်ခြင်း** *pal-phat-chin*
anoint *(v.)* **ဆီဖြင့် လိမ်းသပ်သည်** *si-phit-lain-tat-the*
anomalous *(adj.)* **တစ်မူထူးခြားသော** *ta-mu-htoo-char-taw*
anomaly *(n.)* **မူမမှန်ချက်** *mu-ma-hman-chat*
anon *(adv.)* **မကြာမီ** *ma-kyar-mi*
anonymity *(n.)* **အမည်ဝှက်ထားခြင်း** *a-me-wat-htar-chin*
anonymosity *(n.)* **အမည်ဝှက်ထားခြင်း** *a-me-wat-htar-chin*
anonymous *(adj.)* **အမည်မသိသော** *a-me-ma-thi-taw*
anorak *(n.)* **မိုးလေကာအပေါ်အင်္ကျီ** moe-lay-kar-a-paw-inn-gyi
anorexia *(n.)* **ဝမည်စိုး၍ ဖြစ်သော အစားအသောက်ပျက်ရောဂါ** *wa-me-soe-ywe-phit-taw-a-sar-a-taut-phat-yaw-gar*
anorexic *(adj.)* **ဝမည်စိုး၍ ဖြစ်သော အစားအသောက်ပျက်ရောဂါ ရှိသော** *wa-me-soe-ywe-phit-taw-a-sar-a-taut-phat-yaw-gar-shi-taw*
another *(adj.)* **အခြား** *a-char*
answer *(n.)* **အဖြေ** *a-phyay*
answerable *(adj.)* **ဖြေနိုင်သော** phyay-naing-taw
answering machine *(n.)* **ဖြေစက်** *phyay-set*
ant *(n.)* **ပုရွက်ဆိတ်** *pa-ywet-seik*
antacid *(adj.)* **အစာအိမ်အက်ဆစ်ဓာတ်ချိန်ညှိဆေး** *a-sar-eain-at-sit-dat-chain-nyi-say*
antagonism *(n.)* **ရန်ညိုး** yan-nyo
antagonist *(n.)* **ရန်ဘက်** yan-bat
antagonize *(v.)* **ရန်လုပ်သည်** *yan-lote-the*
antarctic *(adj.)* **တောင်ဝန်ရိုးစွန်းဒေသနှင့်ပတ်သက်သော** *taung-win-yoe-sune-day-ta-nint-pat-thet-taw*
antecardium *(n.)* **အစာအိမ်အချိုင့်နေရာ** *a-sar-eain-a-chyaint-nay-yar*
antecede *(v.)* **ရှေ့ရောက်နှင့်သည်** *shay-yaut-nint-the*
antecedent *(n.)* **ရှေးဦးသာဓက** *shay-oo-thar-da-ka*
antedate *(n.)* **နောက်ကြောင်းပြန်ရက်စွဲတပ်သည်** *naut-kyaung-pyan-yat-swal-tat-the*
antelope *(n.)* **တောဆိတ်မျိုး** *taw-seik-myo*
antenatal *(adj.)* **မီးမဖွားမီ** mee-ma-phwar-mi
antenna *(n.)* **အင်တာနာတိုင်** in-ta-nar-taing

anterior *(adj.)* ရှေ့ပိုင်းကျသော *shay-paing-kya-taw*
anthem *(n.)* ဓမ္မသီချင်း dham-ma-ta-chin
anthology *(n.)* စာညွန့်ပေါင်း *sar-nyunt-paung*
anthrax *(n.)* ထောင့်သန်းရောဂါ *htaung-tan-yaw-gar*
anthropoid *(adj.)* လူနှင့်ဆင်သော *lu-nint-sin-taw*
anthropology *(n.)* မနုဿဗေဒ *ma-note-ta-bay-da*
anti *(pref.)* ဆန့်ကျင်လျက် *sant-kyin-lyat*
anti-ageing *(adj.)* အသက်အရွယ်ကြီးရင့်ခြင်းကို ဆန့်ကျင်သော *a-the-a-ywe-kyi-yint-chin-ko-sant-kyin-taw*
anti-aircraft *(adj.)* လေယာဉ်ပစ် *lay-yin-phit*
antibacterial *(adj.)* ဘက်တီးယီးယားပိုးသတ်သော bat-tee-yee-yar-poe-tat-taw
antibiotic *(n.)* ပဋိဇီဝဆေး pa-di-zi-wa-say
antibody *(n.)* ပဋိပစ္စည်း pa-di-phit-see
antic *(n.)* ထူးခြားဆန်းကျယ်ခြင်း htoo-char-san-kyal-chin
anticipate *(v.)* မျှော်လင့်သည် *myaw-lint-the*
anticipation *(n.)* ကြိုတင်မျှော်မှန်းခြင်း *kyo-tin-hmyaw-man-chin*
anticlimax *(n.)* အဖျားရှူးခြင်း *a-phyar-shue-chin*
anticlockwise *(adv.)* လက်ဝဲရစ် *lat-wal-yit*
antidote *(n.)* ဖြေဆေး phyay-say
antifreeze *(n.)* ရေမခဲဆေး yay-ma-khae-say
antigen *(n.)* အင်တီဂျင် *an-ti-gen*
antinomy *(n.)* အယူအဆနှစ်ခု ဆန့်ကျင်ခြင်း a-yu-a-sa-nit-khu-sant-kyin-chin
antioxidant *(n.)* ဓာတ်တိုးဆန့်ကျင်ပစ္စည်း *dat-toe-sant-kyin-pyit-see*
antipathy *(n.)* ရွံမုန်းမှု *yount-hmone-mu*
antiphony *(n.)* သီဆိုခြင်း၊ တီးခတ်ခြင်း၊ ရွတ်ဆိုခြင်း *thi-so-chin, tee-khat-chin, yut-so-chin*
antipodes *(n.)* အန်တီပိုဒီဒေသ *an-ti-po-de-day-ta*
antiquarian *(adj.)* ရှေးဟောင်းရှားပါးပစ္စည်း *shay-haung-shar-par-pyit-see*
antiquary *(n.)* ရှေးဟောင်းရှားပါးပစ္စည်းစုဆောင်းသူ *shay-haung-shar-par-pyit-see-su-saung-thu*
antiquated *(adj.)* ဘိုးတော်ဘုရားလက်ထက်က *boe-taw-pha-yar-lat-htet-ka*
antique *(adj.)* ရှေးကျ၍ တန်ဖိုးကြီးသော *shay-kya-ywe-tan-phoe-kyi-taw*
antiquity *(n.)* ရှေးပဝေသဏီ shay-pa-way-tha-ni
antiseptic *(n.)* ပိုးသတ်ဆေး *poe-tat-say*
antisocial *(adj.)* လူမှုရေး ခေါင်းပါးသော *lu-mu-yay-khaung-par-taw*
antithesis *(n.)* ဆန့်ကျင်ဘက် *sant-kyin-bat*
antler *(n.)* သမင်ချို *ta-min-gyo*
antonym *(n.)* ဆန့်ကျင်ဘက်စကား *sant-kyin-bat-sa-gar*
anus *(n.)* စအို *sa-o*
anvil *(n.)* ပေ *pay*
anxiety *(n.)* ပူပန်မှု *pu-pan-mu*
anxious *(adj.)* ပူပန်သော *pu-pan-taw*
anxiously *(adv.)* ပူပန်စွာ *pu-pan-swar*
any *(adj.)* တစ်စုံတစ်ရာ *ta-sone-ta-yar*
anybody *(pron.)* တစ်စုံတစ်ယောက် *ta-sone-ta-yauk*

anyhow *(adv.)* **ထို့ပြင်** *htoe-pyin*

anyone *(pron.)* **တစ်စုံတစ်ယောက်** *ta-sone-ta-yauk*

anyplace *(pron.)* **တစ်နေရာရာ** *ta-nay-yar-yar*

anything *(pron.)* **တစ်ခုခု** *ta-khu-khu*

anytime *(adv.)* **တစ်ချိန်ချိန်** ta-chain-chain

anyway *(adv.)* **တစ်နည်းနည်း** *ta-nee-nee*

anywhere *(adv.)* **တစ်နေရာရာ** *ta-nay-yar-yar*

aorta *(n.)* **သွေးကြောမကြီး** *tway-kyaw-ma-kyi*

apace *(adv.)* **မြန်မြန်ဆန်ဆန်** *myan-myan-san-san*

apart *(adv.)* **ဝေးကွာလျက်** *way-kwar-lyat*

apartheid *(n.)* **လူမျိုးရေးခွဲခြားမှု** *lu-myo-yay-kwal-char-mu*

apartment *(n.)* **တိုက်ခန်း** *tite-khan*

apathy *(n.)* **စိတ်မပါခြင်း** *sait-ma-par-chin*

ape *(n.)* **မျောက်ဝံ** *myauk-wun*

aperture *(n.)* **အလင်းဝင်ပေါက်** *a-linn-win-pauk*

apex *(n.)* **ထိပ်** *hteik*

aphasia *(n.)* **အသံမထွက်နိုင်ခြင်း** *a-tan-ma-htwat-naing-chin*

aphorism *(n.)* **ဆောင်ပုဒ်** *saung-pote*

apiary *(n.)* **ပျားမွေးမြူရာဌာန** *pyar-mway-my-yay-htar-na*

apiculture *(n.)* **ပျားမွေးမြူရေး** *pyar-mway-my-yay*

apiece *(adv.)* **တစ်ဖက်စီ** *ta-phat-si*

aplenty *(adj.)* **အများအပြား** *a-myar-a-pyar*

aplogetic *(adj.)* **ဝန်ချတောင်းပန်** *win-cha-taung-pan*

apnoea *(n.)* **အိပ်နေစဉ် ရုတ်တရက် အသက်ရှူခဏရပ်ခြင်း** *aik-pyaw-nay-zin-yote-ta-yat-a-tet-shu-ka-na-yat-chin*

apologize *(v.)* **တောင်းပန်သည်** *taung-pan-the*

apology *(n.)* **တောင်းပန်ခြင်း** *taung-pan-chin*

apostle *(n.)* **ထောက်ခံအားပေးသူ** *htauk-khan-arr-pay-thu*

apostrophe *(n.)* **ပိုင်ဆိုင်မှုပြ သင်္ကေတ** *paing-saing-mu-pya-tin-kay-ta*

apotheosis *(n.)* **အထွတ်အထိပ်** *a-htut-a-hteik*

app *(n.)* **အက်ပ်** *ap*

appal *(v.)* **တုန်လှုပ်ချောက်ချားစေသည်** *tone-hlote-chauk-char-say-the*

apparatus *(n.)* **ကိရိယာ** *ka-yi-yar*

apparel *(n.)* **အဝတ်အစား** *a-wut-a-sar*

apparent *(adj.)* **ထင်ရှားသော** *htin-shar-taw*

appeal *(v.)* **မေတ္တာရပ်သည်** *myit-tar-yat-the*

appear *(v.)* **ပေါ်လာသည်** *paw-lar-the*

appearance *(n.)* **ပေါ်လာခြင်း** *pay-lar-chin*

appease *(v.)* **နှစ်သိမ့်သည်** *hnit-theint-the*

appellant *(n.)* **အယူခံဝင်သည်** *a-yu-khan-win-the*

append *(v.)* **ပူးတွဲပေးလိုက်သည်** *pu-twe-pay-lite-the*

appendage *(n.)* **အဖြည့်ခံ** *a-phyae-khan*

appendicitis *(n.)* **အူအတက်ရောင်ခြင်း** *au-a-tat-yaung-chin*

appendix *(n.)* **အူအတက်** *au-a-tat*

appetite *(n.)* **စားချင်စိတ်** *sar-chin-seik*

appetizer *(n.)* **နှုတ်မြိန်စာ** *note-myine-sar*

applaud *(v.)* လက်ခုပ်ဩဘာပေးသည် lat-khote-aw-bar-pay-the
applause *(n.)* လက်ခုပ်ဩဘာသံ *lat-khote-aw-bar-tan*
apple *(n.)* ပန်းသီး *pan-thee*
appliance *(n.)* ကိရိယာ *ka-yi-yar*
applicable *(adj.)* သက်ဆိုင်သော *thet-saing-taw*
applicant *(n.)* လျှောက်ထားသူ *shaut-htar-thu*
application *(n.)* လျှောက်လွှာတင်ခြင်း *shaut-lwar-tin-chin*
applied *(adj.)* လက်တွေ့အသုံးချ *lat-tway-a-tone-cha*
apply *(v.)* လျှောက်သည် *shaut-the*
appoint *(v.)* ခန့်ထားသည် *khant-htar-the*
appointment *(n.)* ချိန်းဆိုချက် *chein-so-chat*
apportion *(v.)* ခွဲဝေပေးသည် *kwal-way-pay-the*
apposite *(adj.)* ဆန့်ကျင်ဘက် *sant-kyin-bat*
appraise *(v.)* တန်ဖိုးဖြတ်သည် *tan-phoe-phat-the*
appreciable *(adj.)* သိသာသော *ti-tar-taw*
appreciate *(v.)* အသိအမှတ်ပြုသည် *a-ti-a-mat-pyu-the*
appreciation *(n.)* အသိအမှတ်ပြုခြင်း *a-ti-a-mat-pyu-chin*
apprehend *(v.)* ဖမ်းမိသည် *hpan-mi-the*
apprehension *(n.)* ဖမ်းမိခြင်း *hpan-mi-chin*
apprehensive *(adj.)* စိုးရိမ်သော *soe-yein-taw*
apprentice *(n.)* အလုပ်သင် *a-lote-tin*
apprise *(v.)* အသိပေးသည် *a-ti-pay-the*
approach *(v.)* ချဉ်းကပ်သည် *chee-kat-the*
approachable *(adj.)* ဖော်ရွေသော *phaw-yway-taw*
approbation *(n.)* ခွင့်ပြုခြင်း *kwint-pyu-chin*
appropriate *(adj.)* သင့်လျော်သော *tint-lyaw-taw*
appropriation *(n.)* လျာထားငွေ *lyar-htar-ngwe*
approval *(n.)* အတည်ပြုချက် *a-ti-pyu-chat*
approve *(v.)* အတည်ပြုသည် *a-ti-pyu-the*
approximate *(adj.)* ခန့်မှန်းခြေ *khant-man-chay*
approximately *(adv.)* ခန့်မှန်းခြေအားဖြင့် *khant-man-chay-arr-phyint*
apricot *(n.)* ဘင်္ဂလားဆီးသီး *bin-ga-lar-zee-thee*
April *(n.)* ဧပြီလ *a-pri-la*
apron *(n.)* ရှေ့ဖုံးခါးစည်း *shay-hpone-khar-see*
apt *(adj.)* ဆီလျော်သော *si-lyaw-taw*
aptitude *(n.)* ပင်ကိုစွမ်းရည် *pin-ko-swan-yay*
aptitude test *(n.)* ပင်ကိုစွမ်းရည်စစ်ဆေးခြင်း *pin-ko-swan-yay-sit-say-chin*
aquarium *(n.)* ငါးပြတိုက် *ngar-pya-tite*
aquarius *(n.)* ကုံရာသီဖွား *kone-yar-thi-phwar*
aquatic *(adj.)* ရေနေ၊ ရေပျော် *yay-nay, yay-pyaw*
aquatint *(n.)* အရောင်ပါရေ *a-yaung-par-yay*
aqueduct *(n.)* ရေသွယ်တံတား yay-thwe-ta-dar
Arab *(n.)* အာရပ် ar-yat
arable *(adj.)* သီးနှံဖြစ်ထွန်းသော *thee-nan-phit-htun-taw*
arbiter *(n.)* စီရင်ပိုင်သူ *si-yin-paing-thu*

arbitrary *(adj.)* **တစ်ဖက်သတ်** *ta-phat-tat*

arbitrate *(v.)* **ကြားဝင်စေ့စပ်ပေးသည်** kyar-win-say-sat-pay-the

arbitration *(n.)* **ခုံသမာဓိဖြင့်စီရင်ဆုံးဖြတ်ခြင်း** *khone-ta-mar-di-phint-see-yin-sone-phat-chin*

arbitrator *(n.)* **ခုံသမာဓိ** *khone-ta-mar-di*

arbour *(n.)* **ရုက္ခကွန်းသာ** *yoke-kha-kun-thar*

arc *(n.)* **စက်ဝန်းပြတ်** *sat-wun-phyat*

arcade *(n.)* **အမိုးခုံးပါရုံ** *a-moe-khone-par-yone*

arcane *(adj.)* **လျို့ဝှက်ဆန်းကြယ်သော** *shoe-wat-san-kyal-taw*

arch *(n.)* **အခုံး** *a-khone*

archaeologist *(n.)* **ရှေးဟောင်းသုသေတနပညာရှင်** *shay-haung-thu-tay-ta-na-pyin-nyar-shin*

archaeology *(n.)* **ရှေးဟောင်းသုသေတနပညာ** *shay-haung-thu-tay-ta-na-pyin-nyar*

archaic *(adj.)* **အလွန်ရှေးဆန်သော** *a-lun-shay-san-taw*

archbishop *(n.)* **ဂိုဏ်းချုပ်** *gaing-choke*

archer *(n.)* **မြားသမား** *myar-ta-mar*

archery *(n.)* **လေးအတတ်** *lay-a-tat*

architect *(n.)* **ဗိသုကာ** *bi-thu-kar*

architecture *(n.)* **ဗိသုကာပညာ** *bi-thu-kar-pyin-nyar*

archive *(n.)* **မော်ကွန်းတိုက်** *maw-khun-tite*

Arctic *(adj.)* **အာတိတ်ဒေသ** *ar-tate-day-ta*

ardent *(adj.)* **အလွန်တက်ကြွသော** *a-lun-tat-kwa-taw*

ardour *(n.)* **စိတ်ဇော** *seik-zaw*

arduous *(adj.)* **ခက်ခဲကြမ်းတမ်းသော** *khat-khae-kyan-tan-taw*

area *(n.)* **ဧရိယာ** *aye-ri-yar*

arena *(n.)* **အားကစားကွင်း** *ar-ka-sar-kwin*

argil *(n.)* **ရွှံ့** *shwunt*

arguable *(adj.)* **ငြင်းခုံဆွေးနွေးနိုင်သော** *nyin-khone-sway-nway-naing-taw*

argue *(v.)* **ငြင်းခုံဆွေးနွေးသည်** *nyin-khone-sway-nway-the*

argument *(n.)* **အငြင်းအခုံ** *a-nyin-a-khone*

arid *(adj.)* **ခြောက်သွေ့သော** *kyauk-tway-taw*

aries *(n.)* **မိဿရာသီဖွား** *meik-ta-yar-the-phwar*

aright *(adv.)* **မှန်ကန်စွာ** *man-kan-swar*

arise *(v.)* **ပေါ်လာသည်** *paw-lar-the*

aristocracy *(n.)* **မင်းမျိုးစိုးနွယ်** *min-myo-soe-nwe*

aristocrat *(n.)* **မင်းမျိုးစိုးနွယ်** *min-myo-soe-nwe*

arithmetic *(n.)* **ဂဏန်းသင်္ချာ** *ga-nan-tin-char*

ark *(n.)* **သမ္မာကျမ်းစာပါ လှေကြီး** *than-mar-kyan-sar-par-hlay-gyi*

arm *(n.)* **လက်မောင်း** *lat-maung*

armada *(n.)* **စစ်သင်္ဘောစု** *sit-tin-baw-su*

armament *(n.)* **လက်နက်ကြီးများ** *lat-nat-kyi-myar*

armature *(n.)* **ဒိုင်နမိုပတ်ကြေးကြိုးခွေ** *dai-na-mo-pat-kyay-kyoe-khway*

armchair *(n.)* **လက်တင်ကုလားထိုင်** *lat-tin-ka-la-htaing*

armed *(adj.)* **လက်နက်အသုံးပြုသော** *lat-nat-kyi-a-tone-pyu-taw*

armed forces *(n.)* **ကြည်းရေလေတပ်မတော်** *kyee-yay-lay-tat-ma-taw*

armhole *(n.)* **အင်္ကျီလက်ပေါက်** *inn-gyi-lat-pauk*

armistice *(n.)* စစ်ဆိုင်းကာလ *sit-saing-kar-la*
armlet *(adj.)* လက်ပတ် *lat-pat*
armour *(n.)* ချပ်ဝတ်တန်ဆာ *chat-wut-ta-sar*
armoury *(n.)* လက်နက်တိုက် *lat-nat-tite*
armpit *(n.)* ချိုင်းကြား *kyaing-gyar*
armrest *(n.)* လက်တင်အဖုံး *lat-tin-a-hpone*
army *(n.)* စစ်တပ် *sit-tat*
aroma *(n.)* ရနံ့ *ya-nant*
aromatherapy *(n.)* ရနံ့ကုထုံး *ya-nant-khu-htone*
around *(adv.&prep.)* ပတ်လည် *pat-lal*
arouse *(v.)* နှိုးကြွစေသည် *hnoe-kywa-say-the*
arrabbiata *(adj.)* အစပ်အချဉ်ရည် *a-sat-a-chin-yay*
arraign *(v.)* ရုံးတင်သည် *yone-tin-the*
arrange *(v.)* စီစဉ်သည် *si-zin-the*
arrangement *(n.)* အစီအစဉ် *a-si-a-sin*
arrant *(adj.)* ကမ်းကုန်အောင် ဆိုးဝါးသော *kan-kone-aung-soe-war-taw*
array *(n.)* စီစဉ်ခင်းကျင်းသည် *si-sin-khin-kyin-the*
arrears *(n.pl.)* ကြွေးကျန် *kyway-kyan*
arrest *(v.)* ဖမ်းစီးသည် *hpan-see-the*
arrival *(n.)* ရောက်ရှိခြင်း *yauk-shi-chin*
arrive *(v.)* ရောက်ရှိသည် *yauk-shi-the*
arrogance *(n.)* အထက်စီးဆန်ခြင်း *a-htet-see-san-chin*
arrogant *(adj.)* အထက်စီးဆန်သော *a-htet-see-san-taw*
arrow *(n.)* မြား *myar*
arrowroot *(n.)* အာဒါလွတ် *ar-dar-hlut*
arsenal *(n.)* လက်နက်တိုက် *lat-nat-tite*
arsenic *(n.)* စိန်အဆိပ် *sein-a-seik*
arson *(n.)* ရှို့မီး *shooet-mee*
art *(n.)* အနုပညာ *a-nu-pyin-nyar*
art direction *(n.)* အနုပညာဦးတည်ချက် *a-nu-pyin-nyar-oo-tee-chat*
art form *(n.)* အနုပညာရပ် *a-nu-pyin-nyar-yat*
artefact *(n.)* ရှေးလူ့အသုံးအဆောင်ပစ္စည်း *shay-lu-a-tone-a-saung-pyit-see*
artery *(n.)* သွေးလွှတ်ကြော *thway-hlut-kyaw*
artesian *(adj.)* အဝိစိ a-wi-si
artful *(adj.)* ဉာဏ်များသော *nyan-myar-taw*
arthritis *(n.)* အဆစ်ရောင်နာ a-sit-yaung-nar
artichoke *(n.)* ပဲပိုးတိ *pae-poe-ti*
article *(n.)* ဆောင်းပါး *saung-par*
articulate *(adj.)* ရှင်းလင်းစွာပြောဆိုနိုင်သော *shin-lin-swar-pyaw-so-naing-taw*
artifice *(n.)* စကားသံထုတ်မှု *sa-kar-tan-htoke-mu*
artificial *(adj.)* အတု *a-tu*
artificial intelligence *(n.)* အသိဉာဏ်အတု *a-ti-nyan-a-tu*
artillery *(n.)* အမြောက် *a-myauk*
artisan *(n.)* လက်မှုပညာ *lat-mu-pyin-nyar*
artist *(n.)* အနုပညာရှင် *a-nu-pyin-nyar-shin*
artistic *(adj.)* ရသကို ခံစားတတ်သော *ya-ta-ko-khan-sar-tat-taw*
artless *(adj.)* ဟန်ဆောင်မှု ကင်းသော *han-saung-mu-kin-taw*
as *(adv.)* ကဲ့သို့ *kae-tho*

asafoetida *(n.)* **ဆေးဘက်ဝင်အနံ့ဆိုးအစေး** *say-bat-win-a-nant-soe-a-say*
asbestos *(n.)* **ကျောက်ဂွမ်း** *kyauk-goon*
ascend *(v.)* **တက်သွားသည်** *tat-twar-the*
ascendancy *(n.)* **အထက်စီးရခြင်း** *a-htet-see-ya-chin*
ascent *(n.)* **တက်ခြင်း** *tat-chin*
ascertain *(v.)* **သေချာအောင် လေ့လာစိစစ်သည်** *tay-char-aung-lay-lar-si-sit-the*
ascetic *(n.)* **ခြိုးခြံသော အကျင့်ရှိသူ** choe-chan-taw-a-kyint-shi-thu
ascribe *(v.)* **အကြောင်းတရားအဖြစ် မှတ်ယူသည်** *a-kyaung-ta-yar-a-phit-mat-yu-the*
aseptic *(adj.)* **ပိုးမွှားကင်းသော** *poe-mwar-kin-thaw*
asexual *(adj.)* **လိင်မဲ့** lain-mae
ash *(n.)* **ပြာ** pyar
ashamed *(adj.)* **ရှက်သော** shat-taw
ashen *(adj.)* **ဖြူဖပ်ဖြူရော်** *phyu-phat-phyu-yaw*
ashore *(adv.)* **ကမ်းပေါ်သို့** *kan-paw-tho*
aside *(adv.)* **ဘေးဘက်တွင်** bay-bat-twin
asinine *(adj.)* **မိုက်မဲသော** *mite-mae-taw*
ask *(v.)* **မေးမြန်းသည်** may-myan-the
asleep *(adv.)* **အိပ်ပျော်နေသော** aik-pyaw-nay-taw
asparagus *(n.)* **ကညွတ်** *ka-nyut*
aspect *(n.)* **ကဏ္ဍ** *kan-da*
aspersion *(n.)* **ဂုဏ်သရေ ထိပါးသော စကား** *gon-tha-yay-hti-par-taw-sa-gar*
asphyxia *(n.)* **မွန်းခြင်း** *moon-chin*
asphyxiate *(v.)* **မွန်းစေသည်** *moon-say-the*
aspirant *(n.)* **အမြင့်မှန်းသူ** *a-myint-hman-thu*
aspiration *(n.)* **ပြင်းပြသော ဆန္ဒ** *pyin-pya-taw-san-da*
aspire *(v.)* **ဆန္ဒပြင်းပြသည်** *san-da-pyin-pya-the*
ass *(n.)* **လူနုံ** *lu-hnon*
assail *(v.)* **ပြင်းပြင်းထန်ထန် အကြိမ်ကြိမ် ရန်ပြုသည်** *pyin-pyin-htan-htan-a-kyein-kyein-yan-pyu-the*
assassin *(n.)* **လုပ်ကြံသူ** *lote-kyan-thu*
assassinate *(v.)* **လုပ်ကြံသည်** *lote-kyan-the*
assassination *(n.)* **လုပ်ကြံခြင်း** *lote-kyan-chin*
assault *(n.)* **ကိုယ်ထိလက်ရောက်ကျူးလွန်မှု** *ko-hti-lat-yauk-kyu-loon-mu*
assemble *(v.)* **စုဝေးသည်** *su-way-the*
assembly *(n.)* **စုဝေးပွဲ** su-way-pwe
assent *(n.)* **သဘောတူညီမှု** *ta-baw-thu-nyi-mu*
assert *(v.)* **အခိုင်အမာဆိုသည်** *a-khaing-a-mar-so-the*
assertive *(adj.)* **မိမိကိုယ်ကို ယုံကြည်လွန်းသော** *mi-mi-ko-ko-yone-kyi-loon-taw*
assess *(v.)* **အကဲဖြတ်သည်** *a-kae-phat-the*
assessment *(n.)* **အကဲဖြတ်ခြင်း** *a-kae-phat-chin*
asset *(n.)* **ကျွမ်းကျင်လိမ်မာမှု** *kywan-kyin-lain-mar-mu*
assibilate *(v.)* **အသံရှည်ဆုံးဖြင့် အသံထွက်သည်** a-tan-shay-sone-phint-a-tan-htwat-the
assign *(v.)* **တာဝန်ပေးသည်** tar-win-pay-the
assignee *(n.)* **တာဝန်ပေးခံရသူ** *tar-win-pay-khan-ya-thu*

assignment *(n.)* တာဝန်ပေးခြင်း *tar-win-pay-chin*
assimilate *(v.)* လက်ခံသည် lat-khan-the
assimilation *(n.)* လက်ခံခြင်း lat-khan-chin
assist *(v.)* ကူညီသည် *ku-nyi-the*
assistance *(n.)* အကူအညီ *a-ku-a-nyi*
assistant *(n.)* လက်ထောက် *lat-htauk*
associate *(v.)* ဆက်စပ်သည် *set-sat-the*
association *(n.)* အဖွဲ့အစည်း *a-phwe-a-see*
assort *(v.)* အမျိုးတူစုသည် *a-myo-thu-su-the*
assorted *(adj.)* အမည်တူအမျိုးစုံ *a-me-tu-a-myo-sone*
assortment *(n.)* အမျိုးမျိုးသော ပစ္စည်းစု *a-myo-myo-taw-pyit-see-su*
assuage *(v.)* သက်သာစေသည် *thet-tar-say-the*
assume *(v.)* ယူဆသည် *yu-sa-the*
assumption *(n.)* ယူဆချက် *yu-sa-chat*
assurance *(n.)* ယုံကြည်စိတ်ချမှု *yone-kyi-seik-cha-mu*
assure *(v.)* အခိုင်အမာဆိုသည် *a-khaing-a-mar-so-the*
astatic *(adj.)* မတည်ငြိမ်သော *ma-te-nyein-taw*
asterisk *(n.)* ခရေပွင့်သင်္ကေတ *kha-yay-pwint-tin-kay-ta*
asterism *(n.)* ခရေပွင့်သင်္ကေတအစု *kha-yay-pwint-tin-kay-ta-a-su*
asteroid *(v.)* ဂြိုလ်သိမ်ဂြိုလ်မွှား *gyo-thein-gyo-mwar*
asthma *(n.)* ပန်းနာ *pan-nar*
astigmatism *(n.)* မျက်စိဆုံချက်မညီခြင်း *myat-si-sone-chat-ma-nyi-chin*
astonish *(v.)* အလွန်အံ့အားသင့်စေသည် *a-lun-ant-arr-tint-say-the*
astonishment *(n.)* အလွန်အံ့သြခြင်း *a-lun-aunt-aw-chin*
astound *(v.)* မှင်တက်မိသည် *hmin-thet-mi-the*
astral *(adj.)* ကြယ်များနှင့် သက်ဆိုင်သော *Kyal-myar-nint-thet-saing-taw*
astray *(adv.)* သွေဖည်လျက် *thway-phal-lyat*
astride *(prep.& adv.)* ခွလျက် *khwa-lyat*
astringent *(adj.)* မညာတာသော *ma-hnyar-tar-taw*
astrolabe *(n.)* ဂြိုလ်၊ ကြယ်တိုင်းကိရိယာ *gyo-kyal-tine-ka-ri-yar*
astrologer *(n.)* နက္ခဗေဒင်ဆရာ *nat-khat-bay-din-sa-yar*
astrology *(n.)* နက္ခဗေဒင် *nat-khat-bay-din*
astronaut *(n.)* အာကာသယဉ်မှူး *arr-kar-ta-yin-hmu*
astronomer *(n.)* နက္ခတ္တဗေဒပညာရှင် *nat-khat-ta-pyin-nyar-shin*
astronomy *(n.)* နက္ခတ္တဗေဒ *nat-khat-ta-bay-da*
astute *(adj.)* လာဘ်မြင်သော *lat-myin-taw*
asylum *(n.)* ခိုလှုံခွင့် *kho-hlon-kwint*
asymmetrical *(adj.)* အချိုးမညီသော *a-choe-ma-nyi-taw*
asymmetry *(n.)* အချိုးမညီခြင်း *a-choe-ma-nyi-chin*
at *(prep.)* မှာ၊ တွင် *mar, twin*
atheism *(n.)* ဘုရားမဲ့ဝါဒ *phar-yar-mae-wa-da*
atheist *(n.)* ဘုရားမဲ့ဝါဒီ *phar-yar-mae-wa-di*
athirst *(adj.)* စိတ်ဆန္ဒပြင်းပြသော *seik san-da-pyin-pya-taw*
athlete *(n.)* အားကစားသမား *arr-ka-sar-ta-mar*

athletic *(adj.)* **န်းမာကြံ့ခိုင်ဖျတ်လတ်သော** *kyan-mar-kyant-khaing-phyat-lat-taw*
athwart *(prep.)* **တစ်ဖက်တွင်** *ta-phat-twin*
atlas *(n.)* **မြေပုံစာအုပ်** *myay-bone-sar-oak*
atmosphere *(n.)* **လေထု** *lay-htu*
atmospheric *(adj.)* **လေထုနှင့်ဆိုင်သော** *lay-htu-nint-saing-taw*
atoll *(n.)* **သန္တာကျောက်ကျွန်း** *tan-dar-kyauk-kyun*
atom *(n.)* **အက်တမ်** *at-tan*
atomic *(adj.)* **အဏုမြူ** *a-nu-my*
atone *(v.)* **အပြစ်ပြေအောင်ပြုလုပ်သည်** *a-pyit-pyay-aung-pyu-lot-the*
atonement *(n.)* **အပြစ်ပြောအောင်ပြုလုပ်ခြင်း** *a-pyit-pyay-aung-pyu-lot-chin*
atopic *(adj.)* **ထိပ်ဖျားတွင်ဖြစ်သော** *hteik-phyar-twin-phit-taw*
atrium *(n.)* **သွေးလွှတ်ခန်း** *thway-hlut-khan*
atrocious *(adj.)* **အလွန်ကြမ်းကြုတ်သော** *a-lun-kyan-kyoke-taw*
atrocity *(n.)* **ယုတ်မာသော လုပ်ရပ်** *yote-mar-taw-lote-yatt*
atrophy *(v.)* **သိမ်သွားခြင်း** *thein-twar-chin*
attach *(v.)* **ပူးတွဲသည်** *pu-twal-the*
attache *(n.)* **သံမှူး** tan-muu
attachment *(n.)* **သံယောဇဉ်** tan-yaw-zin
attack *(v.)* **တိုက်ခိုက်သည်** tite-khaik-the
attain *(v.)* **ကြိုးပန်းရရှိသည်** *kyo-pan-ya-shi-the*
attainment *(n.)* **အောင်မြင်စွာ ရယူနိုင်ခြင်း** *aung-myin-swar-ra-yu-naing-chin*
attaint *(v.)* **အောင်မြင် ရရှိသည်** aung-myin-ya-shi-the
attempt *(v.)* **ကြိုးစားသည်** kyo-sar-the
attend *(v.)* **တက်ရောက်သည်** tat-yauk-the
attendance *(n.)* **တက်ရောက်သူဦးရေ** tat-yauk-thu-oo-yay
attendant *(n.)* **အစောင့်** a-saunt
attention *(n.)* **အာရုံစိုက်ခြင်း** *ar-yone-seik-chin*
attentive *(adj.)* **အာရုံစိုက်သော** *ar-yone-seik-taw*
attenuance *(n.)* **ဆုံးရှုံးခြင်းအပါအဝင် စုပ်ယူခြင်း** *sone-shone-chin-a-par-a-win-sote-yu-chin*
attest *(v.)* **သက်သေပြုသည်** thet-tay-pyu-the
attic *(n.)* **အမိုးအောက်ထပ်ခိုး** a-moe-aut-htet-kho
attire *(n.)* **အဝတ်အစား** *a-wut-a-sar*
attitude *(n.)* **သဘောထား** ta-baw-htar
attorney *(n.)* **ရှေ့နေ** *shay-nay*
attract *(v.)* **ဆွဲဆောင်သည်** *swal-saung-the*
attraction *(n.)* **ဆွဲဆောင်ခြင်း** *swal-saung-chin*
attractive *(adj.)* **ဆွဲဆောင်မှုရှိသော** *swal-saung-mu-shi-taw*
attribute *(v.)* **မှတ်ယူသည်** *mat-yu-the*
atypic *(adj.)* **ပုံမှန်မဟုတ်သော** pone-man-ma-hote-taw
aubergine *(n.)* **ခရမ်းသီး** kha-yan-thee
auburn *(adj.)* **နီညိုရောင်** *ni-nyo-yaung*
auction *(n.)* **လေလံပွဲ** *lay-lan-pwe*
audacious *(adj.)* **ရဲတင်းသော** *ye-tin-taw*
audacity *(n.)* **ရဲတင်းမှု** *ye-tin-mu*
audible *(adj.)* **ကြားနိုင်သော** *kyar-naing-taw*
audience *(n.)* **ပရိသတ်** *pa-yeik-tat*
audio *(n.)* **အသံ** *a-tan*

audiovisual *(adj.)* ရုပ်သံဆိုင်ရာ *yoke-than-saing-yar*

audit *(n.)* စာရင်းစစ် *sa-yin-sit*

audition *(n.)* စမ်းသပ်ကြည့်ရှုခြင်း *san-that-kyi-shu-chin*

auditive *(adj.)* အကြားစွမ်းရည်အဓိကဖြင့်သင်ယူနိုင်သော သူ *a-kyar-swan-yay-a-di-ka-phint-tin-yu-naing-taw-thu*

auditor *(n.)* စာရင်းစစ် sa-yin-sit

auditorium *(n.)* ဇာတ်ရုံတွင်ပရိတ်သတ်ထိုင်ရာနေရာ zat-yone-twin-pa-yeik-thet-htaing-yar-nay-yar

auger *(n.)* လွန်စူး lun-sue

aught *(n.)* မည်သည့်အရာမဆို me-the-a-yar-ma-so

augment *(v.)* တိုးပွားစေသည် toe-pwar-say-the

augmentation *(n.)* တိုးပွားစေခြင်း *toe-pwar-say-chin*

august *(adj.)* ကြီးကျယ်ခမ်းနားလေးစားဖွယ်ဖြစ်သော *kyi-kyal-khan-nar-lay-sar-phwal-phit-taw*

aunt *(n.)* အန်တီ *an-ti*

aura *(n.)* ရောင်ဝါလက္ခဏာ *yaung-war-lat-kha-nar*

auriform *(adj.)* နားကဲ့သို့ ပုံတူသော *nar-kae-tho-pone-thu-taw*

aurilave *(n.)* နားဖာကလော် *na-phar-ka-lar*

aurora *(n.)* မိုးသောက်ပန်း *moe-taut-pan*

auspicate *(v.)* မင်္ဂလာစကားပြောသည် *min-ga-lar-sa-gar-pyaw-the*

auspice *(n.)* ဦးဆောင်၍ oo-saung-ywe

auspicious *(adj.)* မင်္ဂလာရှိသော *min-ga-lar-shi-taw*

austere *(adj.)* အကျင့်ခြိုးခြံသော *a-kyint-choe-chan-taw*

authentic *(adj.)* စစ်မှန်သော *sit-man-taw*

authenticate *(v.)* စစ်မှန်ကြောင်းသက်သေပြသည် sit-man-kyaung-thet-tay-pya-the

authentication *(n.)* စစ်မှန်ကြောင်းသက်သေပြခြင်း *sit-man-kyaung-thet-tay-pya-chin*

author *(n.)* စာရေးသူ *sar-yay-thu*

authoritative *(adj.)* ခိုင်လုံသော *khaing-lon-taw*

authority *(n.)* လုပ်ပိုင်ခွင့် lote-paing-kwint

authorize *(v.)* လုပ်ပိုင်ခွင့်လွှဲအပ်သည် *lote-paing-kwint-hlwal-at-the*

autism *(n.)* ဆက်သွယ်တုံ့ပြန်မှုနှေးရောဂါ *sat-thwal-tont-pyan-mu-hnay-yaw-gar*

autistic *(adj.)* ဆက်သွယ်တုံ့ပြန်မှုနှေးရောဂါရှိသူ *sat-thwal-tont-pyan-mu-hnay-yaw-gar-shi-thu*

autobiography *(n.)* ကိုယ်တိုင်ရေးအတ္ထုပ္ပတ္တိ *ko-taing-yay-at-htoke-pat-ti*

autocorrect *(n.)* အလိုအလျောက်ပြင်ဆင်ခြင်း *a-lo-a-lyaut-pyin-sin-chin*

autocracy *(n.)* သက်ဦးဆံပိုင်စနစ် *thet-oo-san-paing-sa-nit*

autocrat *(n.)* သက်ဦးဆံပိုင်မင်း *thet-oo-san-paing-sa-min*

autocratic *(adj.)* သက်ဦးဆံပိုင်အုပ်ချုပ်သော *thet-oo-san-paing-oat-choke-taw*

autofocus *(n.)* အလိုအလျောက်ဆုံချက်ချိန်ညှိခြင်း *a-lo-a-lyaut-sone-chat-chein-nyi-chin*

autograph *(n.)* အမှတ်တရလက်မှတ် *a-mat-ta-ya-lat-mat*

automate *(v.)* လူအစားစက်ကိုအစားထိုးသုံးသည် *lu-a-sar-sat-ko-a-sar-htoe-tone-the*

automatic *(adj.)* အလိုအလျောက် *a-lo-a-lyaut*

automatically *(adv.)* **အလိုအလျောက်** *a-lo-a-lyaut*

automation *(n.)* **အလိုအလျောက်လုပ်စက်ကိရိယာသုံးခြင်း** *a-lo-a-lyaut-lote-sat-ka-yi-yar-tone-chin*

automobile *(n.)* **မော်တော်ကား** *maw-taw-kar*

autonomous *(adj.)* **ကိုယ်ပိုင်အုပ်ချုပ်ခွင့်ရှိသော** *ko-paing-oat-choke-kwint-shi-taw*

autopilot *(n.)* **အလိုအလျောက်လေယာဉ်မောင်းခြင်း** *a-lo-a-lyaut-lay-yin-maung-chin*

autopsy *(n.)* **အလောင်းကို ခွဲစိတ်စစ်ဆေးခြင်း** *a-laung-ko-kwal-seik-sit-say-chin*

autumn *(n.)* **ဆောင်းဦးရာသီ** *saung-oo-yar-thi*

auxiliary *(adj.)* **အကူ** *a-khu*

avail *(v.)* **အသုံးချသည်** *a-tone-cha-the*

available *(adj.)* **ရနိုင်သော** *ya-naing-taw*

avalanche *(n.)* **ကြီးမားသော နှင်းခဲ** *kyi-mar-taw-hnin-khae*

avarice *(n.)* **မတော်လောဘ** *ma-taw-law-ba*

avenge *(v.)* **ဒဏ်ခတ်သည်** *dan-khat-the*

avenue *(n.)* **ရိပ်သာလမ်း** *yeik-tar-lan*

average *(n.)* **ပျမ်းမျှ** *pyin-mya*

averse *(adj.)* **ငြင်းပယ်သော** *nyin-pal-taw*

aversion *(n.)* **မနှစ်သက်ခြင်း** *ma-hnit-thet-chin*

avert *(v.)* **မျက်နှာလွှဲသည်** *myat-nar-hlwal-the*

aviary *(n.)* **ငှက်ရုံ** ngyat-yone

aviation *(n.)* **လေယာဉ်မောင်းအတတ်** lay-yin-maung-a-tat

avid *(adj.)* **စိတ်အားထက်သန်သော** seik-arr-htet-tan-taw

avidly *(adv.)* **စိတ်အားထက်သန်စွာ** seik-arr-htet-tan-swar

avocado *(n.)* **ထောပတ်သီး** *htaw-pat-thi*

avoid *(v.)* **ရှောင်သည်** *shaung-the*

avoidance *(n.)* **ရှောင်ခြင်း** *shaung-chin*

avow *(v.)* **အတိအလင်းဝန်ခံသည်** a-ti-a-lin-win-khan-the

avulsion *(n.)* **အသားလှန်ခြင်း** *a-thar-hlan-chin*

await *(v.)* **စောင့်မျှော်သည်** *saung-myaw-the*

awake *(v.)* **နိုးသည်** *noe-the*

awakening *(n.)* **သတိပြုမိခြင်း** *tha-di-pyu-mi-chin*

award *(n.)* **ဆု** hsu

aware *(adj.)* **သတိပြုမိသော** *tha-di-pyu-mi-taw*

awareness *(n.)* **အသိရှိခြင်း** *a-thi-shi-chin*

away *(adv.)* **အဝေး** a-way

awesome *(adj.)* **အံ့ဩဖွယ်** *aunt-aw-phwal*

awful *(adj.)* **အလွန်အမင်းဆိုးရွားသော** *a-lun-a-min-soe-ywar-taw*

awhile *(adv.)* **ခဏတ္တ** *khit-ta*

awkward *(adj.)* **အချိုးမကျသော** *a-choe-ma-kya-taw*

axe *(n.)* **ပုဆိန်** *pa-sein*

axial *(adj.)* **ဝန်ရိုးကျသော** wun-yoe-kya-taw

axillary *(adj.)* **အကူ** *a-khu*

axis *(n.)* **ဝင်ရိုး** *win-yoe*

axle *(n.)* **ဝင်ရိုး** *win-yoe*

Ayurveda *(n.)* **အာယုဗေဒဆေးပညာ** *ar-yu-bay-da-say-pyin=nyar*

azote *(n.)* **အစုဓာတ်ငွေ့** *a-zu-dat-ngwe*

azure *(n.)* **မိုးပြာရောင်** *moe-pyar-yaung*

B

babble *(n.)* ဗလုံးဗထွေးစကားသံ *Ba-lone-ba-htway-sa-kar-tan*
babble *(v.)* ဗလုံးဗထွေးပြောသည် *ba-lone-ba-htway-pyaw-the*
babe *(n.)* ကလေးငယ် *ka-lay-nge*
babel *(n.)* လူသံဆူညံနေသော နေရာ *lu-tan-su-nyan-nay-taw-nay-yar*
baboon *(n.)* ဘာဘွန်းမျောက် *bar-boon-myaut*
baby *(n.)* ကလေးငယ် *ka-lay-nge*
baby bump *(n.)* ဗိုက်စထွက်လာခြင်း *bite-sa-htwat-lar-chin*
baby carriage *(n.)* ကလေးလက်တွန်းလှည်း *ka-lay-lat-toon-lal*
baby corn *(n.)* ပြောင်းအသေး *pyaung-a-thay*
baby food *(n.)* ကလေးအစားအသောက် *ka-lay-a-sar-a-taut*
babyface *(n.)* ကလေးမျက်နှာ *ka-lay-myat-nyar*
babyproof *(adj.)* ကလေးများအတွက် ထိတွေ့ရန်လုံခြုံအောင်ပြုလုပ်ပေးထားသော *ka-lay-myar-a-thwat-hti-tway-yan-lon-chon-aung-pyu-lote-pay-htar-taw*
babysit *(v.)* မိဘအပြင်သွားခိုက်ကလေးကြည့်ပေးသည် *mi-ba-a-pyin-twar-khite-ka-lay-kyi-pay-the*
babysitting *(n.)* မိဘအပြင်သွားခိုက်ကလေးကြည့်ပေးခြင်း *mi-ba-a-pyin-twar-khite-ka-lay-kyi-pay-chin*
baccalaureate *(n.)* အခြေခံပညာအဆင့် နောက်ဆုံးစာမေးပွဲ *a-chay-khan-pyin-nyar-a-sint-naut-sone-sar-may-pwe*
bacchanal *(adj.)* ဘတ်ကတ်နှင့် က်ဆိုင်သော *bat-kat-nint-tat-sai-taw*
bachelor *(n.)* လူပျို၊ တက္ကသိုလ် ပထမဘွဲ့ *lu-pyo, tat-ka-do-pa-hta-ma-bwe*
bachelor party *(n.)* လူပျိုချွတ်ပါတီ *lu-pyo-chut-par-ti*
bachelorette *(n.)* လက်မထက်ရသေးသော မိန်းမငယ် *lat-ma-htet-ya-tay-taw-mein-ma-nge*
back *(n.)* နောက်ကျော *naut-kyaw*
backbencher *(n.)* ပါလီမန်အမတ် *par-li-man-a-mat*
backbiting *(n.)* အတင်းချခြင်း *a-tin-cha-chin*
backbone *(n.)* ကျောရိုး *kyaw-yoe*
backdate *(v.)* နောက်ကြောင်းပြန်ရက်စွဲတပ်သည် *naut-kyaung-pyan-yat-swal-tat-the*
backdrop *(v.)* နောက်ခံဖြစ်ရပ် *naut-khan-phit-yat*
backfire *(v.)* အိတ်ဇောပေါက်သည် *ait-zaw-paut-the*
background *(n.)* နောက်ခံအကြောင်း *naut-khan-a-kyaung*
backhand *(n.)* လက်ပြန် *lat-pyan*
backing *(n.)* အထောက်အပံ့ *a-htaut-a-pant*
backlash *(n.)* လူမှုရေး၊ နိုင်ငံရေးကိစ္စရပ်များအပေါ် လူအများ၏ တုံ့ပြန်ချက် lu-mu-yay, nai-ngan-yay-kait-sa-yat-myar-a-paw-lu-a-myar-ei-tont-pyan-chat
backlight *(n.)* နောက်မှ မီးထိုးခြင်း *naut-ma-mee-htoe-chin*
backlog *(n.)* အလုပ်ကြွေး *a-lote-kyway*
backpack *(n.)* ကျောပိုးအိတ်ကြီး *kyaw-poe-aik-kyi*

backpacker *(n.)* ကျောပိုးအိတ်ဖြင့် ခရီးထွက်သူ *kyaw-poe-aik-phit-kha-yee-htwat-thu*
backslide *(v.)* အခြေအနေကောင်းလာပြီးမှ ဒုံရင်းအတိုင်း ပြန်ဖြစ်ခြင်း *a-chay-a-nay-kaung-lar-pee-ma-don-yin-a-tine-pyan-phyit-chin*
backstage *(adv.)* ဇာတ်စင်နောက်သို့ zat-sin-naut-tho
backstairs *(n.)* အိမ်နောက်ဘက် လှေကား eain-naut-bat-hlay-kar
backtrack *(v.)* လာလမ်းအတိုင်းပြန်သည် lar-lan-a-tine-pyan-the
backup *(n.)* အရန်၊ အကူအညီ *a-yan, a-khu-a-nyi*
backward *(adj.)* နောက်ပြန် *naut-pyan*
backwash *(n.)* ဂယက် *ga-yat*
bacon *(n.)* ဝက်ဆားနယ်ခြောက် *wat-sar-nal-chyauk*
bacteria *(n.)* ဗက်တီးရီးယားပိုး *bat-tee-yee-yar-poe*
bad *(adj.)* ဆိုးသော *soe-taw*
badge *(n.)* တံဆိပ် *ta-seik*
badger *(n.)* ခွေးတူဝက်တူ *khway-tu-wat-tu*
badly *(adv.)* ဆိုးဝါးစွာ *soe-war-swar*
badminton *(n.)* ကြက်တောင် kyat-taung
baffle *(v.)* ခေါင်းခြောက်စေသည် *gaung-chyauk-say-the*
bag *(n.)* အိတ် *aik*
bag *(v.)* အိတ်ထဲ ထည့်သည် aik-htae-htae-teh
bagel *(n.)* ပေါင်မုန့်အကွင်း *paung-mont-a-kwin*
baggage *(n.)* အထုတ်အပိုး *a-htoke-a-poe*
bagpiper *(n.)* အိတ်ပလွေမှုတ်သမား *aik-pa-lway-hmote-ta-mar*
baguette *(n.)* ပေါင်မုန့်ရှည် *paung-hmont-shay*
bail *(n.)* အာမခံငွေ *ar-ma-khan-ngwe*
bailable *(adj.)* အာမခံငွေထုတ်ရန် သတ်မှတ်ချက်ပြည့်မီသော *ar-ma-khan-ngwe-htoke-yan-tat-mat-chat-pyae-mi-taw*
bailey *(n.)* အပြင်ဘက်ဆုံးနံရံ *a-pyin-bat-sone-nan-yan*
bailiff *(n.)* တရားရုံးပစ္စည်းထိန်းစာရေး *ta-yar-yone-pyit-see-htein-sar-yay*
bailout *(n.)* လဲပြိုလုလုကုမ္ပဏီကို ငွေကြေးအကူအညီပေးခြင်း *lal-pyo-lu-lu-com-pa-nee-ko-ngwe-kyay-a-khu-a-nyi-pay-chin*
bait *(n.)* တည်ကြက် *the-kyat*
bake *(v.)* ဖုတ်သည် *hpoke-the*
baker *(n.)* ပေါင်မုန့်ဖုတ်သူ *paung-mont-hpoke-thu*
bakery *(n.)* မုန့်တိုက် *mont-tite*
balaclava *(n.)* သိုးမွှေးခေါင်းစွပ် thoe-hmway-gaung-sut
balafon *(n.)* ပတ္တလားကြီး pat-ta-lar-kyi
balance *(n.)* လက်ကျန်ငွေ၊ နှစ်ဖက်ညီမျှမှု *lat-kyan-ngwe, na-phat-nyi-hmya-hmu*
balance sheet *(n.)* ငွေလက်ကျန်ရှင်းတမ်း *ngwe-lat-kyan-shin-tan*
balanced *(adj.)* မျှတသော *hmya-ta-taw*
balcony *(n.)* လသာဆောင် *la-thar-saung*
bald *(adj.)* ထိပ်ပြောင်သော *hteik-pyaung-taw*
bale *(n.)* ဘေထုပ် *bay-htoke*
baleen *(n.)* ဝေလငါး၏ အထက်မေးရိုးမှ ရသော အရိုးကဲ့သို့ အမျှင် *way-la-ngar-ei-a-htet-may-yoe-ma-ya-taw-a-yoe-kae-doe-a-hmyin*
ball *(n.)* ဘောလုံး *baw-lone*

ball bearing *(n.)* ဘောဘယ်ယာရင် *baw-bal-yar-yin*
ballad *(n.)* ဇာတ်လမ်းကဗျာ *zat-lan-la-byar*
ballerina *(n.)* ဘဲလေးကချေသည် *bal-lay-ka-chay-the*
ballet *(n.)* ဘဲလေးအက *bal-lay-a-ka*
ballistics *(n.)* ဒုံး၊ ကျည်စသည့် ပစ်လွှတ်ရသည်တို့ကို လေ့လာသည့် ပညာ *doon-kyi-sa-the-pyit-hlut-ya-the-doe-ko-lay-lar-the-pyin-nyar*
balloon *(n.)* ပူဖောင်း *buu-hpaung*
ballot *(n.)* လျှို့ဝှက်မဲပေးစနစ် *Hlyoe-hwat-mae-pay-sa-nit*
ballot paper *(n.)* ဆန္ဒမဲပေးလွှာ san-da-mae-pay-hlwar
ballroom *(n.)* ကပွဲခန်းမ ka-pwe-khan-ma
balm *(n.)* ဆေးဖက်ဝင်ဆီမွှေး *say-phat-win-si-hmway*
balsam *(n.)* ဒန်းတလက် *dan-ta-lat*
bamboo *(n.)* ဝါး *war*
ban *(v.)* ပိတ်ပင်သည် *pait-pin-the*
banal *(adj.)* ရိုးသော *yoe-taw*
banana *(n.)* ငှက်ပျောသီး *hnyat-pyaw-thee*
band *(n.)* တီးဝိုင်း၊ သိုင်းကြိုး၊ အကွင်း *tee-wine, taing-kyo, a-kwin*
bandage *(n.)* ပတ်တီး pat-thee
Band-Aid *(n.)* ဆေးပလတ်စတာ *say-pa-lat-sa-tar*
bandana *(n.)* လည်သိုင်း အရောင်တောက် လက်ကိုင်ပဝါ *lal-thaing-a-yaung-taut-lat-kaing-pa-war*
bandit *(n.)* ဓားပြ *dar-pya*
bandwagon *(n.)* ရေပန်းစားနေသော အလုပ် *yay-pan-sar-nay-taw-a-lote*
bandwidth *(n.)* ကွန်ရက်မြန်နှုန်း *kun-yat-myan-hnone*
bane *(n.)* ပြဿနာ *pyat-ta-nar*
bang *(n.)* အုန်းခနဲ မြည်အောင် ထုရိုက်သည် ohn-kha-nal-me-aung-htu-yite-the
bangle *(n.)* လက်ကောက်၊ ခြေချင်း *lat-kauk, chay-chin*
banish *(v.)* ပြည်နှင်ဒဏ်ပေးသည် *pyi-hnin-dan-pay-the*
banishment *(n.)* ပြည်နှင်ဒဏ်ပေးခြင်း *pyi-hnin-dan-pay-chin*
banjo *(n.)* ဘင်ဂျို *bin-gyo*
bank *(v.)* ငွေအပ်သည် *ngwe-at-the*
bank holiday *(n.)* ဘဏ်ပိတ်ရက် *ban-pait-yat*
banker *(n.)* ဘဏ်လုပ်ငန်းရှင် ban-lote-ngan-shin
banknote *(n.)* ငွေစက္ကူ *ngwe-sat-khu*
bankrupt *(adj.)* အကြွေးမဆပ်နိုင်သော *a-kyway-ma-sat-naing-taw*
bankruptcy *(n.)* ဒေဝါလီခံရခြင်း *day-war-li-khan-ya-chin*
banner *(n.)* နဖူးစည်းစာတန်း *na-hpoo-see-sar-tan*
bannister *(n.)* လှေကားလက်ရန်း *hlay-kar-lat-yan*
banquet *(n.)* ဂုဏ်ပြုထမင်းစားပွဲ *gon-pyu-hta-min-sar-pwe*
bantam *(n.)* ကြက်တိန်ညင် *kyat-tain-nyin*
banter *(n.)* ကျီစယ်စကား *kyi-sal-sa-kar*
bantling *(n.)* ကလေးငယ် *ka-lay-nge*
banyan *(n.)* ညောင်မုတ်ဆိတ် *nyaung-mote-seik*
baptism *(n.)* ရေဖျန်းခြင်းမင်္ဂလာ *yay-phyan-min-ga-lar*
baptize *(v.)* ရေဖျန်းခြင်းမင်္ဂလာပြု၍ ခရစ်ယာန်ဖြစ်စေသည် *yay-phyan-min-ga-lar-ywe-kha-yit-yan-phit-say-the*

bar *(n.)* **အဖျော်ယမကာကောင်တာ** *a-phyaw-ya-ma-kar-kaung-tar*
barb *(n.)* **မခံချိမခံသာစကား၊ ဆူးထစ်** *a-khan-chi-ma-khan-tar-sa-kar, sue-htit*
barbarian *(n.)* **အရိုင်းအစိုင်း** a-yai-a-sai
barbaric *(adj.)* **ရိုင်းစိုင်းသော** yai-sai-taw
barbarism *(n.)* **အရိုင်းအစိုင်းဘဝ** a-yai-a-sai-ba-wa
barbarity *(n.)* **ရက်စက်မှု** yat-sat-hmu
barbarous *(adj.)* **ရိုင်းပျသော** *yaing-pya-taw*
barbecue *(n.)* **အသားကင်** *a-tar-kin*
barbed *(adj.)* **ဆူးထစ်ပါသော၊ နာကြည်းစေသော** *sue-htit-par-taw, nar-kyi-say-taw*
barbed wire *(n.)* **သံဆူးကြိုး** tan-sue-kyo
barber *(n.)* **ဆံပင်ညှပ်သမား** san-pin-nyat-ta-mar
barcode *(n.)* **ဘားကုတ်** bar-cote
bard *(n.)* **ကဗျာစာဆို** *ka-byar-sar-so*
bare *(adj.)* **တုံးလုံး၊ ဗလာ** *tone-lone, ba-lar*
barefoot *(adj.)* **ခြေဗလာ** *khyay-ba-lar*
barely *(adv.)* **ရုံမျှသာ** *yone-mya-tar*
bargain *(n.)* **အပေးအယူ** *a-pay-a-yu*
barge *(n.)* **ဖောင်တော်** *hpaung-taw*
baritone *(n.)* **အသံအော** *a-tan-aw*
barium *(n.)* **ဗေရီယမ်ဒြပ်စင်** *bay-yee-yan-drat-sin*
bark *(n.)* **သစ်ခေါက်၊ ဟောင်သံ** *tit-khaut, haung-tan*
barley *(n.)* **မုယောစပါး** *mu-yaw-sa-par*
barman *(n.)* **စားပွဲထိုး** *sa-pwe-htoe*
barn *(n.)* **ကျီ** *kyi*
barnacle *(n.)* **ခရင်းကောင်** *kha-yin-kaung*
barometer *(n.)* **လေဖိအားတိုင်းကိရိယာ** *lay-hpi-arr-taing-ka-yi-yar*
baron *(n.)* **မှူးမတ်** *hmue-mat*
baroness *(n.)* **မှူးမတ်ကတော်** *hmue-mat-ka-taw*
baroque *(adj.)* **ဆန်းကြယ်သော အနုပညာလက်ရာ** *san-kyal-taw-a-nu-pyin-nyar-lat-yar*
barouche *(n.)* **မြင်းလှည်း** *myin-hlae*
barrack *(n.)* **ကန့်ကွက်သည်** *kant-kwat-the*
barrage *(n.)* **တရစပ်ပစ်ခတ်ခြင်း၊ မေးခြင်း** *ta-ya-sat-pyit-khat-chin, may-chin*
barrel *(n.)* **စည်ပိုင်း** *si-pai*
barren *(adj.)* **ကျတ်တီးမြေ** *kyat-tee-myay*
barricade *(n.)* **အတားအဆီး** *a-tar-a-see*
barrier *(n.)* **အတားအဆီး** *a-tar-a-see*
barring *(prep.)* **မှတစ်ပါး** *hma-ta-par*
barrister *(n.)* **ဝတ်လုံတော်ရ ရှေ့နေ** *wit-lone-taw-ya-shay-nay*
bartender *(n.)* **လက်တွန်းလှည်း** *lat-ton-lal*
barter *(v.)* **ကုန်ချင်းဖလှယ်သည်** kon-chin-hpa-hlal-the
basal *(adj.)* **အောက်ခြေ** aut-chay
base *(n.)* **အောက်ခံ** aut-khan
base camp *(n.)* **ဌာနချုပ်စခန်း** htar-na-chote-sa-khan
baseless *(adj.)* **အခြေအမြစ်မရှိသော** *a-chay-a-myit-ma-shi-taw*
basement *(n.)* **မြေအောက်ခန်း** *myay-aut-khan*
bash *(n.)* **ထုနှက်ချက်** htu-hnat-chat
bashful *(adj.)* **ရှက်သော** *shat-taw*
basic *(adj.)* **အခြေခံ** *a-chay-khan*
basically *(adv.)* **အခြေခံအားဖြင့်** *a-chay-khan-arr-phyit*

basil *(n.)* ပင်စိမ်း *pin-sein*

basin *(n.)* ဇလုံ *za-lon*

basis *(n.)* အခြေခံအကြောင်းရင်း *a-chay-khan-a-kyaung-yin*

bask *(v.)* နေပူဆာလှုံသည် *nay-pu-sar-hlon-the*

basket *(n.)* တောင်း taung

basketball *(n.)* ဘတ်စကက်ဘော bat-sa-kat-baw

bass *(n.)* ဘေ့စ်သံ *bae-tan*

bastard *(n.)* အယုတ်တမာကောင် a-yote-ta-mar-kaung

bastion *(n.)* ခုခံကာကွယ်ပေးသူ *khu-khan-kar-kwal-pay-thu*

bat *(n.)* ဘတ်တံ bat-tan

batch *(n.)* အစုအတွဲ a-su-a-twe

bath *(n.)* ရေချိုးခြင်း *yay-choe-chin*

bathe *(v.)* ရေချိုးသည် yay-choe-the

bathrobe *(n.)* ရေသုတ်ကုတ်အင်္ကျီ yay-tote-coat-inn-gyi

baton *(n.)* အချက်ပြတုတ်တံ *a-chat-pya-dote-tan*

batsman *(n.)* ရိုက်လှည့်ကျသူ *yite-hlae-mya-thu*

battalion *(n.)* တပ်ရင်း *tat-yin*

batten *(n.)* ဇလီ *za-li*

batter *(n.)* ဂျုံမှုန့်၊ ကြက်ဥ၊ နို့ရည်ရောထားသော အနှစ် *gyon-mont-kyat-au-noe-yae-yaw-htar-taw-a-hnit*

battery *(n.)* ဘက်ထရီ bat-hta-yee

battle *(n.)* တိုက်ပွဲ tite-pwe

battlefield *(n.)* စစ်မြေပြင် sit-myay-pyin

battlefront *(n.)* ရှေ့တန်းစစ်မြေပြင် shay-tan-sit-myay-pyin

baulk *(n.)* တုံ့ဆိုင်းသည် *tont-sai-the*

bawl *(v.)* ကုန်းအော်သည် *kone-aw-the*

bay *(n.)* ပင်လယ်အော် *pin-lal-aw*

bayonet *(n.)* လှံစွပ် *hlan-sut*

bayside *(adj.)* ပင်လယ်ကမ်းခြေ *pan-lal-kan-chay*

bazaar *(n.)* ဈေး *zay*

bazooka *(n.)* ဘဇူကာဒုံးလောင်ချာ *ba-zu-kar-don-laung-char*

be *(v.)* ရှိသည်၊ ဖြစ်သည် *shi-the, phit-the*

beach *(n.)* *ကမ်းခြေ* kan-chay

beach ball *(n.)* *ကမ်းခြေတွင် ကစားရန် ရောင်စုံဘောလုံး* kan-chay-twin-ka-sar-yan-yaung-son-baw-lone

beachfront *(adj.)* *ကမ်းခြေရှေ့* kan-chay-shay

beachside *(adj.)* *ကမ်းခြေဘေး* kan-chay-bay

beacon *(n.)* *အချက်ပြမီး၊ မီးပြတိုက်* a-chat-pya-mee, mee-pya-tite

bead *(n.)* *ပုတီးစေ့* pa-tee-say

beadle *(n.)* ဘုရားကျောင်းအစောင့်ရှိ *hpa-ya-kyaung-a-yar-shi*

beady *(adj.)* စူးရှသော *sue-sha-taw*

beak *(n.)* ငှက်နှုတ်သီး *nyat-note-thee*

beaker *(n.)* နှုတ်သီးပါဖန်ခွက် *note-thee-par-hpan-khwat*

beam *(n.)* ရောင်ခြည်တန်း yaung-chee-tan

bean *(n.)* ပဲတောင့်ပင်၊ ပဲသီးတောင့် *pal-taunt-pin, pal-thee-taunt*

bear *(v.)* ပါသည်၊ တာဝန်ယူသည်၊ ခေါင်းခံသည်၊ မွေးသည် *par-the, tar-win yu-the, gaung-khan-the, mway-the*

beard *(n.)* မုတ်ဆိတ် *mote-seik*

bearing *(n.)* ဟန်၊ အမူအယာ *han, a-mu-a-yar*

beast *(n.)* တောကောင်ကြီး *taw-kaung-gyi*

beastly *(adj.)* လူမဆန်သော *lu-ma-san-taw*

beat *(v.)* ရိုက်သည် *yite-the*

beatific *(adj.)* ပီတိလျှမ်းသော *pi-ti-hlyan-taw*

beatification *(n.)* ချီးကျူးဂုဏ်ပြုခြင်း chee-kyuu-gon-pyu-chin

beatitude *(n.)* ပီတိ pi-ti

beautiful *(adj.)* လှပသော hla-pa-taw

beautify *(v.)* အလှပြင်သည် a-hla-pyin-the

beauty *(n.)* အလှအပ *a-hla-a-pa*

beaver *(n.)* ဖျံကြီးတစ်မျိုး *hpyan-gyi-ta-myo*

beaverskin *(n.)* ဖျံအရေပြား *hpyan-a-yay-pyar*

becalm *(v.)* လေငြိမ်၍ မရွေ့နိုင်သော လှေကို စွန့်ခွာသည် *lay-nyien-ywe-ma-ywe-nai-taw-hlay-ko-sount-khwar-the*

because *(conj.)* သောကြောင့် *thaw-kyaunt*

beck *(n.)* စမ်းချောင်းကလေး *san-chaung-ka-lay*

beckon *(v.)* လက်ယပ်ခေါ်သည် *lat-yat-khaw-the*

become *(v.)* ဖြစ်လာသည် *phit-lar-the*

bed *(n.)* အိပ်ရာ *aik-yar*

bed sheet *(n.)* အိပ်ရာခင်း aik-yar-khin

bedcover *(n.)* အိပ်ရာဖုံး *aik-yar-hpone*

bedding *(n.)* မွေ့ရာနှင့် အိပ်ရာခင်း *mway-yar-hnint-aik-yar-khin*

bedevil *(v.)* ဒုက္ခပင်လယ်ဝေသည် *dote-kha-pin-lal-wai-the*

bedridden *(adj.)* ရောဂါကြောင့် အိပ်ရာမှ မထနိုင်သော *yaw-gar-kyaunt-aik-yar-hma-ma-hta-nai-taw*

bedrobe *(n.)* ညအိပ်ဝတ်ရုံ *nya-aik-wut-yone*

bedroom *(n.)* အိပ်ခန်း *aik-khan*

bedsore *(n.)* အိပ်ရာနာ *aik-yar-nar*

bee *(n.)* ပျား *pyar*

beech *(n.)* ဘိချ်သစ်ပင် bi-thit-pin

beef *(n.)* အမဲသား a-mae-tar

beefy *(adj.)* တုတ်ခိုင်သန်မာသော tote-khaing-tan-mar-taw

beehive *(n.)* ပျားအုံ pyar-ohn

beekeeper *(n.)* ပျားမွေးမြူသူ pyar-mway-myu-thu

beep *(n.)* တတီတီမြည်သံ ta-ti-ti-myi-tan

beer *(n.)* ဘီယာ bee-yar

beet *(n.)* မုန်လာဥနီ hmone-lar-u-nee

beetle *(n.)* ပိုးတောင့်မာ poe-taunt-mar

beetroot *(n.)* မုန်လာဥနီ *hmone-lar-u-nee*

befall *(v.)* ပေါ်ပေါက်သည် *paw-paut-the*

befit *(v.)* သင့်လျော်သည် *tint-lyaw-the*

before *(prep. &adv.)* မတိုင်မီ *me-tine-mee*

beforehand *(adv.)* ကြိုတင်၍ *kyo-tin-ywe*

befriend *(v.)* မိတ်ဆွေဖြစ်လာသည် *meit-swe-phit-lar-the*

beg *(v.)* အလှူခံသည် *a-hlyu-khan-the*

beget *(v.)* ဖခင်ဖြစ်သည် *pha-khin-phit-the*

beggar *(n.)* သူတောင်းစား thu-taung-sar

begin *(v.)* စတင်သည် *sa-tin-the*

beginner *(n.)* လက်သင် lat-tin

beginning *(n.)* အစ *a-sa*

begrudge *(v.)* တွန့်တိုသည် *twant-toe-the*

beguile *(v.)* ပျော်ရွှင်စေသည် *pyaw-shwin-say-the*

behalf *(n.)* ကိုယ်စား *koe-sar*

behave *(v.)* ပြုမူသည် *pyu-mu-the*

behaviour *(n.)* အပြုအမူ *a-pyu-a-mu*

behead *(v.)* ခေါင်းဖြတ်ကွပ်မျက်သည် *gaung-phat-kwat-myat-the*

behest *(n.)* အမိန့်အရ *a-maint-a-ya*

behind *(prep.& adv.)* နောက်မှာ *naut-mar*

behold *(v.)* ရှုမြင်သည် *shu-myin-the*

being *(n.)* ဖြစ်တည်ခြင်း *phit-the-chin*

belabour *(v.)* အပိုချဲ့ပြောသည် *a-po-chae-pyaw-the*

belated *(adj.)* အချိန်နှောင်းသော *a-chain-hnaung-taw*

belch *(v.)* လေတက်သည် *lay-tat-the*

beleaguered *(adj.)* ရန်သူအဝိုင်းခံရသော *yan-thu-a-wine-khan-ya-taw*

belie *(v.)* အမှန်ကို ဖုံးကွယ် လှည့်စားသည် *a-man-ko-hpone-kwal-hlae-sar-the*

belief *(n.)* ယုံကြည်ချက် *yone-kyi-chat*

believe *(v.)* ယုံကြည်သည် *yone-kyi-the*

belittle *(v.)* သေးသိမ်စေသည် *tay-tain-say-the*

bell *(n.)* ခေါင်းလောင်း *khaung-laung*

bellboy *(n.)* ဟော်တယ်အစောင့် ho-tal-a-saunt

belle *(n.)* အချောအလှ *a-chaw-a-hla*

bellhop *(n.)* ဟော်တယ်အစောင့် ho-tal-a-saunt

bellicose *(adj.)* ရန်လိုသော yan-lo-taw

belligerent *(adj.)* ရန်လိုသော *yan-lo-taw*

bellow *(v.)* နွားကဲ့သို့ အော်သည် nwar-kae-tho-aw-the

bellowing *(n.)* နွားကဲ့သို့ အော်ခြင်း *nwar-kae-tho-aw-chin*

bellows *(n.)* ဖားဖို *phar-pho*

belly *(n.)* ဗိုက်သား *bite-tar*

belong *(v.)* ပိုင်ဆိုင်သည် *pai-sai-the*

belongings *(n.)* ပိုင်ဆိုင်ပစ္စည်း *pai-sai-pyit-see*

beloved *(adj.)* ချစ်လှစွာသော *chit-hla-swar-taw*

belt *(n.)* ခါးပတ် *khar-pat*

belvedere *(n.)* ရှုခင်းကြည့် အဆောက်အအုံငယ် *shyu-khin-kyi-a-saut-a-ohn-nge*

bemoan *(v.)* ဝမ်းနည်းကြောင်းပြောသည် *wan-nae-kyaung-pyaw-the*

bemused *(adj.)* နားမလည်နိုင်သော *nar-ma-lal-nai-taw*

bench *(n.)* ခုံတန်းလျား khon-tan-lyar

bend *(v.)* ကွေးသည် kway-the

beneath *(adv.)* အောက်မှာ *aut-hmar*

benediction *(n.)* ခရစ်ယာန်ဘုန်းတော်ကြီး၊ သီလရှင် *kha-yit-yan-hpone-taw-kyi, thi-la-shin*

benefaction *(n.)* အလှူ *a-hlyu*

benefactor *(n.)* အလှူရှင် *a-hlyu-shin*

benefic *(adj.)* စေတနာကောင်းသော say-ta-nar-kaung-taw

benefice *(n.)* ရစ်ယာန်ဘုန်းတော်ကြီး၏ ရာထူးနှင့် လစာ kha-yit-yan-hpone-taw-kyi-ei-yar-htoo-nint-la-sar

beneficial *(adj.)* အကျိုးရှိသော a-kyo-shi-taw

beneficiary *(n.)* အကျိုးခံစားသူ *a-kyo-khan-sar-thu*

benefit *(v.)* အကျိုး *a-kyo*

benevolence *(n.)* စေတနာ၊ သဒ္ဓါတရား *say-ta-nar, ta-dar-ta-yar*

benevolent *(adj.)* အကျိုးပြုသော *a-kyo-pyu-taw*

benight *(v.)* **အသိဉာဏ်၊ ကျင့်ဝတ်၊ လူမှု အမှောင်ထု လွှမ်းခြုံသည်** *a-thi-nyan-kyint-wut-lu-mu-a-hmaung-htu-hlwan-chon-the*
benign *(adj.)* **ဒုက္ခမပေးသော** *dote-kha-ma-pay-taw*
bent *(n.)* **အထုံပါရမီ** *a-hton-pa-ra-mi*
benzene *(n.)* **ဘန်ဇင်းဓာတ်ဆေးရည်** *ban-zin-dat-say-yae*
bequeath *(v.)* **သေတမ်းစာဖြင့် ပေးခဲ့သည်** *tay-tan-sar-phyit-pay-khae-the*
bequest *(n.)* **သေတမ်းစာဖြင့် ပေးသည့် အမွေ** tay-tan-sar-phyit-pay-the-amway
berate *(v.)* **ဒေါသဖြင့် ဝေဖန်သည်** daw-tha-phit-wai-phan-the
bereaved *(adj.)* **ဆွေမျိုးရင်းချာ ဆုံးပါးသည်** *swe-myo-yin-char-sone-par-the*
bereavement *(n.)* **ပူဆွေးသောက ရောက်ခြင်း** *pu-sway-thaw-ka-yauk-chin*
bereft *(adj.)* **အရည်အသွေးမဲ့သော** *a-yay-a-thway-mae-thaw*
beseech *(v.)* **အရေးတကြီး တောင်းခံသည်** *a-yay-ta-gyi-taung-khan-the*
beseeching *(n.)* **အသနားခံသော** *a-ta-nar-khan-taw*
beshame *(v.)* **ရှက်သည်** *shat-the*
beside *(prep.)* **ဘေးမှာ** bay-mar
besiege *(v.)* **စစ်တပ်ဖြင့် ဝိုင်းထားသည်** sit-tat-phit-wine-htar-the
beslaver *(v.)* **ဖော်လံဖားသည်** *phaw-lan-phar-the*
besmirch *(v.)* **နာမည်ဖျက်သည်** *nan-mal-phat-the*
besotted *(adj.)* **အရူးအမူးဖြစ်သော** *a-yuu-a-muu-phit-taw*
bespeak *(v.)* **သက်သေဖြစ်သည်၊ ညွှန်ပြသည်၊ အမိန့်ပေးသည်** *thet-tay-phit-the, nyun-pya-the, a-maint-pay-the*
bespectacled *(adj.)* **မျက်မှန်တပ်ထားသော** *myat-hman-tat-htar-taw*
bespoke *(adj.)* **ကိုယ်တိုင်းနှင့် ချုပ်ထားသော** *ko-tai-nint-choke-htar-taw*
best *(adj.)* **အကောင်းဆုံး** *a-kaung-sone*
bestial *(adj.)* **ကြမ်းကြုတ်သော** *kyan-kyoke-taw*
bestow *(v.)* **နှင်းအပ်သည်** *hnin-at-the*
bestride *(v.)* **ခွနေသည်** *kwa-nay-the*
bestseller *(n.)* **ရောင်းအားအကောင်းဆုံး** *yaung-arr-a-kaung-sone*
bet *(v.)* **လောင်းကစားသည်** *laung-ka-sar-the*
beta *(adj.)* **ဘီတာ** *be-ta*
betide *(v.)* **ဖြစ်ပျက်သည်** *phit-pyat-the*
betray *(v.)* **သစ္စာဖောက်သည်** *tit-sar-phaut-the*
betrayal *(n.)* **သစ္စာဖောက်ခြင်း** *tit-sar-phaut-chin*
betroth *(v.)* **တရားဝင်စေ့စပ်သည်** *ta-yar-win-say-sat-the*
betrothal *(n.)* **လက်ထပ်ရန် သဘောတူမှု** *lat-htet-yan-ta-baw-thu-mu*
betrothed *(adj.)* **စေ့စပ်ထားသော** *say-sat-htar-thaw*
better *(adj.)* **ပိုကောင်းသော** *po-kaung-taw*
betterment *(n.)* **တိုးတက်ကောင်းမွန်ခြင်း** *toe-tat-kaung-mon-chin*
betting *(adj.)* **လောင်းကစားခြင်း** *laung-ka-sar-chin*
bettor *(n.)* **လောင်းကစားသမား** *laung-ka-sar-ta-mar*
between *(prep.)* **အကြား** *a-kyar*
betwixt *(prep.)* **စကောစက** *sa-kaw-sa-ka*

beverage *(n.)* အဖျော်ယမကာ *a-phaw-ya-ma-kar*
bevy *(n.)* အစု၊ အသိုက် *a-su, a-tite*
bewail *(v.)* ဝမ်းနည်းပက်လက်ပြောသည် *wan-nae-pat-lat-pyaw-the*
beware *(v.)* သတိထားသည် *ta-di-htar-the*
bewilder *(v.)* စိတ်ရှုပ်ထွေးစေသည် *seik-shoke-htway-say-the*
bewilderment *(n.)* စိတ်ရှုပ်ထွေးခြင်း seik-shoke-htway-chin
bewind *(v.)* အသက်မရှူနိုင်ဖြစ်သည် *a-thet-ma-shu-nai-phit-the*
bewitch *(v.)* ပြုစားသည် pyu-sar-the
beyond *(prep.& adj.)* လွန်၍ *lun-ywe*
bi *(adj.)* နှစ်ခုဖြစ်သော *na-khu-phit-taw*
biangular *(adj.)* ထောင့်နှစ်ခုဖြစ်သော *Htaung-na-khu-phit-taw*
biannual *(adj.)* တစ်နှစ်နှစ်ကြိမ် ta-nit-na-kyein
biannually *(adv.)* တစ်နှစ်နှစ်ကြိမ် *ta-nit-na-kyein*
biantennary *(adj.)* ဦးမှင်နှစ်ခုပါသော *u-min-na-khu-par-taw*
bias *(n.)* ဘက်လိုက်ခြင်း *bat-lite-chin*
biased *(adj.)* ဘက်လိုက်သော *bat-lite-taw*
biaxial *(adj.)* ဝန်ရိုးနှစ်ခုပါသော *win-yoe-na-khu*
bib *(n.)* သွားရည်ခံ twar-yee-khan
bibber *(n.)* အချိုရည်တစ်ခုတည်းကို ပုံမှန်သောက်သူ *a-cho-yay-ta-khu-tae-ko-pon-man-taut-thu*
bible *(n.)* သမ္မာကျမ်းစာ *ta-mar-kyan-sar*
bibliographer *(n.)* စာအုပ်ပုံနှိပ်သမိုင်းဆရာ *sar-oak-pon-nait-ta-mai-sa-yar*
bibliography *(n.)* စာအုပ်ပုံနှိပ်သမိုင်း *sar-oak-pon-nait-ta-mai*
bibliophile *(n.)* စာရူး *sar-yuu*
bicentenary *(adj.)* နှစ် ၂၀၀ ပြည့်ပွဲ *nit 200 pyae-pwe*
biceps *(n.)* လက်ရုံးကြွက်သား *lat-yone-kwat-tar*
bicker *(v.)* ဘာမဟုတ်တာကို ငြင်းခံသည် *bar-ma-hote-tar-ko-nyin-khan-the*
bicycle *(n.)* စက်ဘီး *sat-bee*
bid *(v.)* လေလံဆွဲသည် *lay-lan-swal-the*
bidder *(n.)* လေလံဆွဲသူ *lay-lan-swal-thu*
bide *(v.)* အခွင့်ကောင်းစောင့်သည် *a-khwint-kaung-saunt-the*
bidet *(n.)* အင်တုံ *inn-ton*
bidimensional *(adj.)* ရှုထောင့်နှစ်ခု *shu-htaunt-na-khu*
biennial *(adj)* နှစ်နှစ်တစ်ကြိမ် *na-nit-ta-kyein*
bier *(n.)* အလောင်းစင် *a-laung-sin*
bifacial *(adj.)* မျက်နှာနှစ်ခု ရှိသော myat-nar-na-khu-shi-taw
biff *(v.)* ပိတ်ထိုးသည် *pait-htoe-the*
bifocal *(adj.)* အဝေးကြည့်အနီးကြည့် ပါဝါမျက်မှန် a-way-kyi-a-nee-kyi-pa-war-myat-man
biformity *(n.)* ပုံစံနှစ်ခုရှိခြင်း pon-san-na-khu-shi-chin
bifurcate *(v.)* နှစ်ခွ ဖြစ်သွားသည် *na-khwa-phit-twar-the*
bifurcation *(n.)* နှစ်ခွ ဖြစ်သွားခြင်း *na-khwa-phit-twar-chin*
big *(adj.)* ကြီးမားသော *kyi-mar-taw*
bigamist *(n.)* အိမ်ထောင်ရှိလျက် နောက်တစ်ယောက်နှင့် လက်ထပ်သူ *eain-htaung-shi-lyat-naut-ta-yaut-nint-lat-htet-thu*

bigamous *(adj.)* **အိမ်ထောင်ရှိလျက် နောက်တစ်ယောက်နှင့် လက်ထပ်ခြင်းအပြစ်ရှိသော** *eain-htaung-shi-lyat-naut-ta-yaut-nint-lat-htet-chin-a-pyit-shi-taw*
bigamy *(n.)* **အိမ်ထောင်ရှိလျက် နောက်တစ်ယောက်နှင့် လက်ထပ်ခြင်းအပြစ်** *eain-htaung-shi-lyat-naut-ta-yaut-nint-lat-htet-chin-a-pyit*
bighead *(n.)* **ဘဝင်မြင့်သူ** *ba-win-myint-thu*
bighearted *(adj.)* **သဘောထားကြီးသော** *ta-baw-htar-kyi-taw*
bight *(n.)* **အတွင်းဟိုက်ကမ်းရိုးကွေ့** a-twin-hite-kan-yoe-kway
bigot *(n.)* **တစ်ယူသန်** ta-yu-tan
bigotry *(n.)* **တစ်ယူသန်သဘောထား** *ta-yu-tan-ta-baw-htar*
bike *(n.)* **စက်ဘီး၊ ဆိုင်ကယ်** *sat-bee, sai-kal*
biker *(n.)* **ဆိုင်ကယ်၊ စက်ဘီး ရွယ်တူစီးသူ လူငယ်** *sai-kal-sat-bee-ywal-thu-see-thu-lu-ngal*
bikini *(n.)* **ဘီကီနီ** *bi-ki-ni*
bilateral *(adj.)* **နှစ်ဦးနှစ်ဖက်ပါဝင်သော** *na-oo-na-phat-par-win-taw*
bile *(n.)* **သည်းခြေရည်** *tae-chay-yay*
bilingual *(adj.)* **နှစ်ဘာသာ** *na-bar-tar*
bill *(n.)* **ကျသင့်ငွေတောင်းခံလွှာ** *kya-tint-ngwe-taung-khan-hlwar*
billable *(adj.)* **ကျသင့်ငွေတောင်းခံနိုင်သော** *kya-tint-ngwe-taung-khan-nai-taw*
billboard *(n.)* **လမ်းဘေးကြော်ငြာဆိုင်းဘုတ်** *lan-bay-kyar-nyar-sai-board*
billiard table *(n.)* **ဘိလိယက်ခုံ** *bi-li-yat-khon*
billiards *(n.)* **ဘိလိယက်** *bi-li-yat*
billion *(n.)* **သန်းတစ်ထောင်** tan-ta-htaung
billionaire *(n.)* **သန်းပေါင်းထောင်ချီချမ်းသာသူ** tan-paung-htaungchi-chan-tar thu
billow *(v.)* **လှိုင်းတံပိုး** *hlaing-ta-poe*
bimonthly *(adj.)* **နှစ်လတစ်ကြိမ်** *na-la-ta-kyein'*
bin *(n.)* **ပုံး** *pon*
binary *(adj.)* **နှစ်ခုအစုံ** *na-khu-a-sone*
bind *(v.)* **ချည်နှောင်သည်** *chi-naung-the*
binding *(n.)* **စာအုပ်ဖုံး** sar-oak-hpone
binge *(n.)* **ပွဲတော်ကြီးနှင့် တိုးချိန်** *pwe-taw-gyi-nint-toe-chein*
bingo *(n.)* **ဘင်ဂိုလောင်းကစား** *bin-go-laung-ka-sar*
binocular *(adj.)* **မှန်ပြောင်း** man-pyaung
binoculars *(n.)* **စုံမှန်ပြောင်း** zone-man-pyaung
bioactivity *(n.)* **ဇီဝသက်ရှိအပေါ်အကျိုးသက်ရောက်သော** zi-wa-thet-shi-a-paw-a-kyo-thet-yaut-taw
bioagent *(n.)* **အန္တရာယ်ရှိသော ဇီဝအေးဂျင့်** *an-ta-yal-shi-taw-zi-wa-aye-gent*
biochemical *(adj.)* **ဇီဝဓာတုဗေဒနှင့် ဆိုင်သော** *zi-wa-dar-tu-bay-da-nint-sai-taw*
biochemistry *(n.)* **ဇီဝဓာတုဗေဒပညာ** zi-wa-dar-tu-bay-da-pyin-nyar
bioclimate *(n.)* **ဇီဝသက်ရှိမှ လွှမ်းမိုးသော ရာသီဥတု** zi-wa-thet-shi-ma-hlwan-moe-taw-yar-thi-u-tu
biodegradation *(n.)* **ဗက်တီးရီးယားပိုးဖြင့် ဆွေးမြည့်နိုင်ခြင်း** bat-te-ri-yar-poe-phit-sway-myae-naing-chin
bioengineering *(n.)* **ဇီဝအင်ဂျင်နီယာပညာ** zi-wa-in-gyin-nee-yar-pyin-nyar
biofuel *(n.)* **ဇီဝလောင်စာ** *zi-wa-laung-zar*
biogas *(n.)* **ဇီဝဓာတ်ငွေ့** *zi-wa-dat-ngwe*

biographer *(n.)* အတ္ထုပ္ပတ္တိရေးသူ *at-htoke-pat-ti-yay-thu*

biography *(n.)* အတ္ထုပ္ပတ္တိ *at-htoke-pat-ti*

biohazardous *(adj.)* ဇီဝအန္တရာယ်ရှိသော *zi-wa-an-da-yal-shi-taw*

biological *(adj.)* ဇီဝဗေဒနှင့် ဆိုင်သော *zi-wa-bay-da-nint-sai-taw*

biologically *(adv.)* ဇီဝဗေဒဆိုင်ရာ *zi-wa-bay-da-sai-yar*

biologist *(n.)* ဇီဝဗေဒပညာရှင် *zi-wa-bay-da-pyin-nyar-shin*

biology *(n.)* ဇီဝဗေဒ *zi-wa-bay-da*

biomass *(n.)* သတ်မှတ်ထုထည်အတွင်း သက်ရှိအရေအတွက် *tat-mat-htu-htal-a-twin-thet-shi-a-yay-a-thwat*

biometric *(adj.)* ဇီဝအချက်အလက်ဆိုင်ရာ *zi-wa-a-chat-a-lat-sai-yar*

bionic *(adj.)* စက်ရုပ်အင်္ဂါတုတပ်ဆင်ထားသော *sat-yoke-in-gar-tu-tat-sin-htar-taw*

biopic *(n.)* အတ္ထုပ္ပတ္တိရုပ်ရှင်ကား *at-htoke-pat-ti-yoke-shin-kar*

biopsy *(n.)* အသားစ ဓာတ်ခွဲစစ်ဆေးခြင်း *a-tar-sa-dat-khwal-sit-say-chin*

biorhythm *(n.)* ရုပ်ပိုင်း၊ စိတ်ပိုင်း စည်းဝါးကျကျ ဖြစ်ပေါ်ခြင်း *yoke-pai-seik-pai-see-war-kya-kya-phit-paw-chin*

bioscope *(n.)* ရုပ်ရှင်ရုံ *yoke-shin-yone*

bioscopy *(n.)* အသားစ ဓာတ်ခွဲစစ်ဆေးခြင်း *a-tar-sa-dat-khwal-sit-say-chin*

bipartisan *(adj.)* နှစ်ပါတီ *na-par-ti*

bipolar *(adj.)* အစွန်းနှစ်ဖက်ရောက်ခြင်းဆိုင်ရာ *a-soon-na-phat-yaut-chin-saing-yar*

biracial *(adj.)* လူမျိုးနှစ်ခုပါဝင်သော အဖွဲ့ဝင်များဆိုင်ရာ *lu-myo-na-khu-par-win-taw-a-phwe-win-myar-saing-yar*

birch *(n.)* ဘုဇပတ်ပင် bu-za-pat-pin

bird *(n.)* ငှက် *nget*

birdlime *(n.)* စေးကပ်ကပ်အရာဝတ္ထုဖြင့်ပြုလုပ်သော ငှက်ထောင်ချောက် *say-kat-kat-a-yar-wut-htu-phit-pyu-lote-taw-nget-htaung-chauk*

birth *(n.)* မွေးဖွားခြင်း mway-phwar-chin

birthdate *(n.)* မွေးနေ့ mway-nae

birthday *(n.)* မွေးနေ့ *mway-nae*

birthmark *(n.)* မွေးရာပါ အမှတ်အသား *mway-yar-par-a-mat-a-tar*

biscuit *(n.)* ဘီစကစ် *bee-sa-kit*

bisect *(v.)* ထက်ဝက်ပိုင်းသည် *htet-wat-pai-the*

bisexual *(adj.)* နှစ်ဖက်ချွန် *na-phat-choon*

bishop *(n.)* ခရစ်ယာန်ဘုန်းတော်ကြီး *kha-yit-yan-bhone-taw-gyi*

bison *(n.)* အမေရိကန်ပြောင် a-may-ri-kan-pyaung

bisque *(n.)* ပုစွန်တုတ်စွပ်ပြုတ် *pa-zoon-htoke-sut-pyoke*

bistro *(n.)* စားသောက်ဆိုင်ငယ် *sar-taut-sai-nge*

bit *(n.)* အပိုင်းအစ *a-pai-a-sa*

bitch *(n.)* ခွေးမ *khway-ma*

bitcoin *(n.)* ဘစ်ကွိုင်ဒစ်ဂျစ်တယ်ငွေစနစ် *bit-coi-dit-git-tal-ngwe-sa-nit*

bite *(v.)* ကိုက်သည် *kait-the*

biting *(adj.)* ရင့်သီးသော၊ ပက်စက်သော *yint-the-taw, pat-sat-taw*

bitter *(adj.)* ခါးသော၊ ခါးသီးသော *khar-taw, khar-thee-taw*

bitterness *(n.)* ခါးခြင်း၊ ခါးသီးခြင်း *khar-chin, khar-thee-chin*

bi-weekly *(adj.)* **နှစ်ပတ်တစ်ကြိမ်၊ တစ်ပတ်နှစ်ကြိမ်** *na-pat-ta-kyein, ta-pat-na-kyein*
bizarre *(adj.)* **ထူးခြားဆန်းကြယ်သော** thoo-char-san-kyal-taw
blab *(v.)* **လွှတ်ခနဲ ထွက်သွားသည်** hlut-kha-nal-htwat-twar-the
blabber *(n.)* **ရှူးကြောင်ကြောင်၊ လက်လွတ်စပယ်စကား** *yuu-kyaung-kyaung-lat-lut-sa-pal-sa-kar*
black *(adj.)* **အမဲ** a-mal
blackbird *(n.)* **ငှက်မည်း** *nget-mal*
blackboard *(n.)* **ကျောက်သင်ပုန်း** *kyauk-tin-bone*
blacken *(v.)* **မည်းစေသည်** mal-say-the
blacklist *(n.)* **အမည်ပျက်စာရင်းသွင်းသည်** *a-me-pyat-sa-yin-thwin-the*
blackmail *(n.)* **ခြိမ်းခြောက်ငွေညှစ်သည့် လုပ်ရပ်** chain-chauk-ngwe-hnyit-the-lote-yat
blackmailer *(n.)* **ခြိမ်းခြောက်ငွေညှစ်သူ** chain-chauk-ngwe-hnyit-thu
blackout *(n.)* **မှတ်ဉာဏ်ပျောက်သွားခြင်း** *mat-nyan-pyauk-twar-chin*
blacksmith *(n.)* **ပန်းပဲသမား** *pan-pae-ta-mar*
bladder *(n.)* **ဆီးအိမ်** *see-eain*
blade *(n.)* **ဘလိတ်ဓား** *ba-lade-dar*
blame *(v.)* **အပြစ်တင်သည်** *a-pyit-tin-the*
blanch *(v.)* **သွေးဆုတ်သွားသည်** *thway-sote-twar-the*
bland *(adj.)* **ပုံပန်းလက္ခဏာမထူးခြားသော** *pon-pan-lat-kha-nar-ma-htoo-char-taw*
blank *(adj.)* **အလွတ်** *a-hlut*
blanket *(n.)* **စောင်** *saung*
blare *(v.)* **ကျယ်လောင်စူးရှသော အသံမြည်သည်** *kyal-laung-sue-sha-taw-a-tan-myi-the*
blaspheme *(n.)* **ကျိန်ဆဲသည်** *kyein-sal-the*
blasphemy *(n.)* **ကျိန်ဆဲသော စကားအသုံးအနှုန်း** *kyein-sal-taw-sa-kar-a-tone-a-hnone*
blast *(n.)* **ပေါက်ကွဲမှု** *pauk-kwal-mu*
blatant *(adj.)* **ပေါ်တင်** *paw-tin*
blaze *(n.)* **မီးကြီး** *mee-kyi*
blazer *(n.)* **ဘလေဇာကုတ်** *ba-lay-zar-cote*
blazing *(adj.)* **ချစ်ချစ်တောက်** chit-chit-taut
blazon *(v.)* **စာတမ်းထိုးသည်** *sar-tan-htoe-the*
bleach *(v.)* **အရောင်ကျွတ်သည်** *a-yaung-kyut-the*
bleak *(adj.)* **အလွန်အေး၍ ဆိုးဝါးသော** *a-lun-aye-ywe-soe-war-taw*
bleary *(adj.)* **ရီဝေသော** *yee-wai-taw*
bleat *(v.)* **ဆိတ်၊ သိုး အော်သံ** *seik-toe-aw-tan*
bleb *(n.)* **သေးငယ်သော မီးလောင်ဖု** *tay-ngwe-taw-mee-laung-phu*
bleed *(v.)* **သွေးထွက်သည်** *thway-htwat-the*
blemish *(n.)* **အစွန်းအထင်း** *a-soon-a-htin*
blench *(v.)* **လန့်ပြီး ဆတ်ခနဲ တွန့်သည်** *lant-pyi-sat-kha-nae-twant-the*
blend *(v.)* **ရောစပ်သည်** *yaw-sat-the*
blender *(n.)* **မွှေစက်** *hmway-sat*
bless *(v.)* **ဆုတောင်းပေးသည်** *su-taung-pay-the*
blessed *(adj.)* **မြတ်သော** *myat-taw*
blessing *(n.)* **ဘုရားသခင်၏ ကောင်းချီးမင်္ဂလာ** *pha-yar-tha-khin-ei-kaung-chee-min-ga-lar*

blight *(n.)* အပင်ရောဂါ *a-pin-yaw-gar*

blind *(adj.)* မျက်မမြင် *myat-ma-myin*

blindage *(n.)* ကာကွယ်သော စခရင် သို့မဟုတ် အဆောက်အအုံ *kar-kwal-taw-sa-kha-yin-thoe-ma-hote-a-sawt-a-ohn*

blindfold *(n.)* မျက်စိကို အဝတ်ဖြင့် ပိတ်စည်းသည် *myat-si-ko-a-wut-phit-pait-see-the*

blindness *(n.)* မျက်မမြင် *myat-ma-myin*

bling *(n.)* တန်ဖိုးကြီး အဝတ်အထည်၊ လက်ဝတ်ရတနာ *tan-phoe-kyi-a-wut-a-htal-lat-wut-ya-da-nar*

blink *(v.)* မျက်တောင်ခတ်သည် *myat-taung-khat-the*

blip *(n.)* ရေဒါဖန်သားပြင်ပေါ်မှ အလင်းပြောက် *yay-dar-phan-tar-pyin-paw-ma-a-lin-pyauk*

bliss *(n.)* ချမ်းမြေ့ပျော်ရွှင်မှု *khyan-myay-pyaw-shwin-mu*

blister *(n.)* ရည်ကြည်ဖု *yay-kyi-phu*

blithe *(adj.)* အပူအပင်မရှိသော *a-pu-a-pin-ma-shi-taw*

blitz *(n.)* လေကြောင်းမှ အလုံးအရင်း ရုတ်တရက် စစ်ဆင်ခြင်း *lay-kyaung-ma-a-lone-a-yin-yote-ta-yat-sit-sin-chin*

blizzard *(n.)* နှင်းမုန်တိုင်း *hnin-hmone-tai*

bloat *(v.)* လေ၊ အရည်ကြောင့် ဝမ်းရောင်ခြင်း *lay-a-yay-kyaunt-wan-yaung-chin*

blob *(n.)* ဆေးစက် *say-sat*

bloc *(n.)* အုပ်စု *oat-su*

block *(n.)* အောက်ခံတုံး *awt-khan-tone*

blockage *(n.)* ပိတ်ဆို့ခြင်း *pait-soe-chin*

blockbuster *(n.)* အလွန်လူကြိုက်များသည့် ရုပ်ရှင်၊ ဝတ္ထု *a-lun-lu-kyaik-myar-the-yoke-shin-wut-htu*

blockhead *(n.)* ငတုံး *nga-tone*

blog *(n.)* ဘလော့ *ba-lot*

blogger *(n.)* ဘလော့ဂါ *ba-lot-gar*

blogging *(v.)* ဘလော့ရေးခြင်း *ba-lot-yay-chin*

blood *(n.)* သွေး *thway*

bloodshed *(n.)* သွေးထွက်သံယိုမှု *thway-htwat-tan-yo-mu*

bloody *(adj.)* သွေးထွက်နေသော *thway-thwat-nay-taw*

bloom *(v.)* ပန်းပွင့်သည် *pan-pwint-the*

bloomer *(n.)* ကြီးသော အမှား *kyi-taw-a-hmar*

blot *(n.)* အစွန်း၊ အစက် *a-soon-a-sat*

blotted *(adj.)* ထင်ရှားသော *htin-shar-taw*

blouse *(n.)* ဘလောက်အင်္ကျီ *ba-laut-inn-gyi*

blow *(v.)* မှုတ်သည်၊ လေတိုက်သည် *hmot-the, lay-tite-the*

blowout *(n.)* ကားဘီးပေါက်ခြင်း *car-bee-pauk-the*

blowsy *(adj.)* ကြမ်းတမ်းနီမြန်းသည့်မျက်နှာရှိသော *kyan-tan-ni-myan-the-myat-nar-shi-taw*

blue *(n.)* အပြာရောင် *a-pyar-yaung*

bluetooth *(n.)* ဘလူးတု *ba-lu-tut*

bluff *(v.)* ဖြီးသည်၊ ဖြန်းသည် *phee-the, phyan-the*

blunder *(n.)* ဆိုးဝါးသော အမှား *soe-war-taw-a-mar*

blundering *(adj.)* ခပ်တုံးတုံး၊ ခပ်ညံ့ညံ့အမှားများဖြင့် ပြုလုပ်သော *khat-tone-tone-khat-nyant-nyant-a-mar-myar-phint-pyu-lote-taw*

blunt *(adj.)* တုံးသော *tone-taw*

bluntly *(adv.)* ဘွင်းဘွင်း၊ တဲ့တိုး *bwin-bwin, tae-doe*

blur *(v.)* မှုန်ဝါးသည် *hmone-war-the*

blurb *(n.)* အကြောင်းအရာ အကျဉ်းချုပ် *a-kyaung-a-yar-a-kyin-choke*

blurt *(v.)* ရှေ့နောက်မစဉ်းစားဘဲ ပြောချသည် *shay-naut-ma-sin-sar-bae-pyaw-cha-the*

blush *(v.)* မျက်နှာနီမြန်းသွားသည် *myat-nar-ne-myan-thwar-the*

blusher *(n.)* ပါးနီ *par-ni*

bluster *(v.)* သကြိုန်အမြောက်ဖောက်သည် *tha-gyan-a-myauk-phaut-the*

boa *(n.)* စပါးကြီးမြွေ *sa-par-gyi-mway*

boar *(n.)* တောဝက်ထီး *taw-wat-htee*

board *(n.)* ပျဉ်ချပ် *pyin-chat*

board game *(n.)* စစ်တုရင်၊ ကျား။ *sit-tu-yin, kyar*

boarding *(n.)* ပျဉ်ချပ် pyin-chat

boarding school *(n.)* ကျောင်းအိပ်ကျောင်းစားလက်ခံသည့်ကျောင်း kyaung-aik-kyaung-sar-lat-khan-the-kyaung

boast *(v.)* ကြွားသည် kwar-the

boat *(n.)* လှေ *hlay*

boathouse *(n.)* လှေရုံ *hlay-yone*

boatman *(n.)* ကူးတို့သမား *ku-toe-ta-mar*

bob *(v.)* ညိတ်သည် *nyeik-the*

bobbin *(n.)* ရစ်လုံးငယ် *yit-lone-nge*

bobble *(n.)* သိုးမွေး ပန်းဖွားလုံး *toe-mway-pan-phwar-lone*

bodice *(n.)* ဘော်လီအင်္ကျီ *baw-li-inn-gyi*

bodily *(adv.)* ကိုယ်ခန္ဓာ *ko-khan-dar*

body *(n.)* ခန္ဓာကိုယ် *khan-dar-ko*

bodyguard *(n.)* ကိုယ်ရံတော် *ko-yan-taw*

bog *(n.)* စိမ့်မြေ *seint-myay*

bogland *(n.)* စိမ့်မြေထူသောကုန်းမြေ *seint-myay-htu-taw-kone-myay*

boglet *(n.)* သေးငယ်သော စိမ့်မြေကွက် *tay-nge-taw-seint-myay-kwat*

bogus *(adj.)* အယောင်ဆောင် *a-yaung-saung*

bohemian *(adj.)* အနုပညာသည် *a-nu-pyin-nyar-the*

boil *(v.)* ပြုတ်သည် *pyoke-the*

boiler *(n.)* ဘွိုင်လာအိုး *boi-lar-oh*

boist *(n.)* သေတ္တာ *tit-tar*

boisterous *(adj.)* မြူးတူးသောင်းကျန်းသော my-tu-taung-kyan-taw

bold *(adj.)* ရဲရင့်သော *ye-yint-taw*

boldly *(adv.)* ရဲရင့်စွာ ye-yint-swar

boldness *(n.)* ရဲရင့်မှု ye-yint-mu

bolero *(n.)* စပိန်အက *sa-pain-a-ka*

bollard *(n.)* လမ်းပိတ်ငုတ်တိုင် lan-pait-ngote-tai

bollocks *(n.)* ဝှေးစေ့ wai-say

bolt *(n.)* မင်းတုပ် *min-htoke*

bomb *(n.)* ဗုံး *bone*

bombard *(v.)* ဗုံးကြဲတိုက်ခိုက်သည် *bone-kywal-tite-khaik-the*

bombardier *(n.)* အမြောက်တပ်သား *a-myauk-tat-tar*

bombardment *(n.)* အမြောက်၊ ဗုံး၊ ဒုံးဖြင့် ဆက်တိုက် တိုက်ခိုက်ခြင်း *a-myauk-bone-doon-phit-sat-tite-tite-khaik-chin*

bomber *(n.)* ဗုံးကြဲလေယာဉ် *bone-kywal-lay-yin*

bonafide *(adj.)* အစစ်၊ တရားဝင် *a-sit, ta-yar-win*

bonanza *(n.)* ပွဲပေါက် *pwa-pauk*

bond *(n.)* ငွေချေးစာချုပ်၊ သံယောဇဉ် *ngwe-chay-sar-choke, tan-yar-zin*

bondage *(n.)* အကျဉ်းသားဘဝ *a-kyin-tar-ba-wa*

bonds *(n.pl.)* **သံကြိုး၊ နှောင်ကြိုး** *tan-kyo, naung-kyo*
bone *(n.)* **အရိုး** *a-yoe*
boneless *(adj.)* **အရိုးမဲ့သော** *a-yoe-mae-taw*
bonfire *(n.)* **မီးပုံ** *mee-pon*
bonnet *(n.)* **ကားစက်ဖုံး** *car-sat-phone*
bonus *(n.)* **အပိုဆု** *a-po-su*
book *(v.)* **ကြိုတင်လက်မှတ်ဖြတ်သည်** *kyo-tin-lat-mat-phat-the*
bookie *(n.)* **ဒိုင်** *dai*
bookish *(adj.)* **စာဖတ်ဝါသနာကြီးသော** *sar-phat-war-ta-nar-kyi-taw*
book-keeper *(n.)* **စာရင်းကိုင်** *sa-yin-kaing*
booklet *(n.)* **စာစောင်** *sar-saung*
bookmaker *(n.)* **ဒိုင်** *dai*
bookmark *(n.)* **စာညှပ်၊ မှတ်ခြင်း** *sar-nyat, mote-chin*
bookseller *(n.)* **စာအုပ်ရောင်းသူ** *sar-oak-yaung-thu*
bookshop *(n.)* **စာအုပ်ဆိုင်** *sar-oak-sai*
bookstall *(n.)* **စာအုပ်စင်** *sar-oak-sin*
bookworm *(n.)* **စာဂျပိုး** sar-gya-poe
boom *(n.)* **မြည်ဟိန်းသည်** myi-hein-the
boon *(n.)* **ကျက်သရေမင်္ဂလာ** *kyat-tha-yay-min-ga-lar*
boor *(n.)* **လူကြမ်းလူရိုင်း** *lu-kyan-lu-yai*
boost *(n.)* **မြှင့်တင်ခြင်း** *hmyint-tin-chin*
booster *(n.)* **မြှင့်တင်ပေးသောအရာ** *hmyint-tin-pay-taw-a-yar*
boot *(n.)* **ဘွတ်ဖိနပ်** *boot-pha-nat*
booth *(n.)* **ရုံငယ်** *yone-nge*
booty *(n.)* **စစ်အတွင်းအဓမ္မလုယူသော ပစ္စည်း** *sit-a-twin-a-dhamma-lu-yu-taw-pyit-see*
booze *(v.)* **မူးယစ်သောက်စားသည်** *mu-yit-taut-sar-the*
border *(n.)* **နယ်နိမိတ်** nal-ni-meik
bore *(v.)* **ထွင်းဖောက်သည်** htwin-hpaut-the
born *(adj.)* **မွေးရာပါ** mway-yar-par
borne *(adj.)* **ပါရှိသော** *par-shi-taw*
borough *(n.)* **လွှတ်တော်ကိုယ်စားလှယ်ရှိသော မြို့ ခရိုင်** hlut-taw-ko-sa-lal-shi-taw-myo-kha-yai
borrow *(v.)* **ချေးငှားသည်** *chay-ngar-the*
bosom *(n.)* **ရင်ဘတ်** *yin-bat*
boss *(n.)* **သူဌေး၊ လူကြီး** *tha-htay, lu-gyi*
bossy *(adj.)* **ဆရာကြီးလုပ်သော** *sa-yar-gyi-lote-taw*
botanical *(adj.)* **ရုက္ခဗေဒဆိုင်ရာ** *yoke-kha-bay-da-sai-yar*
botany *(n.)* **ရုက္ခဗေဒ** *yoke-kha-bay-da*
botch *(v.)* **ဖြစ်ကတတ်ဆန်းလုပ်သည်** *phit-ka-tat-san-lote-the*
both *(adj & pron.)* **နှစ်ခုလုံး** *na-khu-lone*
bother *(v.)* **နှောင့်ယှက်သည်** *naut-shat-the*
botheration *(n.)* **ပူပန်မှု၊ အခက်အခဲ၊ စိတ်အနှောင့်အယှက်** *pu-pan-mu, a-khat-a-khae, seik-a-naut-a-shat*
bottle *(n.)* **ပုလင်း** *pa-lin*
bottom *(n.)* **အောက်ခြေ** *aut-chay*
bough *(n.)* **ကိုင်းမ** kai-ma
boulder *(n.)* **ရေ၊ လေတိုက်စားခံ ကျောက်တုံးကြီး** yay-lay-tite-sar-khan-kyauk-tone-gyi
boulevard *(n.)* **လမ်းမကျယ်** *lan-ma-kyal*
bounce *(v.)* **ပြန်ကန်ထွက်သည်** *pyan-kan-htwat-the*

bouncer *(n.)* ဆိုင်များတွင် လူရမ်းကားများကို ဆွဲထုတ်ရန် ငှားထားသူ *sai-myar-twin-lu-yan-kar-myar-ko-swal-htoke-yan-hngar-htar-thu*

bound *(v.)* ခုန်ပေါက်သွားသည် *khone-pauk-twar-the*

boundary *(n.)* နယ်နိမိတ်မျဉ်း *nal-ni-meik-myin*

bountiful *(adj.)* ပေါများသော၊ ရက်ရောသော *paw-myar-taw, yat-yaw-taw*

bounty *(n.)* ဆုလာဘ် *su-lat*

bouquet *(n.)* ပန်းစည်း *pan-zee*

bourgeois *(adj.)* အရင်းရှင်ဝါဒီ၊ လူလတ်တန်းစား *a-yin-shin-war-di, lu-lat-tan-sar*

bourgeoise *(n.)* အရင်းရှင်လူတန်းစား *a-yin-shin-lu-tan-sar*

bout *(n.)* ဖုတ်ပူမီးတိုက်အချိန် *phoke-pu-mee-tite-a-chein*

boutique *(n.)* ဖက်ရှင်စတိုး *phat-shin-sa-toe*

bow *(n.)* လေး *lay*

bowel *(n.)* အူသိမ်အူမ au-tain-au-ma

bower *(n.)* အရိပ်ကောင်းသော နေရာ a-yeik-kaung-taw-nay-yar

bowl *(n.)* ပန်းကန်လုံး pan-kan-lone

bowler *(n.)* ဘောလုံးပစ်သူ baw-lone-pyit-thu

box *(n.)* သေတ္တာ *tit-tar*

boxer *(n)* လက်ဝှေ့သမား *lat-hwai-ta-mar*

boxing *(n.)* လက်ဝှေ့ *lat-hwai*

boy *(n.)* ကောင်ကလေး *kaung-ka-lay*

boycott *(v.)* သပိတ်မှောက်သည် *tha-paik-hmaut-the*

boyhood *(n.)* ကောင်ကလေးငယ်စဉ်ဘဝ *kaung-ka-lay-nge-sin-ba-wa*

boyish *(adj.)* ကောင်ကလေးကဲ့သို့ kaung-ka-lay-kae-tho

bra *(n.)* ဘာရာဇီယာ ba-yar-zi-yar

brace *(n.)* အထိန်း a-htein

bracelet *(n.)* လက်ကောက် lat-kauk

braces *(n.)* ဘောင်းဘီသိုင်းကြိုး *baung-bi-thai-kyo*

bracing *(adj.)* အေးမြလတ်ဆတ်သော *aye-mya-lat-sat-taw*

bracken *(n.)* ဒရင်ကောက်ပင်ကြီးတစ်မျိုး *da-yin-kauk-pin-gyi-ta-myo*

bracket *(n.)* ဒေါက်၊ ဝိုက်ကွင်း *daut, wite-kwin*

brackish *(adj.)* ငန်ငြိငြိ *ngan-nyi-nyi*

brag *(v.)* လေလုံးထွားသည် *lay-lone-htwar-the*

braggart *(n.)* ငကြွား *nga-kywar*

braid *(n.)* ဖွတ်မြီးကြိုး *phut-myee-kyo*

braille *(n.)* မျက်မမြင်စာ *myat-ma-myin-sar*

brain *(n.)* ဦးနှောက် *oo-naut*

brainchild *(n.)* ပင်ကိုစိတ်ကူးဉာဏ် *pin-ko-seik-ku-nyan*

brainstorm *(n.)* ကောင်းစွာ မစဉ်းစား မတွေးတောနိုင်ချိန်၊ အတွေးညစ်ထုတ်ခြင်း *kaung-swar-ma-sin-sar-ma-thway-taw-nai-chein, a-thway-nyit-htoke-the*

brainy *(adj.)* ဉာဏ်သွားသော *nyan-twar-taw*

braise *(v.)* အိုးလုံပိတ်၍ နှပ်သည် oh-lon-pait-ywe-nat-the

brake *(n.)* ဘရိတ် *ba-rake*

bran *(n.)* ဖွဲနု *phwe-nu*

branch *(n.)* အကိုင်း၊ အဖွဲ့ခွဲ *a-kai, a-phwe-khwal*

brand *(n.)* ကုန်အမှတ်တံဆိပ် *kone-a-mat-ta-seik*
branding *(n.)* ကုန်အမှတ်တံဆိပ်မိတ်ဆက်တင်ပြခြင်း *kone-a-mat-ta-seik-meik-sat-tin-pya-chin*
brandish *(v.)* ဝှေ့ရမ်းသည် *hwai-yan-the*
brandy *(n.)* ဘရန်ဒီအရက် *ba-yan-di-a-yat*
brangle *(v.)* ဆူညံငြင်းခုံသည် *su-nyan-nyin-khon-the*
brash *(adj.)* မထီတရီ *ma-thi-ta-yee*
brass *(n.)* ကြေးဝါ *kyay-war*
brasserie *(n.)* ဘီယာဆိုင် *bi-yar-sai*
brat *(n.)* ကောင်ဆိုးကလေး *kaung-soe-ka-lay*
bravado *(n.)* သကြဲ့န်အမြောက်ပစ်ခြင်း tha-gyan-a-myauk-phaut-chin
brave *(adj.)* ရဲရင့်သော *ye-yint-taw*
bravery *(n.)* ရဲရင့်မှု *ye-yint-mu*
brawl *(n.)* ရန်ပွဲ *yan-pwe*
brawn *(n.)* ခွန်အား *khun-arr*
bray *(n.)* မြည်းဟီသံ *myie-hee-tan*
braze *(v.)* ကြေးဝါဖြင့် ပြုလုပ်သည်၊ ကြေးဝါကဲ့သို့ လုပ်သည်၊ ကြေးဝါဖြင့် အလှဆင်သည် *kyay-war-phit-pyu-lote-the, kyay-war-kae-tho-lote-the, kyay-war-phit-a-hla-sin-the*
breach *(v.)* ဖောက်သည် phaut-the
bread *(n.)* ပေါင်မုန့် *paung-hmont*
breadcrumb *(n.)* ပေါင်မုန့်သားအပဲ့ *paung-hmont-tar-a-pae*
breaded *(adj.)* ပေါင်မုန့်သားအပဲ့ဖြင့် အုပ်သော *paung-hmont-tar-a-pae-phyint-oak-taw*
breadth *(n.)* အနံ *a-nan*
breadwinner *(n.)* ရှာကျွေးသူ *shar-kway-thu*
break *(v.)* ကျိုးသည်၊ ကွဲသည် kyo-the, kwal-the
break point *(n.)* နိုင်မှတ် *naing-mat*
breakage *(n.)* ကျိုးပဲ့ခြင်း kyo-pae-chin
breakdown *(n.)* စက်ပျက်ခြင်း၊ စိတ်ကျန်းမာရေး ချို့ယွင်းခြင်း sat-pyat-chin, seik-kyan-mar-yay-choe-ywin-chin
breakfast *(n.)* မနက်စာ *ma-nat-sar*
breakfront *(n.)* စာအုပ်စင် *sar-oak-sin*
breaking *(n.)* ကျိုးပဲ့ခြင်း *kyo-pae-chin*
break-off *(n.)* ရပ်တန့်ခြင်း *yat-tant-chin*
breakout *(n.)* ထောင်ဖောက်ပြေးခြင်း *htaung-phaut-pyay-chin*
breaktime *(n.)* ခေတ္တနားချိန် *khit-ta-nar-chein*
breakup *(n.)* ပျက်ခြင်း၊ ပြိုကွဲခြင်း *pyat-chin, pyo-kwal-chin*
breast *(n.)* ရင် yin
breastfeed *(v.)* နို့တိုက်သည် no-tite-the
breath *(n.)* အသက်ရှူခြင်း a-thet-shu-chin
breathe *(v.)* အသက်ရှူသည် a-thet-shu-the
breathtaking *(adj.)* ရင်သပ်ရှုမောဖွယ် *yin-thet-shu-maw-phwal*
breech *(n.)* သေနတ်ပြောင်းရင်း *ta-nat-pyaung-yin*
breed *(v.)* သားပေါက်သည် *tar-pauk-the*
breeze *(n.)* လေညင်း *lay-nyin*
breviary *(n.)* ဘုရင်ကြီးဘုရားစာအုပ် *ba-yin-gyi-pha-yar-sar-oak*
brevity *(n.)* ကျစ်လျစ်မှု *kyit-lyit-mu*
brew *(v.)* ဘီယာချက်သည် *be-yar-chat-the*
brewery *(n.)* ဘီယာချက်စက်ရုံ *be-yar-chat-sat-yone*

bribe *(v.)* လာဘ်ထိုးသည် *lat-htoe-the*

brick *(n.)* အုတ် *oak*

bridal *(adj.)* သတို့သမီး *tha-doe-tha-mee*

bride *(n.)* သတို့သမီး *tha-doe-tha-mee*

bridegroom *(n.)* သတို့သား *the-doe-tar*

bridesmaid *(n.)* အပျိုရံ *a-pyo-yan*

bridge *(n.)* တံတား ta-dar

bridle *(n.)* မြင်းဇက်ကြိုး *myin-zat-kyo*

brief *(adj.)* အကျဉ်းချုပ် *a-kyin-choke*

briefcase *(n.)* ရုံးသုံးလက်ဆွဲအိတ် *yone-tone-lat-swal-aik*

briefing *(n.)* လုပ်ငန်းအသေးစိတ် ရှင်းပြခြင်း *lote-ngan-a-thay-seik-shin-pya-chin*

brigade *(n.)* တပ်မဟာ *tat-ma-har*

brigadier *(n.)* ဗိုလ်မှူးချုပ် *bo-hmu-gyoke*

brigand *(n.)* တောပုန်းဓားပြ *taw-pon-dar-pya*

bright *(adj.)* တောက်ပသော taut-pa-ta

brighten *(v.)* တောက်ပသည် *taut-pa-ta*

brightness *(n.)* တောက်ပခြင်း *taut-pa-chin*

brilliance *(n.)* ဉာဏ်ကောင်းခြင်း *nyan-kaung-chin*

brilliant *(adj.)* ဉာဏ်ကောင်းသော nyan-kaung-taw

brim *(n.)* ပန်းကန်နှုတ်ခမ်း pan-kan-note-khan

brine *(n.)* ဆားရည်၊ ပင်လယ်ရေ *sar-yay, pin-lal-yay*

bring *(v.)* ယူလာသည် yu-lar-the

brinjal *(n.)* ခရမ်းသီး kha-yan-thee

brink *(n.)* ချောက်နှုတ်ခမ်း chauk-note-khan

briquet *(n.)* အုတ်အသေး oak-a-thay

brisk *(adj.)* သွက်လက်ဖျတ်လတ်သော thwat-lat-phat-lat-taw

bristle *(n.)* မာကြမ်းသော အမွေးတို mar-kyan-taw-a-mway-tho

british *(adj.)* ဗြိတိသျှ *byi-ti-sha*

brittle *(adj.)* ကြွပ်ဆတ်သော *kyut-sat-taw*

broad *(adj.)* ကျယ်ပြန့်သော kyal-pyant-taw

broadband *(n.)* မြန်နှုန်းမြင့်ကွန်ရက် *myanm-hnone-myint-kun-yat*

broadcast *(v.)* အသံလွှင့်သည် *a-tan-hlwint-the*

broadway *(n.)* အဓိပတိလမ်း *a-di-pa-ti-lan*

brocade *(n.)* ဘရိုကိတ်စ *ba-ro-kaik-sa*

broccoli *(n.)* ပန်းဂေါ် ဖီစိမ်း *pan-gaw-phi-sein*

brochure *(n.)* လက်ကမ်းစာစောင် lat-kan-sar-saung

broke *(adj.)* ဘိုင်ကျသော *bai-kya-taw*

broken *(v.)* ကျိုးနေသော၊ ကွဲနေသော *kyo-nay-taw, kwal-nay-taw*

broker *(n.)* ပွဲစား *pwe-sar*

brokerage *(n.)* အကျိုးဆောင်ခ *a-kyo-saung-kha*

bromide *(n.)* ဘရိုမိုက်ဒြပ်ပေါင်း *ba-ro-mite-drat-paung*

bronchial *(adj.)* အသက်ရှူပြွန်နှင့် ဆိုင်သော *a-thet-shu-pywun-nint-sai-taw*

bronchitis *(n.)* ချောင်းဆိုးရင်ကျပ်နာ *chaung-soe-yin-kyat-nar*

bronze *(n.)* ကြေးညို *kyay-nyo*

brooch *(n.)* ရင်ထိုး *yin-htoe*

brood *(n.)* သားသမီးတစ်အုပ် *tar-ta-mee-ta-oak*

brook *(n.)* စမ်းချောင်းကလေး *san-chaung-ka-lay*

broom *(n.)* တံမြက်စည်း *ta-myat-see*

broth *(n.)* အသားငါးရွက်ပြုတ်ဟင်းချို *a-tar-ngar-ywat-pyoke-hin-cho*

brothel *(n.)* ဆောင်ကြာမြိုင် *saung-kyar-hmyaing*

brother *(n.)* အစ်ကို၊ ညီ *a-ko, nyi*

brotherhood *(n.)* ညီအစ်ကို တော်စပ်ခြင်း *nyi-a-ko-taw-sat-chin*

brow *(n.)* တောင်ကုန်းထိပ် *taung-kone-hteik*

brown *(adj.)* အညို a-nyo

browse *(v.)* မြည်းစမ်းသည်၊ ရှာဖွေလေ့လာသည် pyie-san-the, shar-phway-lay-lar-the

browser *(n.)* ဘရောက်ဇာ ba-yaut-zar

bruise *(n.)* ပွန်းပဲ့ဒဏ်ရာ pon-pae-dan-yar

brunch *(n.)* မနက်နေ့လည်စာ ma-nat-nae-lal-sar

brunette *(n.)* ဆံပင်နက်လူဖြူအမျိုးသမီး *sa-pin-nat-lu-phyu-a-myo-ta-mee*

brunt *(n.)* အဆိုးဆုံးအပိုင်း *a-soe-sone-a-pai*

brush *(n.)* သွားပွတ်တံ၊ ဝက်မှင်ဘီး *twar-put-tan, wat-hmin-bee*

brusque *(adj.)* တိုးတိ tone-ti

brustle *(v.)* မာကြမ်းသော အမွေးတိုပါရှိသည် *mar-kyan-taw-a-mway-tho-par-shi-taw*

brutal *(adj.)* လူမဆန်သော *lu-ma-san-taw*

brutalize *(v.)* အကြင်နာမဲ့စေသည် *a-kyin-nar-mae-say-the*

brute *(n.)* ဘီလူး *ba-lu*

brutify *(v.)* အသည်းမာစေသည် *a-the-mar-say-the*

brutish *(adj.)* အရိုင်းအစိုင်းကဲ့သို့သော *a-yai-a-sai-kae-tho-taw*

bubble *(n.)* ပူဖောင်း *pu-hpaung*

bubble wrap *(n.)* ပူဖောင်းပလပ်စတစ် *pu-hpaung-pa-lat-sa-tit*

bubblegum *(n.)* ကပ်စေးနဲ့ပူဖောင်း *kat-see-nae-pu-hpaung*

buck *(n.)* သမင်ဖို *tha-min-pho*

bucket *(n.)* ဆွဲပုံး *swal-pone*

bucket list *(n.)* နောက်ဆုံးဆန္ဒစာရင်း *naut-sone-san-da-sa-yin*

buckle *(n.)* ခါးပါတ်ခေါင်း khar-pat-khaung

bud *(n.)* အစို့၊ အဖူး *a-soe, a-phoo*

budding *(adj.)* ဖူးသစ်စ *phoo-tit-sa*

buddy *(n.)* အပေါင်းအသင်း *a-paung-a-tin*

budge *(v.)* လှုပ်သည်ဆိုရုံမျှ လှုပ်သည် *hloke-the-so-yone-mya-hloke-the*

budget *(n.)* ရသုံးမှန်းခြေစာရင်း ya-tone-man-chay-sa-yin

buff *(n.)* ခိုင်မာနူးညံ့သော အဝါနုရောင်အသားအရေ *khai-mar-nu-nyant-taw-a-war-nu-yaung-a-thar-a-yay*

buffalo *(n.)* ကျွဲ *kywe*

buffer *(n.)* ကြားခံအရာ၊ ဒဏ်ခံ *kyar-khan-a-yar, dan-khan*

buffer zone *(n.)* ကြားခံဒေသ *kyar-khan-day-ta*

buffet *(n.)* ဘူဖေး *bu-phae*

buffoon *(n.)* လူပြက် *lu-pyat*

bug *(n.)* ပိုးကောင်ကလေး poe-kaung-ka-lay

buggy *(n.)* စက်တပ်ယာဉ်၊ ရထားလုံး sat-tat-yin, ya-htar-lone

bugle *(n.)* စစ်ခရာ *sit-kha-yar*

build *(v.)* တည်ဆောက်သည် *the-saut-the*

builder *(n.)* တည်ဆောက်သူ *the-saut-thu*

building *(n.)* အဆောက်အဦး *a-saut-a-oo*

bulb *(n.)* မီးသီး၊ ဥ *mee-thee, oo*

bulbous *(adj.)* ဝဝလုံးလုံး၊ အဖုပုံစံရှိသော *wa-wa-lone-lone, a-phu-pone-san-shi-taw*
bulge *(n.)* ဖောင်းကားနေသည့် အရာ၊ အဖု၊ အဖောင်း *hpaung-kar-nay-the-a-yar-a-phu-a-hpaung*
bulimia *(n.)* ပုံမမှန် ဆက်တိုက်ဖြစ်နေသော အစာအငမ်းမရဖြစ်ခြင်း *pon-ma-man-sat-tite-phit-nay-taw-a-sar-a-nyan-ma-ya-phit-chin*
bulk *(n.)* အများစု *a-myar-su*
bulky *(adj.)* ဝန်ကျယ်သော wun-kyal-taw
bull *(n.)* နွားထီး *ngwar-htee*
bull's eye *(n.)* စက်ကွင်းချက်မ *sat-kwin-chat-ma*
bulldog *(n.)* ခွေးဘီလူး *khway-ba-lu*
bulldozer *(n.)* မြေထိုးစက် *myay-htoe-sat*
bullet *(n.)* ကျည်ဆံ kyi-san
bullet train *(n.)* ကျည်ဆံရထား *kyi-san-ya-htar*
bulletin *(n.)* တရားဝင် ထုတ်ပြန်ကြေညာချက် *ta-yar-win-htoke-pyan-kyay-nyar-chat*
bulletproof *(adj.)* ကျည်ကာ *kyi-kar*
bullion *(n.)* ရွှေချောင်း၊ ငွေချောင်း *shwe-chaung, ngwe-chaung*
bullish *(adj.)* မိမိကိုယ်ကို ယုံကြည်လွန်းသော *mi-mi-ko-ko-yone-kyi-loon-taw*
bullock *(n.)* သင်းပြီးနွား *tin-pi-nwar*
bully *(n.)* အနိုင်ကျင့်သူ *a-nai-kyint-thu*
bulwark *(n.)* မြေကတုတ် *myay-ka-htoke*
bumble *(v.)* ဗလုံးဗထွေး မပီမသ ပြောဆိုသည် *ba-lone-ba-htway-ma-pi-ma-ta-pyaw-so-the*
bump *(n.)* တိုးတိုက် ဆောင့်မိသည် *toe-tite-saunt-mi-the*
bumper *(n.)* ကားဘန်ပါ kar-ban-par
bumpkin *(n.)* တောသားလူနုံ taw-dar-lu-hnon
bun *(n.)* ဘန်းမုန့် *banp-hmont*
bunch *(n.)* အစည်း၊ အတွဲ၊ အခိုင်၊ အဖီး *a-see, a-twal, a-khai, a-phee*
bundle *(n.)* အစည်း၊ အထုပ် *a-see, a-htoke*
bungalow *(n.)* ဘန်ဂလို ban-ga-lo
bungee jumping *(n.)* ဘန်ဂီခုန်ခြင်း ban-gee-khone-chin
bungle *(v.)* မအောင်မြင်ဖြစ်သည် *ma-aung-myin-phit-the*
bunk *(n.)* နံရံကပ်အိပ်စင် *nan-yan-kat-aik-sin*
bunk bed *(n.)* နှစ်ထပ်အိပ်စင် *na-htat-aik-sin*
bunker *(n.)* ကတုတ်ကျင်း *ka-htoke-kyin*
buoy *(n.)* ရေကြောင်းပြဖော်ယာ *yay-kyaung-pya-baw-yar*
buoyant *(adj.)* ရေပေါ်ပေါ် နိုင်သော *yay-paw-paw-nai-taw*
burble *(v.)* ရေပွက်သကဲ့သို့ မြည်သည် *yay-pwat-tha-kae-tho-myae-the*
burden *(n.)* ဝန်ထုတ်ဝန်ပိုး *wun-htoke-wun-poe*
burdensome *(adj.)* ဖိစီးသော *phi-see-taw*
bureacuracy *(n.)* ဗျူရိုကရေစီစနစ် *byu-ro-ka-yay-si-sa-nit*
bureau *(n.)* အစိုးရဌာန၊ ဗီရိုစားပွဲ *a-soe-ya-htar-na, bi-ro-sa-pwe*
bureaucrat *(n.)* ဗျူရိုကရက်အရာရှိ *byu-ro-ka-yat-a-yar-shi*
burgeon *(v.)* လျင်မြန်စွာ ကြီးထွားဖွံ့ဖြိုးလာသည် *lyin-myan-swar-kyi-htwar-phwint-phoe-lar-the*
burger *(n.)* ဘာဂါ *bar-gar*
burglar *(n.)* ဖောက်ထွင်းသူခိုး *hpaut-htwin-tha-khoe*

burglar alarm *(n.)* သူခိုးလှန့် ခေါင်းလောင်း *tha-khoe-hlant-khaung-laung*
burglary *(n.)* ဖောက်ထွင်းမှု *phaut-htwin-mu*
burial *(n.)* မြေမြှုပ်သင်္ဂြိုဟ်ခြင်း *myay-myoke-tha-gyo-chin*
burke *(v.)* တိတ်တဆိတ် သွယ်ဝိုက် ဖိနှိပ်ခြင်း *tate-ta-seik-thwal-wide-phi-neikchin*
burlesque *(n.)* စာဖျက် *sar-phat*
burn *(v.)* မီးလောင်သည်၊ မီးရှို့သည် *mee-laung-the, mee-shoe-the*
burner *(n.)* မီးတောက်ထွက်ရာ အပိုင်း *mee-taut-htwat-yar-a-pai*
burning *(adj.)* အလွန်ပြင်းပြသော *a-loon-pyin-pya-taw*
burp *(v.)* လေတက်သည် *lay-tat-the*
burrow *(n.)* လိုဏ်ခေါင်း *hlaing-khaung*
bursary *(n.)* ကောလိပ်ငွေစာရင်းမှူး *kaw-leik-ngwe-sa-yin-hmu*
burst *(v.)* ပေါက်ကွဲသည် *pauk-kwal-the*
bury *(v.)* မြေမြှုပ်သင်္ဂြိုဟ်သည် *myay-myoke-tha-gyo-the*
bus *(n.)* ဘတ်စကား *bat-sa-kar*
bus shelter *(n.)* မှတ်တိုင်တွင် ခရီးသည်များ နားခိုရာ mat-tai-twin-kha-yee-the-myar-nar-kho-yar
bus stop *(n.)* ဘတ်စကားမှတ်တိုင် bat-sa-kar-mat-tai
bush *(n.)* ချုံပုတ် chone-boke
bushy *(adj.)* ချုံထူသော၊ အမွေးထူသော chone-htu-taw, a-hmway-htu-taw
business *(n.)* စီးပွားရေး *see-pwar-yay*
business card *(n.)* လိပ်စာကတ် *leik-sar-kat*
business class *(n.)* အဆင့်မြင့်တန်း *a-sint-myint-tan*
business plan *(n.)* စီးပွားစီမံချက် *see-pwar-see-man-chat*
businessman *(n.)* စီးပွားရေးသမား *see-pwar-yay-ta-mar*
bustle *(v.)* ပျာယာခတ်သည် pyar-yar-khat-the
busy *(adj.)* အလုပ်များသော *a-lote-myar-taw*
but *(conj.)* သို့သော် *tho-thaw*
butcher *(n.)* သားသတ်သမား *tar-tat-ta-mar*
butler *(n.)* ဘဏ္ဍာစိုး ban-nar-soe
butt *(v.)* ဝှေ့သည်၊ ခတ်သည် *hwai-the, khat-the*
butter *(n.)* ထောပတ် *htaw-pat*
butterfly *(n.)* လိပ်ပြာ *leik-pyar*
butterhead *(n.)* ဆလပ်ရွက် sa-lat-ywet
buttermilk *(n.)* ထောပတ်ထုတ်ပြီး နို့ရည် htaw-pat-htoke-p-noe-yee
buttock *(n.)* တင်ပါး tin-par
button *(n.)* ကြယ်သီး kyal-thee
buy *(v.)* ဝယ်သည် wal-the
buyer *(n.)* ဝယ်သူ *wal-thu*
buzz *(n.)* တဝီဝီမြည်သံ ta-wi-wi-myi-tan
buzzer *(n.)* တကျည်ကျည်အသံပေးသည့် လျှပ်စစ်ကိရိယာ *ta-kyi-kyi-a-tan-pay-the-lyat-sit-ka-yi-yar*
by *(prep.)* အားဖြင့် *arr-phyint*
bye *(interj.)* နှုတ်ဆက်ပါတယ် note-sat-par-tal
by-election *(n.)* ကြားဖြတ်ရွေးကောက်ပွဲ *kyar-phyat-ywe-kauk-pwe*
bygone *(adj.)* ဖြစ်ပြီးသွားသော *phit-pi-twar-taw*

bylaw, bye-law *(n.)* ဒေသအာဏာပိုင်မှ ထုတ်ပြန်သည့် ဥပဒေစည်းမျဉ်း day-da-arr-nar-pai-ma-htoke-pyan-the-oo-pa-day-see-myin

bypass *(n.)* လမ်းလွှဲ *lan-hlwal*

by-product *(n.)* ဘေးထွက်ပစ္စည်း *bay-htwat-pyit-see*

byre *(n.)* နွားတင်းကုပ် *nwar-tin-gote*

byte *(n.)* ဘိုက် *bite*

byway *(n.)* ဘာသာရပ်တစ်ခုတွင် လူသိမများလှသည့် နယ်ပယ် *bar-tar-yat-ta-khu-twin-lu-thi-ma-myar-hla-the-nal-pal*

byword *(n.)* လူသုံးများသော စကားလုံး lu-tone-myar-taw-sa-kar-lone

C

cab *(n.)* ယာဉ်မောင်းထိုင်ရာ နေရာ *yin-maung-htai-yar-nay-yar*

cabana *(n.)* အဝတ်လဲတဲ *a-wut-lal-tae*

cabaret *(n.)* ဆိုက ဖျော်ဖြေခြင်း *so-ka-phyaw-phae-chin*

cabbage *(n.)* ဂေါ်ဖီထုပ် *gaw-phee-htoke*

cabby *(n.)* တက္ကစီယာဉ်မောင်း tat-ka-see-yin-maung

cabin *(n.)* အခန်းငယ်၊ တဲ *a-khan-nge, the*

cabinet *(n.)* အစိုးရဝန်ကြီးအဖွဲ့၊ ဗီရို *a-soe-ya-win-gyi-a-phwe, bi-ro*

cable *(n.)* ကေဘယ်ကြိုး *kay-bal-kyo*

cable car *(n.)* ကေဘယ်ကား *kay-bal-kar*

cable television *(n.)* ကေဘယ်ရုပ်မြင်သံကြား *kal-bal-yoke-myin-tan-kyar*

cache *(n.)* ဝှက်ထားသော လက်နက်၊ အစားအစာ၊ ငွေ *hwat-htar-taw-lat-nat-a-sar-a-sar-ngwe*

cachet *(n.)* လေးစားခြင်း *lay-sar-chin*

cackle *(v.)* ကတော်သံ *ka-taw-tan*

cactus *(n.)* ရှားစောင်းပင် shar-saung-pin

cad *(n.)* ကွန်ပျူတာဖြင့် ဒီဇိုင်းထုတ်ခြင်း *koon-pyu-taw-phit-di-zine-htoke-chin*

cadaver *(n.)* လူသေအလောင်း lu-tay-a-laung

cadaverous *(adj.)* ဖြူဖပ်ဖြူရော်နှင့် ပိန်သော *phyu-phat-phyu-yar-nint-pai-taw*

cadence *(n.)* စီးချက်ကျ အစီအစဉ် see-chat-kya-a-si-a-sin

cadet *(n.)* ဗိုလ်လောင်း bo-laung

cadge *(v.)* ကပ်ရပ်တောင်းသည် *kat-yat-taung-the*

cadmium *(n.)* ကက်ဒမီယံဒြပ်စင် *kat-da-mi-yan-drat-sin*

cafe *(n.)* ကဖေး *ka-fay*

cafeteria *(n.)* စားသောက်ဆိုင် *sar-tauk-sai*

caffeine *(n.)* ကဖိန်းဓာတ် *ka-fein-dat*

cage *(n.)* လှောင်အိမ် *laung-ain*

cajole *(v.)* ချော့မော့မြှောက်ပင့်နားချသည် *chawt-mawt-hmyauk-pint-nar-cha-the*

cake *(n.)* ကိတ်မုန့် *kait-hmont*

cakewalk *(v.)* လွယ်ကူစွာ အောင်ပွဲခံသည် *lwal-khu-swar-aung-pwe-khan-the*

calamity *(n.)* ကပ်ဘေး *kat-bay*

calcium *(n.)* ကယ်လစီယမ်ဓာတ် *kal-la-see-yan-dat*

calculate *(v.)* တွက်ချက်သည် *twat-chat-the*

calculation *(n.)* တွက်ချက်ခြင်း *twat-chat-chin*

calculator *(n.)* **တွက်စက်** twat-sat

calendar *(n.)* **ပြက္ခဒိန်** *pyat-kha-dain*

calf *(n.)* **ခြေသလုံးကြွက်သား၊ နွားငယ်ကလေး** chay-ta-lone-kywat-tar, ngwar-nge-ka-lay

calibrate *(v.)* **စံကိုက်ချိန်ညှိသည်** *san-kaik-chain-hnyi-the*

calibration *(n.)* **စံကိုက်ချိန်ညှိခြင်း** *san-kaik-chain-hnyi-chin*

calibre *(n.)* **ပြွန်၊ သေနတ်ပြောင်းအချင်း** *pyun-ta-nat-pyaung-a-chin*

call *(v.)* **ခေါ်သည်** *khaw-the*

call *(n.)* **ခေါ်ခြင်း** *khaw-chin*

call centre *(n.)* **ဖုန်းခေါ်စင်တာ** phone-khaw-cen-tar

caller *(n.)* **တယ်လီဖုန်းခေါ်သူ** tal-li-phone-khaw-thu

calligraphy *(n.)* **လက်ရေးအတတ်** lat-yay-a-tat

calling *(n.)* **အသက်မွေးပညာ** a-thet-mway-pyin-nyar

callous *(adj.)* **စာနာစိတ်ကင်းသော** sar-nar-seik-kin-taw

callow *(adj.)* **ရင့်ကျက်ခြင်းမရှိသော** *yint-kyat-chin-ma-shi-taw*

calm *(adj.)* **တည်ငြိမ်သော** *ti-nyein-taw*

calmative *(adj.)* **စိတ်ငြိမ်စေသည့် အာနိသင်ရှိသော** seik-nyein-say-the-ar-ni-tin-shi-taw

calmness *(n.)* **တည်ငြိမ်ခြင်း** ti-nyein-chin

calorie *(n.)* **ကယ်လိုရီ** kal-lo-yee

calorific *(adj.)* **အပူဓာတ်ပေးသော** *a-pu-dat-pay-taw*

calumniate *(v.)* **မှားယွင်းပြီး ဂုဏ်သိက္ခာကျစေသော ထုတ်ပြန်ချက် ပြုလုပ်သည်** *hmar-ywin-pi-gon-tate-khar-kya-say-taw-htoke-pyan-chat-pyu-lote-the*

calumny *(n.)* **အသရေဖျက်မှု** *a-tha-yay-phat-mu*

camel *(n.)* **ကုလားအုတ်** ka-lar-oak

cameo *(n.)* **စာညွှန့်** sar-nyunt

camera *(n.)* **ကင်မရာ** *ka-ma-yar*

camlet *(n.)* **ကုလားအုတ်မွေးအထည်** *ka-lar-oak-hmway-a-htal*

camouflage *(n.)* **ပုံဖျက်ခြင်း** *pon-phat-chin*

camp *(n.)* **စခန်း** *sa-khan*

campaign *(n.)* **တိုက်ပွဲစဉ်၊ လှုံ့ဆော်ခြင်း** *tite-pwe-zin, lont-sar-chin*

camper *(n.)* **စခန်းချသူ** *sa-khan-cha-thu*

campfire *(n.)* **မီးပုံပွဲ** *mee-pon-pwe*

camphor *(n.)* **ပရုတ်** *pa-yoke*

campsite *(n.)* **စခန်းချရာနေရာ** *sa-khan-cha-yar-nay-yar*

campus *(n.)* **တက္ကသိုလ်ပရဝုဏ်** *tat-ka-tho-pa-ra-won*

can *(v.)* **စည်သွတ်သည်** *si-thut-the*

can *(n.)* **စည်သွတ်ဘူး** *si-thut-bu*

canal *(n.)* **တူးမြောင်း** *tu-myaung*

canard *(n.)* **ကောလာဟလ** *kaw-la-ha-la*

canary *(n.)* **စာဝါငှက်** *sar-war-ngat*

cancel *(v.)* **ဖျက်သည်** *phat-the*

cancellation *(n.)* **ဖျက်ခြင်း** *phat-chin*

cancer *(n.)* **ကင်ဆာရောဂါ** *kin-sar-yaw-gar*

candid *(adj.)* **ပွင့်လင်းသော** *pwint-lin-taw*

candidacy *(n.)* **ကိုယ်စားလှယ်လောင်းအဖြစ်** *ko-sa-lal-laung-a-phit*

candidate *(n.)* **ကိုယ်စားလှယ်လောင်း** ko-sa-lal-laung

candle *(n.)* **ဖယောင်းတိုင်** pha-yaung-tai

candlelight *(n.)* **ဖယောင်းတိုင်မီး** pha-yaung-tai-mee

candour *(n.)* အပြောအဆိုပွင့်လင်းခြင်း a-pyaw-a-so-pwint-lin-chin
candy *(n.)* ချိုချဉ် cho-chin
cane *(n.)* ကြံ *kyan*
canine *(adj.)* ခွေးနှင့်ဆိုင်သော *khway-nint-sai-taw*
canister *(n.)* လက်ဖက်ရည်ဘူး *la-phat-yay-bu*
cannabis *()* ဆေးခြောက် *say-chauk*
cannibal *(n.)* လူသားစားသူ *lu-tar-sar-thu*
cannibalise *(v.)* မျိုးတူပစ္စည်းကို ဖြုတ်ယူသုံးစွဲသည် *myo-thu-pyit-see-ko-phoke-yu-tone-swal-the*
cannon *(n.)* အမြောက် *a-myauk*
cannonade *(v.)* အမြောက်ကြီးအဆက်မပြတ်ပစ်ခတ်ခြင်း *a-myauk-kyi-a-sat-ma-pyat-pyit-khat-chin*
canny *(adj.)* စီးပွားရေး ပိုင်နိုင်စွာ လုပ်နိုင်သော *see-pwar-yay-pai-nai-swar-lote-nai-taw*
canon *(n.)* စည်းမျဉ်း၊ နိယာမ see-myin, ni-yar-ma
canonize *(v.)* သေဆုံးသူသည် သူတော်စဉ်ဖြစ်ကြောင်း တရားဝင် ပြောကြားသည် *tay-sone-thu-the-thu-taw-zin-phit-kyaung-ta-yar-wiin-pyaw-kyar-the*
canopy *(n.)* ကန့်လန့်ကာ *ka-nu-pee-hlay*
canteen *(n.)* ကန်တင်း *kan-teen*
canter *(n.)* မြင်းအသားကျပြေးခြင်း *myin-a-tar-kya-pyay-chin*
canton *(n.)* ဆွစ်ဇလန်ရှိ ဒေသစိတ်နယ်မြေ *swit-za-lan-shi-day-ta-seik-nal-myay*
cantonment *(n.)* စစ်စခန်း sit-sa-khan
canvas *(n.)* ကင်းပတ်စ *kin-pat-sa*
canvass *(v.)* နိုင်ငံရေးမဲဆွယ်သည် *nai-ngan-yay-mae-swal-the*
canyon *(n.)* နက်ရှိုင်းသော ချောက်ကြီး *nat-shine-taw-chauk-gyi*
cap *(v.)* ဖုံးသည် *hpone-the*
cap *(n.)* ကက်ဦးထုပ် *kat-oo-htoke*
capability *(n.)* လုပ်နိုင်စွမ်း *lote-nai-swan*
capable *(adj.)* လုပ်နိုင်သော *lote-nai-taw*
capacious *(adj.)* ကျယ်ဝန်းသော *kyal-win-taw*
capacity *(n.)* လုပ်နိုင်စွမ်း *lote-nai-swan*
cape *(n.)* အငူ *a-ngu*
capillary *(n.)* ဆံခြည်မျှင်သွေးကြော *san-chi-myin-tway-kyaw*
capital *(n.)* မြို့တော် *myo-taw*
capitalism *(n.)* အရင်းရှင်ဝါဒ *a-yin-shin-wa-da*
capitalist *(n.)* အရင်းရှင် *a-yin-shin*
capitalize *(v.)* စာလုံးကြီးဖြင့် ရေးသည် *sar-lone-kyi-phit-yay-the*
capitation *(n.)* လူခွန် *lu-khun*
capitulate *(v.)* အရှုံးပေးသည် *a-shone-pay-the*
cappuccino *(n.)* ကပူချီနိုကော်ဖီ *ka-pu-chi-no-kaw-phi*
caprice *(n.)* အပြောင်းအလဲလွယ်ခြင်း *a-pyaung-a-lal-lwal-chin*
capricious *(adj.)* မတည်တံ့သော *a-the-tant-taw*
capricorn *(n.)* မကရရာသီဖွား *ma-ka-ya-yar-thi-phwar*
capsicum *(n.)* ငရုတ်မျိုး *nga-yoke-myo*
capsize *(v.)* မှောက်သည် *maut-the*
capsular *(adj.)* အတောင့်ဖြစ်သော *a-taunt-phit-taw*
capsule *(n.)* ဆေးတောင့် *say-taunt*
captain *(n.)* ကပ္ပတိန် *kat-pa-tein*

captaincy *(n.)* **ခေါင်းဆောင်အဖြစ်** *kaung-saung-a-phit*
captcha *(n.)* **ကပ်ချာ** *kat-char*
caption *(n.)* **ခေါင်းစီး** *kaung-see*
captivate *(v.)* **ဆွဲဆောင်သည်** *swal-saung-the*
captive *(adj.)* **ဖမ်းထားသော** *phan-htar-taw*
captive *(n.)* **အကျဉ်းသား** *a-kyin-tar*
captivity *(n.)* **အကျဉ်းချခံရခြင်း** *a-kyin-cha-khan-ya-chin*
capture *(n.)* **ဖမ်းခြင်း** hpan-chin
capture *(v.)* **ဖမ်းယူသည်** *hpan-yu-the*
car *(n.)* **ကား** kar
carabine *(n.)* **မြင်းစီးသေနတ်** *myin-see-tay-nat*
caramel *(n.)* **သကြားလုံးအမာ** *ta-gyar-lone-a-mar*
carat *(n.)* **ကရက်** *ka-rat*
caravan *(n.)* **နောက်တွဲလူနေယာဉ်** *naut-twal-lu-nay-yin*
carbide *(n.)* **ကာဗိုက်** *kar-bite*
carbon *(n.)* **ကာဗွန်** *kar-boon*
carbon copy *(n.)* **မင်ခံမိတ္တူ** *min-khan-mait-thu*
carbonate *(n.)* **ကာဗွန်နိတ်** *kar-boon-nate*
carbonization *(n.)* **ကာဗွန်ပြောင်းဖြစ်စဉ်** *kar-boon-pyaung-phit-sin*
carbonize *(v.)* **ကာဗွန်အဖြစ်ပြောင်းလဲသည်** *kar-boon-a-phit-pyaung-lal-the*
card *(n.)* **ကတ်** *kat*
card reader *(n.)* **ကတ်ဖတ်စက်** lat-phat-sat
cardamom *(n.)* **ဖာလာစေ့** *pha-lar-say*
cardboard *(n.)* **ကတ်ထူပြား** *kat-htu-pyar*
cardholder *(n.)* **ကတ်ကိုင်ဆောင်သူ** *kat-kai-saung-thu*
cardiac *(adj.)* **နှလုံးနှင့်ဆိုင်သော** *na-hlone-nint-sai-taw*
cardiac arrest *(n.)* **နှလုံးရပ်ခြင်း** *na-hlone-yat-chin*
cardigan *(n.)* **ရင်ကွဲသိုးမွေးအင်္ကျီ** *yin-kwal-tho-mway-inn-gyi*
cardinal *(n.)* **ဂဏာန်းခြေ** *ga-nan-chay*
cardiograph *(n.)* **နှလုံးစက်** *na-lone-sat*
cardiology *(n.)* **နှလုံးရောဂါပညာ** *na-lone-yaw-gar-pyin-nyar*
care *(v.)* **စောင့်ရှောက်သည်** *saunt-shaut-the*
care *(n.)* **စောင့်ရှောက်မှု** *saunt-shaut-mu*
career *(n.)* **သက်မွေးလုပ်ငန်း** *thet-mway-lote-ngan*
carefree *(adj.)* **စိုးရိမ်ပူပန်မှုကင်းသော** *soe-yein-pu-pan-mu-kin-taw*
careful *(adj.)* **စေ့စပ်သေချာသော၊ ဂရုစိုက်သော** *say-sat-tay-char-taw, ga-yu-site-taw*
careless *(adj.)* **မစေ့စပ်မသေချာသော၊ ဂရုမစိုက်သော** *ma-say-sat-ma-tay-char-taw, ga-yu-ma-site-taw*
carer *(n.)* **လူနာစောင့်** *lu-nar-saunt*
caress *(v.)* **ကြင်နာစွာထွေးပိုက်ခြင်း** *kyin-nar-swar-htway-pite-chin*
caretaker *(n.)* **အစောင့်** *a-saunt*
cargo *(n.)* **သင်္ဘော၊ လေယာဉ်ဖြင့် ပို့သော ကုန်ပစ္စည်း** *tin-baw-lay-yin-phit-poe-taw-kone-pyit-see*
caricature *(n.)* **ကယ်ရီကေချာရုပ်ပြောင်** *kal-re-kay-char-yote-pyaung*
carious *(adj.)* **သွားပိုးစားသော** *twar-poe-sar-taw*
carlock *(n.)* **ကားနေရာရှာစက်** *kar-nay-yar-shar-sat*
carnage *(n.)* **အစုအပြုံလိုက် လူသတ်ခြင်း** a-su-a-pyone-lite-lu-tat-chin

carnal *(adj.)* သွေးသားဆန္ဒနှင့် ဆိုင်သော *thway-tar-san-da-nint-sai-taw*
carnival *(n.)* ဘရင်ဂျီဝါဝင်ပွဲ *ba-yin-gyi-wa-win-pwe*
carnivore *(n.)* သားစားတိရိစ္ဆာန် *tar-sar-ta-yeik-san*
carol *(n.)* နာတာလူးသီချင်း *nar-tar-lu-tha-chin*
carouse *(v.)* ဆူညံစွာ အရက်သောက်သည် *su-nyan-swar-a-yat-taut-the*
carousel *(n.)* လေဆိပ်ရှိ ပစ္စည်းတင် တွန်းလှည်း *lay-seik-shi-pyit-see-tin-toon-lal*
carp *(n.)* ငါးကြင်းငါးသိုင်း *ngar-gyin-ngar-thai*
carpel *(n.)* ပန်း၏ အမမျိုးပွားအင်္ဂါ *pan-ei-a-ma-myo-pwar-in-gar*
carpenter *(n.)* လက်သမား *lat-ta-mar*
carpentry *(n.)* လက်သမားအတတ် *lat-ta-mar-a-tat*
carpet *(n.)* ကော်ဇော *kaw-zaw*
carpool *(n.)* အတူတကွ ခရီးသွားသူ လူစု *a-thu-ta-gwa-kha-yee-twar-thu-lu-su*
carrack *(n.)* စပိန်ရွက်သင်္ဘော *sa-pain-ywet-tin-baw*
carriage *(n.)* လူစီးတွဲ *lu-see-twe*
carrier *(n.)* သယ်ဆောင်ပေးသူ *tal-saung-pay-thu*
carrot *(n.)* မုန်လာဥဝါ *hmone-lar-u-war*
carry *(v.)* သယ်ဆောင်သည် *tal-saung-the*
carsick *(adj.)* ကားမူးသော *kar-mu-taw*
cart *(n.)* လှည်း *hlal*
cartage *(n.)* လှည်းဖြင့် တိုက်ခြင်း ဖြစ်စဉ်၊ ကုန်ကျစရိတ် *hlal-phit-tite-chin-phit-sin, kone-kya-sa-yeik*
cartel *(n.)* လုပ်ငန်းပူးပေါင်းလုပ်ဆောင်သူများ *lote-ngan-pu-baung-lote-saung-thu-myar*
cartilage *(n.)* အရိုးနု *a-yoe-nu*
cartographer *(n.)* မြေပုံဆွဲသူ *myay-pon-swal-thu*
carton *(n.)* ကတ်ထူ *kat-htu*
cartoon *(n.)* ကာတွန်း *kar-toon*
cartoonist *(n.)* ကာတွန်းရေးသူ *kar-toon-yay-thu*
cartridge *(n.)* ကတ်ထရစ်တောင့် *kat-hta-rit-taunt*
carve *(v.)* ပန်းပုထုသည် *pan-pu-htu-the*
carving *(n.)* ပန်းပုရုပ် *pan-pu-yoke*
cascade *(n.)* ရေတံခွန် *yay-ta-khun*
case *(n.)* ကိစ္စ၊ ဖြစ်ရပ် *keik-sa, phit-yat*
casern *(n.)* စစ်သားများနေထိုင်ရန်နေရာ *sit-tar-myar-nay-htai-yan-nay-yar*
cash *(n.)* ငွေသား *ngwe-tar*
cashback *(n.)* ငွေပြန်ပေးခြင်း *ngwe-pyan-pay-chin*
cashew *(n.)* သီဟိုဠ်သရက်ပင် *thi-ho-tha-yat-pin*
cashier *(n.)* ငွေကိုင် *ngwe-kai*
cashmere *(n.)* ဆိတ်မွေးဖြင့် လုပ်ထားသည့် နူးညံ့သော အထည် *seik-hmway-phit-lote-htar-the-nu-nyant-taw-a-htae*
casing *(n.)* အခွံ၊ အဖုံး *a-khoon, a-hpone*
casino *(n.)* ကာစီနို *kar-si-no*
cask *(n.)* စည် *si*
casket *(n.)* ကြုတ်၊ သေတ္တာ *kyoke, tit-tar*
casserole *(n.)* အဖုံးပါအိုးစောက် *a-hpone-par-oh-saut*
cassette *(n.)* ကက်ဆက် *kat-sat*

cast *(n.)* ပုံစံခွက်ထဲ လောင်းခြင်း၊ သရုပ်ဆောင်အားလုံး *pon-san-khwat-htae-laung-chin, tha-yoke-saung-arr-lon*
caste *(n.)* အမျိုးဇာတ် *a-myo-zat*
castellan *(n.)* ရဲတိုက်အုပ်ချုပ်ရေးမှူး *yae-tite-oak-choke-yay-hmue*
caster *(n.)* ပရိဘောဂအောက်ရှိ ဘီးငယ် *pa-yi-baw-ga-awt-shi-bi-nge*
castigate *(v.)* အပြစ်ပေးသည် *a-pyit-pay-the*
casting *(n.)* သရုပ်ဆောင်စေခြင်း *tha-yoke-saung-say-chin*
castle *(n.)* ရဲတိုက် *yae-tite*
castor *(n.)* ပရိဘောဂအောက်ရှိ ဘီးငယ် *pa-yi-baw-ga-awt-shi-bi-nge*
castor oil *(n.)* ကြက်ဆူဆီ *kyat-su-si*
casual *(adj.)* တမင်မဟုတ်သော၊ ဂရုတစိုက်မဟုတ်သော *ta-min-ma-hote-taw, ga-yu-ta-seik-ma-hote-taw*
casualty *(n.)* မတော်တဆ ထိခိုက်ပျက်စီးပျောက်ဆုံးသော အရာ ma-taw-ta-sa-hti-kheik-pyat-see-pyauk-sone-taw-a-yar
cat *(n.)* ကြောင် kyaung
cataclysm *(n.)* ရုတ်တရက်ကျရောက်သော ကပ်ဆိုး *yote-ta-yat-kya-yauk-taw-kat-soe*
catacomb *(n.)* လူသေမြုပ်မြေအောက်လိုဏ်ခေါင်း *lu-tay-myoke-myay-awt-hlaing-khaung*
catalogue *(n.)* စာရင်း *sa-yin*
catalyse *(v.)* ဓာတ်ကူသည် dat-khu-the
catalyst *(n.)* ဓာတ်ကူပစ္စည်း *dat-khu-pyit-see*
catalyzer *(n.)* ဓာတ်ကူပစ္စည်း *dat-khu-pyit-see*
catapult *(n.)* လောက်လေးခွ၊ ကျောက်တုံးပစ်ကိရိယာ *laut-lay-kwa, kyauk-tone-pyit-ka-yi-yar*
cataract *(n.)* အတွင်းတိမ် *a-twin-tain*
catastrophe *(n.)* ရုတ်တရက်ဖြစ်ပွားသော ကပ်ဘေး yote-ta-yat-phyit-pwar-taw-kat-bay
catastrophic *(adj.)* ကြီးမားသော kyi-mar-taw
catch *(v.)* ဖမ်းသည် *phan-the*
catching *(adj.)* ကူးစက်လွယ်သော *khu-sat-lwal-taw*
categorical *(adj.)* ပြတ်သားတိကျသော *pyat-tar-ti-kya-taw*
category *(n.)* အမျိုးအစား *a-myo-a-sar*
cater *(v.)* လိုအပ်သည်ကို ဖြည့်တင်းပေးသည် *lo-at-the-ko-pyae-tin-pay-the*
caterer *(n.)* အကျွေးအမွေးတာဝန်ယူရသူ *a-kyay-a-mway-tar-win-yu-ya-thu*
caterpillar *(n.)* ခူကောင် *khu-kaung*
catfight *(n.)* မိန်းမခြင်း ရန်ဖြစ်ခြင်း *main-ma-chin-yan-phit-chin*
catfish *(n.)* ငါးခူမျိုး *ngar-khu-myo*
catharsis *(n.)* ခံစားချက်ကို အနုပညာဖြင့် ဖြေဖျောက်ခြင်း *khan-sar-chat-ko-a-nu-pyin-nyar-phit-phyay-phyauk-chin*
cathedral *(n.)* ခရစ်ယာန်ဘုရားရှိခိုးကျောင်း *kha-yit-yan-pha-yar-shi-kho-kyaung*
catholic *(adj.)* ခရစ်ယာန်ဘာသာအားလုံးနှင့် ဆိုင်သော *kha-yit-yan-bar-tar-ar-lone-nint-sai-taw*
catholicism *(n.)* ဘရင်ဂျီဘာသာ *ba-yin-gyi-bar-tar*
cattle *(n.)* ကျွဲနွားတိရိစ္ဆာန် *kywe-nwar-ta-yeik-san*
catwalk *(n.)* ဖက်ရှင်လျှောက်လမ်း *phat-shin-shauk-lan*

caudal *(adj.)* အမြီးပိုင်း *a-myi-pai*

cauldron *(n.)* ဒယ်စောက် *dal-saut*

cauliflower *(n.)* ပန်းဂေါ် ဖီ *pan-gaw-phi*

causal *(adj.)* ကြောင်းကျိုးဆက်နွယ်နေသော *kyaung-kyo-sat-hnwe-nay-taw*

causality *(n.)* ကြောင်းကျိုးဆက်နွယ်မှု *kyuang-kyo-sat-hnwe-mu*

causation *(n.)* အကျိုးတရားကို ဖြစ်စေခြင်း *a-kyo-ta-yar-ko-phit-say-chin*

cause *(v.)* အကြောင်းခံသည် *a-kyaung-khan-the*

cause *(n.)* အကြောင်းတရား *a-kyaung-ta-yar*

causeway *(n.)* တာရိုးလမ်း *tar-yoe-lan*

caustic *(adj.)* လောင်တတ်သော၊ ငေါ့သော *laung-tat-taw, ngawt-taw*

caution *(n.)* သတိ *tha-di*

cautionary *(adj.)* သတိပေးသော *tha-di-pay-taw*

cautious *(adj.)* သတိရှိသော *tha-di-shi-taw*

cavalry *(n.)* မြင်းတပ်၊ သံချပ်ကာယန္တရားတပ် *myin-tat, tan-chat-kar-yan-da-yar-tat*

cave *(n.)* ဂူ *gyu*

caveat *(n.)* မလုပ်မီ စဉ်းစားရန် သတိပေးခြင်း *ma-lote-mu-sin-sar-yan-ta-di-pay-chin*

cavern *(n.)* လိုဏ်ဂူကြီး *hlaing-gu-gyi*

caviar *(n.)* ငါးဥဆားနယ် *ngar-oo-sar-nal*

cavil *(v.)* မလိုအပ်ပဲ ကြေးများသည် *ma-lo-at-pal-kyay-myar-the*

cavity *(n.)* ခေါင်းပေါက် *kaung-pauk*

cavort *(v.)* ခုန်ပေါက်မြူးထူးသည် *khone-pauk-my-htoo-the*

cavorting *(n.)* ခုန်ပေါက်မြူးထူးခြင်း *khone-pauk-my-htoo-chin*

caw *(v.)* ကျီးအာသံ *kyi-arr-than*

cease *(v.)* ရပ်စဲသည် yat-sal-the

ceasefire *(n.)* အပစ်အခတ်ရပ်စဲခြင်း *a-pyit-a-khat-yat-sal-chin*

ceaseless *(adj.)* ရပ်စဲခြင်းမရှိသော *yat-sal-chin-ma-shi-taw*

cedar *(n.)* သစ်ကတိုး *tit-ka-toe*

cede *(v.)* ပေးအပ်လိုက်ရသည် *pay-at-lite-ya-the*

ceiling *(n.)* မျက်နှာကြက် *myat-nar-kyat*

celebrate *(v.)* အခမ်းအနားကျင်းပသည် *a-khan-a-nar-kyin-pa-the*

celebration *(n.)* အောင်ပွဲခံခြင်း *aung-pwe-khan-chin*

celebrity *(n.)* လူသိများသူ *lu-thi-myar-thu*

celerity *(n.)* အရှိန် *a-shein*

celery *(n.)* တရုတ်နံနံကြီး *ta-yoke-nan-nan-gyi*

celestial *(adj.)* အာကာသ *ar-kar-tha*

celibacy *(n.)* ဗြဟ္မစရိယကျင့်ခြင်း *bwa-ma-sa-yi-yar-kyint-chin*

celibate *(adj.)* အိမ်ထောင်မပြုသော *eain-htaung-ma-pyu-taw*

cell *(n.)* ဆဲလ်၊ အခန်းငယ် *sal, a-khan-nge*

cell phone *(n.)* ဆဲလ်ဖုန်း *sal-phone*

cellar *(n.)* မြေအောက်ခန်း *myay-awt-khan*

cello *(n.)* တယောကြီး *ta-yaw-gyi*

cellophane *(n.)* မှန်ကြည်စက္ကူ *man-kyi-sat-kyu*

cellular *(adj.)* ဆယ်လူလာ၊ ဆဲလ်များဖြင့်ဖွဲ့စည်းထားသော *sal-lu-lar, sal-myar-phyint-phwe-see-htar-taw*

cellulite *(n.)* ဆဲလ်လူလိုက် *sal-lu-lite*

celluloid *(n.)* ရုပ်ရှင်ဖလင် *yoke-shin-pha-lin*

Celsius *(adj.)* ဆဲလ်စီယပ် *sal-see-yat*

cement *(n.)* ဘိလပ်မြေ *bi-lat-myay*

cemetery *(n.)* သင်္ချိုင်း *tin-gyai*

cense *(v.)* အမွှေးနံ့သာ လောင်ကျွမ်းသည် *a-mway-nant-tar-laung-kywan-the*

censer *(n.)* အမွှေးတိုင်ထွန်းခွက် *a-mway-tai-htun-khwat*

censor *(n.)* ဆင်ဆာလူကြီး *sin-sar-lu-gyi*

censorious *(adj.)* အခြားသူအား ပြင်းထန်စွာ ဝေဖန်သော *a-char-thu-arr-pyin-htan-swar-wai-phan-taw*

censorship *(n.)* ဆင်ဆာဖြတ်ခြင်း *sin-sar-phat-chin*

censure *(v.)* ပြင်းထန်စွာ ဝေဖန်သည် *pyin-than-swar-wai-hpan-the*

census *(n.)* သန်းခေါင်စာရင်း ta-khaung-sar-yin

cent *(n.)* ဆင့် *sint*

centaur *(n.)* လူခေါင်းနှင့် မြင်းကိုယ် *lu-gaung-nint-myin-ko*

centenarian *(n.)* ရာကျော်ဘိုးဘွား *yar-kyaw-boe-bwar*

centenary *(n.)* ရာပြည့်ပွဲ *yar-pyae-pwe*

centennial *(n.)* နှစ်တစ်ရာမှ တစ်ခါဖြစ်သော nit-ta-yar-ma-ta-khar-phit-taw

center *(n.)* စင်တာ *cin-tar*

centigrade *(adj.)* စင်တီဂရိတ် cin-te-ga-yeik

centimetre *(n.)* စင်တီမီတာ cin-te-mi-tar

centipede *(n.)* ကင်းခြေများ kin-chay-myar

central *(adj.)* အလယ် a-lal

central locking *(n.)* ဗဟိုသော့စနစ် ba-ho-taw-sa-nit

centralize *(v.)* ဗဟိုက ချုပ်ကိုင်သည် *ba-ho-ga-choke-kai-the*

centre *(n.)* အလယ်၊ အုပ်ချုပ်ရေးဗဟို *a-lal, oak-choke-yay-ba-ho*

centrical *(adj.)* မြို့လယ် *myo-lal*

centrifugal *(adj.)* ဗဟိုမှ ခွာသော *ba-ho-ma-khwar-taw*

centuple *(adj.)* တစ်ရာဆဖြစ်သော *ta-yar-sa-phit-taw*

century *(n.)* ရာစု *yar-su*

cephaloid *(adj.)* ရုတ်တရက်ကြီးလာသော *yote-ta-yat-kyi-lar-taw*

ceramics *(n.)* ကြွေထည်မြေထည် *kyway-htae-myay-htae*

cerated *(adj.)* ဖယောင်းဖြင့် ဖုံးထားသော *pha-yaung-phit-hpone-htar-taw*

cereal *(n.)* နံ့စားပင် *nan-sar-pin*

cerebellum *(n.)* ဦးနှောက်ငယ် oo-naut-nge

cerebral *(adj.)* ဦးနှောက်နှင့် ဆိုင်သော *oo-naut-nint-sai-taw*

ceremonial *(adj.)* အခမ်းအနား *a-khan-a-nar*

ceremonious *(adj.)* ဟိတ်ဟန်ပါသော *heik-han-par-taw*

ceremony *(n.)* အခမ်းအနား၊ သဘင်၊ ဟိတ်ဟန် *a-khan-a-nar, ta-bin, heik-han*

certain *(adj.)* သေချာသော *tay-char-taw*

certainly *(adv.)* မုချ *mote-cha*

certainty *(n.)* ကေန်ဖြစ်သောအရာ *a-kan-phit-taw-a-yar*

certificate *(n.)* အသိအမှတ်ပြုလက်မှတ် *a-ti-a-mat-pyu-lat-mat*

certify *(v.)* မှန်ကန်ကြောင်း တရားဝင်ဖော်ပြသည် *man-kan-kyaung-ta-yar-win-phaw-pya-the*

certitude *(n.)* သေချာခြင်း *tay-char-chin*

cerumen *(n.)* နာဖာချေး *na-phar-chee*

cervical *(adj.)* သားအိမ်ခေါင်းနှင့် ဆိုင်သော *tar-eain-kaung-nint-sai-taw*

cesarean *(n.)* ခွဲမွေးခြင်း *khwal-mway-chin*

cessation *(n.)* ရပ်ခြင်း၊ ဖြတ်ခြင်း *yat-chin, phat-chin*
cesspool *(n.)* အကျင့်ပျက်ချစားသော နေရာ *a-kyint-pyat-cha-sar-taw-nay-yar*
cetin *(n.)* စီတင် *see-tin*
cetylic *(adj.)* စီတိုင်လစ်အရက်ပြန် *see-tai-lit-a-yat-pyan*
chain *(n.)* ချိန်းကြိုး၊ သံကြိုး *chain-kyo, tan-kyo*
chair *(n.)* ကုလားထိုင် *ka-lar-htai*
chairman *(n.)* ဥက္ကဋ္ဌ *oak-ka-hta*
chaise *(n.)* မြင်းလှည်း *myin-lal*
chalet *(n.)* တောင်ပေါ်သစ်သားအိမ် *taung-paw-tit-tar-eain*
chalice *(n.)* စပျစ်ရည်ထည့်သည့် ဖလား *sa-pyit-yay-htae-the-pha-lar*
chalk *(v.)* မြေဖြူဖြင့် ရေးသည် *myay-phyu-phyint-yay-the*
chalkdust *(n.)* မြေဖြူမှုန့် *myay-phyu-hmont*
challenge *(n.)* စိန်ခေါ်ချက် sein-khaw-chat
chamber *(n.)* အခန်း a-khan
chamberlain *(n.)* ဘုရင့်အိမ်တော်ဝန် ba-yint-eain-taw-win
champagne *(n.)* ရှန်ပိန်ဝိုင် shan-pain-wine
champion *(n.)* ချန်ပီယံ *chan-pi-yan*
chance *(n.)* အခွင့်အရေး *a-khwint-a-yay*
chancellor *(n.)* အဓိပတိ *a-di-pa-ti*
chancery *(n.)* တရားဝန်ကြီးချုပ်ရုံး *ta-yar-win-gyi-choke-yone*
chandelier *(n.)* မီးပန်းဆိုင်း *mee-pan-sai*
change *(n.)* အပြောင်းအလဲ *a-pyaung-a-lal*
change *(v.)* ပြောင်းလဲသည် *pyaung-lal-the*
channel *(n.)* ရေလက်ကြား၊ လမ်းကြောင်း၊ ဦးတည်ရာ *yay-lat-kyar, lan-kyaung, oo-the-yar*
chant *(n.)* ကြွေးကြော်သံ *kway-kyaw-tan*
chaos *(n.)* ပရမ်းပတာဖြစ်ခြင်း *ba-yan-ba-tar-phit-chin*
chaotic *(adv.)* ပရမ်းပတာဖြစ်သော *ba-yan-ba-tar-phit-taw*
chapel *(n.)* ဘုရားကျောင်းတွင် သီးသန့် ဝတ်ပြုရာ နေရာ *pha-ya-kyaung-twin-thee-tant-wut-pyu-yar-nay-yar*
chaperone *(n.)* မိန်းမဖော် *main-ma-phaw*
chaplain *(n.)* ကျောင်း၊ စစ်တပ်၊ ထောင်တွင် အမှုထမ်းသူ ခရစ်ယာန်ဘုန်းကြီး *kyaung-sit-tat-htaung-twin-a-mu-htan-thu-kha-yit-yan-hpone-gyi*
chapter *(n.)* အခန်း *a-khan*
character *(n.)* စရိုက် *za-yite*
charade *(n.)* ဟန်ဆောင်မှု *han-saung-mu*
charcoal *(n.)* မီးသွေး *mee-thway*
charge *(n.)* အဖိုးအခ *a-phoe-a-kha*
charge *(v.)* ကျသင့်ငွေတောင်းခံသည် *kya-tint-ngwe-taung-khan-the*
charger *(n.)* အားသွင်းတုံး *arr-twin-tone*
chariot *(n.)* စစ်ရထား *sit-ya-htar*
charisma *(n.)* သြဇာတိက္ကမနှင့် ပြည့်စုံခြင်း *aw-zar-taik-ka-ma-nint-pyae-zone-chin*
charismatic *(adj.)* သြဇာတိက္ကမနှင့် ပြည့်စုံသော *aw-zar-taik-ka-ma-nint-pyae-zone-taw*
charitable *(adj.)* ကုသိုလ်ဖြစ် *ku-tho-phit*
charity *(n.)* ဒါန *dar-na*
charm *(n.)* ညှို့ဓာတ် *hnyo-dat*

charming *(adj.)* **နှစ်လိုဖွယ်အလွန်ကောင်းသော** nit-lo-phwal-a-lun-kaung-taw
chart *(v.)* **ဇယားကွက်** *za-yar-kwat*
chartbuster *(n.)* **အောင်မြင်သော အဆိုတော်** *aung-myin-taw-a-so-taw*
charter *(n.)* **ပဋိညာဉ်စာတမ်း** pa-dain-nyin-sar-tan
chartered *(adj.)* **အမိန့်ဖြင့် ဖွဲ့စည်းထားသော အဖွဲ့အစည်း၏ သတ်မှတ်ချက် ပြည့်မီသော** a-maint-phit-phwe-see-htar-taw-a-phwe-a-see-ei-tat-mat-chat-pyae-mi-taw
chase *(v.)* **လိုက်သည်** lite-the
chaser *(n.)* **အတားအဆီးကျော်ပြေးပွဲတွင် စီးသော မြင်း** *a-tar-a-see-kyaw-pyay-pwe-twin-see-taw-myin*
chaste *(adj.)* **ကာမေသုမိစ္ဆာစာရကို ရှောင်ကြဉ်သော** kar-may-thu-meik-sar-sar-ya-ko-shaung-kyin-taw
chasten *(v.)* **ဦးကျိုးစေသည်** *oo-kyo-say-the*
chastise *(v.)* **ဝေဖန်ပြစ်တင်သည်** *wai-phan-pyit-tin-the*
chastity *(n.)* **ဗြဟ္မစရိယကျင့်ခြင်း** *bwa-ma-sa-yi-yar-kyint-chin*
chat *(v.)* **စကားပြောသည်** sa-kar-pyaw-the
chat room *(n.)* **စကားပြောခန်း** sa-kar-pyaw-khan
chat show *(n.)* **တီဗီတွင် လူသိများသူတို့နှင့် ပရိသတ် ရင်းရင်းနှီးနှီး တွေ့ဆုံခန်း** *TV-twin-lu-ti-myar-thu-doe-nint-pa-yeik-tat-yin-yin-nee-nee-tway-sone-khan*
chateau *(n.)* **ပြင်သစ်အိမ်၊ ရဲတိုက်** pyin-thit-eain, ye-tite
chatter *(v.)* **ရောက်တတ်ရာရာပြောသည်** yauk-tat-yar-yar-pyaw-the
chauffeur *(n.)* **လူကြီး၏ ယာဉ်မောင်း** lu-gyi-ei-yin-maung
chauvinism *(n.)* **လူမျိုးကြီးဝါဒ** lu-myo-gyi-wa-da
chauvinist *(adj.& n.)* **လူမျိုးကြီးဝါဒီ** lu-myo-gyi-wa-di
cheap *(adj.)* **ဈေးပေါသော** zay-paw-taw
cheapen *(v.)* **ဈေးကျအောင် လုပ်သည်** *zay-kya-aung-lote-the*
cheat *(n.)* **လိမ်နည်း** *lain-nee*
cheat *(v.)* **လိမ်သည်** *lain-the*
cheater *(n.)* **လူလိမ်** *lu-lain*
check *(n.)* **စစ်ဆေးခြင်း** *sit-say-chin*
check *(v.)* **စစ်ဆေးသည်** *sit-say-the*
checker *(n.)* **ကုန်ပစ္စည်း စစ်ဆေးသူ** *kone-pyit-see-sit-say-thu*
check-in *(n.)* **အမည်စာရင်းသွင်းသည်** *a-me-sa-yin-thwin-the*
checklist *(n.)* **စာရင်း** sa-yin
checkmate *(n.)* **မရှုမလှုရှုံးခြင်း** ma-shu-ma-hla-shone-chin
checkout *(n.)* **ထွက်ခွာသည်** thwat-khwar-the
checkpoint *(n.)* **စစ်ဆေးရေးဂိတ်** *sit-say-yay-gate*
cheddar *(n.)* **အဝါရောင် ဒိန်ခဲမာတစ်မျိုး** *a-war-yaung-dain-khae-mar-ta-myo*
cheek *(n.)* **ပါး** *par*
cheep *(v.)* **ကျည်ကျည်ကျာကျာ မြည်သည်** *kyi-kyi-kyar-kyar-myi-the*
cheer *(v.)* **သြဘာပေးသည်** *aw-bar-pay-the*
cheerful *(adj.)* **ရွှင်ပျသော** *shwin-pya-taw*
cheerleader *(n.)* **အားတက်အောင် ဦးဆောင်အားပေးသူ** arr-tat-aung-oo-saung-arr-pay-thu
cheerless *(adj.)* **စိတ်မကြည်လင်ဖွယ်ဖြစ်သော** seik-ma-kyi-lin-phwal-phit-taw

cheese *(n.)* ဒိန်ခဲ *dain-khae*

cheesecake *(n.)* ဒိန်ခဲကိတ် *dain-khae-kate*

cheesy *(adj.)* ဒိန်ခဲကဲ့သို့ အနံ့အရသာရှိသော *dain-khae-kae-tho-a-nant-a-ya-tar-shi-taw*

cheetah *(n.)* သစ်ကျုတ် tite-kyoke

chef *(n.)* စားဖိုမှူး *sa-pho-hmu*

chemical *(n.)* ဓာတုဗေဒ *da-tu-bay-da*

chemical *(adj.)* ဓာတုဗေဒနှင့်ဆိုင်သော *da-tu-bay-da-nint-sai-taw*

chemise *(n.)* ရှင်မီးအင်္ကျီ *shin-mee-inn-gyi*

chemist *(n.)* ဓာတုဗေဒပညာရှင် *da-tu-bay-da-pyin-nyar-shin*

chemistry *(n.)* ဓာတုဗေဒ *da-tu-bay-da*

chemotherapy *(n.)* ကင်ဆာကုထုံး *kin-sar-ku-htone*

cheque *(n.)* ချက်လက်မှတ် *chat-lat-mat*

cherish *(v.)* ချစ်ခင်မြတ်နိုးသည် *chit-khin-myat-noe-the*

cheroot *(n.)* ဆေးပေါ့လိပ် *say-pot-late*

cherry *(n.)* ချယ်ရီပင်၊ ချယ်ရီသီး *cherry-pin, cherry-thee*

chess *(n.)* စစ်တုရင် *sit-tu-yin*

chessboard *(n.)* စစ်တုရင်ခုံ *sit-tu-yin-khone*

chest *(n.)* ရင်ဘတ် *yin-bat*

chestnut *(n.)* သစ်အယ်ပင် *tit-al-pin*

chew *(v.)* ဝါးသည် *war-the*

chic *(adj.)* ခေတ်ဆန်ကြော့မော့သော *khit-san-kyawt-mawt-thaw*

chick *(n.)* ကြက်၊ ငှက်ပေါက်စ *kyat-nget-paut-sa*

chicken *(n.)* ကြက် *kyat*

chickpea *(n.)* ကုလားပဲ *ka-lar-pal*

chide *(v.)* အပြစ်ဆိုသည် a-pyit-so-the

chief *(adj.)* အရေးပါသော a-yay-par-taw

chiefly *(adv.)* အဓိက *a-di-ka*

chieftain *(n.)* မျိုးနွယ်စုအကြီးအကဲ myo-nwe-su-a-kyi-a-kal

child *(n.)* ကလေး ka-lay

childbirth *(n.)* မီးဖွားခြင်း *mee-phwar-chin*

childcare *(n.)* ကလေးသူငယ်စောင့်ရှောက်ခြင်း အလုပ် *ka-lay-thu-ngal-saunt-shaut-chin-a-lote*

childhood *(n.)* ကလေးဘဝ *ka-lay-ba-wa*

childish *(adj.)* ကလေးဆန်သော *ka-lay-san-taw*

chill *(n.)* အေးစိမ့်ခြင်း *aye-saint-chin*

chilli *(n.)* ငရုတ်သီး *nga-yote-thee*

chilly *(adj.)* အေးစိမ့်သော aye-saint-taw

chime *(n.)* သံစုံခေါင်းလောင်းသံ *tan-sone-khaung-laung-than*

chimera *(n.)* ပေါက်ကရစိတ်ကူး *pauk-ka-ya-seik-khu*

chimney *(n.)* မီးခိုးခေါင်းတိုင် *mee-kho-khaung-tai*

chimpanzee *(n.)* ချင်ပန်ဇီမျောက် *chin-pan-zi-myauk*

chin *(n.)* မေးစေ့ *may-sae*

china *(n.)* ကြွေထည်ပစ္စည်း *kway-htae-pyit-see*

chink *(n.)* အက်ကြောင်း at-kyaung

chip *(n.)* အပဲ့၊ ပဲ့ရာ *a-pae, pae-yar*

chipping *(n.)* လမ်းခင်းကျောက်ဆန်ကွဲ *lan-khin-kyauk-san-kwe*

chirp *(v.)* ကျည်ကျည်ကျာကျာ မြည်သံ *kyi-kyi-kyar-kyar-myi-than*

chirpy *(adj.)* မြူးကြွသော *my-kwa-taw*

chisel *(n.)* ဆောက် *saut*

chit *(n.)* လူကြီးသူမမှန်း မသိသော မိန်းကလေး *lu-kyi-thu-ma-man-ma-thi-taw-main-ka-lay*
chivalrous *(adj.)* အမျိုးသမီးအပေါ် ညှာတာထောက်ထားသော *a-myo-ta-mi-a-paw-nyar-tar-htauk-htar-taw*
chivalry *(n.)* အမျိုးသမီးအပေါ် ညှာတာထောက်ထားခြင်း *a-myo-ta-mi-a-paw-nyar-tar-htauk-htar-chin*
chlorine *(n.)* ကလိုရင်းဓာတ် *ka-lo-yin-dat*
chloroform *(n.)* ကလိုရိုဖောင်း မေ့ဆေး *ka-lo-ro-phaung-mae-say*
chocolate *(n.)* ချောကလက် *chaw-ka-lat*
choice *(n.)* ရွေးချယ်မှု yway-chal-mu
choir *(n.)* ခရစ်ယာန်ဓမ္မတေးသံစုံကျူးအဖွဲ့ kha-yit-yan-dhamma-tay-tan-sone-kyu-a-phwe
choke *(v.)* မွန်းသည် *hmune-the*
cholera *(n.)* ကာလဝမ်းရောဂါ *kar-la-wan-yaw-gar*
choleric *(adj.)* စိတ်ဆိုးလွယ်သော *seik-soe-lwal-taw*
cholesterol *(n.)* ကိုလက်စရောအဆီဓာတ် *ko-lat-sa-yaw-a-si-dat*
choose *(v.)* ရွေးချယ်သည် *ywe-chal-the*
choosy *(adj.)* ဇီဇာကြောင်သော *zi-zar-kyaung-taw*
chop *(v.)* ခုတ်သည် *khote-the*
chopper *(n.)* ပုဆိန်တို၊ ရဟတ်ယာဉ် *pa-sein-toe, ya-hat-yin*
chopstick *(n.)* တူ *thu*
chord *(n.)* ကော့ဒ် *kawt*
choreograph *(v.)* ကကွက်စီစဉ်ဖန်တီးသည် *ka-kwat-si-sin-phan-thee-the*
choreography *(n.)* အကဗေဒ *a-ka-bay-da*
chorus *(n.)* သံပြိုင်အပိုဒ် *tan-pyaing-a-pite*
Christ *(n.)* ခရစ်တော်၏ ပုံတော် *kha-yit-taw-ei-pon-taw*
Christendom *(n.)* ခရစ်ယာန်လောက kha-yit-yan-law-ka
Christian *(adj.)* ခရစ်ယာန် kha-yit-yan
Christianity *(n.)* ခရစ်ယာန်အယူ *kha-yit-yan-a-yu*
Christmas *(n.)* ခရစ်စမတ်ပွဲတော် kha-yit-sa-mat-pwe-taw
chrome *(n.)* ခရိုမီယမ်စိမ်ထားသော သတ္တုထည် *kha-ro-mi-yan-sein-htar-taw-tat-thu-htal*
chromosome *(n.)* ခရိုမိုဆုမ်း *kha-ro-mo-sone*
chronic *(adj.)* နာတာရှည် *nar-tar-shay*
chronicle *(n.)* သမိုင်းမှတ်တမ်း *tha-mai-mat-than*
chronological *(adj.)* နှစ်ကာလအလိုက် စီစဉ်ထားသော *nit-kar-la-a-lite-si-sin-htar-taw*
chronology *(n.)* သမိုင်းဖြစ်ရပ်ကို ခေတ်ကာလအလိုက် သတ်မှတ်သည့် ပညာရပ် *tha-mai-phit-yat-ko-khit-kar-la-a-lite-tat-mat-the-pyin-nyar*
chrysalis *(n.)* ပိုးရုပ်ဖုံး *poe-yoke-phone*
chubby *(adj.)* ဝဝကစ်ကစ် *wa-wa-kit-kit*
chuckle *(v.)* တခစ်ခစ်ရယ်သည် *ta-khit-khit-yal-the*
chum *(n.)* မိတ်ဆွေ *meit-swe*
chunk *(n.)* အတုံးအတစ် *a-tone-a-tit*
church *(n.)* ခရစ်ယာန်ဘုရားကျောင်း *kha-yit-yan-pha-yar-kyaung*
churchyard *(n.)* ခရစ်ယာန်ဘုရားကျောင်းဝန်းအတွင်း သင်္ချိုင်း *kha-yit-yan-pha-yar-kyaung-win-a-twin-tin-gyaing*
churlish *(adj.)* ရိုင်းပျသော *yai-pya-taw*

churn *(v.)* နို့ပုံး noe-pone

cicada *(n.)* ပုစဥ်းရင်ကွဲ *pa-zin-yin-kwe*

cider *(n.)* ပန်းသီးအရက် *pan-thee-a-yat*

cigar *(n.)* ဆေးပြင်းလိပ် *say-pyin-leik*

cigarette *(n.)* စီးကရက် *see-ka-rat*

cinema *(n.)* ရုပ်ရှင်ရုံ *yoke-shin-yone*

cinematic *(adj.)* ရုပ်ရှင်နှင့် ပတ်သက်သော *yoke-shin-nint-pat-tat-taw*

cinematography *(n.)* ရုပ်ရှင်ရိုက်ကူးရေးပညာ *yoke-shin-yite-khu-yay-pyin-nyar*

cineplex *(n.)* ရုပ်ရှင်ရုံကြီး *yoke-shin-yone-gyi*

cinnamon *(n.)* သစ်ကြံပိုးခေါက် *tit-kyan-poe-khaut*

cipher(or cypher) *(n.)* စာဝှက်ရေးနည်း *sar-wat-yay-nee*

circle *(n.)* စက်ဝိုင်း *sat-wine*

circuit *(n.)* လျှပ်စီးပတ်လမ်း *hlyat-see-pat-lan*

circular *(adj.)* ဝိုင်းသော *wine-taw*

circulate *(v.)* လှည့်ပတ်သည် *hlae-pat-the*

circulation *(n.)* သွေးလှည့်ပတ်ခြင်း *thway-hlae-pat-chin*

circumcise *(v.)* လိင်တံထိပ်အရေပြားဖြတ်သည် *lain-tan-hteik-a-yay-pyar-phat-the*

circumference *(n.)* စက်ဝန်းမျဉ်း *sat-win-myin*

circumstance *(n.)* အခြေအနေ *a-chay-a-nay*

circumstantial *(adj.)* အသေးစိတ်ဖော်ပြသော *a-tay-seik-phaw-pya-taw*

circumvent *(v.)* ရှောင်သည် *shaung-the*

circus *(n.)* ဆပ်ကပ်အဖွဲ့ *sat-kat-a-phwe*

cirrhosis *(n.)* အသည်းခြောက်ရောဂါ *a-the-chauk-yaw-gar*

cirrus *(n.)* တိမ်မျှင် *tein-hmyin*

cisco *(n.)* ဆစ်စကိုကွန်ရက်ပညာ *sit-sa-ko-kun-yat-pyun-nyar*

cist *(n.)* ကျောက်ခေါင်းတလား *kyauk-khaung-ta-lar*

cistern *(n.)* ခေါင်မိုးတင်ရေတိုင်ကီ *khaung-moe-tin-yay-tai-gi*

citadel *(n.)* ခံတပ်၊ ရဲတိုက် *khan-tat, ye-tite*

citation *(n.)* ကိုးကားခြင်း *koe-kar-chin*

cite *(v.)* တိုက်ရိုက်ကိုးကားသည် *tite-yite-koe-kar-the*

citizen *(n.)* နိုင်ငံသား *nai-ngan-thar*

citizenship *(n.)* နိုင်ငံသားအဖြစ် *nai-ngan-thar-a-phit*

citric *(adj.)* ချဉ်သော *chin-taw*

citrine *(n.)* ဖန်ဝါရောင် သလင်းကျောက် *phan-war-yaung-tha-lin-kyauk*

citrus *(n.)* ရှောက်၊ သံပရာမျိုးဝင် အသီးများ *shaut-tan-pa-yar-myo-win-a-thee-myar*

city *(n.)* မြို့ *myo*

civic *(adj.)* နိုင်ငံသားနှင့် ဆိုင်သော nai-ngan-tar-nint-sai-taw

civics *(n.)* ပြည်သူ့နီတိ pyi-thu-ni-ti

civil *(adj.)* အများပြည်သူနှင့် ဆိုင်သော *a-myar-pyi-thu-nint-sai-taw*

civilian *(n.)* အရပ်သား *a-yat-tar*

civilization *(n.)* ယဥ်ကျေးမှု ဖွံ့ဖြိုးလာခြင်း *yin-kyay-mu-phwint-phyo-lar-chin*

civilize *(v.)* ယဥ်ကျေးမှု ဖွံ့ဖြိုးလာသည် *yin-kyay-mu-phwint-phyo-lar-the*

clack *(v.)* တဖောက်ဖောက်မြည်သံ *ta-taut-taut-myi-tan*

clad *(adj.)* ဝတ်ဆင်ထားသော *wit-sin-htar-taw*

cladding *(n.)* ထပ်အုပ်ထားသော အဖုံး၊ အကာ *htet-oak-htar-taw-a-hpone-a-kar*
claim *(v.)* အခိုင်အမာဆိုသည်၊ တောင်းဆိုသည် *a-khai-a-mar-so-the, taung-so-the*
claimant *(n.)* တောင်းဆိုသူ *taung-so-thu*
clam *(n.)* ခုံးကောင် gon-kaung
clamber *(v.)* ဖက်တက်သည် phat-tat-the
clammy *(adj.)* စေးထန်းထန်း *say-htan-htan*
clamour *(n.)* ပွက်ပွက်ညံသံ *pwat-pwat-nyan-nyan*
clamp *(n.)* ညှပ်၊ ပြုတ်တူ *hnyat, pyoke-tu*
clan *(n.)* မျိုးနွယ်စု *myo-nwe-su*
clandestine *(adj.)* ပုန်းလျှိုးကွယ်လျှိုး *pon-shyo-kwal-sho*
clap *(v.)* လက်ခုပ်တီးသည် *lat-khote-tee-the*
clapper *(n.)* ခလောက်ဆန် *kha-laut-san*
claque *(n.)* အငှားပရိသတ် *a-nyar-pa-yeik-tat*
clarification *(n.)* ရှင်းလင်းခြင်း *shin-lin-chin*
clarify *(v.)* ရှင်းလင်းသည် *shin-lin-the*
clarinet *(n.)* ကလယ်ရီနက် *ka-lal-ri-nat*
clarity *(n.)* ကြည်လင်ပြတ်သားခြင်း *kyi-lin-pyat-tar-chin*
clash *(v.)* ရင်ဆိုင်တိုက်ခိုက်သည် *yin-sai-tite-khite-the*
clasp *(v.)* ချိတ် *cheik*
class *(n.)* အတန်း *a-tan*
classic *(adj.)* အထူးခြားဆုံး၊ ဖြစ်ရိုးဖြစ်စဉ် *a-htoo-char-sone, phit-yoe-phit-sin*
classical *(adj.)* ခိုင်မာနေပြီဖြစ်သော *khai-mar-nay-p-phit-taw*
classification *(n.)* အမျိုးအစားခွဲခြင်း *a-myo-a-sar-khwal-chin*
classified *(adj.)* အုပ်စုအလိုက် ခွဲထားသော *oak-su-a-lite-kwal-htar-taw*
classify *(v.)* အုပ်စုခွဲသည် *oak-su-kwal-the*
classmate *(n.)* အတန်းဖော် *a-tan-phaw*
classroom *(n.)* စာသင်ခန်း *sar-tin-khan*
clatter *(n.)* ဂလောက်ဂလောက်မြည်သံ *ga-laut-ga-laut-myi-tan*
clause *(n.)* အပိုဒ်ငယ် a-pike-ngal
claustrophobia *(n.)* ပိတ်လှောင်ကြောက်လွန်စိတ်ရောဂါ *pait-laung-kyauk-loon-seik-yaw-gar*
clave *(n.)* တီးခေါက်ရန် တုတ်နှစ်ချောင်း *tee-khaut-yan-doke-na-khyaung*
claw *(n.)* လက်သည်း *lat-the*
clay *(n.)* ရွှံ့စေး *shwunt-say*
clean *(v.)* သန့်ရှင်းသည် *tant-shin-the*
clean *(adj.)* သန့်စင်သော *tant-sin-taw*
cleaner *(n.)* သန့်ရှင်းရေးသမား၊ သန့်စင်ဆေး၊ *tant-shin-yay-ta-mar, tant-sin-say*
cleanliness *(n.)* သန့်ရှင်းမှု *tant-shin-mu*
cleanse *(v.)* သန့်ရှင်းစေသည် *tant-shin-say-the*
clear *(adj.)* ကြည်လင်သော *kyi-lin-taw*
clearance *(n.)* ခွင့်ပြုမိန့်၊ ဖယ်ထုတ်ပစ်ခြင်း *khwint-pyu-maint, phal-htoke-pyit-chin*
clearly *(adv.)* ကြည်ကြည်လင်လင် *kyi-kyi-lin-lin*
cleat *(n.)* တောင့်တင်းအောင် ပိုးထားသည့် တန်း *taunt-tin-aung-poe-htar-the-tan*
cleavage *(n.)* အကွဲ *a-lwal*
cleave *(v.)* ခုတ်ပိုင်းသည် *khote-pai-the*
cleft *(n.)* အက်ကွဲကြောင်း *at-kwal-kyaung*
clemency *(n.)* သက်ညှာခြင်း *tat-nyar-chin*
clement *(adj.)* ငြိမ်သက်သာယာသော *nyein-thet-tar-yar-taw*

clementine *(n.)* လိမ္မော်သီး *lain-maw-thee*

clench *(v.)* ကျစ်ကျစ်ဆုပ်သည် *kyit-kyit-sote-the*

clergy *(n.)* ခရစ်ယာန်ဘုန်းတော်ကြီး *kha-yit-yan-bone-daw-gyi*

clerical *(adj.)* စာရေးစာချီနှင့်ဆိုင်သော *sar-yay-sar-chi-nint-sai-taw*

clerk *(n.)* စာရေး *sar-yay*

clever *(adj.)* တော်သော *taw-thaw*

clew *(n.)* ချည်လုံး၊ ကြိုးလုံး *che-lone*

cliché *(n.)* ဖန်တစ်ရာတေနေသော စကားလုံး phan-ta-yar-tay-nay-taw-sa-kar-lone

click *(n.)* ကလစ် မြည်သံ *ka-lit-myi-tan*

client *(n.)* ဖောက်သည် *phaut-the*

cliff *(n.)* ချောက်ကမ်းပါး *chauk-kan-par*

climate *(n.)* ရာသီဥတု yar-thi-oo-tu

climate change *(n.)* ရာသီဥတုပြောင်းလဲခြင်း yar-thi-oo-tu-pyaung-lal-chin

climate control *(n.)* ရာသီဥတုထိန်းသိမ်းခြင်း yar-thi-oo-tu-htein-tain-chin

climax *(n.)* အထွတ်အထိပ် *a-htut-a-hteik*

climb *(v.)* တက်သည် tat-the

climber *(n.)* တောင်တက်သမား taung-tat-ta-mar

clinch *(v.)* အတည်ပြုသည် *a-the-pyu-the*

cling *(v.)* တွယ်ဖက်ထားသည် *twal-phat-htar-the*

clingy *(adj.)* တွယ်ဖက်ထားသော *twal-phat-htar-thaw*

clinic *(n.)* ဆေးခန်း *say-khan*

clinical *(adj.)* ကုသခြင်းနှင့် ဆိုင်သော khu-ta-chin-nint-sai-taw

clink *(n.)* ချွင်ချွင်မြည်သံ chwan-chwan-myi-tan

clip *(n.)* ကလစ် ka-lit

clipper *(n.)* ရွက်သင်္ဘော၊ ကတ်ကြေး၊ လက်သည်းညှပ် ywet-tin-baw, kat-kyay, lat-the-nyat

clipping *(n.)* ဖြတ်စ၊ ညှပ်စ *phat-sa, nyat-sa*

clive *(v.)* တက်သည် tat-the

cloak *(n.)* ဝတ်ရုံ၊ ခြုံထည် wit-yone, chone-htal

cloakroom *(n.)* သန့်စင်ခန်း *tant-sin-khan*

clobber *(n.)* အဝတ်အစား၊ အသုံးအဆောင် *a-wit-a-sar, a-tone-a-saung*

clock *(n.)* နာရီ *nar-yee*

clockwise *(adv.)* လက်ယာရစ် *lat-yar-yit*

clod *(n.)* မြေခဲရွှံ့ခဲ *myay-khae-shwunt-khae*

cloister *(n.)* အမိုးပါစင်္ကြံ *a-moe-par-sin-gyan*

clone *(n.)* ကိုယ်ပွား *koe-pwar*

close *(adj.)* နီးကပ်သော *nee-kat-taw*

close *(n.)* အဆုံး *a-sone*

closet *(n.)* ဗီရို၊ စတိုခန်းငယ် *bi-yo, sa-to-khan-nge*

closure *(n.)* ပိတ်ခြင်း pait-chin

clot *(n.)* ခဲခြင်း *khal-chin*

cloth *(n.)* အထည် *a-htal*

clothe *(v.)* ဝတ်သည် *wit-the*

clothes *(n.)* အဝတ်အစား *a-wit-a-sar*

clothing *(n.)* အဝတ်အထည် *a-wit-a-htal*

cloud *(n.)* တိမ် *tain*

cloudburst *(n.)* မိုးပုဆိန် *moe-pa-sein*

cloudy *(adj.)* တိမ်ထူသော *tain-htoo-taw*

clove *(n.)* လေးညှင်းပွင့် lay-nyin-pwint

clown *(n.)* လူပြက် lu-byat

club *(n.)* ကလပ် *ka-lat*

clue *(n.)* သဲလွန်စ *the-lun-sa*

clueless *(adj.)* သဲလွန်စမရှိသော *the-lun-sa-ma-shi-taw*

clumsy *(adj.)* ဆိုးဝါးသော *soe-war-taw*

cluster *(n.)* အပြွတ်၊ အခိုင်၊ အစုအပြုံ *a-phywut, a-khai, a-su-a-pyon*

clutch *(n.)* ကလပ် *ka-lat*

clutter *(v.)* ရှုပ်ပွနေသည် *shote-pwa-nay-the*

coach *(n.)* ရထားလုံး *ya-thar-lon*

coal *(n.)* ကျောက်မီးသွေး *kyauk-mee-thway*

coalition *(n.)* ယာယီညွန့်ပေါင်းအဖွဲ့ *yar-yee-nyunt-paung-a-phwe*

coarse *(adj.)* ကြမ်းထော်သော *kyan-htaw-taw*

coast *(n.)* ပင်လယ်ကမ်းခြေ *pin-lal-kan-chay*

coastal *(adj.)* ပင်လယ်ကမ်းခြေ pin-lal-kan-chay

coaster *(n.)* ကမ်းရိုးတန်းသွား သင်္ဘော *kan-yoe-tan-twar-tin-baw*

coastguard *(n.)* ကမ်းရိုးတန်းရဲ *kan-yoe-tan-ye*

coastline *(n.)* ကမ်းရိုးတန်း *kan-yoe-tan*

coat *(n.)* ကုတ်အင်္ကျီ *kote-inn-gyi*

coating *(n.)* အလွှာ *a-hlwar*

coax *(v.)* ချော့သည်၊ နူးသည် *chawt-the, nu-the*

coaxial *(n.)* ဝင်ရိုးအလယ်မှတ် *win-yoe-a-lal-mat*

cobalt *(n.)* ကိုဗော့သတ္တု *ko-bawt-tat-tu*

cobble *(n.)* လမ်းခင်းကျောက်လုံး *lan-khin-kyauk-lone*

cobbler *(n.)* ဖိနပ်ချုပ်သမား *phi-nat-choke-ta-mar*

cobblestone *(n.)* လမ်းခင်းကျောက်လုံး *lan-khin-kyauk-lone*

cobra *(n.)* မြွေဟောက် *mway-hauk*

cobweb *(n.)* ပင့်ကူအိမ် *pint-khu-eain*

cocaine *(n.)* ကိုကင်း *ko-kin*

cock *(n.)* ကြက်ဖ *kyat-pha*

cockade *(n.)* ဖဲတံဆိပ် *phal-ta-seik*

cocker *(v.)* နားရွက်ဖား ခွေးစုတ်ဖွား *nar-ywet-phar-khway-sote-phwar*

cockle *(v.)* ချင်း *chin*

cockpit *(n.)* လေယာဉ်မှူးအခန်း *lay-yin-muu-a-khan*

cockroach *(n.)* ပိုးဟပ် *poe-hat*

cocktail *(n.)* ကော့တေးအရက် *kawt-tay-a-yat*

cocoa *(n.)* ကိုကိုးမှုန့် *ko-koe-hmont*

coconut *(n.)* အုန်းသီး *ohn-thee*

cocoon *(n.)* ပိုးအိမ် *poe-eain*

cod *(n.)* ငါးကြီးဆီထုတ် ပင်လယ်ငါးကြီး *nga-gyi-see-htoke-pin-lal-ngar-gyi*

code *(n.)* သင်္ကေတဝှက်စာ၊ ကိုဒဥပဒေ၊ ကျင့်ဝတ်စည်းကမ်း *tin-kay-ta-hwat-sar, ko-da-oo-pa-day, kyint-wit-see-kan*

coding *(n.)* ကုတ်နံပါတ်ထားခြင်း ဖြစ်စဉ် *kote-nan-pat-htar-chin-phit-sin*

co-education *(n.)* ကျားမ အတူသင်ကြားသော *kyar-ma-a-tu-tin-kyar-taw*

coefficient *(n.)* မြှောက်ဖော်ကိန်း *hmyaut-phaw-kein*

coerce *(v.)* အကျပ်ကိုင်သည် *a-kyat-kai-the*

coexist *(v.)* အတူနေထိုင်သည် *a-thu-nay-htain-the*

coexistence *(n.)* ငြိမ်းချမ်းစွာ အတူနေထိုင်ခြင်း *nyein-chan-swar-a-thu-nay-htain-chin*
coffee *(n.)* ကော်ဖီ *kof-fee*
coffee bean *(n.)* ကော်ဖီစေ့ *kof-fee-say*
coffee break *(n.)* ကော်ဖီသောက် နားချိန် *kof-fee-taut-nar-chain*
coffee maker *(n.)* ကော်ဖီဖျော်စက် *kof-fee-phyaw-sat*
coffer *(n.)* ဘဏ္ဍာသေတ္တာ *ban-dar-tit-tar*
coffin *(n.)* အခေါင်း *a-khaung*
cog *(n.)* ခွေးသွားစိတ် *khway-twar-seik*
cogent *(adj.)* ခိုင်လုံသော *khine-lon-taw*
cognate *(adj.)* ရင်းမြစ်တူသော yit-myit-thu-taw
cognition *(n.)* သိမြင်ခြင်း ti-myin-chin
cognitive *(adj.)* သိမြင်တတ်သော *ti-myin-tat-taw*
cognizance *(n.)* အသိ၊ သတိရှိမှု *a-thi, ta-di-shi-mu*
cohabit *(v.)* လက်မထပ်ဘဲ အတူနေသည် *lat-ma-htet-pae-a-thu-nay-the*
cohere *(v.)* ဆက်စပ်မှု ရှိသည် *sat-sat-mu-shi-the*
coherent *(adj.)* အဆီအငေါ်တည့်သော *a-si-a-ngaw-tae-taw*
cohesion *(n.)* အဆက်အစပ် *a-sat-a-sat*
cohort *(n.)* စိတ်တူကိုယ်တူ လူသိုက် *seik-tu-koe-tu-lu-theik*
coiffure *(n.)* ဆံပင်ထုံးဖွဲ့မှု *san-pin-htone-phwe-mu*
coil *(n.)* အခွေ *a-khway*
coin *(n.)* အကြွေစေ့ *a-kyway-say*
coinage *(n.)* ဒင်္ဂါးသွန်းခြင်း *din-gar-thoon-chin*
coincide *(v.)* တိုက်ဆိုင်သည် *tite-sai-the*
coincidence *(n.)* တိုက်ဆိုင်မှု *tite-sai-mu*
coir *(n.)* အုန်းဆံမျှင် *ohn-san-hmyin*
coke *(v.)* ကုတ်မီးသွေး *kote-mee-thway*
cold *(adj.)* အေးသော *aye-taw*
coleslaw *(n.)* ဂေါ် ဖီလက်သုပ် gaw-phi-lat-toke
colic *(n.)* လေထိုးလေအောင့်နာ *lay-htoe-lay-aunt-nar*
collaborate *(v.)* ပူးပေါင်းသည် poe-paung-the
collaboration *(n.)* ပူးပေါင်းခြင်း poe-paung-chin
collagen *(n.)* ကိုလာဂျင် *ko-lar-gin*
collapse *(v.)* ပြိုလဲသည် *pyo-lae-the*
collar *(n.)* ကော်လာ *kaw-lar*
collate *(v.)* ကောက်နုတ်စုစည်းသည် *kaut-note-su-see-the*
collateral *(n.)* အပေါင်ပစ္စည်း *a-paung-pyit-see*
colleague *(n.)* လုပ်ဖော်ကိုင်ဖက် *lote-phaw-kai-phat*
collect *(v.)* စုစည်းသည် *su-see-the*
collection *(n.)* စုစည်းခြင်း su-see-chin
collective *(adj.)* စုပေါင်းသော *su-paung-taw*
collector *(n.)* စုဆောင်းသူ *su-paung-thu*
college *(n.)* ကောလိပ်ကျောင်း *kaw-lait-kyung*
collide *(v.)* တိုက်မိသည် *tite-mi-the*
collision *(n.)* တိုက်မိခြင်း *tite-mi-chin*
colloquial *(adj.)* အရပ်သုံး a-yat-tone
colloquialism *(n.)* အရပ်သုံးစကား *a-yat-tone-sa-kar*

collude *(v.)* လိမ်လည် လှည့်ဖျားရန် ပေါင်းကြံသည် *lain-lal-lae-pyar-yan-paung-kyan-the*
collusion *(n.)* ပူးပေါင်းလိမ်လည်ရန် ညှိထားခြင်း *pu-paung-lain-lal-yan-nyi-htar-chin*
cologne *(n.)* အော်ဒီကလုန်းရေမွှေး *aw-di-ka-lone-yay-mywe*
colon *(n.)* အူမ *aw-ma*
colonel *(n.)* ဗိုလ်မှူးကြီး *bo-mu-gyi*
colonial *(adj.)* ကိုလိုနီနှင့် ဆိုင်သော *ko-lo-ni-nint-sai-taw*
colony *(n.)* ကိုလိုနီ *ko-lo-ni*
colossal *(adj.)* ရောမ *a-yar-ma*
colour *(n.)* အရောင် *a-yaung*
colour-blind *(adj.)* အရောင်ကန်းသော *a-yaung-kan-taw*
colourful *(adj.)* အရောင်စုံသော *a-yaung-sone-taw*
column *(n.)* ကော်လံ *kaw-lan*
columnist *(n.)* ပင်တိုင်ဆောင်းပါးရှင် *pin-tai-saung-par-shin*
coma *(n.)* မေ့မြောခြင်း *mae-myaw-chin*
comatose *(adj.)* သတိမေ့မြောနေသော ta-di-mae-myaw-nay-taw
comb *(n.)* ဘီး *bee*
combat *(n.)* တိုက်ပွဲ *tite-pwe*
combatant *(n.)* တိုက်ပွဲဝင်စစ်သည် *tite-pwe-win-sit-the*
combative *(adj.)* တိုက်ခိုက်ရန် အသင့်ရှိသော *tite-khite-yan-a-tint-shi-taw*
combination *(n.)* ပေါင်းစပ်ခြင်း *paung-sat-chin*
combine *(v.)* ပေါင်းစပ်သည် paung-sat-the
combust *(v.)* လောင်ကျွမ်းသည် *laung-kywan-the*
combustible *(adj.)* မီးလောင်လွယ်သော *mee-laung-lwal-taw*
combustion *(n.)* လောင်ကျွမ်းခြင်း *laung-kywan-chin*
come *(v.)* လာသည် *lar-the*
comedian *(n.)* လူရွှင်တော် *lu-shwin-taw*
comedy *(n.)* ဇာတ်မြူး *zat-my*
comely *(adj.)* လှပတင့်တယ်သော *hla-pa-tint-tal-taw*
comet *(n.)* ကြယ်တံခွန် *kyal-ta-khun*
comfit *(n.)* ချိုချဉ် *cho-chin*
comfort *(n.)* သက်သောင့်သက်သာ ရှိခြင်း *tat-taunt-tat-tar-shi-chin*
comfortable *(adj.)* သက်သောင့်သက်သာ ရှိသော *tat-taunt-tat-tar-shi-taw*
comfy *(adj.)* ဇိမ်ရှိသော zain-shi-taw
comic *(n.)* ကာတွန်း၊ လူရွှင်တော် kar-toon, lu-shwin-taw
comic *(adj.)* ဟာသ *har-ta*
comical *(adj.)* ရယ်စရာကောင်းသော *yal-sa-yar-kaung-taw*
comma *(n.)* ပုဒ်ရပ်သင်္ကေတ *poke-yat-tin-kay-ta*
command *(v.)* အမိန့်ပေးသည် *a-maint-pay-the*
commandant *(n.)* တပ်မှူးချုပ် *tat-mu-gyoke*
commander *(n.)* တပ်မှူး *tat-mu*
commandment *(n.)* ပညတ်တော် ဆယ်ပါးအနက် တစ်ပါးပါး pyit-nyat-taw-sal-par-a-nat-ta-par-par
commando *(n.)* ကွန်မန်ဒိုတပ်ဖွဲ့ koon-man-do-tat-phwe
commemorate *(v.)* အထိမ်းအမှတ်အဖြစ် အမှတ်တရ ကျင်းပသည် *a-htain-a-mat-a-phit-a-mat-ta-ya-kyin-pa-the*

commemoration *(n.)* အထိမ်းအမှတ်ပွဲ *a-htain-a-mat-pwe*
commence *(v.)* စတင်သည် *sa-tin-the*
commencement *(n.)* အစပြုခြင်း၊ ဘွဲ့နှင်းသဘင် *a-sa-pyu-chin, bwe-hnin-ta-bin*
commend *(v.)* ချီးကျူးသည် *chee-kyu-the*
commendable *(adj.)* ချီးကျူးထိုက်သော *chee-kyu-htike-taw*
commendation *(n.)* ချီးကျူးခြင်း *chee-kyu-chin*
comment *(n.)* မှတ်ချက်ပေးသည် *mat-chat-pay-the*
commentary *(n.)* ရှင်းလင်းချက်မှတ်စု *shin-lin-chat-mat-su*
commentator *(n.)* မျက်မှောက်ရေးရာ လေ့လာသုံးသပ်သူ *myat-mauk-yay-yar-lay-lar-tone-tat-thu*
commerce *(n.)* ကုန်သွယ်မှု *kone-twal-mu*
commercial *(adj.)* ကုန်သွယ်မှုနှင့် ဆိုင်သော *kone-twal-mu-nint-sai-taw*
commiserate *(v.)* စာနာစကားပြောသည် *sar-nar-sa-kar-pyaw-the*
commission *(n.)* ကော်မရှင်ခ *kaw-ma-shin-kha*
commissioner *(n.)* ကော်မရှင်အဖွဲ့ဝင် *kaw-ma-shin-a-phwe-win*
commissure *(n.)* အရိုးနှစ်ခုကြားအဆက် *a-yoe-na-khu-kyar-a-sat*
commit *(v.)* ကျူးလွန်သည် *kyu-loon-the*
commitment *(n.)* ကတိပေးပြီး အလုပ် *ka-di-pay-pi-a-lote*
committee *(n.)* ကော်မတီ *kaw-ma-tee*
commode *(n.)* ဗိုလ်ထိုင် *bo-htai*
commodity *(n.)* လူသုံးကုန် lu-tone-kone
common *(adj.)* အများနှင့် ဆိုင်သော *a-myar-nint-sai-taw*
commoner *(n.)* အရပ်သား *a-yat-tar*
commonplace *(adj.)* ရိုးနေပြီဖြစ်သော *yoe-nay-pi-phit-taw*
commonwealth *(n.)* ဓနသဟာယနိုင်ငံများ *da-na-tha-har-ya-nai-ngan-myar*
commotion *(n.)* ဆူညံသောင်းကျန်းခြင်း *su-nyan-taung-gyan-chin*
communal *(adj.)* အများသုံး *a-myar-tone*
commune *(n.)* ဘုံအဖွဲ့ *bon-a-phwe*
communicate *(v.)* ဆက်သွယ်သည် *sat-thwal-the*
communication *(n.)* ဆက်သွယ်ခြင်း *sat-thwal-chin*
communion *(n.)* အတူခံစားခြင်း *a-thu-khan-sar-chin*
communique *(n.)* တရားဝင် ကြေညာချက် *ta-yar-win-kyay-nyar-chat*
communism *(n.)* ကွန်မြူနစ်ဝါဒ *kun-myu-nit-war-da*
communist *(n.)* ကွန်မြူနစ်ဝါဒီ *kun-myu-nit-war-di*
community *(n.)* လူစု၊ ရပ်ကွက် *lu-su, yat-kwat*
commute *(v.)* ပြစ်ဒဏ်လျှော့ပေါ့သည် *pyit-dan-shawt-pawt-the*
compact *(adj.)* သိပ်သည်းသော *taik-the-taw*
companion *(n.)* အဖော် *a-phaw*
company *(n.)* ကုမ္ပဏီ *kone-pa-ni*
comparative *(adj.)* နှိုင်းယှဉ်လေ့လာသော *hnai-shin-lay-lar-taw*
compare *(v.)* နှိုင်းယှဉ်သည် *hnai-shin-the*
comparison *(n.)* နှိုင်းယှဉ်ခြင်း *hnai-shin-chin*
compartment *(n.)* အခန်း a-khan
compass *(n.)* သံလိုက်အိမ်မြှောင် tan-lite-ain-hmyaung

compassion *(n.)* ကရုဏာ *ka-yu-nar*

compatible *(adj.)* သဟဇာတဖြစ်သော *ta-ha-zar-ta-phit-taw*

compel *(v.)* အတင်းအကျပ်ခိုင်းသည် *a-tin-a-kyat-khai-the*

compendious *(adj.)* တိုတိုနှင့် ပြည့်စုံပြီး အရေးကြီးသော အချက်များ အားလုံးပါဝင်သော *toe-toe-nint-pyae-zone-p-a-yay-kyi-taw-a-chat-myar-arr-lone-par-win-taw*

compensate *(v.)* အလျော်ပေးသည် *a-yaw-pay-the*

compensation *(n.)* လျော်ကြေး *yaw-kyay*

compete *(v.)* ပြိုင်ဆိုင်သည် pyai-sai-the

competence *(n.)* လုပ်ရည်ကိုင်ရည် *lote-yay-kai-yay*

competent *(adj.)* အရည်အချင်းရှိသော *a-yay-a-chin-shi-taw*

competition *(n.)* ပြိုင်ပွဲ *pyai-pwe*

competitive *(adj.)* အများနှင့် ယှဉ်ပြိုင်ရသော *a-myar-nint-yin-pyai-ya-taw*

competitor *(n.)* ပြိုင်ဘက် *pyai-bat*

compilation *(n.)* ကျမ်းပြုခြင်း *kyan-pyu-chin*

compile *(v.)* စုဆောင်းသည် *su-saung-the*

complacent *(adj.)* မိမိဘာသာ အားရကျေနပ်သော *mi-mi-bar-tar-arr-ya-kyay-nat-taw*

complain *(v.)* တိုင်ကြားသည် *tai-kyar-the*

complaint *(n.)* တိုင်ကြားချက် *tai-kyar-chat*

complaisance *(n.)* သိတတ်ခြင်း *ti-tat-chin*

complaisant *(adj.)* သိတတ်သော *ti-tat-taw*

complement *(n.)* အဖြည့် *a-phyae*

complementary *(adj.)* လိုက်ဖက်သော *lite-phat-taw*

complete *(adj.)* ပြည့်စုံသော *pyae-zone-taw*

completion *(n.)* အပြီးသတ်ခြင်း *a-pi-tat-chin*

complex *(adj.)* ခက်ခဲရှုပ်ထွေးသော *khat-khae-shote-htway-taw*

complexion *(n.)* အသားအရေ *a-tar-a-yay*

compliance *(n.)* လေးစားလိုက်နာခြင်း *lay-sar-lite-nar-chin*

compliant *(adj.)* လိုက်လျောလွန်းသော *lite-lyaw-loon-taw*

complicate *(v.)* ခက်ခဲရှုပ်ထွေးစေသည် *khat-khae-shote-htway-the*

complication *(n.)* ပိုမိုရှုပ်ထွေးသော အရာ *po-mo-shote-htway-taw-a-yar*

complicity *(n.)* ကြံရာပါခြင်း *kyan-yar-par-chin*

compliment *(n.)* ချီးမွမ်းခြင်း *chee-moon-chin*

complimentary *(adj.)* ချီးမွမ်းသော *chee-moon-taw*

comply *(v.)* လိုက်နာသည် *lite-nar-the*

component *(adj.)* အစိတ်အပိုင်းဖြစ်သော *a-seik-a-pai-phit-taw*

compose *(v.)* စပ်ဆိုသည် *sat-so-the*

composite *(adj.)* အမျိုးမျိုးပါဝင်သော *a-myo-myo-par-win-taw*

composition *(n.)* ရေးစပ်သီကုံးခြင်း၊ ပါဝင်ပစ္စည်းများ *yay-sat-thi-kone-chin, par-win-pyit-see-myar*

compositor *(n.)* စာစီသမား *sar-si-ta-mar*

compost *(n.)* သစ်ရွက်ဆွေးမြေဩဇာ tat-ywet-sway-myay-aw-zar

composure *(n.)* တည်ငြိမ်အေးဆေးမှု the-nyein-aye-say-mu

comprehend *(v.)* နားလည်သည် *nar-lal-the*
comprehension *(n.)* တတ်သိနားလည်မှု *tat-ti-nar-lal-mu*
comprehensive *(adj.)* ပြည့်စုံသော *pyae-zone-taw*
compress *(v.)* ဖိသည် *phi-the*
compressor *(n.)* ဖိစက် phi-sat
comprise *(v.)* ပါဝင်သည် par-win-the
compromise *(n.)* ညှိခြင်း *nyi-chin*
compulsion *(n.)* မလုပ်မနေ လုပ်ရခြင်း *ma-lote-ma-nay-lote-ya-chin*
compulsory *(adj.)* မလုပ်မနေ လုပ်ရသော *ma-lote-ma-nay-lote-ya-taw*
compunction *(n.)* လိပ်ပြာမလုံခြင်း *lake-pyar-ma-lon-chin*
computation *(n.)* တွက်ချက်ခြင်း *twat-chat-chin*
compute *(v.)* တွက်ချက်သည် *twat-chat-the*
computer *(n.)* ကွန်ပျူတာ *kun-pyu-tar*
computerize *(v.)* ကွန်ပျူတာကို လုပ်ငန်းတွင် သုံးသည် *kun-pyu-tar-ko-lote-ngan-twin-tone-the*
comrade *(n.)* ရဲဘော်ရဲဘက် *ye-baw-ye-bat*
concave *(adj.)* ခွက်သော *khwat-taw*
conceal *(v.)* ဖုံးကွယ်သည် *hpone-kwal-the*
concealer *(n.)* ကွန်စီလာ *kun-see-lar*
concede *(v.)* ဝန်ခံသည် *win-khan-the*
conceit *(n.)* ဘဝင်မြင့်ခြင်း *ba-win-myint-chin*
conceive *(v.)* အကြံရသည်၊ ကိုယ်ဝန်ဆောင်သည် a-kyan-ya-the, ko-win-saung-the
concentrate *(v.)* အာရုံစူးစိုက်သည် *arr-yone-sue-site-the*
concentration *(n.)* အာရုံစူးစိုက်ခြင်း *arr-yone-sue-site-chin*
concentric *(adj.)* ဗဟိုတူသော *ba-ho-tu-taw*
concept *(n.)* အယူအဆ *a-yu-a-sa*
conception *(n.)* စိတ်ကူးခြင်း၊ သန္ဓေတည်ခြင်း seik-khu-chin, ta-day-tal-chin
concern *(v.)* သက်ဆိုင်သည်၊ စိုးရိမ်သည် *thet-sai-the, soe-yein-the*
concerned *(adj.)* ပူပန်သော *pu-pan-taw*
concerning *(prep.)* နှင့်ပတ်သက်၍ *nint-pat-thet-ywe*
concert *(n.)* တေးဂီတဖြေဖျော်ပွဲ *tay-gi-ta-phit-phyay-phyaw-pwe*
concerted *(adj.)* ညီညွတ်စွာ ပူးပေါင်းဆောင်ရွက်သော *nyi-nyut-swar-pu-paung-saung-ywet-taw*
concession *(n.)* လိုက်လျောချက် *lite-lyaw-chat*
conch *(n.)* ခရုသင်း *kha-yu-tin*
conciliate *(v.)* ရင်ကြားစေ့သည် *yin-gyar-say-the*
concise *(adj.)* တိကျသော *ti-kya-taw*
conclude *(v.)* နိဂုံးချုပ်သည် *ni-gon-choke-the*
conclusion *(n.)* နိဂုံး *ni-gon*
conclusive *(adj.)* ပြည့်စုံခိုင်လုံသော *pyae-sone-khai-lon-taw*
concoct *(v.)* အမျိုးမျိုး ရောနှော ဖော်စပ်သည် a-myo-myo-yaw-naw-phaw-sat-the
concoction *(n.)* လုပ်ဇာတ် *lote-zat*
concord *(n.)* သင့်မြတ်ခြင်း tint-myat-chin
concordance *(n.)* ဝေါဟာရစာရင်း *wor-ha-ya-sa-yin*
concourse *(n.)* လူစု *lu-su*

concrete *(n.)* **ခိုင်လုံသော၊ လက်ဆုပ်လက်ကိုင်ပြနိုင်သော** *khai-lon-taw, lat-sote-lat-khai-pya-nai-taw*

concubine *(n.)* **ကိုယ်လုပ်တော်** *ko-lote-taw*

concur *(v.)* **သဘောတိုက်ဆိုင်သည်** *ta-baw-tite-sai-the*

concurrent *(adj.)* **တစ်ပြိုင်တည်းဖြစ်ပေါ်သော** ta-pyai-the-phit-paw-taw

concussion *(n.)* **ခေါင်းထိခိုက်၍ သတိမေ့သွားခြင်း** gaung-hti-khite-ywe-ta-di-mae-twar-chin

condemn *(v.)* **ရှုတ်ချသည်၊ ပြစ်တင်ဝေဖန်သည်** shote-cha-the, pyit-tin-wai-phan-the

condemnation *(n.)* **ပြစ်တင်ဝေဖန်ရှုတ်ချခြင်း** *pyit-tin-wai-phan-shote-cha-chin*

condensate *(n.)* **ငွေ့ရည်ဖွဲ့ခြင်းမှ ရသော အရည်** *ngwe-yay-phwe-chin-ma-ya-taw-a-yay*

condense *(v.)* **ပျစ်အောင် ကျိုသည်** *pyit-aung-kyo-the*

condition *(n.)* **အခြေအနေ** *a-chay-a-nay*

conditional *(adj.)* **အခြေအနေအရဖြစ်သော** *a-chay-a-nay-a-ya-phit-taw*

condole *(v.)* **ဝမ်းနည်းသည်** wan-nae-the

condolence *(n.)* **ဝမ်းနည်းစကား** wan-nae-sa-kar

condonation *(n.)* **ခွင့်လွှတ်ခြင်းအနုပညာ** khwint-hlut-chin-a-nu-pyin-nyar

condone *(v.)* **ခွင့်လွှတ်သည်** *khwint-hlut-the*

condor *(n.)* **လင်းတအကြီးစား** *lon-ta-a-kyi-sar*

conduce *(v.)* **ဦးဆောင်သည်** *oo-saung-the*

conduct *(n.)* **အပြုအမူ** *a-pyu-a-mu*

conduction *(n.)* **လျှပ်ကူးခြင်း** *lyat-ku-chin*

conductor *(n.)* **တွဲစောင့်၊ ဘတ်စ်လက်မှတ်ရောင်း၊ လျှပ်ကူးပစ္စည်း** *twal-saunt, bat-lat-mat-yaung, lyat-ku-pyit-see*

cone *(n.)* **ကတော့၊ ထင်းရှူးသီး** *ka-taw, htin-shu-thee*

confection *(n.)* **အချိုခဲဖွယ်** *a-cho-khae-pwal*

confectionery *(n.)* **မုန့်တိုက်** hmont-tite

confederation *(n.)* **အပြန်အလှန်အကျိုးစီးပွားအတွက် ပူးပေါင်းထားသော နိုင်ငံအဖွဲ့အစည်း** *a-pyan-a-lan-a-lyo-see-pwar-a-twat-pu-paung-thar-taw-nai-ngan-a-phwe-a-see*

confer *(v.)* **အပ်နှင်းသည်** *at-hnin-the*

conference *(n.)* **ညီလာခံ** *nyi-lar-khan*

confess *(v.)* **ဖြောင့်ချက်ပေးသည်** *pyaunt-chat-pay-the*

confession *(n.)* **ဖြောင့်ချက်ပေးခြင်း** *pyaunt-chat-pay-chin*

confidant *(n.)* **လူယုံ** *lu-yone*

confide *(v.)* **အတွင်းစကားပြောပြသည်** *a-twin-sa-kar-pyaw-pya-the*

confidence *(n.)* **ယုံကြည်မှု** *yone-kyi-mu*

confident *(adj.)* **ယုံကြည်သော** *yone-kyi-taw*

confidential *(adj.)* **လျှို့ဝှက်** *sho-hwat*

configuration *(n.)* **အစီအစဉ်စနစ်** *a-si-a-sin-sa-nit*

configure *(v.)* **သီးသန့်စီစဉ်ထားရှိသည်** *thee-tant-si-sin-htar-shi-the*

confine *(v.)* **ကန့်သတ်သည်** *kant-tat-the*

confinement *(n.)* **အကျဉ်းကျခြင်း** *a-kyin-kya-chin*

confirm *(v.)* **အတည်ပြုသည်** *a-the-pyu-the*

confirmation *(n.)* အတည်ပြုချက် *a-the-pyu-the*
confiscate *(v.)* သိမ်းယူသည် *thein-yu-the*
confiscation *(n.)* သိမ်းယူခြင်း *thein-yu-chin*
conflict *(n.)* ပဋိပက္ခ *pa-ni-at-kha*
confluence *(n.)* မြစ်ဆုံ၊ ပေါင်းဆုံခြင်း *myit-sone, paung-sone-chin*
confluent *(adj.)* ပေါင်းစုံသော *paung-sone-taw*
conform *(v.)* ထုံးတမ်းစဉ်လာနောက်လိုက်သည် *hton-tan-sin-lar-naut-lite-the*
conformist *(n.)* လမ်းရိုးသမား *lan-yoe-ta-mar*
conformity *(n.)* ထုံးတမ်းနှင့် ကိုက်ညီမှု *hton-tan-nint-kite-nyi-mu*
confound *(v.)* ဝေခွဲမရဖြစ်သည် *wai-kwal-ma-ya-phit-taw*
confront *(v.)* ရင်ဆိုင်တွေ့သည် *yin-sai-tway-the*
confuse *(v.)* စိတ်ရှုပ်ထွေးသည် *seik-shote-htway-the*
confusion *(n.)* စိတ်ရှုပ်ထွေးခြင်း seik-shote-htway-chin
confute *(v.)* မှားကြောင်း သက်သေပြသည် mar-kyaung-thet-tay-pya-the
congeal *(v.)* ခဲသည် *khae-the*
congenial *(adj.)* စရိုက်တူသော *sa-yeik-tu-taw*
congested *(adj.)* ပြည့်ကျပ်နေသော *pyae-kyat-nay-taw*
congestion *(n.)* ပိတ်ဆို့ခြင်း *pait-soe-chin*
conglomerate *(n.)* အစုအပေါင်း *a-su-a-paung*
congratulate *(v.)* ဝမ်းမြောက်ကြောင်းပြောသည် *wan-myauk-kyaung-pyaw-the*
congratulation *(n.)* ဝမ်းမြောက်ကြောင်းပြောခြင်း *wan-myauk-kyaung-pyaw-chin*
congregate *(v.)* စုရုံးလာသည် *su-yone-lar-the*
congregation *(n.)* လူစု *lu-su*
congress *(n.)* ကွန်ကရက် *kon-ka-yat*
congruent *(adj.)* ထပ်တူညီသော *htet-thu-nyi-taw*
conical *(adj.)* ကတော့ပုံ *ka-taw-pon*
conjecture *(n. & v.)* ထင်ကြေးပေးသည် *htin-jay-pay-the*
conjoin *(v.)* ပေါင်းစည်းသည် *paung-see-the*
conjugal *(adj.)* အိမ်ထောင်ရေး *eain-htaung-yay*
conjugate *(v.)* ကြိယာသဏ္ဍာန်ပြောင်းသည် *kyi-yar-tha-htan-pyaung-the*
conjunct *(adj.)* ပူးတွဲသော pu-twal-taw
conjunction *(n.)* သမ္ဗန္ဓ tan-ban-da
conjunctivitis *(n.)* မျက်စိနာ *myit-si-hnar*
conjure *(v.)* မျက်လှည့်ပြသည် myat-hlae-pya-the
connect *(v.)* ဆက်သွယ်သည် sat-twal-the
connection *(n.)* ဆက်သွယ်ခြင်း *sat-twal-chin*
connivance *(n.)* မသိကျိုးကျွန်ပြုခြင်း *a-ti-kyoe-kyun-pyu-chin*
connive *(v.)* လျစ်လျူရှုသည် *lyit-lyu-shu-the*
conniving *(adj.)* ဒုက္ခပေးသော *doke-kha-pay-taw*
connoisseur *(n.)* အနုပညာကို ခံစားနားလည်သူ *a-nu-pyin-nyar-ko-khan-sar-nar-lal-thu*
connote *(v.)* ဂယက်အနက်ရှိသည် *ga-yat-a-nat-shi-the*
conquer *(v.)* အောင်နိုင်သည် *aung-nai-the*

conquerer *(n.)* အောင်နိုင်သူ *aung-nai-thu*

conquest *(n.)* အောင်နိုင်ခြင်း *aung-nai-chin*

conscience *(n.)* ကောင်းဆိုးပိုင်းခြားသိမြင်သော အသိဉာဏ် *kaung-soe-pai-char-ti-myin-taw-a-ti-nyan*

conscious *(adj.)* သတိရှိသော *ta-di-shi-taw*

consecrate *(v.)* လှူသည် *hlu-the*

consecutive *(adj.)* ဆက်တိုက် *sat-tite*

consensual *(adj.)* နှစ်ဦးသဘောတူချက်ကို အခြေပြုသော *na-oo-ta-baw-tu-chat-ko-a-chay-pyu-taw*

consensus *(n.)* အများသဘော *a-myar-ta-baw*

consent *(n.)* ခွင့်ပြုခြင်း *khwint-pyu-chin*

consequence *(n.)* အကျိုးဆက် *a-kyo-sat*

consequent *(adj.)* အကျိုးဆက်ဖြစ်သော *a-kyo-sat-phyit-taw*

conservation *(n.)* ထိန်းသိမ်းစောင့်ရှောက်ခြင်း *htain-tain-saunt-shaut-chin*

conservative *(adj.)* ရှေးရိုးစွဲ *shay-yoe-swal*

conservator *(n.)* ထိခိုက်ခြင်း၊ အကြမ်းဖက်ခြင်းမှ ကာကွယ်သော သူ *hti-khaik-chin-a-kyan-phat-chin-ma-kar-kwal-taw-thu*

conservatory *(n.)* အပင်စိုက်ရန် မှန်လုံဆောင် *a-pin-site-yan-man-hlone-saung*

conserve *(v.)* ထိန်းသိမ်းစောင့်ရှောက်သည် *htain-tain-saunt-shaut-the*

consider *(v.)* သုံးသပ်သည် *tone-tat-the*

considerable *(adj.)* အတန်များသော *a-tan-myar-taw*

considerate *(adj.)* ထောက်ထားညှာတာသော *htauk-htar-nyar-tar-taw*

consideration *(n.)* သုံးသပ်ခြင်း *tone-tat-chin*

considering *(prep.)* သော်လည်း *taw-lal*

consign *(v.)* လွှဲအပ်သည် *hlwal-at-the*

consignment *(n.)* ပို့ကုန် *poe-kone*

consist *(v.)* ပါဝင်သည် *par-win-the*

consistency *(n.)* တစ်သမတ်တည်းဖြစ်ခြင်း၊ ရှေ့နောက်ညီညွတ်ခြင်း *ta-ta-mat-the-phit-chin, shay-naut-nyi-nyut-chin*

consistent *(adj.)* တစ်သမတ်တည်းဖြစ်သော *ta-tat-mat-the-phit-taw*

consolation *(n.)* နှစ်သိမ့်မှု *nit-theint-mu*

console *(v.)* နှစ်သိမ့်သည် *nit-theint-the*

consolidate *(v.)* ခိုင်မာတောင့်တင်းလာသည် *khai-mar-taunt-tin-lar-the*

consolidation *(n.)* ခိုင်မာတောင့်တင်းလာခြင်း *khai-mar-taunt-tin-lar-chin*

consonance *(n.)* ကိုက်ညီခြင်း kite-nyi-chin

consonant *(n.)* ဗျည်းသံ pyi-tan

consort *(n.)* ကြင်ရာတော် *kyin-yar-taw*

conspectus *(n.)* အကြမ်းဖော်ပြချက် *a-kyan-phaw-pya-chat*

conspicuous *(adj.)* ထင်ရှားသော *htin-shar-taw*

conspiracy *(n.)* လျှို့ဝှက်ပူးပေါင်းကြံစည်ချက် sho-hwat-pu-paung-kyan-see-chat

conspirator *(n.)* ပူးပေါင်းကြံစည်သူ *pu-paung-kyan-see-thu*

conspire *(v.)* လျှို့ဝှက်ပူးပေါင်းကြံစည်သည် sho-hwat-pu-paung-kyan-see-the

constable *(n.)* ရဲတပ်ဖွဲ့ *ye-tat-phwe*

constant *(adj.)* **မပြောင်းလဲသော** *ma-pyaung-lal-taw*
constellation *(n.)* **တာရာ** *tar-yar*
consternation *(n.)* **အံ့သြတုန်လှုပ်ခြင်း** *ant-aw-ton-lote-chin*
constipation *(n.)* **ဝမ်းချုပ်ခြင်း** *wan-choke-chin*
constituency *(n.)* **မဲဆန္ဒနယ်** ma-san-da-nal
constituent *(adj.)* **အစိတ်အပိုင်းတစ်ရပ်အဖြစ် ပါဝင်သော** *a-seik-a-pai-ta-yat-a-phit-par-win-taw*
constitute *(v.)* **ပါဝင်သည်** *par-win-the*
constitution *(n.)* **ဖွဲ့စည်းပုံအခြေခံဥပဒေ** *phwe-see-pon-a-chay-khan-au-pa-day*
constrain *(v.)* **ဘောင်ခတ်သည်၊ ကျဉ်းမြောင်းစေသည်** *baung-khat-the, kyin-myaung-say-the*
constraint *(n.)* **အကန့်အသတ်၊ ဖိအား** *a-kant-a-tat, phi-arr*
constrict *(v.)* **ညှစ်သည်၊ ဖျစ်သည်** *nyit-the, phit-the*
construct *(v.)* **တည်ဆောက်သည်** *ti-saut-the*
construction *(n.)* **ဆောက်လုပ်ရေး** saut-lote-yay
constructive *(adj.)* **အပြုသဘောဆောင်သော** a-pyu-ta-baw-saung-taw
construe *(v.)* **နားလည်သည်** *nar-lal-the*
consul *(n.)* **ကောင်စစ်ဝန်** *kaung-sit-win*
consular *(adj.)* **ကောင်စစ်ဝန်နှင့် ဆိုင်သော** *kaung-sit-win-nint-sai-taw*
consulate *(n.)* **ကောင်စစ်ဝန်ရုံး** *kaung-sit-win-yone*
consult *(v.)* **တိုင်ပင်သည်** *tai-pin-the*
consultant *(n.)* **အတိုင်ပင်ခံ** *a-thai-pin-khan*
consultation *(n.)* **တိုင်ပင်ခြင်း** *tai-pin-chin*
consume *(v.)* **စားသုံးသည်** *sar-tone-the*
consumer *(n.)* **စားသုံးသူ** *sar-tone-thu*
consumption *(n.)* **စားသုံးခြင်း** *sar-tone-chin*
contact *(n.)* **အဆက်အသွယ်** *a-sat-a-twal*
contact *(v.)* **ဆက်သွယ်သည်** *sat-twal-the*
contact lens *(n.)* **မျက်ကပ်မှန်** *myat-kat-man*
contagion *(n.)* **ရောဂါကူးစက်ခြင်း** *yaw-gar-ku-sat-chin*
contagious *(adj.)* **ကူးစက်တတ်သော** *ku-sat-tat-taw*
contain *(v.)* **ပါဝင်သည်** *par-win-the*
container *(n.)* **ခွက်** *khwat*
containment *(n.)* **ကန့်သတ် ထိန်းချုပ်မှု** *kant-tat-htain-choke-mu*
contaminate *(v.)* **ညစ်ညမ်းစေသည်** *nyat-nyan-say-the*
contemplate *(v.)* **ချိန်ဆသည်** *chain-sa-the*
contemplation *(n.)* **ချိန်ဆခြင်း** *chain-sa-chin*
contemporary *(adj.)* **ခေတ်ပြိုင်** *khit-pyai*
contempt *(n.)* **အထင်သေးခြင်း** *a-htin-tay-chin*
contemptuous *(adj.)* **အထင်သေးသော** *a-htin-tay-taw*
contend *(v.)* **ဖက်ပြိုင်သည်** *phat-pyai-the*
contender *(n.)* **ပြိုင်ပွဲဝင်** *pyai-pwe-win*
content *(adj.)* **ရောင့်ရဲသော** *yaunt-ye-taw*
contention *(n.)* **ယှဉ်ပြိုင်မှု** *yin-pyai-mu*
contentment *(n.)* **ရောင့်ရဲခြင်း** *yaunt-ye-chin*
contest *(n.)* **ပြိုင်ပွဲ** *pyai-pwe*
contestant *(n.)* **ပြိုင်ပွဲဝင်** pyai-pwe-win

context *(n.)* စကားစပ် *sa-kar-sat*

contiguous *(adj.)* ထိနေသော hti-nay-taw

continent *(n.)* တိုက် tite

continental *(adj.)* ကုန်းမြေထုနှင့် ဆိုင်သော *kone-myay-htu-nint-sai-taw*

contingency *(n.)* အရေးပေါ် a-yay-paw

contingent *(n.)* အားထားနေရသော ar-htar-nay-ya-taw

continual *(adj.)* ထပ်တလဲလဲဖြစ်သော htet-ta-lal-lal-phit-taw

continuation *(n.)* ဆက်လက်လုပ်ဆောင်ခြင်း *sat-lat-lote-saung-chin*

continue *(v.)* ဆက်လက်လုပ်ဆောင်သည် *sat-lat-lote-saung-the*

continuous *(adj.)* ဆက်တိုက်ဖြစ်သော *sat-tite-phit-taw*

continuum *(n.)* ဆက်တိုက် *sat-tite*

contour *(n.)* ကောက်ကြောင်း *kauk-kyaung*

contra *(pref.)* ဆန့်ကျင်အနက်ရှိ ရှေ့ဆက်စကားလုံး *sant-kyin-a-nat-shi-shay-sat-sa-kar-lone*

contraband *(n.)* တရားမဝင် ပို့ကုန်၊ သွင်းကုန် *ta-yar-ma-win-poe-kone-twin-kone*

contraception *(n.)* ကိုယ်ဝန်တားခြင်း *ko-win-tar-chin*

contraceptive *(n.)* ကိုယ်ဝန်တားဆေး *ko-win-tar-say*

contract *(n.)* စာချုပ် *sar-choke*

contraction *(n.)* ကျုံ့ခြင်း၊ ချုံ့ခြင်း *kyont-chin, chont-chin*

contractor *(n.)* ကန်ထရိုက်တာ *kan-hta-rite-tar*

contradict *(v.)* ဆန့်ကျင်ဘက် ပြောသည် *sant-kyin-bat-pyaw-the*

contradiction *(n.)* ဆန့်ကျင်ဘက် ပြောခြင်း *sant-kyin-bat-pyaw-chin*

contrary *(adj.)* ဆန့်ကျင်ဘက် ဖြစ်သော *sant-kyin-bat-phit-taw*

contrast *(n.)* ယှဉ်ကြည့်သည် *yin-kyi-the*

contribute *(v.)* ထောက်ပံ့သည်၊ ထည့်ဝင်သည် *htauk-pant-the, htae-win-the*

contribution *(n.)* ငွေကြေးပစ္စည်း ထည့်ဝင်ခြင်း *ngwe-kyay-pyit-see-htae-win-chin*

contributor *(n.)* ကူညီထောက်ပံ့ထည့်ဝင်သူ *ku-nyi-htauk-ant-htae-win-thu*

contrive *(v.)* ဖန်တီးသည် *phan-tee-the*

control *(n.)* ထိန်းချုပ်ခြင်း *htain-choke-chin*

controller *(n.)* ထိန်းသိမ်းကြီးကြပ်သူ *thain-thein-kyi-kyat-thu*

controversial *(adj.)* အငြင်းပွားဖွယ် *a-nyin-pwar-phwal*

controversy *(n.)* အငြင်းပွားမှု *a-nyin-pwar-mu*

contuse *(v.)* အတွင်းဒဏ်ထိသည် *a-twin-dan-hti-the*

contusion *(n.)* အတွင်းကြေ *a-twin-kyay*

conundrum *(n.)* ပဟေဠိ *pa-hay-hli*

convalesce *(v.)* နာလန်ထသည် *na-lan-hta-the*

convalescence *(n.)* နာလန်ထကာလ *na-lan-hta-kar-la*

convalescent *(adj.)* နာလန်ထ na-lan-hta

convection *(n.)* အပူစီးကူးခြင်း a-pu-see-kyu-chin

convene *(v.)* စုဝေးရန် ဖိတ်ကြားသည် *su-way-yan-phite-kyar-the*

convener *(n.)* ဆော်ဩသူ *saw-aw-the*

convenience *(n.)* အဆင်ပြေမှု *a-sin-pyay-mu*

convenient *(adj.)* **အဆင်ပြေသော** a-sin-pyay-taw

convent *(n.)* **ခရစ်ယာန်သီလရှင်ကျောင်း** kha-yit-yan-thi-la-shin-kyaung

convention *(n.)* **ညီလာခံ၊ ထုံးနည်း** nyi-lar-khan, htone-nee

conventional *(adj.)* **သမားရိုးကျ** *ta-mar-yoe-kya*

converge *(v.)* **လာဆုံသည်၊ အလားတူဖြစ်သည်** *lar-sone-the, a-lar-tu-phit-the*

convergence *(n.)* **ဆုံမှတ်** *sone-mat*

convergent *(adj.)* **တစ်နေရာတည်းတွင်ဆုံသော** *ta-nay-yar-te-twin-son-taw*

conversant *(adj.)* **ဗဟုသုတရှိသော** *ba-hu-thu-ta-shi-taw*

conversation *(n.)* **စကားစမြည်** *sa-kar-sa-mie*

converse *(v.)* **စကားစမြည်ပြောသည်** *sa-kar-sa-mie-pyaw-the*

conversion *(n.)* **ပြောင်းလဲခြင်း** *pyaung-lal-chin*

convert *(v.)* **ပြောင်းလဲသည်** *pyaung-lal-the*

convertible *(n.)* **ခေါက်အမိုးကား** *khauk-a-moe-kar*

convey *(v.)* **သယ်ဆောင်သည်** *thal-saung-the*

conveyance *(n.)* **သယ်ယူပို့ဆောင်မှု** *tal-yu-poe-saung-mu*

conveyor *(n.)* **သယ်ပို့ပေးသည့် အရာ** *tal-poe-pay-the-a-yar*

convict *(v.)* **စီရင်ချက်ချသည်** si-yin-chat-cha-the

conviction *(n.)* **ပြစ်မှုထင်ရှား စီရင်ခြင်း** *pyit-mu-htin-shar-si-yin-chin*

convince *(v.)* **လက်ခံယုံကြည်စေသည်** *lat-khan-yone-kyi-say-the*

convivial *(adj.)* **အပေါင်းအသင်းမင်သော** *a-paung-a-thin-min-taw*

convocation *(n.)* **ဘွဲ့နှင်းသဘင်** *bwe-hnin-tha-bin*

convoke *(v.)* **အစည်းအဝေးဖိတ်သည်** *a-see-a-way-phate-the*

convolve *(v.)* **ရစ်ပတ်သည်** *yit-pat-the*

convoy *(n.)* **တပ်အစောင့်အရှောက်ပါယာဉ်တန်း** *tat-a-saunt-a-shaut-par-yin-tan*

convulse *(v.)* **သိမ့်သိမ့်တုန်သည်** *theint-theint-tone-the*

convulsion *(n.)* **တက်ခြင်း** *tat-chin*

cook *(v.)* **ချက်ပြုတ်သည်** *chat-pyoke-the*

cook *(n.)* **ထမင်းချက်** *hta-min-chat*

cooker *(n.)* **ထမင်းပေါင်းအိုး** *hta-min-paung-oh*

cookie *(n.)* **ကွတ်ကီး** *kwut-kee*

cool *(adj.)* **အေးသော** *aye-taw*

coolant *(n.)* **အအေးပေးရာတွင် သုံးသောအရည်** *a-aye-pay-yar-twin-tone-a-yae*

cooler *(n.)* **အအေးခံဘူး** *a-aye-khan-bu*

cooperate *(v.)* **ပူးပေါင်းဆောင်ရွက်သည်** *pu-paung-saung-ywet-the*

cooperation *(n.)* **ပူးပေါင်းဆောင်ရွက်ခြင်း** *pu-paung-saung-ywet-chin*

cooperative *(adj.)* **ဖက်စပ်** *phat-sat*

coordinate *(v.)* **ကိုဩဒိနိတ်** *ko-aw-di-nate*

coordination *(n.)* **ညှိနှိုင်းဆောင်ရွက်ခြင်း** *nyi-nai-saung-ywet-chin*

coot *(n.)* **ရေကြက်ဒုံ** *yay-kyat-don*

cope *(v.)* **နိုင်နိုင်နင်းနင်း ကိုင်တွယ်ဖြေရှင်းသည်** *nai-nai-ning-ning-kai-twal-phyay-shin-the*

copier *(n.)* **မိတ္တူကူးစက်** *meik-thu-ku-sat*

coping *(n.)* တံတိုင်းခေါင် *ta-dai-khaung*

copious *(adj.)* များပြားသော *myar-pyar-taw*

copper *(n.)* ကြေးနီ *kyay-ni*

coppice *(n.)* သစ်ပင်ချုံနွယ်ထူသော နေရာ *tit-pin-chon-nwe-htu-taw-nay-yar*

copulate *(v.)* မိတ်လိုက်သည် *meik-lite-the*

copy *(n.)* မိတ္တူ *meik-tu*

copy *(v.)* မိတ္တူကူးသည် *meik-tu-ku-the*

copyright *(n.)* မူပိုင်ခွင့် *mu-pai-kwint*

coquette *(n.)* နန့်တန့်တန့် မိန်းမ *nant-tant-tant-main-ma*

coral *(n.)* သန္တာ *tan-dar*

corbel *(n.)* တိုးစီခုံး *toe-si-khone*

cord *(n.)* ကြိုးလုံး *kyo-lone*

cordial *(adj.)* လှိုက်လှဲသော *lite-hlae-taw*

cordless *(adj.)* ကြိုးမဲ့ *kyoe-mae*

cordon *(n.)* ရဲစသည့် အပိတ်အဆို့ *ya-sa-the-a-pait-a-soe*

corduroy *(n.)* ချည်ကတ္တီပါ *chi-ka-di-par*

core *(n.)* အူတိုင် *au-thai*

coriander *(n.)* နံနံပင် *nan-nan-pin*

cork *(n.)* ဖော့ *phort*

cormorant *(n.)* တင်ကျီးငှက် *tin-kyi-nget*

corn *(n.)* ပြောင်းဖူး *pyaung-hpoo*

cornea *(n.)* မျက်ကြည်လွှာ myat-kyi-hlwar

corner *(n.)* ထောင့် htaunt

cornet *(n.)* ကောနက် *taw-nat*

cornicle *(n.)* အဆီခဲထုတ်အတံ *a-si-khar-htoke-a-tan*

corollary *(n.)* သဘာဝအကျိုးဆက် *ta-bar-wa-a-kyo-sat*

coronation *(n.)* နန်းတက်ပွဲ *nan-tat-pwe*

coronet *(n.)* သရဖူငယ် *ta-ya-phu-nge*

corporal *(adj.)* တပ်ကြပ် *tat-kyat*

corporate *(adj.)* ကော်ပိုရေးရှင်းနှင့် ဆိုင်သော *kor-po-yay-shin-nint-sai-taw*

corporation *(n.)* ကော်ပိုရေးရှင်း *kor-po-yay-shin*

corps *(n.)* တပ်မကြီး *tat-ma-gyi*

corpse *(n.)* အလောင်း *a-laung*

correct *(v.)* ပြင်ပေးသည် pyin-pay-the

correction *(n.)* ပြင်ခြင်း pyin-chin

correlate *(v.)* ဆက်နွယ်သည် *sat-nwe-the*

correlation *(n.)* ဆက်နွယ်ခြင်း *sat-nwe-chin*

correspond *(v.)* တူညီသည် *thu-nyi-the*

correspondence *(n.)* စာအဆက်အသွယ် *sar-a-sat-a-twal*

correspondent *(n.)* သတင်းထောက် *ta-tin-htauk*

corridor *(n.)* စင်္ကြံလမ်း *sin-kyan-lan*

corroborate *(v.)* အတည်ပြုသည် *a-the-pyu-the*

corroborative *(adj.)* ခိုင်မာစေသော *khai-mar-say-the*

corrosive *(adj.)* စားတတ်သော *sar-tat-taw*

corrugated *(adj.)* အမြောင်းပုံ ဖော်ထားသော a-hmyaung-pon-phaw-htar-taw

corrupt *(adj.)* အကျင့်ပျက်သည် a-kyint-phat-the

corruption *(n.)* အကတတိလိုက်စားခြင်း *a-ka-ti-lite-sar-chin*

cortege *(n.)* ဈာပနာပို့ယဉ်တန်း *zar-pa-nar-poe-yin-tan*

cortisone *(n.)* ကော်တီဇုန်းဓာတ် *kor-ti-zone-dat*

cosmetic *(adj.)* အမြင်လှအောင် ခွဲစိတ်ပြုပြင်သော *a-myin-hla-aung-kwal-seik-pyu-pyin-taw*
cosmic *(adj.)* စကြာဝဠာနှင့်ဆိုင်သော *sa-kya-wa-lar-nint-sai-taw*
cosmopolitan *(adj.)* လူမျိုးပေါင်းစုံရှိသော *lu-myo-paung-sone-shi-taw*
cosmos *(n.)* စကြာဝဠာ *sa-kya-wa-lar*
cost *(v.)* ကုန်ကျသည် *kone-kya-the*
costal *(adj.)* နံရိုးနှင့်ဆိုင်သော *nan-yoe-nint-sai-taw*
costly *(adj.)* တန်ဖိုးကြီးသော *tan-phoe-kyi-taw*
costume *(n.)* အခမ်းအနားဝတ်စုံ *a-khan-a-nar-wut-sone*
cosy *(adj.)* ဇိမ်ရှိသော *zain-shi-taw*
cot *(n.)* ကလေးခုတင် *ka-lay-ka-tin*
cotemporal *(adj.)* တစ်ချိန်တည်းဖြစ်သော *ta-chain-tal-phit-taw*
cottage *(n.)* တစ်ထပ်တိုက်ကလေး *ta-htat-tite-ka-lay*
cotton *(n.)* ချည်ထည် *chee-htal*
couch *(n.)* ဆိုဖာ *so-far*
cough *(v.)* ချောင်းဆိုးသည် *chaung-sek-the*
could *(v.)* နိုင်သည် *naing-the*
council *(n.)* ကောင်စီ *kaung-si*
councillor *(n.)* ကောင်စီဝင် *kaung-si-win*
counsel *(n.)* အကြံဉာဏ် *a-kyan-nyan*
counsellor *(n.)* အတိုင်ပင်ခံပုဂ္ဂိုလ် *a-tine-pin-khan-poke-ko*
count *(v.)* ရေတွက်သည် *yay-twat-the*
countable *(adj.)* ရေတွက်နိုင်သော *yay-twat-nai-taw*
countdown *(n.)* သတ်မှတ်ချိန် သုညထား၍ တစက္ကန့်စီ နောက်ပြန် ရေတွက်ခြင်း *tat-mat-chain-ton-nyay-htar-ywe-ta-sat-kant-si-naut-pyan-yay-twat-chin*
countenance *(n.)* မျက်နှာထား *myat-na-htar*
counter *(n.)* ကောင်တာ *kaung-tar*
counteract *(v.)* တိုက်ဖျက်သည် *tite-phat-the*
counter-attack *(n.)* တန်ပြန်တိုက်ခိုက်မှု *tan-yina-tite-kite-mu*
counterfeit *(adj.)* အတု *a-tu*
counterfeiter *(n.)* အတုလုပ်သူ *a-tu-lote-thu*
counterfoil *(n.)* လက်ခံဖြတ်ပိုင်း *lat-khan-phat-pai*
countermand *(v.)* ထုတ်ပြီး အမိန့်ကို အမိန့်သစ်ဖြင့် ပယ်ဖျက်အစားထိုးသည် *htoke-pi-a-maint-ko-a-maint-tit-phint-pal-phat-a-sar-htoe-the*
counterpart *(n.)* အဆင့်တူ ပုဂ္ဂိုလ် *a-sint-thu-poke-ko*
countersign *(v.)* ထပ်ဆင့် လက်မှတ်ထိုးသည် *htet-sint-lat-mat-htoe-the*
countess *(n.)* မြို့စားကတော် *myo-sar-ka-taw*
countless *(adj.)* မရေတွက်နိုင်သော *ma-yay-twat-nai-taw*
country *(n.)* တိုင်းပြည် *tai-pyi*
county *(n.)* စီရင်စု *si-yin-su*
coup *(n.)* အာဏာသိမ်းမှု *ar-nar-tain-mu*
couple *(n.)* အတွဲ *a-twal*
couple *(v.)* ပူးတွဲနေသည် *pu-twal-nay-the*
couplet *(n.)* အဆုံးကာရန်တူ နှစ်ကြောင်းကဗျာ *a-sone-kar-yan-thu-nit-kyaung-ka-byar*
coupon *(n.)* ဖြတ်ပိုင်း *phat-pai*
courage *(n.)* ရဲရင့်ခြင်း *ye-yint-chin*

courageous *(adj.)* ရဲဝံ့သော *ye-wint-taw*

courier *(n.)* ညှော်လမ်းညွှန် *ae-lan-hnyun*

course *(n.)* လမ်းကြောင်း *lan-kyaung*

court *(n.)* တရားရုံး *ta-yar-yone*

courteous *(adj.)* ယဉ်ကျေးသည် yin-kyay-the

courtesan *(n.)* ပြည်ကြီးဒါလီ pyi-gyi-dar-li

courtesy *(n.)* ယဉ်ကျေးသည် *yin-kyay-the*

courtier *(n.)* နန်းတွင်းသူ နန်းတွင်းသား *nan-twin-thu-nan-twin-tar*

courtship *(n.)* လူပျိုလှည့်ခြင်း *lu-byo-lae-chin*

courtyard *(n.)* ဝင်း *win*

cousin *(n.)* တစ်ဝမ်းကွဲ *ta-wan-kwal*

couture *(n.)* အဝတ်အစား ဖက်ရှင်ဒီဇိုင်းထွင်ခြင်း *a-wit-a-sar-phat-shin-de-zine-htwin-chin*

cove *(n.)* ပင်လယ်ကွေ့ငယ် *pin-lal-kway-nge*

covenant *(n.)* ပဋိညာဉ် *pa-dain-nyin*

cover *(v.)* ဖုံးသည် *hpone-the*

coverage *(n.)* အကျုံးဝင်မှု၊ လွှမ်းခြုံနိုင်မှု *a-kyone-win-mu, hlwan-chon-nai-mu*

coverlet *(n.)* အိပ်ရာဖုံး *aik-yar-hpone*

covert *(adj.)* တိတ်တိတ်ပုံး *tate-tate-pone*

covet *(v.)* အငမ်းမရဖြစ်သည် *a-ngan-ma-ya-phit-the*

cow *(n.)* နွား *nwar*

coward *(n.)* ငကြောက် *nga-kyauk*

cowardice *(n.)* သူရဲဘောနည်းခြင်း *ta-ye-baw-nae-chin*

cower *(v.)* တွန့်ဆုတ်သည် *twunt-sote-the*

co-worker *(n.)* လုပ်ဖော်ကိုင်ဘက် *lote-phaw-kai-phat*

coy *(adj.)* ရှက်ဟန်ဆောင်သော *shat-han-saung-taw*

cozy *(adj.)* ဇိမ်ရှိသော *zain-shi-taw*

crab *(n.)* ဂဏန်း *ga-nan*

crack *(n.)* အက်ကြောင်း *at-kyaung*

crackdown *(n.)* ဖြိုခွင်းသည် *phyo-kwin-the*

cracker *(n.)* ခရက်ကာမုန့်၊ ဗြောက်အိုး *ka-rat-kar-hmont, byauk-oh*

crackle *(v.)* တဖျစ်ဖျစ်မြည်သည် *ta-phit-phit-myi-the*

cradle *(n.)* ကလေးပုခက် *ka-lay-pa-khat*

craft *(n.)* လက်မှုပညာ *lat-mu-pyin-nyar*

craftsman *(n.)* လက်မှုပညာသည် *lat-mu-pyin-nyar-the*

crafty *(adj.)* လည်သော *lal-taw*

cram *(v.)* သိပ်ထည့်သည် *tate-htae-the*

cramp *(n.)* ကြွက်တက်ခြင်း *kywat-tat-chin*

crane *(n.)* ကြိုးကြာ၊ ကရိန်းကား *kyo-kyar, ka-rain-kar*

crankle *(v.)* တွန့်လိပ်သည် *twunt-laik-the*

crash *(v.)* ယာဉ်တိုက်ခြင်း *yin-tite-chin*

crasis *(n.)* အစိတ်အပိုင်းပေါင်းစုခြင်း *a-seik-a-pai-paung-su-chin*

crass *(adj.)* စာနာစိတ်ကင်းသော *sar-nar-seik-kin-taw*

crate *(n.)* ကုန်သေတ္တာ *kone-tit-tar*

crater *(n.)* မီးတောင်ဝ *mee-taung-wa*

crave *(v.)* အငမ်းမရဖြစ်သည် *a-ngan-ma-ya-phit-the*

craven *(adj.)* အကြောက်ကြီးသော *a-kyauk-kyi-taw*

craving *(n.)* ပြင်းထန်သော၊ ပုံမမှန်သော အရေးတကြီး စိတ်ဆန္ဒ *pyan-htan-taw-pon-ma-man-taw-a-yay-ta-kyi-seik-san-da*

craw *(n.)* ငှက်စလုတ် nget-sa-lote

crawl *(v.)* တွားသွားသည် twar-twar-the

crayfish *(n.)* ကျောက်ပုစွန် *kyauk-pa-zon*

crayon *(n.)* ရောင်စုံခဲတံ *yaung-zon-khae-tan*

craze *(n.)* ပေါ်ပေါ်ပင်လိုက်၍ အရူးထခြင်း *paw-pin-lite-ywe-a-yu-hta-chin*

crazy *(adj.)* ရူးသွပ်သော *yu-thwut-taw*

creak *(v.)* ကျွီခနဲ မြည်သည် *kywi-kha-nae-myi-the*

cream *(n.)* မလိုင်၊ ခရင် *ma-hlai, kha-yin*

crease *(n.)* ခေါက်ရိုး *khauk-yoe*

create *(v.)* တီထွင်သည် *ti-htwin-the*

creation *(n.)* တီထွင်မှု *ti-htwin-mu*

creative *(adj.)* တီထွင်ဉာဏ်ရှိသော *ti-htwin-nyan-shi-taw*

creator *(n.)* တီထွင်သူ၊ ဖန်တီးရှင် *ti-htwin-thu, phan-ti-shin*

creature *(n.)* သက်ရှိ *thet-shi*

credential *(n.)* သင့်တော်သော အရည်အချင်း *tint-taw-thaw-a-yay-a-chin*

credible *(adj.)* ယုံကြည်စိတ်ချရသော *yone-kyi-seik-cha-ya-taw*

credit *(n.)* လေးစားမှု၊ ကြွေးရှင်စာရင်း *lay-sar-mu, kyway-shin-sa-yin*

credit card *(n.)* ခရက်ဒစ်ကတ် *kha-rat-dit-card*

creditable *(adj.)* ချီးမွမ်းထိုက်သော *chee-mon-htike-taw*

creditor *(n.)* ကြွေးရှင် *kyway-shin*

credulity *(n.)* ယုံစားလွယ်ခြင်း *yone-sar-lwal-chin*

credulous *(adj.)* ယုံလွယ်လွန်းသော *yone-lwal-loon-taw*

creed *(n.)* ဘာသာ *bar-tar*

creek *(n.)* ချောင်းစွယ် *chaung-swal*

creep *(v.)* မီးတောင်ဝ *mee-taung-wa*

creeper *(n.)* နွယ်ပင် *nwe-pin*

creepy *(adj.)* ကျောချမ်းဖွယ် *kyaw-chan-phwal*

cremate *(v.)* မီးသဂြိုဟ်သည် *mee-tha-gyo-the*

cremation *(n.)* မီးသဂြိုဟ်ခြင်း *mee-tha-gyo-chin*

crematorium *(n.)* မီးသဂြိုဟ်ရုံ *mee-tha-gyo-yone*

creole *(n.)* နှစ်ဘာသာနှောစကား *nit-bar-tar-naw-sa-kar*

crepe *(n.)* ပိုးတွန့် *poe-twunt*

crepitate *(v.)* တဖျစ်ဖျစ်အသံပြုသည် ta-phit-phit-a-tan-pyu-the

crepitation *(n.)* တဖျစ်ဖျစ်အသံပြုခြင်း ta-phit-phit-a-tan-pyu-chin

crescent *(n.)* လခြမ်းကွေး la-chan-kway

crest *(n.)* အထွတ်၊ လှိုင်းခေါင်းဖြူ *a-htwut, hlaing-gaung-phyu*

cretin *(n.)* ငတုံး nga-tone

crevet *(n.)* ပုဇွန် pa-zon

crew *(n.)* အမှုထမ်း *a-mu-htan*

crib *(n.)* စားခွက် *sar-khwat*

cricket *(n.)* ခရစ်ကက် *kha-rit-kat*

crime *(n.)* မှုခင်း *mu-khin*

criminal *(n.)* ပြစ်မှုကျူးလွန်သော *pyit-mu-kyu-loon-taw*

crimp *(n.)* ခေါက်သည် *khaut-the*

crimple *(v.)* တွန့်ကျေသည်၊ ရှုံ့တွသည်၊ ကောက်သည် *twunt-kyay-the, shont-twa-the, kauk-the*

crimson *(n.)* ကြက်သွေးရောင် *kyat-tway-yaung*

cringe *(v.)* ကြောက်ရွံ့တွန့်ဆုတ်သည် kyauk-shwunt-twunt-sote-the

crinkle *(v.)* အတွန့်အလိပ် a-twunt-a-laik

cripple *(n.)* မသန်မစွမ်းသူ *ma-tan-ma-swan-thu*

crisis *(n.)* ဘေးကျပ်နံကျပ်ကာလ *bay-kyat-nan-kyat-kar-la*

crisp *(adj.)* ကြွပ်သော *kywut-taw*

crispen *(v.)* ကြွပ်အောင်လုပ်သည် *kywut-aung-lote-the*

criterion *(n.)* စံ၊ မှတ်ကျောက် *san, mat-kyauk*

critic *(n.)* ဝေဖန်သူ *wai-phan-thu*

critical *(adj.)* ဆန်းစစ်ဝေဖန်သော *san-sit-wai-phan-taw*

criticism *(n.)* ဝေဖန်ချက် *wai-phan-chat*

criticize *(v.)* ဝေဖန်သည် *wai-phan-the*

critique *(n.)* ဆန်းစစ်ဝေဖန်မှု *san-sit-wai-phan-mu*

croak *(n.)* ဖားမြည်သံကဲ့သို့ အသံ *phar-myi-tan-kae-tho-a-tan*

crochet *(n.)* တစ်ချောင်းထိုး *ta-chaung-htoe*

crockery *(n.)* ပန်းကန်ခွက်ယောက် *pan-kan-khwat-yauk*

crocodile *(n.)* မိကျောင်း *mi-kyaung*

croft *(n.)* စိုက်ပျိုးမွေးမြူရေးခြံငယ် *site-pyo-mway-my-yay-chan-nge*

croissant *(n.)* လခြမ်းကွေးပေါင်မုန့် *la-chan-kway-paung-hmont*

crome *(n.)* ချိတ် *chaik*

crone *(n.)* အရုပ်ဆိုးဆိုး အဖွားကြီး *a-yoke-soe-soe-a-phwar-gyi*

crook *(n.)* လူလိမ်လူညစ် *lu-lain-lu-nyit*

crooked *(adj.)* လိမ်ဖည်သော *lain-phal-taw*

croon *(v.)* သီချင်းညည်းသည် tha-chin-nyee-the

crop *(n.)* ကောက်ပဲသီးနှံ kauk-pal-thee-nan

cross *(n.)* ကြက်ခြေခတ် *kyat-chway-khat*

crossbar *(n.)* ဂိုးတိုင်ဘားတန်း *go-tai-bar-tan*

crossfire *(n.)* ညှပ်ပူးညှပ်ပိတ်ပစ်ခတ်ခြင်း *nyat-poo-nyat-paik-pyit-khat-chin*

crossing *(n.)* လမ်းဆုံ *lan-son*

crossroads *(n.)* လမ်းဆုံ *lan-son*

crotch *(n.)* ခွကြား *khwa-kyar*

crotchet *(n.)* အကန့်တစ်ကန့်၏ လေးစိတ်တစ်စိတ် တန်ဖိုးရှိသော နရီချိန်သင်္ကေတ *a-kant-ta-kant-ei-lay-seik-ta-seik-tan-phoe-shi-taw-na-yee-chain-tin-kay-ta*

crouch *(v.)* ဝပ်သည် *wut-the*

crow *(n.)* ကျီးကန်း *kyee-kan*

crowbar *(n.)* သံတူးရွင်း *tan-ta-ywin*

crowd *(n.)* လူအုပ် *lu-oak*

crowded *(adj.)* လူပြည့်ကျပ်သည် lu-pyae-kyat-the

crowdfunding *(n.)* အွန်လိုင်းလူ့အဖွဲ့အစည်းမှ စုပေါင်းလှူဒါန်းခြင်း on-line-lu-a-phwe-a-see-ma-su-paung-hlu-dan-chin

crown *(n.)* သရဖူ ta-ya-phu

crowned *(adj.)* သရဖူဆောင်းသော *ta-ya-phu-saung-taw*

crucial *(adj.)* အရေးပါလှသော *a-yay-par-hla-taw*

crucified *(adj.)* ညှင်းပန်းနှိပ်စက်သော *nyin-pan-nate-sat-taw*

crucifix *(n.)* လက်ဝါးကပ်တိုင် တင်ထားသော ခရစ်တော်ပုံ lat-war-kat-tai-tin-htar-taw-kha-yit-taw-pon

crucify *(v.)* ကားစင်တင်၍ အဆုံးစီရင်သည် *kar-sin-tin-ywe-a-sone-si-yin-the*

crude *(adj.)* အရိုင်း a-yai

cruel *(adj.)* ရက်စက်သော *yat-sat-taw*

cruelty *(n.)* ရက်စက်ခြင်း yat-sat-chin

cruise *(v.)* အရှိန်နှုန်းမှန်မှန် မောင်းနှင်သည် *a-shein-hnone-man-man-maung-hnin-the*

cruiser *(n.)* ကရူဇာစစ်သင်္ဘောကြီး *ka-yu-zar-sit-tin-baw-gyi*

crumb *(n.)* အစအန *a-sa-a-na*

crumble *(v.)* ဖဲ့သည်၊ ပဲ့သည် *phae-the, pae-the*

crump *(v.)* ကျယ်လောင်စွာ ပေါက်ကွဲသည် *kyal-laung-swar-pauk-kwal-the*

crumple *(v.)* တွန့်ကြေသည် *twunt-kyay-the*

crunch *(v.)* တကျွတ်ကျွတ်ဝါးသည် *ta-kywut-kywut-war-the*

crusade *(n.)* ခရူးဆိတ် စစ်ပွဲ *kha-ru-sate-sit-pwe*

crusader *(n.)* ခရူးဆိတ် စစ်ပွဲတွင် ပါဝင်တိုက်ခိုက်သူ *kha-ru-sate-sit-pwe-twin-par-win-tite-khite-thu*

crush *(v.)* ဖိသည်၊ ထုသည်၊ ခြေသည် hpi-the, htu-the, chay-the

crust *(n.)* ပေါင်မုန့် အကာသား *paung-hmont-a-kar-tar*

crutch *(n.)* ချိုင်းထောက်တစ်မျိုး chai-htauk-ta-myo

cry *(v.)* ငိုကြွေးသည် *nyo-kway-the*

cryogenics *(n.)* အအေးလွန် *a-aye-lun*

cryptic *(adj.)* အသိခက်သော *a-ti-khat-taw*

cryptography *(n.)* ဝှက်စာဖော်နည်း၊ ရေးနည်း *hwat-sar-phaw-nee, yay-nee*

crystal *(n.)* သလင်းကျောက် *tha-lin-kyauk*

crystalize *(v.)* ပုံပေါ်လာသည် *pon-paw-lar-the*

cub *(n.)* သားပေါက် *tar-pauk*

cube *(n.)* ကုဗ *ku-ba*

cubical *(adj.)* ကုဗပုံဖြစ်သော *ku-ba-pon-phit-taw*

cubicle *(n.)* အခန်းငယ် *a-khan-nge*

cubit *(n.)* လက်မောင်းအရှည်ကို မူတည်သော ရှေးဟောင်းအရှည်တိုင်းတာမှု *lat-maung-a-shay-ko-mu-the-taw-shay-haung-a-shay-tine-tar-mu*

cuckold *(n.)* မျောက်မထားသော မိန်းမ၏ လင်ယောကျ်ား *myauk-ma-htar-taw-mein-ma-ei-lin-yauk-kyar*

cuckoo *(n.)* ဥသြငှက် *oat-aw-nget*

cucumber *(n.)* သခွားသီး *ta-kwar-thee*

cuddle *(v.)* ပွေ့ဖက်သည် *pway-phat-the*

cudgel *(n.)* တင်းပုတ် *tin-poke*

cue *(n.)* ဇာတ်အချိတ်အဆက်စကား *zat-a-chake-a-sat-sa-gar*

cuff *(n.)* လက်ရှည်အင်္ကျီ လက်အနားခေါက် *lat-shay-inn-gyi, lat-a-nar-khauk*

cuisine *(n.)* ချက်ပြုတ်နည်း *chat-pyoke-nee*

culinary *(adj.)* အချက်အပြုတ်ဆိုင်ရာ a-chat-a-pyoke-sai-yar

cullet *(n.)* ကျိုးပဲ့သော မသုံးတော့သော ဖန်များကို ဖန်ချက်လုပ်ငန်းတွင် အသုံးချခြင်း *kyo-pae-taw-ma-tone-taw-taw-phan-myar-ko-phan-chat-lote-ngan-twin-tone-chin*

culminate *(v.)* အဆုံးသတ်သည် *a-sone-tat-the*

culpable *(adj.)* တာဝန်ရှိသည် *tar-win-shi-the*

culprit *(n.)* တရားခံ *ta-yar-khan*

cult *(n.)* ယုံကြည်မှုဆိုင်ရာ ကျင့်ထုံး *yone-kyi-mu-sai-yar-kyint-htone*

cultivate *(v.)* စိုက်ပျိုးသည်၊ ထွန်ယက်သည် *site-pyo-the, htun-yat-the*

cultivation *(n.)* စိုက်ပျိုးထွန်ယက်ခြင်း *site-pyo-htun-yat-chin*

cultural *(adj.)* ယဉ်ကျေးမှုနှင့် ဆိုင်သော *yan-kyay-mu-nint-sai-taw*

culture *(n.)* ယဉ်ကျေးမှု *yin-kyay-mu*

culvert *(n.)* မြေအောက်မြောင်း myay-awt-myaung

cumulative *(adj.)* များလာသော *myar-lar-taw*

cunning *(adj.)* ကလိမ်ကျတတ်သော *ka-alin-kya-tat-taw*

cup *(n.)* ခွက် *khwat*

cupboard *(n.)* ကြောင်အိမ် kyaung-eain

cupid *(n.)* ဖူးစာရေးနတ် *phoo-sar-yay-nat*

cupidity *(n.)* လောဘ *law-ba*

cupon *(n.)* ကူပွန်ငွေ *cu-pon-ngwe*

curable *(adj.)* ကုရ၍ ရသော *ku-ywe-ya-taw*

curator *(n.)* ပြတိုက်မှူး pya-tite-hmyu

curb *(v.)* အထိန်းအချုပ် *a-htain-a-choke*

curcumin *(n.)* ကာကူမင်းဒြပ်ပေါင်း *ka-ku-min-drat-paung*

curd *(n.)* ဒိန် *dain*

curdle *(v.)* ဒိန်ချဉ်ဖောက်သည် *dain-chin-hpauk-the*

cure *(v.)* ကုသသည် *khu-ta-the*

curfew *(n.)* ညမထွက်ရ အမိန့် *nya-ma-htwat-ya-a-maint*

curiosity *(n.)* စူးစမ်းစိတ် *sue-san-seik*

curious *(adj.)* စပ်စုသော *sat-su-taw*

curl *(v.)* အခွေအလိပ် *a-khway-a-ote*

curly *(adj.)* တွန့်သော *twunt-taw*

currant *(n.)* စပျစ်သီးခြောက် *sa-pyit-thee-kyauk*

currency *(n.)* ငွေကြေးစနစ် *ngwe-kyay-sa-nit*

current *(n.)* လျှပ်စီး၊ စီးကြောင်း *hlyat-see, see-kyaung*

current *(adj.)* မျက်မှောက်၊ ယခု *myat-mawk, ya-khu*

current account *(n.)* စာရင်းရှင်အပ်ငွေ *sa-yin-shin-at-ngwe*

curriculum *(n.)* သင်ရိုးညွှန်းတမ်း *tin-yoe-nyoon-tan*

curse *(n.)* ဆဲရေးစကား၊ ကျိန်ဆဲစကား *sal-yay-sa-gar, kyein-sal-sa-kar*

cursive *(adj.)* လက်ရေးဆက် *lat-yay-sat*

cursor *(n.)* ကာဆာ *kar-sar*

cursory *(adj.)* ပြီးစလွယ် pyi-sa-lwal

curt *(adj.)* တိုးတိ *tone-ti*

curtail *(v.)* လျှော့သည် hlyawt-the

curtain *(n.)* လိုက်ကာ lite-kar

curvature *(n.)* အကွေး a-kway

curve *(n.)* မျဉ်းခုံး *myin-khon*

curve *(v.)* ကွေးသည်၊ ကောက်သည် *kway-the, kauk-the*

cushion *(n.)* ကူရှင် *ku-shin*

cusp *(n.)* အဖျားချွန်း a-phar-chun

custard *(n.)* ကြက်ဥနို့ပေါင်း kyat-u-noe-paung

custodian *(n.)* ထိန်းသိမ်းစောင့်ရှောက်သူ *htain-tain-saunt-shaut-thu*

custody *(n.)* ထိန်းသိမ်းစောင့်ရှောက်မှု *htain-tain-saunt-shaut-mu*

custom *(n.)* ဓလေ့ *da-lay*

customary *(adj.)* ဓလေ့ထုံးတမ်းနှင့်ညီသော *da-lay-htone-tan-nint-nyi-taw*

customer *(n.)* ဈေးဝယ် *zay-wal*

cut *(n.)* ပြတ်ရှခြင်း၊ ဖြတ်ခြင်း *pyat-sha-chin, phat-chin*

cute *(adj.)* **ချစ်စဖွယ်ကောင်းသော၊ ပါးနပ်သော၊ လည်သော** *chit-sa-phwal-kaung-taw, par-nat-taw, lal-taw*
cutlery *(n.)* **ဇွန်း၊ ခက်ရင်း၊ ဓား** *zoon, khat-yin, dar*
cutlet *(n.)* **ကက်သလိတ်** *kat-ta-laik*
cut-off *(n.)* **နောက်ပိတ်ဆုံး** *naut-pate-sone*
cutter *(n.)* **ခုတ်ဖြတ်သူ** *khote-phat-thu*
cutting *(n.)* **ဖြတ်စ** *phat-sa*
cuvette *(n.)* **ဓာတ်ခွဲခန်းသုံးထည့်စရာအကြည်** *dat-khwal-khan-tone-htae-sa-yar-a-kyi*
cyan *(n.)* **စိမ်းပြာရောင်** *sein-pyar-yaung*
cyanide *(n.)* **ဆိုင်ယာနိုက်အဆိပ်** sai-yar-nide-a-seik
cyber *(adj.)* **ဆိုင်ဘာ** sai-bar
cyberbullying *(n.)* **ဆိုင်ဘာအနိုင်ကျင့်ခြင်း** *sai-bar-a-nai-kyint-chin*
cybercafé *(n.)* **ဆိုင်ဘာကဖေး** *sai-bar-ka-fay*
cyberchat *(n.)* **ဆိုင်ဘာစကားပြောခြင်း** *sai-bar-sa-kar-pyaw-chin*
cybercrime *(n.)* **ဆိုင်ဘာမှုခင်း** *sai-bar-mu-khin*
cycle *(n.)* **စက်ဝန်း၊ စက်ဘီး၊ မော်တော်ဆိုင်ကယ်** *sat-win, sat-bain, maw-taw-sai-kal*
cyclic *(adj.)* **သံသရာလည်နေသော** *tan-ta-yar-lal-nay-taw*
cyclist *(n.)* **စက်ဘီးစီးသမား** *sat-bain-see-ta-mar*
cyclone *(n.)* **ဆိုင်ကလုန်းမုန်တိုင်း** *sai-ka-lone-mone-tai*
cyclops *(n.)* **လူသန်ကြီး** lu-than-gyi
cyclostyle *(n.)* **ရှေးခေတ်မိတ္တူပွားစက်** shay-khit-meik-thu-pwar-sat
cylinder *(n.)* **ဆလင်ဒါပုံ** sa-lin-dar-pon
cylindrical *(adj.)* **ဆလင်ဒါပုံရှိသော** sa-lin-dar-pon-shi-taw
cynic *(n.)* **အဆိုးမြင်ဝါဒီ** a-soe-myin-wa-di
cynical *(adj.)* **အဆိုးမြင်သော** a-soe-myin-taw
cypher *(n.)* **စာဝှက်ရေးနည်း** *sar-hwat-yay-nee*
cypress *(n.)* **ဆိုက်ပရက်ပင်** *site-pa-ress-pin*
cyst *(n.)* **အရည်အိတ်** *a-yay-aik*

D

dabble *(v.)* **ဟိုစပ်စပ် ဒီစပ်စပ် လုပ်သည်** *ho-sat-sat-di-sat-sat-lote-the*
dacoit *(n.)* **ဓားပြအဖွဲ့ဝင်** *da-mya-a-phwe-win*
dacoity *(n.)* **ဓားပြတိုက်ခြင်း** *da-mya-tite-chin*
dad (or daddy) *(n.)* **အဖေ** a-hpay
daffodil *(n.)* **အဝါရောင်ပန်း** a-war-yaung-pan
daft *(adj.)* **ပေါကြောင်ကြောင်နိုင်သော** paw-kyaung-kyaung-nai-taw
dagger *(n.)* **ဓားမြှောင်** da-hmyaung
daily *(adj. & adv.)* **နေ့စဉ်** nay-sin
dainty *(adj.)* **နုနုလှလှ** nu-nu-hla-hla
dairy *(n.)* **နို့ထွက်ပစ္စည်း ချက်ရာနေရာ၊ အရောင်းဆိုင်** *no-htwat-pyit-see-chat-yar-nay-yar, a-yaung-sai*
dairy product *(n.)* **နို့ထွက်ပစ္စည်း** *no-htwat-pyit-see*
dais *(n.)* **တရားဟောစင်** *ta-yar-haw-sin*
daisy *(n.)* **ဒေစီပန်း** *dai-si-pan*

dale *(n.)* တောင်ကြား *taung-gyar*

dally *(v.)* အချိန်ဆွဲသည် *a-chain-swal-the*

dam *(n.)* ရေကာတာ၊ ဆည် *yay-kar-tar, sal*

damage *(n.)* ထိခိုက်ခြင်း *hti-khaik-chin*

damage control *(n.)* ထိခိုက်မှုကို ထိန်းချုပ်ခြင်း hti-khaik-chin-ko-htein-choke-chin

damaging *(adj.)* ထိခိုက်နစ်နာစေသော hti-khaik-nit-nar-say-taw

damask *(n.)* နှစ်ဖက်လှ ပိုးထည်ချည်ထည် *na-phat-hla-poe-htae-chi-htae*

dame *(n.)* သူကောင်းဘွဲ့ *thu-kaung-bwe*

damn *(v.)* ငရဲတွင် ကျခံစေသည် *nga-ye-twin-kya-khan-say-the*

damnable *(adj.)* အလွန့်အလွန် ဆိုးဝါးသော *a-lwunt-a-lun-soe-war-thaw*

damnation *(n.)* ငရဲသစ်ငုတ်ဘဝ *nga-ye-tit-ngote-ba-wa*

damned *(adj.)* အပြည့်အဝ *a-pyae-a-wa*

damp *(adj.)* စိုသော၊ ထိုင်းသော *so-taw, htai-taw*

dampen *(v.)* စိုထိုင်းသည် *so-htai-the*

damsel *(n.)* မိန်းမပျို *main-ma-pyo*

dance *(n.)* ကခြင်း *ka-chin*

dancer *(n.)* ကချေသည်၊ ကပြသူ *ka-chay-tal, ka-pya-thu*

dancing *(adj.)* ကခုန်သော *ka-khone-taw*

dandelion *(n.)* အဝါရောင်အလေ့ကျပန်း *a-war-yaung-a-lay-kya-pan*

dandle *(v.)* ကလေးကို ဒူးပေါ်လက်ပေါ်တင် မြှောက်ကာ မြှူသည် ka-lay-ko-du-paw-lat-paw-hmyauk-kar-hmyu-the

dandruff *(n.)* ဗောက် *bauk*

dandy *(n.)* ဝတ်ကောင်းစားလှဖြင့် ရှိုးထုတ်လွန်းသူ *wut-kaung-sar-hla-phint-sho-htoke-lun-thu*

danger *(n.)* အန္တရာယ် *an-da-yal*

dangerous *(adj.)* အန္တရာယ်များသော *an-da-yal-myar-taw*

dangle *(v.)* တွဲလဲဆွဲထားသည် *twal-lal-swal-htar-the*

dangling *(adj.)* တွဲလဲဆွဲထားခြင်း *twal-lal-swal-htar-chin*

dank *(adj.)* စိမ့်စိုအေးစက်သော *seint-so-aye-sat-taw*

dap *(v.)* ညင်သာစွာနှစ်သည် nyin-tar-swar-nit-the

dapper *(adj.)* ကျစ်လျစ်သွက်လက်သော *kyit-lyit-twat-lat-taw*

dapple *(v.)* အစက်များဖြင့် မှတ်သားသည် a-sat-myar-phint-mat-tar-the

dare *(v.)* ဝံ့သည် wint-the

daredevil *(n.)* မိုက်ရူးရဲ mite-yu-ye

daring *(n.)* ရဲရင့်ခြင်း ye-yint-chin

dark *(adj.)* မှောင်သော *hmaung-taw*

darken *(v.)* မှောင်သည် *hmaung-the*

darkle *(v.)* ပိုမှောင်လာသည် *po-hmaung-lar-the*

darkness *(n.)* အမှောင်ထု *a-hmaung-htu*

darling *(n.)* ဒါလင်၊ အချစ် *da-lin, a-chit*

dart *(n.)* လှံတို၊ မြားငယ် *lan-to, myar-nge*

dartboard *(n.)* စက်ကွင်း *sat-kwin*

darting *(n.)* ရုတ်တရက်ပစ်ခြင်း yote-ta-yat-pyit-chin

dash *(v.)* တရကြမ်းသွားခြင်း *ta-ra-kyan-twar-chin*

dashboard *(n.)* ဒက်ရှ်ဘုတ် *dat-sh-bote*

dashing *(adj.)* နှစ်လိုဖွယ်ကောင်းသော *nit-lo-phwal-kaung-taw*

data *(n.)* အချက်အလက် *a-chat-a-lat*

databank *(n.)* ဒေတာဘဏ်တိုက် *da-tar-ban-tide*

database *(n.)* အချက်အလက်စာရင်း *a-chat-a-lat-sa-yin*

date *(n.)* နေ့စွဲ *nae-swal*

dated *(adj.)* နေ့စွဲတပ်ထားသော *nae-swal-tat-htar-taw*

daub *(n.)* လိမ်းသည် *lain-the*

daughter *(n.)* သမီး *ta-mee*

daunt *(v.)* လန့်သည် *lant-the*

daunting *(adj.)* လန့်စရာကောင်းသော *lant-sa-yar-kaung-taw*

dauntless *(adj.)* မတွန့်မဆုတ်သော *a-twunt-ma-sote-taw*

dawdle *(v.)* အချိန်ဆွဲသည် *a-chain-swal-the*

dawdler *(n.)* အချိန်ဆွဲသူ a-chain-swal-thu

dawn *(v.)* အရုဏ်ကျင်းသည် *ar-yone-kyin-the*

dawnlight *(n.)* အရုဏ်ကျင်းအလင်းရောင် *ar-yone-kyin-a-lin-yaung*

day *(n.)* နေ့၊ ရက် *nae, yat*

daybreak *(n.)* အရုဏ်ဦး *ar-yone-oo*

daylight *(n.)* နေ့အလင်းရောင် *nae-a-lin-yaung*

daze *(v.)* မှူးဝေသည် *mu-wai-the*

dazed *(adj.)* တွေဝေသော *tway-wai-taw*

daziness *(n.)* မှူးဝေသော အခြေအနေ *mu-wai-taw-a-chay-a-nay*

dazzle *(v.)* ပြာသွားသည် *pyar-twar-the*

dazzling *(adj.)* ထူးချွန်ပြောင်မြောက်သော *htoo-chon-pyaung-myauk-taw*

dazzlingly *(adv.)* ထူးချွန်ပြောင်မြောက်စွာ *htoo-chon-pyaung-myauk-swar*

deacon *(n.)* ဂိုဏ်းထောက်ဘုန်းတော်ကြီး *gai-htauk-bone-taw-gyi*

deactivate *(v.)* ပိတ်သည် *pate-the*

deactivation *(n.)* ပိတ်ခြင်း *pate-chin*

deactivator *(n.)* ပိတ်သည့်အရာ *pate-the-a-yar*

dead *(n.)* လူသေ *lu-thay*

deadbolt *(n.)* တံခါးသော့ *ta-khar-taw*

deadline *(n.)* ပြီးစီးရန်သတ်မှတ်ချိန် *pi-see-yan-tat-mat-chain*

deadlock *(n.)* မဆုတ်သာ မတိုးသာ အခြေအနေ *ma-sote-tar-ma-toe-tar-a-chay-a-nay*

deadly *(adj.)* သေလုနီးသော *tay-lu-nee-taw*

deaf *(adj.)* နားပင်းသော *nar-pin-taw*

deafen *(v.)* နားပင်းစေသည် *nar-pin-say-the*

deafening *(adj.)* အလွန်ကျယ်လောင်သော *a-lun-kyal-laung-taw*

deal *(n.)* သဘောတူညီမှု *ta-baw-tu-nyi-mu*

deal *(v.)* ဖဲဝေသည် *phal-wai-the*

dealer *(n.)* ကုန်သည် *kone-thal*

dealership *(n.)* ကုန်သွယ်မှု *kone-thwal-mu*

dealings *(n.)* အရောင်းအဝယ် *a-yaung-a-wal*

dealmaker *(n.)* ညှိနှိုင်းရေးသမား *nyi-nai-yay-ta-mar*

dean *(n.)* မဟာဌာနမှူး *ma-har-htar-na-hmu*

dear *(adj.)* ချစ်လှစွာသော *chit-hla-swar-taw*

dearest *(adj.)* အချစ်ဆုံး *a-chit-sone*

dearth *(n.)* နည်းပါးမှု *nae-par-mu*

death *(n.)* သေဆုံးခြင်း *tay-sone-chin*

deathly *(adj.)* **အသေကောင်လို၊ သုသာန်တစပြင်ပမာ** *a-tay-kaung-lo, tote-tan-ta-sa-pyin-pa-mar*
debacle *(n.)* **အရှုံးကြီးရှုံးခြင်း** *a-shone-gyi-shone-chin*
debar *(v.)* **ထုတ်ပယ်သည်၊ တားမြစ်သည်၊** *htoke-pal-the, tar-myit-the*
debase *(v.)* **ဖျက်သည်၊ တန်ဖိုးလျော့စေသည်** *phat-the, tan-phoe-shawt-say-the*
debate *(n.)* **စကားရည်လုပွဲ** *sa-kar-yay-lu-pwe*
debauch *(v.)* **သူတစ်ပါး သားပျိုသမီးပျိုကို ဖျက်ဆီးသည်** *thu-ta-par-tar-pyo-ta-mee-pyo-ko-phat-see-the*
debauchee *(n.)* **အပျော်အပါး ကျူးသူ** *a-pyaw-a-par-kyu-thu*
debauchery *(n.)* **ကာမရာဂလိုက်စားမှု** *kar-ma-yar-ga-lite-sar-mu*
debenture *(n.)* **ဒီဘင်ချာ ငွေချေးလက်မှတ်** *de-bin-char-ngway-chee-lat-mat*
debile *(adj.)* **အားပျော့သော** *arr-pyawt-taw*
debilitant *(n.)* **အားပျော့သူ** *arr-pyawt-thu*
debilitate *(v.)* **အားလျော့စေသည်** *arr-shawt-say-the*
debilitating *(adj.)* **အားလျော့စေသော** *arr-shawt-say-taw*
debilitation *(n.)* **အားလျော့စေခြင်း** *arr-shawt-say-chin*
debility *(n.)* **ချည့်နဲ့ခြင်း** chae-nae-chin
debit *(n.)* **ပေးငွေ** *pay-ngwe*
debit card *(n.)* **ဒီဘစ်ကတ်** *de-bit-kat*
debonaire *(adj.)* **ကြော့ကြော့မော့မော့ ရှိသော** *kyawt-kyawt-mawt-mawt-shi-taw*
debrief *(v.)* **ပြန်လည် အစီရင်ခံစေသည်** *pyan-lal-a-si-yin-khan-say-the*
debris *(n.)* **အပျက်အစီး** *a-pyat-a-see*
debt *(n.)* **အကြွေး** *a-kyway*
debt-free *(adj.)* **ကြွေးမီကင်းသော** *kyway-mee-kin-taw*
debtor *(n.)* **မြီစား** *myie-sar*
debuff *(n.)* **ဂိမ်းပုံထွက်ကျစေသည့် သက်ရောက်မှု** *gain-pone-htwat-kya-say-the-thet-yauk-mu*
debug *(v.)* **ကွန်ပျူတာပရိုဂရမ်တွင် အပြစ်ကို ရှာဖွေဖယ်ရှားသည်** *kun-pyu-tar-pa-ro-ga-ran-twin-a-pyit-ko-shar-phway-phal-shar-the*
debunk *(v.)* **မမှန်သည်ကို ဖွင့်ချသည်** *ma-man-the-ko-phwint-cha-the*
debut *(n.)* **ပထမအကြိမ်လုပ်ဆောင်ရာတွင် ရှိသော စွမ်းရည်** *pa-hta-ma-a-kyein-lote-saung-yar-twin-shi-taw-swan-yay*
debutante *(n.)* **လူ့အဖွဲ့အစည်းတွင် ဝင်ရောက်သော လူချမ်းသာ မိန်းမပျို** *lu-a-phwe-a-see-twin-win-yauk-taw-lu-chan-tar-mein-ka-lay*
decade *(n.)* **ဆယ်စုနှစ်** *sal-su-nit*
decadent *(adj.)* **ယိုယွင်းသော** *yo-ywin-taw*
decalcification *(n.)* **ကယ်စီယမ်ဓာတ်နည်းခြင်း** *kal-see-yan-dat-nae-chin*
decalcifiy *(v.)* **ကယ်စီယမ်ဓာတ်နည်းသည်** *kal-see-yan-dat-nae-the*
decalibrate *(v.)* **ချိန်ညှိမှုကို ဖယ်ရှားသည်** *chein-nyi-mu-ko-phal-shar-the*
decamp *(v.)* **လစ်သွားသည်** *lat-twar-the*
decapitate *(v.)* **ခေါင်းဖြတ်သည်** *gaung-phat-the*
decay *(v.)* **ယိုယွင်းပျက်စီးသည်** *yo-ywin-pyat-see-the*
decay *(n.)* **ယိုယွင်းပျက်စီးခြင်း** *yo-ywin-pyat-see-chin*
decease *(n.)* **ကွယ်လွန်ခြင်း** *kwal-lun-chin*

deceased *(adj.)* **ကွယ်လွန်သွားသော** *kwal-lun-twar-taw*
deceit *(n.)* **လိမ်ညာမှု** *lain-nyar-mu*
deceitful *(adj.)* **လိမ်လည်လှည့်ဖြားသော** *lain-lal-hlae-phyar-taw*
deceive *(v.)* **လိမ်သည်၊ လှည့်ဖြားသည်** *lain-the, hlae-phyar-the*
decelerate *(v.)* **အရှိန်လျှော့သည်** *a-shein-shawt-the*
deceleration *(n.)* **အရှိန်လျှော့ခြင်း** *a-shein-shawt-chin*
december *(n.)* **ဒီဇင်ဘာလ** *de-zin-bar-la*
decency *(n.)* **သင့်တင့်လျောက်ပတ်ယဉ်ကျေးဖွယ်ရာ ရှိခြင်း** *tint-tint-shaut-pat-yin-kyay-phwal-yar-shi-chin*
decennary *(n.)* **၁၀ နှစ်ကာလ** *10 nit-tar-kar-la*
decent *(adj.)* **သင့်တော်သော** *tint-taw-thaw*
decentralize *(v.)* **အာဏာကို ဒေသအစိုးရသို့ ခွဲဝေပေးသည်** *arr-nar-ko-day-tha-a-soe-ya-tho-khwal-wai-pay-the*
decentre *(v.)* **ဗဟိုချက်ပျောက်သည်** *ba-ho-chat-pyauk-the*
deception *(n.)* **လိမ်လည်လှည့်ဖြားခြင်း** *lain-lal-hlae-phyar-chin*
deceptive *(adj.)* **လှည့်ဖြားတတ်သော** hlae-phyar-tat-taw
decibel *(n.)* **ဒက်ဆီဘယ်** dat-si-bal
decide *(v.)* **ဆုံးဖြတ်သည်** *sone-phat-the*
decided *(adj.)* **တိကျပြတ်သားသော** *ti-kya-pyat-tar-taw*
decidedly *(adv.)* **တိကျပြတ်သားစွာ** ti-kya-pyat-tar-swar
decimal *(adj.)* **ဆယ်လီစိတ်ဖြစ်သော** *sal-li-seik-phit-taw*
decimal point *(n.)* **ဒသမကိန်းကို ဖော်ပြသော အစက်ငယ်** *dat-ta-ma-kain-ko-phaw-pya-taw-a-sat-nge*
decimate *(v.)* **အများအပြား သေကျေပြုန်းတီးသည်** *a-myar-a-pyar-tay-kyay-pyone-tee-the*
decimation *(v.)* **ပြုန်းတီးမှု** *pyone-tee-mu*
decipher *(v.)* **ဝှက်စာဖော်သည်** *hwat-sar-phaw-the*
decision *(n.)* **ဆုံးဖြတ်ချက်** *sone-phat-chat*
decisive *(adj.)* **နောက်ဆုံးဖြစ်သော၊ တိကျပြတ်သားသော** *naut-sone-phit-taw, ti-kya-pyat-tar-taw*
deck *(n.)* **သင်္ဘောကုန်းပတ်** *tin-baw-kone-pat*
declaration *(n.)* **ကြေညာခြင်း** *kyay-nyar-chin*
declare *(v.)* **ကြေညာသည်** kyay-nyar-the
declassify *(v.)* **လျှို့ဝှက်အဆင့်အတန်း လျှော့ချသတ်မှတ်သည်** *sho-hwat-a-sint-a-tan-shawt-cha-tat-mat-the*
decline *(v.)* **ငြင်းဆိုသည်** *nyin-so-the*
declivity *(n.)* **အောက်သို့တိမ်းစောင်းခြင်း** *awt-tho-tain-saung-chin*
declutter *(v.)* **ဖြုပ်စဖျင်းတောင်းဖယ်ရှားသည်** *byoke-sa-byin-taung-phal-shar-the*
decoction *(n.)* **ပြုတ်ခြင်းမှရသော အနှစ်** *pyoke-chin-ma-ya-taw-a-nit*
decode *(v.)* **ဝှက်စာဖော်သည်** *hwat-sar-phaw-the*
decoder *(n.)* **ဝှက်စာဖော်သူ** *hwat-sar-phaw-thu*
decolonization *(n.)* **ကိုလိုနီနိုင်ငံကို လွတ်လပ်ရေးပေးခြင်း** *ko-lo-ni-nai-ngan-ko-hlut-lat-yay-pay-chin*

decolonize *(v.)* ကိုလိုနီနိုင်ငံကို လွတ်လပ်ရေးပေးသည် *ko-lo-ni-nai-ngan-ko-hlut-lat-yay-pay-the*
decommission *(v.)* ပယ်ဖျက်သည် *pal-phat-the*
decompose *(v.)* ပုပ်သိုးသည် *poke-thoe-the*
decomposition *(n.)* ပုပ်သိုးခြင်း *poke-thoe-chin*
decompress *(v.)* ဖိအားတဖြည်းဖြည်း လျှော့ပေးသည် *phi-arr-ta-phyae-phyae-shawt-pay-the*
decompression *(n.)* ဖိအားတဖြည်းဖြည်း လျှော့ပေးခြင်း *phi-arr-ta-phyae-phyae-shawt-pay-chin*
decongest *(v.)* ပိတ်ဆို့မှုကို လျှော့ချသည် *pate-so-mu-ko-shawt-cha-the*
deconstruct *(v.)* တိုက်ဆိုင်စိစစ်သည် *tite-sai-si-sit-the*
deconstruction *(n.)* တိုက်ဆိုင်စိစစ်ခြင်း *tite-sai-si-sit-chin*
deconstructively *(adv.)* ဖျက်ဆီးသည့် စိတ်ထားဖြင့် *pyat-see-the-seik-htar-phyint*
decontrol *(v.)* ထိန်းချုပ်မှု မဲ့သည် *thain-choke-mu-mae-the*
decor *(n.)* အိမ်တွင်းပုံစံ *eain-twin-pon-san*
decorate *(v.)* အလှဆင်သည် *a-hla-sin-the*
decoration *(n.)* အလှဆင်ခြင်း *a-hla-sin-chin*
decorative *(adj.)* လှပစေသော *hla-pa-say-taw*
decorum *(n.)* ဗိုင်းကောင်းကျောက်ဖိ *bai-kaung-kyauk-phi*
decoy *(n.)* တည်ကြက် *tae-kyat*
decrease *(v.)* နည်းသည် *nae-the*
decreasingly *(adv.)* နည်းပါးစွာ *nae-par-swar*
decree *(n.)* အမိန့်၊ ဥပဒေ *a-maint, oo-pa-day*
decrement *(n.)* အရေအတွက်၊ အရည်အသွေး တဖြည်းဖြည်းကျဆင်းခြင်း *a-yay-a-twat-a-yay-a-thway-ta-phyae-phyae-kya-sin-chin*
decrepitate *(v.)* ကွဲသံထွက်သည်အထိ အပူပေးသည် *kwal-tan-htwat-the-a-hti-a-pu-pay-the*
decrepitation *(n.)* ကွဲသံထွက်သည်အထိ အပူပေးခြင်း *kwal-tan-htwat-the-a-hti-a-pu-pay-chin*
decriminalization *(n.)* ဥပဒေပြောင်းလိုက်သောကြောင့် တစ်စုံတစ်ရာသည် မှုခင်းမဖြစ်တော့ခြင်း *oo-pa-day-pyaung-lite-taw-kyaunt-ta-sone-ta-yar-the-mu-khin-ma-phit-taw-chin*
decriminalize *(v.)* တစ်စုံတစ်ရာသည် မှုခင်းမဖြစ်တော့ရန် ဥပဒေပြောင်းသည် *ta-sone-ta-yar-the-mu-khin-ma-phit-say-yan-oo-pa-day-pyaung-the*
decry *(v.)* ဝေဖန်သည်၊ ရှုတ်ချသည် *wai-phan-the, shoke-cha-the*
decrypt *(n.)* ဖြည်ခြင်း *phyay-chin*
decryption *(n.)* ဖြည်ခြင်း phyay-chin
dedicate *(v.)* နှစ်မြှုပ်ထားသည် *nit-hmyoke-htar-the*
dedication *(n.)* စူးစိုက်နှစ်မြှုပ်ထားမှု *sue-site-nit-hmyoke-htar-mu*
deduce *(v.)* အဖြေထုတ်သည် *a-phyay-htoke-the*
deduct *(v.)* နုတ်သည် *note-the*
deduction *(n.)* ထုတ်ယူ ဆင်ခြင်ခြင်း *htoke-yu-sin-chin-chin*
deed *(n.)* ဆောင်ရွက်ချက် *saung-ywet-chat*
deem *(v.)* ယူဆသည် *yu-sa-the*

deep *(adj.)* **နက်သော** nat-taw

deepen *(v.)* **နက်သည်** *nat-taw*

deeply *(adv.)* **နက်နက်ရှိုင်းရှိုင်း** *nat-nat-shine-shine*

deer *(n.)* **သမင်** *ta-min*

deface *(v.)* **အလှပျက်စေသည်** *a-hla-pyat-say-the*

defamation *(n.)* **အသရေဖျက်မှု** *a-tha-yay-phat-mu*

defamatory *(adj.)* **အသရေပျက်စေသော** *a-tha-yay-pyat-say-taw*

defame *(v.)* **အသရေဖျက်သည်** *a-tha-yay-phat-the*

default *(n.)* **နဂိုပုံစံ** *na-go-pon-san*

defeat *(v.)* **အနိုင်ယူသည်** a-nai-yu-the

defecate *(v.)* **မစင်စွန့်သည်** ma-sin-sunt-the

defect *(n.)* **ချွတ်ယွင်းချက်** *chut-ywin-chat*

defective *(adj.)* **ချွတ်ယွင်းသော** *chut-ywin-taw*

defence *(n.)* **ကာကွယ်ခြင်း** *kar-kwal-chin*

defenceless *(adj.)* **အကာအကွယ်မဲ့သော** *a-kar-a-kwal-mae-taw*

defend *(v.)* **ကာကွယ်သည်** *kar-kwal-the*

defendant *(n.)* **တရားခံ** *ta-ya-khan*

defensive *(adj.)* **ကာကွယ်ရေး** *kar-kwal-yay*

defer *(v.)* **ရွှေ့ဆိုင်းသည်** *shwe-saing-the*

deference *(n.)* **လေးစားလိုက်နာခြင်း** *lay-sar-lite-nar-chin*

defiance *(n.)* **အာခံခြင်း** *ar-khan-chin*

defiant *(adj.)* **အာခံသော** *ar-khan-taw*

deficiency *(n.)* **လျော့နည်းခြင်း** *shawt-nae-chin*

deficient *(adj.)* **မပြည့်ဝသော** *ma-pyae-wa-taw*

deficit *(n.)* **လိုငွေ** lo-ngwe

defile *(n.)* **ညစ်ညမ်းစေသည်** *nyit-nyan-say-the*

define *(v.)* **သတ်မှတ်သည်** tat-mat-the

definite *(adj.)* **တိကျသော** *ti-kya-taw*

definition *(n.)* **အဓိပ္ပါယ်ဖွင့်ဆိုချက်** a-date-pal-phwint-so-chat

definitive *(adj.)* **ခိုင်မာသော** *khai-mar-taw*

deflate *(v.)* **လေလျှော့သည်** *lay-shawt-the*

deflation *(n.)* **လျှော့ခြင်း** *shawt-chin*

deflect *(v.)* **ဦးတည်ချက်မှ သွေဖည်စေသည်** *oo-the-chat-ma-thway-phal-say-the*

deflection *(n.)* **လွဲချော်မှု တိမ်းစောင်းမှု ပမာဏ** *lwal-chaw-mu-tain-saung-mu-pa-mar-na*

deflesh *(v.)* **အသားကို ဖယ်ရှားသည်** a-tar-ko-phal-shar-the

deflower *(v.)* **ပန်းဦးပန်သည်** *pan-oo-pan-the*

defoliant *(n.)* **သစ်ရွက်ခြွေဓာတုပစ္စည်း** tit-ywet-chway-dar-tu-pyit-see

defoliate *(v.)* **သစ်ရွက်များကို ကြွေစေသည်** tit-ywet-myar-ko-kyway-say-the

deforest *(v.)* **သစ်တောပြုန်းစေသည်** *tit-taw-pyone-say-the*

deforestation *(n.)* **သစ်တောပြုန်းတီးခြင်း** *tit-taw-pyone-tee-chin*

deform *(v.)* **ပုံပန်းပျက်စေသည်** *pon-pan-pyat-say-the*

deformity *(n.)* **အနေအထားမမှန်မှု** *a-nay-a-htar-ma-man-mu*

defragment *(v.)* **ဖိုင်ကွဲခြင်းကို လျော့ချသည်** *phai-kwal-chin-ko-shawt-cha-the*

defragmentation *(n.)* **ဖိုင်ကွဲခြင်းကို လျော့ချခြင်း** *phai-kwal-chin-ko-shawt-cha-chin*

defrost *(v.)* ရေခဲသေတ္တာမှ ရေခဲကို ဖယ်ရှင်းသည် *yay-khae-tit-tar-ma-yay-khae-ko-phal-shar-the*
deft *(adj.)* ကျင်လည်သော *kyin-lal-taw*
defunct *(adj.)* ခေတ်ကုန်သွားပြီဖြစ်သော *khit-kone-twar-p-phit-taw*
defuse *(v.)* စနက်တံ ဖြုတ်သည် *sa-nat-tan-phyoke-the*
defy *(v.)* အာခံသည် ar-khan-the
degenerate *(v.)* ယိုယွင်းသည် *yo-ywin-the*
deglutination *(n.)* ဂလူတန်ကို စစ်ထုတ်ခြင်း *ga-lu-tan-ko-sit-htoke-chin*
degrade *(v.)* အရိုအသေတန်စေသည် *a-yo-a-tay-tan-say-the*
degrading *(adj.)* အရှက်ရစေသော *a-shat-ya-say-taw*
degree *(n.)* ဒီဂရီ *di-ga-ree*
degustation *(n.)* အစားအသောက်ပေါင်းစုံကို မြည်းစမ်းခြင်း *a-sar-a-thaut-paung-sone-ko-myae-san-chin*
dehort *(v.)* မလုပ်ရန် တားမြစ်သည် *ma-lote-yan-tar-myit-the*
dehumidify *(v.)* အစိုဓာတ်ကို ဖယ်ရှားသည် *a-soe-dat-ko-phal-shar-the*
dehydrate *(v.)* အရည်ဓာတ် ခန်းခြောက်စေသည် *a-yay-dat-khan-kyauk-say-the*
dehydration *(n.)* အရည်ဓာတ် ခန်းခြောက်ခြင်း *a-yay-dat-khan-kyauk-say-chin*
deify *(v.)* နတ်အဖြစ် ကိုးကွယ်သည် *nat-a-phit-koe-kwal-the*
deign *(v.)* အရေးတယူလုပ်သည် *a-yay-ta-yu-lote-the*
deism *(n.)* အထွတ်အထိပ်ပုဂ္ဂိုလ်ရှိကြောင်း ယုံကြည်ခြင်း *a-htut-a-htaik-poke-ko-shi-kyaung-yone-kyi-chin*
deist *(n.)* အထွတ်အထပ်ပုဂ္ဂိုလ်ရှိကြောင်း ယုံကြည်သူ *a-htut-a-htaik-poke-ko-shi-kyaung-yone-kyi-thu*
deity *(n.)* နတ်သမီး *nat-ta-mee*
deject *(v.)* စိတ်ဖိစီးသည် *seik-phi-see-the*
dejection *(n.)* စိတ်ပျက်လက်ပျက်ဖြစ်ခြင်း *seik-pyat-lat-pyat-phit-chin*
delay *(n.)* နှောင့်နှေးခြင်း *naunt-nay-chin*
delectability *(n.)* အလွန် စိတ်ကျေနပ်ခြင်း *a-lun-seik-kyay-nat-chin*
delectable *(adj.)* ပျော်ရွှင်ဖွယ်ကောင်းသော *pyaw-shwin-phwal-kaung-taw*
delegacy *(n.)* တာဝန်ခွဲဝေခြင်းအနုပညာ *tar-win-kwal-wai-chin-a-nu-pyin-nyar*
delegalize *(v.)* အာဏာကို ဖယ်ရှားသည် *ar-nar-ko-phal-shar-the*
delegate *(n.)* ကိုယ်စားလှယ် *ko-sa-lal*
delegation *(n.)* ကိုယ်စားလှယ်အဖွဲ့ *ko-sa-lal-a-phwe*
delegator *(n.)* တာဝန်ခွဲဝေသူ tar-win-kwal-wai-thu
deletable *(adj.)* ဖျက်၍ ရသော *pyat-ywe-ya-taw*
delete *(v.)* ဖျက်သည် *pyat-the*
deliberate *(adj.)* တမင်သက်သက် ဖြစ်သော *ta-min-thet-thet-phit-taw*
deliberation *(n.)* ချိန်ဆခြင်း *chain-sa-chin*
delicacy *(n.)* သိမ်မွေ့နူးညံ့ခြင်း *tein-mway-nu-nyant-chin*
delicate *(adj.)* နူးညံ့သော *nu-nyant-taw*
delicatessen *(n.)* အသင့်စားဖွယ် *a-tint-sar-phwal*
delicious *(adj.)* အရသာရှိသော *a-ya-tar-shi-taw*
delight *(v.)* သာယာကြည်နူးခြင်း tar-yar-kyi-nu-chin
delightedly *(adv.)* ကြည်နူးစွာ kyi-nu-swar

delightful *(adj.)* **ကြည်နူးဖွယ်ကောင်းသော** *kyi-nu-phwal-kaung-taw*
delimit *(v.)* **အနားသတ်သည်** *a-nar-tat-the*
delimitate *(v.)* **အကန့်အသတ်ဖယ်ရှားသည်** *a-kant-a-thet-phal-shar-the*
delimitation *(n.)* **အကန့်အသတ်ဖယ်ရှားခြင်း** *a-kant-a-thet-phal-shar-chin*
delineate *(v.)* **အသေးစိတ်ချပြသည်** *a-tay-seik-cha-pya-the*
delinquency *(n.)* **လူငယ်များ ကျူးလွန်သော ပြစ်မှုများ** *lu-ngal-myar-kyu-lun-taw-pyit-mu*
delinquent *(n.)* **ဆိုးသွမ်းလူငယ်** *soe-twan-lu-nge*
delipidate *(v.)* **အဆီဖယ်ရှားသည်** *a-si-phal-shar-the*
delipidation *(n.)* **အဆီဖယ်ရှားခြင်း** *a-si-phal-shar-chin*
deliriant *(n.)* **ဂယောင်ဂတမ်းဖြစ်စေသောဆေး** *ga-yaung-ga-tan-phit-say-taw-say*
delirium *(n.)* **ဂယောင်ဂတမ်း ညည်းတွားခြင်း** *ga-yaung-ga-tan-nyie-twar-chin*
deliver *(v.)* **ဟောပြောသည်၊ ပေးအပ်သည်** *haw-pyaw-the, pay-at-the*
deliverance *(n.)* **လွတ်မြောက်ခြင်း** hlut-myauk-chin
delivery *(n.)* **စာဝေခြင်း၊ ပေးပို့ခြင်း၊ မီးဖွားခြင်း** sar-wai-chin, pay-poe-chin, mee-phwar-chin
delta *(n.)* **မြစ်ဝကျွန်းပေါ်ဒေသ** myit-wa-kyun-paw-day-ta
deltoid *(n.)* **ပခုံးကြွက်သား** pa-khone-kyat-tar
delude *(v.)* **လှည့်စားသည်** *hlae-sar-the*
deluge *(n.)* **ရေလွှမ်းမိုးခြင်း** yay-hlwan-moe-chin
delusion *(n.)* **ထင်ယောင်ထင်မှားဖြစ်ခြင်း** *htin-yaung-htin-mar-phit-chin*
delusional *(adj.)* **ထင်ယောင်ထင်မှားဖြစ်သော** *htin-yaung-htin-mar-phit-taw*
deluxe *(adj.)* **အလွန်ကောင်းသော** *a-lun-kaung-taw*
delve *(v.)* **နှိုက်၍ ရှာသည်** *nite-ywe-shar-the*
demagnetize *(v.)* **သံလိုက်ဓာတ်ဖယ်ရှားသည်** *tan-lite-dat-phal-shar-the*
demagogue *(n.)* **ပရိသတ်ကျအောင် နှိုးဆွလှုံ့ဆော်နိုင်သော နိုင်ငံရေးသမားခေါင်းဆောင်** pa-yeik-tat-kya-aung-noe-swa-lont-saw-naing-taw-nai-ngan-yay-ta-mar-gaung-saung
demagogy *(n.)* **နိုင်ငံရေးအဟောအပြောနည်းပရိယာယ်** *nai-ngan-yay-a-haw-a-pyaw-nee-pa-yee-yal*
demand *(n.)* **တောင်းဆိုချက်၊ လိုအပ်ချက်** *taung-so-chat, ko-at-chat*
demanding *(adj.)* **မရမနေခိုင်းတတ်သော** *ma-ya-ma-nay-khai-tat-taw*
demarcate *(v.)* **ပိုင်းခြားသတ်မှတ်သည်** *pai-char-tat-mat-the*
demarcation *(n.)* **ပိုင်းခြင်းသတ်မှတ်ခြင်း** *pai-char-tat-mat-chin*
demasculinization *(n.)* **ဝေ့းစေ့ဖယ်ရှားသည်** *wai-say-phal-shar-the*
dematerialisation *(n.)* **ပျောက်သွားခြင်း** *pyauk-twar-chin*
dematerialize *(v.)* **ပျောက်သွားသည်** *pyauk-twar-the*
demean *(v.)* **သိက္ခာချသည်** *taik-khar-cha-the*
demeaning *(adj.)* **ဂုဏ်ငယ်စေသော** *gon-nge-say-the*
dement *(v.)* **အကြောင်းပြချက် ပိတ်ပင်သည်** *a-kyaung-pya-chat-pate-pin-the*

demented *(adj.)* ရူးသော *yu-taw*
dementia *(n.)* ဦးနှောက်ထိခိုက်ဒဏ်ရာရမှု *oo-naut-hti-khaik-dan-yar-ya-mu*
demerit *(n.)* အပြစ် *a-pyit*
demicircle *(n.)* စက်ဝိုင်းခြမ်း *sat-wai-chan*
demilitarized *(adj.)* စစ်တပ်အင်အားလျော့ချသော *sit-tat-inn-ar-shawt-cha-taw*
demise *(n.)* သေခြင်း *tay-chin*
demobilization *(n.)* စစ်မှုထမ်းအဖြစ်မှ ထွက်ခွင့်ပြုခြင်း *sit-mu-htan-a-phit-ma-htwat-kwint-pyu-chin*
demobilize *(v.)* စစ်မှုတမ်းအဖြစ်မှ ထွက်ခွင့်ပြုသည် *sit-mu-htan-a-phit-ma-htwat-kwint-pyu-the*
democracy *(n.)* ဒီမိုကရေစီစနစ် *de-mo-ka-yay-see-sa-nit*
democrat *(n.)* ဒီမိုကရက်၊ ဒီမိုကရေစီဝါဒီ *de-mo-ka-rat, de-mo-ka-yay-see-war-di*
democratic *(adj.)* ဒီမိုကရေစီဝါဒအခြေခံသော *de-mo-ka-yay-see-wa-da-a-kyay-khan-taw*
demographic *(adj.)* လူဦးရေလေ့လာခြင်းနှင့် ဆိုင်သော *lu-oo-yay-lay-lar-chin-nint-sai-taw*
demolish *(v.)* ဖြိုချသည် *phyo-cha-the*
demolition *(n.)* ဖြိုချခြင်း *phyo-cha-chin*
demon *(n.)* မကောင်းဆိုးဝါး *ma-kaung-soe-war*
demonetize *(v.)* ငွေကြေးစံအဖြစ်မှ ရပ်တန့်သည် *ngwe-kyay-san-a-phit-ma-yat-tant-the*
demonize *(v.)* မိစ္ဆာအဖြစ် ပြောင်းသွားသည် *meik-sar-a-phit-pyaung-twar-the*
demonstrate *(v.)* သရုပ်ပြသည် *ta-yoke-pya-the*
demonstration *(n.)* သရုပ်ပြခြင်း *ta-yoke-pya-chin*
demoralize *(v.)* စိတ်ဓာတ်ကျဆင်းစေသည် *seik-dat-kya-sin-say-the*
demote *(v.)* ရာထူးချသည် *yar-htoo-cha-the*
demur *(n.)* ကန့်ကွက်သည် *kant-kwat-the*
demure *(adj.)* အနေအထိုင်ပိပြားသော *a-nay-a-htai-pi-pyar-taw*
demurrage *(n.)* သင်္ဘောနောက်ကျခြင်း *tin-baw-naut-kya-chin*
demystify *(v.)* ရှင်းရှင်းလင်းလင်း ဖြစ်စေသည် *shin-shin-bwin-bwin-phit-say-the*
den *(n.)* သားရဲတွင်း *tar-ye-twin*
denationalize *(v.)* နိုင်ငံပိုင်အဖြစ်မှ ပုဂ္ဂလိကပိုင်အဖြစ် ပြောင်းသည် *nai-ngan-pai-a-phit-ma-poke-ga-li-ka-a-phit-pyaung-the*
dengue *(n.)* တုတ်ကွေး *toke-kway*
denial *(n.)* ငြင်းဆိုချက် *nyin-soe-chat*
denominate *(v.)* သတ်မှတ်သည် *tat-mat-the*
denomination *(n.)* ဘာသာရေးဂိုဏ်း *bar-tar-yay-gai*
denote *(v.)* ဆိုလိုသည် *so-lo-the*
denounce *(v.)* လူသိရှင်ကြား စွပ်စွဲ ရှုတ်ချသည် *lu-thi-shin-kyar-sut-swal-shoke-cha-the*
dense *(adj.)* ထူထပ်သော *htu-htat-taw*
density *(n.)* သိပ်သည်းခြင်း *tate-tae-chin*
dentist *(n.)* သွားဆရာဝန် *twar-sa-yar-win*
denude *(v.)* ကင်းမဲ့သည် *kin-mae-the*
denunciation *(n.)* စွပ်စွဲရှုတ်ချခြင်း *sut-swal-shoke-cha-chin*
deny *(v.)* ငြင်းသည် *nyin-the*

deodorant *(n.)* ချွေးနံ့ပျောက်ဆေး *chway-nant-pyauk-say*
deodrize *(v.)* ချွေးနံ့ပျောက်စေသည် *chway-nant-pyauk-say-the*
deontology *(n.)* တာဝန်၊ ကတိကဝတ်ဆိုင်ရာ ကျင့်ဝတ်ပညာရပ်ခွဲ *tar-win-ka-ti-ka-wut-sai-yar-kyint-wut-pyin-nyar-yat-kwal*
deoxidation *(n.)* ပျော်ဝင်အောက်ဆိုဒ်မှ အောက်ဆီဂျင် ထုတ်ယူခြင်း *pyaw-win-awt-cide-ma-awt-see-gyin-htoke-yu-chin*
depart *(v.)* ထွက်ခွာသည် *htwat-khwar-the*
department *(n.)* ဌာန *htar-na*
departmentalization *(n.)* ဌာနများ ခွဲခြင်း *htar-na-myar-kwal-chin*
departure *(n.)* ထွက်ခွာခြင်း *htwat-khwar-chin*
depauperate *(v.)* ဆုတ်ယုတ်ကုန်ခန်းစေသည် *sote-yote-kone-khan-say-the*
depend *(v.)* မှီခိုသည် *mi-kho-the*
dependant *(n.)* မှီခိုသူ *mi-kho-thu*
dependence *(n.)* မှီခိုနေရခြင်း *mi-kho-nay-ya-chin*
dependent *(adj.)* စွဲနေသော၊ အားထားနေရသော *swal-nay-taw, ar-htar-nay-ya-taw*
depict *(v.)* ပုံရေးဆွဲပြသည် *pon-yay-swal-pya-the*
depiction *(n.)* ပုံရေးဆွဲပြခြင်း *pon-yay-swal-pya-chin*
depilatory *(adj.)* အမွေးချွတ်သော *a-mway-chyut-taw*
deplete *(v.)* ကုန်ခန်းစေသည် *kon-khan-say-the*
depleted *(adj.)* ကုန်ခန်းသော *kon-khan-taw*
depletion *(n.)* ကုန်ခန်းခြင်း *kon-khan-chin*
deplorable *(adj.)* မနှစ်မြို့ဖွယ် *ma-nit-myo-phwal*
deplore *(v.)* အံ့ဩတုန်လှုပ်သည် *ant-aw-ton-lote-the*
deploy *(v.)* တပ်ဖြန့်သည် *tat-phyant-the*
depolarize *(v.)* သံလိုက်ဓာတ်ဖယ်ရှားသည် *tan-lite-dat-phal-shar-the*
deponent *(n.)* သက်သေပေးသူ *thet-tay-pay-thu*
deport *(v.)* ပြည်နှင်ဒဏ်ပေးသည် *pyi-nin-dan-pay-the*
depose *(v.)* ဖြုတ်ချသည် *phyoke-cha-the*
deposit *(n.)* ထည့်သည်၊ နှုန်းတင်သည် *htae-the, hnone-tin-the*
deposition *(n.)* နန်းချခြင်း *nan-cha-chin*
depository *(n.)* ပစ္စည်းသိုလှောင်ထားရာ နေရာ *pyit-see-tho-hlaung-htar-yar-nay-yar*
depot *(n.)* ကုန်လှောင်ရုံ *kon-hlaung-yone*
depravation *(n.)* အကျင့်ပျက်ချစားခြင်း a-kyint-pyat-cha-sar-chin
deprave *(v.)* အကျင့်စာရိတ္တပျက်ပြားစေသည် *a-kyint-sar-yeik-ta-pyat-pyar-say-the*
deprecate *(v.)* အပြစ်ဆိုသည် *a-pyit-soe-the*
depreciate *(v.)* တန်ဖိုးလျော့ကျသည် *tan-pho-shawt-kya-the*
depreciating *(adj.)* အချိန်နှင့်အမျှ တန်ဖိုးကျသော *a-chein-nint-a-mya-tan-pho-kya-taw*
depreciatory *(adj.)* အချိန်နှင့်အမျှ တန်ဖိုးကျသော *a-chein-nint-a-mya-tan-pho-kya-taw*
depredate *(v.)* ထိခိုက်ပျက်စီးမှု *hti-khite-pyat-see-mu*
depress *(v.)* စိတ်ဓာတ်ကျဆင်းသည် *seik-dat-kya-sin-say-the*

depression *(n.)* စိတ်ဓာတ်ကျခြင်း *seik-dat-kya-chin*
deprive *(v.)* ပိတ်ပင်ထားသည် *pate-pin-htar-the*
depth *(n.)* အနက် *a-nat*
deputation *(n.)* ကိုယ်စားလှယ်အဖွဲ့ *ko-sar-lal-a-phwe*
depute *(v.)* ကိုယ်စားလှယ်လွှဲသည် *ko-sar-lal-hlwal-the*
deputy *(n.)* လက်ထောက် *lat-htauk*
derail *(v.)* ရထားကို လမ်းချော်စေသည် *ya-htar-ko-lan-chaw-say-the*
derailment *(n.)* ရထားကို လမ်းချော်စေခြင်း *ya-htar-ko-lan-chaw-say-chin*
deranged *(adj.)* စိတ်ဖောက်ပြန်သော *seik-phaut-pyan-taw*
deregulate *(v.)* ကန့်သတ်ထိန်းချုပ်မှုမှ ကင်းလွတ်စေသည် *kant-tat-htein-choke-mu-ma-kin-hlut-say-the*
deride *(v.)* ပြက်ရယ်ပြုသည် *pyat-yal-pyu-the*
derivative *(adj.)* ပြက်ရယ်ပြုမှု *pyat-yal-pyu-mu*
derive *(v.)* ရရှိသည် *ya-shi-the*
dermabrasion *(n.)* ပွတ်တိုက်ခြင်းဖြင့် ပျက်စီးနေသော အသားအရည်ကို ပြုပြင်ခြင်း *put-tite-chin-phit-pyat-see-nay-taw-a-tar-a-yay-ko-pyu-pyin-chin*
dermatology *(n.)* အရေပြားရောဂါဗေဒ *a-yay-pyar-yaw-gar-bay-da*
derogatory *(adj.)* နိမ့်ကျသော *naint-kya-taw*
derrick *(n.)* ဝန်ချီစက် *win-chi-sat*
desalt *(v.)* ဆားဖယ်ရှားသည် *sar-phal-shar-the*
descale *(v.)* ကြေးချွတ်သည် *kyay-chwut-the*
descend *(v.)* ဆင်းသက်သည် *sin-thet-the*
descendant *(n.)* ဆင်းသက်လာသူ *sin-thet-lar-thu*
descent *(n.)* အဆင်း *a-sin*
describe *(v.)* ဖော်ပြသည် *phaw-pya-the*
description *(n.)* ဖော်ပြချက် *phaw-pya-chat*
descriptive *(adj.)* ဖော်ပြသော *phaw-pya-taw*
desert *(n.)* သဲကန္တာရ *the-kan-dar-ya*
deserve *(v.)* ထိုက်တန်သည် *htike-tan-the*
design *(n.)* ဒီဇိုင်း၊ ပုံစံ *de-zine, pon-san*
designate *(v.)* သတ်မှတ်သည် *tat-mat-the*
designated *(adj.)* သတ်မှတ်သော *tat-mat-taw*
designer *(n.)* ဒီဇိုင်နာ၊ ပုံစံထုတ်သူ *de-zai-nar, pon-zan-htoke-thu*
designing *(adj.)* ပုံစံထုတ်ခြင်း၊ ဒီဇိုင်းဆွဲခြင်းပညာ *pon-zan-htoke-chin, de-zai-swal-chin-pyin-nyar*
desirable *(adj.)* လိုချင်ဖွယ်ရာဖြစ်သော *lo-chin-phwal-yar-phit-taw*
desire *(v.)* လိုချင်သည် *lo-chin-the*
desirous *(adj.)* ဆန္ဒရှိသော *san-da-shi-taw*
desist *(v.)* စွန့်သည် *sunt-the*
desk *(n.)* စာရေးစားပွဲ *sar-yay-sa-pwe*
desktop *(n.)* စာရေးစားပွဲမျက်နှာပြင် *sar-yay-sa-pwe-myat-nar-pyi*
desocialization *(n.)* လူမှုလောကမှ ဖယ်ရှားခြင်း ဖြစ်စဉ် *lu-mu-law-ka-ma-phal-shar-chin-phit-sin*
desolate *(adj.)* လူသူကင်းမဲ့သော *lu-thu-kin-mae-taw*
desolvate *(v.)* ပျော်ရည်ဖယ်ရှားသည် *pyaw-yay-phal-shar-the*

despair *(n.)* မျှော်လင့်ချက်ပျက်သုဉ်းခြင်း *hmyaw-lint-chat-pyat-tone-chin*
desperate *(adj.)* ရမ်းကားကြမ်းတမ်းသော *yan-kar-kyan-tan-taw*
despicable *(adj.)* စက်ဆုပ်ဖွယ်ကောင်းသော *sat-sote-phwal-kaung-taw*
despise *(v.)* အထင်အမြင်သေးသည် *a-htin-a-myin-tay-the*
despiteful *(adj.)* မုန်းခြင်းကို ဖော်ပြသော *mone-chin-ko-phaw-pya-taw*
despondent *(adj.)* မျှော်လင့်ချက်ကုန်နေသော *myaw-lint-chat-kone-nay-taw*
despot *(n.)* သက်ဦးဆံပိုင်ဘုရင် thet-oo-san-pai-ba-yin
dessert *(n.)* အချိုတည်းစရာ *a-cho-te-sa-yar*
destabilization *(n.)* မတည်မငြိမ်ဖြစ်စေခြင်း *ma-the-ma-nyein-phit-say-chin*
destabilize *(v.)* မတည်မငြိမ်ဖြစ်စေသည် *ma-the-ma-nyein-phit-say-the*
destination *(n.)* ခရီးပန်းတိုင် *kha-yee-pan-tai*
destiny *(n.)* ကံတရား *kan-ta-yar*
destitute *(adj.)* ခိုကိုးရာမဲ့ဖြစ်သော *kho-ko-yar-mae-phit-taw*
destress *(v.)* ဖိစီးမှု လျှော့ချသည် *phi-see-mu-shawt-cha-the*
destroy *(v.)* ဖျက်ဆီးသည် *phat-see-the*
destroyer *(n.)* ဖျက်ဆီးသူ *phat-see-thu*
destruction *(n.)* ဖျက်ဆီးခြင်း *phat-see-chin*
detach *(v.)* ဖြုတ်သည် *pyoke-the*
detachment *(n.)* အစွဲကင်းခြင်း၊ ဘက်မလိုက်ခြင်း၊ လျစ်လျူရှုခြင်း *a-swal-kin-chin, bat-ma-lite-chin, lyit-lyu-shu-chin*
detail *(n.)* အသေးစိတ် *a-tay-seik*
detain *(v.)* ချုပ်ထားသည် *choke-htar-the*
detect *(v.)* တွေ့ရှိသည်၊ သတိပြုမိသည် *tway-shi-the, ta-di-pyu-mi-the*
detective *(n.)* စုံထောက် *sone-htauk*
detention *(n.)* အကျဉ်းကျခြင်း *a-kyin-kya-chin*
detergent *(n.)* ဆပ်ပြာမှုန့် *sat-pyar-hmont*
deteriorate *(v.)* ယိုယွင်းသည် *yo-ywin-the*
determination *(n.)* စိတ်ပိုင်းဖြတ်ခြင်း *seik-pai-phat-chin*
determine *(v.)* အဆုံးအဖြတ်ပေးသည် *a-sone-a-phat-pay-the*
detest *(v.)* အလွန်မုန်းတီးသည် *a-lun-hmon-tee-the*
dethrone *(v.)* နန်းချသည် *nan-cha-chin*
detonate *(v.)* ပြင်းထန်စွာ ပေါက်ကွဲသည် *pyin-htan-swar-pauk-kwal-the*
detoxication *(n.)* အဆိပ်ဖယ်ရှားခြင်း *a-seik-phal-shar-chin*
detract *(v.)* ရှုတ်ချပြောသည် *shoke-cha-pyaw-the*
detractor *(n.)* ရှုတ်ချပုတ်ခတ်သူ *shoke-cha-poke-khat-thu*
detriment *(n.)* မထိခိုက်မနစ်နာစေဘဲ *ma-hti-khaik-ma-nit-nar-say-bal*
deturpation *(n.)* ပြုလုပ်သော ပြစ်ဒဏ် *pyu-lote-taw-pyit-dan*
devalue *(v.)* ငွေတန်ဖိုး လျှော့ချသည် *ngwe-tan-pho-shawt-cha-the*
devastate *(v.)* မွှေနှောက်ဖျက်ဆီးသည် *hmway-naut-phat-see-the*
develop *(v.)* ဖွံ့ဖြိုးသည် *phwint-phoe-the*
developer *(n.)* ဆော့ဝဲရေးသူ၊ ဖွံ့ဖြိုးရေး လုပ်သူ *sot-wal-yay-thu, phwint-phyoe-yay-lote-thu*
development *(n.)* ဖွံ့ဖြိုးရေး *phwint-phoe-yay*

deviate *(v.)* လမ်းလွဲသွားသည် *lan-hlwal-twar-the*

deviation *(n.)* လမ်းလွဲခြင်း *lan-hlwal-chin*

device *(n.)* ကိရိယာ *ka-ri-yar*

devil *(n.)* မာရ်နတ်၊ နတ်ဆိုး man-nat, nat-soe

devilry *(n.)* ဆိုးယုတ်ခြင်း *soe-yoke-chin*

devise *(v.)* တီထွင်သည် *ti-htwin-the*

devoid *(adj.)* ကင်းမဲ့သော *kin-mae-taw*

devote *(v.)* အစဉ်ချစ်ခင်၍ သစ္စာရှိသော *a-sin-chit-khin-ywe-tit-sar-shi-taw*

devotee *(n.)* ဝါသနာအိုး *wa-ta-nar-oh*

devotion *(n.)* အချစ်ကြီးမှု *a-chit-kyi-mu*

devour *(v.)* အငမ်းမရစားသည် *a-ngan-ma-ya-sar-the*

devout *(adj.)* ရိုးသားဖြူစင်သော *yoe-tar-phyu-sin-taw*

dew *(n.)* နှင်းပေါက်၊ နှင်းစက် *hnin-pauk, hnin-sat*

diabetes *(n.)* ဆီးချို *sie-cho*

diagnose *(v.)* ရောဂါအမည်တပ်သည် *yaw-gar-a-me-tat-the*

diagnosis *(n.)* ရောဂါအမည်တပ်ခြင်း *yaw-gar-a-me-tat-chin*

diagonal *(adj.)* ထောင့်ဖြတ်မျဉ်း *htaunt-phat-myin*

diagram *(n.)* ပုံကြမ်း၊ ပုံစံ *pon-kyan, pon-san*

dial *(n.)* နာရီဒိုင်ခွက်၊ ဖုန်းခလုတ် *nar-yi-dai-khwat, phone-ka-lote*

dialect *(n.)* ဒေသိယစကား *day-ti-ya-sa-kar*

dialogue *(n.)* အပြန်အလှန် ဆွေးနွေးခြင်း *a-pyan-a-lan-sway-nway-chin*

dialysis *(n.)* ကျောက်ကပ်သန့်စင်ခြင်း *kyauk-kat-tant-sin-chin*

diameter *(n.)* အချင်း *a-chin*

diamond *(n.)* စိန် *sein*

diaper *(n.)* သေးခံ tay-khan

diarrhea *(n.)* ဝမ်းလျှောခြင်း *wan-shaw-chin*

diary *(n.)* နေ့စဉ်မှတ်တမ်း *nay-zin-mat-tan*

diaspora *(n.)* နိုင်ငံပေါင်းစုံတွင် ပြန့်ကျဲနေထိုင်သော လူမျိုး *nai-ngan-paung-sone-twin-pyant-kyal-nay-htai-taw-lu-myo*

dibble *(v.)* ကျွမ်းတူးဆူးဖြင့် အပင်စိုက်သည် *kyun-tu-sue-phit-a-pin-site-the*

dice *(n.)* အန်စာတုံး *an-sar-tone*

dicey *(adj.)* အန္တရာယ်များသော *an-da-yal-myar-taw*

dictate *(v.)* သတ်ပုံခေါ်သည် *tat-pon-khaw-the*

dictation *(n.)* သတ်ပုံခေါ်ခြင်း *tat-pon-khaw-chin*

dictator *(n.)* အာဏာရှင် *ar-nar-shin*

diction *(n.)* စကားပြောဟန် *sa-kar-pyaw-han*

dictionary *(n.)* အဘိဓာန် *a-bi-dan*

dictum *(n.)* အဆိုအမိန့် *a-so-a-maint*

didactic *(adj.)* ပညာပေး *pyin-nyar-pay*

die *(v.)* သေသည် *tay-the*

diehard *(n.)* ပျောက်နိုင်ခဲသည် *pyauk-nai-khae-the*

diesel *(n.)* ဒီဇယ် *di-sal*

diet *(v.)* ကိုယ်အလေးချိန်လျော့အောင် ချင့်ချိန်စားသည် *ko-a-lay-chein-yawt-aung-chint-chain-sar-the*

dietician *(n.)* အာဟာရဗေဒပညာရှင် *a-har-ra-pyin-nyar-shin*

differ *(v.)* ခြားနားသည် *char-nar-the*

difference *(n.)* ခြားနားချက် *char-nar-chat*

different *(adj.)* ခြားနားသော *char-nar-taw*

difficult *(adj.)* ခက်ခဲသော *khat-khae-taw*

difficulty *(n.)* အခက်အခဲ *a-khat-a-khae*

diffident *(adj.)* မဝံ့မရဲဖြစ်သော *ma-wint-ma-ye-phit-taw*

diffuse *(v.)* ပျံ့နှံ့သည် *pyant-nant-the*

dig *(v.)* တူးသည် *tu-the*

digest *(v.)* အစာခြေသည် *a-sar-chay-the*

digestion *(n.)* အစာခြေခြင်း a-sar-chay-chin

digit *(n.)* ဂဏန်း *ga-nan*

digital *(adj.)* ဒစ်ဂျစ်တယ်၊ ဂဏန်းခြေစနစ်ကို သုံးသော *dit-gyit-tal, ga-nan-chay-sa-nit-ko-tone-taw*

digitalize *(v.)* ဒစ်ဂျစ်တယ်စနစ် ပြောင်းသည် *dit-gyit-tal-sa-nit-ko-pyaung-the*

dignify *(v.)* ခံ့ညားစေသည် *khant-nyar-say-the*

dignitary *(n.)* လူကြီး *lu-gyi*

dignity *(n.)* ဂုဏ်သိက္ခာ *gon-taik-khar*

digress *(v.)* မူလအကြောင်းမှ ဘေးချော်သွားသည် *mu-la-a-kyaung-ma-bay-chaw-twar-the*

digression *(n.)* မူလအကြောင်းမှ ဘေးချော်သွားခြင်း *mu-la-a-kyaung-ma-bay-chaw-twar-chin*

dilaceration *(n.)* တစ်စုံတစ်ရာ စုတ်ဖြဲခြင်းဖြစ်စဉ် *ta-sone-ta-yar-sote-phwal-chin-phit-sin*

dilapidation *(n.)* ကျိုးပဲ့ပျက်စီးနေခြင်း *kyo-pae-pyat-see-nay-chin*

dilate *(v.)* ကျယ်လာသည် *kyal-lar-the*

dilemma *(n.)* အကျပ်ရိုက်ခြင်း *a-kyat-yite-chin*

diligence *(n.)* လုံ့လဝီရိယ *lont-la-wi-ri-ra*

diligent *(adj.)* လုံ့လဝီရိယရှိသော *lont-la-wi-ri-ra-shi-taw*

dilute *(v.)* ရေရောသည် *yay-yaw-the*

dilution *(n.)* အရည်ရောခြင်း *a-yay-yaw-chin*

dim *(adj.)* မှန်သော *man-taw*

dimension *(n.)* အတိုင်းအတာ *a-tai-a-tar*

diminish *(v.)* လျော့လာသည်၊ နည်းလာသည် *yawt-lar-the, nae-lar-the*

diminution *(n.)* လျော့နည်းလာခြင်း *yawt-nae-lar-chin*

diminutive *(adj.)* အလွန်သေးငယ်သော a-lun-tay-nge-taw

dimly *(adv.)* မှုန်မှုန်မွှားမွှား *hmone-hmone-hmwar-hmwar*

dimness *(n.)* အလင်းမှိန်ခြင်း *a-lin-main-chin*

din *(n.)* စီစီညံညံအသံ *si-si-nyan-nyan-a-tan*

dine *(v.)* ညစာစားသည် *nya-sar-sar-the*

diner *(n.)* ရထားစားသောက်တွဲ *ya-htar-sar-taut-twe*

dingy *(adj.)* ညစ်ပတ်၍ မှောင်သော *nyit-pat-ywe-hmaung-taw*

dinner *(n.)* ညစာ *nya-sar*

diocese *(n.)* ခရစ်ယာန်ဂိုဏ်းအုပ်နယ်ပယ် *kha-yit-yan-gai-oak-nal-pal*

dioxide *(n.)* ဒိုင်အောက်ဆိုက် *dai-aut-cide*

dip *(v.)* နိမ့်သွားသည်၊ တို့သည်၊ နှိုက်သည် *naint-twar-the, toe-the, hnaik-the*

diploma *(n.)* ဒစ်ပလိုမာ *dit-pa-lo-mar*

diplomacy *(n.)* သံခင်းတမန်ခင်း *tan-khin-ta-man-khin*

diplomat *(n.)* သံတမန် *tan-ta-man*

diplomatic *(adj.)* သံတမန်ရေးရာ *tan-ta-man-yay-yar*

dire *(adj.)* ကြောက်မက်ဖွယ်ဖြစ်သော *kyauk-mat-phwal-phit-taw*
direct *(adj.)* တိုက်ရိုက် *tite-yite*
direction *(n.)* ဦးတည်ချက် *oo-the-chat*
directive *(n.)* ညွှန်ကြားချက် *hnyun-kyar-chat*
director *(n.)* ဒါရိုက်တာ *dar-yite-tar*
directory *(n.)* လမ်းညွှန် *lan-hnyun*
dirt *(n.)* အညစ်အကြေး *a-nyit-a-kyay*
dirty *(adj.)* ညစ်ပတ်သော *nyit-pat-taw*
disability *(n.)* မသန်စွမ်းမှု *ma-tan-swan-mu*
disable *(v.)* မသန်စွမ်းဖြစ်သည် *ma-tan-swan-phit-the*
disabled *(adj.)* မသန်စွမ်းသော ma-tan-swan-taw
disadvantage *(n.)* ဆိုးကျိုး *soe-kyo*
disagree *(v.)* သဘောကွဲလွဲသည် ta-baw-kwe-lwal-the
disagreeable *(adj.)* မနှစ်သက်စရာဖြစ်သော *ma-nit-thet-sa-yar-phit-taw*
disallow *(v.)* ခွင့်မပြု *khwint-ma-pyu*
disappear *(v.)* ပျောက်ကွယ်သည် *pyauk-kwal-the*
disappearance *(n.)* ပျောက်နေခြင်း *pyauk-nay-chin*
disappoint *(v.)* စိတ်ပျက်ရသည် *seik-pyat-ya-the*
disapprove *(v.)* သဘောမတူ *ta-baw-ma-tu*
disarm *(v.)* လက်နက်သိမ်းသည် *lat-nat-thein-the*
disarmament *(n.)* လက်နက်သိမ်းခြင်း *lat-nat-thein-chin*
disarrange *(v.)* ဖရိုဖရဲဖြစ်စေသည် *pha-yo-pha-ye-phit-say-the*
disarray *(n.)* ဖရိုဖရဲဖြစ်ခြင်း *pha-yo-pha-ye-phit-chin*
disaster *(n.)* ဘေးအန္တရာယ် *bay-an-da-yal*
disastrous *(adj.)* ဆိုးဝါးသော *soe-war-taw*
disband *(v.)* ဖျက်သိမ်းသည် *phat-tain-the*
disbelief *(n.)* မယုံနိုင်ခြင်း *ma-yone-nai-chin*
disbelieve *(v.)* မယုံကြည် *ma-yone-kyi*
disburse *(v.)* ငွေပေးဝေသည် *ngwe-pay-wai-the*
disc *(n.)* ဒစ်ပြား *dit-pyar*
discard *(v.)* စွန့်ပစ်သည်၊ လွှင့်ပစ်သည် *sunt-pyit-the, hlwint-pyit-the*
discharge *(v.)* ထွက်ခွာခွင့်ပြုသည်၊ ထွက်ခွင့်ပြုသည် *htwat-khwar-khwint-pyu-the, htwat-khwint-pyu-the*
disciple *(n.)* တပည့် *ta-pyae*
discipline *(n.)* စည်းကမ်း *see-kan*
disclaim *(v.)* မသက်ဆိုင်ကြောင်း ငြင်းဆိုသည် *ma-thet-sai-kyaung-nyin-soe-the*
disclose *(v.)* ဖွင့်ဟပြောဆိုသည် *phwint-ha-pyaw-soe-the*
discolour *(v.)* အရောင်ကျွတ်သည် *a-yaung-kyut-the*
discomfit *(v.)* အနေခက်စေသည် *a-nay-khat-say-the*
discomfort *(n.)* မသက်မသာဖြစ်ခြင်း *ma-thet-ma-tar-phit-chin*
disconnect *(v.)* ဖြတ်တောက်သည် *phat-taut-the*
discontent *(n.)* မကျေနပ်ခြင်း *ma-kyay-nat-chin*
discontinue *(v.)* ရပ်ဆိုင်းသည် *yat-sai-the*
discord *(n.)* သဘောထားကွဲလွဲခြင်း *ta-baw-htar-kwal-lwalchin*

discotheque *(n.)* ဒစ္စကိုကပွဲ *dit-sa-ko-ka-pwe*
discount *(n.)* လျှော့ဈေး *shawt-zay*
discourage *(v.)* စိတ်ဓာတ်ကျသည် *seik-dat-kya-the*
discourse *(n.)* အလေးအနက် အကျယ်တဝင့်ပြောဟောချက် *a-lay-a-nat-a-kyal-ta-wint-haw-pyaw-chat*
discourteous *(adj.)* မယဉ်ကျေးသော *ma-yin-kyay-taw*
discover *(v.)* စတင်တွေ့ရှိသည် *sa-tin-tway-shi-the*
discovery *(n.)* စူးစမ်းရှာဖွေခြင်း *su-san-shar-phway-chin*
discredit *(v.)* သိက္ခာချသည် *tate-khar-cha-the*
discreet *(adj.)* မသိမသာ *ma-ti-ma-thar*
discrepancy *(n.)* ခြားနားချက် *char-nar-chat*
discretion *(n.)* လိမ္မာသိုသိပ်မှု *lain-mar-tho-tate-mu*
discriminate *(v.)* ခွဲခြား ဆက်ဆံသည် *kwal-char-sat-san-the*
discrimination *(n.)* ခွဲခြား ဆက်ဆံခြင်း kwal-char-sat-san-chin
discuss *(v.)* ဆွေးနွေးသည် *sway-nway-the*
disdain *(v.)* အထင်သေးသည် *a-htin-tay-the*
disease *(n.)* ရောဂါ yaw-gar
disembody *(v.)* တပ်မှ ထုတ်သည် tat-ma-htoke-the
disenchant *(v.)* စိတ်ပျက်သည် seik-pyat-the
disengage *(v.)* ပြုတ်အောင် ဖြုတ်သည် *pyoke-aung-pyoke-the*
disfigure *(v.)* ပုံပျက်အောင် လုပ်သည် *pon-pyat-aung-lote-the*
disgrace *(n.)* အသရေပျက်ခြင်း *a-tha-yay-pyat-chin*
disgruntled *(adj.)* မပျော်ရွှင်သော၊ တုန်လှုပ်သော *ma-pyaw-shwin-taw, ton-hloke-taw*
disguise *(v.)* ရုပ်ဖျက်သည် *yoke-phat-the*
disgust *(n.)* မနှစ်မြို့ခြင်း *ma-nit-myo-chin*
dish *(n.)* ပန်းကန် *pa-gan*
dishearten *(v.)* စိတ်ပျက်အားလျော့သည် *seik-pyat-arr-shawt-the*
dishonest *(adj.)* မရိုးသားသော *ma-yoe-tar-taw*
dishonesty *(n.)* မရိုးသားမှု *ma-yoe-tar-mu*
dishonour *(n.)* အရှက်ရခြင်း *a-shat-ya-chin*
disillusion *(v.)* အမှန်အတိုင်း မြင်သိစေသည် *a-man-a-tai-myin-ti-say-the*
disinclined *(adj.)* ဆန္ဒမရှိသော *san-da-ma-shi-taw*
disinfect *(v.)* ပိုးသတ်သည် *poe-tat-the*
disjunction *(n.)* ကွဲခြင်း *kwal-chin*
dislike *(n.)* မနှစ်သက်ခြင်း *ma-nit-thet-chin*
dislocate *(v.)* အရိုး အဆစ်လွဲသည် *a-yoe-a-sit-lwal-the*
dislodge *(v.)* ဖဲ့ထုတ်သည် *phae-htoke-the*
disloyal *(adj.)* သစ္စာမရှိသော *tit-sar-ma-shi-taw*
dismal *(adj.)* စိတ်ပျက်စရာ *seik-pyat-sa-yar*
dismantle *(v.)* ဖြိုဖျက်သည် *phyo-phat-the*
dismay *(n.)* တုန်လှုပ်ချောက်ချားမှု *ton-hloke-chauk-char-mu*
dismiss *(v.)* ဖယ်ပစ်သည် *phal-pyit-the*
dismissal *(n.)* ထုတ်ခြင်း *htoke-chin*

disobey *(v.)* မနာခံဘဲနေသည် *ma-nar-khan-bae-nay-the*
disorder *(n.)* ကစဥ့်ကလျားဖြစ်ခြင်း ka-sint-ka-lyar-phit-chin
disorganize *(v.)* စည်းစနစ် ဖျက်သည် *see-sa-nit-phat-the*
disorient *(v.)* သိမှုပျောက်ဆုံးသည် *ti-mu-pyauk-sone-the*
disown *(v.)* စွန့်လွှတ်သည် *sunt-hlut-the*
disparate *(adj.)* ခြားနားလွန်း၍ နှိုင်းယှဥ်မရသော char-nar-lun-ywe-hnine-shin-ma-ya-taw
disparity *(n.)* ခြားနားချက် *char-nar-chat*
dispatch *(v.)* စေလွှတ်သည် say-hlut-the
dispensary *(n.)* ဆေးပေးခန်း say-pay-khan
dispense *(v.)* ဝေပေးသည်၊ ထုတ်ပေးသည် *sai-pay-the, htoke-pay-the*
disperse *(v.)* ပျံ့နှံ့သည် *pyant-nant-the*
displace *(v.)* အစားဝင်၍ နေရာယူသည် *a-sar-win-ywe-nay-yar-yu-the*
display *(n.)* ခင်းကျင်းပြသသည် *khin-kyin-pya-tha-the*
displease *(v.)* သဘောမကျဖြစ်စေသည် *ta-baw-ma-kya-phit-say-the*
displeasure *(n.)* မကျေမနပ်ဖြစ်ခြင်း *ma-kyay-nat-phit-chin*
disposal *(n.)* ဖယ်ရှားပစ်ခြင်း *phal-shar-pyit-chin*
dispose *(v.)* နေရာချထားသည် *nay-yar-cha-htar-the*
disproportion *(n.)* အချိုးမကျခြင်း *a-choe-ma-kya-chin*
disprove *(v.)* မဟုတ်မမှန်ကြောင်း ထင်ရှားစေသည် *ma-hote-ma-man-kyaung-htin-shar-say-the*
disputation *(n.)* စောဒကတက်ခြင်း *say-da-ma-tat-chin*
dispute *(v.)* အငြင်းအခုံ *a-nyin-a-khone*
disqualification *(n.)* ပိတ်ပင်ခံရခြင်း *pate-pin-khan-ya-chin*
disqualify *(v.)* ပိတ်ပင်ခံရသည် *pate-pin-khan-ya-the*
disquiet *(n.)* ပူပန်မှု *pu-pan-mu*
disregard *(v.)* လျစ်လျူရှုသည် *lyit-lyu-shu-the*
disrepute *(n.)* နာမည်ပျက်ခြင်း *nan-mal-pyat-chin*
disrespect *(n.)* ရိုင်းပျခြင်း *yai-pya-chin*
disrupt *(v.)* နှောင့်ယှက်သည် *naut-shat-the*
dissatisfaction *(n.)* ကျေနပ်မှု မရှိခြင်း *kyay-nat-mu-ma-shi-chin*
dissatisfy *(v.)* ကျေနပ်မှု မရှိ *kyay-nat-mu-ma-shi*
dissect *(v.)* ခွဲစိတ်လေ့လာသည် *khwal-seik-lay-lar-the*
dissection *(n.)* ခွဲစိတ်လေ့လာခြင်း *khwal-seik-lay-lar-chin*
dissimilar *(adj.)* မတူသော *ma-tu-taw*
dissipate *(v.)* ကွယ်ပျောက်စေသည် *kwal-pyauk-say-the*
dissolve *(v.)* အရည်ပျော်စေသည် *a-yay-pyaw-say-the*
dissuade *(v.)* မလုပ်ရန် ဖျောင်းဖျသည် *ma-lote-yan-hpaung-pya-the*
distance *(n.)* အကွာအဝေး *a-kwar-a-way*
distant *(adj.)* ဝေးကွာသော *way-kwar-taw*
distil *(v.)* ပေါင်းခံသည် paung-khan-the
distillery *(n.)* အရက်ချက်စက်ရုံ *a-yat-chat-sat-yone*
distinct *(adj.)* ထင်ရှားသော *htin-shar-taw*
distinction *(n.)* ဂုဏ်ထူး၊ ကွဲပြားခြင်း *gon-htoo, kwal-pyar-chin*

distinctive *(adj.)* **ထင်ရှားသော** *htin-shar-taw*
distinguish *(v.)* **ခွဲခြားသိမြင်သည်** *khwal-char-ti-myin-the*
distort *(v.)* **ရွဲ့စောင်းသည်** *ywe-saung-the*
distraction *(n.)* **အာရုံအနှောင့်အယှက်** *arr-yone-a-naut-a-shat*
distraught *(adj.)* **စိတ်နောက်ကျိသော** seik-naut-kyi-taw
distress *(n.)* **ဆင်းရဲဒုက္ခ** sin-ye-doke-kha
distress *(v.)* **စိတ်သောကရောက်သည်** *seik-taw-ka-yauk-the*
distribute *(v.)* **ဖြန့်ဖြူးရောင်းချသည်** *phyant-phyu-yaung-cha-the*
distribution *(n.)* **ဖြန့်ဖြူးရောင်းချခြင်း** *phyant-phyu-yaung-cha-chin*
district *(n.)* **ခရိုင်** *kha-yai*
distrust *(n.)* **မယုံကြည်မှု** *ma-yone-kyi-mu*
disturb *(v.)* **နှောင့်ယှက်သည်** *naut-shat-the*
ditch *(n.)* **မြောင်း** *myaung*
ditto *(n.)* **၎င်း** *la-kaung*
dive *(v.)* **ဒိုင်ဗင်ထိုးသည်** *dai-bin-htoe-the*
dive *(n.)* **ဒိုင်ဗင်ထိုးခြင်း** *dai-bin-htoe-chin*
diverse *(adj.)* **ထွေပြားသော** *htway-pyar-taw*
diversify *(v.)* **သုံးလေးမျိုး စသည် ခွဲလုပ်သည်** *tone-lay-myo-sa-the-khwal-lote-the*
divert *(v.)* **လမ်းလွှဲသည်** *lan-hlwal-the*
divide *(v.)* **ခွဲခြားသည်** *kwal-char-the*
dividend *(n.)* **အစုပေါ်အမြတ်** *a-su-paw-a-myat*
divine *(adj.)* **ဘုရားသခင်** *pha-yar-ta-khin*
divinity *(n.)* **ဘုရားသခင်၏ ဂုဏ်တော်ကျေးဇူး** *pha-yar-ta-khin-ei-gon-taw-kyay-zu*
division *(n.)* **တိုင်း၊ ခွဲဝေခြင်း** *tai, kwal-wai-chin*
divorce *(n.)* **ကွာရှင်းခြင်း** *kwar-shin-chin*
divulge *(v.)* **ပေါက်ကြားစေသည်** *pauk-kyar-say-the*
do *(v.)* **ပြုလုပ်သည်** *pyu-lote-the*
doable *(adj.)* **ပြုလုပ်နိုင်သော** *pyu-lote-nai-taw*
doating *(adj.)* **အရမ်းချစ်သော** *a-yan-chit-taw*
dob *(v.)* **ထည့်ဝင်သည်** *htae-win-the*
doc *(n.)* **ဒေါက်တာ** *daut-tar*
docent *(n.)* **ဆရာ** *sa-yar*
docile *(adj.)* **သိမ်မွေ့သော** *tein-mway-taw*
dock *(v.)* **ဆိုက်ကပ်သည်** *site-kat-the*
docket *(n.)* **စာရင်းစာရွက်** *sa-yin-sar-ywet*
dockmaster *(n.)* **သင်္ဘောကျင်းကြီးကြပ်** *tin-baw-kyin-kyi-kyat*
dockworker *(n.)* **သင်္ဘောကျင်းအလုပ်သမား** *tin-baw-kyin-a-lote-ta-mar*
dockyard *(n.)* **သင်္ဘောကျင်း** *tin-baw-kyin*
doctor *(n.)* **ဆရာဝန်** *sa-yar-win*
doctorate *(n.)* **ပါရဂူဘွဲ့** *par-ya-gu-bwe*
doctored *(adj.)* **ပြောင်းလဲသော၊ လိမ်လည်သော** *pyaung-lal-taw, lain-lal-taw*
doctrine *(n.)* **ဩဝါဒ** *aw-war-da*
document *(n.)* **စာရွက်စာတမ်း** *sar-ywet-sar-tan*
documentary *(n.)* **မှတ်တမ်းရုပ်ရှင်** *mat-tan-yoke-shin*
dodge *(v.)* **ရှောင်သည်** shaung-the
dodo *(n.)* **ဒိုဒိုငှက်** *do-do-nget*
doe *(n.)* **သမင်မ** *ta-min-ma*

doer *(n.)* လက်တွေ့လုပ်သူ *lat-thway-lote-tu*

doeskin *(n.)* ယုန်သားရေ *yone-ta-yay*

dog *(n.)* ခွေး *khway*

dog *(v.)* တကောက်ကောက်လိုက်သည် *a-kauk-kauk-lite-the*

dogbreath *(n.)* အနိုင်ကျင့်ကာလ *a-nai-kyint-kar-la*

dogfight *(n.)* လေယာဉ်ချင်း အနီးကပ်တိုက်ပွဲ *lay-yin-chin-a-nee-kat-tite-pwe*

doghole *(n.)* စုတ်ပျက်သော နေအိမ်နေရာ *sote-pyat-taw-nay-eain-nay-yar*

doghouse *(n.)* ခွေးအိမ် *khway-eain*

dogma *(n.)* တရားသေလက်ခံထားသော ဝါဒ *ta-yar-tay-lat-khan-htar-taw-war-da*

dogmatic *(adj.)* တစ်ယူသန်ဖြစ်သော *ta-yu-tan-phit-taw*

dole *(n.)* နိုင်ငံတော်၏ ထောက်ပံ့ကြေး *nai-ngan-taw-ei-htauk-pant-kyay*

doll *(n.)* ကစားစရာ လူရုပ် *ka-sar-sa-yar-lu-yoke*

dollar *(n.)* ဒေါ်လာ *daw-lar*

dolman *(n.)* ဒိုလ်မန်ဂျာကင် do-man-gyar-kin

dolmen *(n.)* ရှေးခေတ်သင်္ချိုင်းမှတ်တိုင် *shay-khit-tin-gyai-mat-tai*

dolorous *(adj.)* ဝမ်းနည်းပူဆွေးသော *wan-nae-pu-swae-taw*

dolphin *(n.)* လင်းပိုင် lin-pai

domain *(n.)* ပိုင်နက် *pai-nat*

dome *(n.)* အမိုးခုံး *a-moe-khone*

domestic *(adj.)* မိသားစုနှင့် သက်ဆိုင်သော *mi-tar-su-nint-thet-sai-taw*

domestic *(n.)* အိမ်စေ *eain-say*

domestical *(adj.)* မိသားစုနှင့် သက်ဆိုင်သော *mi-tar-su-nint-thet-sai-taw*

domesticate *(v.)* အိမ်တွင်းမှုကိစ္စများကို စိတ်ပါဝင်စားစေသည် *eain-twin-mu-kaik-sa-myar-ko-seik-pay-win-sar-say-the*

domesticator *(n.)* အိမ်တွင်းမှုကိစ္စစိတ်ဝင်စားသူ *eain-twin-mu-kaik-sa-seik-pay-win-sar-thu*

domicile *(n.)* တရားဝင် အတည်တကျ နေထိုင်ရာ နိုင်ငံ၊ မြို့ ရွာ *ta-yar-win-a-the-ta-kya-nay-htai-yar-nai-ngan-myo-ywar*

domiciled *(adj.)* အတည်တကျ နေထိုင်သော *a-the-ta-kya-nay-htai-taw*

domiciliary *(adj.)* အိမ်တိုင်ရာရောက်သွားသော *eain-tai-yar-yauk-twar-taw*

dominant *(adj.)* အဓိက ဖြစ်သော *a-di-ka-phit-taw*

dominate *(v.)* ကြီးစိုးသည် *kyi-soe-the*

domination *(n.)* မြင့်မားစိုးမိုးခြင်း *myint-mar-soe-moe-chin*

dominion *(n.)* စိုးမိုးမှု *soe-moe-mu*

domino *(n.)* ကက်ဖဲ *kat-phae*

donate *(v.)* လှူသည် *hlu-the*

donation *(n.)* လှူဒါန်းခြင်း hlu-dan-chin

donkey *(n.)* မြည်း *myae*

donor *(n.)* အလှူရှင် *a-hlu-shin*

doodle *(v.)* တောင်ခြစ်မြောက်ခြစ်လုပ်သည် *taung-chit-myauk-chit-lote-the*

doom *(v.)* ကံဆိုးမိုးမှောင်ကျသည် kan-soe-moe-hmaung-kya-the

doomed *(adj.)* ကံဆိုးမိုးမှောင်ကျသော *kan-soe-moe-hmaung-kya-thaw*

doomsday *(n.)* ကမ္ဘာပျက်သော နေ့ *ka-bar-pyat-taw-nae*

door *(n.)* တံခါး *ta-khar*

doorbell *(n.)* လူခေါ်ခေါင်းလောင်း *lu-khaw-khaung-laung*

doorknob *(n.)* တံခါးလက်ကိုင်ဖု *ta-khar-lat-khai-phu*
doormat *(n.)* ခြေသုတ်ဖုံ *chay-tote-hpon*
dope *(n.)* မူးယစ်ဆေးဝါး *mu-yit-say-war*
doped *(adj.)* ဆေးသုံးထားသော *say-tone-htar-thaw*
dopey *(adj.)* ထုံထိုင်းနေသော *hton-htai-nay-taw*
dorky *(adj.)* မိုက်မိုက်မဲမဲ တုံးအသော *mite-mite-mae-mae-ton-aa-taw*
dormant *(adj.)* ငြိမ်နေသော *nyein-nay-taw*
dormitory *(n.)* အိပ်ဆောင် *aik-saung*
dorsal *(adj.)* ကျောနှင့် ဆိုင်သော *kyaw-nint-sai-taw*
dosage *(n.)* ဆေးညွှန်း *say-hnyun*
dose *(n.)* တစ်ခါသောက်ဆေးပမာဏ *ta-khar-taut-say-pa-mar-na*
dot *(n.)* အစက် *a-sat*
double *(adj.)* နှစ်ဆ *na-sa*
double *(v.)* နှစ်ဆတက်သည် *ma-sa-tat-the*
doubt *(n.)* သံသယ *tan-da-ya*
doubt *(v.)* သံသယဖြစ်သည် *tan-da-ya-phit-the*
doubtful *(adj.)* မသေချာသော *ma-tay-char-taw*
doubtless *(adj.)* သေချာသလောက် *tay-char-ta-laut*
dough *(n.)* ဂျုံမုန့်ညက် *gyon-mont-nyat*
doughnut *(n.)* ဒိုးနတ် *doe-nat*
dour *(adj.)* မှုန်ဆန်သော *hmone-san-taw*
douse *(v.)* ရေနှစ်သည် *yay-nit-the*
dove *(n.)* ချိုးငှက် cho-nget
dowery *(n.)* သတို့သမီးက သတို့သားဘက်ပေးရသော အတွင်းပစ္စည်း *ta-do-ta-mee-ka-ta-do-tar-bat-pay-ya-taw-a-twin-pyit-see*
down *(v.)* ကျိုက်ချသည် *kyaik-cha-the*
down *(prep.)* အမြင့်မှ အနိမ့်သို့ *a-myint-ma-a-naint-tho*
down and out *(adj.)* အလုပ်၊ ငွေ၊ နေစရာ မဲ့သော *a-lote-ngwe-nay-sa-yar-mae-taw*
downfall *(n.)* ကျဆုံးခြင်း *kya-sone-chin*
download *(v.)* အချက်အလက် လွှဲပြောင်းသည် *a-chat-a-lat-hlwal-pyaung-the*
downpour *(n.)* မိုးပုဆိန် *moe-pa-sein*
downright *(adj.)* စစ်စစ် *sit-sit*
downstairs *(adj.)* အောက်ထပ်မှာဖြစ်သော *aut-htet-mar-phit-taw*
downward *(adj.)* နိမ့်ဆင်းသော *naint-sin-taw*
downwards *(adv.)* နိမ့်ရာသို့ *naint-yar-tho*
doze *(v.)* ငိုက်မျဉ်းသည် *nyeik-myae-the*
dozen *(n.)* ဒါဇင် *dar-zin*
drab *(adj.)* ငြီးငွေ့ဖွယ် ခြောက်ကပ်သော *ngyi-ngwe-phwal-chauk-kat-taw*
draconic *(adj.)* နဂါးနှင့်ဆိုင်သော na-gar-nint-sai-taw
draft *(n.)* မူကြမ်း *mu-kyan*
draftsman *(adj.)* ပုံဆွဲဆရာ *pon-swal-sa-yar*
drafty *(adj.)* လေစိမ်းတိုက်သော *lay-sein-tite-taw*
drag *(n.)* အတားအဆီး *a-tar-a-see*
drag *(v.)* တရွတ်တိုက်ဆွဲသည် *ta-yut-tite-swal-the*
dragon *(n.)* နဂါး *na-gar*
dragonfly *(n.)* ပုစဉ်း pa-zin
drain *(v.)* စီးဆင်းသွားသည် *see-sin-twar-the*

drainage *(n.)* ရေနုတ်မြောင်း *yay-note-myaung*
drainpipe *(n.)* ရေဆင်းပိုက် *yay-sin-pipe*
dram *(n.)* ဝီစကီအနည်းငယ် *wi-sa-ki-a-nae-ngal*
drama *(n.)* ပြဇာတ် *pya-zat*
dramatic *(adj.)* ပြဇာတ်နှင့် ဆိုင်သော *pya-zat-nint-sai-taw*
dramatist *(n.)* ပြဇာတ်ဆရာ *pya-zat-sa-yar*
drape *(n.)* ခန်းဆီးရှည်ကြီး *khan-see-shay-gyi*
draper *(n.)* အထည်သည် a-htae-the
drapery *(adj.)* ကုန်ခြောက် kon-chauk
drastic *(n.)* ပြင်းထန်သော *pyin-htan-taw*
draught *(n.)* လေစိမ်း *lay-sein*
draw *(n.)* မဲနှိုက်ခြင်း *mae-hnite-chin*
draw *(v.)* ပုံဆွဲသည် *pon-swal-the*
drawback *(n.)* ချွတ်ယွင်းချက် *chyut-ywin-chat*
drawbridge *(n.)* နင်းကြမ်းတံတား *nin-kyan-ta-tar*
drawer *(n.)* အံဆွဲ *an-swal*
drawing *(n.)* ပုံဆွဲပညာ *pon-swal-pyin-nyar*
drawing-room *(n.)* ဧည့်ခန်း *ae-khan*
dread *(n.)* စိုးရိမ်ပူပန်ခြင်း *soe-yein-pu-pan-chin*
dread *(adj.)* ဆိုးဝါးသော *soe-war-taw*
dreadful *(adj.)* အလွန်ဆိုးဝါးသော a-lun-soe-war-taw
dreadfully *(adv.)* အလွန် a-lun
dreadlock *(n.)* ဆံကျစ်အချောင်းချောင်းကျနေသည့် ဆံပင်ပုံ san-kyit-a-khyaung-khyaung-kya-nay-the-san-pin-pon
dream *(n.)* အိပ်မက် aik-mat
dreamcatcher *(n.)* အိပ်မက်ဖမ်းပစ္စည်း *aik-mat-phan-pyit-see*
dreamer *(n.)* အိပ်မက်မက်သူ *aik-mat-mat-thu*
dreamily *(adv.)* အိပ်မက်ဆန်ဆန် *aik-mat-san-san*
dreamworld *(n.)* စိတ်ကူးယဉ်ဘဝ seik-khu-yin-ba-wa
dreamy *(adj.)* အိပ်ချင်မူးတူး *aik-chin-mu-tu*
drench *(v.)* ရွှဲရွှဲစိုသည် *shwe-shwe-so-the*
dress *(n.)* အဝတ်အစား *a-wit-a-sar*
dress *(v.)* အဝတ်ဝတ်သည် *a-wit-wit-the*
dressing *(n.)* ပတ်တီး၊ အဝတ်အစားဝတ်ဆင်ခြင်း *pat-thee, a-wit-a-sar-wit-sin-chin*
dressing table *(n.)* မှန်တင်ခုံ *man-tin-khone*
dressmaker *(n.)* အမျိုးသမီးဝတ်စုံချုပ်သူ *a-myo-ta-mee-wit-sone-choke-thu*
drib *(n.)* အစက် *a-sat*
dribble *(n.)* အစက် a-sat
dried *(adj.)* ခြောက်သွေ့သော chauk-thway-thaw
drift *(n.)* တသွင်သွင်စီးဆင်းခြင်း *ta-twin-twin-see-sin-chin*
drill *(n.)* လွန် lun
drink *(n.)* သောက်ဖွယ် *taut-phwal*
drinking chocolate *(n.)* ချောကလက်ရည် chaw-ka-lat-yay
drinking water *(n.)* သောက်ရည် *taut-yay*
drip *(n.)* တစ်စက်တစ်စက်ကျခြင်း *ta-sat-ta-sat-kya-chin*
drive *(n.)* တွန်းအားပေးမှု၊ ကားမောင်းခြင်း *tun-ar-pya-mu, kar-maung-chin*

drive *(v.)* မောင်းနှင်သည်၊ တွန်းအားပေးသည် *maung-hnin-the-, tun-arr-pay-the*
driver *(n.)* ယာဉ်မောင်း yin-maung
drizzle *(n.)* မိုးဖွဲ *moe-phwe*
drizzle *(v.)* မိုးတဖွဲဖွဲရွာသည် *moe-ta-phwe-phwe-ywar-the*
droid *(n.)* စက်ရုပ် *sat-yoke*
drone *(n.)* မောင်းသူမဲ့လေယာဉ် *maung-thu-mae-lay-yin*
drool *(n)* သွားရည် *twar-yay*
droop *(n.)* ညွတ်ကျနေခြင်း *nyut-kya-nay-chin*
droopy *(adj.)* ညွတ်ကျနေသော *nyut-kya-nay-taw*
drop *(v.)* ကျသည်၊ ချပေးသည် *kya-the, cha-pay-the*
drop *(n.)* အစက်အပေါက် *a-sat-a-paut*
drop box *(n.)* ပြန်အပ်စာအုပ် လက်ခံရာနေရာ *pyan-at-sar-oak-lat-khan-yar-nay-yar*
drop-in *(adj.)* ချိန်းဆိုခြင်းမရှိဘဲလာရောက်သော *chain-so-chin-ma-shi-bal-lar-yauk-taw*
drop-off *(n.)* ကျခြင်း၊ နည်းခြင်း *kya-chin, nae-chin*
dropout *(n.)* ပညာတစ်ပိုင်းတစ်စနှင့်ကျောင်းထွက်သူ *pyin-nyar-ta-pai-ta-sa-nint-kyaung-htwat-thu*
dropzone *(n.)* ချရန်နေရာ *cha-yan-nay-yar*
drought *(n.)* မိုးခေါင်ခြင်း *moe-khaung-chin*
drown *(v.)* ရေနစ်သည် *yay-nit-the*
drug *(n.)* ဆေး *say*
drug addict *(n.)* ဆေးစွဲခြင်း *say-swal-chin*
druggist *(n.)* ဆေးရောင်းဆိုင် *say-yaung-sai*
druid *(n.)* ဆဲလ်တစ်ဘုန်းကြီး *sal-tit-phone-gyi*
drum *(n.)* ဒရမ် *da-ran*
drum kit *(n.)* ဒရမ်ပစ္စည်း *da-ran-pyit-see*
drumbeat *(n.)* ဒရမ်တီးချက် *da-ran-tee-chat*
drumfish *(n.)* ဒရမ်ငါး *da-ran-ngar*
drunk *(adj.)* အရက်မူးသော *a-yat-mu-taw*
drunkard *(n.)* အရက်မူးသမား *a-yat-mu-ta-mar*
dry *(v.)* ခြောက်သွေ့သည် *chauk-thway-the*
dry-clean *(v.)* အခြောက်လျှော်သည် *a-chauk-shaw-the*
dryer *(n.)* အခြောက်ခံစက် *a-chauk-khan-sat*
dual *(adj.)* နှစ်ခုဖြစ်သော *na-khu-phit-taw*
duality *(n.)* လက္ခဏာနှစ်ရပ် ဒွန်တွဲနေမှု *lat-kha-nar-na-yat-dun-twe-nay-mu*
dual-purpose *(adj.)* နှစ်မျိုးသုံး *na-myo-tone*
dub *(n.)* မူလဘာသာစကားအစားအခြားဘာသာစကားဖြင့် အသံသွင်းသည် *mu-la-bar-tar-sa-kar-a-sar-a-char-bar-tar-sa-kar-phyint-a-tan-twin-the*
dubious *(adj.)* သံသယရှိသော *tan-ta-ya-shi-taw*
ducat *(n.)* ဝင်ခွင့်လက်မှတ် *win-khwint-lat-mat*
duchess *(n.)* မြို့စားကတော် *myo-sar-ka-taw*
duck *(v.)* ဆတ်ခနဲ ငုံ့၍ ပုန်းသည် *sat-kha-nae-ngont-ywe-pon-the*
duct *(n.)* ပြွန် *pyun*
duct tape *(n.)* တိတ် *tate*
dude *(n.)* ငကြွား *nga-kywar*

due *(adv.)* စူးစူး *sue-sue*

duel *(n.)* စီးချင်းထိုးခြင်း *si-chin-htoe-chin*

duel *(v.)* စီးချင်းထိုးသည် *see-chin-htoe-the*

duet *(n.)* နှစ်ယောက်ဝိုင်း na-yauk-wine

duffel bag *(n.)* လက်ဆွဲအိတ် *lat-swal-aik*

duke *(n.)* မြို့စားကြီး *myo-sar-gyi*

dull *(adj.)* ပျင်းစရာကောင်းသော *pyin-sa-yar-kaung-taw*

dull *(v.)* မှိန်သွားသည် လျော့စေသည် *main-twar-the-shawt-say-the*

duly *(adv.)* မှန်မှန်ကန်ကန် *man-man-kan-kan*

dumb *(adj.)* ဆွံ့အသော *sunt-aa-taw*

dum-bell *(n.)* ဒမ်ဘယ် *dan-ble*

dumbfound *(v.)* မှင်သက်မိသည် *hmin-thet-mi-the*

dumbfounded *(adj.)* မှင်သက်မိသော *hmin-thet-mi-thaw*

dumbo *(n.)* ငပိန်း *nga-pain*

dummy *(n.)* ကိုယ်တိုင်းရုပ် *koe-tai-yoke*

dump *(n.)* အမှိုက်ပုံ a-mite-pon

dumpster *(n.)* အမှိုက်ပုံးကြီး *a-mite-pone-gyi*

dunce *(n.)* ဉာဏ်ထိုင်းသောသူ *nyan-htai-taw-thu*

dune *(n.)* သဲတောင်ပူစာ *the-taung-pu-sar*

dung *(n.)* တိရစ္ဆာန်ချေး ta-yeik-san-chay

dungeon *(n.)* မြေအောက်အကျဉ်းတိုက် myay-aut-a-kyin-tite

dunk *(n.)* နှစ်ခြင်း၊ တို့ခြင်း *nit-chin, toe-chin*

duo *(n.)* သရုပ်ဆောင် နှစ်ယောက်တွဲ *ta-yoke-saung-na-yauk-twe*

dup *(v.)* ဖွင့်သည် phwint-the

dupe *(v.)* ညာခိုင်းသည် *nyar-khai-the*

duplex *(n.)* နှစ်လုံးတွဲ *na-lone-twe*

duplicate *(adj.)* မိတ္တူ *meik-thu*

duplicity *(n.)* တမင်လိမ်လည်လှည့်စားခြင်း ta-min-lain-lal-hlae-sar-chin

durability *(n.)* ကြာရှည် အသုံးခံနိုင်စွမ်း *kyar-shay-a-ton-khan-nai-swan*

durable *(adj.)* ကြာရှည် အသုံးခံသော *kyar-shay-a-ton-khan-nai-taw*

duration *(n.)* ကာလ kar-la

during *(prep.)* အတောအတွင်း *a-taw-a-twin*

dusk *(n.)* နေဝင်ဆည်းဆာ *nay-win-see-sar*

dust *(n.)* ဖုန် *hpone*

duster *(n.)* ဖုန်သုတ်အဝတ် *hpone-tote-a-wit*

dutiful *(adj.)* တာဝန်ကျေသော tar-win-kyay-taw

duty *(n.)* တာဝန် *tar-win*

duty-free *(adj.)* အကောက်မဲ့ a-kauk-mae

duvet *(n.)* လွှမ်းဖုံ *hlwan-hpone*

dwarf *(n.)* လူပု *lu-pu*

dwell *(v.)* နေထိုင်သည် *nay-htai-the*

dwelling *(n.)* နေအိမ် *nay-eain*

dwindle *(v.)* တစ်စတစ်စလျော့ပါးသည် *ta-sa-ta-sa-yawt-par-the*

dye *(n.)* ဆိုးဆေး *soe-say*

dynamic *(adj.)* အင်တိုက်အားတိုက်ဖြစ်သော *inn-tite-arr-tite-phit-taw*

dynamics *(n.)* ဒိုင်းနမစ်ပညာ dai-na-mit-pyin-nyar

dynamite *(n.)* ဒိုင်းနမိုက် dai-na-mite

dynamo *(n.)* ဒိုင်နမို *dai-na-mo*

dynasty *(n.)* မင်းဆက် *min-sat*

dysentery *(n.)* ဝမ်းကိုက်ရောဂါ *wan-kite-yaw-gar*

dystopia *(n.)* ဆိုးနိုင်သမျှ ဆိုးသော စိတ်ကူးသက်သက် နေရာ *soe-nai-ta-mya-soe-taw-seik-ku-thet-thet-nay-yar*

E

each *(pron.)* တစ်ခုစီ ta-khu-si

each *(adv.)* တစ်ခုစီ *ta-khu-si*

eager *(adj.)* စိတ်အားထက်သန်သော *seik-arr-htet-tan-taw*

eagle *(n.)* လင်းယုန်ငှက် *lin-yone-nget*

ear *(n.)* နား nar

earbud *(n.)* နားကြပ်၊ နားဆို့ *nar-kyat, nar-soe*

early *(adj.)* စောစီးစွာ *saw-see-swar*

earn *(v.)* ဝင်ငွေရှာသည် win-ngwe-shar-the

earnest *(adj.)* အလွန်အလေးအနက်ထားသော *a-lun-a-lay-a-nat-htar-taw*

earth *(n.)* ကမ္ဘာမြေကြီး *ka-bar-myay-gyi*

earthen *(adj.)* မြေကြီးနှင့် လုပ်သော *myay-gyi-nint-lote-taw*

earthenware *(n.)* မြေထည်ပစ္စည်း *myay-htae-pyit-see*

earthly *(adj.)* လက်တွေ့ဘဝနှင့် သက်ဆိုင်သော *lat-tway-ba-wa-nint-thet-sai-taw*

earthquake *(n.)* ငလျင် *nga-lin*

ease *(n.)* လွယ်ကူခြင်း lwal-ku-chin

east *(adv.)* အရှေ့ဘက် *a-shay-bat*

east *(n.)* အရှေ့ a-shay

easter *(n.)* အီစတာပွဲတော် *e-sa-tar-pwe-taw*

eastern *(adj.)* အရှေ့ *a-shay*

easy *(adj.)* လွယ်ကူသော lwal-ku-taw

easy-to-use *(adj.)* အသုံးပြုရန်လွယ်ကူသော *a-ton-pyu-yan-lwal-khu-taw*

eat *(v.)* စားသည် *sar-the*

eatable *(adj.)* စားရ၍ ရသော sar-ywe-ya-taw

eave *(n.)* တံစက်မြိတ် ta-sat-myeik

eavesdrop *(v.)* ခိုးနားထောင်သည် *kho-nar-htaung-the*

ebb *(n.)* ဒီရေကျချိန် *di-yay-kya-chain*

ebb *(v.)* ဒီရေကျသည် *di-yay-kya-the*

ebony *(n.)* အသားမည်းနက်မာကျောသော ရင်းတိုက်ပင် *a-tar-mae-nat-mar-kyaw-taw-yin-tite-pin*

e-book *(n.)* အီလက်ထရောနစ်စာအုပ် *e-lat-hta-yaw-nit-sar-oak*

ebulliate *(v.)* ခွန်အားအပြည့်နှင့် တက်ကြွသည် *khun-ar-a-pyae-nint-tat-kwa-the*

ebullience *(n.)* ခွန်အားအပြည့်နှင့် တက်ကြွခြင်း *khun-ar-a-pyae-nint-tat-kwa-chin*

ebullient *(adj.)* ခွန်အားအပြည့်နှင့် တက်ကြွသော *khun-ar-a-pyae-nint-tat-kwa-taw*

eccentric *(adj.)* အများနှင့် မတူ တစ်မူထူးသော *a-myar-nint-ma-tu-ta-mu-htoo-taw*

ecclesiast *(n.)* ဓမ္မဆရာ dhamma-sa-yar

ecclesiastical *(adj.)* ခရစ်ယာန်အသင်းနှင့် ဆိုင်သော *kha-yit-yan-a-tin-nint-sai-taw*

echinid *(n.)* အီချီးနစ်ပင် *e-chee-nit-pin*

echo *(n.)* ပဲ့တင်ထပ်ခြင်း *pae-tin-htet-chin*

echocardiogram *(n.)* နှလုံးအက်ကိုးရိုက်စက် *na-lone-at-kho-yite-sat*

eclampsia *(n.)* ကိုယ်ဝန်ဆိပ်တက်ခြင်း *koe-win-seik-tat-chin*
eclectic *(n.)* နှံ့နှံ့စပ်စပ် ချယ်တတ်ခြင်း nant-nant-sat-sat-ywe-chal-tat-chin
eclipse *(n.)* ကြတ်ခြင်း၊ လငပုပ်ဖမ်းခြင်း kyat-chin, la-nga-poke-phan-chin
eclipsis *(n.)* စကားလုံးချန်လှပ်ခြင်း sa-kar-lon-chan-hlat-chin
ecological *(adj.)* ဂေဟဗေဒနှင့် ဆိုင်သော *gay-ha-bay-da-nint-sai-taw*
ecologist *(n.)* ဂေဟဗေဒပညာရှင် *gay-ha-bay-da-pyin-nyar-shin*
ecology *(n.)* ဂေဟဗေဒ *gay-ha-bay-da*
e-commerce *(n.)* အီလက်ထရောနစ်စီးပွားရေး *e-lat-hta-yaw-nit-see-pwar-yay*
economic *(adj.)* စီးပွားရေး၊ တွက်ခြေကိုက်သော see-pwar-yay, twat-chay-kite-taw
economical *(adj.)* တွက်ခြေကိုက်သော *twat-chay-kite-taw*
economics *(n.)* ဘောဂဗေဒ *baw-ga-bay-da*
economy *(n.)* စီးပွားရေး *see-pwar-yay*
ecosystem *(n.)* ဂေဟစနစ် gay-ha-sa-nit
ecoterrorism *(n.)* ဂေဟဗေဒဆိုင်ရာ အကြမ်းဖက်မှု လုပ်ဆောင်ခြင်း *gay-ha-bay-da-sai-yar-a-kyan-phat-mu-lote-saung-chin*
ecstasy *(n.)* ပီတိ *pi-ti*
ecstatic *(adj.)* ပီတိဖြာသော *pi-ti-pyar-taw*
ectopia *(n.)* ခန္ဓာကိုယ်အစိတ်အပိုင်း မွေးရာပါ နေရာမှားခြင်း khan-dar-koe-a-seik-a-pai-mway-yar-par-nay-yar-hmar-chin
ectoplasm *(n.)* စုန်းပူးချိန်တွင် ကူးစက်လာသော ဓာတ်တစ်မျိုး sone-pu-chain-twin-khu-sat-lar-taw-dat-ta-myo
ecumenic *(adj.)* ခရစ်ယာန်အသင်းတော်အမျိုးမျိုးမှ အသင်းသားများပါသော *kha-yit-yan-a-tin-taw-a-myo-myo-ma-a-tin-tar-myar-par-taw*
ecumenical *(adj.)* ခရစ်ယာန်အသင်းတော်အမျိုးမျိုးမှ အသင်းသားများပါသော kha-yit-yan-a-tin-taw-a-myo-myo-ma-a-tin-tar-myar-par-taw
eczema *(n.)* နှင်းခူနာ hnin-khu-nar
edema *(n.)* ရောင်ရမ်းခြင်း *yaung-yan-chin*
edge *(n.)* အစွန်း *a-sun*
edible *(adj.)* စားကောင်းသော *sar-kaung-taw*
edict *(n.)* အမိန့်ပြန်တမ်း *a-maint-pyan-tan*
edificant *(adj.)* တည်ဆောက်သော *the-saut-thaw*
edification *(n.)* စိတ်ဓာတ်မြှင့်တင်ရေး *seik-dat-hmyint-tin-yay*
edifice *(n.)* ဗိမာန် *baik-man*
edify *(v.)* စိတ်ဓာတ်မြှင့်တင်သည် *seik-dat-hmyint-tin-the*
edit *(v.)* တည်းဖြတ်သည် the-phat-the
edition *(n.)* ပုံနှိပ်ခြင်း *pon-neik-chin*
editor *(n.)* တည်းဖြတ်သူ *the-phat-thu*
editorial *(adj.)* အယ်ဒီတာနှင့် ဆိုင်သော al-di-tar-nint-sai-taw
editorial *(n.)* အယ်ဒီတာအာဘော် *al-di-tar-ar-baw*
educate *(v.)* ပညာပေးသည် *pyin-nyar-pay-the*
education *(n.)* ပညာရေး *pyin-nyar-yay*
eel *(n.)* ငါးရှဉ့် *ngary-shint*
eerie *(adj.)* ချောက်ချားဖွယ် ဖြစ်စေသော *chauk-char-phwal-phit-say-taw*

effable *(adj.)* **ဖော်ပြနိုင်သော** *phaw-pya-naing-taw*
effably *(adv.)* **ဖော်ပြနိုင်သော နည်းလမ်းဖြင့်** *phaw-pya-naing-taw-nee-lan-phit*
efface *(v.)* **မှေးမှိန်ကွယ်ပျောက်စေသည်** *may-maing-kwal-pyauk-say-the*
effect *(n.)* **အကျိုးတရား** *a-kyo-ta-yar*
effective *(adj.)* **ထိရောက်သော** *hti-yauk-taw*
effeminate *(adj.)* **မိန်းမဆန်သော** *mein-ma-san-taw*
efficacy *(n.)* **အစွမ်းထက်မှု** *a-swan-htet-mu*
efficiency *(n.)* **ထိထိရောက်ရောက် လုပ်နိုင်စွမ်း** *hti-hti-yauk-yauk-lote-nai-swan*
efficient *(adj.)* **ကျွမ်းကျင်သော၊ တော်သော** *kyun-kyin-taw, taw-thaw*
effigy *(n.)* **ရုပ်တု** *yoke-htu*
effort *(n.)* **အားထုတ်မှု** *arr-htoke-mu*
effortless *(adj.)* **သက်တောင့်သက်သာ** *thet-taunt-thet-tar*
effusive *(adj.)* **ခံစားမှု ကဲလွန်းသော** *khan-sar-mu-khae-loon-taw*
egg *(n.)* **ကြက်ဥ** *kyat-au*
ego *(n.)* **အတ္တ** *at-ta*
egocentric *(adj.)* **အတ္တကြီးသော** *at-ta-kyi-taw*
egotism *(n.)* **ကိုယ်ကျိုးကြည့်ခြင်း** *koe-kyo-kyi-chin*
eight *(n.)* **ရှစ်** *shit*
eighteen *(n.)* **ဆယ့်ရှစ်** *sat-shit*
eighty *(n.)* **ရှစ်ဆယ်** *shit-sal*
either *(pron.)* **နှစ်ခုအနက် တစ်ခု** *na-khu-a-net-ta-khu*
either *(adv.)* **တစ်ခုမဟုတ် တစ်ခု** *ta-khu-ma-hote-ta-khu*
ejaculate *(n.)* **သုက်လွှတ်ခြင်း** *toke-hlut-chin*
ejaculation *(n.)* **သုက်လွှတ်ခြင်း** *toke-hlut-chin*
ejaculatory *(adj.)* **သက်လွှတ်သော** *toke-hlut-taw*
eject *(v.)* **ထုတ်သည်၊ မောင်းထုတ်သည်** *htoke-the, muang-htoke-the*
elaborate *(adj.)* **အသေးစိတ် စီစဉ် ပြင်ဆင်ထားသော** *a-tay-seik-si-sin-pyin-sin-htar-taw*
elapse *(v.)* **ကုန်လွန်သွားသည်** *kon-lun-twar-the*
elastic *(adj.)* **ကျုံ့ဆန့်နိုင်သော** *kyont-sant-nai-taw*
elasticity *(n.)* **ကျုံ့ဆန့်နိုင်စွမ်း** *kyont-sant-nai-swan*
elate *(adj.)* **ဘဝင်ခိုက်နေသော** *ba-win-khaik-nay-taw*
elated *(adj.)* **ဘဝင်ခိုက်နေသော** *ba-win-khaik-nay-taw*
elation *(n.)* **ပီတိ** *pi-ti*
elbow *(n.)* **တံတောင်ဆစ်** *ta-daung-sit*
elder *(adj.)* **အကြီးဖြစ်သော** *a-kyi-phit-taw*
elder *(n.)* **အကြီးဖြစ်သူ** a-kyi-phit-thu
elderly *(adj.)* **သက်ကြီး** *thet-kyi*
elect *(v.)* **ရွေးကောက်သည်** *yway-kauk-the*
election *(n.)* **ရွေးကောက်ပွဲ** *yway-kauk-pwe*
electorate *(n.)* **မဲဆန္ဒရှင်များ** *mae-sanda-shin-myar*
electric *(adj.)* **လျှပ်စစ်ဓာတ်အားသုံး** lyat-sit-dat-ar-tone
electricity *(n.)* **လျှပ်စစ်ဓာတ်အား** *lyat-sit-dat-ar*

electrify *(v.)* လျှပ်စစ်ဓာတ်အားလွှတ်ထားသည် lyat-sit-dat-ar-hlut-htar-the
electrocute *(v.)* ဓာတ်လိုက်သေသည် dat-lite-tay-the
electrocution *(n.)* ဓာတ်လိုက်သေခြင်း *dat-lite-tay-chin*
electrolyte *(n.)* လျှပ်လိုက်ရည် *lyat-lite-yay*
electron *(n.)* အီလက်ထရွန် *e-lat-hta-ron*
electronic *(adj.)* အီလက်ထရွန်နစ် *e-lat-hta-yaw-nit*
elegance *(n.)* ကြော့ရှင်းခြင်း *kyaut-shin-chin*
elegant *(adj.)* ကြော့ရှင်းသော *kyaut-shin-taw*
elegy *(n.)* တမ်းချင်း *tan-chin*
element *(n.)* ဒြပ်စင်၊ လိုအပ်ချက် *drat-sin, lo-at-chat*
elemental *(adj.)* ပြင်းထန်ကြမ်းတမ်းသော *pyin-htan-kyan-tan-taw*
elementary *(adj.)* အခြေခံ *a-chay-khan*
elephant *(n.)* ဆင် *sin*
elephantine *(adj.)* ဆင်ခန္ဓာဝက်ကိုယ်လုံး *sin-khandar-wat-koe-lone*
elevate *(v.)* မြှင့်တင်သည် *hmyint-tin-the*
elevation *(n.)* မြှင့်တင်ခြင်း *hmyint-tin-chin*
elevator *(n.)* စက်လှေကား *sat-hlay-kar*
eleven *(n.)* ဆယ့်တစ် *sat-tit*
elf *(n.)* နတ်သူငယ် *nat-thu-ngal*
elicitate *(v.)* အစ်ထုတ်သည် *it-htoke-the*
eligibility *(n.)* အရည်အသွေးသတ်မှတ်ချက် *a-yay-a-thway-tat-mat-chat*
eligible *(adj.)* အရည်အသွေးပြည့်မီသော *a-yay-a-thway-pyae-mi-taw*
eliminate *(v.)* ဖယ်ထုတ်သည် *phal-htoke-the*
elimination *(n.)* ရှင်းလင်းသုတ်သင်ခြင်း *shin-lin-toke-tin-chin*
eliminator *(n.)* ရှင်းလင်းသုတ်သင်သူ shin-lin-toke-tin-thu
eliminatory *(adj.)* ရှင်းလင်းသုတ်သင်သော *shin-lin-toke-tin-taw*
elision *(n.)* အသံဖျောက်ဆိုခြင်း *a-than-phyauk-so-chin*
elite *(adj.)* လူမှုအဆင့်မြင့်သော *lu-mu-a-sint-myint-taw*
elitism *(n.)* အီလိုက်ဝါဒ *e-lite-war-da*
elitist *(n.)* အီလိုက်ဝါဒီ *e-lite-war-di*
elixir *(n.)* သက်စောင့်ဆေး *tat-saunt-say*
elk *(n.)* သမင်ကြီး *ta-min-gyi*
ellipse *(n.)* ဘဲဥပုံ *bae-oo-pon*
elliptic *(adj.)* ဘဲဥပုံရှိသော bae-oo-pon-shi-taw
elocution *(n.)* ရှင်းလင်းထိရောက်စွာပြောဆိုနိုင်ခြင်း *shin-lin-hti-yauk-swar-pyaw-soe-nai-chin*
elope *(v.)* ခိုးရာလိုက်ပြေးသည် *kho-yar-lite-pyay-the*
eloquence *(n.)* ခိုးရာလိုက်ပြေးခြင်း *kho-yar-lite-pyay-chin*
eloquent *(adj.)* ခိုးရာလိုက်သော *kho-yar-lite-taw*
else *(adj.)* နောက်ထပ် *naut-htet*
elucidate *(v.)* ရှင်းပြသည် *shin-pya-the*
elude *(v.)* လွတ်မြောက်သည် hlut-myauk-the
elusion *(n.)* တိမ်းရှောင်ခြင်း *tain-shaung-chin*
elusive *(adj.)* အရှာရခက်သော *a-shar-ya-khat-taw*
emaciate *(v.)* ပိန်ချုံးချည့်နဲ့သည် *pain-chone-chae-nae-the*

emaciated *(adj.)* **ပိန်ချုံးချည့်နဲ့သော** *pain-chone-chae-nae-taw*
email *(n.)* **အီးမေးလ်** *e-male*
emanate *(v.)* **ပေါ်ထွက်သည်** *paw-htwat-the*
emanation *(n.)* **ပေါ်ထွက်ခြင်း** *paw-htwat-chin*
emancipate *(v.)* **လွတ်မြောက်စေသည်** hlut-myauk-say-the
emancipation *(n.)* **လွတ်မြောက်စေခြင်း** *hlut-myauk-say-chin*
emasculate *(v.)* **အရာမရောက်** *a-yar-ma-yauk*
emasculation *(n.)* **အရာမရောက်ခြင်း** *a-yar-ma-yauk-chin*
embalm *(v.)* **လူကို မပုတ်သိုးအောင် ဆေးရည်စိမ်သည်** *lu-ko-ma-poke-tho-aung-say-yay-sein-the*
embalming *(n.)* **လူကို မပုတ်သိုးအောင် ဆေးရည်စိမ်ခြင်း** *lu-ko-ma-poke-tho-aung-say-yay-sein-chin*
embank *(v.)* **ကာကွယ်သည်** *kar-kwal-the*
embankment *(n.)* **ရေကာတာ** yay-kar-tar
embargo *(n.)* **ကုန်သွယ်မှု ပိတ်ပင်မိန့်** *kone-twal-mu-pate-pin-maint*
embark *(v.)* **လေယာဉ်ပေါ်သို့ တက်သည်** *lay-yin-paw-tho-tat-the*
embarrass *(v.)* **ရှက်ကိုးရှက်ကန်း ဖြစ်သည်** *shat-koe-shat-kan-phit-the*
embarrassing *(adj.)* **ရှက်ကိုးရှက်ကန်း ဖြစ်သော** *shat-koe-shat-kan-phit-taw*
embarrassment *(n.)* **ရှက်ကိုးရှက်ကန်း ဖြစ်ခြင်း** *shat-koe-shat-kan-phit-chin*
embassy *(n.)* **သံရုံး** *tan-yone*
embellish *(v.)* **တန်ဆာဆင်သည်** *ta-sar-sin-the*
embitter *(v.)* **နာကြည်းသည်** *nar-kyi-the*
emblem *(n.)* **အမှတ်တံဆိပ်** *a-mat-ta-seik*
embodiment *(n.)* **ပြယုဂ်** *pya-yoke*
embody *(v.)* **ပုံဖော်သည်** *pon-phaw-the*
embolden *(v.)* **ရဲဆေးတင်သည်** *ye-say-tin-the*
embrace *(n.)* **ပွေ့ဖက်ခြင်း** pway-phat-chin
embroidery *(n.)* **ပန်းထိုးအတတ်** pan-htoe-a-tat
embryo *(n.)* **သန္ဓေသား** *ta-day-tar*
embryonic *(adj.)* **ကနဦးအဆင်၊ သန္ဓေသားနှင့် ဆိုင်သော** *ka-na-oo-a-sint, ta-day-tar-nint-sai-taw*
embush *(v.)* **ခြုံခိုတိုက်သည်** chon-kho-tite-the
emend *(v.)* **စာအမှားပြင်သည်** sar-a-mar-pyin-the
emendate *(v.)* **စာအမှားပြင်သည်** *sar-a-mar-pyin-the*
emerald *(n.)* **မြ** *mya*
emerge *(v.)* **ပေါ်ထွက်လာသည်** *paw-htwat-lar-the*
emergency *(n.)* **အရေးပေါ်** *a-yay-paw*
emigrate *(v.)* **အခြားနိုင်ငံတွင် ပြောင်းရွှေ့နေထိုင်သည်** *a-char-nai-ngan-twin-pyaung-shway-nay-htai-the*
emigration *(n.)* **အခြားနိုင်ငံတွင် ပြောင်းရွှေ့နေထိုင်ခြင်း** *a-char-nai-ngan-twin-pyaung-shway-nay-htai-chin*
eminence *(n.)* **ထင်ပေါ်ခြင်း** *htin-paw-chin*
eminent *(adj.)* **ထင်ပေါ်သော** htin-paw-taw
emissary *(n.)* **တမန်** ta-man
emission *(n.)* **ထုတ်လုပ်ခြင်း** htoke-lote-chin
emit *(v.)* **ထုတ်လွှတ်သည်** htoke-hlut-the

emittance *(n.)* **ထုတ်လွှတ်ခြင်း** *htoke-hlut-chin*

emmet *(n.)* **ပုရွတ်ဆိတ်** *pa-ywat-seik*

emoji *(n.)* **ခံစားမှုပြပုံ** *khan-sar-mu-pya-pon*

emolument *(n.)* **လုပ်ခငွေ** *lote-kha-ngwe*

emote *(v.)* **ခံစားချက်ဖွင့်ဟသည်** khan-sar-chat-hpwint-ha-the

emoticon *(n.)* **ခံစားချက်ပြပုံ** khan-sar-chat-pya-pon

emotion *(n.)* **စိတ်ခံစားမှု** *seik-khan-sar-mu*

emotional *(adj.)* **စိတ်လှုပ်ရှားစေသော** *seik-lote-shar-say-taw*

emotive *(adj.)* **စိတ်ကိုလှုပ်ရှားထိခိုက်စေနိုင်သော** seik-ko-lote-shar-hti-khaik-say-nai-taw

empath *(n.)* **မျှဝေခံစားသူ** mya-wai-khan-sar-thu

empathic *(adj.)* **မျှဝေခံစားသော** mya-wai-khan-sar-taw

empathy *(n.)* **မျှဝေခံစားခြင်း** mya-wai-khan-sar-chin

emperor *(n.)* **ကေရာဇ်** *a-ka-rit*

emphasis *(n.)* **ဖိရွတ်ခြင်း၊ အလေးပေးခြင်း** *phi-yut-chin, a-lay-pay-chin*

emphasize *(v.)* **အလေးပေးသည်** *a-lay-pay-the*

emphatic *(adj.)* **အလေးအနက်ပြောသော** *a-lay-a-nat-pyaw-taw*

empire *(n.)* **အင်ပါယာ** in-par-yar

empirical *(adj.)* **လက်တွေ့မျက်မြင်ကိုအခြေခံသော** lat-tway-myat-myin-ko-a-chay-khan-taw

empiricism *(n.)* **ကိုယ်တွေ့မျက်မြင်အခြေစိုက်ဒဿန** *koe-tway-myat-myin-a-chay-site-dat-ta-na*

empiricist *(n.)* **ကိုယ်တွေ့မျက်မြင်အခြေစိုက်ဝါဒီ** *koe-tway-myat-myin-a-chay-site-war-di*

employ *(v.)* **အလုပ်ခန့်သည်** *a-lote-khant-the*

employee *(n.)* **ဝန်ထမ်း** *win-htan*

employer *(n.)* **အလုပ်ရှင်** *a-lote-shin*

employment *(n.)* **အလုပ်ခန့်ခြင်း** *a-lote-khant-chin*

empower *(v.)* **စွမ်းဆောင်ရည်မြင့်တင်သည်** *swan-saung-yay-myint-tin-the*

empress *(n.)* **ကေရီဘုရင်မ** *a-ka-ri-ba-yin-ma*

empty *(v.)* **ထုတ်ပစ်သည်** htoke-pyit-the

empty *(adj.)* **ဗလာ** ba-lar

empty-handed *(adj.)* **လက်ဗလာ** *lat-ba-lar*

emulate *(v.)* **အတုယူသည်** a-tu-yu-the

emulation *(n.)* **အတုယူခြင်း** a-tu-yu-chin

emulsifier *(n.)* **ရေဆေးဆွဲရန် ကူညီပေးသောအရာ** *yay-say-swal-yan-ku-nyi-pay-taw-a-yar*

emulsify *(v.)* **ရေဆေးဖြင့် ပြုလုပ်သည်** yay-say-phint-pyu-loat-the

en route *(adv.)* **လမ်းခရီးတွင်** *lan-kha-yee-twin*

enable *(v.)* **တတ်နိုင်သည်** tat-nai-the

enact *(v.)* **သရုပ်ဆောင်သည်** ta-yoke-saung-the

enamel *(n.)* **ကြွေ** *kway*

enamour *(v.)* **စွဲမက်သည်** swal-mat-the

enamoured *(adj.)* **စွဲမက်သော** *swal-mat-taw*

enamourment *(n.)* **စွမက်ခြင်း** *swal-mat-chin*

encage *(v.)* **အကျဉ်းချသည်** *a-kyin-cha-the*

encapsulate *(v.)* **အချုပ်ကို ထုတ်ပြသည်** *a-choke-ko-htoke-pya-the*
encase *(v.)* **ဖုံးထားသည်** *hpone-htar-the*
enchant *(v.)* **နှစ်သက်ကြည်နူးစေသည်** *nit-thet-kyi-ku-say-the*
encircle *(v.)* **ဝန်းရံသည်၊ ဝိုင်းထားသည်** *win-yan-the, wine-htar-the*
enclose *(v.)* **ပူးတွဲထည့်သည်** pu-twe-htae-the
enclosure *(n.)* **ခြံ၊ ခြံခတ်ခြင်း** *chan,chan-khat-chin*
encompass *(v.)* **အကျုံးဝင်စေသည်** *a-kyone-win-say-the*
encounter *(n.)* **တွေ့ဆုံခြင်း** *tway-sone-chin*
encourage *(v.)* **အားပေးသည်** *arr-pay-the*
encouragement *(n.)* **အားပေးခြင်း** *arr-pay-chin*
encroach *(v.)* **ကျူးကျော်သည်** *kyu-kyaw-the*
encrust *(v.)* **အုပ်ထားသည်၊ ဖွဲ့စည်းသည်** *oak-htar-the, phwe-see-the*
encrusted *(adj.)* **ဖုံးထားသော** *hpone-htar-taw*
encrypt *(v.)* **ဖုံးကွယ်သည်** *hpone-kwal-the*
encrypted *(adj.)* **ဖုံးကွယ်သော** *hpone-kwal-taw*
encryption *(n.)* **ဖုံးကွယ်သည်** *hpone-kwal-the*
encumber *(v.)* **ဝန်ပိသည်** *win-pi-the*
encyclopedia *(n.)* **စွယ်စုံကျမ်း** *swal-sone-kyan*
end *(n.)* **အဆုံး** *a-sone*
endanger *(v.)* **အန္တရာယ်ဖြစ်စေသည်** *an-ta-yal-phit-say-the*
endangered *(adj.)* **အန္တရာယ်ဖြစ်စေသော** *an-ta-yal-phit-say-taw*
endear *(v.)* **ချစ်ခင်စေသည်** chit-khin-say-the
endearment *(n.)* **အချစ်အကြင်နာစကား** a-chit-a-kyin-nar-sa-kar
endeavour *(v.)* **ကြိုးပမ်းသည်** *kyo-pan-the*
endemic *(n.)* **နေရာတစ်ခုတွင် အတွေ့များသည့် မျိုးစိတ်** nay-yar-ta-khu-twin-a-tway-myar-the-myo-seik
endemiology *(n.)* **အဖြစ်များရောဂါလေ့လာသောပညာ** *a-phit-myar-yaw-gar-lay-lar-thaw-pyin-nyar*
endless *(adj.)* **အဆုံးမဲ့** a-sone-mae
endorse *(v.)* **အတည်ပြုချက်ပေးသည်** *a-tin-pyu-chat-pay-the*
endorsement *(n.)* **ထောက်ခံချက်** *htauk-khan-chat*
endorser *(n.)* **အတည်ပြုချက်ပေးသူ** *a-the-pyu-chat-pay-thu*
endoscopic *(adj.)* **ခန္ဓာကိုယ်အတွင်းပိုင်းကြည့်ခြင်းဆိုင်ရာ** *khan-dar-ko-a-twin-pine-kyi-chin-sai-yar*
endoscopy *(n.)* **ခန္ဓာကိုယ်အတွင်းပိုင်းကြည့်ပညာ** *khan-dar-ko-a-twin-pine-kyi-pyin-nyar*
endow *(v.)* **ငွေပဒေသာပင် စိုက်ထူပေးသည်** ngwe-pa-day-tar-pin-seik-thu-pay-the
endowed *(adj.)* **ထောက်ပံ့လှူဒါန်းသော** *htauk-pant-hlu-dan-taw*
endowment *(n.)* **ထောက်ပံ့လှူဒါန်းခြင်း** *htauk-pant-hlu-dan-chin*
endurable *(adj.)* **သည်းခံနိုင်သော** *thee-khan-nai-taw*
endurance *(n.)* **ခံနိုင်ရည်** *khan-nai-yay*
endure *(v.)* **ကြံ့ကြံ့ခံသည်** *khyant-khyant-khan-the*
enemy *(n.)* **ရန်သူ** yan-thu

energetic *(adj.)* **အားစိုက်လုပ်ရသော၊ တက်ကြွသော** *arr-site-lote-ya-taw, tat-kwa-taw*

energize *(v.)* **အားထုတ်သည်** *arr-htoke-the*

energy *(n.)* **စွမ်းအင်** swan-in

enervate *(v.)* **အားကုန်စေသည်** arr-kone-say-the

enervated *(adj.)* **အားကုန်စေသော** arr-kone-say-taw

enfeeble *(v.)* **ချည့်နဲ့သည်** chi-nae-the

enforce *(v.)* **အာဏာတည်စေသည်** ar-nar-the-say-the

enfranchise *(v.)* **မဲဆန္ဒပေးပိုင်ခွင့်ရသည်** *mae-sanda-pay-pai-khwint-ya-the*

engage *(v.)* **ခန့်သည်၊ ဆွဲဆောင်သည်၊ အာရုံစိုက်သည်** *khant-the, swal-saung-the, ar-yone-seik-the*

engagement *(n.)* **စေ့စပ်ကြောင်းလမ်းခြင်း၊ ချိန်းဆိုချက်** say-sat-kyaung-lan-chin, chain-so-chat

engaging *(adj.)* **ထိတွေ့မှု ရှိသော** hti-tway-mu-shi-taw

engine *(n.)* **အင်ဂျင်စက်** *in-gyin-sat*

engineer *(n.)* **အင်ဂျင်နီယာ** *in-gyin-na-yar*

engineering *(n.)* **အင်ဂျင်နီယာပညာ** *in-gyin-na-yar-pyin-nyar*

enginous *(adj.)* **စက်နှင့်ဆိုင်သော** *sat-nint-sai-taw*

English *(n.)* **အင်္ဂလိပ်** *in-ga-late*

englobe *(v.)* **တစ်ကမ္ဘာလုံးကဲ့သို့ လွှမ်းခြုံသည်** *ta-ka-bar-lone-kae-tho-hlwan-chon-the*

engorge *(v.)* **ငမ်းငမ်းတက်စားသည်** *ngan-ngan-tat-sar-the*

engrave *(v.)* **ထွင်းထုသည်** htwin-htu-the

engross *(v.)* **စိတ်ဝင်စားသည်** seik-win-sar-the

engulf *(v.)* **လွှမ်းမိုးသည်** *hlwan-moe-the*

enhance *(v.)* **တိုးမြှင့်သည်** *toe-myint-the*

enhancement *(n.)* **တိုးမြှင့်ခြင်း** *toe-myint-chin*

enigma *(n.)* **ပုစ္ဆာ** poke-sar

enigmatic *(adj.)* **နားလည်ရန် ခက်သော** nar-lal-yan-khat-taw

enigmatical *(adj.)* **ပဟေဠိဆန်သော** *pa-hay-li-san-taw*

enigmatically *(adv.)* **ပဟေဠိဆန်ဆန်** pa-hay-li-san-san

enjoy *(v.)* **နှစ်သက်သည်၊ ကြည်နူးသည်** *nit-thet-the, kyi-nu-the*

enjoyability *(n.)* **ပျော်ရွှင်ကြည်နူးနိုင်စွမ်း** *pyaw-shwin-kyi-nu-nai-swan*

enjoyable *(adj.)* **ပျော်ရွှင်ကြည်နူးဖွယ်ကောင်းသော** *pyaw-shwin-kyi-nu-phwal-kaung-taw*

enjoyment *(n.)* **ပျော်ရွှင်မှု** *pyaw-shwin-mu*

enlarge *(v.)* **တိုးချဲ့သည်** *toe-chae-the*

enlighten *(v.)* **ဉာဏ်အလင်းရစေသည်** *nyan-a-lin-ya-say-the*

enlist *(v.)* **စစ်ထဲဝင်သည်** *sit-htae-win-the*

enliven *(v.)* **စိတ်ဝင်တစားရှိစေသည်** seik-win-ta-sar-shi-say-the

enmity *(n.)* **ရန်လိုမှု** yan-lo-mu

ennoble *(v.)* **သူကောင်းပြုသည်** *thu-kaung-pyu-the*

enormous *(adj.)* **ကြီးမားသော** *kyi-mar-taw*

enough *(adj.)* **လုံလောက်သော** *lon-lauk-thaw*

enquiry *(n.)* **စုံစမ်းခြင်း** *sone-san-chin*

enrage *(v.)* **ဒေါသထွက်စေသည်** daw-ta-htwat-say-the

enrapture *(v.)* **ပီတိဖြစ်စေသည်** pi-ti-phit-say-the

enrich *(v.)* **ကြွယ်ဝချမ်းသာစေသည်** *kywal-wa-chan-tar-say-the*

enrichment *(n.)* **ကြွယ်ဝချမ်းသာစေခြင်း** *kywal-wa-chan-tar-say-chin*

enrol *(v.)* **စာရင်းသွင်းသည်** *sa-yin-thwin-the*

ensemble *(n.)* **တေးဂီတအဖွဲ့** *tay-gi-ta-a-phwe*

enshrine *(v.)* **ဌာပနာသည်** *htar-pa-nar-the*

enslave *(v.)* **ကျွန်ပြုသည်** *kyun-pyu=the*

ensue *(v.)* **ရလဒ်ပေါ်ထွက်သည်** ya-lat-par-htwat-the

ensure *(v.)* **သေချာစေသည်** *tay-char-say-the*

entangle *(v.)* **ရစ်ပတ်နေသည်** *yit-pat-nay-the*

enter *(v.)* **ဝင်သည်** *win-the*

enterprise *(n.)* **လုပ်ငန်း** *lote-ngan*

entertain *(v.)* **ဖျော်ဖြေသည်** *phyaw-phyay-the*

entertainment *(n.)* **ဖျော်ဖြေပွဲ** *phyaw-phyay-pwe*

enthral *(v.)* **ပီတိဖြစ်သည်** *pi-ti-phit-the*

enthrone *(v.)* **နန်းတင်သည်** *nan-tin-the*

enthusiasm *(n.)* **စိတ်အားထက်သန်မှု** *seik-arr-htet-tan-mu*

enthusiastic *(adj.)* **စိတ်အားထက်သန်သော** *seik-arr-htet-tan-taw*

entice *(v.)* **သွေးဆောင်ဖြားယောင်းသည်** *thway-saung-phyar-yaung-the*

enticement *(n.)* **ဆွဲဆောင်မှု** *swal-saung-mu*

enticer *(n.)* **ဆွဲဆောင်အားကောင်းသူ** *swal-saung-arr-kaung-thu*

enticing *(adj.)* **ဆွဲဆောင်အားကောင်းသော** swal-saung-arr-kaung-taw

entire *(adj.)* **တစ်ခုလုံး** *ta-khu-lone*

entirely *(adv.)* **လုံးဝ** *lone-wa*

entitle *(v.)* **ခေါင်းစဉ်တပ်သည်** *gaung-zin-tat-the*

entity *(n.)* **အဆောက်အအုံ၊ အစုအဖွဲ့** a-saut-a-ohn, a-su-a-phwe

entomb *(v.)* **မြေမြှုပ်သည်** *myay-hmyoke-the*

entomology *(n.)* **ပိုးမွှားဗေဒ** *poe-hmywar-bay-da*

entrails *(n.)* **ကလီစာ** *ka-li-zar*

entrance *(n.)* **ဝင်ပေါက်၊ ဝင်ခွင့်** *win-pauk, win-khwint*

entrap *(v.)* **ပိတ်လှောင်သည်** *pait-hlaung-the*

entrapment *(n.)* **ထောင်ချောက်ဆင်ဖမ်းခြင်း** *htaung-chauk-sin-phan-chin*

entreat *(v.)* **အနူးအညွတ်တောင်းပန်သည်** *a-nu-a-nyut-taung-pan-the*

entreaty *(n.)* **အသနားခံခြင်း** *a-ta-nar-khan-chin*

entrench *(v.)* **အမြစ်တွယ်နေသည်** a-myit-twal-nay-the

entrenchment *(n.)* **အမြစ်တွယ်ခြင်း** a-myit-twal-chin

entrepreneur *(n.)* **စွန့်ဦးတည်ထွင်လုပ်ငန်းရှင်** *shwunt-oo-the-htwin-lote-ngan-shin*

entropic *(adj.)* **အင်ထရိုပီနှင့်ဆိုင်သော** en-ta-ro-pi-nint-sai-taw

entropy *(n.)* **အင်ထရိုပီ** en-ta-ro-pi

entrust *(v.)* **အပ်နှံသည်** *at-nan-the*

entry *(n.)* **အဝင်** *a-win*

entry form *(n.)* **ဝင်ခွင့်ပုံစံ** *win-khwint-pon-san*

entry-level *(adj.)* **အဝင်အဆင့်** *a-win-a-sint*

enumerable *(adj.)* **ရေတွက်နိုင်သော** yay-thwat-nai-taw

enumerate *(v.)* **ရေတွက်သည်** yay-thwat-the

enumerative *(adj.)* **ရေတွက်ခြင်းနှင့်သက်ဆိုင်သော** *yay-thwat-chin-nint-thet-sai-taw*

enunciate *(v.)* **ပီသစွာ ရွတ်သည်** pi-ta-swar-yut-the

enunciation *(n.)* **ရှင်းလင်းစွာ ဖော်ထုတ်ခြင်း** shin-lin-swar-phaw-htoke-chin

enunciatory *(adj.)* **ရှင်းလင်းစွာဖော်ထုတ်သော** shin-lin-swar-phaw-htoke-taw

envelop *(v.)* **ပတ်ရံသည်၊ ရုံသည်** pat-yan-the, yone-the

envelope *(n.)* **စာအိတ်** sar-aik

envelopment *(n.)* **အကာ** a-kar

enviable *(adj.)* **မနာလိုစရာကောင်းသော** ma-nar-lo-sa-yar-kaung-taw

envious *(adj.)* **မနာလိုဖြစ်သော** ma-nar-lo-phit-taw

environment *(n.)* **ပတ်ဝန်းကျင်** *pat-win-kyin*

environmental *(adj.)* **သဘာဝပတ်ဝန်းကျင်** *ta-bar-wa-pat-win-kyin*

environmentalism *(n.)* **ဝန်းကျင်ထိန်းသိမ်းရေးဝါဒ** *win-kyin-htain-thein-yay-wa-da*

environmentalist *(n.)* **ဝန်းကျင်ထိန်းသိမ်းရေးဝါဒီ** *win-kyin-htain-thein-yay-wa-di*

envisage *(v.)* **မှန်းကြည့်သည်** *man-kyi-the*

envision *(v.)* **တစ်စုံတစ်ယောက်စိတ်ထဲဝင်ကြည့်သည်** *ta-sone-ta-yauk-seik-htae-win-kyi-the*

envoy *(n.)* **တမန်** *ta-man*

envy *(v.)* **အားကျသည်** *arr-kya-the*

enzyme *(n.)* **အင်ဇိုင်း** *in-zai*

enzymic *(adj.)* **အင်ဇိုင်းနှင့်ဆိုင်သော** in-zai-nint-sai-taw

eon *(n.)* **ကပ်ကမ္ဘာ** *kat-ka-bar*

ephemera *(n.)* **ပေါပြင်ပစ္စည်း** *paw-pin-pyit-see*

ephemeral *(adj.)* **ပေါပြင်** *paw-pin*

ephemeric *(adj.)* **ပေါပြင်** *paw-pin*

epic *(n.)* **သံပိုင်းမော်ကွန်း** *tan-pai-maw-gun*

epical *(adj.)* **ချီးကျူးမှတ်တမ်းတင်ထိုက်သော** *chee-kyu-mat-tan-tin-htike-taw*

epicene *(adj.)* **လိင်နှစ်မျိုးလုံးလက္ခဏာရှိသော** *lain-na-myo-lone-lat-kha-nar-shi-taw*

epicentre *(n.)* **ငလျင်ဗဟိုချက်** *nga-lin-ba-ho-chat*

epicure *(n.)* **အစားကောင်းကြိုက်သူ** *a-sar-kaung-kyaik-taw*

epicurean *(adj.)* **စားကောင်းသောက်ဖွယ်အလျှံပယ်ဖြစ်သော** *sar-kaung-thaut-phwal-a-hlyan-pal-phit-taw*

epidemic *(n.)* **ကူးစက်ရောဂါ** ku-sat-yaw-gar

epidural *(n.)* **ဂျူရာမေတာအပြင်ဘက်တွင်ရှိသော** *ju-ra-may-ta-a-pyin-bat-twin-shi-taw*

epiglottis *(n.)* **အသံအိုးဖုံး** *a-tan-o-phone*

epigram *(n.)* **ဟာသစာတိုစာစ** *har-ta-sar-toe-sar-sa*

epilate *(v.)* **ခန္ဓာကိုယ်မှ အမွေးကိုဖယ်ရှားသည်** khan-dar-koe-ma-a-mway-ko-phal-shar-the

epilepsy *(n.)* **အတက်ရောဂါ** *a-tat-yaw-gar*

epileptic *(adj.)* **တက်သော** *tat-taw*

epilogue *(n.)* **နိဂုံး** *ni-gone*

epiphany *(n.)* ခရစ်တော်ထံ မက်ဂီလာခြင်း အထိမ်းအမှတ်ပွဲ *kha-yit-taw-htan-mag-gi-lar-chin-a-htain-a-mat-pwe*
episode *(n.)* ဖြစ်ရပ်၊ အပိုင်း phit-yat, a-pai
epitaph *(n.)* သင်္ချိုင်းစာ *thin-gyai-sar*
epitome *(n.)* စံနမူနာ san-na-mu-nar
epoch *(n.)* ခေတ် *khit*
epoxy *(n.)* အီပေါက်စီအစေး e-pauk-si-a-say
equal *(n.)* တူညီခြင်း *tu-nyi-chin*
equal *(adj.)* တူညီသော *tu-nyi-taw*
equal *(v.)* တူညီသည် *tu-nyu-the*
equality *(n.)* တန်းတူမှု *tan-tu-mu*
equalize *(v.)* တူညီအောင် လုပ်သည် *tu-nyu-aung-lote-the*
equate *(v.)* တန်းတူထားသည် *tan-tu-htar-the*
equation *(n.)* ညီမျှခြင်း *nyi-mya-chin*
equator *(n.)* အီကွေတာ *e-quay-tar*
equilateral *(adj.)* သုံးနားညီ *tone-nar-nyi*
equinox *(n.)* နေ့တာနှင့် ညတာ ညီမျှသော ကာလ *nay-tar-nint-nya-tar-nyi-mya-taw-mar-la*
equip *(v.)* တပ်ဆင်သည် *tat-sin-the*
equipment *(n.)* ကိရိယာ ka-yi-yar
equitable *(adj.)* သာတူညီမျှဖြစ်သော *tar-tu-nyi-mya-phit-taw*
equivalent *(adj.)* ညီမျှသော *nyi-mya-taw*
equivocal *(adj.)* မပြတ်မသားမရေမရာ *ma-phat-ma-tar-ma-yay-ma-yar*
era *(n.)* ခေတ် *khit*
eradicate *(v.)* အမြစ်ဖြတ်သည် *a-myit-phat-the*
eradication *(n.)* အမြစ်ဖြတ်ခြင်း *a-myit-phat-chin*
eradicator *(n.)* အမြစ်ဖြတ်သူ *a-myit-phat-thu*
erase *(v.)* ဖျက်သည် *phat-the*
eraser *(n.)* ခဲဖျက် *khae-phat*
erect *(v.)* ထောင်မတ်သည် *htaung-mat-the*
erectile *(adj.)* ထောင်မတ်နိုင်သော *htaung-mat-naing-taw*
erection *(n.)* ထောင်မတ်ခြင်း *htaung-mat-chin*
erode *(v.)* တိုက်စားသည် *tite-sar-the*
erosion *(n.)* တိုက်စားခြင်း tite-sar-chin
erosive *(adj.)* တိုက်စားသော *tite-sar-taw*
erotic *(adj.)* ကာမရာဂနိုးဆွသော *kar-ma-yar-ga-noe-swa-taw*
erotica *(n.)* အညှိအဟောက် *a-hnyi-a-haut*
eroticism *(n.)* ရမ္မက်နှိုးဆွမှု yan-mat-hnoe-swa-mu
eroticize *(v.)* ရမ္မက်နှိုးဆွသည် *yan-mat-hnoe-swa-the*
err *(v.)* မှားသည် *hmar-the*
errand *(n.)* လက်တိုလက်တောင်း *lat-to-lat-taung*
erroneous *(adj.)* မမှန်ကန်သော *ma-hman-kan-taw*
error *(n.)* အမှား *a-hmar*
erupt *(v.)* ပေါက်ကွဲသည် *pauk-kwal-the*
eruption *(n.)* ပေါက်ကွဲခြင်း *pauk-kwal-chin*
escalate *(v.)* အရှိန်မြှင့်သည်၊ မြင့်တက်သည် a-shain-hmyint-the, myint-tat-the
escalator *(n.)* စက်လှေကား *sat-hlay-kar*
escapability *(n.)* လွတ်မြောက်နိုင်စွမ်း *lut-myauk-naing-swan*
escapable *(adj.)* လွတ်မြောက်နိုင်သော lut-myauk-naing-taw

escape *(n.)* **လွတ်မြောက်ခြင်း** *lut-myauk-chin*

escapee *(n.)* **ထောင်ပြေး** htaung-pyay

escapism *(n.)* **လွတ်မြောက်ရောက်ရှိခြင်း** *lut-myauk-yauk-shi-chin*

escapist *(n.)* **လွတ်မြောက်ရောက်ရှိသူ** *lut-myauk-yauk-shi-thu*

escapology *(n.)* **လွတ်မြောက်မှုနည်းပညာ** *lut-myauk-mu-nee-pyin-nyar*

escargot *(n.)* **ခရုအပါအဝင် ပြင်သစ်ဟင်းလျာတစ်ခွက်** *kha-yu-a-par-a-win-pyin-tit-hin-lyar-ta-khwat*

eschew *(v.)* **ရှောင်ရှားသည်** *shaung-shar-the*

eschewment *(n.)* **ရှောင်ရှားခြင်း** shaung-shar-chin

escort *(v.)* **စောင့်ရှောက်သည်၊ လိုက်ပို့သည်** *saunt-shaut-the, lite-poe-the*

escorted *(adj.)* **လိုက်ပါစောင့်ရှောက်သော** *lite-par-saunt-shaut-taw*

escrow *(v.)* **ငွေကြိုတင်ထည့်ထားသည်** *ngwe-kyo-tin-htae-htar-the*

esophageal *(adj.)* **အစာရေမြို ပြွန်နှင့် ဆိုင်သော** *a-sar-yay-myo-pyun-nint-sai-taw*

esoteric *(adj.)* **နက်နဲသော** *nat-nae-taw*

esoterism *(n.)* **ယုံကြည်မှု၊ ဘာသာတရား၏ အတွင်းပုံစံ** *yone-kyi-mu, bar-tar-ta-yar-ei-a-twin-pon-san*

espace *(n.)* **လေဟာနယ်** *lay-har-nal*

especial *(adj.)* **အထူး** *a-htoo*

especially *(adv.)* **အထူးသဖြင့်** *a-htoo-ta-phit*

espouse *(v.)* **ထောက်ခံသည်** *htauk-khan-the*

essay *(n.)* **အက်ဆေး၊ စာတမ်းတို၊ စာစီစာကုံး** at-say, sar-tan-toe, sar-si-sar-kone

essayist *(n.)* **စာတမ်းရှင်** *sar-tan-shin*

essence *(n.)* **အနှစ်သာရ** a-nit-tar-ya

essential *(adj.)* **မရှိမဖြစ် အရေးပါသော** *ma-shi-ma-phit-a-yay-par-taw*

establish *(v.)* **တည်ထောင်သည်** *the-htaung-the*

establishment *(n.)* **တည်ထောင်ခြင်း** *the-htaung-chin*

estate *(n.)* **ခြံဝင်း** *chan-win*

estate agent *(n.)* **အိမ်ခြံမြေအကျိုးဆောင်** ain-chan-myay-a-kyo-saung

esteem *(n.)* **အထင်ကြီးခြင်း** *a-htin-kyi-chin*

esteem *(v.)* **အထင်ကြီးသည်** *a-htin-kyi-the*

estimate *(n.)* **ခန့်မှန်းခြေ** *khant-man-chay*

estimate *(v.)* **ခန့်မှန်းသည်** *khant-man-the*

estimation *(n.)* **ထင်မြင်ယူဆချက်** htin-myin-yu-sa-chat

estimative *(adj.)* **အကြမ်းဖျင်းခန့်မှန်းဖြစ်သော** *a-kyan-phin-khant-man-phit-taw*

estragon *(n.)* **အာရာဂွမ်ပင်** ar-yar-gwin-pin

estrange *(v.)* **ခပ်တန်းတန်းဖြစ်သွားသည်** khat-tan-tan-phit-twar-the

estranged *(adj.)* **ခွာပြဲနေသော** khwar-pyal-nay-thaw

estrogen *(n.)* **အီစတိုဂျင်ဟော်မုန်း** *e-sa-to-gyin-haw-hmone*

estuary *(n.)* **မြစ်ဝ** *myit-wa*

etcetera *(adv.)* **အစရှိသဖြင့်** *a-sa-shi-ta-phit*

etch *(v.)* **သတ္တုပြားပေါ်တွင် ငရဲမီးဖြင့် စား၍ ပုံဖော်သည်** *tat-tu-pyar-paw-twin-nga-ye-mee-phit-sar-ywe-pon-phaw-the*

etched *(adj.)* **သတ္တုပြားပေါ်တွင် ငရဲမီးဖြင့် စား၍ ပုံဖော်သော** tat-tu-pyar-paw-twin-nga-ye-mee-phit-sar-ywe-pon-phaw-taw

etching *(adj.)* **သတ္တုပြားပေါ်တွင် ငရဲမီးဖြင့် စား၍ ပုံဖော်သော အတတ်ပညာ** tat-tu-pyar-paw-twin-nga-ye-mee-phit-sar-ywe-pon-phaw-taw-a-tat-pyin-nyar
eternal *(adj.)* **အဆုံးအစမရှိ** *a-sone-a-sa-ma-shi*
eternalize *(v.)* **ထာဝရဖြစ်အောင် လုပ်သည်** *htar-wa-ya-phit-aung-lote-the*
eternally *(adv.)* **ထာဝရ** *htar-wa-ya*
eternity *(n.)* **ထာဝရ** *htar-wa-ya*
ether *(n.)* **အီသာ** *e-thar*
ethical *(adj.)* **ကျင့်ဝတ်နှင့် ဆိုင်သော** *kyint-wit-nint-sai-taw*
ethics *(n.)* **ကျင့်ဝတ်** kyint-wit
ethnic *(adj.)* **လူမျိုးစုနှင့် ဆိုင်သော** *lu-myo-su-nint-sai-taw*
ethnicity *(n.)* **လူမျိုးစု** *lu-myo-su*
ethos *(n.)* **အသိုင်းအဝိုင်း** *a-thai-a-wai*
etiquette *(n.)* **ကျင့်ဝတ်ထုံးတမ်း** *kyint-wit-htone-tann*
etymology *(n.)* **ရင်းမြစ်ဗေဒ** *yin-myit-bay-da*
eucalypt *(n.)* **ယူကလစ်ပင်** *u-ka-lit-pin*
eunuch *(n.)* **မိန်းမစိုး** *mein-ma-soe*
euphemistic *(adj.)* **စကားလှသော** *sa-kar-hla-taw*
euphoria *(n.)* **ဝမ်းသာပီတိ** *wan-tar-pi-ti*
eureka *(int.)* **ဟူးရေး** *huu-yay*
euthanize *(v.)* **သက်သောင့်သက်သာ သေဆုံးခွင့်ပေးသည်** tat-taunt-tat-tar-tay-sone-khwint-pay-the
evacuate *(v.)* **ဘေးကင်းရာသို့ ပြောင်းရွှေ့ပေးသည်** bay-kin-yar-tho-shway-pyaung-pay-the
evacuation *(n.)* **ဘေးကင်းရာသို့ ပြောင်းရွှေ့ပေးခြင်း** bay-kin-yar-tho-shway-pyaung-pay-chin
evade *(v.)* **ရှောင်တိမ်းသည်** *shaung-tein-the*
evaluate *(v.)* **အကဲဖြတ်သည်** a-kae-phat-the
evangel *(n.)* **ခရစ်ယာန်ဧဝံဂေလိတရား** *kha-yit-yan-a-win-gay-li-ta-yar*
evangelic *(adj.)* **ခရစ်ယာန်ဧဝံဂေလိတရားနှင့် ဆိုင်သော** *kha-yit-yan-a-win-gay-li-ta-yar-nint-sai-taw*
evaporate *(v.)* **အငွေ့ပြသည်** *a-ngae-pya-the*
evasion *(n.)* **ရှောင်တိမ်းမှု** *shaung-tein-mu*
evasive *(adj.)* **မပွင့်လင်းသော** *ma-pwint-lin-taw*
even *(adj.)* **ညီညာသော** *nyi-nyar-taw*
evening *(n.)* **ညနေခင်း** *nya-nay-khin*
evenly *(adv.)* **ညီမျှစွာ** *nyi-mya-swar*
event *(n.)* **အဖြစ်အပျက်** *a-phit-a-pyat*
eventually *(adv.)* **နောက်ဆုံးမှာ** naut-sone-mar
ever *(adv.)* **တစ်ချိန်ချိန်တွင်၊ အမြဲ** *ta-chain-chain-twin, a-myae*
everglade *(n.)* **စိမ့်မြေ** *saint-myay*
evergreen *(adj.)* **အမြဲစိမ်း** *a-myae-sein*
everlasting *(adj.)* **ထာဝရ** *htar-wa-ya*
ever-ready *(adj.)* **အမြဲ အဆင်သင့်** *a-myae-a-sin-tint*
evert *(v.)* **အပြင်ဘက်ရွှေ့သည်** *a-pyin-bat-shway-the*
every *(adj.)* **အားလုံး၊ တိုင်း** arr-lone, tine
everybody *(pron.)* **လူတိုင်း** *lu-tine*
everyday *(adj.)* **နေ့တိုင်း** *nay-tine*

everyone *(pron.)* **တစ်စုံတစ်ယောက်** *ta-sone-ta-yauk*
everything *(pron.)* **တစ်စုံတစ်ခု** *ta-sone-ta-khu*
everywhere *(pron.)* **တစ်နေရာရာ** *ta-nay-yar-yar*
eve-teasing *(n.)* **လိင်ပိုင်းဆိုင်ရာ အနှောင့်အယှက်ပေးခြင်း** *lain-pai-sai-yar-a-naut-a-shat-pay-chin*
evict *(v.)* **နှင်ထုတ်သည်** *hnin-htoke-the*
eviction *(n.)* **နှင်ထုတ်ခြင်း** *hnin-htoke-chin*
evictor *(n.)* **နှင်ထုတ်သူ** hnin-htoke-thu
evidence *(n.)* **သက်သေ** *thet-tay*
evident *(adj.)* **ပေါ်လွင်သော** *paw-lwin-taw*
evil *(adj.)* **ယုတ်မာသော** *yoke-mar-taw*
evil *(n.)* **ဆိုးယုတ်ခြင်း** soe-yoke-chin
evince *(v.)* **စိတ်ထားကို ပြသည်** *seik-htar-ko-pya-the*
eviscerate *(v.)* **ကလီစာကို ထုတ်သည်** *ka-li-zar-ko-htoke-the*
evisceration *(n.)* **ကလီစာကို ထုတ်ခြင်း** *ka-li-zar-ko-htoke-chin*
evitability *(n.)* **ရှောင်တိမ်းနိုင်သော အခြေအနေ** *shaung-tain-nai-taw-a-chay-a-nay*
evocate *(v.)* **ပြန်လည် အမှတ်ရစေသည်** *pyan-lal-a-mat-ya-say-the*
evocation *(n.)* **ပြန်လည် အမှတ်ရစေခြင်း** *pyan-lal-a-mat-ya-say-chin*
evocative *(adj.)* **ပြန်လည် အမှတ်ရစေသော** *pyan-lal-a-mat-ya-say-taw*
evoke *(v.)* **ဖြစ်ပေါ်စေသည်** *phit-pyaw-say-the*
evolution *(n.)* **ဆင့်ကဲဖြစ်စဉ်** *sint-kae-phit-sin*
evolutionary *(adv.)* **ဆင့်ကဲဖြစ်စဉ်နှင့် ဆိုင်သော** *sint-kae-phit-sin-nint-sai-taw*
evolve *(v.)* **ပြောင်းလဲ ဖြစ်ပေါ်လာသည်** *pyaung-lal-phit-paw-lar-the*
ewe *(n.)* **သိုးမ** *thoe-ma*
exact *(adj.)* **တိကျသော** ti-kya-taw
exactly *(adv.)* **တိတိကျကျ** ti-ti-kya-kya
exaggerate *(v.)* **ချဲ့ကားပြောသည်** chae-kar-pyaw-the
exaggeration *(n.)* **ချဲ့ကားခြင်း** *chae-kar-chin*
exalt *(v.)* **မြှင့်တင်သည်** *hmyint-tin-the*
examination *(n.)* **စာမေးပွဲ** *sar-may-pwe*
examine *(v.)* **စစ်ဆေးသည်** sit-say-the
examinee *(n.)* **ဖြေဆိုသူ** *phyay-soe-thu*
examiner *(n.)* **စာစစ်** *sar-sit*
example *(n.)* **ဥပမာ** *oo-pa-mar*
excavate *(v.)* **တူးဖော်သည်** *tu-phaw-the*
excavation *(n.)* **တူးဖော်မှု** *tu-phaw-mu*
exceed *(v.)* **ပိုလွန်သည်** *poe-lun-the*
excel *(v.)* **ထူးချွန်သည်** *htoo-chon-the*
excellence *(n.)* **အကောင်းဆုံး** *a-kaung-sone*
excellency *(n.)* **သံအမတ်ကြီးခင်ဗျား** *tan-a-mat-kyi-khin-myar*
excellent *(adj.)* **အကောင်းဆုံးဖြစ်သော** a-kaung-sone-phit-taw
except *(v.)* **ချန်လှပ်သည်** *chan-hlat-the*
exception *(n.)* **ချွင်းချက်** *chwin-chat*
exceptional *(adj.)* **ထူးခြားသော** *htoo-char-taw*
excerpt *(n.)* **ကောက်နုတ်ချက်** *kauk-note-chat*
excess *(adj.)* **ပိုသော** *po-taw*

excess baggage *(n.)* ဝန်ပို *win-po*

excessive *(adj.)* လွန်ကဲသော *lun-kae-taw*

exchange *(n.)* လဲလှယ်ခြင်း *lae-lal-chin*

exchange rate *(n.)* ငွေလဲနှုန်း *ngwe-lal-hnone*

excise *(n.)* ယစ်မျိုးခွန် *yit-myo-khun*

excite *(v.)* စိတ်လှုပ်ရှားစေသည် *sate-hloat-shar-say-the*

exclaim *(v.)* အံ့အားသင့်စွာ ပြောသည် *ant-arr-tint-swar-pyaw-the*

exclamation *(n.)* အာမေဍိတ် *arr-may-daik*

exclude *(v.)* ဖယ်ရှားသည် *phal-shar-the*

exclusive *(adj.)* သီးသန့်ဖြစ်သော *the-tant-phit-taw*

excommunicate *(v.)* ခရစ်ယာန်အသင်းတော်ဝင်အဖြစ်မှ ကြဉ်သည် *kha-yit-yan-a-tin-taw-win-a-phit-ma-kyin-the*

excursion *(n.)* အပျော်ခရီး *a-pyaw-kha-yee*

excuse *(v.)* ခွင့်ပြုသည် *khwint-pyu-the*

execute *(v.)* ကွပ်မျက်သည် *kwat-myat-the*

execution *(n.)* သေဒဏ်စီရင်ခြင်း *tay-dan-si-yin-chin*

executioner *(n.)* အာဏာပါးကွက်သား *ar-nar-par-kwat-tar*

executive *(adj.)* စီရင်ဆုံးဖြတ်ခွင့် အာဏာရှိသော *si-yin-sone-phat-khwint-ar-nar-shi-taw*

exemplar *(n.)* စံပြ *san-pya*

exempt *(v.)* လွတ်ငြိမ်းခွင့်ရသည် *lut-nyein-khwint-ya-the*

exercise *(n.)* လေ့ကျင့်ခန်း *lay-kyint-khan*

exfoliate *(v.)* သစ်ပင်မှ အရွက်ခြွေသည် *thit-pin-ma-a-ywet-chway-the*

exhaust *(v.)* ပင်ပန်းနွမ်းနယ်သည် pin-pan-nwan-nal-the

exhibit *(n.)* ပြတိုက်ပစ္စည်း *pya-tite-pyit-see*

exhibition *(n.)* ခင်းကျင်းပြသခြင်း *khin-kyin-pya-ta-chin*

exile *(n.)* ပြည်နှင်ဒဏ်ခံရခြင်း *pyi-hnin-dan-khan-ya-chin*

exist *(v.)* တည်ရှိသည် *the-shi-the*

existence *(n.)* တည်ရှိခြင်း *the-shi-chin*

existential *(adj.)* လူ့ဘဝနှင့် ဆိုင်သော *lu-ba-wa-nint-sai-taw*

existentialism *(n.)* အတ္တဘဝအမှန်ဝါဒ *at-ta-ba-wa-a-man-wa-da*

exit *(v.)* ထွက်ခွာသည် *htwat-khwar-the*

exotic *(adj.)* တိုင်းတစ်ပါးမှ လာသော *tai-ta-par-ma-lar-taw*

expand *(v.)* ကျယ်ပြန့်သည် *kyal-pyant-the*

expansion *(n.)* ကျယ်ပြန့်လာခြင်း *kyal-pyant-lar-chin*

ex-parte *(adv.)* တစ်ဖက်တည်းမှ ယူလျက် *ta-phat-tae-ma-yu-lyat*

expect *(v.)* မျှော်လင့်သည် *hmyaw-lint-the*

expectation *(n.)* မျှော်လင့်ချက် *hmyaw-lint-chat*

expedient *(adj.)* သင့်တော်လျော်ကန်သော *tint-taw-lyaw-kan-taw*

expedite *(v.)* အလုပ်တွင်စေသည် *a-lote-twin-say-the*

expedition *(n.)* စူးစမ်းလေ့လာရေးခရီး *su-san-lay-lar-yay-kha-yee*

expel *(v.)* ထုတ်ပယ်သည် htoke-pal-the

expend *(v.)* သုံးစွဲသည် *tone-swal-the*

expenditure *(n.)* အသုံးစရိတ် *a-tone-sa-yeik*

expense *(n.)* စရိတ် *sa-yeik*

expensive *(adj.)* ဈေးကြီးသော *zay-kyi-taw*
experience *(n.)* အတွေ့အကြုံ *a-tway-a-kyone*
experiment *(n.)* လက်တွေ့သုတေသန *lat-thway-thu-tay-ta-na*
expert *(adj.)* ကျွမ်းကျင် *kywan-kyin*
expert *(n.)* ကျွမ်းကျင်သူ *kywan-kyin-thu*
expire *(v.)* သက်တမ်းကုန်ဆုံးသည် *thet-tan-kone-sone-the*
expiry *(n.)* သက်တမ်းကုန်ဆုံးခြင်း thet-tan-kone-sone-chin
explain *(v.)* ရှင်းပြသည် *shin-pya-the*
explanation *(n.)* ရှင်းပြချက် *shin-pya-chat*
explicit *(adj.)* တိကျပြတ်သားသော ti-kya-pyat-tar-taw
explode *(v.)* ပေါက်ကွဲသည် *pauk-kwal-the*
exploit *(n.)* စွန့်စားခန်း *sunt-sar-khan*
exploration *(n.)* ရှာဖွေခြင်း *shar-phwe-chin*
explore *(v.)* ရှာဖွေခြင်း *shar-phwe-chin*
explosion *(n.)* ပေါက်ကွဲခြင်း *pauk-kwal-chin*
explosive *(adj.)* ပေါက်ကွဲတတ်သော *pauk-kwal-tat-taw*
exponent *(n.)* ထောက်ခံအားပေးသူ *htauk-khan-arr-pay-thu*
export *(v.)* ပြည်ပသို့ ကုန်တင်ပို့သည် *pyi-pa-poe-kone-tin-poe-the*
export *(n.)* ပြည်ပပို့ကုန် *pyi-pa-poe-kone*
expose *(v.)* ပြသသည် *pya-ta-the*
express *(v.)* ဖော်ပြသည် *phaw-pya-the*
expression *(n.)* မျက်နှာထား၊ ဖော်ပြခြင်း *myat-nar-htar, phaw-pya-chin*
expressive *(adj.)* အသက်ပါသော a-thet-par-taw
expulsion *(n.)* နှင်ထုတ်ခြင်း *hnin-htoke-chin*
exquisite *(adj.)* အလွန်လှပ သိမ်မွေ့သော *a-lun-hla-pa-thein-mway-taw*
exquisitive *(adj.)* စူးစမ်းသော *sue-san-taw*
extend *(v.)* ချဲ့သည်၊ ဆန့်သည် chae-the, sant-the
extent *(n.)* ပမာဏ၊ အတိုင်းအတာ pa-mar-na, a-tine-a-tar
external *(adj.)* ပြင်ပနှင့် ဆိုင်သော *pyin-pa-nint-sai-taw*
extinct *(adj.)* မျိုးသုဉ်းသွားသော *myo-tone-twar-taw*
extinguish *(v.)* ငြိမ်းသည်၊ ကွယ်ပျောက်စေသည် *nyein-the, kwal-pyauk-say-the*
extol *(v.)* ထောပနာပြုသည် *htaw-pa-nar-pyu-the*
extortion *(n.)* ခြိမ်းခြောက်၍ ငွေညှစ်ခြင်း *chein-chauk-ywe-ngwe-hnyit-chin*
extra *(adj.)* အပို *a-po*
extract *(v.)* နှိုက်ယူသည်၊ ကောက်နုတ်ဖော်ပြသည် *hnike-yu-the, kauk-note-phaw-pya-the*
extrajudicial *(adj.)* တရားရုံးအာဏာပြင်ပတွင် ရှိသော *ta-yar-yone-ar-nar-pyin-pa-twin-shi-taw*
extramarital *(adj.)* ဖောက်ပြန်သော *hpauk-pyan-taw*
extranet *(n.)* အင်တာနက် *inn-tar-net*
extraordinary *(adj.)* သာမန်ထက် လွန်ကဲသော *tar-man-htet-lun-kae-taw*
extrapolate *(v.)* တွက်ချက် ခန့်မှန်းသည် twat-chat-khant-man-the
extrapolation *(n.)* တွက်ချက် ခန့်မှန်းခြင်း *twat-chat-khant-man-chin*

extraspecial *(adj.)* **ထူးကဲကောင်းမွန်သော** *htoo-kae-kaung-mon-taw*
extraterrestrial *(n.)* **တစ်ခြားကမ္ဘာမှ သက်ရှိများ** ta-char-ka-bar-ma-thet-shi-myar
extravagance *(n.)* **ဖြုန်းတီးမှု** *hpyone-tee-mu*
extravagant *(adj.)* **အသုံးအဖြုန်းကြီးသော** *a-tone-a-hpyone-kyi-taw*
extreme *(adj.)* **ထူးကဲသော၊ ပြင်းထန်သော** *htoo-kae-taw, pyin-htan-taw*
extremist *(n.)* **အစွန်းရောက်ဝါဒီ** *a-sun-yauk-war-di*
extremity *(n.)* **အစွန်အဖျား** *a-sun-a-pyar*
extricate *(v.)* **ကယ်ထုတ်သည်** *kal-htoke-the*
extrinsic *(adj.)* **နဂိုရှိရင်း မဟုတ်သော** *na-go-shi-yin-ma-hoke-taw*
extrinsically *(adv.)* **မူလအတိုင်းမဟုတ်သော ပုံစံဖြင့်** *mu-la-a-tine-ma-hoke-taw-pon-san-phint*
extrovert *(n.)* **ဘွင်းဘွင်းပျော်ပျော်သမား** bwin-bwin-pyaw-pyaw-ta-mar
exude *(v.)* **ထွက်သည်** *htwat-the*
exult *(v.)* **ပျော်ရွှင်မြူးတူးသည်** *pyaw-shwin-my-tu-the*
exultant *(adj.)* **မြူးတူးပျော်ရွှင်နေသော** *my-tu-pyaw-shin-nay-taw*
eye *(n.)* **မျက်လုံး** *myat-lone*
eyeball *(n.)* **မျက်ဆန်** myat-san
eyebrow *(n.)* **မျက်ခုံး** *myat-khone*
eyecatcher *(n.)* **အမြင်တွင် ဆွဲဆောင်မှု ရှိသော သူ၊ အရာဝတ္ထု** *a-myin-twin-swal-saung-mu-shi-taw-thu-a-yar-wut-htu*
eye-catching *(adj.)* **ထင်းခနဲမြင်သာသော** *htin-kha-nae-myin-tar-taw*
eyeglass *(n.)* **မျက်မှန်** myat-man
eyelash *(n.)* **မျက်တောင်** myat-taung
eyelet *(n.)* **နဖားပေါက်** na-phar-pauk
eyelid *(n.)* **မျက်ခွံ** *myat-khun*
eyeliner *(n.)* **လိုင်နာတောင့်** *lai-nar-taunt*
eye-opener *(n.)* **အမြင်ကျယ်စေသော အတွေ့အကြုံ** *a-myin-kyal-say-taw-a-tway-a-kyone*
eyespot *(n.)* **ဒေါင်းမြီးရှိ မျက်လုံးကဲ့သို့ အမှတ်** *daung-myi-shi-myat-lone-kae-tho-a-mat*
eyewash *(n.)* **ပေါက်တတ်ကရစကား** *pauk-tat-ka-ya-sa-kar*

F

fable *(n.)* **ဒဏ္ဍာရီပုံပြင်** *dan-dar-yi-pone-pyin*
fabric *(n.)* **အထည်သား** *a-htal-tar*
fabricate *(v.)* **လုပ်ကြံပြောဆိုသည်** *lote-kyan-pyaw-so-the*
fabrication *(n.)* **လုပ်ကြံစွပ်စွဲခြင်း** lote-kyan-sut-swal-chin
fabulous *(adj.)* **အံ့ဖွယ်** *ant-phwal*
facade *(n.)* **အဆောက်အအုံမျက်နှာစာ** *a-saut-a-ohn-myat-nar-sar*
face *(n.)* **မျက်နှာ** *myat-nar*
Face cream *(n.)* **မိုးပွင့်** *moe-pwint*
face mask *(n.)* **မျက်နှာအကာ** *myat-nar-a-kar*
facelift *(n.)* **မျက်နှာ နုပျိုအောင် ခွဲစိတ်ကုသမှု** myat-nar-nu-pyo-aung-khwal-seik-ku-ta-mu
facet *(v.)* **မျက်နှာပြင်ညီဖြတ်သည်** *myat-nar-pyin-nyi-phat-the*

facial *(adj.)* **မျက်နှာနှင့် ဆိုင်သော** *myat-nar-nint-sai-taw*
facile *(adj.)* **အလေးအနက် မရှိသော** *a-lay-a-net-ma-shi-taw*
facilitate *(v.)* **လွယ်ကူချောမောစေသည်** *lwal-khu-chaw-maw-say-the*
facilitation *(n.)* **လွယ်ကူချောမောစေခြင်း** *lwal-khu-chaw-maw-say-chin*
facility *(n.)* **ပါရမီ၊ အထောက်အပံ့ပစ္စည်း** *pa-ra-mi, a-htauk-a-pnat-pyit-see*
facsimile *(n.)* **မိတ္တူ၊ ပုံတူ** *meik-tu, pon-tu*
fact *(n.)* **အချက်အလက်** *a-chat-a-lat*
faction *(n.)* **အုပ်စု** *oak-su*
factious *(adj.)* **အုပ်စုကြောင့်ဖြစ်သော** *oak-su-kyaunt-phit-taw*
factor *(n.)* **အကြောင်းခံ** a-kyaung-khan
factory *(n.)* **စက်ရုံ** sat-yone
faculty *(n.)* **မဟာဌာန** ma-har-htar-na
fad *(n.)* **ပေါ်ပင်** paw-pin
fade *(v.)* **အရောင်လွင့်သည်၊ မှိန်သွားသည်** *a-yaung-lwint-the, mein-twar-the*
faggot *(n.)* **ထင်းစည်း** *htin-see*
Fahrenheit *(adj.)* **ဖာရင်ဟိုက်** *phar-yin-hike*
fail *(n.)* **ကျရှုံးခြင်း** *kya-shone-chin*
failure *(n.)* **အရှုံး** *a-shone*
faint *(v.)* **သတိလစ်သည်** *ta-di-lit-the*
fair *(adj.)* **တရားမျှတသော** *ta-yar-mya-ta-taw*
fair game *(n.)* **ပြောင်စရာ၊ နောက်စရာ** *pyaung-sa-yar, naut-sa-yar*
fair trade *(n.)* **မျှတသော ကုန်သွယ်မှု** *mya-ta-taw-kone-twal-mu*
fairground *(n.)* **ပွဲခင်း** *pwe-khin*
fairly *(adv.)* **မျှတစွာ** *mya-ta-swar*
fairy *(n.)* **နတ်သမီး** *nat-ta-mee*
faith *(n.)* **ယုံကြည်မှု** *yone-kyi-mu*
faithful *(adj.)* **သစ္စာရှိသော** *tit-sar-shi-taw*
fake *(n.)* **အတု** *a-tu*
falcon *(n.)* **သိမ်းငှက်** thein-hnget
fall *(n.)* **ကျခြင်း** *kya-chin*
fallacy *(n.)* **အတွေးမှားခြင်း** *a-tway-mar-chin*
fallen *(n.)* **ကျခြင်း** kya-chin
fallout *(n.)* **ရေဒီယိုဓာတ်သတ္တိကြွအမှုန်များ** ra-di-yo-dat-tat-ti-kwa-a-hmone-myar
fallow *(v.)* **ထည့်ထိုးသည်၊ ထွန်ယက်သည်** htae-htoe-the, htun-yat-the
falls *(n.)* **ရေတံခွန်** *yay-tan-khun*
false *(adj.)* **မှားသော** *hmar-taw*
falsehood *(n.)* **မုသား၊ အမှား** mu-tar, a-mar
falsetto *(n.)* **သီချင်းဆိုရာတွင် အလွန်မြင့်သော အသံ** thi-chin-so-yar-twin-a-lun-myint-taw-a-tan
falsification *(n.)* **မမှန်မကန် ပြုလုပ်ထားမှု** ma-hman-ma-kan-pyu-lote-htar-mu
falsify *(v.)* **လိမ်သည်** lain-the
falter *(v.)* **အခြေအနေယိုင်သည်** *a-chay-a-nay-yai-the*
fame *(n.)* **ဂုဏ်သတင်း** *gone-ta-din*
familiar *(adj.)* **ရင်းနှီးသော** *yin-hnee-taw*
family *(n.)* **မိသားစု** *mi-tar-su*
famine *(n.)* **ငတ်မွတ်ခြင်းဘေးကြီး** *ngat-mut-chin-bay-gyi*
famous *(adj.)* **ကျော်ကြားသော** *kyaw-kyar-taw*
fan *(n.)* **ပန်ကာ** pan-kar
fanatic *(n.)* **အရူးအမူးဖြစ်သူ** *a-yu-a-mu-phit-thu*

fanciful *(adj.)* **စိတ်ကူးယဉ်တတ်သော** seik-ku-yin-tat-taw

fancy *(n.)* **စိတ်ကူး၊ ဖန်စီပစ္စည်း** *seik-ku, phan-si-pyit-see*

fantastic *(adj.)* **အလွန်ကောင်းသော** *a-lun-kaung-taw*

fantasy *(n.)* **စိတ်ကူးယဉ်အိပ်မက်** *seik-ku-yin-eain-mat*

far *(adv.)* **ဝေးဝေး** *way-way*

faraway *(adj.)* **ဝေးကွာသော** *way-kwar-taw*

farce *(n.)* **ဟာသသက်သက်** *har-tat-thet-thet*

fare *(n.)* **ယာဉ်စီးခ** *yin-see-kha*

farewell *(interj.)* **ခွဲခွာခါနီးနှုတ်ဆက်စကား** *kwal-kwar-khar-nee-note-set-sa-kar*

farm *(n.)* **စိုက်ပျိုးမွေးမြူရေးခြံ** *seik-pyo-mway-my-yay-chan*

farmaceutical *(adj.)* **စိုက်ပျိုးရေးဆေးနှင့်ဆိုင်သော** *seik-pyo-yay-say-nint-sai-taw*

farmer *(n.)* **လယ်သမား** *lal-ta-mar*

farmhouse *(n.)* **လယ်သမားနေအိမ်** *lal-ta-mar-nay-eain*

fascinate *(v.)* **စွဲမက်စေသည်** *swal-mat-say-the*

fascination *(n.)* **စွဲလမ်းခြင်း** *swal-lan-chin*

fashion *(n.)* **ဖက်ရှင်** *fas-shin*

fashionable *(adj.)* **ခေတ်ဆန်သော** *khit-san-taw*

fast *(v.)* **မြန်ဆန်သည်** *myan-san-the*

fast food *(n.)* **အသင့်စားအစားအစာ** a-tint-sar-a-sar-a-sar

fasten *(v.)* **ချည်နှောင်သည်** *chi-naung-the*

fat *(adj.)* **ဝသော** *wa-taw*

fatal *(adj.)* **သေစေနိုင်သော** *tay-say-nai-taw*

fatalism *(n.)* **ကံကြမ္မာပဓာနဝါဒ** *kan-kyan-mar-pa-dar-na-wa-da*

fatality *(n.)* **အသေအပျောက်** *a-tay-a-pyauk*

fate *(n.)* **ကံကြမ္မာ** *kan-kyan-mar*

father *(v.)* **ကလေးအဖေဖြစ်သည်** *ka-lay-a-hpay-phit-the*

fathom *(n.)* **ရေအနက်တစ်လံ** *yay-a-net-ta-lan*

fathom *(v.)* **နားလည်သဘောပေါက်သည်** *nar-lal-ta-baw-pauk-the*

fatigue *(n.)* **ပင်ပန်းနွမ်းနယ်မှု** pin-pan-nwan-nal-mu

faucet *(n.)* **ဘုံပိုင်ခေါင်း** bon-bai-gaung

fault *(n.)* **အမှား** a-hmar

faulty *(adj.)* **ချွတ်ယွင်းသော** *chwut-ywin-taw*

fauna *(n.)* **ဒေသရင်း တိရစ္ဆာန်** *day-ta-yin-ta-yeik-san*

favour *(n.)* **ထောက်ခံမှု** htauk-khan-mu

favour *(v.)* **ထောက်ခံသည်** *htauk-khan-the*

favourable *(adj.)* **ထောက်ခံသော၊ အလေးပေးသော** *htauk-khan-taw, a-lay-pay-taw*

favourite *(adj.)* **အကြိုက်ဆုံး** *a-kyaik-sone*

fax *(n.)* **ဖက်စ်** phat

fealty *(n.)* **သစ္စာစောင့်သိခြင်း** *tit-sar-saunt-ti-chin*

fear *(n.)* **ကြောက်ရွံ့ခြင်း** *kyauk-shunt-chin*

fearful *(adj.)* **ကြောက်စရာကောင်းသော** *kyauk-sa-yar-kaung-taw*

feasible *(adj.)* **ဖြစ်နိုင်သော** phit-naing-taw

feast *(n.)* **စားပွဲ** *za-pwe*

feat *(n.)* **စွမ်းဆောင်မှု** swan-saung-mu

feather *(n.)* **ငှက်မွေး** *ngat-mway*

feature *(n.)* **အင်္ဂါရပ်** in-gar-yat

febrile *(adj.)* **ပျားပန်းခပ်မှုဖြစ်သော** *pyar-pan-khat-mya-phit-taw*

February *(n.)* **ဖေဖော်ဝါရီလ** *hpay-pha-war-yee-la*

fecal *(adj.)* **မစင်နှင့် ဆိုင်သော** *ma-sin-nint-sai-taw*

feces *(n.)* **မစင်** *ma-sin*

fecund *(adj.)* **မျိုးပွားနိုင်သော** *myo-pwar-nai-taw*

fecundation *(n.)* **မျိုးပွားနိုင်ခြင်း** *myo-pwar-nai-chin*

federal *(adj.)* **ဖက်ဒရယ်နှင့် ဆိုင်သော** *fat-da-ral-nint-sai-taw*

federation *(n.)* **အဖွဲ့ချုပ်** *a-phwe-choke*

fee *(n.)* **ဝန်ဆောင်ခ** *win-saung-kha*

feeble *(adj.)* **အားနည်းသော၊ ချည့်နဲ့သော** *arr-nae-taw, chi-nae-taw*

feed *(n.)* **ကျွေးချိန်** *kyway-chein*

feel *(v.)* **ခံစားသည်** *khan-sar-the*

feeling *(n.)* **ခံစားခြင်း** *khan-sar-chin*

feign *(v.)* **ဟန်ဆောင်သည်** *han-saung-the*

felicitate *(v.)* **ဂုဏ်ပြုသည်** *gon-pyu-the*

felicitations *(int.)* **ချီးကျူးထောမနာသြဘာစကား** *chee-kyu-htaw-pa-nar-aw-bar-sa-gar*

felicity *(n.)* **ကျွမ်းကျင်မှု၊ ပျော်ရွှင်ခြင်း** *kyun-kyin-mu, pyaw-shwin-chin*

feline *(adj.)* **ကြောင်ကဲ့သို့သော** *kyaung-kae-tho-taw*

felinity *(n.)* **ကြောင်ကဲ့သို့ဖြစ်ခြင်း** *kyaung-kae-tho-phit-chin*

fell *(v.)* **ခုတ်လှဲသည်** *kote-hlae-the*

fellatio *(n.)* **လိင်တံကို စုပ်၍ နိုးကြွစေသည်** *lain-tan-ko-sote-ywe-noe-kwa-say-the*

fellow *(n.)* **အဖော်၊ အပေါင်းအသင်း** *a-hpaw, a-paung-a-tin*

fellowship *(n.)* **ဖော်ရွေစွာ ဆက်ဆံခြင်း၊ သုတေသန ထောက်ပံ့ကြေး** hpaw-yway-swar-sat-san-chin, thu-tay-ta-na-htauk-pant-kyay

felony *(n.)* **ကြီးလေးသော ပြစ်မှု** *kyi-lay-taw-pyit-mu*

female *(n.)* **အမ** *a-ma*

feminine *(adj.)* **မိန်းမဆန်သော** *mein-ma-san-taw*

feminism *(n.)* **အမျိုးသမီးဝါဒ** a-myo-ta-mee-wa-da

feminist *(adj.)* **အမျိုးသမီးဝါဒကို ထောက်ခံသော** a-myo-ta-mee-wa-da-ko-htauk-khan-taw

femur *(n.)* **ပေါင်ရိုး** *paung-yoe*

fence *(n.)* **ခြံစည်းရိုး** *chan-see-yoe*

fencer *(n.)* **ဓားရေးပြိုင်သည်** *dar-yay-pyine-the*

fencing *(n.)* **ဓားရေးယှဉ်ပြိုင်ကစားနည်း** dar-yay-shin-pyine-ka-sar-nee

fend *(v.)* **ကိုယ့်ဝမ်းကိုယ်ကျောင်းသည်** *koe-wan-ko-kyaung-the*

fengshui *(n.)* **ဖုန်းရွှေ** hpone-shway

fennel *(n.)* **စမုန်နက်** *sa-hmone-nat*

ferment *(n.)* **လှုပ်လှုပ်ရွရွဖြစ်ခြင်း** hloke-hloke-ywa-ywa-phit-chin

fermentation *(n.)* **အချဉ်ဖောက်ခြင်း** a-chin-phauk-chin

fern *(n.)* **ဖန်းပင်** *hpan-pin*

ferocious *(adj.)* **ကြမ်းကြုတ်ရက်စက်သော** *kyan-kyoke-yat-sat-taw*

ferret *(n.)* **မြွေပါကတိုးဖြူ** *mway-par-ka-toe-phyu*

ferry *(v.)* **ကြိုပို့လုပ်သည်** *kyo-po-lote-the*

ferryboat *(n.)* **ဖယ်ရီလှေ** phal-re-lay

fertile *(adj.)* **မျိုးအောင်သော** *myo-aung-taw*

fertility *(n.)* မျိုးအောင်ခြင်း *myo-aung-chin*
fertilize *(v.)* မျိုးစပ်သည် myo-sat-the
fertilizer *(n.)* မြေသြဇာ *myay-aw-zar*
fervent *(adj.)* ထက်သန်သော htet-tan-taw
fervour *(n.)* စိတ်အားထက်သန်မှု seik-ar-htet-tan-mu
fester *(v.)* ပြည်တည်သည် *pyi-te-the*
festival *(n.)* ပွဲတော် *pwal-taw*
festive *(adj.)* တောက်ပသော၊ ပွဲတိုးသော *taut-pa-taw, pwe-toe-taw*
festivity *(n.)* ပွဲလမ်းသဘင် *pwal-lan-ta-bin*
festoon *(n.)* ပန်းကုံး၊ ပန်းဆိုင်း *pan-kone, pan-sai*
fetal *(adj.)* သေနိုင်သော *tay-naing-taw*
fetch *(v.)* ခေါ်လာသည် *khaw-lar-the*
fetish *(n.)* အစွဲအလမ်းကြီးခြင်း a-swal-a-lan-kyi-chin
fetishism *(n.)* ဝတ္ထုစွဲကာမစိတ် wut-htu-swal-kar-ma-seik
fetter *(n.)* ထူးကွင်း *htoo-kwin*
feud *(v.)* ရန်စ *yan-sa*
feud *(n.)* ကမ္ဘာ့ရန်ဖြစ်သည် *ka-bar-yan-phit-the*
feudal *(adj.)* မြေရှင်ပဒေသရာဇ်စနစ်နှင့် ဆိုင်သော *myay-shin-pa-day-ta-yit-sa-nit-nint-sai-taw*
feudalism *(n.)* ကံကျွေးချစနစ် *kan-kyway-cha-sa-nit*
fever *(n.)* အဖျား *a-phyar*
feverish *(adj.)* အဖျားရှိနေသော *a-phyar-shi-nay-taw*
few *(adj.)* အနည်းငယ် *a-nae-ngal*
fiancé *(n.)* စေ့စပ်ထားသော ယောကျာ်း *say-sat-htar-taw-yauk-kyar*
fiasco *(n.)* အရှုံးကြီး ရှုံးခြင်း *a-shone-gyi-shone-chin*
fibre *(n.)* ဖိုင်ဘာ၊ အမျှင် *phi-bar, a-myin*
fibreglass *(n.)* ဖန်မျှင်ထည် phan-hmyin-htae
fibre-optic *(adj.)* ဖန်မျှင်နန်းကြိုး phan-hmyin-nan-kyo
fibrillate *(v.)* ပုံမမှန် မြန်ဆန်စွာ ရွေ့လျားသည် pon-ma-hman-myan-san-swar-ywe-lyar-the
fibroid *(adj.)* ဖိုက်ဘရွိုက် *phite-ba-roid*
fibromuscular *(adj.)* ကြွက်သား၊ အမျှင်တစ်ရှူးနှင့် ဆိုင်သော kywat-tar-a-hmyin-tit-shu-nint-sai-taw
fibrosis *(n.)* အင်္ဂါတစ်ခုတွင် အမျှင်တစ်ရှူးဖြစ်ပေါ်ခြင်း in-gar-ta-khu-twin-a-hmyin-tit-shu-phit-paw-chin
fibrosity *(n.)* အမျှင်အရည်အသွေး *a-hmyin-a-yay-a-thway*
fibrous *(adj.)* အမျှင်နှင့်ဆိုင်သော *a-hmyin-nint-sai-taw*
fickle *(adj.)* ပြောင်းလဲလွယ်သော *pyaung-lal-lwal-taw*
fiction *(n.)* ဝတ္ထု wut-htu
fictional *(adj.)* ဝတ္ထုဆန်သော wut-htu-san-taw
fictitious *(adj.)* စိတ်ကူးဖြင့် ဖန်တီးသော *seik-ku-phit-phan-tee-taw*
fiddle *(v.)* ကလိသည် ka-li-the
fiddle *(n.)* တယော ta-yaw
fidelity *(n.)* သစ္စာရှိခြင်း *tit-sar-shi-chin*
fidget *(v.)* ဂနာမငြိမ် *ga-nar-ma-nyein*
fie *(interj.)* မနှစ်မြို့ခြင်းကို ဖော်ပြသံ *ma-nit-myo-chin-ko-phaw-pya-tan*
field *(n.)* ကွင်းပြင် *kwin-pyin*

fiend *(n.)* မကောင်းဆိုးဝါး ma-kaung-soe-war
fierce *(adj.)* ကြမ်းတမ်းသော kyan-tan-taw
fiery *(adj.)* မီးကဲ့သို့သော mee-kae-tho-taw
fifteen *(n.)* ဆယ့်ငါး *sae-ngar*
fifty *(n.)* ငါးဆယ် *ngar-sal*
fig *(n.)* သဖန်းသီး၊ ကတွတ်သီး ta-phan-tee, ka-tut-tee
fight *(n.)* တိုက်ခိုက်ခြင်း *tite-khite-chin*
figment *(n.)* စိတ်ကူးသက်သက် *seik-ku-thet-thet*
figurative *(adj.)* တင်စားထားသော *tin-sar-htar-taw*
figure *(v.)* ပါဝင်သည်၊ ထည့်သည် par-win-the, htae-the
filament *(n.)* နန်းမျှင်၊ အမျှင် nan-hmyin, a-hmyin
filamentation *(n.)* အမျှင်ကြီးထွားလာခြင်း a-hmyin-kyi-htwar-lar-chin
filamented *(adj.)* အမျှင်နှင့်ဆိုင်သော *a-hmyin-nint-sai-taw*
file *(v.)* တိုင်ချက်ဖွင့်သည်၊ ဖိုင်ဖွင့်သည် *tine-chat-phwint-the, fai-phwint-the*
fillet *(n.)* အရိုးထွင်ပြီးသား ငါး၊ အသား *a-yoe-htwin-pi-tar-ngar-a-tar*
film *(n.)* ရုပ်ရှင် *yoke-shin*
filmmaker *(n.)* ရုပ်ရှင်ရိုက်ကူးသူ *yoke-shin-yite-ku-thu*
filter *(n.)* စစ်ထုတ်ကိရိယာ *sit-htoke-ka-yi-yar*
filth *(n.)* အညစ်အကြေး *a-nyit-a-kyay*
filthy *(adj.)* ညစ်ပတ်ပေရေသော *nyit-pat-pay-yay-taw*
fin *(n.)* ဆူးတောင် su-taung
final *(adj.)* နောက်ဆုံး naut-sone
finale *(n.)* ဇာတ်သိမ်းပိုင်း zat-thein-pai
finance *(v.)* ငွေကြေးထောက်ပံ့သည် *ngwe-kyay-htauk-pant-the*
financial *(adj.)* ငွေရေးကြေးရေး *ngwe-yay-kyay-yay*
financier *(n.)* ငွေရှင် *ngwe-shin*
find *(v.)* ရှာဖွေသည် *shar-phway-the*
fine *(adj.)* ကောင်းသော *kaung-taw*
finger *(v.)* ကိုင်သည်၊ စမ်းသည် *kai-the, san-the*
fingernail *(n.)* လက်သည်း lat-the
fingerpaint *(n.)* လက်ညှိုးပန်းချီ lat-nyo-pan-chi
fingerprint *(n.)* လက်ဗွေ lat-bway
fingerstick *(n.)* လက်ထိပ်ဖောက်ခြင်း lat-htike-phauk-chin
finish *(n.)* ပြီးဆုံးခြင်း *pyi-sone-chin*
finish *(v.)* ပြီးဆုံးသည် pyi-sone-the
finite *(adj.)* ကန့်သတ်ချက်ရှိသော *kant-tat-chat-shi-taw*
fir *(n.)* ထင်းရှူးပင် *htin-shu-pin*
fire *(n.)* မီး mee
fire engine *(n.)* မီးသတ်ကား mee-tat-kar
fire exit *(n.)* မီးလောင်လျှင် ထွက်ပေါက် mee-laung-lyin-htwat-pauk
fire extinguisher *(n.)* မီးသတ်ဘူး mee-tat-bu
fire station *(n.)* မီးသတ်စခန်း mee-tat-sa-khan
fireball *(n.)* မီးလုံး mee-lone
firefight *(n.)* မီးသတ်ခြင်း *mee-tat-chin*
firefighter *(n.)* မီးသတ်သမား *mee-tat-ta-mar*
firehose *(n.)* မီးသတ်ပိုက် *mee-tat-pike*
firehouse *(n.)* မီးသတ်စခန်း *mee-tat-sa-khan*

firepit *(n.)* မီးဖို mee-pho

fireproof *(adj.)* မီးခံ *mee-khan*

fire-resistant *(adj.)* မီးဒဏ်ခံ mee-dan-khan

firesuit *(n.)* မီးဒဏ်ခံဝတ်စုံ *mee-dan-khan-wit-sone*

firetruck *(n.)* မီးသတ်ကား *mee-tat-kar*

fireworks *(n.)* မီးရှူးမီးပန်း *mee-shu-mee-pan*

firm *(n.)* စီးပွားရေး လုပ်ငန်း *see-pwar-yay-lote-ngan*

firm *(adj.)* ခိုင်မာသော *khai-mar-taw*

firmament *(n.)* မိုးကောင်းကင် *moe-kaung-kin*

firmness *(n.)* ခိုင်မြဲတည်ကြည်မှု khai-myal-the-kyi-mu

first *(adj.)* ပထမ pa-hta-ma

first aid *(n.)* ရှေးဦးသူနာပြုစုခြင်း shay-oo-thu-nar-pyu-su-chin

fiscal *(adj.)* ဘဏ္ဍာရေး *ban-nar-yay*

fish *(n.)* ငါး *ngar*

fisherman *(n.)* တံငါသည် *tan-ngar-the*

fissure *(n.)* အကွဲကြောင်း *a-kwal-kyaung*

fist *(n.)* လက်သီး lat-thee

fistula *(n.)* ပုံမမှန်လမ်းကြောင်း *pon-ma-hman-lan-kyaung*

fit *(adj.)* ကျန်းမာသော *kyan-mar-taw*

fit *(v.)* သင့်လျော်သည်၊ မှန်ကန်သည် *tint-lyaw-the, hman-kan-the*

fitful *(adj.)* ထုံ့ပိုင်းထုံ့ပိုင်း *htont-pai-htont-pai*

fitness test *(n.)* ကြံ့ခိုင်မှု စမ်းသပ်ခြင်း kyant-khai-mu-san-tat-chin

fitness tracker *(n.)* ကြံ့ခိုင်မှု မှတ်တမ်း kyant-khai-mu-mat-tan

fitness training *(n.)* ကြံ့ခိုင်မှု သင်တန်း kyant-khai-mu-tin-than

fitter *(n.)* စက်ဆရာ *sat-sa-yar*

fitting room *(n.)* အဝတ်လဲခန်း a-wut-lae-khan

five *(n.)* ငါး ngar

fix *(v.)* တပ်ဆင်သည် *tat-sin-the*

fixer-upper *(n.)* ပြင်ဆင်ရန်လိုသည့် ပိုင်ဆိုင်မှုများ pyin-sin-yan-lo-the-pai-sai-mu-myar

fixture *(n.)* ရက်ချိန်း yat-chain

fizz *(n.)* အမြှုပ်တစီစီ ထွက်ခြင်း a-hmyoke-ta-si-si-htwat-chin

fizzy *(adj.)* အမြှုပ်တက်သော *a-hmyoke-tat-taw*

flabbergast *(n.)* အံ့အားသင့်သွားခြင်း *ant-arr-tint-twar-chin*

flabbergasted *(adj.)* အံ့အားသင့်သွားသော *ant-arr-tint-twar-taw*

flabby *(adj.)* မခိုင်မာသော၊ ဝမ်းပျဉ်းကျသော ma-khaing-mar-taw, wan-pyin-kya-taw

flag *(n.)* အလံ *a-lan*

flagrant *(adj.)* ပြောင်ပြောင်တင်းတင်း ကျူးလွန်သော *pyaung-pyaung-tin-tin-kyue-loon-taw*

flake *(n.)* အပွင့်အဖတ် a-pwint-a-phat

flaking *(adj.)* ပွင့်ချပ်လွှာကွာကျသော *pwint-chat-hlwar-kwar-kya-taw*

flambé *(adj.)* ဘရန်ဒီလောင်း၍ မီးရှို့လောင်မြိုက်စေပြီးမှ စားရသော *ba-yan-di-laung-ywe-mee-sho-laung-hmyike-pay-pyi-ma-sar-ya-taw*

flamboyance *(n.)* ဝင့်ကြွားမှု wint-kywar-mu

flamboyant *(n.)* ဝင့်ဝါလွန်းခြင်း wint-war-lun-chin

flame *(v.)* **တောက်လောင်သည်** taut-laung-the
flamenco *(n.)* **စပိန်ဂီတာတေးသံအက** sa-pain-gi-tar-tay-tan-a-ka
flank *(v.)* **တစ်ဖက်တစ်ချက်တွင် ရံသည်** *ta-phat-ta-chat-twin-yan-the*
flannel *(n.)* **ဖလန်နယ်စ** pha-lan-nal-sa
flap *(v.)* **တဖျပ်ဖျပ် လှုပ်သည်** ta-phat-phat-hlote-the
flapper *(n.)* **ခေတ်ဆန်၍ ခေတ်ကို တက်တက်ကြွကြွ တော်လှန်သော မိန်းမပျို** khit-san-ywe-khit-ko-tat-tat-kwa-kwa-taw-lan-taw-mein-ma-pyo
flapping *(adj.)* **တဖြတ်ဖြတ် လှုပ်ခတ်သော** *ta-phat-phat-hlote-khat-taw*
flare *(v.)* **ရုတ်တရက် ထတောက်၍ လင်းဖြာသည်** *yoke-ta-yat-hta-tauk-ywe-lin-phar-the*
flash *(v.)* **ပြက်သည်၊ လက်သည်** *pyat-the-, let-the*
flashback *(n.)* **နောက်ကြောင်းပြန် ပြကွက်** *naut-kyaung-pyan-pya-kwat*
flashbulb *(n.)* **လျှပ်တစ်ပြက် မီးသီး** *hlyat-ta-pyat-meet-thee*
flashcard *(n.)* **စာလုံးရုပ်ပုံပါကတ်** *sar-lone-yoke-pon-par-kat*
flasher *(n.)* **မတော်တရော် လိင်တံ လှစ်ပြသူ** *ma-taw-ta-yaw-lain-tan-hlit-pya-thu*
flashing *(n.)* **သတ္တုပြား** *tat-tu-pyar*
flashlight *(n.)* **ဓာတ်မီး** *dat-mee*
flask *(n.)* **သိပ်ပွဲခန်းသုံး ပုလင်း** *tate-pan-khan-tone-pa-lin*
flat *(n.)* **တိုက်ခန်း** tite-khan
flat screen *(n.)* **စခရင်အပြား** *sa-kha-rin-a-pyar*
flatbed *(adj.)* **တွဲကား သို့မဟုတ် စကင်နာပါရှိသော** *twe-kar-toe-ma-hoke-sa-kan-nar--par-shi-taw*
flatbread *(n.)* **ဘီစကွတ်မွမွ** *bi-sa-kwut-mwa-mwa*
flatfoot *(n.)* **ခြေဖဝါးအပြား** chay-pha-war-a-pyar
flatland *(n.)* **မြေပြန့်** myay-pyant
flatter *(v.)* **မျက်နှာချိုသွေးသည်** *myat-nar-cho-thway-the*
flattery *(n.)* **မြှောက်လုံးပင့်လုံး** *hmyauk-lone-pint-lon*
flatulence *(n.)* **လေပွခြင်း** *lay-pwa-chin*
flatulent *(adj.)* **လေပွသော** lay-pwa-taw
flaunt *(v.)* **ကြွားလုံးထုတ်သည်** kywar-lone-htoke-the
flaunter *(n.)* **ငကြွား** *nga-kywar*
flavour *(n.)* **အနံ့အရသာ** a-nant-a-ya-tar
flaw *(n.)* **အပြစ်၊ အနာ** a-phit, a-nar
flawless *(adj.)* **ချို့ယွင်းချက် မရှိသော** *choe-ywin-chat-ma-shi-taw*
flea *(n.)* **လှေး** *hlae*
flea market *(n.)* **လဟာပြင်ဈေး** *la-har-pyin-zay*
flee *(v.)* **ထွက်ပြေးသည်** *htwat-pyay-the*
fleece *(v.)* **လှီးသည်၊ ရိတ်သည်** *hlee-the, yate-the*
fleet *(n.)* **ရေတပ်သင်္ဘောစု** *yay-tat-tin-baw-su*
flesh *(n.)* **အသား** *a-tar*
flexible *(adj.)* **ပြောင်းလွယ်ပြင်လွယ်ရှိသော** *pyaung-lwal-pyin-lwal-shi-taw*
flicker *(n.)* **ဆတ်ခနဲ ဆတ်ခနဲ လှုပ်ရှားခြင်း** *sat-kha-nae-sat-kha-nae-hlote-shar-chin*
flicker *(v.)* **မှိတ်တုတ်မှိတ်တုတ်လင်းသည်** maik-toke-maik-toke-lin-the

flight *(n.)* ပျံသန်းရေး၊ လေယာဉ်ခရီး *pyan-tan-yay, lay-yin-kha-yee*
flimsy *(adj.)* ပါးလျပေါ့ပါးသော par-lya-pawt-par-taw
fling *(v.)* ပစ်ပေါက်သည် pyit-pauk-the
flip *(adj.)* ကရော်ကမည်ပြောသော၊ လုပ်သော *ka-yau-ka-mal-pyaw-taw, lote-taw*
flippancy *(n.)* အလေးမထားခြင်း *a-lay-ma-htar-chin*
flirt *(v.)* ပရောပရည် လုပ်သည် *pa-yaw-pa-yee-lote-the*
float *(v.)* ပေါလောပေါ်သည် *paw-law-paw-the*
flock *(n.)* လူအုပ်၊ ငှက်အုပ် *lu-oak, hnget-oak*
flog *(v.)* ကြိမ်ဒဏ်ပေးသည် kyein-dan-pay-the
flood *(n.)* ရေကြီးခြင်း yay-kyi-chin
flood gate *(n.)* ရေတံခါး *yay-ta-khar*
floodlight *(n.)* မီးမောင်း mee-maung
floor *(n.)* ကြမ်းခင်း kyan-khin
flop *(v.)* ဖုတ်ခနဲ ကျသည် hpoke-kha-nae-kya-the
flora *(n.)* ဒေသရင်း အပင်များ *day-da-yin-a-pin-myar*
florist *(n.)* ပန်းသည် *pan-the*
floss *(v.)* ပိုးကြိုးမျှင်သုံး၍ သွားသန့်စင်သည် moe-kyo-hmyin-tone-ywe-twar-tant-sin-the
flour *(n.)* ဂျုံမှုန့် gyone-hmont
flourish *(v.)* ဂျုံမှုန့်ပါးပါးဖြူးသည် *gyone-hmont-par-par-phyue-the*
flow *(v.)* စီးဆင်းသည် *see-sin-the*
flow chart *(n.)* လုပ်ငန်းစဉ်အဆင့်ဆင့်ပြကားချပ် *lote-ngan-sin-a-sint-sint-pya-kar-chat*
flower *(n.)* ပန်း *pan*
flowery *(adj.)* ပန်းများ ဝေဆာနေသော *pan-myar-wai-sar-nay-taw*
fluctuate *(v.)* အတက်အကျ ရှိသည် a-tat-a-kya-shi-the
fluent *(adj.)* ကျွမ်းကျွမ်းကျင်ကျင် ပြောနိုင်သော *kywan-kywan-kyin-kyin-pyaw-nai-taw*
fluid *(adj.)* စီးဆင်းနိုင်သော၊ ပြေပြစ်ကြော့ရှင်းသော *see-sin-nai-taw, pyay-pyit-kyawt-shin-taw*
fluorescent *(adj.)* အလင်းထွက်သော a-linn-htwat-thaw
flush *(n.)* မျက်နှာ သွေးရောင်ဖြန်းခြင်း၊ ရေဆွဲခြင်း *myat-nar-thway-yaung-phyan-chin, yay-swal-chin*
flute *(n.)* ပလွေ *pa-lway*
flutter *(n.)* တဖျပ်ဖျပ် ခတ်ခြင်း၊ ပျာယာခတ်ခြင်း ta-phat-phat-khat-chin, pyar-yar-khat-chin
flutter *(v.)* တဖျပ်ဖျပ်ပျံသည်၊ တောင်ပံခတ်သည် *ta-phat-phat-khat-the, pyar-yar-khat-the*
fly *(n.)* ပျံသန်းခြင်း *pyan-tan-chin*
flyer *(n.)* လေယာဉ်မှူး၊ လက်ကမ်းကြော်ငြာစာ lay-yin-hmue, lat-kan-kyaw-nyar-sar
foal *(n.)* မြင်းပေါက်စ *myin-pauk-sa*
foam *(n.)* အမြှုပ် *a-hmyoke*
foam *(v.)* အမြှုပ်ထသည် *a-hmyoke-hta-the*
foamy *(adj.)* အမြှုပ်တစီစီထနေသော *a-hmyoke-ta-se-se-hta-nay-taw*
focal *(adj.)* ရုပ်ပုံကြည်သော ဆုံချက်၊ ဆုံချက်ဆိုင်ရာ *yoke-pon-kyi-taw-sone-chat, sone-chat-sai-yar*
focalization *(n.)* ဆုံချက်ဖြတ်ခြင်း sone-chat-phat-chin

focalize *(v.)* ဆုံချက်ဖြတ်သည် sone-chat-phat-the
focus *(n.)* ဗဟို၊ အချက်အချာ၊ ဆုံချက် *ba-ho, a-chat-a-char, sone-chat*
focus *(v.)* အာရုံစိုက်သည်၊ စူးစိုက်သည် *arr-yone-site-the, sue-site-the*
focused *(adj.)* အာရုံစူးစိုက်သော *arr-yone-sue-site-the*
focusing *(adj.)* စူးစိုက်ထားသော sue-site-htar-taw
fodder *(n.)* ကျွဲစာနွားစာ kywe-sar-nwar-sar
foe *(n.)* ရန်သူ yan-thu
foetus *(n.)* သန္ဓေသား *ta-day-tar*
fog *(n.)* မြူထူ myu-htu
fogbank *(n.)* မြူထူထပ်ခြင်း *myu-htu-htet-chin*
foggy *(adj.)* မြူပိတ်သော myu-htu-taw
foil *(v.)* ဖျက်လိုဖျက်ဆီး လုပ်သည်၊ နှောင့်ယှက်သည် phat-lo-phat-see-lote-the, naut-shat-the
fold *(v.)* ခေါက်သည်၊ တွန့်သည် khauk-the, twunt-the
folder *(n.)* စာတွဲ၊ ဖိုလ်ဒါ *sar-twe, fo-dar*
folding *(n.)* ခေါက်ခြင်း khauk-chin
foldup *(adj.)* အရှုံးပေးသော a-shone-pay-taw
foliage *(n.)* သစ်ရွက် *thit-ywet*
foliate *(v.)* ပြားနေအောင် ထုရိုက်သည် *pyar-nay-aung-htu-yike-the*
foliation *(n.)* ပြားနေအောင် ထုရိုက်ခြင်း *pyar-nay-aung-htu-yike-chin*
folic *(adj.)* သစ်ရွက်နှင့် ဆိုင်သော thit-ywet-nint-sai-taw
folio *(n.)* တစ်ခေါက်ခေါက်ထားသော စက္ကူ *ta-khauk-khauk-htar-taw-sat-khu*
folk *(adj.)* ရိုးရာ *yoe-yar*
folklore *(n.)* ရှေးရိုးစဉ်လာ၊ ပုံပြင်၊ ဓလေ့လေ့လာမှု *shay-yoe-sin-lar, pon-pyin, da-lay-lay-lar-mu*
folkloric *(adj.)* ရှေးရိုးစဉ်လာ၊ ပုံပြင်၊ ဓလေ့လေ့လာမှုနှင့် ဆိုင်သော shar-yoe-sin-lar, pon-pyin, da-lay-lay-lar-mu-nint-sai-taw
follies *(n.)* မိုက်မဲမှုများ mike-mae-mu-myar
follow *(v.)* နောက်လိုက်သည် *naut-lite-the*
follower *(n.)* နောက်လိုက် *naut-lite*
follow-up *(n.)* နောက်ဆက်တွဲ naut-sat-twe
folly *(n.)* မိုက်မဲမှု mite-mae-mu
foment *(v.)* လှုံ့ဆော်သည် *lont-saw-the*
fond *(adj.)* နှစ်သက်သော *nit-the-taw*
fondant *(n.)* ပျော့အိအိ သကြားလျှောပေါ်ဝဲ *pyaw-ei-ei-tha-kyar-shar-paw-wae*
fondle *(v.)* ယုယုယယ ပွတ်သပ်သည် *yu-yu-ya-ya-put-tat-the*
fondler *(n.)* ယုယုယယ ပွတ်သပ်သူ *yu-yu-ya-ya-put-tat-thu*
fondling *(n.)* ယုယုယယ ပွတ်သပ်ခြင်း *yu-yu-ya-ya-put-tat-chin*
font *(n.)* ကျောက်အင်တုံ၊ စာလုံးဖောင့်ပုံစံ kyauk-inn-tone, sar-lone-font-pon-san
food *(n.)* အစားအစာ *a-sar-a-sar*
fool *(v.)* လှည့်စားသည်၊ ကလိသည် *hlae-sar-the, ka-li-the*
foolish *(adj.)* မိုက်မဲသော *mite-mae-taw*
foolscap *(n.)* ဖူးစကက် phoo-sa-khat
foot *(v.)* ကန်သည် *kan-taw*
footage *(n.)* ရုပ်ရှင်ကား yoke-shin-kar
football *(n.)* ဘောလုံးပွဲ *baw-lone-pwe*
foothold *(n.)* ခြေကုပ် *chay-coke*
footloose *(adj.)* လူလွတ်ဖြစ်သော lu-lut-phit-taw

footman *(n.)* **ငယ်ကျွေ** *ae-kyo*

footmark *(n.)* **ခြေရာ** *chay-yar*

footnote *(n.)* **အောက်ခြေမှတ်ချက်** aut-chay-mat-chat

footpath *(n.)* **လူသွားလမ်း** lu-twar-lan

footprint *(n.)* **ခြေရာ** chay-yar

footsore *(adj.)* **ခြေကုန်သော** *khay-kone-taw*

footwear *(n.)* **ဖိနပ်** *pha-nat-*

footwork *(n.)* **ခြေလှမ်းကွက်** *chay-hlan-kwat*

for *(conj.)* **ကြောင့်** *kyaunt*

forage *(n.)* **မြင်းစာ၊ ကျွဲနွားစာ** *myin-sar, kywe-sar*

forager *(n.)* **လိုက်ရှာသူ** lite-shar-thu

foraging *(n.)* **လိုက်ရှာခြင်း** lite-shar-chin

foray *(n.)* **ချင်းနင်းဝင်ရောက်ခြင်း** *chin-nin-win-yauk-chin*

forbear *(v.)* **သည်းခံသည်၊ အောင့်အည်းသည်** the-khan-the, aung-ae-the

forbearance *(n.)* **စိတ်ရှည်ခြင်း** *seik-shay-chin*

forbid *(v.)* **တားမြစ်သည်** *tar-myit-the*

forbidden *(adj.)* **တားမြစ်ထားသော** *tar-myit-htar-taw*

force *(n.)* **ခွန်အား** *khun-arr*

forceful *(adj.)* **အားမာန်ပါသော** *arr-man-par-taw*

forceps *(n.)* **ညှပ်** *hnyat*

forcible *(adj.)* **အတင်းအဓမ္မ** *a-tin-a-da-ma*

forearm *(v.)* **ခုခံကာကွယ်ရန် အသင့်ပြင်ထားသည်** *khu-khan-kar-kwe-yan-a-tint-pyin-htar-the*

forecast *(n.)* **ကြိုတင်ခန့်မှန်းချက်၊ ဟောကိန်း** *kyo-tin-khant-hman-chat, haw-kein*

forecourt *(n.)* **မျက်နှာစာ** *myat-nar-sar*

forefather *(n.)* **ဘိုး၊ ဘေး၊ ဘီ၊ ဘင်** *bo, bay, bi, bin*

forefinger *(n.)* **လက်ညှိုး** lat-hnyo

forehead *(n.)* **နဖူး** *na-phoo*

foreign *(adj.)* **နိုင်ငံခြား** *nai-ngan-char*

foreigner *(n.)* **နိုင်ငံခြားသား** *nai-ngan-char-thar*

foreknowledge *(n.)* **ကြိုတင် သိမြင်ခြင်း** *kyo-tin-ti-myin-chin*

foreleg *(n.)* **ရှေ့ခြေ၊ လက်** *shay-chay, lat*

forelock *(n.)* **နဖူးပေါ် ဝဲကျနေသော ဦးစွန်းဖုတ်** *na-phoo-paw-wal-kya-nay-taw-oo-sun-hpoke*

foreman *(n.)* **အလုပ်ကြပ်** *a-lote-kyat*

foremost *(adj.)* **အထင်ကရ** *a-htin-ka-ya*

forenoon *(n.)* **မနက်ခင်း** *ma-nat-khin*

forensic *(adj.)* **မှုခင်းဆေးပညာဆိုင်ရာ** *mu-khin-say-pyin-nyar-sai-yar*

forerunner *(n.)* **ရှေ့တော်ပြေး** *shay-taw-pyay*

foresee *(v.)* **ကြိုမြင်သည်** *kyo-myin-the*

foresight *(n.)* **မြော်မြင်မှု** *myaw-myin-mu*

forest *(n.)* **သစ်တော** *tit-taw*

forestall *(v.)* **ကြိုတင်ဟန့်တားသည်** *kyo-tin-hant-tar-the*

forester *(n.)* **တောအုပ်** taw-oak

forestry *(n.)* **သစ်တောပညာ** *tit-taw-pyin-nyar*

foretell *(v.)* **ဟောကိန်းထုတ်သည်** haw-kain-htoke-the

forethought *(n.)* **အမြော်အမြင်** a-myaw-a-myin

forever *(adv.)* **ထာဝရ** htar-wa-ya

forewarn *(v.)* ကြိုတင်သတိပေးခြင်း *kyo-tin-ta-di-pay-chin*
foreword *(n.)* စကားချီး *sa-kar-chee*
forfeit *(n.)* ဒဏ်ကြေး *dan-kyay*
forfeiture *(n.)* ပြစ်ဒဏ်အဖြစ် အသိမ်းသော *pyit-dan-a-phit-thein-taw*
forge *(n.)* ပန်းပဲဖို *pan-pae-pho*
forgery *(n.)* လိမ်လည်အတုပြုမှု lain-lae-a-tu-pyu-mu
forget *(v.)* မေ့လျော့သည် *mae-lyaw-the*
forgetful *(adj.)* မေ့လျော့သော mae-lyaw-thaw
forgive *(v.)* ခွင့်လွှတ်သည် khwint-hlut-the
forgo *(v.)* စွန့်လွှတ်သည် sunt-hlut-the
forlorn *(adj.)* အထီးကျန်ဖြစ်သော *a-htee-kyan-phit-taw*
form *(v.)* ပုံသွင်းသည်၊ ပုံဖော်သည် pon-twin-the, pon-phaw-the
formal *(adj.)* သမားရိုးကျဆန်သော *ta-ma-yoe-kya-san-taw*
formality *(n.)* လုပ်ရိုးလုပ်စဉ် lote-yoe-lote-sin
format *(n.)* ပုံစံ *pon-san*
formation *(n.)* ဖွဲ့စည်းခြင်း *phwe-see-chin*
former *(adj.)* ယခင် *ya-khin*
formerly *(adv.)* ယခင်က ya-khin-ka
formidable *(adj.)* ခံ့ညားလောက်သော *khant-nyar-laut-taw*
formula *(n.)* ဖော်မြူလာ *phaw-myu-lar*
formulate *(v.)* ဖော်ထုတ်သည် *phaw-htoke-the*
forsake *(v.)* ကျောခိုင်းသည် *kyaw-khai-the*
forswear *(v.)* အပြီးအပိုင် စွန့်သည် *a-pee-a-pai-sunt-the*
fort *(n.)* ခံတပ် *khan-tat*
forte *(n.)* သန်သည့်ကိစ္စ tan-the-kait-sa
forth *(adv.)* ခရီး *kha-yee*
forthcoming *(adj.)* လာမည့် lar-mae
forthwith *(adv.)* ချက်ခြင်း *chat-chin*
fortify *(v.)* ခံစစ်ပြင်သည် *khan-sit-phin-the*
fortitude *(n.)* ခံနိုင်ရည် *khan-nai-yay*
fortnight *(n.)* ရက်သတ္တနှစ်ပတ် *yat-tat-ta-na-pat*
fortress *(n.)* ခံတပ်ကြီး *khan-tat-kyi*
fortunate *(adj.)* ကံကောင်းသော *kan-kaung-taw*
fortune *(n.)* ကံ *kan*
forty *(n.)* လေးဆယ် *lay-sal*
forum *(n.)* ဖိုရမ်၊ ဆွေးနွေးပွဲ *pho-ran, swe-nwe-pwe*
forward *(v.)* တစ်ဆင့်ကမ်းသည် ta-sint-khan-the
fossil *(n.)* ကျောက်ဖြစ်ရုပ်ကြွင်း *kyauk-phit-yoke-kywin*
foster *(v.)* အားပေးသည်၊ မွေးစားသည် *arr-pay-the, mway-sar-the*
foster care *(n.)* မွေးစားသားသမီးစောင့်ရှောက်ခြင်း mway-sar-tar-ta-mee-saunt-shaut-chin
foul *(adj.)* ဆိုးရွားသော soe-ywar-thaw
foul play *(n.)* ပြစ်ဒဏ်ကျူးလွန်သည် pyit-dan-kyu-lun-the
found *(v.)* တည်ထောင်သည် *ti-htaung-the*
foundation *(n.)* ဖောင်ဒေးရှင်း၊ တည်ထောင်ခြင်း၊ အုတ်မြစ် *phaung-day-shin, the-htaung-chin, oak-myit*
founder *(n.)* တည်ထောင်သူ *te-htaung-thu*
foundry *(n.)* သတ္တုပုံလောင်းစက်ရုံ *tat-tu-pon-laung-sat-yone*
fountain *(n.)* ရေပန်း *yay-pan*

four *(n.)* **လေး** *lay*

fourteen *(n.)* **ဆယ့်လေး** *sal-lay*

fowl *(n.)* **ကြက်ငှက်၊ ကြက်သား** *kyat-nget, kyat-tar*

fowler *(n.)* **တောကြက်လိုက်သူ** *taw-kyat-lite-thu*

fox *(n.)* **မြေခွေး** *myay-khway*

fraction *(n.)* **အစိတ်အပိုင်း** *a-seik-a-pai*

fracture *(n.)* **ကျိုးခြင်း၊ အက်ခြင်း** *kyo-chin, at-chin*

fragile *(adj.)* **ကွဲတတ်သော၊ နုသော၊ အထိအရှမခံသော** *kwal-tat-taw, nu-taw, a-hti-a-sha-ma-khan-taw*

fragment *(n.)* **အပိုင်းအစ** *a-pai-a-sa*

fragrance *(n.)* **ရနံ့၊ ရေမွှေး** *ya-nant, yay-mway*

fragrant *(adj.)* **မွှေးသော၊ ကြိုင်သော** *hmway-taw, kyaing-taw*

frail *(adj.)* **နုသော၊ ချည့်နဲ့သော** *nu-taw, chae-nae-taw*

frame *(n.)* **ဘောင်** *baung*

framework *(n.)* **အောက်ခံဘောင်၊ အဆောက်အအုံ၊ ဘောင်ကန့်သတ်ချက်** aut-khan-baung, a-saut-a-ohn, baung-kant-tat-chat

franchise *(n.)* **မဲဆန္ဒပေးပိုင်ခွင့်၊ လုပ်ပိုင်ခွင့်** *mae-san-da-pay-pai-khwint, lote-pai-khwint*

frank *(adj.)* **ပွင့်လင်းသော** *pwint-lin-taw*

frankly *(adv.)* **ပွင့်ပွင့်လင်းလင်း** pwint-pwint-lin-lin

frantic *(adj.)* **ဗျာများနေသော** *byaw-myar-nay-taw*

fraternal *(adj.)* **ညီရင်းအစ်ကို ပမာဖြစ်သော** *nyi-yin-a-ko-pa-mar-phit-taw*

fraternity *(n.)* **အသိုင်းအဝိုင်း၊ အသင်း၊ ကလပ်၊ သဟာယစိတ်ဓာတ်** *a-thai-a-wai, a-tin, ka-lat, ta-har-ya-seik-dat*

fratricide *(n.)* **ညီအစ်ကိုချင်းသတ်မှု** nyi-a-ko-chin-tat-mu

fraud *(n.)* **လိမ်လည်မှု** lain-lal-mu

fraudulent *(adj.)* **မမှန်မကန်သော** *ma-hman-ma-kan-taw*

fraught *(adj.)* **အတိပြီးသော** a-ti-pi-taw

fray *(n.)* **တိုက်ပွဲ** *tite-pwe*

freak *(adj.)* **ထူးဆန်းသော** htoo-san-taw

freak-out *(n.)* **ပေါက်သည်၊ ဖြောင်းဆန်သည်** *pauk-the, byaung-san-the*

free *(adj.)* **လွတ်လပ်သော** *lut-lat-taw*

freedom *(n.)* **လွတ်လပ်မှု** *lut-lat-mu*

freelancer *(n.)* **အလွတ်တန်းပညာရှင်** *a-lut-tan-pyin-nyar-shin*

freewheel *(v.)* **ဖရီးရိုက်သည်** pha-ree-rite-the

freeze *(v.)* **အေးခဲသည်** *aye-khae-the*

freight *(n.)* **ကုန်စည်** *kon-se*

French *(adj.)* **ပြင်သစ်** *pyin-thit*

French *(n.)* **ပြင်သစ်** *pyin-thit*

frenzy *(n.)* **သွေးရူးသွေးတန်းဖြစ်ခြင်း** *tway-yu-tway-tan-phit-chin*

frequency *(n.)* **ကြိမ်နှုန်း** *kyein-hnone*

frequent *(n.)* **မကြာခဏ** *ma-kyar-kha-na*

fresh *(adj.)* **အသစ်၊ လတ်လတ်ဆတ်ဆတ်** a-thit, lat-lat-sat-sat

fret *(n.)* **စိုးရိမ်ပူပန်ခြင်း** soe-yein-pu-pan-chin

friction *(n.)* **ပွတ်တိုက်အား** *put-tite-arr*

Friday *(n.)* **သောကြာနေ့** *taut-kyar-nae*

fridge *(n.)* **ရေခဲသေတ္တာ** *yay-khae-tit-tar*

friend *(n.)* သူငယ်ချင်း *thu-nge-chin*

fright *(n.)* လန့်ဖျပ်ခြင်း *lant-phat-chin*

frighten *(v.)* အထိတ်တလန့်ဖြစ်စေသည် *a-hteik-ta-lant-phit-say-the*

frigid *(adj.)* ကာမဆန္ဒနည်းသော *kar-ma-san-da-nae-taw*

frill *(n.)* အနားတွန့် *a-nar-tunt*

fringe *(n.)* ဆံရစ် san-yit

frivolous *(adj.)* လေးအနက်မထားသော *a-lay-a-nat-ma-htar-taw*

frock *(n.)* ဂါဝန် *gar-win*

frog *(n.)* ဖား *phar*

frolic *(n.)* မြူးခြင်း *myu-chin*

frolic *(v.)* မြူးထူးဆော့ကစားသည် *myu-tu-saw-ka-sar-the*

from *(prep.)* မှ *hma*

front *(v.)* မျက်နှာပြုသည် *myat-nar-pyu-the*

front page *(n.)* မျက်နှာဖုံးသတင်း myat-hnar-phone-ta-din

frontier *(n.)* နယ်ခြား၊ နယ်စပ် *nal-char, nal-sat*

frontside *(adj.)* ရှေ့ဘက် *shay-bat*

frost *(n.)* နှင်းခဲ hnin-khae

frosting *(n.)* သကြားလွှာ *tha-kyar-hlwar*

frown *(v.)* မျက်မှောင်ကြုတ်သည် *myat-hmaung-kyoke-the*

frozen *(adj.)* အလွန်အေးသော *a-lun-aye-taw*

frugal *(adj.)* ချွေတာသော *chway-tar-taw*

fruit *(n.)* သစ်သီး tit-thee

fruitful *(adj.)* သီးအပွင့်ဖြစ်ထွန်းသော၊ အကျိုးများသော၊ လှိုင်လှိုင်သီးသော *a-thee-a-pwint-phit-htun-taw, a-kyo-myar-taw, hlaing-hkaing-thee-taw*

frustrate *(v.)* နှောင့်ယှက်သည် *naut-shat-the*

frustration *(n.)* အားမလိုအားမရဖြစ်ခြင်း *arr-am-lo-arr-ma-ya-phit-chin*

fry *(v.)* ကြော်သည် *kyaw-the*

fuel *(n.)* လောင်စာဆီ *laung-sar-si*

fugitive *(n.)* တရားခံပြေး *ta-ya-khan-pyay*

fulfil *(v.)* ဖြည့်စွမ်းသည် *phyae-swan-the*

fulfilment *(n.)* စိတ်ချမ်းသာမှု seik-chan-tar-mu

full *(adv.)* တည့်တည့်၊ ကောင်းကောင်း *tae-tae, kaung-kaung*

full moon *(n.)* လပြည့် *la-pyae*

full name *(n.)* နာမည်အပြည့်အစုံ na-mal-a-pyae-a-son

full stop *(n.)* အဆုံးပြ သင်္ကေတ a-sone-pya-tin-kay-ta

fullness *(n.)* ပြည့်ခြင်း pyae-chin

fully *(adv.)* အပြည့်အဝ *a-pyae-a-wa*

fumble *(v.)* စမ်းတဝါးဝါး ဖြစ်နေသည် *san-ta-war-war-phit-nay-the*

fun *(n.)* အပျော် *a-pyaw*

function *(n.)* လုပ်ငန်းဆောင်တာ *lote-ngan-saung-tar*

functionary *(n.)* အရာထမ်း *a-yar-htan*

fund *(n.)* ရန်ပုံငွေ *yan-pon-ngwe*

fundamental *(adj.)* အခြေခံကျသော *a-chay-khan-kya-taw*

fundraise *(v.)* ရန်ပုံငွေတိုးအောင်လုပ်သည် *yan-pon-ngwe-toe-aung-lote-the*

funeral *(n.)* အသုဘ *a-thu-ba*

fungus *(n.)* မှိုတက်ခြင်း *hmo-tat-the*

funny *(n.)* ရယ်စရာကောင်းသော *yal-sa-yar-kaung-taw*

fur *(n.)* အမွေး *a-hmway*

furious *(adj.)* ပြင်းထန်သော *pyin-htan-taw*

furl *(v.)* လိပ်သည် *lait-the*

furlong *(n.)* ဖာလုံ *phar-lon*

furnace *(n.)* ဖို *pho*

furnish *(v.)* ပရိဘောဂ ခင်းကျင်းသည် *pa-yi-baw-ga-khin-kyin-the*

furniture *(n.)* ပရိဘောဂ *pa-yi-baw-ga*

furrow *(n.)* ထယ်ကြောင်း *htal-kyaung*

further *(adv.)* ထိုထက် *hto-htet*

fury *(n.)* အမျက်သည်းခြင်း *a-myat-thae-chin*

fuse *(n.)* ဖျူးကြိုး *phyue-kyo*

fusion *(n.)* ပေါင်းခြင်း *paung-chin*

fuss *(n.)* ဇာချဲ့ခြင်း *zar-chae-chin*

futile *(adj.)* အချည်းနှီးဖြစ်သော *a-chee-nee-phit-taw*

futility *(n.)* အချည်းနှီးဖြစ်ခြင်း *a-chee-nee-phit-chin*

future *(adj.)* အနာဂါတ် *a-nar-gat*

future *(n.)* အနာဂါတ် *a-nar-gat*

futuristic *(adj.)* အစဉ်အလာမှ လမ်းခွဲ၍ ခေတ်ဆန်လွန်းသော a-sin-a-lar-ma-lan-kwal-ywe-khit-san-lun-taw

futurology *(n.)* အနာဂါတ်လေ့လာမှုပညာ *a-nar-gat-lay-lar-mu-pyin-nyar*

fuzz *(v.)* မထင်မရှားဖြစ်သည် *ma-htin-ma-shar-phit-the*

fuzzy *(adj.)* အမွေးပွသော a-mway-pwa-taw

gabble *(v.)* ဗလုံးဗထွေးပြောသည် *ba-lone-ba-htway-pyaw-the*

gadfly *(n.)* မှက်၊ ထိုးနှက် ဝေဖန်သူ *hmat, htoe-nat-wai-phan-thu*

gadget *(n.)* ကိရိယာ *ka-yi-yar*

gaffe *(n.)* အပြုမှား၊ အပြောမှား *a-pyu-hmar, a-pyaw-hmar*

gag *(v.)* ပါးစပ်ကို ဆို့သည်၊ စည်းသည် *pa-sat-ko-soe-the, see-the*

gaiety *(n.)* ပျော်ပွဲ *pyaw-pwe*

gain *(n.)* အမြတ်အစွန်း *a-myat-a-sune*

gain *(v.)* ရရှိသည် *ya-shi-the*

gainful *(adj.)* အမြတ်ထွက်သော a-myat-htwat-taw

gainly *(adj.)* သင့်လျော်သော *tint-lyaw-taw*

gainsay *(v.)* ငြင်းပယ်သည် *nyin-pal-the*

gait *(n.)* လမ်းလျှောက်ဟန် *lan-shaut-han*

gala *(n.)* ပြိုင်ပွဲ၊ ပျော်ပွဲရွှင်ပွဲ *pyai-pwe, pyaw-pwe-shwin-pwe*

galactic *(adj.)* ကြယ်စုနှင့် သက်ဆိုင်သော *kyal-su-nint-thet-sai-taw*

galaxy *(n.)* ကြယ်စု *kyal-su*

gale *(n.)* လေပြင်းမုန်တိုင်း *lay-pyin-hmone-tai*

gallant *(adj.)* ရဲရင့်သော *ye-yint-taw*

gallantry *(n.)* သူရသတ္တိ *thu-ra-that-ti*

gallery *(n.)* ပြခန်း *pya-khan*

gallon *(n.)* ဂါလန် *gar-lan*

gallop *(n.)* ကဆုန်ပေါက်ပြေးခြင်း *ka-sone-pauk-pyay-chin*

gallows *(n.)* ကြိုးစင် *kyo-sin*

galore *(adv.)* ပေါများစွာ *paw-myar-swar*

galvanize *(v.)* သွပ်ရည်စိမ်သည် *tut-yay-sein-the*
galvanometer *(n.)* ပ်စီးတိုင်းကိရိယာ *hlyat-see-tai-ka-yi-yar*
galvanoscope *(n.)*လျှပ်စီးစမ်းကိရိယာ *hlyat-see-san-ka-yi-yar*
gambit *(n.)* အကွက်ဆင်ခြင်း *a-kwat-sin-chin*
gamble *(n.)* လောင်းကစား *laung-ka-sar*
gambler *(n.)* လောင်းကစားသမား *laung-ka-sar-ta-mar*
game *(n.)* ကစားနည်း *ka-sar-nee*
game changer *(n.)* အမြော်အမြင်ရှိ၊ တီထွင်ဉာဏ်ကောင်းသော သူ *a-myaw-a-myin-shi-ti-htwin-nyan-kaung-taw-thu*
game point *(n.)* နိုင်မှတ် *nai-mat*
gamemaster *(v.)* သရုပ်ဖော်ကစားပွဲကျင်းပသည် *ta-yoke-phaw-ka-sar-pwe-kyin-pa-the*
gamepad *(n.)* ဂိမ်းခလုတ် *game-kha-lote*
gameplayer *(n.)* ဂိမ်းကစားသမား *game-ka-sar-ta-mar*
gamespace *(n.)* ဂိမ်းကစားရာ နေရာ *game-ka-sar-yar-nay-yar*
gamma *(n.)* တတိယဂရိအက္ခရာ *ta-ti-ya-ga-yi-at-kha-yar*
gander *(n.)* ငန်းဖို *ngan-pho*
gang *(n.)* လူဆိုးဂိုဏ်း lu-soe-gai
gangrene *(n.)* သွေးမလျှောက်၍ ခြေထောက် ပုပ်ပွပျက်စီးခြင်း *tway-ma-shaut-ywe-chay-htaut-poke-pwa-pyat-see-chin*
gangster *(n.)* လူဆိုးဂိုဏ်းဝင် *lu-soe-gai-win*
gap *(n.)* အပေါက်၊ ကွက်လပ်၊ ကွာဟချက်၊ လိုအပ်ချက် *a-pauk, kwat-lat, kwar-ha-chat, lo-at-chat*
gape *(v.)* ပါးစပ်အဟောင်းသား ငေးကြည့်သည် *pa-sat-a-haung-tar-ngay-kyi-the*
garage *(n.)* ကားဂိုဒေါင် *kar-go-daung*
garb *(n.)* သတ်မှတ် ဝတ်စုံ *tat-mat-wit-sone*
garbage *(n.)* အမှိုက်ပုံး၊ ပေါက်ကရစကား *a-hmite-pone, pauk-ka-ya-sa-kar*
garden *(n.)* ပန်းခြံ *pan-chan*
gardener *(n.)* ဥယျာဉ်မှူး *au-yin-hmue*
gargle *(v.)* ပလုတ်ကျင်းသည် *pa-hlote-kyin-the*
garland *(n.)* ပန်းကုံး pan-kone
garlic *(n.)* ကြက်သွန်ဖြူ *kyat-toon-phyu*
garlicky *(adj.)* ကြက်သွန်ဖြူစော်နံသော *kyat-toon-phyu-saw-nan-the*
garment *(n.)* အဝတ် *a-wit*
garnish *(n.)* ဖြူးစရာ *phyue-sa-yar*
garnishment *(n.)* ဖြူးစရာ *phyue-sa-yar*
garrotte *(v.)* ကြိုးဖြင့် လည်ပင်းညှစ်သတ်သည် *kyo-phyint-lal-pin-nyit-tat-the*
garrotter *(n.)* လည်ပင်းကို ကြိုးဖြင့် ညှစ်သတ်သူ *lal-pin-ko-kyo-phyint-nyit-tat-thu*
garter *(n.)* သားရေကွင်း၊ မျှော့ကွင်း *ta-yay-kwin, myawt-kwin*
gas *(n.)* ဓာတ်ငွေ့ *dat-ngwe*
gasesous *(adj.)* ဓာတ်ငွေ့နှင့် တူသော *dat-ngwe-nint-tu-taw*
gash *(n.)* ဟက်တက်ကွဲ ဒဏ်ရာ *hat-tat-kwal-dan-yar*
gashing *(adj.)* ဟက်တက်ကွဲသော *hat-tat-kwal-taw*
gasification *(n.)* ဓာတ်ငွေ့ပြောင်းခြင်း *dat-ngwe-pyaung-chin*

gasified *(adj.)* **ဓာတ်ငွေ့ပြောင်းသော** *dat-ngwe-pyaung-taw*
gasify *(v.)* **ဓာတ်ငွေ့ပြောင်းသည်** *dat-ngwe-pyaung-the*
gasket *(n.)* **ဂတ်စကက်** *gat-sa-kat*
gasmask *(n.)* **ဓာတ်ငွေ့ကာ** *dat-ngwe-kar*
gasoline *(n.)* **ဓာတ်ဆီ** *dat-see*
gasp *(n.)* **ပင့်သက်ရှိုက်ခြင်း** *pint-thet-shite-chin*
gassy *(adj.)* **ဓာတ်ငွေ့ပါသော** *dat-ngwe-par-taw*
gastric *(adj.)* **အစာအိမ်နှင့် သက်ဆိုင်သော** a-sar-eain-nint-thet-sai-taw
gastronomy *(n.)* **အစားအသောက်ကောင်းရွေးနည်း၊ ချက်ပြုတ်နည်း၊ စားခြင်း** *a-sar-a-taut-kaung-ywe-nee, chat-pyoke-nee, sar-chin*
gate *(n.)* **ဂိတ်** *gait*
gatehouse *(n.)* **ဂိတ်စောင့်တဲ** *gait-saunt-tae*
gatekeeper *(n.)* **ဂိတ်စောင့်** gait-saunt
gatepost *(n.)* **ခြံတံခါးတိုင်** *chan-ta-khar-tai*
gateway *(n.)* **အဝင်ဝတံခါး** *a-win-wa-ta-khar*
gather *(v.)* **စုသည်** *su-the*
gaudy *(adj.)* **ကြောင်လွန်းသော** *kyaung-lun-taw*
gauge *(n.)* **စံ အထုအပါး** *san-a-htu-a-par*
gaunt *(adj.)* **ပိန်လှီသော** *pain-hlee-taw*
gauntlet *(n.)* **သတ္တုလက်အိတ်** *tat-tu-lat-aik*
gawk *(v.)* **ငမ်းသည်** *ngan-the*
gawky *(adj.)* **ကလန်ကလားနိုင်သော** ka-lan-ka-lar-nai-taw
gay *(n.)* **လိင်တူချင်း ဆက်ဆံသူ** *lain-tu-chin-sat-san-thu*
gaze *(n.)* **ငေးစိုက်ကြည့်ခြင်း** *ngay-site-kyi-chin*
gazelle *(n.)* **ဂဇဲဆိတ်** *ga-zae-seik*
gazette *(n.)* **ဂေဇက်** *gay-zat*
gazillion *(n.)* **ကြီးမားသော ဂဏန်း** *kyi-mar-taw-ga-nan*
gear *(n.)* **ဂီယာ** *gi-yar*
gearbox *(n.)* **ဂီယာအုံ** *gi-yar-ohn*
gearset *(n.)* **ဂီယာအစုံလိုက်** *gi-yar-a-sone-lite*
gearwheel *(n.)* **ဂီယာဘီး** *gi-yar-bee*
geek *(v.)* **ချောင်းသည်၊ ကြည့်သည်** *chaung-the, kyi-the*
geeksville *(n.)* **ကြီးကျယ်သည်ဟု ထင်ရသော နေရာ** *kyi-kyal-the-hu-htin-ya-taw-nay-yar*
geekwear *(n.)* **ဂုရုဝတ်အင်္ကျီ** *gu-yu-wit-in-gyi*
geeky *(adj.)* **ဂုရုအကျင့်အကြံရှိသော** *gu-yu-a-kyint-a-kyan-shi-taw*
geisha *(n.)* **ဂေရှားမယ်** *gay-shar-mal*
gel *(n.)* **ခေါင်းလိမ်းဂျယ်** *kaung-lain-gyal*
gelatin *(n.)* **စေးပျစ်သည့် အရာ** *say-pyit-the-a-yar*
gelatinize *(v.)* **စေးပျစ်ပျစ် ဖြစ်သော** *say-pyit-pyit-phit-taw*
gelatinous *(adj.)* **ကျောက်ကျောကဲ့သို့ ပျစ်ခဲသော** *kyauk-kyaw-kae-tho-pyit-taw*
geld *(v.)* **သင်းသည်** *thin-the*
gelded *(adj.)* **သင်းကွပ်သော** *thin-kwut-taw*
gelding *(n.)* **သင်းကွပ်ခြင်း** *thin-kwut-chin*
gem *(n.)* **ကျောက်မျက်ရတနာ** *kyauk-myat-ya-da-nar*

geminal *(adj.)* တူညီသော အက်တမ်ကို ဖော်ပြသော tu-nyi-taw-at-tam-ko-phaw-pya-taw
geminate *(v.)* အတွဲဖြင့် စီသည် *a-twe-phit-see-the*
Gemini *(n.)* မေထုန်ရာသီဖွား may-htone-yar-ti-phwar
gemmology *(n.)* ကျောက်မျက်ဗေဒ kyauk-myat-bay-da
gender *(n.)* လိင် *lain*
gene *(n.)* မျိုးရိုးဗီဇ *myo-yoe-bi-za*
genealogical *(adj.)* မျိုးရိုးဗီဇဆိုင်ရာ *myo-yoe-bi-za-sai-yar*
genealogy *(n.)* မျိုးရိုးဗီဇပညာ *myo-yoe-bi-za-pyin-nyar*
generable *(adj.)* ထုတ်နိုင်သော *htoke-nai-taw*
general *(adj.)* အထွေထွေ၊ အားလုံး၊ ယေဘုယျ *a-htway-htway, arr-lone, yay-buu-ya*
generally *(adv.)* ယေဘုယျအားဖြင့် *yay-buu-ya-arr-phit*
generate *(v.)* ထုတ်လုပ်သည် *htoke-lote-the*
generation *(n.)* မျိုးဆက် *myo-sat*
generator *(n.)* ဂျင်နရေတာ၊ မီးစက် gyan-na-rat-tor, mee-sat
generosity *(n.)* ရက်ရောမှု *yat-yaw-mu*
generous *(adj.)* ရက်ရောသော yat-yaw-taw
genetic *(adj.)* မျိုးရိုးဗီဇနှင့်ဆိုင်သော *myo-yoe-bi-za-nint-sai-taw*
geneticist *(n.)* မျိုးရိုးဗီဇပညာရှင် *myo-yoe-bi-za-pyin-nyar-shin*
genial *(adj.)* ခင်မင်တတ်သော *khin-min-tat-taw*
geniality *(n.)* ခင်မင်တတ်ခြင်း *khin-min-tat-chin*
genie *(n.)* ဂျီနီနတ်သမီး *gi-ni-nat-ta-mee*
genital *(adj.)* လိင်အင်္ဂါနှင့်ဆိုင်သော *lain-in-gar-nint-sai-taw*
genitalia *(n.)* လိင်အင်္ဂါ *lain-in-gar*
genius *(n.)* ပါရမီရှင် *pa-ra-mi-shin*
genocide *(n.)* လူမျိုးတုံးသတ်ဖြတ်ခြင်း *lu-myo-tone-tat-phat-chin*
genome *(n.)* ဂျီနုန်း *ge,hnone*
genre *(n.)* အနုပညာအမျိုးအစား *a-nu-pyin-nyar-a-myo-a-sar*
genteel *(adj.)* ယဉ်မွန်သော *yi-mon-taw*
gentility *(n.)* ယဉ်မွန်ခြင်း *yi-mon-chin*
gentle *(adj.)* ညင်သာနူးညံ့သော *nyin-tar-nu-nyant-taw*
gentleman *(n.)* လူကြီးလူကောင်း *lu-gyi-lu-gaung*
gentry *(n.)* လူ့ရတတ် *lu-ya-hat*
genuine *(adj.)* စစ်မှန်သော *sit-man-taw*
geographer *(n.)* ပထဝီဝင်ပညာရှင် *pa-hta-wi-win-pyin-nyar-shin*
geographical *(adj.)* ပထဝီဝင် *pa-hta-wi-win*
geography *(n.)* ပထဝီဝင် *pa-hta-wi-win*
geological *(adj.)* ဘူမိဗေဒနှင့် ဆိုင်သော *bu-mi-bay-da-nint-sai-taw*
geologist *(n.)* ဘူမိဗေဒပညာရှင် *bu-mi-bay-da-pyin-nyar-shin*
geology *(n.)* ဘူမိဗေဒ *bu-mi-bay-da*
geometrical *(adj.)* ဂဲသြမေထြီဆိုင်ရာ *gae-aw-may-tree-sai-yar*
geometry *(n.)* ဂဲသြမေထြီ *gae-aw-may-tree*
geopolitical *(adj.)* ပထဝီဝင် နိုင်ငံရေးပညာ *pa-hta-wi-win-nai-ngan-yay-pyin-nyar*
geothermal *(adj.)* မြေကမ္ဘာနှင့် အပူဆိုင်ရာ *myay-ka-bar-nint-a-pu-sai-yar*
geranium *(n.)* ကြွေပန်း *kyay-pan*

germ *(n.)* ရောဂါပိုး *yaw-gar-poe*

germicide *(n.)* ပိုးသတ်ဆေး *poe-tat-say*

germin *(n.)* ဂျာမင်း *gyar-min*

germinate *(v.)* အညှောက်ပေါက်သည် *a-hnyauk-pauk-the*

germination *(n.)* အညှောက်ပေါက်ခြင်း *a-hnyauk-pauk-chin*

gerund *(n.)* ကြိယာနမ် *kyi-yar-nan*

gesture *(n.)* လက်ဟန်ခြေဟန် *lat-han-chay-han*

get *(v.)* ရရှိသည် ya-shi-the

geyser *(n.)* ရေပူစမ်း yay-pu-san

ghastly *(adj.)* ကြမ်ကျက်ဖွယ်ကောင်းသော *kyauk-mat-phwal-kaung-taw*

ghetto *(n.)* လူတန်းစားနိမ့်သော သူများ နေထိုင်ရာ ရပ်ကွက် lu-tan-sar-naint-taw-thu-myar-nay-htai-yar-yat-kwat

ghost *(n.)* သရဲ *ta-ye*

ghost town *(n.)* မြို့ဆိုး myo-soe

ghostwriter *(n.)* ရှဲဒိုးရေးသူ *shal-doe-yay-thu*

ghoul *(n.)* ဖုတ်ကောင် *phoke-kaung*

ghoulish *(adj.)* ဖုတ်ကောင်ဆန်သော *phoke-kaung-san-taw*

giant *(n.)* ဘီလူး *ba-lu*

giantess *(n.)* ဘီလူးမ *ba-lu-ma*

gib *(v.)* ကြောင်ကို ကြိုးချည်ထားသည် *kyaung-ko-kyo-chi-htar-the*

gibber *(n.)* ဗလုံးဗထွေးပြောခြင်း *ba-lone-ba-htway-pyaw-chin*

gibberish *(n.)* ကယောက်ကယက်စကား *ka-yauk-ka-yat-sa-kar*

gibbon *(n.)* မျောက်လွှဲကျော် *myauk-hlwal-kyaw*

gibe *(n.)* လှောင်လုံး၊ ပြောင်လုံး *htaung-lone, pyaung-lone*

giddy *(adj.)* မူးဝေသော *mu-wai-taw*

gift *(n.)* လက်ဆောင် *lat-saung*

gifted *(adj.)* အထုံပါရမီရှိသော *a-htone-pa-ra-mi-shi-taw*

giftwrap *(v.)* လက်ဆောင်ပစ္စည်း လှလှပပ ထုပ်ပေးသည် *lat-saung-pyit-see-hla-hla-pa-pa-htoke-pay-the*

gig *(n.)* တီးမှုတ်ဖျော်ဖြေမှု *tee-moke-phyaw-phyay-mu*

gigabit *(n.)* ဂီဂါဘစ် *gi-ga-bit*

gigabyte *(n.)* ဂီဂါဘိုက် *gi-ga-bite*

gigantic *(adj.)* အလွန်ကြီးမားသော *a-lun-kyi-mar-taw*

giggle *(v.)* တခစ်ခစ်ရယ်သည် *ta-khit-kht-yal-the*

gild *(v.)* ရွှေချသည် *shwe-cha-the*

gilt *(adj.)* ရွှေရည်စိမ်သော *shwe-ch-sein-taw*

gimmick *(v.)* ထွင်လုံး လုပ်သည် *htwin-lone-lote-the*

gimmickry *(n.)* ထွင်လုံး *htwin-lone*

gimp *(n.)* ခြေဆာနေသော သူ *chay-sar-nay-thaw-thu*

gin *(n.)* ဂျင်အရက် *gyin-a-yat*

ginger *(n.)* ချင်းတက် *gyin-tat*

ginger ale *(n.)* ချင်းနံ့သင်းဘီလပ်ရည် *gyin-nant-tin-bi-lat-yay*

gingerbread *(n.)* ချင်းနံ့သင်းပေါင်မုန့် *gyin-nant-tin-paung-hmont*

giraffe *(n.)* သစ်ကုလားအုပ် *tit-ka-lar-oak*

gird *(v.)* ပါတ်သည် *pat-the*

girder *(n.)* ရက်မ *yat-ma*

girdle *(n.)* ခါးစည်းကြိုး *khar-see-kyo*

girl *(n.)* မိန်းကလေး mein-ka-lay

girlish *(adj.)* ကန္ဒဲ့ကလျ ကဗျာဟန် ka-nwe-ka-lya-ka-byar-han

gist *(n.)* အကျဉ်းချုပ် *a-kyin-choke*

give *(v.)* ပေးသည် *pay-the*

gizmo *(n.)* ကိရိယာ *ka-ri-yar*

glacier *(n.)* ရေခဲမြစ် *yay-khae-myit*

glad *(adj.)* ဝမ်းမြောက်သော *wan-myauk-taw*

gladden *(v.)* ဝမ်းမြောက်ဝမ်းသာဖြစ်စေသည် *wan-myauk-wan-tar-phit-say-the*

glade *(n.)* တောတွင်းလဟာ taw-twin-la-har

gladiator *(n.)* ရောမခေတ် တိရစ္ဆာန်နှင့် သတ်ပုတ် ဖျော်ဖြေရသူ yaw-ma-khit-ta-yeik-san-nint-tat-poke-phyaw-phyay-ya-thu

gladiatorial *(adj.)* ရောမခေတ် တိရစ္ဆာန်နှင့် သတ်ပုတ် ဖျော်ဖြေရသော yaw-ma-khit-ta-yeik-san-nint-tat-poke-phyaw-phyay-ya-taw

gladly *(adv.)* ဝမ်းမြောက်စွာ wan-myauk-swar

glam *(adj.)* စွဲလမ်းခြင်း *swal-lan-chin*

glamour *(n.)* မက်မောဖွယ်ရာ *mat-maw-phal-yar*

glance *(v.)* ဖျက်ခနဲ ကြည့်သည် *phat-kha-nae-kyae-the*

gland *(n.)* ဂလင်း *ga-lin*

glare *(v.)* စူးရှတောက်ပသည် *su-sha-taut-pa-the*

glass *(n.)* ဖန် phan

glasses *(n.)* မျက်မှန် *myat-man*

glasshouse *(n.)* ဖန်လုံအိမ် *phan-lon-eain*

glassify *(v.)* ဖန်အဖြစ် ပြောင်းလဲသည် *hpan-aphit-pyaung-lal-the*

glassmaker *(n.)* ဖန်ချက်သူ *phan-chat-thu*

glaucoma *(n.)* ရေတိမ် *yay-tein*

glaze *(n.)* စဋ္ဌ *sint*

glazier *(n.)* မှန်တပ်သမား mam-tat-ta-mar

gleam *(v.)* ဝင်းလက်သည် *win-latt-the*

gleaming *(adj.)* ဝင်းလက်သော *win-lat-taw*

glee *(n.)* အူမြူးခြင်း *au-myue-chin*

gleeful *(adj.)* ပျော်ရွှင်သော *pyaw-shwin-taw*

gleefully *(adv.)* အားရဝမ်းသာ *arr-ya-wan-tar*

glide *(v.)* ညက်ညောစွာ ရွေ့လျားသည် nyat-nyaw-swar-shwe-lyar-the

glider *(n.)* စက်မဲ့လေယာဉ် *sat-mae-lay-yin*

glimmer *(v.)* ခပ်မှိန်မှိန်လင်းသည် *khat-mein-mein-lin-the*

glimpse *(n.)* ရိပ်ခနဲမြင်ခြင်း *yeik-kha-nae-myin-chin*

glitch *(n.)* စွန့်စားမှု *sunt-sar-khan*

glitter *(n.)* ပြိုးပြိုးပြက်ပြက်လက်ခြင်း *pyo-pyo-pyat-pyat-lat-chin*

gloat *(n.)* ပီတိတဖွားဖွားဖြစ်ခြင်း *pi-ti-ta-phwar-phwar-phit-chin*

gloatingly *(adv.)* ဝင့်ကြွားစွာ *wint-kywar-swar*

global *(adj.)* ကမ္ဘာအနှံ့ *ka-bar-a-nant*

global warming *(n.)* ကမ္ဘာကြီး ပူနွေးလာခြင်း *ka-bar-kyi-pu-nway-lar-chin*

globally *(adv.)* တစ်ကမ္ဘာလုံး *ta-ka-bar-lone*

globe *(n.)* ကမ္ဘာလုံး ka-bar-lone

globetrotter *(n.)* ကမ္ဘာလှည့်ခရီးသည် *ka-bar-hlae-kha-yee-the*

gloom *(n.)* မှုန်မှိုင်းနေခြင်း *hmone-hmine-nay-chin*

gloomy *(adj.)* မှုန်မှိုင်းနေသော *hmone-hmine-nay-taw*

glorification *(n.)* အမွှမ်းတင်ခြင်း *a-hmun-tin-chin*
glorify *(v.)* အမွှမ်းတင်သည် *a-hmun-tin-the*
glorious *(adj.)* မွန်မြတ်သော *mon-myat-taw*
glory *(n.)* ထင်ပေါ်ကျော်ကြားမှု *htin-paw-kyaw-kyar-mu*
gloss *(n.)* ရွှန်းလဲ့တောက်ပခြင်း *shun-lae-taut-pa-chin*
glossary *(n.)* ခက်ဆစ် khat-sit
glossy *(adj.)* ချောမွေ့တောက်ပသော chaw-mway-taut-pa-taw
glove *(n.)* လက်အိတ် *lat-aik*
glovebox *(n.)* လက်အိတ်ဘူး *lat-aik-bu*
glow *(v.)* တောက်သည် *taut-the*
glow *(n.)* ခပ်မှိန်မှိန်လင်းခြင်း၊ နီမြန်းခြင်း *khat-mein-mein-lin-chin, ni-myan-chin*
glucose *(n.)* ဂလူးကို့စ် *ga-lu-kose*
glue *(n.)* ကော် *kaw*
glue stick *(n.)* ကော်ထောင့် *kaw-htaunt*
glut *(n.)* အလျှံပယ်ပေါခြင်း a-hlyan-pal-paw-chin
gluten-free *(adj.)* ဂလူတန်ကင်းသော *ga-lu-tan-kin-taw*
glutton *(n.)* အစားကြီးသူ *a-sar-kyi-thu*
gluttony *(n.)* အစားကြူးခြင်း *a-sar-kyu-chin*
glycerine *(n.)* အလှဆီ *a-hla-se*
gnarl *(v.)* ထုံးသည်၊ လိမ်သည် *htone-the, lain-the*
gnaw *(v.)* ကိုက်ဝါးသည် *kite-war-the*
gnome *(n.)* ဒဏ္ဍာရီလာ ဥစ္စာစောင့်လူပုလေး *dan-tar-yee-lar-oak-sar-saunt-lu-pu-lay*
go *(v.)* သွားသည် *twar-the*
goad *(n.)* နှင်တံ *hnin-tan*
goal *(n.)* ပန်းတိုင်၊ ဂိုးပေါက် *pan-tai, goe-pauk*
goalkeeper *(n.)* ဂိုးစောင့် *goe-saunt*
goalpost *(n.)* ဂိုးတိုင် *goe-tai*
goalscoring *(n.)* ဂိုးရခြင်း *goe-ya-chin*
goanna *(n.)* ဂိုအန်းနားပုတ်သင် *go-an-na-poke-tin*
goat *(n.)* ဆိတ် *seik*
gobble *(n.)* အငမ်းမရ မျိုချသည် *a-ngan-ma-ya-myo-cha=the*
goblet *(n.)* ဝိုင်ကလပ်ခွက် *wai-ka-lat-khwat*
god *(n.)* နတ်ဘုရား *nat-pha-yar*
goddess *(n.)* နတ်ဘုရားမ *nat-pha-yar-ma*
godfather *(n.)* ခေါင်းကိုင်အဖ *kaung-kai-a-pha*
godhead *(n.)* ဘုရားသခင် *pha-yar-ta-khin*
godly *(adj.)* ဘုရားတရားကိုင်းရှိုင်းသော *pha-yar-ta-yar-kai-shai-taw*
godown *(n.)* ကုန်လှောင်ရုံ *kone-hlaung-yone*
godsend *(n.)* ဘုရားမခြင်း *pha-yar-ma-chin*
goggles *(n.)* လေကာရေကာမျက်မှန် *lay-kar-yay-kar-myat-man*
gold *(n.)* ရွှေ *shwe*
golden *(adj.)* ရွှေသား၊ ရွှေရောင် *shwe-tar, shwe-yaung*
goldsmith *(n.)* ရွှေပန်းထိမ် *shwe-pan-htein*
golf *(n.)* ဂေါက် *gauk*
golf cart *(n.)* ဂေါက်တွန်းလှည်း *gauk-toon-hlae*
golf course *(n.)* ဂေါက်ကွင်း *gauk-kwin*
gonads *(n.)* မျိုးပွားအင်္ဂါ myo-pyaw-inn-gar

gondola *(n.)* ဂွန်ဒိုလာလှေ *goon-doo-lar-hlay*
gong *(n.)* မောင်း *maung*
goo *(v.)* ကပ်သည်၊ သုတ်သည် *kat-the, tote-the*
good *(adj.)* ကောင်းသော *kaung-taw*
good-bye *(interj.)* နှုတ်ဆက်ပါတယ် *hnote-sat-par-the*
goodness *(n.)* ကောင်းခြင်း၊ ကြင်နာမှု kaung-chin, kyin-nar-mu
goodwill *(n.)* စိတ်ကောင်းစေတနာ *seik-kaung-say-ta-nar*
goof *(n.)* ငတုံး၊ ငအ *nga-tone, nga-a*
goofy *(adj.)* ကြောင်တောင်တောင် *kyaung-taung-taung*
google *(v.)* ဂူဂဲလ်တွင် ရှာဖွေသည် *goo-gal-twin-shar-phway-the*
gooney *(n.)* လူအ *lu-aa*
goose *(n.)* ဘဲငန်း *bae-ngan*
gooseberry *(n.)* ကုလားဆီးဖြူ *ka-lar-see-phyu*
gore *(n.)* သွေးထွက်သံယို *thway-htwat-tan-yo*
gorge *(n.)* ချောက်နက် chauk-nat
gorgeous *(adj.)* ထူးထူးကဲကဲ ကောင်းမွန်သော *htoo-htoo-kae-kae-kaung-mon-taw*
gorilla *(n.)* ဂေါ် ရီလာမျောက်ဝံ *gaw-ri-lar-myauk-win*
gospel *(n.)* ခရစ်ဝင်ကျမ်း *kha-yit-win-kyan*
gossip *(n.)* အတင်းအဖျင်းစကား *a-tin-a-phyin-sa-kar*
gothic *(n.)* ဂေါ့တစ်ဗိသုကာလက်ရာပုံစံ *got-tit-bi-thu-kar-lat-yar-pon-san*
gouda *(n.)* ဒတ်ချ်ဒိန်ခဲ *dat-dain-khae*
gourd *(n.)* ဘူးသီး *bu-thee*
gout *(n.)* ဂေါက်နာ *gauk-nar*
govern *(v.)* အုပ်ချုပ်သည် *oak-choke-the*
governance *(n.)* အုပ်ချုပ်ပုံ *oak-choke-pon*
governess *(n.)* ကလေးထိန်းဆရာမ *ka-lay-htein-sa-yar-ma*
government *(n.)* အစိုးရ *a-soe-ya*
governor *(n.)* ဘုရင်ခံ *ba-yin-khan*
gown *(n.)* ပွဲတက်ဂါဝန် *pwe-tat-gar-win*
grab *(v.)* ဆုပ်ကိုင်သည် *sote-kai-the*
grace *(n.)* ကျက်သရေ *kyat-ta-yay*
graceful *(adj.)* တင့်တယ်သော *tint-the-taw*
gracious *(adj.)* ယဉ်ကျေးသိမ်မွေ့သော *yin-kyay-tint-mway-taw*
gradation *(n.)* အဆင့်ဆင့် *a-sint-sint*
grade *(n.)* အဆင့်အတန်း *a-sint-a-tan*
gradual *(adj.)* ဖြည်းညင်းသော *phyae-nyin-taw*
graduate *(v.)* ဘွဲ့ရသည် *bwe-ya-the*
graduation ceremony *(n.)* ဘွဲ့နှင်းသဘင် *bwe-hnin-ta-bin*
graffiti *(v.)* နံရံပေါ်တွင် ဆွဲသောပုံ *nan-yan-paw-twin-swal-taw-pon*
graft *(n.)* ကိုင်းဆက်ကူးခြင်း *kai-set-ku-chin*
grain *(n.)* ဂျုံ၊ စပါး *gyone, sa-par*
grammar *(n.)* သဒ္ဒါ *ta-dar*
grammarian *(n.)* သဒ္ဒါပညာရှင် *ta-dar-pyin-nyar-shin*
gramme *(n.)* ဂရမ် ga-ran
gramophone *(n.)* အသံဖမ်းစက် *a-tan-phan-sat*
granary *(n.)* ကျီ၊ စပါးကျီ *kyi, sa-par-kyi*
grand *(adj.)* ကြီးကျယ်ခမ်းနားသော *kyi-kyal-khan-nar-taw*

grand finale *(n.)* နောက်ဆုံးဗိုလ်လုပွဲ *naut-sone-bo-lu-pwe*

grandeur *(n.)* ကြီးကျယ်ခမ်းနားခြင်း *kyi-kyal-khan-nar-chin*

grant *(v.)* ဂရန့် ချပေးသည် ga-rant-cha-pay-the

grape *(n.)* စပျစ်သီး *sa-pyit-thee*

graph *(n.)* ဂရပ် *ga-rat*

graphic *(adj.)* ပုံရေးခြင်းဆိုင်ရာ *pon-yay-chin-sai-yar*

grapple *(n.)* လုံးထွေးသတ်ပုတ်ခြင်း lone-htway-tat-poke-chin

grasp *(v.)* ဆုပ်ကိုင်သည် *sote-kai-the*

grass *(n.)* မြက် *myat*

grassland *(n.)* မြက်ခင်းပြင် myat-khin-pyin

grate *(v.)* ခြစ်သည် *chit-the*

grateful *(adj.)* ကျေးဇူးတင်သော *kyay-zuu-tin-taw*

grater *(n.)* ခြစ်ခုံ *chit-khone*

gratification *(n.)* ဝမ်းမြောက်ခြင်း *wan-myauk-chin*

gratis *(adv.)* အခမဲ့ a-kha-mae

gratitude *(n.)* ကျေးဇူးတရား *kyay-zuu-ta-yar*

gratuity *(n.)* လုပ်သက်ဆု *lote-thet-su*

grave *(adj.)* လေးနက်သော *lay-nat-taw*

gravitate *(v.)* ဦးတည်သည် *oo-the-the*

gravitation *(n.)* ဆွဲငင်အား swal-ngin-arr

gravity *(n.)* ကမ္ဘာ့ဆွဲအား ka-bar-swal-ngin-arr

graze *(v.)* စားကျက်တွင် မြက်စားသည် *sar-kyat-twin-myat-sar-the*

grease *(n.)* အမဲဆီ၊ ချောဆီ *a-mae-si, chaw-si*

grease *(v.)* ဆီသုတ်သည် *si-toke-the*

greasy *(adj.)* ဆီပေကျံနေသော *si-pay-kyan-nay-taw*

great *(adj.)* ကြီးမားသော *kyi-mar-taw*

greed *(n.)* အစားလောဘကြီးမှု *a-sar-law-ba-kyi-mu*

greedy *(adj.)* လောဘကြီးသော *law-ba-kyi-taw*

Greek *(n.)* ဂရိနိုင်ငံသား၊ ဂရိဘာသာစကား *ga-ri-nai-ngan-tar, ga-ri-bar-tar-sa-kar*

Greek *(adj.)* ဂရိနှင့် ဆိုင်သော *ga-ri-nint-sai-taw*

green *(adj.)* စိမ်းသော *sein-taw*

green *(n.)* အစိမ်း *a-sein*

greenery *(n.)* အလှစိုက် စိမ်းလန်းသော သစ်ပင်၊ ခြုံနွယ် *a-hla-site-sein-lan-taw-tit-pin-chon-nwe*

greenhouse *(n.)* ဖန်လုံအိမ် phan-lon-eain

greet *(v.)* ကြိုဆို နှုတ်ဆက်သည် *kyo-so-note-sat-the*

grenade *(n.)* ဗုံး *bone*

grey *(adj.)* မီးခိုးရောင် *me-kho-yaung*

grey market *(n.)* အစု ရှယ်ယာများကို တရားဝင် ထုတ်မပေးမီ ရောင်းချခြင်း *a-su-shal-yar-myar-ko-ta-yar-win-htoke-ma-pay-mi-yaung-cha-chin*

greyhound *(n.)* ခွေးသမင် *khway-ta-min*

grief *(n.)* ပူဆွေးမှု *pu-sway-mu*

grievance *(n.)* နစ်နာချက် *nit-nar-chat*

grieve *(v.)* ဝမ်းနည်းကြေကွဲသည် *wan-nae-kyay-kwal-the*

grievous *(adj.)* ဝမ်းနည်းကြေကွဲဖွယ်ရာ wan-nae-kyay-kwal-phwal-yar

grim *(adj.)* မဆုတ်မနစ်သော *ma-sote-ma-nit-taw*

grind *(v.)* ကြိတ်ခြေသည် kyate-chay-the

grinder *(n.)* ကြိတ်စက် *kyate-sat*

grip *(v.)* ဆုပ်ကိုင်သည် *sote-kai-the*

groan *(n.)* ညည်းသံ *nyee-than*

grocer *(n.)* ကုန်စုံဆိုင်ရှင် *kone-sone-sai-shin*

grocery *(n.)* စားသောက်ကုန် *sar-taut-kone*

groom *(v.)* မြင်းကို ပြုစုစောင့်ရှောက်သည် *myin-ko-pyu-su-saunt-shaut-the*

groove *(n.)* မြောင်း *myaung*

grope *(v.)* လိုက်စမ်းသည် *lite-san-the*

gross *(n.)* ၁၂ ဒါဇင် *12 da-zin*

grotesque *(adj.)* မတော်တရော်ဖြစ်သော *ma-taw-ta-yaw-phit-taw*

ground *(n.)* မြေကြီး myay-gyi

ground attack *(n.)* မြေပြင်တိုက်ခိုက်ခြင်း *myay-pyin-tite-khite-chin*

ground clearance *(n.)* မြေပြင်ရှင်းလင်းခြင်း myay-pyin-shin-lin-chin

group *(v.)* အဖွဲ့ဖွဲ့သည် *a-phwe-phwe-the*

grow *(v.)* ကြီးထွားသည် *kyi-htwar-the*

grower *(n.)* စိုက်ပျိုးသူ *site-pyo-thu*

growl *(v.)* မာန်ဖီသည် *man-phi-the*

growth *(n.)* ကြီးထွားမှု *kyi-htwar-mu*

grudge *(v.)* နှမြောသည် *hna-myaw-the*

grumble *(v.)* ညည်းသည် *nyee-the*

grunt *(n.)* အစ်အစ် မြည်သံ *it-it-tan-myee-tan*

grunt *(v.)* တအစ်အစ် မြည်သည် *ta-it-it-myee-tan*

guarantee *(n.)* အာမခံချက် *arr-ma-khan-chat*

guard *(v.)* စောင့်ကြပ်သည်၊ *saunt-kyat-the*

guardian *(n.)* ကာကွယ်စောင့်ရှောက်သူ *kar-kwal-saunt-shaut-thu*

guava *(n.)* မာလကာသီး *ma-la-kar-thee*

guerilla *(n.)* ပြောက်ကျား pyauk-kyar

guess *(n.)* မှန်းဆချက် *man-hsa-chat*

guest *(n.)* ဧည့်သည် ae-the

guest list *(n.)* ဧည့်သည်စာရင်း *ae-the-sa-yin*

guest room *(n.)* ဧည့်သည် အိပ်ခန်း *ae-the-aik-khan*

guidance *(n.)* လမ်းညွှန်ချက် *lan-hnyun-chat*

guide *(v.)* လမ်းညွှန်သည် *lin-hnyun-the*

guide *(n.)* လမ်းပြ *lan-pya*

guideline *(n.)* လမ်းညွှန်ချက် lan-hnyun-chat

guild *(n.)* အစည်းအရုံး a-see-a-yone

guile *(n.)* ပရိယာယ်၊ မာယာ *pa-yi-yal, mar-yar*

guilt *(n.)* အပြစ်ရှိခြင်း *a-pyit-shi-chin*

guilt-free *(adj.)* အပြစ်ကင်းသော a-pyit-kin-taw

guilty *(adj.)* အပြစ်ရှိသော *a-pyit-shi-taw*

guise *(n.)* အယောင်ဆောင်ထားသော အသွင် *a-yaung-saung-htar-taw-a-twin*

guitar *(n.)* ဂီတာ *gi-tar*

gulf *(n.)* ပင်လယ်ကွေ့ *pin-lal-kway*

gull *(n.)* စင်ရော်မျိုး *sin-yaw-myo*

gulp *(n.)* တစ်ကျိုက်၊ တစ်ငုံ ta-kyaik, ta-ngon

gum *(n.)* သွားဖုံး *twar-hpone*

gumboot *(n.)* ရော်ဘာဘွတ်ဖိနပ်ရှည် yaw-bar-boot-phi-nat-shay

gun *(n.)* သေနတ် *ta-nat*

gunpoint *(n.)* သေနတ်ဖြင့် တေ့၍ ta-nat-phint-tay-ywe

gust *(n.)* လေပြင်း *lay-pyin*

gutter *(n.)* ရေတံလျှောက် *yay-ta-shaut*

guttural *(adj.)* လည်ချောင်းသံ *lal-chaung-tan*
gymnasium *(n.)* အားကစားရုံ *arr-ka-sar-yone*
gymnast *(n.)* ကျွမ်းဘားသမား kyun-bar-ta-mar
gymnastic *(adj.)* ကျွမ်းဘားနှင့် ဆိုင်သော *kyun-bar-nint-sai-taw*
gymnastics *(n.)* ကျွမ်းဘားပညာလေ့ကျင့်မှု *kyun-bar-pyin-nyar-lay-kyint-mu*

H

habeas corpus *(n.)* အမိန့်စာ၊ စာချွန်တော်၊ ရုံးထုတ်မိန့် *a-maint-sar, sar-chun-taw, yone-htoke-maint*
habit *(n.)* အကျင့် *a-kyint*
habitable *(adj.)* နေထိုင်ရန် သင့်လျော်သော nay-htai-yan-tint-yaw-taw
habitat *(n.)* နေထိုင်ရာနေရာ nay-htai-yar-nay-yar
habitation *(n.)* နေထိုင်မှု *nay-htai-mu*
habituate *(v.)* အလေ့ပါအောင် ကျင့်ယူသည် *a-lay-par-aung-kyint-yu-the*
hack *(v.)* ခုတ်ထစ်သည် *khote-htit-the*
hacker *(n.)* ဟက်ကာ *hat-kar*
haemoglobin *(n.)* ဟီမိုဂလိုဗင်သွေးဆဲလ် hae-mo-ga-lo-bin-tway-sal
hag *(n.)* ကုန်းမအို *kone-ma-oh*
haggard *(adj.)* မျက်တွင်းကျသော *myat-twin-kya-taw*
haggle *(v.)* ဈေးဆစ်သည် *zay-sit-the*
hail *(n.)* မိုးသီး *moe-thee*
hailstorm *(n.)* မိုးသီးမုန်တိုင်း *moe-thee-mon-tine*
hair *(n.)* ဆံပင် *sa-pin*
hairbrush *(n.)* ဘီး *bee*
hairdryer *(n.)* ဆံပင်အခြောက်ခံစက် *san-pin-a-chauk-khan-sat*
hale *(adj.)* ကျန်းမာသန်စွမ်းသော *kyan-mar-tan-swan-taw*
half *(n.)* တစ်ဝက် *ta-wat*
half-day *(n.)* နေ့တစ်ဝက် nay-ta-wat
half-hearted *(adj.)* စိတ်မပါ့တပါ seik-ma-par-ta-par
hall *(n.)* အိမ်ဦးခန်း၊ ခန်းမကြီး *eain-oo-khan, khan-ma-gyi*
hallmark *(n.)* ဝိသေသလက္ခဏာ wi-tay-ta-lat-kha-nar
hallow *(v.)* သန့်ရှင်းစင်ကြယ်စေသည် tant-shin-sin-kyal-say-the
hallucination *(n.)* စိတ်အာရုံချောက်ချားခြင်း seik-arr-yone-chauk-char-chin
halt *(n.)* ရပ်တန့်ခြင်း *yat-tant-chin*
halve *(v.)* တစ်ဝက်ဝက်သည် *ta-wat-wat-the*
hamlet *(n.)* ဇနပုဒ် *za-na-poke*
hammer *(n.)* တူ tu
hammer *(v.)* တူနှင့် ထုသည် tu-nint-htu-the
hand *(v.)* ပေးသည်၊ ဝေသည် *pay-the, wai-the*
hand baggage *(n.)* လက်ဆွဲအိတ် *lat-swal-aik*
hand lotion *(n.)* လက်လိမ်းလိုးရှင်း *lat-lain-lo-shin*
hand luggage *(n.)* လက်ဆွဲအိတ် *lat-swal-aik*
handbill *(n.)* လက်ကမ်းကြော်ငြာ *lat-khan-kyaw-nyar*
handbook *(n.)* လက်စွဲ *lat-swal*

handbrake *(n.)* လက်ဆွဲဘရိတ် *lat-swal-ba-rate*
handcuff *(n.)* လက်ထိပ် *lat-htaik*
handful *(n.)* လက်တစ်ဆုပ်စာ *lat-ta-soke-sar*
handicap *(n.)* အနှောင့်အယှက် *a-naut-a-shat*
handicap *(v.)* အဟန့်အတားဖြစ်သည် *a-hant-a-tar-phit-the*
handicraft *(n.)* လက်မှုပညာ *lat-mu-pyin-nyar*
handiwork *(n.)* လက်ရာ *lat-yar*
handkerchief *(n.)* လက်ကိုင်ပဝါ *lat-kai-pa-war*
handle *(v.)* ကိုင်တွယ်သည် *kai-twal-the*
handsome *(adj.)* ရုပ်ဖြောင့်သော *yauk-phaunt-taw*
handy *(adj.)* အသုံးဝင်သော a-tone-win-taw
hang *(v.)* ချိတ်ဆွဲသည် *chait-swal-the*
hanker *(v.)* တောင့်တသည် *taunt-ta-the*
haphazard *(adj.)* စနစ်တကျမရှိသော *sa-nit-ta-kya-ma-shi-taw*
happen *(v.)* ဖြစ်ပွားသည် *phit-pwar-the*
happening *(n.)* အဖြစ်အပျက် *a-phit-a-pyat*
happiness *(n.)* ပျော်ရွှင်မှု *pyaw-shwin-mu*
happy *(adj.)* ပျော်ရွှင်သော *pyaw-shwin-taw*
harass *(v.)* အနှောင့်အယှက်ပေးသည် *a-naut-a-shat-pay-the*
harassment *(n.)* အနှောင့်အယှက် *a-naut-a-shat*
harbour *(n.)* ဆိပ်ကမ်း *seik-kan*
hard *(adv.)* ခက်ခက်ခဲခဲ *khat-khat-khae-khae*
harden *(v.)* အရေထူသည်၊ မာကျောစေသည် *a-yay-htu-the, mar-kyaw-say-the*
hardihood *(n.)* အလွန်အမင်းခက်ခဲမှုကို ခံနိုင်စွမ်း *a-lun-a-min-khat-khae-mu-ko-lat-khan-nai-swan*
hardly *(adv.)* ခက်ခက်ခဲခဲ khat-khat-khae-khae
hardship *(n.)* ဆင်းရဲဒုက္ခ *sin-ye-dote-kha*
hardware *(n.)* ကွန်ပျူတာအမာထည် *kon-pyu-tar-a-mar-htae*
hard-working *(adj.)* အလုပ်ကြိုးစားသော *a-lote-kyo-sar-taw*
hardy *(adj.)* ကျန်းမာသန်စွမ်းသော kyan-mar-tan-swan-taw
hare *(n.)* တောယုန် taw-yone
harm *(v.)* ထိခိုက်နစ်နာစေသည် *hti-khite-nit-nar-say-the*
harmful *(adj.)* အန္တရာယ်ရှိသော *an-da-yal-shi-taw*
harmless *(adj.)* အန္တရာယ် မရှိသော *an-da-yal-ma-shi-taw*
harmonious *(adj.)* သဟဇာတဖြစ်သော၊ သင့်မြတ်သော ta-ha-zar-ta-phit-taw, tint-myat-taw
harmonium *(n.)* အော်ဂင် *aw-gan*
harmony *(n.)* ဟာမိုနီ၊ သဟဇာတဖြစ်ခြင်း *har-mo-ni, ta-ha-zar-ta-phit-chin*
harness *(n.)* ကကြိုး *ka-kyo*
harp *(n.)* စောင်း *saung*
harsh *(adj.)* ကြမ်းတမ်းသော *kyan-tan-taw*
harvest *(n.)* သီးနှံရိတ်သိမ်းခြင်း *thee-nan-yeik-thein-chin*
harvester *(n.)* သီးနှံရိတ်သိမ်းသူ *thee-nan-yeik-thein-thu*
haste *(n.)* အမြန်လုပ်ဆောင်ခြင်း a-myan-lote-saung-chin

hasten *(v.)* အမြန်ပြီးစေသည် *a-myan-pi-say-the*
hasty *(adj.)* အလောတကြီး ပြောဆို၊ ပြုမူသည် a-law-ta-gyi-pyaw-se-pyu-mu-the
hat *(n.)* ဦးထုတ် oo-htoke
hatch *(n.)* ကုန်တင်ကုန်ချပေါက်၊ မလွယ်ပေါက် *kone-tin-kone-cha-pauk, ma-lwal-pauk*
hatchet *(n.)* ပုဆိန် *pa-sein*
hate *(v.)* မုန်းသည် hmone-the
hat-trick *(n.)* တစ်ပွဲတွင် သွင်းသော ဂိုးသုံးဂိုး *ta-pwe-twin-twin-taw-goe-tone-goe*
haughty *(adj.)* မာနကြီးသော *ma-na-kyi-taw*
haunt *(v.)* ခြောက်သည် *chauk-the*
have *(v.)* ရှိသည် *shi-the*
haven *(n.)* ကွန်းခိုရာ *kun-kho-yar*
havoc *(n.)* ဖြောင်းဆန်ခြင်း *byaung-san-chin*
hawk *(n.)* သိမ်းငှက် *thein-nget*
hawker *(n.)* ခေါင်းရွက်ဗျပ်ထိုးဈေးသည် *kaung-ywet-byat-htoe-zay-the*
hawthorn *(n.)* ဟော့သွန်းဆူးပင် *hot-toon-su-pin*
hay *(n.)* မြက်ခြောက် *myat-chauk*
hazard *(n.)* ဘေး၊ အန္တရာယ် *bay, an-da-yal*
haze *(n.)* မှုန်ဝါးဝါးဖြစ်ခြင်း *hmone-war-war-phit-chin*
hazy *(adj.)* မြူဆိုင်းသော *myu-sai-taw*
he *(pron.)* သူ *thu*
head *(n.)* ဦးခေါင်း *oo-kaung*
headache *(n.)* ခေါင်းကိုက်ခြင်း *gaung-kite-chin*
headband *(n.)* ခေါင်းစည်း gaung-see
heading *(n.)* ခေါင်းစီး *gaung-see*
headlight *(n.)* ရှေ့မီး *shay-mee*
headline *(n.)* ခေါင်းစီး gaung-see
headlong *(adv.)* ဦးစောက်ကျွမ်းပြန် *oo-saut-kyun-pyan*
headquarter *(v.)* ဌာနချုပ် *htar-na-choke*
headstrong *(adj.)* ခေါင်းမာသော *gaung-mar-taw*
heal *(v.)* ကုသသည် *ku-ta-the*
health *(n.)* ကျန်းမာရေး *kyan-mar-yay*
healthy *(adj.)* ကျန်းမာသော *kyan-mar-taw*
heap *(v.)* စုပုံသည် *su-pon-the*
hear *(v.)* ကြားသည် *kyar-the*
hearsay *(n.)* အကြားသက်သေ *a-kyaw-thet-tay*
heart *(n.)* နှလုံးသား *na-lone-tar*
heartbeat *(n.)* နှလုံးခုန်သံ *na-lone-khone-tan*
heartbreak *(n.)* အသည်းကွဲခြင်း *a-tal-kwe-chin*
hearth *(n.)* မီးလင်းဖို *mee-lin-pho*
heartily *(adv.)* လှိုက်လှဲစွာ *hlite-lal-swar*
heat *(v.)* ပူသည် *pu-the*
heat-resistant *(adj.)* အပူဒဏ်ခံနိုင်သော a-pu-dan-khan-nai-taw
heatstroke *(n.)* အပူကြောင့် လေဖြတ်ခြင်း a-pu-kyaunt-lay-phat-chin
heave *(v.)* ပင့်မသည် *pint-ma-the*
heaven *(n.)* ကောင်းကင်ဘုံ *kaung-kin-bon*
heavenly *(adj.)* ကောင်းကင်ဘုံနှင့် ဆိုင်သော *kaung-kin-bon-nint-sai-taw*
heavily *(adv.)* လေးလံစွာ lay-lan-swar
heavy *(adj.)* လေးလံသော lay-lay-taw

hedge *(n.)* ချုံတန်းစည်းရိုး *chon-tan-see-yoe*
heed *(n.)* ဂရုစိုက်ခြင်း *ga-yu-site-chin*
heel *(n.)* ခြေဖနှောင့် *chay-pha-naut*
hefty *(adj.)* ထွားကျိုင်းသန်မာသော *htwar-kyaing-tan-mar-taw*
height *(n.)* အမြင့် *a-myint*
heighten *(v.)* မြှင့်သည် *hmyint-the*
heinous *(adj.)* အလွန်ယုတ်မာသော *a-lun-yoke-mar-taw*
heir *(n.)* အမွေခံ *a-mway-khan*
heiress *(n.)* အမွေခံအမျိုးသမီး a-mway-khan-a-myo-ta-mee
hell *(n.)* ငရဲ *nga-yee*
helm *(n.)* ပဲ့ထိန်းလက်ကိုင်ဘီး *pae-htain-lat-kai-bee*
helmet *(n.)* ဟဲလ်မတ်ဦးထုပ် *hel-mat-oo-htoke*
help *(n.)* အကူအညီ *a-ku-a-nyi*
helpful *(adj.)* ကူညီတတ်သော *ku-nyi-tat-taw*
helpless *(adj.)* အကူအညီမဲ့သော *a-ku-a-nyi-mae-taw*
helpmate *(n.)* အိမ်ထောင်ဖက်၊ အကူအညီပေးသူ *ain-htaung-phat, a-ku-a-nyi-pay-thu*
hemisphere *(n.)* စက်လုံးခြမ်း *sat-lone-chan*
hemp *(n.)* ပိုက်ဆံလျှော်ပင် *pike-san-shaw-pin*
hen *(n.)* ကြက် *kyat*
hence *(adv.)* ဤအကြောင်းကြောင်းကြောင့် e-a-kyaung-kyaung-kyaunt
henceforth *(adv.)* ဤအချိန်မှစ၍ နောင်တွင် e-a-chain-ma-sa-ywe-naung-twin
henceforward *(adv.)* ဤအချိန်မှစ၍ နောင်တွင် *e-a-chain-ma-sa-ywe-naung-twin*
henchman *(n.)* လူယုံတော် *lu-yone-taw*
henpeck *(v.)* မိန်းမအနိုင်ခံရသည် *mein-ma-a-nai-khan-ya-the*
her *(pron.)* သူမ *thu-ma*
herald *(v.)* ကြေညာသည် *kyay-nyar-the*
herb *(n.)* အပင်ပျော့ *a-pin-pawt*
herculean *(adj.)* အင်အားကြီးမားသော *in-arr-kyi-mar-taw*
herd *(n.)* အုပ် *oak*
herdsman *(n.)* အုပ်ကို ထိန်းကျောင်းသူ *oak-ko-htain-kyaung-thu*
here *(adv.)* ဒီမှာ *di-mar*
hereabouts *(adv.)* အနီးအနားတွင် *a-nee-a-nar-twin*
hereafter *(n.)* အနာဂတ်ကာလတွင် *a-nar-gat-kar-la-twin*
hereditary *(adj.)* မျိုးရိုးလိုက်သော *myo-yoe-lite-taw*
heredity *(n.)* မျိုးရိုး *myo-yoe*
heritable *(adj.)* မျိုးရိုးဆက်ခံနိုင်သော *myo-yoe-sat-khan-nai-taw*
heritage *(n.)* အမွေအနှစ် *a-mway-a-nit*
hermit *(n.)* ရသေ့ *ya-thae*
hermitage *(n.)* ရသေ့သင်္ခမ်းကျောင်း *ya-thae-tin-khan-kyaung*
hernia *(n.)* အူကျွံနာ *oo-kywun-nar*
hero *(n.)* သူရဲကောင်း *thu-ye-gaung*
heroic *(adj.)* ရဲစွမ်းသတ္တိရှိသော *ye-swan-tat-ti-shi-taw*
heroine *(n.)* ဘိန်းဖြူ *bain-phyu*
heroism *(n.)* သူရဲကောင်းကိုးကွယ်ဝါဒ *thu-ye-gaung-koe-kwal-war-da*

herring *(n.)* ငါးသလောက် *ngar-ta-laut*

hesitant *(adj.)* တုံ့ဆိုင်းတုံ့ဆိုင်းဖြစ်သော *tont-sai-tont-sai-phit-taw*

hesitate *(v.)* တုံ့ဆိုင်းသည် *tont-sai-the*

hesitation *(n.)* တုံ့ဆိုင်းခြင်း *tont-sai-chin*

hew *(v.)* ခုတ်ဖြတ်သည် *khote-phat-the*

heyday *(n.)* ကောင်းစားချိန် *kaung-sar-chain*

hibernation *(n.)* ဆောင်းခိုခြင်း saung-kho-chin

hiccup *(n.)* ကြို့ထိုးသံ *kyo-htoe-tan*

hide *(v.)* ပုန်းကွယ်သည် *pone-kwal-the*

hideous *(adj.)* ကြောက်မက်ဖွယ်ကောင်းသော *kyauk-mat-phwal-kaung-taw*

hierarchy *(n.)* ရာထူးဂုဏ်သိမ်အဆင့်ဆင့် yar-htoo-gon-tein-a-sint-sint

high *(adj.)* မြင့်သော *myint-taw*

higher education *(n.)* အဆင့်မြင့်ပညာရေး a-sint-myint-pyin-nyar-yay

highlight *(n.)* မြင်သာအောင် လုပ်ခြင်း *myin-tar-aung-lote-chin*

highly *(adv.)* မြင့်မားစွာ *myint-mar-swar*

Highness *(n.)* မင်းညီမင်းသားသုံး စကားလုံး *min-nyi-min-tar-tone-sa-kar-lone*

highway *(n.)* ဟိုင်းဝေးလမ်းမကြီး *hai-way-lan-ma-gyi*

hilarious *(adj.)* အလွန်ရယ်ဖွယ်ကောင်းသည် *a-lun-ye-phwal-kaung-the*

hilarity *(n.)* မြူးတူးပျော်ရွှင်ခြင်း *my-tu-pyaw-shwin-chin*

hill *(n.)* တောင်ကုန်း၊ တောင်တန်း *taung-kone, taung-tan*

hillock *(n.)* တောင်ပူစာ taung-pu-zar

him *(pron.)* သူ *thu*

hinder *(v.)* တားဆီးသည် *tar-see-the*

hindrance *(n.)* အဟန့်အတား *a-hant-a-tar*

hint *(v.)* စကားရိပ်သန်းသည် sa-kar-yeik-tan-the

hip *(n.)* တင်ပါး tin-bar

hire *(v.)* ငှားသည် *hngar-the*

hireling *(n.)* အငှားလိုက်သူ *a-hngar-lite-thu*

his *(pron.)* သူ၏ *thu-ae*

hiss *(n.)* ရှူးရှူးမြည်သံ *shu-shu-myee-tan*

historian *(n.)* သမိုင်းပညာရှင် *ta-mai-pyin-nyar-shin*

historic *(adj.)* သမိုင်းဝင် *ta-mai-win*

historical *(adj.)* သမိုင်းနှင့်ဆိုင်သော *ta-mai-nint-sai-taw*

history *(n.)* သမိုင်း *ta-mai*

hit *(n.)* ထိမှန်ခြင်း *hti-hman-chin*

hit *(v.)* ထိုးနှက်သည်၊ ထိသည် *htoe-nat-the, hti-the*

hitch *(n.)* အခက်အခဲ *a-hat-a-khae*

hither *(adv.)* ဤနေရာသို့ *e-nay-yar-tho*

hitherto *(adv.)* ဤအချိန်အထိ *e-a-chain-a-hti*

hive *(n.)* ပျားအုံ *pyae-ohn*

hoarse *(adj.)* အသံပြာသော *a-tan-pyar-taw*

hoax *(v.)* နောက်ပြောင်လိမ်လည်သည် *naut-pyaung-lain-lal-the*

hobby *(n.)* ဝါသနာ *war-ta-nar*

hobbyhorse *(n.)* စိတ်ကြိုက်ဘာသာရပ် *seik-kyaik-bar-tar-yat*

hobnob *(v.)* အကျွမ်းတဝင်ပြုသည် a-kyuwn-ta-wiwn-pyu-the

hockey *(n.)* ဟော်ကီ *hor-ky*

hoist *(v.)* မြှောက်ပင့်သည် *hmyaut-pint-the*

hold *(n.)* ဆုပ်ကိုင်ခြင်း *sote-kai-chin*

holdback *(n.)* **ကန့်သတ်ချက်** *kant-thet-chat*
hole *(v.)* **ဖောက်သည်** *phauk-the*
holiday *(n.)* **အားလပ်ရက်** *arr-lat-yat*
hollow *(n.)* **တွင်းကြီး၊ ချိုင့်ကြီး** twin-kyi, gyaint-kyi
holocaust *(n.)* **ကပ်ဆိုက်ခြင်း** *kat-site-chin*
holograph *(n.)* **သုံးဖက်မြင်ဓာတ်ပုံ** *tone-phat-myn-dat-pon*
holy *(adj.)* **ထာဝရဘုရားနှင့် ဆိုင်သော** *htar-wa-ya-pha-yar-nint-sai-taw*
homage *(n.)* **ဂါရဝပြုခြင်း** *gar-ra-wa-pyu-chin*
home *(n.)* **အိမ်** *eain*
home-made *(adj.)* **အိမ်တွင်းလုပ်** eain-twin-lote
homeopath *(n.)* **ဓာတ်ကြမ်းကုဆရာ** *dat-kyan-ku-sa-yar*
homeopathy *(n.)* **ဓာတ်ကြမ်းကုသနည်း** *dat-kyan-ku-ta-nee*
homesick *(adj.)* **အိမ်လွမ်းသော** *eain-luan-taw*
homicide *(n.)* **လူသတ်မှု** lu-tat-mu
homogeneous *(adj.)* **မျိုးတူဖြစ်သော** *myo-tu-phit-taw*
honest *(adj.)* **ရိုးသားသော** *yoe-tar-taw*
honesty *(n.)* **ရိုးသားမှု** yoe-tar-mu
honey *(n.)* **ပျားရည်၊ အချစ်** *pyar-yay, a-chit*
honeycomb *(n.)* **ပျားလပို့** *pyar-la-poe*
honeymoon *(n.)* **ပျားရည်စမ်းခရီး** *pyar-yay-san-kha-yee*
honorarium *(n.)* **ညာဏ်ပူဇော်ခ** *nyan-pu-zaw-kha*
honorary *(adj.)* **ဂုဏ်ထူးဆောင်** *gon-htoo-saung*
honour *(n.)* **ဂုဏ်ပြုခြင်း** *gon-pyu-chin*
honour *(v.)* **ဂုဏ်ပြုသည်** gon-pyu-the
honourable *(adj.)* **ဂုဏ်သရေရှိသော** *gon-ta-ya-shi-taw*
hood *(n.)* **ခြုံထည်၊ ခေါင်းစွပ်မျက်နှာဖုံး** *chon-htae, gaung-sut-myat-nar-hpone*
hoodwink *(v.)* **လိမ်လည်သည်** *lain-lae-the*
hoof *(n.)* **ခွာ** khwar
hook *(n.)* **ချိတ်** *chaik*
hooligan *(n.)* **လမ်းသရဲ** *lan-ta-ye*
hoot *(n.)* **ဟစ်ရယ်သံ** *hit-yal-tan*
hop *(n.)* **ခြေတစ်ပေါင်ကျိုးခုန်ခြင်း** *chay-ta-paung-kyo-khone-chin*
hope *(n.)* **မျှော်လင့်ချက်** *myaw-lint-chat*
hopeful *(adj.)* **မျှော်လင့်သော** *myaw-lint-taw*
hopeless *(adj.)* **မျှော်လင့်ချက်မရှိသော** *myaw-lint-chat-ma-shi-taw*
horde *(n.)* **လူစုလူဝေး** *lu-su-lu-way*
horizon *(n.)* **မိုးကုပ်စက်ဝိုင်း** *moe-kote-sat-wine*
horn *(n.)* **ဦးချို** *oo-cho*
hornet *(n.)* **ပျားတူ** *pyaw-tu*
horrible *(adj.)* **ကြောက်မက်ဖွယ်ကောင်းသော** *kyauk-mat-phwal-kaung-taw*
horrify *(v.)* **ထိတ်လန့်သည်** *htaik-lant-the*
horror *(n.)* **ကြောက်ရွံ့ခြင်း** *kyauk-shount-chin*
horse *(n.)* **မြင်း** *myin*
horseshoe *(n.)* **မြင်းသံခွာ** myin-tan-kwar
horticulture *(n.)* **ဥယျာဉ်စိုက်ခြင်းအတတ်** *oo-yin-site-chin-a-tat*
hose *(n.)* **ပိုက်လုံး** *pike-lone*
hosiery *(n.)* **ပိုက်လုံး** *pike-lone*

hospitable *(adj.)* သက်တောင့်သက်သာရှိသော tat-taunt-tat-tar-shi-taw

hospital *(n.)* ဆေးရုံ *say-yone*

hospitality *(n.)* ဧည့်ဝတ်ကျေပွန်မှု *ae-wit-kyay-pon-mu*

host *(n.)* အိမ်ရှင်၊ တစ်ပြုံတစ်ခေါင်း *eain-shin, ta-pyone-ta-khaung*

hostage *(n.)* ဓားစာခံ *da-sar-khan*

hostel *(n.)* ဘော်ဒါဆောင် *baw-dar-saung*

hostile *(adj.)* ရန်လိုသော၊ အပြင်းအထန်ဆန့်ကျင်သော *yan-lo-taw, a-pyin-a-htan-sant-kyin-taw*

hostility *(n.)* ရန်လိုစိတ် *yan-lo-seik*

hot *(adj.)* ပူသော pu-taw

hotchpotch *(n.)* သောင်းပြောင်း *taung-pyaung*

hotel *(n.)* ဟိုတယ် *ho-tal*

hound *(n.)* အမဲလိုက်ခွေး *a-me-lite-khway*

hour *(n.)* နာရီ *nar-yee*

house *(n.)* အိမ် *eain*

household *(n.)* အိမ်ထောင်စု *eain-htaung-su*

how *(adv.)* ဘယ်လို *bal-lo*

however *(adv.)* ဒါပေမယ့် *dar-pay-mae*

however *(conj.)* သော်ငြားလည်း *daw-nyar-lal*

howl *(n.)* အူသံ၊ အော်သံ *au-tan, aw-tan*

hub *(n.)* ပုံတောင်း *pon-taung*

hubbub *(n.)* ပွက်လောရိုက်သံ *pwat-law-yite-tan*

huge *(adj.)* ကြီးမားသော kyi-mar-taw

hum *(n.)* တစီစီမြည်သံ *a-wi-wi-myae-tan*

human *(adj.)* လူသား *lu-tar*

humane *(adj.)* လူဆန်သော *lu-san-thaw*

humanitarian *(adj.)* လူသားချင်းစာနာသော *lu-tar-chin-sar-nar-taw*

humanity *(n.)* လူသား *lu-tar*

humanize *(v.)* စာနာတတ်သည် *sar-nar-tat-the*

humble *(adj.)* နှိမ့်ချမှုရှိသော *naint-cha-mu-shi-taw*

humdrum *(adj.)* ငြီးငွေ့ပျင်းရိဖွယ်ကောင်းသော *nyee-ngwe-pyint-yi-phwal-kaung-taw*

humid *(adj.)* စိုထိုင်းသော *soe-htai-taw*

humidity *(n.)* စိုထိုင်းစ *soe-htai-sa*

humiliate *(v.)* အရှက်ခွဲသည် *a-shat-kwal-the*

humiliation *(n.)* မျက်နှာပျက်ရခြင်း *myat-nar-pyat-ya-chin*

humility *(n.)* နှိမ့်ချခြင်း naint-cha-chin

humorist *(n.)* ဟာသဉာဏ်ရွှင်သူ *har-ta-nyan-shwin-thu*

humorous *(adj.)* ဟာသဉာဏ်ရှိသော *har-ta-nyan-shwin-taw*

humour *(n.)* ဟာသ *har-ta*

hunch *(n.)* စိတ်ထင် *seik-htin*

hundred *(n.)* တစ်ရာ ta-yar

hunger *(n.)* ဆာလောင်ခြင်း sar-laung-chin

hungry *(adj.)* ဆာလောင်သော *sar-laung-taw*

hunt *(v.)* တောလိုက်သည် *taw-lite-the*

hunter *(n.)* မုဆိုး mote-soe

huntsman *(n.)* မုဆိုး mote-soe

hurdle *(n.)* တန်း tan

hurl *(v.)* ပစ်သည် *pyit-the*

hurrah *(interj.)* ဟူးရေ hoo-yay

hurricane *(n.)* ဟာရီကိန်းမုန်တိုင်း *har-yee-kain-mone-tine*

hurry *(v.)* **လောသည်** *law-the*

hurt *(n.)* **နာကျင်ခြင်း** *nar-kyin-chin*

husband *(n.)* **ခင်ပွန်း** *khin-pon*

husbandry *(n.)* **စိုက်ပျိုးမွေးမြူရေး** *site-pyo-mway-my-yay*

hush *(n.)* **ငြိမ်သက်ခြင်း** *nyein-thet-chin*

husk *(n.)* **အခွံ** *a-khun*

husky *(adj.)* **အက်ကွဲသော** *at-kwal-taw*

hustle *(v.)* **တွန်းထုတ်သည်** *tun-htoke-the*

hut *(n.)* **တဲ** tae

hyaena, hyena *(n.)* **ဟိုင်အီးနားတိရစ္ဆာန်** *hai-ei-nar-ta-yeik-san*

hybrid *(n.)* **ကပြား** *ka-pyar*

hydrogen *(n.)* **ဟိုက်ဒရိုဂျင်ဒြပ်** *hai-da-ro-gyin-drat*

hygiene *(n.)* **တစ်ကိုယ်ရေသန့်ရှင်းရေး** *ta-koe-yay-tant-shint-yay*

hygienic *(adj.)* **သန့်ရှင်းပြီး ရောဂါမဖြစ်စေနိုင်သော** *tant-shin-pi-yaw-gar-ma-phit-say-nai-taw*

hymn *(n.)* **ဓမ္မတေး** *da-ma-tay*

hyperbole *(n.)* **အတိဝုတ္တိ** *a-ti-woke-ti*

hypnotism *(n.)* **စိတ်ညှို့ပညာ** *seik-nyo-pyin-nyar*

hypnotize *(v.)* **ညှို့သည်** *nyo-the*

hypocrisy *(n.)* **သူတော်ကောင်းဟန်ဆောင်ခြင်း** *thu-taw-kaung-han-saung-chin*

hypocrite *(n.)* **ကြောင်သူတော်** *kyaung-thu-daw*

hypocritical *(adj.)* **ကြောင်သူတော်** *kyaung-thu-daw*

hypothesis *(n.)* **အနုမာန အယူအဆ** *a-nu-mar-na-a-yu-a-sa*

hypothetical *(adj.)* **အနုမာန အယူအဆကို အခြေခံသော** a-nu-mar-na-a-yu-a-sa-ko-a-chay-khan-taw

hysteria *(n.)* **စိတ်ချောက်ချားရောဂါ** *seik-chauk-char-yay-gar*

hysterical *(adj.)* **ကယောင်ချောက်ချားဖြစ်သော** *ka-yaung-chauk-char-phit-taw*

I

I *(pron.)* **ကျွန်ုပ်** *kyone-note*

iambic *(adj.)* **နရီစည်းဝါး** *na-yee-see-war*

ice *(v.)* **ရေခဲသည်** *yay-khae-the*

ice *(n.)* **ရေခဲ** *yay-khae*

ice bucket *(n.)* **ရေခဲပုံး** yay-khae-pone

ice cream *(n.)* **ရေခဲမုန့်** *yay-khae-hmont*

iceberg *(n.)* **ရေခဲစိုင်ကြီး** *yay-khae-sai-gyi*

iceblock *(n.)* **ရေခဲတုံး** *yay-khae-tone*

icebreaker *(n.)* **ရေခဲပြင်ခွဲသင်္ဘော** *yay-khae-pyin-khwal-tin-baw*

icecap *(n.)* **ရေခဲထာဝစဉ် ဖုံးလွှမ်းခြင်း** *yay-khae-htar-wa-zin-phone-hlwan-chin*

ice-cold *(adj.)* **ရေခဲတမျှ အေးသော** yay-khae-ta-hmya-aye-taw

iced *(adj.)* **ရေခဲစိမ်** *yay-khae-sein*

icicle *(n.)* **ရေခဲပန်းဆွဲ** *yay-khae-pan-swal*

icon *(n.)* **အိုင်ကွန်** *ai-kon*

iconic *(adj.)* **အိုင်ကွန်ဖြစ်သော၊ အထိန်းအမှတ်ဖြစ်သော** *ai-kon-phit-taw, a-htein-a-mat-phit-taw*

iconoclastic *(adj.)* **အများလက်ခံထားသော ဓလေ့များကို ပုတ်ခတ်ပြောဆိုသော** *a-myaw-*

lat-khan-htar-taw-da-lay-myar-ko-poke-khat-pyaw-soe-taw

icy *(adj.)* **အလွန်အေးသော** a-lun-aye-taw

idea *(n.)* **အိုင်ဒီယာ၊ အယူအဆ** *ai-de-ya, a-yu-a-sa*

ideal *(n.)* **စံ** *san*

idealism *(n.)* **စိတ်ကူးယဉ်ဝါဒ** *seik-ku-yin-wa-da*

idealist *(n.)* **အတွေးအမြင် ပဓာနဝါဒီ** *a-tway-a-myin-pa-dar-na-wa-di*

idealistic *(adj.)* **အတွေးအမြင် ပဓာနဖြစ်သော** a-tway-a-myin-pa-dar-na-phit-taw

idealize *(v.)* **စံပြုသည်** *san-pyu-the*

ideate *(v.)* **အိုင်ဒီယာထုတ်သည်** i-de-ya-htoke-the

identical *(adj.)* **ထပ်တူဖြစ်သော** *htet-tu-phit-taw*

identification *(n.)* **ခွဲခြားရွေးထုတ်ခြင်း၊ သက်သေခံကတ်ပြား** *kwal-char-yway-htoke-chin, thet-tay-khan-kat-pyar*

identify *(v.)* **ဖော်ထုတ်သည်၊ ရွေးထုတ်သည်၊ ခွဲခြားနိုင်သည်** *phaw-htoke-the, yway-htoke-the, kwal-char-nai-the*

identity *(n.)* **ကိုယ်ပိုင်လက္ခဏာ** *ko-pai-lat-kha-nar*

identity card *(n.)* **သက်သေခံကတ်ပြား** *tat-tay-khan-kat-pyar*

idiocy *(n.)* **မိုက်မဲမှု** *mite-mae-mu*

idiom *(n.)* **ဓလေ့သုံးစကား** *da-lay-tone-sa-kar*

idiomatic *(adj.)* **ဓလေ့သုံးဆန်သော** *da-lay-tone-san-taw*

idiot *(n.)* **ငတုံး** *nga-tone*

idiotic *(adj.)* **ငတုံးဖြစ်သော** *nga-tone-phit-taw*

idle *(adj.)* **အသုံးမကျသော** *a-tone-ma-kya-taw*

idleness *(n.)* **အလုပ်လက်မဲ့ဖြစ်ခြင်း** *a-lote-lat-mae-phit-chin*

idler *(n.)* **လူပျင်း** *lu-pyin*

idol *(n.)* **အသည်းစွဲ** *a-the-swal*

idolater *(n.)* **ရုပ်တု ကိုးကွယ်သူ** *yoke-htu-koe-kwal-thu*

if *(conj.)* **အကယ်၍** *a-kal-ywe*

igloo *(n.)* **သံခမောက်ပုံအိမ်ငယ်** *tan-kha-mauk-pon-eain-nge*

ignite *(v.)* **လောင်သည်** *laung-the*

ignition *(n.)* **မီးပေးရသော အပိုင်း** *mee-pay-ya-taw-a-pai*

ignoble *(adj.)* **ယုတ်ညံ့သော** yoke-nyant-taw

ignorance *(n.)* **မသိခြင်း** *ma-thi-chin*

ignorant *(adj.)* **ပညာမဲ့သော** *pyin-nyar-mae-taw*

ignore *(v.)* **လျစ်လျူရှုသည်** *lyit-lyu-shu-the*

ill *(adj.)* **နေမကောင်းသော** *nay-ma-kaung-taw*

ill *(adv.)* **မမှန်မကန်** *ma-hman-ma-kan*

illegal *(adj.)* **တရားမဝင်သော** *ta-yar-ma-win-taw*

illegibility *(n.)* **တရားမဝင်ခြင်း၏ လက္ခဏာ** *ta-yar-ma-win-chin-ei-lat-kah-nar*

illegible *(adj.)* **ဖတ်မရသော** *phat-ma-ya-taw*

illegitimate *(adj.)* **တရားမဝင်သော** *ta-yar-ma-win-taw*

illicit *(adj.)* **ဥပဒေက ခွင့်မပြုသော** *au-pa-day-ka-khwint-ma-pyu-taw*

illiteracy *(n.)* **စာမတတ်ခြင်း** *sar-ma-tat-chin*

illiterate *(adj.)* **စာမတတ်သော** *sar-ma-tat-taw*

illness *(n.)* မကျန်းမာခြင်း *ma-kyan-mar-chin*
illogical *(adj.)* ယုတ္တိမရှိသော *yoke-ti-ma-shi-taw*
ill-treat *(v.)* ဆိုးဝါးစွာ ဆက်ဆံသည် *soe-war-swar-sat-san-the*
illuminate *(v.)* အလင်းရောင်ပေးသည် *a-lin-yaung-pay-the*
illumination *(n.)* အလင်းရောင် *a-lin-yaung*
illusion *(n.)* အတွေးမှား *a-tway-hmar*
illustrate *(v.)* ပုံဆောင်သည် *pon-saung-the*
illustration *(n.)* သာဓကပြခြင်း၊ ပုံဆောင်ခြင်း *tar-da-ka-pyu-chin, pon-saung-chin*
image *(n.)* ပုံ *pon*
imagery *(n.)* နိမိတ်ပုံ na-meik-pon
imaginary *(adj.)* စိတ်ကူးသက်သက် *seik-ku-tat-tat*
imagination *(n.)* စိတ်ကူးစိတ်သန်း seik-ku-seik-tan
imaginative *(adj.)* စိတ်ကူးဉာဏ်ရှိသော *seik-ku-nyan-shi-taw*
imagine *(v.)* စိတ်ကူးယဉ်သည် *seik-ku-yin-the*
imbalance *(n.)* မညီမျှခြင်း *ma-nyi-mya-chin*
imitate *(v.)* အတုခိုးသည် *a-tu-khoe-the*
imitation *(n.)* အတုခိုးခြင်း *a-tu-khoe-chin*
imitator *(n.)* အတုခိုးသူ *a-tu-khoe-thu*
immaterial *(adj.)* အရေးမကြီးသော၊ ဒြပ်မရှိသော *a-yay-ma-kyi-taw, drat-ma-shi-taw*
immature *(adj.)* ရင့်ကျက်မှုမရှိသော *yint-kyat-mu-ma-shi-taw*
immaturity *(n.)* ရင့်ကျက်မှုမရှိခြင်း *yint-kyat-mu-ma-shi-chin*
immeasurable *(adj.)* အတိုင်းမသိ *a-tine-ma-ti*
immediate *(adj.)* ချက်ခြင်း *chat-chin*
immemorial *(adj.)* ရှေးအတီတေ shay-a-te-tay
immense *(adj.)* ရောမ *a-yar-ma*
immensity *(n.)* အလွန်ကြီးမားသော ပမာဏ a-lun-kyi-mar-taw-pa-mar-na
immerse *(v.)* စိမ်သည်၊ နှစ်မြှုပ်သည် *sein-the, nit-hmyoke-the*
immersion *(n.)* နှစ်မြှုပ်ခြင်း *nit-hmyoke-chin*
immigrant *(n.)* ပြောင်းရွှေ့နေထိုင်သူ *pyaung-shwe-nay-htai-thu*
immigrate *(v.)* ပြောင်းရွှေ့နေထိုင်သည် *pyaung-shwe-nay-htai-the*
immigration *(n.)* လူဝင်မှု *lu-win-mu*
imminent *(adj.)* ဖြစ်အံ့ဆဲဆဲ phit-ant-sal-sal
immodest *(adj.)* ဣန္ဒြေမဲ့သော *ain-dray-mae-taw*
immodesty *(n.)* ဣန္ဒြေမဲ့ခြင်း *ain-dray-mae-chin*
immoral *(adj.)* အကျင့်ပျက်သော *a-kyint-pyat-taw*
immorality *(n.)* အကျင့်ပျက်ခြင်း၊ မကောင်းမှု *a-kyint-pyat-chin, ma-kaung-mu*
immortal *(adj.)* ထာဝရရှင်သန်သော *htar-wa-ya-shin-tan-taw*
immortality *(n.)* ထာဝရရှင်သန်ခြင်း *htar-wa-ya-shin-tan-chin*
immortalize *(v.)* မော်ကွန်းတင်အပ်သည် *maw-kun-tin-at-taw*
immovable *(adj.)* မရွေ့ရှားနိုင်သော *ma-shway-shar-nai-taw*
immune *(adj.)* ကိုယ်ခံအားရှိသော *ko-khan-ar-shi-taw*

immunity *(n.)* ခံနိုင်ရည် *khan-nai-yay*

immunize *(v.)* ကာကွယ်ဆေးထိုးနှံသည် *kar-kwal-say-htoe-nan-the*

impact *(n.)* အကျိုးသက်ရောက်မှု *a-kyo-tat-yauk-mu*

impart *(v.)* ပေးသည် *pay-the*

impartial *(adj.)* ဘက်မလိုက်သော *bat-ma-lite-taw*

impartiality *(n.)* ဘက်မလိုက်ခြင်း *bat-ma-lite-chin*

impassable *(adj.)* ဖြတ်သန်းသွားလာရန် မဖြစ်နိုင်သော *phat-tan-twar-lar-yan-ma-phit-nai-taw*

impasse *(n.)* ချောင်ပိတ်မိခြင်း *chaung-pate-mi-chin*

impatience *(n.)* စိတ်မရှည်ခြင်း *seik-ma-shay-chin*

impatient *(adj.)* စိတ်မရှည်သော *seik-ma-shay-taw*

impeach *(v.)* စွပ်စွဲပြစ်တင်သည် *sut-swal-pyit-tin-the*

impeachment *(n.)* စွပ်စွဲပြစ်တင်ခြင်း *sut-swal-pyit-tin-chin*

impeccable *(adj.)* စင်းလုံးချော *sin-lon-chaw*

impede *(v.)* ကြန့်ကြာစေသည် *kyant-kyar-say-the*

impediment *(n.)* အဟန့်အတား *a-hant-a-tar*

impenetrable *(adj.)* ပိတ်ဆီးနေသော *pate-see-nay-taw*

imperative *(adj.)* အမိန့်ပေးသော *a-meint-pay-taw*

imperfect *(adj.)* မပြည့်စုံသော *ma-pyae-sone-taw*

imperfection *(n.)* အပြစ်အနာအဆာ *a-pyit-a-nar-a-sar*

imperial *(adj.)* အင်ပါယာနှင့် ဆိုင်သော *in-par-yar-nint-sai-taw*

imperialism *(n.)* နယ်ချဲ့ဝါဒ *nal-chae-wa-da*

imperil *(v.)* အန္တရာယ်ပေးသည် *an-da-yal-pay-the*

imperishable *(adj.)* မပျက်စီးနိုင်သော *ma-pyat-see-nai-taw*

impermissible *(adj.)* ခွင့်မပြုနိုင်သော *khwint-ma-pyu-nai-taw*

impersonal *(adj.)* အေးတိအေးစက်နိုင်သော *aye-ti-aye-sat-nai-taw*

impersonate *(v.)* တူအောင် တုသည် *tu-aung-tu-the*

impersonation *(n.)* တုပြခြင်း *tu-pya-chin*

impertinence *(n.)* ရိုင်းစိုင်းမှု *yai-sai-mu*

impertinent *(adj.)* ရိုင်းစိုင်းသော *yai-sai-taw*

impetuosity *(n.)* စိတ်မြန်လက်မြန်လုပ်ခြင်း *seik-myan-lat-myan-lote-chin*

impetuous *(adj.)* စိတ်မြန်လက်မြန်လုပ်သော *seik-myan-lat-myan-lote-taw*

implement *(n.)* ကိရိယာ၊ တန်ဆာပလာ *ka-yi-yar, ta-zar-pa-lar*

implicate *(v.)* ငြိစွန်းသည် *nyi-sun-the*

implication *(n.)* ဂယက်ရိုက်ခတ်မှု *ga-yat-yite-khat-mu*

implicit *(adj.)* သွယ်ဝိုက်သော twal-wite-taw

implore *(v.)* ပန်ကြားသည် *pan-kyar-the*

imply *(v.)* သွယ်ဝိုက်ညွှန်းဆိုသည် *twal-wite-hnyun-soe-the*

impolite *(adj.)* ရိုင်းပျသော yai-pya-taw

import *(v.)* တင်သွင်းသည် *tin-twin-the*

importance *(n.)* အရေးကြီးခြင်း *a-yay-kyi-chin*

important *(adj.)* **အရေးကြီးသော** *a-yay-kyi-taw*
impose *(v.)* **သတ်မှတ်သည်၊ စည်းကြပ်သည်** *tat-mat-the, see-kyat-the*
imposing *(adj.)* **အဟန့်ကောင်းသော** *a-hant-kaung-taw*
imposition *(n.)* **သတ်မှတ်ခြင်း** *tat-mat-chin*
impossibility *(n.)* **ဖြစ်နိုင်ချေမရှိခြင်း** *phit-nai-chay-ma-shi-chin*
impossible *(adj.)* **မဖြစ်နိုင်သော** *ma-phit-nai-taw*
impostor *(n.)* **အယောင်ဆောင်** a-yaung-saung
imposture *(n.)* **အယောင်ဆောင်၍ လိမ်လည်ခြင်း** a-yaung-saung-ywe-lain-lal-chin
impotence *(n.)* **ပန်းသေခြင်း** *pan-tay-chin*
impotent *(adj.)* **ပန်းသေသော** pan-tay-taw
impoverish *(v.)* **ဆင်းရဲစေသည်** *sin-ye-say-the*
impracticability *(n.)* **လက်တွေ့မကျခြင်း** lat-tway-ma-kya-chin
impracticable *(adj.)* **လက်တွေ့မကျသော** *lat-tway-ma-kya-taw*
impress *(v.)* **အထင်ကြီးစေသည်** *a-htin-kyi-say-the*
impression *(n.)* **ထင်မြင်ချက်၊ ခံစားချက်** *htin-myin-chat, khan-sar-chat*
impressive *(adj.)* **အထင်အမြင်ကြီးလောက်သော** *a-htin-a-myin-kyi-laut-taw*
imprint *(n.)* **ဖိရာ** phi-yar
imprison *(v.)* **ထောင်ချသည်** htaung-cha-the
improper *(adj.)* **မမှန်သော၊ မသင့်လျော်သော** *ma-man-taw, ma-tint-lyaw-taw*
impropriety *(n.)* **မရိုးသားမှု** *ma-yoe-tar-mu*
improve *(v.)* **တိုးတက်သည်** *toe-tat-the*
improvement *(n.)* **တိုးတက်ခြင်း** *toe-tat-chin*
imprudence *(n.)* **မလိမ္မာခြင်း** *ma-lain-mar-chin*
imprudent *(adj.)* **မလိမ္မာသော** *ma-lain-mar-taw*
impulse *(n.)* **စိတ်ပေါက်ခြင်း** *seik-pauk-chin*
impulsive *(adj.)* **စိတ်လိုက်မာန်ပါ ပြုလုပ်တတ်သော** *seik-lite-man-par-pyu-lote-tat-taw*
impunity *(n.)* **ဒဏ်ခတ်မခံရခြင်း** *dan-khat-ma-khan-ya-chin*
impure *(adj.)* **မသန့်စင်သော** *ma-tant-sin-taw*
impurity *(n.)* **မသန့်စင်ခြင်း** *ma-tant-sin-chin*
impute *(v.)* **စွပ်စွဲသည်** *sut-swal-the*
in *(prep.)* **မှာ** *hmar*
inability *(n.)* **မတတ်နိုင်ခြင်း** ma-tat-nai-chin
inaccurate *(adj.)* **မတိကျသော** ma-ti-kya-taw
inaction *(n.)* **အရေးယူရန် ပျက်ကွက်မှု** a-yay-yu-yan-pyat-kwat-mu
inactive *(adj.)* **မလှုပ်ရှားသော၊, သေသော** *ma-hlote-shar-taw, tay-taw*
inadequate *(adj.)* **မလုံလောက်သော** *ma-lon-laut-taw*
inadmissible *(adj.)* **လက်မခံနိုင်သော** *lat-ma-khan-nai-taw*
inanimate *(adj.)* **သက်မဲ့** *thet-mae*
inapplicable *(adj.)* **မဆီမဆိုင်ဖြစ်သော** *ma-si-ma-sai-phit-taw*

inattentive *(adj.)* စိတ်မပါသော *seik-ma-par-taw*
inaudible *(adj.)* မကြားရသော *ma-kyaw-ya-taw*
inaugural *(adj.)* အဖွင့် *a-phwint*
inauguration *(n.)* အဖွင့် *a-phwint*
inauspicious *(adj.)* မင်္ဂလာမရှိသော *min-ga-lar-ma-shi-taw*
inborn *(adj.)* မွေးရာပါ *mway-yar-par*
inbound *(adj.)* အတွင်းဘက်လှည့်သော၊ ဝင်လာသော *a-twin-bat-hlae-taw, win-lar-taw*
inbox *(n.)* စာဝင်ပုံး *sar-win-pone*
incalculable *(adj.)* မရေတွက်နိုင်သော *ma-yay-twat-nai-taw*
incapable *(adj.)* မတတ်နိုင်သော *ma-tat-nai-taw*
incapacity *(n.)* မစွမ်းဆောင်နိုင်ခြင်း *ma-swan-saung-nai-chin*
incarnate *(v.)* ဖော်ဆောင်သည် *phaw-saung-the*
incarnation *(n.)* လူ့အဖြစ်ဝင်စားခြင်း *lu-a-phit-win-sar-chin*
incense *(v.)* ဒေါသထွက်စေသည် *daw-da-htwat-say-the*
incense *(n.)* အမွှေးနံ့သာ *a-hmway-nant-taw*
incentive *(n.)* မက်လုံး *mat-lone*
inception *(n.)* ကနဦး *ka-na-oo*
inch *(n.)* လက်မ *lat-ma*
incharge *(n.)* တာဝန်ခံ *tar-win-khan*
incident *(n.)* ဖြစ်ပွားမှုပမာဏ *phit-pwar-mu-pa-mar-na*
incidental *(adj.)* အသေးအဖွဲ *a-thway-a-phwe*
incite *(v.)* လှုံ့ဆော်သည် *lont-saw-the*
inclination *(n.)* လိုအင်ဆန္ဒ *lon-inn-san-da*
incline *(v.)* စောင်းသည်၊ ငဲ့သည်၊ ညွတ်သည် *saung-the, nge-the, nyut-the*
include *(v.)* ပါဝင်သည် *par-win-the*
inclusion *(n.)* ပါဝင်ခြင်း *par-win-chin*
inclusive *(adj.)* ပါဝင်သော *par-win-taw*
incoherent *(adj.)* ဗလုံးဗထွေးပြောသော *ba-lone-ba-htway-pyaw-thaw*
income *(n.)* ဝင်ငွေ *win-ngwe*
incomparable *(adj.)* ပြိုင်ဘက်ကင်းသော *pyai-bat-kin-taw*
incompetent *(adj.)* မကျွမ်းကျင်သော *ma-kyun-kyin-taw*
incomplete *(adj.)* မပြည့်စုံသော *ma-pyae-sone-taw*
inconsiderate *(adj.)* မစာနာသော *ma-sar-nar-taw*
inconvenient *(adj.)* အဆင်မပြေသော *a-sin-ma-pyay-taw*
incorporate *(v.)* ဖြည့်သွင်းသည် *pyae-twin-the*
incorporation *(n.)* သိမ်းသွင်းခြင်း *tain-twin-chin*
incorrect *(adj.)* မမှန်ကန်သော *ma-hman-kan-taw*
incorrigible *(adj.)* ပြုပြင်မရသော *pyu-pyin-ma-ya-taw*
incorruptible *(adj.)* ဖျက်ဆီးမရနိုင်သော *phat-see-ma-ya-nai-taw*
increase *(n.)* တိုးတက်ခြင်း *toe-tat-chin*
increase *(v.)* တိုးတက်သည် *toe-tat-the*
incredible *(adj.)* မယုံကြည်နိုင်လောက်သော *ma-yone-kyi-nai-laut-taw*
increment *(n.)* နှစ်တိုးလစာ *nit-toe-la-sar*
incriminate *(v.)* အပြစ်ကျူးလွန်သူဖြစ်ကြောင်း ထွက်ဆိုသည်

a-pyit-kyu-lun-thu-phit-kyaung-htwat-soe-the
incubate *(v.)* ဝပ်သည် *wit-the*
inculcate *(v.)* စွဲမှတ်အောင် သွန်သင်သည် *swal-mat-aung-toon-tin-the*
incumbent *(n.)* တာဝန်ထမ်းဆောင်ဆဲပုဂ္ဂိုလ် *tar-winn-htan-saung-sal-poke-ko*
incur *(v.)* ကျရောက်သည်၊ တည်ရှိသည် *kya-yauk-the, the-shi-the*
incurable *(adj.)* ကုစား၍ မရနိုင်သော *ku-sar-ywe-ma-ya-nai-taw*
indebted *(adj.)* အကြွေးတင်ရှိသော *a-kyay-tin-shi-taw*
indecency *(n.)* မတော်တရော်ပြုမူခြင်း *ma-taw-ta-yaw-pyu-mu-chin*
indecent *(adj.)* မတော်တရော်ဖြစ်သော *ma-taw-ta-yaw-pyu-mu-taw*
indecision *(n.)* ချီတုံချတုံဖြစ်ခြင်း *chi-tone-cha-tone-phit-chin*
indeed *(adv.)* ဟုတ်ပါ့၊ တကယ်ပါပဲ *hoke-pa, ta-kal-par-pal*
indefensible *(adj.)* မကာကွယ်နိုင်သော *ma-kar-kwal-nai-taw*
indefinite *(adj.)* အချိန်အကန့်အသတ်မရှိသော *a-chain-a-kant-a-tat-ma-shi-taw*
indemnity *(n.)* လျော်ကြေးငွေ *lyaw-kyay-ngwe*
independence *(n.)* လွတ်လပ်ရေး *lut-lat-yay*
independent *(adj.)* လွတ်လပ်သော *lut-lat-taw*
indescribable *(adj.)* ပြောမပြနိုင်လောက်အောင် *pyan-ma-pyaw-nai-laut-taw*
index *(n.)* အညွှန်း *a-hnyun*
Indian *(adj.)* အိန္ဒိယ *eain-di-ya*
indicate *(v.)* ညွှန်ပြသည် hnyun-pya-the
indication *(n.)* အမှတ်အသား၊ လက္ခဏာ a-mat-a-tar, lat-kha-nar
indicative *(adj.)* ညွှန်ပြသော *hnyun-pya-taw*
indicator *(n.)* အညွှန်း *a-hnyun*
indict *(v.)* စွဲချက်တင်သည် *swal-chat-tin-the*
indictment *(n.)* စွဲချက်တင်ခြင်း *swal-chat-tin-chin*
indifference *(n.)* စိတ်မဝင်စားခြင်း *seik-ma-win-sar-chin*
indifferent *(adj.)* စိတ်ဝင်စားမှု မရှိသော *seik-win-sar-mu-ma-shi-taw*
indigenous *(adj.)* ဒေသခံ *day-ta-khan*
indigestible *(adj.)* အစာမကျေသော *a-sar-ma-kyay-taw*
indigestion *(n.)* အစာမကျေခြင်း *a-sar-ma-kyay-chin*
indignant *(adj.)* မခံမရပ်နိုင်ဖြစ်သော *ma-khan-ma-yat-nai-phit-taw*
indignation *(n.)* မခံမရပ်နိုင်ဖြစ်ခြင်း *ma-khan-ma-yat-nai-phit-chin*
indigo *(n.)* မဲနယ်ရောင် *mae-nal-yaung*
indirect *(adj.)* သွယ်ဝိုက် *twal-wite*
indiscipline *(n.)* စည်းကမ်းမဲ့ခြင်း *see-kan-mae-chin*
indiscreet *(adj.)* နှုတ်မစောင့်သော၊ အဆင်ခြင်မဲ့သော *hnote-ma-saunt-taw, a-sin-chin-mae-taw*
indiscretion *(n.)* နှုတ်မစောင့်ခြင်း *hnote-ma-saunt-chin*
indiscriminate *(adj.)* အရမ်းကာရော ပြုမူသော *a-yan-kar-yaw-pyu-mu-taw*
indispensable *(adj.)* မရှိမဖြစ်သော *ma-shi-ma-phit-taw*
indisposed *(adj.)* နာမကျန်းသော *nar-ma-kyan-taw*

indisputable *(adj.)* မငြင်းနိုင်သော *ma-nyin-nai-taw*
indistinct *(adj.)* မရှင်းလင်းသော၊ မပြတ်သားသော *ma-shin-lin-taw, ma-pyat-tar-taw*
individual *(adj.)* တစ်ဦးချင်း၊ သီးခြား *ta-oo-chin, thee-char*
individualism *(n.)* ကိုယ်ပိုင်မှု *ko-pai-mu*
individuality *(n.)* ပင်ကိုလက္ခဏာ *pin-ko-lat-kha-nar*
indivisible *(adj.)* ခွဲခြမ်း၍ မရနိုင်သော *kwal-chan-ywe-ma-ya-nai-taw*
indolent *(adj.)* ပျင်းရိသော pyin-yi-taw
indomitable *(adj.)* အနိုင်မခံ အရှုံးမပေးသော a-nai-ma-khan-a-shone-ma-pay-taw
indoor *(adj.)* အိမ်တွင်း *eain-twin*
indoors *(adv.)* အမိုးအောက် *a-moe-aut*
induce *(v.)* တိုက်တွန်းသည် *tite-tun-the*
inducement *(n.)* မက်လုံး *mat-lone*
induct *(v.)* ရာထူးအပ်နှင်းသည် *yar-htoo-at-hnin-the*
induction *(n.)* ဝင်ရောက်ခြင်း *win-yauk-chin*
indulge *(v.)* အရသာတွေ့သည် *a-ya-tar-tway-the*
indulgence *(n.)* အလိုလိုက်ခံရခြင်း *a-lo-lite-khan-ya-chin*
indulgent *(adj.)* အလိုလိုက်ခံရသော *a-lo-lite-khan-ya-taw*
industrial *(adj.)* စက်မှုလုပ်ငန်းနှင့် ဆိုင်သော *sat-mu-lote-ngan-nint-sai-taw*
industrious *(adj.)* အလုပ်ကြိုးစားသော *a-lote-kyo-sar-taw*
industry *(n.)* စက်မှုလုပ်ငန်း *sat-mu-lote-ngan*
ineffective *(adj.)* မထိရောက်သော ma-hti-yauk-taw
inert *(adj.)* ဓာတ်မပြုသော *dat-ma-pyu-taw*
inertia *(n.)* အီနားရှားဂုဏ်သတ္တိ *e-nar-shar-gon-tat-ti*
inevitable *(adj.)* ကေန်ဖြစ်သော *aye-kan-phit-taw*
inexact *(adj.)* မတိကျသော ma-ti-kya-taw
inexorable *(adj.)* ရှောင်လွှဲမရသော *shaung-hlwal-ma-ya-taw*
inexpensive *(adj.)* တန်ဖိုးနည်းသော *tan-pho-nae-taw*
inexperience *(n.)* အတွေ့အကြုံမရှိခြင်း *a-tway-a-kyone-ma-shi-chin*
inexplicable *(adj.)* နားလည်ရခက်သော *nar-lal-ya-khat-taw*
infallible *(adj.)* အမှားကင်းသော *a-hmar-kin-taw*
infamous *(adj.)* သတင်းဆိုးဖြင့် ကျော်ကြားသော *ta-tin-soe-phyint-kyaw-kyar-taw*
infamy *(n.)* ယုတ်မာမှု *yote-mar-mu*
infancy *(n.)* မွေးကင်းစ၊ အစပျိုးစ *mway-kin-sa, a-sa-pyo-sa*
infant *(n.)* နို့စို့ကလေး *no-so-ka-lay*
infanticide *(n.)* ကလေးသတ်မှု *ka-lay-tat-mu*
infantile *(adj.)* မွေးကင်းစများ *myay-kin-sa-myar*
infantry *(n.)* ခြေလျင်တပ် *chay-lin-tat*
infatuate *(v.)* အရူးအမူးစွဲလမ်းသော *a-yu-a-mu-swal-lan-taw*
infatuation *(n.)* အရူးအမူးစွဲလမ်းမှု *a-yu-a-mu-swal-lan-mu*
infect *(v.)* ရောဂါပိုးဝင်သည် *yaw-gar-poe-win-the*

infection *(n.)* ရောဂါပိုးဝင်ခြင်း *yaw-gar-poe-win-chin*
infectious *(adj.)* ကူးစက်တတ်သော *ku-sat-tat-taw*
infer *(v.)* ကောက်ချက်ချသည် *kauk-note-chat-cha-the*
inference *(n.)* ကောက်ချက် *kauk-chat*
inferior *(adj.)* ညံ့သော *nyant-taw*
inferiority *(n.)* သိမ်ငယ်ခြင်း *thein-nge-chin*
infernal *(adj.)* ငရဲ *nga-ye*
infertile *(adj.)* မြုံသော *myone-taw*
infest *(v.)* ဖိစီးသည် *phi-see-the*
infinite *(adj.)* မရေမတွက်နိုင်သော *ma-yay-ma-twat-nai-taw*
infinity *(n.)* အနန္တ *a-nan-da*
infirm *(adj.)* အိုမင်းမစွမ်းသော *oh-min-ma-swan-taw*
infirmity *(n.)* အိုမင်းမစွမ်းခြင်း *oh-min-ma-swan-chin*
inflame *(v.)* လှုံ့ဆော်သည် *hlont-saw-the*
inflammable *(adj.)* မီးလောင်လွယ်သော *mee-laung-lwal-thaw*
inflammation *(n.)* ရောင်ရမ်းခြင်း *yaung-yan-chin*
inflammatory *(adj.)* ရောင်ရမ်းသော *yaung-yan-taw*
inflation *(n.)* ငွေကြေးဖောင်းပွခြင်း *ngwe-kyay-hpaung-pwa-chin*
inflexible *(adj.)* မလိုက်လျောသော *ma-lite-lyaw-taw*
inflict *(v.)* ဒုက္ခပေးသည် *doke-kha-pay-the*
influence *(v.)* သြဇာလွှမ်းမိုးသည် *aw-zar-hlwan-moe-the*
influential *(adj.)* သြဇာ ညောင်းသော *aw-zar-hlwan-moe-taw*
influenza *(n.)* တုတ်ကွေး *toke-kway*
influx *(n.)* စုပြုံကျလာခြင်း *su-pyone-kya-lar-chin*
inform *(v.)* အကြောင်းကြားသည် *a-kyaung-kyar-the*
informal *(adj.)* ရင်းနှီးဖော်ရွေသော၊ ရိုးရိုး *yin-hnee-hpaw-yway-taw, yoe-yoe*
information *(n.)* သတင်းအချက်အလက် *ta-din-a-chat-a-lat*
informative *(adj.)* ဗဟုသုတပေးသော *ba-hu-tu-ta-pay-taw*
informer *(n.)* သတင်းပေး ta-din-pay
infringe *(v.)* ချိုးဖောက်သည် *choe-hpauk-the*
infringement *(n.)* ချိုးဖောက်မှု *choe-hpauk-mu*
infuriate *(v.)* ဒေါသထွက်စေသည် *daw-ta-htwat-say-the*
infuse *(v.)* သွင်းပေးသည် twin-pay-the
infusion *(n.)* ဖြည့်သွင်းခြင်း *phyae-twin-chin*
ingrained *(adj.)* အရိုးစွဲသော *a-yoe-swal-taw*
ingratitude *(n.)* ကျေးဇူးမသိတတ်ခြင်း *kyay-zu-ma-ti-tat-chin*
ingredient *(n.)* ပါဝင်ပစ္စည်း *par-win-pyit-see*
inhabit *(v.)* နေထိုင်သည် *nay-htai-the*
inhabitable *(adj.)* အခြေချနေထိုင်နိုင်သော *a-chay-cha-nay-htai-nai-taw*
inhabitant *(n.)* နေထိုင်သူ *nay-htai-thu*
inhale *(v.)* ရှူသွင်းသည် *shu-twin-the*
inherent *(adj.)* မွေးရာပါ၊ ဝမ်းတွင်းပါ *mway-yar-par, wan-twin-par*
inherit *(v.)* အမွေဆက်ခံသည် *a-myay-sat-khan-the*
inheritance *(n.)* အမွေဆက်ခံခြင်း *a-myay-sat-khan-chin*

inhibit *(v.)* **ဟန့်တားသည်** *hant-tar-the*

inhibition *(n.)* **အရှက်အကြောက်၊ ချုပ်ချယ်ခြင်း** *a-shat-a-kyauk, choke-chal-chin*

inhospitable *(adj.)* **မဖော်ရွေသော** *ma-phaw-yway-taw*

inhuman *(adj.)* **လူမဆန်သော** *lu-ma-san-taw*

inimical *(adj.)* **မလိုလားသော** *ma-lo-lar-taw*

inimitable *(adj.)* **မတုပနိုင်သော** *ma-tu-pa-nai-taw*

initial *(adj.)* **ကနဦး** *ka-na-oo*

initial *(v.)* **လက်မှတ်တိုထိုးသည်** *lat-mat-toe-htoe-the*

initiate *(v.)* **စတင်သည်** *sa-tin-the*

initiative *(n.)* **ပဏာမခြေလှမ်း** *pa-nar-ma-chay-lan*

inject *(v.)* **ထိုးသည်** *htoe-the*

injection *(n.)* **ထိုးဆေး၊ ထိုးခြင်း** *htoe-say, htoe-chin*

injudicious *(adj.)* **မသင့်မတင့်** *ma-tint-ma-tint*

injunction *(n.)* **တရားဝင်အမိန့်** *ta-yar-win-a-meint*

injure *(v.)* **ဒဏ်ရာရသည်** *dan-yar-ya-the*

injurious *(adj.)* **ထိခိုက်စေသော** *hti-khaik-say-taw*

injury *(n.)* **ဒဏ်ရာ** *dan-yar*

injustice *(n.)* **တရားမျှတမှု မရှိခြင်း** ta-yar-mya-ta-mu-ma-shi-chin

ink *(n.)* **မင်** *min*

inkling *(n.)* **အရိပ်အခြည်** *a-yeik-a-chay*

inland *(adv.)* **ကုန်းတွင်းပိုင်းကျကျ** *kone-twin-pai-kya-kya*

inland *(adj.)* **ကုန်းတွင်းပိုင်းကျသော** *kone-twin-pai-kya-taw*

in-laws *(n.)* **အိမ်ထောင်ဖက်၏ မိသားစုဝင်များ** *eain-htaung-phat-ei-mi-tar-su-win-myar*

inmate *(n.)* **ထောင်ကဲ့သို့ နေရာတွင် အတူနေသူ** *htaung-kae-thoe-nay-yar-twin-a-tu-nay-tu*

inmost *(adj.)* **အတွင်းရေးအကျဆုံး** *a-twin-yay-a-kya-sone*

inn *(n.)* **အဆေးစားဟိုတယ်** *a-tay-sar-ho-tal*

innate *(adj.)* **ဝမ်းတွင်းပါ** *wan-twin-par*

inner *(adj.)* **အတွင်းဘက်** a-twin-bat

innermost *(adj.)* **အတွင်းဘက်ဆုံး** *a-twin-bat-sone*

innings *(n.)* **ဘက်တံဖြင့် ရိုက်ရသည့် အလှည့်** *bat-tan-phit-yite-ya-the-a-hlae*

innocence *(n.)* **အပြစ်ကင်းခြင်း** a-pyit-kin-chin

innocent *(adj.)* **အပြစ်ကင်းသော** *a-pyit-kin-taw*

innovate *(v.)* **အသစ်ထွင်သည်** a-thit-htwin-the

innovation *(n.)* **ဆန်းသစ်တီထွင်ခြင်း** *san-tit-ti-htwin-chin*

innovator *(n.)* **တီထွင်သူ** *ti-htwin-thu*

innumerable *(adj.)* **အသင်္ချေ** *a-tin-chay*

inoculate *(v.)* **ကာကွယ်ဆေးထိုးသည်** *kar-kwal-say-htoe-the*

inoculation *(n.)* **ကာကွယ်ဆေးထိုးခြင်း** *kar-kwal-say-htoe-chin*

inoperative *(adj.)* **တရားမဝင်သော** *ta-yar-ma-win-taw*

inopportune *(adj.)* **အဆင်မပြေသော** *a-sin-ma-pyay-taw*

input *(n.)* **ဖြည့်သွင်းသော အချက်အလက်၊ ဖြည့်သွင်းခြင်း** *phyae-twin-taw-a-chat-a-let, phyae-twin-chin*

inquest *(n.)* သေမှုသေခင်း စုံစမ်းစစ်ဆေးခြင်း *tay-mu-tay-khin-sone-san-sit-say-chin*

inquire *(v.)* မေးမြန်းသည် *may-myan-the*

inquiry *(n.)* စုံစမ်းမေးမြန်းသည် *sone-san-may-myan-the*

inquisition *(n.)* စစ်ကြောမှု *sit-kyaw-mu*

inquisitive *(adj.)* စုပ်စုသော *sat-su-taw*

insane *(adj.)* စိတ်မနှံ့သော *seik-ma-hnant-taw*

insanity *(n.)* ရူးခြင်း *yuu-chin*

insatiable *(adj.)* မတင်းတိမ်သော *ma-tin-tain-taw*

inscribe *(v.)* ဖော်ပြသည် *phaw-pya-the*

inscription *(n.)* ဖော်ပြခြင်း *phaw-pya-chin*

insect *(n.)* အင်းဆက်ပိုး *in-set-poe*

insecticide *(n.)* အင်းဆက်သတ်ဆေး *in-set-tat-say*

insecure *(adj.)* မလုံခြုံသော *ma-hlone-chone-taw*

insecurity *(n.)* မလုံခြုံမှု *ma-hlone-chone-mu*

insensibility *(n.)* သတိကင်းမဲ့သော အခြေအနေ *ta-di-kin-mae-taw-a-chay-a-nay*

insensible *(adj.)* သတိကင်းမဲ့သော *ta-di-kin-mae-taw*

insensitive *(adj.)* စာနာစိတ်ကင်းမဲ့သော *sar-nar-seik-kin-mae-taw*

inseparable *(adj.)* ခွဲထုတ်မရသော *kwal-htoke-ma-ya-taw*

insert *(v.)* ထည့်သွင်းသည် *htae-twin-the*

insertion *(n.)* ထည့်သွင်းခြင်း *htae-twin-chin*

inside *(prep.)* အတွင်း *a-twin*

inside *(n.)* အတွင်းပိုင်း *a-twin-pai*

insight *(n.)* ထိုးထွင်းသိမြင်စွမ်းသော ဉာဏ် *htoe-htwin-ti-myin-swan-taw-nyan*

insignificance *(n.)* အရေးမပါခြင်း *a-yay-ma-par-chin*

insignificant *(adj.)* အရေးမပါသော *a-yay-ma-par-taw*

insincere *(adj.)* မရိုးသားသော *ma-yoe-tar-taw*

insincerity *(n.)* သစ္စာမရှိခြင်း *tit-sar-ma-shi-chin*

insinuate *(v.)* စောင်းမြောင်းသည် *saung-myaung-the*

insinuation *(n.)* စောင်းပါးရိပ်ခြေပြောခြင်း *saung-par-yeik-chay-pyaw-chin*

insipid *(adj.)* အရသာမရှိသော *a-ya-tar-ma-shi-taw*

insipidity *(n.)* ပေါ့ရှုတ်ရှုတ်နိုင်ခြင်း *pot-shyut-shyut-nai-chin*

insist *(v.)* အပြင်းအထန်တောင်းဆိုသည် *a-pyin-a-htan-taung-so-the*

insistence *(n.)* မရမကတောင်းဆိုခြင်း *ma-ya-ma-ka-taung-so-chin*

insistent *(adj.)* မရမကတောင်းဆိုသော *ma-ya-ma-ka-taung-so-taw*

insolence *(n.)* မိုက်ရိုင်းမှု *mite-yai-mu*

insolent *(adj.)* မိုက်ရိုင်းသော *mite-yai-taw*

insoluble *(n.)* မပျော်ဝင်နိုင်သော *ma-pyaw-win-nai-taw*

insolvency *(n.)* လူမွဲစာခံခြင်း *lu-mwe-sar-khan-chin*

insolvent *(adj.)* အကြွေးမဆပ်နိုင်သော *a-kyay-ma-sat-nai-taw*

inspect *(v.)* စစ်ဆေးသည် *sit-say-the*

inspection *(n.)* စစ်ဆေးခြင်း *sit-say-chin*

inspector *(n.)* ရဲအုပ် *ye-oak*

inspiration *(n.)* ဉာဏ်ကွန့်မြူးမှု *nyan-kyunt-my-mu*

inspire *(v.)* လှုံ့ဆော်သည် *lont-saw-the*

instability *(n.)* တည်ငြိမ်မှု မရှိခြင်း *the-nyein-mu-ma-shi-chi*

install *(v.)* တပ်ဆင်သည် tat-sin-the

installation *(n.)* တပ်ဆင်ခြင်း *tat-sin-chin*

instalment *(n.)* အရစ်ကျ ငွေပေးချေခြင်း *a-yit-kya-ngwe-pay-chay-chin*

instance *(n.)* ဖြစ်စဉ် *phit-sin*

instant *(n.)* ချက်ချင်း *chat-chin*

instantaneous *(adj.)* အချိန်မဆိုင်း *a-chain-ma-sai*

instantly *(adv.)* ချက်ချင်း *chat-chin*

instigate *(v.)* လှုံ့ဆော်သည် *hlont-saw-the*

instigation *(n.)* လှုံ့ဆော်ချက် *hlont-saw-chat*

instil *(v.)* သွတ်သွင်းပေးသည် *twat-twin-pay-the*

instinct *(n.)* ဗီဇ *bi-za*

instinctive *(adj.)* အလိုအလျောက် *a-lo-hlyaut*

institute *(n.)* တက္ကသိုလ်၊ အသင်း၊ အဖွဲ့အစည်း *tat-ka-do, a-tin, a-phwe-a-see*

institution *(n.)* အဖွဲ့အစည်း၊ အထင်ကရ ပုဂ္ဂိုလ်၊ အလေ့အထ *a-phwe-a-see, a-htin-ka-ya-poke-ko, a-lay-a-hta*

instruct *(v.)* ညွှန်ကြားသည်၊ သင်ပေးသည် *hnyun-kyar-the, tin-pay-the*

instruction *(n.)* ညွှန်ကြားချက်၊ သင်ကြားပို့ချမှု *hnyun-kyar-chat, tin-kyar-poe-cha-mu*

instructor *(n.)* ဆရာ၊ တက္ကသိုလ်ဆရာ *sa-yar, tat-ka-doe-sa-yar*

instrument *(n.)* ကိရိယာ၊ လက်နက်၊ တူရိယာ *ka-yi-yar, lat-nat, tu-yi-yar*

instrumental *(adj.)* အတီးသက်သက်ဖြစ်သော၊ အရေးပါသော *a-tee-tat-tat-phit-taw, a-yay-par-taw*

instrumentalist *(n.)* အတီးအမှုတ်သမား *a-tee-a-hmoke-ta-mar*

insubordinate *(adj.)* အမိန့်မနာခံသော *a-meint-ma-nar-khan-chin*

insubordination *(n.)* အမိန့်မနာခံခြင်း *a-meint-ma-nar-khan-chin*

insufficient *(adj.)* မလုံလောက်သော *ma-lon-laut-taw*

insular *(adj.)* ကျဉ်းမြောင်းသော *kyin-myar-taw*

insularity *(n.)* တသီးတခြား ဖြစ်ခြင်း *ta-thee-ta-char-phit-chin*

insulate *(v.)* တားဆီးသည်၊ ကာကွယ်သည် *tar-see-the, kar-kwal-the*

insulation *(n.)* ကာကွယ်ပေးမှု *kar-kwal-pay-mu*

insulator *(n.)* လျှပ်စစ်၊ အပူကာ ပစ္စည်း *lyat-sit, a-pyu-kar-pyit-see*

insult *(n.)* စော်ကားခြင်း *saw-kar-chin*

insupportable *(adj.)* မထမ်းနိုင်သော၊ မခံနိုင်သော *ma-htan-nai-taw, ma-khan-nai-taw*

insurance *(n.)* အာမခံ *arr-ma-khan*

insure *(v.)* အာမခံသည် *arr-ma-khan-the*

insurgent *(n.)* သောင်းကျန်းသူ *taung-kyan-thu*

insurgent *(adj.)* အစိုးရဆန့်ကျင်သော *a-soe-ya-sant-kyin-taw*

insurmountable *(adj.)* မကျော်လွှားနိုင်သော *ma-kyaw-hlwar-nai-taw*

insurrection *(n.)* ပုန်ကန်မှု၊ ဆူပူအုံကြွမှု *pon-kan-mu, su-pu-ohn-kwa-mu*

intact *(adj.)* ပကတိအတိုင်း *pa-ka-ti-a-tai*

intangible *(adj.)* ကိုင်တွယ်မရသော *hti-tway-kai-twal-ma-ya-taw*

integral *(adj.)* တစ်သားတည်း စ်သော *ta-tar-the-phit-taw*

integrate *(v.)* ပေါင်းသည် *paung-the*

integrity *(n.)* ပေါင်းစပ်ခြင်း *paung-sat-chin*

intellect *(n.)* အသိဉာဏ် *a-ti-nyan*

intellectual *(adj.)* အသိဉာဏ် *a-ti-nyan*

intellectual *(n.)* ပညာရှင် *pyin-nyar-shin*

intelligence *(n.)* အသိဉာဏ် *a-ti-nyan*

intelligent *(adj.)* ဉာဏ်ရည်ဉာဏ်စွမ်းရှိသော *nyan-yay-nyan-swan-shi-taw*

intelligentsia *(n.)* တတ်လူတန်းစား *pyin-nyar-tat-lu-tan-sar*

intelligible *(adj.)* နားလည်နိုင်သော *nar-lal-nai-taw*

intend *(v.)* ရည်ရွယ်သည် *yee-ywal-the*

intense *(adj.)* ပြင်းထန်သော၊ ထက်သန်သော *pyin-htan-taw, htet-tan-taw*

intensify *(v.)* အရှိန်မြှင့်သည် *a-shein-hmyint-the*

intensity *(n.)* ပြင်းအား *pyin-arr*

intensive *(adj.)* အချိန်တိုအတွင်း ပြင်းပြင်းထန်ထန် ကြိုးပမ်းရသော *a-chain-to-a-twin-pyin-pyin-htan-htan-kyoe-pan-ya-taw*

intent *(adj.)* စူးစူးစိုက်စိုက် *sue-sue-site-site*

intention *(n.)* ရည်ရွယ်ချက် *yee-ywal-chat*

intentional *(adj.)* တမင် လုပ်သော *ta-min-lote-taw*

interactive *(adj.)* အတုံ့အပြန် ရှိသော *a-tont-a-pyan-shi-taw*

intercept *(v.)* ကြားဖြတ်တိုက်သည် *kyar-phat-tite-the*

interception *(n.)* ဖြတ်ယူခြင်း *phat-yu-chin*

interchange *(n.)* ဖလှယ်ခြင်း *pha-lal-chin*

intercourse *(n.)* ဆက်ဆံမှု *sat-san-mu*

interdependence *(n.)* အပြန်အလှန် မှီခိုသည် *a-pyan-a-hlyan-mi-kho-the*

interdependent *(adj.)* အပြန်အလှန် မှီခိုသော *a-pyan-a-hlyan-mi-kho-taw*

interest *(n.)* စိတ်ဝင်စားမှု၊ အကျိုး၊ အတိုး *seik-win-sar-mu, a-kyo, a-toe*

interested *(adj.)* စိတ်ဝင်စားသော *seik-win-sar-taw*

interesting *(adj.)* စိတ်ဝင်စားဖွယ်ကောင်းသော *seik-win-sar-phwal-kaung-taw*

interfere *(v.)* နှောင့်ယှက်သည် *naut-shat-the*

interference *(n.)* ဝင်ရောက်စွက်ဖက်ခြင်း *win-yauk-swat-phat-chin*

interim *(n.)* ကြားကာလ *kyar-kar-la*

interior *(adj.)* အတွင်းပိုင်း *a-twin-pai*

interjection *(n.)* အာမေဋိတ် *arr-may-daik*

interlock *(v.)* ချိတ်ဆက်ထားသည် *chate-sat-htar-the*

interlude *(n.)* နားချိန် *nar-chain*

intermediary *(n.)* ကြားမှ ဖျန်ဖြေသူ *kyar-ma-pyan-pyay-thu*

intermediate *(adj.)* အလယ်အလတ်ဖြစ်သော *a-lal-a-lat-phit-taw*

interminable *(adj.)* မဆုံးနိုင်သော *ma-sone-nai-taw*

intermingle *(v.)* ထွေးရောယှက်တင်ပြုသည် *htway-yaw-yat-tin-pyu-the*

intern *(n.)* ထိန်းသိမ်းထားသည် *htein-tain-htar-the*
internal *(adj.)* အတွင်းဘက် *a-twin-bat*
international *(adj.)* အပြည်ပြည်ဆိုင်ရာ *a-pyi-pyi-sai-yar*
internet *(n.)* အင်တာနက် *in-tar-net*
interplay *(n.)* အပြန်အလှန် သက်ရောက်မှု *a-pyan-a-lan-thet-yauk-mu*
interpret *(v.)* ဘာသာပြန်သည်၊ အဓိပ္ပါယ်ကောက်သည် *bar-tar-pyan-the, a-dait-pal-kauk-the*
interpreter *(n.)* စကားပြန် *sa-kar-pyan*
interrogate *(v.)* စိစစ်သည်၊ စစ်မေးသည် *si-sit-the, sit-may-the*
interrogation *(n.)* စိစစ်ခြင်း၊ စစ်မေးခြင်း *si-sit-chin, sit-may-chin*
interrogative *(adj.)* မေးမြန်းသော *may-myan-taw*
interrupt *(v.)* ကြားဖြတ်သည် *kyar-phat-the*
interruption *(n.)* အနှောင့်အယှက် *a-naut-a-shat*
intersect *(v.)* ဖြတ်သည် *phat-the*
intersection *(n.)* လမ်းဆုံ *lan-sone*
interval *(n.)* အကြား၊ ကြားကာလ *a-kyar, kyar-kar-la*
intervene *(v.)* ကြားဝင်ဖျန်ဖြေသည် *kyar-win-phyan-pyay-the*
intervention *(n.)* ကြားဝင်စွက်ဖက်ခြင်း *kyar-win-swat-phat-chin*
interview *(n.)* လူတွေ့မေးမြန်းခြင်း၊ အင်တာဗျူး *lu-tway-may-myan-chin, in-ter-byu*
intestinal *(adj.)* အူတွင်းဖြစ်သော *au-twin-phit-taw*
intestine *(n.)* အူ *au*
intimacy *(n.)* ရင်းနှီးမှု *yin-nee-mu*
intimate *(adj.)* ရင်းနှီးသော *yin-nee-taw*
intimation *(n.)* အရိပ်အမြွက် *a-yeik-a-mywat*
intimidate *(v.)* ခြိမ်းခြောက်သည် *chain-chauk-the*
intimidation *(n.)* ခြိမ်းခြောက်ခြင်း *chain-chauk-chin*
into *(prep.)* ထဲ၊ အထဲ *htae, a-htae*
intolerable *(adj.)* သည်းမခံနိုင်သော *tee-ma-khan-nai-taw*
intolerance *(n.)* လွတ်လပ်ခွင့်မပေးခြင်း *lut-lat-khwint-ma-pay-chin*
intolerant *(adj.)* သည်းမခံသော *tee-ma-khan-taw*
intoxicant *(n.)* မူးယစ်စေတတ်သော အရာ *mu-yit-say-tat-taw-a-yar*
intoxicate *(v.)* မူးယစ်သည် *mu-yit-the*
intoxication *(n.)* မူးယစ်ခြင်း *mu-yit-chin*
intransitive *(adj. (verb))* ကံပုဒ်မရှိသော *kan-poke-ma-shi-taw*
intrepid *(adj.)* သတ္တိပြောင်သော *tat-ti-pyaung-taw*
intrepidity *(n.)* သတ္တိပြောင်ခြင်း *tat-ti-pyaung-chin*
intricate *(adj.)* ရှုပ်ထွေးသော *shoke-htway-taw*
intrigue *(v.)* စိတ်ဝင်စားသည်၊ ခြေပုန်းခုတ်သည် *seik-win-sar-the, chay-pone-khote-the*
intrinsic *(adj.)* ကိုယ်ပိုင် *ko-pai*
introduce *(v.)* မိတ်ဆက်သည် *meik-sat-the*
introduction *(n.)* မိတ်ဆက် *meik-sat*
introductory *(adj.)* နိဒါန်း *ni-dan*
introspect *(v.)* မိမိကိုယ်ကို ပြန်လည်ဆန်းစစ်သည် *mi-mi-ko-ko-pyan-lal-san-sit-the*

introspection *(n.)* မိမိကိုယ်ကို ပြန်လည်ဆန်းစစ်ခြင်း *mi-mi-ko-ko-pyan-lal-san-sit-chin*
introvert *(n.)* ဘာသိဘာသာနေတတ်ခြင်း *bar-ti-bar-tar-nay-tat-chin*
intrude *(v.)* ကျူးကျော်သည် *kyu-kyaw-the*
intrusion *(n.)* ကျူးကျော်ခြင်း *kyu-kyaw-chin*
intuition *(n.)* အလိုလိုသိခြင်း *a-lo-lo-ti-chin*
intuitive *(adj.)* အလိုလိုသိသော *a-lo-lo-ti-taw*
invade *(v.)* ထိုးဖောက်သည် *htoe-phauk-the*
invalid *(adj.)* တရားမဝင်သော *ta-yar-ma-win-taw*
invalid *(n.)* လူမမာ၊ ဒုက္ခိတ *lu-ma-mar, dote-khi-ta*
invalidate *(v.)* ပျက်ပြယ်စေသည် *pyat-pyal-say-the*
invaluable *(adj.)* တန်ဖိုးမဖြတ်နိုင်သော *tan-phoe-ma-phat-nai-taw*
invasion *(n.)* ထိုးဖောက်ဝင်ရောက်ခြင်း *htoe-phauk-win-yauk-chin*
invective *(n.)* ဆဲရေးတိုင်းထွာခြင်း *sal-yay-tai-htwar-chin*
invent *(v.)* တီထွင်သည် *ti-htwin-the*
invention *(n.)* တီထွင်မှု *ti-htwin-mu*
inventive *(adj.)* တီထွင်တတ်သော *ti-htwin-tat-taw*
inventor *(n.)* တီထွင်သူ *ti-htwin-thu*
invert *(v.)* ဇောက်ထိုးထားသည် *zaut-htoe-htar-the*
invest *(v.)* ရင်းနှီးမြှုပ်နှံသည် *yin-nee-hmyoke-nan-the*
investigate *(v.)* စုံစမ်းစစ်ဆေးသည် *sone-san-sit-say-the*
investigation *(n.)* စုံစမ်းစစ်ဆေးခြင်း *sone-san-sit-say-chin*
investment *(n.)* ရင်းနှီးမြှုပ်နှံခြင်း *yin-nee-hmyoke-nan-chin*
invigilate *(v.)* စာမေးပွဲစောင့်သည် *sar-may-pwe-saunt-the*
invigilation *(n.)* စာမေးပွဲစောင့်ခြင်း *sar-may-pwe-saunt-chin*
invigilator *(n.)* စာမေးပွဲစောင့်သူ *sar-may-pwe-saunt-thu*
invincible *(adj.)* မလွှမ်းမိုးနိုင်သော *ma-hlwan-moe-nai-taw*
inviolable *(adj.)* မချိုးဖောက်အပ်သော *ma-choe-hpauk-at-taw*
invisible *(adj.)* မမြင်ရသော *ma-myin-ya-taw*
invitation *(n.)* ဖိတ်ကြားခြင်း *phate-kyar-chin*
invite *(v.)* ဖိတ်ကြားသည် *phate-kyar-the*
invocation *(n.)* ကိုးကားသည်၊ မှီငြမ်းသည် *koe-kar-the, mee-nyan-the*
invoice *(n.)* ကုန်ပို့လွှာ *kone-poe-hlwar*
invoke *(v.)* ကိုးကားသည်၊ မှီငြမ်းသည် *koe-kar-the, mee-nyan-the*
involve *(v.)* ပါဝင်သည် *par-win-the*
inward *(adj.)* အတွင်း *a-twin*
inwards *(adv.)* အတွင်းသို့ *a-twin-thoe*
irate *(adj.)* အလွန်စိတ်ဆိုးသော *a-lun-seik-soe-taw*
ire *(n.)* အမျက် *a-myat*
Irish *(adj.)* အိုင်ယာလန်နိုင်ငံနှင့် ဆိုင်သော *i-ra-land-nai-ngan-nint-sai-taw*
irk *(v.)* စိတ်ဆိုးစေသည် *seik-soe-say-the*
irksome *(adj.)* စိတ်တိုစရာ *seik-toe-sa-yar*
iron *(v.)* မီးပူတိုက်သည် *mee-pu-tite-the*
ironic *(adj.)* ရွဲ့သော *ywe-taw*

ironical *(adj.)* ငေါ့သော *ngot taw*

irony *(n.)* ဇောက်ထိုးစကား *zaut-htoe-sa-kar*

irradiate *(v.)* ရောင်ခြည်တစ်ခုခုပေးသည် *yaung-che-ta-khu-khu-pay-the*

irrational *(adj.)* ယုတ္တိမရှိခြင်း *yote-ti-ma-shi-chin*

irreconcilable *(adj.)* ညှိ၍ မရသော *hnyi-ywe-ma-ya-taw*

irrecoverable *(adj.)* ပြန်မရနိုင်သော *pyan-ma-ya-nai-taw*

irrefutable *(adj.)* မငြင်းနိုင်သော *ma-nyin-nai-taw*

irregular *(adj.)* ပုံမမှန်သော *pon-ma-hman-taw*

irregularity *(n.)* ပုံမှန်မဟုတ်ခြင်း *pon-hman-ma-hote-chin*

irrelevant *(adj.)* မဆီလျော်သော *ma-se-lyaw-taw*

irresistible *(adj.)* မအောင့်အည်းနိုင်သော *ma-aung-ae-nai-taw*

irrespective *(adj.)* ဂရုမထားဘဲ *ga-yu-ma-htar-pal*

irresponsible *(adj.)* တာဝန်မဲ့သော *tar-win-mae-taw*

irrigate *(v.)* ဆည်ရေပေးသည် *sal-yay-pay-the*

irrigation *(n.)* ဆည်မြောင်းသွယ်ခြင်း *sal-myaung-thwe-chin*

irritable *(adj.)* ကသိကအောက်ဖြစ်သော *ka-ti-ka-aut-phit-taw*

irritant *(adj.)* ကသိကအောက်ဖြစ်စေသော *ka-ti-ka-aut-phit-say-taw*

irritate *(v.)* ဒေါသထွက်သည် *daw-ta-htwat-the*

irritation *(n.)* ဒေါသ *daw-ta*

irruption *(n.)* ထိုးဖောက်ဝင်ရောက်ခြင်း *htoe-hpauk-win-yauk-chin*

island *(n.)* ကျွန်း *kyun*

isle *(n.)* ကျွန်း *kyun*

isobar *(n.)* ဖိအားတူမျဉ်း *phi-arr-tu-myin*

isolate *(v.)* သီးခြားထားသည်၊ ခွဲထားသည် *thee-char-htar-the, kwal-htar-the*

isolation *(n.)* သီးသန့်ထားခြင်း *tee-tant-htar-chin*

issue *(n.)* ကိစ္စရပ်၊ ထုတ်ဝေခြင်း *kait-sa-yat, htoke-wai-chin*

it *(pron.)* ၄င်း *la-gaung*

Italian *(adj.)* အီတလီနှင့်ဆိုင်သော *ae-ta-li-nint-sai-taw*

Italian *(n.)* အီတလီနိုင်ငံသား *ae-ta-li-nai-ngan-tar*

italic *(adj.)* အစောင်း *a-saung*

italics *(n.)* စာလုံးစောင်း *sar-lone-saung*

itch *(n.)* ယားခြင်း *yar-chin*

item *(n.)* အချက်၊ ပစ္စည်း၊ သတင်းတစ်ပုဒ် *a-chat, pyit-see, ta-din-ta-poke*

itinerary *(n.)* ခရီးစဉ် *kha-yee-sin*

ivory *(n.)* ဆင်စွယ်ရုပ်ထု *sin-swal-yoke-htu*

ivy *(n.)* တိုင်ကပ်နွယ်ပင် *tai-kat-nwe-pin*

jab *(v.)* ဆတ်သည်၊ ထိုးသည် *sat-the, htoe-the*

jabber *(v.)* ဗလုံးဗထွေးပြောသည် *ba-lon-ba-htway-pyaw-the*

jack *(v.)* ဂျိုက်ဖြင့် မသည် *gyaik-phint-ma-the*

jackal *(n.)* ခွေးအ *khway-a*

jacket *(n.)* အပေါ်အင်္ကျီ *a-paw-in-gyi*

jackpot *(n.)* အလယ်ပုံ *a-lal-pon*

jade *(n.)* ကျောက်စိမ်း *kyauk-sein*

jail *(n.)* ထောင် *htaung*

jailer *(n.)* ထောင်မှူး *htaung-hmu*

jam *(v.)* ညပ်သပ်သည် *nyat-tat-the*

jam-packed *(adj.)* ငါးပိသိပ် ငါးချဉ်သိပ် ပြည့်ကျပ်နေသော *ngar-pi-tate-ngar-chin-tat-pyae-kyat-nay-taw*

janitor *(n.)* အစောင့် *a-saunt*

January *(n.)* ဇန်နဝါရီလ *zan-na-war-ree-la*

jar *(n.)* အိုး *oh*

jargon *(n.)* ဗန်းစကား *ban-sa-kar*

jasmine, jessamine *(n.)* စံပယ်ပန်း *sa-pal-pan*

jaundice *(n.)* အသားဝါခြင်း *a-tar-war-chin*

javelin *(n.)* လှံတံ *hlan-tan*

jaw *(n.)* မေးရိုး *mae-yoe*

jay *(n.)* ဗွတ်ကုလား *bwat-ka-lar*

jealous *(adj.)* မနာလိုသော *ma-nar-lo-taw*

jealousy *(n.)* မနာလိုမှု *ma-nar-lo-mu*

jean *(n.)* ဂျင်းအင်္ကျီ *gyin-in-gyi*

jeer *(v.)* လှောင်ပြောင်သည် *hlaung-paung-the*

jelly *(n.)* ဂျယ်လီ *jal-lee*

jeopardize *(v.)* ထိခိုက်သည် *hti-khite-the*

jeopardy *(n.)* အန္တရာယ် *an-ta-yal*

jerk *(n.)* ဆတ်ခနဲ လှုပ်ရှားမှု *sat-kha-nae-lote-shar-mu*

jerkin *(n.)* ဂျာကင်အင်္ကျီ *jar-kin-in-gyi*

jerky *(adj.)* ဆတ်တောက်ဆတ်တောက် သွားသော *sat-taut-sat-taut-twar-taw*

jersey *(n.)* ဂျာဆီနို့စားနွားမမျိုး *jar-si-noe-sar-nwar-ma-myo*

jest *(n.)* ပြက်လုံး *pyat-lone*

jet *(n.)* ဂျက်လေယာဉ် *jat-lay-yin*

jet engine *(n.)* ဂျက်အင်ဂျင် *jat-in-gyin*

jew *(n.)* ဂျူးဗရှူး *ju-ba-yu*

jewel *(n.)* ကျောက်မျက် *kyauk-myat*

jeweller *(n.)* စိန်ရွှေရတနာဆိုင်ရှင် *sein-shwe-ya-da-nar-sine-shin*

jewellery *(n.)* လက်ဝတ်လက်စား *lat-wit-lat-sar*

jiggle *(v.)* နန့်သည် *nant-the*

jigsaw *(n.)* ဂျစ်ဆောအရုပ်ဆက်ခြင်း *jit-saw-a-yike-sat-chin*

jingle *(n.)* ချူသံ *chu-tan*

job *(n.)* အလုပ် *a-lote*

jobber *(n.)* အလုပ်ခန့်သောသူ *a-lote-khant-taw-thu*

jobbery *(n.)* မသင့်လျော်သော၊ ချစားသော အပြုအမူ *ma-tint-lyaw-taw-cha-sar-taw-a-pyu-a-mu*

jobless *(adj.)* အလုပ်လက်မဲ့ *a-lote-lat-mae*

jockey *(n.)* ဂျော်ကီ *jaw-ki*

jocular *(adj.)* အပြောင်အပြက် *a-pyaung-a-pyat*

jog *(v.)* ရွရွ ပြေးသည် *ywa-ywa-pyay-the*

join *(v.)* ချိတ်ဆက်သည် *chate-sat-the*

joiner *(n.)* ကျည်းပေါင်သမား *kyi-paung-ta-mar*

joint *(adj.)* ပူးတွဲ *pu-twal*

joint effort *(n.)* ပူးတွဲအားထုတ်ခြင်း *pu-twal-arr-htoke-chin*

jointly *(adv.)* ပူးတွဲ *pu-twal*

joke *(n.)* ရယ်စရာ၊ ဟာသ *yal-sa-yar, har-ta*

joker *(n.)* ဂျိုကာ *jo-ker*

jollity *(n.)* ပျော်ရွှင်ခြင်း *pyaw-shwin-chin*

jolly *(adj.)* ပျော်ရွှင်သော *pyaw-shwin-taw*

jolt *(v.)* တွန်းသည်၊ လှုပ်သည် *tun-the, hlote-the*

jostle *(n.)* တွန်းမိတိုက်မိခြင်း *tun-mi-tite-mi-chin*

jot *(n.)* အနည်းငယ် *a-nae-ngal*

jot *(v.)* တို့သည်၊ မှတ်သည် *toe-the, mat-the*

journal *(n.)* ဂျာနယ် *jar-nal*

journalism *(n.)* သတင်းစာပညာ *ta-din-sar-pyin-nyar*

journalist *(n.)* သတင်းထောက် *ta-din-htauk*

journey *(n.)* ခရီး *kha-yee*

jovial *(adj.)* ပျော်ပျော်ရွှင်ရွှင် *pyaw-pyaw-shwin-shwin*

joviality *(n.)* ပျော်ရွှင်ခြင်း *pyaw-shwin-chin*

joy *(n.)* ဝမ်းသာခြင်း *wan-tar-chin*

joyful *(adj.)* ပျော်စရာ *pyaw-sa-yar*

joyous *(n.)* ပျော်စရာရွှင်စရာ *pyaw-sa-yar-shwin-sa-yar*

jubilant *(adj.)* ဝင့်ကြွား ဝမ်းမြောက်သော *wint-kywar-wan-myauk-taw*

jubilation *(n.)* ဂုဏ်ယူဝင့်ကြွားခြင်း *gon-yu-wint-kywar-chin*

jubilee *(n.)* နှစ်ပတ်လည် *nit-pat-lal*

judge *(v.)* ချင့်ချိန်သည် *chint-chain-the*

judgement *(n.)* ဝေဖန်ပိုင်းခြားနိုင်စွမ်း *wai-phan-pai-char-nai-swan*

judicature *(n.)* တရားစီရင်မှု *ta-yar-si-yin-mu*

judicial *(adj.)* တရားရေး *ta-yar-yay*

judiciary *(n.)* တရားစီရင်ရေး *ta-yar-si-yin-yay*

judicious *(adj.)* အမြော်အမြင်ရှိသော *a-myaw-a-myin-shi-taw*

jug *(n.)* ရေချိုင့် *yay-chaint*

juggle *(v.)* လက်လှည့်အစွမ်းပြသည် *lat-hlae-a-swan-pya-the*

juggler *(n.)* လက်လှည့်ဆရာ *lat-hlae-sa-yar*

juice *(n.)* သစ်သီးရည် *tit-tee-yay*

juicy *(adj.)* အရည်ရွှမ်းသော *a-yay-shwan-taw*

jukebox *(n.)* ဂီတသေတ္တာ *gi-ta-tit-tar*

jumble *(n.)* ဗရပွ *ba-ra-pwa*

jumble *(v.)* ရောပုံထားသည် *yaw-pon-htar-the*

jump *(n.)* ခုန်ခြင်း *kone-chin*

junction *(n.)* လမ်းဆုံ *lan-sone*

juncture *(n.)* အဆုံ *a-sone*

jungle *(n.)* ထူထပ်သောတော *htu-htat-taw-taw*

junior *(adj.)* ငယ်သော *hgal-taw*

junk *(n.)* ဗြုတ်စဗျင်းတောင်း *byoke-sa-byin-taung*

jupiter *(n.)* ကြာသပတေးဂြိုလ် *kyar-ta-pa-tay-gyo*

jurisdiction *(n.)* တရားစီရင်ပိုင်ခွင့် *ta-yar-si-yin-pai-khwint*

jurisprudence *(n.)* ဥပဒေသိပ္ပံပညာ *au-pa-day-tate-pan-pyin-nyar*

jurist *(n.)* ဥပဒေပညာရှင် *au-pa-day-pyin-nyar-shin*

juror *(n.)* ဂျူရီအဖွဲ့ဝင်လူကြီး *ju-re-a-phwe-win-lu-gyi*

jury *(n.)* ဂျူရီလူကြီးအဖွဲ့ *ju-re-lu-gyi-a-phwe*

juryman *(n.)* ဂျူရီလူကြီး *ju-re-lu-gyi*

just *(adj.)* တရားသော *ta-yar-taw*

justice *(n.)* တရားမျှတမှု *ta-yar-mya-ta-mu*

justifiable *(adj.)* လျော်ကန်သော *lyaw-kan-taw*

justification *(n.)* ကျိုးကြောင်းပြချက် *kyo-kyaung-pya-chat*

justified *(adj.)* တရားသော *ta-yar-taw*

justify *(v.)* ရှင်းချက်ထုတ်သည် *shin-chat-htoke-the*

justly *(adv.)* မှန်မှန်ကန်ကန် *man-man-kan-kan*

jute *(n.)* ဂုန်လျှော် *gon-shaw*

juvenile *(adj.)* လူငယ်လူရွယ် *lu-ngal-lu-ywe*

juxtapose *(v.)* တစ်ခုနှင့် တစ်ခု ယှဉ်တွဲပြသည် *ta-khu-nint-ta-khu-yin-twe-pya-the*

juxtaposed *(adj.)* တစ်ခုနှင့် တစ်ခု ယှဉ်တွဲပြသော *ta-khu-nint-ta-khu-yin-twe-pya-taw*

juxtaposition *(n.)* ယှဉ်တွဲ ခိုင်းနှိုင်းခြင်း *shin-twe-khai-nai-chin*

K

kaffir *(n.)* လူမည်း *lu-me*

kaki *(n.)* ကာကီရောင် *ka-ki-yaung*

kaleidoscope *(n.)* ရုပ်စုံမှန်ပြောင်း *yoke-sone-man-pyaung*

kamikaze *(n.)* အသက်ကို ပဓာနမထားဘဲ တဇောက်ကန်း လုပ်ဆောင်သော *a-tat-ko-pa-dar-na-ma-htar-bae-ta-zaut-kan-lote-saung-taw*

kangaroo *(n.)* သားပိုက်ကောင် *tar-bike-kaung*

karat *(n.)* ကရက် *ka-rat*

keen *(adj.)* စူးရှသော၊ စိတ်ဝင်စားသော *su-sha-taw, seik-win-sar-taw*

keenness *(n.)* ထက်မြက်ခြင်း၊ ပြင်းပြခြင်း *htet-myat-cin, pyin-pya-chin*

keep *(v.)* သိမ်းသည် *thein-the*

keeper *(n.)* အစောင့် *a-saunt*

keepsake *(n.)* အမှတ်တရ လက်ဆောင် *a-mat-ta-ya-lat-saung*

kennel *(n.)* ခွေးအိမ် *khway-eain*

kerchief *(n.)* ခေါင်းစည်းပဝါ *gaung-see-pa-war*

kernel *(n.)* အဆန်၊ အစေ့ *a-san, a-say*

kerosene *(n.)* ရေနံဆီ *yay-nan-si*

ketchup *(n.)* ဆော့ *sawt*

kettle *(n.)* ရေနွေးကရား *yay-nway-ka-yar*

key *(n.)* သော့၊ သော့ချက် *tot, tot-chat*

keyboard *(n.)* ကီးဘုတ် *kee-bote*

keyhole *(n.)* သော့ပေါက် *tot-pauk*

keypad *(n.)* ခလုတ်ခုံအငယ်စား *kha-lote-khon-a-nge-sar*

keysmith *(n.)* သော့ဖျက်သူ *taw-phat-thu*

keystone *(n.)* အချက်အချာ၊ သော့ချက် *a-chat-a-char, tot-chat*

keyword *(n.)* အဓိက စကားလုံး *a-di-ka-sa-kar-lone*

kick *(n.)* ကန်ခြင်း *kan-chin*

kick-start *(v.)* ကစ်ဖြင့် စက်နိုးသည် *kit-phit-sat-noe-the*

kid *(n.)* ကလေး *ka-lay*

kidnap *(v.)* ပြန်ပေးဆွဲသည် *pyan-pay-swal-the*

kidney *(n.)* ကျောက်ကပ် *kyauk-kat*

kill *(n.)* သတ်ခြင်း *tat-chin*

kiln *(n.)* ဖိုကြီး *pho-gyi*

kilo *(n.)* ကီလို *ki-lo*

kilogram *(n.)* ကီလိုဂရမ် *ki-lo-gram*

kilt *(n.)* ဒူးဆစ်ရောက် ရိုးရာ ခါးဝတ် *du-sit-yauk-yoe-yar-khar-wit*

kin *(n.)* မိမိ မိသားစုနှင့် ဆွေမျိုးသားချင်း *mi-mi-mi-tar-su-nint-swe-myo-tar-chin*

kind *(adj.)* ကြင်နာသော *kyin-nar-taw*

kindergarten *(n.)* သူငယ်တန်း *thu-ngal-tan*

kind-hearted *(adj.)* ကြင်နာစိတ် ရှိသော *kyin-nar-seik-shi-taw*

kindle *(v.)* မီးမွှေးသည်၊ နှိုးဆွသည် *mee-hmway-the, noe-swa-the*

kindly *(adv.)* ကြင်နာစွာ *kyin-nar-swar*

kindness *(n.)* ကြင်နာမှု *kyin-nar-mu*

kinetic *(adj.)* အရွေ့ *a-shway*

king *(n.)* ဘုရင် *ba-yin*

kingdom *(n.)* ဘုရင့်နိုင်ငံတော် *ba-yin-nai-ngan-taw*

kinship *(n.)* သွေးသားတော်စပ်မှု *tway-tar-taw-sat-mu*

kiosk *(n.)* အများသုံး တယ်လီဖုန်းရုံ၊ ဆိုင်ငယ် *a-myar-tone-tal-le-phone-yone, sai-ngal*

kiss *(v.)* နမ်းသည် *nan-the*

kit *(n.)* ပစ္စည်းကိရိယာ *pyit-see-ka-ri-yar*

kitchen *(n.)* မီးဖိုချောင် *mee-pho-chaung*

kite *(n.)* စွန် *soon*

kith *(n.)* ဆွေမျိုးမိတ်သင်္ဂဟ *sway-myo-meik-tin-ga-har*

kitten *(n.)* ကြောင်ပေါက်စ *kyaung-pauk-sa*

knave *(n.)* လူယုတ်မာ *lu-yoke-mar*

knavery *(n.)* လိမ်ညာလှည့်ဖျားမှု *lain-nyar-lae-hpyar-mu*

knead *(v.)* နယ်သည်၊ နှိပ်နယ်ပေးသည် *nal-the, nate-nal-pay-the*

knee *(n.)* ဒူး *du*

kneel *(v.)* ဒူးထောက်သည် *du-htauk-the*

knife *(n.)* ဓား *dar*

knight *(v.)* ဆာဘွဲ့ဖြင့် သူကောင်းပြုသည် *sar-bwe-phint-thu-gaung-pyu-the*

knit *(v.)* သိုးမွေးထိုးသည် *toe-mway-htoe-the*

knock *(v.)* ခေါက်သည် *khauk-the*

knockout *(n.)* ရှုံးထွက်ပြိုင်ပွဲ *shone-htwat-pyai-pwe*

knot *(n.)* အထုံး *a-htone*

knot *(v.)* ထုံးသည် *htone-the*

know *(v.)* သိသည် *ti-the*

knowledge *(n.)* အသိပညာ *a-ti-pyin-nyar*

knowledgeable *(adj.)* အသိပညာကြွယ်သော *a-ti-pyin-nyar-kywe-taw*

knuckle *(n.)* လက်ဆစ် *lat-sit*

koala *(n.)* ကိုအာလာဝက်ဝံ *ko-ar-lar-wat-win*

koi *(n.)* ရွှေငါး *shwe-ngar*

krill *(n.)* ပုစွန်ဆိတ်ငယ် *pa-sun-seik-ngal*

L

label *(n.)* လေဘယ်လ်ကတ် *lay-bal-kat*

labial *(adj.)* နှုတ်ခမ်းဆိုင်ရာ *note-khan-sai-yar*

laboratory *(n.)* ဓာတ်ခွဲခန်း *dat-kwal-khan*

laborious *(adj.)* လက်ဝင်သော *lat-win-taw*

labour *(v.)* အလုပ်လုပ်သည် *a-lote-lote-the*

labour *(n.)* အလုပ်ကြမ်း *a-lote-kyan*

laboured *(adj.)* ခက်ခဲ ပင်ပန်းသော *khat-khae-pin-pan-taw*

labourer *(n.)* အလုပ်ကြမ်းသမား *a-lote-kyan-ta-mar*

labyrinth *(n.)* ဝင်္ကပါ *win-ka-bar*

lac, lakh *(n.)* သိန်း *thein-the*

lace *(v.)* ချည်သည် *chi-the*

lace *(n.)* ဇာပန်းထည် *zar-pan-htal*

lacerate *(v.)* ပြဲသည် *pyae-the*

lachrymose *(adj.)* အငိုလွယ်သော *a-nyo-lwal-the*

lack *(v.)* ချို့တဲ့သည် *choe-tae-the*

lackey *(n.)* လက်ပါးစေ *lat-par-say*

lacklustre *(adj.)* ထိုင်းမှိုင်းသော *htai-mai-taw*

laconic *(adj.)* နှုတ်နည်းသော *note-nae-taw*

lactate *(v.)* နို့ထုတ်သည် *noe-nae-taw*

lactic *(adj.)* နို့နှင့် သက်ဆိုင်သော *noe-nint-thet-sai-taw*

lactometer *(n.)* နို့တွင်ခရင်ပါနှုန်းတိုင်းကိရိယာ *noe-twin-kha-rin-par-hnone-tai-ka-ri-ya*

lactose *(n.)* လက်တို့သကြား *lat-toe-ta-kyar*

lacuna *(n.)* စာကျန်၊ အကျအပေါက် *sar-kyan,a-kya-pauk*

lacy *(adj.)* ဇာဖြင့် ပြီးသော *zar-phint-pi-taw*

lad *(n.)* လူငယ် *lu-ngal*

ladder *(n.)* လှေကား *hlay-kar*

lade *(v.)* ဖြည့်သည် *pyae-the*

ladle *(n.)* ယောက်ချို *yauk-cho*

ladle *(v.)* ဟင်းလိုက်သည် *hin-lite-the*

lady *(n.)* အမျိုးသမီး *a-myo-ta-mee*

lag *(v.)* နောက်ကျ ကျန်ရစ်သည် *naut-kya-kyan-yit-the*

laggard *(n.)* ဖင့်နွှဲလေးကန်သူ *phint-nwe-kan-the*

lagoon *(n.)* ပင်လယ်ထုံးအိုင် *pin-lal-htone-ai*

laid-back *(adj.)* အေးအေးလူလူ *aye-aye-lu-lu*

lair *(n.)* သားရဲတွင်း *tar-ye-twin*

lake *(n.)* ရေကန် *yay-kan*

lakefront *(n.)* ကန်ရှေ့ *kan-shay*

lama *(n.)* လားမားဘုန်းတော်ကြီး *lar-ma-phone-taw-gyi*

lamb *(n.)* သိုးငယ် *toe-ngal*

lambaste *(v.)* ပယ်ပယ်နယ်နယ်ဝေဖန်ရှုတ်ချသည် *pal-pal-ne-ne-wai-hpan-shoke-cha-the*

lambkin *(n.)* သိုးငယ် *thoe-ngal*

lame *(adj.)* ခြေကျိုးနေသော *chay-kyo-nay-taw*

lament *(n.)* **ကြေကွဲဝမ်းနည်းခြင်း** *kyay-kwal-wan-nae-chin*
lament *(v.)* **ကြေကွဲဝမ်းနည်းသည်** *kyay-kwal-wan-nae-the*
lamentable *(adj.)* **စိတ်ပျက်ဖွယ်ကောင်းသော** *seik-pyat-phwal-kaung-taw*
lamentation *(n.)* **ငိုမြည်တမ်းတခြင်း** *ngo-mye-tan-ta-chin*
laminate *(v.)* **အပြားခတ်သည်** *a-pyar-khat-the*
lamp *(n.)* **မီးအိမ်** *mee-eain*
lampoon *(n.)* **သရော်စာ** *ta-yaw-sar*
lance *(v.)* **ဖောက်သည်၊ ခွဲသည်** *hpaut-the, khwal-the*
lancer *(n.)* **လှံသမား** *lan-ta-mar*
lancet *(adj.)* **အပ်** *at*
land *(n.)* **ကုန်းမြေ** *kone-myay*
landing *(n.)* **မြေပြင်သို့ ဆင်းသက်ခြင်း** *myay-pyin-toe-sin-thet-chin*
landline *(n.)* **အထိုင်ဖုန်း** *a-htai-phone*
landlord *(n.)* **မြေပိုင်ရှင်** *myay-pai-shin*
landmark *(n.)* **အထင်ကရနေရာ** *a-htin-ka-ya-nay-nar*
landscape *(n.)* **ရှုခင်း** *shu-khin*
lane *(n.)* **လမ်း** *lan*
language *(n.)* **ဘာသာစကား** *bar-tar-sa-kar*
languish *(v.)* **အားအင်လျော့လာသည်** *arr-inn-shawt-lar-the*
languor *(n.)* **နွမ်းလျခြင်း** *nwan-hlya-chin*
lank *(adj.)* **ကြမ်းကြမ်းတောင့်တောင့်** *kyan-kyan-taunt-taunt*
lantern *(n.)* **လက်ဆွဲမီးအိမ်** *lat-swal-mee-eain*
lanugo *(n.)* **နူးညံ့ပျော့ပျောင်းသော ဆံသား** *nu-nyant-pawt-pyaung-taw-san-tar*
lap *(n.)* **ပေါင်ခွင်၊ ပေါင်** *paung-kwin, paung*
lapse *(v.)* **သက်တမ်းလွန်သွားသည်** *thet-tan-lun-twar-the*
laptop *(n.)* **လက်ဆွဲကွန်ပျူတာ** *lat-swal-kun-pyu-tar*
lard *(n.)* **ဝက်ဆီ** *wat-si*
large *(adj.)* **ကြီးမားသော** *kyi-mar-taw*
largesse *(n.)* **အပေးအကမ်းရက်ရောမှု** *a-pay-a-kan-yat-yaw-mu*
lark *(n.)* **ဘီလုံးငှက်** *bi-lone-nget*
lascivious *(adj.)* **တဏှာကြီးသော** *ta-nar-kyi-taw*
lash *(n.)* **ကျာပွတ်** *kyar-put*
lass *(n.)* **မိန်းကလေး** *mein-ka-lay*
last *(adj.)* **နောက်ဆုံး** *naut-sone*
last *(v.)* **ကြာသည်** *kyar-the*
lasting *(adj.)* **ကြာသော** *kyaw-taw*
lastly *(adv.)* **နောက်ဆုံး** *naut-sone*
latch *(n.)* **တံခါးကျင်** *ta-khar-kyin*
late *(adj.)* **နောက်ကျသော** *naut-kya-taw*
lately *(adv.)* **ခုတစ်လော** *khu-ta-law*
latent *(adj.)* **အောင်းနေသော၊ ငုပ်နေသော** *aung-nay-taw, ngoke-nay-thaw*
lath *(n.)* **ပျဉ်ချပ်ပါး** *pyin-chat-par*
lathe *(n.)* **ပွတ်ခုံ** *put-khone*
lather *(n.)* **ဆပ်ပြာမြှုပ်** *sat-pyar-hmyoke*
latitude *(n.)* **လတ္တီတွဒ်** *lat-ti-tut*
latrine *(n.)* **အိမ်သာ** *eain-tar*
latter *(adj.)* **နောက်ပိုင်း** *naut-pai*
lattice *(n.)* **ရာဇမတ်ကွက်** *ya-za-mat-hwat*
laud *(n.)* **ချီးမြှောက်ခြင်း** *chee-hmyauk-chin*
laudable *(adj.)* **ချီးကျူးထိုက်သော** *chee-kyu-htike-taw*

laugh *(n.)* ရယ်မောခြင်း၊ ရယ်သံ *yal-maw-chin, yal-tan*
laughable *(adj.)* ရယ်ဖွယ်ဖြစ်သော *yal-phwal-phit-taw*
laughter *(n.)* ရယ်မောခြင်း၊ ရယ်သံ *yal-maw-chin, yal-tan*
launch *(v.)* စတင်ဆောင်ရွက်သည် *sa-tin-saung-ywet-the*
launder *(v.)* လျှော်ဖွပ်သည် *shaw-hput-the*
laundress *(n.)* ဒိုဘီသည် *do-be-sal*
laundry *(n.)* ဒိုဘီဆိုင် *do-be-sai*
laureate *(n.)* စာဆိုတော် *sar-so-taw*
laurel *(n.)* လော်ရယ်ပင် *law-yal-pin*
lava *(n.)* ချော်ရည် *chaw-yay*
lavatory *(n.)* အိမ်သာ *eain-tar*
lavender *(n.)* လာဗင်ဒါပန်း *la-vin-dar-pan*
lavish *(adj.)* ဖောဖောသီသီ သုံးစွဲသော *phaw-phaw-ti-ti-tone-swal-taw*
lavish *(v.)* ရက်ရောသည် *yat-yaw-the*
law *(n.)* ဥပဒေ *au-pa-day*
lawful *(adj.)* တရားဝင်ဖြစ်သော *ta-yar-win-phit-taw*
lawless *(adj.)* ဥပဒေမဲ့ *au-pa-day-mae*
lawn *(n.)* မြက်ခင်း *myat-khin*
lawyer *(n.)* ရှေ့နေ *shay-nay*
lax *(adj.)* လျော့ရဲသော *yawt-ye-thaw*
laxative *(n.)* ဝမ်းပျော့ဆေး *wan-pyawt-say*
laxative *(adj.)* ဝမ်းသွားစေသော *wan-twar-say-the*
laxity *(n.)* တင်းအား နည်းခြင်း၊ ကိုယ်ကျင့် အားနည်းခြင်း *tin-arr-nae-chin, ko-kyint-arr-nae-chin*
lay *(n.)* လိုင်ဆက်ဆံဖက် *lain-sat-san-phat*
lay *(v.)* ချခင်းသည်၊ တာဝန်ပေးသည် *cha-khin-the, tar-win-pay-the*
layer *(n.)* အလွှာ *a-hlwar*
layman *(n.)* လူသာမန် *lu-tar-man*
lay-off *(n.)* အလုပ်ပြုတ်သူ *a-lote-pyoke-thu*
layout *(n.)* အခင်းအကျင်းပုံစံ *a-khin-a-kyin-pon-san*
laze *(v.)* နားနားနေနေ နေသည် *nar-nar-nay-nay-nay-the*
laziness *(n.)* ပျင်းရိခြင်း *pyin-yi-chin*
lazy *(adj.)* ပျင်းရိသော *pyin-yi-taw*
lea *(n.)* ကွင်းပြင် *kwin-pyin*
leach *(v.)* ပျော်ဝင်ပါသွားသည် *pyaw-win-par-twar-the*
lead *(n.)* ခေါင်းဆောင်မှု၊ ခဲသတ္တု *gaung-saung-mu, khae-tat-tu*
lead *(v.)* ဦးဆောင်သည် *au-saung-the*
leaden *(adj.)* ထိုင်းမှိုင်းသော *htai-mai-taw*
leader *(n.)* ခေါင်းဆောင် *gaung-saung*
leadership *(n.)* ခေါင်းဆောင်မှုပညာ *gaung-saung-mu-pyin-nyar*
leaf *(n.)* သစ်ရွက် *tit-ywet*
leaflet *(n.)* လက်ကမ်းစာစောင် *lat-kan-sar-saung*
leafy *(adj.)* အရွက်ဝေဆာသော *a-ywet-wai-sar-taw*
league *(n.)* အသင်း၊ အဖွဲ့ချုပ် *a-tin, a-phwe-chike*
leak *(n.)* စိမ့်ပေါက် *seint-pauk*
leakage *(n.)* သတင်းပေါက်ကြားမှု၊ ယိုစိမ့်မှု *ta-din-pauk-kyar-mu, yoe-seint-mu*
lean *(v.)* မှီသည် *hmi-the*
leap *(n.)* ခုန်လွှားခြင်း *khone-hlwar-chin*
learn *(v.)* လေ့လာသည် *lay-lar-the*
learned *(adj.)* လေ့လာသော *lay-lat-taw*

learner *(n.)* လေ့လာသင်ယူသူ *lay-lar-tin-yu-thu*

learning *(n.)* လေ့လာသင်ယူခြင်း *lay-lar-tin-yu-chin*

lease *(v.)* စာချုပ်နှင့် ငှားသည် *sar-choke-nint-ngar-the*

least *(adv.)* အနည်းဆုံး *a-ne-sone*

leather *(n.)* သားရေ *ta-yay*

leave *(n.)* ခွင့် *khwint*

lecture *(n.)* ပို့ချခြင်း *poe-cha-chin*

lecture *(v.)* ပို့ချသည် *poe-cha-the*

lecturer *(n.)* ကထိက *ka-hti-ka*

ledger *(n.)* စာရင်းစာအုပ် *sa-yin-sar-oak*

lee *(n.)* လေကွယ် *lay-kwal*

leech *(n.)* မျှော့၊ ပိုင်းလုံး *myawt, pine-lone*

leek *(n.)* ကြက်သွန်မြိတ် *kyat-toon-myeik*

left *(n.)* ပစ္စည်းခေတ္တအပ်နှံရာနေရာ *pyit-see-khit-ta-at-nan-yar-nay-yar*

leftist *(n.)* လက်ဝဲဝါဒီ *lat-wal-wa-di*

leftover *(n.)* အကြွင်းအကျန် *a-kywin-a-kyan*

leg *(n.)* ခြေထောက် *chay-htauk*

legacy *(n.)* အမွေအနှစ် *a-mway-a-nit*

legal *(adj.)* ဥပဒေဆိုင်ရာ *au-pa-day-sai-yar*

legal action *(n.)* ဥပဒေနှင့်အညီ အရေးယူခြင်း *au-pa-day-nint-a-nyi-a-yay-yu-chin*

legality *(n.)* တရားဥပဒေနှင့် ညီညွတ်ခြင်း *ta-yar-au-pa-day-nint-nyi-nyut-chin*

legalize *(v.)* တရားဝင်ဖြစ်စေသည် *ta-yar-win-phit-say-the*

legend *(n.)* ရိုးရာပုံပြင်၊ အကျော်ဇေယျ *yoe-yar-pon-pyin, a-kyaw-zay-ya*

legendary *(adj.)* အထင်ကရဖြစ်သော *a-htin-ka-ya-phit-taw*

leghorn *(n.)* လက်ဟွန်းကြက် *lat-hone-kyat*

legible *(adj.)* ဖတ်၍ ရနိုင်သော *phat-ywe-ya-nai-taw*

legibly *(adv.)* ပီပီသသ *pi-pi-ta-ta*

legion *(n.)* ကြေးစားစစ်တပ် *kyay-sar-sit-tat*

legionary *(n.)* ကြေးစားတပ်ဖွဲ့ဝင် *kyay-sar-tat-phwe-win*

legislate *(v.)* ဥပဒေပြုသည် *au-pa-day-pyu-the*

legislation *(n.)* ဥပဒေ *au-pa-day*

legislative *(adj.)* ဥပဒေပြု *au-pa-day-pyu*

legislator *(n.)* ဥပဒေပြု လွှတ်တော်အမတ် *au-pa-day-pyu-hlut-taw-a-mat*

legislature *(n.)* ဥပဒေပြု လွှတ်တော် *au-pa-day-pyu-hlut-taw*

legitimacy *(n.)* တရားဝင်ဖြစ်ခြင်း *ta-yar-win-phit-chin*

legitimate *(adj.)* တရားဝင်ဖြစ်သော *ta-yar-win-phit-taw*

leisure *(n.)* အားလပ်ချိန် *arr-lat-chain*

leisurely *(adj.)* အေးအေးဆေးဆေး *aye-aye-say-say*

lemon *(n.)* လီမွန်သီး၊ ရှောက်သီး *li-mon-thee, shaut-thee*

lemonade *(n.)* လင်မနစ် *lin-ma-nit*

lend *(v.)* ငှားသည်၊ ချေးသည် *ngar-the, chay-the*

length *(n.)* အရှည် *a-shay*

lengthen *(v.)* ရှည်လာသည် *shay-lar-the*

lengthy *(adj.)* ရှည်ရှည်လျားလျား *shay-shay-lyar-lyar*

lenience *(n.)* သက်ညှာခြင်း *tat-nyar-chin*

leniency *(n.)* သက်ညှာမှု *tat-nyar-mu*

lenient *(adj.)* သက်ညှာသော *tat-nyar-taw*

lens *(n.)* မှန်ဘီလူး *hman-ba-lu*

lentil *(n.)* ပဲနီကလေး *pae-ni-ka-lay*

Leo *(n.)* သိဟ်ရာသီဖွား *theik-yar-thee-phwar*

leonine *(adj.)* ခြင်္သေ့နှင့် တူသော *chin-tay-nint-tu-taw*

leopard *(n.)* ကျားသစ် *kyar-tit*

leper *(n.)* အနာကြီးရောဂါသည် *a-nar-gyi-yaw-gar-the*

leprosy *(n.)* အနာကြီးရောဂါ *a-nar-gyi-yaw-gar*

leprous *(adj.)* အနာကြီးရောဂါရှိသော *a-nar-gyi-yaw-gar-shi-taw*

less *(adj.)* နည်းနည်း *nae-nae*

lessee *(n.)* အိမ်ငှား *eain-ngar*

lessen *(v.)* လျော့ပါးသည် *yawt-par-the*

lesser *(adj.)* လျော့နည်းသော *yawt-ne-taw*

lesson *(n.)* သင်ခန်းစာ *tin-khan-sar*

lest *(conj.)* စိုးရိမ်၍ *soe-yein-ywe*

let *(v.)* ခွင့်ပြုသည် *khwint-pyu-the*

lethal *(adj.)* သေစေသော *tay-say-taw*

lethargic *(adj.)* ထိုင်းမှိုင်းသော *htai-mai-taw*

lethargy *(n.)* ထိုင်းမှိုင်းခြင်း *htai-mai-chin*

let-out *(n.)* ကယ်ပေါက် *kal-pauk*

letter *(n.)* စာ *sar*

letterhead *(n.)* စာခေါင်းစည်း *sar-gaung-see*

level *(v.)* ညှိသည် *nyi-the*

lever *(n.)* ကုတ်၊ မောင်းသံ *kote, maung-tan*

leverage *(n.)* ကုတ်အား၊ ကန်အား *kote-arr, kan-arr*

levity *(n.)* ပြက်ရယ်ပြုခြင်း *pyat-yal-pyu-chin*

levy *(n.)* စည်းကြပ်ခြင်း *see-kyat-chin*

lewd *(adj.)* ညစ်ညမ်းသော၊ ရိုင်းပျသော *nyit-nyan-taw, yai-pya-taw*

lexicography *(n.)* အဘိဓာန်ပြုစုမှု *a-bi-dan-pyu-su-mu*

lexicon *(n.)* ဝေါဟာရစာရင်း *wor-har-ya-sa-yin*

liability *(n.)* တာဝန်ရှိခြင်း *tar-win-shi-chin*

liable *(adj.)* တာဝန်ရှိသော *tar-win-shi-taw*

liaison *(n.)* ဆက်ဆံရေး *sat-san-yay*

liar *(n.)* လူလိမ်၊ လူညာ *lu-lain, lu-nyar*

libel *(v.)* အသရေဖျက်သည် *a-ta-yay-phat-the*

liberal *(adj.)* လစ်ဘရယ်၊ အစွန်းမရောက်သော *lit-ba-ral, a-sun-ma-yauk-taw*

liberalism *(n.)* လစ်ဘရယ်ဝါဒ *lit-ba-ral-war-da*

liberality *(n.)* လစ်ဘရယ်ဆန်ဆန် *lit-ba-ral-san-san*

liberate *(v.)* လွတ်မြောက်စေသည် *lut-myauk-say-the*

liberation *(n.)* လွတ်မြောက်စေမှု *lut-myauk-say-mu*

liberator *(n.)* လွတ်မြောက်စေသူ *lut-myauk-say-thu*

libertine *(n.)* အကျင့်သီလမဲ့သူ *a-kyint-thi-la-mae-thu*

liberty *(n.)* လွတ်လပ်ရေး *lut-lat-yay*

librarian *(n.)* စာကြည့်တိုက်မှူး *sar-kyi-tite-hmu*

library *(n.)* စာကြည့်တိုက် *sar-kyi-tite*

licence *(n.)* လိုင်စင် *hlai-sin*

license *(v.)* လိုင်စင်ထုတ်ပေးသည် *hlai-sin-htoke-pay-the*

licensee *(n.)* လိုင်စင်ရသူ *hlai-sin-ya-thu*

licentious *(adj.)* လိင်ကိစ္စများတွင် ကိုယ်ကျင့်သိက္ခာ ကင်းမဲ့သော *lain-kait-sa-myar-twin-koe-kyint-theik-khar-kin-mae-taw*

lick *(v.)* လျက်သည် *lyat-the*

lick *(n.)* လျက်ခြင်း *lyat-chin*

lid *(n.)* အဖုံး *a-hpone*

lie *(n.)* လိမ်ညာခြင်း *lain-nyar-chin*

lie *(v.)* လိမ်ညာသည် *lain-nyar-the*

lien *(n.)* အကြွေးမဆပ်နိုင်၍ ပိုင်ဆိုင်ပစ္စည်းကို လက်ဝယ်ထားခွင့် *a-kyay-a-sat-nai-ywe-pai-sai-pyit-see-ko-lat-wal-htar-khwint*

lieu *(n.)* အစား *a-sar*

lieutenant *(n.)* ဗိုလ်ကြီး *bo-gyi*

life *(n.)* ဘဝ *ba-wa*

life jacket *(n.)* အသက်ကယ်အင်္ကျီ *a-thet-kal-in-gyi*

life support *(n.)* အသက်အထောက်အကူ *a-thet-a-htauk-a-ku*

lifeless *(adj.)* အသက်မဲ့သော *a-thet-mae-taw*

lifelong *(adj.)* တစ်ဘဝလုံး *ta-ba-wa-lone*

lifestyle *(n.)* ဘဝလူနေမှုပုံစံ *ba-wa-lu-nay-mu-pon-san*

lift *(n.)* ဓာတ်လှေကား *dat-lay-kar*

ligament *(n.)* အရွတ် *a-yut*

light *(v.)* မီးညှိသည်၊ မီးစွဲသည် *mee-nyi-the, mee-swal-the*

lighten *(v.)* ဝန်လျော့သည်၊ ပေါ့ပါးသွားသည် *win-yawt-the, pot-par-twar-the*

lightening *(n.)* ဝန်လျော့ခြင်း၊ ပေါ့ပါးသွားခြင်း *win-yawt-chin, pot-par-twar-chin*

lighter *(n.)* မီးခြစ် *mee-chit*

lightly *(adv.)* ပေါ့ပါးသွက်လက်စွာ *pot-par-thwat-lat-swar*

lignite *(n.)* ကျောက်မီးသွေးညို *kyauk-mee-tway-nyo*

like *(v.)* နှစ်သက်သည် *nit-thet-the*

like *(prep.)* ကဲ့သို့ *kae-tho*

likelihood *(n.)* ဖြစ်နိုင်ခြေ *phit-nai-chay*

likely *(adj.)* ဖြစ်နိုင်သော *phit-nai-taw*

liken *(v.)* ပုံနှိုင်းလေ့ရှိသည် *pon-khai-lay-shi-the*

likeness *(n.)* တူခြင်း *tu-chin*

likewise *(adv.)* အလားတူ *a-lar-tu*

liking *(n.)* အကြိုက် *a-kyaik*

lilac *(n.)* ခရမ်းဖျော့ရောင် *kha-yan-phawt-yaung*

lily *(n.)* လီလီပန်း *li-li-pan*

limb *(n.)* ခြေလက် *chay-lat*

limber *(n.)* အကြောလျှော့ လေ့ကျင့်ခန်း *a-kyaw-shawt-lay-kyint-khan*

lime *(n.)* ထုံး *htone*

limelight *(n.)* ထင်ရှားကျော်ကြားမှု *htin-shar-kyaw-kyar-mu*

limit *(n.)* ကန့်သတ်ခြင်း *kant-tat-chin*

limitation *(n.)* အကန့်အသတ် *a-kant-a-thet*

limited *(adj.)* ကန့်သတ်သော *kant-thet-taw*

limitless *(adj.)* အကန့်အသတ်မဲ့သော *a-kant-a-thet-mae-taw*

line *(v.)* မျဉ်းတားထားသည် *myin-tar-htar-the*

lineage *(n.)* မျိုးရိုး *myo-yoe*

linen *(n.)* ပိတ် *pate*

linger *(v.)* တရစ်ဝဲဝဲနေသည် *ta-yit-wal-wal-nay-the*

lingo *(n.)* ဘာသာခြားစကား *bar-tar-char-sa-gar*

lingual *(adj.)* ဘာသာစကားနှင့် ဆိုင်သော *bar-tar-sa-kar-nint-sai-taw*

linguist *(n.)* ဘာသာဗေဒပညာရှင် *bar-tar-bay-da-pyin-nyar-shin*

linguistic *(adj.)* ဘာသာစကားနှင့် ဆိုင်သော *bar-tar-sa-kar-nint-sai-taw*

linguistics *(n.)* ဘာသာဗေဒ *bar-tar-bay-da*

lining *(n.)* အနားကွပ် *a-nar-kut*

link *(n.)* အဆက်အသွယ်၊ ကွင်းဆက် *a-sat-a-thwe, kwin-sat*

link *(v.)* ဆက်သွယ်သည် *sat-thwe-the*

linseed *(n.)* နှမ်းကြတ် *hnan-kyat*

lintel *(n.)* ပြတင်းထုပ် *pya-tin-htoke*

lion *(n.)* ခြင်္သေ့ *chin-tay*

lioness *(n.)* ခြင်္သေ့မ *chin-tay-ma*

lip *(n.)* နှုတ်ခမ်း *hnote-khan*

liquefy *(v.)* အရည်ဖြစ်အောင် လုပ်သည် *a-yay-phit-aung-lote-the*

liquid *(n.)* အရည် *a-yay*

liquidate *(v.)* စာရင်းရှင်း ဖျက်သိမ်းသည် *sa-yin-shin-phat-thein-the*

liquidation *(n.)* စာရင်းရှင်း ဖျက်သိမ်းခြင်း *sa-yin-shin-phat-thein-chin*

liquor *(n.)* အရက်ပြင်း *a-yat-pyin*

lisp *(n.)* မပီကလာ ပီကလာ ပြောခြင်း *ma-pi-ka-lar-pi-ka-lar-pyaw-chin*

list *(n.)* စာရင်း *sa-yin*

listen *(v.)* နားထောင်သည် *nar-htaung-the*

listener *(n.)* နားထောင်သူ *nar-htaung-thu*

listless *(adj.)* နုံးချည့်သော *hnone-chee-taw*

literacy *(n.)* စာတတ်မြောက်ခြင်း *sar-tat-myauk-chin*

literal *(adj.)* တိုက်ရိုက် *tite-yite*

literary *(adj.)* စာပေ *say-pay*

literate *(adj.)* စာတတ်မြောက်သော *sar-tat-myauk-taw*

literature *(n.)* စာပေ *sar-pay*

litigant *(n.)* အမှုသည် *a-mu-the*

litigate *(v.)* တရားစွဲဆိုသည် *ta-yar-swal-so-the*

litigation *(n.)* တရားစွဲခြင်း *ta-yar-swal-chin*

litre *(n.)* လီတာ *li-tar*

litter *(v.)* ပြန့်ကျဲနေသည် *pyant-kyae-nay-the*

litter *(n.)* အမှိုက်သရိုက် *a-hmite-ta-yite*

litterateur *(n.)* စာပေဝေဖန်ရေးသမား *sar-pay-wai-phan-yay-ta-mar*

little *(n.)* အနည်းငယ် *a-ne-ngal*

little *(adv.)* နည်းနည်း *ne-ne*

littoral *(adj.)* ပင်လယ်ကမ်းခြေဒေသ *pin-lal-kan-chay-tay-ta*

liturgical *(adj.)* ခရစ်ယာန်ကဲ့သို့ ဝတ်ပြုသော *kha-yit-yan-kae-tho-wit-pyu-taw*

live *(adv.)* တိုက်ရိုက် *tite-yite*

livelihood *(n.)* အသက်မွေးဝမ်းကျောင်း *a-thet-mway-wan-kyaung*

lively *(adj.)* ရွှင်ပျသော *shwin-pya-taw*

liver *(n.)* အသည်း *a-tae*

livery *(n.)* အမှတ်တံဆိပ် *a-mat-ta-seik*

living *(n.)* အသက်မွေးမှု *a-thet-mway-mu*

lizard *(n.)* အိမ်မြှောင် *eain-hmyaung*

load *(v.)* တင်သည်၊ ထည့်သည် *tin-the, htae-the*

loadstar *(n.)* လမ်းပြကြယ် *lan-pya-kyal*

loadstone *(n.)* သံလိုက်ကျောက် *tan-lite-kyauk*

loaf *(n.)* ပေါင်မုန့်လုံး *paung-hmont-lone*

loaf *(v.)* အချိန်ဖြုန်းသည် *a-chain-hpyone-the*

loafer *(n.)* လူလေလူလွင့် *lu-lay-lu-lwint*

loan *(n.)* ချေးငွေ *chay-ngwe*

loath *(adj.)* မနှစ်မြို့သော *ma-nit-hmyo-taw*

loathe *(v.)* ရွံရှာသည် *yon-shar-the*

loathsome *(adj.)* ရွံစရာကောင်းသော *yon-sa-yar-kaung-taw*

lobby *(n.)* ဧည့်ခန်း *ae-khan*

lobe *(n.)* အပိုင်း *a-pai*

lobster *(n.)* ပုစွန်တုပ်ကြီး *pa-sun-htoke-gyi*

local *(adj.)* ဒေသတွင်း *day-ta-twin*

locale *(n.)* ပင်ရင်းဒေသ *pin-yin-day-ta*

locality *(n.)* တည်နေရာ *the-nay-yar*

localize *(v.)* ကွက်၍ ဖြစ်ပွားသည်၊ ဒေသပုံစံဖြစ်အောင် ပြုလုပ်သည် *kwat-ywe-phit-pwar-the, day-ta-pon-san-phit-aung-pyu-lote-the*

locate *(v.)* ရှာသည် *shar-the*

location *(n.)* တည်နေရာ *ti-nay-yar*

lock *(v.)* သော့ခတ်သည် *tot-kha-the*

locker *(n.)* အံဆွဲ၊ ဗီရိုငယ် *an-swal, bi-yo-ngwe*

locket *(n.)* လော့ကက်သီး *lot-kat-thee*

locomotive *(n.)* ရွေ့လျားနိုင်မှု *ywe-lyar-nai-mu*

locus *(n.)* တည်ရာ *te-yar*

locust *(n.)* ကျိုင်းကောင် *kyai-kaung*

locution *(n.)* ပြောနည်းဆိုနည်း *pyaw-nee-so-nee*

lodge *(n.)* ခြံဝင်းဝ *chan-win-wa*

lodge *(v.)* တင်သည်၊ တိုင်သည် *tin-the, tai-the*

lodging *(n.)* တည်းခိုခန်း *te-kho-khan*

loft *(n.)* အမိုးအောက် ထပ်ခိုး *a-moe-awt-htet-kho*

lofty *(adj.)* အလွန်မြင့်သော *a-lun-myint-taw*

log *(v.)* သစ်ပင်ခုတ်လှဲသည် *tit-pin-khote-hlae-the*

logarithm *(n.)* လော်ဂရစ်သမ် *law-ga-rit-tan*

loggerhead *(n.)* ငတုံး *nga-tone*

logic *(n.)* ယုတ္တိဗေဒ *yoke-ti-bay-da*

logical *(adj.)* ယုတ္တိရှိသော *yoke-ti-shi-taw*

logician *(n.)* ယုတ္တိဗေဒပညာရှင် *yoke-ti-bay-da-pyin-nyar-shin*

logout *(n.)* ထွက်သည် *htwat-the*

loin *(n.)* ပေါင်ရင်းသား *paung-yin-tar*

loiter *(v.)* ယောင်ပေပေ လုပ်သည် *yaung-pay-pay-lote-the*

loll *(v.)* တွဲလဲကျသည် *twal-lae-kya-the*

lollipop *(n.)* လိုလီပေါ့ *lo-li-pot*

lone *(adj.)* အထီးကျန်သော၊ တစ်ခုတည်း *a-htee-kyan-taw, ta-khu-tae*

loneliness *(n.)* အထီးကျန်ခြင်း *a-htee-kyan-chin*

lonely *(adj.)* အထီးကျန်သော *a-htee-kyan-taw*

lonesome *(adj.)* အဖော်မဲ့ စိတ်အားငယ်သော *a-phaw-mae-seik-arr-ngal-taw*

long *(adv.)* ကြာကြာ *kyar-kyar*

long *(adj.)* ရှည်သော *shay-taw*

longevity *(n.)* အသက်ရှည်ခြင်း *a-thet-shay-chin*

longing *(n.)* တောင့်တခြင်း *taunt-ta-chin*

longitude *(n.)* လောင်ဂျီတွဒ် *laung-gi-tut*

long-term *(adj.)* ရေရှည် *yay-shay*

look *(v.)* ကြည့်သည် *kyi-the*

loom *(v.)* ဘွားခနဲပေါ်လာသည် *bwar-kha-nae-paw-lar-the*

loop *(n.)* လျှပ်စီးပတ်လမ်း *hlyat-see-pat-lan*

loop-hole *(n.)* ကယ်ပေါက် *kal-pauk*

loose *(adj.)* ချောင်သော၊ လွတ်နေသော *chaung-taw, hlut-nay-taw*

loose end *(n.)* လက်စသတ်စရာ *lat-sa-tat-sa-yar*

loosen *(v.)* ချောင်စေသည် *chaung-say-the*

loot *(v.)* ခေတ်ပျက်တွင် ဖောက်ထွင်းပစ္စည်းယူသည် *khit-pyat-twin-phauk-htwin-pyit-see-yu-the*

lop *(v.)* သစ်ပင်ချိုင်သည် *tit-pin-chai-the*

lord *(n.)* ရှင်ဘုရင်၊ သူကောင်းမျိုး *shin-ba-yin, thu-kaung-myo*

lordly *(adj.)* ဟိတ်ဟန်များသော *hate-han-myar-taw*

lordship *(n.)* လော့ဒ်ဘွဲ့ရ *lot-bwe-ya*

lore *(n.)* အစဉ်အလာစကား *a-sin-a-lar-sa-kar*

lorry *(n.)* လော်ရီကား *lor-yi-kar*

lose *(v.)* ဆုံးရှုံးသည် *sone-shone-the*

loss *(n.)* ဆုံးရှုံးခြင်း *sone-shone-chin*

lost *(v.)* ပျောက်သည် *pyauk-the*

lot *(n.)* အားလုံး၊ များစွာ *arr-lone, myar-swar*

lotion *(n.)* လိမ်းဆေး၊ လိုးရှင်း *lane-say, lo-shin*

lottery *(n.)* ထီ *hti*

lotus *(n.)* ကြာပင် *kyar-pin*

loud *(adj.)* ကျယ်လောင်သော *kyal-laung-taw*

lounge *(v.)* လတ်လျားလတ်လျားနေသည် *lat-lyar-lat-lyar-nay-the*

louse *(n.)* သန်း *tan*

lovable *(adj.)* ချစ်ဖွယ်ကောင်းသော *chit-phwal-kaung-taw*

love *(v.)* ချစ်သည် *chit-the*

lovely *(adj.)* ချစ်စဖွယ် *chit-sa-phwal*

lover *(n.)* ချစ်သူ *chit-thu*

loving *(adj.)* ချစ်သော *chit-taw*

low *(adv.)* နိမ့်နိမ့် *naint-naint*

low *(n.)* နွားအော်သံ *nwar-aw-than*

lower *(v.)* အောက်ချသည်၊ *awt-cha-the*

low-fat *(adj.)* အဆီနည်းသော *a-see-nae-taw*

lowliness *(n.)* အရေးမပါခြင်း *a-yay-ma-par-chin*

lowly *(adj.)* အရေးမပါသော *a-yay-ma-par-taw*

loyal *(adj.)* သစ္စာရှိသော *tit-sar-shi-taw*

loyalist *(n.)* သစ္စာခံ *tit-sar-khan*

loyalty *(n.)* သစ္စာခံယူခြင်း *tit-sar-khan-yu-chin*

lubricant *(n.)* ချောဆီ *chaw-si*

lubricate *(v.)* ချောဆီထည့်သည် *chaw-si-htae-the*

lubrication *(n.)* ချောဆီထည့်ခြင်း *chaw-si-htae-chin*

lucent *(adj.)* အလင်းထုတ်သော *a-lin-htoke-taw*

lucerne *(n.)* လူဆန်ပဲပင် *lu-san-pae-pin*

lucid *(adj.)* နားလည်လွယ်သော *nar-lal-lwal-taw*

lucidity *(n.)* ရှင်းလင်းပြတ်သားမှု *shin-lin-pyat-tar-mu*

luck *(n.)* ကံ *kan*

luckily *(adv.)* ကံကောင်းစွာဖြင့် *kan-kaung-swar-phint*
luckless *(adj.)* မအောင်မြင်သော၊ ကံဆိုးသော *ma-aung-myin-taw, kan-soe-taw*
lucky *(adj.)* ကံကောင်းသော *kan-kaung-taw*
lucrative *(adj.)* အကျိုးရှိသော *a-kyo-shi-taw*
lucre *(n.)* ငွေ *ngwe*
luggage *(n.)* ခရီးဆောင်အိတ် *kha-yee-saung-aite*
lukewarm *(adj.)* ကြက်သီးနွေး *kyat-thee-nway*
lull *(n.)* ခေတ္တစဲချိန် *khit-ta-sal-chain*
lullaby *(n.)* ကလေးချော့တေး *ka-lay-chawt-tay*
luminary *(n.)* အထင်ကရ *a-htin-ka-ya*
luminous *(adj.)* တောက်ပသော *taut-pa-taw*
lump *(v.)* စုပေါင်းသည်၊ ရောသည် *su-paung-the, yaw-the*
lump sum *(n.)* တစ်လုံးတစ်ခဲတည်း *ta-hlone-ta-khae-tae*
lunacy *(n.)* ရူးသွပ်ခြင်း *yu-tut-chin*
lunar *(adj.)* လနှင့်ဆိုင်သော *la-nint-sai-taw*
lunatic *(n.)* ငမိုက်သား *nga-mite-tar*
lunch *(v.)* နေ့လည်စာစားသည် *nae-lal-sar-sar-the*
lunch *(n.)* နေ့လည်စာ *nae-lal-sar*
lung *(n.)* အဆုတ် *a-sote*
lunge *(v.)* ရှေ့သို့ဆတ်ခနဲ လှမ်းခြင်း *shay-tho-sat-kha-nae-hlan-chin*
lurch *(v.)* ပစ်ထားသည် *pyit-htar-the*
lure *(v.)* သွေးဆောင်သည် *tway-saung-the*
lurk *(v.)* ချောင်းသည်၊ ခိုသည် *chaung-the, kho-the*
luscious *(adj.)* အနံ့အရသာရှိသော *a-nant-a-ya-tar-shi-taw*
lush *(adj.)* စိမ်းလန်းစိုပြည်သန်စွမ်းသော *sein-lan-so-pyay-tan-swan-taw*
lust *(n.)* တပ်မက်ခြင်း *tat-mat-chin*
lustful *(adj.)* တဏှာကြီးသော *ta-nar-kyi-taw*
lustre *(n.)* အရောင်စိုခြင်း *a-yaung-so-chin*
lustrous *(adj.)* အရောင်စိုသော *a-yaung-so-taw*
lusty *(adj.)* ကြံ့ခိုင်သော *kyant-khai-taw*
lute *(n.)* ဗျပ်စောင်းတူရိယာ *byat-saung-tu-ri-yar*
luxuriance *(n.)* ထူထဲခြင်း *htu-htae-chin*
luxuriant *(adj.)* ထူထဲသော *htu-htae-taw*
luxurious *(adj.)* တန်ဖိုးကြီးသော *tan-phoe-kyi-taw*
luxury *(n.)* ဇိမ်ခံပစ္စည်း *zain-khan-pyit-see*
lynch *(v.)* သေဒဏ်ပေးသည် *tay-dan-pay-the*
lyre *(n.)* ရှေးခေတ်စောင်း *shay-khit-saung*
lyric *(n.)* စာသား *sar-tar*
lyric *(adj.)* ခံစားချက်ပါသော *khan-sar-chat-par-taw*
lyrical *(adj.)* ခံစားချက်ပါသော *khan-sar-chat-par-taw*
lyricist *(n.)* တေးရေး *tay-yay*

M

macadamia *(n.)* ကာဓားမီးယားအသီး *ma-kar-dar-mee-yar-a-thee*

macaroon *(n.)* ဘီစကွတ် *bi-sa-kut*

mace *(n.)* ကျိုင်း *kyai*

machinate *(v.)* စက်ပုန်းခုတ်သည် *sat-pone-khote-the*

machination *(n.)* စက်ပုန်းခုတ်ခြင်း *sat-pone-khote-chin*

machine *(n.)* စက် *sat*

machine-made *(adj.)* စက်ဖြင့် လုပ်သော *sat-phint-lote-taw*

machinery *(n.)* စက်ယန္တရား *sat-yan-da-yar*

machinist *(n.)* စက်မောင်း *sat-maung*

mack *(n.)* နှုတ်ဖြင့် လိင်စိတ်နိုးဆွကျမ်းကျင်သူ *hnote-phyint-lain-seik-noe-swa-kyan-kyin-thu*

macro *(adj.)* ကြီးသော *kyi-taw*

macrobiotic *(adj.)* အာဟာရသိပ္ပံ *a-har-ya-tait-pan*

macrocephaly *(n.)* ခေါင်းကြီးသော *gaung-gyi-taw*

macrofibre *(n.)* အမျှင်ကြီး *a-myin-gyi*

macrosphere *(n.)* နိုင်းရ ကြီးမားသော အလုံး *nai-ya-kyi-mar-taw-a-lone*

maculate *(adj.)* မသန့်စင်သော *ma-tant-sin-taw*

mad *(adj.)* ရူးသော *yu-taw*

madam *(n.)* မဒမ် *ma-dan*

madden *(v.)* စိတ်အနှောင့်အယှက်ဖြစ်စေသည် *seik-a-naut-a-shat-phit-say-the*

maddening *(adj.)* စိတ်တိုစရာကောင်းသော *seik-to-sa-yar-kaung-taw*

madhouse *(n.)* ဝရုန်းသုန်းကားနိုင်သော နေရာ *wa-yone-tone-kar-nai-taw-nay-yar*

madness *(n.)* ရူးသွပ်ခြင်း *yu-tut-chin*

mafia *(n.)* မာဖီးယား *mar-phee-yar*

magazine *(n.)* မဂ္ဂဇင်း *ma-ga-zin*

mage *(n.)* မှော်ဆရာ *maw-sa-yar*

maggot *(n.)* လောက် *laut*

magic *(n.)* မှော်၊ မျက်လှည့် *maw, myat-hlae*

magical *(adj.)* မှော်ဆန်သော၊ မျက်လှည့်ဆန်သော *maw-san-taw, myat-hlae-san-taw*

magician *(n.)* မျက်လှည့်ပညာရှင်၊ မှော်ပညာရှင် *myat-hlae-pyin-nyar-shin, maw-pyin-nyar-shin*

magisterial *(adj.)* ဩဇာအာဏာရှိသော *aw-zar-ar-nar-shi-taw*

magistracy *(n.)* အောက်ရုံး *awt-yone*

magistrate *(n.)* အောက်ရုံးတရားသူကြီး *awt-yone-ta-yar-thu-gyi*

magistrature *(n.)* အောက်ရုံး *awt-yone*

magma *(n.)* ကျောက်ရည်ပူ *kyauk-yay-pu*

magnanimity *(n.)* သဘောထားကြီးခြင်း *ta-baw-htar-kyi-chin*

magnanimous *(adj.)* သဘောထားကြီးသော *ta-baw-htar-kyi-taw*

magnate *(n.)* စီးပွားရေး လုပ်ငန်းရှင်ကြီး *see-pwar-yay-lote-ngan-shin-gyi*

magnet *(n.)* သံလိုက် *tan-lite*

magnetic *(adj.)* သံလိုက်သတ္တိ *tan-lite-tat-ti*

magnetism *(n.)* သံလိုက်ဓာတ် *tan-lite-dat*

magnificent *(adj.)* ခမ်းနားသော *khan-nar-taw*

magnify *(v.)* ပုံကြီးချဲ့သည် *pon-gyi-chae-the*
magnitude *(n.)* ပမာဏ *pa-mar-na*
magpie *(n.)* ငှက်ကျား *nget-kyar*
mahogany *(n.)* မဟော်ဂနီသစ်၊ နီညိုရောင် *ma-haw-ga-ni-tit, ni-nyo-yaung*
mahout *(n.)* ဆင်ထိန်း *sin-htein*
maid *(n.)* အိမ်ဖော် *eain-phaw*
maiden *(adj.)* ပွဲဦးထွက် *pwe-oo-htwat*
mail *(n.)* စာ *sar*
main *(n.)* မိန်းကြိုး၊ *mein-kyo*
mainly *(adv.)* အဓိကအားဖြင့် *a-di-ka-arr-phyint*
mainstay *(n.)* အဓိကပံ့ပိုးမှု *a-di-ka-pant-poe-mu*
maintain *(v.)* ထိန်းသိမ်းသည် *htein-tain-the*
maintenance *(n.)* ထိန်းသိမ်းမှု *htein-tain-mu*
maize *(n.)* ပြောင်းဖူး *pyaung-hpoo*
majestic *(adj.)* ကြီးကျယ်ခမ်းနားသော *kyi-kyal-khan-nar-taw*
majesty *(n.)* ဘုရင့်ဘုန်းတန်ခိုး *ba-yint-hpone-ta-kho*
major *(n.)* အဓိက *a-di-ka*
majority *(n.)* အများစု *a-myar-su*
make *(n.)* ဆောက်လုပ်မှုပုံစံ *saut-lote-mu-pon-san*
makeover *(n.)* အဓိက အပြောင်းအလဲ *a-di-ka-a-pyaung-a-hlae*
maker *(n.)* ပြုလုပ်သူ *pyu-lote-thu*
make-up *(n.)* မိတ်ကပ် *meik-kat*
maladjustment *(n.)* ပတ်ဝန်းကျင်နှင့် အံချော်ခြင်း *pat-win-kyin-nint-an-chaw-chin*
maladministration *(n.)* အုပ်ချုပ်မှုညံ့ခြင်း *oak-choke-mu-nyant-chin*
maladroit *(adj.)* မကျွမ်းကျင်သော *ma-kyun-kyin-taw*
malady *(n.)* ရောဂါ *yaw-gar*
malaise *(n.)* မအီမသာဖြစ်ခြင်း *ma-ei-ma-tar-phit-chin*
malaria *(n.)* ငှက်ဖျား *nget-phyar*
malcontent *(n.)* မကျေနပ်သူ *ma-kyay-nat-thu*
male *(adj.)* အထီး *a-htee*
malediction *(n.)* ဆဲခြင်း၊ ကျိန်စာတိုက်ခြင်း *sal-chin, kyain-sar-tite-chin*
malefactor *(n.)* အမှားပြုလုပ်သူ *a-hmar-pyu-lote-thu*
maleficent *(adj.)* ထိခိုက်စေသော *hti-khite-say-taw*
malfunction *(v.)* လုပ်ဆောင်ချက်ချွတ်ယွင်းသည် *lote-saung-chat-chut-ywin-the*
malice *(n.)* အငြိုး *a-nyoe*
malicious *(adj.)* အငြိုးထားသော၊ အန္တရာယ်ရှိသော *a-nyoe-htar-taw, an-da-yal-shi-taw*
malign *(adj.)* ဆိုးဝါးသော *soe-war-taw*
malignancy *(n.)* ကင်ဆာ *kin-sar*
malignant *(adj.)* ကင်ဆာဖြစ်သော *kin-sar-phit-taw*
malignity *(n.)* ဆိုးဝါးခြင်း၊ ကင်ဆာဖြစ်နိုင်သော *soe-war-taw, kin-sar-phit-nai-taw*
malleable *(adj.)* အလွယ်တကူပုံသွင်း၍ ရသော *a-lwal-ta-ku-pon-twin-ywe-ya-taw*
malmsey *(n.)* ပြုပြင်ထားသည့် ချိုမြသော ဝိုင် *pyu-pyin-htar-the-cho-mya-taw-win*

malnourished *(adj.)* အာဟာရချို့တည့်သော *a-har-ya-choe-tae-taw*
malnutrition *(n.)* အာဟာရချို့တည့်ခြင်း *a-har-ya-choe-tae-chin*
malpractice *(n.)* အကျင့်မှား *a-kyint-hmar*
malt *(n.)* မုယော *mu-yaw*
mal-treatment *(n.)* မှားယွင်းစွာ ပြုကျင့်ခြင်း *mar-ywin-swar-pyu-kyint-chin*
mamma *(n.)* မေမေ *may-may*
mammal *(n.)* နို့တိုက်သတ္တဝါ *noe-tite-tat-ta-war*
mammary *(adj.)* နို့ *noe*
mammon *(n.)* ဥစ္စာဓနေ၏ ဆိုးကျိုး *oak-sar-da-na-ei-soe-kyo*
mammoth *(n.)* အမွေးရှည်ဆင် *a-mway-shay-sin*
man *(v.)* တာဝန်ယူသည် *tar-win-yu-the*
man *(n.)* ယောကျာ်း *yauk-kyar*
manage *(v.)* စီမံသည် *si-man-the*
manageable *(adj.)* ပိုင်နိုင်သော၊ စီမံနိုင်သော *pai-nai-taw, si-man-nai-taw*
management *(n.)* စီမံခြင်း *si-man-chin*
manager *(n.)* မန်နေဂျာ *man-nay-gyar*
managerial *(adj.)* စီမံခန့်ခွဲရေးနှင့် ဆိုင်သော *si-man-khant-kwal-yay-nint-sai-taw*
mandate *(n.)* လုပ်ပိုင်ခွင့် *lote-pai-khwint*
mandatory *(adj.)* မလုပ်မဖြစ်သော *ma-lote-ma-phit-taw*
mane *(n.)* ဆံပင်ရှည် *san-pin-shay*
manes *(n.)* ထူထဲရှည်လျားသော ဆံပင် *htoo-htae-shay-lyar-taw-san-pin*
manful *(adj.)* ဇွဲသတ္တိနှင့် ပြည့်စုံသော *zwe-tat-ti-nint-pyae-sone-taw*
manganese *(n.)* မန်ဂနိ *man-ga-ni*
manger *(n.)* စားခွက် *sar-khwat*
mangle *(v.)* ရုပ်ပျက်ဆင်းပျက် ဖြစ်သည် *yoke-pyat-sin-pyat-phit-the*
mango *(n.)* သရက်သီး *ta-yat-thee*
manhandle *(v.)* လူအားဖြင့် ရွှေ့သည် *lu-arr-phint-shwae-the*
manhole *(n.)* လူဆင်းပေါက် *lu-sin-pauk*
manhood *(n.)* ယောကျာ်းဘဝ *yauk-kyar-ba-wa*
mania *(n.)* စွဲလမ်းခြင်း *swal-lan-chin*
maniac *(n.)* အရူး *a-yuu*
manicure *(n.)* လက်သည်းထိုးခြင်း *lat-thae-htoe-chin*
manifest *(v.)* ပေါ်လွင်သည် *paw-lwin-the*
manifestation *(n.)* သရုပ်သကန် *ta-yoke-ta-kan*
manifesto *(n.)* မူဝါဒ ကြေညာစာတမ်း *mu-war-da-kyay-nyar-sar-tan*
manifold *(adj.)* အမျိုးစုံသော *a-myo-sone-taw*
manipulate *(v.)* ကျွမ်းကျင်စွာ ကိုင်တွယ်သည် *kyun-kyin-swar-kai-twal-the*
manipulation *(n.)* ကျွမ်းကျင်စွာ ကိုင်တွယ်ခြင်း *kyun-kyin-swar-kai-twal-chin*
mankind *(n.)* လူသား *lu-thar*
manlike *(adj.)* ယောကျာ်းကဲ့သို့ *yaut-kyar-kae-tho*
manliness *(n.)* ယောကျာ်းဆန်ခြင်း *yauk-kyar-san-chin*
manly *(adj.)* ယောကျာ်းဆန်သော *yauk-kyar-san-taw*
manna *(n.)* နတ်သုဓာ၊ မန်နာ *nat-tode-dar, man-nar*
mannequin *(n.)* လူပုံစံရုပ် *lu-pon-san-yoke*

manner *(n.)* အပြုအမူ *a-pyu-a-mu*

mannerism *(n.)* ဟန်အမူအရာ *han-a-mu-a-yar*

mannerly *(adj.)* သိမ်မွေ့သော ကိုယ်အမူအရာဖြင့် *thein-mway-taw-koe-a-mu-a-yar-phint*

manoeuvre *(v.)* ကိုင်တွယ်သည်၊ စီးနင်းသည်၊ မောင်းနှင်သည်၊ ကြောင်းပေးသည် *kai-twal-the, see-hnin-the, maung-hnin-the, kyaung-pay-the*

manor *(n.)* ရဲစခန်းပိုင်နက်၊ အိမ်ကြီးရခိုင် *ye-sa-khan-pai-net, eain-kyi-ya-khine*

manorial *(adj.)* အိမ်ကြီးရခိုင်နှင့် ဆိုင်သော *eain-gyi-ra-khine-nint-sai-taw*

mansion *(n.)* အိမ်ကြီးရခိုင် *eain-gyi-ra-khine*

mantel *(n.)* ကျပ်ခိုးစင် *kyat-khoe-sin*

mantle *(v.)* ဖုံးကွယ်သည် *phone-kwal-the*

manual *(n.)* လက်စွဲ *lat-swal*

manufacture *(n.)* ထုတ်လုပ်ခြင်း *htoke-lote-chin*

manufacturer *(n.)* ထုတ်လုပ်သူ *htoke-lote-thu*

manumission *(n.)* ကျွန်အဖြစ်မှ လွတ်ခြင်း *kyun-a-phit-ma-hlut-chin*

manumit *(v.)* ကျွန်အဖြစ်မှ လွတ်သည် *kyun-a-phit-ma-hlut-the*

manure *(n.)* မြေဩဇာ *myay-aw-zar*

manuscript *(n.)* လက်ရေးစာမူ *lat-yay-sar-mu*

many *(adj.)* များစွာ *myar-swar*

map *(v.)* မြေပုံထုတ်သည် *myay-pon-htoke-the*

map *(n.)* မြေပုံ *myay-pon*

mar *(v.)* ဖျက်သည် *phat-the*

marathon *(n.)* မာရသွန် *mar-ra-thon*

maraud *(v.)* ညှ်လှည်သောင်းကျန်းသည် *hlae-lal-taung-kyan-the*

marauder *(n.)* လှည့်လည်သောင်းကျန်းသူ *hlae-lal-taung-kyan-thu*

marble *(n.)* စကျင်ကျောက် *sa-kyin-kyauk*

march *(n.)* ချီတက်ခြင်း *chee-tat-chin*

mare *(n.)* မြင်းမ *myin-ma*

margarine *(n.)* မာဂျရင်း *mar-gya-yin*

margin *(n.)* ဘေးမျဉ်း၊ မာဂျင်၊ အနားသတ်မျဉ်း *bay-myin, mar-gyin, a-nar-tat-myin*

marginal *(adj.)* မာဂျင်ထဲတွင် ရေးထားသော၊ မဖြစ်စလောက် *mar-gyin-htae-twin-yay-htar-taw, ma-phit-sa-laut*

marigold *(n.)* ထပ်တစ်ရာပန်း *htet-ta-yar-pan*

marine *(adj.)* ပင်လယ်နှင့် ဆိုင်သော *pin-lal-nint-sai-taw*

mariner *(n.)* သင်္ဘောသား *tin-baw-tar*

marionette *(n.)* ရုပ်သေးရုပ် *yoke-tay-yoke*

marital *(adj.)* အိမ်ထောင်နှင့်ဆိုင်သော *eain-htaung-nint-sai-taw*

maritime *(adj.)* ပင်လယ်ပိုင်း *pin-lal-pai*

mark *(n.)* အမှတ် *a-hmat*

marker *(n.)* အမှတ်မှတ်သူ *a-hmat-mat-thu*

market *(n.)* ဈေးကွက်၊ ဈေး *zay-kwat, zay*

market research *(n.)* ဈေးကွက်သုတေသန *zay-kwat-thu-tay-ta-na*

market share *(n.)* ဈေးကွက်ပမာဏ *zay-kwat-pa-mar-na*

marketable *(adj.)* ရောင်းပန်းလှသော *yaung-pan-hla-taw*

marksman *(n.)* လက်ဖြောင့်သူ *lat-phaunt-thu*

marl *(n.)* ထုံးမြေစေးကျောက် *htone-myay-say-kyauk*

marmalade *(n.)* ယို *yo*

maroon *(n.)* နီညိုရင့်ရောင် *ni-nyo-yint-yaung*

marriage *(n.)* လက်ထပ်ခြင်း *lat-htet-chin*

marriageable *(adj.)* လက်ထပ်နိုင်သော *lat-htet-nai-taw*

marrow *(n.)* ခြင်ဆီ *chin-si*

marry *(v.)* လက်ထပ်သည် *lat-htet-the*

Mars *(n.)* အင်္ဂါဂြိုလ် *in-gar-gyo*

marsh *(n.)* စိမ့်မြေ *saint-myay*

marshal *(n.)* ထိပ်တန်းအရာရှိ၊ ပွဲထိန်း *hteik-tan-a-yar-shi, pwe-htein*

marshal *(v.)* ထိန်းကျောင်းသည် *htain-kyaung-the*

marshy *(adj.)* ဗွက်ပေါက်သော *bwat-pauk-taw*

marsupial *(n.)* အိတ်ဖြင့် သားငယ်ကို သယ်သော သားပိုက်ကောင်ကဲ့သို့ နို့တိုက်သတ္တဝါ *aik-phint-tar-nge-ko-tal-taw-tar-pike-kaung-kae-tho-noe-tite-tat-ta-war*

mart *(n.)* ဈေးပွဲ *zay-pwe*

marten *(n.)* အသားစားကောင် *a-tar-sar-kaung*

martial *(adj.)* စစ် *sit*

martinet *(n.)* စည်းကမ်းတင်းကြပ်သူ *see-kan-tin-kyat-thu*

martyr *(n.)* အာဇာနည် *ar-zar-ne*

martyrdom *(n.)* အာဇာနည်အဖြစ် *ar-zar-ne-a-phit*

marvel *(v.)* လက်ဖျားခါသည် *lat-phyar-khar-the*

marvellous *(adj.)* အံ့ဩဖွယ်ကောင်းသော သူ *ant-aw-phwal-kaung-taw-thu*

mascot *(n.)* လာဘ်ကောင် *lat-kaung*

masculine *(adj.)* ယောကျ်ားရုပ်သွင် ရှိသော *yauk-kyar-yoke-twin-shi-taw*

mash *(v.)* ချေသည် *chay-the*

mash *(n.)* အာလူးပြုတ်ထောင်း *arr-lu-pyoke-htaung*

mask *(n.)* မျက်နှာဖုံး *myat-nar-hpone*

mason *(n.)* ပန်းရန်ဆရာ *pa-yan-sa-yar*

masonry *(n.)* အင်္ဂတေ *in-ga-day*

masquerade *(n.)* ဟန်ဆောင်ခြင်း *han-saung-chin*

mass *(v.)* စုသည် *su-the*

massacre *(n.)* အစုလိုက်အပြုံလိုက်သတ်ဖြတ်ခြင်း *a-su-lite-a-pyone-lite-tat-phat-chin*

massage *(n.)* နှိပ်နယ်ပေးခြင်း *nate-nal-pay-chin*

masseur *(n.)* အနှိပ်သည် *a-nate-the*

massive *(adj.)* အများအပြား *a-myar-a-pyar*

massy *(adj.)* လေးလံသော *lay-lan-taw*

mast *(n.)* ရွက်တိုင် *ywet-tai*

master *(v.)* တစ်ဖက်ကမ်းခပ်သည် *ta-phat-kan-khat-the*

master class *(n.)* က်ရွေးစင်သင်ခန်းစာ *lat-yway-sin-tin-khan-sar*

master copy *(n.)* မူရင်း *mu-yin*

masterly *(adj.)* ပိုင်နိုင်သော *pai-nai-taw*

masterpiece *(n.)* အပြောင်မြောက်ဆုံးလက်ရာ *a-pyuang-myauk-sone-lat-yar*

mastery *(n.)* တစ်ဖက်ကမ်းခပ်ခြင်း *ta-phat-kan-khat-chin*

masticate *(v.)* ဝါးသည် *war-the*

masturbate *(v.)* မိမိလက်ဖြင့် အာသာဖြေခြင်း *mi-mi-lat-phint-ar-tar-phyay-chin*

mat *(n.)* ဖျာ *pyar*

matador *(n.)* နွားရိုင်းသတ်သူ *nwar-yine-tat-thu*

match *(v.)* ယှဉ်ပြိုင်သည် *yin-pyai-the*

match *(n.)* ပြိုင်ပွဲ *pyai-pwe*

matchless *(adj.)* ပြိုင်ဘက်ကင်းသော *pyai-bat-kin-taw*

matchmaker *(n.)* အောင်သွယ် *aung-twal*

mate *(v.)* မိတ်လိုက်သည် *meik-lite-the*

material *(n.)* ပစ္စည်း *pyit-see*

materialism *(n.)* ရုပ်ဝါဒ *yoke-war-da*

materialize *(v.)* ပေါ်ပေါက်လာသည် *paw-pauk-lar-the*

maternal *(adj.)* မိခင်နှင့်ဆိုင်သော *mi-khin-nint-sai-taw*

maternity *(n.)* မိခင်ဘဝ *mi-khin-ba-wa*

mathematical *(adj.)* သင်္ချာ *tin-char*

mathematician *(n.)* သင်္ချာပညာရှင် *tin-char-pyin-nyar-shin*

mathematics *(n.)* သင်္ချာပညာ *tin-char-pyin-nyar*

matinee *(n.)* နေ့ပွဲ *nae-pwe*

matriarch *(n.)* အမျိုးသမီးခေါင်းဆောင် *a-myo-ta-mee-kaung-saung*

matricidal *(adj.)* အမိကိုသတ်သော *a-mi-ko-tat-taw*

matricide *(n.)* အမိကိုသတ်ခြင်း *a-mi-ko-tat-chin*

matriculate *(v.)* တက္ကသိုလ်ဝင်ခွင့်ရသည် *tat-ka-do-win-khwint-ya-the*

matriculation *(n.)* တက္ကသိုလ်ဝင်ခွင့် *tat-ka-do-win-khwint*

matrimonial *(adj.)* အိမ်ထောင်ရေး *eain-htaung-yay*

matrimony *(n.)* လက်ထပ်ထိမ်းမြားခြင်း *lat-htet-htein-myar-chin*

matrix *(n.)* ကွန်ရက် *kun-yat*

matron *(n.)* သူနာပြုအုပ် *thu-nar-pyu-oak*

matter *(n.)* ကိစ္စ *kait-sa*

mattock *(n.)* ပေါက်တူး *pauk-tu*

mattress *(n.)* မွေ့ရာ *mway-yar*

mature *(adj.)* ရင့်ကျက်သော *yint-kyat-taw*

maturity *(n.)* ရင့်ကျက်ခြင်း *yint-kyat-chin*

maudlin *(adj.)* မူး၍ တငိုငိုတရီရီ ဖြစ်နေသော *mu-ywe-a-ngo-ngo-ta-ye-ye-phit-nay-taw*

maul *(v.)* ကိုက်ဖဲ့သည် *kite-phae-the*

maulstick *(n.)* နားကြပ်တံကဲ့သို့ တုတ်ချောင်းငယ်

maunder *(v.)* လျှော့မွေးနှင့် ဗာရာဏသီချဲ့သည် *shaw-mway-nint-bar-yar-na-the-chae-the*

mausoleum *(n.)* ဂူဗိမာန် *gu-baik-man*

mawkish *(adj.)* မပိမရိ အလွမ်းသယ်သော *ma-pi-ma-yi-a-lwan-tal-thaw*

maxilla *(n.)* မဇီလာရိုး *ma-zi-lar-yoe*

maxim *(n.)* ဆိုရိုး *so-yoe*

maximize *(v.)* အကောင်းဆုံးအသုံးချသည် *a-kaung-sone-a-tone-cha-the*

maximum *(n.)* အကောင်းဆုံး *a-kaung-sone*

maximum *(adj.)* အကောင်းဆုံး *a-kaung-sone*

may *(v.)* နိုင်သည် *nai-the*

mayor *(n.)* မြို့တော်ဝန် *myo-taw-win*

maze *(n.)* ဝင်္ကပါ *win-ka-bar*

me *(pron.)* ကျွန်တော့်ကို *kyun-taw-ko*

mead *(n.)* ပျားရည်အရက် *pyar-yay-a-yat*

meadow *(n.)* မြက်ခင်းပြင် *myat-khin-pyin*

meagre *(adj.)* နည်းပါးသော *nae-par-taw*

meal *(n.)* အစားအသောက် *a-sar-a-taut*

mealy *(adj.)* အစားအစာနှင့် တူသော *a-sar-a-sar-nint-tu-taw*

mean *(v.)* အဓိပ္ပါယ်ရသည်၊ ဆိုလိုသည် *a-dait-pal-ya-the, so-lo-the*

mean *(adj.)* တွန့်တိုသော၊ ကုတ်ကတ်သော *tunt-to-taw, kote-kat-taw*

meander *(v.)* ကောက်ကောက်ကွေ့ကွေ့စီးဆင်းသည် *kauk-kauk-kway-kway-see-sin-the*

meaning *(n.)* အနက် *a-nat*

meaningful *(adj.)* အဓိပ္ပါယ်ရှိသော *a-dait-pal-shi-taw*

meaningless *(adj.)* အဓိပ္ပါယ်မဲ့သော *a-dait-pal-mae-taw*

meanness *(n.)* ကပ်စီးနည်းခြင်း *kat-see-ne-chin*

means *(n.)* နည်းစနစ် *ne-sa-nit*

meanwhile *(adv.)* အချိန်အတောအတွင်း *a-chain-a-taw-a-twin*

measles *(n.)* ဝက်သက် *wat-that*

measurable *(adj.)* တိုင်းတာ၍ ရသော *tine-tar-ywe-ya-taw*

measure *(v.)* တိုင်းတာသည် *tine-tar-the*

measure *(n.)* အတိုင်းအတာ *a-tai-a-tar*

measureless *(adj.)* အတိုင်းအတာမဲ့သော *a-tai-a-tar-mae-taw*

measurement *(n.)* အတိုင်းအတာ *a-tai-a-tar*

meat *(n.)* အသား *a-tar*

mechanic *(n.)* စက်ပြင် *sat-pyin*

mechanical *(adj.)* စက်နှင့်ဆိုင်သော *sat-nint-sai-taw*

mechanics *(n.)* မက္ကင်းနစ်ပညာ *ma-kan-nit-pyin-nyar*

mechanism *(n.)* စက်ကိရိယာ *sat-ka-yi-yar*

medal *(n.)* ဆုတံဆိပ် *su-ta-seik*

medallist *(n.)* ဆုတံဆိပ်ရှင် *su-ta-seik-shin*

meddle *(v.)* စွက်ဖက်သည် *swat-phat-the*

median *(adj.)* ပျမ်းမျှဖြစ်သော *pyan-mya-phit-taw*

mediate *(v.)* ဖျန်ဖြေသည် *phyan-phyay-the*

mediation *(n.)* ဖျန်ဖြေခြင်း *phyan-phyay-chin*

mediator *(n.)* ဖျန်ဖြေသူ *phyan-phyay-thu*

medic *(n.)* ဆေးကျောင်းသား၊ ဆရာဝန် *say-kyaung-tar, sa-yar-win*

medical *(adj.)* ဆေးဘက်ဆိုင်ရာ *say-bat-sai-yar*

medicament *(n.)* ဆေးဝါး *say-war*

medicinal *(adj.)* ဆေးဖက်ဝင်သော *say-phat-win-taw*

medicine *(n.)* ဆေးပညာ *say-pyin-nyar*

medieval *(adj.)* အလယ်ခေတ် *a-lal-khit*

mediocre *(adj.)* သာမန်မျှ *tar-man-mya*

mediocrity *(n.)* သာမညောင်ည *tar-ma-nyaung-nya*

meditate *(v.)* တရားထိုင်သည် *ta-yar-htai-the*

meditation *(n.)* တရားထိုင်ခြင်း *ta-yar-htai-chin*

meditative *(adj.)* တရားထိုင်သော *ta-yar-htai-taw*

medium *(n.)* ကြားခံ *kyar-khan*

meek *(adj.)* အောက်ကျို့တတ်သော *awt-kyo-tat-taw*

meet *(n.)* တွေ့ဆုံခြင်း *tway-sone-chin*

meeting *(n.)* အစည်းအဝေး *a-see-a-way*

megalith *(n.)* ရောမကျောက်တုံးကြီး *a-yar-ma-kyauk-tone-kyi*
megalithic *(adj.)* ရောမကျောက်တုံးကြီးဖြင့်တည်ဆောက်ထားသော *a-yar-ma-kyauk-tone-kyi-phint- te-saut-htar-taw*
megaphone *(n.)* အော်လန် *aww-lan*
megastore *(n.)* စတိုင်းဆိုင်ကြီး *sa-toe-sai-gyi*
melancholia *(n.)* မှိုင်တွေရောဂါ *hmai-tway-yaw-gar*
melancholic *(adj.)* မှိုင်တွေသော *hmai-tway-taw*
melancholy *(n.)* ညှိုးငယ်ခြင်း *nyoe-ngal-chin*
melee *(n.)* လက်နက်မဲ့တိုက်ခိုက်ခြင်း *lat-nat-mae-tite-khite-chin*
meliorate *(v.)* ပိုကောင်းအောင်လုပ်သည် *po-kaung-aung-lote-the*
mellow *(adj.)* ရင့်မှည့်သော *yint-mae-taw*
melodious *(adj.)* သာယာကြည်နူးဖွယ် *taw-yar-kyi-nu-phwal*
melodrama *(n.)* ဇာတ်ဆန်လွန်းခြင်း *zat-san-lun-chin*
melodramatic *(adj.)* ဇာတ်ဆန်လွန်းသော *zat-san-lun-taw*
melody *(n.)* တေးသွား *tay-twar*
melon *(n.)* ဖရဲသီး *pha-ye-thee*
melt *(v.)* အရည်ပျော်သည် *a-yay-pyaw-the*
member *(n.)* အဖွဲ့ဝင် *a-phwe-win*
membership *(n.)* အဖွဲ့ဝင်ဖြစ်ခြင်း *a-phwe-win-phit-chin*
membrane *(n.)* အမြှေးပါး *a-myay-par*
memento *(n.)* အမှတ်တရပစ္စည်း *a-mat-ta-ya-pyit-see*
memoir *(n.)* ကိုယ်တွေ့မှတ်တမ်း *ko-tway-mat-tan*
memorable *(adj.)* အမှတ်တရဖြစ်သော *a-mat-ta-ya-pyit-taw*
memorandum *(n.)* မှတ်စု၊ မှတ်တမ်း *mat-su, mat-tan*
memorial *(n.)* အထိမ်းအမှတ် *a-htein-a-mat*
memory *(n.)* မှတ်ဉာဏ် *mat-nyan*
menace *(v.)* ခြိမ်းခြောက်သည် *chain-chauk-the*
mend *(v.)* ပြင်ဆင်သည် *pyin-sin-the*
mendacious *(adj.)* လိမ်သော *lain-taw*
menial *(n.)* အစေအပါး *a-say-a-par*
meningitis *(n.)* ဦးနှောက်အမြှေးရောင်ရောဂါ *oo-naut-a-myay-yaung-yaw-gar*
menopause *(n.)* သွေးဆုံးခြင်း *tway-sone-chin*
menses *(n.)* ရာသီသွေး *yar-thi-tway*
menstrual *(adj.)* ရာသီနှင့် ဆိုင်သော *yar-thi-nint-sai-taw*
menstruation *(n.)* ရာသီလာခြင်း *yar-thi-lar-chin*
mental *(adj.)* စိတ်ပိုင်းဆိုင်ရာ *seik-pai-sai-yar*
mentality *(n.)* စိတ်နေသဘောထား *seik-nay-ta-bar-htar*
mention *(v.)* ဖော်ပြသည် *phaw-pya-the*
mentor *(n.)* ညွှန်ပြသူ *hnyun-pya-thu*
menu *(n.)* မီနူး *mee-nu*
mercantile *(adj.)* ကုန်သွယ်မှုဆိုင်ရာ *kone-twal-mu-sai-yar*
mercenary *(adj.)* ကြေးစား *kyay-sar*
merchandise *(n.)* ကုန်စည် *kone-se*
merchant *(n.)* ကုန်သည် *kone-the*
merciful *(adj.)* သက်ညှာသော *thet-nyar-taw*

merciless *(adj.)* မသနားတတ်သော *ma-ta-nar-tat-taw*
mercurial *(adj.)* စိတ်အပြောင်းအလဲမြန်သော *seik-a-pyaung-a-lal-myan-taw*
mercury *(n.)* ပြဒါး *pya-dar*
mercy *(n.)* သက်ညှာမှု *thet-nyar-mu*
mere *(adj.)* မျှသာ *mya-tar*
merge *(v.)* ပေါင်းသည် *paung-the*
merger *(n.)* ကုမ္ပဏီချင်းပေါင်းခြင်း *kone-pa-ni-chin-paung-chin*
meridian *(n.)* လောင်ဂျီတွဒ်မျဉ်း *laung-gyi-tut-myin*
merit *(n.)* ကောင်းမြတ်ခြင်း *kaung-myat-chin*
meritorious *(adj.)* ချီးမွမ်းထိုက်သော *chee-mun-htike-taw*
mermaid *(n.)* ရေသူမ *yay-thu-ma*
merman *(n.)* ရေသူထီး *yay-thu-htee*
merriment *(n.)* ရွှင်မြူးကြည်နူးဖွယ် *shwin-myi-kyi-nu-phwal*
merry *(adj.)* ပျော်ရွှင်သော *pyaw-shwin-taw*
mesh *(n.)* ကွန်ရက် *kyun-yat*
mesmerism *(n.)* ညို့နည်းဖြင့် စိတ်ညို့ထားသော အခြေအနေ *nyo-ne-phint-sate-nyo-htar-taw-a-chay-nay*
mesmerize *(v.)* ညို့သည် *nyo-the*
mess *(n.)* ညစ်ပတ်ခြင်း *nyit-pat-chin*
message *(n.)* စာတို *sar-to*
messenger *(n.)* စာပို့တမန် *sar-po-ta-man*
messiah *(n.)* ကယ်တင်ရှင် *kal-tin-shin*
Messrs *(n.)* အာလုပ်စကား *ar-lote-sa-kar*
metabolism *(n.)* ဇီဝဖြစ်စဉ် *zi-wa-phit-sin*
metal *(n.)* သတ္တု *tat-tu*
metallic *(adj.)* သတ္တုနှင့်တူသော *tat-tu-nint-tu-taw*
metallurgy *(n.)* သတ္တုဗေဒ *tat-tu-bay-da*
metamorphosis *(n.)* အသွင်ပြောင်းလဲခြင်း *a-twin-pyaung-lal-chin*
metaphor *(n.)* တင်စားမှု *tin-sar-mu*
metaphysical *(adj.)* ရုပ်လွန်ပညာနှင့်ဆိုင်သော *yoke-lun-pyin-nyar-nint-sai-taw*
metaphysics *(n.)* ရုပ်လွန်ပညာ *yoke-lun-pyin-nyar*
mete *(v.)* စီရင်သည် *si-yin-the*
meteor *(n.)* ဥက္ကာပျံ *oak-kar-pyan*
meteoric *(adj.)* တစ်ရှိန်ထိုး၊ ဥက္ကာပျံနှင့်ဆိုင်သော *ta-shein-htoe, oak-kar-pyan-nint-sai-taw*
meteorologist *(n.)* မိုးလေဝသပညာရှင် *moe-lay-wa-ta-pyin-nyar-shin*
meteorology *(n.)* မိုးလေဝသပညာ *moe-lay-wa-ta-pyin-nyar*
meter *(n.)* မီတာ *mi-tar*
method *(n.)* နည်းလမ်း *nee-lan*
methodical *(adj.)* နည်းစနစ်ကျနသော *nee-sa-nit-kya-na-taw*
meticulous *(adj.)* စေ့စပ်သော *say-sat-taw*
metre *(n.)* မီတာ *mi-tar*
metric *(adj.)* မက်ထရစ်စနစ် *mat-hta-rit-sa-nit*
metrical *(adj.)* နရီသွား *na-yee-twar*
metro *(n.)* မြေအောက်ရထားစနစ် *myay-awt-ya-htar-sa-nit*
metropolis *(n.)* မြို့ကြီး *myo-kyi*
metropolitan *(adj.)* မြို့တော် *myo-taw*
mettle *(n.)* သတ္တိသွေး *tat-ti-thway*
mettlesome *(adj.)* သတ္တိသွေးကောင်းသော *tat-ti-thway-kaung-taw*

mew *(n.)* ကြောင်အော်သံ *kyaung-aw-tan*

mew *(v.)* ကြောင်အော်သည် *kyaung-aw-the*

mezzanine *(n.)* ထပ်ခိုး *htet-kho*

mica *(n.)* လချေး *la-chay*

microbrewery *(n.)* ဘီယာချက်စက်ရုံငယ် *bee-yar-chat-sat-yone-ngal*

microfilm *(n.)* မိုက်ခရိုဖလင် *mite-kha-ro-pha-lin*

micrology *(n.)* မျိုးနွယ်စုငယ်အကြောင်းလေ့လာမှုပညာ *myo-nwe-su-ngal-a-kyaung-lay-lar-mu-pyin-nyar*

micrometer *(n.)* မိုက်ခရိုမီတာ *mite-ka-ro-me-ter*

microphone *(n.)* မိုက်ခွက် *mite-khwat*

microprint *(n.)* အလွန်သေးငယ်စာ ပုံနှိပ်ခြင်း *a-lun-tay-ngal-swar-pon-nate-chin*

microprocessor *(n.)* မိုက်ခရိုပရော်ဆက်ဆာ *mite-kha-ro-pa-yaw-sat-sar*

microscope *(n.)* အဏုကြည့်မှန်ပြောင်း *a-nu-kyi-man-pyaung*

microscopic *(adj.)* သေးငယ်မှုန်မွှားသော *tay-nge-hmone-hmwar-taw*

microwave *(n.)* မိုက်ခရိုဝေ့ဖ် *mite-kha-ro-wave*

mid *(adj.)* အလယ် *a-lal*

midday *(n.)* နေ့လည် *nae-lal*

middle *(n.)* အလယ် *a-lal*

middle *(adj.)* အလယ် *a-lal*

middleman *(n.)* တစ်ဆင့်ခံ ရောင်းသူ *ta-sint-khan-yaung-thu*

middling *(adj.)* အလယ်အလတ် *a-lal-a-lat*

midget *(n.)* သက်ကြီးပု *thet-kyi-pyu*

midland *(n.)* မြေလတ်ပိုင်း *myay-lat-pai*

midnight *(n.)* ညသန်းခေါင် *nya-tan-khaung*

mid-off *(n.)* အလယ်အပြင်ဘက် *a-lal-a-pyin-bat*

mid-on *(n.)* အလယ်အတွင်းဘက် *a-lal-a-twin-bat*

midriff *(n.)* ဝမ်းဗိုက် *wan-bike*

midst *(n.)* အလယ်တွင် *a-lal-twin*

midsummer *(n.)* နွေလယ်ကာလ *nway-lal-kar-a*

midwife *(n.)* သားဖွား *tar-phwar*

miffed *(adj.)* ကျွဲမြီးတိုသော *kywe-mee-toe-taw*

might *(n.)* ကြီးမားသော ခွန်အား *kyi-mar-taw-khun-arr*

mighty *(adj.)* ခွန်အားကြီးမားသော *khun-arr-kyi-mar-taw*

migraine *(n.)* ခေါင်းတစ်ခြမ်းကိုက်ရောဂါ *khaung-ta-chan-kite-yaw-gar*

migrant *(n.)* ရွှေ့ပြောင်း *shway-pyaung*

migrate *(v.)* ပြောင်းရွှေ့နေထိုင်သည် *pyaung-shway-nay-htai-the*

migration *(n.)* ပြောင်းရွှေ့နေထိုင်ခြင်း *pyaung-shway-nay-htai-chin*

milch *(adj.)* နွားကို ရည်ညွှန်းသော *nwar-ko-yee-nyun-taw*

mild *(adj.)* ပျော့ပျောင်းသော *pyawt-pyaung-taw*

mildew *(n.)* ဖားး၊ မှို *hpar, hmoe*

mile *(n.)* မိုင် *mai*

mileage *(n.)* ခရီးမိုင်ပေါင်း *kha-yee-mai-paung*

milestone *(n.)* သမိုင်းမှတ်တိုင် *ta-mai-mat-tai*

milieu *(n.)* ပတ်ဝန်းကျင်၊ အသိုင်းအဝိုင်း *pat-win-kyin, a-tine-a-wine*

militant *(n.)* ရန်လိုသူ *yan-lo-thu*

military *(n.)* စစ် *sit*

militate *(v.)* ဟန့်တားသည် *hant-tar-the*

militia *(n.)* စစ်ဝန်ထမ်း *sit-win-htan*

milk *(v.)* နို့တက်သည် *noe-thet-the*

milk *(n.)* နို့၊ နို့ရည် *noe, noe-yay*

milk powder *(n.)* နို့မှုန့် *noe-hmont*

milky *(adj.)* နို့ပါသော *noe-par-taw*

mill *(v.)* ကြိတ်ခွဲသည် *kyaik-kwal-the*

mill *(n.)* သီးနှံကြိတ်ခွဲစက် *thee-nan-kyaik-kwal-sat*

millennium *(n.)* ထောင်စုနှစ် *htaung-su-nit*

miller *(n.)* ဂျုံစက်ပိုင်ရှင် *gyone-sat-pai-shin*

millet *(n.)* ကောက်နှံပင် *kauk-hnan-pin*

milliner *(n.)* အမျိုးသမီး ရောင်းသူ *a-myo-ta-mee-yaung-thu*

millinery *(n.)* အမျိုးသမီး ဦးထုပ်လုပ်ငန်း *a-myo-ta-mee-oo-htoke-lote-ngan*

million *(n.)* သန်း *tan*

millionaire *(n.)* သန်းကြွယ်သူဌေး *tan-kywe-ta-htay*

millipede *(n.)* ပိုးနားသန် *poe-na-tan*

mime *(n.)* သဘင်အတတ် *ta-bin-a-tat*

mimesis *(n.)* အစစ်အမှန်ကမ္ဘာကို စာပေထဲရှိ အတုကိုယ်စားပြုမှု *a-sit-a-man-ka-bar-ko-sar-pay-htae-shi-a-tu-a-yaung-koe-sar-pyu-mu*

mimic *(v.)* တုသည် *tu-the*

mimicry *(n.)* တုပ၍ ဖြေဖျော်မှုအတတ် *tu-pa-ywe-pyaw-phyay-mu-a-tat*

minaret *(n.)* ဗလီမျှော်စင် *ba-li-myaw-sin*

mince *(v.)* နုပ်နုပ်စင်းသည် *note-note-sin-the*

mind *(n.)* စိတ် *seik*

mind-blowing *(adj.)* လက်ဖျားခါလောက်သော *lat-pyar-khar-laut-taw*

mindful *(adj.)* သတိရှိသော *ta-di-shi-taw*

mindless *(adj.)* သတိမဲ့သော *ta-di-mae-taw*

mindset *(n.)* တွေးခေါ်မှုအလေ့အထ *tway-khaw-mu-a-lay-a-hta*

mine *(pron.)* ကျွန်တော်၏ ဟာ *kyun-taw-ei-har*

miner *(n.)* မိုင်းအလုပ်သမား *mai-a-lote-ta-mar*

mineral *(adj.)* တွင်းထွက်ပစ္စည်းနှင့် ဆိုင်သော *twin-htwat-pyit-see-nint-sai-taw*

mineral *(n.)* တွင်းထွက်ပစ္စည်း *twin-htwat-pyit-see*

mineralogist *(n.)* တွင်းထွက်ဓာတ်သတ္တုပညာရှင် *twin-htwat-dat-tat-tu-pyin-nyar-shin*

mineralogy *(n.)* တွင်းထွက်ဓာတ်သတ္တုပညာ *twin-htwat-dat-tat-tu-pyin-nyar*

mingle *(v.)* ရောသည်၊ နှောသည် *yaw-the, naw-the*

miniature *(adj.)* အသေးစား *a-tay-zar*

miniature *(n.)* ပန်းချီကားအသေးစား *pan-chi-kar-a-tay-sar*

minim *(n.)* တစ်ဝက်ပြဂီတသင်္ကေတ *ta-wat-pya-gi-ta-tin-kay-ta*

minimal *(adj.)* အနည်းဆုံး *a-nae-sone*

minimize *(v.)* နည်းအောင် လုပ်သည် *nae-aung-lote-the*

minimum *(adj.)* အနည်းဆုံး *a-nae-sone*

minimum *(n.)* အနည်းဆုံး *a-nae-sone*

minion *(n.)* လက်ပါးစေ *lat-par-say*

minister *(v.)* ပြုစုသည် *pyu-su-the*

minister *(n.)* ဝန်ကြီး *win-gyi*

ministrant *(adj.)* စီမံအုပ်ချုပ်သူ *see-man-oak-choke-thu*

ministry *(n.)* ဝန်ကြီးဌာန *win-gyi-htar-na*

mink *(n.)* မြွေပါ *mway-par*

minor *(n.)* သာမည *tar-ma-nya*

minor *(adj.)* အရေးမပါသော *a-yay-ma-par-taw*

minority *(n.)* အနည်းစု *a-nae-su*

minster *(n.)* ခရစ်ယာန် ဘုရားရှိခိုးကျောင်း *kha-yit-yan-pha-yar-shi-kho-kyaung*

mint *(v.)* ဒင်္ဂါးသွန်းလုပ်သည် *din-gar-thoon-lote-the*

minus *(adj.)* အနုတ် *a-note*

minus *(prep.)* အနုတ် *a-note*

minuscule *(adj.)* မှုန်မွှားသော *hmone-hmwar-taw*

minute *(n.)* မိနစ် *mi-nit*

minutely *(adv.)* အနုစိတ် *a-nu-seik*

minx *(n.)* ဆတ်ဆတ်လူး စွာတေးမ *sat-sat-lu-swar-tay-ma*

miracle *(n.)* အံ့ဖွယ်သရဲ *ant-phwe-ta-ye*

miraculous *(adj.)* အံ့ဖွယ်သရဲ *ant-phwe-ta-ye*

mirage *(n.)* တံလျှပ် *tan-hlyat*

mire *(v.)* နွံနစ်နေသည် *non-nit-nay-the*

mire *(n.)* စိမ့်မြေ *seint-myay*

mirror *(v.)* ပုံရိပ်ထင်သည် *pon-yeik-htin-the*

mirror *(n.)* ကြေးမုံ *kyay-mone*

mirror image *(n.)* ကြေးမုံပုံရိပ် *kyay-mone-pon-yeik*

mirth *(n.)* ဟာသ *har-ta*

mirthful *(adj.)* ဟာသဖြစ်သော *har-ta-phit-taw*

misadventure *(n.)* ကံဆိုးခြင်း *kan-soe-chin*

misalliance *(n.)* အသင့်လျော်သော မဟာမိတ် *ma-tint-lyaw-thaw-ma-har-mate*

misanthrope *(n.)* လူကို မုန်း၍ လူ့အသိုင်းအဝိုင်းကို ရှောင်ကြဉ်သော သူ *lu-ko-hmone-ywe-lu-a-tine-a-win-ko-shaung-kyin-taw*

misapplication *(n.)* လွဲမှားစွာ အသုံးချခြင်း *lwal-mar-swar-a-tone-cha-chin*

misapprehend *(v.)* မှားယွင်းစွာ ယူဆသည် *mar-ywin-swar-yu-sa-the*

misapprehension *(n.)* မှားယွင်းစွာ ယူဆခြင်း *mar-ywin-swar-yu-sa-chin*

misappropriate *(v.)* ငွေအလွဲသုံးစားပြုသည် *ngwe-a-lwal-tone-sar-pyu-the*

misappropriation *(n.)* ငွေအလွဲသုံးစားပြုခြင်း *ngwe-a-lwal-tone-sar-pyu-chin*

misbehave *(v.)* လွဲမှားစွာ ပြုမူသည် *lwal-mar-swar-pyu-mu-the*

misbehaviour *(n.)* လွဲမှားစွာ ပြုမူခြင်း *lwal-mar-swar-pyu-mu-chin*

misbelief *(n.)* တလွဲ အယုံအကြည် *ta-lwal-a-yone-a-kyi*

miscalculate *(v.)* မှားတွက်သည် *mar-twat-the*

miscalculation *(n.)* မှားတွက်ခြင်း *mar-twat-chin*

miscall *(v.)* မှားခေါ်သည် *mar-khaw-the*

miscarriage *(n.)* ကိုယ်ဝန်ပျက်ခြင်း *ko-win-pyat-chin*

miscarry *(v.)* ကိုယ်ဝန်ပျက်သည် *ko-win-pya-the*

miscellaneous *(adj.)* အမျိုးမျိုး *a-myo-myo*

miscellany *(n.)* သောင်းပြောင်းထွေလာ *taung-pyaung-htway-lar*

mischance *(n.)* ကံဆိုးခြင်း *kan-soe-chin*

mischief *(n.)* ဒုက္ခပေးခြင်း *doke-kha-pay-chin*

mischievous *(adj.)* ကျီစယ်တတ်သော *kyi-sal-tat-taw*
misconceive *(v.)* နားလည်မှု လွဲသည် *nar-lal-mu-lwal-the*
misconception *(n.)* နားလည်မှု လွဲခြင်း *nar-lal-mu-lwal-chin*
misconduct *(n.)* အုပ်ချုပ်ရေး ညံ့ဖျင်းမှု *oak-choke-yay-nyant-pyin-mu*
misconstrue *(v.)* အဓိပ္ပါယ်ကောက်လွဲသည် *a-dait-pal-kauk-lwal-the*
miscreant *(n.)* ကိုယ်ကျင့်တရား ပျက်သူ *ko-kyint-ta-yar-pyat-thu*
misdeed *(n.)* အကုသိုလ် *a-ku-do*
misdemeanour *(n.)* သေးအဖွဲ့အမှား *a-tay-a-phwe-a-hmar*
misdiagnose *(v.)* ရောဂါအမည်မှားတပ်သည် *yaw-gar-a-me-mar-tat-the*
misdirect *(v.)* တလွဲပို့သည် *ta-lwal-poe-the*
misdirection *(n.)* တလွဲလမ်းညွှန်ခြင်း *ta-lwal-lan-hnyun-chin*
miser *(n.)* ကပ်စေးနဲ၊ ကော်တရာ *kat-say-nae, kaw-ta-yar*
miserable *(adj.)* မသက်မသာ ဖြစ်သော *ma-thet-ma-tar-phit-taw*
miserly *(adj.)* ကပ်စေးနဲသော *kat-say-nae-taw*
misery *(n.)* ဝေဒနာ *wai-da-nar*
misfire *(v.)* လိုရင်းမရောက် *lo-yin-ma-yauk*
misfit *(n.)* လူခွစာ *lu-khwa-sar*
misfortune *(n.)* ကံဆိုးခြင်း *kan-soe-chin*
misgive *(v.)* သံသယဖြစ်သည်၊ မှားယွင်းပေးသည် *tan-ta-ya-phit-the, mar-ywin-pay-the*
misgiving *(n.)* သို့လော သို့လော ဖြစ်ခြင်း *tho-law-tho-law-phit-chin*
misguide *(v.)* လွဲမှားစွာ ဆုံးဖြတ်သည် *lwal-mar-swar-sone-phat-the*
mishap *(n.)* ကံခေခြင်း *kan-khay-chin*
misjudge *(v.)* ထင်မြင်ယူဆချက် လွဲသည် *htin-myin-yu-sa-chat-lwal-the*
mislead *(v.)* လှည့်စားသည် *hlae-sar-the*
mismanagement *(n.)* လွဲမှားစွာ စီမံခန့်ခွဲခြင်း *lwal-mar-swar-si-man-khant-khwal-chin*
mismatch *(v.)* လိုက်ဖက်မညီ *lite-phat-ma-nyi*
misnomer *(n.)* မဆီလျော်သည့် အမည် *ma-si-hlyaw-the-a-mee*
misperception *(n.)* လွဲမှားစွာသိမြင်ခြင်း *lwal-mar-swar-ti-myin-chin*
misplace *(v.)* နေရာမှားထားသည် *nay-yar-mar-htar-the*
misprint *(v.)* ပုံနှိပ်မှားသည် *pon-nate-hmar-the*
misrepresent *(v.)* မှားယွင်းစွာ တင်ပြသည် *hmar-ywin-swar-tin-pya-the*
misrepsentation *(n.)* မှားယွင်းစွာ တင်ပြခြင်း *hmar-ywin-swar-tin-pya-chin*
misrule *(n.)* ဖရိုဖရဲ ဖြစ်ခြင်း *pha-yo-pha-ye-phit-chin*
miss *(v.)* သတိရသည် *ta-di-ya-the*
miss *(n.)* အလှမယ်ဘွဲ့၊ ကောင်မလေး၊ ကလေးမ၊ သူငယ်မကို ရည်ညွှန်းသော စကား *a-hla-mal-bwe, kaung-ma-lay, ka-lay-ma, thu-nge-ma-ko-yay-hnyun-taw-sa-gar*
missile *(n.)* ဒုံးလက်နက် *dote-lat-nat*
missing *(adj.)* ပျောက်နေသော *pyauk-nay-taw*
mission *(n.)* မစ်ရှင် *mit-shin*
missionary *(n.)* သာသနာပြုအဖွဲ့ *tar-ta-nar-pyu-a-phwe*
missis, missus *(n.)* ဇနီး *za-nee*

missive *(n.)* စာ၊ သဝဏ်လွှာ *sar, ta-win-hlwar*
mist *(n.)* မြူ၊ မြူခိုး *myu, my-khoe*
mistake *(v.)* မှားယွင်းသည် *hmar-ywin-the*
mistake *(n.)* အမှားအယွင်း *a-hmar-a-ywin*
mister *(n.)* မစ်စတာ၊ အမျိုးသားကို ရည်ညွှန်းပြောသော စကား *mit-sa-tar-a-myo-tar-ko-yay-hnyum-pyaw-taw-sa-kar*
mistletoe *(n.)* ကျီးပေါင်းပင်တစ်မျိုး *kyee-paung-pin-ta-myo*
mistreat *(v.)* အကိုင်ကြမ်းသည် *a-kai-kyan-the*
mistress *(n.)* အိမ်ရှင်မ *eain-shin-ma*
mistrust *(v.)* ယုံကြည်မှု ကင်းသည် *yone-kyi-mu-kin-the*
mistrust *(n.)* မယုံကြည် *ma-yone-kyi*
misty *(adj.)* မြူဖြင့်ဖုံးလွှမ်းထားသော *my-phint-hpone-hlwan-htar-taw*
misunderstand *(v.)* နားလည်မှု လွဲသည် *nar-lal-mu-lwal-the*
misunderstanding *(n.)* နားလည်မှု လွဲခြင်း *nar-lal-mu-lwal-chin*
misuse *(n.)* တလွဲသုံးခြင်း *ta-lwal-tone-chin*
mite *(n.)* ပုလုကွေးလေး *pu-lu-kway-lay*
mithridate *(n.)* အဆိပ်အလုံးစုံဖြေဆေး *a-seik-a-lone-sone-hpyay-say*
mitigate *(v.)* သက်သာစေသည် *thet-tar-say-the*
mitigation *(n.)* သက်သာစေခြင်း *thet-tar-say-chin*
mitre *(n.)* သင်္ကန်းထောင့်ချိုးဆက် *tin-khan-htaunt-choe-sat*
mitten *(n.)* နှစ်ကန့် အနွေးလက်အိတ် *not-khant-a-nway-lat-aik*
mix *(v.)* ရောနှောသည် *yaw-hnaw-the*
mixture *(n.)* အရောအနှော *a-yaw-a-hnaw*
mnemonic *(adj.)* မှတ်ဉာဏ်ကူ *mat-nyan-ku*
mnemonization *(n.)* မှတ်ဉာဏ်ကူ အတိုမှတ်ခြင်း *mat-nyan-ku-a-to-mat-chin*
moan *(n.)* ညည်းသံ *nyee-tan*
moat *(n.)* ကျုံး *kyone*
mob *(n.)* လူအုပ် *lu-oak*
mobile *(adj.)* ရွှေ့ပြောင်းနိုင်သော *shway-pyaung-nai-taw*
mobility *(n.)* ရွှေ့လျားနိုင်မှု *shway-lyar-nai-mu*
mobilize *(v.)* စစ်စည်းရုံးသည် *sit-si-yone-the*
mock *(v.)* ရယ်သွေးလွှမ်းသည် *ywal-thway-lwan-the*
mockery *(n.)* သရော်ခြင်း *ta-yaw-chin*
mocktail *(n.)* မော့တေးလ်အရက် *mot-tay-a-yat*
modality *(n.)* အာရုံတစ်ပါးပါး *arr-yone-ta-par-par*
mode *(n.)* နည်းလမ်း *nee-lan*
model *(v.)* နမူနာယူသည် *na-mu-nar-yu-the*
model *(n.)* ပုံစံငယ် *pon-san-nge*
moderate *(v.)* လျှော့စေသည် *shaw-zay-the*
moderation *(n.)* အစွန်းမရောက်ခြင်း *a-sun-ma-yauk-chin*
modern *(adj.)* ပစ္စုပ္ပန် *pyit-sote-pan*
modernity *(n.)* ခေတ်မီခြင်း *khit-mi-chin*
modernization *(n.)* ခေတ်မီအောင် ပြုလုပ်ခြင်း *khit-mi-aung-pyu-lote-chin*
modernize *(v.)* ခေတ်မီသည် *khit-mi-the*

modest *(adj.)* အသင့်အတင့် ဖြစ်သော *a-tint-a-tint-phyit-taw*
modesty *(n.)* သင့်ရှိမှု *tint-yone-mya*
modicum *(n.)* အနည်းငယ် *a-ne-ngal*
modification *(n.)* ပြုပြင်မွမ်းမံခြင်း *pyu-pyin-moon-man-chin*
modify *(v.)* ပြုပြင်မွမ်းမံသည် *pyu-pyin-moon-man-the*
modular *(adj.)* မော်ဂျူးပုံစံ *maw-ju-pon-san*
modulate *(v.)* ညှိသည် *nyi-the*
module *(n.)* မော်ဂျူး *maw-ju*
moil *(v.)* အလုပ်ကြိုးစားသည် *a-lote-kyo-sar-the*
moist *(adj.)* စိုစွတ်သော *so-sut-taw*
moisten *(v.)* ဆွတ်သည် *sut-the*
moisture *(n.)* အစိုဓာတ် *a-so-dat*
molar *(adj.)* အံသွားနှင့်ဆိုင်သော *an-twar-nint-sai-taw*
molar *(n.)* အံသွား *an-twar*
molasses *(n.)* သကာ *ta-kar*
mole *(n.)* မှဲ့ *mae*
molecular *(adj.)* မော်လီကျူးဆိုင်ရာ *maw-li-kyu-sai-yar*
molecule *(n.)* မော်လီကျူး *maw-li-kyu*
molest *(v.)* ကိုယ်ထိလက်ရောက် စော်ကားသည် *ko-hti-lat-yauk-saw-kar-the*
molestation *(n.)* ဗလက္ကာရ *ba-lat-kar-ya*
mollusc *(n.)* ခရုမျိုး *ka-yu-myo*
molluscous *(adj.)* ခရုမျိုးနှင့် ဆိုင်သော *kha-yu-myo-nint-sai-taw*
molten *(adj.)* အရည်ကျိုထားသော *a-yay-kyo-htar-taw*
moment *(n.)* တဒင်္ဂ *da-din-ga*
momentary *(adj.)* ခဏမျှဖြစ်သော *kha-na-mya-phit-taw*
momentous *(adj.)* အလွန်အရေးပါသော *a-lun-a-yay-par-taw*
momentum *(n.)* အဟုန် *a-hon*
monarch *(n.)* ကေရာဇ် *a-ka-yit*
monarchy *(n.)* သက်ဦးဆံပိုင်စနစ် *thet-oo-san-pai-sa-nit*
monastery *(n.)* ဘုန်းကြီးကျောင်း *hpone-gyi-kyaung*
monasticism *(n.)* ရဟန်းဘဝ *ya-han-ba-wa*
Monday *(n.)* တနင်္လာနေ့ *ta-nin-lar-nay*
monetary *(adj.)* ငွေရေးကြေးရေး *ngwe-yay-kyay-kya*
money *(n.)* ငွေ *ngwe*
money laundering *(n.)* ငွေကြေး ခဝါချခြင်း *ngwe-kyay-kha-war-cha-chin*
monger *(n.)* မလိုလားသော အရာတစ်ခုကို ကြော်ငြာသည် *ma-lo-lar-taw-a-yar-ta-khu-ko-kyaw-nyar-the*
mongoose *(n.)* မြွေပါ *myway-par*
mongrel *(n.)* ရောကျော်ခွေး *yaw-kyaw-khway*
monitor *(n.)* စောင့်ကြည့်၊ မှတ်သား၊ စစ်ဆေးပေးသော ကိရိယာ *saunt-kyi-mat-tar-sit-say-htar-taw-ka-yi-yar*
monitory *(adj.)* ထောက်လှမ်းသော *htauk-hlan-taw*
monk *(n.)* ဘုန်းကြီး *phone-gyi*
monkey *(n.)* မျောက် *myauk*
monochromatic *(adj.)* တရောင်ထဲပါသော *ta-yaung-htae-par-taw*
monocle *(n.)* တစ်ဖက်တည်းမျက်မှန် *ta-phat-te-myat-man*

monocular *(adj.)* တစ်ဖက်တည်းဖြစ်သော *ta-phat-te-phit-taw*
monody *(n.)* ရတုကဗျာ *ya-tu-ka-byar*
monoestrous *(adj.)* တစ်နှစ်တစ်ကြိမ်ဖြစ်သော *ta-nit-ta-kyein-phit-taw*
monogamy *(n.)* တစ်လင်မယားစလေ့ *ta-lin-ma-yar-da-lay*
monogram *(n.)* လုံးကောက် ပန်းစာလုံး *lone-kauk-pan-sar-lone*
monograph *(n.)* အကြောင်းအရာတစ်ရပ်ကို ပြုစုထားသော စာတမ်း *a-kyung-a-yar-ta-yat-ko-pyu-su-htar-taw-sar-tan*
monogynous *(adj.)* ပစ်စတေးတံ တစ်ခုတည်းပါသော *pit-sa-til-tan-ta-khu-tae-par-taw*
monolatry *(n.)* ဘုရားတစ်ပါးတည်းကိုးကွယ်ခြင်း *phayar-ta-bar-tae-koe-kwal-chin*
monolith *(n.)* ကျောက်သားတိုင်ကြီး *kyauk-tar-tai-gyi*
monologue *(n.)* တစ်ဦးတည်း ရှည်လျားစွာ ပြောသော စကား *ta-oo-the-shay-lyar-swar-pyaw-taw-sakar*
monopolist *(n.)* တစ်ဦးတည်း ဈေးကွက်ချုပ်ကိုင်ခွင့်ရ ကုမ္ပဏီ *ta-oo-the-zay-kwat-choke-kai-khwint-ya-kon-pa-ni*
monopolize *(v.)* လက်ဝါးကြီး အုပ်သည် *lat-war-gyi-oak-the*
monopoly *(n.)* လက်ဝါးကြီးအုပ် ချုပ်ကိုင်မှုစနစ် *lat-war-gyi-oak-choke-kai-mu-sa-nit*
monorail *(n.)* တစ်လမ်းပြေးရထား *ta-lan-pyay-ya-htar*
monosyllabic *(adj.)* ကေဝဏ္ဏ *a-ka-wunna*
monosyllable *(n.)* ကေဝဏ္ဏ စကားလုံး *a-ka-wunna-sa-kar-lone*
monotheism *(n.)* ဘုရားတစ်ဆူတည်း ကိုးကွယ်သော ဝါဒ *pha-yar-ta-su-the-ko-kwal-taw-war-da*
monotheist *(n.)* ဘုရားတစ်ဆူတည်း ကိုးကွယ်သော သူ *pha-yar-ta-su-the-ko-kwal-taw-thu*
monotonous *(adj.)* ငြီးငွေ့ဖွယ်ကောင်းသော *nyee-ngway-phwal-kaung-taw*
monotony *(n.)* ရိုးအီနေခြင်း *yoe-e-nay-chin*
monsoon *(n.)* မုတ်သုံလေ *mote-thon-lay*
monster *(n.)* ဘီလူး *ba-lu*
monstrous *(adj.)* ကြောက်ခမန်းလိလိ *kyauk-kha-an-li-li*
month *(n.)* လ *la*
monthly *(adv.)* လစဉ် *la-sin*
monthly *(adj.)* လစဉ် *la-sin*
monument *(n.)* အထိမ်းအမှတ် အဆောက်အအုံ *a-htein-a-mat-a-saut-a-ohn*
monumental *(adj.)* အထိမ်းအမှတ် အဆောက်အအုံနှင့် ဆိုင်သော *a-htein-a-mat-a-saut-a-ohn-nint-sai-taw*
moo *(v.)* ဘွတ်အဲဟု အော်သည် *boot-ae-hu-aw-the*
mood *(n.)* စိတ်နေစိတ်ထား *seik-nay-seik-htar*
moody *(adj.)* စိတ်ပြောင်းလွယ်သော *seik-pyaung-lwal-taw*
moon *(n.)* လ *la*
moonlight *(n.)* လရောင် *la-yaung*
moor *(v.)* ကွဲသတ်သည် *kwal-tat-the*
moorings *(n.)* ကွဲသတ်ကြိုး *kwal-tat-kyo*

moot *(n.)* အဆိုပြုသည် *a-so-pyu-the*

mop *(v.)* ကြမ်းတိုက်သုတ်ဖတ်ဖြင့် ကြမ်းတိုက်သည် *kyan-tite-toke-phat-phyint-kyan-tite-the*

mop *(n.)* ကြမ်းတိုက်သုတ်ဖတ် *kyan-tite-toke-phat*

mope *(v.)* မှိုင်တွေသည် *hmai-tway-the*

moral *(n.)* ကိုယ်ကျင့်တရား *ko-kyint-ta-yar*

moral *(adj.)* အကျင့်သိက္ခာရှိသော *a-kyiint-taik-khar-shi-taw*

morale *(n.)* စိတ်ဓာတ် *seik-dat*

moralist *(n.)* ဘုရားဖြစ်မည့် အုတ်ခဲ *pha-yar-phit-mae-oak-nee-khae*

morality *(n.)* အကျင့်စာရိတ္တဆိုင်ရာ *a-kyint-sar-yeik-ta-sai-yar*

moralize *(v.)* အကျင့်သိက္ခာနှင့် ပတ်သက်၍ ဟောပြော ရေးသားသည် *a-kyint-take-khar-nint-pat-tat-ywe-haw-pyaw-yay-tar-the*

morbid *(adj.)* ဥပါဒါန် *au-par-dan*

morbidity *(n.)* မကျန်းမာမှု *ma-kyan-mar-mu*

more *(adv.)* နောက်ထပ် *naut-htet*

more *(adj.)* နောက်ထပ် *naut-htet*

moreover *(adv.)* ထို့အပြင် *htoe-a-pyin*

morganatic *(adj.)* လက်ထပ်ခြင်းကို ဒီဇိုင်းလုပ်သော *lat-htet-chin-ko-ta-zai-lote-taw*

morgue *(n.)* ရင်ခွဲရုံ *yin-khwal-yone*

moribund *(adj.)* ပျက်သုဥ်းလုနီးပါး *pyat-tone-lu-ni-par*

morning *(n.)* မနက်ခင်း *ma-nat-khin*

moron *(n.)* ငတုံး *nga-tone*

morose *(adj.)* သုန်မှုန်သော *ton-hmone-taw*

morph *(n.)* ပုံစံ *pon-san*

morphia *(n.)* မော်ဖိန်း *maw-fane*

morphine *(n.)* မော်ဖင်း *maw-phine*

morphology *(n.)* ရုပ်သွင်ပညာ *yoke-twin-pyi-nyar*

morrow *(n.)* မနက်ဖြန် *ma-nat-phan*

morse *(n.)* ချိတ် *chate*

morsel *(n.)* တစ်လုတ်စာ *ta-lote-sar*

mortal *(n.)* လူ *lu*

mortal *(adj.)* သေမျိုးဖြစ်သော *tay-myo-phit-taw*

mortality *(n.)* သေနှုန်း *tay-hnone*

mortar *(v.)* အင်္ဂတေ *in-ga-tay*

mortgage *(v.)* အပေါင်ထားသည် *a-paung-htar-the*

mortgage *(n.)* အပေါင်စာချုပ် *a-puang-sar-choke*

mortgagee *(n.)* အပေါင်ခံသူ *a-paung-khan-thu*

mortgagor *(n.)* အပေါင်ထားသူ *a-paung-htar-thu*

mortify *(v.)* အရှက်ရစေသည် *a-shat-ya-say-the*

mortuary *(n.)* ရင်ခွဲရုံ *yin-khwal-yone*

mosaic *(n.)* မှန်စီရွှေချ *man-si-shway-cha*

mosque *(n.)* ဗလီ *ba-li*

mosquito *(n.)* ခြင် *chin*

moss *(n.)* ရေညှိ *yay-nyi*

most *(n.)* အများစု *a-myar-su*

mostly *(adv.)* အများအားဖြင့် *a-myar-arr-phint*

mote *(n.)* မြူမှုန် *myu-hmone*

motel *(n.)* မိုတယ် *mi-the*

moth *(n.)* ဖလံ *pah-lan*

mother *(v.)* မိခင်ကဲ့သို့ ဂရုစိုက်သည် *mi-khin-kae-tho-ga-yu-site-the*
mother *(n.)* မိခင် *mi-khin*
motherhood *(n.)* မိခင်ဘဝ *mi-khin-ba-wa*
motherlike *(adj.)* မိခင်ကဲ့သို့ *mi-khin-kae-tho*
motherly *(adj.)* မိခင်ကဲ့သို့သော *mi-khin-kae-tho-taw*
motif *(n.)* အလှတန်ဆာ *a-hla-tan-sar*
motion *(v.)* လက်ရိပ်ပြသည် *lat-yeik-pya-the*
motion *(n.)* ရွေ့လျားမှု *shway-lyar-mu*
motionless *(adj.)* ရွေ့လျားမှု မရှိသော *shway-lyar-mu-ma-shi-taw*
motivate *(v.)* စိတ်အားတက်ကြွသည် *seik-arr-tat-kwa-the*
motivation *(n.)* စိတ်ပါဝင်စားမှု *seik-par-win-sar-mu*
motive *(n.)* အကြောင်းရင်း *a-kyaung-yin*
motley *(adj.)* သောင်းပြောင်းထွေလာ *taung-pyaung-htway-lar*
motor *(v.)* ကားဖြင့် အပျော်ခရီးထွက်သည် *kar-phint-a-pyaw-kha-yee-htwat-the*
motor *(n.)* မော်တာစက် *maw-tar-sat*
motorist *(n.)* ဆိုင်ကယ်မောင်းသမား *sai-kal-maung-ta-mar*
mottle *(n.)* အရောင်ကွက်ကျား *a-yaung-kwat-kyar*
motto *(n.)* ဆောင်ပုဒ် *saung-poke*
mould *(v.)* ပုံသွင်းသည် *pon-twin-the*
mould *(n.)* ပုံစံခွက် *pon-san-khwat*
mouldy *(adj.)* မှိုတက်သော *hmo-tat-taw*
moult *(v.)* အမွေးချသည် *a-mway-cha-he*
mound *(n.)* တောင်ပို့ *taung-po*
mount *(v.)* တက်သည်၊ တင်သည် *tat-the, tin-the*
mount *(n.)* မြင်း *myin*
mountain *(n.)* တောင်တန်း *taung-tan*
mountaineer *(n.)* တောင်တက်သမား *taung-tat-ta-mar*
mountainous *(adj.)* တောင်ထူထပ်သော *taung-htu-htet-taw*
mourn *(v.)* ကြေကွဲသည် *kyay-kwal-the*
mourner *(n.)* အသုဘပို့လိုက်သူ *a-tu-ba-boe-lite-thu*
mournful *(n.)* ဝမ်းနည်းကြေကွဲသော *wan-nae-kyay-kwe-taw*
mourning *(n.)* ဝမ်းနည်းကြေကွဲခြင်း *wan-nae-kyay-kwe-chin*
mouse *(n.)* ကြွက် *kywat*
moustache *(n.)* နှုတ်ခမ်းမွေး *hnote-khan-mway*
mouth *(v.)* တီးတိုးရေရွတ်သည် *ti-toe-yay-yut-the*
mouth *(n.)* ပါးစပ် *par-sat*
mouthful *(n.)* ပါးစပ်အပြည့် *par-sat-a-pyae*
movable *(adj.)* ရွှေ့ပြောင်းနိုင်သော *shway-pyaung-nai-taw*
movables *(n.)* ရွှေ့ပြောင်းနိုင်သော ပစ္စည်းများ *shway-pyaung-nai-taw-pyit-see*
move *(n.)* ရွှေ့ပြောင်းခြင်း *shway-pyaung-chin*
movement *(n.)* လှုပ်ရှားမှု *lote-shar-mu*
mover *(n.)* သွားလာလှုပ်ရှားတတ်သူ *twar-lar-lote-shar-tat-thu*
movies *(n.)* ရုပ်ရှင် *yoke-shin*
mow *(v.)* ရိတ်သည်၊ ဖြတ်သည် *yeik-the, phat-the*
much *(adv.)* များများ *myar-myar*

much *(adj.)* များပြားသော *myar-pyar-taw*
mucilage *(n.)* စေးကပ်ကပ်အရာ *say-kat-kat-a-yar*
muck *(n.)* တိရစ္ဆာန်ချေး *ta-yeik-san-chay*
mucous *(adj.)* အကျိအချွဲဖြစ်သော *a-kyi-a-chwe-phit-taw*
mucus *(n.)* အကျိအချွဲ *a-kyi-a-chwe*
mud *(n.)* ရွှံ့ *shwunt*
muddle *(v.)* ကမောက်ကမဖြစ်စေသည် *ka-mauk-ka-ma-phit-say-the*
muddle *(n.)* စိတ်ရှုပ်ခြင်း *seik-shoke-chin*
muffle *(v.)* ခြုံသည်၊ ထွေးသည် *chone-the, htway-the*
muffler *(n.)* ခြုံခြင်း *chon-chin*
mug *(n.)* မတ်ခွက် *mat-khwat*
muggy *(adj.)* အိုက်စပ်စပ်ဖြစ်သော *aik-sat-sat-phit-taw*
mulatto *(n.)* လူဖြူလူမည်းကပြား *lu-phyu-lu-mae-ka-pyar*
mulberry *(n.)* ပိုးစာပင် *poe-sar-pin*
mule *(n.)* လား *lar*
mulish *(adj.)* ခေါင်းမာသော *gaung-mar-taw*
mull *(n.)* အချိန်ယူစဉ်းစားခြင်း *a-chain-yu-sin-sar-chin*
mullah *(n.)* မွတ်စလင် ဘာသာရေးခေါင်းဆောင် *mu-sa-lin-bar-tar-yay-gaung-saung*
mullion *(n.)* ဒေါင်လိုက် ပြတင်းတိုင် *daung-lite-pya-tin-tai*
multifarious *(adj.)* အထူးထူး အပြားပြားဖြစ်သော *a-htoo-htoo-a-pyar-pyar-phit-taw*
multiform *(n.)* ပုံစံအမျိုးမျိုး *pon-san-a-myo-myo*
multilateral *(adj.)* နှစ်ဦးနှစ်ဖက် *na-oo-na-phat*
multilingual *(adj.)* ဘာသာစကားပေါင်းစုံ ပြောသော *bar-tar-sa-kar-paung-sone-pyaw-taw*
multiparous *(adj.)* ကလေးနှစ်ယောက်ထက် ပိုရှိသော *ka-lay-na-yaut-htet-po-shi-taw*
multiped *(n.)* ခြေများသော သတ္တဝါ *kyay-myar-taw-tat-ta-war*
multiple *(n.)* ဆတိုးကိန်း *sa-toe-kein*
multiple *(adj.)* ပေါင်းစုံ *paung-sone*
multiplex *(adj.)* ရှုပ်ရှင်ရုံကြီး *yoke-shin-yone-gyi*
multiplicand *(n.)* အခြားဂဏန်းနှင့် မြှောက်ခံရသော ဂဏန်း *a-char-ga-nan-nint-myaut-khan-ya-taw-ga-nan*
multiplication *(n.)* မြှောက်ခြင်း၊ ဆတိုးခြင်း *hmauk-chin, sa-toe-chin*
multiplicity *(n.)* မျိုးစုံ *moe-sone*
multiply *(v.)* မြှောက်သည်၊ တိုးပွားသည် *hmyauk-the, toe-pwar-the*
multitude *(n.)* အမြောက်အမြား *a-myauk-a-myar*
mum *(adj.)* နှုတ်ဆိတ်သော *note-seik-taw*
mumble *(v.)* မပွင့်တပွင့် ပြောသည် *ma-pwint-ta-pwint-pyaw-the*
mummer *(n.)* စကားမပြောဘဲ ကပြသည့် ရှေးပုံစံပြဇာတ်တွင် သရုပ်ဆောင်သူ *sa-kar-ma-pyaw-bae-ka-pya-the-shay-pon-san-pya-zat-twin-ta-yoke-saung-thu*
mummy *(n.)* မေမေ *may-may*
mumps *(n.)* ပါးချိတ်ရောင်နာ *par-chate-yaung-nar*
munch *(v.)* မြုံ့သည် *myone-the*
mundane *(adj.)* သူလိုငါလို *thu-lo-ngar-lo*

municipal *(adj.)* စည်ပင်သာယာ *si-pin-tar-yar*
municipality *(n.)* စည်ပင်သာယာရေးအဖွဲ့ *si-pin-tar-yar-yay-a-phwe*
munificent *(adj.)* အလွန်ရက်ရောသော *a-lun-yat-yaw-thaw*
munitions *(n.)* စစ်လက်နက် ပစ္စည်း *sit-lat-nat-pyit-see*
mural *(n.)* နံရံဆေးရေးပန်းချီ *nan-yan-say-yay-pan-chee*
mural *(adj.)* နံရံဆေးရေး *nan-yan-say-yay*
murder *(n.)* လူသတ်မှု *lu-tat-mu*
murderer *(n.)* လူသတ်သမား *lu-tat-ta-mar*
murderous *(adj.)* လူသတ်ရန် ဝန်မလေးသော *lu-tat-yan-win-ma-lay-taw*
murmur *(v.)* တီးတိုးစကား *ti-toe-sa-kar*
murmur *(n.)* တီးတိုးပြောသည် *ti-toe-pyaw-the*
muscle *(n.)* ကြွက်သား *kywat-tar*
muscovite *(n.)* အဖြိုက်ကျောက် *a-phyike kyauk*
muscular *(adj.)* ကြွက်သားဆိုင်ရာ *kywat-tar-sai-yar*
muse *(n.)* အနုပညာစျန်ဝင်စားခြင်း *a-nu-pyin-nyar-zan-win-sar-chin*
museum *(n.)* ပြတိုက် *pya-tite*
mush *(n.)* ပျော့ပြဲသော အရာ *pyawt-pyae-taw-a-yar*
mushroom *(n.)* မှို *hmo-tat-taw*
music *(n.)* ဂီတ *gi-ta*
musical *(adj.)* ဂီတနှင့် ဆိုင်သော *gi-ta-nint-sai-taw*
musician *(n.)* ဂီတပညာရှင် *gi-ta-pyin-nyar-shin*
musk *(n.)* ကတိုး *ka-toe*
musket *(n.)* ပြောင်းချောသေနတ် *pyaung-chaw-ta-nat*
musketeer *(n.)* ပြောင်းချောသေနတ်ကိုင်စစ်သား *pyaung-chaw-ta-nat-kai-sit-tar*
muslim *(adj.)* မူစလင်ဘာသာဝင် *mu-sa-lin-bar-tar-win*
muslin *(n.)* ခါသာပိတ်သား *khar-tar-pate-tar*
must *(n.)* မဖြစ်မနေ လုပ်ရမည့် အရာ *ma-phit-ma-nay-lote-ya-me-a-yar*
mustache *(n.)* နှုတ်ခမ်းမွေး *note-khan-hmway*
mustang *(n.)* အမေရိကန် မြင်းရိုင်း *a-may-ri-kan-myine-yai*
mustard *(n.)* အဝါဖျော့ရောင် *a-war-phaw-yaung*
muster *(n.)* လူစုခြင်း *lu-su-chin*
muster *(v.)* စစ်သားများ တန်းစီသည် *sit-tar-myar-tan-si-the*
musty *(adj.)* အောက်သော၊ သိုးသော *awt-taw, toe-taw*
mutation *(n.)* သန္ဓေပြောင်းခြင်း *ta-day-pyaung-chin*
mutative *(adj.)* သန္ဓေပြောင်းသော *ta-day-pyaung-taw*
mute *(n.)* ဆွံ့အသူ *sunt-a-thu*
mutidisciplinary *(adj.)* ဘာသာရပ်ပေါင်းစုံမှ ပါဝင်သော *bar-tar-yat-paung-sone-ma-par-win-taw*
mutilate *(v.)* ပုံပျက်အောင် ဖျက်ဆီးသည် *pon-pyat-aung-phat-see-the*
mutilation *(n.)* အင်္ဂါချွတ်ယွင်းခြင်း *in-gar-chyut-ywin-chin*
mutinous *(adj.)* အာဏာဖီဆန်သော *ar-nar-phi-san-taw*
mutiny *(v.)* သူပုန်ထသည် *ta-pon-hta-the*

mutiny *(n.)* ပုန်ကန်မှု *pon-kan-mu*

mutter *(v.)* ရေရွတ်သည် *yay-yut-the*

mutton *(n.)* သိုးသား *toe-dar*

mutual *(adj.)* အပြန်အလှန် *a-pyan-a-lan*

muzzle *(v.)* နှုတ်စွပ်စွပ်သည်၊ နှုတ်ပိတ်သည် *note-sut-sut-the, note-pate-the*

muzzle *(n.)* နှုတ်သီးစွပ်၊ သေနတ်ပြောင်းဝ *note-thee-sut, tay-nat-pyaung-wa*

my *(adj.)* ကျွန်တော်၏ *kyun-taw-ei*

myalgia *(n.)* ကြွက်သားနာကျင်ခြင်း *kywat-tar-nar-kyin-chin*

myopia *(n.)* အဝေးမှုန်ခြင်း *a-way-hmone-chin*

myopic *(adj.)* အဝေးမှုန်သော *a-way-hmone-taw*

myosis *(n.* မျက်လုံးကြွက်သားကျုံ့ခြင်း *myat-lone-kwyat-tar-kyont-chin*

myriad *(adj.)* အမြောက်အမြား *a-myauk-a-myar*

myriad *(n.)* အနန္တ *a-nan-da*

myrrh *(n.)* မုရန်စေး *mu-yan-say*

myrtle *(n.)* ချုံပင် *chon-pin*

myself *(pron.)* ကျွန်တော်ကိုယ်တိုင် *kyun-taw-ko-tai*

mysterious *(adj.)* ထူးဆန်းသော *htoo-san-taw*

mystery *(n.)* ဆန်းဆန်းပြားပြား အရာ *san-san-pyar-pyar-ayar*

mystic *(n.)* အသိဉာဏ်ထူးကို ရသော ပုဂ္ဂိုလ် *a-ti-nyan-htoo-ko-ya-taw-poke-ko*

mystic *(adj.)* ထူးခြားဆန်းပြားသော *htoo-char-san-pyar-taw*

mysticism *(n.)* ထူးခြားသော ဉာဏ်အမြင်ကို ယုံကြည်သက်ဝင်မှု *htoo-char-taw-nyan-a-myin-ko-yone-kyi-tat-win-mu*

mystify *(v.)* မှင်သက်မိစေသည် *hmin-tat-mi-say-the*

mystique *(n.)* တန်းခိုး၏ သွင်ပြင် *tan-kho-ei-twin-pyin*

myth *(n.)* ဒဏ္ဍာရီ *dan-tar-yi*

mythical *(adj.)* ဒဏ္ဍာရီလာ *dan-tar-yi-lar*

mythological *(adj.)* ဒဏ္ဍာရီလာ *dan-tar-yi-lar*

mythology *(n.)* ဒဏ္ဍာရီ *dan-tar-yi*

N

nab *(v.)* ဖမ်းသည် *phan-the*

nabob *(n.)* အလွန်ချမ်းသာသူ *a-lun-chan-tar-thu*

nacho *(n.)* မက္ကဆီကို ချာပါတီ *ma-si-ko-char-par-tee*

nack *(v.)* အပျက်သဘောဆန်ဆန် အသိအမှတ်ပြုသည် *a-pyat-ta-baw-san-san-ta-ti-a-mat-pyu-the*

nacre *(n.)* နာကာမုတ်ကောင် *na-kar-mote-kaung*

nadger *(n.)* ဝေးစေ့ *way-sae*

nadir *(n.)* အောက်ဆုံး *awt-sone*

nag *(v.)* နားပူနားဆာလုပ်သည် *na-pu-na-sar-lote-the*

nag *(n.)* မြင်းအိုမြင်းနာ *myin-oh-myin-nar*

nagging *(adj.)* ခပ်ပျော့ပျော့ဆက်တိုက်နာသော *khat-pyawt-pyawt-sat-tite-nar-taw*

nail *(v.)* ဖမ်းဆီးသည် *phan-see-the*

nail *(n.)* လက်သည်း၊ သံ *lat-the, tan*

naive *(adj.)* အတွေ့အကြုံမရှိသော *a-tway-a-kyone-ma-shi-taw*

naivete *(n.)* နုံအခြင်း *hnon-a-chin*

naivety *(n.)* နုံအခြင်း *hnon-a-chin*

naked *(adj.)* ကိုယ်တုံးလုံး *ko-tone-lone*

name *(n.)* နာမည် *na-mal*

namely *(adv.)* အတိအကျပြောရသော် *a-ti-a-kya-pyaw-ya-taw*

nameplate *(n.)* နာမည်တံဆိပ်ပြား *na-mal-ta-seik-pyar*

namesake *(n.)* နာမည်တူ *na-mal-thu*

nanism *(n.)* ပုံမမှန်စွာ သေးငယ်ခြင်း *pon-ma-man-tay-nge-taw*

nanite *(n.)* နာနိုစက်ရုပ် *na-no-sat-yoke*

nanny *(n.)* ကလေးထိန်း *ka-lay-htein*

nano *(n.)* နာနိုနည်းပညာ *na-no-nee-pyin-nyar*

nanobiology *(n.)* နာနိုဇီဝဗေဒ *na-no-zi-wa-bay-da*

nanobot *(n.)* နာနိုစက်ရုပ် *na-no-sat-yoke*

nanochip *(n.)* နာနိုဆားကစ်ပြား *na-no-sar-kit-pyar*

nanocircuitry *(n.)* နာနိုလျှပ်စစ်ပတ်လမ်းစနစ် *na-no-hlyat-sit-pat-lan-sa-nit*

nanocomponent *(n.)* နာနိုအစိတ်အပိုင်း *na-no-a-seit-a-pai*

nanocomputer *(n.)* နာနိုကွန်ပျူတာ *na-no-kun-pyu-tar*

nanoengineer *(n.)* နာနိုအင်ဂျင်နီယာ *na-no-in-gyin-na-yar*

nanohertz *(n.)* နာနိုဟတ် *na-no-hat*

nanomechanics *(n.)* နာနိုမက္ကင်းနစ်ပညာ *na-no-ma-kin-nit-pin-nyar*

nanoparticle *(n.)* နာနိုအမှုန် *na-no-a-hmone*

nanoplasma *(n.)* နာနိုသွေးရည်ကြည် *na-no-thway-yay-kyi*

nanotransistor *(n.)* နာနိုထရန်စစ္စတာ *na-no-hta-ran-sis-sa-tar*

nap *(n.)* တစ်မှေးအိပ်ခြင်း *ta-may-ate-chin*

nape *(n.)* ကုပ်ပိုး *gote-poe*

naphthalene *(n.)* ပရုပ်လုံး *pa-yoke-lone*

napkin *(n.)* လက်ကိုင်ပဝါ *lat-kai-pa-war*

narcissism *(n.)* အတ္တပေမဝါဒ *at-ta-pay-ma-war-da*

narcissus *(n.)* ဥပေါက်အပင် *au-pauk-a-pin*

narcosis *(n.)* ဆေး၊ ဓာတုပစ္စည်းကြောင့် သတိမေ့ခြင်း *say-dar-tu-pyit-see-kyaunt-ta-di-mae-chin*

narcotic *(n.)* မူးယစ်ဆေးဝါး *mu-yit-say-war*

narrate *(v.)* ဇာတ်ကြောင်းပြန်ပြောသည် *zat-kyaung-pyan-pyaw-the*

narration *(n.)* ဇာတ်ကြောင်းပြန်ခြင်း *zat-kyaung-pyan-chin*

narrative *(adj.)* ဇာတ်လမ်း *zat-lan*

narrative *(n.)* ဇာတ်လမ်း *zat-lan*

narrator *(n.)* ဇာတ်ကြောင်းပြန်ပြောသူ *zat-lan-pyan-pyaw-thu*

narrow *(v.)* ကျဉ်းသည် *kyin-the*

narrow *(adj.)* ကျဉ်းသော *kyin-thaw*

nasal *(n.)* နှာခေါင်း *hnar-khaung*

nascent *(adj.)* ဖွံ့ဖြိုးစ *phwint-phyo-sa*

nasty *(adj.)* မနှစ်မြို့ဖွယ် *ma-nit-myo-phwal*

natal *(adj.)* မွေးဖွားခြင်းနှင့်ဆိုင်သော *mway-phwar-chin-nint-sai-taw*

natant *(adj.)* ပေါလောပေါ်ခြင်း၊ ရေကူးခြင်း *paw-law-paw-chin, yay-ku-chin*

nation *(n.)* နိုင်ငံ *nai-ngan*

national *(adj.)* နိုင်ငံဆိုင်ရာ *nai-ngan-sai-yar*

nationalism *(n.)* နိုင်ငံချစ်စိတ်ဓာတ် *nai-ngan-chit-seik-dat*

nationalist *(n.)* အမျိုးသားရေး *a-myo-tar-yay*

nationality *(n.)* နိုင်ငံသား *nai-ngan-tar*

nationalization *(n.)* နိုင်ငံပိုင်ပြုခြင်း *nai-ngan-pai-pyu-chin*

nationalize *(v.)* နိုင်ငံပိုင်ပြုသည် *nai-ngan-pai-pyu-the*

native *(n.)* ဇာတိ *zar-ti*

native *(adj.)* ဇာတိ *zar-ti*

nativity *(n.)* ခရစ်တော် ဖွားမြင်ခန်းရုပ်ပုံ *kha-yit-taw-phwar-myin-khan-yoke-pon*

natural *(adj.)* သဘာဝ *ta-bar-wa*

naturalist *(n.)* သဘာဝလောကပညာရှင် *ta-bar-wa-law-ka-pyin-nyar-shin*

naturalize *(v.)* နိုင်ငံသားအဖြစ် ခံယူသည် *nai-ngan-tar-a-phit-khan-yu-the*

naturally *(adv.)* သဘာဝအားဖြင့် *ta-bar-wa-ar-phint*

nature *(n.)* သဘာဝ *ta-bar-wa*

naughty *(adj.)* ဆိုးသော *soe-taw*

nausea *(n.)* ပျို့ခြင်း *pyoe-chin*

nautic(al) *(adj.)* သင်္ဘော ရေကြောင်းနှင့် ဆိုင်သော *tin-baw-yay-kyaung-nint-sai-taw*

naval *(adj.)* ရေတပ်နှင့် ဆိုင်သော *yay-tat-nint-sai-taw*

nave *(n.)* ခရစ်ယာန်ဘုရားရှိခိုးသူ ထိုင်ရာ နေရာ *kha-yit-yan-pha-yar-shi-kho-thu-htai-yar-nay-yar*

navigable *(adj.)* လှေ၊ သင်္ဘောများ သွားလာနိုင်သော *hlay-tin-baw-myar-twar-lar-nai-taw*

navigate *(v.)* လမ်းညွှန်အတိုင်း သွားသည် *lan-nyun-a-tai-twar-the*

navigation *(n.)* မောင်းနှင်သွားလာခြင်း *maung-hnin-twar-lar-chin*

navigator *(n.)* လေကြောင်းပြ၊ လမ်းညွှန် *lay-kyaung-pya, lan-hnyun*

navy *(n.)* ရေတပ် *yay-tat*

nay *(adv.)* ထိုမျှမက *hto-mya-ma-ka*

neap *(adj.)* ရေသေ *yay-tay*

near *(v.)* နီးသည် *nee-the*

near *(adj.)* နီးသော *nee-taw*

nearly *(adv.)* လုနီးပါး *lu-nee-par*

neat *(adj.)* သပ်ရပ်သော *tat-yat-taw*

nebula *(n.)* နက်ဗျူလာဓာတ်ငွေ့ထု *nat-byu-lar-dat-ngwe-htu*

necessary *(adj.)* လိုအပ်သော *lo-at-taw*

necessary *(n.)* လိုအပ်သော အရာများ *lo-at-taw-a-yar-myar*

necessitate *(v.)* လိုအပ်လာသည် *lo-at-lar-the*

necessity *(n.)* လိုအပ်ခြင်း *lo-at-chin*

neck *(n.)* လည်ပင်း *lal-pin*

necklace *(n.)* လည်ဆွဲ *lal-swal*

necklet *(n.)* လည်ဆွဲ *lal-swal*

necromancer *(n.)* အောက်လမ်းဆရာ *awt-lan-sa-yar*

necropolis *(n.)* ရှေးသင်္ချိုင်းကြီး *shay-tin-gyai-gyi*

nectar *(n.)* ဝတ်ရည် *wit-yay*

need *(v.)* လိုအပ်သည် *lo-at-the*

need *(n.)* လိုအပ်ချက် *lo-at-chat*

needful *(adj.)* လိုအပ်သော *lo-at-taw*

needle *(n.)* အပ် *at*

needless *(adj.)* မလိုအပ်သော *ma-lo-at-taw*

needs *(adv.)* လိုအပ်ချက်များ *lo-at-chat-myar*

needy *(adj.)* ဆင်းရဲသော *sin-ye-taw*

nefarious *(adj.)* ယုတ်မာသော *yoke-mar-taw*
negate *(v.)* အချည်းနှီးဖြစ်စေသည် *a-chee-nee-phit-say-the*
negation *(n.)* ဆန့်ကျင်ခြင်း *sant-kyin-chin*
negative *(v.)* ဆန့်ကျင်သည် *sant-kyin-the*
negative *(adj.)* ဆန့်ကျင်သော *sant-kyin-taw-sa-kar*
neglect *(n.)* ပစ်ထားခြင်း *pyit-htar-chin*
negligence *(n.)* ပေ့ါဆမှု *pot-sa-mu*
negligent *(adj.)* ပေ့ါဆသော *pot-sa-taw*
negligible *(adj.)* မပြောပလောက်သော *ma-pyaw-pa-laut-taw*
negotiable *(adj.)* ညှိနှိုင်းနိုင်သော *nyi-nai-nai-taw*
negotiate *(v.)* စေ့စပ်ဆွေးနွေးသည် *say-sat-sway-nway-the*
negotiation *(n.)* စေ့စပ်ဆွေးနွေးခြင်း *say-sat-sway-nway-chin*
negotiator *(n.)* စေ့စပ်ဆွေးနွေးသူ *say-sat-sway-nway-thu*
negress *(n.)* နီဂရိုးမ *ne-ga-ro-ma*
negro *(n.)* နီဂရိုး *ne-ga-ro*
neigh *(n.)* ဟီသံ *hi-tan*
neigh *(v.)* ဟီသည် *hi-the*
neighbour *(n.)* အိမ်နီးချင်း *eain-nee-chin*
neighbourhood *(n.)* ရပ်ကွက် *yat-kwat*
neighbourly *(adj.)* ရိုင်းပင်းခင်မင်တတ်သော *yin-pin-khin-min-tat-taw*
neither *(conj.)* ဘယ်သူမျှ၊ တစ်ခုမျှ *bal-thu-mya, ta-khu-mya*
nemesis *(n.)* အကုသိုလ် ဝိပါက် *a-ku-tho-wi-pat*
neolithic *(adj.)* ကျောက်ခေတ်သစ် *kyauk-khit-tit*
neon *(n.)* နီယွန်ဓာတ်ငွေ့ *ni-yoon-dat-ngwe*
nephew *(n.)* တူ *tu*
nepotism *(n.)* ဆွေမျိုးကောင်းစားရေးဝါဒ *sway-myo-kaung-sar-yay-war-da*
Neptune *(n.)* နက်ပကျွန်းဂြိုလ် *nat-pa-kyun-gyo*
nerve *(n.)* အာရုံကြော *ar-yone-gyaw*
nerveless *(adj.)* ခွန်အားမရှိသော *khun-ar-ma-shi-taw*
nervous *(adj.)* ကြောက်ရွံ့သော *kyauk-shunt-taw*
nescience *(n.)* အသိပညာနည်းခြင်း *a-ti-pin-nyar-nae-chin*
nest *(n.)* အသိုက် *a-thaik*
nestle *(v.)* ထွေးပိုက်သည် *htway-pike-the*
nestling *(n.)* မပျံနိုင်သေးသော ငှက်ပေါက်စ *ma-pyan-nai-tay-taw-ngat-pauk-sa*
net *(v.)* ဖမ်းမိသည် *phan-mi-the*
net *(n.)* ပိုက်၊ ပိုက်ကွန် *pike, pike-kun*
nether *(adj.)* အောက်ပိုင်း *awt-pai*
netizen *(n.)* နက်လူ့အဖွဲ့အစည်း *net-lu-a-phwe-a-see*
nettle *(v.)* ဆွပေးသည် *swa-pay-the*
network *(n.)* ကွန်ရက် *kun-yat*
neurologist *(n.)* ဦးနှောက်နှင့် အာရုံကြောပါရဂူ *oo-naut-nint-arr-yone-kyaw-pa-ra-gu*
neurology *(n.)* အာရုံကြောဆိုင်ရာ ဆေးပညာ *arr-yone-kyaw-sai-yar-say-pyin-nyar*
neurosis *(n.)* စိတ်မူမမှန်သည့် စိတ်ရောဂါ *seik-mu-ma-hman-the-seik-yaw-gar*
neuter *(adj.)* နပုလ္လိင် *na-pone-lain*
neutral *(adj.)* ဘက်မလိုက် *bat-ma-lite*
neutralize *(v.)* အာနိသင်လျော့ပါးစေသည် *arr-ni-tin-shawt-par-say-the*

neutron *(n.)* နျူထရွန် *nyu-hta-ron*

never *(adv.)* ဘယ်တော့မှ *bal-taw-ma*

never-ending *(adj.)* မပြီးနိုင် မဆုံးနိုင်သော *ma-pi-nai-ma-sone-nai-taw*

nevertheless *(conj.)* မည်သို့ပင်ဖြစ်စေ *me-tho-pin-phit-say*

new *(adj.)* အသစ် *a-thit*

newborn *(adj.)* မွေးကင်းစ *mway-kin-sa*

news *(n.)* သတင်း *ta-din*

newspaper *(n.)* သတင်းစာ *ta-din-sar*

next *(adv.)* နောက် *naut*

next *(adj.)* ထို့နောက် *htoe-naut*

nib *(n.)* ကလောင်သွား *ka-laung-twar*

nibble *(n.)* တစ်တိတစ်တိစားခြင်း *ta-ti-ta-ti-sar-chin*

nibble *(v.)* တစ်တိတစ်တိစားသည် *ta-ti-ta-ti-sar-the*

nice *(adj.)* ကောင်းသော *kaung-aw*

nicely *(adv.)* သပ်သပ်ရပ်ရပ် *tat-tat-yat-yat*

nicety *(n.)* အတိအကျ *a-ti-a-kya*

niche *(n.)* နံရံကလိုင်ပေါက် *nan-yan-ka-hlai-pauk*

nick *(n.)* အနည်းငယ်ဖြတ်ညှပ်ခြင်း *a-nae-ngal-phyat-nyat-chin*

nickel *(n.)* နီကယ်ဒြပ်စင် *nee-kal-drat-sin*

nickname *(v.)* နာမည်ပြောင်ခေါ်သည် *na-mal-pyaung-khaw-the*

nickname *(n.)* နာမည်ပြောင် *nar-mal-pyaung*

nicotine *(n.)* နီကိုတင်းဓာတ် *ni-ko-tin-dat*

niece *(n.)* တူမ *tu-ma*

niggard *(n.)* နှမြောတွန့်တိုခြင်း *na-myaw-tunt-to-chin*

niggardly *(adj.)* နှမြောတွန့်တိုသော *na-myaw-tunt-to-chin*

nigger *(n.)* လူမည်း luu-mae

nigh *(adv.)* နီးပြီ nee-pye

night *(n.)* ည nya

night shelter *(n.)* ညအိပ်အဆောက်အအုံ *nya-aik-a-saut-a-ohn*

nightie *(n.)* ညအိပ်ဝတ်စုံ *nya-aik-wit-sone*

nightingale *(n.)* ညတေးသီငှက် nya-tayy-te-nghaat

nightly *(adv.)* ညစဉ်ညတိုင်း nya-hcain-nya-tine

nightmare *(n.)* အိပ်မက်ဆိုး ain-mat-soe

nihilism *(n.)* ဘုရားမဲ့ဝါဒ pha-yar-mae-war-da

nil *(n.)* မရှိ ma-shi

nimble *(adj.)* သွက်လက်ကျွမ်းကျင်သော twat-lat-kyan-kyin-taw

nimbus *(n.)* မိုးမည်းတိမ်တောင် moe-mae-tain-taung

nine *(n.)* ကိုး koe

nineteen *(n.)* တစ်ဆယ့်ကိုး ta-sae-koe

nineteenth *(adj.)* တစ်ဆယ့်ကိုးခုမြောက် ta-sae-koe-hku-myauk

ninetieth *(adj.)* ကိုးဆယ်ခုမြောက် koe-sal-hku-myauk

ninety *(n.)* ကိုးဆယ် koe-sal

ninth *(adj.)* ကိုးခုမြောက် koe-hku-myauk

nip *(v.)* ဖျစ်သည် hpyit-te

nipple *(n.)* နို့သီး nhoe-tee

nitrogen *(n.)* နိုက်ထရိုဂျင်ဓာတ်ငွေ့ nite-hta-ro-gyin-dhat-ngwae

no *(adj.)* မရှိ ma-shi

nobility *(n.)* မြင့်မြတ်ခြင်း myint-myat-chin

noble *(n.)* ဆွေကြီးမျိုးကြီး sway-kyee-myoe-kyee

nobleman *(n.)* **ဆွေကြီးမျိုးကြီး** sway-kyee-myoe-kyee
nobly *(adv.)* **မြင့်မြတ်စွာ** myint-myat-swar
nobody *(pron.)* **မည်သူမှ** me-tuu-mha
nocturnal *(adj.)* **ညမှ ကျက်စားသော** nya-mha-kyet-sarr-taw
nod *(n.)* **ခေါင်းညိတ်ခြင်း** hkaung-gnyate-chin
noddle *(v)* **ဆက်တိုက်ခေါင်းညိတ်ခြင်း** *sat-tite-hkaung-gnyate-chin*
node *(n.)* **အဖုငယ်** a-hpu-ngaal
noise *(n.)* **ဆူညံသံ** suu-nyan-tan
noiseless *(adj.)* **မသံမထွက်သော** ma-tan-ma-htwat-taw
noisy *(adj.)* **ဆူညံသော** suu-nyan-taw
nomad *(n.)* **ရေကြည်ရာမြက်နုရာ လှည့်လည်နေထိုင်သူ** yay-kyi-yar-myat-nu-yar-hlae-lal-nay-htine-tuu
nomadic *(adj.)* **ရေကြည်ရာမြက်နုရာ လှည့်လည်နေထိုင်သော** yay-kyi-yar-myat-nu-yar-hlae-lal-nay-htine-taw
nomenclature *(n.)* **အမည်ပေးစနစ်** a-me-pay-sa-nit
nominal *(adj.)* **အမည်ခံ** a-me-hkan
nominate *(v.)* **အဆိုပြုသည်** a-so-pyu-te
nomination *(n.)* **အဆိုပြုခြင်း** a-so-pyu-chin
nominee *(n.)* **အဆိုပြုခံရသူ** a-so-pyu-hkan-ya-tuu
non-alcoholic *(adj.)* **အရက်မပါသော** a-yat-ma-par-taw
non-alignment *(n.)* **ဘက်မလိုက်ရေးဝါဒ** bhat-ma-lite-ray-war-da
nonchalance *(n.)* **မတူညီခြင်း၊ ဂရုမစိုက်ခြင်း** *ma-tu-nyi-chin, ga-yu-ma-site-chin*
nonchalant *(adj.)* **မတူညီသော၊ ဂရုမစိုက်သော** *ma-tu-nyi-taw, ga-yu-ma-site-taw*
non-disclosure *(n.)* **ထုတ်ဖော်မပြောခြင်း** *htoke-hpaw-ma-pyaw-chin*
none *(adv.)* **ဘာမျှ ထူးပြီး** Bhar-mya-htuu-pyee
none *(pron.)* **တစ်ယောက်မျှ** Ta-yout-mya
nonentity *(n.)* **အညတြ** a-nya-ta-ya
nonetheless *(adv.)* **မည်သို့ပင်ဖြစ်စေ** me-toe-pin-hpyit-say
nonpareil *(n.)* **ပြိုင်စံရှား** pyaine-san-sharr
nonpareil *(adj.)* **ပြိုင်စံရှား** pyaine-san-sharr
nonplus *(v.)* **မှင်သက်မိသည်** hmin-tat-mi-te
non-profit *(adj.)* **အကျိုးအမြတ်မပါသော** a-kyoe-a-myat-ma-par-taw
nonsense *(n.)* **အဓိပ္ပါယ်မဲ့စကား** a-date-pal-mae-sa-karr
nonsensical *(adj.)* **အဓိပ္ပါယ်မဲ့သော** a-date-pal-mae-taw
non-stick *(adj.)* **မကပ်သော** ma-kat-taw
non-stop *(adj.)* **ဆက်တိုက်** sat-tite
noodle *(n.)* **ခေါက်ဆွဲ** hkout-swal
nook *(n.)* **ချောင်ကြိုချောင်ကြား** kyaung-kyo-kyaung-kyarr
noon *(n.)* **မွန်းတည့်** mwann-tae
noose *(n.)* **ကြိုးကွင်း** kyoe-kwin
nor *(conj.)* **သော်လည်းကောင်း** taw-lae-kaung
Nordic *(adj.)* **စကင်ဒီနေးဗီးယားနှင့်ဆိုင်သော** sa-kan-de-nayy-bee-yarr-nint-sine-taw
norm *(n.)* **စံ** san
normal *(adj.)* **သာမန်** tar-man

normalcy *(n.)* **နဂိုအခြေအနေ** na-go-a-chay-a-nay
normalization *(n.)* **ပုံမှန်ပြန်ဖြစ်အောင်လုပ်ခြင်း** pone-maan-pyan-hpyit-aung-lote-chinn
normalize *(v.)* **ပုံမှန်ပြန်ဖြစ်အောင်လုပ်သည်** pone-maan-pyan-hpyit-aung-lote-tai
north *(adj.)* **မြောက်ဘက်** myauk-bhat
north *(n.)* **မြောက်အရပ်** myauk-a-yat
northerly *(adv.)* **မြောက်ဘက်သို့** myauk-bhaat-thoet
northerly *(adj.)* **မြောက်ဘက်သွား** myauk-bhaat-twarr
northern *(adj.)* **မြောက်ဘက်** myauk-bhaat
nose *(v.)* **အနံ့ခံသည်** a-nant-hkan-te
nose *(n.)* **နှာခေါင်း** nhar-hkaung
nosegay *(n.)* **ပန်းစည်း** pann-saee
nosey *(adj.)* **စပ်စုသော** sat-su-taw
nostalgia *(n.)* **အတိတ်ကို တသလွမ်းဆွတ်ခြင်း** a-tate-ko-ta-ta-lwan-sut-chinn
nostril *(n.)* **နှာပေါက်** nhar-pout
nostrum *(n.)* **ရမ်းကုဆေး** yan-ku-say
nosy *(adj.)* **စပ်စုသော** sat-su-taw
not *(adv.)* **မဟုတ်** ma-hote
notability *(n.)* **ထင်ရှားသော ပုဂ္ဂိုလ်** htin-shar-taw-poke-ko
notable *(adj.)* **ထင်ရှားသော** htin-shar-taw
notary *(n.)* **နိုထရီ** no-hta-re
notation *(n.)* **သင်္ကေတစနစ်** tin-kay-ta-sa-nit
notch *(n.)* **အထစ်** a-htait
note *(v.)* **ဂရုပြုသည်** ga-ru-pyu-te
note *(n.)* **မှတ်စု** mhat-su
noteworthy *(adj.)* **သတိပြုဖွယ်** ta-ti-pyu-hpwal
nothing *(adv.)* **နတ္ထိ** nat-hti
nothing *(n.)* **မရှိ** ma-shi
notice *(v.)* **သတိပြုမိသည်** ta-ti-pyu-mi-te
notice *(n.)* **အာရုံစိုက်ခြင်း** ar-yone-site-chinn
notification *(n.)* **ဆင့်ခေါ်စာ** sint-hkaw-sar
notify *(v.)* **အကြောင်းကြားသည်** a-kyaung-kyar-te
notion *(n.)* **အယူအဆ** a-yuu-a-sa
notional *(adj.)* **အထင်အရ** a-htin-a-ya
notoriety *(n.)* **နာမည်ဆိုးဖြင့် ကျော်ကြားခြင်း** na-mal-soe-hpyint-kyaw-kyar-chinn
notorious *(adj.)* **နာမည်ဆိုးဖြင့် ကျော်ကြားသော** na-mai-soe-hpyint-kyaw-kyarr-taw
notwithstanding *(prep.)* **ပါလျက်** par-lyet
nought *(n.)* **သုည** ton-nya
noun *(n.)* **နာမ်** narm
nourish *(v.)* **အာဟာရ ဖြစ်စေသည်** a-har-hpyit-say-te
nourishment *(n.)* **အာဟာရဓာတ်** a-har-a-dhat
novel *(adj.)* **ဆန်းသစ်သော** san-tit-taw
novelette *(n.)* **ဝတ္ထုလတ်** wut-htu-lat
novelist *(n.)* **ဝတ္ထုရေးဆရာ** wit-htu-yay-sa-yar
novelty *(n.)* **အသစ်အဆန်း** a-tit-a-san
November *(n.)* **နိုဝင်ဘာလ** no-win-bhar-la
novice *(n.)* **လက်သင်** lat-tin
now *(conj.)* **လို့မို့** loet-mhoet
now *(adv.)* **ယခုအချိန်** ya-hku-a-chane

nowhere *(adv.)* ဘယ်မှာမှ bal-mar-mha

noxious *(adj.)* အန္တရာယ်ရှိသော an-ta-yal-shi-taw

nozzle *(n.)* နော်ဇယ် naw-zal

nuance *(n.)* မသိမသာကွဲပြားချက် ma-ti-ma-tar-kwal-pyar-chet

nubile *(adj.)* မက်စဖွယ် mat-sa-hpwal

nuclear *(adj.)* နျူကလီးယား nyuu-ka-lee-yarr

nuclear family *(n.)* မိဘနှစ်ပါးနှင့် သားသမီးများသာပါသော မိသားစု mi-bha-na-par-nint-tar-ta-mee-myar-tar-par-taw mi-tarr-su

nucleus *(n.)* နျူကလိယ nyuu-ka-li-ya

nude *(n.)* အဝတ်ဗလာအနုပညာ a-wut-ba-lar-a-nu-pyin-nyar

nudge *(v.)* တံတောင်ဖြင့် တွတ်သည် tan-daung-hpyint-twat-te

nudity *(n.)* အဖော်အချွတ် a-hpaw-a-chyaut

nugget *(n.)* မြေမှရသော သတ္တုအတုံးအခဲ myay-mha-ya-taw-tat-tu-a-tone-a-hkae

nuisance *(n.)* စိတ်ငြိုငြင်စရာ sate-ngyo-ngyin-sa-yar

null *(adj.)* တရားမဝင်သော ta-yar-ma-win-taw

nullification *(n.)* ပယ်ဖျက်ခြင်း pal-hpyet-chinn

nullify *(v.)* ပယ်ဖျက်သည် pal-hpyet-te

numb *(adj.)* ထုံသော htone-taw

number *(v.)* နံပါတ်တပ်သည် nan-pat-tat-tai

number *(n.)* ကိန်း၊ ဂဏန်း၊ နံပါတ် kein, ga-nan, nan-pat

numberless *(adj.)* မရေမတွက်နိုင်သော ma-yay-ma-twat-nine-taw

numeral *(n.)* ဂဏန်းခြေ ga-nan-chay

numerator *(n.)* ပိုင်းဝေ pine-way

numerical *(adj.)* ကိန်းဂဏန်းနှင့် သက်ဆိုင်သော kein-ga-nan-nint-tat-sine-taw

numerous *(adj.)* အမြောက်အမြား a-myauk-a-myar

nun *(n.)* သီလရှင် te-la-shin

nunnery *(n.)* သီလရှင်ကျောင်း te-la-shin-kyaung

nuptial *(adj.)* အိမ်ထောင်ပြုခြင်းနှင့် ဆိုင်သော ain-htaung-pyu-chin-hnint-sine-taw

nuptials *(n.)* မင်္ဂလာဆောင်ခြင်း main-ga-lar-saung-chinn

nurse *(v.)* သူနာပြုစုသည် tu-nar-pyu-su-tai

nurse *(n.)* သူနာပြု tu-nar-pyu

nursery *(n.)* ကလေးထိန်းကျောင်း ka-lay-htein-kyaung

nurture *(v.)* ပြုစုပျိုးထောင်သည် pyu-su-pyoe-htaung-tai

nurture *(n.)* စောင့်ရှောက်ခြင်း saunt-shout-chinn

nut *(v.)* ဒေါသူပုန်ထသည် daw-ta-pone-hta-tai

nutcase *(n.)* ငရူး nga-ruu

nuthouse *(n.)* အရူးထောင် a-ruu-htaung

nutmeg *(n.)* ဇာတိပ္ဖိုလ်သီး zar-tip-hpol-tee

nutrient *(n.)* အာဟာရဓာတ် a-har-a-dat

nutrition *(n.)* အာဟာရ a-har-ra

nutritious *(adj.)* အာဟာရဖြစ်သော a-har-ra-hpyit-taw

nutritive *(adj.)* အာဟာရ a-har-ra

nutty *(adj.)* ဆိမ့်သော seint-taw

nuzzle *(v.)* ပွတ်သီးပွတ်သပ်လုပ်သည် put-tee-put-tat-lote-tai

nylon *(n.)* နိုင်လွန် nine-lwan

nymph *(n.)* မြစ်စောင့်နတ်သမီး myit-saunt-nat-ta-mee

nymphet *(n.)* ယောကျာ်းများ ပစ်ကျရသည့် ချာတိတ်မ yauk-kyar-myar-pyit-kya-ya-taeet-char-tate-ma

nymphomaniac *(adj.)* ရာဂလွန်ကဲသော yar-ga-lwan-kell-taw

oaf *(n.)* အချိုးမပြေသူ a-choe-ma-pyay-tuu

oafish *(adj.)* ထုံအအ htone-a-a

oak *(n.)* ဝက်သစ်ချပင် wat-tit-cha-pin

oaktree *(n.)* ဝက်သစ်ချပင် wat-tit-cha-pin

oar *(n.)* ခတ်တက် hkat-tat

oarsman *(n.)* တက်ခတ်သမား tat-hkat-ta-mar

oasis *(n.)* အိုအေစစ် o-a-sit

oat *(n.)* မြင်းစားဂျုံ myin-sar-gyone

oath *(n.)* ကျမ်းသစ္စာ kyan-tit-sar

oathbreaker *(n.)* ကျမ်းသစ္စာဖောက်ဖျက်သူ kyan-tit-sar-hpout-hpyet-tuu

oathbreaking *(adj.)* ကျမ်းသစ္စာဖောက်ဖျက်ခြင်း kyan-tit-sar-hpout-hpyet-chin

oatmeal *(n.)* အုတ်ဂျုံမှုန့် ote-gyone-mone

obduct *(v.)* ဆွဲယူသည် swal-yu-the

obduction *(n.)* ဆွဲယူခြင်း swal-yu-chin

obduracy *(n.)* ခေါင်းမာခြင်း hkaung-mar-chinn

obdurate *(adj.)* ခေါင်းမာသော hkaungg - mar-taw

obedience *(n.)* နာခံခြင်း nar-hkan-chinn

obedient *(adj.)* နာခံတတ်သော nar-hkan-tat-taw

obeisance *(n.)* အရိုအသေ a-yo-a-tay

obese *(adj.)* အလွန်ဝသော a-lwan-wa-taw

obesity *(n.)* အလွန်ဝခြင်း a-lwan-wa-chinn

obey *(v.)* နာခံသည် nar-hkan-tai

obituary *(adj.)* နာရေးကြော်ငြာ nar-ray-kyay-nyar

object *(v.)* ကန့်ကွက်သည် kant-kwat-tai

objection *(n.)* ကန့်ကွက်ချက် kant-kwat-chet

objectionable *(adj.)* ကန့်ကွက်စရာ kant-kwat-sa-rar

objective *(adj.)* ဓမ္မဓိဌာန်ကျသော dham-ma-date-htan-kya-taw

oblation *(n.)* လှူဒါန်းခြင်း hlu-dan-chin

obligation *(n.)* တာဝန် tar-wan

obligatory *(adj.)* ဆောင်ရွက်ရန် တာဝန်ရှိသော saung-ywat-ran-tar-wan-shi-taw

oblige *(v.)* မလွှဲသာဖြစ်သည် ma-lwal-tar-hpyit-tai

oblique *(adj.)* တိုက်ရိုက်မဟုတ်သော tite-rite-ma-hote-taw

obliterate *(v.)* ချေဖျက်သည် chay-hpyet-tai

obliteration *(n.)* ချေဖျက်ခြင်း chay-hpyet-chinn

oblivion *(n.)* သတိလွတ်ခြင်း ta-ti-lwat-chinn

oblivious *(adj.)* သတိမမူသော ta-ti-ma-mu-taw

oblong *(adj.)* ထောင့်မှန်ပုံရှည် htaunt - mhan-pone-shay

obnoxious *(adj.)* စက်ဆုပ်ရွံရှာဖွယ် sat-sote-ywan-shar-hpwal

obscene *(adj.)* ညစ်ညမ်းသော nyit-nyam-taw
obscenity *(n.)* မဖွယ်မရာ ma-hpwal-ma-rar
obscure *(v.)* ပိတ်သည် pate-tai
obscure *(adj.)* မှေးမှိန်သော mhay-mhein-taw
obscurity *(n.)* မထင်ပေါ်ခြင်း ma-htain-paw-chinn
observance *(n.)* လိုက်နာခြင်း lite-nar-chinn
observant *(adj.)* မျက်စိရှင်သော myet-si-shin-taw
observation *(n.)* စောင့်ကြည့်ခြင်း sawnt-kyi-chinn
observatory *(n.)* စောင့်ကြည့်လေ့လာရာအဆောက်အအုံ saunt-kyi-lay-lar-rar-a-sout-a-ohn
observe *(v.)* စောင့်ကြည့်သည် saunt-kyi-tai
obsess *(v.)* စွဲလမ်းသည် swal-lam-tai
obsession *(n.)* စွဲလမ်းခြင်း swal-lam-chinn
obsessive *(adj.)* အစွဲအလမ်းကြီးလွန်းသော a-swal-a-lam-kyee-lwan-taw
obsolete *(adj.)* အသုံးမဝင်တော့သော a-tone-ma-win-tot-taw
obstacle *(n.)* အတားအဆီး a-tar-a-see
obstetric *(adj.)* သားဖွားပညာ tar-hpwar-pyin-nyar
obstetrician *(n.)* သားဖွားဆရာဝန် tar-hpwar-sa-rar-wan
obstinacy *(n.)* ခေါင်းမာခြင်း hkaung-mar-chinn
obstinate *(adj.)* ခေါင်းမာသော hkaung-mar-taw
obstruct *(v.)* ပိတ်ဆို့သည် pate-shoet-tai
obstruction *(n.)* ပိတ်ဆို့ခြင်း pate-shoet-chinn
obstructive *(adj.)* ပိတ်ဆို့သော pate-shoet-taw
obtain *(v.)* ရရှိသည် ra-shi-tai
obtainable *(adj.)* ရနိုင်သော ra-nine-taw
obtuse *(adj.)* ထူသော htuu-taw
obvious *(adj.)* ထင်ရှားပေါ်လွင်သော htain-shar-paw-lwin-taw
obviously *(adv.)* သိသိသာသာ ti-ti-tar-tar
occasion *(v.)* ဖြစ်ပေါ်စေသည် hpyit-paw-say-tai
occasion *(n.)* အခါ၊ အခိုက် a-hkar, a-hkite
occasional *(adj.)* အခါအားလျော်စွာ a-hkar-ar-lyaw-swar
occasionally *(adv.)* ရံဖန်ရံခါ ran-hpan-ran-hkar
occident *(n.)* အနောက်တိုင်း a-nout-tine
occidental *(adj.)* အနောက်တိုင်း a-nout-tine
occipital *(adj.)* နောက်စေ့ nout-sae
occlude *(v.)* စုပ်ယူသည်၊ ပိတ်သည် sote-yu-the, pate-the
occlusive *(adj.)* စုပ်ယူသော၊ ပိတ်သော sote-yu-taw, pate-taw
occult *(v.)* မြင်ကွင်းပိတ်သည် myin-kwin-pate-the
occupancy *(n.)* နေထိုင်မှု nay-htine-mhu
occupant *(n.)* အိမ်သူအိမ်သား ain-tuu-ain-tar
occupation *(n.)* အလုပ်အကိုင် a-lote-a-kine
occupied *(adj.)* သုံးစွဲနေသော tone-swal-nay-taw
occupier *(n.)* နေထိုင်သူ nay-htine-tuu
occupy *(v.)* သိမ်းပိုက်သည်၊ နေသည် taim-pite-tai, nay-tai
occur *(v.)* ဖြစ်ပွားသည် hpyit-pwar-tai

occurrence *(n.)* **အဖြစ်အပျက်** a-hpyit-a-pyet
ocean *(n.)* **သမုဒ္ဒရာ** ta-mode-ta-rar
oceanfront *(n.)* **သမုဒ္ဒရာရှေ့ရှိ ပိုင်ဆိုင်မှု** ta-mode-ta-rar-shae-shi-pai-sai-mu
oceanic *(adj.)* **အဏ္ဏဝါ** an-na-war
oceanographer *(n.)* **အဏ္ဏဝါဗေဒပညာရှင်** an-na-war-bay-da-pyin-nyar-shin
oceanographic *(adj.)* **အဏ္ဏဝါဗေဒနှင့်ဆိုင်သော** an-na-war-bay-da-nint-sine-taw
oceanologist *(n.)* **အဏ္ဏဝါဗေဒပညာရှင်** an-na-war-bay-da-pyin-nyar-shin
oceanology *(n.)* **အဏ္ဏဝါဗေဒ** an-na-war-bay-da
octagon *(n.)* **အဋ္ဌဂံ** a-hta-gan
octane *(n.)* **အောက်တိန်းဆီ** out-tein-se
octangular *(adj.)* **အနားရှစ်ထောင့်ရှိသော** a-narr-shit-htaunt-shi-taw
octave *(n.)* **ရှစ်သံတွဲ** shit-tan-twal
October *(n.)* **အောက်တိုဘာလ** out-to-bhar-la
octogenarian *(adj.)* **အသက် ၈၀ ကျော် ၉၀ အောက်ဖြစ်သော** a-tat-80-kyaw-90-out-hpyit-taw
octogenarian *(n.)* **အသက် ၈၀ ကျော် ၉၀ အောက်** a-tat-80-kyaw-90-out
octonionics *(n.)* **အတိုင်းအတာရှစ်ခုဆိုင်ရာ အသုံးချသင်္ချာပညာ** a-tine-a-tar-shit-khu-sai-yar-a-tone-cha-tin-cha-pyin-nyar
octopede *(n.)* **ခြေရှစ်ချောင်းပါသတ္တဝါ** chay-shit-chaung-par-tat-ta-war
octopus *(n.)* **ရေဘဝဲ** ray-bha-well
octopussy *(n.)* **ရေဘဝဲ** ray-bha-well
octuple *(v.)* **ရှစ်ခုထိတိုးသည်** shit-khu-hti-toe-the
octuplicate *(n.)* **တူညီသောအရာ ရှစ်ခု** tu-nyi-taw-a-yar-shit-khu
octyne *(n.)* **ကာဗွန်ရှစ်လုံး၊ အဆက်သုံးခုပါ အယ်ကိုင်း** car-bon-shit-lon-a-sat-tone-khu-par-al-kine
ocular *(adj.)* **မျက်မြင်** myet-myin
oculist *(n.)* **မျက်စိအထူးကု** myet-si-a-htu-ku
odd *(adj.)* **တစ်မူထူးသော** ta-mu-htu-taw
oddity *(n.)* **တစ်မူထူးခြင်း** ta-mu-htuu-chinn
odds *(n.)* **အလားအလာ** a-lar-a-lar
ode *(n.)* **ရတုကဗျာ** ra-tu-ka-byar
odious *(adj.)* **မသတီစရာ** ma-ta-te-sa-rar
odium *(n.)* **ကဲ့ရဲ့ခြင်း** kae-rae-chinn
odometer *(n.)* **မိုင်တိုင်းကိရိယာ** mine-tine-ka-ri-yar
odontologist *(n.)* **သွားဆရာဝန်** twar-sa-yar-win
odontology *(n.)* **သွားလေ့လာမှုပညာ** twar-lae-lar-mu-pin-nyar
odorous *(adj.)* **ရနံ့သင်းသော** ra-nant-tin-taw
odour *(n.)* **အနံ့** a-nant
of *(prep.)* **၏** eat
off *(prep.)* **မှ၊ က** mha, ka
off balance *(adj.)* **အံ့သြသော၊ ရုပ်ပိုင်းညီမျှမှုမရှိသော** ant-aw-taw, yoke-pai-nyi-mya-mu-ma-shitaw
offbeat *(adj.)* **တစ်မူထူးသော** ta-muu-htuu-taw
offence *(n.)* **ပြစ်မှု** pyit-mhu
offend *(v.)* **စော်ကားရာရောက်သည်** saw-karr-rar-rout-tai
offender *(n.)* **ဥပဒေချိုးဖောက်သည်** u-pa-day-choe-hpout-tai

offensive *(n.)* တိုက်စစ် tite-sit

offensive *(adj.)* စော်ကားသော saw-kar-taw

offer *(n.)* ကမ်းလှမ်းချက် kam-lam-chet

offer *(v.)* ကမ်းလှမ်းသည်၊ ပေးသည် kam-lam-tai, pay-tai

offering *(n.)* လက်ဆောင်၊ လှူဖွယ်ပစ္စည်း lat-saung, hlu-hpwal-pyit-see

office *(n.)* ရုံး yone

officer *(n.)* အရာရှိ a-rar-shi

official *(n.)* အရာရှိ a-rar-shi

official *(adj.)* တရားဝင် ta-rar-win

officially *(adv.)* တရားဝင် ta-rar-win

officiate *(v.)* ကြီးမှူးသည် kyee-mhuu-tai

officious *(adj.)* စွက်ဖက်တတ်သော swat-hpat-tat-taw

offing *(n.)* အလားအလာရှိသည် a-lar-a-lar-shi-tai

offline *(adj.)* အော့ဖ့်လိုင်းဖြစ်သော aot-pha-line-hpyit-taw

off-road *(adj.)* ပုံမှန်လမ်းမခင်းထားသော ကားမောင်းရန်၊ ရပ်ရန် လမ်း pone-man-lan-ma-khin-htar-taw-kar-maung-yan-kar-yat-yan-lan

offset *(n.)* အော့ဖ့်ဆက်စက် off-sat-sat

offset *(v.)* ထေသည် htay-tai

offshoot *(n.)* အတက် a-tat

offspring *(n.)* သားသမီး tar-ta-mee

oft *(adv.)* မကြာခဏ ma-kyar-hka-na

often *(adv.)* မကြာခဏ ma-kyar-hka-na

ogle *(n.)* ငမ်းခြင်း ngan-chin

oil *(n.)* ဆီ se

oil paint *(n.)* ဆီဆေးပန်းချီ se-say-pan-chee

oil rig *(n.)* ရေနံတူးစင် ray-nan-tuu-sin

oily *(adj.)* ဆီကဲ့သို့သော se-kae-shoet-taw

oink *(n.)* အွန့် awnt

oinker *(n.)* အွန့်ခနဲ့ မြည်သူ ommt-kha-nae-myae-thu

ointment *(n.)* လိမ်းဆေး laim-say

okay *(int.)* ကောင်းပြီ kaung-pye

okayish *(adj.)* အိုကေသော ok taw

okra *(n.)* ရုံးပတီ rone-pa-te

old *(n.)* သက်ကြီးရွယ်အို tat-kyee-rwal-ao

old age *(n.)* သက်ကြီးရွယ်အို tat-kyee-rwal-ao

oleaceous *(adj.)* အိုလေးရှားမျိုးနှင့် ဆိုင်သော o-le-shar-myo-nint-sine-taw

oleaginous *(adj.)* ကျိချွဲသော kyi-chwal-taw

oleochemical *(n.)* သဘာဝဆီမှ ရသော ဒြပ်ပေါင်း ta-bar-wa-see-ma-ya-tawdat-paung

olfactic *(adj.)* အနံ့အာရုံနှင့် ဆိုင်သော a-nant-arr-yone-nint-sine-taw

olfactics *(n.)* ရနံ့ဗေဒ ya-nant-bay-da

olfactory *(adj.)* ဂန္ဓာရုံ gan-dhar-rone

oligarch *(n.)* လူနည်းစုကို ကိုယ်စားပြုနိုင်ငံသား lu-nae-su-ko-sar-pyu-nine-ngan-tar

oligarchal *(adj.)* လူနည်းစုကို ကိုယ်စားပြုအစိုးရနှင့် ဆိုင်သော lu-nae-su-ko-sar-pyu-a-soe-ya-nint-sine-taw

oligarchy *(n.)* လူနည်းစုကို ကိုယ်စားပြုသော အစိုးရ lu-nae-su-ko-ko-sar-pyu-taw-a-soe-ra

olive *(n.)* သံလွင်သီး tan-lwin-tee

olympiad *(n.)* မျက်မှောက်ခေတ် အိုလံပစ်ပွဲတော် myet-maut-hkit-ao-lan-pit-pwal-taw
omega *(n.)* အိုမီဂါ ao-me-gar
omelette *(n.)* ကြက်ဥခေါက်ကြော် kyat-u-kout-kyaw
omen *(n.)* နိမိတ် na-mate
ominous *(adj.)* မကောင်းသော ma-kaung-taw
omission *(n.)* ချန်ထားခြင်း chan-htar-chinn
omit *(v.)* ချန်ထားသည် chan-htar-tai
omittance *(n.)* ချန်လှပ်ခြင်း chan-lat-chin
omitter *(n.)* ချန်လှပ်သည် chan-lat-the
omnibenevolence *(n.)* အလုံးစုံကောင်းမွန်နှစ်သက်ဖွယ်ဖြစ်ခြင်း a-lone-sone-kaung-mon-nit-tat-phwal-phit-chin
omnibenevolent *(adj.)* အလုံးစုံကောင်းမွန်နှစ်သက်ဖွယ်ဖြစ်သော a-lone-sone-kaung-mon-nit-tat-phwal-phit-taw
omnibus *(n.)* ပေါင်းချုပ် paung-chote
omnicompetence *(n.)* ဘက်စုံတော်ခြင်း bat-sone-taw-chin
omnicompetent *(adj.)* ဘက်စုံတော်သော bat-sone-taw-taw
omnidirectional *(adj.)* ဘက်ပေါင်းစုံဦးတည်သော bat-paung-sone-u-te-taw
omnidirectionality *(n.)* ဘက်ပေါင်းစုံဦးတည်ခြင်း bat-paung-sone-u-te-chin
omniform *(adj.)* ပုံစံမျိုးစုံဖြစ်သော pon-san-myo-sone-phit-taw
omniformity *(n.)* ပုံစံမျိုးစုံဖြစ်ခြင်း pon-san-myo-sone-phit-chin
omnilingual *(n.)* ဘာသာစကားပေါင်းစုံပြောခြင်း bar-tar-sa-kar-paung-sone-pyaw-chin
omnipotence *(n.)* အရာရာ စွမ်းခြင်း a-rar-rar-swam-chinn
omnipotent *(adj.)* အရာရာ စွမ်းသော a-rar-rar-swam-taw
omnipresence *(n.)* အနှံ့အစပ် a-nant-a-sat
omnipresent *(adj.)* နေရာတိုင်းမှာ nay-rar-tine-mhar
omniscience *(n.)* သဗ္ဗညုတဉာဏ် tab-ba-nyu-ta-nyarn
omniscient *(adj.)* သဗ္ဗညုတ tab-ba-nyu-ta
omnivore *(n.)* အစုံစားသတ္တဝါ *a-sone-sar-tat-ta-war*
omnivorous *(adj.)* အစုံစားသော a-sone-sar-taw
omophagia *(n.)* အသားစိမ်းစားခြင်း *a-tar-sein-sar-chin*
on *(adv.)* ဆက်၍ sat-ywe
once *(adv.)* တစ်ကြိမ်က ta-kyain-ka
oncogene *(n.)* ကင်ဆာဆဲလ် အဖြစ်ပြောင်းအောင် လုပ်နိုင်သောဂျင်းများ kin-sar-sel-a-phit-pyaung-aung lote-nine-taw-gin-myar
oncogenic *(adj.)* ကင်ဆာဆဲလ်ဖြစ်လာနိုင်ခြေရှိသော kin-sar-sel-phit-lar-nine-chay-shi-taw
oncologist *(n.)* ကင်ဆာဆရာဝန် kin-sar-sa-rar-wan
oncology *(n.)* ကင်ဆာပညာရပ် kin-sar-pyin-nyar-rat
one *(pron.)* တစ်ခု ta-hku
one *(adj.)* တစ်ခု ta-hku
oneness *(n.)* တစ်သားတည်းဖြစ်ခြင်း ta-tar-tae-hpyit-chinn

onerous *(adj.)* ကြီးလေးသော kyee-lay-taw

one-sided *(adj.)* တစ်ဖက်သတ် ta-hpat-tat

one-way *(adj.)* တစ်လမ်းမောင်း ta-lam-maung

ongoing *(adj.)* နေဆဲ nay-sell

onion *(n.)* ကြက်သွန်နီ kyat-twan-ne

online *(adj.)* အွန်လိုင်းဖြစ်သော on-line-hpyit-taw

on-looker *(n.)* ပရိသတ် pa-rait-sat

only *(conj.)* ဒါပေမယ့် dar-pay-mae

only *(adj.)* မျှသာ mya-tar

onology *(n.)* မိုက်မှားသောဟောပြောချက် mite-mar-taw-haw-pyaw-chat

onomancy *(n.)* အမည်ပါစာလုံးဖြင့်အနာဂတ်ဟောခြင်း a-mee-par-sar-lone-phint-a-nar-gat-haw-chin

onomast *(n)* အမည်ဗေဒပညာရှင် a-mee-bay-da-pin-nyar-shin

onomastic *(adj.)* အမည်၏ သမိုင်း၊ မူလအစလေ့လာချက်ဆိုင်ရာ a-mee-ei-ta-mine-mu-la-a-sa-lae-lar-chat-sine-yar

onomatologist *(n.)* အမည်သမိုင်းကျွမ်းကျင်သူ a-mee-ta-mine-kyun-kyin-thu

onomatology *(n.)* အမည်ဗေဒပညာ a-mee-bay-da-pin-nyar

onomatope *(n.)* သာဒကဖြစ် ဖွဲ့စည်းသောစကားလုံး tar-da-ka-phint-phwal-see-taw-sa-kar-lone

onomatopoeia *(n.)* သာဒက tar-da-ka

on-road *(adj.)* ပုံမှန်လမ်းပေါ်တွင် ကားမောင်းရန် ရပ်ရန် လမ်း pone-man-lan-paw-twin-kar-maung-yan-kar-yat-yan-lan

onrush *(n.)* တစ်ဟုန်ထိုး တက်ခြင်း Ta-hone-htoe-tat-chinn

on-screen *(adj.)* စခရင်ပေါ်တွင် sa-kha-rin-paw-twin

onset *(n.)* အစ a-sa

onslaught *(n.)* အပြင်းအထန်တိုက်ခိုက်ခြင်း a-pyin-a-htan-tite-hkite-chinn

ontogenic *(adj.)* သက်ရှိမျိုးဆက်နှင့် ဖွံ့ဖြိုးခြင်းနှင့် ဆိုင်သော thet-shi-myo-sat-nint-phwint-phyoe-chin-nint-sai-taw

ontogeny *(n.)* သက်ရှိမျိုးဆက်နှင့် ဖွံ့ဖြိုးခြင်း thet-shi-myo-sat-nint-phwint-phyoe-chin

ontologic *(adj.)* ရှိမှုပညာနှင့် ဆိုင်သော shi-mhu-pyin-nyar-nint-sine-taw

ontological *(adj.)* ရှိမှုပညာနှင့် ဆိုင်သော shi-mhu-pyin-nyar-nint-sine-taw

ontologism *(n.)* ဘုရားသခင်ရှိမှုကို ထိန်းသိမ်းသော အယူအဆ pha-rar-ta-khin-shi-mu-ko-htein-tain-taw-a-yu-a-sa

ontologist *(n.)* ရှိမှုပညာရှင် shi-mhu-pyin-nyar-shin

ontology *(n.)* ရှိမှုပညာ shi-mhu-pyin-nyar

onus *(n.)* တာဝန် tar-wan

onward *(adj.)* ရှေ့သို့ shae-thoet

onwards *(adv.)* ရှေ့သို့ shae-thoet

ooze *(v.)* စိမ့်သည် saint-tai

ooze *(n.)* ရွှံ့နွံ shwan-nit

opacity *(n.)* အလင်းပိတ်မှု a-lin-pate-mhu

opal *(n.)* မဟူရာဖလား ma-huu-ra-pha-lar

opaque *(adj.)* အလင်းပိတ်သော a-lin-pate-taw

open *(v.)* ဖွင့်သည် hpwint-tai

open *(adj.)* ဖွင့်သော hpwint-taw

opening *(n.)* အပေါက် a-pout

openly *(adv.)* ပွင့်ပွင့်လင်းလင်း pwint-pwint-lin-lin

opera *(n.)* အော်ပရာ aw-pa-rar

operability *(n.)* **လုပ်ဆောင်နိုင်စွမ်း** loat-saung-nine-swan
operable *(adj.)* **ခွဲစိတ်ကုသ၍ ရနိုင်သော** kwal-sate-ku-ta-ywe-ya-nine-taw
operate *(v.)* **အလုပ်လုပ်သည်၊ မောင်းသည်** a-lote-lote-tai, maung-tai
operation *(n.)* **ခွဲစိတ်ကုသခြင်း** kwal-sate-ku-ta-chinn
operative *(adj.)* **အသက်ဝင်သော၊ အကျိုးသက်ရောက်သော** a-tat-win-taw, a-kyoe-tat-rout-taw
operator *(n.)* **အော်ပရေတာ၊ လုပ်ငန်းရှင်** aw-pa-ray-tar, lote-ngan-shin
operetta *(n.)* **ဇာတ်မြူး** zat-myuu
ophtalmic *(adj.)* **မျက်စိဆိုင်ရာ** myet-si-sine-rar
ophtalmologic *(adj.)* **မျက်စိပညာနှင့်ဆိုင်သော** myet-si-pyin-nyar-nint-sine-taw
ophtalmologist *(n.)* **မျက်စိကုပညာရှင်** myet-si-ku-pyin-nyar-shin
ophtalmology *(n.)* **မျက်စိကုပညာ** myet-si-ku-pyin-nyar
ophtalmoscope *(n.)* **မျက်စိကြည့်မှန်ပြောင်း** myet-si-kyi-mhan-pyaung
opiate *(adj.)* **ဘိန်းပါသော** bane-par-taw
opinator *(n.)* **အယူအဆစုပ်ကိုင်ထားသူ** a-yu-a-sa-sote-kine-htar-thu
opine *(v.)* **ထင်မြင်ယူဆချက်ထုတ်ပြောသည်** htin-myin-yu-sa-chet-htoke-pyaw-the
opinion *(n.)* **ထင်မြင်ယူဆချက်** htin-myin-yu-sa-chet
opinionate *(v.)* **ခေါင်းမာသည်** kaung-mar-tai
opinionated *(adj.)* **ခေါင်းမာသော** kaung-mar-taw
opinionless *(adj.)* **ထင်မြင်ယူဆချက်မရှိသော** htin-myin-yu-sa-chet-ma-shi-taw
opinionnaire *(n.)* **ထင်မြင်ယူဆချက်မေးခွန်းလွှာ** htin-myin-chat-maykhun-lwar
opium *(n.)* **ဘိန်း** bhein
opponent *(n.)* **ပြိုင်ဘက်** pyaine-bhat
opportune *(adj.)* **အချိန်သင့်** a-chane-tint
opportunism *(n.)* **အခွင့်သမားဝါဒ** a-chaung-ta-mar-war-da
opportunity *(n.)* **အခွင့်အရေး** a-kwint-a-ray
oppose *(v.)* **ကန့်ကွက်သည်** kant-kwat-tai
opposite *(adj.)* **ဆန့်ကျင်ဘက်** sant-kyin-bhat
opposition *(n.)* **အတိုက်အခံပြုခြင်း** a-tite-a-hkan-pyu-chinn
oppress *(v.)* **ဖိနှိပ်သည်** hpi-nate-tai
oppression *(n.)* **ဖိနှိပ်ခြင်း** hpi-nate-chinn
oppressive *(adj.)* **ဖိနှိပ်သော** hpi-nate-taw
oppressor *(n.)* **ဖိနှိပ်သူ** hpi-nate-tuu
opt *(v.)* **ဆုံးဖြတ်သည်** sone-hpyat-tai
optic *(adj.)* **မျက်စိ** myet-si
optician *(n.)* **မျက်မှန်ကျွမ်းကျင်သူ** myet-mhan-kyam-kyin-tuu
optimism *(n.)* **အကောင်းမြင်ခြင်း** a-kaung-myin-chinn
optimist *(n.)* **အကောင်းမြင်ဝါဒီ** a-kaung-myin-war-de
optimistic *(adj.)* **အကောင်းမြင်သော** a-kaung-myin-taw
optimum *(adj.)* **အသင့်ဆုံးဖြစ်သော** a-tint-sone-hpyit-taw
optimum *(n.)* **အသင့်ဆုံး** a-tint-sone
option *(n.)* **ရွေးစရာ** rway-sa-rar
optional *(adj.)* **စိတ်ကြိုက်** sate-kyaite
opulence *(n.)* **ခမ်းနားထည်ဝါခြင်း** hkam-narr-htai-war-chinn

opulent *(adj.)* **ခမ်းနားထည်ဝါသော** hkam-narr-htai-war-taw

oracle *(n.)* **နိမိတ်စကား** na-mate-sa-karr

oracular *(adj.)* **သိုက်** tite

oral *(adj.)* **ခံတွင်း** hkan-twin

orally *(adv.)* **ပြောစကားဖြင့်** pyaw-sa-kar-hpyint

orange *(adj.)* **လိမ္မော်ရောင်** laim-maw-raung

orange *(n.)* **ကမ္ဘလာသီး** kam-ba-lar-tee

oration *(n.)* **မိန့်ခွန်း** meint-hkwan

orator *(n.)* **အဟောအပြောကောင်းသူ** a-haw-a-pyaw-kaung-tuu

oratorical *(adj.)* **အဟောအပြော** a-haw-a-pyaw

oratory *(n.)* **ဘုရားစင်** pha-rar-sin

orb *(n.)* **စက်လုံး** sat-lone

orbit *(n.)* **ပတ်လမ်း** pat-lam

orbital *(adj.)* **ပတ်လမ်း** pat-lam

orbituary *(n.)* **မြို့ပတ်လမ်း** *myoe-pat-lam*

orca *(n.)* **ဝေလငါး** *way-la-ngar*

orchard *(n.)* **သစ်သီးခြံ** tit-tee-chan

orchestra *(n.)* **သံစုံတီးဝိုင်း** tan-sone-tee-wine

orchestral *(adj.)* **သံစုံသီးဝိုင်းဆိုင်ရာ** tan-sone-tee-wine-sine-rar

ordain *(v.)* **သိက္ခာတော်ဘွဲ့အပ်နှင်းသည်၊ ပဇ္ဇင်းတက်ပေးသည်** hteik-hkar-taw-bhwal-at-hnin-tai, pa-zin-tat-pay-tai

ordained *(adj.)* **ဘုရားကျောင်းဝန်ကြီးဌာနသို့ ဝင်ခွင့်ပေးသော** *pha-rar-kyaung-win-gyi-htar-na-tho-win-khwint-pay-taw*

ordeal *(n.)* **ဒုက္ခသုက္ခ** duk-hka -tuk-hka

order *(v.)* **အမိန့်ပေးသည်၊ အော်ဒါမှာသည်** a-meint-pay-tai, aw-dar-mhar-tai

order *(n.)* **စီစဉ်တကျ၊ အမှာစာ** se-zin-ta-kya, a mhar sar

orderly *(n.)* **ဆေးရုံအထွေထွေလုပ်သား** say-rone-a-htway-htway-lote-tarr

orderly *(adj.)* **အစီတကျဖြစ်သော** a-se-ta-kya-hpyit-taw

ordinance *(n.)* **အမိန့်၊ စည်းမျဉ်း၊ စည်းကမ်း၊ ဥပဒေ** a-meint, see-myain, see-kam, u-pa-day

ordinarily *(adv.)* **ပုံမှန်** pone-man

ordinary *(adj.)* **ပုံမှန်** pone-man

ordnance *(n.)* **စစ်လက်နက်ပစ္စည်း** sit-lat-nat-pyit-see

ore *(n.)* **သတ္တုရိုင်း** tat-tu-rine

organ *(n.)* **အင်္ဂါ** in-gar

organic *(adj.)* **ကိုယ်အင်္ဂါဆိုင်ရာ** ko-in-gar-sine-rar

organism *(n.)* **သက်ရှိ** tat-shi

organization *(n.)* **အဖွဲ့အစည်း** a-hpw-a-see

organize *(v.)* **စုစည်းသည်၊ စည်းရုံးသည်** su-see-tai, see-rone-tai

organography *(n.)* **သက်ရှိအင်္ဂါ၏ သိပ္ပံနည်းကျဖွဲ့စည်းပုံနှင့် လုပ်ငန်းဆောင်တာ** thet-shi-inn-gar-ei-tate-pan-nee-kya-phwe-see-pone-nint-lote-ngan-saung-tar-phaw-pya-chat

organza *(n.)* **ပါးလွှာသောပိုးထည်** par-lwar-taw-poe-htal

orgasm *(n.)* **လိင်အထွတ်အထိပ်** lain-a-htwat-a-hteik

orgasmic *(adj.)* **လိင်အထွတ်အထိပ်ရောက်သော** lain-a-htwat-a-hteik-yauk-taw

orgy *(n.)* **ရမ်းရမ်းကားကားပျော်ပွဲ** ram-ram-kar-kar-pyaw-pwal

orient *(v.)* **စိတ်ကိုင်းညွတ်မှု ရှိသည်** sate-kine-nyut-mhu-shi-tai

orient *(n.)* အရှေ့တိုင်း a-shae-tine

oriental *(n.)* အရှေ့တိုင်းသား a-shae-tine-tarr

oriental *(adj.)* အရှေ့တိုင်း a-shae-tine

orientate *(v.)* စိတ်ကိုင်းညွတ်မှု ရှိသည် sate-kine-nyut-mhu-shi-tai

orientational *(adj.)* ပတ်ဝန်းကျင်အသားကျအောင် လုပ်သော pat-wan-kyin-a-tar-kya-aung-lote-taw

oriented *(adj.)* တိကျသော စိတ်ညွတ်ကိုင်းမှု ရှိသော ti-kya-taw-seik-kine-nyut-mu-shi-taw

orifice *(n.)* အပေါက် a-pout

orificial *(adj.)* ကိုယ်ခန္ဓာပေါက်များနှင့် ဆိုင်သော koe-khan-dar-pauk-myar-nint-sine-taw

origami *(n.)* စက္ကူခေါက်ပညာ sat-ku-khaut-pin-nyar

origin *(n.)* မူလ၊ အစ mu-la, a-sa

original *(n.)* မူလ၊ ပင်ရင်း mu-la , pin-rinn

original *(adj.)* မူလ၊ ပင်ရင်း mu-la , pin-rinn

originality *(n.)* ကိုယ်ပိုင်ဟန် ko-pine-han

originate *(v.)* ပေါ်ပေါက်လာသည်၊ တီထွင်သည် paw-pout-lar-tai, te-htwin-tai

originator *(n.)* တီထွင်သူ te-htwin-tuu

orl *(n.)* ယန်ဖော်ပင် yan-baw-pin

orn *(v.)* ဥုံဟု ရွတ်သည် *ohn-hu-yut-the*

ornament *(v.)* တန်ဆာဆင်သည် taan-sar-sin-tai

ornamental *(adj.)* အလှတန်ဆာ a-hla-taan-sar

ornamentation *(n.)* အဆင်တန်ဆာ a saintaansar

ornithologist *(n.)* သကုဏဗေဒပညာရှင် ta-ku-na-bay-da-pyin-nyar-shin

ornithology *(n.)* သကုဏဗေဒပညာ ta-ku-na-bay-da-pyin-nyar

ornithoscopy *(n.)* ငှက်ကြည့်ခြင်း ngat-kyi-chin

orogen *(n.)* မြေတွန့်ခေါက်ခြင်းဖြင့် ပုံပန်းပျက်သွားသော ကျောက် myay-twunt-khaut-chin-phyint-pone-pan-pyat-twar-taw-kyauk

orogenic *(adj.)* မြေတွန့်ခေါက်ခြင်းနှင့် ဆိုင်သော myay-twunt-khaut-chin-nint-sai-taw

orologist *(n.)* တောင်နှင့် တောင်ဖြစ်ပေါ်မှုဆိုင်ရာ ပညာရှင် taung-nint-taung-phit-paw-mu-sine-yar-pin-nyar-shin

orphan *(v.)* မိဘမဲ့ဖြစ်သွားသည် mi-bha-mae-hpyit-twar-tai

orphan *(n.)* မိဘမဲ့ mi-bha-mae

orphanage *(n.)* မိဘမဲ့ ကလေးဂေဟာ mi-bha-mae-ka-layy-gay-har

orthodox *(adj.)* သမားရိုးကျ ta-mar-roe-kya

orthodoxy *(n.)* သမားရိုးကျ အတွေးအကျင့် sa-mar-roe-kya-a-tway-a-kyint

orthograph *(n.)* မြေပုံ၊ ဗိသုကာတွင် သုံးသော အစွန်းများ myay-pon-bi-tu-kar-twin-tone-taw-a-sune-myar

orthographer *(n.)* စာလုံးပေါင်းဆိုင်ရာ ပညာရှင် sar-lone-paung-sine-yar-pin-nyar-shin

orthographic *(adj.)* စာလုံးပေါင်းဆိုင်ရာ ပညာ sar-lone-paung-sine-yar-pin-nyar

orthopaedia *(n.)* အရိုးရောဂါကုပညာ a-roe-raw-gar-ku-pyin-nyar

orthopaedical *(adj.)* အရိုးရောဂါနှင့် ဆိုင်သော a-roe-raw-gar-nint-sine-taw

orthopaedics *(n.)* အရိုးရောဂါကုပညာ a-roe-raw-gar-ku-pyin-nyar
oscillate *(v.)* လှုးလာဆန်ခတ်လှုပ်ရှားသည် luu-lar-san-hkaat-lote-shar-tai
oscillation *(n.)* အတက်အကျဖြစ်ပေါ်ခြင်း a-tat-a-kya-hpyit-paw-chin
oscillograph *(n.)* လျှပ်စစ်လှိုင်းတိုင်းကိရိယာ lyat-sis-hline-tine-ka-yi-yar
oscillometric *(adj.)* အတက်အကျတိုင်းကိရိယာ a-tat-a-kya-tine-ka-yi-yar
oscilloscope *(n.)* လှိုင်းပုံကြည့်ကိရိယာ hlaine-pone-kyi-ka-ri-yar
osculant *(adj.)* နမ်းသော nan-taw
oscular *(adj.)* ပါးစပ်နှင့်ဆိုင်သော pa-sat-nint-sine-taw
osculate *(v.)* တစ်ခုခုကို နမ်းသည် ta-khu-khu-ko-nan-the
osmobiosis *(n.)* သက်ရှိနေထိုင်သော အရည်ပျစ်လာပြီးမှ အစပြုသော သက်ရှိစုဖွဲ့ဖြစ်ပေါ်ခြင်း thet-shi-nay-htine-taw-a-yay-pyit-lar-pi-ma-a-sa-pyu-taw-thet-shi-su-phwe-phit-paw-chin
osmobiotic *(adj.)* သက်ရှိနေထိုင်သော အရည်ပျစ်လာပြီးမှ အစပြုသော သက်ရှိစုဖွဲ့ဖြစ်ပေါ်ခြင်းဆိုင်ရာ thet-shi-nay-htine-taw-a-yay-pyit-lar-pi-ma-a-sa-pyu-taw-thet-shi-su-phwe-phit-paw-chin-sine-yar
osmose *(v.)* စိမ့်ဝင်ပျံ့နှံ့ခြင်းနည်းဖြင့် ပျံ့နှံ့စေသည် seint-win-pyant-nant-chinn-nae-phint-pyant-nant-say-the
osmosis *(n.)* စိမ့်ဝင်ပျံ့နှံ့ခြင်း seint-win-pyant-nant-chinn
ossify *(v.)* အရိုးဖြစ်သွားသည် a-roe-hpyit-twar-tai
ostensibility *(n.)* ပြသနိုင်စွမ်း pya sanine-swam
ostensible *(adj.)* အကြောင်းပြသော a-kyaung-pya-taw
ostensibly *(adv.)* အပြင်ပန်းအားဖြင့် a-pyin-pan-ar-hpyint
ostension *(n.)* ပြသခြင်း၊ ဆန္ဒထုတ်ဖော်ခြင်း pyasahkyinn , sandahtotehpawchinn
ostentation *(n.)* ဝင့်ကြွားခြင်း wint-kyar-chinn
ostentatious *(adj.)* ပြစားသော pya-sar-taw
ostracize *(v.)* ဝိုင်းပယ်သည် wine-pal-tai
ostrich *(n.)* ငှက်ကုလားအုတ် nghaat-ka-lar-aote
other *(pron.)* အခြား a-charr
otherwise *(conj.)* တစ်နည်းအားဖြင့် ta-nee-ar-hpyint
otherwise *(adv.)* သို့မဟုတ်လျှင် thoet-ma-hote-hlyin
otherworld *(n.)* သေဆုံးပြီးနောက်ဘဝ saysonepyeenoutbhaw
otherworldliness *(n.)* အခြားဘဝကူးပြောင်းနိုင်စွမ်း aahkyarr bhaw kuu-pyaungg-nineswam
otoscope *(n.)* နားတွင်းကြည့်မှန်ပြောင်း narr twin kyany mhaanpyaungg
otoscopis *(adj.)* နားတွင်းကြည့်မှန်ပြောင်းနှင့်ဆိုင်သော narr twin kyany mhaan pyaungg-nint sinesaw
otoscopy *(n.)* နားတွင်း မှန်ပြောင်းနှင့်ကြည့်ရှုစစ်ဆေးခြင်း narrtwin mhaan pyaunggnhang kyi shu-sitsayy-chinn
otter *(n.)* ဖျံ hpyaan
ottoman *(n.)* ဖုံကွပ်သေတ္တာ hpone-kwut-tayt-tar
ouch *(n.)* နာကျင်မှုကို ဖော်ပြသံ narkyinmhuko hpawpyasan

ought *(v.)* **သင့်သည်** tint-tai

ounce *(n.)* **အောင်စ** aung-sa

our *(pron.)* **ကျွန်တော်တို့၏** kyun-taw-thoet-eat

oust *(v.)* **ထုတ်သည်** htote-tai

out *(prep.)* **အပြင်ဘက်** aapyin-bhaat

outage *(n.)* **လျှပ်စစ်ဓာတ်အားပြတ်တောက်သော ကာလ** lyat-sit-dhat-ar-pyat-tout-taw-kar-la

outback *(n.)* **ကုန်းခေါင်ရေဝေးအရပ်** kone-hkaung-ray-way-a-rat

out-balance *(v.)* **သာသည်** sar-sai

outbid *(v.)* **လေလံအရ ဆွဲသွားသည်** lay-lan-a-ra-swal-twar-tai

outbound *(adj.)* **အရပ်တစ်ပါး** a-rat-ta-par

outbreak *(n.)* **ပေါ်ပေါက်ခြင်း** paw-pout-chinn

outburst *(n.)* **ဝါးလုံးကွဲ** war-lone-kwal

outcast *(adj.)* **အပယ်ခံဖြစ်သော** a-paal-hkan-hpyit-taw

outcast *(n.)* **အပယ်ခံ** a-paal-hkan

outcome *(n.)* **အကျိုး** a-kyoe

outcry *(adj.)* **အုတ်အော်သောင်းသဲဆဲသံ** aote-aw-taung-tell-sell-tan

outdated *(adj.)* **ခေတ်မမီတော့သော** khit-ma-me-tot-taw

outdo *(v.)* **သူများထက် သာအောင် လုပ်သည်** tuu-myar-htat-ta-aung-lote-tai

outdoor *(adj.)* **အိမ်အပြင်ဘက်** ain-a-pyin-bhat

outer *(adj.)* **အပြင်ဘက်** a-pyin-bhat

outfit *(v.)* **ဝတ်စုံ** waat-sone

outgrow *(v.)* **ဖျောက်သည်၊ လွန်မြောက်သည်** hpyaut-tai, lwan-myaut-tai

outhouse *(n.)* **အိမ်မမှ ခွဲထုတ်ထားသော အိမ်သာ** ain-ma-mha-hkwal-htote-htar-taw-ain-tar

outing *(n.)* **အပျော်ခရီးတို** a-pyaw-hka-ree-to

outlandish *(adj.)* **ကိုးရိုးကားရားနိုင်သော** koe-roe-karr-rar-nine-saw

outlaw *(v.)* **ဝရမ်းပြေးကြော်ညာသည်** wa-ram-pyay-kyaw-nyar-tai

outlaw *(n.)* **ဝရမ်းပြေး** wa-ram-pyay

outlet *(n.)* **ဆိုင်** sine

outline *(v.)* **လိုရင်းအချုပ်ဖော်ပြသည်** lo-rinn-a-chaote-hpaw-pya-tai

outline *(n.)* **ကောက်ကြောင်း၊ အကြမ်းဖော်ပြချက်** kout-kyaung, a-kyam-hpaw-pya-chet

outlive *(v.)* **ထက် ပိုနေရသည်** htaat-po-nay-ra-tai

outlook *(n.)* **သဘောထားအမြင်** ta-bhaw-htar-a-myin

outmoded *(adj.)* **ခေတ်မမီတော့သော** khit-ma-me-tot-taw

outnumber *(v.)* **ပိုများသည်** po-myar-tai

outpatient *(n.)* **ပြင်ပလူနာ** pyin-pa-luu-nar

outpost *(n.)* **တပ်စခန်း** tat-sa-hkan

output *(n.)* **ထုတ်လုပ်ပေးသည့် ပမာဏ** htote-lote-pay-teet-pa-mar-na

outrage *(n.)* **နာကြည်းမှု၊ ရက်စက်ရမ်းကားမှု** nar-kyi-mhu, rat-sat-ram-kar-mhu

outright *(adj.)* **လုံးလုံးလျားလျား** lone-lone-lyarr-lyarr

outright *(adv.)* **ဘွင်းဘွင်းရှင်းရှင်း** bhwin bhwinhlyinnhlyinn

outrun *(v.)* **ကျော်သည်၊ တစ်ပန်းသာသည်** kyaw-tai, ta-pan-tar-tai

outset *(n.)* **အစမှ** a-sa-mha

outshine *(v.)* ထူးထူးခြားခြားချွန်သည် htuu-htuu-charr-charr-chun-tai
outside *(prep.)* အပြင် a-pyin
outside *(adj.)* အပြင်ပန်း a-pyin-pan
outsider *(n.)* အပြင်လူ a-pyin-luu
outsize *(adj.)* သာမန်ထက်ကြီးသော sar-man-htat-kyee-taw
outskirts *(n.)* ဆင်ခြေဖုံး sin-chay-hpone
outspoken *(adj.* မကွယ်မဝှက်သော ma-kwal-ma-what-taw
outstanding *(adj.)* ထူးချွန်သော htuu-chun-taw
outward *(adv.)* အပြင်ဘက်သို့ a-pyin-bhat-thoet
outward *(adj.)* အထွက်၊ အပြင်ပန်း a-htwat, a-pyin-pan
outwardly *(adv.)* အမြင်အားဖြင့် a-myin-ar-hpyint
outwards *(adv.)* အပြင်ဘက်သို့ a-pyin-bhat-thoet
outweigh *(v.)* အလေးသာသည် a-lay-tar-tai
outwit *(v.)* တစ်ပတ်ရိုက်သည် ta-pat-rite-tai
outworld *(n.)* ပြင်ပကမ္ဘာ pyinpa-kambhar
ouzo *(n.)* အူဇိုအရက်ပြင်း auu-zo-a-rat-pyinn
oval *(n.)* ဘဲဥပုံ bhell-u-pone
oval *(adj.)* ဘဲဥပုံ bhell-u-pone
ovary *(n.)* သားအိမ် tar-ain
ovation *(n.)* ဩဘာပေးခြင်း aw-bhar-pay-chinn
oven *(n.)* ဖို hpo
over *(n.)* အလုံးစုံ a-lone-sone
over *(prep.)* အထက်တွင် a-htat-twin
overact *(v.)* သရုပ်ဆောင်ရာတွင် ပိုလွန်းသည် tar-yote-saung-rar-twin-polwan-tai
overall *(adj.)* စုစုပေါင်း၊ အဘက်ဘက် tu-tu-paung, a-bhat-bhat
overall *(n.)* အပေခံ အပေါ်ရုံကုတ် a-pay-hkan-a-paw-rone-kote
overawe *(v.)* ရှိန်သွားသည် shein-swar-tai
overboard *(adv.)* ဗွမ်းခနဲ bwam-hka-nell
overburden *(v.)* ဝန်ပိသည် wan-pi-tai
overcast *(adj.)* တိမ်ဖုံးသော tain-hpone-taw
overcharge *(n.)* ပြေစာတွင် ပိုတောင်းခြင်း pyay-sar-twin-po-taung-chinn
overcoat *(n.)* အပေါ်ရုံ ကုတ်အင်္ကျီရှည် a-paw-rone-kote-ain-kyae-shay
overcome *(v.)* ကျော်လွှားသည် kyaw-hlar-tai
overcrowd *(v.)* ပြည့်သိပ်သည် pyi-tate-tai
overdo *(v.)* ပိုလွန်းသည် po-lwan-tai
overdose *(v.)* ဆေးချိန်လွန်သည် say-chane-lwan-tai
overdose *(n.)* ဆေးချိန်လွန်ခြင်း say-chane-lwan-chinn
overdraft *(n.)* မိမိဘဏ်စာရင်းရှိငွေထက် ပိုထုတ်ခြင်း mi-mi-bhan-sar-rin-shi-ngway-htat-po-htote-chinn
overdraw *(v.)* မိမိဘဏ်စာရင်းရှိငွေထက် ပိုထုတ်သည် mi-mi-bhan-sar-rin-shi-ngway-htat-po-htote-tai
overdue *(adj.)* အချိန်နှောင်းသော a-chane-nhaung-taw
overhaul *(n.)* အလုံးစုံ စစ်ဆေးခြင်း a-lone-sone-sit-say-chinn
overhaul *(v.)* အလုံးစုံ စစ်ဆေးသည် a-lone-sone-sit-say-tai
overhear *(v.)* နားစွန်နားဖျားကြားသည် narr-swan-narr-hpyar-kyar-tai
overjoyed *(adj.)* အလွန် ဝမ်းသာသော a-lwan-wam-tar-taw

overlap *(n.)* ထပ်နေသည့်ပမာဏ htat-nay-teet-pa-mar-na
overlap *(v.)* အစွန်းချင်းထပ်သည် a-swan-chinn-htaut-tai
overleaf *(adv.)* တစ်ဖက်စာမျက်နှာတွင် ta-hpat-sar-myet-nhar-twin
overload *(n.)* မတန်တဆပမာဏ ma-tan-ta-sa-pa-mar-na
overload *(v.)* မတန်တဆဝန်တင်သည် ma-taan-ta-sa-wan-tin-tai
overlook *(v.)* မျက်စိလျှမ်းသည် myet-si-shan-tai
overnight *(adj.)* ညတွင်းချင်း၊ တစ်ညတာ nya-twin-chinn , ta-nya-tar
overnight *(adv.)* ညတွင်းချင်း၊ တစ်ညတာ nya-twin-chinn, ta-nya-tar
overpower *(v.)* ထိန်းနိုင်သည် htein-nine-tai
overrate *(v.)* အထင်ကြီးလွန်းသည် a-htin-kyee-lwan-tai
overrule *(v.)* ကျော်လွန်ပယ်ချသည် kyaw-lwan-pal-cha-tai
overrun *(v.)* သောင်းကျန်းသည် saung-kyan-tai
oversee *(v.)* ကြီးကြပ်သည် kyee-kyaut-tai
overseer *(n.)* ကြီးကြပ်ရေးမှူး kyee-kyaut-ray-mhuu
overshadow *(v.)* လောင်းရိပ်မိသည် laung-yeik-mi-tai
oversight *(n.)* သတိမမူမိခြင်း ta-ti-ma-mu-mi-chinn
oversleep *(v.)* အအိပ်လွန်သည် a-ait-lwan-tai
overt *(adj.)* ပြောင်ကျသော byaung-kya-taw
overtake *(v.)* ကျော်တက်သွားသည် kyaw-tat-twar-tai
overthrow *(n.)* ဖြုတ်ချခြင်း hpyoke-cha-chinn
overthrow *(v.)* ဖြုတ်ချသည် hpyoket-cha-tai
overtime *(n.)* အချိန်ပို a-chane-po
overtime *(adv.)* အချိန်ပို a-chane-po
overture *(n.)* ပဏာမတေး pa-nar-ma-tayy
overweight *(adj.)* ဝလွန်းသော၊ ဝန်ပိုသော wa-lwan-taw, wan-po-taw
overwhelm *(v.)* စီးနင်းသည် see-nin-tai
overwork *(n.)* အလုပ်ပိခြင်း a-lote-pi-chinn
oviferous *(adj.)* ဥဥသော u u-saw
ovular *(adj.)* သားဥနှင့် ဆိုင်သော sarr u-nint sine-saw
ovulate *(v.)* ဥတည်သည် u-tai-tai
ovum *(n.)* သား၊ ဥ tarr, u
owe *(v.)* အကြွေးတင်သည် a-kyay-tin-tai
owl *(n.)* ဇီးကွက် zee-kwat
owlery *(n.)* ဇီးကွက်အောင်းသံ jeekwat-aaw-san
owly *(adj.)* ဇီးကွက်ပုံစံရှိသော jeekwat pone-sanshisaw
own *(v.)* ပိုင်ဆိုင်သည် pine-sine-tai
own *(adj.)* ပိုင်ဆိုင်သော pine-sine-taw
owner *(n.)* ပိုင်ရှင် pine-shin
ownership *(n.)* ပိုင်ဆိုင်မှု pine-sine-mhu
ox *(n.)* နွားထီး nwar-htee
oxbird *(n.)* ငှက် nghaat
oxcart *(n.)* လှည်းယဉ် hlaee-yain
oxidant *(n.)* ဓာတ်တိုးအေးဂျင့် dhat toe aayy gyint
oxidate *(v.)* ဓာတ်တိုးသည် dhat toesai
oxidation *(n.)* ဓာတ်တိုးခြင်း Dhat-toe-chinn
oxide *(n.)* အောက်ဆိုက် aout-site

oxidization *(n.)* သံချေးတက်ခြင်း san-chay-taat-chinn

oxyacid *(n.)* အောက်ဆီဂျင်ပါသော အက်ဆစ် aout-segyin parsaw at-sait

oxygen *(n.)* အောက်ဆီဂျင် aout-se-gyin

oxygenate *(v.)* အောက်ဆီဂျင်ထည့်သည် aout-segyin htaeetsai

oxygenated *(adj.)* အောက်ဆီဂျင်ပါသော aout-segyin parsaw

oxygenation *(n.)* အောက်ဆီဂျင်ထည့်ခြင်း aout-segyin htaeethkyinn

oyster *(adj.)* ကမာကဲ့သို့ မီးခိုး၊ သနပ်ခါးရောင်ကြား ka mar-kaeshoet meehkoe-sa-nat-hkarr-raungkyarr

oysterling *(n.)* ကမာငယ် ka mar-ngaal

oysterman *(n.)* ကမာဖမ်းသမား ka mar hpam-samarr

ozonate *(n.)* အိုဇုန်းဓာတ်ပေါင်း ao jone dhatpaungg

ozonation *(n.)* အိုဇုန်းဖြစ်ထားခြင်း ao jone hpyat-htarrhkyinn

ozone *(n.)* အိုဇုန်းဓာတ်ငွေ့ ao -zone-dhat-ngwae

ozone layer *(n.)* အိုဇုန်းလွှာ ao-zone-lwhar

P

pace *(v.)* လျှောက်လှမ်းသည် shout-hlam-sai

pace *(n.)* ခြေတစ်လှမ်း chay-ta-hlam

pacemaker *(n.)* ဦးဆောင်ပြေးသူ၊ နှလုံးခုန်နှုန်းမှန်ကိရိယာ u-saung-pyay -suu, nha-lone-hkone-hnone-mhaan-ka-ri-yar

pachidermatous *(adj.)* အရေထူသော a ray htuusaw

pachyderm *(n.)* အရေထူ သတ္တဝါ a-ray-htuu-sat-ta-war

pacific *(adj.)* ငြိမ်းချမ်းသော ngyaim-cham-saw

pacifier *(n.)* ကိုယ်တိုင်းရုပ် ko-tine-rote

pacifism *(n.)* ရန်သူကို မထိပဲ ဂိမ်းနိုင်ရန် နောက်ထပ် စိန်ခေါ်မှု raansuuko ma htipell gaim-nineraan nout-htaut sein-hkaw-mhu

pacifist *(n.)* ငြိမ်းချမ်းရေးမြတ်နိုးသူ ngyeim-cham-rayymyat-noesuu

pacify *(v.)* နှစ်သိမ့်သည်၊ ချွေးသိပ်သည် nhait-seimt-sai, chway-siut-sai

pack *(n.)* ကတ်ထူဘူး kaat-htuu-bhuu

package *(n.)* အထုပ် a-htote

packet *(n.)* ကတ်ထူဘူး၊ အထုပ် kaat-htuu-bhuu, a-htote

packing *(n.)* ပါကင်၊ ထုပ်ပိုးပြင်ဆင်ခြင်း par-kin, htote-poe-pyin-sin-chinn

pact *(n.)* ကတိကဝတ်၊ ပဋိညာဉ် ka-ti-ka-waat, pa-tain-nyin

pad *(v.)* ခုသည်၊ ခံသည် hku-sai , hkan-sai

pad *(n.)* အခု၊ အခံ a-hku, a-hkan

padding *(n.)* အခုအခံ a-hku a-hkan

paddle *(n.)* လှော်တက် hlaaw-taat

paddle *(v.)* လှော်သည် hlaaw-sai

paddy *(n.)* လယ်ကွက် laal-kwat

paediatric *(adj.)* ကလေးနှင့် ပတ်သက်သော ka-layy-nint-paat-saat-saw

paedologist *(n.)* ကလေးအထူးကုဆရာဝန် ka-layy-aa-htuu-ku-sa-rar-waan

paedology *(n.)* မြေကြီးဆိုင်ရာ သိပ္ပံပညာခွဲ myay kyee-sinerar sippan-pin-nyarhkwal

paedophile *(n.)* ကလေးများကို ကာမစိတ်တိမ်းညွတ်သူ ka-layy-myarr-ko-kar-ma-sate-taim-nyut-suu

paedophilia *(n.)* ကလေးများကို ကာမစိတ်တိမ်းညွတ်မှု အခြေအနေ ka-layy-myarr-ko-kar-ma-sate-taim-nytt-mhu-aa-chay-aa-nay
paedophiliac *(n.)* ကလေးငယ်ကို လိင်မှုဆိုင်ရာ ဆွဲဆောင်သူ kalayy-ngaalko lain-mhusinerar swalsaungsuu
pagan *(n.)* ဒိဋ္ဌိ di-hti
paganism *(n.)* ဗာဟီရဝါဒ bar-he-ra-war-da
paganistic *(adj.)* ဗဟုဝါဒကိုးကွယ်သော bahu warda-koekwalsaw
page *(v.)* ပေဂျာဖြင့် ဆက်သွယ်သည် pay-gyaar-hpyint-saat-swal-sai
page *(n.)* စာမျက်နှာ sar-myet-nhar
pageant *(n.)* ခမ်းနားသော ပသာဒ hkam-narr-saw-pa-sar-da
pageantry *(n.)* ခမ်းနားကြီးကျယ်မှု hkam-narr-kyee-kyaal-mhu
pagoda *(n.)* ဘုရား pha-rarr
pail *(n.)* လက်ဆွဲပုံး laat-swal-pone
pain *(v.)* နာကျင်သည် nar-kyin-sai
pain *(n.)* နာကျင်မှု nar-kyin-mhu
pain relief *(n.)* နာကျင်မှု သက်သာခြင်း nar-kyin-mhu-saat-sar-chinn
painful *(adj.)* နာကျင်သော nar-kyin-saw
painstaking *(adj.)* အပင်ပန်းခံသော a-pin-pan-hkan-saw
paint *(v.)* ဆေးသုတ်သည် say-sote-sai
paint *(n.)* ဆေး say
paintbrush *(n.)* စုတ်တံ *sote-tan*
painter *(n.)* ဆေးသုတ်သမား say-sote-sa-marr
painting *(n.)* ပန်းချီ၊ ဆေးသုတ်ခြင်း paann-chae, say-sote-chinn
pair *(n.)* တစ်ရန်၊ တစ်စုံ ta-raan, ta-sone
pal *(n.)* မိတ်ဆွေ mate-sway
palace *(n.)* နန်းတော် naan-taw
palanquin *(n.)* ဝေါယဉ် waw-yin
palatable *(adj.)* အရသာရှိသော aa-ra-sar-shi-saw
palatal *(adj.)* အာခေါင်နှင့် ဆိုင်သော aar-hkaung-nint-sine-saw
palate *(n.)* အာခေါင် aar-hkaung
palatial *(adj.)* နန်းတော်အလား naann-taw-aa-larr
pale *(adj.)* ဖြူရော်သော hpyu-raw-saw
pale *(n.)* ခြံတိုင် chan-tine
paleness *(n.)* ဖြူဖပ်ဖြူရော်ဖြစ်ခြင်း hpyu-hpaut-hpyu-raw-hpyit-chinn
paleobiological *(adj.)* အပင်၊ သတ္တဝါရုပ်ကြွင်းလေ့လာမှုပညာနှင့် ဆိုင်သော a pin , sattawar rote-kywin laelarmhu pinnyar-nint sinesaw
paleobiologist *(n.)* အပင်၊ သတ္တဝါရုပ်ကြွင်းလေ့လာမှုပညာရှင် a pain , sattawar rotekywin laelarmhupin-nyarshin
paleobiology *(n.)* အပင်၊ သတ္တဝါရုပ်ကြွင်းလေ့လာမှုပညာ a pain , sattawar rotekywin laelarmhupin-nyar
paleoecologist *(n.)* ရှေးဟောင်းဂေဟဗေဒပညာရှင် shayyhaungg gay ha bayda-pin-nyarshin
paleoecology *(n.)* ရှေးဟောင်းဂေဟဗေဒ shayyhaungg gay habayda
paleolithic *(n.)* လွန်ခဲ့သော နှစ်နှစ်သန်းခွဲကာလ lwanhkaesaw nit-nha saann hkwal-karla
paleontologist *(n.)* ရုပ်ကြွင်းလေ့လာမှုပညာရှင် rotekyawin laelar-mhupin-nyarshin

paleontology *(n.)* ရုပ်ကြွင်းလေ့လာမှုပညာ rotekyawin laelar-mhupin-nyar
palette *(n.)* ဆေးစပ်ပြား say-saut-pyar
palm *(v.)* လက်ထဲတွင် ဝှက်သည် *laat-htell-twin-whaat-sai*
palmist *(n.)* လက္ခဏာဆရာ lakh-ka-nar-sa-rar
palmistry *(n.)* လက္ခဏာဗေဒင် lakh-ka-nar-bay-din
palpable *(adj.)* ထိသိနိုင်သော hti-si-nine-saw
palpitate *(v.)* တုန်သည် tone-sai
palpitation *(n.)* တဆတ်ဆတ်တုန်ခြင်း ta-saat-saat-tone-chinn
palsy *(n.)* လေဖြတ်ခြင်း lay-hpyat-chinn
paltry *(adj.)* သေးနုပ်သော say-note-saw
pamper *(v.)* အလိုလိုက်သည် a-lo-lite-the
pamphlet *(n.)* လက်ကမ်းစာစောင် lat-khan-sar-saung
pamphleteer *(n.)* လက်ကမ်းစာစောင်ရေးသူ lat-khan-sar-saung-yay-thu
panacea *(n.)* ကုနည်း၊ ကုထုံး ku naee, ku-htone
pandemonium *(n.)* ဝရုန်းသုန်းကား ဖြစ်ခြင်း wa-yone-tone-gar-phit-chin
pane *(n.)* ပြတင်းမှန်တစ်ချပ် pya-tin-man-ta-chat
panegyric *(n.)* ချီးကျူးထောမနာ ဩဘာစကား chee-kyu-htaw-pa-nar-aw-bar-sa-kar
panel *(v.)* အကွက်ဖော်သည် a-kwat-phaw-the
panel *(n.)* မှန်ပုံကွက်၊ ဘောင်ကွက်၊ ဦးဆောင်ဆွေးနွေးသူအဖွဲ့ hman-pon-kwat, baung-kwat, u-saung-sway-nway-thu-a-phwe
pang *(n.)* စိတ်ထိခိုက်ခံစားမှု seik-hti-khite-khan-sar-mu
panic *(n.)* ကြောက်စိတ်မွှန်ခြင်း kyauk-sate-mun-chin
panorama *(n.)* မြင်ကွင်းကျယ် myin-kwin-kyaal
pant *(n.)* မောပန်းကြီး၍ ပါးစပ်ဖြင့် ရှူရှိုက်သောအသက် maw-paann-kyee-ywe-parr-saut-hpyint-shuu-shite-saw-a-saat
pant *(v.)* မောပန်းကြီး၍ ပါးစပ်ဖြင့် ရှူရှိုက်သည် maw-paann-kyee-parr-sat-hpyint-shuu-shite-sai
pantaloon *(n.)* ဘောင်းဘီပုံစံအမျိုးမျိုး bhaung-bhe-pone-san-aa-myoe-myoe
pantheism *(n.)* အရာခပ်သိမ်းကို ဘုရားအဖြစ် ကိုးကွယ်မှု ဝါဒ a-rar-khat-saim-ko-pha-rar-aa-hpyit-koe-kwal-mhu-war-da
pantheist *(n.)* အရာခပ်သိမ်းကို ဘုရားအဖြစ် ကိုးကွယ်မှု ဝါဒီ a-rar-hkat-saim-ko-pha-rar-aa-hpyit-koe-kwal-mhu-war-de
panther *(n.)* သစ်နက် sait-naat
panting *(n.)* ဟောဟဲဟိုက်သူ၏ အပြုအမူ haw hell hite-suueat aapyu-aamuu
pantomime *(n.)* ဇရုတ်သုတ်ခ ဟာသဖြစ်ရပ် Ba-rote-sote-hka-har-sa-hpyit-rat
pantry *(n.)* ဗီရို၊ စင် be-ro, sin
papacy *(n.)* ပုပ်ရဟန်းမင်းကြီးတစ်ဦး၏ လက်ထက် pote-ra-haan-minn-kyee-ta-u-eat-laat-htaat
papal *(adj.)* ပုပ်ရဟန်းမင်းကြီးနှင့် အတူ လုပ်ရန် ရှိသော pote-rahaann-minn-kyee-nint aatuu lote-raan shisaw
paper *(n.)* စာရွက် sarr-rwat
paper bag *(n.)* စာရွက်ထည့်အိတ် sarr-rwat-htaee-ate

par *(n.)* သတ်မှတ်ရိုက်ချက် saat-mhaat-rite-chet
parable *(n.)* ပုံဆောင်ဝတ္ထု pone-saung-wat-htu
parachute *(n.)* လေထီး lay-htee
parachutist *(n.)* လေထီးခုန်သူ lay-htee-hkone-suu
parade *(v.)* စီတန်းလှည့်လည်သည် se-taann-hleet-lal-sai
parade *(n.)* စီတန်းလမ်းလျှောက်ခြင်း se-taann-lam-shout-chinn
paradise *(n.)* နိဗ္ဗာန် nib-ban
paradox *(n.)* ဝိရောဓိ wi-raw-dhi
paradoxical *(adj.)* ဝိရောဓိဖြစ်သော wi-raw-dhi-hpyit-saw
paraffin *(n.)* ရေနံဆီ ray-nan-se
paragon *(n.)* ပြစ်မျိုးမှဲ့မထင်သူ pyit-myoe-mhaae-ma-htin-suu
paragraph *(n.)* စာပုဒ် sar-pike
parallel *(v.)* မျဉ်းပြိုင် myin-pyaine
parallel *(adj.)* ပြိုင်တန်းလျက်ရှိသော pyaine-taann-lyet-shi-saw
parallelism *(n.)* အလားတူမှု aa-larr-tuu-mhu
parallelogram *(n.)* အနားပြိုင်စတုဂံ aa-narr-pyaine-sa-tu-gan
paralyse *(v.)* အကြောသေသည် aa-kyaww-say-sai
paralysis *(n.)* အကြောသေခြင်း aa-kyaww-say-chinn
paralytic *(adj.)* သွက်ချာပါဒ swat-chaar-par-da
paramount *(adj.)* ထိပ်တန်း htaik-taann
paramour *(n.)* တရားမဝင်ချစ်သူ ta-rarr-ma-win-chitsuu
paraphernalia *(n. pl)* ပစ္စည်းပစ္စယ pyit-see-pyit-sa-ya
paraphrase *(v.)* စကားပြေပြန်သည် sa-karr-pyay-pyan-sai
paraphrase *(n.)* စကားပြေပြန်ခြင်း sa-karr-pyay-pyan-chinn
parasite *(n.)* ကပ်ပါးကောင် kaut-parr-kaung
parcel *(v.)* ပါဆယ်ထုပ်သည် par-saal-htote-sai
parcel *(n.)* ပါဆယ်ထုပ် par-saahl-tote
parch *(v.)* လောင်ကျွမ်းစေသည် laungkyamsaysai
pardon *(n.)* ခွင့်လွှတ်ခြင်း hkwint-lwhaat-chinn
pardon *(v.)* ခွင့်လွှတ်သည် hkwint-lwhaat-sai
pardonable *(adj.)* ခွင့်လွှတ်သင့်သော hkwint-lwhaat-saint-saw
parent *(n.)* မိဘ mi-bha
parentage *(n.)* မိဘမျိုးရိုး mi-bha-myoe-roe
parental *(adj.)* မိဘ၏ mi-bha-eat
parenthesis *(n.)* ဝိုက်ကွင်း wite-kwin
parish *(n.)* အသင်းတော်နယ်ပယ် aa-sainn-taw-naal-paal
parity *(n.)* ငွေတန်ဖိုးချင်းတူညီမှု ngway-taan-hpoe-chinn-tuu-nye-mhu
park *(v.)* ခဏထားသည် hka-na-htarr-sai
parking ticket *(n.)* ဒဏ်ငွေဆောင်သတိပေးစာ dann-gway-saung-sa-ti-payy-sar
parlance *(n.)* စကားပြောပုံပြောနည်း sa-karr-pyaww-pone-pyaww-naee
parley *(v.)* ငြိမ်းချမ်းရေး ဆွေးနွေးသည် ngyeim-cham-rayy-sway-nway-sai
parley *(n.)* ငြိမ်းချမ်းရေး ဆွေးနွေးခြင်း ngyeim-cham-rayy-sway-nway-chinn
parliament *(n.)* ပါလီမန် par-le-maan

parliamentarian *(n.)* ပါလီမန်အဖွဲ့ဝင် par-le-maan-aa-hpwal-win
parliamentary *(adj.)* ပါလီမန်နှင့် ဆိုင်သော par-le-maan-nint-sine-saw
parlour *(n.)* ဧည့်ခန်း eeth-kaann
parody *(v.)* သရော်သည် sa-raw-sai
parody *(n.)* သရော်ခြင်း sa-raw-chinn
parole *(v.)* ခံဝန်ချက်ဖြင့် အကျဉ်းသားလွှတ်သည် hkan-waan-chet-hpyint-aa-kyin-sarr-lwhaat-sai
parole *(n.)* ခံဝန်ချက်ဖြင့် အကျဉ်းသားလွှတ်ခြင်း hkan-waan-chet-hpyint-aa-kyin-sarr-lwhaat-chinn
parricide *(n.)* သွေးသားချင်း သတ်ဖြတ်ခြင်း sway-sarr-chinn-saat-hpyat-chinn
parrot *(n.)* ကြက်တူရွေး kyat-tuu-rway
parry *(n.)* ဖယ်ထုတ်မှု hpaal-htote-mhu
parry *(v.)* ခတ်ထုတ်သည် hkaat-htote-sai
parsley *(n.)* တရုတ်နံနံ ta-rote-nan-nan
parson *(n.)* သင်းအုပ်ဆရာ sin-aote-sa-rar
part *(v.)* ခွဲခွာသည် hkwahl-kwar-sai
part *(n.)* အပိုင်း၊ အခန်း aa-pine, aa-hkaann
partake *(v.)* သုံးဆောင်သည် sone-saung-sai
partial *(adj.)* တစ်ပိုင်းတစ်စ ဖြစ်သော ta-pine-ta-sa-hpyit-saw
partiality *(n.)* ဘက်လိုက်မှု bhaat-lite-mhu
participant *(n.)* အဖွဲ့ဝင် aa-hpwal-win
participate *(v.)* ပါဝင်သည် par-win-sai
participation *(n.)* ပါဝင်ခြင်း par-win-chinn
particle *(n.)* အမှုန် aa-hmone
particular *(n.)* အကြောင်းအချက် aa-kyaung-aa-chet
particular *(adj.)* အထူး aa-htuu
particularly *(adv.)* အထူးသဖြင့် aa-htuu-sa-hpyint
partisan *(adj.)* ဘက်လိုက်သော bhaat-lite-saw
partisan *(n.)* တော်လှန်ရေးပြောက်ကျား taw-hlaan-rayy-pyaut-kyarr
partition *(v.)* ကန့်လိုက်သည် kant-lite-sai
partition *(n.)* ပိုင်းခြားခြင်း pine-charr-chinn
partner *(n.)* လုပ်ဖော်ကိုင်ဖက် lote-hpaw-kine-hpaat
partnership *(n.)* စီးပွားဖက်အဖြစ် see-pwarr-hpaat-aa-hpyit
party *(n.)* ပါတီပွဲ၊ ပါတီ par-te pwal, par-te
pass *(n.)* ဖြတ်ကျော်သည် hpyat-kyaw-sai
pass *(v.)* ဖြတ်ကျော်သည် hpyat-kyaw-sai
passage *(n.)* လမ်းကြောင်း၊ စင်္ကြံ၊ ဖြတ်သန်းခြင်း lam-kyaung, sin-kyaan, hpyat-sann-chinn
passenger *(n.)* ခရီးသည် hka-ree-sai
passion *(n.)* စိတ်အားထက်သန်မှု sate-ar-htaat-saan-mhu
passionate *(adj.)* ပြင်းပြသော၊ ချစ်စိတ်ပြင်းပြသော pyinn-pya-saw, chit-sate-pyinn-pya-saw
passive *(adj.)* ပြုသမျှနုသော pyu-sa-mya-nu-saw
passport *(n.)* နိုင်ငံကူးလက်မှတ် nine-ngan-kuu-laat-mhaat
past *(prep.)* ကျော် kyaw
past *(adj.)* ပြီးခဲ့သော pyee-hkae-saw
paste *(v.)* ကပ်သည်၊ ကူးထည့်သည် kaut-sai, kuu-htae-sai
paste *(n.)* ကော် kaw
pastel *(n.)* ရောင်စုံချယ်ပန်းချီကား raung-sone-chaal-pa-chae-karr

pastime *(n.)* ဝါသနာပါ၍ လုပ်သော အလုပ် war-sa-nar-par-ywe-lote-saw-aa-lote

pastoral *(adj.)* ကျေးလက်သဘာဝသရုပ်ဖော်အနုပညာ kyaay-laat-sa-bhar-wa-sa-rote-hpaw-aa-nu-pa-nyar

pastry *(n.)* အဆာသွတ်မုန့် a-sar-swat-mone

pasture *(v.)* စားကျက်တွင် လှန်သည် sarr-kyet-twin-hlaan-sai

pasture *(n.)* စားကျက်မြေ sarr-kyet-myay

pat *(n.)* ဖွဖွပုတ်ခြင်း hpwa-hpwa-pote-chinn

pat *(v.)* ပုတ်သည် pote-sai

patch *(n.)* အဖာ၊ မျက်စိကာ a-hpar, myet-si-kar

patch *(v.)* ဖာထေးသည် hpar-htayy-sai

patch test *(n.)* ဓာတ်မတည့်ပစ္စည်းစမ်းသပ်နည်း dhat ma tae-pyit-see samsat-naee

patent *(n.)* မှတ်ပုံတင်မူပိုင် mhaat-pone-tin-muu-pine

patent *(adj.)* မူပိုင်ခွင့်မှတ်ပုံတင်ပြီးသော muu-pine-hkwint-mhaat-pone-tin-pyee-saw

paternal *(adj.)* ဖခင်၏ hpah-kin-eat

path *(n.)* လမ်းကြောင်း၊ လူသွားလမ်း lam-kyaung, luu-swarr-lam

pathetic *(adj.)* သနားစဖွယ် sa-narr-sa-hpwal

pathology *(n.)* ရောဂါဗေဒ raw-gar-bay-da

pathos *(n.)* ကရုဏာရသ ka-ru-nar-ra-sa

patience *(n.)* စိတ်ရှည်ခြင်း sate-shi-chinn

patient *(n.)* လူနာ luu-nar

patient *(adj.)* စိတ်ရှည်သော sate-shay-saw

patricide *(n.)* ဖခင်ကို သတ်မှု hpa-hkin-ko-saat-mhu

patrimony *(n.)* ဘိုးဘအမွေ bhoe-bha-aa-mway

patriot *(n.)* မျိုးချစ်ပုဂ္ဂိုလ် myoe-chit-poke-gol

patriotic *(adj.)* မျိုးချစ်သော myoe-chit-saw

patriotism *(n.)* မျိုးချစ်စိတ် myoe-chit-sate

patrol *(n.)* ကင်းလှည့်ခြင်း kinn-hlae-chinn

patrol *(v.)* ကင်းလှည့်သည် kinn-hlae-sai

patron *(n.)* အားပေးသူ၊ ဖောက်သည် ar-payy-suu, hpout-sai

patronage *(n.)* အားပေးမှု ar-payy-mhu

patronize *(v.)* အကျောနှင့် ဆက်ဆံသည် a-kyaw-nint-saat-san-sai

pattern *(n.)* ပုံစံ pone-san

paucity *(n.)* ရှားပါးမှု sharr-parr-mhu

pauper *(n.)* သူဆင်းရဲ suu-sinn-rell

pause *(v.)* ရပ်တန့်သည် rat-tant-sai

pause *(n.)* ရပ်တန့်ခြင်း rat-tant-chinn

pave *(v.)* ခင်းသည် hkinn-sai

pavement *(n.)* ပလက်ဖောင်း၊ လူသွားစင်္ကြံ pa-laat-hpaung, luu-swarr-sin-kyaan

pavilion *(n.)* နားနေအဆောက်အအုံ narr-nay-aa-sout-aa-ohn

paw *(v.)* ကုတ်သည်၊ ခြစ်သည် kote-sai, chit-sai

paw *(n.)* ဖဝါး hpa-warr

pay *(n.)* ပုံမှန်လုပ်ခ pone-mhaan-lote-hka

pay *(v.)* ပေးသည် payy-sai

payable *(adj.)* ပေးချေနိုင်သော payy-chaay-nine-saw

payee *(n.)* ငွေလက်ခံသူ ngway-laat-hkan-suu

payment *(n.)* ငွေပေးချေခြင်း ngway-payy-chaay-chinn

payout *(n.)* ငွေများများစားစား ထုတ်ပေးခြင်း ngway-myarr-myarr-sarr-sarr-htote-payy-chinn
pea *(n.)* ပဲစေ့ pell-sae
peace *(n.)* ငြိမ်းချမ်းရေး ngyeim-cham-rayy
peaceable *(adj.)* အေးချမ်းစွာ နေလိုသော aye-cham-swar-nay-lo-saw
peaceful *(adj.)* ငြိမ်းချမ်းသော၊ ငြိမ်းချမ်းရေးလိုလားသော ngyeim-cham-saw, ngyeim-cham-rayy-lo-larr-saw
peach *(n.)* မက်မွန်သီး maat-mwan-see
peacock *(n.)* ဒေါင်းဖို daungg-hpo
peahen *(n.)* ဒေါင်းမ daungg-ma
peak *(n.)* ထိပ် hteik
pear *(n.)* သစ်တော်သီး sit-tawtsee
pearl *(n.)* ပုလဲ pu-lell
peasant *(n.)* လယ်သမား laal-sa-marr
peasantry *(n.)* တောင်သူလယ်သမားထု taung-suu-laal-sa-marr-htu
pebble *(n.)* ကျောက်စရစ်ခဲ kyaut-sa-rit-hkell
peck *(v.)* ဆိတ်သည်၊ ပေါက်သည် sate-sai, pout-sai
peck *(n.)* ပေါက်ခြင်း၊ ဆိတ်ခြင်း pout-chinn, sate-chinn
peculiar *(adj.)* တစ်မူထူးသော ta-muu-htuu-saw
peculiarity *(n.)* ထူးခြားကွဲပြားမှု htuu-charr-kwal-pyarr-mhu
pecuniary *(adj.)* ငွေကြေးအရ ngway-kyay-aa-ra
pedagogue *(n.)* ဆရာ sa-rar
pedagogy *(n.)* သင်ကြားနည်းပညာ sin-kyarr-nee-pa-nyar
pedal *(n.)* ခြေနင်း chay-ninn
pedant *(n.)* ရှေ့တန်းတင်လွန်းသူ shae-taann-tin-lwann-suu
pedantic *(n.)* ခရေစေ့တွင်းကျလိုက်လွန်းသော hka-ray-sae-twin-kya-lite-lwann-saw
pedantry *(n.)* အသေးအဖွဲကို ဇာချဲ့ခြင်း a-sayy-aa-hpwal-ko-jar-chaae-chinn
pedestal *(n.)* တိုင်ခုံ tine-hkone
pedestrian *(n.)* လမ်းသွားလမ်းလာ lam-swarr-lam-lar
pedigree *(n.)* မျိုးရိုးစဉ်ဆက်ပြမှတ်တမ်း myoe-roe-sin-saat-pya-mhaat-tam
peel *(n.)* အခွံ aa-hkwan
peel *(v.)* အခွံနွှာသည် a-hkwan-nwhar-sai
peep *(n.)* ချောင်းကြည့်ခြင်း chaung-kyi-chinn
peep *(v.)* ချောင်းကြည့်သည် chaung-kyi-sai
peer *(n.)* သက်တူ saat-tuu
peerless *(adj.)* ပြိုင်ဘက်ကင်းသော pyaine-bhaat-kin-saw
peg *(v.)* အဝတ်ညှပ်သည် aa-waat-nyat-sai
peg *(n.)* အဝတ်ညှပ် aa-waat-nyat
pelf *(n.)* ငွေ၊ ချမ်းသာမှု၊ ကြွယ်ဝမှု ngway , chamsar mhu , kywal-wamhu
pell-mell *(adv.)* ဝရုန်းသုန်းကား wa-rone-sone-karr
pen *(v.)* စာရေးသည် sar-rayy-sai
pen *(n.)* ကလောင်၊ ဘောပင် ka-laung, bhaw-pin
penal *(adj.)* ပြစ်မှုဆိုင်ရာ pyit-mhu-sine-rar
penalize *(v.)* အပြစ်ပေးသည် aa-pyit-payy-sai
penalty *(n.)* ပြစ်ဒဏ် pyit-dan
pencil *(v.)* ခဲတံဖြင့် ရေးသည် hkell-tan-hpyit-rayy-sai

pencil *(n.)* ခဲတံ hkell-tan

pending *(adj.)* ဆိုင်းငံ့ထားသော sine-ngant-htarr-saw

pendulum *(n.)* ချိန်သီး chane-see

penetrate *(v.)* ထိုးဖောက်သည် htoe-hpout-sai

penetration *(n.)* ထိုးဖောက်ခြင်း htoe-hpout-chinn

penis *(n.)* လိင်တံ lain-tan

penniless *(adj.)* ငွေအနည်းငယ်မျှမရှိသော ngway aa-nae-ngaal mya-mashisaw

penny *(n.)* ပဲနီ pell-ni

pension *(v.)* ပင်စင်ယူသည် pin-sin-yuu-sai

pension *(n.)* ပင်စင်လစာ pin-sin-la-sar

pensioner *(n.)* ပင်စင်စား pin-sin-sarr

pensive *(adj.)* ငေးစိုက်ဆင်ခြင်သော ngayy-site -sin-chin-saw

pentagon *(n.)* ပဥ္စဂံ pin-sa-gan

pentatonic *(adj.)* အသံငါးခုကို အခြေခံသော aa-san ngarr-hkuko aa-chyay-hkansaw

penthouse *(n.)* မိုးထိတိုက်ခန်း moe-hti-tite-hkaann

peon *(n.)* ပီယွန်ပင် pe ywan-pin

people *(v.)* နေထိုင်လျက်ရှိသည် nay-htine-lyet-shi-sai

people *(n.)* လူ luu

pepper *(n.)* ငရုတ်ကောင်း nga-rote-kaungg

pepper-and-salt *(adj.)* ဆား၊ ငရုတ်ကောင်းပါသော sarr, nga-rote-kaung-par-saw

per *(prep.)* လျှင် hlyin

per annum *(adv.)* တစ်နှစ်လျှင် ta-nit-hlyin

per cent *(adv.)* ရာနှုန်းအားဖြင့် rar-hnone-ar-hpyint

perambulator *(n.)* လေးလက်တွန်းလှည်း lay-laat-twann-hlaee

perceive *(v.)* သတိမူမိသည် sa-ti-muu-mi-sai

percentage *(n.)* ရာနှုန်း rar-hnone

perceptible *(adj.)* သိသာသော si-sar-saw

perception *(n.)* သိမြင်နားလည်ခြင်း si-myin-narr-lai-chinn

perceptive *(adj.)* အမြော်အမြင်ရှိသော a-myaw-aa-myin-shi-saw

perch *(v.)* ဆင်းသက်နားနေသည် sinn-saat-narr-nay-sai

perch *(n.)* အမြင့်တွင် ရှိသော နေရာ a-myint-twin-shi-saw-nay-rar

percussion *(n.)* စည်းချက်တူရိယာ see-chet-tuu-ri-yar

perennial *(n.)* ထာဝရ htar-wa-ra

perennial *(adj.)* အမြဲပေါ်ပေါက်သော aa-myaell-paw-pout-saw

perfect *(adj.)* ပြည့်စုံသော pyi-sone-saw

perfection *(n.)* ခြောက်ပြစ်ကင်း သဲလဲစင် chauk-pyit-kinn-selllell-sin

perfidy *(n.)* သစ္စာမဲ့မှု sit-sar-mae-mhu

perforate *(v.)* အပေါက်ဖောက်သည် a-pout-hpout-sai

perforce *(adv.)* မတတ်သာ၍ ma-taat-sar-ywe

perform *(v.)* လုပ်ဆောင်သည် lote-saung-sai

performance *(n.)* ဖျော်ဖြေရေး၊ စွမ်းဆောင်မှု hpyaw-hpyay-rayy, swam-saung-mhu

performer *(n.)* တင်ဆက်သူ၊ သဘင်သည် tin-saat-suu, sa-bhin-sai

perfume *(v.)* မွှေးကြိုင်သည် *hmway-kyaine-sai*

perhaps (*adv.*) ဖြစ်ကောင်းဖြစ်နိုင်သည် hpyit-kaung-hpyit-nine-sai
peril (*v.*) ဘေးသင့်သည် bhayy-sint-sai
peril (*n.*) ဘေးသင့်မှု bhayy-sint-mhu
perilous (*adj.*) အန္တရာယ်များသော aan-ta-ral-myarr-saw
period (*n.*) ကာလ kar-la
periodical (*adj.*) အပတ်စဉ်ဖြစ်သော aa-paat-sin-hpyit-saw
periodical (*n.*) အပတ်စဉ် စာစောင် aa-paat-sin-sar-saung
periphery (*n.*) အစွန်းပိုင်း၊ အဖျားအနား aa-swann-pine, aa-hpyarr-aa-narr
perish (*v.*) ပျက်စီးသည် pyet-see-sai
perishable (*adj.*) ပျက်စီးလွယ်သော pyet-see-lwal-saw
perjure (*v.*) မုသားသက်သေခံသည် mu-sarr-saat-say-hkan-sai
perjury (*n.*) မုသားသက်သေခံခြင်း mu-sarr-saat-say-hkan-chinn
perk (*v.*) အကျိုးခံစားခွင့် aa-kyoe-hkan-sarr-hkwint
permanence (*n.*) တည်မြဲမှု၊ ခိုင်ကျည်မှု tai-myaell-mhu, hkine-kyai-mhu
permanent (*adj.*) အမြဲတမ်း aa-myaell-tam
permissible (*adj.*) လက်သင့်ခံနိုင်သော laat-sint-hkan-nine-saw
permission (*n.*) ခွင့်ပြုချက် hkwint-pyu-chet
permit (*n.*) ခွင့်ပြုချက်၊ ပါမစ် hkwint-pyu-chet, par-mit
permutation (*n.*) ပတ်လည် အတွဲစဉ် paat-lai-aa-twal-sin
pernicious (*adj.*) ပျက်စီးရာ ပျက်စီးကြောင်း စေတနာပါသော pyet-see-rar-pyet-see-kyaungg-say-ta-nar-par-saw
perpendicular (*adj.*) ထောင့်မှန်ကျသော htaunt-mhaan-kya-saw
perpetual (*adj.*) မရပ်မနားသော ma-rat-ma-narr-saw
perpetuate (*v.*) ဆက်လက်တည်တံ့စေသည် saat-laat-tai-tant-say-sai
perplex (*v.*) စိတ်ရှုပ်စေသည် sate-shote-say-sai
perplexity (*n.*) စိတ်ရှုပ်ဖွယ်ရာ sate-shote-hpwal-rar
persecute (*v.*) နှိပ်ကွပ်သည် nate-kwut-sai
persecution (*n.*) ဖိစီးနှိပ်စက်မှု hpi-see-nate-saat-mhu
perseverance (*n.*) ဇွဲလုံ့လ zwe lont-la
persevere (*v.*) အပတ်တကုတ်ကြိုးစားသည် aa-paat-ta-kote-kyoe-sarr-sai
persist (*v.*) ဇွတ်လုပ်သည် zwut-lote-sai
persistence (*n.*) မဆုတ်မနစ် ကြိုးပမ်းမှု ma-sote-ma-nit -kyoe-pam-mhu
persistent (*adj.*) မရမနေ ဇွဲကောင်းသော ma-ra-ma-nay-zwal-kaungg-saw
person (*n.*) လူ luu
personage (*n.*) အကျော်အမော်ပုဂ္ဂိုလ်များ aa-kyaw-aa-maw-poke-gol-myarr
personal (*adj.*) ကိုယ်ရေး ko-rayy
personality (*n.*) ပင်ကိုစရိုက် pin-ko-sa-rite
personification (*n.*) လူပုဂ္ဂိုလ်အဖြစ် တင်စားသုံးနှုန်းမှု luu-poke-gol-aa-hpyit-tin-sarr-sone-hnone-mhu
personify (*v.*) လူပုဂ္ဂိုလ်အဖြစ် တင်စားသုံးနှုန်းသည် luu-poke-gol-aa-hpyit-tin-sarr-sone-hnone-sai
personnel (*n.*) အမှုထမ်း aa-mhu-htam
perspective (*n.*) ရှုထောင့် shu-htaung-
perspiration (*n.*) ချွေးထွက်ခြင်း chway-htwat-chinn

perspire *(v.)* ချွေးထွက်သည် chway-htwat-sai
persuade *(v.)* ဆွဲဆောင်သည် swal-saung-sai
persuasion *(n.)* ဆွဲဆောင်ခြင်း swal-saung-chinn
pertain *(v.)* ဆက်စပ်သည် saat-saut-sai
pertinent *(adj.)* သက်ဆိုင်သော saat-sine-saw
perturb *(v.)* တုန်လှုပ်သည် tone-hlote-sai
perusal *(n.)* ဖတ်ရှုခြင်း hpaat-shu-chinn
peruse *(v.)* ဖတ်ရှုသည် hpaat-shu-sai
pervade *(v.)* ပြည့်နှက်သည် pyi-nhaat-sai
perverse *(adj.)* ကကြိုကကြောင်နိုင်သော ka-kye-ka-kyaung-nine-saw
perversion *(n.)* သွေဖည်မှု sway-hpai-mhu
perversity *(n.)* ပေကတ်ကတ် pay-kaat-kaat
pervert *(v.)* သွေလှန်သည် sway-hlaan-sai
pessimism *(n.)* မကောင်းမြင်ဝါဒ ma-kaungg-myin-war-da
pessimist *(n.)* အဆိုးမြင်ဝါဒီ aa-soe-myin-war-de
pessimistic *(adj.)* အားရစရာ မရှိသော ar-ra-sa-rar-ma-shi-saw
pest *(n.)* ဖျက်ကောင် hpyet-kaung
pesticide *(n.)* ပိုးသတ်ဆေး poe-saat-sayy
pestilence *(n.)* ကပ်ရောဂါ kat-raw-gar
pet *(v.)* တယုတယ ပွတ်သပ်သည် ta-yu-ta-ya-pwut-sat-sai
pet *(n.)* အိမ်မွေးတိရစ္ဆာန် eain-mway-ti-rait-san
petal *(n.)* ပွင့်ချပ် pwint-chaut
petite *(adj.)* သေးသွယ်ကျစ်လျစ်သော say-swal-kyit -lyit-saw
petition *(v.)* အသနားခံသည် aa-sa-narr-hkan-sai
petition *(n.)* အသနားခံစာ aa-sa-narr-hkan-sarr
petitioner *(n.)* အသနားခံသူ aa-sa-narr-hkan-suu
petrify *(v.)* မှင်သက်မိသည် mhin-saat-mi-sai
petrol *(n.)* ဓာတ်ဆီ dhat-se
petroleum *(n.)* ရေနံ ray-nan
petticoat *(n.)* အတွင်းခံစကတ် aa-twin-hkan-sa-kaat
petty *(adj.)* သေးနုပ်သော say-note-saw
petulance *(n.)* စိတ်ချဉ်ပေါက်ခြင်း sate-chin-pout-chinn
petulant *(adj.)* စိတ်ကောက်တတ်သော sate-kaut-taat-taw
phagic *(adj.)* ဘက်တီးယီးရားကို တွယ်ကပ်သော ဗိုင်းရပ်စ်ဆိုင်ရာ bhaat tee yee rarrko twel katsaw bine-rat sinerar
phalange *(n.)* လက်ချောင်းရိုး laat-chaungg-roe
phalanx *(n.)* လူစုလူဝေး luu-su-luu-wayy
phallic *(adj.)* ပုရိသဘာဝအသွင်ရှိသော pu-ri-sa-bhar-wa-aa-swin-shi-saw
phallocentric *(adj.)* လိင်တံကို အဓိကထားသော laintanko aadhikahtarrsaw
phallus *(n.)* ယောက်ျားလိင်တံ yaut-kyaarr-lain-tan
phantasmagoria *(n.)* အိပ်မက်သဖွယ် လှုပ်ရှားမှုမြင်ကွင်း ain-maat-sa-hpwal-hlote-sharr-mhu-myin-kwin
phantasmal *(adj.)* စိတ်လှည့်စားမှုကြောင့် နိမိတ်ထင်မြင်သော sate-hlae-sarr-mhu-kyount-ni-mate-htin-myin-saw
phantom *(n.)* တစ္ဆေ၊ အာရုံ ta-say, ar-rone

pharmaceutic *(adj.)* ဆေးဖော်စပ်၊ ထုတ်လုပ်၊ ဖြန့်ချိမှုနှင့် ဆိုင်သော say-hpaw-sat, htote-lote, hpyant-chai-mhu-nint-sine-saw

pharmaceutical *(n.)* ဆေး၊ ဆေးဝါး sayy, sayywarr

pharmaceutist *(n.)* ဆေးဝါးကျွမ်းကျင် sayywarr-kywam-kyin

pharmacist *(n.)* ဆေးစပ်သမား say-saut-sa-marr

pharmacy *(n.)* ဆေးဆိုင် say-sine

phase *(n.)* လသဏ္ဍာန်အဆင့်ဆင့် la-san-htan-aa-sint-sint

phenomenal *(adj.)* ထူးကဲသော htuu-kell-saw

phenomenon *(n.)* ဖြစ်စဉ် hpyit-sin

phial *(n.)* ဆေးရည်ထည့်ရန် ဖန်ဘူးငယ် say-rai-htaeet-raan-hpaan-bhuu-ngaal

philalethist *(n.)* အမှန်တရားမြတ်နိုးသူ aa-mhaan-ta-rarr-myatnoesuu

philander *(n.)* မိန်းမလိုက်စားခြင်း mein-ma-lite-sarr-chinn

philanderer *(n.)* မိန်းမလိုက်စားသူ mein-ma-lite-sarr-suu

philandry *(n.)* ယောကျ်ားကို သဘောကျသူ yauk-kyaarrko sa-bhawkyasuu

philanthropy *(n.)* ပရဟိတအလုပ် pa-ra-hi-ta-aa-lote

philological *(adj.)* ဝေါဟာရဗေဒနှင့် သက်ဆိုင်သော waw-har-ra-bay-da-nint-saat-sine-saw

philologist *(n.)* ဝေါဟာရဗေဒပညာရှင် waw-har-ra-bay-da-pa-nyar-shin

philology *(n.)* ဝေါဟာရဗေဒ waw-har-ra-bay-da

philosopher *(n.)* ဒဿနိကပညာရှင် dat-ta-ni-ka-pa-nyar-shin

philosophical *(adj.)* ဒဿနိက dat-ta-ni-ka

philosophy *(n.)* ဒဿနိကဗေဒ dat-ta-ni-ka-bay-da

phone *(n.)* ဖုန်း hpone

phonetic *(adj.)* သဒ္ဒဗေဒ sad-da-bay-da

phonetics *(n.)* သဒ္ဒဗေဒ sad-da-bay-da

phosphate *(n.)* ဖော့စဖိတ်ဓာတ် hpot-sa-hpate-dhrat

phosphorus *(n.)* ဖော့စဖရပ်ဓာတ် hpot-sa-hpa-rat-dhrat

photo *(n.)* ဓာတ်ပုံ dhrat-pone

photocopy *(n.)* မိတ္တူ meit-tuu

photogenic *(adj.)* ဓာတ်ပုံစားသော dhrat-pone-sarr-saw

photograph *(n.)* ဓာတ်ပုံ dhrat-pone

photograph *(v.)* ဓာတ်ပုံရိုက်သည် dhrat-pone-rite-sai

photographer *(n.)* ဓာတ်ပုံဆရာ dhrat-pone-sa-rar

photographic *(adj.)* ဓာတ်ပုံရိုက်ရာတွင် သုံးသော dhrat-pone-rite-rar-twin-sone-saw

photography *(n.)* ဓာတ်ပုံပညာ dhrat-pone-pa-nyar

phrase *(v.)* စီကုံးသည် se-kone-sai

phrase *(n.)* ပုဒ်စု pud-su

phraseology *(n.)* စကားအစီအစဉ် sa-karr-aa-se-aa-sin

physic *(v.)* ကုသသည် kusasai

physic *(n.)* ဝမ်းပျော့ဆေး wam pyawt-sayy

physical *(adj.)* ကိုယ်ခန္ဓာ ko-hkan-dhar

physician *(n.)* ဆရာဝန် sa-rar-waan

physicist *(n.)* ရူပဗေဒပညာရှင် ruu-pa-bay-da-pa-nyar-shin

physics *(n.)* ရူပဗေဒ ruu-pa-bay-da

physiognomy *(n.)* ရုပ်လက္ခဏာ rote-lak-hka-nar

physique *(n.)* ကိုယ်လုံးကိုယ်ပေါက် ko-lone-ko-pout

pianist *(n.)* စန္ဒရားဆရာ san-da-rar-sa-rar

piano *(n.)* စန္ဒရား san-da-rar

pick *(n.)* လက်ရွေးစင် laat-rway-sin

pick *(v.)* ကောက်ယူသည် kout-yuu-sai

picket *(v.)* သပိတ်တားသည် sa-pate-tarr-sai

picket *(n.)* သပိတ်တားသူ sa-pate-tarr-suu

pickle *(v.)* ဆားစိမ်သည် sarr-sin-sai

pickle *(n.)* ဆားစိမ်ဟင်းသီးဟင်းရွက် sarr-sein-hinn-see-hinn-rwat

picnic *(v.)* ပျော်ပွဲစားထွက်သည် pyaw-pwal-sar-htwat-sai

picnic *(n.)* ပျော်ပွဲစား pyaw-pwal-sarr

pictorial *(adj.)* ပုံများပါသော pone-myarr-par-saw

picture *(v.)* စိတ်ကူးကြည့်သည် sate-kuu-kyi-sai

picture *(n.)* ပန်းချီကား pan-chae-karr

picturesque *(adj.)* ပသာဒဖြစ်သော pa-sar-da-hpyit-saw

piece *(v.)* တပ်စင်သည် tat sainsai

pier *(n.)* ဆိပ်ခံတံတား seik-hkan-ta-tarr

pierce *(v.)* ဖောက်သည် hpout-sai

piercing *(adj.)* စူးရှသော suu-sha-saw

piety *(n.)* ဘာသာတရားကိုင်းရှိုင်းမှု bhar-sar-ta-rarr-kine-shine-mhu

pig *(n.)* ဝက် waat

pigeon *(n.)* ခို hko

piggy bank *(n.)* စုဘူး su-bhuu

pigment *(n.)* အရောင်ပစ္စည်း aa-raung-pyit-see

pigmy *(n.)* ပစ်ဂမီလူမျိုး pit-ga-me-luu-myoe

pile *(v.)* ပုံသည် pone-sai

pile *(n.)* အပုံ aa-pone

piles *(n.)* လိပ်ခေါင်း leit-hkaung

pilfer *(v.)* ကဲ့ဝှက်သည် kae-whaat-sai

pilgrim *(n.)* ဘုရားဖူး pha-rarr-hpuu

pilgrimage *(n.)* ဘုရားဖူး pha-rarr-hpuu

pill *(n.)* ဆေးပြား say-pyarr

pillar *(n.)* တိုင်လုံးပုံ tine-lone-pone

pillow *(v.)* ခေါင်းအုံးသည် hkaung-aone-sai

pillow *(n.)* ခေါင်းအုံး hkaung-aone

pilot *(v.)* မောင်းသည် maung-sai

pilot *(n.)* လေယာဉ်မှူး lay-rin-mhau

pimple *(n.)* ဝက်ခြံ waat-chaan

pin *(v.)* ပင်အပ်ဖြင့် တွဲသည် pin-at-hpyint-twal-sai

pin *(n.)* ပင်အပ် pin-at

pinch *(n.)* ဆိတ်ခြင်း sate-chinn

pinch *(v.)* ဆိတ်သည် sate-sai

pine *(v.)* ဆွေးသည် sway-sai

pine *(n.)* ထင်းရှူးပင် htinn-shuu-pin

pineapple *(n.)* နာနတ်သီး nar-naat-see

pink *(adj.)* ပန်းရောင် paan-raung

pink *(n.)* ပန်းရောင် paan-raung

pinkish *(adj.)* ပန်းနုရောင် paan-nu-raung

pinnacle *(n.)* အထွတ်အထိပ် aa-htwat-aa-hteik

pioneer *(v.)* တီထွင်သည် te-htwin-sai

pioneer *(n.)* တီထွင်သူ te-htwin-suu

pious *(adj.)* ဘာသာတရားကိုင်းရှိုင်းသော bhar-sar-ta-rarr-kine-shine-saw
pipe *(n.)* ပိုက် pite
piquant *(adj.)* မြက်မြက်စက်စက်ရှိသော myaat-myaat-saat-saat-shi-saw
piracy *(n.)* ပင်လယ်ဓားပြမှု pin-laal-dharr-pya-mhu
pirate *(v.)* မူပိုင်ခွင့်ကို ထိပါး၍ ခိုးချသည် muu-pine-hkwint-ko-hti-parr-hkoe-cha-sai
pirate *(n.)* ပင်လယ်ဓားပြ၊ မူပိုင်ခွင့်ကို ထိပါးခိုးချသူ pin-laal-dharr-pya, muu-pine-hkwint-ko-hti-parr-hkoe-cha-suu
pistol *(n.)* ပစ္စတို pyit-sa-to
piston *(n.)* ပစ္စတင် pyit-sa-tin
pit *(v.)* အချိုင့် ဖြစ်ပေါ်စေသည် a-chaine-hpyit-paw-say-sai
pit *(n.)* ချိုင့်၊ တွင်း၊ ကျင်း chaint, twin, kyinn
pitch *(n.)* ကစားကွင်း ka-sarr-kwin
pitcher *(n.)* ကရား ka-rarr
piteous *(adj.)* သနားစရာ sa-narr-sa-rar
pitfall *(n.)* ကြိုလင့်နေသော ဘေးရန် kyo-lint-nay-saw-bhayy-raan
pitiable *(adj.)* သနားကရုဏာသက်စရာ sa-narr-ka-ru-nar-saat-sa-rar
pitiful *(adj.)* သနားချင့်စဖွယ် sa-narr-chint-sa-hpwal
pitiless *(adj.)* အကြင်နာမဲ့သော aa-kyin-nar-mae-saw
pitman *(n.)* မိုင်းအလုပ်သမား mine-aa-lotesamarr
pittance *(n.)* တစ်ပဲခြောက်ပြား ta-pell-chauk-pyarr
pity *(v.)* သနားသည် sa-narr-sai
pity *(n.)* သနားခြင်း sa-narr-chinn
pivot *(v.)* ချာခနဲ လှည့်သည် chaar-hka-nell-hlae-sai
pixel *(n.)* ပုံပစ်ဇယ် pone-pit-zal
pixelate *(v.)* ပုံကို ပစ်ဇယ်အဖြစ်ခွဲသည် poneko pait jaal aahpyit hkwalsai
pizza *(n.)* ပီဇာ pe-zar
pizzeria *(n.)* ပီဇာမုန့် pe jar mone
placable *(adj.)* ခွင့်လွှတ်လွယ်သော hkwng lwhaat lwalsaw
placard *(n.)* လက်ကိုင်ပိုစတာ laat-kine-po-sa-tar
placate *(v.)* ဖျောင်းဖျသည် hpyaung-hpya-sai
placative *(adj.)* စိတ်အေးချမ်းသော sate aayyhkyamsaw
placatory *(adj.)* ကျေရာကျေကြောင်း kyaay-rar-kyaay-kyaungg
place *(v.)* ထားသည် htarr-sai
place *(n.)* နေရာ nay-rar
placebic *(adj.)* အာနိသင်မဲ့ဆေးကဲ့သို့ အလုပ်လုပ်သော aarnisin mae sayy-kaeshoet aalotelotesaw
placebo *(n.)* အာနိသင်မရှိသောဆေး aar-ni-sin-ma-shi-saw-sayy
placement *(n.)* ထားခြင်း htarr-chinn
placenta *(n.)* အချင်း aa-chinn
placid *(adj.)* တည်ငြိမ်သော tai-ngyein-saw
plague *(v.)* ဒုက္ခပေးသည် duk-hka-payy-sai
plague *(adj.)* ဆက်တိုက် စိတ်ဆိုးစေသည် saat-tite sate-soe-saysai
plain *(adj.)* ပြောင်၊ ပေါ်ပေါ်ထင်ထင် byaung, paw-paw-htin-htin
plaintiff *(n.)* တရားလို ta-rarr-lo
plan *(v.)* စီစဉ်သည် se-sin-sai
plan *(n.)* အစီအစဉ် aa-se-aa-sin

plane *(adj.)* ပြင်ညီ pyin-nye

plane *(n.)* လေယာဉ် lay-rin

planet *(n.)* ဂြိုလ် gyo

planetary *(adj.)* ဂြိုလ်၏ gyo-eat

plank *(v.)* သစ်သားပြားဖြင့် ကာရံသည် saitsarr pyarr-hpyint kar-ransai

plank *(n.)* ပျဉ်ပြား၊ လမ်းစဉ်ရပ်တည်ချက် pyin-pyarr, lam-sin-rat-tai-chet

plant *(v.)* စိုက်သည် *site-sai*

plantain *(n.)* ငှက်ပျော nghaat-pyaww

plantation *(n.)* အခင်း aa-hkainn

plaster *(v.)* သရွတ်ကိုင်သည် sa-rwat-kine-sai

plaster *(n.)* သရွတ်၊ အင်္ဂတေ sa-rwat, eain-ga-tay

plastic *(n.)* ပလတ်စတစ် pa-laat-sa-tit

plate *(v.)* စိမ်သည်၊ သံချပ်ကာသည် sein-sai, san-chat-kar-sai

plateau *(n.)* တိုးတက်မှု တန်းသွားခြင်း၊ ကုန်းပြင်မြင့် toe-taat-mhu-taan-swarr-chinn, kone-pyin-myint

platform *(n.)* စင်မြင့် sin-myint

platinum *(n.)* ပလက်တီနမ် pa-laat-te-nam

platonic *(adj.)* တဏှာကင်းသော ta-nhar-kinn-saw

platoon *(n.)* တပ်စု tat-su

play *(v.)* ကစားသည် ka-sarr-sai

play *(n.)* ပြဇာတ်၊ ကစားခြင်း pya-zat, ka-sarr-chinn

playback *(n.)* ပြန်ဖွင့်ပြခြင်း pyan-hpwint-pya-chinn

playcard *(n.)* ဖဲ hpell

playdate *(n.)* ကြိုစီစဉ်ထားသော အပန်းဖြေမှု kyo sesinhtarrsaw aa-paann-hpyaymhu

player *(n.)* ကစားသူ ka-sarr-suu

playfield *(n.)* ကစားကွင်း ka-sarr-kwin

playful *(adj.)* ဆော့တတ်သော၊ မြူးသော sot-taat-saw, myuu-saw

playground *(n.)* ကစားကွင်း ka-sarr-kwin

playhouse *(n.)* ပြဇာတ်ရုံ pya-zat-rone

plea *(n.)* တောင်းပန်မှု taung-pan-mhu

plead *(v.)* အသနားခံသည် aa-sa-narr-hkan-sai

pleader *(n.)* တရားရုံးတွင် လျှောက်လဲသူ ta-rarrronetwin shout lellsuu

pleasant *(adj.)* နှစ်လိုဖွယ်၊ သာယာသော nit-lo-hpwal, sar-yar-saw

pleasantry *(n.)* စကားစမြည် sa-karr-sa-myi

please *(adv.)* ကျေးဇူးပြု၍ kyaayy-zuu-pyu-ywe

pleasure *(n.)* ပျော်ရွှင်မှု pyaw-shwin-mhu

plebiscite *(n.)* လူထုဆန္ဒ ခံယူပွဲ luu-htu-san-da-hkan-yuu-pwal

pledge *(v.)* ကတိပေးသည် kati-payy-sai

pledge *(n.)* ကတိ၊ သက်သေ ka-ti, saat-say

plenty *(n.)* အများအပြား aa-myarr-aa-pyarr

plight *(n.)* အကျဉ်းအကျပ် aa-kyin-aa-kyat

plod *(v.)* တစ်လှမ်းချင်းရုန်းသည် ta-hlam-chinn-rone-sai

plot *(v.)* ရေးမှတ်သည် ray-mhaat-sai

plot *(n.)* မြေကွက် myay-kwat

plough *(v.)* ထယ်ထိုးသည် htaal-htoe-sai

plough *(n.)* ထယ် htaal

ploughman *(n.)* ထယ်ထိုးသူ htaal-htoe-suu

pluck *(n.)* သတ္တိ sat-ti

pluck *(v.)* ခူးဆွတ်သည် hkuu-swat-sai-

plug *(v.)* ပလတ်ခေါင်းထိုးသည်၊ ပိတ်သည် pa-laat-hkaungg-htoe-sai, pate-sai
plug *(n.)* ပလတ်ခေါင်း pa-laat-hkaungg
plum *(n.)* သပြေမှည့်ရောင် sa-pyay-mhae-raung
plumber *(n.)* ပိုက်ပြင်ဆရာ pite-pyin-sa-yar
plunder *(n.)* လုယက်ယူခြင်း lu-yaat-yuu-chinn
plunder *(v.)* လုယက်ယူသည် lu-yaat-yuu-sai
plunge *(n.)* ထိုးကျသွားခြင်း htoe-kya-swarr-chinn
plunge *(v.)* ထိုးသွင်းသည် htoe-swin-sai
plural *(adj.)* ဗဟုဝုစ် ba-hu-wit
plurality *(n.)* များပြားမှု myarr-pyarr-mhu
plus *(adj.)* အထက် aa-htaat
plus *(n.)* အပေါင်းလက္ခဏာ aa-paungg-lak-hka-nar
plush *(adj.)* ဇိမ်ခံ zain-hkan
plutocrat *(adj.)* ဓနသြဇာကြီးသူ dha-na-aw-zar-kyee-suu
plutonic *(adj.)* ပလူတိုနီယမ်ဓာတ်ပါဝင်သော pa luu to ne yam dhatpar-winsaw
plutonium *(n.)* ပလူတိုနီယမ်ဓာတ် pa-luu-to-ne-yam-dhrat
pluvial *(adj.)* မိုးနှင့် သက်ဆိုင်သော moe-nint sat-sinesaw
pluviometer *(n.)* မိုးရေချိန်တိုင်းကိရိယာ moerayhkyane tinekiriyar
ply *(n.)* အထည်စအလွှာ aa-htai-saa-a-lwhar
ply *(v.)* လွန်းပြန်ပြေးဆွဲသည် lwann-pyan-pyay-swal-sai
plyer *(n.)* ပလာယာ pa laryar
plywood *(n.)* အထပ်သား a-htat-sarr
pneudraulics *(n.)* အငွေ့၊ အရည်နှစ်ခုလုံးဖြစ်သော ငွေ့ရည် သိပ္ပံပညာ aangwae , aarai nhaithku lonehpyitsaw ngwaerai sippanpanyar
pneuma *(n.)* စိတ်ဝိဉာဉ် sate wi nyari
pneumatic *(n.)* လူစီးယဉ် luu seeyin
pneumatological *(adj.)* စိတ်ဝိဉာဉ်၊ ဖြစ်စဉ်များကို လေ့လာသော ပညာနှင့် ဆိုင်သော sate-wi-nyi , hpyit-sin-myarr-ko-lae-lar-saw-pa-nyar-nint-sine-saw
pneumatology *(n.)* စိတ်ဝိဉာဉ်၊ ဖြစ်စဉ်များကို လေ့လာသော ပညာ sate-wi-nyi , hpyit-sin-myarr-ko-lae-lar-saw-pa-nyar
pneumogastric *(adj.)* အဆုတ်၊ အစာအိမ်နှင့် ဆိုင်သော a-sote-a-sar-eain-nint-sine-taw
pneumology *(n.)* အသက်ရှူလမ်းကြောင်းနှင့် အင်္ဂါလေ့လာသော ပညာရပ် a-thet-shu-lan-kyaung-nint-inn-gar-lae-lar-taw-pa-nyar-yat
pneumonia *(n.)* အဆုတ်ရောင်ရောဂါ aa-sote-raung-raw-gar
pneumoniac *(n.)* အဆုတ်ရောင်ရောဂါရှိသူ *aa-sote-raung-raw-gar-shi-thu*
pneumonic *(adj.)* အဆုတ်နှင့် ဆိုင်သော *a-sote-nint-sai-taw*
pneumotherapy *(n.)* လေရှူကုထုံး *lay-shu-ku-htone*
poach *(v.)* ပြုတ်သည်၊ မီးမျှဉ်းမျှဉ်းဖြင့် ချက်သည် pyoke-sai, mee-myin-myin-hpyint-chet-sai
poached *(adj.)* ပြုတ်သော *pyoke-taw*
poacher *(n.)* ခိုးဖမ်းသူ hkoe-hpam-suu
pocket *(v.)* အိတ်ကပ်ထဲ ထည့်လိုက်သည် ate-kat-htel-htae-lite-sai
pocket *(n.)* အိတ်ကပ် ate-kat
pod *(n.)* အသီးတောင့် a-see-taung

podcast *(n.)* **အသံအစီအစဉ်** a-san-a-si-a-sin

podcaster *(n.)* **အသံအစီအစဉ်လွှင့်သူ** a-san-a-si-a-sin-hlwint-suu

podge *(n.)* **ဗွက်အိုင်** bwat-ai

podgy *(adj.)* **ဝတိုသော** wa-to-saw

podiatric *(adj.)* **ခြေဖဝါးနာအထူးကုသော** chay-pha-war-nar-a-htuu-ku-taw

podiatrist *(n.)* **ခြေဖဝါးနာအထူးကု** chay-pha-war-nar-a-htuu-ku

podium *(n.)* **စင်မြင့်** sin-myint

poem *(n.)* **ကဗျာ** ka-byaar

poesy *(n.)* **ကဗျာ** ka-byaar

poet *(n.)* **ကဗျာဆရာ** ka-byaar-sa-rar

poetaster *(n.)* **ခပ်ညံ့ညံ့ကဗျာဆရာ** khat-nyant-nyant-ka-byar-sa-yar

poetess *(n.)* **ကဗျာဆရာမ** ka-byaar-sa-rar-ma

poetic *(adj.)* **ကဗျာဆန်သော** ka-byaar-saan-saw

poetics *(n.)* **ကဗျာသီအိုရီ** ka-byaar-the-o-ree

poetry *(n.)* **ကဗျာ** ka-byaar

poignacy *(n.)* **ဆွတ်ပျံ့ဖွယ်ဖြစ်ခြင်း** swat-pyaan-hpwal-pyit-chinn

poignant *(adj.)* **ဆွတ်ပျံ့ဖွယ်** swat-pyaan-hpwal

point *(v.)* **လက်ညှိုးထိုးသည်၊ ညွှန်ပြသည်** laat-nyoe-htoe-sai, nyun-pya-sai

point blank *(adv.)* **တေ့၊ ပြတ်ပြတ်** tae, pyat-pyat

pointed *(adj.)* **ချွန်သော** chwan-saw

pointedly *(adv.)* **စူးစူးစိုက်စိုက်** suu-suu-site-site

pointedness *(n)* **ချွန်ထက်မှု** chun-htet-mu

pointerless *(adj.)* **ညွှန်တံမရှိသော၊ နည်းပေးလမ်းပြမှု မရှိသော** nyun-tan-ma-shi-saw, naee-payy-lam-pya-mhu-ma-shi-saw

pointful *(adj.)* **ချွန်ထက်သော** chun-htet-thaw

pointillism *(n.)* **အစက်အပြောက်ဖြင့် ပုံဖော်ပန်းချီရေးနည်း** a-saat-a-pyaut-hpyint-pone-hpaw-pan-chae-rayy-nee

pointillist *(n.)* **အစက်အပြောက်ဖြင့် ပုံဖော်ပန်းချီဆရာ** a-saat-a-pyatt-hpyint-pone-hpaw-pan-chae-sa-rar

pointless *(adj.)* **အကျိုးမရှိ** aa-kyoe-ma-shi

pointwork *(n.)* **အမှတ်အစု** a-mat-a-su

poise *(n.)* **ဟန်မူရာ ကြော့မော့ခြင်း** haan-muu-rar-kyaww-mot-chinn

poise *(v.)* **နေသားတကျ ဟန်ထားသည်** nay-sarr-ta-kya-haan-htarr-sai

poison *(v.)* **အဆိပ်ခပ်သည်** aa-seik-hkat-sai

poison *(n.)* **အဆိပ်** aa-seik

poisonous *(adj.)* **အဆိပ်ရှိသော** aa-seik-shi-saw

poke *(n.)* **ထိုးခြင်း** htoe-chinn

poke *(v.)* **ထိုးသည်** htoe-sai

poker *(n.)* **မီးဆွတံ၊ ပိုကာဖဲကစားနည်း** mee-swa-tan, po-kar-hpell-ka-sarr-nee

polar *(adj.)* **ဝင်ရိုးစွန်း** win-roe-swann

polarazing *(adj.)* **ဆန့်ကျင်ဘက်ဖြစ်သော** sant-kyin-bat-phit-taw

polarity *(n.)* **ဆန့်ကျင်ဘက်** saant-kyin-bhaat

polarize *(v.)* **နှစ်ခြမ်းကွဲသည်** na-cham-kwal-sai

polaroid *(n.)* **နေကာအလွှာပါး** nay-kar-aa-lwhar-parr

polary *(adj.)* **ဝင်ရိုးစွန်းတစ်ဘက်သို့ သွားသော** win-roe-swann-ta-bat-thoe-twar-taw

pole *(n.)* **ထိုးဝါး၊ တိုင်၊ ဝင်ရိုးစွန်း** htoe-warr, tine, win-roe-swann

pole dancer *(n.)* တိုင်ပတ်ကချေသယ် tine-pat-ka-chay-sai
polearm *(n.)* လှံချွန်လက်နက် hlaan hkyawan-laatnaat
polecat *(n.)* ဖျံ hpyaan
polemic *(n.)* စကားစစ်ထိုးခြင်း sa-karr-sit-htoe-chinn
polenta *(n.)* ပိုလန်တာအနှစ် polaan tar aanit
police *(v.)* ထိန်းသိမ်းကြပ်မတ်သည် htein-saim-kyat-maat-sai
police beat *(n.)* ရဲကင်းစခန်း rell kinnsahkaann
policeboat *(n.)* ရဲလှေ relllhaay
policeless *(adj.)* ရဲမရှိသော rellmashisaw
policeman *(n.)* ရဲသား rell-sarr
policy *(n.)* မူဝါဒ muu-war-da
polish *(n.)* ပေါ်လစ်တင်ခြင်း paw-lit-tin-chinn
polish *(v.)* ပေါ်လစ်တင်သည် paw-lit-tin-sai
polite *(adj.)* ယဉ်ကျေးသော yin-kyaayy-saw
politeness *(n.)* ယဉ်ကျေးသိမ်မွေ့မှု yin-kyaayy-sin-mwae-mhu
politic *(adj.)* လိမ္မာပါးနပ်သော laim-mar-parr-nat-saw
political *(adj.)* နိုင်ငံရေး nine-ngan-rayy
politician *(n.)* နိုင်ငံရေးသမား nine-ngan-rayy-sa-marr
politics *(n.)* နိုင်ငံရေး nine-ngan-rayy
polity *(n.)* အစိုးရပုံစံနှင့် လုပ်ငန်းစဉ် aa-soe-ra-pone-san-nint-lote-ngaann-sin
poll *(v.)* မဲဆန္ဒရရှိသည် mell-san-da-ra-shi-sai
poll *(n.)* မဲအရေအတွက် mell-aa-ray-aa-twat
pollen *(n.)* ဝတ်မှုန် waat-hmone
pollute *(v.)* ညစ်ညမ်းသည် nyit-nyam-sai
pollution *(n.)* ညစ်ညမ်းခြင်း nyit-nyam-chinn
polo *(n.)* ပိုလို po-lo
polyacetylene *(n.)* ပိုလီအက်ဆီတိုင်လင်းဓာတ် po-le-at-se-tine-linn-dhrat
polyander *(n.)* ပိုလီအန်ဒရီမျိုးနွယ်ဝင် အပင် po-le aaan d re myoe nwalwain aapin
polyandrianism *(n.)* ပိုလီအန်ဒရီမျိုးနွယ် po-le aaan d re myoenwal
polyandry *(n.)* လင်ပြိုင်ယူဓလေ့ lin-pyaine-yuu-dha-lae
polybutene *(n.)* ပိုလီဗြူတင်းဓာတ် po-le-byuu-tinn-dhrat
polybutylene *(n.)* ပိုလီဗြူတိုင်လင်းဓာတ် po-le-byuu-tine-linn-dhrat
polycarbonate *(n.)* ပိုလီကာဘွန်နိတ်ဓာတ် po-le-kar-bhwan nate-dhrat
polycentric *(adj.)* ဗဟိုများစွာ ရှိသော bahomyarrswar shisaw
polycentrism *(n.)* ဗဟိုချက်များစွာရှိသော နိုင်ငံရေး၊ ယဉ်ကျေးမှုစနစ် baho hkyet myarrswarshisaw ninenganrayy , yinkyaayy-mhu-sanit
polychrome *(adj.)* ပိုလီခရုန်းဓာတ် po-le hka ronedhat
polycracy *(n.)* အုပ်ချုပ်သူများစွာဖြင့် အုပ်ချုပ်သည် aotehkyote-suu myarr-swar-hpyang aotehkyotesai
polyene *(n.)* ပိုလီအင်းဒြပ်ပေါင်း pole aainn dyatpaungg
polyform *(n.)* ပိုလီဂွန်ချိတ်ဆက်ခြင်းဖြင့် တည်ဆောက်ထားသော အခဲ po-le gwan chaate-saat-chinn-hpyint tai-sout-htarrsaw aahkell
polygamous *(adj.)* မယားပြိုင် ma-yarr-pyaine

polygamy *(n.)* မယားပြိုင်ယူခြင်း ma-yarr-pyaine-yuu-dha-lae

polyglot *(adj.)* ဘာသာစကားအမျိုးမျိုးပြောနိုင်သော bhar-sar-sa-karr-aa-myoe-myoe-pyaw-nine-saw

polyloquent *(adj.)* စကားများသော sakarr-myarrsaw

polymath *(n.)* ဗဟုသုတနှံ့စပ်သူ bahusut nhaan sautsuu

polymer *(n.)* ပိုလီမာ po-le-mar

polymerize *(v.)* မိုနိုမာကို ပိုလီမာပြောင်းသည် mo no marko polemar pyaunggsai

polymetallic *(adj.)* သတ္တုဓာတ်များစွာပါဝင်သော sattu dhat myarr-swarparwinsaw

polymethine *(n.)* ပိုလီမီတင်းဒြပ်ပေါင်း po-le me tinn dyat-paungg

polymethylene *(n.)* ပိုလီမီတိုင်လင်းဓာတ် po-le me tine linn-dhrat

polymicrobial *(adj.)* ပိုးအမျိုးပေါင်းများစွာနှင့် ဆိုင်သော poe aamyoe paunggmyarr-swar-nint sinesaw

polymolecular *(adj.)* မော်လီကျူးများစွာ maw le kyauumyarr-swar

polymorph *(n.)* ပုံစံများစွာ ponehcanmyarrhcwar

polymorphic *(adj.)* ရုပ်သွင်အဆင့်အမျိုးမျိုးကူးပြောင်းဖြစ်ပေါ်သော rote swin aa-sint aa-myoe-myoe kuu-pyaung-hpyit-paw-saw

polymorphism *(n.)* ပုံစံများစွာ ဆက်လက်ယူနိုင်စွမ်း pone-sanmyarrhcwar saatlaat yuu-nine-swam

polymorphosis *(n.)* ပုံစံများစွာ ဆက်လက်ယူနိုင်စွမ်းရှိခြင်း pone-sanmyarr-swar saatlaat yuu ninehcwmshihkyinn

polynucleate *(adj.)* နယူကလိယများစွာ n yuu k li yamyarr-swar

polypharmacal *(adj.)* ဆေးများများစွာဆိုင်ရာ sayymyarr myarr-swar-sinerar

polypropylene *(n.)* ပိုလီပရိုပိုင်လင်း *Po-le paro pine lin*

polyprotein *(n.)* ပရိုတိန်းဓာတ်များစွာ paro tein dhat myarr-swar

polysemia *(n.)* အဓိပ္ပါယ်များစွာ ဖြစ်နိုင်သော စကားလုံး၊ လက္ခဏာ၊ သင်္ကေတဂုဏ်သတ္တိ aa-dhate-palmyarr-swar hpyit-ninesaw sa-karrlone , lakhkanar , sin-k-tay gonsatti

polytechnic *(adj.)* နည်းပညာမျိုးစုံ naee-pin-nyarmyoe-sone

polytheism *(n.)* ဗဟုနာထဝါဒ bahu nar hta-war-da

polytheist *(n.)* ဗဟုနာထဝါဒီ bahu nar hta-war-de

polytheistic *(adj.)* နတ်ဘုရားတစ်ပါးမက ကိုးကွယ်သော naat pha-rarr ta-parr mak koe-kwal-saw

pomp *(n.)* ခမ်းနားမှု hkam-narrmhu

pomposity *(n.)* ဟိတ်ဟန် hate-haan

pompous *(adj.)* ဟိတ်ဟန်များသော hate haan-myarr-saw

pond *(n.)* ရေကန်ငယ် ray kaan-ngaal

ponder *(v.)* တွေးဆသည် tway sa-sai

pony *(n.)* မြင်းပု myinn-pu

poor *(adj.)* ဆင်းရဲသော sinn-rell-saw

pop *(n.)* ဖောက်ခနဲမြည်သံ hpout hka nell myi-san

pope *(n.)* ပုပ်ရဟန်းမင်းကြီး poterahaannmainnkyee

poplar *(n.)* ပေါ့ပလာပင် pot pa lar-pin

poplin *(n.)* ပေါ်ပလင်ပိတ် paw pa lin-pate

populace *(n.)* လူထု luu-htu

popular *(adj.)* **ထင်ပေါ်သော** htinpawsaw

popularity *(n.)* **ရေပန်းစားမှု** ray-paann-sarr-mhu

popularize *(v.)* **နာမည်ကြီးအောင် လုပ်သည်** narmai-kyee-aaung lote-sai

populate *(v.)* **နေထိုင်သည်** nayhtine-sai

population *(n.)* **လူဦးရေ** luu uray

populous *(adj.)* **လူဦးရေသိပ်သည်းသော** luu u ray seik saee-saw

porcelain *(n.)* **ကြွေထည်** kyay-htai

porch *(n.)* **ဆင်ဝင်** sin-win

pore *(n.)* **ချွေးပေါက်** chwaypout

pork *(n.)* **ဝက်သား** waatsarr

porridge *(n.)* **အုတ်ဂျုံယာဂု** aote gyaone-yar-gu

port *(n.)* **ဆိပ်ကမ်းမြို့** seikkammyoe

portable *(adj.)* **သယ်ရလွယ်သော** saal ra lwalsaw

portage *(n.)* **သယ်ဆောင်ခြင်း** *tal-saung-chin*

portal *(n.)* **မုခ်ဝ** mote-wa

portend *(v.)* **နိမိတ်ပြသည်** na-matepya-sai

porter *(n.)* **အထမ်းသမား** aa-htamsa-marr

portfolio *(n.)* **ရုံးအိတ်၊ အချက်အလက်အစုစု** rone aate, aa-chet-aa-laat-aa-susu

portico *(n.)* **ဆင်ဝင်** sinwin

portion *(v.)* **ခွဲတမ်းချသည်** hkwaltam chasai

portrait *(n.)* **ပုံတူ** pone-tuu

portraiture *(n.)* **ပုံတူရေးပညာ** pone-tuu rayypa-nyar

portray *(v.)* **သရုပ်ဆောင်သည်၊ ဖော်ပြသည်** sa-rotesaung sai, hpawpya-sai

portrayal *(n.)* **သရုပ်ဆောင်မှု** sa-rotesaung-mhu

pose *(n.)* **ကိုယ်ဟန်အနေအထား** ko haan-aa-nay-aa-htarr

position *(n.)* **နေရာ၊ ရာထူး** nayrar, rar-htuu

positive *(adj.)* **အပြုသဘောဆောင်သော** aa-pyu-sa-bhaw-saung-saw

possess *(v.)* **ပိုင်ဆိုင်သည်** pine-sine-sai

possession *(n.)* **ပိုင်ဆိုင်မှု** pine-sine-mhu

possibility *(n.)* **ဖြစ်နိုင်ခြေ** hpyitnine-chay

possible *(adj.)* **ဖြစ်နိုင်သော** hpyitnine-saw

post *(v.)* **ကပ်သည်၊ တင်သည်** kat sai, tinsai

postage *(n.)* **စာပို့ခ** sarphoet-hka

postal *(adj.)* **စာပို့၊ စာတိုက်မှ ပေးပို့သော** sarphoet, sar-tite-mha payy-phoet-saw

post-date *(v.)* **နှောင်းရက်စွဲတပ်သည်** nhaung raat-swal taut-sai

poster *(n.)* **ပိုစတာ** po-sa-tar

posterity *(n.)* **နောင်လာနောက်သား** naung lar nout-sarr

postgraduate *(adj.)* **ဘွဲ့လွန်** bhwal-lwan

posthumous *(adj.)* **ကွယ်လွန်ပြီးမှ ချီးမြှင့်ခံရသော** kwal-lwan-pyeemha chee-myint hkan-ra-saw

postman *(n.)* **စာပို့သမား** sar-phoet-samarr

postmaster *(n.)* **စာတိုက်ဗိုလ်** sar-tite-bo

post-mortem *(n.)* **သေပြီးနောက် စစ်ဆေးခြင်း** *say-pi-naut-sis-say-chinn*

post-office *(n.)* **စာတိုက်** sartite

postpone *(v.)* **ရွှေ့ဆိုင်းသည်** shwae-sine-sai

postponement *(n.)* **ရွှေ့ဆိုင်းခြင်း** shwae-sinechinn

postscript *(n.)* **စာကြွင်း** sar-kywin

posture *(n.)* **ကိုယ်နေဟန်ထား** konay haanhtarr

pot *(n.)* အိုး aoe

potash *(n.)* ပြာဓာတ် pyaar-dhrat

potassium *(n.)* ပိုတက်စီယမ်ဓာတ် po taat se yam-dhrat

potato *(n.)* အာလူး aarluu

potency *(n.)* အာနိသင်၊ ထိရောက်မှု aarnisin, hti-rout-mhu

potent *(adj.)* ပြင်းထန်သော၊ အာနိသင်ရှိသော pyinnhtaansaw , aar-ni-sin-shi-saw

potential *(n.)* အလားအလာ aa-larr-aalar

potential *(adj.)* အလားအလာရှိသော aalarr-aalar-shisaw

potentiality *(n.)* အစွမ်းသတ္တိ aa-swam-satti

potter *(n.)* အိုးထိန်းသည် aoehteinsai

pottery *(n.)* မြေထည် myay-htai

pouch *(n.)* အိတ် aate

poultry *(n.)* ဥစား၊ အသားစား ကြက်၊ ဘဲ u sarr , aa-sarr-sarr kyaat , bhell

pounce *(n.)* ခုန်အုပ်တိုက်ခိုက်သည် *kone-oak-tite-khite-the*

pounce *(v.)* ခုန်အုပ်သည် hkone aote-sai

pound *(n.)* စတာလင်ပေါင်၊ အလေးချိန် ပေါင် sa-tar-lin-paung , aalayychane paung

pound *(v.)* တဒုန်းဒုန်းထုသည် ta done done htusai

pour *(v.)* လောင်းသည် laung-sai

poverty *(n.)* ဆင်းရဲခြင်း sinn-rell-chinn

powder *(v.)* ပေါင်ဒါရိုက်သည် paung dar-ritesai

powder *(n.)* ပေါင်ဒါ၊ အမှုန့် paung dar , a hmont

power *(n.)* ပါဝါ၊ အင်အား parwar , aain-aarr

powerful *(adj.)* အားကောင်းသော၊ အစွမ်းထက်သော၊ ပါဝါရှိသော aarr kaunggsaw , aa-swam-htaat saw , parwarshisaw

practicability *(n.)* လက်တွေ့ကျမှု laat-twae kyamhu

practicable *(adj.)* လက်တွေ့ကျသော laat-twaekyasaw

practical *(adj.)* လက်တွေ့ laat-twae

practically *(adv.)* လက်တွေ့ကျကျ laat-twaekyakya

practice *(n.)* လက်တွေ့ laat-twae

practise *(v.)* လက်တွေ့လုပ်သည် laat-twaelotesai

practitioner *(n.)* အသက်မွေးသူ aa-saat-mway-suu

pragmatic *(adj.)* လက်တွေ့ဆန်သော laat-twaesaansaw

pragmatism *(n.)* လက်တွေ့အကျိုးမျှော်ဝါဒ laat-twae aakyoe myahaawward

praise *(n.)* ချီးကျူးခြင်း chee-kyuu-chinn

praiseworthy *(adj.)* ချီးကျူးထိုက်သော chee-kyuu-htite-saw

pram *(n.)* ကလေးလက်တွန်းလှည်း ka-layy laat twann-hlaee

prank *(n.)* နောက်ပြောင်ကျီစယ်မှု nout pyaung kyae saal-mhu

prattle *(v.)* တတွတ်တွတ်ပြောသည် ta-twat-twat-pyaww-sai

pray *(v.)* ဆုတောင်းသည် su-taungg-sai

prayer *(n.)* ဆုတောင်းခြင်း su-taungg-chinn

preach *(v.)* ဟောပြောသည် haw-pyaww-sai

preacher *(n.)* တရားဟောဆရာ ta-rarr-haw-sarar

preamble *(n.)* နိဒါန်း ni-dann

precaution *(n.)* ကြိုတင်ကာကွယ်မှု kyo-tin-karkwal-mhu

precautionary *(adj.)* ကြိုတင်ကာကွယ်မှု kyo-tin-karkwal-mhu

precede *(v.)* ရှေ့ရောက်သည် shae-rout-sai

precedence *(n.)* ဦးစားပေးမှု u sarr-payy-mhu

precedent *(n.)* သာဓက၊ အစဉ်အလာ sar-dha-ka, a sin aalar

precept *(n.)* စည်းမျဉ်း seemyain

preceptor *(n.)* ကျောင်းအုပ် kyaungg-aote

precious *(adj.)* တန်ဖိုးရှိသော taanhpoe-shisaw

precis *(n.)* အကျဉ်းချုပ်၊ သံခိပ် aa-kyin chote, san hkate

precise *(adj.)* တိကျသော ti-kya-saw

precision *(n.)* အတိအကျ aa-ti-aakya

preclude *(v.)* ဟန့်တားသည် hant tarr-sai

precursor *(n.)* ရှေ့ပြေးနိမိတ် shae-pyayna-mate

predator *(n.)* ခေါင်းပုံဖြတ်အမြတ်ကြီးစား hkaung pone hpyat-aa-myat-kyee-sarr

predecessor *(n.)* အလျင်လူ a lyin-luu

predestination *(n.)* ဘုရားသခင်မှ ကြိုတင်ပြဋ္ဌာန်းသည့်အတိုင်း ဖြစ်သည်ဟူသော ဝါဒ pha-rarrsahkinmha kyotin pyahtann seet-aa-tine hpyit-sai-huu-saw war-da

predetermine *(v.)* ကြိုတင်ဟောကိန်းထုတ်သည် kyo-tin hawkeinhtote-sai

predicament *(n.)* အကျပ်အတည်း aa-kyat-aa-tee

predicate *(n.)* ဝါစက war sa-ka

predict *(v.)* ခန့်မှန်းသည်၊ ဟောကိန်းထုတ်သည် hkaant mhaann sai, hawkein-htotesai

prediction *(n.)* ဟောကိန်း hawkein

predominance *(n.)* လွှမ်းမိုးမှု lwam-moemhu

predominant *(adj.)* လွှမ်းမိုးသော lwam-moesaw

predominate *(v.)* လွှမ်းမိုးသည် lwam-moesai

pre-eminence *(n.)* အလွန်အရေးကြီးခြင်း *a-lun-a-yay-kyi-chin*

pre-eminent *(adj.)* အခြားသူများထက် သာလွန်ခြင်း *a-char-thu-myar-htet-tar-lun-chin*

preemptive *(adj.)* လက်ဦးမှု ရယူသော *lat-oo-mu-ya-yu-taw*

preen *(v.)* တသသ အလှပြင်သည် *ta-ta-ta-a-hla-pyin-the*

preexistence *(n.)* ရှေ့ကတည်းက တည်ရှိခဲ့သော အခြေအနေ *shae-ka-tae-ka-the-shi-khae-taw-a-chay-a-nae*

preface *(n.)* နိဒါန်း ni-dann

prefect *(n.)* ကျောင်းသားခေါင်းဆောင် kyaungg-sarr-hkaung-saung

prefer *(v.)* ပိုနှစ်သက်သည် po-nit-saat-sai

preference *(n.)* လိုလားမှု lolarr-mhu

preferential *(adj.)* ဦးစားပေး u sarrpayy

prefix *(n.)* ရှေ့ဆက်ပုဒ် shae-saat-pote

pregnancy *(n.)* ကိုယ်ဝန်ဆောင်ခြင်း ko-waan-saung-chinn

pregnant *(adj.)* ကိုယ်ဝန်ဆောင်သော ko-waan-saung-saw

prehistoric *(adj.)* သမိုင်းမတင်မီ sa-mine ma tin-me

prejudice *(n.)* မျက်စိမှတ် ဘက်လိုက်ခြင်း myet-si-mate bhaat-lite-chinn

prelate *(n.)* ရာထူးကြီးသော ဘုန်းတော်ကြီး rar-htuu-kyee-saw bhone-taw-kyee

preliminary *(adj.)* အကြို၊ ပဏာမ aa-kyo , pa-nar-ma

prelude *(n.)* ရှေ့ပြေး၊ အတိတ်နိမိတ် shae-pyay, aa-tate-na-mate

premarital *(adj.)* လက်မထပ်မီ laat-ma-htat-me
premature *(adj.)* ပုံမှန်ထက်စောသော pone-mhaan-htaat-saw-saw
premeditate *(v.)* ကြိုတင်ကြံရွယ်ထားသည် kyo-tin kyaan rwahl-tarr-sai
premeditation *(n.)* ကြိုတင်ကြံရွယ်မှု kyo-tin kyaan rwal-mhu
premier *(adj.)* ပထမတန်းစား pa-hta-ma-taann-sarr
premiere *(n.)* ဦးဆုံးပွဲ u sone-pwal
premium *(n.)* ပရီမီယမ်ကြေး pa re me yamkyay
premonition *(n.)* စိတ်လေးခြင်း sate layychinn
preoccupation *(n.)* စိတ်စွဲလမ်းမှု sate swal lam-mhu
preoccupy *(v.)* ဖိစီးသည် hpi see-sai
preparation *(n.)* တင်ကြိုပြင်ဆင်မှု tin kyo-pyin-sin-mhu
preparatory *(adj.)* အကြိုပြုလုပ်သော aakyo-pyulotesaw
prepare *(v.)* ကြိုတင်ပြင်ဆင်သည် kyotin-pyinsinsai
preponderance *(n.)* ပိုလွန်မှု po lwan-mhu
preponderate *(v.)* အလေးသာသည် a-lay-tar-the
preposition *(n.)* ဝိဘတ် wi-bhaat
prerequisite *(adj.)* မရှိမဖြစ် ရှိထားရမည့် mashimahpyit shihtarr ra-meet
prerogative *(n.)* အခွင့်အာဏာ a hkwint-aar-nar
prescience *(n.)* ရှေ့ကို ကြို၍ မြင်နိုင်ခြင်း shae-ko kyo myin-ninechinn
prescribe *(v.)* ညွှန်ကြားသည် nyun-kyarr-sai
prescription *(n.)* ဆေးညွှန်း say-nyunn
presence *(n.)* ရှိနေခြင်း shi-naychinn
present *(adj.)* ရှိနေသော shi-naysaw
presentation *(n.)* တင်ပြချက် tin-pya-chet
presently *(adv.)* မကြာမီ၊ လောလောဆယ် makyaarme, law-lawsaal
preservation *(n.)* ထိန်းသိမ်းထားရှိခြင်း htein-saim-htarr-shichinn
preservative *(adj.)* တာရှည်ခံ tar shay hkan
preserve *(n.)* တာရှည်ခံစေသော အရာ tar shay hkansaysaw aa-rar
preside *(v.)* ဦးဆောင်သည် u saung-sai
president *(n.)* သမ္မတ sam-ma-ta
presidential *(adj.)* သမ္မတ sam-ma-ta
press *(v.)* ဖိနှိပ်သည် hpi nate-sai
pressure *(n.)* ဖိအား၊ လေထုဖိအား hpi-aarr , lay-htu-hpi-aarr
pressurize *(v.)* ဖိအားပေးသည် hpi-aarr-payy-sai
prestige *(n.)* သိက္ခာ sate-hkar
prestigious *(adj.)* ဂုဏ်သိက္ခာမြင့်သော gon-sate-hkar myintsaw
presume *(v.)* မှတ်ယူသည်၊ မှန်းဆသည် mhaat yuu sai, mann-sa-sai
presumption *(n.)* မှတ်ယူခြင်း mhaat-yuu-chinn
presuppose *(v.)* ကြိုတင်ကောက်ချက်ချသည် kyo-tin kout-chetchasai
presupposition *(n.)* ကြိုတင်ကောက်ချက်ချခြင်း kyo-tin kout-chetchachinn
pretence *(n.)* ဟန်ဆောင်မှု haan-saung-mhu
pretend *(v.)* ဟန်ဆောင်သည် haan-saung-sai

pretension *(n.)* အယောင်ဆောင်ခြင်း aa-yaung-saung-chinn
pretentious *(adj.)* လေလုံးထွားသော lay lone htwarr-saw
pretext *(n.)* ယိုးမယ်ဖွဲ့ခြင်း yoe maal hpwalchinn
prettiness *(n.)* အလှ aa-hla
pretty *(adj.)* လှပသော hla-pa-taw
prevail *(v.)* အောင်နိုင်သည်၊ ပျံ့နှံ့သည် aaung nine-sai , pyant-nant-sai
prevalence *(n.)* ပျံ့နှံ့မှု pyant-nant-mhu
prevalent *(adj.)* ပျံ့နှံ့ pyant nant
prevent *(v.)* ကာကွယ်သည် karkwalsai
prevention *(n.)* ကာကွယ်ခြင်း karkwalchinn
preventive *(adj.)* ကာကွယ်သော karkwalsaw
preview *(v.)* ရုံမတင်မီ အထူးပွဲ၊ ကြိုတင်အသိပေးချက် rone ma tin-mhae aahtuu pwal , kyo-tin-aa-si-payy-chet
previous *(adj.)* ယခင် ya-hkin
prey *(n.)* သားကောင် sarr-kaung
price *(n.)* ဈေးနှုန်း zayy-hnone
price list *(n.)* ဈေးနှုန်းစာရင်း zayy-hnone-sar-rinn
priceless *(adj.)* တန်ဖိုးမဖြတ်နိုင်သော tan-hpoe-ma-hpyat-ninesaw
prick *(v.)* ဖောက်သည် hpout-sai
prick *(n.)* ဆူးဖြင့် ထိုးခြင်း *suu-hpyint htoechinn*
pride *(n.)* ဂုဏ်၊ ဂုဏ်ယူခြင်း gon, gonyuu-chinn
priest *(n.)* ခရစ်ယာန်ဘုန်းကြီး hka-rit-yan-bhonekyee
priestess *(n.)* ဘာသာရေးခေါင်းဆောင် bhar-sar-rayy-hkaunggsaung
priesthood *(n.)* သာသနာ့ဘောင် sarsa-narbhaung
prima facie *(adv.)* မြင်ရုံမျှဖြင့် myin rone mya-hpyint
primarily *(adv.)* အဓိကအားဖြင့် aa-dhi-ka-aarr-hpyint
primary *(adj.)* အခြေခံ aa-chay-hkan
prime *(n.)* အရွယ်ကောင်း aar-walkaungg
primer *(n.)* သင်ပုန်းကြီး sin-pone-kyee
primeval *(adj.)* ကမ္ဘာဦး kambhar u
primitive *(adj.)* ရှေးဦး shayy u
prince *(n.)* မင်းသား minn sarr
princely *(adj.)* မင်းသား ကြီးကဲအုပ်စိုးသော minn sarr kyee kell aote-soesaw
princess *(n.)* မင်းသမီး min-sa-mee
principal *(n.)* ကျောင်းအုပ်ကြီး kyaungg-aote-kyee
principle *(n.)* အခြေခံသဘောတရား achay-hkansabhaw-tararr
print *(n.)* ပုံနှိပ်စာလုံး pone-nate-sarlone
printer *(n.)* ပရင်တာစက်၊ ပုံနှိပ်စက် pa rin tar saat , pone-nate-saat
printout *(n.)* ပရင်တာမှ ပုံနှိပ်သော စာရွက် pa rin tar-mha pone-nate-saw sarrwat
prior *(adj.)* ကြိုတင် kyotin
prioress *(n.)* တိုက်အုပ်ဆရာ *tite-oak-sa-rar*
priority *(n.)* ဦးစားပေး u sarr-payy
prison *(n.)* ထောင် htaung
prisoner *(n.)* အကျဉ်းသား aa-kyin-sarr
privacy *(n.)* တစ်ကိုယ်ရေလုံခြုံမှု ta-ko-ray-lone-chon-mhu
private *(adj.)* သီးသန့်၊ ကိုယ်ပိုင် see sant , ko-pine
privation *(n.)* စားဝတ်နေရေး ဆင်းရဲခြင်း sarr-waatnayrayy sinn-rell-chinn

privilege *(n.)* အထူးအခွင့်အရေး aa-htuu-aa-hkwin-aa-rayy
prize *(n.)* ဆု su
prize money *(n.)* ဆုငွေ su-ngway
pro forma *(adj.)* ကြိုတင်ပို့ ကုန်ပို့လွှာ kyo-tin-phoet kone phoet-lwhar
probability *(n.)* ဖြစ်နိုင်ခြေ hpyit-nine-chay
probable *(adj.)* ဖြစ်နိုင်သော hpyitninesaw
probably *(adv.)* ဖြစ်ကောင်းဖြစ်နိုင်စွာ hpyit-kaungg hpyit-nine-swar
probation *(n.)* အစမ်းခန့်ကာလ၊ ခံဝန်ချုပ်ဖြင့် လွှတ်ခြင်း a sam hkaant karla , hkan waan-chote-hpyint lwut-chinn
probationer *(n.)* အစမ်းခန့်ကာလတွင် ရှိသူ၊ ခံဝန်ချုပ်ဖြင့် လွှတ်ခံရသူ *a sam hkaant karla twin shi-thu , hkan waan-chote-hpyint lwut-khan-ya-thu*
probe *(n.)* စမ်းတံ၊ အာကာသ စူးစမ်းရေးယာဉ် sam tan , aarkars suusam rayyyarin
problem *(n.)* ပြဿနာ pyat-tanar
problematic *(adj.)* ခက်ခဲသော *hkaat-hkell-saw*
procedure *(n.)* လုပ်ထုံးလုပ်နည်း၊ ကျင့်ထုံး lotehtone-lote-nee , kyint-htone
proceed *(v.)* ရှေ့ဆက်သည် shae-saatsai
proceeding *(n.)* မှတ်တမ်းထုတ်ပြန်ချက်၊ အစီအစဉ် mhaat-tam htote-pyan-chet , aa-sea-a-sin
proceeds *(n.)* ကောက်ခံရငွေ၊ ရောင်းရငွေ၊ အမြတ်အစွန်း kout-hkan ra ngway, raunggrangway , aamyataaswann
process *(n.)* လုပ်ငန်းစဉ် lote-ngaann-sin
procession *(n.)* တန်းစီသွားခြင်း taann-se-swarr-chinn
processor *(n.)* လုပ်ငန်းဆောင်ရွက်သည့် စက် lote-ngaann saungrwat seet saat
proclaim *(v.)* ကြေညာသည် kyay nyarsai
proclamation *(n.)* ကြော်ညာချက် kyawnyar-chet
proclivity *(n.)* အထုံပါမှု aa-htone par-mhu
procrastinate *(v.)* အချိန်ဆွဲသည် aa-chane-swalsai
procrastination *(n.)* အချိန်ဆွဲခြင်း aa-chane-swalchinn
proctor *(n.)* စာမေးပွဲကြီးကြပ်သူ sarmayypwal kyeekyautsuu
procure *(v.)* ရယူပေးသည် rayuu-payysai
procurement *(n.)* ရယူခြင်း rayuu-chinn
prodigal *(adj.)* အသုံးကြီးသော aa-sone-kyeesaw
prodigality *(n.)* အသုံးအဖြုန်း aa-sone a hpyone
prodigy *(n.)* ပါရမီရှင်ကလေး par-rame-shin-kalayy
produce *(n.)* ခြံထွက်ပစ္စည်း chaan htwatpyit-saee
product *(n.)* ထုတ်ကုန် htote-kone
production *(n.)* ထုတ်လုပ်ခြင်း htote-lote-chinn
productive *(adj.)* ဖြစ်ထွန်းသော hpyit-htwann-saw
productivity *(n.)* ကုန်ထုတ်စွမ်းအား kone-htote-swam-aarr
profane *(v.)* ဘုရားတရားကို စော်ကားသည် pha-rarr ta-rarr-ko saw-karrsai
profane *(adj.)* ဘုရားတရားကို စော်ကားသော pha-rarr ta-rarrko sawkarrsaw
profess *(v.)* ဖွင့်ဟသည် hpwint ha-sai
profession *(n.)* အလုပ်အကိုင်၊ အတတ်ပညာရှင် aa-lote-aakine, aa-taat-pa-nyar-shin

professional *(adj.)* **အတတ်ပညာဆိုင်ရာ** aa-taat-pa-nyar-sine-rar
professor *(n.)* **ပါမောက္ခ** par-mawk-hka
proficiency *(n.)* **ကျွမ်းကျင်မှု** kywam-kyin-mhu
proficient *(adj.)* **ကျွမ်းကျင်သော** kywam-kyin-saw
profile *(n.)* **ဘေးတိုက်ပုံ၊ တစ်စေ့တစ်စောင်း၊ ကိုယ်ရေးအကျဉ်း** bhayy-tite pone, ta-sae-ta-saung , ko-rayy-aa-kyin
profit *(n.)* **အကျိုးအမြတ်** aa-kyoe-aa-myat
profitable *(adj.)* **အမြတ်ထွက်သော၊ အကျိုးရှိသော** aa-myat htwat-saw, aa-kyoe-shi-saw
profiteer *(n.)* **ခေါင်းပုံဖြတ်အမြတ်ကြီးစား** hkaungg pone hpyat-aa-myat-kyee-sarr
profligacy *(n.)* **ဖြုန်းတီးခြင်း** hpyuann tee-chinn
profligate *(adj.)* **ဖြုန်းတီးသော** hpyone tee-saw
profound *(adj.)* **အကြီးအကျယ်** aa-kyee-aa-kyaal
profundity *(n.)* **နက်နဲ သိမ်မွေ့မှု** naatnell sin-mwae-mhu
profuse *(adj.)* **အလွန်အမင်း** aalwan-aa-minn
profusion *(n.)* **တစ်ပုံတစ်ခေါင်း** ta-pone ta-hkaungg
progeny *(n.)* **သားသမီး** sarr-sa-mee
programme *(n.)* **အစီအစဉ်** aa-se-aa-sin
progress *(n.)* **ခရီး၊ တိုးတက်မှု** hkaree , toe-taatmhu
progressive *(adj.)* **တိုးတက်သော** toe-taatsaw
prohibit *(v.)* **တားဆီးသည်** tarr-seesai
prohibition *(n.)* **တားဆီးခြင်း** tarr-seechinn
prohibitive *(adj.)* **ပိတ်ပင်ဟန့်တားရာရောက်သော** pate-pin hant tarr rar-routsaw
prohibitory *(adj.)* **ပိတ်ပင်ရန် လုပ်ဆောင်သော** *pate-pin-yan-lote-saung-taw*
project *(n.)* **စီမံကိန်း** se-man-kein
projectile *(n.)* **ကျည်ဖူး** kyai-hpuu
projection *(n.)* **ခန့်မှန်းခြေ၊ ထိုးပြခြင်း၊ အစွန်း** hkaant mhaann-chay , htoe pya chinn , aaswann
projector *(n.)* **ပရိုဂျက်တာ** pa-rogyet-tar
proliferate *(v.)* **တိုးတက်ပွားများသည်** toe-taat pwarr-myarr-sai
proliferation *(n.)* **တစ်ဟုန်ထိုး တိုးပွားလာခြင်း** ta-hone-htoe toepwarr-larchinn
prolific *(adj.)* **လျင်မြန်စွာ ပေါက်ပွားသော** lyin-myanswar pout pwarr-saw
prologue *(n.)* **ခြေဆင်း** chaysinn
prolong *(v.)* **ရှည်စေသည်** shaysaysai
prolongation *(n.)* **ကြာညောင်းစေခြင်း** kyaar nyaungg say-chinn
prominence *(n.)* **ထင်ပေါ်ကျော်စောခြင်း** htinpaw kyaw sawchinn
prominent *(adj.)* **ထင်ရှားသော** htinsharrsaw
promise *(v.)* **ကတိပြုသည်** kati-pyusai
promise *(n.)* **ကတိ** kati
promising *(adj.)* **အလားအလာကောင်းသော** aalarr-aalar-kaunggsaw
promissory *(adj.)* **ကတိကဝတ်ပြုသော** *ka-ti-ka-wit-pyu-taw*
promote *(v.)* **အရောင်းမြှင့်တင်သည်၊ အားပေးသည်** aaraungg myaha int tinsai , aarrpayysai

promotion *(n.)* ရာထူးတက်ခြင်း၊ အရောင်းမြှင့်တင်ခြင်း rarhtuu taatchinn , aaraungg myint-tinchinn
prompt *(adj.)* ချက်ခြင်း chetchinn
prompter *(n.)* ထောက်ပေးသူ htout payysuu
prone *(adj.)* ဖြစ်လွယ်သော hpyit lwalsaw
pronoun *(n.)* နာမ်စား narm-sarr
pronounce *(v.)* အသံထွက်သည် aa-sanht-watsai
pronunciation *(n.)* အသံထွက် aa-san-htwat
proof *(adj.)* ကာကွယ်ပေးနိုင်စွမ်းသော kar-kwal-payy-nine swamsaw
prop *(v.)* ထောက်ထားသည် htout-htarr-sai
propaganda *(n.)* ဝါဒဖြန့်မှု war-da hpyant-mhu
propagandist *(n.)* ဝါဒဖြန့်ချီရေးသမား war-da hpyant chae rayysamarr
propagate *(v.)* ဖြန့်သည်၊ မျိုးပွားသည် hpya ant sai , myoe pwarr-sai
propagation *(n.)* မျိုးပွားခြင်း myoe pwarr-chinn
propel *(v.)* မောင်းနှင်သည်၊ တွန်းပို့သည် maung-nhin sai , twann phoetsai
proper *(adj.)* သင့်လျော်သော sint lyawsaw
properly *(adv.)* သင့်လျော်စွာ sint lyawswar
property *(n.)* ပိုင်ဆိုင်မှု pine-sinemhu
prophecy *(n.)* ဟောကိန်း haw-kein
prophesy *(v.)* ဟောကိန်းထုတ်သည် haw-kein-htotesai
prophet *(n.)* ဘုရားသခင်၏ တမန်တော် pha-rarr-sa-hkin-eat ta-maan-taw
prophetic *(adj.)* နိမိတ်ဖတ်သော na-mate hpaat-saw
proportion *(v.)* ဝေပုံကျသည် *wai-pon-kya-sai*
proportional *(adj.)* အချိုးကျဖြစ်သော aa-choe-kya-hpyit-saw
proportionate *(adj.)* အချိုးကျ aa-choe-kya
proposal *(n.)* အဆိုပြုချက်၊ ချစ်ရေးဆိုခြင်း aa-so-pyu-chet, chit rayy so-chinn
propose *(v.)* အဆိုပြုသည် a so-pyu-sai
proposition *(n.)* အဆိုပြုချက် aa-so-pyu-chet
propound *(v.)* ဖော်ထုတ်တင်ပြသည် hpaw-htote-tin-pya-sai
proprietary *(adj.)* ပိုင်ဆိုင်မှုနှင့် ပတ်သက်သော pine-sine-mhu-nint paat-saat-saw
proprietor *(n.)* ပိုင်ရှင် pine-shin
propriety *(n.)* ရည်မွန်မှု၊ မှန်ကန်မှု rai-mwan mhu , mhaan-kaan-mhu
prorogue *(v.)* အချိန်ဆွဲသည် *a-chane-swal-the*
prosaic *(adj.)* ကြည်နူးဆွတ်ပျံ့ဖွယ်ရာ ကင်းမဲ့သော၊ ငြီးငွေ့ဖွယ်ကောင်းသော Kyi-nuu sut pyaant hpwal-rar kinn-mae saw , ngyee ngwae hpwal-kaungg-saw
prose *(n.)* စကားပြေ Sa-karr-pyay
prosecute *(v.)* တရားစွဲသည် ta-rarr-swalsai
prosecution *(n.)* တရားစွဲခြင်း tararr swalchinn
prosecutor *(n.)* ဆွဲချ swal-cha
prosody *(n.)* ကဗျာဖွဲ့နည်း ka-byaar hpwal-naee
prospect *(n.)* အလားအလာ၊ မျှော်လင့်ချက် aa-larr-aalar, myaw lint-chet
prospective *(adj.)* ရှေ့လာမည့်၊ မျှော်မှန်းရသော shae lar-meet, myaw mhaann-rasaw
prospectus *(n.)* လမ်းညွှန်စာအုပ် lam-nyun-sar-aote

prosper *(v.)* ကြီးပွားသည်၊ အောင်မြင်သည် kyee pwarr sai, aaung-myinsai

prosperity *(n.)* ချမ်းသာကြွယ်ဝခြင်း cham-sar-kywal-wa-chinn

prosperous *(adj.)* ဖြစ်ထွန်းစည်ပင်သော hpyit-htwann sai-pin-saw

prosthetic *(adj.)* အတုဖြစ်သော aa-tu-hpyit-saw

prostitute *(n.)* ပြည့်တန်ဆာ pyae-taansar

prostitution *(n.)* ပြည့်တန်ဆာမှု pyae taan-sar-mhu

prostrate *(v.)* မှောက်လျက် နေသည် mout-lyet nay-sai

prostration *(n.)* မှောက်လျက်သားနေခြင်း mout lyet sarr-naychinn

protagonist *(n.)* ဇာတ်ကောင်၊ ဇာတ်လိုက် zat-kaung , zat-lite

protect *(v.)* ကာကွယ်သည် kar-kwalsai

protection *(n.)* အကာအကွယ် aa-kar-aakwal

protective *(adj.)* အကာအကွယ်ပေးသော aa-kar-aa-kwalpayysaw

protector *(n.)* ကာကွယ်ပေးသူ kar-kwal-payysuu

protein *(n.)* အသားဓာတ် a sarr-dhrat

protest *(n.)* ကန့်ကွက်ချက် kaant-kwat-chet

protestation *(n.)* အလေးအနက်ပြောခြင်း aa-layy-aa-naatpyaww-chinn

protocol *(n.)* စာတမ်း *sar-tan*

prototype *(n.)* ရှေ့ပြေးပုံစံ Shae-pyay-pone-san

proud *(adj.)* ဂုဏ်ယူသော၊ မာနကြီးသော gon-yuu saw , mar na-kyeesaw

prove *(v.)* သက်သေပြသည် saat-say-pya-sai

proverb *(n.)* စကားပုံ sa-karr-pone

proverbial *(adj.)* စကားပုံလာ sa-karr-pone-lar

provide *(v.)* ထောက်ပံ့သည် htout-pan-sai

providence *(n.)* ဘုရားသခင်က သတ္တဝါအပေါင်းကို ကြည့်ရှုစောင့်ရှောက်ပုံ pha-rarr-sa-hkin-ka-sat-ta-war-aa-paungg-ko kyi shu saunt shout-pone

provident *(adj.)* နောင်ရေးအတွက် ဂရုတစိုက် ကြိုတင်စီမံထားသော naung-rayy-aa-twat garu-tasite kyo-tin seman-htarr-saw

providential *(adj.)* ကံကောင်းထောက်မ kan-kaungg htout-ma

province *(n.)* စီရင်စု se-rinsu

provincial *(adj.)* စီရင်စု se-rinsu

provincialism *(n.)* ဒေသစွဲ day-saswal

provision *(n.)* ထောက်ပံ့ခြင်း htout-panchinn

provisional *(adj.)* ယာယီ yarye

proviso *(n.)* စည်းကမ်းချက် saeekamchet

provocation *(n.)* ရန်စခြင်း raan-sachinn

provocative *(adj.)* ဆွပေးသော swapayysaw

provoke *(v.)* ရန်စသည် raan sasai

prowess *(n.)* ကျွမ်းကျင်လိမ္မာမှု kyawmkyin limmarmhu

proximate *(adj.)* အနီးကပ်ဆုံး aaneekautsone

proximity *(n.)* ထိစပ်မှု hti sat-mhu

proxy *(n.)* ကိုယ်စားလှယ် ko-sarr-hlaal

prude *(n.)* ရှက်ချင်ဟန်ဆောင်ခြင်း shat chin-haan-saung-chinn

prudence *(n.)* ဆင်ခြင်မြော်တွေးမှု sin-chin myaw twaymhu

prudent *(adj.)* နှိုင်းချင့်မျှော်ခေါ်သော nhai chint myaw-hkaw-saw

prudential *(adj.)* နှိုင်းဆချင့်ချိန်သော *nai-sa-chint-chane-taw*
prune *(v.)* ဖြတ်တောက်သည် Hpyat-toutsai
pry *(v.)* စပ်စုသည် sat-susai
psalm *(n.)* ဆာလံကျမ်း sar-lankyam
pseudonym *(n.)* အမည်ဝှက် aamaiwhaat
psyche *(n.)* စိတ်သဘော satesabhaw
psychiatrist *(n.)* စိတ်ရောဂါအထူးကု saterawgaraahtuuku
psychiatry *(n.)* စိတ်ရောဂါကုပညာ saterawgar kupanyar
psychic *(adj.)* စိတ်၊ ဝိညာဉ်ဆိုင်ရာ sate, winyarinsinerar
psychological *(adj.)* စိတ်ပိုင်းဆိုင်ရာ sate-pinesinerar
psychologist *(n.)* စိတ်ပညာရှင် sate-panyarshin
psychology *(n.)* စိတ်ပညာ sate-panyar
psychopath *(n.)* စိတ်ဝေဒနာရှင် sate-waydanarshin
psychosis *(n.)* ပင်ကိုစရိုက်ကို ထိခိုက်စေသည့် စိတ်ဝေဒနာ pin ko sa-riteko htihkite saysaeet sate-waydanar
psychotherapy *(n.)* စိတ်ကုထုံး sate-ku-htone
puberty *(n.)* အပျိုဖော်၊ လူပျိုဖော်ဝင်ခြင်း aa-pyao hpaw , luupyao hpaw wainchinn
public *(adj.)* လူထု၊ ပြည်သူ luu-htu , pyisuu
public transport *(n.)* အများသုံးသယ်ယူပို့ဆောင်ရေး aa-myarr-sonesaalyuuphoetsaungrayy
publication *(n.)* ထုတ်ဝေခြင်း၊ စာအုပ်၊ စာနယ်ဇင်း htoteway chinn , saraote , sarnaaljainn
publicity *(n.)* ကျော်ကြားမှု kyaw-kyarrmhu
publicize *(v.)* ကြော်ငြာသည် kyawng-yaarsai
publish *(v.)* ထုတ်ဝေသည် htote-waysai
publisher *(n.)* ထုတ်ဝေသူ htote-waysuu
pudding *(n.)* ပူတင်း puu-tinn
puddle *(n.)* ဗွက်အိုင် *bwat-ine*
puerile *(adj.)* ကလေး Ka-layy
puff *(v.)* မှုတ်ထုတ်သည် mote htote-sai
pull *(n.)* ဆွဲခြင်း swalchinn
pulley *(n.)* စက်သီး saatsee
pullover *(n.)* ခေါင်းစွပ်ဆွယ်တာ hkaungg swut swaltar
pulp *(n.)* ပျော့စိပျော့နဲ့ အခြေအနေ pyaww si pyawwnell aa-chay-aanay
pulpit *(adj.)* တရားဟောစင်မြင့် tararrhaw sin-myint
pulpy *(adj.)* ပျော့စိပျော့နဲ့ pyaww si pyaww-nell
pulsate *(v.)* တဒုတ်ဒုတ်မြည်သည် ta dote dote myisai
pulsation *(n.)* တဒုတ်ဒုတ်မြည်ခြင်း ta dote dote myichinn
pulse *(v.)* ခုန်သည် hkone-sai
pump *(n.)* စုပ်စက် sotesaat
pumpkin *(n.)* ရွှေဖရုံ shway hparone
pun *(n.)* စကားဖန် sakarr-hpaan
punch *(n.)* ထိုးခြင်း htoe-chinn
punctual *(adj.)* အချိန်မှန်သော aa-chane-mhaansaw
punctuality *(n.)* အချိန်မှန်ခြင်း aa-chane-mhaanchinn
punctuate *(v.)* အလေးအနက်ပြုသည် aalayy-aa-naatpyusai
punctuation *(n.)* ပုဒ်ဖြတ်ပုဒ်ရပ် poke hpyat poke-raut

puncture *(v.)* **ပေါက်သည်** pout-sai

pungency *(n.)* **ပျစ်ပျစ်နှစ်နှစ်ရှိခြင်း** pyit pyit nit-nit-shi-chinn

pungent *(adj.)* **ပျစ်ပျစ်နှစ်နှစ်ရှိသော** pyit pyit nit-nit-shi-saw

punish *(v.)* **အပြစ်ပေးသည်** aapyit-payysai

punishment *(n.)* **ပြစ်ဒဏ်** pyit-dan

punitive *(adj.)* **ဒဏ်ခတ်သော** dan-hkaat-saw

puny *(adj.)* **လှီသော၊ ညှက်သော** hlae saw , nyat-saw

pupil *(n.)* **တပည့်** ta paeet

puppet *(n.)* **ရုပ်သေးရုပ်** rotesayyrote

puppy *(n.)* **ခွေးကလေး** hkway-kalayy

purblind *(n.)* **တစ်စိတ်တစ်ပိုင်း ကန်းသည်** *ta-seik-ta-pine-kan-the*

purchase *(v.)* **ဝယ်ယူသည်** waal-yuusai

purchase *(n.)* **ဝယ်ယူခြင်း** waal-yuuchinn

pure *(adj.)* **သန့်စင်သော** saant sinsaw

purgation *(n.)* **ဝမ်းနုတ်ခြင်း** *wan-note-chin*

purgative *(n.)* **ဝမ်းနုတ်ဆေး** wam notesayy

purgatory *(n.)* **ငရဲ** nga-rell

purge *(v.)* **သုတ်သင်သည်၊ သန့်စင်သည်** sote-sin sai , saant sinsai

purification *(n.)* **သန့်စင်ခြင်း** saant sin-chinn

purify *(v.)* **သန့်စင်သည်** saant sin-sai

purist *(n.)* **စာပေအနုပညာကို မတိမ်းမယွင်း ထိန်းသိမ်းလိုသူ** sar-pay-aanu-pa-nyar-ko ma taim ma-ywin hteinsaim losuu

puritan *(n.)* **ပျူရီတန်ခရစ်ယာန်ဂိုဏ်း** pyuu re taan hka-rit-yan-gai

puritanical *(adj.)* **အကျင့်သိက္ခာစောင့်စည်းမှု တင်းကျပ်လွန်းသော** a kyint sate-hkar saunt see-mhu, tinnkyat lwann-saw

purity *(n.)* **စင်ကြယ်ခြင်း** sin kyaal-chinn

purple *(adj./n.)* **ခရမ်းရောင်** hka-ram-raung

purport *(n.)* **ရည်ရွယ်ချက်** rai-rwal-chet

purpose *(n.)* **ရည်ရွယ်ချက်** rai-rwal-chet

purposely *(adv.)* **တမင်သက်သက်** ta-min-saatsaat

purr *(n.)* **သဲ့သဲ့ပြောသံ** sae sae pyawwsan

purse *(v.)* **နှုတ်ခမ်းကို စုဝိုင်းထားသည်** note-hkam-ko su wine-htarrsai

purse *(n.)* **ပိုက်ဆံအိတ်** pite-sanaate

pursuance *(n.)* **လိုက်နာခြင်း** lite-narchinn

pursue *(v.)* **လိုက်သည်** lite-sai

pursuit *(n.)* **ရှာဖွေမှု** shar-hpwaymhu

purview *(n.)* **ပိုင်နက်** pine-naat

pus *(n.)* **ပြည်** pyi

push *(n.)* **တွန်းခြင်း** twann-chinn

put *(n.)* **ကြိုသတ်မှတ်ထားသောဈေးဖြင့် ရောင်းချခွင့်** *kyo-tat-mat-htar-taw-zay-nint-yaung-cha-khwint*

puzzle *(n.)* **ပဟေဠိ** Pa-hayli

pygmy *(n.)* **ပစ်ဂမီလူမျိုး** pit ga meluumyoe

pyorrhoea *(n.)* **ပြည်ထွက်ခြင်း** *pyi-htwat-chin*

pyramid *(n.)* **ပိရမစ်** pi ramit

pyre *(n.)* **မီးရှို့စင်** mee-shoet-sin

pyromantic *(n.)* **မီးစွမ်းအားရှင်** *mee-swan-arr-shin*

python *(n.)* **စပါးအုံး** sa-ba-aone

Q

quack *(n.)* ဂတ်ဂတ်မြည်သံ၊ ရမ်းကု gaat gaat myi san , ram-ku
quack *(v.)* ဂတ်ဂတ်မြည်သည် gaat gaat myi-sai
quackery *(n.)* ရမ်းကုခြင်း ram ku-chinn
quadrangle *(n.)* လေးထောင့်ပုံမြေကွက်လပ် layy htaunt pone myay-kwatlaut
quadrangular *(adj.)* ထောင့်လေးထောင့်ပါသော *htaunt-lay-htaunt-par-taw*
quadrilateral *(n.)* စတုဂံ sa tu gan
quadruped *(n.)* ခြေလေးချောင်းသတ္တဝါ chay layy chaung-sattawar
quadruple *(adj.)* လေးဆ lay-sa
quail *(n.)* ငုံး ngone
quaint *(adj.)* တစ်မူထူးခြားသော ta-muu-htuu-charr-saw
quake *(n.)* ငလျင် nga-lyin
quake *(v.)* လှုပ်သည် hlote-sai
qualification *(n.)* အရည်အချင်း aa-rai-aa-chinn
qualify *(v.)* အသိအမှတ်ပြုခံရသည် aa-si-aa-mhaat-pyu-hkan-rasai
qualitative *(adj.)* အရည်အချင်းအရ aa-rai-aa-chinn aa-ra
quality *(n.)* အရည်အသွေး aa-rai-aa-sway
quandary *(n.)* ဝေခွဲမရခြင်း way hkwal ma-ra-chinn
quantitative *(adj.)* ရေတွက်တိုင်းတာသော ray-twat tine tarsaw
quantity *(n.)* အရေအတွက် aa-ray-aatwat
quantum *(n.)* ပမာဏ pa-mar-na
quarrel *(v.)* ရန်ဖြစ်သည်၊ စကားများသည် raan hpyit-sai , sakarr-myarrsai
quarrel *(n.)* ခိုက်ရန်ဖြစ်ခြင်း hkite-raan-hpyit-chinn
quarrelsome *(adj.)* ရန်လိုသော raan-lo-saw
quarry *(v.)* ကျောက်တူးသည် kyaut tuusai
quarry *(n.)* သားကောင် sarr-kaung
quarter *(v.)* လေးပိုင်းပိုင်းသည် layy pine pine sai
quarter *(n.)* လေးပုံတစ်ပုံ layypone-ta-pone
quarterly *(adj.)* သုံးလတစ်ကြိမ် sone lata-kyaain
queen *(n.)* ဘုရင်မ ba-rin-ma
queer *(n.)* လိင်တူချင်းဆက်ဆံသော ယောကျ်ား lain-tuuchinn saat-sansaw yout-yarr
quell *(v.)* နှိမ်နင်းသည်၊ ချေမှုန်းသည် nhain-ninn sai , chaay-hmone-sai
quench *(v.)* ရေငတ်ပြေစေသည် ray ngaat pyay-saysai
query *(v.)* မေးမြန်းသည် may-myansai
query *(n.)* မေးခွန်း may-hkwann
quest *(v.)* စူးစမ်းရှာဖွေသည် suusam shar-hpwaysai
question *(v.)* မေးမြန်းသည် may-myansai
question *(n.)* မေးခွန်း may-hkwann
questionable *(adj.)* သံသယဖြစ်ဖွယ်ရာ san sa ra hpyit-hpwalrar
questionnaire *(n.)* စစ်တမ်းမေးခွန်းလွှာ sait-tam-mayy-hkwannlwhar
queue *(v.)* တန်းစီသည် taann-sesai
quibble *(v.)* ကတ်တီးကတ်ဖဲ့ပြောသည် kat tee kat hpae-pyawwsai
quibble *(n.)* ကတ်တီးကတ်ဖဲ့ပြောခြင်း kat tee kat hpae-pyawwchinn

quick *(n.)* လက်ထပ်၊ ခြေထိပ် laat-htaik , chay-hteik
quick *(adj.)* လျင်မြန်သော lyin-myansaw
quick fix *(n.)* ရိုးရှင်းသော အဖြေ *yoe-shin-taw-a-phyay*
quickly *(adv.)* မြန်မြန် myan-myan
quicksand *(n.)* သဲဗွက် sell bwat
quicksilver *(n.)* မာကျူရီ mar-kyuu-re
quiet *(v.)* ငြိမ်သက်သည် ngyein-saatsai
quilt *(n.)* အိပ်ရာလွှမ်း ait-rar-lwam
quinine *(n.)* ကွီနိုင်ဆေး qui-nine-sayy
quintessence *(n.)* အနှစ်သာရ aa-nit-sarra
quintessential *(adj.)* စံပြုလောက်သော san pyu loutsaw
quirky *(adj.)* ဓလေ့ထူး dha-lae-htuu
quit *(v.)* ထွက်သည် htwat-sai
quite *(adv.)* အတော်အတန် aa-taw-aataan
quiver *(v.)* တုန်သည် tone-sai
quiver *(n.)* တုန်လှုပ်ခြင်း၊ မြားကျည်တောက် tone hlote chinn , myarr kyi-tout
quixotic *(adj.)* လက်တွေ့မကျသော laat-twaema-kyasaw
quiz *(v.)* မေးမြန်းစုံစမ်းသည် may-myan sonesamsai
quiz *(n.)* ဉာဏ်စမ်းပဟေဠိပြိုင်ပွဲ nyarn-sam pahay-li-pyaine-pwal
quorum *(n.)* အစည်းအဝေးအထမြောက်ရန် အနည်းဆုံး လိုသည့် ဦးရေ aa-see-aa-wayy a hta-myawt-raan aa-nae-sone lo-seet u-ray
quota *(n.)* ကန့်သတ်ပမာဏ kant saat-pa-marna
quotation *(n.)* ကိုးကားချက်၊ နှုန်းထား koe-karr chet , hnone-htarr
quote *(v.)* ကိုးကားသည် koe-karrsai
quotient *(n.)* အတိုင်းအတာ၊ ပမာဏ aa-tine-aatar , pa-marna

R

rabbi *(n.)* ဂျူးဓမ္မဆရာ juu-dham-ma-sarar
rabbit *(n.)* ယုန် yone
rabble *(n.)* ဝရုန်းသုန်းကား wa-rone-sonekarr
rabies *(n.)* ခွေးရူးပြန်ရောဂါ hkway-ruu pyan-rawgar
race *(v.)* ယှဉ်ပြေးသည် shin pyaysai
race *(n.)* အပြေးပြိုင်ပွဲ a pyay-pyaine-pwal
racial *(adj.)* လူမျိုးရေး luumyoe-rayy
racialism *(n.)* လူမျိုးကြီးဝါဒ luumyoe-kyeewarda
racism *(n.)* လူမျိုးကြီးဝါဒ luumyoe-kyeewarda
racist *(adj.)* လူမျိုးရေးဝါဒီ luumyoe-rayywarde
rack *(n.)* စင် sin
rack *(v.)* ဖိစီးနှိပ်စက်လျက် ရှိသည် hpi see nhate-saatlyet shisai
racket *(n.)* တင်းနစ်ဘောလုံး tinn-nit-bhawlone
radiance *(n.)* ထွန်းလင်းဝင်းပခြင်း htwann-linn winn pachinn
radiant *(adj.)* အလင်း၊ အပူဓာတ် ဖြာထွက်သော aa-lainn , aa-puu-dhrat hpyaar-htwat-saw
radiate *(v.)* ဖြာထွက်သည် hpyaar htwat-sai
radiation *(n.)* ရောင်ခြည်ဖြာခြင်း raung-chi hpyaar-chinn

radical *(adj.)* အရင်းအမြစ်ဖြစ်သော၊ အခြေခံကျသော aa-rinn-aa-myit hpyit-saw , aa-chayhkankyasaw
radio *(n.)* ရေဒီယို ray-deyo
radioactive *(adj.)* ရေဒီယိုသတ္တိကြွသော ray deyo satti kyawsaw
radiogram *(n.)* ရေဒီယိုလှိုင်းမှ ပေးပို့သော စာတို *ray-deyo-hlaing-ma-pay-poe-taw-sar-to*
radiography *(n.)* ဓာတ်မှန်ရိုက်ခြင်း dhat mhaan rite-chinn
radiolocation *(n.)* ရေဒီယိုလှိုင်းမှ ပေးပို့သော တည်နေရာ *ray-deyo-hlaing-ma-pay-poe-taw-te-nay-yar*
radiology *(n.)* ဓာတ်ရောင်ခြည်ပညာ dhat-raung-chi-pin-nyar
radiomercury *(n.)* ရေဒီယိုမာကျူရီ *ray-deyo-mar-cu-ry*
radiommunology *(n.)* ရေဒီယိုရောဂါပြီးပညာ *ray-deyo-yaw-gar-pi-pin-nyar*
radion *(n.)* ရေဒီယမ်ဒြပ်စင် *ray-deyo-dat-sin*
radiophone *(n.)* ရေဒီယိုလှိုင်းသုံးဖုန်း *ray-deyo-hline-tone-phone*
radioscan *(n.)* ရေဒီယိုစကန် *ray-deyo-sa-kan*
radiotelegraphy *(n.)* ရေဒီယိုကြေးနန်း *ray-deyo-kyay-nan*
radious *(adj.)* အလင်း၊ အပူဓာတ် ဖြာထွက်သော *alinn-a-pu-dat-phwar-htwat-taw*
radish *(n.)* မုန်လာဥ mone-lar-u
radium *(n.)* ရေဒီယမ်ဒြပ်စင် ray de yam dyatsin
radius *(n.)* အချင်းဝက် a chinn-waat
rag *(v.)* စသည် sa-sai
rag *(n.)* အဝတ်စုတ် aa-wit-sote
rage *(v.)* ဒေါသူပုန်ထသည် daw sa-ponehtasai
rage *(n.)* ဒေါသူပုန်ထခြင်း daw sa-ponehtachinn
raid *(v.)* အငိုက်ဖမ်းတိုက်ခိုက်သည် a ngite hpam tite-hkitesai
raid *(n.)* အငိုက်ဖမ်းတိုက်ခိုက်ခြင်း a ngite hpam tite-hkitechinn
rail *(v.)* ထိန်းမရ သိမ်းမရ ဖြစ်သွားသည် htein ma-ra saim ma-ra hpyitswarrsai
rail *(n.)* လက်ရန်း laat raann
railing *(n.)* လက်ရန်း laat raann
raillery *(n.)* ကျီစယ်နောက်ပြောင်ခြင်း kyee saal nout pyaung-chinn
railway *(n.)* မီးရထားသံလမ်း၊ ရထားလမ်း mee-ra-htarr sanlam , ra-htarrlam
rain *(n.)* မိုး moe
rain *(v.)* မိုးရွာသည် moe rwar-sai
rainbow *(n.)* သက်တံ့ saat-tan
rainy *(adj.)* မိုးရွာသော moe rwar-saw
raise *(v.)* ထောင်သည်၊ ပင့်သည်၊ တင်ပြသည် htaung sai , pint-sai , tinpyasai
raisin *(n.)* စပျစ်သီးခြောက် sa pyit see-chauk
rally *(n.)* လူထုစည်းဝေးပွဲ luu-htu-see-wayypwal
rally *(v.)* ရှိုင်းပင်းသည် rine pinn-sai
ram *(v.)* ဝင်ဆောင့်သည် win saunt-sai
ram *(n.)* သိုးထီး soehtee
ramble *(n.)* အပျင်းပြေလမ်းလျှောက်ခြင်း aa-pyinn-pyay lam-shoutchinn
ramble *(v.)* အပျင်းပြေလမ်းလျှောက်သည် aa-pyinn-pyay lam-shoutsai

rampage *(n.)* ဝရုန်းသုန်းကား ပြေးလွှားသောင်းကျန်းသည် wa-ronesone-karr pyay-lwar saungg-kyannsai
rampage *(v.)* ဝရုန်းသုန်းကား ပြေးလွှားသောင်းကျန်းခြင်း wa-ronesone-karr pyay-lwar saungg-kyannchinn
rampant *(adj.)* သောင်းကျန်းသော saung-kyannsaw
rampart *(n.)* မြေရိုးတံတိုင်း myay roetantine
ranch *(n.)* မွေးမြူရေးခြံကြီး mway-myuu-rayy chaan-kyee
rancid *(adj.)* ဆီချေးစော်နံသော *se-gyee-zar-nan-taw*
rancidify *(v.)* ဆီချေးစော်နံသည် *se-gyee-zar-nan-the*
rancour *(n.)* အမျက်သိုခြင်း a myet so-chinn
random *(adj.)* ကျပန်း kya-paann
randomise *(v.)* ကျပန်းလုပ်သည် kya-paann-lote-sai
range *(n.)* အပိုင်းအခြား aapine-aa-charr
range *(v.)* အတန်းလိုက် နေရာယူသည် aataann-lite nayraryuusai
ranger *(n.)* တောခေါင်း၊ ရိန်ဂျားတပ်ဖွဲ့ taw hkaungg , rein gyarr-taut-hpwal
rank *(adj.)* သက်သက် saat-saat
rank *(n.)* အဆင့်အတန်း aasint-aataann
ransack *(v.)* အိတ်သွန်ဖာမှောက် ရှာသည် ate swan hpar-mhaout sharsai
ransom *(v.)* ငွေပေး၍ အဖမ်းခံရသူကို ပြန်ရွေးသည် ngway-payy-ywe aah-pham-hkan-ra-suuko pyan rwaysai
ransom *(n.)* ဖမ်းဆီးထားသူကို ပြန်ရွေးရာ၌ ပေးရသည့်ငွေ hpamsee-htarr suuko pyan rwayrar-nite payyr saeetngway
rape *(v.)* မုဒိန်းကျင့်သည် mu-dein kyint-sai
rape *(n.)* မုဒိန်းမှု mu-deinmhu
rapid *(adj.)* မြန်ဆန်သော myan-saansaw
rapidity *(n.)* လျင်မြန်သော အဟုန် lyinmyan-saw a hone
rapier *(n.)* ဓားရှည် dharr-shay
rapport *(n.)* အပေါက်အလမ်းတည့်ခြင်း a pout a lam teet-chinn
rapt *(adj.)* ရွှန်းရွှန်းစားစား shwann shwann sarrsarr
rapture *(n.)* နှစ်ထောင်းအားရရှိခြင်း nit htaungg aarr-ra-shi-chinn
rare *(adj.)* ရှားပါးသော sharr-parrsaw
rarefy *(v.)* ရှားပါးအောင် လုပ်သည် *shar-par-aung-lote-the*
rarely *(adv.)* ရှားပါးစွာ *shar-par-swar*
rareness *(n.)* ရှားပါးမှု *shar-par-mu*
rarity *(n.)* ရှားပါးခြင်း sharr-parrchinn
rascal *(n.)* လူရှုပ်ကလေး luu shotekalayy
rash *(adj.)* မဆင်မခြင်ပြုလုပ်သော ma sin m chin-pyulotesaw
rasp *(n.)* ခြစ်သံ chit-san
raspberry *(n.)* ရတ်စဘယ်ရီသီး *raat sa bhaal re-see*
raspy *(adj.)* ကြမ်းတမ်းသော *kyan-tan-taw*
rasta *(n.)* ရပ်စတာဘာသာဝင် *art-sa-tar-bar-tar-win*
rasure *(n.)* ဆံချခြင်း *san-cha-chin*
rat *(v.)* ကတိဖျက်သည် ka ti hpye-tsai
rate *(n.)* နှုန်း၊ အချိုးအစား hnone , aachoe-aa-sarr
rate *(v.)* တန်ဖိုးခန့်မှန်းသည် taan-hpoe hkaant mhaann-sai
rather *(adv.)* တော်တော် taw-taw
ratify *(v.)* အတည်ပြုသည် aataipyusai
ratio *(n.)* အချိုး aa-choe

ration *(n.)* ခွဲတမ်း hkwal-tam

rational *(adj.)* ယုတ္တိတန်သော yote-ti taan-saw

rationale *(n.)* အကြောင်းပြချက်၊ သဘောတရား aa-kyaungg-pyachet, sa-bhaw-tararr

rationality *(n.)* ဆင်ခြင်တုံတရား sin-chintone-ta-rarr

rationalize *(v.)* အကြောင်းရှာသည် aakyaungg sharsai

rattle *(n.)* ဂျိုးဂျိုးဂျောက်ဂျောက် မြည်သံ gyoe gyoe gyawt gyawt myisan

rattle *(v.)* တဒေါက်ဒေါက်မြည်သည် ta dout-dout myi-sai

raucous *(adj.)* ရုန့်ကြမ်းကျယ်လောင်သော ront kyam kyaal-laungsaw

ravage *(v.)* ဖျက်ဆီးသည် hpyet-seesai

ravage *(n.)* ဖျက်ဆီးမှုဒဏ် hpyet-see mhu-dan

rave *(v.)* ကယောင်ကတမ်း ပြောသည် kayaungkatam pyawwsai

raven *(n.)* ကျီးနက်ကြီး kyaee naatkyee

ravine *(n.)* လျှို၊ မြောင် sho , myaung

raw *(adj.)* အစိမ်း၊ အရိုင်း၊ အကြမ်းထည် aasaim , aarine , aakyam-htai

ray *(n.)* ရောင်ခြည် raung-chi

raze *(v.)* လုံးလုံးလျားလျားဖြိုပစ်သည် lonelone-lyarrlyarr hpyo pyitsai

razor *(n.)* သင်တုန်းဓား sin tone dharr

reabsorb *(v.)* ပြန်စုပ်သည် *pyan-sote-the*

reabsorption *(n.)* ပြန်စုပ်ခြင်း *pyan-sote-chin*

reaccept *(v.)* ပြန်လက်ခံသည် pyan laathkansai

reach *(v.)* ရောက်သည်၊ လှမ်းယူသည် routsai , hlam yuusai

reachable *(adj.)* လှမ်းယူနိုင်သော hlam yuu-ninesaw

react *(v.)* တုံ့ပြန်သည် tone-pyansai

reaction *(n.)* တုံ့ပြန်ချက် tone-pyanchet

reactionary *(adj.)* ဖောက်ပြန်ရေး ဝါဒီ *hpaut-pyan-yay-war-de*

reactionist *(n.)* ဖောက်ပြန်ရေး ဝါဒီ *hpaut-pyan-yay-war-de*

reactivate *(v.)* ပြန်လည် ရှင်သန်စေသည် hpout-pyan-rayy warde

reactivation *(n.)* ပြန်လည် အသက်သွင်းခြင်း pyanlai aasaat swinchinn

reactive *(adj.)* တုံ့ပြန်သော tonepyansaw

reactor *(n.)* အဏုမြူဓာတ်ပေါင်းဖို aanumyauudharatpaungghpo

read *(v.)* ဖတ်သည် hpaatsai

reader *(n.)* စာဖတ်သူ sarhpaatsuu

readily *(adv.)* အဆင်သင့် a sinsint

readiness *(n.)* အဆင်သင့် a sinsint

readjust *(v.)* နေသားတကျ ပြန်ဖြစ်သည် nay-sarrtakya pyan-hpyitsai

ready *(adj.)* အဆင်သင့် a sin-sint

ready-made *(adj.)* အဆင်သင့်ဝတ်ရန် ချုပ်လုပ်ထားသော a sin tint wit-raan chote lote-htarrsaw

reak *(n.)* ထိုးထွက်ခြင်း *htoe-htwat-chin*

real *(adj.)* စစ်မှန်သော sit-mhaansaw

realism *(n.)* အရှိကို အရှိအတိုင်းလက်ခံခြင်း a shiko aashi-aatine-laath-kanchinn

realist *(n.)* ယထာဘူတဝါဒီ yahtar bhuu ta-warde

realistic *(adj.)* လက်တွေ့ကျသော laat-twae-kyasaw

reality *(n.)* အစစ်အမှန် aasait-aamhaan

realization *(n.)* ဖြစ်ထွန်းမှု hpyit-htwann-mhu

realize *(v.)* **အသိတရားရသည်၊ သဘောပေါက်မိသည်** aasitararr rasai , sabhawpout misai
reallocate *(v.)* **ပြန်နေရာချသည်** *pyan-nay-yar-cha-the*
reallocation *(n.)* **ပြန်နေရာချခြင်း** *pyan-nay-yar-cha-chin*
really *(int.)* **တကယ်လား** *ta-kal-lar*
realm *(n.)* **လောက** law-ka
realtor *(n.)* **အိမ်ရာမြေအကျိုးဆောင်** ain rar myay-aa-kyoesaung
realty *(n.)* **ထာဝရဥစ္စာ** htarwa-ra-oak-sar
ream *(v.)* **ရောမွှေ၍ ပစ်ခဲအောင် လုပ်သည်** *yaw-mway-ywe-pyit-khae-aung-lote-the*
reamer *(n.)* **အရစ်ဖော်စက်** *a-yit-phaw-sat*
reamplify *(v.)* **ပြန်ချဲ့သည်** *pyan-chae-the*
reamputation *(n.)* **ထပ်မံခြေလက်ဖြတ်တောက်သည်** *htet-man-chay-lat-phat-taut-the*
reanimate *(v.)* **ပြန်လည်သက်ဝင်လှုပ်ရှားသည်** *pyan-lal-thet-win-lote-shar-the*
reanimation *(n.)* **ပြန်လည်သက်ဝင်လှုပ်ရှားခြင်း** *pyan-lal-thet-win-lote-shar-chin*
reannex *(v.)* **တဖန်ပြန်သိမ်းပိုက်သည်** *ta-phan-pyan-thein-pike-the*
reannexation *(n.)* **တဖန်ပြန်သိမ်းပိုက်ခြင်း** *ta-phan-pyan-thein-pike-chin*
reap *(n.)* **ဂျုံအစည်း** *jone-a-see*
reaper *(n.)* **ကောက်ရိတ်သမား** kout rate-samarr
reappear *(v.)* **ပြန်ပေါ်လာသည်** pyan-pawlarsai
reappearance *(n.)* **ပြန်ပေါ်လာခြင်း** pyan-pawlarchinn
reapplication *(n.)* **ပြန်လည်ကျင့်သုံးခြင်း** pyan-lai kyint sonechinn
reapply *(v.)* **ပြန်လည် ကျင့်သုံးသည်** pyan-lai kyint-sonesai
reappoint *(v.)* **ပြန်လည် ခန့်အပ်သည်** pyan-lai hkaant at-sai
reappraisal *(n.)* **ပြန်လည်သုံးသပ်ခြင်း** pyan-lai-sone-sautchinn
reappraise *(v.)* **ပြန်လည်သုံးသပ်သည်** pyan-laisone-sautsai
reapproach *(v.)* **ပြန်လည်ချဉ်းကပ်သည်** pyan-lai chee kautsai
reappropriate *(v.)* **ပြန်လည်သင့်လျော်စေသည်** pyan-lai sang lyawsaysai
reapproval *(n.)* **ပြန်လည်အတည်ပြုခြင်း** pyan-lai aatai-pyuchinn
rear *(v.)* **ကြီးပြင်းအောင် ကျွေးမွေးစောင့်ရှောက်သည်** kyee pyinn-aung kyway-mway sannt shoutsai
rear *(n.)* **နောက်ဖေး၊ နောက်ကျော** nout hpayy , noutkyaww
rearrange *(v.)* **ပြန်လည်စီစဉ်သည်** pyan-lai se-sinsai
rearticulate *(v.)* **ပြန်လည်ပြောဆိုသည်** pyanlai-pyaww-so-sai
rearview *(adj.)* **ရှေ့မှ မြင်ရသော** *shay-ma-myin-ya-taw*
reason *(v.)* **ဆင်ခြင်သည်၊ နှိုင်းချင့်သည်** sinchin sai , nine chintsai
reason *(n.)* **အကြောင်းပြချက်** aa-kyaunggpya-chet
reasonable *(adj.)* **မျှတသော၊ လက်တွေ့ကျသော** myata-saw , laat-twaekyasaw
reassign *(v.)* **ပြန်လည်တာဝန်ချသည်** pyanlai tarwaan chasai
reassume *(v.)* **ဆက်လုပ်သည်** *sat-lote-the*
reassure *(v.)* **စိတ်ချလက်ချရှိစေသည်** Satecha-laatcha shisaysai

reattach *(v.)* ပြန်လည်ပူးတွဲသည် *pyan-lal-pu-twe-the*
rebate *(n.)* ပေးရန် တန်ဖိုးပေါ် ပြန်အမ်းငွေ payy-raan taan-hpoe paw pyan an-ngway
rebel *(v.)* သူပုန်ထသည် sa-pone-htasai
rebel *(n.)* သူပုန် suu-pone
rebellion *(n.)* သူပုန်ထခြင်း suupone-hta-chinn
rebellious *(adj.)* ပုန်ကန်လိုသော pone-kaan-losaw
rebirth *(n.)* ပြန်လည် ရှင်သန်ခြင်း pyan-lai hlyinsaanchinn
rebound *(v.)* ကိုယ့်ရှူးကိုယ်ပတ်သည် ko shuu ko paat-sai
rebuff *(v.)* ခါးခါးသီးသီးငြင်းပယ်သည် hkarr-hkarr-seesee ngyinnpaalsai
rebuff *(n.)* ခါးခါးသီးသီးငြင်းပယ်ခြင်း hkarrhkarrseesee ngyinnpaalchinn
rebuild *(v.)* ပြန်လည်တည်ဆောက်ခြင်း pyanlaitaisoutchinn
rebuke *(n.)* ပြစ်တင် မောင်းမဲသည် pyit-tin maungg mellsai
rebuke *(v.)* ပြစ်တင်မောင်းမဲသည် pyit-tin maungg mellsai
recall *(n.)* ပြန်လည်ခေါ်ယူခြင်း pyan-lai-hkawyuuchinn
recall *(v.)* ပြန်လည်ခေါ်ယူသည် pyan-lai hkawyuusai
recede *(v.)* ဆုတ်သည် sote-sai
receipt *(n.)* လက်ခံရရှိခြင်း laat-hkan-rashichinn
receive *(v.)* လက်ခံရရှိသည် laat-hkan-rashisai
receiver *(n.)* လက်ခံသူ laat-hkansuu
recent *(adj.)* မကြာသေးမီကဖြစ်သော ma-kyaar-sayyme-kahpyitsaw
recently *(adv.)* တစ်လောက ta-lawka
reception *(n.)* လက်ခံခြင်း laat-hkan-chinn
receptive *(adj.)* သဘောပေါက်လက်ခံလွယ်သော sa-bhawpout laat-hkan lwalsaw
recess *(n.)* ရပ်နားချိန် ratnarr-chane
recession *(n.)* စီးပွားရေးကျဆင်းမှု seepwarr-rayykya-sinn-mhu
recipe *(n.)* ချက်နည်းပြုတ်နည်း chet-nee-pyote-nee
recipient *(n.)* လက်ခံရရှိသူ laat-hkan-rashisuu
reciprocal *(adj.)* အပြန်အလှန် aa-pyan-aahlaan
reciprocate *(v.)* အပြန်အလှန်ပြုလုပ်သည် aapyan-aahlaan-pyu-lotesai
recital *(n.)* ဖြစ်ကြောင်းကုန်စင် ပြန်ပြောပြခြင်း hpyit-kyaung-konesin pyan-pyaww-pyachinn
recitation *(n.)* စာဟောပွဲ sar haw-pwal
recite *(v.)* စာဟောသည် sar-hawsai
reckless *(adj.)* မဆင်မခြင် ma-sin-ma-chin
reckon *(v.)* လက်ခံထားသည် laat-hkan-htarrsai
reclaim *(v.)* ပြန်တောင်းယူသည် pyan taungg yuu-sai
reclamation *(n.)* ဖော်ယူခြင်း၊ ဆယ်တင်ခြင်း hpaw yuu-chinn , saal-tin-chinn
recluse *(n.)* တစ်ကိုယ်တော်သမား ta-kotaw-samarr
recognition *(n.)* အသိအမှတ်ပြုခြင်း aa-si-aa-mhaat-pyu-chinn
recognize *(v.)* မှတ်မိသည် mhaat-mi-sai
recoil *(v.)* တွန့်ဆုတ်သည် twant sotesai
recollect *(v.)* ပြန်လည် သတိရသည် pyan-lai sa-ti-rasai
recollection *(n.)* အမှတ်ရခြင်း aa-mhaat-ra-chinn

recommend *(v.)* အကြံပြုထောက်ခံသည် aa-kyaan-pyu htout-hkansai
recommendation *(n.)* ထောက်ခံချက် htout-hkan-chet
recompense *(n.)* ချီးမြှင့်ငွေ cheemyint-ngway
recompense *(v.)* နစ်နာကြေး၊ ချီးမြှင့်ငွေပေးသည် nitnar-kyay, cheemyint ngway-payysai
reconcile *(v.)* စေ့စပ်ပေးသည် sae-saut-payysai
reconciliation *(n.)* ပြန်လည်စေ့စပ်ညှိနှိုင်းခြင်း pyanlai saesat nyi-nine-chinn
recondensation *(n.)* ပြန်ပစ်အောင်ကျိုသည် *pyan-pyit-aung-kyo-chin*
recondense *(v.)* ပြန်ပစ်အောင်ကျိုခြင်း *pyan-pyit-aung-kyo-the*
recondition *(v.)* ပြုပြင်မွမ်းမံသည် *pyu-pyin mwam-man sai*
reconductor *(v.)* ဆားကစ်ပေါ် ရှိကြိုးပြန်လှဲသည် *sar-kit-paw-shi-kyo-pyan-lal-the*
reconfigurate *(v.)* ပြန်လည်စီစဉ်သည် *pyan-lal-si-sin-the*
reconfiguration *(n.)* ပြန်လည်စီစဉ်ခြင်း *pyan-lal-si-sin-chin*
reconquer *(v.)* ပြန်လည်အောင်နိုင်သည် *pyan-lal-aung-naing-the*
reconsider *(v.)* ပြန်လည်သုံးသပ်သည် pyan-laisone-satsai
reconsolidate *(v.)* ပြန်လည်စုစည်းသည် *pyan-lal-su-see-the*
record *(n.)* မှတ်တမ်း mhaat-tam
recorder *(n.)* ရှပ်၊ အသံ ဖမ်းစက် rote , aa-san hpamsaat
recount *(v.)* အသေးစိတ်ပြန်ပြောပြသည် aasayy-sate pyanpyaw-pyasai
recoup *(v.)* ပြန်ထေမိသည် pyan htay misai
recourse *(n.)* အားကိုးအားထား aarr-koe aarr-htarr
recover *(v.)* ပြန်ကောင်းသည်၊ နလန်ထူသည် pyan kaunggsai , n laan htuu-sai
recovery *(n.)* နာလန်ထူခြင်း narlaan htuu-chinn
recreation *(n.)* အပန်းဖြေမှု aapaan-hpyay-mhu
recreational *(adj.)* အပန်းဖြေ aapaan-hpyay
recreative *(adj.)* အပန်းဖြေသည် *a-pann-phyay-the*
recriminate *(v.)* တန်ပြန်စွပ်စွဲသည် taanpyan swut-swalsai
recrimination *(n.)* တန်ပြန်စွပ်စွဲခြင်း taanpyan swut-swalchinn
recrudency *(n.)* ရောဂါပြန်ထခြင်း *yaw-gar-pyan-hta-chin*
recruit *(v.)* လူသစ်စုဆောင်းသည် luu sit susaunggsai
recruit *(n.)* တပ်သားသစ် tautsarrsait
rectangle *(n.)* ထောင့်မှန်စတုဂံ htaunt mhaan sa tu gan
rectangular *(adj.)* ထောင့်မှန်စတုဂံ htaunt mhaan sa tu gan
rectification *(n.)* ပြုပြင်ခြင်း pyupyinchinn
rectify *(v.)* ပြုပြင်သည် pyupyinsai
rectum *(n.)* စအို sa-ao
recuperate *(v.)* ချွေးသိပ်အားဖြည့်သည် chway seik aarr hpyae-sai
recur *(v.)* ပြန်ဖြစ်သည် pyan-hpyitsai
recurrence *(n.)* အဖန်တလဲလဲ ဖြစ်ခြင်း a hpaan ta lell-lell hpyit-chinn
recurrent *(adj.)* မကြာခဏ ပေါ်ပေါက်သော makyaar-hkan paw-poutsaw
recycle *(v.)* ဆယ်တင်သည် saal-tin-sai

red *(n.)* **အနီ** aa-ne

red *(adj.)* **နီသော** ne-saw

redden *(v.)* **နီမြန်းသည်** ne myan-sai

reddish *(adj.)* **နီကြင်ကြင်** ne kyin-kyin

redeem *(v.)* **အဖတ်ဆယ်သည်** a hpaat saal-sai

redemption *(n.)* **ပေးဆပ်ခြင်း၊ အဖတ်ဆယ်ခြင်း** payy-satchinn , a hpaat saalchinn

redouble *(v.)* **ဆတက်ထမ်းပိုး ပြုလုပ်သည်** sa taat htampoe pyu-lotesai

redress *(n.)* **နစ်နာကြေး၊ အလျော်** nit-narkyay , aalyaw

redress *(v.)* **တရားသဖြင့် ဖြစ်စေသည်** tararr sa-hpyint hpyitsaysai

reduce *(v.)* **လျှော့သည်** shotsai

reduction *(n.)* **လျှော့ချခြင်း** shot-chachinn

redundance *(n.)* **ပိုလျှံခြင်း** *po-lyan-chin*

redundant *(adj.)* **ပိုလျှံသော** po shan-saw

reel *(v.)* **ဒယီးဒယိုင်ဖြစ်သည်** da yee da yine-hpyitsai

refer *(v.)* **ရည်ညွှန်းသည်** ray-nyunn-sai

referee *(n.)* **ဒိုင်လူကြီး** dine-luukyee

reference *(n.)* **ရည်ညွှန်းပြောဆိုခြင်း** rai-nyunn-pyaww-sochinn

referendum *(n.)* **ဆန္ဒခံယူပွဲ** san-da-hkan-yuupwal

refine *(v.)* **သန့်စင်သည်၊ ချက်သည်** saant saan sai , chet-sai

refinement *(n.)* **မွမ်းမံမှု၊ ချက်လုပ်ခြင်း** mwam-man mhu , chet-lotechinn

refinery *(n.)* **ချက်စက်ရုံ** chet-saat-rone

reflect *(v.)* **ပုံရိပ်ထင်သည်၊ ရောင်ပြန်ဟပ်သည်** pone-rate htinsai , raungpyan hatsai

reflection *(n.)* **ပုံရိပ်၊ အရိပ်** pone-rate , aa-yate

reflective *(adj.)* **လေးလေးနက်နက် တွေးတတ်သော** layylayy-naatnaat tway-taatsaw

reflector *(n.)* **ရောင်ပြန်ပြား** raung-pyanpyarr

reflex *(adj.)* **အမှတ်မဲ့ တုံ့ပြန်သော** aamhaat-mae tont-pyansaw

reflex *(n.)* **အမှတ်မဲ့ တုံ့ပြန်မှု** aamhaat-mae tont-pyanmhu

reflexive *(adj.)* **ကတ္တားရည်ညွှန်း** kat tarr-rai-nyunn

reform *(n.)* **ပြုပြင်ပြောင်းလဲမှု** pyu-pyin-pyaungg-lel-mhu

reform *(v.)* **ပြုပြင်ပြောင်းလဲသည်** pyu-pyin-pyaungg-lel-sai

reformation *(n.)* **ပြုပြင်ခြင်း** pyu-pyin-chinn

reformatory *(n.)* **လူငယ်ပြုပြင်ရေးကျောင်း** luungaal pyu-pyin-rayy-kyaungg

reformatory *(adj.)* **ပြုပြင်ပြောင်းလဲမှုနှင့်ဆိုင်သော** *pyu-pyin-pyaung-lal-mu-nint-sai-taw*

reformer *(n.)* **ပြုပြင်ပြောင်းလဲရေးသမား** pyupyin-pyaungg-lellrayy-samarr

refrain *(n.)* **ထပ်ကျော့ပုဒ်၊ သံပြိုင်ကောက်ခြင်း** htat kyaww pote , san-pyaine koutchinn

refrain *(v.)* **အောင့်အည်းထားသည်** awnt aaee-htarrsai

refresh *(v.)* **အားသစ်လောင်းသည်** aarrsit-launggsai

refreshment *(n.)* **အစားအသောက်** aasarr-aasout

refrigerate *(v.)* **ရေခဲရိုက်သည်** ray hkell ritesai

refrigeration *(n.)* **ရေခဲရိုက်ခြင်း** ray hkell ritechinn

refrigerator *(n.)* **ရေခဲသေတ္တာ** rayhkellsit-tar

refuel *(v.)* ဓာတ်ဆီထည့်သည် dhatse htaeetsai
refuge *(n.)* ခိုလှုံရာ hko-hlonrar
refugee *(n.)* ဒုက္ခသည် duk-hkasai
refulgence *(n.)* လင်းထိန်ခြင်း linn hteinchinn
refulgent *(adj.)* လင်းထိန်သော linn hteinsaw
refund *(v.)* ငွေပြန်အမ်းသည် ngway pyan aamsai
refurbish *(v.)* ပြင်ဆင်မွမ်းမံသည် pyinsin mwam-mansai
refusal *(n.)* ငြင်းဆန်ခြင်း ngyinn-saanchinn
refuse *(v.)* ငြင်းဆန်သည် ngyinn-saansai
refutation *(n.)* ငြင်းဆိုခြင်း ngyinn-sochinn
refute *(v.)* ချေပသည် chaay-pya-sai
regal *(adj.)* တော်ဝင်သော taw-winsaw
regard *(n.)* အလေးထားမှု aalayy-htarrmhu
regard *(v.)* လေ့လာသည် laelarsai
regenerate *(v.)* ပြန်လည်သန်စွမ်းတိုးပွားလာစေသည် pyanlai saan swam toepwarrlarsaysai
regeneration *(n.)* ပြန်လည်သန်စွမ်းတိုးပွားလာစေခြင်း pyanlai saan swm toepwarrlar saychinn
regicide *(n.)* ဘုရင်၊ ဘုရင်မကို သတ်မှု ba-rin , ba-rinmako saatmhu
regime *(n.)* အစိုးရစနစ် aa-soe-rasanit
regiment *(n.)* တပ်ရင်းကြီး tat-rinn-kyee
regiment *(v.)* စည်းကမ်းတင်းကျပ်သည် seekam tinnkyatsai
region *(n.)* ဒေသ၊ နယ်မြေ day-sa , naal-myay
regional *(adj.)* ဒေသ day-sa
register *(v.)* စာရင်းသွင်းသည် sarrinn-swinsai
registrar *(n.)* မှတ်ပုံတင်အရာရှိ mhaatpone-tin-aarar-shi
registration *(n.)* မှတ်ပုံတင်ခြင်း mhaatpone-tinchinn
registry *(n.)* မော်ကွန်းထိန်းဌာန mawkwann htein-htarna
regret *(n.)* ဝမ်းနည်းခြင်း wam-naeechinn
regret *(v.)* နောင်တရသည် naung-tarasai
regular *(adj.)* ပုံမှန် ponemhaan
regularity *(n.)* ပုံမှန်ဖြစ်ပေါ်မှု ponemhaan hpyitpawmhu
regulate *(v.)* စည်းမျဉ်းဖြင့် ထိန်းသည် see myin-hpyint hteinsai
regulation *(n.)* စည်းမျဉ်း seemyin
regulator *(n.)* ထိန်းညှိကိရိယာ htein nyi-ka-ri-yar
rehabilitate *(v.)* ပြန်လည် ထူထောင်ပေးသည် pyanlai htuu-htaungpayysai
rehabilitation *(n.)* ပြန်လည် ထူထောင်ခြင်း pyanlai htuu-htaungchinn
rehearsal *(n.)* အစမ်းလေ့ကျင့်ခြင်း a sam lae kyintchinn
rehearse *(v.)* ဇာတ်တိုက်သည် zat titesai
reign *(v.)* မင်းပြုသည် min-pyusai
reimburse *(v.)* ငွေပြန်ထုတ်ပေးသည် ngway pyanhtotepayysai
reimbursement *(n.)* ငွေပြန်ထုတ်ပေးခြင်း ngway pyanhtotepayychinn
rein *(v.)* ဇက်ကိုင်သည် zat kinesai
rein *(n.)* ဇက်ကြိုး zat-kyoe
reinforce *(v.)* အားပေးသည်၊ အားပေးထောက်ခံသည် aarr payysai , aarrpayy htout-hkansai

reinforcement *(n.)* အားပေးခြင်း၊ ထောက်ခံခြင်း aarr-payychinn , htout-hkanchinn
reinstate *(v.)* မူလရာထူး၌ ပြန်လည်ခန့်အပ်သည် mu-la rar-htuu pyanlai hkaant atsai
reinstatement *(n.)* ပြန်လည် အသက်သွင်းခြင်း pyanlai aasaat swin-chinn
reiterate *(v.)* ထပ်လောင်းပြောဆိုသည် htat-laungg-pyawwsosai
reiteration *(n.)* ထပ်လောင်းဖွင့်ဟချက် that-laungg hpwint ha-chet
reject *(v.)* ပယ်ချသည် paal-chasai
rejection *(n.)* ပယ်ချခြင်း paal-chachinn
rejoice *(v.)* ဝမ်းမြောက်ဝမ်းသာဖြစ်သည် wam-myaut wamsar-hpyitsai
rejoin *(v.)* ပြန်ပေါင်းသည် pyan paunggsai
rejoinder *(n.)* ပြန်လှန်ပြောဆိုချက် pyan-hlaan-pyawwsochet
rejuvenate *(v.)* နုပျိုစေသည် nu pyosaysai
rejuvenation *(n.)* အားသစ်လောင်းပေးခြင်း aarr-sitlaungg-payychinn
relapse *(n.)* ပြန်ထခြင်း pyanhta-chinn
relapse *(v.)* ရောဂါပြန်ထခြင်း rawgar pyan-htachinn
relate *(v.)* ဆက်စပ်သည်၊ တည်မှီသည် saat-sat sai , tai mhaesai
relation *(n.)* ဆက်ဆံရေး၊ ဆက်သွယ်မှု saat-sanrayy , saatswalmhu
relative *(n.)* ဆွေမျိုး sway-myoe
relative *(adj.)* နှိုင်းယှဉ်ချက်အရ nhaine yhainchetaar
relax *(v.)* အပန်းဖြေသည် aapaann-hpyaysai
relaxation *(n.)* အပန်းဖြေခြင်း aapaann-hpyaychinn
relay *(n.)* လက်ဆင့်ကမ်းပြိုင်ပွဲ laat sint kam-pyainepwal
release *(n.)* လွှတ်ပေးခြင်း၊ လွတ်ငြိမ်းစေခြင်း၊ ထုတ်ပြန်ချက် lwut-payychinn , lwut-ngyeim say chinn , htote-pyanchet
release *(v.)* လွတ်ငြိမ်းခွင့်ပြုသည် lut-ngyeim hkwint-pyusai
relent *(v.)* အလျှော့ပေးသည် a shot-payysai
relentless *(adj.)* မရပ်မနားဖြစ်သော ma ratmanarr-hpyitsaw
relevance *(n.)* သက်ဆိုင်မှု saat-sinemhu
relevant *(adj.)* ဆီလျော်သော၊ သက်ဆိုင်သော se lyaw saw , saat-sinesaw
reliable *(adj.)* ယုံကြည်အားထားရသော yonekyi-aarrhtarr-rasaw
reliance *(n.)* အားထားမှု၊ မှီခိုခြင်း aarr htarr mhu , mhae-hkochinn
relic *(n.)* အမွေအနှစ် aamway-aanit
relief *(n.)* သက်သာရာရခြင်း saatsar-rar-rachinn
relieve *(v.)* သက်သာရာရစေသည် saatsar-rar rasaysai
religion *(n.)* ဘာသာအယူဝါဒ bharsar-aa-yuuwarda
religious *(adj.)* ဘာသာရေး bhar-sar-rayy
relinquish *(v.)* စွန့်လွှတ်သည် swant lutsai
relish *(n.)* မြိန်မြိန်ရှက်ရှက် myein myein shatshat
relish *(v.)* မြိန်သည် myein-sai
reluctance *(n.)* သဘောမတူခြင်း sabhaw-matuuchinn
reluctant *(adj.)* အင်တင်တင် ဖြစ်နေသော in tintin hpyit-naysaw
rely *(v.)* အမှီပြုသည်၊ အားထားသည် aamhae pyusai , aarr-htarrsai

remain *(v.)* ကျန်သည်၊ ဆက်လက်တည်ရှိသည် kyaan sai , saat-laat-tai-shisai
remainder *(n.)* ကျန်သည့်အပိုင်း kyaan saeet-aapine
remains *(n.)* အကြွင်းအကျန် a-kywin aakyaan
remand *(n.)* ရမန်၊ ချုပ်မိန့် ra maan , chote-meint
remand *(v.)* ရမန်ပေးသည်၊ ချုပ်မိန့်ပေးသည် ra maan payysai , chote meinpayysai
remark *(v.)* မှတ်ချက်ချသည် mhaatchetchasai
remark *(n.)* ဝေဖန်ချက်၊ မှတ်ချက် wayhpaanchet , mhaatchet
remarkable *(adj.)* ထူးခြားသော၊ မှတ်သားဖွယ် htuucharrsaw , mhaat-sarrhpwal
remedial *(adj.)* ကုစားသော၊ ပျောက်ကင်းရေး kusarr saw , pyaut-kinnrayy
remedy *(v.)* ကုသသည် kusasai
remember *(v.)* မှတ်မိသည် mhaat-misai
remembrance *(n.)* သတိရခြင်း၊ အမှတ်တရပစ္စည်း sati-rachinn , aamhaat-tarapyit-saee
remind *(v.)* သတိပေးသည် sati-payysai
reminder *(n.)* သတိပေးချက် sati-payychet
reminiscence *(n.)* ပြန်လည်သတိရခံစားမှု pyanlai satira-hkansarrmhu
reminiscent *(adj.)* ဆင်တူယိုးမှားဖြစ်သော sintuu-yoe-mhar-hpyitsaw
remission *(n.)* လျှော့ပေါ့ခြင်း shot potchinn
remit *(n.)* တရားဝင်လုပ်ပိုင်ခွင့် tararrwin lote pinehkwint
remittance *(n.)* ပို့ငွေ၊ လွှဲပြောင်းပေးငွေ phoet ngway , lwhaellpyaungg payyngway
remorse *(n.)* နောင်တ naungt
remote *(adj.)* ဝေးလံသော wayy lansaw
remould *(v.)* ပန်းပြန်တင်ထားသော တာယာ paann pyantinhtarrsaw taryar
removable *(adj.)* အရှင် aashin
removal *(n.)* ဖယ်ရှားခြင်း၊ ချွတ်ခြင်း hpaalsharr chinn , chyut-chinn
remove *(v.)* ဖယ်ရှားသည် hpaal-sharrsai
remunerate *(v.)* လုပ်ခ၊ ဝန်ဆောင်ခ ရှင်းပေးသည် lotehka , waansaunghka shinnpayysai
remuneration *(n.)* ပေးငွေ payy-ngway
remunerative *(adj.)* ဝင်ငွေ လစာကောင်းသော winngway lasar-kaunggsaw
renaissance *(n.)* ရီနေဆန်းခေတ် re nay saannh-khit
render *(v.)* ဖြစ်စေသည် hpyitsaysai
rendezvous *(n.)* ချိန်းတွေ့ခြင်း chane-twaechinn
renew *(v.)* ပြန်စသည် pyan sasai
renewal *(n.)* အသစ်လဲလှယ်ခြင်း aasit lell-hlaalchinn
renounce *(v.)* ရပိုင်ခွင့် စွန့်လွှတ်သည် rapinehkwint swant lwutsai
renovate *(v.)* အသစ်ပြုပြင်သည် aasit pyupyinsai
renovation *(n.)* အသစ်ပြုပြင် ဆောက်လုပ်ခြင်း aasitpyupyin soutlotechinn
renown *(n.)* ကျော်ကြားမှု kyawkyarrmhu
renowned *(adj.)* ကျော်ကြားသော kyawkyarrsaw
rent *(v.)* ငှားရမ်းသည် ngharramsai

rent *(n.)* ငှားရမ်းခ ngharramhka

renunciation *(n.)* စွန့်လွှတ်ခြင်း swant lwutchinn

repair *(n.)* ပြင်ဆင်ခြင်း pyinsinchinn

repair *(v.)* ပြင်သည် pyinsai

repairable *(adj.)* ပြုပြင်နိုင်သည့် အခြေအနေ ရှိသော pyupyin nine-seet aachay-aanay shisaw

repartee *(n.)* ထက်မြက်သော ရှတ်ခြည်းခွန်းတုံ့လှယ်မှု htaat-myaatsaw rote chi hkwann tone hlaalmhu

repatriate *(n.)* မိခင်နိုင်ငံသားပြန်ဖြစ်ခြင်း *mi-khin-nine-ngan-tar-pyan-phit-chin*

repatriation *(n.)* မိခင်နိုင်ငံသားပြန်ဖြစ်ခြင်း *mi-khin-nine-ngan-tar-pyan-phit-chin*

repay *(v.)* အကြွေးဆပ်သည် aakyaway satsai

repayment *(n.)* ပေးဆပ်ခြင်း payysatchinn

repeal *(n.)* ရုပ်သိမ်းခြင်း rotesaimchinn

repeal *(v.)* ရုပ်သိမ်းသည် rotesaimsai

repeat *(v.)* ထပ်ပြောသည် htatpyawwsai

repel *(v.)* တွန်းလှန်သည် twann hlaansai

repellent *(n.)* ရွံရှာဖွယ်ရာ rwan sharhpwalrar

repellent *(adj.)* စိမ့်မဝင်နိုင်သော seint ma-win-ninesaw

repent *(v.)* နောင်တရသည် naung-tarasai

repentance *(n.)* နောင်တ naung ta

repentant *(adj.)* နောင်တရပုံ naung-ta rapone

repercussion *(n.)* ဂယက်ရိုက်မှု ga-yaat-ritemhu

repertoire *(n.)* တင်ဆက်မှု tin-saatmhu

repetition *(n.)* ပြန်ကျော့ခြင်း pyan kyawt-chinn

replace *(v.)* အစားထိုးသည် aasarr-htoesai

replacement *(n.)* အစားထိုးခြင်း aasarr-htoechinn

replay *(v.)* ပြန်ကစားသည် pyan kasarr-sai

replenish *(v.)* ထပ်ဖြည့်သည် htat hpyae sai

replete *(adj.)* ပြည့်နှက်နေသော pyae nhaat-naysaw

replica *(n.)* ပုံတူ ponetuu

reply *(v.)* ပြန်ကြားသည် pyankyarrsai

report *(n.)* အစီရင်ခံစာ aase-rinhkansar

report *(v.)* အစီရင်ခံသည် aase-rinhkansai

reporter *(n.)* သတင်းထောက် sa-tinn-htout

repose *(v.)* လဲလျောင်းသည် lell lyaungg-sai

repose *(n.)* အိပ်စက်ခြင်း ait-saat-chinn

repository *(n.)* ဘဏ် bhan

represent *(v.)* ကိုယ်စားပြုခြင်း ခံရသည် kosarr-pyuchinn hkanrasai

representation *(n.)* ကိုယ်စားပြုခြင်း kosarr-pyuchinn

representative *(adj.)* သဘောထားကို ထင်ဟပ်သော sabhaw-htarrko htinhautsaw

representative *(n.)* ကိုယ်စားပြုခြင်း kosarr-pyuchinn

repress *(v.)* ချုပ်တည်းသည် chote tae-sai

repression *(n.)* ဖိနှိပ်မှု hpi-natemhu

reprimand *(v.)* အပြစ်ဖော်ဆုံးမသည် aapyit hpaw sone masai

reprimand *(n.)* အပြစ်ဖော်ဆုံးမခြင်း aapyit hpaw-sonemachinn

reprint *(v.)* ထပ်မံရိုက်နှိပ်သည် htatman rite natesai

reproach *(n.)* အပြစ်တင်ခြင်း aapyit-tinchinn

reproach *(v.)* အပြစ်တင်သည် aapyit-tinsai

reproduce *(v.)* မျိုးပွားသည်၊ ပြန်လည်ဖော်ထုတ်သည် myoe pwarr sai , pyanlai-hpaw-htotesai
reproduction *(n.)* မျိုးပွားခြင်း myoe pwarr-chinn
reproductive *(adj.)* မျိုးပွားမှု myoe pwarr-mhu
reproof *(n.)* ပြစ်တင်ကန့်ကွက်ခြင်း pyittin kaantkwatchinn
reptile *(n.)* တွားသွားသတ္တဝါ twarr swarr-sattawar
republic *(n.)* သမ္မတစနစ် sam-mata-sanit
republican *(n.)* ရီပါဗလီကန်ပါတီ re par bale kaanparte
republican *(adj.)* သမ္မတစနစ်လိုလားသော sam-mata sanit-lolarrsaw
repudiate *(v.)* ငြင်းပယ်သည် ngyinn-paalsai
repudiation *(n.)* ငြင်းပယ်ခြင်း ngyinn-paalchinn
repugnance *(n.)* ရွံရှာခြင်း rwan shar-chinn
repugnant *(adj.)* မနှစ်မြို့ ma nit myoet
repulse *(n.)* တွန်းလှန်ခြင်း *twann hlaans-chin*
repulse *(v.)* တွန်းလှန်သည် twann hlaansai
repulsion *(n.)* ရွံရှာမှု rwan sharmhu
repulsive *(adj.)* ရွံရှာဖွယ် rwan sharhpwal
reputation *(n.)* နာမည်၊ ဂုဏ်သတင်း narmai , gonsatinn
repute *(n.)* နာမည်၊ သတင်း narmai , satinn
repute *(v.)* ဂုဏ်သတင်းကျော်ကြားသော *gon-ta-tin-kyaw-kyar-taw*
request *(n.)* တောင်းခံခြင်း taungghkanchinn
request *(v.)* တောင်းခံသည် taungghkansai
requiem *(n.)* ကွယ်လွန်သူ ဝိညာဉ်အတွက် ဆုတောင်းပွဲ kwallwansuu wi-nyin-aatwat sutaungg-pwal
require *(v.)* လိုအပ်သည် lo-atsai
requirement *(n.)* လိုအပ်ချက် lo-atchet
requisite *(n.)* လိုအပ်ချက် lo-atchet
requisite *(adj.)* သတ်မှတ်ထားသော saat-mhaathtarrsaw
requisition *(n.)* ချောဆွဲခြင်း chaww-swalchinn
requite *(v.)* တုံ့ပြန်သည် *tont-pyan-the*
reschedule *(v.)* ရွှေ့ဆိုင်းထားနိုင်ရန် အစီအစဉ် ပြန်လည် ရေးဆွဲသည် shwaesine htarr-nineraan aaseaasin pyanlai rayyswalsai
rescue *(n.)* ကယ်ဆယ်ခြင်း kaal-saalchinn
research *(n.)* သုတေသန sutaysan
resemblance *(n.)* တူခြင်း၊ ဆင်ခြင်း tuu chinn , sinchinn
resemble *(v.)* ဆင်သည် sinsai
resent *(v.)* မကျေနချမ်းနိုင်ဖြစ်သည် ma kyaay ma cham ninehpyitsai
resentment *(n.)* မကျေမချမ်းမှု ma kyaay ma chammhu
reservation *(n.)* ကြိုတင်စာရင်းသွင်းထားခြင်း kyaotin sarrinnswinhtarrchinn
reserve *(v.)* သီးသန့်ထားသည် see saanthtarrsai
reservoir *(n.)* ရေလှောင်ကန် ray hlaawinkaan
reside *(v.)* နေထိုင်သည် nayhtinesai
residence *(n.)* ဂေဟာ gayhar
resident *(adj.)* နေထိုင်သူ nayhtinesuu
residual *(adj.)* အကျန် *a-kyan*

residue *(n.)* အကြွင်းအကျန် aakywin aakyaan
resign *(v.)* နုတ်ထွက်သည် notehtwatsai
resignation *(n.)* နုတ်ထွက်ခြင်း notehtwatchinn
resist *(v.)* ခုခံသည် hkuhkansai
resistance *(n.)* ခုခံခြင်း၊ တော်လှန်ခြင်း hkuhkan chinn, tawhlaanchinn
resistant *(adj.)* ခုခံသော၊ ခုခံအားရှိသော hkuhkan saw, hkuhkanaarr shisaw
resolute *(adj.)* ပြတ်သားသော pyatsarrsaw
resolution *(n.)* ကြံ့ခိုင်မှု kyaanhkinemhu
resolve *(v.)* ဆုံးဖြတ်သည် sonehpyatsai
resonance *(n.)* အသံသြဇာ၊ ဟိန်းသံ aasan sya zar, heinsan
resonant *(adj.)* ဟိန်းသော heinsaw
resort *(n.)* ခိုကိုးရာ hkokoerar
resound *(v.)* ပဲ့တင်ထပ်သည် pae tin htatsai
resource *(n.)* အရင်းအနှီး aarinnaanhaee
resourceful *(adj.)* လုပ်ရည်ကိုင်ရည်ရှိသော lote rai kine raishisaw
respect *(n.)* လေးစားမှု layysarrmhu
respectful *(adj.)* အလေးထားသော aalayyhtarrsaw
respective *(adj.)* အသီးသီး aaseesee
respiration *(n.)* အသက်ရှူခြင်း aasaatshuuchinn
respire *(v.)* အသက်ရှူသည် aasaatshuusai
resplendent *(adj.)* အရောင်အဝါ တောက်ပခဲ့ညားသော aaraung aawar toutp hkan nyarrsaw
respond *(v.)* တုံ့ပြန်သည် tonepyansai
respondent *(n.)* ဖြေကြားသူ hpyay kyarrsuu
response *(n.)* ဖြေကြားချက် hpyaykyarrchet
responsibility *(n.)* တာဝန်ယူခြင်း tarwaanyuuchinn
responsible *(adj.)* တာဝန်ရှိသော tarwaanshisaw
rest *(n.)* အနားယူခြင်း၊ အိပ်စက်ခြင်း *anarr-yuuchinn, ait-saatchinn*
restaurant *(n.)* စားသောက်ဆိုင် sarrsoutsine
restive *(adj.)* လှုပ်လှုပ်ရွရွဖြစ်သော hlotehlote rw rwhpyitsaw
restoration *(n.)* နဂိုအတိုင်း ပြန်လည်မွမ်းမံခြင်း nagoaatine pyanlai mwmmanchinn
restore *(v.)* နဂိုအတိုင်း ပြန်လည် မွမ်းမံသည် nagoaatine pyanlai mwmmansai
restrain *(v.)* ချုပ်ထိန်းသည် chote hteinsai
restrict *(v.)* ကန့်သတ်သည် kant saatsai
restriction *(n.)* ကန့်သတ်ခြင်း kant saatchinn
restrictive *(adj.)* အနေအထိုင်ကျဉ်းကျပ်သော aanayaahtine kyain kyautsaw
result *(n.)* ရလဒ်၊ အကျိုးဆက် ralad , aakyoesaat
resume *(n.)* ကိုယ်ရေးအကျဉ်း korayyaakyain
resumption *(n.)* ပြန်စခြင်း pyan sachinn
resurgence *(n.)* နိုးထလာခြင်း noehtalarchinn
resurgent *(adj.)* နိုးကြားလာသော noe kyarrlarsaw
retail *(v.)* ရောင်းသည် raunggsai
retailer *(n.)* လက်လီဖြန့်ချိသူ laatle hpyant chisuu

retain *(v.)* ထိန်းသိမ်းထားသည် hteinsaimhtarrsai
retaliate *(v.)* လက်တုံ့ပြန်သည် laattonepyansai
retaliation *(n.)* လက်တုံ့ပြန်မှု laattonepyanmhu
retard *(v.)* နှောင့်နှေးစေသည် nhaaw int nhaayysaysai
retardation *(n.)* ဖွံ့ဖြိုးမှုနည်းခြင်း hpwan-hpyoemhu neechinn
retention *(n.)* ထိန်းသိမ်းထားခြင်း hteinsaimhtarrchinn
retentive *(adj.)* ကောင်းသော မှတ်ဉာဏ် kaunggsaw mhaatnyarn
reticence *(n.)* နှုတ်နည်းခြင်း nhuat naeechinn
reticent *(adj.)* လျှို့ထားသော shohtarrsaw
retina *(n.)* မြင်လွှာ myinlwhar
retinue *(n.)* နောက်တော်ပါအဖွဲ့ nouttaw paraahpwal
retire *(v.)* အငြိမ်းစားယူသည် aangyeim-sarr yuusai
retirement *(n.)* အငြိမ်းစားယူခြင်း aangyeim-sarryuuchinn
retort *(n.)* ထက်မြက်၍ဟာသဉာဏ်ရှင်သောပြန်ကြားချက် *htet-myat-ywe-har-ta-nyan-shwin-taw-pyan-kyar-chat*
retouch *(v.)* ခဲထိုးသည် hkell htoesai
retrace *(v.)* ခြေရာပြန်ကောက်သည် chay rar pyan koutsai
retread *(v.)* တာရာပန်းပြန်ထွင်းသည် *tayar-pan-pyan-htwin-the*
retreat *(v.)* ဆုတ်ခွာသည် sotehkwarsai
retrench *(v.)* ကုန်ကျစရိတ် လျှော့ချသည် konekyasarate shotchasai
retrenchment *(n.)* လျှော့ချခြင်း shotchachinn
retrieve *(v.)* ပြန်သိမ်းယူသည် pyan saimyuusai
retrospect *(n.)* ပြန်ပြောင်းမြော်ရှုလိုက်သောအခါ pyanpyaungg myaw shu litesawaahkar
retrospection *(n.)* ပြန်တွေးကြည့်ခြင်း pyantway kyanychinn
retrospective *(adj.)* အတိတ်ခြေရာကောက် aatatechayrarkout
return *(v.)* ပြန်သွားသည် pyanswarrsai
reuse *(v.)* ပြန်သုံးသည် pyansonesai
revaluation *(n.)* တစ်ဖန် တန်ဖိုးဖြတ်ခြင်း taithpaan taanhpoe hpyatchinn
revamp *(v.)* သနပ်ခါးလိမ်းသည် sanauthkarr laimsai
reveal *(v.)* ထုတ်ဖော်ပြောသည် htotehpawpyawwsai
revel *(n.)* ပျော်ပွဲရွှင်ပွဲ pyawpwalshwinpwal
revelation *(n.)* လှစ်ဟ၍ သိမြင်စေခြင်း hlit ha simyin saychinn
reveller *(n.)* သောက်စားမြူးထူးနေသူ soutsarr myauu htuu naysuu
revelry *(n.)* ဆူဆူညံညံ မြူးထူးပျော်ရွှင်ပွဲ suu suunyannyan myuu htuu pyawshwinpwal
revenge *(n.)* လက်စားချေခြင်း laat sarr chaaychinn
revengeful *(adj.)* လက်စားချေလိုစိတ်ပြင်းပြသော laat sarr chaay losate pyinnpyasaw
revenue *(n.)* အခွန်ဘဏ္ဍာ aahkwanbhandar
revere *(v.)* ကြည်ညိုသည်၊ မြတ်နိုးသည် kyinyo sai , myatnoesai
reverence *(n.)* ကြည်ညိုခြင်း kyinyochinn
reverend *(adj.)* သိက္ခာတော်ရ sikhkar tawra

reverent *(adj.)* **ကြည်ညိုလေးစားသော** kyinyolayysarrsaw

reverential *(adj.)* **ရိုသေလေးစားသော** ro saylayysarrsaw

reverie *(n.)* **အတွေးနယ်ချဲ့ခြင်း** aatway naalchaaechinn

reversal *(n.)* **ကပြောင်းကပြန် ဖြစ်စေခြင်း** ka pyaungg kapyan hpyitsaychinn

reverse *(v.)* **နောက်ဆုတ်သည်** noutsotesai

reversible *(adj.)* **ပြောင်းပြန်လှန်နိုင်သော** pyaung pyanhlaanninesaw

revert *(v.)* **ဒုံရင်းအခြေအနေ ပြန်ဆိုက်သည်** done-rinnaachayaanay pyan sitesai

review *(n.)* **ဆန်းစစ်ခြင်း** saannsitchinn

review *(v.)* **ဆန်းစစ်သည်** saannsitsai

revise *(v.)* **ပြည်ဆင်သည်** pyi sinsai

revision *(n.)* **ပြင်ဆင်ခြင်း** pyinsinchinn

revisit *(v.)* **နေရာဟောင်းသို့ အလည်တစ်ပတ် ပြန်ရောက်သည်** nayrar-haunggthoet aalai-ta-paat-pyan-routsai

revival *(n.)* **အားပြန်ကောင်းလာခြင်း** aarrpyankaungglarchinn

revive *(v.)* **သတိပြန်လည်လာသည်** sati pyanlailarsai

revocable *(adj.)* **ပြန်လည် ရုပ်သိမ်းနိုင်စွမ်း** *pyan-lal-yoke-thein-nine-swan*

revocation *(n.)* **ပြန်လည် ရုပ်သိမ်းခြင်း** pyanlai rotesaimchinn

revoke *(v.)* **ပြန်လည် ရုပ်သိမ်းသည်** pyanlai rotesaimsai

revolt *(n.)* **ပုန်ကန်ခြင်း** ponekaanchinn

revolution *(n.)* **တော်လှန်ရေး** tawhlaanrayy

revolutionary *(n.)* **တော်လှန်ရေးသမား** tawhlaanrayysamarr

revolve *(v.)* **လည်ပတ်သည်** laipaatsai

revolver *(n.)* **ခြောက်လုံးပြူးသေနတ်** chauklone pyauusaynaat

reward *(v.)* **ဆုချီးမြှင့်သည်** su chaeemyintsai

rewrite *(v.)* **ပြန်ရေးသည်** *pyan-yay-the*

rhetoric *(n.)* **အာစလျှာစ** aar sa shar-sa

rhetorical *(adj.)* **အလင်္ကာ** aa-linkar

rheumatic *(adj.)* **အဆစ်ရောင်သော** aasit raungsaw

rheumatism *(n.)* **အဆစ်ရောင်ရောဂါ** aasitraungrawgar

rhinoceros *(n.)* **ကြံ့** kyaan

rhyme *(n.)* **ကာရန်** karraan

rhymester *(n.)* **နဘေထပ်ဆရာ** *na-bay-htet-sa-yar*

rhythm *(n.)* **ရစ်သမ်** rit-sam

rhythmic *(adj.)* **စည်းချက်ကျသော** see-chetkyasaw

rib *(n.)* **နံရိုး** nanroe

ribbon *(n.)* **ဖဲပြား** hpellpyarr

rice *(n.)* **စပါးပင်** saparrpin

rich *(adj.)* **ချမ်းသာသော** chamsarsaw

riches *(n.)* **လူချမ်းသာ** luuchamsar

richness *(adj.)* **ချမ်းသာကြွယ်ဝမှု** chamsarkyawalwamhu

rick *(n.)* **ပုံစံတကျပုံထားသော ကောက်လှိုင်းပုံ** ponesan ta kya ponehtarrsaw kout hlinepone

rickets *(n.)* **အရိုးပျော့နာ** aaroe pyaw-nar

rickety *(adj.)* **ခနော်နီခနော်နဲ့** hka naw ne hk nawnae

rickshaw *(n.)* **လန်ချား** laan charr

rid *(v.)* **ပထုတ်သည်** *pa htotesai*

riddle *(n.)* **စကားထာ** sakarrhtar

ride *(n.)* **ယာဉ်စီးနင်းခြင်း** yin seenainnchinn

ride *(v.)* **မြင်းအပျော်စီးသည်** myinn aapyawseesai
rider *(n.)* **မြင်းစီးတတ်သူ၊ နောက်ဆက်တွဲ မှတ်ချက်** myinnsee taat suu , noutsaattwal mhaatchet
ridge *(n.)* **တောင်ကြော** taungkyaww
ridicule *(n.)* **လှောင်ပြောင်သရော်မှု** hlaawinpyaung sarawmhu
ridiculous *(adj.)* **ရယ်ဖွယ်ရာ၊ မဖြစ်နိုင်တာ** raal hpwalrar , mahpyitninetar
rifle *(v.)* **မွှေနှောက်လှန်လှောသည်** mwhaay nhaout hlaan hlaawsai
rift *(n.)* **အကြား၊ အဟ** a kyarr , aah
right *(n.)* **ညာဘက်** nyarbhaat
righteous *(adj.)* **တရားကျသော၊ လမ်းကျသော** tararr kyasaw, lamkyasaw
rigid *(adj.)* **တောင့်သော** taunt saw
rigorous *(adj.)* **ပြင်းထန်သော** pyinnhtaansaw
rigour *(n.)* **ပြင်းထန်မှု** pyinnhtaanmhu
rim *(n.)* **အနားဝန်း** aanarrwaann
ring *(n.)* **လက်စွပ်** laatswut
ringlet *(n.)* **ဆံနွယ်ခွေ** sannwahlkway
ringworm *(n.)* **ပွေး** pway
rinse *(v.)* **ရေဆေးသည်** ray sayysai
riot *(n.)* **အဓိကရုဏ်း** aadhikarun
rip *(v.)* **ဆုတ်ဖြဲသည်** sote hpyaellsai
ripe *(adj.)* **မှည့်သော** mhae saw
ripen *(v.)* **မှည့်လာသည်** mha ny larsai
ripple *(n.)* **လှိုင်းတွန့်** hline twant
rise *(v.)* **တက်သည်** taatsai
risk *(v.)* **စွန့်စားသည်** swant sarrsai
risky *(adj.)* **အန္တရာယ်များသော** aantararalmyarrsaw
rite *(n.)* **ဘာသာရေး၊ ရိုးရာထုံးတမ်းဓလေ့** bharsarrayy , roerar htonetamdhalae
ritual *(adj.)* **ရိုးရာ** roerar
rival *(n.)* **ပြိုင်ဘက်** pyainebhaat
rivalry *(n.)* **ပြိုင်ဆိုင်မှု** pyainesinemhu
river *(n.)* **မြစ်** myit
rivet *(v.)* **သံမှိုနှက်သည်** san mhao nhaatsai
rivulet *(n.)* **ချောင်းငယ်** chaunggngaal
roach *(n.)* **ဥရောပ ရေချိုငါးငယ်** urawp ray cho ngarrngaal
road *(n.)* **လမ်း** lam
road race *(n.)* **လမ်းပေါ်ကားပြိုင်ပွဲ** *lan-paw-kar-pyaing-pwe*
road rage *(n.)* **မထိန်းမသိမ်းနိုင်ကြမ်းတမ်းစွာ ကားမောင်းခြင်း** *ma-htein-ma-thein-ning-kyan-tan-swar-kar-maung-chin*
roadblock *(n.)* **လမ်းဆို့** lamshoet
roadhouse *(n.)* **အမြန်လမ်းမဘေးတွင် ဖွင့်ထားသော စားသောက်ဆိုင်** aamyan lam mabhayytwin hpwint htarrsaw sarrsoutsine
roadkill *(n.)* **လမ်းပေါ်တွင် တရိစ္ဆာန်ကားတိုက်သေခြင်း** *lan-paw-twin-ta-yeik-san-kar-tite-tay-chin*
roadrunner *(n.)* **ဥသြမိသားစုဝင်ငှက်မျိုး** *oat-aw-mi-tar-su-win-ngat-myo*
roadshow *(n.)* **လမ်းဘေးဖျော်ဖြေပွဲ** *lan-bay-phyaw-phyay-pwe*
roadster *(n.)* **ကားအမောင်းများသော ဒရိုင်ဘာ** *kar-a-maung-myar-taw-da-ri-bar*
roam *(v.)* **သဝေထိုးသည်** sawayhtoesai
roar *(n.)* **ဟိန်းသံ** heinsan
roast *(adj.)* **ကင်၊ လှော်၊ ဖုတ်** kin , hlaaw , hpote

rob *(v.)* လုယက်သည် luyaatsai

robber *(n.)* သူခိုးဓားပြ suuhkoedharrpya

robbery *(n.)* လုယက်မှု luyaatmhu

robe *(n.)* ရေလဲဝတ်ရုံ ray lellwaatrone

robot *(n.)* စက်ရုပ် saatrote

robust *(adj.)* သန်မြန်သော saan myansaw

rock *(n.)* ကျောက်တုံး kyawwattone

rock climber *(n.)* ကျောင်တောင်တက်သူ kyaung taungtaatsuu

rock-bottom *(v.)* အနိမ့်ဆုံး a ni msone

rocker *(n.)* ရော့ခ်ကာသမား rothk karsamarr

rocket *(n.)* ဒုံးကျည်၊ ရှူးဒိုင်း donekyai , shuudine

rocket scientist *(n.)* ဒုံးကျည်ပညာရှင် donekyaipanyar-shin

rocketeer *(n.)* ရော့ကက်ဒီဇိုင်းလုပ်သူ၊ ပစ်သူ၊ ဒုံးစီးနင်းသူ *yot-kat-da-zine-lote-thu, pyit-th, done-si-nin-thu*

rocketman *(n.)* ရော့ကက်ဒီဇိုင်းလုပ်သည်၊ ပစ်သည်၊ ဒုံးစီးနင်းသည် *yot-kat-da-zine-lote-the, pyit-the, done-si-nin-the*

rockfall *(n.)* တောင်ပြိုခြင်း *taung-pyo-chin*

rockfish *(n.)* ကျောက်ငါး *kyauk-ngar*

rocking *(adj.)* တုန်သော၊ ခါသော၊ ရှေ့နောက်ခါသည် *tone-taw, khar-taw, shay-naut-khar-the*

rod *(n.)* အချောင်းအတံ a chaungg aatan

rodent *(n.)* ကိုက်ဖြတ်သတ္တဝါ kite hpyatsattawar

roe *(n.)* ငါး ngarr

rogue *(n.)* ဆိုးယုတ်သောသူ soe yotesawsuu

roguery *(n.)* အန္တရာယ်များသော အပြုအမူ *an-da-yal-myar-taw-a-pyu-a-mu*

roguish *(adj.)* ကျီစယ်သော kyae saalsaw

role *(n.)* ကဏ္ဍ၊ ဇာတ်ကောင် kan-da, zatkaung

role model *(n.)* စံနမူနာယူထိုက်သူ sannamuunar yuu htitesuu

roll *(v.)* လိမ့်သည်၊ လိပ်သည် lint sai , lattsai

roll-call *(n.)* လူစစ်ဆေးခြင်း luusitsayychinn

roller *(n.)* တလိမ့်တုံး t lintone

rollicking *(adj.)* သွက်လက်မြူးကြွသော swat laat myauu kyawsaw

romance *(n.)* ကြည်နူးဖွယ်ချစ်ဇာတ်လမ်း kyinuuhpwal chitzatlam

romantic *(adj.)* စိတ်ကူးယဉ်ဆန်သော satekuu yainsaansaw

romp *(n.)* မြူးတူးခုန်ပေါက် ဆော့ကစားခြင်း myauu tuu hkonepout sotkasarrchinn

rood *(n.)* လက်ဝါးကပ်တိုင်ကြီး laatwarrkauttinekyee

roof *(n.)* ခေါင်မိုး hkaungmoe

rooftop *(n.)* အမိုးပေါ် a moepaw

rook *(n.)* ကျီးအ kyaeea

rook *(v.)* ရိတ်သည် ratesai

room *(n.)* အခန်း aahkaann

room-mate *(n.)* အခန်းဖော် aahkaannhpaw

roomy *(adj.)* ကျယ်ကျယ်ဝန်းဝန်းရှိသော kyaalkyaal waann waannshisaw

roost *(n.)* အိပ်တန်း aintaann

root *(n.)* အမြစ် aamyit

rope *(n.)* ကြိုး kyoe

rosary *(n.)* စိတ်ပုတီး sateputee

rose *(n.)* နှင်းဆီပန်း natensepaann

roseate *(adj.)* ပန်းရောင်ရင့် paannraung rint

rostrum *(n.)* တရားဟော စင်မြင့် tararrhaw sinmyint
rosy *(adj.)* နီတျာတျာ ne tyaar tyaar
rot *(v.)* ဆွေးသည်၊ မြည့်သည် sway sai , myae-sai
rotary *(adj.)* လည်ပတ်သော laipaatsaw
rotate *(v.)* လည်သည်၊ အလှည့်ကျဖြစ်သည် lai sai , a hla ny kyahpyitsai
rotation *(n.)* လည်ခြင်း laichinn
rote *(n.)* အလွတ်ကျက်ခြင်း a lwat kyetchinn
rotten *(adj.)* ပုပ်သော၊ ဆိုးရွားသော pote saw , soerwarrsaw
rouble *(n.)* ရုရှားနိုင်ငံသုံးငွေ ရူဘယ် rusharrninengansonengway ruubhaal
rough *(adj.)* ကြမ်းသော၊ လှိုင်းလေထန်သော kyam saw , hline lay htaansaw
round *(n.)* ပုံမှန်ခရီးတစ်ပတ်၊ အလှည့် ponemhaan hkaree ta-paat , a hlae
rouse *(v.)* နှိုးသည် nhoe-sai
rout *(n.)* ခွက်ခွက်လန်ရှုံးခြင်း hkwat hkwat laan shonechinn
route *(n.)* လမ်းကြောင်း lamkyaungg
routine *(n.)* ပုံမှန် ponemhaan
rove *(v.)* လှည့်လည်သွားလာသည် hla ny lai swarrlarsai
rover *(n.)* ခြေရှည်သူ chay shisuu
row *(v.)* လှော်ခတ်သည် hlaaw hkaatsai
rowdy *(adj.)* ဗရုတ် barote
royal *(adj.)* တော်ဝင် tawwin
royalist *(n.)* ဘုရင်စနစ်ကို ထောက်ခံသူ bhurinsanitko htouthkansuu
royalty *(n.)* မင်း မိဖုရားနှင့် မင်းမျိုးမင်းနွယ် min mihpurarrnint min myoeminnwal
rub *(v.)* ပွတ်သည် pwatsai
rubber *(n.)* ရော်ဘာ rawbhar
rubber bullet *(n.)* ရော်ဘာကျည် rawbharkyai
rubber duck *(n.)* ရာဘာ *yar-bar-bal-yoke*
rubber tree *(n.)* ရော်ဘာပင် *rawbharpin*
rubberneck *(n.)* အူကြောင်ကြောင်ခေါင်းကို လှည့်ကြည့်သည် *au-kyuang-kyaung-kaung-ko-hlae-kyi-the*
rubbing *(n.)* ထပ်ကူးခြင်း *htet-ku-pon*
rubbish *(n.)* အမှိုက်သရိုက် aamhaite sarite
rubble *(n.)* အုတ်ကျိုးအုတ်ပဲ့ aote kyoe aote pae
rubblework *(n.)* အုတ်ကျိုးအုတ်ပဲ့စီထားသော အင်္ဂတေ *oak-kyoe-oak-pae-si-htar-taw-in-ga-day*
rubeola *(n.)* ဂျိုက်သိုး *gyaik-thoe*
rubian *(n.)* ရူဘီအန်ဓာတ် *ru-bi-an-dat*
rubicon *(n.)* ကျော်သွားလျှင်ပြန်လှည့်မရနိုင်သော အကန့်အသတ် *kyaw-twar-lyin-pyan-hlae-ma-ya-nine-taw-a-kant-a-thet*
rubify *(v.)* နီလာသည် *ni-lar-the*
rubric *(n.)* မင်နီ သို့မဟုတ် ကျန်စာသားနှင့် ကွဲအောင် ရိုက်နှိပ်ထားသော ခေါင်းစီး၊ ညွှန်ကြားချက်၊ ကျင့်စဉ် mine thoetmahote kyaan sarsarrnint kwalaaung rite natehtarrsaw hkaungg see , nywhaankyarrchet , kyint-sin
rubricate *(v.)* အနီဖြင့် မှတ်သားသည် *a-ni-phint-mat-tar-the*
ruby *(n.)* ပတ္တမြား pat-tamyarr
ruck *(v.)* တွန့်လိပ်တက်သည် twant late taatsai
rucksack *(n.)* ကျောပိုးအိတ် kyawpoeate
ruckus *(n.)* ရုတ်ရုတ်ရုတ်ရုတ် rote rote roterote
rudder *(n.)* တက်မ taat-ma

rudderpost *(n.)* တက်မရိုး *tat-ma-yoe*

ruddy *(adj.)* စိုပြည်နီမြန်းသော so pyi ne myansaw

rude *(adj.)* ရိုင်းစိုင်းသော rinesinesaw

rudiment *(n.)* အခြေခံသဘောတရား aachayhkansabhawtararr

rudimentary *(adj.)* အခြေခံမျှသာ ဖြစ်သော aachayhkanmya-sar hpyitsaw

rue *(v.)* နောင်တရသည် naungtarasai

rueful *(adj.)* မချိသော machaisaw

ruffian *(n.)* လူရမ်းကား luuramkarr

ruffle *(n.)* တွန့်ခေါက်ထားသော အင်္ကျီလက်နား twant hkouthtarrsaw aain kyae laatnarr

rug *(n.)* ကော်ဇော kawzaw

rugged *(adj.)* မျက်နှာပြင် ကြမ်းတမ်းသော myetnharpyin kyamtamsaw

ruin *(n.)* ပျက်စီးခြင်း pyetseechinn

rule *(n.)* စည်းမျဉ်း seemyin

rulebook *(n.)* စည်းမျဉ်းစာအုပ် see myinsaraote

rulebound *(adj.)* စည်းမျဉ်းဖြင့် ချုပ်ကိုင်သော see myinhpyint chotekinesaw

rulebreaking *(n.)* စည်းမျဉ်းချိုးဖောက်သည် *si-myin-choe-hpauk-chin*

ruler *(n.)* အုပ်ချုပ်သူ aote-chotesuu

ruling *(n.)* အုပ်ချုပ်ခြင်း aote-chotechinn

rum *(adj.)* ကြောင်သော kyaungsaw

rumble *(n.)* ခပ်အုပ်အုပ်မြည်ဟည်းသံ khat-aote aote myi haeesan

ruminant *(n.)* စားမြို့ပြန်တိရစ္ဆာန် sarr myuan pyantirate-san

ruminate *(v.)* စားမြို့ပြန်သည် sarr myuanpyansai

rumination *(n.)* စားမြို့ပြန်ခြင်း sarr myuanpyanchinn

rummage *(n.)* ဖွခြင်း hpwa-chinn

rummy *(n.)* ပိုကာ ဖဲကစားနည်း pokar hpellkasarrnaee

rumour *(n.)* ကောလာဟလ kawlarha-la

run *(n.)* ပြေးခြင်း pyaychinn

runabout *(n.)* ပေါ့ပါးသော ကားငယ် pot parrsaw karrngaal

runaway *(n.)* အိမ်ပြေး aainpyay

runback *(n.)* ဘောလုံးနောက်ပြန်လိုက်သည် *baw-lone-naut-pyan-lite-the*

runcation *(n.)* လက်ဖြင့်ပေါင်းသင်သည် *lat-phint-paung-tin-the*

rundown *(n.)* ခေါင်းစဉ်အကြမ်း *hkaung-sin-a-kyan*

rune *(n.)* ရှေးဂျာမန်အက္ခရာ shayy gyaarmaanaakhkarar

rung *(n.)* မြည်ခြင်း myichinn

runner *(n.)* ပြေးသူ *pyay-thu*

runs *(n.)* ဝမ်းလျှောသည် *wan-shaw-the*

rupee *(n.)* ရူပီးငွေ ruupeengway

rupture *(v.)* ပေါက်ကွဲခြင်း poutkwalchinn

rupture *(n.)* သဘောထား ကွဲလွဲမှု sabhawhtarr kwallwalmhu

rural *(adj.)* ကျေးလက်တောနယ် kyaayylaat tawnaal

ruse *(n.)* ဥပါယ်တံမျဉ် au-pal tan myin

rush *(n.)* တစ်ဟုန်ထိုးပြေးခြင်း ta-hone-htoe pyaychinn

rust *(v.)* သံချေးတက်သည် sanchaayytaatsai

rustic *(adj.)* ကျေးတောဆန်သော၊ ရိုးစင်းသော kyaayytaw saansaw , roesinnsaw

rusticate *(v.)* ကျောင်းမှ နားခံရသည်၊ ထုတ်ပယ်ခံရသည် *kyaung-ma-nar-khan-ya-the-htoke-pal-khan-ya-the*
rustication *(n.)* ကျောင်းမှ နားခံရခြင်း၊ ထုတ်ပယ်ခံရခြင်း *kyaung ma-nar-khan-ya-chin-htoke-pal-khan-ya-chin*
rusticity *(n.)* ကျေးလက်ဆန်ခြင်း *kyay-lat-san-chin*
rustle *(v.)* တရှဲရှဲ မြည်သည် ta shellshell myisai
rusty *(adj.)* သံချေးတက်သော sanchaayytaatsaw
rut *(adj.)* ဘီးရာ အပြိုင်းအရိုင်းမွနေသော bheerar a pyaine aa-rine mwa-nay-saw
ruthless *(adj.)* အကြင်နာမဲ့သော aa-kyinnar maesaw
rye *(n.)* ရိုင်းဂျုံ rine-gyaone

S

sabbath *(n.)* ဥပုသ်နေ့ upusnae
sabbatical *(n.)* ခွင့်ကာလ hkwintkar-la
sabotage *(v.)* တမင်ဖျက်ဆီးသည် ta-min hpyetseesai
sabre *(v.)* ဓားရှည်နှင့် ခုတ်သည် *da-shay-nint-khote-sai*
saccharin *(n.)* ဆေးသကြား sayy sakyarr
saccharine *(adj.)* ချွဲနွဲ့လွန်းသော chwal nwal lwannsaw
sachet *(n.)* ရနံ့အိတ်ငယ် ranan aatengaal
sack *(v.)* အလုပ်မှ ထုတ်ပစ်သည် aalotemha htote paitsai
sacrament *(n.)* ခရစ်ယာန်ဓမ္မမင်္ဂလာအမှု hkaraityaran dhamm main g lar aamhu
sacred *(adj.)* အလေးအမြတ်ထားသော a layy aamyathtarrsaw
sacrifice *(n.)* စွန့်လွှတ်ခြင်း swant lwutchinn
sacrificial *(adj.)* စွန့်လွှတ်ရသော swant lwutrasaw
sacrilege *(n.)* မလေးမခန့်ပြုခြင်း ma layy m hkaantpyuchinn
sacrilegious *(adj.)* မလေးမခန့်ပြုသော ma layy m hkaantpyusaw
sacrosanct *(adj.)* အထိမခံသော aa-hti m hkansaw
sad *(adj.)* ဝမ်းနည်းသော wamnaeesaw
sadden *(v.)* ဝမ်းနည်းစေသည် wamnaeesaysai
saddle *(n.)* ကုန်းနှီး kone-nhaee
sadism *(n.)* ရက်စက်ခြင်း၌ သာယာမှု raatsaat chinn-nite saryarmhu
sadist *(n.)* ရက်စက်ခြင်း၌ သာယာသူ raatsaat chinn-nite saryarsuu
sadness *(n.)* ဝမ်းနည်းမှု wamnaeemhu
safari *(n.)* ဓာတ်ပုံရိုက်ရုံ တောလည်ခရီး dhratponeriterone taw laihkaree
safe *(adj.)* လုံခြုံသော lonechuansaw
safe harbour *(n.)* လုံခြုံသော ကွန်းခိုရာ *lone-shone-taw-kun-kho-yar*
safebox *(n.)* မီးခံသေတ္တာ *mee-khan-tit-tar*
safe-conduct *(n.)* အနှောင့်အယှက်မဲ့ သွားပိုင်ခွင့် a nhaut aa-shaatmae swarr pinehkwint
safecracker *(n.)* မီးခံသေတ္တာဖောက်သူ *mee-khan-tit-tar-phaut-thu*
safe-deposit *(n.)* အာမခံသေတ္တာများထားရာ အဆောက်အအုံ aarmahkan sayttar myarr htarrrar aasoutaaaone
safeguard *(v.)* ကာကွယ်ပေးသည် karkwalpayysai

safehouse *(n.)* **လုံခြုံစွာ ခိုင်အောင်းနိုင်သော အိမ်** lonechuanswar hkine aaungnginesaw aain
safekeeping *(n.)* **လုံခြုံစွာ သိမ်းဆည်းထားသည်** *lone-chone-swar-thein-see-htar-the*
safely *(adv.)* **လုံခြုံစွာ** lonechuanswar
safety *(n.)* **လုံခြုံမှု** lonechuanmhu
saffron *(adj.)* **အဝါရောင်** aa-warraung
sag *(n.)* **မြုပ်သည့် အခြေအနေ** *myoke-the-a-chay-a-nay*
saga *(n.)* **ဝတ္ထုရှည်** wathtushay
sagacious *(adj.)* **ဉာဏ်၊ အမြော်အမြင် ကြီးသော** nyarn, a myawaamyin kyeesaw
sagacity *(n.)* **ဉာဏ်၊ အမြော်အမြင် ကြီးမှု** nyarn, a myawaamyin kyeemhu
sage *(n.)* **ကလျာဏီပင်မျိုး၊ ပညာရှိ** kalyaar-ne pin myoe , panyarshi
sagebrush *(n.)* **ချုံပင်** *chone-pin*
sage-green *(n.)* **အစိမ်းညို့ရောင်** *a-sein-nyoe-yaung*
sageness *(n.)* **မျှော်မြင်တွေးခေါ်မှုရှိခြင်း** *myaw-myin-tway-khaw-mu-shi-chin*
saggy *(adj.)* **ပွယောင်းသော** *pwa-yaung-taw*
sagittary *(n.)* **မနွတ်၊ မြားသမား** *ma-nwat-ta, myar-ta-mar*
sahib *(n.)* **အရှင်** aashin
sail *(v.)* **ရွက်လွှင့်သည်** rwat lwint sai
sail *(n.)* **ရွက်** rwat
sailboard *(n.)* **ပင်လယ်လှိုင်းစီးလှေ** pinlaal hline see-hlaay
sailboarder *(n.)* **ပင်လယ်လှိုင်းစီးလှေဖြင့် လှိုင်းစီးသူ** pinlaal hline see hlaayhpyint hline seesuu
sailboat *(n.)* **ရွက်လှေ** rwathlaay
sailboater *(n.)* **ရွက်လှေစီးသူ** rwathlaay seesuu
sailboating *(n.)* **ရွက်လှေစီးခြင်း** rwathlaayseechinn
sailcraft *(n.)* **ရွက်တစ်ခုထက် ပိုပါသော လှေ** *ywet ta-khu-htet-po-par-taw-hlae*
sailing *(n.)* **ရွက်လွှင့်ခြင်း** rwat lwint chinn
sailor *(n.)* **သင်္ဘောသား** sinbhawsarr
saint *(n.)* **သူတော်စင်** suutawsin
saintly *(adj.)* **သူတော်စင်ကဲ့သို့** suutawsinkaethoet
sake *(n.)* **ဘုရားရေ** pha-rar-ray
salable *(adj.)* **ရောင်းနိုင်သော** *yaung-nai-taw*
salad *(n.)* **အသုပ်** aa-sote
salamander *(v.)* **ချက်ပြုတ်ရာတွင် ဆလာမန်သာဥသုံးခြင်း** *chat-pyoke-yar-twin-sa-lar-man-da-oo-tone-chin*
salary *(n.)* **လစာ** lasar
sale *(n.)* **ရောင်းချခြင်း** raunggchachinn
salebrosity *(n.)* **ကြမ်းတမ်းခြင်း** *kyan-tan-chin*
salesforce *(n.)* **အရောင်းအင်အားစု** *a-yaung-inn-arr-su*
salesman *(n.)* **အရောင်းစာရေး** aaraunggsarrayy
salient *(adj.)* **အဓိက** aadhika
saline *(adj.)* **ဆားငန်** sarr ngan
salinity *(n.)* **ဆားဓာတ်ပါဝင်မှု** sarr dhrat-parwinmhu
saliva *(n.)* **တံတွေး** tantway
sally *(n.)* **ခွန်းတုံ့ပြန်ခြင်း၊ ထွက်တိုက်ခြင်း** hkwann tonepyanchinn, htwat titechinn
Salon *(n.)* **အလှပြင်ဆိုင်** aahlapyinsine
saloon *(n.)* **ဆလွန်းကား** salwannkarr

salt *(n.)* ဆား sarr

salty *(adj.)* ဆားငန်သော sarr ngaansaw

salutary *(adj.)* အကျိုးပြုသော aakyoepyusaw

salutation *(n.)* ပဋိသန္ဓာရပြုခြင်း pati san dhar rapyuchinn

salute *(v.)* ဂုဏ်ပြု ခြင်း gonpyu chinn

salvage *(n.)* ဆယ်တင်မှု saal tinmhu

salvation *(n.)* ကယ်တင်ခြင်း kaaltinchinn

samaritan *(n.)* ဒုက္ခရောက်နေသူများကို ကူညီသော အဖွဲ့ dukhkaroutnaysuumyarrko kuunyesaw aahpwal

samba *(v.)* ဆန်ဘာအက saan bhar aak

sambuca *(n.)* ဆန်ဘူကအရက် saan bhuu ka aa-raat

same *(adj.)* တူညီသော tuu-nyesaw

samely *(adv.)* တူညီစွာ tuunyeswar

samite *(n.)* ရွှေချည်ထိုး ပိုးထည်စ shway hkyaihtoe poe htaih-ca

samovar *(n.)* ရေနွေးအိုး raynwayoe

sample *(n.)* နမူနာ namuunar

sampler *(n.)* နမူနာ namuunar

sampling *(n.)* နမူနာ ရွေးချယ်ခြင်းဖြစ်စဉ် na-muunar rway-hkyaal-chinn-hpyit-hcain

samsonite *(n.)* ဆန်မိုနိုက်သတ္တု saan mo nite-sattu

samurai *(n.)* ဆာမူရိုင်း sarmuurine

sanability *(n.)* ကုသနိုင်သော အခြေအနေ kusaninesaw aah-kyay-aa-nay

sanatorium *(n.)* နာတာရှည်ဆေးကုဌာန nartarshi sayykuhtarna

sanctification *(n.)* မှန်ကန်ကြောင်း သက်သေထူခြင်း mhaankaankyaungg saatsay htuuchinn

sanctify *(v.)* မှန်ကန်ကြောင်း သက်သေထူသည် mhaankaankyaungg saatsay htuusai

sanction *(n.)* ခွင့်ပြုမိန့်၊ ခွင့်ပြုချက် hkwin pyu mein , hkwintpyuchet

sanctity *(n.)* မွန်မြတ်သန့်စင်မှု mwanmyat saant sinmhu

sanctuary *(n.)* ခိုလှုံရာ hkohluanrar

sand *(v.)* ကော်ဖတ်စားသည် kaw hpaat sarrsai

sandal *(n.)* ကြိုးသိုင်းဖိနပ် kyaoe sinehpinaut

sandalwood *(n.)* စန္ဒကူး san-da-kuu

sandbank *(n.)* သောင်ခုံ saunghkone

sandboard *(v.)* သဲလျှောစီးဘုတ်စီးသည် sell shaw hcee bhote hcee-sai

sandbox *(n.)* သဲဖြည့်ကျင်း sell hpyay kyinn

sandcastle *(n.)* သဲရဲတိုက် sell rell-tite

sandfish *(n.)* သဲငါး sell-ngarr

sandglass *(n.)* သဲနာရီ sell-nar-re

sandhill *(n.)* သဲတောင်ပူစာ sell taung puu-hcar

sandpaper *(n.)* ကော်ဖတ် kawhpaat

sandpit *(n.)* သဲဖြည့်ကျင်း sell hpyay kyin

sandscape *(n.)* သဲသုံး ရှုခင်း sellsone shu-hkinn

sandstone *(n.)* သဲကျောက် sell-kyaut

sandstorm *(n.)* သဲမုန်တိုင်း sell-monetine

sandwich *(n.)* အသားညှပ်ပေါင်မုန့် a sarr nyhaut paung mone

sandy *(adj.)* သဲထူသော sell htuusaw

sane *(adj.)* စိတ်မှန်သော satemhaansaw

sanely *(adv.)* စိတ်မှန်မှန် satemhaanmhaan

sanguine *(adj.)* မျှော်လင့်ချက်ထားသော myahaaw lint chethtarrsaw

sanitary *(adj.)* သန့်ရှင်းရေး၊ ကျန်းမာရေးနှင့်ညီညွတ်သော saant hlyinn rayy , kyannmarrayynint nyenywatsaw

sanity *(n.)* စိတ်နှံ့ခြင်း sate nhaanchinn

sap *(n.)* သစ်ရည်၊ ပင်ရည်၊ အစေး sit rai , pin rai , aasayy

sap *(v.)* ဆုတ်ယုတ်စေသည်၊ ကုန်ခမ်းစေသည် soteyote saysai , kone hkamsaysai

sapidity *(n.)* အရသာဂုဏ်သတ္တိ aarasar gon-satti

sapience *(n.)* တတ်သိနားလည်ခြင်း taat sinarrlaichinn

sapiens *(n.)* လူသား luu-sarr

sapient *(adj.)* ပညာရှိသော panyarshisaw

sapling *(n.)* ပင်ပျို pinpyo

sapphire *(n.)* နီလာ nelar

sarcasm *(n.)* ထေ့လုံး၊ ငေါ့လုံး htae lone, ngotlone

sarcastic *(adj.)* ငေါ့သော ngae saw

sardonic *(adj.)* လှောင်သော၊ သရော်သော hling saw, sa-rawsaw

satan *(n.)* ဆာတန်မာရ်နတ် sar taanmarrnaat

satanic *(adj.)* ဆာတန်မာရ်နတ်အလား sar taan marrnaat aalarr

satanically *(adv.)* စိတ်ယုတ်စိတ်မာဖြင့် sate yote sate marhpyint

satchel *(n.)* သားရေ sarrray

satellite *(n.)* ဂြိုလ်တု gyaoltu

satiable *(adj.)* ကျေနပ်နိုင်သော kyaay-nat-nine-saw

satiate *(v.)* အီသည်၊ အင့်သည် ae sai , a intsai

satiety *(n.)* ပြည့်အင့်ခြင်း pyae aint-chinn

satin *(n.)* ဖဲ hpell

satire *(n.)* သရောခြင်း၊ သရော်စာ sa raw chinn , sarawsar

satirical *(adj.)* သရော်၊ အထေ့အခေါ့ saraw , a htae a hkaear

satirist *(n.)* သရော်မှုပညာရှင် saraw mhupanyarshin

satirize *(v.)* သရောစာရေးသည် s raw sar-rayysai

satisfaction *(n.)* ကျေနပ်ခြင်း kyaay-nautchinn

satisfactory *(adj.)* ကျေနပ်ဖွယ်ကောင်းသော kyaaynaut hpwalkaunggsaw

satisfy *(v.)* ကျေနပ်သည် kyaaynautsai

saturate *(v.)* စို့ရွှဲစေသည် so shwellsaysai

saturation *(n.)* ပြည့်ဝခြင်း pyae-wachinn

Saturday *(n.)* စနေ sa-nay

sauce *(v.)* ချဉ်ရည်ထည့်သည် hkyain rai htee-tsai

saucer *(n.)* အောက်ခံပန်းကန်ပြား aout-hkanpaannkaanpyarr

saucy *(adj.)* ရှုတ်နောက်နောက် shwat noutnout

sauna *(v.)* ပေါင်းခံချွေးထုတ်ခန်းသုံးသည် paungg hkan hkyaway htote hkaann-sonesai

saunter *(n.)* စိမ်ပြေနပြေ လမ်းလျှောက်ခြင်း sin pyay napyay lamshoutchinn

saunterer *(n.)* စိမ်ပြေနပြေ လမ်းလျှောက်သူ sin pyay napyay lamshoutsuu

sausage *(n.)* ဝက်အူချောင်း waatauuchaungg

saute *(v.)* ဆီပူထိုးသည် se puu htoesai

savable *(adj.)* ကယ်နိုင်သော kaal-nine-saw

savage *(v.)* ရက်ရက်စက်စက် ကိုက်ဖဲ့သည် raatraatsaatsaat kite hpaesai

savagely *(adv.)* ရက်ရက်စက်စက် raatraatsaatsaat

savagery *(n.)* ရက်စက်ကြမ်းကြုတ်မှု raatsaat kyam kyuatmhu

savant *(n.)* ပညာရှိ pyin-nyar-shi

save *(v.)* ကယ်ဆယ်သည်၊ စုဆောင်းသည် kaalsaal sai , susaunggsai

saviour *(n.)* ကယ်တင်ရှင် kaaltinshin

savour *(n.)* အရသာ aa-ra-sar

savoury *(adj.)* အမွှေးအကြိုင်ကဲသော a hmway a kyaine kellsaw

saw *(n.)* လွှ lwa

saw pit *(n.)* လွှဖြင့် သစ်ကို အလယ်ကြားမှ ဖြတ်သည် lwha-hpyint saitko aa-laal-kyarr-mha hpyat-sai

sawbench *(n.)* လွှဖြင့် ဖြတ်လုပ်ထားသော ခုံ lwha-hpyint hpyat lote-htarr-saw hkone

sawbill *(n.)* ရေဘဲ raybhell

sawbones *(n.)* ခွဲစိတ်ဆရာဝန် hkwal-sate-sa-rar-waan

sawbuck *(n.)* လမ်းတား၊ lam tarr ,

sawdust *(n.)* လွှစာ lwhasar

sawfish *(n.)* လွှငါး lwhangarr

sawgrass *(n.)* လွှမြက် lwhamyaat

sawhorse *(n.)* လေးချောင်းထောက်ခုံ layy hkyaungg htouthkone

sawmill *(n.)* သစ်စက် sitsaat

sawtooth *(n.)* လွှသွားပုံ လှိုင်း lwha swarrpone lhaine

sawyer *(n.)* လွှဖြတ်သမား lwha hpyatsamarr

saxophone *(n.)* ဆက်ဆိုဖုန်း saat sohpone

saxophonist *(n.)* ဆက်ဆိုဖုန်းမှုတ်သူ saat so hpone mhuatsuu

say *(n.)* ပြောရေးဆိုခွင့် pyawwrayysohkwint

scab *(n.)* အနာဖေး aanar hpayy

scabbard *(n.)* ဓားအိမ် dharraain

scabies *(n.)* ဝဲ well

scaffold *(n.)* ကြိုးစင် kyaoesin

scale *(v.)* အကြေးထိုးသည် a kyay htoesai

scalp *(n.)* ဦးရေ u-ray

scambling *(n.)* အလောတကြီးဖြစ်သော အစားအစာ a law t kyeehpyitsaw aahcarraahcar

scamper *(v.)* ခုန်ပေါက်ပြေးသည် hkone pout pyaysai

scan *(n.)* ရိုက်ခြင်း၊ စကန်ဖတ်ခြင်း rite chinn , sa kaan hpaatchinn

scandal *(n.)* မကောင်းသတင်း makaunggsatinn

scandalize *(v.)* မျက်စိရှက်စရာ လုပ်ပြသည် myetsishatsarar lotepyasai

scandalous *(adj.)* မျက်စိရှက်စရာ myetsishatsarar

scandalously *(adv.)* မတော်တရော် matawtaraw

scanner *(n.)* စကန်ဖတ်စက် sa kaan hpaatsaat

scant *(n.)* ကျောက်ပြား kyawwatpyarr

scanty *(adj.)* မဖြစ်စလောက် mahpyitsalout

scape *(v.)* လွတ်မြောက်သည် lwatmyawwatsai

scapegoat *(v.)* ပြစ်မှုကြောင့် တစ်စုံတစ်ယောက် ဒဏ်ခတ်ခံရသည် pyitmhukyount taithconetaityout danhkaathkanrasai

scapeless *(adj.)* တိရိစ္ဆာန်၏ အတိုင်တစ်ခုခု မပါသော ti rihc taraneat a tinetaithkuhku maparsaw

scapula *(n.)* လက်ပြင်ရိုး laat pyinroe

scapular *(n.)* ပခုံးရုံဝတ်ရုံ pahkone ronewaatrone

scar *(n.)* အမာရွတ် aamarrwat

scarab *(n.)* ပိုးထောင့်မာ poe htaw intmar

scarce *(adj.)* ရှားပါးသော sharrparrsaw

scarcely *(adv.)* ရှားရှားပါးပါး sharrsharrparrpar

scarcity *(n.)* ရှားပါးမှု sharrparrmhu

scare *(v.)* လန့်သွားသည် lantswarrsai

scarf *(n.)* လည်စည်း lai-see

scary *(adj.)* အလန့်တကြား a lant ta-kyarr

scatter *(v.)* ပြန့်ကျဲသည် pyant kyaell-sai

scatterbrain *(n.)* နမော်နမဲ့ကောင် na-mawnamaekaung

scatterbrained *(adj.)* နမော်နမဲ့နိုင်သော namawnamaeninesaw

scattered *(adj.)* ကျိုးတိုးကျဲတဲ kyoetoekyaelltell

scattergun *(n.)* သေနတ် saynaat

scatteringly *(adv.)* ပြန့်ကျဲလျက် pya ant kyaelllyet

scattery *(adj.)* ပြန်ကျဲလိုသော pyan kyaelllosaw

scatty *(adj.)* ရူးကြောင်ကြောင်ဖြစ်သော ruukyaungkyaunghpyitsaw

scavenge *(v.)* အသေကောင်ရှာစားသည် a say kaung shar sarrsai

scavenger *(n.)* အပုပ်ကောင်စား သားငှက် a pote kaungsarr sarrnghaat

scenario *(n.)* အနာဂတ်ဖြစ်နိုင်ခြေ၊ ဇာတ်ညွှန်း aanargaat hpyitninechay , zatnyun

scenarist *(n.)* ရုပ်ရှင်ဇာတ်ညွှန်းဆရာ roteshinjaratnywhaannsarar

scene *(v.)* ပြကွက်တစ်ကွက်အဖြစ် ပြသည် pyakwat tait kwataahpyit pyasai

scenery *(n.)* သဘာဝရှုခင်း sabharwashuhkinn

scenic *(adj.)* သဘာဝပသာဒ sabharwapata-da

scent *(n.)* ရနံ့ ra-nant

sceptic *(n.)* အယုံအကြည်ကင်းမဲ့သူ aayoneaakyi kinnmaesuu

sceptical *(adj.)* ယုံကြည်မှုကင်းမဲ့သော yonekyimhu kinnmaesaw

scepticism *(n.)* ယုံကြည်မှုကင်းမဲ့ခြင်း yonekyimhukinnmaechinn

sceptre *(n.)* တောင်ဝှေး taungwhaayy

schedule *(v.)* စီစဉ်ထားသည် sesinhtarrsai

schematic *(adj.)* ပုံ၊ ကားချပ်ဖြင့် သရုပ်ဖော်ထားသော pone , karr chauthpyint sarotehpawhtarrsaw

schematically *(adv.)* ဖွဲ့စည်းပုံဇယားကျကျ hpwalhcaeepone jayarrkyakya

schematist *(n.)* စီမံကိန်းအကြမ်း ရေးဆွဲပေးအပ်သော သူ hcemankeinaakyam rayyswalpayyaautsaw suu

scheme *(n.)* စီမံချက်၊ အကြံအစည် semanchet , aakyaanaasai

schemer *(n.)* အကြံသမား aakyaansamarr

schism *(n.)* ဂိုဏ်းကွဲမှု gonkwalmhu

schizophrenia *(n.)* စိတ်ကစဉ့်ကလျားရောဂါ sate ka sink lyarrrawgar

schizophreniac *(n.)* စကီဇိုဖရီးနီးယားစ်ရောဂါနှင့် ဆိုင်သော hc ke jo hparee nee yarr hc rawgarnhang sinesaw

scholar *(n.)* ပညာသင်ဆုရကျောင်းသား၊ ပညာရှင် panyarsinsu r kyaunggsarr , panyarshin

scholarly *(adj.)* ပညာရှင်ဆန်သော panyarshinsaansaw

scholarship *(n.)* ပညာသင်ဆု panyarsinsu

scholastic *(adj.)* ကျောင်းပညာရေး kyaunggpanyarrayy

school *(n.)* ကျောင်း၊ တက္ကသိုလ်၊ အုပ်စု kyaungg , takkasol , aotesu

schoolfellow *(n.)* **ကျောင်းနေဖက်သူငယ်ချင်း** kyaungg nay hpaatsuungaalchinn
schoolhouse *(n.)* **ကျောင်းကလေး** kyaunggkalayy
schoolmaster *(n.)* **ကျောင်းဆရာ** kyaunggsarar
schoolmate *(n.)* **ကျောင်းနေဖက်သူငယ်ချင်း** kyaung nay hpaatsuungaalchinn
schoolteacher *(n.)* **ကျောင်းဆရာ** kyaunggsarar
schoolyard *(n.)* **ကျောင်းဝန်း** kyaunggwaann
schooner *(n.)* **စက်လှေ၊ ဖန်ခွက်ရှည်** saathlaay , hpaanhkwatshi
sciatic *(adj.)* **တင်ပါးဆုံအာရုံကြောနှင့်ဆိုင်သော** tin parr sone aarronekyawwnint sinesaw
sciatica *(n.)* **တင်ပါးဆုံအာရုံကြောနာ** tin parr sone aarronekyawwnar
science *(n.)* **သိပ္ပံပညာ** sippanpanyar
scientific *(adj.)* **သိပ္ပံနည်းကျသော** sippannaeekyasaw
scientist *(n.)* **သိပ္ပံပညာရှင်** sippanpanyarshin
scintillate *(v.)* **တလက်လက်တောက်ပသည်** t laat laat toutpasai
scintillation *(n.)* **လင်းလက်ပြိုးပြက်သော** linnlaat pyoe pyaatsaw
scissors *(n.)* **ကတ်ကြေး** kaatkyay
scoff *(n.)* **ရယ်မှောလှောင်ပြောင်မှု** raal mhaaw lhaawinpyaungmhu
scold *(v.)* **ဆူပူသည်** suupuusai
scooter *(n.)* **စကူတာဆိုင်ကယ်** sa kuu tarsinekaal
scope *(n.)* **အခွင့်အလမ်း၊ နယ်ပယ်** a-hkwint a lam , naalpaal
scorch *(n.)* **မျက်နှာပြင်အပူ** myetnharpyinaapuu
score *(v.)* **ဂိုးသွင်းသည်၊ အမှတ်မှတ်သည်** goeswin sai , aamhaat mhaatsai
scoreboard *(n.)* **အမှတ်သင်ပုန်း** aamhaat sinpone
scorebook *(n.)* **အမှတ်စာအုပ်** aamhaatsaraote
scorebox *(n.)* **အမှတ်ပေးသူ ထိုင်ရာ နေရာ** aamhaatpayysuu htinerar nayrar
scorecard *(n.)* **စခိုးကတ်** hc hkoekaat
scorekeeper *(n.)* **အမှတ်မှတ်သူ** aamhaat mhaatsuu
scorekeeping *(n.)* **အမှတ်မှတ်ခြင်း** aamhaat mhaathkyinn
scorepad *(n.)* **အမှတ်မှတ် စာရွက်** aamhaatmhaat hcarrwat
scorer *(n.)* **အမှတ်မှတ်သူ** aamhaat mhaatsuu
scorn *(n.)* **အထင်သေးခြင်း** a htin sayychinn
scorpion *(n.)* **ကင်းမြီးကောက်** kinn-myee-kout
Scot *(n.)* **စကော့တလန်သား** sakottalaansarr
scotch *(adj.)* **စကော့တလန်** sakottalaan
scot-free *(adj.)* **လွတ်လွတ်ကျွတ်ကျွတ်၊ မထိမရှ** lwatlwat kyawatkyawat , m hti mash
scoundrel *(n.)* **လူလိမ်လူညစ်** luulin luunyait
scourge *(n.)* **ကျာပွတ်** kyaarpwat
scout *(n.)* **ကင်းထောက်** kinnhtout
scowl *(v.)* **သုန်သုန်မှုန်မှုန် ကြည့်သည်** sone sone hmonehmone kyanysai
scragged *(adj.)* **စောင်းသော၊ ကြမ်းတမ်းသော** hcaungg saw , kyamtamsaw
scraggy *(adj.)* **ပိန်တာရိုး** pein tarroe

scramble *(v.)* လက်နှင့်ပါ ကုတ်ကတ်တက်သည် laat nintpar kote kaat taatsai
scrambled *(adj.)* ရောနှောသော rawnhaawsaw
scrap *(v.)* တစ်ပိုင်းတစ်စစီ ဖြုတ်ရောင်းသည် ta-pine-ta-sase hpyuat raunggsai
scrapbook *(n.)* ဖြတ်ညှပ်ကပ်ရန် ဗလာစာအုပ် *hpyat-nyhaut-kat-raan balar-saraote*
scrape *(n.)* ကုတ်ခြစ်သံ kote chitsan
scraper *(n.)* ခြစ်ရန် ကိရိယာ chitraan ka-ri-yar
scratch *(n.)* ကုတ်ရာ၊ ပွန်းရာ kote rar , pwannrar
scratchboard *(n.)* စာထွင်းရွံ့ပြား hcar htwin rwanpyarr
scratched *(adj.)* စာထွင်းသော hcar htwinsaw
scratchpad *(n.)* မှတ်စုစာအုပ် mhaatsusaraote
scratchy *(adj.)* ယားကျိကျိရှိသော yarr kyai kyaishisaw
scrawl *(n.)* သော့ရေးသော လက်ရေး sotrayysaw laatrayy
scrawl *(v.)* သော့ရေးသည် sotrayysai
scream *(n.)* စူးစူးဝါးဝါး အော်သံ suu suu warrwarr aawsan
scream *(v.)* အော်ဟစ်သည် aawhaitsai
screen *(v.)* ကာကွယ်သည် karkwalsai
screen *(n.)* အကာအကွယ်၊ လိုက်ကာ aakaraakwal , litekar
screen name *(n.)* စခရင်အမည် hcahkarainaamai
screenable *(adj.)* ကာကွယ်နိုင်သော karkwalninesaw
screencast *(n.)* စခရင်ဖမ်းယူခြင်း hcahkarain hpamyuuhkyinn
screendoor *(n.)* စခရင်ပေါက် hcahkarainpout
screenprint *(n.)* စခရင်ဖမ်းခြင်း hcahkarain hpamhkyinn
screensaver *(n.)* စခရင်ဆေဗာ hcahkarain saybar
screenshot *(n.)* စခရင်ဖမ်းခြင်း hcahkarain hpamhkyinn
screenwork *(n.)* ရုပ်ရှင်အတွက် အလုပ်ပြီးမြောက်ခြင်း roteshinaatwat a lotepyee myawwathkyinn
screw *(v.)* ဝက်အူစုပ်သည် waat auu sotesai
screw *(n.)* ဝက်အူ၊ လိင်ဆက်ဆံခြင်း၊ လိင်ဆက်ဆံဖော် waat auu , linsaatsanchinn , linsaatsanhpaw
scribble *(n.)* သော့ရေးသော လက်ရေး sotrayysaw laatrayy
scribble *(v.)* သော့ရေးသည် sotrayysai
script *(n.)* ဇာတ်ညွှန်း zat-nyun
scripture *(n.)* ခရစ်ယာန်သမ္မာကျမ်း၊ ဝေဒကျမ်း၊ ပိဋကကျမ်း hkaraityaran sammarkyam, wayd kyam , pitakakyam
scroll *(n.)* အခွေ၊ အလိပ်ပုံ အပြောက်အမွမ်း aahkway , a liutpone a pyaut a mwm
scrooge *(n.)* ကပ်စေးနှဲကော်တရာ kaut sayy nhaell kaw tarar
scrotum *(n.)* ကပ်ပယ်အိတ် kaut paal-ate
scrub *(adj.)* ညှစ်ပေသော nyait paysaw
scrubby *(adj.)* ကြုံလှီသော kyun hlisaw
scruff *(v.)* ဇက်ပိုးအုပ်သည် zaat poe aotesai
scruffiness *(n.)* ကပျစ်ကညစ် k pyit kanyait
scrumble *(n.)* အလွှတ်ပုံစံ ခရိုရှေးအပိုင်းအစ a lwatponehcan hk ro shayyaapineaahc

scrump *(v.)* အသီးခိုးသည် a see hkoesai

scrumptious *(adj.)* ချိုမြိန်ဖွယ် cho myaeinhpwal

scruple *(n.)* သိက္ခာစောင့်စည်းမှု sikhkar sawng saeemhu

scrupleless *(adj.)* သိက္ခာစောင့်စည်းမှု မရှိသော sikhkar hcaung hcaeemhu mashisaw

scrupulous *(adj.)* စေ့စပ်သေချာသော saesatsay-chaarsaw

scrupulously *(adv.)* လုံးဝဥဿုံ lonewa oak-tone

scrutinize *(v.)* စေ့စေ့စပ်စပ်ကြည့်ရှုစစ်ဆေးသည် saesaesatsat kyany shu sitsayysai

scrutiny *(n.)* စိစစ်ခြင်း sisitchinn

scuffle *(v.)* လုံးထွေးသတ်ပုတ်သည် lone htway saatpotesai

scuffle *(n.)* လုံးထွေးသတ်ပုတ်ခြင်း lone htway saatpotechinn

sculpt *(v.)* ထုဆစ်သည် htu sitsai

sculptor *(n.)* ပန်းပုဆရာ paannpusarar

sculptural *(adj.)* ပန်းပု၊ ပန်းတမော့ဆိုင်ရာ paannpu , paann t motsinerar

sculpture *(n.)* ကျောက်တုံးထုဆစ်ပညာ kyauttone htu sitpanyar

sculpturist *(n.)* ပန်းပုဆရာ paannpusarar

scum *(v.)* ရေမျက်နှာပြင် အညစ်အကြေး raymyetnharpyin aanyaitaakyay

scumbag *(n.)* ကွန်ဒုံး kwandone

scurry *(v.)* သုတ်သုတ်ပျာပျာပြေးသည် sote sote pyaar pyaar pyaysai

scuttle *(n.)* ထည့်ခွက် htaeethkwat

scythe *(v.)* ရိတ်သည် ratesai

scythe *(n.)* မြက်ယမ်းစား myaat yamdharr

sea *(n.)* ပင်လယ် pinlaal

sea bass *(n.)* ပင်လယ်ကကတစ်ငါး painlaal k k taitngarr

sea boat *(n.)* ပင်လယ်လှေ painlaallhaay

sea dog *(n.)* ပင်လယ်ဓားပြ painlaaldharrpya

seabeach *(n.)* ပင်လယ်ကမ်းခြေ pinlaalkamchay

seabird *(n.)* ပင်လယ်ပျော်ငှက် pinlaalpyawnghaat

seaborne *(adj.)* သင်္ဘောများဖြင့် သယ်ဆောင်သော sinbhaw-myarrhpyint saalsaungsaw

seacliff *(n.)* ပင်လယ်ကမ်းဘေးကျောက်ဆောင် painlaal kam bhayykyawwatsaung

seafarer *(n.)* သင်္ဘောသား sinbhawsarr

seafloor *(n.)* ပင်လယ်ကြမ်းပြင် painlaalkyampyin

seafoam *(n.)* ပင်လယ်ရေမြှုပ် painlaalraymyuut

seafood *(n.)* ပင်လယ်စာ pinlaalsar

seagull *(n.)* စင်ရော် sin raw

seahorse *(n.)* ရေနဂါး raynagarr

seajack *(n.)* ရေယဉ်ကို တရားမဝင် ထိန်းချုပ်ခြင်း ray yainko tararrmawain hteinhkyaotehkyinn

seajacker *(n.)* ရေယဉ်ကို တရားမဝင် ထိန်းချုပ်သူ ray yainko tararrmawain hteinhkyaotesuu

seajacking *(n.)* ရေယဉ်ကို တရားမဝင် ထိန်းချုပ်ခြင်း ray yainko tararrmawain hteinhkyaotehkyinn

seak *(n.)* ဆပ်ပြာ sautpyaar

seakeeping *(n.)* ပင်လယ်တွင်း သင်္ဘောကောင်းစွာ မောင်းနှင်ခြင်း painlaaltwin sainbhawkaungghcwar maunggnhainhkyinn

seal *(v.)* ချိပ်ပိတ်သည် chainpatesai

seal *(n.)* ချိပ်တံဆိပ်၊ ပင်လယ်ဖျံ chain tanseik, pinlaal hpyaan

sealab *(n.)* ပင်လယ်ရေအောက်ဓာတ်ခွဲခန်း painlaalrayaoutdharathkwalhkaann

sealability *(n.)* ချိပ်ပိတ်နိုင်စွမ်း hkyaiutpateninehcwm

sealant *(n.)* ထေးဆေး htayysayy

sealed *(adj.)* ချိပ်ပိတ်သော hkyaiutpatesaw

sealion *(n.)* ရေခြင်္သေ့ ray hkyinsae

sealskin *(n.)* ပင်လယ်ဖျံရေမှ လုပ်သော အထည် painlaal hpyaan raymha lotesaw aahtai

seam *(v.)* ချုပ်ရိုး choteroe

seam *(n.)* ချုပ်ရိုး hkyaoteroe

seamless *(adj.)* ချုပ်ရာမရှိသော chote rarmashisaw

seamy *(adj.)* ဆိုးယုတ်သော soe yotesaw

sear *(v.)* လောင်မြိုက်သည်၊ မီးဟပ်သည် laung myaite sai, mee hatsai

search *(v.)* ရှာဖွေသည် sharhpwaysai

search *(n.)* ရှာဖွေခြင်း sharhpwaychinn

search warrant *(n.)* ရှာဖွေဝရမ်း sharhpwaywaram

searching *(adj.)* စူးစမ်းသော suusamsaw

searchlight *(n.)* ဆလိုက်မီး sa litemee

seared *(adj.)* မီးလောင်သော meelaungsaw

seashore *(n.)* ပင်လယ်ကမ်းခြေ pinlaalkamchay

season *(v.)* ခတ်သည်၊ အသားသေစေသည် hkaat sai , a sarr saysaysai

season *(n.)* ဥတု u-tu

seasonable *(adj.)* ရာသီပေါ် rarsepaw

seasonal *(adj.)* ရာသီအလိုက် rarseaalite

seat *(v.)* ထိုင်သည် htinesai

seat *(n.)* ထိုင်ခုံ htinehkone

seaweed *(n.)* ကျောက်ပွင့် kyaut pwint

secede *(v.)* ခွဲထွက်သည် hkwaltwatsai

secession *(n.)* ခွဲထွက်ခြင်း hkwaltwatchinn

secessionist *(n.)* ခွဲထွက်ရေးသမား hkwaltwatrayysamarr

seclude *(v.)* ကင်းကင်းနေသည် kinn kinnnaysai

secluded *(adj.)* ချောင်ကျသော chaungkyasaw

seclusion *(n.)* လူသူဝေးရာ luu suuwayyrar

second *(v.)* ထောက်ခံသည် htouthkansai

secondary *(adj.)* သာမည sarmanya

seconder *(n.)* ထပ်ဆင့်ထောက်ခံသူ htaut sainthtouthkansuu

second-hand *(adj.)* တစ်ပတ်ရစ် taitpaatrit

secondly *(adv.)* ပြီးတော့ pyeetot

secrecy *(n.)* လျှို့ဝှက်ခြင်း shoetwhaatchinn

secret *(n.)* လျှို့ဝှက်ချက် shoetwhaatchet

secret *(adj.)* လျှို့ဝှက်သော shhoetwhaatsaw

secretariat *(n.)* အတွင်းဝန်များရုံး aatwinwaan myarrrone

secretary *(n.)* အတွင်းရေးမှူး aatwinrayymhauu

secrete *(v.)* ထုတ်ပေးသည် htotepayysai

secretion *(n.)* အရည်ထုတ်ပေးခြင်း aarai htotepayychinn

secretive *(adj.)* သိုဝှက်သော so whaatsaw

sect *(n.)* ဂိုဏ်းကွဲ gaikwal

sectarian *(adj.)* ဂိုဏ်းဂဏဆိုင်ရာ gai nasinerar

section *(n.)* အပိုင်း aapine

sector *(n.)* ကဏ္ဍ kan-da

secularism *(n.)* လောကီသီးသန့်ဝါဒ law-ke-see saantwarda

secure *(v.)* ရယူနိုင်ခဲ့သည် ra-yuuninehkaesai

security *(n.)* လုံခြုံရေး lonechuanrayy

sedan *(n.)* ထမ်းစင် htamsin

sedate *(v.)* စိတ်ငြိမ်ဆေးတိုက်သည် sate ngyaain sayy titesai

sedate *(adj.)* တည်ငြိမ်သော tingyeinsaw

sedative *(n.)* စိတ်ငြိမ်ဆေး sate ngyeinsayy

sedative *(adj.)* စိတ်ငြိမ်သော sate ngyeinsaw

sedentary *(adj.)* ထိုင်လုပ်ရသော အလုပ် htine loterasaw aalote

sediment *(n.)* အနည်အနှစ် a nai aa-nhit

sedition *(n.)* နိုင်ငံတော်အား အကြည်ညိုပျက်အောင် ပြုခြင်း ninengantawaarr aakyinyopyetaaung pyuchinn

seditious *(adj.)* နိုင်ငံတော်အား အကြည်ညိုပျက်အောင် ပြုသော ninengantawaarr aakyinyopyetaaung pyusaw

seduce *(v.)* သွေးဆောင်ဖြားယောင်းသည် swaysaung hpyarryaunggsai

seduction *(n.)* ဖြားယောင်းသွေးဆောင်မှု hpyarryaungg swaysaungmhu

seductive *(adj.)* ညှို့ယူဖမ်းစားသော nyhahoet yuu hpam sarrsaw

see *(v.)* မြင်သည် myinsai

seed *(n.)* အစေ့ aasae

seek *(v.)* ရှာဖွေသည် sharhpwaysai

seem *(v.)* ထင်ရသည် htinrasai

seemly *(adj.)* ယဉ်ကျေးဖွယ်ရာရှိသော yain kyaayy hpwalrarshisaw

seep *(v.)* ယိုသည်၊ စိမ့်သည် yo sai , seint-sai

seer *(n.)* ရှေ့ဖြစ်ဟောသူ shaehpyit haw suu

seethe *(v.)* အမြုပ်တစီစီထသည် a myoke ta se-se htasai

segment *(v.)* စိတ်ပိုင်းသည် satepinesai

segment *(n.)* အစိတ်၊ အပိုင်း a sate , aapine

segregate *(v.)* ခွဲခြားသည် hkwalcharrsai

segregation *(n.)* ခွဲခြားမှု hkwalcharrmhu

seismic *(adj.)* မြေငလျင် myayngalyin

seismicity *(n.)* ဒေသတစ်ခုတွင် ငလျင်ဖြစ်နိုင်သော အတိုင်းအတာ ဒီဂရီ daysataithkutwin ngalyinhpyitninesaw aatineaatar degare

seismogram *(n.)* ငလျင်လှုပ်ရှားမှုမှတ်တမ်းဂရပ် ngalyin lhuutsharrmhumhaattam garaut

seismograph *(n.)* မြေငလျင်မှတ်စက် myayngalyin mhaatsaat

seismography *(n.)* ငလျင်လှုပ်ရှားမှု၊ မှတ်တမ်း ngalyin lhuutsharrmhu , mhaattam

seismologist *(n.)* မြေငလျင်ပညာရှင် myayngalyinpanyarshin

seismology *(n.)* မြေငလျင်ပညာ myayngalyinpanyar

seismoscope *(n.)* ငလျင်ဖြစ်ပွားမှုကို ပြသော ကိရိယာ ngalyin hpyitpwarrmhuko pyasaw kiriyar

seize *(v.)* ဖမ်းကိုင်သည် hpam kinesai

seizure *(n.)* တက်ခြင်း၊ ဖမ်းဆီးခြင်း taatchinn, hpamseechinn

seldom *(adv.)* ကြုံထောင့်ကြုံခဲ kyone htaunt kyone-hkell

select *(adj.)* ရွေးထားသော rwayhtarrsaw

select *(v.)* ရွေးချယ်သည် rwaychaalsai

selection *(n.)* ရွေးချယ်ခြင်း၊ လက်ရွေးစင် rwaychaalchinn , laatrwaysin
selective *(adj.)* သီးသန့်၊ စိစိစစ်စစ်ရှိသော see saant , si-si-sit sitshisaw
self *(n.)* ကိုယ် ko
self-abuse *(n.)* မိမိကိုယ်ကို ထိခိုက်စေခြင်း mimikoko htihkite hcayhkyinn
self-appointed *(adj.)* မိမိဘာသာ ခန့်အပ်သော mi-mi-bhar-sar hkaantatsaw
self-awareness *(n.)* ကိုယ့်ကိုယ်ကိုယ် သိခြင်း ko koko si-chinn
self-centered *(adj.)* အတ္တဗဟိုပြုသော at ta-bahopyusaw
self-confident *(adj.)* မိမိကိုယ်ကိုယ် ယုံကြည်သော mimikoko yonekyisaw
self-conscious *(adj.)* ကိုယ့်အကြောင်းကိုယ်သိသော ko aakyaungg ko si-saw
self-control *(n.)* စိတ်ထိန်းနိုင်ခြင်း sate hteinninechinn
self-destruct *(v.)* မိမိကိုယ်ကို ဖျက်စီးခြင်း mimikoko hpyethceehkyinn
self-doubt *(n.)* မိမိကိုယ်ကို သံသယရှိခြင်း mimikoko sansayashihkyinn
self-employed *(adj.)* ကိုယ်ပိုင်လုပ်ငန်းလုပ်သော ko-pine lotengaannlotesaw
self-esteem *(n.)* မိမိကိုယ်ကို တန်ဖိုးထားခြင်း mimikoko taanhpoehtarrchinn
selfie *(n.)* ဆက်ဖီဆွဲခြင်း saat hpe swalhkyinn
elf-imposed *(adj.)* မိမိကိုယ်ကိုယ် အကျပ်ကိုင်သော mimikoko a kyat kinesaw
selfish *(adj.)* တစ်ကိုယ်ကောင်းဆန်သော ta-ko kaunggsaansaw
selfless *(adj.)* အတ္တကင်းသော a-ta-kinnsaw
self-proclaimed *(adj.)* မိမိတစ်ဦးတည်း ကြေညာချက်ထုတ်သော mimi tait utaee kyaynyarhkyet htotesaw
self-service *(adj.)* ကိုယ်တိုင်ယူစနစ် ko-tine yuusanit
sell *(v.)* ရောင်းချသည် raunggchasai
seller *(n.)* ရောင်းသူ raunggsuu
sell-out *(n.)* ရောင်းကုန်ခြင်း raunggkonechinn
semblance *(n.)* အသွင်၊ ပုံပန်း aaswin , ponepaann
semen *(n.)* သုက် sote
semester *(n.)* နှစ်ဝက်စာသင်ကာလ nit waat sarsinkarla
semi-amusing *(adj.)* တစ်စိတ်တစ်ပိုင်း ရွှင်မြူးဖွယ် taithcatetaitpine shwin myauuhpwal
semi-finalist *(n.)* အကြိုဗိုလ်လုပွဲတက်သူ aakyao bollupwal taatsuu
semi-formal *(adj.)* တစ်စိတ်တစ်ပိုင်း တရားဝင်ဖြစ်သော taithcatetaitpine tararrwainhpyitsaw
seminal *(adj.)* သုက်နှင့်ဆိုင်သော sote nintsinesaw
seminar *(n.)* ဆွေးနွေးပွဲ swaynwaypwal
senate *(n.)* ဆီးနိတ် seenate
senator *(n.)* လွှတ်တော်အမတ် hluttaw-aa-mat
senatorial *(adj.)* လွှတ်တော်အမတ်နှင့် ပတ်သက်၍ lwhaattawaamaatnhang paatsaat
send *(v.)* ပို့သည် phoet-sai
senile *(adj.)* သူငယ်ပြန်နေသော suu-ngaal-pyannaysaw
senility *(n.)* သူငယ်ပြန်ခြင်း suungaalpyanchinn

senior *(n.)* ကြီးသူ၊ ကျောင်းသားကြီး kyee suu , kyaunggsarrkyee
senior *(adj.)* ရာထူးမြင့်သော ra htuu myintsaw
seniority *(n.)* ဝါရင့်ခြင်း၊ ရာထူး၊ အသက်အားဖြင့် မြင့်သူ warrint chinn , rarhtuu , aasaat aarrhpyint myintsuu
sensation *(n.)* အတွေ့အထိ a twaeaahti
sensational *(adj.)* အုတ်အော်သောင်းတင်း aote aaw saunggtinn
sense *(v.)* ခံစားရသည် hkan-sarr-ra-sai
sense *(n.)* အာရုံ၊ ခံစားတတ်မှု aar-rone , hkan-sarr taat-mhu
senseless *(adj.)* မိုက်မဲသော mite mell-saw
sensibility *(n.)* ရသခံစားနိုင်စွမ်း ra sa hkansarrnineswam
sensible *(adj.)* စဉ်းစားချင့်ချိန်တတ်သော sin sarr chint chane-taatsaw
sensitive *(adj.)* ဆတ်ဆတ်ထိ မခံသော saat saathti ma hkansaw
sensitivity *(n.)* အထိမခံနိုင်ခြင်း aahti ma hkanninechinn
sensual *(adj.)* ကာမဂုဏ်အာရုံ karmagonaarrone
sensualist *(n.)* ကာမဂုဏ်လိုက်စားသူ karmagon litesarrsuu
sensuality *(n.)* ကာမဂုဏ် karmagon
sensuous *(adj.)* စွဲမက်ဖွယ်ကောင်းသော swal maat hpwalkaunggsaw
sentence *(v.)* ပြစ်ဒဏ်ချမှတ်သည် pyitdan chamhaatsai
sentence *(n.)* ဝါကျ၊ စီရင်ချက် warkya , serinchet
sentience *(n.)* စိတ်ထိခိုက်လွယ်ခြင်း hcate htihkite lwalhkyinn
sentient *(adj.)* အသိရှိသော aa-si-shi-saw
sentiment *(n.)* စိတ်ကူးယဉ်ခြင်း satekuu yinchinn
sentimental *(adj.)* စိတ်ကူးယဉ်သော satekuu yainsaw
sentinel *(n.)* ကင်းစောင့် kinnsawnt
sentry *(n.)* ကင်းသမား kinnsamarr
separable *(adj.)* ခွဲခြားနိုင်သော hkwalcharrninesaw
separate *(v.)* ကွဲသည် kwalsai
separation *(n.)* ကွဲခြင်း kwalchinn
sepsis *(n.)* သွေးဆိပ်သင့်ခြင်း sway siut sainthkyinn
September *(n.)* စက်တင်ဘာလ saattinbharla
septic *(adj.)* အနာရင်းသော aanar rinnsaw
sepulchre *(n.)* သင်္ချိုင်းဂူ sin chai-guu
sepulture *(n.)* သင်္ချိုင်းဂူ sain hkyaineguu
sequel *(n.)* အကျိုးဆက် aa-kyoesaat
sequence *(n.)* အစီအစဉ်၊ ဇာတ်ကွက် aaseaasin, zatkwat
sequester *(v.)* သိမ်းယူထားသည် saimyuuhtarrsai
serendipitous *(adj.)* ကံကောင်းသော kankaunggsaw
serendipity *(n.)* မုတ်ဆိတ်ပျားစွဲတတ်သော ပါရမီ motesate pyarr swaltaatsaw parrame
serene *(adj.)* ကြည်လင်အေးငြိမ်းသော kyilin aayy-ngyeim-saw
serenity *(n.)* ငြိမ်ချမ်းခြင်း ngyein cham-chinn
serf *(n.)* မြေကျွန် myaykywan
serge *(n.)* သက္ကလတ်အကြမ်းစား sak ka laat aakyamsarr
sergeant *(n.)* တပ်ကြပ်ကြီး tautkyatkyee

serial *(n.)* အခန်းဆက်ဝတ္ထု aahkansaatwathtu
serial *(adj.)* အစဉ်လိုက်ဖြစ်သော a sin litehpyitsaw
series *(n.)* စာစဉ် sarsin
serious *(adj.)* ပြင်းထန်သော pyinnhtaansaw
sermon *(n.)* ဟောကြားသော တရား hawkyarrsaw tararr
sermonize *(v.)* လက်ချာရိုက်သည် laatchaar ritesai
serpent *(n.)* မြွေကြီး myawaykyee
serpentine *(n.)* မြွေလိမ်မြွေကောက်၊ ဝက်ပါ myway lin myaway kout , win kapar
servant *(n.)* အစေခံ a sayhkan
serve *(n.)* စာပေးခြင်း sarpayychinn
serve *(v.)* အလုပ်အကျွေးပြုသည်၊ အမှုထမ်းသည် aalote a kyaway pyusai , aamhuhtamsai
service *(v.)* ဝန်ဆောင်မှုပေးသည် waansaungmhupayysai
service *(n.)* ဝန်ဆောင်မှု waansaungmhu
serviceable *(adj.)* အသုံးပြုနိုင်သော aasonepyuninesaw
servile *(adj.)* ခယလွန်းသော hka ya lwannsaw
servility *(n.)* ခယဝယလုပ်ခြင်း hka ya wa yalotechinn
servitude *(n.)* ခိုင်းဖတ်ဘဝ hkine hpaatbhawa
sesame *(n.)* နှမ်း nham
sesamin *(n.)* နှမ်းမှ အဆီထုတ်ခြင်း nhammha a se htotehkyinn
session *(n.)* အပိုင်း၊ ဆက်ရှင် aapine , saatshin
sessional *(n.)* ကောလိပ်မှာ ငှားရမ်းထားသော သင်တန်းဆရာ kawliutmhar ngharramhtarrsaw saintaannsarar
sessionless *(adj.)* ဆက်ရှင်မရှိဘဲ saat shinmashibhell
set *(n.)* သတ်မှတ်ချက် saatmhaatchet
set *(v.)* သတ်မှတ်သည် saatmhaatsai
setback *(n.)* အတားအဆီး aatarraasee
setlist *(n.)* သီချင်းစာရင်း sehkyinnhcarrainn
settee *(n.)* ဆိုဖာ sohpar
settle *(v.)* စာရှင်းရှင်းသည်၊ အခြေချသည် sar hlyinnshinn sai, aachaychasai
settlement *(n.)* ပြေငြိမ်းခြင်း၊ ကြွေးဆပ်ခြင်း၊ အခြေချခြင်း pyay ngyaaim chinn , kyaway sat chinn , aachaychachinn
settler *(n.)* နယ်သစ်တွင် အခြေချသူ naal sittwin aachaychasuu
seven *(adj.)* ခုနှစ် hkunit
seven *(n.)* ခုနစ် hkunit
seventeen *(n.)* တစ်ဆယ့်ခုနှစ် ta-sae-hkun-nit
seventeenth *(adj.)* တစ်ဆယ့်ခုနှစ်ခုမြောက် ta-sae-hkun-nit-hku-myaut
seventh *(adj.)* ခုနှစ်ခုမြောက် hkun-nit-khu-myaut
seventieth *(adj.)* ခုနှစ်ဆယ်ခုမြောက် hku nit-saal-ku-myaut
seventy *(n.)* ခုနှစ်ဆယ် hkun-nit-saal
sever *(v.)* ပြတ်သည် pyatsai
several *(adj.)* များပြားသော myarrpyarrsaw
severance *(n.)* ဖြတ်ခြင်း၊ ပြတ်ခြင်း hpyat chinn , pyatchinn
severe *(adj.)* ပြင်းထန်သော pyinnhtaansaw
severity *(n.)* ပြင်းထန်မှု pyinnhtaanmhu

sew *(v.)* ချုပ်သည် chate-sai

sewage *(n.)* အညစ်အကြေး aanyaitaakyay

sewer *(n.)* ရေဆိုးပိုက် ray soepite

sewerage *(n.)* မိလ္လာသိမ်းစနစ် main lar saim-sa-nit

sex *(n.)* လိင်၊ လိင်ဆက်ဆံခြင်း lain, lainsaatsanchinn

sexily *(adv.)* လိင်စိတ်ဖြင့် linsatehpyint

sexual *(adj.)* လိင်မှုဆိုင်ရာ linmhu-sine-rar

sexuality *(n.)* လိင် lin

sexy *(adj.)* ညှို့ဓာတ်အားကောင်းသော nyhahoet dharataarrkaunggsaw

shabby *(adj.)* ဟောင်းနွမ်းစုတ်ပြတ်သော haunggnwm sotepyatsaw

shack *(n.)* တဲကုပ် tell kote

shackle *(v.)* လက်ထိတ်ခတ်သည် laat htate hkaatsai

shackle *(n.)* လက်ထိတ် laat htate

shade *(v.)* အလင်းကာသည် a-linn karsai

shade *(n.)* အရိပ်အာဝါသ a riutaarwarsa

shadow *(v.)* နောက်ယောင်ခံလိုက်သည် nout yaung hkanlitesai

shadow *(n.)* အရိပ် aa-rate

shadowy *(adj.)* အရိပ်ရသော a rate-ra-saw

shaft *(n.)* အရိုး၊ အတံ aaroe, aatan

shake *(n.)* လှုပ်ခြင်း hlotechinn

shake *(v.)* ခါသည်၊ လှုပ်သည် hkar sai , hlotesai

shaky *(adj.)* တုန်တုန်ယင်ယင် ဖြစ်နေသော tone tone yin yin hpyitnaysaw

shallow *(adj.)* တိမ်သော tain-saw

sham *(adj.)* ဟန်ဆောင်သော၊ အတု haan-saung saw, aatu

sham *(v.)* ဟန်ဆောင်သည် haansaungsai

shaman *(n.)* နတ်ဆရာ naatsarar

shamble *(v.)* တရွတ်ဆွဲသွားသည် ta rwat swalswarrsai

shambles *(n.)* ဝက်သိုက် waatsite

shambolic *(adj.)* ဖရိုဖရဲ hparohparell

shame *(v.)* ရှက်သည် shatsai

shame *(n.)* ရှက်စိတ် shatsate

shameful *(adj.)* ရှက်ဖွယ် shathpwal

shameless *(adj.)* အရှက်မဲ့သော aa-shat maesaw

shampoo *(v.)* ခေါင်းလျှော်သည် hkaungg shawsai

shampoo *(n.)* ခေါင်းလျှော်ရည် hkaungg shawrai

shanty *(adj.)* လိုင်စင်မရှိသော အရက်ဆိုင် linehcainmashisaw aaraatsine

shape *(v.)* ပုံဖော်သည် ponehpawsai

shape *(n.)* ပုံ၊ အနေအထား pone , aanayaahtarr

shape up *(v.)* တိုးတက်အောင် ကြိုးစားသည် toetaataaung kyaoesarrsai

shapeless *(adj.)* ပုံပျက်ပန်းပျက် pone pyet paannpyet

shapely *(adj.)* အချိုးကျသော aa-choekyasaw

shapeshift *(v.)* ပုံစံပြောင်းသည် ponehcanpyaunggsai

shard *(n)* အစအန aa-sa-aa-na

share *(n.)* ဝေစု၊ ရှယ်ယာ way su, shalyar

share *(v.)* ဝေသည်၊ မျှသည် way sai, mya-sai

share market *(n.)* ရှယ်ယာဈေးကွက် shal rarsyaayykwat

sharebeam *(n.)* ထယ်သွား htaalswarr

sharecrop *(n.)* အထွက်သီးနှံအပေါ်တွင် ငွေကြေးစီမံခွင့်ရရှိသည် a htwat

seenhaanaapawtwin ngwaykyay hceman hkwngrashisai
shareholder *(n.)* ရှယ်ရာရှင် shal rarshin
shareholding *(n.)* အစုရှယ်ယာပမာဏ aasushalyarpamarna
shark *(n.)* ငါးမန်း ngarrmaann
sharp *(adv.)* တိတိ titi
sharp *(adj.)* ထက်သော၊ ချွန်သော htaat saw, chwansaw
sharpen *(v.)* ချွန်သည်၊ ထက်မြက်စေသည် chawan sai, htaatmyaatsaysai
sharpener *(n.)* ချွန်စက်၊ သွေးစက် chwan saat , swaysaat
sharper *(n.)* လူလိမ် luulain
shatter *(v.)* အစိတ်စိတ်အမြှာမြှာ ကွဲသည် a sate sate aa-mwar mwar kwalsai
shave *(n.)* သင်တုန်းဓားဖြင့် ရိတ်ခြင်း sintone dharrhpyint ratechinn
shave *(v.)* သင်တုန်းဓားဖြင့် ရိတ်သည် sintone dharrhpyint ratesai
shaven *(adj.)* ရိတ်ထားသော ratehtarrsaw
shaving *(n.)* ရိတ်ခြင်း ratechinn
shavings *(n.)* ရွှေပေါ်စာ rway pawsar
shawarma *(n.)* သိုးသားညှပ်မုန့် soe sarr nyhaut mone
shawl *(n.)* ရှောစောင် shawsaung
she *(pron.)* သူမ suu-ma
sheading *(n.)* နယ်မြေ naalmyay
sheaf *(n.)* ကောက်နှံစည်း kout nhaan-see
shear *(v.)* ညှပ်သည် nyat-sai
shears *(n.)* စည်းရိုးညှပ်ကတ်ကြေး see roe nyat kaatkyay
shearwall *(n.)* နံရံတည်ဆောက်ရာတွင် ပါဝင်ပစ္စည်း nanrantaisoutrartwin parwainpahchcaee
sheat *(n.)* ငါးခူမျိုး ngarrhkuumyoe
sheath *(n.)* ဓားအိမ်၊ အစွပ်၊ ကွန်ဒုံး dharr aain, a swut, kwandone
sheathe *(v.)* ဓားအိမ်တွင်း ထိုးသွင်းသည် dharr-ain-twin htoe swin-sai
shed *(n.)* ရုံ rone
shed *(v.)* အရေလဲသည် a ray lellsai
sheep *(n.)* သိုး soe
sheepish *(adj.)* မလုံမလဲ ma lonemalell
sheer *(adj.)* ဖောက်မြင်နိုင်သော၊ မတ်စောက်သော hpout myinnine saw , maat soutsaw
sheet *(v.)* အကျီ၊ အခြားအရာတစ်ခုခုနှင့် ခြုံသည် aain kyae , aahkyarr a rar taithkuhkunhang hkyuansai
sheet *(n.)* အိပ်ရာခင်း ait-rarhkinn
shelf *(n.)* စင် sin
shell *(v.)* အခွံခွာသည် a hkwan hkwarsai
shell *(n.)* အခွံမာ a hkwanmar
shelter *(v.)* ကာသည်၊ ခိုလှုံခွင့်ပေးသည် kar sai , hkohluan hkwintpayysai
shelter *(n.)* အရိပ်အာဝါသ a riutaarwarsa
shelve *(v.)* ချောင်ထိုးလိုက်သည် chaunghtoelitesai
shepherd *(n.)* သိုးထိန်း soehtein
shide *(n.)* ဘုတ်ပြား bhotepyarr
shield *(v.)* ကာကွယ်သည် karkwalsai
shield *(n.)* ဒိုင်း၊ အကာအကွယ် dine , aakaraakwal
shift *(n.)* ပြောင်းလဲမှု၊ အဆိုင်း pyaungglellmhu , aa-sine
shift *(v.)* ရွှေ့ပြောင်းသည် rwaepyaunggsai
shifty *(adj.)* မတည်ကြည်သော ma tai kyisaw
shilly-shally *(v.)* ချီတုံချတုံဖြစ်သည် chae tone cha tonehpyitsai

shilly-shally *(n.)* ချီတုံချတုံဖြစ်ခြင်း chae tone cha tonehpyitchinn

shin *(n.)* ညို့သကျည်း nyoet sa kyee

shine *(n.)* တောက်ပမှု toutpamhu

shine *(v.)* အလင်းရောင်ပေးသည် aalinnraungpayysai

shiny *(adj.)* ပြောင်လက်သော pyaung laatsaw

ship *(v.)* ရေလမ်းဖြင့် ကုန်ပစ္စည်းပို့သည် raylamhpyint konepahchcaee phoetsai

ship *(n.)* သင်္ဘော sinbhaw

shipboard *(adj.)* သင်္ဘောပေါ်၌ ကျင့်သုံးသော sinbhawpaw kyintsonesaw

shipborne *(adj.)* သင်္ဘောပေါ်တင်သော sainbhaw pawtainsaw

shipbuilder *(n.)* သင်္ဘော တည်ဆောက်သူ sinbhaw tai-soutsuu

shiplap *(n.)* ထပ်ရန်အထစ်ပါသော သစ်သားပြား htaut raan a htait parsaw saitsarrpyarr

shipload *(n.)* သင်္ဘောတစ်စီးစာ အပြည့် sinbhaw taitseesar aapyi

shipmaster *(n.)* သင်္ဘောကပ္ပတိန် sainbhawkappatein

shipmate *(n.)* သင်္ဘောတွင် အတူ လုပ်ဖော်ကိုင်ဖက် sinbhawtwin aatuu lotehpawkinehpaat

shipment *(n.)* ကုန်ပစ္စည်း ပို့ဆောင်မှု konepyit-saee phoetsaungmhu

shipowner *(n.)* သင်္ဘောပိုင်ရှင် sinbhawpineshin

shipped *(adj.)* သင်္ဘောနှင့် ထောက်ပံ့ပေးသည် sainbhawnhang htoutpanpayysai

shipping *(n.)* ကုန်စည်ပို့ဆောင်ခြင်း konesai phoetsaungchinn

shipshape *(adj.)* နေထားတကျ nay htarr takya

shipwreck *(n.)* သင်္ဘောပျက်ခြင်း sinbhawpyetchinn

shipyard *(n.)* သင်္ဘောကျင်း sinbhawkyinn

shire *(n.)* မြို့နယ် myoet-naal

shirk *(v.)* ရှောင်သည်၊ အချောင်ခိုသည် shawin sai , a chaung hkosai

shirker *(n.)* ခေါင်းရှောင်သူ hkaungg shawinsuu

shirt *(n.)* အင်္ကျီ aainkyae

shive *(n.)* ပေါင်မုန့်ချပ် paung mu anthkyaut

shiver *(v.)* ခိုက်ခိုက်တုန်သည် hkite hkite tonesai

shoal *(n.)* ငါးအုပ် ngarrote

shock *(v.)* တုန်လှုပ်သည် tonehlotesai

shock *(n.)* စိတ်ချောက်ချားမှု sate chauk charrmhu

shoe *(v.)* သံခွာရိုက်သည် san hkwar ritesai

shoe *(n.)* ခြေနင်း chayninn

shoot *(n.)* အစို့၊ အတက်၊ အမဲပစ်ပွဲ၊ ဓာတ်ပုံရိုက်ခြင်း a shoet, a taat, a mell pait pwal , dharatponeritechinn

shoot *(v.)* ပစ်ခတ်သည်၊ ဓာတ်ပုံရိုက်သည် paithkaat sai , dharatponeritesai

shooting *(n.)* သေနတ်ပစ်ခတ်မှု၊ saynaat paithkaatmhu

shop *(v.)* ဈေးဝယ်သည် syaayywaalsai

shop *(n.)* ဆိုင်ခန်း sinehkaann

shopaholic *(n.)* ဈေးဝယ်စွဲလမ်းသူ hcyaayywaal hcwal lamsuu

shopaholism *(n.)* ဈေးဝယ်စွဲလမ်းခြင်း hcyaayywaalhcwallamhkyinn

shopbook *(n.)* အရောင်းစာရင်းစာအုပ် aaraungg hcarrainnhcaraote

shopfloor *(n.)* စက်ရုံ၊ အလုပ်ရုံ hcaatrone , aaloterone

shopfront *(n.)* ဆိုင်မျက်နှာစာ sinemyetnharsar

shopkeep *(n.)* ဈေးသည် hcyaayysai

shopkeeper *(n.)* ဆိုင်ရှင် sineshin

shoplift *(v.)* အလစ်သုတ်သည် a lait sotesai

shoplifter *(n.)* အလစ်သုတ်သမား a lait sotesamarr

shopowner *(n.)* ဆိုင်ရှင် sineshin

shopping *(n.)* ဈေးဝယ်ခြင်း syaayywaalchinn

shopping cart *(n.)* ဈေးဝယ်လက်တွန်းလှည်း syaayywaal laat twannhlaee

shopping centre *(n.)* ကုန်တိုက် konetite

shopping list *(n.)* ဈေးဝယ်ရန် စာရင်း syaayywaalraan sarrinn

shore *(n.)* ကမ်းခြေ၊ ကမ်းစပ် kamchay, kamsat

shorefront *(n.)* ပင်လယ်ကမ်းခြေ painlaalkamhkyay

shoreline *(n.)* ကမ်းရိုး kamroe

shoreward *(adj.)* ကမ်းခြေဆီသို့ kamhkyayseshoet

shoreweed *(n.)* ပင်လယ်ရေညှိ painlaalraynyhai

short *(adv.)* ရုတ်တရက်၊ အကျဉ်းချုပ် rotetaraat , aakyainhkyaote

short *(n.)* ဆားကစ်အတို sarr kait aato

shortbread *(n.)* ဘီစကွတ်ရွရွ bhe sa kwat rwa-rwa

shortcake *(n.)* ကိတ်မုန့် kate mone

shortcoming *(n.)* အားနည်းချက် aarrnaeechet

shortcut *(n.)* ဖြတ်လမ်း hpyat-lam

shorten *(v.)* တိုအောင် လုပ်သည် toaaung lotesai

shortening *(n.)* ဆီ se

shortfall *(n.)* လိုငွေ၊ အလိုပြခြင်း lo ngway, a lo pyachinn

shorthand *(n.)* လက်ရေးတို laatrayyto

shortish *(adj.)* အတော်အတန်တိုသော aatawaataan tosaw

shortlist *(v.)* ဆန်ခါတင်စာရင်း saanhkartinsarrinn

shortlisted *(adj.)* ဆန်ခါတင်စာရင်းဝင်သော saanhkartin sarrinnwinsaw

shortly *(adv.)* ခဏ၊ အချိန်တိုအတွင်း၊ မကြာမီ hka-na, aachanetoaatwin, makyaarme

shorts *(n. pl.)* ဘောင်းဘီတို၊ အောက်ခံဘောင်းဘီ bhaunggbhe to, aout-hkan-bhaung-bhe

short-term *(adj.)* ရေတို rayto

shot *(int.)* ကျေးဇူးပါ kyaayyjuupar

shotgun *(n.)* ပြောင်းချောသေနတ် pyaungg chawwsaynaat

shotproof *(adj.)* ကျည်မတိုးသော kyai m toesaw

shottie *(n.)* ပြောင်းတိုသေနတ် pyaungg to saytaan

should *(v.)* သင့်သည် sintsai

shoulder *(v.)* လွယ်သည်၊ ပိုးသည် lwal sai , poe-sai

shoulder *(n.)* ပုခုံး၊ အင်္ကျီပုခုံး pu hkone , aain kyee puhkone

shout *(v.)* အော်သည် aawsai

shout *(n.)* အော်သံ aawsan

shove *(n.)* တိုးဝှေ့ခြင်း toe whaaechinn

shove *(v.)* တိုးသည် toesai

shovel *(v.)* ဂေါ်ပြားဖြင့် ကော်သည် gaw pyarrhpyint kawsai

shovel *(n.)* ဂေါ်ပြား gawpyarr

show *(n.)* **ပြပွဲ၊ ဖျော်ဖြေမှု** pyapwal, hpyawhpyaymhu
show *(v.)* **ပြသသည်၊ ထင်ရှားစေသည်** pya sa sai, htinsharrsaysai
showcase *(n.)* **စင်မြင့်၊ ဗန်းပြရာ၊ မှန်ပတ်လည်ဗီရို** sin myint , baann pya rar, mhaan paatlai bero
showdown *(n.)* **အသေအကျေတိုက်ပွဲ** a say a kyaay-tite-pwal
shower *(v.)* **ရေပန်းဖြင့် ချိုးသည်** ray pan-hpyint choesai
shower *(n.)* **ရေပန်း** ray-pan
showerhead *(n.)* **ရေပန်းခေါင်း** ray paannhkaungg
showerless *(adj.)* **ရေမချိုးပဲ** ray m hkyoepell
showerproof *(adj.)* **မိုးရေခံ** moe rayhkan
showery *(adj.)* **ပြတ်တောင်းပြတ်တောင်း ရွာသောမိုး** pyat taungg pyattaungg rwar sawmoe
showpiece *(n.)* **ခင်းကျင်းပြသရန် ရည်ရွယ်၍ ပြုလုပ်ထားသော အရာ** hkainn kyinnpyasaraan rairwal pyulotehtarrsaw aarar
showroom *(n.)* **ပြခန်း** pyahkan
showstopper *(n.)* **ရှေ့ဆက်ခြင်းအတွက် အတားအဆီး** shaesaat hkyinnaatwat aatarraasee
showup *(n.)* **အဖွဲ့ဝင်ရန် တစ်နေရာရာ ရောက်ရှိသည်** aahpwalwainraan taitnayrarrar routshisai
shrapnel *(n.)* **ဗုံးဆန်** bonesan
shred *(v.)* **နုပ်နုပ်စင်းသည်** note note sinnsai
shredder *(n.)* **စက္ကူဖြတ်စက်** sakkuu hpyatsaat
shrew *(n.)* **ကြွက်စုတ်** kyawatsote
shrewd *(adj.)* **လိမ္မာပါးနပ်သော** laimmar parr natsaw
shriek *(v.)* **ဟစ်အော်သည်** hit aawsai
shriek *(n.)* **စီခနဲ အော်သံ** se hkanell aawsan
shrill *(adj.)* **စူးစူးရှရှ** suu suushasha
shrine *(n.)* **အထွတ်အမြတ်ထားရာ ဗိမာန်** aahtwat aamyat htarrrar biman
shrink *(v.)* **ကျုံ့စေသည်** kyaonesaysai
shrinkage *(n.)* **ကျုံ့ခြင်း** kyaonechinn
shroud *(v.)* **ကွယ်သည်၊ ကာဆီးသည်** kwal sai , kar seesai
shroud *(n.)* **အဝတ်စ** aawaat-sa
shrub *(n.)* **ချုံ** chone
shrug *(n.)* **ပခုံးတွန့်ခြင်း** pahkone twantchinn
shrug *(v.)* **ပခုံးတွန့်သည်** pahkone twantsai
shudder *(n.)* **တုန်ခြင်း** tonechinn
shudder *(v.)* **ခိုက်ခိုက်တုန်သည်** hkite hkite tonesai
shuffle *(n.)* **ရှပ်တိုက်ခြင်း** shut titechinn
shuffle *(v.)* **ရှပ်တိုက်လျှောက်သည်** shut tite shoutsai
shun *(v.)* **ရှောင်ဖယ်သည်** shawng hpaalsai
shunt *(v.)* **ချောင်ထိုးသည်** chaunghtoesai
shut *(v.)* **ပိတ်သည်** patesai
shutter *(n.)* **ပြတင်းကာ** pya tinnkar
shuttle *(v.)* **ခေါက်တုံ့ခေါက်ပြန်သွားသည်** hkout tone hkout pyan-swarrsai
shuttle *(n.)* **လွန်း** lwann
shuttlecock *(n.)* **ကြက်တောင်** kyat-taung
shy *(v.)* **ပစ်သည်၊ ပေါက်သည်၊** pait sai , pout sai
shy *(n.)* **ပစ်ခြင်း** paithkyinn

siamese *(adj.)* ထိုင်းနိုင်ငံနှင့် ဆိုင်သော htine-nine-ngannint sinesaw
sibilant *(adj.)* ရှသံပါသော sh san parsaw
sibilate *(v.)* ရှသံပြုသည် sh sonepyusai
sibilating *(n.)* ရှသံပါခြင်း sh san parhkyinn
sibling *(n.)* မောင်နှမအရင်း maung-nha-maa-a-rinn
sich *(n.)* စံမံအုပ်ချုပ်ရေးနှင့် တပ်စင်တာ hcan man aotehkyaoterayynhang tauthcaintar
sick *(adj.)* ဖျားနာသော hpyarr narsaw
sickbag *(n.)* အန်ရန် အိတ် aaanraan aate
sickbay *(n.)* ဖျားနာခန်း hpyarr narhkaann
sickbed *(n.)* ဖျားနာသူ၏ အိပ်ရာ hpyarr narsuueat ait-rar
sicken *(v.)* အော်ဂလီဆန်စေသည် aaw g le saansaysai
sickened *(adj.)* မနှစ်မြို့သော m nhait myahoetsaw
sickle *(n.)* တံစဉ် tansin
sickly *(adj.)* ချူချာသော chauu chaarsaw
sickness *(n.)* နာဖျားမကျန်းဖြစ်ခြင်း nar hpyarr ma kyannhpyitchinn
side *(v.)* ဘေးတစ်ဖက်ယိမ်းသည် bhayy taithpaat yaimsai
side *(n.)* ဘေးဘက်၊ အစွန်း၊ အမြင်၊ ရှုထောင့် bhayy bhaat , aaswann , aamyin , shu htaung
sidearm *(n.)* လက်နက် laatnaat
sideband *(n.)* ကြိမ်နှုန်းလှိုင်း kyaain nhuannlhaine
sidebar *(n.)* ဘေးဘား bhayybharr
sideboard *(n.)* ဗီရို bero
sidebox *(n.)* စာအုပ်တစ်အုပ်တွင် အဓိကစာသားတစ်လျှောက်လို့ အစ်ကပ် hcaraotetaitaotetwin aadhik hcarsarr tait shoutlhoet aaitkaut
sideburn *(n.)* နားသယ်မွေး narr saalmway
sideburns *(n.)* နားသယ်မွေး narr saalmway
sidecar *(n.)* ဘေးတွဲကား bhayy twalkarr
sideline *(v.)* ဘေးထွက်နေရသည် bhayyhtwatnayrasai
sidereal *(adj.)* ကြာများနှင့် သက်ဆိုင်သော kyaar myarrnhang saatsinesaw
side-saddle *(n.)* မြင်းကုန်းနှီး myinn konenhaee
sideshow *(n.)* ပွဲမြှောင် pwal myaung
side-stream *(n.)* ပေါင်းခံခြင်းအလယ်ဆင့်မှ ရရှိသော အရည်စီးကြောင်း paungg hkan hkyinn aalaal saintmha rashisaw aarai hceekyaungg
sidestroke *(n.)* ရေကူးလေဖြတ်ခြင်း ray kuu layhpyathkyinn
sidetrack *(n.)* လမ်းလွှဲခြင်း lam lwhaellchinn
sidewalk *(n.)* ပလက်ဖောင်း palaathpaung
sidewall *(n.)* ဘေးနံရံ bhayynanran
sideway *(adv.)* စောင်း၍ saung-ywe
sidewind *(n.)* ဘေးဘက်ရွှေ့သည် bhayy bhaat rwaesai
siege *(n.)* ဝန်းရံလုပ်ကြံခြင်း waann-ran lotekyaanchinn
siesta *(n.)* တစ်မှေးအိပ်ခြင်း ta-mhaayy ait-chinn
sieve *(v.)* ဆန်ခါချသည် saan hkar chasai
sieve *(n.)* ဆန်ခါ saanhkar
sift *(v.)* အမှုန့်ကို ဆန်ခါချသည် a mhu antko saan hkar chasai
sigh *(v.)* သက်ပြင်းချသည် saatpyinn chasai
sigh *(n.)* သက်ပြင်း saatpyinn
sight *(v.)* တွေ့သည်၊ မြင်သည် twae sai , myinsai
sight *(n.)* အမြင်အာရုံ aamyinaarrone

sightly *(adj.)* အနည်းငယ်သော aanaeengaalsaw

sign *(v.)* လက်မှတ်ထိုးသည် laatmhaathtoesai

sign *(n.)* သင်္ကေတ sin kayta

signal *(v.)* အချက်ပြသည် aachetpyasai

signal *(n.)* အချက်ပြခြင်း aachet pyachinn

signatory *(n.)* လက်မှတ်ပါဝင်ရေးထိုးသူ laatmhaat parwin rayyhtoesuu

signature *(n.)* လက်မှတ် laatmhaat

significance *(n.)* အရေးပါမှု aarayyparmhu

significant *(adj.)* အရေးပါသော aarayyparsaw

signification *(n.)* ဖော်ညွှန်းမှု hpaw nywhaannmhu

signify *(v.)* သဘောဆောင်သည် sabhaw saungsai

signing *(n.)* လက်မှတ်ရေးထိုးခြင်း laatmhaatrayyhtoechinn

silence *(v.)* နှုတ်ဆိတ်စေသည် note satesaysai

silence *(n.)* တိတ်ဆိတ်ခြင်း tatesatechinn

silencer *(n.)* အသံတိတ်ကိရိယာ aasantateka-ri-yar

silent *(adj.)* တိတ်ဆိတ်သော tatesatesaw

silently *(adv.)* တိတ်တိတ်ဆိတ်ဆိတ် tate-tate-sate-sate

silhouette *(n.)* ပုံရိပ်မည်း poneriutmaee

silica *(n.)* ဆီလီကာ se lekar

silicene *(n.)* ဆီလီကွန်အလွှာတစ်လွှာ selekwan aalwhar taitlwhar

silicon *(n.)* ဆီလီကွန်ဒြပ်စင် selekwan drat-sin

silk *(n.)* ပိုး poe

silken *(adj.)* နူးညံ့ချောမွေ့သော nuunyan chawwmwaesaw

silky *(adj.)* ပိုးသားကဲ့သို့ poe sarrkaethoet

silly *(adj.)* မိုက်မဲသော mite mellsaw

silt *(v.)* နုန်းဖြင့် ပိတ်နေသည် nonehpyint patenaysai

silt *(n.)* နုန်း none

silver *(n.)* ငွေ ngway

similar *(adj.)* တူညီသော tuunyesaw

similarity *(n.)* တူညီချက် tuunyechet

simile *(n.)* ဥပမာ upamar

similitude *(n.)* တစ်စုံတစ်ခုနှင့် ဆင်တူခြင်း taithconetaithkunhang saintuuhkyinn

simmer *(v.)* ဆူရုံတည်သည် suu rone taisai

simple *(adj.)* ရိုးရှင်းသော roeshinn-saw

simpleton *(n.)* ငနု၊ ငအ nga na, nga-a

simplicity *(n.)* လွယ်ခြင်း၊ ရိုးခြင်း lwal chinn, roe-chinn

simplification *(n.)* လွယ်အောင် ပြုလုပ်ခြင်း lwal-au pyulotechinn

simplify *(v.)* လွယ်အောင် ပြုလုပ်သည် lwalaaung pyulotesai

simultaneous *(adj.)* တစ်ပြိုင်နက်ဖြစ်သော taitpyainenaathpyitsaw

sin *(v.)* မကောင်းမှုပြုသည် makaunggmhupyusai

sin *(n.)* မကောင်းမှု makaunggmhu

since *(conj.)* ကတည်းက kataeka-

since *(prep.)* ကတည်းက ka-tae-ka

sincere *(adj.)* စစ်မှန်သော sit-mhaan-saw

sincerity *(n.)* မှန်ကန်မှု mhaankaanmhu

sinful *(adj.)* လွဲမှားသော lwalmharsaw

sing *(v.)* သီဆိုသည် se-so-sai

singe *(n.)* မီးမြှိုက်ခြင်း mee myahaitechinn

singe *(v.)* မီးမြှိုက်သည် mee myahaitesai

singer *(n.)* အဆိုတော် aasotaw

single *(v.)* **တစ်ကိုယ်ရေတစ်ကာယဖြစ်သည်** taitkoray tait kar yahpyitsai
single *(adj.)* **တစ်ကိုယ်ရေတစ်ကာယဖြစ်သော** taitkoray tait kar yahpyitsaw
single-handedly *(adv.)* **တစ်ကိုယ်တော်** taitkotaw
singular *(adj.)* **ဧကဝုစ်** eka wote
singularity *(n.)* **ထူးခြားသော လက္ခဏာ** htuucharrsaw lakhkanar
singularly *(adv.)* **ထူးထူးကဲကဲ** htuuhtuukellkell
sinister *(adj.)* **အန္တရာယ်ပြုမည့် လက္ခဏာရှိသော** aanta-ral pyumaeet lakhkanarshisaw
sink *(n.)* **ပန်းကန်ဆေးကန်** paannkaan sayykaan
sink *(v.)* **မြုပ်သည်** myuutsai
sinner *(n.)* **ငမိုက်သား** ngamitesarr
sinuous *(adj.)* **အကွေ့အဝိုက်များသော** aakwae a witemyarrsaw
sip *(n.)* **တစ်ငုံစာ** tait ngone-sar
sip *(v.)* **နည်းနည်းချင်းစီ စုပ်သောက်သည်** neenee-chinnse sotesoutsai
sir *(n.)* **ဆရာ** sarar
siren *(n.)* **အချက်ပေးဥသြ** aachetpayy oak-aw
sister *(n.)* **ညီအစ်မ** nyeaaitma
sisterhood *(n.)* **ညီအစ်မစိတ်ဓာတ်** nyeaaitmasatedhat
sisterly *(adj.)* **ညီအစ်မကဲ့သို့** nyeaaitmakathoet
sit *(v.)* **ထိုင်သည်** htinesai
site *(n.)* **တည်နေရာ၊ ဖြစ်ပွားရာ** tinayrar, hpyitpwarrrar
situation *(n.)* **အခြေအနေ** aachayaanay
six *(n.)* **ခြောက်** chauk
sixteen *(n., adj.)* **ဆယ့်ခြောက်** sae chauk
sixteenth *(adj.)* **ဆယ့်ခြောက်ခုမြောက်** sae chauk-hku-myaut
sixth *(adj.)* **ခြောက်ခုမြောက်** chauk-hku-myaut
sixtieth *(adj.)* **ခြောက်ဆယ်ခုမြောက်** chauk saal-ku-myaut
sixty *(n., adj.)* **ခြောက်ဆယ်** chauk-saal
sizable *(adj.)* **အတော်အတန်ကြီးမားသော** aatawaataankyeemarrsaw
size *(v.)* **ပမာဏကို တိုင်းဆသည်** pamarnako tine sasai
sizzle *(n.)* **ရှဲရှဲမြည်သံ** shell shell myisan
sizzle *(v.)* **ရှဲရှဲမြည်သည်** shell shell myisai
skate *(v.)* **စကိတ်စီးသည်** sa kate seesai
skater *(n.)* **စကိတ်စီးသူ** sa kate seesuu
skein *(n.)* **ချည်အခင်** chai aahkain
skeleton *(n.)* **အရိုး** aa-roe
sketch *(v.)* **ပုံကြမ်းဆွဲသည်** pone-kyaa swalsai
sketch *(n.)* **ပုံကြမ်း** ponekyam
sketchy *(adj.)* **အပေါ်ယံ** aapawyan
skid *(n.)* **ဘီးချော်ခြင်း** bhee chawchinn
skid *(v.)* **ဘီးချော်သည်** bhee chawsai
skilful *(adj.)* **ကျွမ်းကျင်သော** kywankyinsaw
skill *(n.)* **ကျွမ်းကျင်မှု** kywankyinmhu
skin *(v.)* **အရေခွံခွာသည်** a ray hkwan hkwarsai
skin *(n.)* **အရေပြား၊ အခွံ** aaraypyarr, aahkwan
skip *(n.)* **ခုန်ခြင်း** hkone-chinn
skip *(v.)* **လစ်သည်၊ ကျော်သည်** lit sai , kyaw-sai
skipper *(n.)* **မာလိန်မှူး** mar lein-mhauu

skirmish *(v.)* ထိတွေ့သည်၊ အပြန်အလှန်တိုက်ခိုက်သည် hti-twae sai, aapyanaahlaan titehkitesai
skirmish *(n.)* ထိတွေ့ခြင်း၊ ပစ်ခတ်မှုဖြစ်ပွားခြင်း hti-twaechinn, pyit-hkaatmhu hpyitpwarrchinn
skirt *(v.)* ပတ်သွားသည် paat-swarr-sai
skirt *(n.)* စကတ် sakaat
skit *(n.)* ဇာတ်လမ်းတို zatlamto
skull *(n.)* ဦးခွံ u-hkwan
sky *(v.)* မိုးထိအောင် မြှောက်သည် moe-htiaaung myaut-sai
sky *(n.)* ကောင်းကင် kaungg-kin
skyscraper *(n.)* မိုးမျှော်တိုက် moe-myaw-tite
slab *(n.)* အချပ်၊ အပြား a chat, aa-pyarr
slack *(adj.)* မတင်းသော ma tinn-saw
slacken *(v.)* လျှော့ပေးသည်၊ ဖျော့လိုက်သည် shot payy-sai, hpyaw-litesai
slacks *(n.)* ဘောင်းဘီရှည် bhaung-bhe-shay
slake *(v.)* ရေငတ်ပြေစေသည် ray-ngaat-pyay-saysai
slam *(n.)* ဆောင့်ပိတ်ခြင်း saunt-pate-chinn
slam *(v.)* ဆောင့်ပိတ်သည် saunt-pate-sai
slander *(v.)* လုပ်ကြံ၍ အသရေဖျက်သည် lote-kyaan-ywe-a-sa-ray hpyetsai
slanderous *(adj.)* အသရေဖျက်သော a sa ray hpyetsaw
slang *(n.)* ဗန်းစကား baannsakarr
slant *(n.)* ရှုထောင့်၊ အမြင် shu htawnt, aamyin
slant *(v.)* စွေသည်၊ စောင်းသည် sway sai, saungg-sai
slap *(v.)* ရိုက်သည်၊ ပုတ်သည် rite sai, pote-sai
slap *(n.)* ရိုက်ခြင်း၊ ပုတ်ခြင်း rite chinn , pote-chinn
slash *(n.)* ခုတ်ပိုင်းခြင်း hkote pinechinn
slash *(v.)* ခုတ်ထွင်သည် hkote htwinsai
slate *(n.)* သင်ပုန်းကျောက် sin ponekyawt
slather *(v.)* ထူထဲစွာ သုတ်လိမ်းသည် htuu htellhcwar sote laimsai
slattern *(n.)* မသန့်မပြန့် ဖိုသီဖတ်သီ မိန်းမ ma saant ma pyant hpo se hpaatse meinm ma
slatternly *(adj.)* မသန့်မပြန့် ဖိုသီဖတ်သီ ma saant ma pyant hpo se hpaatse
slaughter *(v.)* သတ်ပွဲကျင်းပသည် saat pwalkyinnpa-sai
slaughter *(n.)* လူသတ်ပွဲ luu-saatpwal
slave *(v.)* ပင်ပင်ပန်းပန်း မနားမနေ လုပ်သည် pinpinpaannpaann ma narr manay lotesai
slave *(n.)* ကျွန် kywan
slavery *(n.)* ကျွန်ပြုခြင်း kywanpyuchinn
slavish *(adj.)* ပုံတူခိုးချသော ponetuu hkoe chasaw
slay *(v.)* သတ်ဖြတ်သည် saat-hpyat-sai
sleek *(adj.)* ချောမွတ်တောက်ပြောင်နေသော chaww-mwat tout pyaungnaysaw
sleep *(n.)* အိပ်စက်ခြင်း ait-saat-chinn
sleep *(v.)* အိပ်ပျော်သည် aitpyawsai
sleeper *(n.)* အိပ်နေသူ ait naysuu
sleepy *(adj.)* အိပ်ငိုက်သော ait ngitesaw
sleeve *(n.)* အင်္ကျီလက် ain kye-laat
sleight *(n.)* လက်လှည့်၊ မျက်လှည့် laat hlae, myet hlae
slender *(adj.)* ကျစ်လျစ်သော၊ သွယ်သော kyit lyit saw, swalsaw
slice *(v.)* အချပ်လိုက် အလွှာလိုက် လှီးသည် a chat-lite aa-lwhar-lite hlee-sai
slice *(n.)* အချပ်၊ အယှက် a chat, aa-shaat

slick *(adj.)* သဘောကျလောက်အောင် သွက်လက်သော sabhawkyaloutaaung swat laatsaw
slide *(n.)* ရေခဲလျှောစီး ray hkell shawsee
slide *(v.)* လျှောဆင်းသည် shaw sinnsai
slight *(n.)* စော်ကားမှု sawkarrmhu
slight *(adj.)* သွယ်လျသော၊ ပေါ့တန်သော swal lya saw, pot taansaw
slim *(v.)* ကျစ်လျစ်အောင် လုပ်သည် kyit lyit-aung lotesai
slim *(adj.)* ကျစ်လျစ်သော၊ သွယ်သော kyit lyit saw, swalsaw
slime *(n.)* အကျိအချွဲ aakyi a chwal
slimy *(adj.)* ကျိချွဲသော kyi chwalsaw
sling *(n.)* လည်သိုင်းပတ်တီး lai-sine paattee
slip *(n.)* ခြေချော်ခြင်း chay chawchinn
slip *(v.)* ခြေချော်သည် chay chawsai
slip road *(n.)* ချောသော လမ်း chawwsaw lam
slipper *(n.)* ကွင်းထိုးဖိနပ် kwin htoehpinaut
slippery *(adj.)* ချောသော chawwsaw
slipshod *(adj.)* ပေါ့ပေါ့ဆဆ pot-pot-sa-sa
slit *(v.)* လှီးသည်၊ ခွဲသည် hlee sai, hkwal sai
slit *(n.)* ဟက်တက်ရာ၊ အကွဲ haat taat rar, aakwal
slogan *(n.)* ကြွေးကြော်သံ kyay-kyaw-san
slope *(v.)* လျှောသည်၊ စောင်းသည် shaw sai, saung-sai
slope *(n.)* ကုန်းစောင်း kone-saung
slot *(n.)* အပေါက် aapout
slot. *(v.)* အလိုက်သင့် သွင်းသည် aa-lite-sint swinsai
sloth *(n.)* ပျင်းရိခြင်း pyinn richinn
slothful *(n.)* ပျင်းရိသော pyinn risaw
slough *(v.)* လဲသည်၊ ခွာသည် lell sai, hkwarsai
slough *(n.)* ရွှံ့တော ဗွက်တော shwantaw bwattaw
slovenly *(adj.)* ဖြစ်ကတတ်ဆန်း၊ ပေါက်လွတ်ပဲစား hpyit k taat saann , pout lwut pellsarr
slow *(v.)* အရှိန်လျှော့ချသည် aashein shotchasai
slow *(adj.)* နှေးသော nhaayysaw
slow motion *(n.)* အနှေးရိုက်ချက် a nhaayyritechet
slowly *(adv.)* နှေးကွေးစွာ nhaayykwayswar
slowness *(n.)* နှေးကွေးခြင်း nhaayykwaychinn
sluggard *(n.)* ပျင်းရိလေ့တွဲ့သောသူ pyinn ri lae twalsawsuu
sluggish *(adj.)* နှေးကွေးလေးကန်သော nhaayykway layy kaansaw
sluice *(n.)* ရေလွှဲပေါက် ray lwhaellpout
slum *(n.)* ဆင်းရဲသားရပ်ကွက် sinnrellsarrratkwat
slumber *(n.)* အိပ်စက်ခြင်း၊ အိပ်ရေး ait-saat-chinn, ait-rayy
slumber *(v.)* အိပ်စက်သည်၊ အိပ်မောကျသည် aitsaat sai , ait-maw-kyasai
slump *(v.)* ပစ်ထိုင်သည် pyit htinesai
slump *(n.)* အလုပ်အကိုင် မကောင်းသည့် အချိန် aaloteaakine makaunggsaeet aachane
slur *(n.)* မဟုတ်မတရား စွပ်စွဲ ပြောဆိုချက် mahotematararr swutswal pyawwsochet
slush *(n.)* နှင်းပျော်ဝင်နေသော ရွှံ့ nhinn pyaw winnaysaw shwan

slushy *(adj.)* **နှင်းပျော်ဝင်နေသော** nhinn pyaw winnaysaw
slut *(n.)* **မိန်းမပျက်** mein-ma-pyet
sly *(adj.)* **မရိုးသော** ma roesaw
smack *(v.)* **လက်ဝါးဖြင့် ရိုက်သည်** laatwarrhpyint ritesai
smack *(n.)* **လက်ဝါးဖြင့် ရိုက်ခြင်း** laatwarrhpyint ritechinn
small *(n.)* **ကျဉ်းသော အပိုင်း** kyinsaw aapine
small *(adj.)* **သေးသော၊ နည်းသော၊ ငယ်ရွယ်သော** say-saw , naee saw , ngaalrwalsaw
smallness *(adv.)* **သေးငယ်ခြင်း** sayy ngaalchinn
smallpox *(n.)* **ရေကျောက်** raykyaut
smart *(n.)* **သပ်ရပ်ကြော့မော့ခြင်း** sat rat kyaww motchinn
smart *(adj.)* **သပ်ရပ်ကြော့မော့သော** sat rat kyaww motsaw
smartly *(adv.)* **သပ်ရပ်ကြော့မော့စွာ** sat rat kyaww motswar
smash *(n.)* **ရိုက်ချိုးခြင်း** ritechoechinn
smash *(v.)* **ရိုက်ခွဲသည်** rite hkwalsai
smear *(n.)* **အစွန်းအထင်း** aaswann aahtinn
smear *(v.)* **လူးသည်၊ လိမ်းသည်၊ ပေကျံသည်** luu sai , laim sai , pay kyaansai
smell *(v.)* **အနံ့ရသည်** aananrasai
smell *(n.)* **အနံ့** aanan
smelt *(v.)* **သတ္တုရိုင်းကို အရည်ကျိုသည်** sattu rineko aaraikyaosai
smile *(v.)* **ပြုံးသည်** pyuansai
smile *(n.)* **အပြုံး** aapyuan
smith *(n.)* **ပန်းပဲသမား** paann pellsamarr
smock *(n.)* **သင်တိုင်း** sintine
smog *(n.)* **မီးခိုးမြူ** meehkoemyauu
smoke *(v.)* **မီးခိုးထွက်သည်** meehkoe htwatsai
smoke *(n.)* **မီးခိုး** meehkoe
smoking *(n.)* **ဆေးလိပ်သောက်ခြင်း** sayyliutsoutchinn
smoky *(adj.)* **မီးခိုးအူသော** meehkoe auusaw
smooth *(v.)* **အချောသတ်သည်** a chaww saatsai
smooth *(adj.)* **ချောမွေ့သော** chawwmwaesaw
smoothie *(n.)* **ညက်ညက်နှင့် ပတ်တက်သူ** nyaat nyaat-nint paat taatsuu
smother *(v.)* **တစ်ခုခုနှင့် ဖိသတ်သည်** ta-hku-hku-nint hpi saatsai
smoulder *(v.)* **တငွေ့ငွေ့ လောင်ကျွမ်းသည်** ta ngwae-ngwae laungkyawmsai
smug *(adj.)* **ကိုယ့်ကိုယ်ကိုယ် ဟုတ်လှပြီဟု ဘဝင်ခိုက်နေသော** ko koko hote hla pyehu bha win hkitenaysaw
smuggle *(v.)* **မှောင်ခိုသွင်း၊ ထုတ်သည်** mhaawinhko swin , htotesai
smuggler *(n.)* **မှောင်ခိုသမား** mhaawinhkosamarr
snack *(n.)* **သရေစာ** sa ray-sar
snag *(n.)* **ခလုတ်ကန်သင်း** hkalotekaansinn
snail *(n.)* **ခရု** hkaru
snake *(v.)* **ကွေ့ကောက်သွားသည်** kwae koutswarrsai
snake *(n.)* **မြွေ** myway
snap *(n.)* **ထောက်ခနဲ မြည်သံ** htout hkanell myisan
snap *(v.)* **ထောက်ခနဲ မြည်လျက် ပြတ်သည်** htout hkanell myilyet pyatsai
snapshot *(n.)* **သဘာဝအတိုင်း ဖြတ်ခနဲ ဓာတ်ပုံ ရိုက်ခြင်း** sabharwaaatine hpyathkanell dhratpone ritechinn

snare *(v.)* ညွှတ်ထောင်သည် nywut htaungsai
snare *(n.)* ကျော့ကွင်း kyawwt-kwin
snarl *(v.)* အစွယ်ပြပြီး မာန်ဖီသည် aa-swal pyapyee man hpesai
snarl *(n.)* မာန်ဖီခြင်း man hpe-chinn
snatch *(n.)* ဆတ်ခနဲ ယူငင်ခြင်း saath-kanell yuu ngainchinn
snatch *(v.)* ဆတ်ခနဲ ဆွဲယူသည် saath-kanell swalyuusai
sneak *(n.)* သတ္တိကြောင်သည့် ကလိမ်ကကျစ် satti kyaungsaeet kalinkakyit
sneak *(v.)* အတို့အထောင်လုပ်သည် a thoet a htaunglotesai
sneer *(n.)* အထင်သေးကြောင်းကို ပြသည့် ပုံစံ a htin sayykyaunggko pyasaeet ponesan
sneer *(v.)* လှောင်သည်၊ သရော်သည် hlawng sai, sa-rawsai
sneeze *(n.)* နှာချေခြင်း nhar chaaychinn
sneeze *(v.)* နှာချေသည် nhar chaaysai
sniff *(n.)* နှာရှုပ်ခြင်း nhar shotechinn
sniff *(v.)* နှာရှုပ်သည် nhar shotesai
sniper *(n.)* လက်ဖြောင့် laat hpyount
snob *(n.)* အထက်ဖား အောက်ဖိ aahtaathparr athpi
snobbery *(n.)* ဘဝင်ကိုင်ခြင်း bha win kinechinn
snobbish *(v.)* ဇီဇာကြောင်သော zezar kyaungsaw
snoop *(v.)* ချောင်းသည် chaunggsai
snoot *(n.)* သွေးကြီး မွေးကြီး နိုင်ခြင်း swaykyee mwaykyee ninechinn
snooze *(v.)* တစ်ရေးမှေးသည် ta rayy mhaayysai
snore *(n.)* ဟောက်သံ houtsan
snore *(v.)* ဟောက်သည် houtsai

snort *(n.)* နှာမှုတ်ခြင်း nhar mhuatchinn
snort *(v.)* ရှူသည်၊ နှာမှုတ်သည် shuu sai, nhar mhuatsai
snout *(n.)* နှုတ်သီး nhuatsee
snow *(v.)* နှင်းကျသည် naten kyasai
snow *(n.)* နှင်း naten
snow boot *(n.)* နှင်းဆီးဘွတ်ဖိနပ် naten see bhwathpinaut
snowfall *(n.)* ဆီးနှင်းကျခြင်း see natenkyachinn
snowy *(adj.)* နှင်းဖုံးနေသော naten hponenaysaw
snub *(adj.)* တို၍ ထိပ်လန်နေသော to hteik laannaysaw
snub *(v.)* ပစ်ပယ်သည် pyit paalsai
snuff *(n.)* နှာ nhar
snug *(n.)* အရက်ဆိုင်ရှိ သီးသန့်ထိုင်ရန် နေရာ aaraatsineshi see saant htineraan nayrar
so *(conj.)* ထို့ကြောင့် hthoetkyount
soak *(n.)* ရေစိမ်ခြင်း ray sinchinn
soak *(v.)* စိမ်သည် sinsai
soap *(v.)* ဆပ်ပြာတိုက်သည် satpyaar titesai
soap *(n.)* ဆပ်ပြာ satpyaar
soapy *(adj.)* ဆပ်ပြာပါသော satpyaar parsaw
soar *(v.)* ပျံတက်သည် pyaan taatsai
sob *(n.)* ရှိုက်သံ shitesan
sob *(v.)* ရှိုက်ငိုသည် shite ngosai
sober *(adj.)* အရက်မသောက်သော a raat ma soutsaw
sobriety *(n.)* တည်ကြည်လေးနက်ခြင်း tai kyi layynaatchinn
sociability *(n.)* လူ့ထုံးတမ်း လိုက်နာခြင်း hluhtonetam litenarchinn
sociable *(adj.)* ဖော်ရွေသော hpaw rwaysaw

social *(n.)* လူမှုရေး luumhurayy

socialism *(n.)* ဆိုရှယ်လစ်ဝါဒ soshallaitwar-da

socialist *(n.)* ဆိုရှယ်လစ်ဝါဒီ soshallaitwar-de

socialite *(n.)* ခေတ်ဆန်သော အသိုင်းအဝိုင်းတွင် ရေပန်းစားသူ hkayatsaansaw aasineaawinetwin raypaannsarrsuu

society *(n.)* လူ့အဖွဲ့အစည်း hluaahpwalaasaee

sociology *(n.)* လူမှုဗေဒ luumhubay-da

sock *(n.)* ခြေအိတ် chayaate

socket *(n.)* ပလတ်ပေါက် pa laatpout

sod *(n.)* ငနာ၊ ငနဲ nga nar, nganell

sodomite *(n.)* ဓမ္မတာနှင့် ဆန့်ကျင်၍ ကာမဆက်ဆံသူ dhammatarnint s ant kyin kar m saatsansuu

sodomy *(n.)* ဓမ္မတာနှင့် ဆန့်ကျင်၍ ကာမဆက်ဆံခြင်း dhammatarnint s ant kyin kar masaatsanchinn

sofa *(n.)* ဆိုဖာ sohpar

soft *(adj.)* နူးညံ့သော nuunyansaw

soft copy *(n.)* ကွန်ပျူတာဖိုင် kwanpyauutarhpine

soften *(v.)* ပျော့စေသည် pyawt-saysai

softener *(n.)* ရေစေးချွတ်ဆေး ray sayy chyutsayy

soggy *(adj.)* နူးအိသော nuu aisaw

soil *(v.)* ညစ်သည်၊ ပေသည် nyit sai, paysai

soil *(n.)* မြေကြီး myaykyee

sojourn *(n.)* နေခြင်း၊ သီတင်းသုံးခြင်း naychinn , setinnsonechinn

sojourn *(v.)* နေသည်၊ သီတင်းသုံးသည် naysai , setinnsonesai

solace *(n.)* စိတ်သက်သာမှု satesaatsarmhu

solar *(adj.)* နေရောင်ခြည် nayraungchi

solar panel *(n.)* ဆိုလာကွက် so larkwat

solder *(v.)* ဂဟေဆော်သည် ga hay sawsai

solder *(n.)* ဂဟေ gahay

soldier *(v.)* စစ်သားအဖြစ် ထမ်းဆောင်သည် hcaitsarraahpyit htamsaungsai

soldier *(n.)* စစ်သား sitsarr

sole *(adj.)* တစ်ခုတည်းသော ta-hkutaeesaw

sole *(n.)* ခြေဖဝါး chayhpawarr

solemn *(adj.)* တည်ကြည်လေးနက်သော tai kyi layynaatsaw

solemnity *(n.)* တည်ကြည်လေးနက်မှုရှိခြင်း tai kyi layynaatmhushichinn

solemnize *(v.)* ထုံးတမ်းနှင့်ညီအောင် ပြုလုပ်သည် htonetam nint nyeaaung pyulotesai

solicit *(v.)* တောင်းခံသည် taungghkansai

solicitation *(n.)* အဆိုလွှာတင်ခြင်း a so lwhartainhkyinn

solicitor *(n.)* တရားရုံးရှေ့နေ tararrroneshaenay

solicitous *(adj.)* အရေးတယူရှိသော aarayytayuushisaw

solicitude *(n.)* စာနာမှု sarnarmhu

solid *(n.)* အခဲ aahkell

solid *(adj.)* အခဲ aahkell

solidarity *(n.)* စည်းလုံးညီညွတ်မှု seelonenyenywatmhu

solidify *(v.)* ခဲစေသည် hkell-saysai

soliloquy *(n.)* ဇာတ်ထွက်စကား zat htwatsakarr

solitaire *(n.)* တစ်ပင်တိုင်လက်ဝတ်ရတနာ ta pintinelaatwaatratanar

solitary *(adj.)* တစ်ဦးတည်း ta u-tee

solitude *(n.)* အထီးကျန်ခြင်း aa-hteekyaanchinn
solo *(adj.)* တစ်ကိုယ်တော် ta-kotaw
solo *(n.)* တစ်ကိုယ်တော် ta-kotaw
soloist *(n.)* တစ်ကိုယ်တော်သီဆိုဖြေဖျော်သူ ta-kotaw se-so hpyay hpyawsuu
solubility *(n.)* ပျော်ဝင်သတ္တိ pyaw winsatti
soluble *(adj.)* ပျော်ဝင်နိုင်သော pyaw winninesaw
solution *(n.)* ပျော်ရည်၊ ဖြေရှင်းနည်း pyaw rai, hpyayhlyinnnaee
solve *(v.)* အဖြေရှာသည် aahpyaysharsai
solvency *(n.)* ကြွေးဆပ်နိုင်အား kyway sat nineaarr
solvent *(n.)* ဖျော်ရည် hpyawrai
solvent *(adj.)* ကြွေးကင်းသော kyway kinnsaw
sombre *(adj.)* မှိုင်းသော mhainesaw
some *(pron.)* တစ်ချို့ ta-choet
some *(adj.)* တစ်ချို့ ta-choet
somebody *(n.)* တစ်စုံတစ်ယောက် ta-sonetaityout
somebody *(pron.)* တစ်စုံတစ်ယောက် ta-sonetaityout
somehow *(adv.)* တစ်နည်းနည်းဖြင့် ta- nee-neehpyint
someone *(pron.)* တစ်စုံတစ်ယောက် ta-sone-ta-yout
somersault *(v.)* ကျွမ်းထိုးသည် kyawm htoesai
somersault *(n.)* ကျွမ်းထိုးခြင်း kyawm htoechinn
something *(adv.)* တစ်စုံတစ်ရာ ta-soneta-rar
something *(pron.)* တစ်စုံတစ်ရာ ta-soneta-rar
sometime *(adv.)* တစ်ချိန်ချိန် ta-chanechane
sometimes *(adv.)* တစ်ခါတစ်ရံ ta-hkarta-ran
somewhat *(adv.)* အနည်းငယ် aa-nee-ngaal
somewhere *(adv.)* တစ်နေရာရာ ta-nayrar-rar
somnambulism *(n.)* အိပ်ပျော်လျက်လမ်းလျှောက်ခြင်း aitpyawlyet lamshoutchinn
somnambulist *(n.)* အိပ်ပျော်လျက်လမ်းလျှောက်တတ်သူ aitpyawlyet lamshout taatsuu
somnolence *(n.)* အိပ်ငိုက်ခြင်း ait ngitechinn
somnolent *(adj.)* အိပ်ငိုက်သော ait ngitesaw
son *(n.)* သား sarr
song *(n.)* သီချင်း se-chinn
songster *(n.)* အဆိုတော် aa-sotaw
sonic *(adj.)* အသံလှိုင်း aa-sanhline
sonnet *(n.)* ၁၄ ကြောင်းစပ်လင်္ကာ 14 kyaung sat linkar
sonography *(n.)* ညစာရေးခြင်း nyahcarrayyhkyinn
sonority *(n.)* အသံအောင်ခြင်း aa-sanaaungchinn
soon *(adv.)* မကြာမီ makyaarme
soot *(v.)* မီးခိုးငွေ့လွမ်းသည် meehkoe ngway lwmsai
soot *(n.)* ကျပ်ခိုး kyauthkoe
soothe *(v.)* နှစ်သိမ့်သည် nit teint the
sophism *(n.)* ဒဿနသင်ကြားနည်း dသသnasainkyarrnaee

sophist *(n.)* ဆိုဖစ်အယူအဆ so hpaitaayuuaas
sophisticate *(n.)* ခေတ်မီသူ hkitmesuu
sophisticated *(adj.)* အတွေ့အကြုံများသော aatwaeaakyuanmyarrsaw
sophistication *(n.)* ဆန်းပြားမှု saann pyarrmhu
sorcerer *(n.)* မှော်ဆရာ mhaawsarar
sorcery *(n.)* မှော်အတတ် mhaaw aataat
sordid *(adj.)* ညစ်ပေသော nyit paysaw
sore *(n.)* အနာ aanar
sore *(adj.)* နာသော narsaw
sorrow *(v.)* ဝမ်းနည်းသည်၊ ပူဆွေးသည် wamnaee sai , puuswaysai
sorrow *(n.)* ဝမ်းနည်းခြင်း၊ ပူဆွေးခြင်း wamnaeechinn , puuswaychinn
sorry *(adj.)* ဝမ်းနည်းသော wamnaeesaw
sort *(v.)* မျိုးတူစုသည် myoe tuu susai
soul *(n.)* ဝိညာဉ်၊ လိပ်ပြာ၊ စိတ်ထား wit-nyin, late-pyaar, satehtarr
sound *(v.)* ထင်ရသည်၊ အချက်ပေးသည် htin rasai, aachetpayysai
sound *(adj.)* အကောင်းပကတိ a kaunggpakati
sound system *(n.)* အသံစနစ် aasansanit
soundproof *(adj.)* အသံလုံသော aasan lonesaw
soundtrack *(n.)* နောက်ခံ သီချင်းသံ nouthkan sehkyinnsan
soup *(n.)* စွပ်ပြုတ် swutpyote
sour *(v.)* အချဉ်ပေါက်သည် a chin poutsai
sour *(adj.)* ချဉ်သော၊ စိတ်ကုန်သော chin saw, sate konesaw
source *(n.)* အစ၊ ဇာတိ၊ မြစ်ဖျားခံရာ၊ ရင်းမြစ် a sa, zarti , myithpyarrhkanrar , rinn-myit
south *(adj.)* တောင်ပိုင်း taungpine
southerly *(adj.)* တောင်ဘက်သို့ taungbhaatthoet
southern *(adj.)* တောင်ပိုင်း taungpine
souvenir *(n.)* အမှတ်တရ လက်ဆောင်ပစ္စည်း aa-mhaattara laatsaungpyit-see
sovereign *(adj.)* အချုပ်အခြာ aa-chote-aa-chaar
sovereign *(n.)* နိုင်ငံဦးသျှောင် ninengan u shawn
sovereignty *(n.)* လွတ်လပ်သော အချုပ်အခြာအာဏာ lwatlautsaw aachoteaachaaraarnar
sow *(v.)* ပျိုးသည်၊ မျိုးကြဲသည် pyoe sai, myoe kyaellsai
space *(v.)* ခြားထားသည် charrhtarrsai
space *(n.)* ကြား၊ ကွက်လပ် kyarr , kwatlat
spacecraft *(n.)* အာကာသယာဉ် aarkarsayin
spacious *(adj.)* ကျယ်ဝန်းသော kyaalwaannsaw
spade *(v.)* ဂေါ်ပြားနှင့် မြေကော်သည် gaw pyarrnhang myay kawsai
spade *(n.)* ဂေါ်ပြား gawpyarr
span *(v.)* တံတားခင်းသည် tantarr hkinnsai
span *(n.)* ကာလ၊ အကွာအဝေး kar-la , aakwaraawayy
Spaniard *(n.)* စပိန်နိုင်ငံသား hcapeinninengansarr
spaniel *(n.)* သင်ဘော်ခွေး sinbhawhkway
Spanish *(n.)* စပိန်ဘာသာစကား sapeinbharsarsakarr
Spanish *(adj.)* စပိန် sapein
spanner *(n.)* ခွ hkwa
spare *(n.)* အပို aapo
spare *(v.)* ချမ်းသာပေးသည် chamsarpayysai

spark *(v.)* မီးပွားထွက်သည် mee pwarr htwatsai

spark *(n.)* မီးပွား meepwarr

sparkle *(n.)* လင်းလက်ခြင်း linnlaatchinn

sparkle *(v.)* တလက်လက် တောက်ပသည် ta laatlaat toutpa-sai

sparrow *(n.)* စာကလေး sarkalayy

sparse *(adj.)* ကျဲသော၊ ပါးသော kyaell saw , parrsaw

spasm *(n.)* လျှပ်တစ်ပြက်ဖြစ်ရပ် shuttaitpyaathpyitrat

spasmodic *(adj.)* ပြတ်တောင်းပြတ်တောင်း pyat taungg pyattaungg

spate *(n.)* ရုတ်ခြည်းကျလာခြင်း rote chi kyalarchinn

spatial *(adj.)* အကွာအဝေး aakwaraawayy

spawn *(v.)* ဥ ဥသည် u u-sai

spawn *(n.)* ဥ u

speak *(v.)* စကားပြောသည် sakarrpyawwsai

speaker *(n.)* ပြောသူ၊ လွှတ်တော်ဥက္ကဋ္ဌ pyaww suu, hlut-taw-u-kkaht

spear *(v.)* ထိုးသည် htoe-sai

spear *(n.)* လှံ၊ လှံတံ hlaan, hlaantan

spearhead *(v.)* ဦးဆောင်သည် u saung-sai

spearhead *(n.)* ခေါင်းဆောင်၊ တပ်ဦး hkaung-saung, tat u

special *(adj.)* အထူး aa-htuu

specialist *(n.)* အထူးကျွမ်းကျင်သူ aa-htuukywamkyinsuu

speciality *(n.)* အထူးလုပ်ငန်း aahtuulotengan

specialization *(n.)* အထူးပြုခြင်း aa-htuu-pyu-chinn

specialize *(v.)* အထူးပြုသည် aa-htuu-pyu-sai

species *(n.)* မျိုးစိတ် myoe-sate

specific *(adj.)* တိကျသော ti-kya-saw

specification *(n.)* အသေးစိတ်ဖော်ပြချက် aa-sayy-sate-hpawpyachet

specify *(v.)* သတ်မှတ်သည် saatmhaatsai

specimen *(n.)* နမူနာ namuunar

speck *(n.)* အစက် aasaat

speckle *(n.)* အစက်အပြောက် a saat aapyaut

spectacle *(n.)* ပွဲလမ်းအခမ်းအနား pwal lamaahkamaanarr

spectacular *(adj.)* ခမ်းနားကြီးကျယ်သော hkamnarr kyeekyaalsaw

spectator *(n.)* ပွဲကြည့်ပရိသတ် pwal kyanyparisaat

spectre *(n.)* တစ္ဆေ ta-say

spectrum *(n.)* ရောင်စဉ် raungsin

speculate *(v.)* မှန်းဆသည် mhan-sa sai

speculation *(n.)* မှန်းဆခြင်း mhaannsachinn

speech *(n.)* မိန့်ခွန်း၊ စကား mein hkwan, sakarr

speed *(v.)* အဟုန်မြှင့်သည် a hone myint sai

speed *(n.)* လျင်မြန်ခြင်း lyin-myan-chinn

speedily *(adv.)* မြန်မြန် myan-myan

speedy *(adj.)* မြန်သော myansaw

spell *(v.)* စာလုံးပေါင်းသည် sarlonepaunggsai

spell *(n.)* မန္တန် mantaan

spelling *(n.)* စာလုံးပေါင်း sarlonepaungg

spend *(v.)* အသုံးပြုသည် aasonepyusai

spendthrift *(n.)* လက်ဖွာသူ laat hpwarsuu

sperm *(n.)* သုက် sote

sphere *(n.)* စက်လုံး saatlone

spherical *(adj.)* လုံးသော lonesaw

spice *(v.)* **အမွှေးအကြိုင်ခတ်သည်** a hmway a kyaine-hkaatsai
spice *(n.)* **ဟင်းခတ်အမွှေးအကြိုင်** hinn hkaat a hmway a kyaine
spicy *(adj.)* **စပ်သော၊ အမွှေးအကြိုင်ကဲသော** sat saw, a hmway a kyaine kellsaw
spider *(n.)* **ပင့်ကူ** pintkuu
spike *(v.)* **ငြောင့်စူးသည်** ngyawnt suusai
spike *(n.)* **ငြောင့်** ngyount
spill *(n.)* **လွင့်စဉ်ခြင်း** lwint sinchinn
spill *(v.)* **ဖိတ်သည်** hpate-sai
spin *(n.)* **အလှည့်၊ အမွေ့** a hlae, aa-mwae
spin *(v.)* **လှည့်သည်** hlae sai
spinach *(n.)* **ဒေါက်ခွ** douth-kwa
spinal *(adj.)* **ကျောရိုး** kyawwroe
spindle *(n.)* **ဗိုင်းလိပ်တံ** bine late-tan
spine *(n.)* **ကျောရိုး** kyawwroe
spinner *(n.)* **လှည့်စက်** lha ny hcaat
spinster *(n.)* **အပျိုဟိုင်း** aa-pyohine
spiral *(adj.)* **ရစ်ပတ်နွယ်တက်သော** rit-paat nwal taatsaw
spiral *(n.)* **ရစ်ပတ်ပြေးသည့် မျဉ်း** rit paat pyaysaeet myin
spirit *(n.)* **စိတ်၊ ဝိညာဉ်** sate , winyin
spirited *(adj.)* **မာန်ပါသော** man parsaw
spiritual *(adj.)* **စိတ်ပိုင်းဆိုင်ရာ** satepinesinerar
spiritualism *(n.)* **လိပ်ပြာခေါ်ခြင်း** late-pyaar hkawchinn
spiritualist *(n.)* **မှော်ဆရာ** mhaawsarar
spirituality *(n.)* **ယုံကြည်သက်ဝင်မှု** yonekyi saatwinmhu
spit *(n.)* **တံတွေး** tantway
spit *(v.)* **ထွေးထုတ်သည်** htway htotesai
spite *(n.)* **မလိုမုန်းထားစိတ်** ma lo mone htarrsate
spittle *(n.)* **တံတွေး** tantway
spittoon *(n.)* **ထွေးခံ** htway-hkan
splash *(n.)* **ဗွမ်းခနဲ မြည်သံ** bwam hka-nell myisan
splash *(v.)* **ပက်သည်၊ ဖျန်းသည်** paat sai, hpyannsai
spleen *(n.)* **သရက်ရွက်** sa raatrwat
splendid *(adj.)* **ရှုမောဖွယ်ရာ** shumawhpwalrar
splendour *(n.)* **သားနားမှု၊ ထည်ဝါမှု** sarr narr mhu , htai warmhu
splinter *(v.)* **အပိုင်းပိုင်းအစစ ကွဲသည်** aapine pine a sa-sa-kwalsai
splinter *(n.)* **ပဲ့ထွက်သော အစ** paehtwatsaw aa-sa
split *(n.)* **ခွဲထွက်ခြင်း** hkwal-twatchinn
split *(v.)* **အုပ်စုခွဲသည်** aotesuhkwalsai
spoil *(v.)* **ပျက်စီးစေသည်** pyetseesaysai
spoke *(n.)* **စပုတ်တိုင်** sa pote-tine
spokesman *(n.)* **ပြောရေးဆိုခွင့်ရှိသူ** pyaww-rayysohkwinshisuu
sponge *(v.)* **ရေဖတ်တိုက်သည်** ray hpaat titesai
sponge *(n.)* **ရေမြှုပ်** ray myote
sponsor *(v.)* **ထောက်ပံ့လှူဒါန်းသည်** htout-pan hlauudarannsai
sponsor *(n.)* **စပွန်ဆာပေးသူ** sapwansar payysuu
spontaneity *(n.)* **အလိုအလျောက်သဘောသက်ဝင်ခြင်း** aaloaalyawwat sabhaw saatwinchinn
spontaneous *(adj.)* **အလိုအလျောက်ဖြစ်သော** aaloaalyawwathpyitsaw
spoon *(n.)* **ဇွန်း** zwann

spoonful *(n.)* တစ်ဇွန်းစာ ta zwann-sar

sporadic *(adj.)* ပြတ်တောင်းပြတ်တောင်း pyat taungg pyattaungg

sport *(v.)* ဆင်မြန်းသည်၊ မွေးထားသည် sin myan sai , mway-htarrsai

sport *(n.)* အားကစား aarrkasarr

sportive *(adj.)* အားကစားစိတ်ဝင်စားသော aarrkahcarr hcatewainhcarrsaw

sportsman *(n.)* အားကစားသမား aarrkasarrsamarr

spot *(v.)* ရှာတွေ့သည်၊ ရိပ်စားမိသည် shar twae sai , rate sarr mi-sai

spot *(n.)* အပြောက် aapyawt

spotless *(adj.)* သပ်ရပ်သန့်ရှင်းသော sat rat saant shinn-saw

spotlight *(n.)* မီးမောင်း mee-maungg

spousal *(adj.)* လက်ထပ်ခြင်းနှင့် ဆိုင်သော laathtauthkyinnnhang sinesaw

spouse *(n.)* လင် သို့မဟုတ် မယား lin thoetmahote mayarr

spout *(v.)* ငေါက်ကနဲ ပန်းထွက်သည် ngout ka-nell paann htwatsai

spout *(n.)* နှုတ်သီး၊ ရေပန်း note see, ray-paann

sprain *(n.)* အဆစ်လွဲခြင်း aa-sit-lwal-chinn

spray *(v.)* မှုတ်သည်၊ ဖျန်းသည် mote sai, hpyann-sai

spray *(n.)* အခက်၊ ရေမှုန်ရေမွှား aah-kaat, ray hmone ray mwhar

spread *(n.)* ဖြန့်ကားနိုင်သော အတိုင်းအတာ hpya ant karrninesaw aatineaatar

spread *(v.)* သုတ်သည်၊ ခင်းသည် sote sai , hkinnsai

spree *(n.)* စိတ်လွတ်လက်လွတ် ပြုမူခြင်း sate lwatlaatlwat pyumuuchinn

sprig *(n.)* အခက် aahkaat

sprightly *(adj.)* သန်မြင်သော saan myinsaw

spring *(n.)* စမ်း၊ ပြန်ကန်နိုင်သော သတ္တု၊ စပရိန် sam , pyan kaanninesaw satti , sprein

spring *(v.)* လွှားခနဲ ခုန်သည် lwhar hkanell hkonesai

sprinkle *(v.)* ဖျန်းသည်၊ ဖြူးသည် hpyann sai, hpyuu-sai

sprint *(n.)* တာတိုပြေးပွဲ tar topyaypwal

sprint *(v.)* တာတိုပြေးသည် tar to pyaysai

sprout *(n.)* အစို့အညှောက် a shoet a nyaut

sprout *(v.)* အစို့အညှောက်ထွက်သည် a shoet a nyaut htwatsai

spur *(v.)* ဖနောင့်သံဆူး hpa naut sansuu

spur *(n.)* ဖနောင့်သံဆူး၊ တွန်းအား hpa naut san suu, twann-aarr

spurious *(adj.)* အတုအယောင် aa-tu-aa-yaung

spurn *(v.)* ပစ်ပစ်ခါခါငြင်းသည် pyit-pyit hkar hkar ngyinn-sai

spurt *(n.)* ငေါက်ကနဲ ပန်းထွက်သည် ngout kanell paann htwatsai

spurt *(v.)* ပန်းထွက်သည် paann htwatsai

sputnik *(n.)* လူလုပ်ဂြိုလ်တု luu lote gyaoltu

sputum *(n.)* သလိပ် salate

spy *(v.)* သူလျှိုလုပ်သည် suusholotesai

spy *(n.)* သူလျှို suusho

squad *(n.)* အငယ်ဆုံးအဖွဲ့၊ တပ်ဖွဲ့ငယ် aangaalsone aahpwal , tauthpwalngaal

squadron *(n.)* လေယာဉ်အုပ် lay yin-ote

squalid *(adj.)* ပေရစုတ်ချာသော pay ra sote chaarsaw

squalor *(n.)* ဆင်းရဲနွံ့ချာခြင်း sinnrell none chaarchinn

squander *(v.)* ဖြုန်းတီးသည် hpyone tee-sai

square *(v.)* ကျင်တွက်ကိုက်လုပ်သည် kyin twat kitelote-sai

square *(n.)* စတုရန်း saturaann

squash *(n.)* ငါးပိသိပ်ငါချဉ်သိပ် ngarrpi seik ngar chainseik

squash *(v.)* ဖိခြေသည် hpi chaysai

squat *(v.)* ဆောင့်ကြောင့်ထိုင်သည် saw int kyount htinesai

squeak *(n.)* ကျွီခနဲ မြည်သံ kyai hkanell myisan

squeeze *(v.)* ဖျစ်သည်၊ ညစ်သည် hpyit sai , nyaitsai

squint *(n.)* မျက်စိစွေခြင်း myetsi swaychinn

squint *(v.)* မျက်စိမှေး၍ ကြည့်သည် myetsi mhaayy kyanysai

squire *(n.)* လူကုံထံ luu konehtan

squirrel *(n.)* ရှဉ့် shint

stab *(n.)* ဓားထိုးမှု dharr htoemhu

stab *(v.)* ထိုးသည် htoesai

stability *(n.)* တည်ငြိမ်မှု tingyaainmhu

stabilization *(n.)* တည်ငြိမ်ခြင်း tingyaainchinn

stabilize *(v.)* တည်ငြိမ်သည် tingyaainsai

stable *(v.)* ထားသည် htarrsai

stable *(adj.)* တည်ငြိမ်သော tingyaainsaw

stadium *(n.)* အားကစားရုံ aarrkasarrrone

staff *(v.)* အမှုထမ်းခန့်အပ်သည် aamhuhtam hkaant atsai

staff *(n.)* ဝန်ထမ်း waanhtam

stag *(n.)* ဒရယ်ဖို da-raahpo

stage *(v.)* ပြဇာတ်တင်ဆက်သည် pyajarattinsaatsai

stage *(n.)* ဇာတ်စင် zatsin

stagger *(n.)* ဒယီးဒယိုင်ရွေ့လျားခြင်း d yee d yine rwaelyarrhkyinn

stagger *(v.)* ယိမ်းထိုးလျှောက်သည် yaim htoe shoutsai

stagnant *(adj.)* ရေသေ raysay

stagnate *(v.)* တန့်သည်၊ အိုသည် tant sai, aesai

stagnation *(n.)* တိုးတက်မှု ဆိတ်သုဉ်းခြင်း toetaatmhu sate suinchinn

staid *(adj.)* ဣန္ဒြေတင်းလွန်းသော eain dyay tinn lwannsaw

stain *(v.)* စွန်းထင်းသည် swann htinnsai

stain *(n.)* အစွန်းအထင်း aaswann aahtinn

stainless *(adj.)* အစွန်းခံ aaswannhkan

stair *(n.)* လှေကား hlaaykarr

staircase *(n.)* လှေကားအုံ hlaaykarraone

stake *(v.)* လောင်းကြေးထပ်သည်၊ တိုင်၊ ငုတ်ဖြင့် ထောက်မပေးသည် launggkyay htat sai, tine, ngotehpyint htout mapayysai

stake *(n.)* တိုင်၊ လောင်းကြေး tine , launggkyay

stale *(v.)* ဆီချေးစော်နံသော se hkyaayy hcaw nansaw

stale *(adj.)* ဆီချေးစော်နံသော se chaayy saw nansaw

stalemate *(n.)* မတိုးသာမဆုတ်သာ အခြေအနေ ma toe sar masotesar aachayaanay

stalk *(v.)* တရွေ့ရွေ့ချဉ်းကပ်သည် tarwaerwae chain kautsai

stalk *(n.)* ညှာတံ nyhartan

stall *(v.)* ရှတ်တရက် သေသည် rotetaraat saysai

stall *(n.)* ဆိုင်ခန်းငယ် sinehkaannngaal

stallion *(n.)* မြင်းလား myinnlarr

stalwart *(n.)* အားထားရသူ aarr htarr rasuu

stamina *(n.)* ခံနိုင်ရည် hkanninerai

stammer *(n.)* စကားထစ်ခြင်း sakarr htaitchinn

stamp *(v.)* ခြေဆောင့်နင်းသည် chay saw int nainnsai

stamp *(n.)* တံဆိပ်ခေါင်း tanseikhkaungg

stampede *(v.)* လှန့်သည် hlantsai

stampede *(n.)* ကမ္ဘူးရှူးထိုးထပြေးခြင်း ka muu shuu htoe hta pyaychinn

stand *(n.)* ရပ်တည်ချက်၊ စင် rattaichet, sin

stand *(v.)* ရပ်သည်၊ ထောင်သည်၊ မူတည်သည် rat sai, htaung sai , muu-tai-sai

standard *(adj.)* စံဖြစ်သော၊ စံပြု san hpyit-saw, sanpyu

standard *(n.)* အဆင့်အတန်း၊ စံချိန် aa-sint aa-taann, san-chane

standardization *(n.)* စံညွှန်းထားရှိခြင်း san nyun htarr-shi-chinn

standardize *(v.)* စံသတ်မှတ်သည် sansaatmhaatsai

standing *(n.)* အဆင့်အတန်း၊ သက်တမ်း aasint aataann , saattam

standpoint *(n.)* ရှုထောင့် shu htaung

standstill *(n.)* လုံးဝဥဿုံရပ်ခြင်း lonew oak-tone ratchinn

stanza *(n.)* ကဗျာတစ်ပိုဒ် ka-byaar ta-pote

staple *(v.)* ချုပ်စက်ဖြင့် တွဲသည် chote saathpyint twalsai

staple *(n.)* ချုပ်စက် chotesaat

star *(v.)* ကြယ်ပွင့်ပြသည် kyaal pw intpyasai

star *(n.)* ကြယ် kyaal

starch *(v.)* ကော်တင်သည် kawtinsai

starch *(n.)* ကစီဓာတ် ka se-dhrat

stardom *(n.)* လူထုအသည်းစွဲ luu-htu-aa-see-swal

stare *(n.)* စိုက်ကြည့်ခြင်း site kyany-chinn

stare *(v.)* စိုက်ကြည့်သည် site kyi-sai

stark *(adj.)* အရှိအရှိအတိုင်းဖြစ်သော a shi aa-shi-aa-tine-hpyitsaw

stark *(adv.)* သိသိသာသာ si-si-sar-sar

starry *(adj.)* ကြယ်လင်းလက်သော kyaal-linn-laat-sai

start *(n.)* အစ၊ စတင်ခြင်း a sa , sa-tin-chinn

start *(v.)* စတင်သည် satinsai

startle *(v.)* လန့်စေသည်၊ လှန့်သည် lant saysai , hlant-sai

starvation *(n.)* ငတ်မွတ်ခြင်း ngaattmwat-chinn

starve *(v.)* ငတ်မွတ်သည် ngaat mwatsai

state *(v.)* အဆိုရှိသည် a soshisai

state *(n.)* နိုင်ငံ၊ အစိုးရ nine-ngan , aa-soe-ra

stateliness *(n.)* ခံ့ညားထည်ဝါမှု hkan nyarr htai warmhu

stately *(adj.)* ခံ့ညားသော hkan nyarrsaw

statement *(n.)* ထုတ်ပြန်ချက် htotepyanchet

statesman *(n.)* နိုင်ငံရေးသမား ninengan-rayysamarr

statewide *(adj.)* ပြည်နယ်တစ်ခုလုံးကို သက်ရောက်သော pyinaaltaithkuloneko saatroutsaw

static *(adj.)* တည်ငြိမ်သော tingyaainsaw

statics *(n.)* စတက်တစ်ပညာ sa taat tait-panyar

station *(v.)* နေရာချထားသည် nayrarchahtarrsai

stationary *(adj.)* ရပ်နေသော၊ ပုံသေ rat naysaw , ponesay

stationer *(n.)* စာရေးကိရိယာဆိုင်ရှင် sarrayyka-ri-yarsine-shin

stationery *(n.)* **စာရေးကိရိယာ** sarrayyka-ri-yar
statistical *(adj.)* **ကိန်းဂဏာန်းအချက်အလက်** kein ganarannaachetaalaat
statistician *(n.)* **စာရင်းအင်းပညာရှင်** sarrinnaainnpanyar-shin
statistics *(n.)* **ကိန်းဂဏာန်း** keinganarann
statue *(n.)* **ရုပ်ထု** rotehtu
stature *(n.)* **အရပ်အမောင်း** aa-rat-aa-maung
status *(n.)* **အဆင့်အတန်း** aa-sint-aa-taann
statute *(n.)* **ဥပဒေ** u-paday
statutory *(adj.)* **ပြဋ္ဌာန်းဥပဒေအရ** pyahtann u-paday aa-ra
staunch *(adj.)* **မြဲစွဲစွာ အားကိုးထိုက်သော** myaell swalswar aarrkoehtitesaw
stay *(n.)* **အလည်အပတ်၊ ညအိပ်ခြင်း** aalaiaapaat , nyaainchinn
stay *(v.)* **နေသည်** naysai
steadfast *(adj.)* **တည်မြဲသော** taimyaellsaw
steadiness *(n.)* **မှန်မှန်** mhaanmhaan
steady *(v.)* **တည်ငြိမ်သည်၊ ထိန်းထိန်းသိမ်းသိမ်းရှိသည်** tingyaain sai , htein hteinsaim saimshisai
steady *(adj.)* **တည်ငြိမ်သော၊ ပုံမှန်** tingyaainsaw , ponemhaan
steal *(v.)* **ခိုးသည်** hkoesai
stealthily *(adv.)* **ခိုးကြောင်ခိုးဝှက်** hkoe kyaung hkoewhaat
steam *(v.)* **ကျိုက်ကျိုက်ဆူနေသည်** kyaite kyaite suunaysai
steamer *(n.)* **မီးသင်္ဘော၊ ပေါင်းအိုး** mee sinbhaw , paungg-oe
steed *(n.)* **မြင်း** myinn
steel *(n.)* **သံမဏိ** sanmani
steep *(v.)* **စိမ်သည်** sinsai
steep *(adj.)* **မတ်စောက်သော** maat sout-saw
steeple *(n.)* **ဘုရားရှိခိုးကျောင်းမျှော်စင်** pha-rarrshihkoekyaungg-myaw-sin
steer *(v.)* **ဦးတည်သွားသည်** u taiswarrsai
stellar *(adj.)* **ကြယ်ကဲ့သို့သော** kyaalkaethoetsaw
stem *(v.)* **တိတ်အောင် လုပ်သည်** tate-aung lotesai
stem *(n.)* **ပင်စည်၊ ရိုးတံ** pin se , roetan
stench *(n.)* **အနံ့ဆိုး** aanansoe
stencil *(v.)* **ပုံဖော်သည်** ponehpawsai
stencil *(n.)* **ပန်းဖောက်ပြား** paann hpoutpyarr
stenographer *(n.)* **လက်ရေးတိုလက်နှိပ်စက်** laat-rayy to laatnatesaat
stenography *(n.)* **လက်ရေးတို** laatrayyto
step *(v.)* **လှမ်းသည်** hlamsai
step *(n.)* **ခြေလှမ်း** chayhlam
steppe *(n.)* **မြက်ခင်းလွင်ပြင်** myaat hkinnlwinpyin
stereotype *(v.)* **ပုံသေသတ်မှတ် မြင်သည်** pone saysaatmhaat myinsai
stereotype *(n.)* **ပုံသေကားကျပုံစံ** pone say karr kya
stereotyped *(adj.)* **ပုံသေကားကျ ပုံသွင်းထားသော** pone-say karrkya pone swin-htarrsaw
sterile *(adj.)* **မြုံသော** myone-saw
sterility *(n.)* **မျိုးကန်းခြင်း** myoe kaannchinn
sterilization *(n.)* **သားကြောဖြတ်ခြင်း၊ ပိုးသတ်ခြင်း** sarr kyaww hpyat chinn , poe saatchinn

sterilize *(v.)* **သားကြောဖြတ်သည်၊ ပိုးသတ်သည်** sarr kyaww hpyat sai , poe saatsai
sterling *(n.)* **ပေါင်** paung
sterling *(adj.)* **ပြောင်မြောက်သော** pyaung-myawt-saw
stern *(n.)* **ပဲ့** pae
stern *(adj.)* **တင်းမာသော၊ ပြင်းထန်သော** tinnmar saw , pyinn-htaansaw
steroid *(n.)* **စတီးရွိုက်ဟော်မုန်း** sa tee write-hawmone
stethoscope *(n.)* **နားကြပ်** narr-kyaut
stew *(v.)* **ပြုတ်ချက်ချက်သည်** pyuat chet chetsai
stew *(n.)* **ပြတ်ချက်** pyatchet
steward *(n.)* **သဘော်စားပွဲထိုး၊ ပစ္စည်းထိန်း၊ ကြီးကြပ်သူ၊ ရိက္ခာမှူး** sinbhaw sarrpwahltoe , pyit-saee htein , kyeekyaut suu , rikhkarmhauu
stick *(v.)* **ထိုးသည်၊ စိုက်သည်** htoe sai , sitesai
stick *(n.)* **တုတ်ချောင်း** totechaungg
sticker *(n.)* **စတစ်ကာ** sataitkar
stickler *(n.)* **စည်းကမ်းကလနားကြီးသူ** see-kam ka la narr kyeesuu
sticky *(n.)* **စေးကပ်သော** sayy kautsaw
stiff *(n.)* **လူသေကောင်** luu saykaung
stiffen *(v.)* **တောင့်သည်၊ မာသည်** taunt sai , marsai
stifle *(v.)* **ငြိမ်းသတ်သည်** ngyeim saatsai
stigma *(n.)* **အမည်းစက်** aa-maeesaat
still *(adv.)* **ငြိမ်ငြိမ်သက်သက်** ngyein ngyein-saat-saat
still *(adj.)* **ငြိမ်သော** ngyein-saw
stillness *(n.)* **ငြိမ်ခြင်း** ngyein-chinn
stilt *(n.)* **ကုလားမခြေထောက်** ka-larr-machayhtout
stimulant *(n.)* **အားတက်စေသော အရာ** aarr-taatsaysaw aarar
stimulate *(v.)* **တက်ကြွလာစေသည်** taatkya larsaysai
stimulus *(n.)* **လှုံ့ဆော်ပေးသည့်အရာ** hlont saw payy seet aarar
sting *(n.)* **အဆိပ်ဆူး၊ စပ်ဖျဉ်းဖျဉ်းဖြစ်ခြင်း၊ နာခြင်း** aaseik suu , sat hpyain hpyain hpyitchinn , narchinn
sting *(v.)* **စူးသည်၊ နာကျင်စေသည်** suu sai , narkyinsaysai
stingy *(adj.)* **ကပ်စေးနည်းသော** kat sayy naeesaw
stink *(n.)* **အပုပ်နံ့** a pote-nan
stink *(v.)* **ပုပ်စော်နံသည်** pote-saw nan-sai
stipend *(n.)* **ထောက်ပံ့ကြေးငွေ** htout-pankyay-ngway
stipulate *(v.)* **စည်းကမ်းထားသည်၊ သတ်မှတ်သည်** seekam htarr-sai , saatmhaatsai
stipulation *(n.)* **ပြဋ္ဌာန်းချက်၊ သတ်မှတ်ချက်** pya-htarannchet , saatmhaatchet
stir *(v.)* **မွှေသည်** mwhaay sai
stirrup *(n.)* **ခြေနင်းကွင်း** chay nainnkwin
stitch *(v.)* **ချုပ်သည်၊ သီသည်** chote sai , se-sai
stitch *(n.)* **ချုပ်ခြင်း၊ သီခြင်း** chote chinn , sechinn
stock *(v.)* **တင်သည်** tinsai
stock *(n.)* **ကုန်စည်ပစ္စည်း** konesaipyit-see
stocking *(n.)* **ခြေအိတ်ရှည်** chay aateshay
stoic *(n.)* **လောကဓံတရားကို ကြံ့ကြံ့ခံနိုင်သူ** law-ka-dhan-ta-rarr-ko kyan-kyaanhkan ninesuu
stoke *(v.)* **မီးထိုးသည်** mee htoesai

stoker *(n.)* မီးထိုးသမား mee htoesamarr

stomach *(v.)* သည်းညည်းခံသည်၊ စိတ်ရှည်သည် see nyee hkan sai , sateshi sai

stomach *(n.)* အစာအိမ်၊ ဗိုက် aa-saraain , bite

stone *(v.)* ခဲနှင့် ပေါက်သတ်သည် hkell-nint pout saatsai

stone *(n.)* ကျောက်တုံး kyawt-tone

stony *(adj.)* ကျောက်ခဲထူထပ်သော kyawt-hkell htuu-htat-saw

stool *(n.)* ခွေးခြေ၊ မစင် hkway-chay , masin

stoop *(n.)* ခါးကိုင်းခြင်း hkarr kinechinn

stoop *(v.)* ငုံ့သည်၊ ကိုင်းသည် ngone sai , kinesai

stop *(n.)* မှတ်တိုင်၊ ရပ်တန့်ခြင်း mhaattine , rat-tantchinn

stop *(v.)* ရပ်တန့်သည် rat-tantsai

stoppage *(n.)* သပိတ်မှောက်ခြင်း sapatemhaoutchinn

storage *(n.)* သိုလှောင်မှု so-hlaungmhu

store *(v.)* သိုလှောင်သည် so-hlaungsai

store *(n.)* သိုလှောင်ထားသည့် အရာ so-hlaung-htarr-seet aarar

storey *(n.)* အထပ်၊ အဆင့် a htat , aa-sint

stork *(n.)* ငှက်ကျား ngat-kyarr

storm *(v.)* ဒေါသူပုန်ထသည် daw suuponehtasai

storm *(n.)* မုန်တိုင်း monetine

stormy *(adj.)* မုန်တိုင်းထန်သော monetine htaansaw

story *(n.)* ဇာတ်လမ်း၊ ပုံပြင် zat-lam , ponepyin

stout *(adj.)* ခိုင်ခံ့သော၊ တုတ်ခိုင်သော hkine hkan saw, tote hkinesaw

stove *(n.)* မီးဖို mee-hpo

stow *(v.)* ကောင်းမွန်သေသပ်စွာ ထားသိုသည် kaung-mon say satswar htarr sosai

straggle *(v.)* ဖရိုဖရဲ ပြန့်ကျဲနေသည် hparohparell pyant kyaellnaysai

straggler *(n.)* နောက်ကျန်ရစ်သူ noutkyaanraitsuu

straight *(adv.)* ဖြောင့်ဖြောင့်တန်းတန်း hpyaunt hpyunt taanntaann

straight *(adj.)* ဖြောင့်တန်းသော hpyaunt taannsaw

straighten *(v.)* ဖြောင့်သည် hpyauntsai

straightforward *(adj.)* ဖြောင့်မတ်သော hpyaunt maatsaw

straightway *(adv.)* လမ်းအတည့် lam a taeet

strain *(n.)* ပင်ပန်းမှုဒဏ်၊ ဝန်ပိခြင်း၊ အားအင်ကုန်ခမ်းခြင်း pinpaann mhu dan , waan pi chinn , aarr in kone hkamchinn

strain *(v.)* အားစိုက်သည်၊ တင်းမာစေသည် aarr site sai , tinnmarsaysai

strait *(n.)* ရေလက်ကြား raylaatkyarr

straiten *(v.)* ဆင်းရဲနွမ်းပါးသည် sinnrellnwmparrsai

strand *(n.)* ကမ်းနား kamnarr

strand *(v.)* သောင်တင်သည် saungtinsai

strange *(adj.)* ထူးဆန်းသော htuusaannsaw

stranger *(n.)* လူစိမ်း luu-saim

strangle *(v.)* လည်ညှစ်သတ်သည်၊ လည်ပင်းအစ်သည် lai nyit saat sai , laipinn aaitsai

strangulation *(n.)* ညှစ်ထားခြင်း၊ nyit htarrchinn

strap *(v.)* တုတ်နှောင်သည် tote nhaawinsai

strap *(n.)* လက်ပတ်ကြိုး laatpaatkyoe

stratagem *(n.)* ပရိယာယ် pa-ri-yal

strategic *(adj.)* **မဟာဗျူဟာ** maharbyuuhar
strategist *(n.)* **မဟာဗျူဟာမြောက် တွေးခေါ်သူ** maharbyauuharmyawt tway hkawsuu
strategy *(n.)* **မဟာဗျူဟာ** maharbyauuhar
stratum *(n.)* **အလွှာ** aalwhar
straw *(n.)* **ကောက်ရိုး** kout-roe
strawberry *(n.)* **စတော်ဘယ်ရီ** sa-tawbhaal-re
stray *(adj.)* **လေလွင့်နေသော** lay lw intnaysaw
stray *(v.)* **လေလွင့်သည်၊ လမ်းလွဲသည်၊ စိတ်ကစားသည်** lay-lwint sai , lam lwal sai , sate kasarrsai
stream *(v.)* **အဆက်မပြတ်စီးဆင်းသည်** aa-saatmapyat seesinnsai
stream *(n.)* **စမ်းချောင်း** samchaungg
streamer *(n.)* **ကုက္ကား** kukkarr
streamlet *(n.)* **ချောင်းငယ်** hkyaunggngaal
street *(n.)* **လမ်း** lam
strength *(n.)* **ခွန်အား** hkwan-aarr
strengthen *(v.)* **အားကောင်းလာသည်** aarrkaungglarsai
strenuous *(adj.)* **ပင်ပန်းရသော** pinpaannrasaw
stress *(v.)* **အရေးစိုက်သည်၊ ဖိရွတ်သည်** aa-rayy site sai , hpi rwat-sai
stress *(n.)* **ဖိစီးမှု** hpi see-mhu
stretch *(n.)* **တစ်ကျော့၊ တစ်ကန့်** ta-kyaww , ta-kaant
stretch *(v.)* **ဆွဲသည်၊ ဆန့်သည်** swal sai , santsai
stretcher *(n.)* **လူနာတင်ထမ်းစင်** luu nar tin htamsin
strew *(v.)* **ပြန့်ကျဲနေသည်၊ ဖြန့်သည်** pyant kyaell naysai , hpyantsai
strict *(adj.)* **တင်းကျပ်သော** tinn-kyatsaw
stricture *(n.)* **ပြစ်တင်ရှုတ်ချခြင်း** pyittin shotechachinn
stride *(n.)* **ခြေလှမ်းကျဲ** chayhlamkyaell
stride *(v.)* **ခြေလှမ်းကျဲကျဲ လျှောက်သည်** chayhlam kyaellkyaell shoutsai
strident *(adj.)* **နားငြီးစရာ၊ ကြားပြင်းကတ်စရာကောင်းသော** narr ngyee sarar , kyarr pyinn kaat sararkaunggsaw
strife *(n.)* **ခိုက်ရန်ဒေါသ** hkiteraandawsa
strike *(n.)* **သပိတ်မှောက်ခြင်း** sapatemhaoutchinn
striker *(n.)* **သပိတ်မှောက်သူ** sapatemhaoutsuu
string *(v.)* **ဆွဲသည်၊ သွယ်သည်** swal sai , swalsai
string *(n.)* **ကြိုး** kyoe
stringency *(n.)* **ကျပ်တည်းမှု** kyat teemhu
stringent *(adj.)* **တင်းကျပ်သော** tinnkyatsaw
strip *(v.)* **ခွာသည်၊ ချွတ်သည်** hkwar sai , chwatsai
strip *(n.)* **ဗလာကျင်းခြင်း** balar kyinn-chinn
stripe *(v.)* **အရောင်တစ်ခု၏ ရှည်လျားသော အပိုင်း** aaraungtaithkueat shilyarrsaw aapine
stripe *(n.)* **အစင်း၊ အရေးအကြောင်း** a sinn , aa-rayy-aa-kyaung
strive *(v.)* **ကြိုးပမ်းသည်** kyoe-pam-sai
stroke *(v.)* **ပွတ်သပ်ပေးသည်၊ ရိုက်သည်** pwat sat payysai , ritesai
stroke *(n.)* **ရိုက်ချက်၊ ပွတ်သပ်ခြင်း၊** ritechet , pwat sat chinn

stroll *(n.)* အပန်းဖြေလမ်းလျှောက်ခြင်း aa-paannhpyay lamshoutchinn

stroll *(v.)* အေးအေးလူလူ လမ်းလျှောက်သည် aye-aayy-luuluu lamshoutsai

strong *(adj.)* သန်မာသော saan marsaw

stronghold *(n.)* အမာခံနယ်မြေ aa-marhkannaalmyay

structural *(adj.)* ဖွဲ့စည်းတည်ဆောက်ပုံနှင့်ဆိုင်သော hpwal-see taisout pone nintsinesaw

structure *(n.)* ဖွဲ့စည်းပုံ၊ အဆောက်အအုံ hpwal-see-pone , aa-sout-aa-ohn

struggle *(n.)* ရုန်းကန်ခြင်း ronekaanchinn

struggle *(v.)* ရုန်းကန်သည် ronekaansai

strumpet *(n.)* ပြည့်တန်ဆာမ pyi taansarma

strut *(n.)* ကျား၊ ဒေါက် kyarr , dout

strut *(v.)* ဟန်ပါပါ လျှောက်သည် haan parpar shoutsai

stub *(n.)* အငုတ်၊ ငုတ်တို a ngote , ngote-to

stubble *(n.)* ရိုးပြတ် roepyat

stubborn *(adj.)* ခေါင်းမာသော hkaung-mar-saw

stud *(v.)* စီခြယ်သည် se chaalsai

stud *(n.)* နားကပ်၊ နှိပ်ကြယ်သီး narr kat , nate-kyaal-see

student *(n.)* ကျောင်းသား kyaunggsarr

studio *(n.)* စတူဒီယို satuudeyo

studious *(adj.)* ကြိုးစားသော kyoesarrsaw

study *(n.)* လေ့လာချက်၊ လေ့လာခြင်း laelarchet , laelarchinn

study *(v.)* လေ့လာသည်၊ သင်ယူသည် laelar sai , sinyuusai

stuff *(v.)* ပြည့်ကျပ်နေသည် pyae kyatnaysai

stuff *(n.)* ပစ္စည်း၊ အရာ၊ အစွမ်းအစ pyit-see , a rar , aaswm aa-sa

stuffy *(adj.)* လှောင်သော၊ မွန်းသော hlaung saw , mwann-saw

stumble *(n.)* ခလုတ်တိုက်ခြင်း hka-lote titechinn

stumble *(v.)* ခလုတ်တိုက်သည် hkalote titesai

stump *(v.)* အခက်တွေ့သည်၊ သစ်ငုတ်တို aa-hkaat-twae sai , sit ngote-to

stump *(n.)* သစ်ငုတ်တို sit ngote-to

stun *(v.)* မူးမေ့သတိလစ်သွားစေသည် muu mae satilait swarrsaysai

stunt *(n.)* ထွင်လုံး၊ စတန့် htwin lone , sa tant

stunt *(v.)* ကြီးထွားနှုန်းကို တန့်စေသည် kyee-htwarr hnoneko tant-saysai

stupefy *(v.)* အံ့သြတုန်လှုပ်သည်၊ ထုံထိုင်းတွေဝေသွားသည် ant aw tonehlote sai , htone htine twaywayswarrsai

stupendous *(adj.)* ကြောက်ခမန်းလိလိ၊ အံ့မခန်းဖွယ်ရာ kyawt-hka-maann-lili , ant-ma-hkan-hpwal-rar

stupid *(adj.)* ထုံထိုင်းသော၊ ညံ့ဖျင်းသော htone htine saw , nyan hpyinnsaw

stupidity *(n.)* မိုက်မဲမှု၊ ဆင်ခြင်ဉာဏ်မရှိမှု mite mell mhu , sinchin nyan mashimhu

sturdy *(adj.)* တောင့်သော၊ သန်သော tawnt saw , saansaw

sty *(n.)* မျက်စိစွန်ခြင်း myetsi-swanchinn

stye *(n.)* မျက်လုံးနားတဝိုက် ဘက်တီးရီးယားပိုးဝင်ခြင်း myetlone narrtawite bhaatteereeyarrpoewainhkyinn

style *(n.)* အမူအရာ၊ စတိုင် aamuuarar , satine

stylish *(adj.)* ခေတ်ဆန်သော၊ ဖက်ရှင်ကျသော hkit saan-saw , hpaathlyinkyasaw

subculture *(n.)* သီးခြားစရိုက်လူ့အဖွဲ့အစည်း see charr sa rite-hlu-aa-hpwal-aa-sae

subdivide *(v.)* ထပ်ဆင့်ပိုင်းခြားသည် htat sint pinecharrsai

subdue *(v.)* နှိမ်နင်းသည် nhaainnainnsai

subject *(adj.)* ဖွယ်ရှိသော hpwalshisaw

subject *(v.)* ခံစားစေသည် hkansarrsaysai

subjection *(n.)* အတိုက်အခိုက်ခံရခြင်း aa-tite-aa-hkite-hkan-ra-chinn

subjective *(adj.)* ဘက်လိုက်သော bhaatlitesaw

subjugate *(v.)* လက်အောက်ခံအဖြစ်သွတ်သွင်းသည် laataouthkan aahpyit swat swinsai

subjugation *(n.)* ဖိနှိပ်ချုပ်ချယ်ခြင်း hpinate chotechaalchinn

sublet *(v.)* တစ်ဆင့်ငှားသည် ta-sint ngar-sai

sublimate *(v.)* နူးညံ့သိမ်မွေ့စေသည် nuunyant sinmwaesaysai

sublime *(n.)* မြင့်မြတ်သည့် အရာ myint myatsaeet aarar

sublime *(adj.)* ရင်သပ်ရှုမောဖွယ်ရာ rinsat shumawhpwalrar

sublimity *(n.)* ထူးခြားမှု htuucharrmhu

submarine *(adj.)* ပင်လယ်ရေမျက်နှာပြင်အောက် pinlaalray myetnharpyinawt

submarine *(n.)* ရေငုတ်သင်္ဘော ray ngotesinbhaw

submerge *(v.)* မြှုပ်သည် myahuutsai

submission *(n.)* တင်ပြခြင်း tinpyachinn

submissive *(adj.)* နှိမ့်ချသော naimt chasaw

submit *(v.)* တင်ပြသည် tinpyasai

subordinate *(adj.)* နိမ့်သော naint saw

subordinate *(v.)* ဦးစားမပေး u sarr mapayy

subordination *(n.)* နာခံခြင်း၊ လိုက်နာခြင်း nar hkan chinn , litenarchinn

subscribe *(v.)* ပေးသွင်းသည်၊ မှာယူသည် payyswin sai , mhar yuusai

subscription *(n.)* အသင်းဝင်ကြေး၊ ပုံမှန်အလှူထည့်ဝင်ငွေ aasinnwin kyay , ponemhaan aahluu htaee-win-ngway

subsequent *(adj.)* နောက်ဆက်တွဲဖြစ်သော noutsaattwahlpyitsaw

subservience *(n.)* ခယဝယလုပ်ခြင်း hka ya wa yalotechinn

subservient *(adj.)* ခယဝပ်တွားသော hka ya wut twarrsaw

subside *(v.)* စဲသည်၊ လျော့ကျသွားသည် sell sai , lyaw-kya-swarr-sai

subsidiary *(adj.)* အကူအပံ့သဘောမျှသာဖြစ်သော aakuu-a-pant sabhaw myahasarhpyitsaw

subsidize *(v.)* ထောက်ပံ့ကြေးပေးသည် htoutpankyaypayysai

subsidy *(n.)* ထောက်ပံ့ငွေ htoutpanngway

subsist *(v.)* အသက်ရှင်နေသည် aa-saat-shin-naysai

subsistence *(n.)* အသက်ရှင်နေနိုင်မှု aa-saat-shin nayninemhu

substance *(n.)* အရာ၊ ဟာ၊ အခြေအမြစ် a rar , har , aachayaamyit

substantial *(adj.)* ကိုးလုံသော၊ မည်မည်ရရဖြစ်သော kone lone saw , mai mai ra ra-hpyitsaw

substantially *(adv.)* အများအပြား aa-myarr-aa-pyarr

substantiate *(v.)* သက်သေပြသည် saat-saypyasai

substantiation *(n.)* သက်သေပြခြင်း saatsay pyachinn

substitute *(v.)* အစားထိုးသည် aasarrhtoesai

substitute *(n.)* အစားထိုးသူ aasarrhtoesuu

substitution *(n.)* **အစားထိုးခြင်း** aasarrhtoechinn

subterranean *(adj.)* **မြေအောက်** myay-out

subtle *(adj.)* **သိမ်မွေ့သော** sin-mwae-saw

subtlety *(n.)* **သိမ်မွေ့နက်နဲခြင်း** sinmwae naat nellchinn

subtract *(v.)* **နုတ်သည်** notesai

subtraction *(n.)* **အနုတ်** aa-note

suburb *(n.)* **ဆင်ခြေဖုံး** sinchayhpone

suburban *(adj.)* **ဆင်ခြေဖုံး** sinchayhpone

subversion *(n.)* **ကူညီထောက်ပံ့ငွေ** kuu-nye-htout-pant-ngway

subversive *(adj.)* **အဖျက်အမှောင့်** a hpyet a mhaunt

subvert *(v.)* **ဖြိုဖျက်သည်** hpyo-hpyet-sai

succeed *(v.)* **အောင်မြင်သည်** aung-myin-sai

success *(n.)* **အောင်မြင်မှု** aung-myin-mhu

successful *(adj.)* **အောင်မြင်သော** aung-myin-saw

succession *(n.)* **တစ်ခုပြီး တစ်ခု** ta-hku-pyee ta-hku

successive *(adj.)* **ဆက်တိုက်** sat-tite

successor *(n.)* **ဆက်ခံသူ** saat-hkan-suu

succour *(v.)* **ရိုင်းပင်းကူညီသည်** rine-pinn-kuu-nye-sai

succour *(n.)* **ရိုင်းပင်းကူညီခြင်း** rine-pinn-kuu-nyechinn

succumb *(v.)* **မလွန်ဆန်နိုင်** ma-lwansaannine

such *(pron.)* **ဤသို့ပင်** i-thoet-pin

such *(adj.)* **ကဲ့သို့** kaeshoet

suck *(n.)* **စုပ်ခြင်း** sote-chinn

suck *(v.)* **စုပ်သည်** sote-sai

suckle *(v.)* **နို့တိုက်သည်** noe tite-sai

suckling *(n.)* **နို့တိုက်ခြင်း** noe tite-chinn

sudden *(n.)* **ရုတ်တရက်** rote-ta-raat

suddenly *(adv.)* **ရုတ်တရက်** rote-ta-raat

sue *(v.)* **တရားစွဲသည်** ta-rarrswalsai

suffer *(v.)* **ဝေဒနာခံစားရသည်** waydanarhkansarrrasai

suffice *(v.)* **လုံလောက်သည်** loneloutsai

sufficiency *(n.)* **ပြည့်စုံခြင်း** pyae sonechinn

sufficient *(adj.)* **လုံလောက်သော** loneloutsaw

suffix *(v.)* **နောက်မှ ဆက်သည်** noutmha saatsai

suffix *(n.)* **နောက်ဆက်** noutsaat

suffocate *(v.)* **မွမ်းကျပ်သည်** mwam kyatsai

suffocation *(n.)* **မွမ်းကျပ်ခြင်း** mwam kyat-chinn

suffrage *(n.)* **မဲပေးပိုင်ခွင့်** mell-payy pinehkwint

sugar *(v.)* **သကြားထည့်သည်** sa kyarr htae-sai

sugar *(n.)* **သကြား** sa-kyarr

suggest *(v.)* **အကြံပြုသည်** aakyaanpyusai

suggestion *(n.)* **အကြံပြုခြင်း** aakyaanpyuchinn

suggestive *(adj.)* **အရိပ်အမြွက်ပြသော** aa-rate-aa-myawt-pya-saw

suicidal *(adj.)* **မိမိကိုယ်ကို အဆုံးစီရင်လိုသည့် သဘောရှိသော** mimikoko aasoneserin losaeet sabhawshisaw

suicide *(n.)* **မိမိကိုယ်ကို အဆုံးစီရင်ခြင်း** mimikoko aasoneserinchinn

suit *(v.)* **သင့်လျော်သည်** sint lyawsai

suit *(n.)* **ဝတ်စုံ** waatsone

suitability *(n.)* **သင့်လျော်မှု** sint lyawmhu

suitable *(adj.)* သင့်လျော်သော sint lyawsaw
suite *(n.)* ဧည့်ခန်းပါဟိုတယ်ခန်း et hkan par hotaahlkaann
suitor *(n.)* ချစ်ရေးဆိုသူ chit ray so-suu
sullen *(adj.)* သုန်မှုန်နေသော sone-hmone-nay-saw
sulphur *(n.)* ဆာလ်ဖာ sarhlpar
sulphuric *(adj.)* ဆာလ်ဖာပါသော sarl hpar parsaw
sultry *(adj.)* အိုက်စပ်သော aite sat-saw
sum *(v.)* အကျဉ်းရုံးသည် aa-kyin ronesai
sum *(n.)* ငွေပေါင်း ngway-paung
summarily *(adv.)* အကျဉ်းချုပ်အားဖြင့် aa-kyin chote aarr-hpyint
summarize *(v.)* အကျဉ်းချုပ်သည် aa-kyin chote-sai
summary *(adj.)* အကျဉ်းချုပ် aa-kyin-chote
summary *(n.)* အကျဉ်းချုပ် aa-kyin-chote
summer *(n.)* နွေရာသီ nway-rar-se
summit *(n.)* ထိပ်သီးတွေ့ဆုံပွဲ hteikseetwaesonepwal
summon *(v.)* ဆင့်ခေါ်သည် sinthkawsai
summons *(n.)* ဆင့်ဆိုခြင်း sint sochinn
sumptuous *(adj.)* ခမ်းနားသော၊ ငွေကုန်ကြေးကျများသော hkam-narr-saw , ngwaykone kyay kyamyarrsaw
sun *(v.)* နေပူဆာလှုံသည် nay puu sar hlone-sai
sun *(n.)* နေ nay
sunburn *(n.)* နေလောင်ခြင်း nay-laungchinn
sundae *(n.)* သီးစုံရေခဲမုန့် see sone ray hkell mone
Sunday *(n.)* တနင်္ဂနွေ ta nin ga-nway
sunder *(v.)* ခွဲသည် hkwal-sai
sundry *(adj.)* အမျိုးမျိုး aa-myoe-myoe
sunlight *(n.)* နေရောင် nay-raung
sunny *(adj.)* နေသာသော nay-sar-saw
sunrise *(n.)* နေထွက်ချိန် nay-htwat-chane
sunset *(n.)* နေဝင်ချိန် nay-win-chane
sup *(n.)* တစ်ကျိုက် ta-kyaite
superabundance *(n.)* အလျှံပယ် a-shan-paal
superabundant *(adj.)* အလျှံပယ် a-shan-paal
superb *(adj.)* ထိပ်တန်း hteik-tan
superficial *(adj.)* အပေါ်ယံ aa-paw-yan
superficiality *(n.)* ပေါ့ပြက်ခြင်း pot pyaat-chinn
superfine *(adj.)* အလွန်နူးညံ့ချောမွတ်သော aa-lwan-nuu-nyan-chaw-mwat-saw
superfluity *(n.)* ပိုလျှံခြင်း po-shan-chinn
superfluous *(adj.)* မလိုလားအပ်သော malolarratsaw
superhuman *(adj.)* အာဂ aar-ga
superintend *(v.)* ကြီးကြပ်သည် kyeekyatsai
superintendence *(n.)* ကြီးကြပ်မှု kyeekyatmhu
superintendent *(n.)* ကြီးကြပ်သူ kyeekyatsuu
superior *(adj.)* သာလွန်သော sarlwansaw
superiority *(n.)* ပိုခြင်း၊ သာခြင်း po chinn , sarchinn
superlative *(adj.)* အသာလွန်ဆုံး a sarlwan-sone
superman *(n.)* စူပါမင်း၊ အာဂလူ suuparminn , aar-ga-luu
supernatural *(adj.)* သဘာဝလွန်ဖြစ်သော sabharwalwanhpyitsaw

supersede *(v.)* **အစားထိုးသည်** aasarr-htoe-sai
supersonic *(adj.)* **အသံထက်မြန်သော** aa-san-htat myansaw
superstition *(n.)* **အယူသီးခြင်း** a yuu seechinn
superstitious *(adj.)* **အယူသီးသော** a yuu seesaw
supertax *(n.)* **လက်ရှိမြင့်မားသော အခွန်နှုန်း** laatshi myint marrsaw aahkwannhuann
supervise *(v.)* **ကြီးကြပ်သည်** kyeekyatsai
supervision *(n.)* **ကြီးကြပ်မှု** kyeekyatmhu
supervisor *(n.)* **ကြီးကြပ်သူ** kyeekyatsuu
supper *(n.)* **ညလယ်စာ** nyalaalsar
supple *(adj.)* **ပျော့ပျောင်းသော** pyaww pyaunggsaw
supplement *(n.)* **ဖြည့်စွက်ချက်** hpya ny swatchet
supplementary *(adj.)* **နောက်ဆက်တွဲ** noutsaattwal
supplier *(n.)* **ထောက်ပံ့** htoutpan
supply *(n.)* **ပေးသွင်းခြင်း** payyswinchinn
supply *(v.)* **ထောက်ပံ့သည်** htoutpansai
support *(n.)* **ဝိုင်းဝန်းကူညီမှု** winewaannkuunyemhu
support *(v.)* **အားပေးသည်၊ ချီးမြှင့်သည်** aarr payysai , chaeemyintsai
suppose *(v.)* **ယူဆသည်** yuusasai
supposition *(n.)* **စိတ်မှန်းသက်သက်၊ ကိုထောက်၍** sate mhan saat-saat ko htout-ywe
suppress *(v.)* **နှိမ်နင်းသည်** nhin-ninn-sai
suppression *(n.)* **နှိမ်နှင်းခြင်း** nain-nhinn-chinn
supremacy *(n.)* **သာလွန်မှု** sarlwanmhu
supreme *(adj.)* **အထွတ်အထိပ်** aa-htwat-aa-hteik
surcharge *(v.)* **အပိုကြေးယူသည်** aa-po-kyay-yuu-sai
surcharge *(n.)* **အပိုကြေး** aa-po-kyay
sure *(adj.)* **သေချာသော** say-chaar-saw
surely *(adv.)* **သေချာစွာ** say-chaar-swar
surety *(n.)* **အာမခံ** aar-ma-hkan
surf *(v.)* **ရေလွှာလှိုင်းစီးကစားသည်** ray lwhar hline see-kasarrsai
surface *(v.)* **မံသည်၊ ကျံသည်** man sai , kyaansai
surfeit *(n.)* **လွန်ခြင်း၊ ကြူးခြင်း၊ အလျှံပယ်ဖြစ်ခြင်း** lwan chinn , kyuu chinn , a shan paal hpyit-chinn
surge *(v.)* **တလိပ်လိပ်တက်သည်** ta late late taat-sai
surge *(n.)* **တလိပ်လိပ်တက်ခြင်း** ta late late-taat-chinn
surgeon *(n.)* **ခွဲစိတ်ဆရာဝန်** hkwal-satesararwaan
surgery *(n.)* **ခွဲစိတ်မှု** hkwalsatemhu
surmise *(v.)* **ရမ်းဆသည်** ram sasai
surmise *(n.)* **စိတ်မှန်း** sate-mhan
surmount *(v.)* **ကျော်လွှားသည်** kyawlwharsai
surname *(n.)* **မိသားစုအမည်** misarrsuaamai
surpass *(v.)* **သာလွန်သည်** sarlwansai
surplus *(n.)* **အပိုအလျှံ** a po aashan
surprise *(v.)* **အံ့သြသည်** ant aw-sai
surprise *(n.)* **အံ့အားသင့်ခြင်း** ant-aarr-sint-chinn
surrender *(n.)* **အရှုံးပေးခြင်း** aa-shone-payy-chinn

surrender *(v.)* အရှုံးပေးသည် aa-shone-payy-sai
surround *(v.)* ရံသည်၊ ပတ်သည် ran sai , paatsai
surroundings *(n.)* ပတ်ဝန်းကျင် paat-waannkyin
surtax *(n.)* အပိုခွန် a pohkwan
surveillance *(n.)* စောင့်ကြပ်ခြင်း saunt kyat-chinn
survey *(n.)* ဆန်းစစ်ခြင်း saannsit-chinn
survival *(n.)* ဘေးအန္တရာယ်လွတ်မြောက်ခြင်း bhay-yaantararallwatmyautchinn
survive *(v.)* အသက်ရှင်ကျန်ရစ်သည် aa-saat-shin-kyaan-rit-sai
suspect *(n.)* မသင်္ကာဖွယ်ဖြစ်သူ ma sin kar hpwal-pyit-suu
suspect *(adj.)* စိတ်မချဖွယ် sate-ma-cha-hpwal
suspend *(v.)* ဆိုင်းထားသည် sine-htarr-sai
suspense *(n.)* သည်းထိတ်ခြင်း sae htate-chinn
suspension *(n.)* ဆိုင်းခြင်း sine-chinn
suspicion *(n.)* မသင်္ကာမှု ma-sin karmhu
suspicious *(adj.)* သံသယဖြစ်ဖွယ် sansayahpyithpwal
sustain *(v.)* အကျိုးပြုသည် aakyoepyusai
sustenance *(n.)* အာဟာရ aarhar-ra
swab *(n.)* ဂွမ်းဖတ်၊ သလိပ်နမူနာ gwam hpaat , sa late-na-muunar
swagger *(n.)* ကားကားကားကား လျှောက်ခြင်း karr karr karrkarr shou-tchinn
swagger *(v.)* ကားကားကားကား လျှောက်သည် karr karr karrkarr shoutsai
swallow *(n.)* မြိုချခြင်း myo chachinn
swallow *(v.)* မြိုချသည် myo chasai
swamp *(v.)* ရေလွှမ်းသည် raylwhamsai
swamp *(n.)* စိမ့်၊ ရွှံ့ညွန် seint , shwan-nywan
swan *(n.)* ငန်း ngaann
swarm *(v.)* အုံသည်၊ စွဲသည် ant-sai , swalsai
swarm *(n.)* အစု၊ အအုံ a su , aa-aone
swarthy *(adj.)* ညိုသော nyosaw
sway *(n.)* လှုပ်ယမ်းခြင်း hlote yamchinn
sway *(v.)* ယိမ်းထိုးသည် yaim htoesai
swear *(v.)* ဆဲသည်၊ ဆိုသည် sell sai , sosai
sweat *(v.)* ချွေးထွက်သည် chway htwat-sai
sweat *(n.)* ချွေး chway
sweater *(n.)* ဆွယ်တာ swaltar
sweep *(n.)* တံမြက်လှည်းခြင်း tan myaat hlaeechinn
sweep *(v.)* လှည်းကျင်းသည် hlaee kyinnsai
sweeper *(n.)* တံမြက်လှည်းသမား tan myaat hlaeesamarr
sweet *(n.)* အချို aacho
sweet *(adj.)* ချိုသော chosaw
sweeten *(v.)* ချိုစေသည် chosaysai
sweetmeat *(n.)* အချိုခဲဖွယ် a hkyao hkellhpwal
sweetness *(n.)* ချိုခြင်း chochinn
swell *(n.)* ပူခြင်း၊ စူခြင်း puu chinn , suuchinn
swell *(v.)* ပွသည်၊ ဖောင်းသည် pwa sai , hpaunggsai
swift *(adj.)* လျင်မြန်သော lyinmyansaw
swim *(n.)* ရေကူးခြင်း ray kuuchinn
swim *(v.)* ရေကူးသည် ray kuusai
swimmer *(n.)* ရေကူးသမား ray kuusamarr
swindle *(n.)* လိမ်လည်မှု linlaimhu

swindle *(v.)* **လိမ်သည်** linsai

swindler *(n.)* **လူလိမ်** luulain

swine *(n.)* **လူယုတ်မာ** luuyotemar

swing *(n.)* **လွှဲခြင်း** lwhaellchinn

swing *(v.)* **လွှဲသည်၊ ယမ်းသည်** lwhaell sai , yamsai

swipe *(v.)* **တအားလွှဲရိုက်သည်** ta aarr lwhaell ritesai

swirl *(v.)* **ဝေ့သည်၊ လည်သည်** wae sai , laisai

Swiss *(adj.)* **ဆွစ်ဇာလန်နိုင်ငံ** switzarlaan-nine-ngan

Swiss *(n.)* **ဆွစ်ဇာလန်သား** switzarlaan-sarr

switch *(v.)* **လှည့်သည်၊ ပြောင်းသည်** hlae sai , pyaungsai

switch *(n.)* **ခလုတ်** hka-lote

swoon *(v.)* **အရူးအမူးဖြစ်နေသည်** *aa-ruu-aa-muu-hpyit-nay-sai*

swoon *(n.)* **မူးမော်ခြင်း** muu-maw-chinn

swoop *(v.)* **ထိုးဆင်းသည်** htoe sinnsai

sword *(n.)* **ဓားရှည်** *dharrshay*

sycamore *(n.)* **သဖန်းပိုးစာ** sa hpan-poesar

sycophancy *(n.)* **ကပ်ဖား** katt-hparr

sycophant *(n.)* **ကပ်ဖား** kat-hparr

syllabic *(adj.)* **ဝဏ္ဏပါဝင်သော** wannaparwainsaw

syllable *(n.)* **ဝဏ္ဏ** wan-na

syllabus *(n.)* **သင်ရိုးမာတိကာ** sin-roemar[tikar

sylph *(n.)* **လေ မမြင်ရဘဲ တည်ရှိခြင်း** lay mamyinrabhell taishihkyinn

sylviculturist *(n.)* **သစ်တောသစ်ပင်များကို စိုက်ပျိုးသူ** saittaw saitpainmyarrko hcitepyoesuu

symbiosis *(n.)* **သဟဇီဝ** sa-ha-zee wa

symbiote *(n.)* **အပြန်အလှန်အကျိုးပြုခြင်း** aapyanaalhaan aakyoepyuhkyinn

symbol *(n.)* **သင်္ကေတ** sin kay-ta

symbolic *(adj.)* **သင်္ကေတဖြစ်သော** sin kay tahpyitsaw

symbolism *(n.)* **အမှတ်သညာဖြင့် သရုပ်ဖော်မှု** aa-mhaat sa-nyar-hpyint sarotehpawmhu

symbolize *(v.)* **သညာထားသည်** sanyarhtarrsai

symmetrical *(adj.)* **ခေါက်ချိုးညီ** hkout-choenye

symmetry *(n.)* **ခေါက်ချိုးညီခြင်း** hkoutchoenyechinn

sympathetic *(adj.)* **စာနာသော** sarnarsaw

sympathize *(v.)* **ကြင်နာမှုပြသည်၊ ထောက်ထားသည်** kyinnarmhu pyasai , htouthtarrsai

sympathy *(n.)* **ကရုဏာ** karunar

symphony *(n.)* **သံစုံတီးဝိုင်းအတွက် တေးသွား** san sone teewineaatwat tayyswarr

symposium *(n.)* **စာတမ်းဖတ်ပွဲ** sartamhpaatpwal

symptom *(n.)* **လက္ခဏာ** lakhkanar

symptomatic *(adj.)* **အရိပ်လက္ခဏာ** a riutlakhkanar

synergy *(n.)* **စုပေါင်းညှိနှိုင်းဆောင်ရွက်မှု အကျိုးရလဒ်** supaungg nyhainateesaungrwatmhu aakyoeralad

synonym *(n.)* **ကြောင်းတူသံကွဲ၊ စကားပရိယာယ်** kyaunggtuusankwal , sakarrpariyal

synonymous *(adj.)* **အနက်တူ** aa-naattuu

synopsis *(n.)* **အနှစ်ချုပ်** aanitchote

syntax *(n.)* **ဝါကျဖွဲ့ထုံး** warkya hpwahltone

synthesis *(n.)* စုပေါင်းညှိနှိုင်းမှု supaunggnyhainateemhu
synthetic *(n.)* အတု aatu
synthetic *(adj.)* အတု aatu
syringe *(v.)* ပြွတ်ဖြင့် ဆေးကြောသည် pywat-hpyint sayy kyawwsai
syringe *(n.)* ပြွတ်၊ ဆေးထိုးပြွန် pywat, sayy htoe pywan
syrup *(n.)* သကြားရည် sa kyar-rai
system *(n.)* စနစ် sa-nit
systematic *(adj.)* စနစ်ကျသော sanit-kya-saw
systematize *(v.)* စနစ်ကျစေသည် sanit kya-say-sai

T

table *(v.)* တင်သည် tinsai
table *(n.)* စားပွဲ sarr-pwal
tableau *(n.)* ပြကွက်သရုပ်ဖော်ပြသခြင်း pyakwat sarotehpawpyasachinn
tablet *(n.)* ဆေးပြား sayypyarr
tabloid *(n.)* လူပြိန်းကြိုက်သတင်းစာ luupyaeinkyaitesatinnsar
taboo *(v.)* ဘာသာရေး၊ ယဉ်ကျေးမှုအရ ခွင့်မပြုထားသည့်အရာ bharsarrayy , yainkyaayymhu aar hkwng m pyuhtarr saeet aarar
taboo *(n.)* မပြောအပ်၊ မလုပ်အပ်ဟု တားမြစ်ထားသော အမှု ma pyaww at, malote athu tarrmyithtarrsaw aamhu
tabular *(adj.)* ဇယား zayarr
tabulate *(v.)* ဇယားဆွဲသည် zayarr swalsai
tabulation *(n.)* ဇယားဖြင့် ဆွဲခြင်း zayarr-hpyint swalchinn
tabulator *(n.)* ဇယား ကွက်ခွဲခလုတ် zayarr kwat hkwal-kalote
tacit *(adj.)* အပြန်အလှန်နားလည်မှုဖြင့် သိသာသော aa-pyan-aa-hlaan narr-lai-mhuhpyint si-sarsaw
taciturn *(adj.)* စကားနည်းသော sakarr-nae-saw
tack *(n.)* လမ်းကြောင်း lamkyaungg
tackle *(v.)* ကိုင်တွယ်သည် kine-twalsai
tackle *(n.)* ဘောလုံး ဝင်လုခြင်း၊ ဖျက်ခြင်း bhawlone win lu chinn , hpyetchinn
tact *(n.)* လိမ္မာပါးနပ်မှု laimmar parr nautmhu
tactful *(adj.)* ပါးနပ်သော parr nautsaw
tactician *(n.)* နည်းဗျူဟာပညာရှင် nee-byuuharpanyarshin
tactics *(n.)* နည်းဗျူဟာ neebyauuhar
tactile *(adj.)* အထိအတွေ့ဖြင့် သိသော aa-hti a twaehpyint si-saw
tag *(n.)* စာတန်း၊ ကတ်ပြား sar-taann , kaatpyarr
tail *(v.)* နောက်ယောင်ခံလိုက်သည် nout yaung hkanlitesai
tailor *(v.)* အံဝင်ခွင်ကျ စီမံထားပေးသည် aan-winhkwinkya seman htarrpayysai
tailor *(n.)* အပ်ချုပ်သမား at-chote-samarr
taint *(v.)* ပုပ်သိုးသည်၊ စွန်းထင်းသည် pote soe sai , swann htinnsai
taint *(n.)* အစွန်းအထင်း၊ အမည်းစက် aaswann a htinn , aamaeesaat
take *(v.)* ယူသည်၊ ဆွဲသည် yuu sai , swalsai
takeable *(adj.)* ယူဆောင်နိုင်သော yuusaung-nine-saw
takeaway *(n.)* ပါဆယ် parsaal
taken *(adj.)* သယ်ခဲ့သော saal-kaesaw

take-off *(n.)* ပျံတက်ခြင်း pyaantaatchinn

takeout *(n)* ထုတ်ပစ်ခြင်း htotepyitchinn

takeover *(n.)* လွှဲယူခြင်း lwhaellyuuchinn

taker *(n.)* လက်ခံသူ laathkansuu

tala *(n.)* ပြတ်ခြင်း၊ လဲခြင်း pyat hkyinn , lellhkyinn

talbot *(n.)* အမဲလိုက်ခွေး a mell litehkway

talc *(n.)* ရွှံ့ကျောက် rwankyawwat

tale *(n.)* ပုံပြင် ponepyin

talebear *(v.)* ကောလဟာလဖြန့်သည် kawlaharl hpya antsai

talebearer *(n.)* ကောလဟာလဖြန့်သူ kawlaharl hpya antsuu

talebearing *(n.)* ကောလဟာလပြန့်ခြင်း kawlaharl pya anthkyinn

talebook *(n.)* ပုံပြင်စာအုပ် ponepyinsar-aote

talent *(n.)* ပါရမီရှင် parramehlyin

talisman *(n.)* အဆောင် *aa-saung*

talk *(n.)* ဆွေးနွေးခြင်း swaynwaychinn

talk *(v.)* စကားပြောသည် sakarrpyawwsai

talkative *(adj.)* စကားများသော sakarrmyarrsaw

talkatively *(adv.)* စကားများ sakarrmyarr

talkativeness *(n.)* စကားများခြင်း sakarrmyarrchinn

talkback *(n.)* ပြန်ပက်ခြင်း pyan paatchinn

talkboard *(n.)* စကားပြောခန်း hcakarrpyawwhkaann

tall *(adj.)* ရှည်သော shaysaw

tallow *(n.)* အမဲဆီ a mellse

tally *(v.)* ကိုက်သည် kitesai

tally *(n.)* စာရင်း၊ တာလီ sarrinn , tarle

talon *(n.)* ငှက်ရဲ၏ လက်သည်း ngatrelleat laatsaee

taloned *(adj.)* ငှက်ခြေသည်းရှိသော nghaat hkyaysaeeshisaw

tamarind *(n.)* မန်ကျည်းသီး maan kyaeesee

tame *(v.)* ယဉ်ပါးစေသည် yin parrsaysai

tame *(adj.)* ယဉ်ပါးသော yin parrsaw

tamper *(v.)* ကလိသည်၊ လက်ဆော့သည် ka li sai , laat sotsai

tamperproof *(adj.)* ခွင့်မပြုသော မသင့်လျော်သော ပြင်ဆင်ချက် ပြုလုပ်ခြင်းကို ခံနိုင်ရည်ရှိသော hkwng mapyusaw m saint lyawsaw pyinsainhkyet pyulotehkyinnko hkannineraishisaw

tampon *(v.)* တန်ပွန်ထည့်သည် taan pwan htaeetsai

tan *(adj.)* ကြေးနီရောင်ရှိသော kyay-ne raungshisaw

tan *(n.)* အညိုရောင် aa-nyoraung

tanbark *(n.)* ဝက်သစ်ချအခေါက် waat sait hkyaaaahkout

tandem *(n.)* ထိုင်ခုံနှစ်ခုံ၊ ခြေနင်းနှစ်စုံပါ စက်ဘီးရှည် htine-hkone na hkone , chay ninn na sonepar saatbheeshay

tandoor *(n.)* ဆလင်ဒါပုံ မြေအိုး s lain darpone myayaoe

tang *(n.)* အနံ့စူးစူး aanant suu-suu

tanged *(adj.)* အနံ့စူးသော aanant suu-saw

tangent *(n.)* တန်းဂျင့်မျဉ်း tan gyant-myin

tangible *(adj.)* အမှန်တကယ်ရှိသော aa-mhaan-takaalshisaw

tangle *(v.)* ငြိသည်၊ လိမ်ယှက်သည် ngyai sai , lin yhaatsai

tangle *(n.)* အရှုပ်အထွေး aa-shote aa-htway

tango *(v.)* တန်ဂိုကသည် taan go kasai

tank *(n.)* တိုင်ကီ tineke

tankard *(n.)* မတ်ခွက်ကြီး maat hkwatkyee

tanker *(n.)* ဆီသယ်ကား se saalkarr

tanner *(n.)* ကြေးနီရောင် kyayneraung

tannery *(n.)* ကြေးနီရောင် kyayneraung

tantalize *(v.)* မချင့်မရဲဖြစ်စေသည် ma chint ma relhlpyitsaysai

tantamount *(adj.)* သဘောသက်ရောက်သော sabhaw saatroute-saw

tantra *(n.)* ဟိန္ဒူ hinduu

tantric *(adj.)* ဝိရယနဗုဒ္ဓဘာသာကို ဖော်ပြသော wi r y nabuddhabharsarko hpawpyasaw

tap *(v.)* ဖောက်သည်၊ ထုတ်သည် hpoutsai , htotesai

tape *(v.)* တိပ်ဖြင့် ကပ်သည် tate-hpyint kautsai

tape *(n.)* တိပ် tate

tape player *(n.)* တိတ်ဖွင့်စက် tate hpw ng hcaat

tapeless *(adj.)* တိတ်မပါသော tatemaparsaw

tapeline *(n.)* တိတ်အတိုင်းအတာ tateaatineaatar

taper *(n.)* သေးသွယ်သော ဖယောင်းတိုင်လေး sayy swalsaw hpayaunggtinelayy

taper *(v.)* သွယ်သည်၊ လျော့သည် swal sai , lyawwsai

tapestry *(n.)* ရောင်စုံချည်ဖြင့် ပုံဖော် ထိုးထားသော အထည် raungsone chaihpyint ponehpaw htoehtarrsaw aahtai

tar *(v.)* ကတ္တရာ ခင်းသည်၊ လောင်းသည် kat tarar hkinn sai , launggsai

tar *(n.)* ကတ္တရာ kat tarar

taramite *(n.)* တာရာမိုက်သတ္တု tar rar mitesattu

tarantism *(n.)* ကရန် ပြင်းထန်စွာ လှုံ့ဆော်မှု karaan pyinnhtaanhcwar lhuansaungmhu

tardiness *(n.)* နောက်ကျခြင်း noutkyachinn

tardy *(adj.)* နောက်ကျသော noutkyasaw

target *(n.)* ပန်းတိုင် pantine

tariff *(n.)* ဈေးနှုန်းစာရင်း syaayyhnonesarrinn

tarnish *(v.)* အရောင်မှေးမှိန်သွားသည် aa-raung mhaayy mhaeinswarrsai

task *(v.)* တာဝန်ပေးအပ်သည် tarwaanpayyatsai

task *(n.)* လုပ်ငန်းတာဝန် lotengaanntarwaan

taste *(v.)* အရသာကို ခံသည် aarasarko hkansai

taste *(n.)* အရသာ ခံနိုင်စွမ်း aarasar hkannineswam

taste bud *(n.)* အာရုံခံ အဖု aarronehkan aahpu

tasteful *(adj.)* မျက်စိပသာဒရှိသော myetsi pyit-ardashisaw

tasty *(adj.)* အရသာရှိသော aarasarshisaw

tatter *(v.)* ကြမ်းတမ်းအောင်လုပ်သည် kyamtam aaunglotesai

tatter *(n.)* ပြဲနေသော အင်္ကျီ pyaellnaysaw aainkyae

tattoo *(v.)* တက်တူးထိုးသည် taattuu htoesai

tattoo *(n.)* တက်တူး taattuu

taunt *(n.)* မခံချင်အောင် ပြောသောစကား ma hkan chinaaung pyawwsawsakarr

taunt *(v.)* မခံချင်အောင် ပြောသည် ma hkan chinaaung pyawwsai

taunter *(n.)* မခံချင်အောင် ပြောသူ ma hkan chinaaung pyawwsuu

taunting *(adj.)* မခံချင်အောင် ပြောသော ma hkan chinaaung pyawwsaw

tauntingly *(adv.)* **မခံချင်အောင် ထိကပါးရိကပါး အမူအရာဖြင့်** ma hkan chinaaung hti k parr ri kaparr aamuuaararhpyint
tauromachy *(n.)* **ကျွဲရိုင်းသတ်ပွဲ** kyawal rine saatpwal
taut *(adj.)* **တင်းသော၊ တောင့်သော** tinn saw , tawntsaw
tautly *(adv.)* **အကွက်စေ့စေ့** aakwat saesae
tavern *(n.)* **အရက်ဆိုင်** aaraatsine
taverner *(n.)* **အသေးစားဟိုတယ်ပိုင်ရှင်** aasayyhcarr hotaalpineshin
tavernkeeper *(n.)* **အသေးစားဟိုတယ်စောင့်** aasayyhcarr hotaalhcaung
taw *(n.)* **ဟီဘရူး ၂၃ လုံးမြောက်စာလုံး** he bharuu 2 3 lone myawwathcarlone
tawer *(n.)* **သားရေဆေးဆိုးသူ** sarr ray sayy soesuu
tax *(v.)* **အခွန်စည်းကြပ်သည်** aahkwan saeekyautsai
tax *(n.)* **အခွန်** aahkwan
tax return *(n.)* **အခွန်စည်းကြပ်ရန် ဝင်ငွေစာရင်း** aahkwan saeekyautraan win-ngway-sarrinn
taxable *(adj.)* **အခွန်တော် ဆောင်ရန်** aahkwantaw saungraan
taxation *(n.)* **အခွန်စည်းကြပ်ခြင်း** aahkwan saeekyautchinn
tax-free *(adj.)* **အကောက်အခွန်လွတ်** aakoutaahkwanlwat
taxi *(v.)* **မောင်းနှင်သည်** maunggnhinsai
taxi *(n.)* **တက္ကစီ** takkase
taxibus *(n.)* **တက္ကစီဘတ်စကား** takkase bhaatsakarr
taxicab *(n.)* **တက္ကစီကား** takkahce karr
taxidermal *(adj.)* **တိရိစ္ဆာန်အရေပြားထိန်းသိမ်းစောင့်ရှောက်ခြင်းဆိုင်ရာ** ta rate ran aaraypyarr hteinsaim hcaung shout hkyinnsinerar
taxidermic *(adj.)* **တိရိစ္ဆာန်အရေပြားထိန်းသိမ်းစောင့်ရှောက်ခြင်းဆိုင်ရာ** ta rate ran aaraypyarr hteinsaim hcaung shout hkyinnsinerar
taxidermist *(n.)* **ရုပ်လုံးသွင်းသူ** rote lone swinsuu
taxidermy *(n.)* **ရုပ်လုံးသွင်းပညာ** rote lone swinpanyar
taxpayer *(n.)* **အခွန်ထမ်း** aahkwanhtam
T-bone *(n.)* **ဖြတ်တိုက်ခြင်း** hpyat titehkyinn
tchick *(n.)* **မြင်းမောင်းရန် တောက်ခေါက်သံ** myinn maunggraan tout-hkoutsan
tea *(n.)* **လက်ဖက်ပင်၊ လက်ဖက်ရည်** laathpaat pin , laathpaatrai
tea maker *(n.)* **လက်ဖက်ရည်ဖျော်ဆရာ** laathpaat-rai hpyawsarar
teabag *(n.)* **တစ်ခွက်စာလက်ဖက်ခြောက်အိတ်** taithkwat sar laathpaatchauk-ate
teabox *(n.)* **လက်ဖက်ရည်သယ်ရန် ထည့်ရန် သေတ္တာ** laathpaatrai saalraan htaeet-raan sayttar
teacake *(n.)* **တီးကိတ်မုန့်** tee kate mone
teach *(v.)* **သင်ပေးသည်** sinpayysai
teacheable *(adj.)* **သင်ပြနိုင်သော** sin pyaninesaw
teacher *(n.)* **ဆရာ** sarar
teacher centric *(adj.)* **ဆရာ ဗဟိုပြုသော** sarar bahopyusaw
teaching *(n.)* **စာသင်ပြခြင်း** sarsinpyachinn
teacup *(n.)* **လက်ဖက်ရည်ပန်းကန်လုံး** laathpaatrai paannkaanlone
teagle *(n.)* **ပင့်မစက်** p int ma-saat
teahouse *(n.)* **လက်ဖက်ရည်ဆိုင်** laathpaatraisine

teak *(n.)* ကျွန်းသစ် kyawannsit

team *(n.)* အဖွဲ့ aahpwal

team building *(n.)* အဖွဲ့ဖွဲ့ခြင်း aahpwal hpwalchinn

teamed *(adj.)* အသင်းအဖွဲ့ဖြစ်သော aasinnaahpwal hpyitsaw

teammate *(n.)* အဖွဲ့သား aahpwalsarr

teamwise *(adv.)* တစ်ဖွဲ့လုံး ta-hpwal-lone

teamwork *(n.)* ပူးပေါင်းဆောင်ရွက်မှု puupaunggsaung-rwatmhu

teapot *(n.)* လက်ဖက်ရည်အိုး laathpaatrai-aoe

tear *(n.)* မျက်ရည် myetrai

tear *(v.)* ဆုတ်ဖြဲသည် sote hpyaellsai

tear gas *(n.)* မျက်ရည်ယိုဓာတ်ငွေ့ myet-rai yodhrat-ngwae

teardrop *(n.)* မျက်ရက်စက် myetraatsaat

tearful *(adj.)* မျက်ရည်လည်သော myetrai laisaw

tease *(n.)* စနောက်ခြင်း sa noutchinn

teaser *(n.)* ပဟေဠိ pa hay li

teasing *(n.)* ကျီစယ်ခြင်း kyae saalchinn

teasingly *(adv.)* ကျီစယ်သည့် သဘောဖြင့် kyae saalsaeet sabhawhpyint

teat *(n.)* နို့သီးခေါင်း nhoet seehkaungg

technical *(adj.)* နည်းပညာ naee pin-nyar

technicality *(n.)* လုပ်ထုံးလုပ်နည်း lote-htone-lote-naee

technician *(n.)* နည်းပညာရှင် naeepanyarshin

technique *(n.)* နည်းပညာ naeepanyar

technological *(adj.)* နည်းပညာဆိုင်ရာ naeepanyarsinerar

technologist *(n.)* နည်းပညာရှင် naeepanyarshin

technology *(n.)* နည်းပညာ naeepanyar

technomad *(n.)* နည်းပညာရှူးသွပ်သူ nee-pin-nyar-ruu-swutsuu

technomania *(n.)* နည်းပညာရှူးသွပ်သူ nee-pin-nyar-ruu-swutsuu

technomusic *(n.)* ဂီတနည်းပညာ ge-ta-naee-pa-nyar

technophile *(n.)* နည်းပညာကို ချစ်မြတ်နိုးသူ naee-pa-nyarko chitmyatnoesuu

technophobe *(n.)* နည်းပညာကို ကြောက်ရွံ့သူ naee-pa-nyarko kyawwatrwansuu

techy *(n.)* နည်းပညာကျွမ်းကျင်သူ nee-pin-nyar-kywam-kyin-suu

tect *(n.)* နည်းပညာ nee-pin-nyar

tectonic *(adj.)* တည်ဆောက်ခြင်း၊ ဗိသုကာနှင့် သက်ဆိုင်သော taisout-chinn , bisukar-nint saat-sinesaw

tedious *(adj.)* ငြီးငွေ့ဖွယ် ngyee ngwae-hpwal

tedium *(n.)* ငြီးငွေ့ဖွယ် ngyee ngwae-hpwal

teem *(v.)* မိုးသည်းထန်သည် moesaeehtaansai

teenager *(n.)* ဆယ်ကျော်သက် saalkyawsaat

teens *(n. pl.)* ဆယ်ကျော်သက် saalkyawsaat

teethe *(v.)* သွားပေါက်သည် swarr poutsai

teetotal *(adj.)* သေရည်သေရက် ရှောင်ကြဉ်သော say rai sayraat shaung kyinsaw

teetotaller *(n.)* သေရည်သေရက် ရှောင်ကြဉ်သူ say rai sayraat shawin kyinsuu

telebanking *(n.)* တယ်လီဘဏ်စနစ် taallebhansanit

telecast *(n.)* တယ်လီရုပ်သံလွှင့်ခြင်း taalle rotesan lwint-chinn
telecommunications *(n.)* တယ်လီဆက်သွယ်ရေး taallesaatswalrayy
telecomputing *(n.)* တယ်လီကွန်ပျူတင်း taalle kwan-pyuu-tinn
teleconference *(n.)* တယ်လီကွန်ဖရန့် taalle kwan hpa raant
telecopier *(n.)* တယ်လီမိတ္တူကူးစက် taallemittuukuusaat
telecourse *(n.)* တယ်လီသင်တန်း taallesintaann
telefax *(n.)* တယ်လီဖက်စ် taallehpaatit
telegram *(n.)* သံကြိုးစာ sankyaoesar
telegraph *(v.)* ကြေးနန်းရိုက်သည် kyaynaann ritesai
telegraph *(n.)* ကြေးနန်း kyaynaann
telegraphic *(adj.)* ကြေးနန်းဖြင့် ပို့သော kyaynaannhpyint phoetsaw
telegraphist *(n.)* ကြေးနန်းရိုက်သူ kyaynaann ritesuu
telegraphy *(n.)* ကြေးနန်း kyaynaann
teleguide *(n.)* တယ်လီလမ်းညွှန် taallelamnywhaan
telejournalism *(n.)* တယ်လီသတင်းစာပညာ taallesatinnsarpanyar
telekinesis *(n.)* စိတ်စွမ်းအင်ဖြင့် ပစ္စည်းရွှေ့ခြင်း hcate swmaan-in-hpyint pyit-cee rwae chinn
telekinetic *(adj.)* စိတ်စွမ်းအင်ဖြင့် ပစ္စည်းရွှေ့ခြင်းဆိုင်ရာ hcate swmaan-in-hpyint pyit-cee rwae chinn-sinerar
telemark *(v.)* တယ်လီအမှတ် taalle-aa-mhaat
telemarket *(v.)* တယ်လီဈေးကွက် taalle-zyayy-kwat
telemarketing *(n.)* တယ်လီမားကက်တင်း taalle marr kaattinn
telematic *(adj.)* တယ်လီဆက်သွယ်ရေးနည်းပညာ taalle-saatswalrayynaeepanyar
telemetry *(n.)* တယ်လီတိုင်းတာချက်ပို့စနစ် taalle tine tar chet phoetsanit
teleologic *(adj.)* အကြောင်းအကျိုးအယူအဆရှိသော aakyaunggaakyoe aayuuaasashisaw
teleologist *(n.)* အကြောင်းအကျိုးအယူအဆရှိသူ aakyaunggaakyoe aayuuaasashisuu
teleology *(n.)* အကြောင်းအကျိုးအယူအဆ aakyaunggaakyoeaayuuaas
teleoperator *(n.)* တယ်လီမောင်းနှင်သူ taalle maung-nate-suu
telepathic *(adj.)* မနောနှင့် ဆက်သွယ်သော manaw-nint saatswalsaw
telepathist *(n.)* မနောနှင့် ဆက်သွယ်သူ manaw-nint saatswalsuu
telepathy *(n.)* မနောနှင့် ဆက်သွယ်ခြင်း manaw-nint saatswalchinn
telephone *(n.)* တယ်လီဖုန်း taallehpone
teleport *(n.)* အဝေးပို့ aawayy-phoet
teleportation *(n.)* တစ်နေရာမှ တစ်နေရာသို့ ကြားအကွာအဝေးကို ဖျောက်၍ ချက်ခြင်း ရောက်အောင် ပို့ဆောင်ခြင်း ta-nay-rarmha ta-nayrar-thoet kyarr aa-kwar-aa-wayy-ko hpyawt-ywe-chet-chinn routaaung phoetsaunghkyinn
teleprint *(v.)* အဝေးမှ ပရင့်ထုတ်ခြင်း aa-wayymha print htotechinn
teleprinter *(n.)* တယ်လီပရင်တာ taalle printar
teleprompter *(n.)* စကားထောက်ကိရိယာ sakarr htoutka-ri-yar
telescope *(n.)* အဝေးကြည့်မှန်ပြောင်း aa-wayy-kyi mhaanpyaungg

telescopic *(adj.)* အဝေးကြည့်မှန်ပြောင်း aa-wayy kyi mhaanpyaungg
telescopy *(n.)* တယ်လီစကုပ်တီထွင်အသုံးပြုခြင်း taalle hca kote tehtwin-aa-sone-pyu-chinn
teleshopper *(n.)* တယ်လီဈေးရောင်းသူ taalle syaayyraunggsuu
teleshopping *(n.)* တယ်လီဈေးဝယ်ခြင်း taalle syaayywaalchinn
teletext *(n.)* တယ်လီစာသား taallesarsarr
televise *(v.)* ရုပ်မြင်သံကြားမှ ထုတ်လွှင့်သည် rotemyinsankyarrmha htote lwintsai
television *(n.)* ရုပ်မြင်သံကြား rotemyinsankyarr
tell *(v.)* ပြောသည် pyawwsai
teller *(n.)* ငွေကိုင်တွယ်သူ၊ ပုံပြောသူ ngway kinetwal suu , pone pyawwsuu
telling *(adj.)* ထိရောက်သော htiroutsaw
telling-off *(n.)* ဩဘာ aw-bhar
telltale *(n.)* ဖော်ကောင် hpawkaung
tellural *(adj.)* ကမ္ဘာမြေနှင့်ဆိုင်သော kam-bhar-myay nint-sine-saw
telluric *(adj.)* ကမ္ဘာမြေနှင့်ဆိုင်သော kam-bhar-myay nint-sine-saw
temeritous *(adj.)* ရဲဝံ့သော rellwansaw
temerity *(n.)* ရဲဝံ့ခြင်း rellwanchinn
temper *(v.)* မီးဆေးသည်၊ ဖေးမသည် mee sayy sai , hpayymasai
temper *(n.)* ဒေါသ၊ စိတ် daw-sa , sate
temperament *(n.)* ပင်ကိုစရိုက် pin kosarite
temperamental *(adj.)* စိတ်ဆတ်သော sate saatsaw
temperance *(n.)* ချိုးချံခြင်း choe chaanchinn
temperate *(v.)* အပူအအေးမျှတသည် aapuu aaaayy myahatasai
temperature *(n.)* အပူချိန် aapuuchane
tempest *(n.)* မိုးသက်မုန်တိုင်း moe saatmonetine
tempestuous *(adj.)* မုန်တိုင်းထန်သော monetine htaansaw
templar *(n.)* ဝတ်လုံတော်ရ ရှေ့နေ waat lone tawra shaenay
template *(n.)* ပုံစံ ponesan
temple *(n.)* ဘုရားကျောင်း pha-rarrkyaungg
temporal *(adj.)* အချိန်တခဏသာလျှင်ကြာသော aahkyane tahkan sarshin kyaarsaw
temporary *(adj.)* လောကီရေးရာ lawkerayyrar
tempt *(v.)* ဆွယ်သည်၊ သွေးဆောင်သည် swal sai , swaysaungsai
temptation *(n.)* ဖြားယောင်းမှု hpyarryaunggmhu
tempter *(n.)* ဖြားယောင်းသွေးဆောင်သူ hpyarryaungg swaysaungsuu
ten *(n.)* တစ်ဆယ် taitsaal
tenable *(adj.)* ယုတ္တိတန်သော yutti taansaw
tenacious *(adj.)* ကျားကုတ်ကျားခဲဖြစ်သော kyarrkote kyarr hkelhlpyitsaw
tenacity *(n.)* ဇွဲ zwal
tenancy *(n.)* သီးစားလုပ်ခြင်း see sarrlotechinn
tenant *(n.)* အိမ်ငှား aainnghar
tend *(v.)* ဂရုစိုက်သည် *garusitesai*
tendency *(n.)* ယိမ်းယိုင်မှု yaimyinemhu
tender *(adj.)* ကြင်နာသနားတတ်သော kyinnar sanarrtaatsaw
tender *(n.)* ကြည့်ရှုစောင့်ရှောက်သူ kyi shu saung shoutsuu
tenderfoot *(n.)* အတွေ့အကြုံနည်းသော သူ aa-twae-aa-kyon nee-saw suu

tender-hearted *(adj.)* ကြင်နာသနားတတ်သော kyinnar sanarrtaatsaw
tenderize *(v.)* နှပ်သည် nhautsai
tenderizer *(n.)* အသားနူးအောင်မချက်ခင်ထည့်ရသော အရာ a sarr nuu aaung ma-chet-hkin hteet-rasaw aarar
tenderly *(adv.)* နူးနူးညံ့ညံ့ nuu nuunyannyan
tenderness *(n.)* သိမ်မွေ့ခြင်း sinmwaechinn
tendinitis *(n.)* အရွတ်ရောင်ရမ်းခြင်း a -rwat raung ram-chinn
tendon *(n.)* အရွတ် aa-rwat
tendril *(n.)* နွယ်ပင်နှာမောင်း nwalpin nharmaungg
tenebrose *(adj.)* မှုန်မှိုင်းမှဲမှောင်သော mhone mhaine mhaell mhaung-saw
tenebrosity *(n.)* မှုန်မှိုင်းမှဲမှောင်ခြင်း mhone mhaine mhaell mhaung-chinn
tenebrous *(adj.)* မှုန်မှိုင်းမှဲမှောင်သော mhone mhaine mhaell mhaung-saw
tenent *(n.)* ယုံကြည်မှုရေးရာ ရေသောက်မြစ် yonekyimhurayyrar ray soutmyit
tenet *(n.)* ရေသောက်မြစ် ray soutmyit
tenfold *(adj.)* ဆယ်ဆ saal-sa
tennis *(n.)* တင်းနစ် tinnnit
tenor *(n.)* ပကတိအခြေအနေ pakatiaachayaanay
tense *(v.)* တင်းမာသည် tinnmarsai
tense *(n.)* ကြိယာကာလ kyaiyarkarla
tensely *(adv.)* တင်းမာစွာ tinnmarswar
tensible *(adj.)* ဆွဲဆန့်နိုင်သော swal s ant ninesaw
tensile *(adj.)* ဆန့်နိုင်အား sant nineaarr
tensility *(adj.)* ဆန့်နိုင်အားရှိသော sant nine aarrshi-saw
tension *(v.)* ဆွဲဆန့်ထားသည် swal santhtarrsai
tensioned *(adj.)* ဆွဲဆန့်ထားသော swal santhtarrsaw
tensor *(n.)* တင်းနေသော ကြွက်သား *tin-nay-taw-kywat-tar*
tent *(n.)* ရွက်ဖျင်တဲ rwat hpyintell
tentative *(adj.)* အစမ်း aasam
tentativeness *(n.)* အစမ်း aasam
tenth *(adj.)* ဆယ်ခုမြောက် saahlkumyawt
tentmaker *(n.)* ရွက်ဖျင်တဲထုတ်လုပ်သူ *ywet-phyin-tae-htoke-lote-thu*
tentpole *(n.)* ရွက်ဖျင်တဲ့ ထောင်သော တုတ် *ywet-phyin-tae-htaung-taw-dote*
tenue *(n.)* ထိန်းသိမ်းသည် *htein-tain-the*
tenuous *(adj.)* မခိုင်မာသော ma-hkine-marsaw
tenuously *(adv.)* မခိုင်မာစွာ mahkinemarswar
tenure *(v.)* ရာထူးပေးသည် *yar-thoo-pay-the*
tepid *(adj.)* နွေးရုံမျှရှိသော nway rone myahashisaw
tepidity *(n.)* ကြက်သီးနွေး kyaat seenway
tepidly *(adv.)* စိတ်မပါ့တပါ sate-ma par tapar
tequila *(n.)* တက်ခီလာအရက် taat hke lar aaraat
terabase *(n.)* ထပ်ကိန်း ၁၂ ခု *htet-kein-12-khu-*
terabit *(n.)* တာရာဘစ် *tar-yar-bit*
terabyte *(n.)* တာရာဘိုက် *tar-yar-bite*
terajoule *(n.)* တာရာဂျိုး *tar-yar-jole*
term *(n.)* စကားရပ် sakarrrat

terminable *(adj.)* အဆုံးရှိသော *a-sone-shi-taw*
terminal *(n.)* ဘူတာရုံ၊ ဂိတ် bhuutarrone , gate
terminal *(adj.)* ကျွမ်းနေသော kyawmnaysaw
terminate *(v.)* အဆုံးသတ်သည် aasonesaatsai
termination *(n.)* အဆုံးသတ်ခြင်း aasonesaatchinn
terminological *(adj.)* အသုံးအနှုန်း aasoneaahnone
terminology *(n.)* အသုံးအနှုန်း aasoneaahnone
terminus *(n.)* ကားဂိတ်၊ ရထားလမ်းဆုံးဘူတာ karrgate , rahtarrlam sonebhuutar
termite *(n.)* ခြ cha
termiticide *(n.)* ခြသတ်ဆေး *cha-tat-say*
terp *(v.)* ဆီကို ရောထည့်သည် *si-koyaw-htae-the*
terrace *(v.)* တစ်စုံတစ်ရာကို နေထိုင်ရာ အဖြစ်ပြောင်းသည် *ta-sone-ta-yar-ko-nay-htai-yar-a-phit-pyaung-the*
terracotta *(adj.)* နီညိုရောင် myay nehtai nenyoraung
terraforming *(n.)* ကမ္ဘာကဲ့သို့ တစ်ခြားဂြိုလ်ကို ပုံစံပြောင်းသည် *ka-bar-kae-thoe-a-char-gyo-ko-pon-san-pyaung-the*
terrain *(n.)* မြေအနေအထား myayaanayaahtarr
terrestrial *(n.)* ကမ္ဘာဂြိုလ် kambhar gyol
terrible *(adj.)* ကြောက်မက်ဖွယ်ကောင်းသော kyawt-maat-hpwalkaunggsaw
terrier *(n.)* တယ်ရီယာခွေး taal re yarhkway
terrific *(adj.)* ကြောက်မက်ဖွယ် kyawtmaathpwal
terrify *(v.)* ခြောက်သည် chauksai
territorial *(adj.)* ပိုင်နက် pinenaat
territory *(n.)* ပိုင်နက် pinenaat
terror *(n.)* ထိတ်လန့်ကြောက်ရွံ့ခြင်း htate l antkyawwatrwanchinn
terrorism *(n.)* အကြမ်းဖက်ဝါဒ aakyamhpaatwarda
terrorist *(n.)* အကြမ်းဖက်သမား aakyamhpaatsamarr
terrorize *(v.)* ခြောက်သည် *chauksai*
terse *(adj.)* တိုတိုတောင်းတောင်း to to taunggtaungg
tersely *(adv.)* တိုတိုတောင်းတောင်း to to taunggtaungg
tertian *(n.)* တာရှန်အဖျား *tar-shan-a-phyarr*
tertiary *(n.)* တတိယအဆင့် tatiyaaasint
tesseract *(n.)* ကုဗတုံး ရှစ်ခုပါ လေးဖက်မြင်ပိုလီတုတ် *ku-ba-tone-shit-khu*
test *(n.)* စာမေးပွဲ၊ ဆေးစစ်ခြင်း sarmayypwal , sayysitchinn
test *(v.)* စစ်သည်၊ စစ်ဆေးသည် sitsai , sitsayysai
testament *(n.)* သက်သေ saatsay
testicle *(n.)* ဝှေးစေ့ whaayysae
testify *(v.)* သက်သေခံသည် saatsayhkansai
testimonial *(n.)* ထောက်ခံစာ htouthkansar
testimony *(n.)* သက်သေခံချက် saatsayhkanchet
testosterone *(n.)* တက်စတိုစတီရုန်းဟော်မုန်း taat sa to sa te ronehawmone

tete-a-tete *(n.)* မြတ်နှာချင်းဆိုင် အစည်းအဝေး *myat-na-chin-sine-a-see-a-way*

tether *(v.)* လံထားသည် lanhtarrsai

tether *(n.)* လံကြိုး lankyoe

tetra *(n.)* လေးခု layyhku

text *(n.)* စာသား sarsarr

textbook *(adj.)* စံပြ sanpya

textbookish *(adj.)* ကျမ်းစာအုပ်၏ ဝိသေသလက္ခဏာ *tat-sar-oak-ei-wi-tay-ta-lat-kha-nar*

textile *(n.)* အထည်အလိပ် aahtai-aalate

textile *(adj.)* အဝတ်အစားစွဲလမ်းခြင်း *a-wit-a-sar-swal-lan-thu*

textual *(adj.)* စာသား sarsarr

texture *(n.)* ဖွဲ့စပ်ပုံ၊ အနေအထား hpwal sat pone , aanayaahtarr

thank *(v.)* ကျေးဇူးတင်သည် kyaayyjuutinsai

thankful *(adj.)* ကျေးဇူးတင်သော kyaayyjuutinsaw

thankless *(adj.)* မည်သူကမျှ အသိအမှတ်မပြုသော maisuukamyaha aasiaamhaatmapyusaw

thanks *(n.)* ကျေးဇူးတင်ခြင်း kyaayyjuutinchinn

that *(conj.)* ဆိုတာ sotar

thatch *(v.)* သက်ငယ်ဖြင့် မိုးသည် saat ngaahlpyang moesai

thatch *(n.)* သက်ငယ်အမိုး saat ngaal aamoe

thaw *(n.)* ပျော့ပျောင်းလာသည့် အခြေအနေ pyaww pyaungg larsaeet aachayaanay

theatre *(n.)* ကဇာတ်ရုံ ka zatrone

theatrical *(adj.)* ပြဇာတ် pyazat

theft *(n.)* သူခိုး suuhkoe

their *(adj.)* သူတို့၏ suuthoeteat

theirs *(pron.)* သူတို့၏ ဟာ suuthoeteat har

theism *(n.)* ထာဝရဘုရားသခင်တွင် သက်ဝင်ယုံကြည်ခြင်း htarwar bhurarrsahkaintwin saatwinyonekyichinn

theist *(n.)* ထာဝရဘုရားသခင်တွင် သက်ဝင်ယုံကြည်သူ htarwar phararrsahkaintwin saatwin yonekyisuu

them *(pron.)* သူတို့ကို suuthoetko

thematic *(adj.)* ခေါင်းစဉ်၊ အာဘော်၊ အကြောင်းအရာအလိုက် hkaunggsin , aarbhaw , aakyaunggaararaalite

theme *(n.)* အဓိကဆိုလိုရင်း aadhikasolorinn

then *(adj.)* ထိုအချိန်တွင်ဖြစ်သော *htoe-a-chain-twin-phit-taw*

then *(adv.)* ထိုစဉ် htosin

thence *(adv.)* ထိုမှ htomha

theocracy *(n.)* ဘုရားမှ အုပ်ချုပ်ခြင်း *pa-yar-ma-oak-choke-chin*

theologian *(n.)* ဘာသာရေး ကျွမ်းကျင်သူ bharsarrayy -kyawmkyinsuu

theological *(adj.)* ဘာသာရေးနှင့်ဆိုင်သော bharsarrayy nintsinesaw

theology *(n.)* ထာဝရဘုရားသခင်လေ့လာမှုပညာ htarwar phararrsahkain laelarmhupanyar

theorem *(n.)* သီအိုရမ် se aoram

theoretical *(adj.)* အယူအဆဆိုင်ရာ aayuuaasasinerar

theorist *(n.)* သီအိုရီပညာရှင် seaorepanyarshin

theorize *(v.)* စိတ်ကူးသည် satekuusai

theory *(n.)* သီအိုရီ sea-o-re

therapist *(n.)* ကုထုံးဆရာ kuhtonesarar

therapy *(n.)* ရောဂါကုထုံး rawgarkuhtone

there *(adv.)* ထိုနေရာ htonayrar

thereabouts *(adv.)* သို့မဟုတ် ထိုအနီးဝန်းကျင် thoetmahote hto aaneewaannkyin

thereafter *(adv.)* ထို့နောက် hthoetnout

thereby *(adv.)* ထိုသို့ဖြင့် htothoethpyint

therefore *(adv.)* ထို့ကြောင့် hthoetkyount

thermal *(adj.)* အပူဓာတ်ရှိသော aapuu dharatshisaw

thermometer *(n.)* အပူချိန်တိုင်းကိရိယာ aapuuchane tineka-ri-yar

thermos (flask) *(n.)* ဓာတ်ဘူး dhratbhuu

thesis *(n.)* စာတမ်း sartam

thick *(n.)* ထူခြင်း htuuchinn

thicken *(v.)* ထူပိန်းလာသည် htuu peinlarsai

thicket *(n.)* ချုံပုတ် chone-pote

thief *(n.)* သူခိုး suuhkoe

thigh *(n.)* ပေါင်၊ ပေါင်တံ paung , paungtan

thimble *(n.)* အပ်ထောက် at-htout

thin *(v.)* ပါးသွားသည် parrswarrsai

thin *(adj.)* ပိန်သော၊ ပါးသော pein saw , parrsaw

thing *(n.)* အရာ aa-rar

think *(v.)* တွေးသည် twaysai

thinker *(n.)* အတွေးအခေါ်ပညာရှင် aatwayaahkawpanyarshin

third *(n.)* တတိယ tati-ya

third *(adj.)* တတိယမြောက် tati-ya-myawt

thirdly *(adv.)* တတိယအနေဖြင့် tati-ya a nay hpyint

thirst *(v.)* ရေဆာသည် ray sarsai

thirst *(n.)* ရေဆာခြင်း ray sarchinn

thirsty *(adj.)* ရေဆာသော ray sarsaw

thirteen *(n.)* ဆယ့်သုံး sae-sone

thirteenth *(n.)* ဆယ့်သုံးခုမြောက် sae sone-hkumyawt

thirtieth *(n.)* သုံးဆယ်ခုမြောက် sone-saahl-kumyawt

thirtieth *(adj.)* သုံးဆယ်ခုမြောက် sone-saahl-kumyawt

thirty *(n.)* သုံးဆယ် sone-saal

thistle *(n.)* စကော့တလန် ဆူးလေပင် sakottalaan suulaypin

thither *(adv.)* ထိုအရပ်သို့ hto aarat-thoet

thorax *(n.)* ရင်ဘတ် rin-bhaat

thorn *(n.)* ဆူး suu

thorny *(adj.)* ဆူးရှိသော suushisaw

thorough *(adj.)* အစုံအစေ့ aa-sone-aa-sae

thoroughfare *(n.)* လမ်းမ lam-ma

though *(adv.)* သို့သော်လည်း thoetsawlaee

though *(conj.)* သော်ငြားလည်း saw ngyarrlaee

thought *(n.)* အတွေး aatway

thoughtful *(adj.)* အတွေးနယ်ချဲ့သော aatway naalchaaesaw

thousand *(n.)* ထောင် htaung

thousandth *(adj.)* တစ်ထောင်မြောက် ta-htaungmyawt

thrall *(n.)* ကျွန်ပြုခံရသူ *kyun-pyu-khan-ya-thu*

thralldom *(n.)* ကျွန်ပြုခြင်း *kyun-pyu-chin*

thrash *(v.)* ရိုက်နှက်သည် ritenhaatsai

thread *(v.)* အပ်ပေါက်ထိုးသည် at pout htoesai

thread *(n.)* အပ်ချည် atchai

threadbare *(adj.)* နွမ်းရိပါးလိုက်နေသော nwam ri parr litenaysaw
threat *(n.)* ခြိမ်းခြောက်မှု chaaimchaukmhu
threaten *(v.)* ခြိမ်းခြောက်သည် chaaimchauksai
three *(n.)* သုံး sone
thresh *(v.)* တလင်းနယ်သည် ta linn naalsai
thresher *(n.)* သလင်းနယ်စက် *ta-lin-nal-sat*
threshold *(n.)* ခံနိုင်စွမ်း၊ လက်တစ်ကမ်း hkan nineswm , laattaitkam
thrice *(adv.)* သုံးကြိမ် sonekyain
thrift *(n.)* ချွေတာခြင်း chaway tarchinn
thrifty *(adj.)* ခြိုးခြံချွေတာသော choe chaan chway tarsaw
thrill *(v.)* ရင်ဖိုစေသည် rin hposaysai
thrill *(n.)* ရင်ဖိုခြင်း rin hpochinn
thriller *(n.)* လျှို့ဝှက်သည်းဖိုဇာတ်လမ်း shoetwhaat saee hpo-zatlam
thrive *(v.)* ရှင်သန်သည် shin-saansai
throat *(n.)* လည်ချောင်း lai-chaung
throaty *(adj.)* အသံအောသော *aa-san aaw-saw*
throb *(n.)* တဒုတ်ဒုတ်မြည်သံ ta dote-dote myisan
throb *(v.)* တဒုတ်ဒုတ် ကိုက်ခဲသည် ta dote-dote kite hkellsai
throe *(n.)* မချိတင်ကဲ အခြေအနေ ma-chi tinkell aachayaanay
throne *(v.)* နန်းတင်သည် *nan-tin-the*
throne *(n.)* ထီးနန်း hteenaann
throng *(v.)* စုပြုံသွားသည် su pyuanswarrsai
throttle *(v.)* လည်ပင်းညှစ်သည် laipinn nyhaitsai
throttle *(n.)* လီဗာ lebar
through *(adj.)* တောက်လျှောက် toutshout
through *(prep.)* ဖြတ်၍ hpyat-ywe
throughout *(prep.)* တစ်ဝန်းလုံး ta waannlone
throughout *(adv.)* တောက်လျှောက် toutshout
throw *(n.)* ပစ်ပေါက်ခြင်း pyit poutchinn
throw *(v.)* ပစ်ပေါက်သည် pyit poutsai
thrust *(n.)* ထိုးချက်၊ ထိုးသွင်းခြင်း htoe chet , htoe swinchinn
thrust *(v.)* ထိုးသည် htoesai
thud *(v.)* ဘုတ်ခနဲကျသည် bhote hk nell kyasai
thud *(n.)* ဘုတ်ခနဲ မြည်သံ bhote hkanell myisan
thug *(n.)* လူမိုက် luumite
thumb *(v.)* လက်မဖြင့်ထိသည် *lat-ma-phint-hti-the*
thumb *(n.)* လက်မ laat-ma
thumbprint *(n.)* လက်မဗွေရာ laat-ma bwayrar
thump *(v.)* ထုနှက်သည် htu-nhaatsai
thump *(n.)* ပိတ်ထုခြင်း pate htuchinn
thunder *(v.)* မိုးချုန်းသည် moe chonesai
thunder *(n.)* မိုးခြိမ်းသံ moe chaimsan
thunderous *(adj.)* တဖြောင်းဖြောင်း ta hpyaung-hpyaung
thunderstorm *(n.)* မိုးသက်မုန်တိုင်း moe saatmonetine
Thursday *(n.)* ကြာသပတေးနေ့ kyaarsapatayynae
thus *(adv.)* ထို့ကြောင့် hthoetkyount
thwart *(v.)* ကဖျက်ယဖျက်လုပ်သည် ka hpyet ya hpyetlotesai
tiara *(n.)* ဦးဆောက်ပန်း u soutpaann

tick *(v.)* တချက်ချက်မြည်သည် tachet chet myisai
tick *(n.)* တချက်ချက်မြည်သံ tachet chet myisan
ticket *(n.)* လက်မှတ် laatmhaat
tickle *(v.)* ကလိထိုးသည် ka li htoesai
ticklish *(adj.)* ယားလွယ်သော yarr lwalsaw
tidal *(adj.)* ဒီ de
tide *(n.)* ဒီလှိုင်း dehline
tidiness *(n.)* သေသပ်ခြင်း say satchinn
tidings *(n. pl.)* သတင်းစကား satinnsakarr
tidy *(v.)* သေသပ်သည် say satsai
tidy *(adj.)* သေသပ်သော say satsaw
tie *(v.)* ချည်နှောင်သည် chainhaawinsai
tier *(n.)* အထပ်၊ အဆင့် a htat , aasint
tiger *(n.)* ကျား kyarr
tight *(adj.)* တင်းကြပ်သော tinnkyautsaw
tighten *(v.)* တင်းသည်၊ ကျပ်သည် tinn sai , kyatsai
tigress *(n.)* ကျားမ kyarr-ma
tile *(v.)* ခင်းသည်၊ ကပ်သည် hkinn sai , katsai
tile *(n.)* အုတ်ကြွပ်ပြား aote kywutpyarr
till *(n.)* ငွေထည့်အံဆွဲ ngway htae aan-swal
till *(prep.)* ထိအောင် htiaaung
tilt *(n.)* တိမ်းခြင်း၊ စောင်းခြင်း taim chinn , saungchinn
timber *(n.)* သစ် sit
time *(v.)* အချိန်ကိုက်သည် aachanekitesai
time *(n.)* အချိန် aachane
time limit *(n.)* အချိန်ကန့်သတ်ချက် aachane kant saatchet
timeline *(n.)* အချိန်အလိုက် အဖြစ်အပျက်များ aachaneaalite aahpyitaapyetmyarr
timely *(adj.)* အချိန်မှီ aachanemhae
timid *(adj.)* ကြောက်တတ်သော kyawt-taatsaw
timidity *(n.)* မဝံ့မရဲ ma-want-ma-rell
timorous *(adj.)* အသည်းငယ်သော aa-saee ngaalsaw
tin *(v.)* စည်သွပ်သည် si swut-sai
tin *(n.)* သံဖြူဒြပ်စင် san hpyuu dyatsin
tincture *(v.)* စွန်းထင်းသည် *soon-htin-the*
tincture *(n.)* တင်ချာဆေးရည် tin chaar sayyrai
tinge *(v.)* သန်းသည်၊ စွက်သည် saann sai , swatsai
tinge *(n.)* သန်းခြင်း၊ စွက်ခြင်း saann chinn , swatchinn
tinker *(n.)* ခြေသလုံးအိမ်တိုင် သွားလာနေသူ chay-salone-aaintine swarrlar naysuu
tinsel *(n.)* ကုလားရွှေ kularrshway
tint *(v.)* အရောင်သန်းထားသည် aaraung saannhtarrsai
tint *(n.)* အရောင်သန်းခြင်း aaraung saannchinn
tiny *(adj.)* သေးငယ်သော sayyngaalsaw
tip *(v.)* စောင်းထောင်စေသည် saungg htaungsaysai
tip *(n.)* အဖျား၊ အစွန်း၊ ထိပ် aa-hpyarr , aa-swann , hteik
tip-off *(v.)* ထင်ရှားသော သဲလွန်စ *htin-hsar-taw-tae-lun-sa*
tipsy *(adj.)* ထွေနေသော htwaynaysaw
tirade *(n.)* တဖျစ်တောက်တောက်ပြောခြင်း ta hpyit tout toutpyawwchinn
tire *(n.)* တာယာ taryar

tired *(adj.)* **မောပန်းသော** maw paannsaw

tiresome *(adj.)* **စိတ်ပျက်ဖွယ်ရာ** satepyethpwalrar

tissue *(n.)* **တစ်ရှူး** tit-shuu

titanic *(adj.)* **အလွန်ကြီးကြီးမားမား** aalwankyeekyeemarrmarr

tithe *(n.)* **သသသမေဓအခွန်** sat ta may dhaaahkwan

title *(n.)* **ခေါင်းစဉ်** hkaunggsin

titular *(adj.)* **မည်ကာမတ္တ** mai kar mat-ta

toad *(n.)* **ဖားပြုပ်** hparr pyote

toast *(v.)* **ကင်သည်** kinsai

toast *(n.)* **ပေါင်မုန့်မီးကင်** paung mont meekin

tobacco *(n.)* **ဆေးရွက်ကြီး** sayyrwatkyee

today *(n.)* **ယနေ့** yanae

today *(adv.)* **ယနေ့** yanae

toe *(v.)* **ခြေချောင်းဖြင့် ထိသည်** *chay-chaung-phyint-thi-the*

toe *(n.)* **ခြေချောင်း** chaychaung

toffee *(n.)* **တော်ဖီ** tawhpe

toga *(n.)* **ဝတ်ရုံလွှာ** waatronelwhar

together *(adv.)* **အတူတကွ** aatuutakwa

toil *(v.)* **ပင်ပင်ပန်းပန်း လုပ်သည်** pinpinpaannpaann lotesai

toil *(n.)* **အလုပ်ကြမ်း** aalotekyam

toilet *(n.)* **အိမ်သာ** aain-sar

toils *(n. pl.)* **ထောင်ချောက်** htaungchauk

token *(n.)* **တိုကင်** tokin

tolerable *(adj.)* **ခံသာသော၊ သင့်တင်သော** hkan sar saw , sinttinsaw

tolerance *(n.)* **ခံနိုင်ရည်ရှိခြင်း၊ လက်ခံနိုင်သော ကွာဟချက်** hkan-nine-rai shichinn , laathkanninesaw kwarhachet

tolerant *(adj.)* **သည်းခံနိုင်သော** saeehkanninesaw

tolerate *(v.)* **သည်းခံသည်** saeehkansai

toleration *(n.)* **သည်းခံခြင်း** saeehkanchinn

toll *(v.)* **ခေါင်းလောင်းထိုးသည်** hkaungglaungghtoesai

toll *(n.)* **ဖြတ်သန်းခ၊ ဖုန်းပြောခ** hpyatsaann hka , hpone pyawwhka

tomato *(n.)* **ခရမ်းချဉ်သီး** hkaram chaisee

tomb *(n.)* **အုတ်ဂူ** aoteguu

tomboy *(n.)* **ယောကျ်ားလျာ** yawkyaarrlyaar

tomcat *(n.)* **ကြောင်ထီး** *kyaung-htee*

tome *(n.)* **ကျမ်းကြီးကျမ်းခိုင်** kyam kyee kyamhkine

tomorrow *(adv.)* **မနက်ဖြန်** ma-naathpyan

tomorrow *(n.)* **မနက်ဖြန်** ma-naathpyan

ton *(n.)* **တန်** taan

tone *(v.)* **ပိုခိုင်မြဲအောင်လုပ်သည်** *po-khaing-myae-aung-lote-the*

toned *(adj.)* **အသံရှိသော** aasanshisaw

tongs *(n. pl.)* **ညှပ်** nyေt

tongue *(n.)* **လျှာ** shar

tonic *(n.)* **အားဆေး** aarrsayy

tonic *(adj.)* **အားဆေး** aarrsayy

tonight *(adv.)* **ယနေ့ည** yanaenya

tonight *(n.)* **ယနေ့ည** yanaenya

tonne *(n.)* **မက်ထရစ်တန်** maat hta rittaan

tonsil *(n.)* **အာသီး** aarsee

tonsure *(n.)* **ဆံချခြင်း** san chachinn

too *(adv.)* **လည်းပဲ** laeepell

tool *(n.)* **ကိရိယာ၊ လက်နက်** ka-ri-yar , laatnaat

toolkit *(n.)* ကိရိယာတန်ဆာပလာ ka-ri-yartaansarpalar
tooth *(n.)* သွား swarr
toothache *(n.)* သွားနာခြင်း swarr narchinn
toothsome *(adj.)* စားချင့်စဖွယ် sarr chintsahpwal
top *(v.)* သာလွန်သည် sarlwansai
top *(n.)* ထိပ်ပိုင်း hteikpine
topaz *(n.)* ဥဿဖရားကျောက် oak ta hpararrkyawt
topic *(n.)* ခေါင်းစဉ် hkaung-sin
topical *(adj.)* ရေပန်းစားသော raypaannsarrsaw
topographer *(n.)* မြေမျက်နှာသွင်ပြင်ပညာရှင် myay myetnhar swinpyinpanyarshin
topographical *(adj.)* မြေမျက်နှာသွင်ပြင်နှင့်ဆိုင်သော myay myetnhar swinpyin nintsinesaw
topography *(n.)* မြေမျက်နှာသွင်ပြင် myay myetnharswinpyin
topper *(n.)* ဦးထုတ်မြင့် u htotemyint
topple *(v.)* ပြိုကျသည် pyokyasai
topsy turvy *(adj.)* ထက်အောက် ပြောင်းပြန် htaataout pyaunggpyan
torch *(n.)* ဓာတ်မီး dhratmee
torment *(n.)* ညှဉ်းပန်းမှုဒဏ် nyin paann mhudan
torment *(v.)* နှိပ်စက်သည် nate-saat-sai
tornado *(n.)* လေဆင်နှာမောင်း laysinnharmaungg
torpedo *(v.)* တော်ပီဒိုဖြင့် တိုက်ခိုက်သည် taw pe do-hpyint titehkitesai
torpedo *(n.)* တော်ပီဒို taw pe do
torrent *(n.)* ပြင်းထန်သော ရေစီး pyinn-htaansaw raysee
torrential *(adj.)* တစ်ဟုန်ထိုး ta-honehtoe
torrid *(adj.)* ပူပြင်းခြောက်သွေ့သော puu pyinn chaukswaesaw
tortoise *(n.)* လိပ် late
tortuous *(adj.)* ကွေ့ကောက်သော kwae koutsaw
torture *(v.)* နှိပ်စက်သည် nate-saat-sai
torture *(n.)* နှိပ်စက်ခြင်း nate-saat-chinn
toss *(n.)* မြှောက်ခြင်း myaut-chinn
toss *(v.)* ပစ်ပေးသည် pit-payy-sai
total *(v.)* စာရင်းချုပ်သည် sar-rinn-chote-sai
total *(adj.)* စုစုပေါင်း susupaung
totalitarian *(adj.)* အကြွင်းမဲ့ အာဏာရှင်စနစ် aa-kywin-mae aar-narhlyinsanit
totality *(n.)* အားလုံးပေါင်း aarr-lone-paung
touch *(n.)* ထိခြင်း hti-chinn
touch *(v.)* ထိသည် htisai
touchy *(adj.)* အထိမခံသော aa-hti ma hkansaw
tough *(adj.)* ခိုင်သော hkinesaw
toughen *(v.)* အကြမ်းခံနိုင်စေသည် aa-kyam hkan ninesaysai
tour *(v.)* ခရီးလှည့်လည်သည် hka-ree hlae laisai
tour *(n.)* အလည်ခရီး aa-lai-hka-ree
tourism *(n.)* ခရီးသွားလုပ်ငန်း hka-ree-swarr-lote-ngan
tourist *(n.)* တိုးရစ် toe-rit
tournament *(n.)* ပြိုင်ပွဲ pyaine-pwal
tout *(v.)* ဆွယ်သည် swalsai
tow *(n.)* ဆွဲယူခြင်း swalyuuchinn
towards *(prep.)* ဆီသို့ sethoet
towboat *(n.)* ဆွဲသင်္ဘော *swal-tin-baw*

towel *(v.)* **ပဝါဖြင့် သုတ်သည်** pa warhpyint sotesai
towel *(n.)* **ပဝါ** pawar
tower *(v.)* **မိုးနေသည်** moenaysai
tower *(n.)* **မျှော်စင်** myaw-sin
town *(n.)* **မြို့** myoet
township *(n.)* **မြို့** myoet
toxaemia *(n.)* **သွေးဆိပ်သင့်ခြင်း** sway seik sintchinn
toxic *(adj.)* **အဆိပ်ဖြစ်စေသော** a satehpyitsaysaw
toxicity *(n.)* **အဆိပ်အာနိသင်** aa-seik-aar-ni-sin
toxicologist *(n.)* **အဆိပ်ပညာရှင်** aa-seik-pa-nyarshin
toxicology *(n.)* **အဆိပ်ပညာ** aa-seik-pa-nyar
toxification *(n.)* **အဆိပ်ဖြစ်ခြင်း** *a-seik-phit-chin*
toxin *(n.)* **အဆိပ်** aa-seik
toy *(v.)* **ဆော့သည်** sotsai
toy *(n.)* **ကလေးကစားစရာ** kalayykasarrsarar
toyhouse *(n.)* **အရုပ်အိမ်** *a-yoke-eain*
toymaker *(n.)* **အရုပ်လုပ်သူ** *a-yoke-lote-thu*
toyseller *(n.)* **အရုပ်ရောင်းသူ** a roteraunggsuu
toystore *(n.)* **အရုပ်စတိုး** a rote satoe
trace *(v.)* **လိုက်ရှာသည်** litesharsai
trace *(n.)* **သဲလွန်စ** selllwansa
traceable *(adj.)* **သဲလွန်စလိုက်နိုင်သော** selllwansa liteninesaw
trachea *(n.)* **လေပြွန်** lay pywan
tracheal *(adj.)* **လေပြွန်နှင့် ဆိုင်သော** lay pywan-nint sinesaw
tracheole *(n.)* **လေပြွန်** *lay-pyun*
tracheoscopy *(n.)* **လေပြွန်ကြည့်မှန်ပြောင်း** lay pywan kyi mhaanpyaung
tracing *(n.)* **ရုပ်ပုံ မိတ္တူ** rotepone meittuu
track *(v.)* **ခြေရာခံသည်** chay rar hkansai
track *(n.)* **လမ်းကြောင်း၊ ပြေးလမ်း** lamkyaungg , pyaylam
trackable *(adj.)* **ခြေရာခံနိုင်သော** *chay-yar-khan-nine-taw*
trackback *(n.)* **အလိုအလျောက်အသိပေးချက်** *a-lo-a-lyauk-a-thi-pay-chat*
trackball *(n.)* **အခွက်တွင် ထည့်ထားသော ညွှန်ပြအလုံး** *a-khwat-twin-htae-htar-taw-nyun-pya-a-lone*
tracker *(n.)* **ခြေရာကောက်သူ** chayrarkoutsuu
tracklist *(n.)* **အယ်ဘန်ပါ သီချင်းစာရင်း** *al-ban-par-thi-chin-sa-yin*
tracksuit *(n.)* **အားကစားဝတ်စုံ** aarrkasarrwaatsone
tract *(n.)* **လမ်းကြောင်း** lamkyaungg
traction *(n.)* **ဆွဲအား၊ ကုပ်အား** swal aarr , koteaarr
tractor *(n.)* **ထွန်စက်** htwansaat
trade *(v.)* **ကုန်သွယ်သည်** koneswalsai
trade *(n.)* **ကုန်သွယ်မှု** koneswalmhu
trademark *(n.)* **ကုန်အမှတ်တံဆိပ်** koneaamhaattanseik
trader *(n.)* **ကုန်သည်** konesai
tradesman *(n.)* **ဈေးသည်** zayysai
tradition *(n.)* **ဓလေ့၊ ရိုးရာ** dhalae , roerar
traditional *(adj.)* **အစဉ်အလာ** a sin aalar
traffic *(v.)* **ကုန်ကူးသည်** konekuusai
traffic *(n.)* **ယာဉ်အသွားအလာ** yinaaswarraalar

traffic sign *(n.)* လမ်းပြသင်္ကေတ lampya sin kay-ta
tragedian *(n.)* အလွမ်းပြဇာတ်ရေးဆရာ aalwm pyajarat rayysarar
tragedy *(n.)* အလွမ်းဇာတ်သဘင် aalwmjaratsabhain
tragic *(adj.)* ဝမ်းနည်းစရာ wamnaeesarar
trail *(v.)* တရွတ်ဆွဲသည် ta rwat swalsai
trail *(n.)* တောလမ်း၊ တောင်လမ်း taw lam , taunglam
trailer *(n.)* နောက်တွဲယာဉ် nout twal-yin
train *(v.)* လေ့ကျင့်ပေးသည် lae kyintpayysai
train *(n.)* ရထား rahtarr
trainee *(n.)* သင်တန်းသား sintaannsarr
training *(n.)* သင်တန်း sintaann
trait *(n.)* ဉာဉ်၊ လက္ခဏာ nyin , lakhkanar
traitor *(n.)* သစ္စာဖောက် sit-sar-hpout
tram *(n.)* ဓာတ်ရထား dhrat-ra-htarr
trample *(v.)* နင်းခြေသည် ninn-chay-sai
trance *(n.)* ဘဝင်စိတ်ကျခြင်း bhawin-sate-kyachinn
tranquil *(adj.)* ငြိမ်သက်အေးချမ်းသော ngyeinsaat aayychamsaw
tranquility *(n.)* ငြိမ်သက်ခြင်း ngyeinsaatchinn
tranquillize *(v.)* ငြိမ်ဆိမ်စေသည် ngyein sin saysai
tranquillizer *(n.)* စိတ်ငြိမ်ဆေး sate ngyaainsayy
transact *(v.)* တွေ့တွေ့ဆိုင်ဆိုင် ညှိနှိုင်းသည် tae taesinesine nyhainateesai
transaction *(n.)* လုပ်ငန်း၊ ကိစ္စ၊ အရောင်းအဝယ် lotengan , kait-sa , aaraunggaawaal
transborder *(adj.)* ဘော်ဒါဖြတ်သော *baw-dar-phat-taw*
transboundary *(adj.)* ကန့်သတ်ချက်ဖြတ်သော *kant-tat-chat-phat-taw*
transceive *(v.)* ဆက်သွယ်ချက်လွှင့်သည်၊ လက်ခံသည် *sat-thwal-chat-lwint-the-lat-khan-the*
transceiver *(n.)* ဆက်သွယ်ချက် လွှင့်သည့်၊ လက်ခံသည့် စက် *sat-thwal-chat-lwint-the-lat-khan-the-sat*
transcend *(v.)* ကျော်လွန်သည် *kyawlwansai*
transcendent *(adj.)* ထူးကဲသာလွန်သော အထွတ်အထိပ် *htu-kae-tar-lun-thaw-a-htut-ahteik*
transcendental *(adj.)* လောကသဘာဝနှင့် သာမန်လူတို့ မမီနိုင်သော *law-ka-ta-barwanint-tar-man-lu-thoe-ma-minine-taw*
transcendentally *(adv.)* ထူးကဲသာလွန်လျက် htuu kell sarlwansaw
transcendingly *(adv.)* ကျော်လွန်လျက် aahtwataahteik
transcribe *(v.)* ကူးပြောင်းပေးသည် lawkasabharwanint sarmaanluuthoet ma meninesaw
transcriber *(n.)* အသံကို စာအဖြစ် နားထောင်ပြောင်းပေးသူ htuu kell sarlwanlyet
transcription *(n.)* အသံကို စာအဖြစ် နားထောင်ပြောင်းပေးခြင်း kyawlwanlyet
transfer *(v.)* ပြောင်းသည် kuupyaunggpayysai
transfer *(n.)* လွှဲခြင်း aasanko saraahpyit narrhtaung pyaunggpayysuu
transferable *(adj.)* လွှဲပြောင်းပေးနိုင်သော aasanko saraahpyit narrhtaung pyaunggpayychinn

transfiguration *(n.)* ပြောင်းလဲသွားခြင်း pyaungsai
transfigure *(v.)* ပြောင်းလဲသွားသည် lwhaellchinn
transform *(v.)* အသွင်ပြောင်းသည် lwhaellpyaungpayyninesaw
transformation *(n.)* အသွင်ပြောင်းခြင်း pyaunglellswarrchinn
transgress *(v.)* ကျူးကျော်သည် pyaunglellswarrsai
transgression *(n.)* ကျူးကျော်ခြင်း aaswinpyaunggsai
transit *(v.)* ကူးပြောင်းသည် kyauukyawsai
transition *(n.)* အကူးအပြောင်း kyauukyawchinn
transitive *(adj.)* ကံရှိ a kuu aapyaung
transitory *(adj.)* အချိန်ပိုင်းမျှသာခံသော kuupyaunggsai
translate *(v.)* ဘာသာပြန်သည် a kuu aapyaungg
translation *(n.)* ဘာသာပြန်ခြင်း kanshi
transmigration *(n.)* ခန္ဓာသစ်ကို ဝိညာဉ်ကူးပြောင်းမှီတွယ်ခြင်း aachanepine myahasar hkansaw
transmission *(n.)* တစ်ဆင့်ပို့ပေးခြင်း bharsarpyansai
transmit *(v.)* လွှင့်သည် bharsarpyanchinn
transmitter *(n.)* အသံလွှင့်စက် hkandhar sitko winyin kuupyaungg mhae twalchinn
transparent *(adj.)* ဖောက်ထွင်းမြင်နိုင်သော ta-sint phoetpayychinn
transplant *(n.)* အစားထိုးကုသချက် aa-san hlwint-saat
transplantation *(n.)* အစားထိုးကုသခြင်း hpouth-twin-myin-nine-saw
transplantee *(n.)* အစားထိုးကုသမှု ခံယူသူ aa-sarr-htoe ku-sai
transport *(n.)* သယ်ယူပို့ဆောင်ရေး aa-sarrhtoe kusachet
transport *(v.)* သယ်ယူပို့ဆောင်သည် aasarrhtoekusachinn
transportation *(n.)* သယ်ယူပို့ဆောင်ရေး aasarrhtoekusamhu hkanyuusuu
trap *(v.)* ပိတ်မိသည်၊ ငြိနေသည် saalyuuphoetsaungrayy
trap *(n.)* ထောင်ချောက် saalyuu phoetsaungsai
trapdoor *(n.)* အံဝှက်တံခါး saalyuuphoetsaungrayy
trapeze *(n.)* ကောင်းကင်ဘား pate mi sai , ngyainaysai
trapezist *(n.)* ကောင်းကင်ကျွမ်းဘားသမား an what-tanhkarr
trapezoid *(n.)* အနားမပြိုင်စတုဂံ kaunggkainbharr
trapline *(n.)* ထောင်ချောက်လိုင်း *htaung-chauk-line*
trash *(n.)* အညှစ်စား a nyantsarr
trashed *(adj.)* ရမ်းကားဖျက်ဆီးသော ramkarr hpyetseesaw
trauma *(n.)* စိတ်ဒဏ်ရာ satedanrar
traumatic *(adj.)* စိတ်ဒဏ်ရာရသော satedanrarrasaw
traumatism *(n.)* ထိခိုက်မှုကြောင့် ရုပ်ပိုင်းစိတ်ပိုင်း ဒဏ်ရာရခြင်း *hti-khait-mu-kyaunt-yoke-pine-seik-pine-dan-yar-ya-chin*
traumatology *(n.)* ထိခိုက်မှုကို လေ့လာသည့် ပညာ *hti-khait-mu-ko-lae-lar-the-pin-nyar*
traunch *(n.)* တစ်စုံ *ta-zone*
travel *(n.)* ခရီးသွားခြင်း hkareeswarrchinn
traveller *(n.)* ခရီးသွား hkareeswarr

travelogue *(n.)* ခရီးသွားမှတ်တမ်း hkareeswarrmhaattam
traveltime *(n.)* ခရီးသွားချိန် hkareeswarrchane
traversable *(adj.)* ဖြတ်ကျော်နိုင်သော *phat-kyaw-nine-taw*
traverse *(n.)* ကန့်လန့်ဖြတ်တက်ခြင်း kant lant hpyattaatchinn
trawl *(n.)* ပိုက်စိပ်တိုက်လိုက်ခြင်း pite seik titelitechinn
trawlboat *(n.)* ပိုက်စိတ်ဖြင့် ငှားဖမ်းသောလှေ *pike-seit-pyint-ngar-phan-taw-hlay*
tray *(v.)* ဗန်းထဲ ထည့်သည် *ban-htae-htae-the*
treacherous *(adj.)* သစ္စာဖောက်သော sit-sar-hpout-saw
treachery *(n.)* သစ္စာဖောက်မှု *sit-sarhpoutmhu*
tread *(n.)* လမ်းလျှောက်ဟန် lamshouthaan
tread *(v.)* နင်းသည်၊ လျှောက်သည် ninn sai , shoutsai
treader *(n.)* နင်းသူ *nin-thu*
treadmill *(n.)* ပုံသေအလုပ်၊ စက်ခါးပတ် pone say aa-lote , saat hkarrpaat
treadplate *(n.)* သတ္တုကြမ်းခင်း *tat-tu-kyan-khin*
treadwheel *(n.)* ပြေးစက် *pyay-sat*
treason *(n.)* နိုင်ငံတော်သစ္စာဖောက်မှု nine-ngantaw sit-sarhpoutmhu
treasure *(v.)* တန်ဖိုးထားသည် taanhpoehtarrsai
treasure *(n.)* ရတနာ ratanar
treasurer *(n.)* ဘဏ္ဍာရေးမှူး bhandarrayymhauu
treasury *(n.)* ဘဏ္ဍာတိုက် bhandartite
treat *(v.)* ဆက်ဆံသည်၊ ဒကာခံသည် saatsan sai , dakar hkansai
treatise *(n.)* ကျမ်း kyam
treatment *(n.)* ကုထုံး kuhtone
treaty *(n.)* နိုင်ငံအချင်းချင်း သဘောတူစာအုပ် ninenganaachinnchinn sabhawtuusaraote
tree *(n.)* သစ်ပင် sitpin
trek *(n.)* ခြေကျင်ခရီးကြမ်း chay kyinhkareekyam
trek *(v.)* ခရီးကြမ်းနှင်သည် hkareekyam natesai
tremble *(v.)* တုန်သည် tonesai
tremendous *(adj.)* ကြီးမားသော kyeemarrsaw
tremor *(n.)* တုန်တုန်ယင်ယင်ဖြစ်ခြင်း tone tone yin yinhpyitchinn
trench *(v.)* ထိုးဖောက်ဝင်ရောက်သည် *htoe-hpauk-win-yauk-the*
trench *(n.)* ကတုတ်ကျင်း ka totekyinn
trend *(n.)* ဦးတည်ရာ u tairar
trespass *(n.)* ကျူးကျော်ဝင်ရောက်မှု kyuukyawwinroutmhu
trespass *(v.)* ကျူးကျော်သည် kyuukyawsai
trial *(n.)* စစ်ဆေးစီရင်ခြင်း sitsayy serinchinn
triangle *(n.)* တြိဂံ tyai gan
triangular *(adj.)* သုံးပွင့်ဆိုင် sone pwintsine
tribal *(adj.)* လူမျိုးနွယ်စု luumyoenwalsu
tribe *(n.)* မျိုးနွယ်စု myoenwalsu
tribulation *(n.)* အတိဒုက္ခ aatidukhka
tribunal *(n.)* ခုံအဖွဲ့ hkoneaahpwal
tributary *(n.)* လက်တက် laattaat
tribute *(n.)* ချီးကျူးဂုဏ်ပြုခြင်း cheekyuugonpyuchinn
trick *(v.)* လိမ်သည် linsai

trick *(n.)* လှည့်စားမှု hlae sarrmhu

trickery *(n.)* လိမ်လည်လှည့်စားမှု linlai hlae sarrmhu

trickle *(v.)* စီးကျသည် see kyasai

trickster *(n.)* လူလိမ် luulin

tricky *(adj.)* သိမ်မွေ့သော sinmwaesaw

tricolour *(n.)* သုံးရောင်ခြယ်အလံ soneraungchaalaalan

tricolour *(adj.)* သုံးရောင်ခြယ်သော soneraungchaalsaw

tricycle *(n.)* သုံးဘီးစက်ဘီး sonebheesaatbhee

trifle *(v.)* ယီးတီးယားတားလုပ်သည် yee tee yarr tarrlotesai

trifle *(n.)* အသေးအဖွဲ a sayyaahpwal

trigger *(n.)* ခလုတ်၊ မောင်း hkalote , maungg

trim *(n.)* ဆံပင်တိပေးခြင်း sanpin tipayychinn

trim *(adj.)* သွယ်လျသော၊ ကြော့ရှင်းသော swal lya saw , kyaww hlyinnsaw

trimester *(n.)* သုံးလအပိုင်းအခြား sone laaapineaacharr

trinity *(n.)* သုံးယောက်အစု soneyout aasu

trio *(n.)* သုံးယောက်တွဲ အဆိုအတီး soneyouttwal a so aatee

trip *(n.)* ခရီးတို hkareeto

trip *(v.)* ခလုတ်တိုက်သည် hkalote titesai

tripartite *(adj.)* သုံးပိုင်းရှိသော sone pineshisaw

triple *(v.)* သုံးဆတိုးသည် sone-sa toesai

triplicate *(n.)* မိတ္တူသုံးစောင် meittuu sonesaung

triplicate *(adj.)* မိတ္တူသုံးစောင်ကူးသော meittuu sone saung kuusaw

triplication *(n.)* မိတ္တူသုံးစောင်ကူးခြင်း meittuu sone saung kuuchinn

tripod *(n.)* သုံးချောင်းထောက် sone chaungghtout

triumph *(v.)* အောင်နိုင်သည် aaungninesai

triumph *(n.)* အောင်ပွဲ aaungpwal

triumphal *(adj.)* အောင်ပွဲခံ aaungpwahlkan

triumphant *(adj.)* ထူးထူးကဲကဲ အောင်မြင်သော htuuhtuukellkell aaungmyinsaw

trivial *(adj.)* အရေးမပါလှသော aarayy ma parhlasaw

troop *(v.)* ပြုံသည် pyone-sai

troop *(n.)* စစ်သည် sitsai

trooper *(n.)* သံချပ်ကာတပ် sanchautkartat

trophy *(n.)* ဖလားဆု hpalarrsu

tropic *(n.)* ယဉ်စွန်းတန်း yin swanntaann

tropical *(adj.)* အပူပိုင်းဒေသ aapuupineday-sa

trot *(n.)* ရှုရှားတော်လှန်ရေးခေါင်းဆောင် ထရော့စကီး၏ နောက်လိုက် rusharr tawhlaanrayyhkaunggsaung hta rot sa kee-eat nout-lite

trot *(v.)* ထောင့်ဖြတ် ခွာကျရွရွပြေးသည် htaunt-hpyat hkwar kya rwa rwa pyaysai

trouble *(v.)* သောကရောက်စေသည် saw ka routsaysai

trouble *(n.)* ဒုက္ခ duk-hka

troublesome *(adj.)* ဒုက္ခပေးသော duk-hka-payysaw

troupe *(n.)* အဖွဲ့ aa-hpwal

trousers *(n. pl.)* ဘောင်းဘီ bhaung-bhe

trowel *(n.)* သံလက် san-laat

truce *(n.)* အတိုက်အခိုက်ရပ်စဲခြင်း aa-titeaahkite ratsellchinn

truck *(n.)* ကုန်တင်ကား konetinkarr

true *(adj.)* မှန်ကန်သော mhaankaansaw

trump *(v.)* ကျယ်သည်၊ တစ်ပန်းသာအောင် လုပ်သည် kyaal sai , ta pan sar-aung lotesai

trump *(n.)* နိုင်ဖဲ၊ ဝှက်ဖဲ nine hpell , whaat-hpell

trumpet *(v.)* အာရိုက်သည် aar ritesai

trumpet *(n.)* ခရာ hka-rar

trunk *(n.)* ပင်စည် pin-sai

trust *(v.)* ယုံကြည်သည် yone-kyisai

trust *(n.)* ယုံကြည်ခြင်း yonekyi-chinn

trustee *(n.)* အုပ်ထိန်းသူ aote thein-suu

trustful *(adj.)* ယုံကြည်ရသော *yone-kyi-ya-taw*

trustworthy *(adj.)* ယုံကြည်စိတ်ချရသော yone-kyi-sate-cha-ra-saw

trusty *(adj.)* အားထားရသော ar-htarr-ra-saw

truth *(n.)* အမှန်တရား aa-mhaan-ta-rarr

truthful *(adj.)* မှန်ကန်သော mhaan-kaan-saw

try *(n.)* စမ်းကြည့်ခြင်း sam-kyi-chinn

try *(v.)* ကြိုးစားသည် kyoe-sarrsai

trying *(adj.)* သည်းခံရခက်သော saee-hkan-ra-hkaatsaw

tryst *(n.)* ပဋိညာဉ် *pa-dain-nyin*

tub *(n.)* စည်ပိုင်း sai-pine

tube *(n.)* ပြွန် pywan

tuberculosis *(n.)* အဆုတ်တီဘီရောဂါ aasotetebherawgar

tubular *(adj.)* ပြွန်ပုံ pywanpone

tug *(v.)* ဆွဲသည်၊ သုတ်သည် swal sai , sotesai

tuition *(n.)* ကျူရှင်ပေးခြင်း၊ ကျောင်းလခ kyuushin payychinn , kyaunglahka

tumble *(n.)* တလိမ့်ခေါက်ကွေးကျခြင်း ta lint hkout kwaykyachinn

tumble *(v.)* ကျွမ်းထိုးမှောက်ခုံကျသည် kywam htoe mhaout hkone kyasai

tumbler *(n.)* ကျည်ပုံဖန်ခွက် kyi pone hpaan-hkwat

tumour *(n.)* အသားပို a sarrpo

tumult *(n.)* အုတ်အုတ်ကျက်ကျက်အသံ aote aote kyet kyet-aa-san

tumultuous *(adj.)* ဝရုန်းသုန်းကား wa-ronesonekarr

tune *(v.)* ကြိုးညှိသည် kyoe nyhaisai

tune *(n.)* တီးလုံး teelone

tunnel *(v.)* လိုဏ်ခေါင်းဖောက်သည် lonhkaungghpoutsai

tunnel *(n.)* လိုဏ်ခေါင်း lonhkaungg

turban *(n.)* ခေါင်းပေါင်း hkaunggpaungg

turbine *(n.)* တာဘိုင် tarbhine

turbulence *(n.)* ဆူပူမှု suupuumhu

turbulent *(adj.)* ဆူဆူပူပူ suu suupuupuu

turf *(n.)* မြက်လွှာ myaatlwhar

turkey *(n.)* ကြက်ဆင် kyat-sin

turmeric *(n.)* နနွင်း na-nwam

turmoil *(n.)* ဝရုန်းသုန်းကားအခြေအနေ waronesonekarraachayaanay

turn *(n.)* လှည့်ခြင်း hlae-chinn

turn *(v.)* လှည့်သည် hlae sai

turner *(n.)* လှည့်သူ *hlae-thu*

turnip *(n.)* ခါးဖုဖြူ hkarr hpuhpyuu

turn-off *(n.)* လမ်းခွဲ lamhkwal

turnout *(n.)* ပရိသတ် pa-rate-sat

turpentine *(n.)* တာပင်တိုင်ဆီ tapintine-se

turtle *(n.)* လိပ် late

tusk *(n.)* အစွယ် aaswal

tussle *(v.)* နပန်းသတ်သည် na paann saatsai

tussle *(n.)* နပန်းပွဲ na paannpwal

tutor *(n.)* နည်းပြဆရာ naeepyasarar

tutorial *(n.)* ကျူတိုရီရယ် kyuu to reraal

tutorial *(adj.)* ကျူတိုရီရယ် kyuu to reraal

twelfth *(n.)* ဆယ့်နှစ်ခုမြောက် sae nit-hkumyawt

twelfth *(adj.)* ဆယ့်နှစ်ခုမြောက် sae nit-hkumyawt

twelve *(n.)* ဆယ့်နှစ် sae-nit

twentieth *(n.)* နှစ်ဆယ်ခုမြောက် nit-saahl-kumyawt

twentieth *(adj.)* နှစ်ဆယ်ခုမြောက် nit-saahl-kumyawt

twenty *(n.)* နှစ်ဆယ် nit-saal

twice *(adv.)* နှစ်ကြိမ် nit-kyain

twig *(n.)* သစ်ခက် sit-hkat

twilight *(n.)* ညနေဆည်းဆာ nya-nay-see-sar

twin *(adj.)* အမြွှာ aa-mywar

twin *(n.)* အမြွှာ aa-mywar

twinkle *(n.)* မှိတ်တုတ်မှိတ်တုတ်အလင်းရောင် mate-tote matetoteaalinnraung

twinkle *(v.)* မှိတ်တုတ်မှိတ်တုတ်လင်းသည် mhaatetote mhaatetote linnsai

twist *(n.)* လိမ်ခြင်း၊ လှည့်ခြင်း lin chinn , hlae chinn

twist *(v.)* ရစ်သည် ritsai

twitter *(v.)* တွတ်ထိုးသည် twat htoesai

twitter *(n.)* တွစ်တာလူမှုကွန်ရက်၊ စိုးစီစိုးစီမြည်သံ twittar luumhukwanraat , soe se soe se myisan

two *(n.)* နှစ်ခု na-hku

twofold *(adj.)* နှစ်ဆ na-sa

type *(v.)* အုပ်စုခွဲသည် aote-su-hkwal-sai

type *(n.)* အမျိုးအစား aamyoeaasarr

typhoid *(n.)* အူရောင်ငန်းဖျား auu raung ngaannhpyarr

typhoon *(n.)* တိုင်ဖွန်းမုန်တိုင်း tinehpwannmonetine

typhus *(n.)* တိုက်ဖတ်ရောဂါ tite hpaatrawgar

typical *(adj.)* နမူနာအားဖြင့် namuunar aarrhpyint

typify *(v.)* ကိုယ်စားပြုသည် kosarrpyusai

typist *(n.)* လက်နှိပ်စက်ရိုက်သူ laat natesaat ritesuu

tyranny *(n.)* မင်းဆိုးမင်းညစ်၏ အုပ်ချုပ်မှု၊ ကြီးစိုးဖိစီးမှု min soe min nyaiteat aotechotemhu , kyeesoe hpi seemhu

tyrant *(n.)* အာဏာရှင် aarnarshin

tyre *(n.)* တာယာ taryar

U

uber *(adv.)* အလွန် *a-loon*

ubergeek *(n.)* ထိတ်တန်းကျွမ်းကျင်သူ *htate-tan-kywan-kyin-thu*

uberous *(adj.)* အကျိုးများသော *a-kyo-myar-taw*

ubersexual *(n.)* လိင်ကွဲစိတ်ဝင်စားသူဖြစ်သော *lain-kwal-seik-win-sar-thu-phit-taw*

ubicity *(n.)* တည်နေရာ *the-nay-yar*

ubiquitous *(adj.)* နေရာတိုင်းမှာ nay-rar-tinemhar

ubiquity *(n.)* နေရာအနှံ့ရှိခြင်း nay-raraanhaanshichinn

udder *(n.)* နွားမ၏ နို့အုံ nwarr-ma-eat nhoet-aone
ufo *(n.)* အမည်မသိယာဥ်ပျံ aa-mai-ma-si yinpyaan
ufologist *(n.)* အမည်မသိယာဥ်ပျံဆိုင်ရာ ပညာရှင် aa-mai-ma-si yin pyaansinerar panyarshin
ufology *(n.)* အမည်မသိယာဥ်ပျံ လေ့လာမှု aa-mai-ma-si yinpyaan laelarmhu
uglify *(v.)* ရုပ်ဆိုးအောင်လုပ်သည် *yoke-soe-aung-lote-sai*
ugliness *(n.)* အရုပ်ဆိုးခြင်း a rote-soechinn
ugly *(adj.)* အရုပ်ဆိုးသော a rotesoesaw
ukelele *(n.)* လေးကြိုးတပ်ဂစ်တာ *lay-kyo-tat-gittar*
ukeleleist *(n.)* လေးကြိုးတပ်ဂစ်တာပညာရှင် *lay-kyo-tat-gittar-pyin-nyar-shin*
ulcer *(n.)* အနာ aa-nar
ulcerous *(adj.)* အနာနှင့်ဆိုင်သော *a-nar-nint-sine-taw*
ulterior *(adj.)* ဖုံးကွယ်ထားသော hpone-kwahltarrsaw
ultimate *(adj.)* နောက်ဆုံး noutsone
ultimately *(adv.)* နောက်ဆုံးတွင် noutsonetwin
ultimatum *(n.)* ရာဇသံ rar-za-san
ultra *(n.)* အလွန်အကျွံ aa-lwan-aa-kywan
ultracasual *(adj.)* အလွန်အမှတ်မထင်ဖြစ်သော aa-lwan-aa-mhaatmahtinhpyitsaw
ultracompact *(adj.)* အလွန်သိပ်သည်းသော aa-lwan seik saeesaw
ultraconservative *(n.)* ရှေးရိုးအလွန်ဆန်သူ shayy roe aalwan saansuu
ultrasecure *(adj.)* အလွန်လုံခြုံသော aalwan lonechon-saw
ultrasonic *(adj.)* နှုန်းလွန်အသံ hnone lawn-aa-san
ultrasonics *(n.)* နှုန်းလွန်အသံလှိုင်း hnone lawn-aa-san-hline
ultrasound *(n.)* နှုန်းလွန်အသံလှိုင်း hnone lwan aasanhline
ultraviolet *(adj.)* ခရမ်းလွန် hkaramlwan
ululate *(v.)* မြည်တမ်းသည် myi tamsai
ululation *(n.)* မြည်ကြွေးခြင်း myi kywaychinn
umbrella *(n.)* ထီး htee
umpire *(n.)* ဒိုင်လူကြီး dineluukyee
unabashed *(adj.)* မရှက်သော ma shat-saw
unabashedly *(adv.)* မရှက်မကြောက် ma shatmakyawt
unable *(adj.)* မနိုင်သော ma-nine-saw
unabridged *(adj.)* မူရင်းအတိုင်းဖြစ်သော muurinnaatinehpyitsaw
unacceptable *(adj.)* လက်မခံနိုင်သော laat-mahkanninesaw
unaccessible *(adj.)* ဝင်ခွင့်မရသော win hkwintmarasaw
unaccommodating *(adj.)* ထည့်သွင်းမစဉ်းစားသော htae swin ma sin sarrsaw
unaccountable *(adj.)* ရှင်းမပြနိုင်သော shinn ma pya-ninesaw
unaccurate *(adj.)* မတိကျသော ma ti-kya-saw
unachievable *(adj.)* မအောင်မြင်နိုင်သော ma-aung-myin ninesaw
unacquainted *(adj.)* မရင်းနှီးသော ma-rinn-nee-saw
unadapted *(adj.)* ကျင့်သားမရသော kyint-sar-ma-ra-saw
unadjusted *(adj.)* အနေအထားမပြုပြင်နိုင်သော a-nay-a-htarr ma pyu-pyin-ninesaw

unaffected *(adj.)* **ထိခိုက်ခြင်းမရှိ** htihkite chinnmashi
unaffectionate *(adj.)* **မချစ်ခင်သော** ma chit-hkin-saw
unaided *(adj.)* **အကူအညီမပါဘဲဖြစ်သော** aa-kuu-aa-nye ma-parbhelhlpyitsaw
unambiguous *(adj.)* **ပြတ်သားသော** pyat-sarrsaw
unambivalence *(n.)* **စိတ်နှစ်ခွမဖြစ်ခြင်း** sate na hkwa ma-hpyit-chinn
unamused *(adj.)* **မပျော်ရွှင်ခြင်း** ma-pyaw-shwinchinn
unanimity *(n.)* **စည်းလုံးမှု** see-lone-mhu
unanimous *(adj.)* **တညီတညွတ်တည်း** ta-nye-ta-nywat-tee
unannounced *(adj.)* **မပြောမဆို** ma pyaw maso
unappealing *(adj.)* **စိတ်မပါသော** sate-ma-parsaw
unapproved *(adj.)* **ခွင့်မပြုသော** hkwint mapyusaw
unarmed *(adj.)* **လက်နက်မဲ့သော** laat-naatmaesaw
unauthorized *(adj.)* **ခွင့်မပြုသော** hkwint mapyusaw
unavoidable *(adj.)* **မရှောင်နိုင်သော** ma shaung-ninesaw
unaware *(adj.)* **သတိမပြုမိသော** sa-ti-mapyumisaw
unawares *(adv.)* **အလစ်** aa-lit
unbearable *(adj.)* **သည်းမခံနိုင်သော** see ma hkan-ninesaw
unbeaten *(adj.)* **ရှုံးပွဲမရှိသော** shone pwalmashisaw
unbelievable *(adj.)* **ယုံကြည်မှုမရှိသော** yonekyimhumashisaw
unburden *(v.)* **ရင်ဖွင့်သည်** rin-hpwint sai
uncanny *(adj.)* **မသိုးမသန့်ဖြစ်သော** ma soe ma saanthpyitsaw
uncertain *(adj.)* **မသေချာသော** masaychaarsaw
uncivilized *(adj.)* **မယဉ်ကျေးသော** ma yin kyaayysaw
uncle *(n.)* **ဦးလေး** ulayy
unclear *(adj.)* **မရှင်းလင်းသော** ma-shinnlinnsaw
uncomfortable *(adj.)* **သက်သောင့်သက်သာမရှိသော** saat saunt-saat-sar mashisaw
uncouth *(adj.)* **ရိုင်းစိုင်းသော** rinesinesaw
undecided *(adj.)* **မဆုံးဖြတ်နိုင်သော** ma sonehpyatninesaw
undefeated *(adj.)* **မရှုံးနိမ့်နိုင်သော** ma shone-nint-ninesaw
under *(adj.)* **အောက်** aout
undercurrent *(n.)* **အတွင်းအောင်း** aa-twinaaungg
underdog *(n.)* **အနိုမ်ခံလူတန်းစား** aa-nain-hkan-luu-taan-sarr
undergo *(v.)* **ကြုံရသည်** kyone-ra-sai
undergraduate *(n.)* **ကောလိပ်ကျောင်းသား** kaw-late-kyaung-sarr
underhand *(adj.)* **လက်သီးပုန်းထိုးသော** laat-see pone htoesaw
underline *(v.)* **အောက်မျဉ်းသားသည်** aout myin sarr-sai
undermine *(v.)* **အောက်ခြေက လှိုက်စားသည်** aout-chay-ka hlite sarrsai
underneath *(prep.)* **အောက်** aout
underpriviledged *(adj.)* **နွမ်းပါးသော** nwam parrsaw
understand *(v.)* **နားလည်သည်** narrlaisai
undertake *(v.)* **တာဝန်ယူသည်** tarwaanyuusai

undertone *(n.)* တီးတိုးလေသံ teetoe laysan
underwear *(n.)* အတွင်းခံဘောင်းဘီ aatwin hkanbhaunggbhe
underworld *(n.)* မြေအောက်ကမ္ဘာ myay-aoutkambhar
undo *(v.)* မလုပ်ပါ malotepar
undue *(adj.)* ပိုကဲသော po kellsaw
undulate *(v.)* တအိအိလှုပ်သည် ta-ai-ai hlotesai
undulation *(n.)* တအိအိလှုပ်သည် ta-ai-ai hlotesai
unearth *(v.)* တူးဖော်ရရှိသည် tuuhpawrashisai
uneasy *(adj.)* မလွယ်ကူသော ma-lwal-kuusaw
uneducated *(adj.)* ပညာမတတ်သော pa-nyar mataatsaw
uneven *(adj.)* မညီညာသော ma nye nyarsaw
unfair *(adj.)* မတရားသော matararrsaw
unfold *(v.)* ဖြန့်သည် hpyant-sai
unfortunate *(adj.)* ကံမကောင်းသော kanmakaunggsaw
ungainly *(adj.)* ကိုးရိုးကားရားနိုင်သော koe roe karr rarr-ninesaw
unhappy *(adj.)* မပျော်ရွှင်သော mapyawshwinsaw
unhealthy *(adj.)* မကျန်းမာသော ma kyannmarsaw
unification *(n.)* ပေါင်းစီးခြင်း *paung-see-chin*
uninspired *(adj.)* ဈာန်မဝင်သော zan mawinsaw
uninstall *(adj.)* ဖြုတ်သည် hpyote-sai
uninterrupted *(adj.)* အနှောင့်အယှက်ကင်းသော a naut a-shat kinnsaw
union *(n.)* ပြည်ထောင်စု pyi-htaung-su
unionist *(n.)* အလုပ်သမားသမဂ္ဂဝင် aa-lote-samarrsamaggawin
unique *(adj.)* ထူးခြားသော htuucharrsaw
unison *(n.)* ညီညာခြင်း nye nyarchinn
unit *(n.)* ယူနစ် yuunit
unite *(v.)* စည်းလုံးသည် seelonesai
unity *(n.)* စည်းလုံးခြင်း saeelonechinn
universal *(adj.)* အားလုံးနှင့်ဆိုင်သော aarrlone nintsinesaw
universality *(n.)* ကမ္ဘာလုံးပျံ့နှံ့မှု kambharlone pyaannhaanmhu
universe *(n.)* အနန္တစကြဝဠာ aanantasakyawalar
university *(n.)* တက္ကသိုလ် takkasol
unjust *(adj.)* မတရားသော matararrsaw
unknown *(adj.)* မသိသော masisaw
unless *(conj.)* မဖြစ်ခဲ့လျှင် ma hpyithkaehlyin
unlike *(adj.)* တစ်ခြားစီ ta-charr-se
unlikely *(adj.)* အလားအလာမရှိ aalarraalarmashi
unmanned *(adj.)* လူက ထိန်းရန် မလိုသော luuk hteinraan malosaw
unmannerly *(adj.)* ရိုင်းသော rinesaw
unnecessary *(adj.)* မလိုအပ်သော maloatsaw
unofficial *(adj.)* တရားမဝင်သော tararrmawinsaw
unplanned *(adj.)* အစီအစဉ်မရှိ aaseaasinmashi
unprincipled *(adj.)* မူမရှိသော muumashisaw
unquote *(adj.)* မကိုးကားသော *ma-koe-kar-taw*

unread *(adj.)* **မဖတ်ရသေးသော** mahpaatrasayysaw
unreliable *(adj.)* **စိတ်မချရသော** satemacharasaw
unrest *(n.)* **အုံကြွမှု၊ ဆူပူမှု** aonekyawmhu , suupuumhu
unruly *(adj.)* **ထိန်းမနိုင်သိမ်းမရသော** htein ma nine saimmarasaw
unsalted *(adj.)* **ဆားမပါသော** sarrmaparsaw
unsettle *(v.)* **နေသားမကျဖြစ်စေသည်** nay sarr m kyahpyitsaysai
unsheathe *(v.)* **ဓားအိမ်မှ ထုတ်သည်** *dar-eain-ma-htoke-the*
unsold *(adj.)* **မရောင်းသော** ma raunggsaw
until *(conj.)* **တိုင်အောင်** tineaaung
untoward *(adj.)* **ဆိုးရွားသော** soerwarrsaw
unwanted *(adj.)* **မလိုချင်သော** malochinsaw
unwell *(adj.)* **နေထိုင်မကောင်းသော** nayhtinemakaunggsaw
unwittingly *(adv.)* **မတော်တဆ** matawta-sa
up *(prep.)* **ထသည်၊ ထောင်သည်၊ တက်သည်** hta sai , htaung sai , taatsai
upbraid *(v.)* **ကြိမ်းမောင်းသည်** kyaaimmaunggsai
upgrade *(v.)* **အဆင့်မြှင့်သည်** aasintmyahaintsai
upheaval *(n.)* **ကသောင်းကနင်းဖြစ်မှု** ka saungg ka ninnhpyitmhu
uphold *(v.)* **အတည်ပြုသည်** aataipyusai
upkeep *(n.)* **ထိန်းသိမ်းစရိတ်** hteinsaimsarate
uplift *(n.)* **စိတ်ဓာတ်တက်လာခြင်း** satedhrat taat-larchinn
upload *(v.)* **တင်သည်** tinsai
upon *(prep.)* **အပေါ်မှာ** aapaw-mhar
upper *(adj.)* **အပေါ်** aa-paw
upright *(adj.)* **ထောင်လျက်ရှိသော၊ တည့်မတ်သော** htaung lyetshisaw , tae maat-saw
uprising *(n.)* **သူပုန်ထခြင်း** suuponehtachinn
uproar *(n.)* **အုတ်အုတ်ကျက်ကျက်ဖြစ်ခြင်း** aote aote kyet kyethpyitchinn
uproarious *(adj.)* **သောင်းသောင်းသဲသဲ** saunggsaunggsellsell
uproot *(v.)* **အမြစ်ပြုတ်သည်** aamyit pyote-sai
upset *(v.)* **ဝမ်းနည်းသည်** wamnaeesai
upshot *(n.)* **ရလဒ်** ralad
upstart *(n.)* **နောက်မှ ပေါ်သည့် ရှေ့ကြာပင်** noutmha paw-seet shway kyaarpin
up-to-date *(adj.)* **ခေတ်မီသော** hkitt-mesaw
upward *(adj.)* **မော့၍ ကြည့်သော** mot-ywe kyi-saw
upwards *(adv.)* **မော့၍ ထောင်၍** mot-ywe htaung-ywe
urban *(adj.)* **မြို့ပြ** myoe-pya rai-mwansaw
urbane *(adj.)* **ရည်မွန်သော** raimwanmhu
urbanity *(n.)* **ရည်မွန်မှု** lay lwintsuungaal
urchin *(n.)* **လေလွင့်သူငယ်** titetwannsai
urge *(v.)* **တိုက်တွန်းသည်** pyinnpyinn pya paysan-da
urgency *(n.)* **အရေးတကြီး** aarayytakyee
urgent *(adj.)* **အရေးတကြီး** see swarrhkaann
urinal *(n.)* **ဆီးသွားခန်း** see nintsinesaw
urinary *(adj.)* **ဆီးနှင့်ဆိုင်သော** seeswarrsai
urinate *(v.)* **ဆီးသွားသည်** seeswarrchinn

urination *(n.)* ဆီးသွားခြင်း see

urine *(n.)* ဆီး aaroeaoe

urn *(n.)* အရိုးအိုး aasonepyuninesaw

usable *(adj.)* အသုံးပြုနိုင်သော aasoneaahnone

usage *(n.)* အသုံးအနှုန်း aasonepyuchinn

use *(n.)* အသုံးပြုခြင်း aasonepyusai

used *(adj.)* အသုံးပြုသော aasonewinsaw

useful *(adj.)* အသုံးဝင်သော eet-kyo

usher *(v.)* ခရီးဦးကြိုပြု၍ နေရာချပေးသည် htonesanaatinehpyitsaw

usual *(adj.)* ထုံးစံအတိုင်းဖြစ်သော htonesanaatine

usually *(adv.)* ထုံးစံအတိုင်း a toe kyeehpyint ngway toe chasuu

usurer *(n.)* အတိုးကြီးဖြင့် ငွေတိုးချသူ lu yuusai

usurp *(v.)* လုယူသည် matararrsaimyuuchinn

usurpation *(n.)* မတရားသိမ်းယူခြင်း a toe kyeesarr ngway toe chachinn

usury *(n.)* အတိုးကြီးစား၍ ငွေတိုးချခြင်း aasoneaasaung

utensil *(n.)* အသုံးအဆောင် sarraain

uterus *(n.)* သားအိမ် kaungkyoepyumhu shayyshusaw

utilitarian *(adj.)* ကောင်းကျိုးပြုမှု ရှေးရှုသော aasonewin chinn , aasonewaansaungmhulotengaann

utility *(n.)* အသုံးဝင်ခြင်း၊ အသုံးဝန်ဆောင်မှုလုပ်ငန်း aasonepyuchinn

utilization *(n.)* အသုံးပြုခြင်း aasonepyasai

utilize *(v.)* အသုံးပြုသည် a myintsone

utmost *(n.)* အစွမ်းကုန် satekuu yinlawk

utopia *(n.)* စိတ်ကူးယဉ်လောက satekuu yinsaansaw

utopian *(adj.)* စိတ်ကူးယဉ်ဆန်သော htwatsai

utter *(v.)* ထွက်သည် aakywin-mae

utterance *(n.)* ဖွင့်ဟခြင်း lonelonelyarrlyarr

utterly *(adv.)* လုံးလုံးလျားလျား aalote laitlautmhu

vacancy *(n.)* အလုပ်လစ်လပ်မှု aalote laitlautsaw

vacant *(adj.)* အလုပ်လစ်လပ်သော htwatsai

vacate *(v.)* ထွက်သည် aarrlautraat

vacation *(n.)* အားလပ်ရက် karkwalsayy htoesai

vaccinate *(v.)* ကာကွယ်ဆေးထိုးသည် karkwalsayy htoechinn

vaccination *(n.)* ကာကွယ်ဆေးထိုးခြင်း karkwalsayy htoe payysuu

vaccinator *(n.)* ကာကွယ်ဆေးထိုးပေးသူ karkwalsayy

vaccine *(n.)* ကာကွယ်ဆေး mapyat ma sarrhpyitsai

vacillate *(v.)* မပြတ်မသားဖြစ်သည် layharnaal

vacuum *(v.)* ဖုန်စုပ်စက်ဖြင့် စုပ်သည် lay lwint saw

vagabond *(adj.)* လေလွင့်သော luu lay luu lwint

vagabond *(n.)* လူလေလူလွင့် pyaungglell taatchinn

vagary *(n.)* ပြောင်းလဲတတ်ခြင်း mwaylamkyaungg

vagina *(n.)* မွေးလမ်းကြောင်း ma sell kwalsaw

vague *(adj.)* မသဲကွဲသော ma sell makwal

vagueness *(n.)* မသဲမကွဲ sate kyeewinsaw

vain *(adj.)* စိတ်ကြီးဝင်သော mar na htaung lwannsaw

vainglorious *(adj.)* မာနထောင်လွှန်းသော mar na htaung lwannchinn

vainglory *(n.)* မာနထောင်လွှန်းခြင်း a chaeenhaee

vainly *(adv.)* အချည်းနှီး chaine , taungkyarr

vale *(n.)* ချိုင့်၊ တောင်ကြား youtyarr a say aaparr

valet *(n.)* ယောက်ျားအစေအပါး rell swam sattishisaw

valiant *(adj.)* ရဲစွမ်းသတ္တိရှိသော aasaatwinsaw

valid *(adj.)* အသက်ဝင်သော aasaatwinaaung lotesai

validate *(v.)* အသက်ဝင်အောင် လုပ်သည် hkine lone chinn , tararrwinhpyitchinn

validity *(n.)* ခိုင်လုံခြင်း၊ တရားဝင်ဖြစ်ခြင်း taungkyarr

valley *(n.)* တောင်ကြား rell swmsatti

valour *(n.)* ရဲစွမ်းသတ္တိ taanhpoeshisaw

valuable *(adj.)* တန်ဖိုးရှိသော taanhpoe hpyatchinn

valuation *(n.)* တန်ဖိုးဖြတ်ခြင်း taanhpoehtarrsai

value *(v.)* တန်ဖိုးထားသည် taanhpoe

value *(n.)* တန်ဖိုး a thoet-shin

valve *(n.)* အဆို့ရှင် baankarr

van *(n.)* ဗန်ကား laat saram hpyet-seesai

vandalize *(v.)* လက်သရမ်း ဖျက်ဆီးသည် pyawt-kwalswarrsai

vanish *(v.)* ပျောက်ကွယ်သွားသည် wint warchinn

vanity *(n.)* ဝင့်ဝါခြင်း nhaainnainnsai

vanquish *(v.)* နှိမ်နင်းသည် aangwaepyansai

vaporize *(v.)* အငွေ့ပြန်သည် aangwae pyansaw

vaporous *(adj.)* အငွေ့ပြန်သော aangwae

vapour *(n.)* အငွေ့ pyaungglellsaw

variable *(adj.)* ပြောင်းလဲသော kwallwalchet

variance *(n.)* ကွဲလွဲချက် aapyaungaalell

variation *(n.)* အပြောင်းအလဲ kwalsaw

varied *(adj.)* ကွဲသော aamyoeaasarr sone linchinn

variety *(n.)* အမျိုးအစားစုံလင်ခြင်း aamyoemyoesaw

various *(adj.)* အမျိုးမျိုးသော aaraungtinsai

varnish *(v.)* အရောင်တင်သည် aaraung tinse

varnish *(n.)* အရောင်တင်ဆီ charrnarrsai

vary *(v.)* ခြားနားသည် paan-oe

vase *(n.)* ပန်းအိုး youtyarr sarr kyaww hpyatchinn

vasectomy *(n.)* ယောက်ျားသားကြောဖြတ်ခြင်း baat salin

vaseline *(n.)* ဗက်ဆလင် kyaal-pyawwsaw

vast *(adj.)* ကျယ်ပြောသော tote htout hkonesai

vault *(v.)* တုတ်ထောက်ခုန်သည် a-moepaunggkuu

vault *(n.)* အမိုးပေါင်းကူး baat tar , nyun rat , rawgar saalsaungsaw tirassaran

vector *(n.)* ဗက်တာ၊ ညွှန်ရပ်၊ ရောဂါသယ်ဆောင်သော တိရစ္ဆာန်
vectorial *(adj.)* ဗက်တာနှင့်ဆိုင်သော *vat-tar-nint-sine-taw*
vegan *(adj.)* သတ်သတ်လွတ်စားသော saatsaatlwat sarrsaw
vegetable *(adj.)* အသီးအရွက် aaseeaarwat
vegetable *(n.)* အသီးအရွက် aaseeaarwat
vegetarian *(n.)* သတ်သတ်လွတ်စားသူ saatsaatlwat sarrsuu
vegetation *(n.)* သဘာဝပေါက်ပင် sabharwapoutpin
vehemence *(n.)* ပြင်းထန်ခြင်း pyinnhtaanchinn
vehement *(adj.)* ပြင်းထန်သော pyinnhtaansaw
vehicle *(n.)* ယာဉ် yin
vehicular *(adj.)* ယာဉ် yin
veil *(v.)* ဖုံးအုပ်သည် hpone aote-sai
veil *(n.)* မျက်နှာလွှားဇာ myetnhar lwharjar
vein *(v.)* သွေးကြောကဲ့သို့ ပုံစံ *thway-kyaw-kae-tho-pon-san*
velocity *(n.)* အရှိန် aa-shein
velvet *(n.)* ကတ္တီပါ kat tepar
velvety *(adj.)* ကတ္တီပါလို kat te parlo
venal *(adj.)* ငွေမက်သော ngway maatsaw
venality *(n.)* လောဘဇော lawbhazaw
vendor *(n.)* ပျံ့ကျဈေးသည် pyaan kyasyaayysai
venerable *(adj.)* ကြည်ညိုကိုင်းရှိုင်းဖွယ်ရာ kyinyo kine hlyinehpwalrar
venerate *(v.)* အမွန်အမြတ်ထားသည် a mwan aamyathtarrsai
veneration *(n.)* ကြည်ညိုကိုင်းရှိုင်းမှု kyinyo kine hlyinemhu
vengeance *(n.)* ကလဲ့စားချေခြင်း kalaesarr chaaychinn
venial *(adj.)* အရေးမယူလောက်သော aarayymayuu loutsaw
venom *(n.)* အဆိပ်၊ အငြိုး aaseik, aangyaoe
venomous *(adj.)* အဆင်ရှိသော a sinshisaw
vent *(n.)* လေဝင်လေထွက်အပေါက် laywinlayhtwat aapout
ventilate *(v.)* လေဝင်လေထွက်ကောင်းသည် laywinlayhtwat kaunggsai
ventilation *(n.)* လေဝင်လေထွက် laywinlayhtwat
ventilator *(n.)* လေဝင်ပေါက် laywinpout
ventriloquism *(n.)* မိမိအသံကို တစ်ခြားမှ ထွက်ပေါ်လာဟန် ဖန်တီးဖျော်ဖြေမှု mimiaasanko taitcharrmha htwatpawlarhaan hpaanteehpyawhpyaymhu
ventriloquist *(n.)* မိမိအသံကို တစ်ခြားမှ ထွက်ပေါ်လာဟန် ဖန်တီးဖျော်ဖြေသူ mimiaasanko taitcharrmha htwatpawlarhaan hpaantee hpyawhpyaysuu
ventriloquistic *(adj.)* မိမိအသံကို တစ်ခြားမှ ထွက်ပေါ်လာဟန် ဖန်တီးဖျော်ဖြေသော mimiaasanko taitcharrmha htwatpawlarhaan hpaantee hpyawhpyaysaw
ventriloquize *(v.)* မိမိအသံကို တစ်ခြားမှ ထွက်ပေါ်လာဟန် ဖန်တီးဖျော်ဖြေသည် mimiaasanko taitcharrmha htwatpawlarhaan hpaantee hpyawhpyaysai
venture *(v.)* သွားသည်၊ ပြောသည်၊ စွန့်သည် swarrsai , pyawwsai , swunt-sai
venture *(n.)* လုပ်ငန်း lotengaann
venturesome *(adj.)* စွန့်ရဲသော swant rellsaw
venturous *(adj.)* စွန့်ရဲသော *sunt-yaal-taw*

venue *(n.)* နေရာ nayrar

veracity *(n.)* မှန်ကန်ခြင်း mhaankaanchinn

veranda *(n.)* ဝရန်တာ waraantar

verb *(n.)* ကြိယာ kyari-yar

verbal *(adj.)* အပြော aa-pyaww

verbally *(adv.)* နှုတ်ဖြင့် nhuat-hpyint

verbatim *(adj.)* လုံးချင်း lonechinn

verbose *(adj.)* လေရှည်သော lay shisaw

verbosity *(n.)* စကားတံရှည်ခြင်း sakarr tan shichinn

verdant *(adj.)* စိမ်းလန်းသော saimlaannsaw

verdict *(n.)* ဆုံးဖြတ်ချက် sonehpyatchet

verge *(n.)* လမ်းပခုံး lampahkone

verification *(n.)* စိစစ်ခြင်း၊ အတည်ပြုခြင်း sisit chinn , aataipyuchinn

verify *(v.)* စိစစ်သည်၊ အတည်ပြုသည် sisit sai , aataipyusai

verisimilitude *(n.)* သဏ္ဍာန်လုပ်သရုပ်တူခြင်း san daran lote sarote tuuchinn

veritable *(adj.)* သဖွယ်ဖြစ်သော sahpwahlpyitsaw

vermillion *(adj.)* ဟင်္သပဒါး hin sa pa darr

vermillion *(n.)* ဟင်္သပဒါး hin sa pa darr

vernacular *(adj.)* ဒေသန္တရတိုင်း daysantaratine

vernacular *(n.)* ဒေသဝေါဟာရ daysawawharr

vernal *(adj.)* နွေဦး nway u

versatile *(adj.)* စွယ်စုံရသော swalsonerasaw

versatility *(n.)* သပ္ပာယရှိခြင်း sap par yashichinn

verse *(n.)* ကဗျာ kabyaar

versed *(adj.)* တတ်မြောက်သော taat myawtsaw

versification *(n.)* ကဗျာဖွဲ့ခြင်း kabyaar hpwalchinn

versify *(v.)* ကဗျာဖွဲ့သည် kabyaar hpwalsai

version *(n.)* ဗားရှင်း barrhlyinn

versus *(prep.)* နှင့် nint

vertical *(adj.)* မတ်စောက်သော maat soutsaw

verve *(n.)* မာန်ပါခြင်း man parchinn

very *(adj.)* အလွန် aa-lwan

vessel *(n.)* သွေးကြော sway-kyaww

vest *(v.)* အပ်နှင်းသည် atnatensai

vest *(n.)* စွပ်ကျယ်အင်္ကျီ swut kyaal aainkyae

vested *(adj.)* ဝတ်ရုံခြုံသည် *wut-yone-chone-taw*

vestige *(n.)* လက်စလက်န laat sa laatna

vestment *(n.)* ဝတ်ရုံ waatrone

veteran *(adj.)* စစ်ပြန် sitpyan

veteran *(n.)* စစ်ပြန် sitpyan

veterinary *(adj.)* တိရစ္ဆာန်ဆေးကု tirassaransayyku

veto *(v.)* ဗီတိုအာဏာသုံး၍ ပယ်ချသည် betoaarnarsone paalchasai

veto *(n.)* ဗီတိုအာဏာ betoaarnar

vex *(v.)* စိတ်ဆိုးသည် satesoesai

vexation *(n.)* စိတ်အနှောင့်အယှက် sate a naut-aa-shaat

via *(prep.)* မှတစ်ဆင့်ဖြင့် mha-ta-sint-hpyint

viable *(adj.)* အလားအလာရှိသော aalarraalarshisaw

vial *(n.)* ဖန်ဘူးငယ် hpaan bhuungaal

vibrate *(v.)* တုန်ခါသည် tone hkarsai

vibration *(n.)* တုန်ခါခြင်း tone hkarchinn

vicar *(n.)* ခရစ်ယာန်ဘုန်းကြီး hkaraityaranbhonekyee

vicarious *(adj.)* တစ်ဆင့်ခံ taitsinthkan

vice *(n.)* မကောင်းမှု makaunggmhu

viceroy *(n.)* ဘုရင်ခံ bhurinhkan

vice-versa *(adv.)* အပြန်အလှန် aapyanaahlaan

vicinity *(n.)* အနီး aanee

vicious *(adj.)* ရက်စက်သော raatsaatsaw

vicissitude *(n.)* လောကဓံတရား lawkadhantararr

victim *(n.)* ခံရသူ hkanrasuu

victimize *(v.)* မတရားဖိနှိပ်ခံရသည် matararr hpinatehkanrasai

victor *(n.)* အောင်နိုင်သူ aaungninesuu

victorious *(adj.)* အောင်မြင်သော aaungmyinsaw

victory *(n.)* အောင်မြင်မှု aaungmyinmhu

victuals *(n. pl)* စားသောက်စရာ sarrsoutsarar

video *(n.)* ဗီဒီယို bedeyo

videoblogger *(n.)* ဗီဒီယိုဘလော့ကာ bedeyobhalotkar

videobook *(n.)* ဗီဒီယိုစာအုပ် bedeyosaraote

videocassette *(n.)* ဗီဒီယိုကက်ဆက် bedeyo kaatsaat

videogaming *(n.)* ဗီဒီယိုဂိမ်း bedeyogaim

videotape *(n.)* ဗီဒီယိုတိတ်ခွေ bedeyotatehkway

videotelephone *(n.)* ဗီဒီယိုဖုန်းခေါ်ခြင်း bedeyo hponehkawchin

vie *(v.)* ပြိုင်သည် pyaine-sai

view *(n.)* မြင်ကွင်း၊ ရှုခင်း myinkwin , shuhkinn

vigil *(n.)* အိပ်စက်ခြင်း မပြုဘဲ နေခြင်း aitsaatchinn mapyubhell naychinn

vigilance *(n.)* နိုးနိုးကြားကြားရှိခြင်း noenoe kyarr kyarrshichinn

vigilant *(adj.)* နိုးနိုးကြားကြားရှိသော noenoe kyarr kyarrshisaw

vigorous *(adj.)* အားမာန်ပါသော aarrmarn parsaw

vile *(adj.)* မသတီစရာ ma sa te-sa-rar

vilify *(v.)* အမနာပ ပြောသည် aamanarp pyawwsai

villa *(n.)* မြို့ပြင် အိမ်ကြီးရခိုင် myoet-pyin aainkyeerahkine

village *(n.)* ရွာ rwar

villager *(n.)* ရွာသား rwar-sarr

villain *(n.)* ဗီလိန် belein

vindicate *(v.)* သက်ာရှင်းသည် sin kar shinn-sai

vindication *(n.)* သက်သေထူခြင်း saatsay htuuchinn

vine *(n.)* စပျစ်ပင် sa pyitpin

vinegar *(n.)* ရှလကာရည် sha la karrai

vintage *(n.)* ထုတ်လုပ်သောနှစ် htotelotesawnit

violate *(v.)* ချိုးဖောက်သည် choehpoutsai

violation *(n.)* ချိုးဖောက်ခြင်း choehpoutchinn

violence *(n.)* အကြမ်းဖက်မှု aakyamhpaatmhu

violent *(adj.)* ကြမ်းကြုတ်သော kyam kyuatsaw

violet *(n.)* နီလာပန်း၊ ခရမ်းရောင် nelar paann , hkaramraung

violin *(n.)* တယော tayaw

violinist *(n.)* တယောသမား tayawsamarr

viral *(adj.)* ဗိုင်းရပ်စ်နှင့်ဆိုင်သော bineratit nintsinesaw

virgin *(adj.)* ပကတိ pakati

virgin *(n.)* အပျိုစင် aapyosin

virginity *(n.)* အပျိုစစ်စစ်ဖြစ်ခြင်း aapyo sitsithpyitchinn

virile *(adj.)* သန်သော၊ သန်မာသော saan saw , saan marsaw

virility *(n.)* ခွန်အားဗလ hkwanaarrbala

virtual *(adj.)* ပုံရိပ်ယောင် poneriutyaung

virtue *(n.)* သူတော်ကောင်းတရား suutawkaunggtararr

virtuous *(adj.)* မွန်မြတ်သော mwanmyatsaw

virulence *(n.)* ပြင်းပြင်းထန်ထန်၊ ခါးခါးသီးသီး pyinnpyinnhtaanhtaan , hkarrhkarrseesee

virulent *(adj.)* သေနိုင်လောက်အောင် ပြင်းထန်သော say nineloutaaung pyinnhtaansaw

virus *(n.)* ဗိုင်းရပ်စ် binerat

visage *(n.)* မျက်နှာ myetnhar

visibility *(n.)* မြင်ကွင်း myinkwin

visible *(adj.)* မြင်နိုင်သော myin-nine-saw

vision *(n.)* မျှော်မှန်းချက် myaw-mhaannchet

visionary *(n.)* စိတ်ကူးကောင်းသူ satekuu kaunggsuu

visionary *(adj.)* အမြော်အမြင်ရှိသော a myaw aamyinshisaw

visit *(n.)* လည်ပတ်ခြင်း laipaatchinn

visitor *(n.)* ခရီးသည် hkareesai

vista *(n.)* ရှုခင်း shuhkinn

visual *(adj.)* စက္ခုအာရုံ sakhkuaarrone

visualize *(v.)* တွေးကြည့်သည်၊ မြင်ယောင်သည် tway kyany sai , myinyaungsai

vital *(adj.)* မရှိမဖြစ်လိုအပ်သော mashimahpyitloatsaw

vitality *(n.)* အသက်ပါခြင်း aasaat parchinn

vitalize *(v.)* အသက်ပါသည် aasaatparsai

vitamin *(n.)* ဗီတာမင်အားဆေး betarmain aarrsayy

vitiate *(v.)* ဖျက်ဆီးသည်၊ သိမ်ဖျင်းစေသည် hpyetsee sai , sin hpyinnsaysai

viva voce *(adj.)* နှုတ်ဖြေ note-hpyay

viva voce *(adv.)* နှုတ်ဖြေ note-hpyay

vivacious *(adj.)* သွက်လက်သော swat laatsaw

vivacity *(n.)* မြူးကြွခြင်း myuu kywachinn

vivid *(adj.)* ဝင်းလက်သော winn laatsaw

vixen *(n.)* မြေခွေးမ myayhkwayma

vocabulary *(n.)* ဝေါဟာရ waw-har-ra

vocal *(adj.)* အသံ aa-san

vocalist *(n.)* အဆိုတော် aa-sotaw

vocation *(n.)* မွေးရာပါတာဝန်ဟု ခံယူချက် mwayrarpar tarwaanhu hkanyuuchet

vogue *(n.)* ခေတ်ထခြင်း hkit htachinn

voice *(v.)* ထုတ်ဖော်သည် htotehpawsai

voice *(n.)* အသံ aasan

void *(v.)* ဆီးဝမ်းသွားသည် see wamswarrsai

void *(adj.)* ဟာသော harsaw

volcanic *(adj.)* မီးတောင် mee-taung

volcano *(n.)* မီးတောင် mee-taung

volition *(n.)* သဘော sabhaw

volley *(v.)* ဘောလုံး မြေမကျမီ ရိုက်သည် bhawlone myay ma kyame ritesai

volley *(n.)* တရစပ်၊ ဘောလုံးမြေမကျမီ ရိုက်ခြင်း tarasat , bhawlone myay ma kyame ritechinn

volt *(n.)* ဗို့ bhoet

voltage *(n.)* ဗို့အား bhoetaarr

volume *(n.)* အတွဲ aatwal

voluminous *(adj.)* ပွပွရောင်းရောင်း pwa pwa raunggraungg

voluntarily *(adv.)* မိမိသဘောဆန္ဒဖြင့် mimi sabhaw sandahpyint

voluntary *(adj.)* မိမိသဘောဆန္ဒအရဖြစ်သော mimi sabhaw sandaaarahpyitsaw

volunteer *(v.)* စေတနာ့ဝန်ထမ်းသည် saytanarwaanhtamsai

volunteer *(n.)* စေတနာ့ဝန်ထမ်း saytanarwaanhtam

voluptuary *(n.)* ဇိမ်ယစ်သူ zain yitsuu

voluptuous *(adj.)* ဇိမ်ယစ်သော zain yitsaw

vomit *(n.)* အန်ဖတ် aaanhpaat

vomit *(v.)* အန်သည် aaansai

voracious *(adj.)* အစားကြီးသော aasarrkyeesaw

vortex *(n.)* ဝဲ well

votary *(n.)* ဆည်းကပ်သူ saee kutsuu

vote *(v.)* မဲပေးသည် mellpayysai

vote *(n.)* မဲ mell

voter *(n.)* မဲပေးသူ mellpayysuu

vouch *(v.)* အာမခံသည် aarmahkansai

voucher *(n.)* အာမခံသူ aarmahkansuu

vouchsafe *(v.)* သဒ္ဓါတော်မူသည် saddhar taw muusai

vow *(v.)* အဓိဋ္ဌာန်ပြုသည် aadhihtaranpyusai

vow *(n.)* အဓိဋ္ဌာန် aadhihtaran

vowel *(n.)* သရအက္ခရာ sa raaakhkarar

voyage *(v.)* ခရီးရှည် ထွက်သည် hkareeshay htwatsai

voyage *(n.)* ခရီးရှည် hkareeshqy

voyager *(n.)* ခရီးသည် hkareesai

voyeur *(n.)* လိင်ကိစ္စကို ခိုးကြည့်ရသည်ကို မွေ့လျော်သူ linkissako hkoe kyi rasaiko mwae lyawsuu

voyeurism *(n.)* လိင်ကိစ္စကို ခိုးကြည့်ရသည်ကို မွေ့လျော်ခြင်း linkissako hkoe kyi rasaiko mwae lyawchinn

vulgar *(adj.)* အောက်တန်းကျသော aout taannkyasaw

vulgarity *(n.)* အောက်တန်းကျခြင်း aout taannkyachinn

vulnerable *(adj.)* ထိလွယ်ရှလွယ်သော hti lwal sh lwalsaw

vulture *(n.)* လင်းတငှက် linntanghaat

wabble *(v.)* ရှေ့နောက် ရွှေ့သည် *shay-naut-shae-sai*

wabbly *(adj.)* ရှေ့နောက်ရွှေ့လိုသော *shay-naut-shae-lo-taw*

wack *(adj.)* ရူးသော *yuu-taw*

wacko *(adj.)* ရှင်မြူး၍ တမူထူးသူ *shwin-myu-ywe-ta-mu-htoo-thu*

waddle *(v.)* ဘဲသွားသွားသည် bhell swarrswarrsai

wade *(v.)* ခက်ခက်ခဲခဲ ကူးဖြတ်သည် hkaathkaathkelhlkell kuu hpyatsai

waft *(n.)* လေနှင့်ပါလာသော အနံ့ lay nintparlarsaw aanant

waft *(v.)* လေနှင့်ပါလာသည် lay nint parlarsai

wag *(n.)* လှုပ်ခြင်း hlotechinn

wag *(v.)* ယမ်းသည် *yamsai*

wage *(n.)* လုပ်အားခ loteaarrhka

wage *(v.)* ဆင်နွှဲသည် sinnwhaellsai

wager *(v.)* လောင်းသည် launggsai

wager *(n.)* အလောင်းအစား aalaunggaasarr

wagon *(n.)* ပက်လက်တွဲ paatlaattwal

wail *(n.)* အော်ငိုခြင်း aaw ngochinn

wail *(v.)* ဆွဲဆွဲငင်ငင် ငိုကြွေးသည် swal swal ngainngain ngokyawaysai

wain *(n.)* လေးဘီးလှည်း *lay-bi-lal*

waist *(n.)* ခါး hkarr

waistband *(n.)* ခါးစည်း hkarrsaee

waistcoat *(n.)* ဝေ့စကုတ်အင်္ကျီ waist-kote aainkyae

wait *(n.)* စောင့်ဆိုင်းခြင်း saunt since-hinn

wait *(v.)* စောင့်ဆိုင်းသည် sawnt sine-sai

waiter *(n.)* စားပွဲထိုး sarr-pwahl-toe

waitress *(n.)* စားပွဲထိုး sarr-pwahl-toe

waive *(v.)* သက်ညှာခွင့်ပေးသည် saatnyhar hkwintpayysai

waiver *(n.)* စွန့်လွှတ်ကြောင်း တရားဝင်စာ swunt-lwut-kyaungg-tararrwinsar

wake *(n.)* နိုးထခြင်း *noe-hta-chin*

wake *(v.)* အိပ်ရာမှ ထသည် ait-rar-mha htasai

wakeful *(adj.)* အိပ်မရသော aitmarasaw

walk *(n.)* လမ်းလျှောက်ခြင်း lamshoutchinn

walk *(v.)* လမ်းလျှောက်သည် lamshoutsai

wall *(v.)* တံတိုင်းခတ်သည် tantine hkaatsai

wall *(n.)* တံတိုင်း tantine

wallet *(n.)* ပိုက်ဆံအိတ် pitesanaate

wallop *(v.)* ထိုးသည်၊ ရိုက်သည် htoe sai , ritesai

wallow *(v.)* ရွှံ့လူးသည် shwan luusai

walnut *(n.)* သစ်ကြားသီး sit kyarrsee

walrus *(n.)* ပင်လယ်ဖျံကြီးမျိုး pinlaal hpyaan kyeemyoe

wan *(adj.)* လူမမာရုပ်ပေါက်နေသော luu m mar rote poutnaysaw

wand *(n.)* ဆေးကြိမ်လုံး sayy kyaainlone

wander *(v.)* လှည့်လည်သွားလာသည် hlae lai swarrlarsai

wane *(n.)* လဆုတ် lasote

wane *(v.)* လဆုတ်သည် la sotesai

want *(n.)* အလိုဆန္ဒ a losanda

want *(v.)* ဆန္ဒရှိသည် sanda-shisai

wanton *(adj.)* အကြောင်းမဲ့ aa-kyaunggmae

war *(v.)* စစ်တိုက်သည် sit titesai

war *(n.)* စစ်မက် sitmaat

warble *(n.)* တွန်မြည်သီကျူးသော အသံ twan myi se kyauusaw aasan

warble *(v.)* တွန်မြည်သီကျူးသည် twan myi se kyauusai

warbler *(n.)* တေးဆိုငှက် tayysonghaat

ward *(v.)* တားဆီးကာကွယ်သည် tarrsee karkwalsai

ward *(n.)* လူနာဆောင် luunarsaung

warden *(n.)* ကြီးကြပ်ကွပ်ကဲသူ၊ ထောင်ပိုင် kyeekyaut kwut kell suu , htaungpine

warder *(n.)* ထောင်ကြပ် htaungkyaut

wardrobe *(n.)* မတ်ရပ်ဗီရို maat rat bero

wardship *(n.)* ရပ်ကွက်အဖြစ် သတ်မှတ်ခြင်း rat-kwataahpyit saatmhaatchinn

ware *(n.)* အိုးလုပ်ငန်း aoe-lotengaann

warehouse *(n.)* ကုန်လှောင်ရုံ kone hlaawinrone

warfare *(n.)* အချင်းများခြင်း aachinnmyarrchinn
warlike *(adj.)* စစ်ရေးကျွမ်းသော sitrayy kyawmsaw
warm *(v.)* နွေးသည် nwhaayysai
warmth *(n.)* နွေးထွေးခြင်း nwayhtwaychinn
warn *(v.)* သတိပေးသည် satipayysai
warning *(n.)* သတိပေးချက် satipayychet
warrant *(v.)* လုံလောက်စေသည် loneloutsaysai
warrant *(n.)* အမိန့်စာ a meinsar
warrantee *(n.)* ဝရမ်းထုတ်ခံရသူ waram htotehkanrasuu
warrantor *(n.)* ဝရမ်းထုတ်သူ waram htotesuu
warranty *(n.)* အာမခံ aarmahkan
warren *(n.)* ယုန်တွင်း စနစ် *yone-twin-sa-nit*
warrior *(n.)* စစ်သည် sitsai
wart *(n.)* ကြွက်နို့ kywatnhoet
wary *(adj.)* သတိရှိသော sati-shi-saw
wash *(n.)* ရေဆေးခြင်း ray say-chinn
wash *(v.)* လျှော်သည် shawsai
washable *(adj.)* လျှော်နိုင်သော shawninesaw
washer *(n.)* ဝါရှာ warshar
wasp *(n.)* နကျယ်ကောင် na kyaalkaung
waspish *(adj.)* နားဝင်မချိုသော narr win machaosaw
wassail *(n.)* မြူးတူးပျော်ရွှင်သော *myu-tu-pyaw-shwin-pwe*
wastage *(n.)* လေလွင့်ဆုံးရှုံးမှု lay lwint soneshonemhu
waste *(n.)* စွန့်ပစ်ပစ္စည်း swunt paitpyit-saee
waste *(adj.)* လူသူလေးပါးမနေသော luu suu lay-parr manaysaw
wasteful *(adj.)* ဖြုန်းတီးသော hpyonn teesaw
watch *(n.)* စောင့်ကြည့်သူ၊ လက်ပတ်နာရီ saunt kyi suu, laat-paat-narre
watch *(v.)* ကြည့်သည် kyisai
watchful *(adj.)* ဂရုစိုက်ကြည့်သော garusite kyisaw
watchword *(n.)* ဆောင်ပုဒ် saungpud
water *(v.)* ရေလောင်းသည် ray launggsai
water *(n.)* ရေ ray
waterfall *(n.)* ရေတံခွန် raytanhkwan
water-melon *(n.)* ဖရဲသီး hparellsee
waterproof *(n.)* ရေစိမ်ခံ raysinhkan
waterproof *(adj.)* ရေလုံသော ray lonesaw
watertight *(adj.)* ရေလုံသော ray lonesaw
watery *(adj.)* ရေကဲ့သို့သော raykaethoetsaw
watt *(n.)* ဝပ် waut
wave *(v.)* တလူလူလွင့်သည် taluuluu lwint sai
wave *(n.)* လှိုင်းလုံး hlinelone
waver *(v.)* ယိမ်းယိုင်သည် yaimyinesai
wavy *(adj.)* ကောက်သော koutsaw
wax *(v.)* ဖယောင်းဖြင့် အရောင်တင်သည် hpayaungghpyint aaraungtinsai
wax *(n.)* ပျားဖယောင်း pyarrhpayaungg
way *(n.)* နည်းလမ်း naeelam
wayfarer *(n.)* ခြေကျင်ခရီးသည် chay kyinhkareesai
waylay *(v.)* လမ်းက ဆီး၍ စောင့်သည် lamk see saungsai
wayward *(adj.)* ရိုင်းသော rinesaw

weak *(adj.)* **အားနည်းသော** aarrnaeesaw

weaken *(v.)* **အားနည်းသည်** aarrnaeesai

weakling *(n.)* **ငပျော့** ngapyaww

weakness *(n.)* **အားနည်းခြင်း** aarrnaeechinn

weal *(n.)* **အရှိုး** aashoe

wealth *(n.)* **ချမ်းသာခြင်း** chamsarchinn

wealthy *(adj.)* **ချမ်းသာသော** chamsarsaw

wean *(v.)* **နို့ဖြတ်သည်** nhoet hpyatsai

weapon *(n.)* **လက်နက်** laatnaat

wear *(v.)* **ဝတ်ဆင်သည်** waatsinsai

weary *(v.)* **ပင်ပန်းစေသည်** pinpaannsaysai

weather *(v.)* **မိုးဒဏ်လေဒဏ်ကြောင့် လွင့်ပြယ်သည်** moe dan laydankyount lwint pyaalsai

weave *(v.)* **ရက်လုပ်သည်** raatlotesai

weaver *(n.)* **ရက်ကန်းသမား** raatkaannsamarr

web *(n.)* **ပင့်ကူအိမ်** pint kuuaain

web page *(n.)* **ဝဘ်စာမျက်နှာ** wabhsarmyetnhar

web store *(n.)* **ဝဘ်စတိုး** wabh satoe

webby *(adj.)* **ဝဘ်ဆိုက်တစ်ခုရှိသော** *web-site-ta-khu-shi-taw*

webcam *(n.)* **ဝဘ်ကင်မရာ** wabhkinmarar

webcasting *(n.)* **အင်တာနက်ပေါ်တွင် အသံလွှင့်ခြင်း** *in-ter-net-paw-twin a-tan-lwint-chin*

webinar *(n.)* **ဝဘ်ဆွေးနွေးပွဲ** wabhswaynwaypwal

webisode *(n.)* **ဝဘ်အပိုင်းတွဲ** wabh aapinetwal

webmaster *(n.)* **ဝဘ်မာစတာ** wabhmarsatar

wed *(v.)* **လက်ထပ်သည်** laathtatsai

wedding *(n.)* **လက်ထပ်ခြင်း** laathtatchinn

wedge *(v.)* **သပ်လျှိုသည်** satshosai

wedge *(n.)* **သပ်** sat

wedlock *(n.)* **ထိမ်းမြားလက်ထပ်ခြင်း** htaim myarrlaathtatchinn

Wednesday *(n.)* **ဗုဒ္ဓဟူး** buddhahuu

weed *(v.)* **ပေါင်းသင်သည်** paungg sinsai

weed *(n.)* **ပေါင်းပင်** paunggpin

week *(n.)* **တစ်ပတ်** taitpaat

weekly *(adv.)* **အပတ်စဉ်** aapaatsin

weekly *(adj.)* **အပတ်စဉ်ဖြစ်သော** aapaat sinhpyitsaw

weep *(v.)* **မျက်ရည်ကျသည်** myetrai kyasai

weevil *(n.)* **ဆန်ပိုး၊ ကောက်နှံပိုး** saan poe , kout nhaanpoe

weigh *(v.)* **ချိန်သည်၊ ချိန်တွယ်သည်** chane sai , chanetwalsai

weight *(n.)* **အလေးချိန်** aa-layychane

weightage *(n.)* **အပိုထောက်ပံ့ကြေး** *a-po-htaut-pant-jay*

weighty *(adj.)* **လေးနက်သော** layynaatsaw

weir *(n.)* **ဆည်၊ တာတမံ** sai , tartaman

weird *(adj.)* **ထူးထူးဆန်းဆန်း ထိတ်လန့်ဖွယ်ကောင်းသော** htuuhtuusaannsaann htate l ant hpwalkaunggsaw

welcome *(n.)* **ကြိုဆိုခြင်း** kyaosochinn

welcome *(adj.)* **ကြိုဆိုသော** kyaososaw

weld *(n.)* **ဂဟေအဆက်** ga hay aasaat

weld *(v.)* **ဂဟေဆော်သည်** ga hay sawsai

welfare *(n.)* **ကောင်းကျိုးချမ်းသာ** kaunggkyoechamsar

well *(adv.)* **ကောင်းကောင်း** kaunggkaungg

well *(adj.)* ကောင်းသော၊ ကျန်းမာသော kaunggsaw , kyannmarsaw
well off *(adj.)* ချမ်းသာသော chamsarsaw
wellington *(n.)* ဘွတ်ဖိနပ်ရှည် bhwat hpinautshay
well-known *(adj.)* လူသိများသော luusimyarrsaw
wellness *(n.)* ချမ်းသာခြင်း chamsarchinn
well-read *(adj.)* ကောင်းစွာဖတ်သော kaunggswar hpaatsaw
well-timed *(adj.)* အချိန်သင့်သော၊ မှန်ကန်စွာဖြစ်သော *a-chane-tint-taw-man-kan-swar-phit-taw*
well-to-do *(adj.)* လုပ်သင့်သော lote sangsaw
welt *(n.)* ပြင်းထန်စွာ ထုရိုက်သည် *pyin-htan-swar-htu-yite-the*
welter *(n.)* တစ်ထွေးကြီး ta htwaykyee
wen *(n.)* အရေပြားအရေအိတ် *a-yay-pyar-a-yay-ate*
wench *(n.)* ကညာပျို kanyarpyo
west *(adj.)* အနောက်ဘက် aanoutbhaat
west *(n.)* အနောက်ဘက် aanoutbhaat
westerly *(adv.)* အနောက်မှ တိုက်သော aanoutmha titesaw
westerly *(adj.)* အနောက်မှ တိုက်သော aanoutmha titesaw
western *(adj.)* အနောက်တိုင်း aanouttine
wet *(v.)* စိုစွပ်သည် so swutsai
wet *(adj.)* စိုစွပ်သော so swutsaw
wetness *(n.)* စိုစွပ်ခြင်း so swutchinn
whack *(v.)* ဗုန်းခနဲ ရိုက်သည် bone hkanell ritesai
whale *(n.)* ဝေလငါး waylangarr
wharfage *(n.)* ဆိပ်ခံတံတား အသုံးပြုခ *seik-khan-ta-dar-a-tone-pyu-kha*

what *(pron.)* ဘယ်အရာ bhaalaarar
whatever *(pron.)* ဘာပဲဖြစ်ဖြစ် bharpelhlpyithpyit
wheat *(n.)* ဂျုံ gyaone
wheedle *(v.)* နားပူနားဆာလုပ်သည် narr puu narr sarlotesai
wheel *(v.)* ဘီးလှည့်သည် bhee hlae sai
wheel *(n.)* ဘီး bhee
whelm *(v.)* မြုပ်သည်၊ ကာသည် *myoke-the, kar-the*
whelp *(n.)* သားပေါက် sarrpout
when *(conj.)* သောအခါ sawaahkar
when *(adv.)* သောအခါ sawaahkar
whence *(adv.)* သည့်အရပ် seet-a-rat
whenever *(conj.)* ဘယ်အချိန်မဆို bhal-aa-chane maso
where *(conj.)* သည့်အရပ် seet-aa-rat
where *(adv.)* ဘယ်မှာ bhaal-mhar
whereabout *(adv.)* ဘယ်နား bhaalnarr
whereas *(conj.)* တကယ်တော့ takaaltot
whereat *(conj.)* ထိုနေရာတွင် *htoe nay-yar-twin*
wherein *(adv.)* သည့်နေရာတွင် saeetnayrartwin
whereupon *(conj.)* သည်နှင့် sinint
wherever *(adv.)* ဘယ်နေရာမဆို bhaalnayrarmaso
whet *(v.)* သွားရေယိုစေသည် swarr ray yosaysai
whether *(conj.)* လား လား larr larr
which *(adj.)* ဘယ် bhaal
whichever *(pron.)* မည်သည့်အရာ mai saeet aarar
whiff *(n.)* ဝေ့ခနဲ ရသော အနံ့ wae hkanell rasaw aanan

while *(conj.)* စဉ်တွင် sintwin

while *(n.)* ကာလ kar-la

whim *(n.)* ပေါက်ပေါက်ရှာရှာစိတ်ကူး poutpoutsharsharsatekuu

whimper *(v.)* အသံတအီအီ ပြုသည် aasantaaiai pyusai

whimsical *(adj.)* တစ်မျိုးစီဖြစ်သော်လည်း နှစ်သက်ဖွယ်ကောင်းသော *ta-myoe sehpyit-sawlaee nit-saat-hpwal-kaunggsaw*

whine *(n.)* ရှည်လျားစူးရှသော အသံ shay-lyarr suushsaw aasan

whine *(v.)* ရှည်လျားစူးရှသော အသံ ပြုသည် shay-lyarr suushsaw aasan pyusai

whip *(n.)* ကျာပွတ် kyaar-pwat

whip *(v.)* ကျာပွတ်နှင့် ရိုက်သည် kyaar pwat-nint rite-sai

whipcord *(n.)* ချုပ်ကြိုး *choke-kyo*

whir *(n.)* တဝီဝီလည်သံ ta wewe laisan

whirl *(n.)* လည်ပတ်ခြင်း laipaat-chinn

whirl *(v.)* ချာချာလည်သည် chaar-chaar-laisai

whirligig *(n.)* ဂျင် gyin

whirlpool *(n.)* ဝဲ၊ ဝဲကတော့ well , well-ka-tot

whirlwind *(n.)* လေပွေ laypway

whisk *(n.)* ခလောက်တံ hka louttan

whisk *(v.)* ရုတ်ခြည်းသယ်ယူသွားသည် rote chi saalyuuswarrsai

whisker *(n.)* နှုတ်ခမ်းမွေး note-hkam-mway

whisky *(n.)* ဝီစကီအရက် we-sa-ke aa-raat

whisper *(n.)* တီးတိုးသံ teetoesan

whisper *(v.)* တိုးတိုးပြောသည် toetoepyawwsai

whistle *(n.)* ဝီစီ wese

whistle *(v.)* ရွှီခနဲ အသံပြုသည် shwe hkanell aasanpyusai

white *(n.)* အဖြူ aahpyuu

white *(adj.)* ဖြူသော hpyuusaw

whiten *(v.)* ဖြူလာသည် hpyuularsai

whitewash *(v.)* ထုံးသုတ်သည် htone sotesai

whitewash *(n.)* ထုံးဖြူမှုန့် htone hpyauu hmonet

whither *(adv.)* ဘယ်ဆီသို့ bhaalsethoet

whitish *(adj.)* ဖြူတူတူ hpyauutuutuu

whittle *(v.)* ရွေသည် rwaysai

whiz *(v.)* ဝှီးခနဲ မြည်၍ သွားသည် whaee hkanell myi swarrsai

who *(pron.)* ဘယ်သူ bhaalsuu

whoever *(pron.)* မည်သူဖြစ်စေ mai suuhpyitsay

whole *(n.)* တစ်ခုလုံး ta-hkulone

whole *(adj.)* တစ်ခုလုံး ta-hkulone

whole-hearted *(adj.)* လှိုက်လှိုက်လှဲလှဲ *hlite-hlite-hlae-hlae*

wholesale *(adv.)* လက်ကားဈေးဖြင့် laat karrsyaayyhpyint

wholesale *(n.)* လက်ကား laatkarr

wholesaler *(n.)* လက်ကားရောင်းသူ laat karrraunggsuu

wholesome *(adj.)* အာဟာရပြည့်ဝသော aarharr pyany wasaw

wholly *(adv.)* အပြည့်အဝ a pyi aawa

whom *(pron.)* မည်သူ maisuu

whore *(n.)* မိန်းမပျက် mein-ma-pyet

whose *(pron.)* မည်သူ၏ maisuueat

why *(adv.)* ဘာကြောင့် bharkyount

wick *(n.)* မီးစာ mee-sar

wicked *(adj.)* ကောက်ကျစ်စဉ်းလဲသော kout kyit sin lellsaw

wicker *(n.)* အသုံးအဆောင် ပရိဘောဂ aasoneaasaung paribhawg

wicket *(n.)* ငုတ်တန်း ngote-taann

wide *(adv.)* အကျယ် aakyaal

wide *(adj.)* ကျယ်သော kyaal-saw

widen *(v.)* ကျယ်အောင် ချဲ့သည် kyaal-aung chaae-sai

widespread *(adj.)* ပျံ့နှံ့နေသော pyant-hnant-nay-saw

widow *(v.)* မုဆိုးမ၊ မုဆိုးဖိုဖြစ်သည် musoe-ma , mu-soe hpohpyitsai

widow *(n.)* မုဆိုးမ musoe-ma

widower *(n.)* မုဆိုးဖို musoe-hpo

width *(n.)* အကျယ် aa-kyaal

wield *(v.)* ကိုက်စွဲသည် kite swal-sai

wife *(n.)* မိန်းမ mein-ma

wig *(n.)* ဆံပင်တု sanpintu

wigwam *(n.)* တဲ tell

wild *(adj.)* ရိုင်းသော rine-saw

wilderness *(n.)* ရိုင်းခြင်း rine-chinn

wildfire *(n.)* တောမီး taw-mee

wile *(n.)* မာယာ mar-yar

will *(v.)* လိမ့်မည် lin-mai

will *(n.)* သေတမ်းစာ၊ စိတ်စွမ်းအား၊ စိတ်သဘော say-tam-sar , sateswmaarr , satesabhaw

willing *(adj.)* ဆန္ဒရှိသော san-da-shi-saw

willingness *(n.)* စိတ်ဆန္ဒ sate-san-da

willow *(n.)* မိုးမခပင် moe-ma-hka-pin

wily *(adj.)* ဉာဏ်များသော nyarn-myarr-saw

wimble *(n.)* မဝတ်ခေါင်းစွပ် ma-waat-hkaung-swut

win *(n.)* အနိုင်ရခြင်း a-nine-ra-chinn

win *(v.)* အနိုင်ရသည် aa-nine-ra-sai

wince *(v.)* ရှုံ့မဲ့မဲ့ဖြစ်သည် shone-mae-mae-hpyit-sai

winch *(n.)* ဝန်ချီစက် waan-chaesaat

wind *(v.)* အသက်မရှူနိုင်ဖြစ်သည် aa-saat ma shuu ninehpyitsai

wind *(n.)* လေ lay

windbag *(n.)* လေပေါ lay-paw

winder *(n.)* လေမှုတ်စက် *lay-mote-sat*

windlass *(n.)* ဝန်ချီစက် waan chaesaat

windmill *(n.)* လေရဟတ် lay-ra-haat

window *(n.)* ပြတင်းပေါက် pya-tinn-pout

windscreen *(n.)* လေကာမှန် lay kar-mhaan

windy *(adj.)* လေတိုက်သော lay-tite-saw

wine *(n.)* ဝိုင်အရက် wine aa-raat

wing *(n.)* အတောင်ပံ aa-taung-pan

wink *(n.)* မျက်စိတစ်ဖက်မှိတ်ပြခြင်း myetsi taithpaat mhaate pyachinn

winner *(n.)* အနိုင်ရသူ aaninerasuu

winnow *(v.)* လှေ့သည် hlaaesai

winsome *(adj.)* ဆွဲဆောင်မှု ရှိသော swalsaungmhu shisaw

winter *(v.)* ဆောင်းခိုသည် saungg hkosai

winter *(n.)* ဆောင်းရာသီ saunggrarse

wintry *(adj.)* ဆောင်းနှင့် တူသော saunggnint tuusaw

wipe *(n.)* သုတ်ခြင်း sotechinn

wipe *(v.)* သုတ်သည် sotesai

wire *(v.)* ဝိုင်ယာနှင့် ပူးချည်သည် wine yarnint puu chaisai

wire *(n.)* နန်းကြိုး naannkyaoe

wireless *(n.)* ကြိုးမဲ့ကြေးနန်း kyaoemaekyaynaann

wireless *(adj.)* ဝိုင်ယာလက် wine yarlaat

wiring *(n.)* လျှပ်စစ်ကြိုးသွယ်တန်းတပ်ဆင်မှု shutsit kyaoe swaltaann tautsinmhu

wisdom *(n.)* ဉာဏ်ပညာ nyarnpanyar

wisdom-tooth *(n.)* အံဆုံး aansone

wise *(adj.)* ပညာရှိသော panyarshisaw

wish *(v.)* ဆန္ဒရှိသည် sandashisai

wish *(n.)* ဆန္ဒ san-da

wishful *(adj.)* ဖြစ်ချင်သော hpyitchinsaw

wisp *(n.)* အမျှင်စု aa-myin-su

wistful *(adj.)* ကြေကွဲသော kyay kwalsaw

wit *(n.)* ဟာသဉာဏ် harsanyarn

witch *(n.)* စုန်းမ sone-ma

witchcraft *(n.)* စုန်းကဝေအတတ် sone-k-way aa-taat

witchery *(n.)* စုန်းပညာ sone-pyin-nyar

with *(prep.)* နှင့်အတူ nint-aa-tuu

withal *(adv.)* အားလုံးထည့်သွင်းစဉ်းစား *arr-lone-thae-twin-sin-sar*

withdraw *(v.)* ရုပ်သိမ်းသည် rote-saim-sai

withdrawal *(n.)* ရုပ်သိမ်းခြင်း rotesaimchinn

withe *(n.)* ပျော့ပြီး သွယ်သော အကိုင်း *pyawt-pee-twal-taw-a-kai*

wither *(v.)* ခြောက်သွေ့ညှိုးနွမ်းသည် chaukswae nyhaoenwmsai

withhold *(v.)* ထုတ်မပေးဘဲ ထားသည် htotemapayybhell htarrsai

within *(adv.)* အတွင်းမှ aatwinmha

within *(prep.)* အတွင်း aatwin

without *(adv.)* မပါဘဲ maparbhell

without *(prep.)* မပါဘဲ maparbhell

withstand *(v.)* ကြံ့ကြံ့ခံနိုင်သည် kyaankyaanhkanninesai

witless *(adj.)* မိုက်မဲသော mite mellsaw

witness *(v.)* မျက်မြင်တွေ့သည် myet myintwaesai

witness *(n.)* သက်သေ saatsay

witticism *(n.)* ဟာသမြောက်သော စကား har-sa myawt-saw sa-karr

witty *(adj.)* ဟာသဉာဏ်ရွှင်သော har-sa nyarn shwin-saw

wizard *(n.)* မှော်ဆရာ mhaw-sa-rar

wobble *(v.)* လှုပ်သည်၊ နဲ့သည် hlote sai , naesai

woe *(n.)* ပူဆွေးသောက puusway sawka

woebegone *(adj.)* မရွှင်ပျသော ma shwin pyasaw

woeful *(n.)* ဝမ်းနည်းပူဆွေးသော wam-naee puuswaysaw

wolf *(n.)* ဝံပုလွေ wanpulway

woman *(n.)* မိန်းမ mein-ma

womanhood *(n.)* မိန်းမဘဝ mein-ma-bha-wa

womanise *(v.)* မိန်းမလိုက်စားသည် mein-ma lite-sarr-sai

womaniser *(n.)* မိန်းမလိုက်စားသူ mein-ma lite-sarr-suu

womanish *(adj.)* မိန်းမဆန်သော mein-ma-saan-saw

womb *(n.)* သားအိမ် sarraain

wonder *(v.)* စူးစမ်းမိသည် suu sam misai

wonder *(n.)* ရင်သပ်ရှုမော အံ့သြခြင်း rinsatshumaw aan syachinn

wonderful *(adj.)* အံ့သြဖွယ်ကောင်းသော aan aw hpwal-kaung-saw

wondrous *(adj.)* အံ့သြဖွယ် aan aw-hpwal-

wont *(n.)* အကျင့် aa-kyint

wont *(adj.)* အကျင့်ရှိသော a-kyintshisaw

wonted *(adj.)* ဓလေ့ထုံးတမ်းအားဖြင့် *da-lae-hton-tan-arr-phint*

woo *(v.)* ဆွယ်သည် swal-sai

wood *(n.)* သစ်သား sit-sarr

wooden *(adj.)* သစ်သားနှင့် လုပ်သော sit-sarr-nint lotesaw

woodland *(n.)* သစ်တော ဖုံးလွှမ်းနေသော နယ်မြေ sittaw hpone lwhamnaysaw naalmyay

woods *(n.)* သစ်တော sittaw

woof *(n.)* ခွေးဟောင်သံ hkway haungsan

wool *(n.)* သိုးမွေး soemway

woollen *(n.)* သိုးမွေးနှင့် လုပ်သော soe mway-nint lotesaw

woollen *(adj.)* အမွေးထူ aa-mwayhtuu

word *(v.)* စကားလုံးရွေးချယ်သုံးနှုန်းသည် sakarrlone rwaychaal sone hnonesai

word *(n.)* စကားလုံး sakarrlone

wordy *(adj.)* စကားလုံးဖောင်းပွသော sakarrlone hpaunggpwsaw

work *(v.)* အလုပ်လုပ်သည် aa-lote-lote-sai

work *(n.)* အလုပ် aa-lote

workable *(adj.)* လုပ်၍ ဖြစ်နိုင်သော lote-ywe hpyitninesaw

workaday *(adj.)* သာမန် sar-maan

worker *(n.)* အလုပ်သမား aa-lote-sa-marr

workman *(n.)* ကာယလုပ်သား kar ya-lotesarr

workmanship *(n.)* လုပ်ငန်းကျွမ်းကျင်၊ နိုင်နင်းမှု lote-ngan kywam-kyin , nine ninn-mhu

workshop *(n.)* အလုပ်ရုံ၊ ဝပ်ရှော့ aa-lote-rone , wautshot

world *(n.)* ကမ္ဘာ kam-bhar

worldling *(n.)* ကမ္ဘာ့ရေးရာတွင် နစ်မြုပ်နေသော သာမန်လူ *ka-bar-yay-yar-twin-nit-myoke-nay-taw-tar-hman lu*

worldly *(adj.)* လောက law-ka

worm *(n.)* တီကောင် te-kaung

wormwood *(n.)* သစ်နံကိုင်းပင် sit-nan-kine-pin

worn *(adj.)* ဖတ်ဖတ်မော၊ ဖန်တစ်ရာတေအောင် သုံးထား၍ စုတ်ချာနေသော hpant-hpaat maw , hpaan taitrar tayaaung sonehtarr sote chaarnaysaw

worry *(v.)* စိုးရိမ်သည် soerinsai

worry *(n.)* စိုးရိမ်ခြင်း soerinchinn

worsen *(v.)* ပိုဆိုးလာသည် posoelarsai

worship *(v.)* ကိုးကွယ်သည် koekwalsai

worship *(n.)* ကိုးကွယ်ခြင်း koekwalchinn

worshipper *(n.)* ကိုးကွယ်သူ koekwalsuu

worst *(v.)* ရှုံးသည်၊ အရေးနိမ့်သည် shone sai , aa-rayy naint-sai

worsted *(n.)* သိုးမွေးအထည်စ thoe mway aa-htai-sa

worth *(adj.)* တန်သော taan-saw

worth *(n.)* အဖိုးငွေပမာဏ aahpoengwaypamarn

worthless *(adj.)* သုံးမရသော sonemarasaw

worthy *(adj.)* ထိုက်တန်သော htitetaansaw

would-be *(adj.)* နောင်ဖြစ်လာမည့် naung hpyitlarmaeet

wound *(v.)* ဒဏ်ရာရသည် danrarrasai

wound *(n.)* ထိခိုက်ဒဏ်ရာ htihkitedanrar

wrack *(n.)* စင် sin

wraith *(n.)* **တစ္ဆေ** tassay

wrangle *(n.)* **ရှည်လျား ရှုပ်ထွေးသော အငြင်းအခုံ** shilyarr shotehtway-saw aangyinn-aahkone

wrangle *(v.)* **အော်ကြီးဟစ်ကျယ်ငြင်းခုံသည်** aaw kyee hait kyaal ngyinn hkonesai

wrap *(n.)* **ခြုံလွှာ** chuanlwhar

wrap *(v.)* **လွှမ်းခြုံသည်** lwhamchuansai

wrapper *(n.)* **ထုပ်ပိုးပစ္စည်း** htote poepyit-saee

wrath *(n.)* **အမျက်ဒေါသ** a myetdawsa

wreath *(n.)* **ပန်းခွေ** paannhkway

wreathe *(v.)* **ဖုံးလွှမ်းသည်** hpone lwhamsai

wreck *(v.)* **သင်္ဘောပျက်သည်** sinbhawpyetsai

wreck *(n.)* **သင်္ဘောပျက်** sinbhawpyet

wreckage *(n.)* **အပျက်အစီး** aapyetaasee

wrecker *(n.)* **ဖျက်ဆီးသူ** hpyetseesuu

wren *(n.)* **နှံပြီစုတ်ငှက်** nhaan pye sotenghaat

wrench *(v.)* **တအားဆွဲဖြုတ်သည်** ta aarr swal hpyuatsai

wrench *(n.)* **ဆောင့်ဆွဲခြင်း** saunt swalchinn

wrest *(v.)* **ဆွဲလုသည်** swal lusai

wrestle *(v.)* **နပန်းလုံးသည်** na pan lonesai

wrestler *(n.)* **နပန်းလုံးခြင်း** na paann lonechinn

wretch *(n.)* **ကံဆိုးသူ** kan soesuu

wretched *(adj.)* **စိတ်မချမ်းသာသော** satemachamsarsaw

wrick *(n.)* **လှည့်သည်** *hlae-the*

wriggle *(n.)* **တွန့်လိမ်ခြင်း** twunt lainchinn

wriggle *(v.)* **တွန့်လိမ်သည်** twunt linsai

wring *(v.)* **အရည်ညှစ်သည်** aarai nyit-sai

wrinkle *(v.)* **နှာခေါင်းရှုံ့သည်** nhar-hkaungg shone sai

wrinkle *(n.)* **အတွန့်ကြောင်း** a twunt-kyaung

wrist *(n.)* **လက်ကောက်ဝတ်** laatkoutwaat

writ *(n.)* **အမိန့်စာချွန်** a mein sarchwan

write *(v.)* **ရေးသည်၊ စီကုံးသည်** rayysai , se konesai

writer *(n.)* **စာရေးဆရာ** sarrayysarar

writhe *(v.)* **ထွန့်ထွန့်လူးသည်** htwunt htwunt luusai

wrong *(v.)* **မတရားသဖြင့် ခံရသည်** ma-ta-rarr sa-hpyint hkan-ra-sai

wrong *(adj.)* **မှားယွင်းသော** mhar-ywin-saw

wrongful *(adj.)* **မတရား** matararr

wry *(adj.)* **ခနဲ့တဲ့တဲ့** hka nae taetae

X

xenobiology *(n.)* **ပြင်ပသက်ရှိဇီဝဗေဒ** *ka-bar-pyin-pa-thet-shi-zi-wa-bay-da*

xenogenesis *(n.)* **ပြင်ပရင်းမြစ်** *pyin-pa-yin-myit*

xenomania *(n.)* **သူစိမ်းနှင့် ပတ်သက်၍ စိတ်စွဲလမ်းခြင်း** *ta-zein-nint- pat-thet-ywe-seik-swal-lan-chin*

xenomorph *(n.)* **ထူးဆန်းပုံစံ** *htoo-san-pon-san*

xenophile *(n.)* **နိုင်ငံခြားသားနှင့် ယဉ်ကျေးမှုကို ချစ်သူ** *nine-ngan-char-tar-nint-yin-kyay-mu-ko-chitsuu*

xenophobe *(n.)* နိုင်ငံခြားသားနှင့် ယဉ်ကျေးမှုကို ကြောက်သူ *nine-ngan-char-tar-nint-yin-kyay-mu-ko-kyauk-suu*
xenophobia *(n.)* သူစိမ်းကြောက်ခြင်း sasaim kyawwatchinn
xerox *(n.)* ဓာတ်ပုံမိတ္တူကူး dhrat-pone meit-tuu-kuu
Xmas *(n.)* ခရစ်စမတ် hka-rit-samaat
x-ray *(n.)* ဓာတ်မှန် dhrat-mhaan
xylophilous *(adj.)* သစ်သားပေါ်တွင် ရှိသော *tit-tar-paw-twin-shi-taw*
xylophone *(n.)* ပတ္တလား pat talarr

yacht *(v.)* ရွက်လွှင့်သည် *ywet-lwint-the*
yak *(n.)* တိဗက်နွား ti-baat-nwarr
yap *(n.)* အသံစူးစူးဖြင့် ဟောင်သံ aa-san suu-suu-hpyint haungsan
yap *(v.)* အသံစူးစူးဖြင့် ဟောင်သည် aasan suu suuhpyint haungsai
yard *(n.)* ဝင်းခြံ winnchaan
yarn *(n.)* ချည်ခင် chaihkin
yawn *(n.)* သမ်းဝေခြင်း sam waychinn
year *(n.)* နှစ် nhit
yearly *(adj.)* နှစ်စဉ် nhit-sin
yearn *(v.)* တမ်းတသည် tamtasai
yearning *(n.)* တမ်းတခြင်း tamtachinn
yeast *(n.)* တဆေး tasayy
yell *(n.)* စူးစူးဝါးဝါးအော်သံ suu suu warr war-aawsan
yellow *(v.)* ဝါရော်သည် war raw sai
yellowish *(adj.)* ဝါကြင့်ကြင့် war kyint kyint
Yen *(n.)* ယန်းငွေ yaann-ngway
yes *(adv.)* ဟုတ်သည် hote-sai
yesterday *(n.)* မနေ့က ma-nae-ka
yet *(adv.)* ယခုတိုင် ya-hku-tine
yield *(n.)* ထွက်ရှိသည့်ပမာဏ htwat-shi saeet-pa-mar-na
yodel *(v.)* သီချင်းကို အသံ အဆုံးထိမြှင့်တင်၍ ပြန်ချဆိုသည် se-chinnko aa-san aasonehti myaha inttin pyan cha-sosai
yoga *(n.)* ယောဂဒဿန yaw-ga-dattana
yoghurt *(n.)* ဒိန်ချဉ် dein-chin
yogi *(n.)* ယောဂနည်းပြဆရာ yaw-ga naee-pya-sarar
yoke *(v.)* ထမ်းပိုးတပ်သည် htam poe tat-sai
yolk *(n.)* အနှစ် aa-nit
yonder *(adj.)* ဟိုနား honarr
You Tube *(v.)* ယူကျု yuu-kyu
young *(adj.)* ငယ်ရွယ်သော ngaal-rwal-saw
youngster *(n.)* ကလေး၊ လူငယ်၊ ချာတိတ် kalayy , luungaal , chaartate
yourself *(pr.)* သင်ကိုယ်တိုင် sin-ko-tine
youth *(n.)* လူငယ် luu-ngaal
youthful *(adj.)* ငယ်ရွယ်သော၊ ပျိုမျစ်သော ngaal-rwal-saw , pyo myitsaw

Z

zany *(adj.)* တစ်မူထူးသော ta muu htuusaw

zeal *(n.)* စိတ်အားထက်သန်ခြင်း sate-aarr htaat saan-chinn

zealot *(n.)* တက်ကြွလွန်းသူ taat-kya-lwann-suu

zealous *(adj.)* စိတ်အားထက်သန်သော sate-aarr htaat saansaw

zeb *(v.)* ကျောက်တုန်း kyawt-tone

zebra *(n.)* မြင်းကျား myinn-kyarr

zebra crossing *(n.)* လူကူးမျဉ်းကျား luu-kuu-myin-kyarr

zenith *(n.)* အထွတ်အထိပ် aa-htwat-aa-hteik

zephyr *(n.)* ညင်းလေပြည် nyinn-lay-pyi

zero *(n.)* သုည su-nya

zest *(n.)* နှစ်ခြိုက်သာယာခြင်း nit-chite sar-yar-chinn

zesty *(adj)* စူးရှရှ အရသာရှိသော suu-sha-sha aa-rasarshi-saw

zig *(v.)* အပြောင်းအလဲလုပ်သည် aa-pyaungg-aa-lell-lote-sai

zigzag *(n.)* မြွေလိမ်မြွေကောက် myway lain myway-kout

zinc *(n.)* ဇင့်ဓာတ် zint-dhrat

zip *(n.)* ဇစ် zit

ziplock *(adj.)* ဇစ်ပိတ်ထားသော zit-pate-htarr-saw

zipper *(n.)* ဇစ် zit

zodiac *(n.)* ဆယ့်နှစ်ရာသီခွင် sae na-rar-se-hkwin

zonal *(adj.)* ဇုန်နယ်အလိုက် zone naal-aa-lite

zone *(n.)* ဇုန် zone

zoo *(n.)* တိရိစ္ဆာန်ရုံ ta-rate-san-rone

zoological *(adj.)* သတ္တဗေဒနှင့် ဆိုင်သော sat-ta-bay-da-nint sinesaw

zoologist *(n.)* သတ္တဗေဒပညာရှင် sat-ta-bay-da-pa-nyar-shin

zoology *(n.)* သတ္တဗေဒ sat-ta-bay-da

zoom *(v.)* တဟုန်ထိုးသွားသည် tahonehtoeswarrsai

Zorb *(n.)* လေကူရှင်ခံ လူဝင်နိုင်သော ဘောလုံး lay kuu hlyinhkan luu win-nine-saw bhaw-lone

Burmese (Myanmar) - English

က

ကံ kan *(n.)* **fortune**

ကံကျွေးချစနစ် kan-kyway-cha-sa-nit *(n.)* **feudalism**

ကံကြမ္မာ kan-kyan-mar *(n.)* **fate**

ကံကြမ္မာပဓာနဝါဒ kan-kyan-mar-pa-dar-na-wa-da *(n.)* **fatalism**

ကံကောင်းစွာဖြင့် kan-kaung-swar-phint *(adv.)* **luckily**

ကံကောင်းထောက်မ kan-kaungg htout-ma *(adj.)* **providential**

ကံကောင်းသော kankaunggsaw *(adj.)* **serendipitous**

ကံခေခြင်း kan-khay-chin *(n.)* **mishap**

ကံဆိုးခြင်း kan-soe-chin *(n.)* **misadventure**

ကံဆိုးမိုးမှောင်ကျသည် kan-soe-moe-hmaung-kya-the *(v.)* **doom**

ကံဆိုးမိုးမှောင်ကျသော kan-soe-moe-hmaung-kya-thaw *(adj.)* **doomed**

ကံဆိုးသူ kan soesuu *(n.)* **wretch**

ကံတရား kan-ta-yar *(n.)* **destiny**

ကံပုဒ်မရှိသော kan-poke-ma-shi-taw *(adj. (verb))* **intransitive**

ကံမကောင်းသော kanmakaunggsaw *(adj.)* **unfortunate**

ကံရှိ a kuu aapyaung *(adj.)* **transitive**

ကကြိုး ka-kyo *(n.)* **harness**

ကကြိုးဆင်သည် ka-kyo-sin-the *(v.)* **harness**

ကကြီးကကြောင်နိုင်သော ka-kye-ka-kyaung-nine-saw *(adj.)* **perverse**

ကကွက်စီစဉ်ဖန်တီးသည် ka-kwat-si-sin-phan-thee-the *(v.)* **choreograph**

ကက်ဆက် kat-sat *(n.)* **cassette**

ကက်ဒမီယံဒြပ်စင် kat-da-mi-yan-drat-sin *(n.)* **cadmium**

ကက်ဖဲ kat-phae *(n.)* **domino**

ကက်သလိတ် kat-ta-laik *(n.)* **cutlet**

ကက်ဦးထုပ် kat-oo-htoke *(n.)* **cap**

ကချေသည်၊ ကပြသူ ka-chay-tal, ka-pya-thu *(n.)* **dancer**

ကခြင်း ka-chin *(n.)* **dance**

ကခုန်သော ka-khone-taw *(adj.)* **dancing**

ကင်းကင်းနေသည် kinn kinnnaysai *(v.)* **seclude**

ကင်းကွာသည် kin-kwar-the *(v.)* **alienate**

ကင်းခြေများ kin-chay-myar *(n.)* **centipede**

ကင်းစောင့် kinnsawnt *(n.)* **sentinel**

ကင်းထောက် kinnhtout *(n.)* **scout**

ကင်းပတ်စ kin-pat-sa *(n.)* **canvas**

ကင်းမြီးကောက် kinn-myee-kout *(n.)* **scorpion**

ကင်းမဲ့သည် kin-mae-the *(v.)* **denude**

ကင်းမဲ့သော kin-mae-taw *(adj.)* **devoid**

ကင်းလှည့်ခြင်း kinn-hlae-chinn *(n.)* **patrol**

ကင်းလှည့်သည် kinn-hlae-sai *(v.)* **patrol**

ကင်းသမား kinnsamarr *(n.)* **sentry**

ကင်၊ လှော်၊ ဖုတ် kin , hlaaw , hpote *(adj.)* **roast**

ကင်ဆာ kin-sar *(n.)* **malignancy**

ကင်ဆာကုထုံး kin-sar-ku-htone *(n.)* **chemotherapy**

ကင်ဆာဆရာဝန် kin-sar-sa-rar-wan *(n.)* **oncologist**

ကင်ဆာဆဲလ် အဖြစ်ပြောင်းအောင် လုပ်နိုင်သောဂျင်းများ kin-sar-sel-a-phit-pyaung-aung lote-nine-taw-gin-myar *(n.)* **oncogene**
ကင်ဆာဆဲလ်ဖြစ်လာနိုင်ခြေရှိသော kin-sar-sel-phit-lar-nine-chay-shi-taw *(adj.)* **oncogenic**
ကင်ဆာပညာရပ် kin-sar-pyin-nyar-rat *(n.)* **oncology**
ကင်ဆာဖြစ်သော kin-sar-phit-taw *(adj.)* **malignant**
ကင်ဆာရောဂါ kin-sar-yaw-gar *(n.)* **cancer**
ကင်မရာ ka-ma-yar *(n.)* **camera**
ကင်သည် kinsai *(v.)* **roast**
ကစဉ့်ကလျားဖြစ်ခြင်း ka-sint-ka-lyar-phit-chin *(n.)* **disorder**
ကစားကွင်း ka-sarr-kwin *(n.)* **pitch**
ကစားစရာ လူရုပ် ka-sar-sa-yar-lu-yoke *(n.)* **doll**
ကစားနည်း ka-sar-nee *(n.)* **game**
ကစားသည် ka-sarr-sai *(v.)* **play**
ကစားသူ ka-sarr-suu *(n.)* **player**
ကစီဓာတ် ka se-dhrat *(n.)* **starch**
ကစ်ဖြင့် စက်နိုးသည် kit-phit-sat-noe-the *(v.)* **kick-start**
ကဆုန်ပေါက်ပြေးခြင်း ka-sone-pauk-pyay-chin *(n.)* **gallop**
ကဆုန်ပေါက်ပြေးသည် ka-sone-pauk-pyay-the *(v.)* **gallop**
ကဇာတ်ရုံ ka zatrone *(n.)* **theatre**
ကညွတ် ka-nyut *(n.)* **asparagus**
ကညာပျို kanyarpyo *(n.)* **wench**
ကဏ္ဍ kan-da *(n.)* **aspect**
ကဏ္ဍ၊ ဇာတ်ကောင် kan-da, zatkaung *(n.)* **role**
ကတည်းက kataeka- *(conj.)* **since**
ကတိ kati *(n.)* **promise**
ကတိ၊ သက်သေ ka-ti, saat-say *(n.)* **pledge**
ကတိကဝတ်၊ ပဋိညာဉ် ka-ti-ka-waat, pa-tain-nyin *(n.)* **pact**
ကတိကဝတ်ပြုသော ka-ti-ka-wit-pyu-taw *(adj.)* **promissory**
ကတိပြုသည် kati-pyusai *(v.)* **promise**
ကတိပေးပြီး အလုပ် ka-di-pay-pi-a-lote *(n.)* **commitment**
ကတိပေးသည် kati-payy-sai *(v.)* **pledge**
ကတိဖျက်သည် ka ti hpye-tsai *(v.)* **rat**
ကတိုး ka-toe *(n.)* **musk**
ကတုတ်ကျင်း ka totekyinn *(n.)* **trench**
ကတော့၊ ထင်းရှူးသီး ka-taw, htin-shu-thee *(n.)* **cone**
ကတော့ပုံ ka-taw-pon *(adj.)* **conical**
ကတော်သံ ka-taw-tan *(v.)* **cackle**
ကတ္တရာ kat tarar *(n.)* **tar**
ကတ္တရာ ခင်းသည်၊ လောင်းသည် kat tarar hkinn sai , launggsai *(v.)* **tar**
ကတ္တားရည်ညွှန်း kat tarr-rai-nyunn *(adj.)* **reflexive**
ကတ္တီပါ kat tepar *(n.)* **velvet**
ကတ္တီပါလို kat te parlo *(adj.)* **velvety**
ကတ် kat *(n.)* **card**
ကတ်ကြေး kaatkyay *(n.)* **scissors**
ကတ်ကိုင်ဆောင်သူ kat-kai-saung-thu *(n.)* **cardholder**
ကတ်တီးကတ်ဖဲ့ပြောခြင်း kat tee kat hpae-pyawwchinn *(n.)* **quibble**
ကတ်တီးကတ်ဖဲ့ပြောသည် kat tee kat hpae-pyawwsai *(v.)* **quibble**

ကတ်ထရစ်တောင့် kat-hta-rit-taunt *(n.)* **cartridge**
ကတ်ထူ kat-htu *(n.)* **carton**
ကတ်ထူပြား kat-htu-pyar *(n.)* **cardboard**
ကတ်ထူဘူး kaat-htuu-bhuu *(n.)* **pack**
ကတ်ထူဘူး၊ အထုပ် kaat-htuu-bhuu, a-htote *(n.)* **packet**
ကတ်ဖတ်စက် lat-phat-sat *(n.)* **card reader**
ကထိက ka-hti-ka *(n.)* **lecturer**
ကနွဲ့ကလျ ကဗျာဟန် ka-nwe-ka-lya-ka-byar-han *(adj.)* **girlish**
ကနဦး ka-na-oo *(n.)* **inception**
ကနဦးအဆင်၊ သန္ဓေသားနှင့် ဆိုင်သော ka-na-oo-a-sint, ta-day-tar-nint-sai-taw *(adj.)* **embryonic**
ကနူးပီလေ့ ka-nu-pee-hlay *(n.)* **canopy**
ကန့်ကွက်ချက် kaant-kwat-chet *(n.)* **protest**
ကန့်ကွက်စရာ kant-kwat-sa-rar *(adj.)* **objectionable**
ကန့်ကွက်သည် kaant-kwatsai *(v.)* **protest**
ကန့်လန့်ဖြတ်တက်ခြင်း kant lant hpyattaatchinn *(n.)* **traverse**
ကန့်လိုက်သည် kant-lite-sai *(v.)* **partition**
ကန့်သတ် ထိန်းချုပ်မှု kant-tat-htain-choke-mu *(n.)* **containment**
ကန့်သတ်ချက် kant-thet-chat *(n.)* **holdback**
ကန့်သတ်ချက်ဖြတ်သော kant-tat-chat-phat-taw *(adj.)* **transboundary**
ကန့်သတ်ချက်ရှိသော kant-tat-chat-shi-taw *(adj.)* **finite**
ကန့်သတ်ခြင်း kant saatchinn *(n.)* **restriction**
ကန့်သတ်ထိန်းချုပ်မှုမှ ကင်းလွတ်စေသည် kant-tat-htein-choke-mu-ma-kin-hlut-say-the *(v.)* **deregulate**
ကန့်သတ်ပမာဏ kant saat-pa-marna *(n.)* **quota**
ကန့်သတ်သည် kant saatsai *(v.)* **restrict**
ကန့်သတ်သော kant-thet-taw *(adj.)* **limited**
ကန်ခြင်း kan-chin *(n.)* **kick**
ကန်တင်း kan-teen *(n.)* **canteen**
ကန်ထရိုက်တာ kan-hta-rite-tar *(n.)* **contractor**
ကန်ရှေ့ kan-shay *(n.)* **lakefront**
ကန်သည် kan-taw *(v.)* **foot**
ကပျစ်ကညစ် k pyit kanyait *(n.)* **scruffiness**
ကပြား ka-pyar *(n.)* **hybrid**
ကပြောင်းကပြန် ဖြစ်စေခြင်း ka pyaungg kapyan hpyitsaychinn *(n.)* **reversal**
ကပွဲခန်းမ ka-pwe-khan-ma *(n.)* **ballroom**
ကပူချီနိုကော်ဖီ ka-pu-chi-no-kaw-phi *(n.)* **cappuccino**
ကပ္ပတိန် kat-pa-tein *(n.)* **captain**
ကပ်ကမ္ဘာ kat-ka-bar *(n.)* **aeon**
ကပ်ချာ kat-char *(n.)* **captcha**
ကပ်ခြင်း kat-chin *(n.)* **adhesion**
ကပ်စီးနည်းခြင်း kat-see-ne-chin *(n.)* **meanness**
ကပ်စေးနည်းသော kat sayy naeesaw *(adj.)* **stingy**
ကပ်စေးနှဲကော်တရာ kaut sayy nhaell kaw tarar *(n.)* **scrooge**
ကပ်စေးနှဲပူဖောင်း kat-see-nae-pu-hpaung *(n.)* **bubblegum**
ကပ်စေးနှဲ၊ ကော်တရာ kat-say-nae, kaw-ta-yar *(n.)* **miser**
ကပ်စေးနှဲသော kat-say-nae-taw *(adj.)* **miserly**

ကပ်ဆိုက်ခြင်း kat-site-chin *(n.)* **holocaust**

ကပ်ပယ်အိတ် kaut paal-ate *(n.)* **scrotum**

ကပ်ပါးကောင် kaut-parr-kaung *(n.)* **parasite**

ကပ်ဖား kat-hparr *(n.)* **sycophant**

ကပ်ဘေး kat-bay *(n.)* **calamity**

ကပ်ရပ်တောင်းသည် kat-yat-taung-the *(v.)* **cadge**

ကပ်ရောဂါ kat-raw-gar *(n.)* **pestilence**

ကပ်လျက် kat-lyat *(adj.)* **adjacent**

ကပ်လျက် တည်ရှိသည် kat-kyat-the-shi-the *(v.)* **adjoin**

ကပ်သည် kat-the *(v.)* **adhere**

ကပ်သည်၊ ကူးထည့်သည် kaut-sai, kuu-htae-sai *(v.)* **paste**

ကပ်သည်၊ တင်သည် kat sai, tinsai *(v.)* **post**

ကပ်သည်၊ သုတ်သည် kat-the, tote-the *(v.)* **goo**

ကပ်သော kat-taw *(n.)* **adhesive**

ကဖျက်ယဖျက်လုပ်သည် ka hpyet ya hpyetlotesai *(v.)* **thwart**

ကဖိန်းဓာတ် ka-fein-dat *(n.)* **caffeine**

ကဖေး ka-fay *(n.)* **cafe**

ကဗျာ ka-byaar *(n.)* **poem**

ကဗျာစာဆို ka-byar-sar-so *(n.)* **bard**

ကဗျာစာပိုဒ် ka-byar-sar-baik *(n.)* **acrostic**

ကဗျာဆန်သော ka-byaar-saan-saw *(adj.)* **poetic**

ကဗျာဆရာ ka-byaar-sa-rar *(n.)* **poet**

ကဗျာဆရာမ ka-byaar-sa-rar-ma *(n.)* **poetess**

ကဗျာတစ်ပိုဒ် ka-byaar ta-pote *(n.)* **stanza**

ကဗျာဖွဲ့ခြင်း kabyaar hpwalchinn *(n.)* **versification**

ကဗျာဖွဲ့နည်း ka-byaar hpwal-naee *(n.)* **prosody**

ကဗျာဖွဲ့သည် kabyaar hpwalsai *(v.)* **versify**

ကဗျာသီအိုရီ ka-byaar-the-o-ree *(n.)* **poetics**

ကမကထပြုခြင်း ka-ma-ka-hta-pyu-chin *(n.)* **aegis**

ကမာကဲ့သို့ မီးခိုး၊ သနပ်ခါးရောင်ကြား ka mar-kaeshoet meehkoe-sa-nat-hkarr-raungkyarr *(adj.)* **oyster**

ကမာငယ် ka mar-ngaal *(n.)* **oysterling**

ကမာဖမ်းသည် ka mar hpam-sai *(v.)* **oyster**

ကမာဖမ်းသမား ka mar hpam-samarr *(n.)* **oysterman**

ကမူးရှူးထိုးထပြေးခြင်း ka muu shuu htoe hta pyaychinn *(n.)* **stampede**

ကမောက်ကမဖြစ်စေသည် ka-mauk-ka-ma-phit-say-the *(v.)* **muddle**

ကမ္ဗလာသီး kam-ba-lar-tee *(n.)* **orange**

ကမ္ဘာ kam-bhar *(n.)* **world**

ကမ္ဘာ့ဆွဲအား ka-bar-swal-ngin-arr *(n.)* **gravity**

ကမ္ဘာ့ရန်ဖြစ်သည် ka-bar-yan-phit-the *(n.)* **feud**

ကမ္ဘာ့ရေးရာတွင် နစ်မြုပ်နေသော သာမန်လူ ka-bar-yay-yar-twin-nit-myoke-nay-taw-tar-hman lu *(n.)* **worldling**

ကမ္ဘာကြီး ပူနွေးလာခြင်း ka-bar-kyi-pu-nway-lar-chin *(n.)* **global warming**

ကမ္ဘာကဲ့သို့ တစ်ခြားဂြိုလ်ကို ပုံစံပြောင်းသည် ka-bar-kae-thoe-a-char-gyo-ko-pon-san-pyaung-the *(n.)* **terraforming**

ကမ္ဘာဂြိုလ် kambhar gyol *(n.)* **terrestrial**

ကမ္ဘာပျက်သော နေ့ ka-bar-pyat-taw-nae *(n.)* **doomsday**

ကမ္ဘာပျက်သော နေ့ဆိုင်ရာ ka-bar-pyat-taw-nae-sai-yar *(adj.)* **doomsday**

ကမ္ဘာပြင်ပသက်ရှိဇီဝဗေဒ ka-bar-pyin-pa-thet-shi-zi-wa-bay-da *(n.)* **xenobiology**
ကမ္ဘာမြေကြီး ka-bar-myay-gyi *(n.)* **earth**
ကမ္ဘာမြေနှင့်ဆိုင်သော kam-bhar-myay nint-sine-saw *(adj.)* **tellural**
ကမ္ဘာလှည့်ခရီးသည် ka-bar-hlae-kha-yee-the *(n.)* **globetrotter**
ကမ္ဘာလုံး ka-bar-lone *(n.)* **globe**
ကမ္ဘာလုံးပျံ့နှံ့မှု kambharlone pyaannhaanmhu *(n.)* **universality**
ကမ္ဘာအနှံ့ ka-bar-a-nant *(adj.)* **global**
ကမ္ဘာဦး kambhar u *(adj.)* **primeval**
ကမ်းကုန်အောင် ဆိုးဝါးသော kan-kone-aung-soe-war-taw *(adj.)* **arrant**
ကမ်းခြေ kan-chay *(n.)* **beach**
ကမ်းခြေ၊ ကမ်းစပ် kamchay, kamsat *(n.)* **shore**
ကမ်းခြေဆီသို့ kamhkyayseshoet *(adj.)* **shoreward**
ကမ်းခြေတွင် ကစားရန် ရောင်စုံဘောလုံး kan-chay-twin-ka-sar-yan-yaung-son-baw-lone *(n.)* **beach ball**
ကမ်းခြေဘေး kan-chay-bay *(adj.)* **beachside**
ကမ်းခြေရှေ့ kan-chay-shay *(adj.)* **beachfront**
ကမ်းစပ်ဆီသို့ kam sat sethoet *(adv.)* **shoreward**
ကမ်းနား kamnarr *(n.)* **strand**
ကမ်းပေါ်သို့ kan-paw-tho *(adv.)* **ashore**
ကမ်းရိုး kamroe *(n.)* **shoreline**
ကမ်းရိုးတန်း kan-yoe-tan *(n.)* **coastline**
ကမ်းရိုးတန်းရဲ kan-yoe-tan-ye *(n.)* **coastguard**
ကမ်းရိုးတန်းသွား သင်္ဘော kan-yoe-tan-twar-tin-baw *(n.)* **coaster**
ကမ်းလှမ်းချက် kam-lam-chet *(n.)* **offer**
ကမ်းလှမ်းသည်၊ ပေးသည် kam-lam-tai, pay-tai *(v.)* **offer**
ကယောက်ကယက်စကား ka-yauk-ka-yat-sa-kar *(n.)* **gibberish**
ကယောက်ကယက်ဖြစ်သော ka-yauk-ka-yat-phit-taw *(adj.)* **gibberish**
ကယောင်ကတမ်း ပြောသည် kayaungkatam pyawwsai *(v.)* **rave**
ကယောင်ချောက်ချားဖြစ်သော ka-yaung-chauk-char-phit-taw *(adj.)* **hysterical**
ကယ်စီယမ်ဓာတ်နည်းခြင်း kal-see-yan-dat-nae-chin *(n.)* **decalcification**
ကယ်စီယမ်ဓာတ်နည်းသည် kal-see-yan-dat-nae-the *(v.)* **decalcifiy**
ကယ်ဆယ်ခြင်း kaal-saalchinn *(n.)* **rescue**
ကယ်ဆယ်သည် kaal-saalsai *(v.)* **rescue**
ကယ်ဆယ်သည်၊ စုဆောင်းသည် kaalsaal sai , susaunggsai *(v.)* **save**
ကယ်တင်ခြင်း kaaltinchinn *(n.)* **salvation**
ကယ်တင်ရှင် kaaltinshin *(n.)* **saviour**
ကယ်ထုတ်သည် kal-htoke-the *(v.)* **extricate**
ကယ်နိုင်သော kaal-nine-saw *(adj.)* **savable**
ကယ်ပေါက် kal-pauk *(n.)* **let-out**
ကယ်ရီကေချာရုပ်ပြောင် kal-re-kay-char-yote-pyaung *(n.)* **caricature**
ကယ်လစီယမ်ဓာတ် kal-la-see-yan-dat *(n.)* **calcium**
ကယ်လိုရီ kal-lo-yee *(n.)* **calorie**
ကျက်သရေ kyat-ta-yay *(n.)* **grace**
ကျက်သရေမင်္ဂလာ kyat-tha-yay-min-ga-lar *(n.)* **boon**
ကျခြင်း kya-chin *(n.)* **fall**
ကျခြင်း၊ နည်းခြင်း kya-chin, nae-chin *(n.)* **drop-off**

ကျင့်ယူသည် kyint-yu-the *(v.)* **acquire**

ကျင့်ဝတ် kyint-wit *(n.)* **ethics**

ကျင့်ဝတ်ထုံးတမ်း kyint-wit-htone-tann *(n.)* **etiquette**

ကျင့်ဝတ်နှင့် ဆိုင်သော kyint-wit-nint-sai-taw *(adj.)* **ethical**

ကျင့်သားမရသော kyint-sar-ma-ra-saw *(adj.)* **unadapted**

ကျင့်သားရသည် kyint-tar-ya-the *(v.)* **accustom**

ကျင်တွက်ကိုက်လုပ်သည် kyin twat kitelote-sai *(v.)* **square**

ကျင်လည်သော kyin-lal-taw *(adj.)* **deft**

ကျစ်ကျစ်ဆုပ်သည် kyit-kyit-sote-the *(v.)* **clench**

ကျစ်လျစ်မှု kyit-lyit-mu *(n.)* **brevity**

ကျစ်လျစ်သွက်လက်သော kyit-lyit-twat-lat-taw *(adj.)* **dapper**

ကျစ်လျစ်သော၊ သွယ်သော kyit lyit saw, swalsaw *(adj.)* **slender**

ကျစ်လျစ်အောင် လုပ်သည် kyit lyit-aung lotesai *(v.)* **slim**

ကျဆုံးခြင်း kya-sone-chin *(n.)* **downfall**

ကျဉ်းမြောင်းသော kyin-myar-taw *(adj.)* **insular**

ကျဉ်းသည် kyin-the *(v.)* **narrow**

ကျဉ်းသော kyin-thaw *(adj.)* **narrow**

ကျဉ်းသော အပိုင်း kyinsaw aapine *(n.)* **small**

ကျည် kyi *(n.)* **ammunition**

ကျည်းပေါင်သမား kyi-paung-ta-mar *(n.)* **joiner**

ကျည်ကျည်ကျာကျာ မြည်သံ kyi-kyi-kyar-kyar-myi-than *(v.)* **chirp**

ကျည်ကျည်ကျာကျာ မြည်သည် kyi-kyi-kyar-kyar-myi-the *(v.)* **cheep**

ကျည်ကာ kyi-kar *(adj.)* **bulletproof**

ကျည်ဆံ kyi-san *(n.)* **bullet**

ကျည်ဆံရထား kyi-san-ya-htar *(n.)* **bullet train**

ကျည်ပုံဖန်ခွက် kyi pone hpaan-hkwat *(n.)* **tumbler**

ကျည်ဖူး kyai-hpuu *(n.)* **projectile**

ကျည်မတိုးသော kyai m toesaw *(adj.)* **shotproof**

ကျတ်တီးမြေ kyat-tee-myay *(adj.)* **barren**

ကျန်းမာကြံ့ခိုင်ဖျတ်လတ်သော kyan-mar-kyant-khaing-phyat-lat-taw *(adj.)* **athletic**

ကျန်းမာရေး kyan-mar-yay *(n.)* **health**

ကျန်းမာသန်စွမ်းသော kyan-mar-tan-swan-taw *(adj.)* **hale**

ကျန်းမာသော kyan-mar-taw *(adj.)* **fit**

ကျန်သည့်အပိုင်း kyaan saeet-aapine *(n.)* **remainder**

ကျန်သည်၊ ဆက်လက်တည်ရှိသည် kyaan sai , saat-laat-tai-shisai *(v.)* **remain**

ကျပန်း kya-paann *(adj.)* **random**

ကျပန်းလုပ်သည် kya-paann-lote-sai *(v.)* **randomise**

ကျပ်ခိုး kyauthkoe *(n.)* **soot**

ကျပ်ခိုးစင် kyat-khoe-sin *(n.)* **mantel**

ကျပ်တည်းမှု kyat teemhu *(n.)* **stringency**

ကျမ်း kyam *(n.)* **treatise**

ကျမ်းကျိန်လွှာ kyan-kyein-hlwar *(n.)* **affidavit**

ကျမ်းကြီးကျမ်းခိုင် kyam kyee kyamhkine *(n.)* **tome**

ကျမ်းစာအုပ်၏ ဝိသေသလက္ခဏာ tat-sar-oak-ei-wi-tay-ta-lat-kha-nar *(adj.)* **textbookish**

ကျမ်းပြုခြင်း kyan-pyu-chin *(n.)* **compilation**
ကျမ်းသစ္စာ kyan-tit-sar *(n.)* **oath**
ကျမ်းသစ္စာဖောက်ဖျက်ခြင်း kyan-tit-sar-hpout-hpyet-chin *(adj.)* **oathbreaking**
ကျမ်းသစ္စာဖောက်ဖျက်သူ kyan-tit-sar-hpout-hpyet-tuu *(n.)* **oathbreaker**
ကျယ်ကျယ်ဝန်းဝန်းရှိသော kyaalkyaal waann waannshisaw *(adj.)* **roomy**
ကျယ်ပြန့်လာခြင်း kyal-pyant-lar-chin *(n.)* **expansion**
ကျယ်ပြန့်သည် kyal-pyant-the *(v.)* **expand**
ကျယ်ပြန့်သော kyal-pyant-taw *(adj.)* **broad**
ကျယ်ပြောသော tote htout hkonesai *(adj.)* **vast**
ကျယ်လာသည် kyal-lar-the *(v.)* **dilate**
ကျယ်လောင်စွာ ပေါက်ကွဲသည် kyal-laung-swar-pauk-kwal-the *(v.)* **crump**
ကျယ်လောင်စူးရှသော အသံ မြည်သည် kyal-laung-sue-sha-taw-a-tan-myi-the *(v.)* **blare**
ကျယ်လောင်သော kyal-laung-taw *(adj.)* **loud**
ကျယ်ဝန်းသော kyaalwaannsaw *(adj.)* **spacious**
ကျယ်သည်၊ တစ်ပန်းသာအောင် လုပ်သည် kyaal sai , ta pan sar-aung lotesai *(v.)* **trump**
ကျယ်သော kyaal-saw *(adj.)* **wide**
ကျယ်အောင် ချဲ့သည် kyaal-aung chaae-sai *(v.)* **widen**
ကျရှုံးခြင်း kya-shone-chin *(n.)* **fail**
ကျရောက်သည်၊ တည်ရှိသည် kya-yauk-the, the-shi-the *(v.)* **incur**
ကျွန် kywan *(n.)* **slave**
ကျွန်း kyun *(n.)* **island**
ကျွန်းသစ် kyawannsit *(n.)* **teak**
ကျွန်တော့်ကို kyun-taw-ko *(pron.)* **me**
ကျွန်တော်၏ kyun-taw-ei *(adj.)* **my**
ကျွန်တော်၏ ဟာ kyun-taw-ei-har *(pron.)* **mine**
ကျွန်တော်ကိုယ်တိုင် kyun-taw-ko-tai *(pron.)* **myself**
ကျွန်တော်တို့၏ kyun-taw-thoet-eat *(pron.)* **our**
ကျွန်ပြုခံရသူ kyun-pyu-khan-ya-thu *(n.)* **thrall**
ကျွန်ပြုခြင်း kyun-pyu-chin *(n.)* **thralldom**
ကျွန်ပြုသည် kyun-pyu=the *(v.)* **enslave**
ကျွန်အဖြစ်မှ လွှတ်ခြင်း kyun-a-phit-ma-hlut-chin *(n.)* **manumission**
ကျွန်အဖြစ်မှ လွှတ်သည် kyun-a-phit-ma-hlut-the *(v.)* **manumit**
ကျွန်ုပ် kyone-note *(pron.)* **I**
ကျွမ်းကျင် kywan-kyin *(adj.)* **expert**
ကျွမ်းကျင်စွာ ကိုင်တွယ်ခြင်း kyun-kyin-swar-kai-twal-chin *(n.)* **manipulation**
ကျွမ်းကျင်စွာ ကိုင်တွယ်သည် kyun-kyin-swar-kai-twal-the *(v.)* **manipulate**
ကျွမ်းကျင်မှု kywam-kyin-mhu *(n.)* **proficiency**
ကျွမ်းကျင်မှု၊ ပျော်ရွှင်ခြင်း kyun-kyin-mu, pyaw-shwin-chin *(n.)* **felicity**
ကျွမ်းကျင်လိမ္မာမှု kyawmkyin limmarmhu *(n.)* **prowess**
ကျွမ်းကျင်လိမ္မာသော kywan-kyin-lain-mar-taw *(adj.)* **adroit**
ကျွမ်းကျင်လိမ်မာမှု kywan-kyin-lain-mar-mu *(n.)* **asset**
ကျွမ်းကျင်သူ kywan-kyin-thu *(n.)* **expert**
ကျွမ်းကျင်သော kywam-kyin-saw *(adj.)* **proficient**

ကျွမ်းကျင်သော၊ တော်သော kyun-kyin-taw, taw-thaw *(adj.)* **efficient**
ကျွမ်းကျွမ်းကျင်ကျင် ပြောနိုင်သော kywan-kywan-kyin-kyin-pyaw-nai-taw *(adj.)* **fluent**
ကျွမ်းတူးဆူးဖြင့် အပင်စိုက်သည် kyun-tu-sue-phit-a-pin-site-the *(v.)* **dibble**
ကျွမ်းထိုးခြင်း kyawm htoechinn *(n.)* **somersault**
ကျွမ်းထိုးမှောက်ခုံကျသည် kywam htoe mhaout hkone kyasai *(v.)* **tumble**
ကျွမ်းထိုးသည် kyawm htoesai *(v.)* **somersault**
ကျွမ်းနေသော kyawmnaysaw *(adj.)* **terminal**
ကျွမ်းဘားကစားခြင်း kywan-bar-ka-sar-chin *(n.)* **acrobatics**
ကျွမ်းဘားနှင့် ဆိုင်သော kyun-bar-nint-sai-taw *(adj.)* **gymnastic**
ကျွမ်းဘားနှင့်ဆိုင်သော kywan-bar-nint-saing-taw *(adj.)* **acrobatic**
ကျွမ်းဘားပညာလေ့ကျင့်မှု kyun-bar-pyin-nyar-lay-kyint-mu *(n.)* **gymnastics**
ကျွမ်းဘားပြစားသူ kywan-bar-pya-sar-thu *(n.)* **acrobat**
ကျွမ်းဘားသမား kyun-bar-ta-mar *(n.)* **gymnast**
ကျွီခနဲ မြည်သံ kyai hkanell myisan *(n.)* **squeak**
ကျွီခနဲ မြည်သည် kyai hkanell myisai *(v.)* **squeak**
ကျွီခနဲ မြည်သည် kywi-kha-nae-myi-the *(v.)* **creak**
ကျွေးချိန် kyway-chein *(n.)* **feed**
ကျွေးသည် kyway-the *(v.)* **feed**
ကျွဲ kywe *(n.)* **buffalo**
ကျွဲစာနွားစာ kywe-sar-nwar-sar *(n.)* **fodder**
ကျွဲနွားတိရိစ္ဆာန် kywe-nwar-ta-yeik-san *(n.)* **cattle**
ကျွဲနွားတိရိစ္ဆာန်ခိုးယူခြင်း kywe-nwar-ta-yeik-san-kho-yu-chin *(n.)* **abactor**
ကျွဲနွားတိရိစ္ဆာန်ခိုးယူသူ kywe-nwar-ta-yeik-san-kho-yu-thu *(n.)* **abacus**
ကျွဲမြီးတိုသော kywe-mee-toe-taw *(adj.)* **miffed**
ကျွဲရိုင်းသတ်ပွဲ kyawal rine saatpwal *(n.)* **tauromachy**
ကျသင့်ငွေတောင်းခံသည် kya-tint-ngwe-taung-khan-the *(v.)* **charge**
ကျသင့်ငွေတောင်းခံနိုင်သော kya-tint-ngwe-taung-khan-nai-taw *(adj.)* **billable**
ကျသင့်ငွေတောင်းခံလွှာ kya-tint-ngwe-taung-khan-hlwar *(n.)* **bill**
ကျသည် kya-the *(v.)* **fall**
ကျသည်၊ ချပေးသည် kya-the, cha-pay-the *(v.)* **drop**
ကျသော kya-taw *(adj.)* **fallen**
ကျား kyarr *(n.)* **tiger**
ကျား၊ ဒေါက် kyarr , dout *(n.)* **strut**
ကျားကုတ်ကျားခဲဖြစ်သော kyarrkote kyarr hkelhlpyitsaw *(adj.)* **tenacious**
ကျားမ kyarr-ma *(n.)* **tigress**
ကျားမ အတူသင်ကြားသော kyar-ma-a-tu-tin-kyar-taw *(n.)* **co-education**
ကျားသစ် kyar-tit *(n.)* **leopard**
ကျာပွတ် kyaarpwat *(n.)* **scourge**
ကျာပွတ်နှင့် ရိုက်သည် kyaar pwatnint ritesai *(v.)* **scourge**
ကျာပွတ်ဖြင့်ရိုက်သည် kyar-put-phint-yite-the *(v.)* **lash**
ကျိချွဲသော kyi chwalsaw *(adj.)* **slimy**
ကျိန်ဆဲသည် kyein-sal-the *(n.)* **blaspheme**

ကျိန်ဆဲသော စကားအသုံးအနှုန်း kyein-sal-taw-sa-kar-a-tone-a-hnone *(n.)* **blasphemy**
ကျိုးကြောင်းပြချက် kyo-kyaung-pya-chat *(n.)* **justification**
ကျိုးခြင်း၊ အက်ခြင်း kyo-chin, at-chin *(n.)* **fracture**
ကျိုးတိုးကျဲတဲ kyoetoekyaelltell *(adj.)* **scattered**
ကျိုးနေသော၊ ကွဲနေသော kyo-nay-taw, kwal-nay-taw *(v.)* **broken**
ကျိုးပဲ့ခြင်း kyo-pae-chin *(n.)* **breakage**
ကျိုးပဲ့ပျက်စီးနေခြင်း kyo-pae-pyat-see-nay-chin *(n.)* **dilapidation**
ကျိုးပဲ့သော မသုံးတော့သော ဖန်များကို ဖန်ချက်လုပ်ငန်းတွင် အသုံးချခြင်း kyo-pae-taw-ma-tone-taw-taw-phan-myar-ko-phan-chat-lote-ngan-twin-tone-chin *(n.)* **cullet**
ကျိုးသည်၊ ကွဲသည် kyo-the, kwal-the *(v.)* **break**
ကျိုးသည်၊ အက်သည် kyo-the, at-the *(v.)* **fracture**
ကျိုက်ကျိုက်ဆူနေသည် kyaite kyaite suunaysai *(v.)* **steam**
ကျိုက်ချသည် kyaik-cha-the *(v.)* **down**
ကျိုင်း kyai *(n.)* **mace**
ကျိုင်းကောင် kyai-kaung *(n.)* **locust**
ကျိုင်းဖြင့် ရိုက်သည် kyai-phyint-yite-the *(v.)* **mace**
ကျီ kyi *(n.)* **barn**
ကျီးကန်း kyee-kan *(n.)* **crow**
ကျီးနက်ကြီး kyaee naatkyee *(n.)* **raven**
ကျီးပေါင်းပင်တစ်မျိုး kyee-paung-pin-ta-myo *(n.)* **mistletoe**
ကျီးအ kyaeea *(n.)* **rook**
ကျီးအာသံ kyi-arr-than *(v.)* **caw**
ကျီ၊ စပါးကျီ kyi, sa-par-kyi *(n.)* **granary**
ကျီစယ်ခြင်း kyae saalchinn *(n.)* **teasing**
ကျီစယ်စကား kyi-sal-sa-kar *(n.)* **banter**
ကျီစယ်တတ်သော kyi-sal-tat-taw *(adj.)* **mischievous**
ကျီစယ်နောက်ပြောင်ခြင်း kyee saal nout pyaung-chinn *(n.)* **raillery**
ကျီစယ်သည့် သဘောဖြင့် kyae saalsaeet sabhawhpyint *(adv.)* **teasingly**
ကျီစယ်သော kyae saalsaw *(adj.)* **roguish**
ကျုံ့ခြင်း kyaonechinn *(n.)* **shrinkage**
ကျုံ့ခြင်း၊ ချုံ့ခြင်း kyont-chin, chont-chin *(n.)* **contraction**
ကျုံ့ဆန့်နိုင်စွမ်း kyont-sant-nai-swan *(n.)* **elasticity**
ကျုံ့ဆန့်နိုင်သော kyont-sant-nai-taw *(adj.)* **elastic**
ကျုံး kyone *(n.)* **moat**
ကျုံးဖြင့် ပတ်သည် kyone-phyint-pat-the *(v.)* **moat**
ကျုံ့စေသည် kyaonesaysai *(v.)* **shrink**
ကျူးကျော်ခြင်း aaswinpyaunggsai *(n.)* **transgression**
ကျူးကျော်ဝင်ရောက်မှု kyuukyawwinroutmhu *(n.)* **trespass**
ကျူးကျော်သည် kyu-kyaw-the *(v.)* **encroach**
ကျူးကျော်သူ kyu-kyaw-thu *(n.)* **aggressor**
ကျူးလွန်သည် kyu-loon-the *(v.)* **commit**
ကျူတိုရီရယ် kyuu to reraal *(n.)* **tutorial**
ကျူရှင်ပေးခြင်း၊ ကျောင်းလခ kyuushin payychinn , kyaunglahka *(n.)* **tuition**
ကျေးဇူးတင်ခြင်း kyaayyjuutinchinn *(n.)* **thanks**
ကျေးဇူးတင်သည် kyaayyjuutinsai *(v.)* **thank**

ကျေးဇူးတင်သော kyaayyjuutinsaw *(adj.)* **thankful**
ကျေးဇူးတရား kyay-zuu-ta-yar *(n.)* **gratitude**
ကျေးဇူးပြု၍ kyaayy-zuu-pyu-ywe *(adv.)* **please**
ကျေးဇူးပါ kyaayyjuupar *(int.)* **shot**
ကျေးဇူးမသိတတ်ခြင်း kyay-zu-ma-ti-tat-chin *(n.)* **ingratitude**
ကျေးတောဆန်သော၊ ရိုးစင်းသော kyaayytaw saansaw , roesinnsaw *(adj.)* **rustic**
ကျေးတောသား kyaayytawsarr *(n.)* **rustic**
ကျေးလက်ဆန်ခြင်း kyay-lat-san-chin *(n.)* **rusticity**
ကျေးလက်တောနယ် kyaayylaat tawnaal *(adj.)* **rural**
ကျေးလက်သဘာဝသရုပ်ဖော်အနုပညာ kyaay-laat-sa-bhar-wa-sa-rote-hpaw-aa-nu-pa-nyar *(adj.)* **pastoral**
ကျေနပ်ခြင်း kyaay-nautchinn *(n.)* **satisfaction**
ကျေနပ်စေသည် kyaay-nat-say-sai *(v.)* **please**
ကျေနပ်နိုင်သော kyaay-nat-nine-saw *(adj.)* **satiable**
ကျေနပ်ဖွယ်ကောင်းသော kyaaynaut hpwalkaunggsaw *(adj.)* **satisfactory**
ကျေနပ်မှု မရှိ kyay-nat-mu-ma-shi *(v.)* **dissatisfy**
ကျေနပ်မှု မရှိခြင်း kyay-nat-mu-ma-shi-chin *(n.)* **dissatisfaction**
ကျေနပ်သည် kyaaynautsai *(v.)* **satisfy**
ကျေရာကျေကြောင်း kyaay-rar-kyaay-kyaungg *(adj.)* **placatory**
ကျော့ကွင်း kyawwt-kwin *(n.)* **snare**
ကျောက်ကပ် kyauk-kat *(n.)* **kidney**
ကျောက်ကပ်သန့်စင်ခြင်း kyauk-kat-tant-sin-chin *(n.)* **dialysis**
ကျောက်ကျောက်ကဲ့သို့ ပျစ်ခဲသော kyauk-kyaw-kae-tho-pyit-taw *(adj.)* **gelatinous**
ကျောက်ချရပ်နားရာ kyauk-cha-yat-nar-yar *(n.)* **anchorage**
ကျောက်ခေတ်သစ် kyauk-khit-tit *(adj.)* **neolithic**
ကျောက်ခေါင်းတလား kyauk-khaung-ta-lar *(n.)* **cist**
ကျောက်ခဲထူထပ်သော kyawt-hkell htuu-htat-saw *(adj.)* **stony**
ကျောက်ဂွမ်း kyauk-goon *(n.)* **asbestos**
ကျောက်ငါး kyauk-ngar *(n.)* **rockfish**
ကျောက်စရစ်ခဲ kyaut-sa-rit-hkell *(n.)* **pebble**
ကျောက်စိမ်း kyauk-sein *(n.)* **jade**
ကျောက်ဆူး kyauk-sue *(n.)* **anchor**
ကျောက်တုံး kyawt-tone *(n.)* **stone**
ကျောက်တုံးထုဆစ်ပညာ kyauttone htu sitpanyar *(n.)* **sculpture**
ကျောက်တုန်း kyawt-tone *(v.)* **zeb**
ကျောက်တူးသည် kyaut tuusai *(v.)* **quarry**
ကျောက်ပြား kyawwatpyarr *(n.)* **scant**
ကျောက်ပွင့် kyaut pwint *(n.)* **seaweed**
ကျောက်ပုစွန် kyauk-pa-zon *(n.)* **crayfish**
ကျောက်ဖြစ်ရုပ်ကြွင်း kyauk-phit-yoke-kywin *(n.)* **fossil**
ကျောက်ဖြူနု kyauk-phyu-nu *(n.)* **alabaster**
ကျောက်မျက် kyauk-myat *(n.)* **jewel**
ကျောက်မျက်ဗေဒ kyauk-myat-bay-da *(n.)* **gemmology**
ကျောက်မျက်ရတနာ kyauk-myat-ya-da-nar *(n.)* **gem**

ကျောက်မီးသွေး kyauk-mee-thway *(n.)* **coal**

ကျောက်မီးသွေးညို kyauk-mee-tway-nyo *(n.)* **lignite**

ကျောက်ရည်ပူ kyauk-yay-pu *(n.)* **magma**

ကျောက်သင်ပုန်း kyauk-tin-bone *(n.)* **blackboard**

ကျောက်သားတိုင်ကြီး kyauk-tar-tai-gyi *(n.)* **monolith**

ကျောက်အင်တုံ၊ စာလုံးဖောင့်ပုံစံ kyauk-inn-tone, sar-lone-font-pon-san *(n.)* **font**

ကျောချမ်းဖွယ် kyaw-chan-phwal *(adj.)* **creepy**

ကျောခိုင်းသည် kyaw-khai-the *(v.)* **forsake**

ကျောင်း၊ စစ်တပ်၊ ထောင်တွင် အမှုထမ်းသူခရစ်ယာန်ဘုန်းကြီး kyaung-sit-tat-htaung-twin-a-mu-htan-thu-kha-yit-yan-hpone-gyi *(n.)* **chaplain**

ကျောင်း၊ တက္ကသိုလ်၊ အုပ်စု kyaungg , takkasol , aotesu *(n.)* **school**

ကျောင်းကလေး kyaunggkalayy *(n.)* **schoolhouse**

ကျောင်းဆရာ kyaunggsarar *(n.)* **schoolmaster**

ကျောင်းတိုက် kyaung-tite *(n.)* **abbey**

ကျောင်းတိုက်ဆရာတော် kyaung-tite-sa-ya-taw *(n.)* **abbot**

ကျောင်းနေဖက်သူငယ်ချင်း kyaung nay hpaatsuungaalchinn *(n.)* **schoolmate**

ကျောင်းပညာရေး kyaunggpanyarrayy *(adj.)* **scholastic**

ကျောင်းမှ နားခံရခြင်း၊ ထုတ်ပယ်ခံရခြင်း kyaung ma-nar-khan-ya-chin-htoke-pal-khan-ya-chin *(n.)* **rustication**

ကျောင်းမှ နားခံရသည်၊ ထုတ်ပယ်ခံရသည် kyaung-ma-nar-khan-ya-the-htoke-pal-khan-ya-the *(v.)* **rusticate**

ကျောင်းဝန်း kyaunggwaann *(n.)* **schoolyard**

ကျောင်းသား kyaunggsarr *(n.)* **student**

ကျောင်းသားခေါင်းဆောင် kyaungg-sarr-hkaung-saung *(n.)* **prefect**

ကျောင်းအိပ်ကျောင်းစားလက်ခံသည့်ကျောင်း kyaung-aik-kyaung-sar-lat-khan-the-kyaung *(n.)* **boarding school**

ကျောင်းအုပ် kyaungg-aote *(n.)* **preceptor**

ကျောင်းအုပ်ကြီး kyaungg-aote-kyee *(n.)* **principal**

ကျောက်တောင်တက်သူ kyaung taungtaatsuu *(n.)* **rock climber**

ကျောနှင့် ဆိုင်သော kyaw-nint-sai-taw *(adj.)* **dorsal**

ကျောပိုးအိတ် kyawpoeate *(n.)* **rucksack**

ကျောပိုးအိတ်ကြီး kyaw-poe-aik-kyi *(n.)* **backpack**

ကျောပိုးအိတ်ဖြင့် ခရီးထွက်သူ kyaw-poe-aik-phit-kha-yee-htwat-thu *(n.)* **backpacker**

ကျောရိုး kyawwroe *(adj.)* **spinal**

ကျောသည်၊ တစ်ပန်းသာသည် kyaw-tai, ta-pan-tar-tai *(v.)* **outrun**

ကျော် kyaw *(prep.)* **past**

ကျော်ကြားမှု kyaw-kyarrmhu *(n.)* **publicity**

ကျော်ကြားသော kyawkyarrsaw *(adj.)* **renowned**

ကျော်တက်သွားသည် kyaw-tat-twar-tai *(v.)* **overtake**

ကျော်လွန်ပယ်ချသည် kyaw-lwan-pal-cha-tai *(v.)* **overrule**

ကျော်လွန်လျက် aahtwataahteik *(adv.)* **transcendingly**

ကျော်လွန်သည် kyawlwansai *(v.)* **transcend**

ကျော်လွှားသည် kyaw-hlar-tai *(v.)* **overcome**
ကျော်သွားလျှင်ပြန်လှည့်မရနိုင်သော အကန့်အသတ် kyaw-twar-lyin-pyan-hlae-ma-ya-nine-taw-a-kant-a-thet *(n.)* **rubicon**
ကျဲသော၊ ပါးသော kyaell saw , parrsaw *(adj.)* **sparse**
ကရက် ka-rat *(n.)* **carat**
ကရန် ပြင်းထန်စွာ လှုံ့ဆော်မှု karaan pyinnhtaanhcwar lhuansaungmhu *(n.)* **tarantism**
ကရား ka-rarr *(n.)* **pitcher**
ကရုဏာ karunar *(n.)* **sympathy**
ကရုဏာရသ ka-ru-nar-ra-sa *(n.)* **pathos**
ကရုဇာစစ်သင်္ဘောကြီး ka-yu-zar-sit-tin-baw-gyi *(n.)* **cruiser**
ကရော်ကမည်ပြောသော၊ လုပ်သော ka-yau-ka-mal-pyaw-taw, lote-taw *(adj.)* **flip**
ကြံ kyan *(n.)* **cane**
ကြံ့ kyaan *(n.)* **rhinoceros**
ကြံ့ကြံ့ခံနိုင်သည် kyaankyaanhkanninesai *(v.)* **withstand**
ကြံ့ကြံ့ခံသည် khyant-khyant-khan-the *(v.)* **endure**
ကြံ့ခိုင်မှု kyaanhkinemhu *(n.)* **resolution**
ကြံ့ခိုင်မှု စမ်းသပ်ခြင်း kyant-khai-mu-san-tat-chin *(n.)* **fitness test**
ကြံ့ခိုင်မှု မှတ်တမ်း kyant-khai-mu-mat-tan *(n.)* **fitness tracker**
ကြံ့ခိုင်မှု သင်တန်း kyant-khai-mu-tin-than *(n.)* **fitness training**
ကြံ့ခိုင်သော kyant-khai-taw *(adj.)* **lusty**
ကြံရာပါ kyan-yar-par *(n.)* **accomplice**
ကြံရာပါခြင်း kyan-yar-par-chin *(n.)* **complicity**

ကြက် kyat *(n.)* **chicken**
ကြက်၊ ငှက်ပေါက်စ kyat-nget-paut-sa *(n.)* **chick**
ကြက်ခြေခတ် kyat-chway-khat *(n.)* **cross**
ကြက်ငှက်၊ ကြက်သား kyat-nget, kyat-tar *(n.)* **fowl**
ကြက်ဆင် kyat-sin *(n.)* **turkey**
ကြက်ဆူဆီ kyat-su-si *(n.)* **castor oil**
ကြက်ဥအကာ kyat-au-a-karr *(n.)* **albumen**
ကြက်တိန်ညင် kyat-tain-nyin *(n.)* **bantam**
ကြက်တူရွေး kyat-tuu-rway *(n.)* **parrot**
ကြက်တောင် kyat-taung *(n.)* **badminton**
ကြက်ဖ kyat-pha *(n.)* **cock**
ကြက်သွန်နီ kyat-twan-ne *(n.)* **onion**
ကြက်သွန်ဖြူ kyat-toon-phyu *(n.)* **garlic**
ကြက်သွန်ဖြူစော်နံသော kyat-toon-phyu-saw-nan-the *(adj.)* **garlicky**
ကြက်သွန်မြိတ် kyat-toon-myeik *(n.)* **leek**
ကြက်သွေးရောင် kyat-tway-yaung *(n.)* **crimson**
ကြက်သီးနွေး kyaat seenway *(n.)* **tepidity**
ကြက်ဥ kyat-au *(n.)* **egg**
ကြက်ဥခေါက်ကြော် kyat-u-kout-kyaw *(n.)* **omelette**
ကြက်ဥနို့ပေါင်း kyat-u-noe-paung *(n.)* **custard**
ကြင်နာစွာ kyin-nar-swar *(adv.)* **kindly**
ကြင်နာစွာထွေးပိုက်ခြင်း kyin-nar-swar-htway-pite-chin *(v.)* **caress**
ကြင်နာစိတ် ရှိသော kyin-nar-seik-shi-taw *(adj.)* **kind-hearted**
ကြင်နာမြတ်နိုးမှု kyin-nar-myat-noe-mu *(n.)* **adoration**
ကြင်နာမှု kyin-nar-mu *(n.)* **kindness**

ကြင်နာမှုပြသည်၊ ထောက်ထားသည် kyinnarmhu pyasai , htouthtarrsai *(v.)* **sympathize**
ကြင်နာသနားတတ်သော kyinnar sanarrtaatsaw *(adj.)* **tender**
ကြင်နာသော kyin-nar-taw *(adj.)* **affectionate**
ကြင်ရာတော် kyin-yar-taw *(n.)* **consort**
ကြည့်ရှုစောင့်ရှောက်သူ kyi shu saung shoutsuu *(n.)* **tender**
ကြည့်သည် kyi-the *(v.)* **look**
ကြည့်သည် kyisai *(v.)* **watch**
ကြည်းရေလေတပ်မတော် kyee-yay-lay-tat-ma-taw *(n.)* **armed forces**
ကြည်ကြည်လင်လင် kyi-kyi-lin-lin *(adv.)* **clearly**
ကြည်ညိုကိုင်းရှိုင်းဖွယ်ရာ kyinyo kine hlyinehpwalrar *(adj.)* **venerable**
ကြည်ညိုကိုင်းရှိုင်းမှု kyinyo kine hlyinemhu *(n.)* **veneration**
ကြည်ညိုခြင်း kyinyochinn *(n.)* **reverence**
ကြည်ညိုလေးစားသော kyinyolayysarrsaw *(adj.)* **reverent**
ကြည်ညိုသည်၊ မြတ်နိုးသည် kyinyo sai , myatnoesai *(v.)* **revere**
ကြည်နူးစွာ kyi-nu-swar *(adv.)* **delightedly**
ကြည်နူးဆွတ်ပျံ့ဖွယ်ရာ ကင်းမဲ့သော၊ ငြီးငွေ့ဖွယ်ကောင်းသော Kyi-nuu sut pyaant hpwal-rar kinn-mae saw , ngyee ngwae hpwal-kaungg-saw *(adj.)* **prosaic**
ကြည်နူးဖွယ်ကောင်းသော kyi-nu-phwal-kaung-taw *(adj.)* **delightful**
ကြည်နူးဖွယ်ချစ်ဇာတ်လမ်း kyinuuhpwal chitzatlam *(n.)* **romance**
ကြည်လင်ပြတ်သားခြင်း kyi-lin-pyat-tar-chin *(n.)* **clarity**
ကြည်လင်သော kyi-lin-taw *(adj.)* **clear**
ကြည်လင်အေးငြိမ်းသော kyilin aayy-ngyeim-saw *(adj.)* **serene**
ကြတ်ခြင်း၊ လငပုပ်ဖမ်းခြင်း kyat-chin, la-nga-poke-phan-chin *(n.)* **eclipse**
ကြတ်သည် kyat-the *(v.)* **eclipse**
ကြန့်ကြာစေသည် kyant-kyar-say-the *(v.)* **impede**
ကြမ်းကြမ်းတောင့်တောင့် kyan-kyan-taunt-taunt *(adj.)* **lank**
ကြမ်းကြုတ်ရက်စက်သော kyan-kyoke-yat-sat-taw *(adj.)* **ferocious**
ကြမ်းကြုတ်သော kyam kyuatsaw *(adj.)* **violent**
ကြမ်းခင်း kyan-khin *(n.)* **floor**
ကြမ်းတမ်းခြင်း kyan-tan-chin *(n.)* **salebrosity**
ကြမ်းတမ်းနီမြန်းသည့်မျက်နှာရှိသော kyan-tan-ni-myan-the-myat-nar-shi-taw *(adj.)* **blowsy**
ကြမ်းတမ်းသော kyan-tan-taw *(adj.)* **fierce**
ကြမ်းတမ်းအောင်လုပ်သည် kyamtam aaunglotesai *(v.)* **tatter**
ကြမ်းတိုက်သုတ်ဖတ် kyan-tite-toke-phat *(n.)* **mop**
ကြမ်းတိုက်သုတ်ဖတ်ဖြင့် ကြမ်းတိုက်သည် kyan-tite-toke-phat-phyint-kyan-tite-the *(v.)* **mop**
ကြမ်းထော်သော kyan-htaw-taw *(adj.)* **coarse**
ကြမ်းသော၊ လှိုင်းလေထန်သော kyam saw , hline lay htaansaw *(adj.)* **rough**
ကြယ် kyaal *(n.)* **star**
ကြယ်ကဲ့သို့သော kyaalkaethoetsaw *(adj.)* **stellar**
ကြယ်စု kyal-su *(n.)* **galaxy**

ကြယ်စုနှင့် သက်ဆိုင်သော kyal-su-nint-thet-sai-taw *(adj.)* **galactic**

ကြယ်တံခွန် kyal-ta-khun *(n.)* **comet**

ကြယ်ပွင့်ပြသည် kyaal pw intpyasai *(v.)* **star**

ကြယ်များနှင့် သက်ဆိုင်သော Kyal-myar-nint-thet-saing-taw *(adj.)* **astral**

ကြယ်လင်းလက်သော kyaal-linn-laat-sai *(adj.)* **starry**

ကြယ်သီး kyal-thee *(n.)* **button**

ကြွက် kywat *(n.)* **mouse**

ကြွက်စုတ် kyawatsote *(n.)* **shrew**

ကြွက်တက်ခြင်း kywat-tat-chin *(n.)* **cramp**

ကြွက်နို့ kywatnhoet *(n.)* **wart**

ကြွက်သား kywat-tar *(n.)* **muscle**

ကြွက်သား၊ အမျှင်တစ်ရှူးနှင့် ဆိုင်သော kywat-tar-a-hmyin-tit-shu-nint-sai-taw *(adj.)* **fibromuscular**

ကြွက်သားဆိုင်ရာ kywat-tar-sai-yar *(adj.)* **muscular**

ကြွက်သားနာကျင်ခြင်း kywat-tar-nar-kyin-chin *(n.)* **myalgia**

ကြွပ်ဆတ်သော kyut-sat-taw *(adj.)* **brittle**

ကြွပ်သော kywut-taw *(adj.)* **crisp**

ကြွပ်အောင်လုပ်သည် kywut-aung-lote-the *(v.)* **crispen**

ကြွယ်ဝ၍ လွှမ်းမိုးနိုင်သူ kywe-wa-ywe-hlwan-moe-naing-thu *(n.)* **affluential**

ကြွယ်ဝချမ်းသာစေခြင်း kywal-wa-chan-tar-say-chin *(n.)* **enrichment**

ကြွယ်ဝချမ်းသာစေသည် kywal-wa-chan-tar-say-the *(v.)* **enrich**

ကြွယ်ဝခြင်း kywe-wa-chin *(n.)* **affluence**

ကြွယ်ဝသော kywe-wa-taw *(adj.)* **affluent**

ကြွားလုံးထုတ်သည် kywar-lone-htoke-the *(v.)* **flaunt**

ကြွားသည် kwar-the *(v.)* **boast**

ကြွေ kway *(n.)* **enamel**

ကြွေးကင်းသော kyway kinnsaw *(adj.)* **solvent**

ကြွေးကျန် kyway-kyan *(n.pl.)* **arrears**

ကြွေးကြော်သံ kway-kyaw-tan *(n.)* **chant**

ကြွေးဆပ်နိုင်အား kyway sat nineaarr *(n.)* **solvency**

ကြွေးမီကင်းသော kyway-mee-kin-taw *(adj.)* **debt-free**

ကြွေးရှင် kyway-shin *(n.)* **creditor**

ကြွေထည် kyay-htai *(n.)* **porcelain**

ကြွေထည်ပစ္စည်း kway-htae-pyit-see *(n.)* **china**

ကြွေထည်မြေထည် kyway-htae-myay-htae *(n.)* **ceramics**

ကြွေပန်း kyay-pan *(n.)* **geranium**

ကြား၊ ကွက်လပ် kyarr , kwatlat *(n.)* **space**

ကြားကာလ kyar-kar-la *(n.)* **interim**

ကြားခံ kyar-khan *(n.)* **medium**

ကြားခံဒေသ kyar-khan-day-ta *(n.)* **buffer zone**

ကြားခံအရာ၊ ဒဏ်ခံ kyar-khan-a-yar, dan-khan *(n.)* **buffer**

ကြားဆက်ကိရိယာ kyar-set-ka-yi-yar *(n.)* **adaptor**

ကြားနိုင်သော kyar-naing-taw *(adj.)* **audible**

ကြားဖြတ်တိုက်သည် kyar-phat-tite-the *(v.)* **intercept**

ကြားဖြတ်ရွေးကောက်ပွဲ kyar-phyat-ywe-kauk-pwe *(n.)* **by-election**

ကြားဖြတ်သည် kyar-phat-the *(v.)* **interrupt**

ကြားမှ ဖျန်ဖြေသူ kyar-ma-pyan-pyay-thu *(n.)* **intermediary**

ကြားဝင်စွက်ဖက်ခြင်း kyar-win-swat-phat-chin *(n.)* **intervention**
ကြားဝင်စေ့စပ်ပေးသည် kyar-win-say-sat-pay-the *(v.)* **arbitrate**
ကြားဝင်ဖျန်ဖြေသည် kyar-win-phyan-pyay-the *(v.)* **intervene**
ကြားသည် kyar-the *(v.)* **hear**
ကြာကြာ kyar-kyar *(adv.)* **long**
ကြာညောင်းစေခြင်း kyaar nyaungg say-chinn *(n.)* **prolongation**
ကြာပင် kyar-pin *(n.)* **lotus**
ကြာများနှင့် သက်ဆိုင်သော kyaar myarrnhang saatsinesaw *(adj.)* **sidereal**
ကြာရှည် အသုံးခံနိုင်စွမ်း kyar-shay-a-ton-khan-nai-swan *(n.)* **durability**
ကြာရှည် အသုံးခံသော kyar-shay-a-ton-khan-nai-taw *(adj.)* **durable**
ကြာသည် kyar-the *(v.)* **last**
ကြာသပတေးဂြိုလ် kyar-ta-pa-tay-gyo *(n.)* **jupiter**
ကြာသပတေးနေ့ kyaarsapatayynae *(n.)* **Thursday**
ကြာသော kyaw-taw *(adj.)* **lasting**
ကြိတ်ခြေသည် kyate-chay-the *(v.)* **grind**
ကြိတ်ခွဲသည် kyaik-kwal-the *(v.)* **mill**
ကြိတ်စက် kyate-sat *(n.)* **grinder**
ကြိမ်းမောင်းသည် kyaaimmaunggsai *(v.)* **upbraid**
ကြိမ်ဒဏ်ပေးသည် kyein-dan-pay-the *(v.)* **flog**
ကြိမ်နှုန်း kyein-hnone *(n.)* **frequency**
ကြိမ်နှုန်းလှိုင်း kyaain nhuannlhaine *(n.)* **sideband**
ကြိယာ kyari-yar *(n.)* **verb**
ကြိယာကာလ kyaiyarkarla *(n.)* **tense**
ကြိယာနာမ် kyi-yar-nan *(n.)* **gerund**
ကြိယာဝိသေသန kri-yar-wi-tay-ta-na *(n.)* **adverb**
ကြိယာဝိသေသနပါသော kri-yar-wi-tay-ta-na-par-taw *(adj.)* **adverbial**
ကြိယာသဏ္ဍာန်ပြောင်းသည် kyi-yar-tha-htan-pyaung-the *(v.)* **conjugate**
ကြို့ထိုးသံ kyo-htoe-tan *(n.)* **hiccup**
ကြိုး kyoe *(n.)* **rope**
ကြိုးကြာ၊ ကရိန်းကား kyo-kyar, ka-rain-kar *(n.)* **crane**
ကြိုးကွင်း kyoe-kwin *(n.)* **noose**
ကြိုးကွင်းစွပ်သည် kyoe-kwin-swut-te *(v.)* **noose**
ကြိုးစင် kyaoesin *(n.)* **scaffold**
ကြိုးစားသည် kyoe-sarrsai *(v.)* **try**
ကြိုးစားသော kyoesarrsaw *(adj.)* **studious**
ကြိုးညှိသည် kyoe nyhaisai *(v.)* **tune**
ကြိုးပန်းရရှိသည် kyo-pan-ya-shi-the *(v.)* **attain**
ကြိုးပမ်းသည် kyoe-pam-sai *(v.)* **strive**
ကြိုးပမ်းအားထုတ်မှု kyo-pan-arr-htoke-mu *(n.)* **endeavour**
ကြိုးဖြင့် လည်ပင်းညှစ်သတ်သည် kyo-phyint-lal-pin-nyit-tat-the *(v.)* **garrotte**
ကြိုးမဲ့ kyoe-mae *(adj.)* **cordless**
ကြိုးမဲ့ကြေးနန်း kyaoemaekyaynaann *(n.)* **wireless**
ကြိုးလုံး kyo-lone *(n.)* **cord**
ကြိုးသိုင်းဖိနပ် kyaoe sinehpinaut *(n.)* **sandal**
ကြိုစီစဉ်ထားသော အပန်းဖြေမှု kyo sesinhtarrsaw aa-paann-hpyaymhu *(n.)* **playdate**

ကြိုဆို နှုတ်ဆက်သည် kyo-so-note-sat-the *(v.)* **greet**
ကြိုဆိုခြင်း kyaosochinn *(n.)* **welcome**
ကြိုဆိုသည် kyaososai *(v.)* **welcome**
ကြိုဆိုသော kyaososaw *(adj.)* **welcome**
ကြိုတင် kyotin *(adj.)* **prior**
ကြိုတင် ကောက်ချက်ချခြင်း kyo-tin kout-chetchachinn *(n.)* **presupposition**
ကြိုတင် ကောက်ချက်ချသည် kyo-tin kout-chetchasai *(v.)* **presuppose**
ကြိုတင် စာရင်းသွင်းထားခြင်း kyaotin sarrinnswinhtarrchinn *(n.)* **reservation**
ကြိုတင် သိမြင်ခြင်း kyo-tin-ti-myin-chin *(n.)* **foreknowledge**
ကြိုတင်၍ kyo-tin-ywe *(adv.)* **beforehand**
ကြိုတင်ကြံရွယ်ထားသည် kyo-tin kyaan rwahl-tarr-sai *(v.)* **premeditate**
ကြိုတင်ကြံရွယ်မှု kyo-tin kyaan rwal-mhu *(n.)* **premeditation**
ကြိုတင်ကာကွယ်မှု kyo-tin-karkwal-mhu *(n.)* **precaution**
ကြိုတင်ခန့်မှန်းချက်၊ ဟောကိန်း kyo-tin-khant-hman-chat, haw-kein *(n.)* **forecast**
ကြိုတင်ခန့်မှန်းသည်၊ ဟောကိန်းထုတ်သည် kyo-tin-khant-hman-the, haw-kein-htoke-the *(v.)* **forecast**
ကြိုတင်ပြင်ဆင်သည် kyotin-pyinsinsai *(v.)* **prepare**
ကြိုတင်ပို့ ကုန်ပို့လွှာ kyo-tin-phoet kone phoet-lwhar *(adj.)* **pro forma**
ကြိုတင်ဖော်ပြထားသော kyo-tin-phaw-pya-htar-taw *(adj.)* **aforementioned**
ကြိုတင်မျှော်မှန်းခြင်း kyo-tin-hmyaw-man-chin *(n.)* **anticipation**
ကြိုတင်လက်မှတ်ဖြတ်သည် kyo-tin-lat-mat-phat-the *(v.)* **book**
ကြိုတင်သတိပေးခြင်း kyo-tin-ta-di-pay-chin *(v.)* **forewarn**
ကြိုတင်ဟန့်တားသည် kyo-tin-hant-tar-the *(v.)* **forestall**
ကြိုတင်ဟောကိန်းထုတ်သည် kyo-tin hawkeinhtote-sai *(v.)* **predetermine**
ကြိုပို့လုပ်သည် kyo-po-lote-the *(v.)* **ferry**
ကြိုမြင်သည် kyo-myin-the *(v.)* **foresee**
ကြိုလင့်နေသော ဘေးရန် kyo-lint-nay-saw-bhayy-raan *(n.)* **pitfall**
ကြိုသတ်မှတ်ထားသောဈေးဖြင့် ရောင်းချခွင့် kyo-tat-mat-htar-taw-zay-nint-yaung-cha-khwint *(n.)* **put**
ကြီးကျယ်ခမ်းနား လေးစားဖွယ်ဖြစ်သော kyi-kyal-khan-nar-lay-sar-phwal-phit-taw *(adj.)* **august**
ကြီးကျယ်ခမ်းနားခြင်း kyi-kyal-khan-nar-chin *(n.)* **grandeur**
ကြီးကျယ်ခမ်းနားသော kyi-kyal-khan-nar-taw *(adj.)* **grand**
ကြီးကျယ်သည်ဟု ထင်ရသော နေရာ kyi-kyal-the-hu-htin-ya-taw-nay-yar *(n.)* **geeksville**
ကြီးကြပ်ကွပ်ကဲသူ၊ ထောင်ပိုင် kyeekyaut kwut kell suu , htaungpine *(n.)* **warden**
ကြီးကြပ်မှု kyeekyatmhu *(n.)* **superintendence**
ကြီးကြပ်ရေးမှူး kyee-kyaut-ray-mhuu *(n.)* **overseer**
ကြီးကြပ်သည် kyeekyatsai *(v.)* **superintend**
ကြီးကြပ်သူ kyeekyatsuu *(n.)* **superintendent**
ကြီးကောင်ဝင်ချိန် kyi-kaung-win-chein *(n.)* **adolescence**
ကြီးစိုးသည် kyi-soe-the *(v.)* **dominate**
ကြီးထွားနှုန်းကို တန့်စေသည် kyee-htwarr hnoneko tant-saysai *(v.)* **stunt**

ကြီးထွားမှု kyi-htwar-mu *(n.)* **growth**

ကြီးထွားသည် kyi-htwar-the *(v.)* **grow**

ကြီးပြင်းအောင် ကျွေးမွေးစောင့်ရှောက်သည် kyee pyinn-aung kyway-mway sannt shoutsai *(v.)* **rear**

ကြီးပွားသည်၊ အောင်မြင်သည် kyee pwarr sai, aaung-myinsai *(v.)* **prosper**

ကြီးမှူးသည် kyee-mhuu-tai *(v.)* **officiate**

ကြီးမားမှု kyi-mar-mu *(n.)* **amplitude**

ကြီးမားသော kyeemarrsaw *(adj.)* **tremendous**

ကြီးမားသော ခွန်အား kyi-mar-taw-khun-arr *(n.)* **might**

ကြီးမားသော ဂဏန်း kyi-mar-taw-ga-nan *(n.)* **gazillion**

ကြီးမားသော နှင်းခဲ kyi-mar-taw-hnin-khae *(n.)* **avalanche**

ကြီးလေးသော kyee-lay-taw *(adj.)* **onerous**

ကြီးလေးသော ပြစ်မှု kyi-lay-taw-pyit-mu *(n.)* **felony**

ကြီးသူ၊ ကျောင်းသားကြီး kyee suu , kyaunggsarrkyee *(n.)* **senior**

ကြီးသော kyi-taw *(adj.)* **macro**

ကြီးသော အမှား kyi-taw-a-hmar *(n.)* **bloomer**

ကြုံထောင့်ကြုံခဲ kyone htaunt kyone-hkell *(adv.)* **seldom**

ကြုံရသည် kyone-ra-sai *(v.)* **undergo**

ကြံ့လှီသော kyun hlisaw *(adj.)* **scrubby**

ကြုတ်၊ သေတ္တာ kyoke, tit-tar *(n.)* **casket**

ကြေးချွတ်သည် kyay-chwut-the *(v.)* **descale**

ကြေးစား kyay-sar *(adj.)* **mercenary**

ကြေးစားစစ်တပ် kyay-sar-sit-tat *(n.)* **legion**

ကြေးစားတပ်ဖွဲ့ဝင် kyay-sar-tat-phwe-win *(n.)* **legionary**

ကြေးညို kyay-nyo *(n.)* **bronze**

ကြေးနန်း kyaynaann *(n.)* **telegraph**

ကြေးနန်းဖြင့် ပို့သော kyaynaannhpyint phoetsaw *(adj.)* **telegraphic**

ကြေးနန်းရိုက်သည် kyaynaann ritesai *(v.)* **telegraph**

ကြေးနန်းရိုက်သူ kyaynaann ritesuu *(n.)* **telegraphist**

ကြေးနီ kyay-ni *(n.)* **copper**

ကြေးနီရောင် kyayneraung *(n.)* **tannery**

ကြေးနီရောင်ရှိသော kyay-ne raungshisaw *(adj.)* **tan**

ကြေးမုံ kyay-mone *(n.)* **mirror**

ကြေးမုံပုံရိပ် kyay-mone-pon-yeik *(n.)* **mirror image**

ကြေးဝါ kyay-war *(n.)* **brass**

ကြေးဝါဖြင့် ပြုလုပ်သည်၊ ကြေးဝါကဲ့သို့ လုပ်သည်၊ ကြေးဝါဖြင့် အလှဆင်သည် kyay-war-phit-pyu-lote-the, kyay-war-kae-tho-lote-the, kyay-war-phit-a-hla-sin-the *(v.)* **braze**

ကြေကွဲဝမ်းနည်းခြင်း kyay-kwal-wan-nae-chin *(n.)* **lament**

ကြေကွဲဝမ်းနည်းသည် kyay-kwal-wan-nae-the *(v.)* **lament**

ကြေကွဲသည် kyay-kwal-the *(v.)* **mourn**

ကြေကွဲသော kyay kwalsaw *(adj.)* **wistful**

ကြေညာချက် kyaw-nyar-chat *(n.)* **announcement**

ကြေညာခြင်း kyay-nyar-chin *(n.)* **declaration**

ကြေညာသည် kyaw-nyar-the *(v.)* **announce**

ကြေညာသူ kyaw-nyar-thu *(n.)* **announcer**

ကြော့ကြော့မော့မော့ ရှိသော kyawt-kyawt-mawt-mawt-shi-taw *(adj.)* **debonaire**

ကြော့ရှင်းခြင်း kyaut-shin-chin *(n.)* **elegance**
ကြော့ရှင်းသော kyaut-shin-taw *(adj.)* **elegant**
ကြောက်ခမန်းလိလိ kyauk-kha-an-li-li *(adj.)* **monstrous**
ကြောက်ခမန်းလိလိ၊ အံ့မခန်းဖွယ်ရာ kyawt-hka-maann-lili , ant-ma-hkan-hpwal-rar *(adj.)* **stupendous**
ကြောက်စရာကောင်းသော kyauk-sa-yar-kaung-taw *(adj.)* **fearful**
ကြောက်စိတ်မွှန်ခြင်း kyauk-sate-mun-chin *(n.)* **panic**
ကြောက်တတ်သော kyawt-taatsaw *(adj.)* **timid**
ကြောက်မက်ဖွယ် kyawtmaathpwal *(adj.)* **terrific**
ကြောက်မက်ဖွယ်ကောင်းသော kyauk-mat-phwal-kaung-taw *(adj.)* **ghastly**
ကြောက်မက်ဖွယ်ဖြစ်သော kyauk-mat-phwal-phit-taw *(adj.)* **dire**
ကြောက်ရွံ့ခြင်း kyauk-shunt-chin *(n.)* **fear**
ကြောက်ရွံ့တွန့်ဆုတ်သည် kyauk-shwunt-twunt-sote-the *(v.)* **cringe**
ကြောက်ရွံ့သော kyauk-shunt-taw *(adj.)* **nervous**
ကြောက်ရွံ့ခြင်း kyauk-shount-chin *(n.)* **horror**
ကြောက်သည် kyauk-the *(v.)* **fear**
ကြော်ငြာ kyaw-nyar *(n.)* **advertisement**
ကြောင် kyaung *(n.)* **cat**
ကြောင့် kyaunt *(conj.)* **for**
ကြောင်းကျိုးဆက်နွယ်မှုမရှိသော kyaung-kyo-sat-new-mu-ma-shi-taw *(adj.)* **acausal**
ကြောင်းကျိုးဆက်နွယ်နေသော kyaung-kyo-sat-hnwe-nay-taw *(adj.)* **causal**
ကြောင်းကျိုးဆက်နွယ်မှု kyuang-kyo-sat-hnwe-mu *(n.)* **causality**
ကြောင်းတူသံကွဲ၊ စကားပရိယာယ် kyaunggtuusankwal , sakarrpariyal *(n.)* **synonym**
ကြောင်ကို ကြိုးချည်ထားသည် kyaung-ko-kyo-chi-htar-the *(v.)* **gib**
ကြောင်ကဲ့သို့ဖြစ်ခြင်း kyaung-kae-tho-phit-chin *(n.)* **felinity**
ကြောင်ကဲ့သို့သော kyaung-kae-tho-taw *(adj.)* **feline**
ကြောင်တောင်တောင် kyaung-taung-taung *(adj.)* **goofy**
ကြောင်တောင်တောင်ဖြစ်နေသော kyaung-taung-taung-phit-nay-taw *(adj.)* **addled**
ကြောင်ထီး kyaung-htee *(n.)* **gib**
ကြောင်ပေါက်စ kyaung-pauk-sa *(n.)* **kitten**
ကြောင်လွှန်းသော kyaung-lun-taw *(adj.)* **gaudy**
ကြောင်သူတော် kyaung-thu-daw *(n.)* **hypocrite**
ကြောင်သော kyaungsaw *(adj.)* **rum**
ကြောင်အိမ် kyaung-eain *(n.)* **cupboard**
ကြောင်အော်သံ kyaung-aw-tan *(n.)* **mew**
ကြောင်အော်သည် kyaung-aw-the *(v.)* **mew**
ကြော်ငြာသည် kyawng-yaarsai *(v.)* **publicize**
ကြော်ညာချက် kyawnyar-chet *(n.)* **proclamation**
ကြော်သည် kyaw-the *(v.)* **fry**
ကလစ် ka-lit *(n.)* **clip**
ကလစ် မြည်သံ ka-lit-myi-tan *(n.)* **click**
ကလန်ကလားနိုင်သော ka-lan-ka-lar-nai-taw *(adj.)* **gawky**
ကလပ် ka-lat *(n.)* **club**

ကလယ်ရီနက် ka-lal-ri-nat *(n.)* **clarinet**
ကလျာဏီပင်မျိုး၊ ပညာရှိ kalyaar-ne pin myoe , panyarshi *(n.)* **sage**
ကလိထိုးသည် ka li htoesai *(v.)* **tickle**
ကလိမ်ကျတတ်သော ka-alin-kya-tat-taw *(adj.)* **cunning**
ကလိသည် ka-li-the *(v.)* **fiddle**
ကလိသည်၊ လက်ဆော့သည် ka li sai , laat sotsai *(v.)* **tamper**
ကလိုရင်းဓာတ် ka-lo-yin-dat *(n.)* **chlorine**
ကလိုရိုဖောင်း မေ့ဆေး ka-lo-ro-phaung-mae-say *(n.)* **chloroform**
ကလီစာ ka-li-zar *(n.)* **entrails**
ကလီစာကို ထုတ်ခြင်း ka-li-zar-ko-htoke-chin *(n.)* **evisceration**
ကလီစာကို ထုတ်သည် ka-li-zar-ko-htoke-the *(v.)* **eviscerate**
ကလေး ka-lay *(n.)* **child**
ကလေး၊ လူငယ်၊ ချာတိတ် kalayy , luungaal , chaartate *(n.)* **youngster**
ကလေးကစားစရာ kalayykasarrsarar *(n.)* **toy**
ကလေးကို ဒူးပေါ်လက်ပေါ်တင် မြှောက်ကာ မြှူသည် ka-lay-ko-du-paw-lat-paw-hmyauk-kar-hmyu-the *(v.)* **dandle**
ကလေးချော့တေး ka-lay-chawt-tay *(n.)* **lullaby**
ကလေးခုတင် ka-lay-ka-tin *(n.)* **cot**
ကလေးငယ် ka-lay-nge *(n.)* **babe**
ကလေးငယ်ကို လိင်မှုဆိုင်ရာ ဆွဲဆောင်သူ kalayy-ngaalko lain-mhusinerar swalsaungsuu *(n.)* **paedophiliac**
ကလေးငယ်ကို လိင်မှုဆိုင်ရာ ဆွဲဆောင်သော kalayy-ngaalko lain-mhusinerar swalsaungsaw *(adj.)* **paedophiliac**
ကလေးဆန်သော ka-lay-san-taw *(adj.)* **childish**
ကလေးထိန်း ka-lay-htein *(n.)* **nanny**
ကလေးထိန်းကျောင်း ka-lay-htein-kyaung *(n.)* **nursery**
ကလေးထိန်းဆရာမ ka-lay-htein-sa-yar-ma *(n.)* **governess**
ကလေးနှင့် ပတ်သက်သော ka-layy-nint-paat-saat-saw *(adj.)* **paediatric**
ကလေးနှစ်ယောက်ထက် ပိုရှိသော ka-lay-na-yaut-htet-po-shi-taw *(adj.)* **multiparous**
ကလေးပုခက် ka-lay-pa-khat *(n.)* **cradle**
ကလေးဖွားခြင်း ka-lay-phwar-chin *(n.)* **accouchement**
ကလေးဘဝ ka-lay-ba-wa *(n.)* **childhood**
ကလေးမျက်နှာ ka-lay-myat-nyar *(n.)* **babyface**
ကလေးများကို ကာမစိတ်တိမ်းညွတ်မှု အခြေအနေ ka-layy-myarr-ko-kar-ma-sate-taim-nytt-mhu-aa-chay-aa-nay *(n.)* **paedophilia**
ကလေးများကို ကာမစိတ်တိမ်းညွတ်သူ ka-layy-myarr-ko-kar-ma-sate-taim-nyut-suu *(n.)* **paedophile**
ကလေးများအတွက် ထိတွေ့ရန် လုံခြုံအောင် ပြုလုပ်ပေးထားသော ka-lay-myar-a-thwat-hti-tway-yan-lon-chon-aung-pyu-lote-pay-htar-taw *(adj.)* **babyproof**
ကလေးလက်တွန်းလှည်း ka-lay-lat-toon-lal *(n.)* **baby carriage**
ကလေးသတ်မှု ka-lay-tat-mu *(n.)* **infanticide**
ကလေးသူငယ်စောင့်ရှောက်ခြင်း အလုပ် ka-lay-thu-ngal-saunt-shaut-chin-a-lote *(n.)* **childcare**
ကလေးအစားအသောက် ka-lay-a-sar-a-taut *(n.)* **baby food**
ကလေးအထူးကုဆရာဝန် ka-layy-aa-htuu-ku-sa-rar-waan *(n.)* **paedologist**

ကလေးအဖေဖြစ်သည် ka-lay-a-hpay-phit-the *(v.)* **father**
ကလောင်၊ ဘောပင် ka-laung, bhaw-pin *(n.)* **pen**
ကလောင်သွား ka-laung-twar *(n.)* **nib**
ကလဲ့စားချေခြင်း kalaesarr chaaychinn *(n.)* **vengeance**
ကွက်၍ ဖြစ်ပွားသည်၊ ဒေသပုံစံ ဖြစ်အောင် ပြုလုပ်သည် kwat-ywe-phit-pwar-the, day-ta-pon-san-phit-aung-pyu-lote-the *(v.)* **localize**
ကွင်းထိုးဖိနပ် kwin htoehpinaut *(n.)* **slipper**
ကွင်းပြင် kwin-pyin *(n.)* **field**
ကွတ်ကီး kwut-kee *(n.)* **cookie**
ကွန်းခိုရာ kun-kho-yar *(n.)* **haven**
ကွန်ကရက် kon-ka-yat *(n.)* **congress**
ကွန်စီလာ kun-see-lar *(n.)* **concealer**
ကွန်ဒုံး kwandone *(n.)* **scumbag**
ကွန်ပျူတာ kun-pyu-tar *(n.)* **computer**
ကွန်ပျူတာကို လုပ်ငန်းတွင် သုံးသည် kun-pyu-tar-ko-lote-ngan-twin-tone-the *(v.)* **computerize**
ကွန်ပျူတာပရိုဂရမ်တွင် အပြစ်ကို ရှာဖွေဖယ်ရှားသည် kun-pyu-tar-pa-ro-ga-ran-twin-a-pyit-ko-shar-phway-phal-shar-the *(v.)* **debug**
ကွန်ပျူတာဖြင့် ဒီဇိုင်းထုတ်ခြင်း koon-pyu-taw-phit-di-zine-htoke-chin *(n.)* **cad**
ကွန်ပျူတာဖိုင် kwanpyauutarhpine *(n.)* **soft copy**
ကွန်ပျူတာအမာထည် kon-pyu-tar-a-mar-htae *(n.)* **hardware**
ကွန်မန်ဒိုတပ်ဖွဲ့ koon-man-do-tat-phwe *(n.)* **commando**

ကွန်မြူနစ်ဝါဒ kun-myu-nit-war-da *(n.)* **communism**
ကွန်မြူနစ်ဝါဒီ kun-myu-nit-war-di *(n.)* **communist**
ကွန်ရက် kun-yat *(n.)* **matrix**
ကွန်ရက်မြန်နှုန်း kun-yat-myan-hnone *(n.)* **bandwidth**
ကွပ်မျက်သည် kwat-myat-the *(v.)* **execute**
ကွယ်ပျောက်စေသည် kwal-pyauk-say-the *(v.)* **dissipate**
ကွယ်လွန်ခြင်း kwal-lun-chin *(n.)* **decease**
ကွယ်လွန်ပြီးမှ ချီးမြှင့်ခံရသော kwal-lwan-pyeemha chee-myint hkan-ra-saw *(adj.)* **posthumous**
ကွယ်လွန်သွားသော kwal-lun-twar-taw *(adj.)* **deceased**
ကွယ်လွန်သူ ဝိညာဉ်အတွက် ဆုတောင်းပွဲ kwallwansuu wi-nyin-aatwat sutaungg-pwal *(n.)* **requiem**
ကွယ်သည်၊ ကာဆီးသည် kwal sai , kar seesai *(v.)* **shroud**
ကွာရှင်းခြင်း kwar-shin-chin *(n.)* **divorce**
ကွာရှင်းသည် kwar-shin-the *(v.)* **divorce**
ကွီနိုင်ဆေး qui-nine-sayy *(n.)* **quinine**
ကွေ့ကောက်သွားသည် kwae koutswarrsai *(v.)* **snake**
ကွေ့ကောက်သော kwae koutsaw *(adj.)* **tortuous**
ကွေးသည် kway-the *(v.)* **bend**
ကွေးသည်၊ ကောက်သည် kway-the, kauk-the *(v.)* **curve**
ကွဲခြင်း kwal-chin *(n.)* **disjunction**
ကွဲတတ်သော၊ နုသော၊ အထိအရှမခံသော kwal-tat-taw, nu-taw, a-hti-a-sha-ma-khan-taw *(adj.)* **fragile**
ကွဲလွဲချက် aapyaungaalell *(n.)* **variance**

ကွဲသံထွက်သည်အထိ အပူပေးခြင်း kwal-tan-htwat-the-a-hti-a-pu-pay-chin *(n.)* **decrepitation**
ကွဲသံထွက်သည်အထိ အပူပေးသည် kwal-tan-htwat-the-a-hti-a-pu-pay-the *(v.)* **decrepitate**
ကွဲသည် kwalsai *(v.)* **separate**
ကွဲသတ်ကြိုး kwal-tat-kyo *(n.)* **moorings**
ကွဲသတ်သည် kwal-tat-the *(v.)* **moor**
ကွဲသော aamyoeaasarr sone linchinn *(adj.)* **varied**
ကသိကအောက်ဖြစ်စေသော ka-ti-ka-aut-phit-say-taw *(adj.)* **irritant**
ကသိကအောက်ဖြစ်စေသော အရာ ka-ti-ka-aut-phit-say-taw-a-yar *(n.)* **irritant**
ကသိကအောက်ဖြစ်သော ka-ti-ka-aut-phit-taw *(adj.)* **irritable**
ကသောင်းကနင်းဖြစ်မှု ka saungg ka ninnhpyitmhu *(n.)* **upheaval**
ကား kar *(n.)* **car**
ကားကားကားကား လျှောက်ခြင်း karr karr karrkarr shou-tchinn *(n.)* **swagger**
ကားကားကားကား လျှောက်သည် karr karr karrkarr shoutsai *(v.)* **swagger**
ကားဂိတ်၊ ရထားလမ်းဆုံးဘူတာ karrgate , rahtarrlam sonebhuutar *(n.)* **terminus**
ကားဂိုဒေါင် kar-go-daung *(n.)* **garage**
ကားစက်ဖုံး car-sat-phone *(n.)* **bonnet**
ကားစင်တင်၍ အဆုံးစီရင်သည် kar-sin-tin-ywe-a-sone-si-yin-the *(v.)* **crucify**
ကားနေရာရှာစက် kar-nay-yar-shar-sat *(n.)* **carlock**
ကားဖြင့် အပျော်ခရီးထွက်သည် kar-phint-a-pyaw-kha-yee-htwat-the *(v.)* **motor**
ကားဘန်ပါ kar-ban-par *(n.)* **bumper**
ကားဘီးပေါက်ခြင်း car-bee-pauk-the *(n.)* **blowout**
ကားမူးသော kar-mu-taw *(adj.)* **carsick**
ကားအမောင်းမြန်သော ဒရိုင်ဘာ kar-a-maung-myar-taw-da-ri-bar *(n.)* **roadster**
ကာကွယ်ခြင်း kar-kwal-chin *(n.)* **defence**
ကာကွယ်စောင့်ရှောက်သူ kar-kwal-saunt-shaut-thu *(n.)* **guardian**
ကာကွယ်ဆေး mapyat ma sarrhpyitsai *(n.)* **vaccine**
ကာကွယ်ဆေးထိုးခြင်း kar-kwal-say-htoe-chin *(n.)* **inoculation**
ကာကွယ်ဆေးထိုးနှံသည် kar-kwal-say-htoe-nan-the *(v.)* **immunize**
ကာကွယ်ဆေးထိုးပေးသူ karkwalsayy *(n.)* **vaccinator**
ကာကွယ်ဆေးထိုးသည် kar-kwal-say-htoe-the *(v.)* **inoculate**
ကာကွယ်နိုင်သော karkwalninesaw *(adj.)* **screenable**
ကာကွယ်ပေးနိုင်စွမ်းသော kar-kwal-payy-nine swamsaw *(adj.)* **proof**
ကာကွယ်ပေးမှု kar-kwal-pay-mu *(n.)* **insulation**
ကာကွယ်ပေးသည် karkwalpayysai *(v.)* **safeguard**
ကာကွယ်ပေးသူ kar-kwal-payysuu *(n.)* **protector**
ကာကွယ်ရေး kar-kwal-yay *(adj.)* **defensive**
ကာကွယ်သည် karkwalsai *(v.)* **prevent**
ကာကွယ်သော karkwalsaw *(adj.)* **preventive**
ကာကွယ်သော စခရင် သို့မဟုတ် အဆောက်အအုံ kar-kwal-taw-sa-kha-yin-thoe-ma-hote-a-sawt-a-ohn *(n.)* **blindage**
ကာကီရောင် ka-ki-yaung *(n.)* **kaki**

ကာကူမင်းဒြပ်ပေါင်း ka-ku-min-drat-paung (*n.*) **curcumin**
ကာစီနို kar-si-no (*n.*) **casino**
ကာဆာ kar-sar (*n.*) **cursor**
ကာတွန်း kar-toon (*n.*) **cartoon**
ကာတွန်း၊ လူရွှင်တော် kar-toon, lu-shwin-taw (*n.*) **comic**
ကာတွန်းရေးသူ kar-toon-yay-thu (*n.*) **cartoonist**
ကာဗိုက် kar-bite (*n.*) **carbide**
ကာဗွန် kar-boon (*n.*) **carbon**
ကာဗွန်နိတ် kar-boon-nate (*n.*) **carbonate**
ကာဗွန်ပြောင်းဖြစ်စဉ် kar-boon-pyaung-phit-sin (*n.*) **carbonization**
ကာဗွန်ရှစ်လုံး၊ အဆက်သုံးခုပါ အယ်ကိုင်း car-bon-shit-lon-a-sat-tone-khu-par-al-kine (*n.*) **octyne**
ကာဗွန်အဖြစ်ပြောင်းလဲသည် kar-boon-a-phit-pyaung-lal-the (*v.*) **carbonize**
ကာမဂုဏ် karmagon (*n.*) **sensuality**
ကာမဂုဏ်လိုက်စားသူ karmagon litesarrsuu (*n.*) **sensualist**
ကာမဂုဏ်အာရုံ karmagonaarrone (*adj.*) **sensual**
ကာမဆန္ဒနည်းသော kar-ma-san-da-nae-taw (*adj.*) **frigid**
ကာမရာဂနှိုးဆွသော kar-ma-yar-ga-noe-swa-taw (*adj.*) **erotic**
ကာမရာဂလိုက်စားမှု kar-ma-yar-ga-lite-sar-mu (*n.*) **debauchery**
ကာမေသုမိစ္ဆာစာရကို ရှောင်ကြဉ်သော kar-may-thu-meik-sar-sar-ya-ko-shaung-kyin-taw (*adj.*) **chaste**
ကာယလုပ်သား kar ya-lotesarr (*n.*) **workman**
ကာရန် karraan (*n.*) **rhyme**
ကာလ kar-la (*n.*) **duration**
ကာလ၊ အကွာအဝေး kar-la , aakwaraawayy (*n.*) **span**
ကာလဝမ်းရောဂါ kar-la-wan-yaw-gar (*n.*) **cholera**
ကာသည်၊ ခိုလှုံခွင့်ပေးသည် kar sai , hkohluan hkwintpayysai (*v.*) **shelter**
ကိစ္စ kait-sa (*n.*) **affair**
ကိစ္စ၊ ဖြစ်ရပ် keik-sa, phit-yat (*n.*) **case**
ကိစ္စရပ်၊ ထုတ်ဝေခြင်း kait-sa-yat, htoke-wai-chin (*n.*) **issue**
ကိတ်မုန့် kait-hmont (*n.*) **cake**
ကိန်း၊ ဂဏာန်း၊ နံပါတ် kein, ga-nan, nan-pat (*n.*) **number**
ကိန်းဂဏာန်း keinganarann (*n.*) **statistics**
ကိန်းဂဏာန်းနှင့် သက်ဆိုင်သော kein-ga-nan-nint-tat-sine-taw (*adj.*) **numerical**
ကိန်းဂဏာန်းအချက်အလက် kein ganarannaachetaalaat (*adj.*) **statistical**
ကိရိယာ ka-ri-yar (*n.*) **device**
ကိရိယာ၊ တန်ဆာပလာ ka-yi-yar, ta-zar-pa-lar (*n.*) **implement**
ကိရိယာ၊ လက်နက် ka-ri-yar , laatnaat (*n.*) **tool**
ကိရိယာ၊ လက်နက်၊ တူရိယာ ka-yi-yar, lat-nat, tu-yi-yar (*n.*) **instrument**
ကိရိယာတန်ဆာပလာ ka-ri-yartaansarpalar (*n.*) **toolkit**
ကိုး koe (*n.*) **nine**
ကိုးကွယ်ခြင်း koekwalchinn (*n.*) **worship**
ကိုးကွယ်သည် koekwalsai (*v.*) **worship**
ကိုးကွယ်သူ koekwalsuu (*n.*) **worshipper**
ကိုးကားချက်၊ နှုန်းထား koe-karr chet , hnone-htarr (*n.*) **quotation**
ကိုးကားခြင်း koe-kar-chin (*n.*) **citation**

ကိုးကားသည် koe-karrsai *(v.)* **quote**

ကိုးကားသည်၊ မှီငြမ်းသည် koe-kar-the, mee-nyan-the *(n.)* **invocation**

ကိုးခုမြောက် koe-hku-myauk *(adj.)* **ninth**

ကိုးဆယ် koe-sal *(n.)* **ninety**

ကိုးဆယ်ခုမြောက် koe-sal-hku-myauk *(adj.)* **ninetieth**

ကိုးရိုးကားရားနိုင်သော koe roe karr rarr-ninesaw *(adj.)* **ungainly**

ကိုကင်း ko-kin *(n.)* **cocaine**

ကိုကိုးမှုန့် ko-koe-hmont *(n.)* **cocoa**

ကိုက်ခဲသည် keik-khae-the *(v.)* **ache**

ကိုက်စွဲသည် kite swal-sai *(v.)* **wield**

ကိုက်ညီခြင်း kite-nyi-chin *(n.)* **accordance**

ကိုက်ဖြတ်သတ္တဝါ kite hpyatsattawar *(n.)* **rodent**

ကိုက်ဖဲ့သည် kite-phae-the *(v.)* **maul**

ကိုက်ဝါးသည် kite-war-the *(v.)* **gnaw**

ကိုက်သည် kait-the *(v.)* **bite**

ကိုင်းဆက်ကူးခြင်း kai-set-ku-chin *(n.)* **graft**

ကိုင်းဆက်ကူးသည် kai-set-ku-the *(v.)* **graft**

ကိုင်းမ kai-ma *(n.)* **bough**

ကိုင်တွယ်သည် kai-twal-the *(v.)* **handle**

ကိုင်တွယ်သည်၊ စီးနင်းသည်၊ မောင်းနှင်သည်၊ ကြောင်းပေးသည် kai-twal-the, see-hnin-the, maung-hnin-the, kyaung-pay-the *(v.)* **manoeuvre**

ကိုင်သည်၊ စမ်းသည် kai-the, san-the *(v.)* **finger**

ကိုဗော့သတ္တု ko-bawt-tat-tu *(n.)* **cobalt**

ကိုယ် ko *(n.)* **self**

ကိုယ့်ကိုယ်ကိုယ် သိခြင်း ko koko si-chinn *(n.)* **self-awareness**

ကိုယ့်ကိုယ်ကိုယ် ဟုတ်လှပြီဟု ဘဝင်ခိုက်နေသော ko koko hote hla pyehu bha win hkitenaysaw *(adj.)* **smug**

ကိုယ့်ရှူးကိုယ်ပတ်သည် ko shuu ko paat-sai *(v.)* **rebound**

ကိုယ့်ဝမ်းကိုယ်ကျောင်းသည် koe-wan-ko-kyaung-the *(v.)* **fend**

ကိုယ့်အကြောင်းကိုယ်သိသော ko aakyaungg ko si-saw *(adj.)* **self-conscious**

ကိုယ်ကျင့်တရားမဲ့သော ko-kyint-ta-yar-mae-taw *(adj.)* **acratic**

ကိုယ်ကျင့်တရား ko-kyint-ta-yar *(n.)* **moral**

ကိုယ်ကျင့်တရား ပျက်သူ ko-kyint-ta-yar-pyat-thu *(n.)* **miscreant**

ကိုယ်ကျိုးကြည့်ခြင်း koe-kyo-kyi-chin *(n.)* **egotism**

ကိုယ်ကျိုးမငဲ့သော ko-kyo-ma-nge-taw *(adj.)* **altruistic**

ကိုယ်ခံအားကျ ကူးစက်ရောဂါ koe-khan-arr-kya-khu-set-yaw-gar *(n.)* **AIDS**

ကိုယ်ခံအားရှိသော ko-khan-ar-shi-taw *(adj.)* **immune**

ကိုယ်ခန္ဓာ ko-hkan-dhar *(adj.)* **physical**

ကိုယ်ခန္ဓာပေါက်များနှင့် ဆိုင်သော koe-khan-dar-pauk-myar-nint-sine-taw *(adj.)* **orificial**

ကိုယ်စား koe-sar *(n.)* **behalf**

ကိုယ်စားပြုခြင်း kosarr-pyuchinn *(n.)* **representation**

ကိုယ်စားပြုခြင်း ခံရသည် kosarr-pyuchinn hkanrasai *(v.)* **represent**

ကိုယ်စားပြုသည် kosarrpyusai *(v.)* **typify**

ကိုယ်စားလှယ် ko-sa-lal *(n.)* **delegate**

ကိုယ်စားလှယ်လွှဲသည် ko-sar-lal-hlwal-the *(v.)* **depute**

ကိုယ်စားလှယ်လောင်း ko-sa-lal-laung *(n.)* **candidate**

ကိုယ်စားလှယ်လောင်းအဖြစ် ko-sa-lal-laung-a-phit *(n.)* **candidacy**
ကိုယ်စားလှယ်အဖွဲ့ ko-sa-lal-a-phwe *(n.)* **delegation**
ကိုယ်တွေ့မျက်မြင် အခြေစိုက်ဒဿန koe-tway-myat-myin-a-chay-site-dat-ta-na *(n.)* **empiricism**
ကိုယ်တွေ့မျက်မြင် အခြေစိုက်ဝါဒီ koe-tway-myat-myin-a-chay-site-war-di *(n.)* **empiricist**
ကိုယ်တွေ့ မှတ်တမ်း ko-tway-mat-tan *(n.)* **memoir**
ကိုယ်တိုင်းနှင့် ချုပ်ထားသော ko-tai-nint-choke-htar-taw *(adj.)* **bespoke**
ကိုယ်တိုင်းရုပ် koe-tai-yoke *(n.)* **dummy**
ကိုယ်တိုင်ယူစနစ် ko-tine yuusanit *(adj.)* **self-service**
ကိုယ်တိုင်ရေးအတ္ထုပ္ပတ္တိ ko-taing-yay-at-htoke-pat-ti *(n.)* **autobiography**
ကိုယ်တုံးလုံး ko-tone-lone *(adj.)* **naked**
ကိုယ်ထိလက်ရောက် စော်ကားသည် ko-hti-lat-yauk-saw-kar-the *(v.)* **molest**
ကိုယ်ထိလက်ရောက်ကျူးလွန်မှု ko-hti-lat-yauk-kyu-loon-mu *(n.)* **assault**
ကိုယ်နေဟန်ထား konay haanhtarr *(n.)* **posture**
ကိုယ်ပွား koe-pwar *(n.)* **clone**
ကိုယ်ပိုင် ko-pai *(adj.)* **intrinsic**
ကိုယ်ပိုင်မှု ko-pai-mu *(n.)* **individualism**
ကိုယ်ပိုင်လက္ခဏာ ko-pai-lat-kha-nar *(n.)* **identity**
ကိုယ်ပိုင်လုပ်ငန်းလုပ်သော ko-pine lotengaannlotesaw *(adj.)* **self-employed**
ကိုယ်ပိုင်ဟန် ko-pine-han *(n.)* **originality**
ကိုယ်ပိုင်အုပ်ချုပ်ခွင့်ရှိသော ko-paing-oat-choke-kwint-shi-taw *(adj.)* **autonomous**
ကိုယ်ရံတော် ko-yan-taw *(n.)* **bodyguard**
ကိုယ်ရေး ko-rayy *(adj.)* **personal**
ကိုယ်ရေးအကျဉ်း korayyaakyain *(n.)* **resume**
ကိုယ်လက်သန့်စင်ခန်း ko-lat-thant-sin-khan *(n.)* **ablution**
ကိုယ်လုံးကိုယ်ပေါက် ko-lone-ko-pout *(n.)* **physique**
ကိုယ်လုပ်တော် ko-lote-taw *(n.)* **concubine**
ကိုယ်ဝန်ဆိပ်တက်ခြင်း koe-win-seik-tat-chin *(n.)* **eclampsia**
ကိုယ်ဝန်ဆောင်ခြင်း ko-waan-saung-chinn *(n.)* **pregnancy**
ကိုယ်ဝန်ဆောင်သော ko-waan-saung-saw *(adj.)* **pregnant**
ကိုယ်ဝန်တားခြင်း ko-win-tar-chin *(n.)* **contraception**
ကိုယ်ဝန်တားဆေး ko-win-tar-say *(n.)* **contraceptive**
ကိုယ်ဝန်ပျက်ခြင်း ko-win-pyat-chin *(n.)* **miscarriage**
ကိုယ်ဝန်ပျက်သည် ko-win-pya-the *(v.)* **miscarry**
ကိုယ်ဝန်ဖျက်ချသူ ko-win-phat-cha-thu *(n.)* **abortionist**
ကိုယ်ဝန်ဖျက်ခြင်း ko-win-phat-chin *(n.)* **abortion**
ကိုယ်ဝန်ဖျက်သည် ko-win-phat-the *(v.)* **abort**
ကိုယ်ဟန်အနေအထား ko haan-aa-nay-aa-htarr *(n.)* **pose**
ကိုယ်အင်္ဂါဆိုင်ရာ ko-in-gar-sine-rar *(adj.)* **organic**
ကိုယ်အလေးချိန်လျော့အောင် ချင့်ချိန်စားသည် ko-a-lay-chein-yawt-aung-chint-chain-sar-the *(v.)* **diet**

ကိုလက်စရောအဆီဓာတ် ko-lat-sa-yaw-a-si-dat *(n.)* **cholesterol**
ကိုလာဂျင် ko-lar-gin *(n.)* **collagen**
ကိုလိုနီ ko-lo-ni *(n.)* **colony**
ကိုလိုနီနှင့် ဆိုင်သော ko-lo-ni-nint-sai-taw *(adj.)* **colonial**
ကိုလိုနီနိုင်ငံကို လွတ်လပ်ရေးပေးခြင်း ko-lo-ni-nai-ngan-ko-hlut-lat-yay-pay-chin *(n.)* **decolonization**
ကိုလိုနီနိုင်ငံကို လွတ်လပ်ရေးပေးသည် ko-lo-ni-nai-ngan-ko-hlut-lat-yay-pay-the *(v.)* **decolonize**
ကိုဩဒိနိတ် ko-aw-di-nate *(v.)* **coordinate**
ကိုအာလာဝက်ဝံ ko-ar-lar-wat-win *(n.)* **koala**
ကီးဘုတ် kee-bote *(n.)* **keyboard**
ကီလို ki-lo *(n.)* **kilo**
ကီလိုဂရမ် ki-lo-gram *(n.)* **kilogram**
ကုံရာသီဖွား kone-yar-thi-phwar *(n.)* **aquarius**
ကုံလုံသော၊ မည်မည်ရရဖြစ်သော kone lone saw , mai mai ra ra-hpyitsaw *(adj.)* **substantial**
ကုစ္ဆ ရသော ku-ywe-ya-taw *(adj.)* **curable**
ကုက္ကား kukkarr *(n.)* **streamer**
ကုစားစ္ဆ မရနိုင်သော ku-sar-ywe-ma-ya-nai-taw *(adj.)* **incurable**
ကုစားသော၊ ပျောက်ကင်းရေး kusarr saw , pyaut-kinnrayy *(adj.)* **remedial**
ကုတ်၊ မောင်းသံ kote, maung-tan *(n.)* **lever**
ကုတ်ခြစ်သံ kote chitsan *(n.)* **scrape**
ကုတ်နံပါတ်ထားခြင်း ဖြစ်စဉ် kote-nan-pat-htar-chin-phit-sin *(n.)* **coding**
ကုတ်ဖြင့် ကော်သည် kote-phint-kaw-the *(v.)* **lever**
ကုတ်မီးသွေး kote-mee-thway *(v.)* **coke**
ကုတ်ရာ၊ ပွန်းရာ kote rar , pwannrar *(n.)* **scratch**
ကုတ်သည်၊ ခြစ်သည် kote-sai, chit-sai *(v.)* **paw**
ကုတ်သည်၊ ရေးခြစ်သည်၊ ပယ်ဖျက်သည် kote sai , rayy chit sai , paahlpyetsai *(v.)* **scratch**
ကုတ်အင်္ကျီ kote-inn-gyi *(n.)* **coat**
ကုတ်အား၊ ကန်အား kote-arr, kan-arr *(n.)* **leverage**
ကုထုံး kuhtone *(n.)* **treatment**
ကုထုံးဆရာ kuhtonesarar *(n.)* **therapist**
ကုနည်း၊ ကုထုံး ku naee, ku-htone *(n.)* **panacea**
ကုန်း၊ ကြည်း kone , kyi *(adj.)* **terrestrial**
ကုန်းခေါင်ရေဝေးအရပ် kone-hkaung-ray-way-a-rat *(n.)* **outback**
ကုန်းစောင်း kone-saung *(n.)* **slope**
ကုန်းတွင်းပိုင်းကျကျ kone-twin-pai-kya-kya *(adv.)* **inland**
ကုန်းတွင်းပိုင်းကျသော kone-twin-pai-kya-taw *(adj.)* **inland**
ကုန်းနှီး kone-nhaee *(n.)* **saddle**
ကုန်းနှီးတင်သည် kone nhee-tinsai *(v.)* **saddle**
ကုန်းမြေ kone-myay *(n.)* **land**
ကုန်းမြေထုနှင့် ဆိုင်သော kone-myay-htu-nint-sai-taw *(adj.)* **continental**
ကုန်းမအို kone-ma-oh *(n.)* **hag**
ကုန်းရေနေဖြစ်သော kone-yay-nay-phit-taw *(adj.)* **amphibious**
ကုန်းရေနေသတ္တဝါ kone-yay-nay-tat-ta-war *(n.)* **amphibian**
ကုန်းအော်သည် kone-aw-the *(v.)* **bawl**
ကုန်ကျစရိတ် လျှော့ချသည် konekyasarate shotchasai *(v.)* **retrench**

ကုန်ကျသည် kone-kya-the *(v.)* **cost**

ကုန်ကူးသည် konekuusai *(v.)* **traffic**

ကုန်ခန်းခြင်း kon-khan-chin *(n.)* **depletion**

ကုန်ခန်းစေသည် kon-khan-say-the *(v.)* **deplete**

ကုန်ခန်းသော kon-khan-taw *(adj.)* **depleted**

ကုန်ချင်းဖလှယ်သည် kon-chin-hpa-hlal-the *(v.)* **barter**

ကုန်ခြောက် kon-chauk *(adj.)* **drapery**

ကုန်စည် kone-se *(n.)* **merchandise**

ကုန်စည်ပစ္စည်း konesaipyit-see *(n.)* **stock**

ကုန်စည်ပို့ဆောင်ခြင်း konesai phoetsaungchinn *(n.)* **shipping**

ကုန်စုံဆိုင်ရှင် kone-sone-sai-shin *(n.)* **grocer**

ကုန်တင်ကား konetinkarr *(n.)* **truck**

ကုန်တင်ကုန်ချပေါက်၊ မလွယ်ပေါက် kone-tin-kone-cha-pauk, ma-lwal-pauk *(n.)* **hatch**

ကုန်တိုက် konetite *(n.)* **shopping centre**

ကုန်ထုတ်စွမ်းအား kone-htote-swam-aarr *(n.)* **productivity**

ကုန်ပစ္စည်း စစ်ဆေးသူ kone-pyit-see-sit-say-thu *(n.)* **checker**

ကုန်ပစ္စည်း ပို့ဆောင်မှု konepyit-saee phoetsaungmhu *(n.)* **shipment**

ကုန်ပို့လွှာ kone-poe-hlwar *(n.)* **invoice**

ကုန်လွန်သွားသည် kon-lun-twar-the *(v.)* **elapse**

ကုန်လှောင်ရုံ kone hlaawinrone *(n.)* **warehouse**

ကုန်သည် konesai *(n.)* **trader**

ကုန်သွယ်မှု koneswalmhu *(n.)* **trade**

ကုန်သွယ်မှု ပိတ်ပင်မိန့် kone-twal-mu-pate-pin-maint *(n.)* **embargo**

ကုန်သွယ်မှုဆိုင်ရာ kone-twal-mu-sai-yar *(adj.)* **mercantile**

ကုန်သွယ်မှုနှင့် ဆိုင်သော kone-twal-mu-nint-sai-taw *(adj.)* **commercial**

ကုန်သွယ်သည် koneswalsai *(v.)* **trade**

ကုန်သေတ္တာ kone-tit-tar *(n.)* **crate**

ကုန်အမှတ်တံဆိပ် koneaamhaattanseik *(n.)* **trademark**

ကုန်အမှတ်တံဆိပ်မိတ်ဆက်တင်ပြခြင်း kone-a-mat-ta-seik-meik-sat-tin-pya-chin *(n.)* **branding**

ကုပ်ပိုး gote-poe *(n.)* **nape**

ကုဗ ku-ba *(n.)* **cube**

ကုဗတုံး ရှစ်ခုပါ လေးဖက်မြင်ပိုလီတုတ် ku-ba-tone-shit-khu *(n.)* **tesseract**

ကုဗပုံဖြစ်သော ku-ba-pon-phit-taw *(adj.)* **cubical**

ကုမ္ပဏီ kone-pa-ni *(n.)* **company**

ကုမ္ပဏီချင်းပေါင်းခြင်း kone-pa-ni-chin-paung-chin *(n.)* **merger**

ကုလားဆီးဖြူ ka-lar-see-phyu *(n.)* **gooseberry**

ကုလားထိုင် ka-lar-htai *(n.)* **chair**

ကုလားပဲ ka-lar-pal *(n.)* **chickpea**

ကုလားမခြေထောက် ka-larr-machayhtout *(n.)* **stilt**

ကုလားရွှေ kularrshway *(n.)* **tinsel**

ကုလားအုတ် ka-lar-oak *(n.)* **camel**

ကုလားအုတ်မွေးအထည် ka-lar-oak-hmway-a-htal *(n.)* **camlet**

ကုသခြင်းနှင့် ဆိုင်သော khu-ta-chin-nint-sai-taw *(adj.)* **clinical**

ကုသနိုင်သော အခြေအနေ kusaninesaw aah-kyay-aa-nay *(n.)* **sanability**

ကုသသည် khu-ta-the *(v.)* **cure**

ကုသိုလ်ဖြစ် ku-tho-phit *(adj.)* **charitable**

ကူးစက်တတ်သော ku-sat-tat-taw *(adj.)* **contagious**

ကူးစက်ရောဂါ ku-sat-yaw-gar *(n.)* **epidemic**

ကူးစက်လွယ်သော khu-sat-lwal-taw *(adj.)* **catching**

ကူးတို့သမား ku-toe-ta-mar *(n.)* **boatman**

ကူးပြောင်းပေးသည် lawkasabharwanint sarmaanluuthoet ma meninesaw *(v.)* **transcribe**

ကူးပြောင်းသည် kyauukyawsai *(v.)* **transit**

ကူညီတတ်သော ku-nyi-tat-taw *(adj.)* **helpful**

ကူညီထောက်ပံ့ငွေ kuu-nye-htout-pant-ngway *(n.)* **subversion**

ကူညီထောက်ပံ့ထည့်ဝင်သူ ku-nyi-htauk-ant-htae-win-thu *(n.)* **contributor**

ကူညီသည် ku-nyi-the *(v.)* **assist**

ကူပွန်ငွေ cu-pon-ngwe *(n.)* **cupon**

ကူရှင် ku-shin *(n.)* **cushion**

ကေဘယ်ကြိုး kay-bal-kyo *(n.)* **cable**

ကေဘယ်ကား kay-bal-kar *(n.)* **cable car**

ကေဘယ်ရုပ်မြင်သံကြား kal-bal-yoke-myin-tan-kyar *(n.)* **cable television**

ကော့တေးအရက် kawt-tay-a-yat *(n.)* **cocktail**

ကော့ဒ် kawt *(n.)* **chord**

ကောက်ကျစ်စဉ်းလဲသော kout kyit sin lellsaw *(adj.)* **wicked**

ကောက်ကြောင်း kauk-kyaung *(n.)* **contour**

ကောက်ကြောင်း၊ အကြမ်းဖော်ပြချက် kout-kyaung, a-kyam-hpaw-pya-chet *(n.)* **outline**

ကောက်ကောက်ကွေ့ကွေ့စီးဆင်းသည် kauk-kauk-kway-kway-see-sin-the *(v.)* **meander**

ကောက်ခံရငွေ၊ ရောင်းရငွေ၊ အမြတ်အစွန်း kout-hkan ra ngway, raunggrangway , aamyataaswann *(n.)* **proceeds**

ကောက်ချက် kauk-chat *(n.)* **inference**

ကောက်ချက်ချသည် kauk-note-chat-cha-the *(v.)* **infer**

ကောက်နံ့စည်း kout nhaan-see *(n.)* **sheaf**

ကောက်နံ့ပင် kauk-hnan-pin *(n.)* **millet**

ကောက်နုတ်ချက် kauk-note-chat *(n.)* **excerpt**

ကောက်နုတ်စုစည်းသည် kaut-note-su-see-the *(v.)* **collate**

ကောက်ပဲသီးနှံ kauk-pal-thee-nan *(n.)* **crop**

ကောက်ယူသည် kout-yuu-sai *(v.)* **pick**

ကောက်ရိတ်သမား kout rate-samarr *(n.)* **reaper**

ကောက်ရိုး kout-roe *(n.)* **straw**

ကောက်သော koutsaw *(adj.)* **wavy**

ကောင်းကင် kaungg-kin *(n.)* **sky**

ကောင်းကင်ကျွမ်းဘားသမား an what-tanhkarr *(n.)* **trapezist**

ကောင်းကင်ကြိုး kaung-kin-kyoe *(n.)* **aerial**

ကောင်းကင်ဘား pate mi sai , ngyainaysai *(n.)* **trapeze**

ကောင်းကင်ဘားပေါ်တွင် ကစားသော htaungchauk *(v.)* **trapeze**

ကောင်းကင်ဘုံ kaung-kin-bon *(n.)* **heaven**

ကောင်းကင်ဘုံနှင့် ဆိုင်သော kaung-kin-bon-nint-sai-taw *(adj.)* **heavenly**

ကောင်းကျိုးချမ်းသာ kaunggkyoechamsar *(n.)* **welfare**

ကောင်းကျိုးပြုမှု ရှေးရှုသော aasonewin chinn, aasonewaansaungmhulotengaann *(adj.)* **utilitarian**

ကောင်းကောင်း kaunggkaungg *(adv.)* **well**

ကောင်းခြင်း၊ ကြင်နာမှု kaung-chin, kyin-nar-mu *(n.)* **goodness**

ကောင်းစွာ မစဉ်းစား မတွေးတောနိုင်ချိန်၊ အတွေးညစ်ထုတ်ခြင်း kaung-swar-ma-sin-sar-ma-thway-taw-nai-chein, a-thway-nyit-htoke-the *(n.)* **brainstorm**

ကောင်းစွာဖတ်သော kaunggswar hpaatsaw *(adj.)* **well-read**

ကောင်းစားချိန် kaung-sar-chain *(n.)* **heyday**

ကောင်းဆိုးပိုင်းခြားသိမြင်သော အသိဉာဏ် kaung-soe-pai-char-ti-myin-taw-a-ti-nyan *(n.)* **conscience**

ကောင်းထောက်သည် kaungg htoutsai *(v.)* **scout**

ကောင်းပြီ kaung-pye *(int.)* **okay**

ကောင်းမြတ်ခြင်း kaung-myat-chin *(n.)* **merit**

ကောင်းမွန်သေသပ်စွာ ထားသိုသည် kaung-mon say satswar htarr sosai *(v.)* **stow**

ကောင်းသော kaung-aw *(adj.)* **nice**

ကောင်းသော မှတ်ဉာဏ် kaunggsaw mhaatnyarn *(adj.)* **retentive**

ကောင်းသော၊ ကျန်းမာသော kaunggsaw , kyannmarsaw *(adj.)* **well**

ကောင်ကလေး kaung-ka-lay *(n.)* **boy**

ကောင်ကလေးကဲ့သို့ kaung-ka-lay-kae-tho *(adj.)* **boyish**

ကောင်ကလေးငယ်စဉ်ဘဝ kaung-ka-lay-nge-sin-ba-wa *(n.)* **boyhood**

ကောင်စစ်ဝန် kaung-sit-win *(n.)* **consul**

ကောင်စစ်ဝန်နှင့် ဆိုင်သော kaung-sit-win-nint-sai-taw *(adj.)* **consular**

ကောင်စစ်ဝန်ရုံး kaung-sit-win-yone *(n.)* **consulate**

ကောင်စီ kaung-si *(n.)* **council**

ကောင်စီဝင် kaung-si-win *(n.)* **councillor**

ကောင်ဆိုးကလေး kaung-soe-ka-lay *(n.)* **brat**

ကောင်တာ kaung-tar *(n.)* **counter**

ကောနက် taw-nat *(n.)* **cornet**

ကောလဟာလပြန့်ခြင်း kawlaharl pya anthkyinn *(n.)* **talebearing**

ကောလဟာလဖြန့်သည် kawlaharl hpya antsai *(v.)* **talebear**

ကောလဟာလဖြန့်သူ kawlaharl hpya antsuu *(n.)* **talebearer**

ကောလာဟလ kaw-la-ha-la *(n.)* **canard**

ကောလာဟလပြောသည် kaw-la-har-la-pyaw-the *(v.)* **rumour**

ကောလိပ်ကျောင်း kaw-lait-kyung *(n.)* **college**

ကောလိပ်ကျောင်းသား kaw-late-kyaung-sarr *(n.)* **undergraduate**

ကောလိပ်ငွေစာရင်းမှူး kaw-leik-ngwe-sa-yin-hmu *(n.)* **bursary**

ကောလိပ်မှာ ငှားရမ်းထားသော သင်တန်းဆရာ kawliutmhar ngharramhtarrsaw saintaannsarar *(n.)* **sessional**

ကော် kaw *(n.)* **glue**

ကော်ကပ်သည် kaw-kat-the *(v.)* **glue**

ကော်ဇော kaw-zaw *(n.)* **carpet**

ကော်တင်သည် kawtinsai *(v.)* **starch**

ကော်တီဇုန်းဓာတ် kor-ti-zone-dat *(n.)* **cortisone**

ကော်ထောင့် kaw-htaunt *(n.)* **glue stick**

ကော်ပိုရေးရှင်း kor-po-yay-shin *(n.)* **corporation**

ကော်ပိုရေးရှင်းနှင့် ဆိုင်သော kor-po-yay-shin-nint-sai-taw *(adj.)* **corporate**
ကော်ဖတ် kawhpaat *(n.)* **sandpaper**
ကော်ဖတ်စားသည် kaw hpaat sarrsai *(v.)* **sand**
ကော်ဖတ်တိုက်သည် kaw hpaat titesai *(v.)* **sandpaper**
ကော်ဖီ kof-fee *(n.)* **coffee**
ကော်ဖီစေ့ kof-fee-say *(n.)* **coffee bean**
ကော်ဖီဖျော်စက် kof-fee-phyaw-sat *(n.)* **coffee maker**
ကော်ဖီသောက် နားချိန် kof-fee-taut-nar-chain *(n.)* **coffee break**
ကော်မတီ kaw-ma-tee *(n.)* **committee**
ကော်မရှင်ခ kaw-ma-shin-kha *(n.)* **commission**
ကော်မရှင်အဖွဲ့ဝင် kaw-ma-shin-a-phwe-win *(n.)* **commissioner**
ကော်လံ kaw-lan *(n.)* **column**
ကော်လာ kaw-lar *(n.)* **collar**
ကဲ့ရဲ့ခြင်း kae-rae-chinn *(n.)* **odium**
ကဲ့ဝှက်သည် kae-whaat-sai *(v.)* **pilfer**
ကဲ့သို့ kaeshoet *(adj.)* **such**

ခံ့ညားစေသည် khant-nyar-say-the *(v.)* **dignify**
ခံ့ညားလောက်သော khant-nyar-laut-taw *(adj.)* **formidable**
ခံစစ်ပြင်သည် khan-sit-phin-the *(v.)* **fortify**
ခံစားချက်ကို အနုပညာဖြင့် ဖြေဖျောက်ခြင်း khan-sar-chat-ko-a-nu-pyin-nyar-phit-phyay-phyauk-chin *(n.)* **catharsis**
ခံစားချက်ပြပုံ khan-sar-chat-pya-pon *(n.)* **emoticon**
ခံစားချက်ပါသော khan-sar-chat-par-taw *(adj.)* **lyric**
ခံစားချက်ဖွင့်ဟသည် khan-sar-chat-hpwint-ha-the *(v.)* **emote**
ခံစားခြင်း khan-sar-chin *(n.)* **feeling**
ခံစားစေသည် hkansarrsaysai *(v.)* **subject**
ခံစားမှု ကဲလွန်းသော khan-sar-mu-khae-loon-taw *(adj.)* **effusive**
ခံစားမှုပြပုံ khan-sar-mu-pya-pon *(n.)* **emoji**
ခံစားရသည် hkan-sarr-ra-sai *(v.)* **sense**
ခံစားသည် khan-sar-the *(v.)* **feel**
ခံညားထည်ဝါမှု hkan nyarr htai warmhu *(n.)* **stateliness**
ခံညားသော hkan nyarrsaw *(adj.)* **stately**
ခံတပ် khan-tat *(n.)* **fort**
ခံတပ်၊ ရဲတိုက် khan-tat, ye-tite *(n.)* **citadel**
ခံတပ်ကြီး khan-tat-kyi *(n.)* **fortress**
ခံတွင်း hkan-twin *(adj.)* **oral**
ခံနိုင်စွမ်း၊ လက်တစ်ကမ်း hkan nineswm , laattaitkam *(n.)* **threshold**
ခံနိုင်ရည် hkanninerai *(n.)* **stamina**
ခံနိုင်ရည်ရှိခြင်း၊ လက်ခံနိုင်သော ကွာဟချက် hkan-nine-rai shichinn , laathkanninesaw kwarhachet *(n.)* **tolerance**
ခံရသူ hkanrasuu *(n.)* **victim**
ခံဝန်ချက်ဖြင့် အကျဉ်းသားလွှတ်ခြင်း hkan-waan-chet-hpyint-aa-kyin-sarr-lwhaat-chinn *(n.)* **parole**
ခံဝန်ချက်ဖြင့် အကျဉ်းသားလွှတ်သည် hkan-waan-chet-hpyint-aa-kyin-sarr-lwhaat-sai *(v.)* **parole**

ခံသာသော၊ သင့်တင်သော hkan sar saw , sinttinsaw (*adj.*) **tolerable**
ခက်ခက်ခဲခဲ khat-khat-khae-khae (*adv.*) **hard**
ခက်ခက်ခဲခဲ ကူးဖြတ်သည် hkaathkaathkelhlkell kuu hpyatsai (*v.*) **wade**
ခက်ခဲ ပင်ပန်းသော khat-khae-pin-pan-taw (*adj.*) **laboured**
ခက်ခဲကြမ်းတမ်းသော khat-khae-kyan-tan-taw (*adj.*) **arduous**
ခက်ခဲရှုပ်ထွေးစေသည် khat-khae-shote-htway-the (*v.*) **complicate**
ခက်ခဲရှုပ်ထွေးသော khat-khae-shote-htway-taw (*adj.*) **complex**
ခက်ခဲသော hkaat-hkell-saw (*adj.*) **problematic**
ခက်ဆစ် khat-sit (*n.*) **glossary**
ခင်းကျင်းပြသခြင်း khin-kyin-pya-ta-chin (*n.*) **exhibition**
ခင်းကျင်းပြသရန် ရည်ရွယ်၍ ပြုလုပ်ထားသော အရာ hkainn kyinnpyasaraan rairwal pyulotehtarrsaw aarar (*n.*) **showpiece**
ခင်းကျင်းပြသသည် khin-kyin-pya-tha-the (*n.*) **display**
ခင်းသည် hkinn-sai (*v.*) **pave**
ခင်းသည်၊ ကပ်သည် hkinn sai , katsai (*v.*) **tile**
ခင်ပွန်း khin-pon (*n.*) **husband**
ခင်မင်တတ်ခြင်း khin-min-tat-chin (*n.*) **geniality**
ခင်မင်တတ်သော khin-min-tat-taw (*adj.*) **genial**
ခဏ၊ အချိန်တိုအတွင်း၊ မကြာမီ hka-na, aachanetoaatwin, makyaarme (*adv.*) **shortly**
ခဏထားသည် hka-na-htarr-sai (*v.*) **park**
ခဏမျှဖြစ်သော kha-na-mya-phit-taw (*adj.*) **momentary**
ခတ်တက် hkat-tat (*n.*) **oar**
ခတ်ထုတ်သည် hkaat-htote-sai (*v.*) **parry**
ခတ်သည်၊ အသားသေစေသည် hkaat sai , a sarr saysaysai (*v.*) **season**
ခနော်နီခနော်နဲ့ hka naw ne hk nawnae (*adj.*) **rickety**
ခနဲ့တဲ့တဲ့ hka nae taetae (*adj.*) **wry**
ခန္ဓာကိုယ် khan-dar-ko (*n.*) **body**
ခန္ဓာကိုယ်မှ အမွေးကို ဖယ်ရှားသည် khan-dar-koe-ma-a-mway-ko-phal-shar-the (*v.*) **epilate**
ခန္ဓာကိုယ်အစိတ်အပိုင်း မွေးရာပါ နေရာမှားခြင်း khan-dar-koe-a-seik-a-pai-mway-yar-par-nay-yar-hmar-chin (*n.*) **ectopia**
ခန္ဓာကိုယ်အတွင်းပိုင်းကြည့်ခြင်းဆိုင်ရာ khan-dar-ko-a-twin-pine-kyi-chin-sai-yar (*adj.*) **endoscopic**
ခန္ဓာကိုယ်အတွင်းပိုင်းကြည့်ပညာ khan-dar-ko-a-twin-pine-kyi-pyin-nyar (*n.*) **endoscopy**
ခန္ဓာဗေဒ khan-dar-bay-da (*n.*) **anatomy**
ခန္ဓာသစ်ကို ဝိညာဉ်ကူးပြောင်း မှီတွယ်ခြင်း aachanepine myahasar hkansaw (*n.*) **transmigration**
ခန့်ထားသည် khant-htar-the (*v.*) **appoint**
ခန့်မှန်းခြေ khant-man-chay (*adj.*) **approximate**
ခန့်မှန်းခြေ၊ ထိုးပြခြင်း၊ အစွန်း hkaant mhaann-chay , htoe pya chinn , aaswann (*n.*) **projection**
ခန့်မှန်းခြေအားဖြင့် khant-man-chay-arr-phyint (*adv.*) **approximately**
ခန့်မှန်းသည် khant-man-the (*v.*) **estimate**
ခန့်မှန်းသည်၊ ဟောကိန်းထုတ်သည် hkaant mhaann sai, hawkein-htotesai (*v.*) **predict**

ခန့်သည်၊ ဆွဲဆောင်သည်၊ အာရုံစိုက်သည် khant-the, swal-saung-the, ar-yone-seik-the *(v.)* **engage**

ခန်းဆီးရှည်ကြီး khan-see-shay-gyi *(n.)* **drape**

ခပ်ညံ့ညံ့ကဗျာဆရာ khat-nyant-nyant-ka-byar-sa-yar *(n.)* **poetaster**

ခပ်တန်းတန်းဖြစ်သွားသည် khat-tan-tan-phit-twar-the *(v.)* **estrange**

ခပ်တုံးတုံး၊ ခပ်ညံ့ညံ့အမှားများဖြင့် ပြုလုပ်သော khat-tone-tone-khat-nyant-nyant-a-mar-myar-phint-pyu-lote-taw *(adj.)* **blundering**

ခပ်ပျော့ပျော့ဆက်တိုက်နာသော khat-pyawt-pyawt-sat-tite-nar-taw *(adj.)* **nagging**

ခပ်မှိန်မှိန်လင်းခြင်း၊ နီမြန်းခြင်း khat-mein-mein-lin-chin, ni-myan-chin *(n.)* **glow**

ခပ်မှိန်မှိန်လင်းသည် khat-mein-mein-lin-the *(v.)* **glimmer**

ခပ်အုပ်အုပ်မြည်ဟည်းသံ khat-aote aote myi haeesan *(n.)* **rumble**

ခမ်းနားကြီးကျယ်မှု hkam-narr-kyee-kyaal-mhu *(n.)* **pageantry**

ခမ်းနားကြီးကျယ်သော hkamnarr kyeekyaalsaw *(adj.)* **spectacular**

ခမ်းနားထည်ဝါခြင်း hkam-narr-htai-war-chinn *(n.)* **opulence**

ခမ်းနားထည်ဝါသော hkam-narr-htai-war-taw *(adj.)* **opulent**

ခမ်းနားမှု hkam-narrmhu *(n.)* **pomp**

ခမ်းနားသော khan-nar-taw *(adj.)* **magnificent**

ခမ်းနားသော ပသာဒ hkam-narr-saw-pa-sar-da *(n.)* **pageant**

ခမ်းနားသော၊ ငွေကုန်ကြေးကျများသော hkam-narr-saw , ngwaykone kyay kyamyarrsaw *(adj.)* **sumptuous**

ခယလွန်းသော hka ya lwannsaw *(adj.)* **servile**

ခယဝပ်တွားသော hka ya wut twarrsaw *(adj.)* **subservient**

ခယဝယလုပ်ခြင်း hka ya wa yalotechinn *(n.)* **servility**

ချက်ချင်း chat-chin *(n.)* **instant**

ချက်ခြင်း chat-chin *(adv.)* **forthwith**

ချက်ခြင်းလက်ငင်း chat-chin-lat-ngin *(n.)* **ado**

ချက်စက်ရုံ chet-saat-rone *(n.)* **refinery**

ချက်နည်းပြုတ်နည်း chet-nee-pyote-nee *(n.)* **recipe**

ချက်ပြုတ်နည်း chat-pyoke-nee *(n.)* **cuisine**

ချက်ပြုတ်ရာတွင် ဆလာမန်သာဥသုံးခြင်း chat-pyoke-yar-twin-sa-lar-man-da-oo-tone-chin *(v.)* **salamander**

ချက်ပြုတ်သည် chat-pyoke-the *(v.)* **cook**

ချက်လက်မှတ် chat-lat-mat *(n.)* **cheque**

ချခင်းသည်၊ တာဝန်ပေးသည် cha-khin-the, tar-win-pay-the *(v.)* **lay**

ချင့်ချိန်သည် chint-chain-the *(v.)* **judge**

ချင်း chin *(v.)* **cockle**

ချင်းတက် gyin-tat *(n.)* **ginger**

ချင်းနံ့သင်းပေါင်မုန့် gyin-nant-tin-paung-hmont *(n.)* **gingerbread**

ချင်းနံ့သင်းဘီလပ်ရည် gyin-nant-tin-bi-lat-yay *(n.)* **ginger ale**

ချင်းနံ့သင်းသော gyin-a-nant-tin-taw *(adj.)* **ginger**

ချင်းနင်းဝင်ရောက်ခြင်း chin-nin-win-yauk-chin *(n.)* **foray**

ချင်ပန်ဇီမျောက် chin-pan-zi-myauk *(n.)* **chimpanzee**

ချစ်ကြည်မှု chit-kyi-mu *(n.)* **amity**

ချစ်ကြည်သော chit-kyi-taw *(adj.)* **amicable**

ချစ်ခင်စေသည် chit-khin-say-the *(v.)* **endear**

ချစ်ခင်မြတ်နိုးသည် chit-khin-myat-noe-the *(v.)* **cherish**

ချစ်ခင်မှု chit-khin-mu *(n.)* **affection**

ချစ်ချစ်တောက် chit-chit-taut *(adj.)* **blazing**

ချစ်စဖွယ် chit-sa-phwal *(adj.)* **lovely**

ချစ်စဖွယ်ကောင်းသော၊ ပါးနပ်သော၊ လည်သော chit-sa-phwal-kaung-taw, par-nat-taw, lal-taw *(adj.)* **cute**

ချစ်စရာကောင်းသော chit-sa-yar-kaung-taw *(adj.)* **adorable**

ချစ်ဖွယ်ကောင်းသော chit-phwal-kaung-taw *(adj.)* **lovable**

ချစ်ရေးဆိုသူ chit ray so-suu *(n.)* **suitor**

ချစ်လှစွာသော chit-hla-swar-taw *(adj.)* **beloved**

ချစ်သည် chit-the *(v.)* **love**

ချစ်သူ chit-thu *(n.)* **lover**

ချစ်သော chit-taw *(adj.)* **loving**

ချဉ်းကပ်မြူဆွယ်သည် chee-kat-myu-swal-the *(v.)* **accost**

ချဉ်းကပ်သည် chee-kat-the *(v.)* **approach**

ချဉ်ရည်ထည့်သည် hkyain rai htee-tsai *(v.)* **sauce**

ချဉ်သော chin-taw *(adj.)* **citric**

ချဉ်သော၊ စိတ်ကုန်သော chin saw, sate konesaw *(adj.)* **sour**

ချည့်နဲ့သည် chi-nae-the *(v.)* **enfeeble**

ချည့်နဲ့ခြင်း chae-nae-chin *(n.)* **debility**

ချည်ကတ္တီပါ chi-ka-di-par *(n.)* **corduroy**

ချည်ခင် chaihkin *(n.)* **yarn**

ချည်ထည် chee-htal *(n.)* **cotton**

ချည်နှောင်သည် chainhaawinsai *(v.)* **rope**

ချည်လုံး၊ ကြိုးလုံး che-lone *(n.)* **clew**

ချည်သည် chi-the *(v.)* **lace**

ချည်အခင် chai aahkain *(n.)* **skein**

ချန်ထားခြင်း chan-htar-chinn *(n.)* **omission**

ချန်ထားသည် chan-htar-tai *(v.)* **omit**

ချန်ပီယံ chan-pi-yan *(n.)* **champion**

ချန်လှပ်ခြင်း chan-lat-chin *(n.)* **omittance**

ချန်လှပ်သည် chan-hlat-the *(v.)* **except**

ချပ်ဝတ်တန်ဆာ chat-wut-ta-sar *(n.)* **armour**

ချမ်းမြေ့ပျော်ရွှင်မှု khyan-myay-pyaw-shwin-mu *(n.)* **bliss**

ချမ်းသာကြွယ်ဝခြင်း cham-sar-kywal-wa-chinn *(n.)* **prosperity**

ချမ်းသာကြွယ်ဝမှု chamsarkyawalwamhu *(adj.)* **richness**

ချမ်းသာခြင်း chamsarchinn *(n.)* **wealth**

ချမ်းသာပေးသည် chamsarpayysai *(v.)* **spare**

ချမ်းသာသော chamsarsaw *(adj.)* **rich**

ချယ်ရီပင်၊ ချယ်ရီသီး cherry-pin, cherry-thee *(n.)* **cherry**

ချရန်နေရာ cha-yan-nay-yar *(n.)* **dropzone**

ချွင်းချက် chwin-chat *(n.)* **exception**

ချွင်ချွင်မြည်သံ chwan-chwan-myi-tan *(n.)* **clink**

ချွတ်ယွင်းချက် chut-ywin-chat *(n.)* **defect**

ချွတ်ယွင်းသော chut-ywin-taw *(adj.)* **defective**

ချွန်စက်၊ သွေးစက် chwan saat , swaysaat *(n.)* **sharpener**

ချွန်ထက်မှု chun-htet-mu *(n)* **pointedness**

ချွန်ထက်သော chun-htet-thaw *(adj.)* **pointful**
ချွန်သည်၊ ထက်မြက်စေသည် chawan sai, htaatmyaatsaysai *(v.)* **sharpen**
ချွန်သော chwan-saw *(adj.)* **pointed**
ချွေး chway *(n.)* **sweat**
ချွေးထွက်ခြင်း chway-htwat-chinn *(n.)* **perspiration**
ချွေးထွက်သည် chway htwat-sai *(v.)* **sweat**
ချွေးနံ့ပျောက်စေသည် chway-nant-pyauk-say-the *(v.)* **deodrize**
ချွေးနံ့ပျောက်ဆေး chway-nant-pyauk-say *(n.)* **deodorant**
ချွေးပေါက် chwaypout *(n.)* **pore**
ချွေးသိပ်အားဖြည့်သည် chway seik aarr hpyae-sai *(v.)* **recuperate**
ချွေတာခြင်း chaway tarchinn *(n.)* **thrift**
ချွေတာသော chway-tar-taw *(adj.)* **frugal**
ချွဲနွဲ့လွန်းသော chwal nwal lwannsaw *(adj.)* **saccharine**
ချာခနဲ လှည့်သည် chaar-hka-nell-hlae-sai *(v.)* **pivot**
ချာချာလည်သည် chaar-chaar-laisai *(v.)* **whirl**
ချိတ် chaik *(n.)* **crome**
ချိတ်ဆက်ထားသည် chate-sat-htar-the *(v.)* **interlock**
ချိတ်ဆက်မိသည် chate-sat-mi-the *(v.)* **mesh**
ချိတ်ဆက်သည် chate-sat-the *(v.)* **join**
ချိတ်ဆွဲသည် chait-swal-the *(v.)* **hang**
ချိန်းကြိုး၊ သံကြိုး chain-kyo, tan-kyo *(n.)* **chain**
ချိန်းဆိုချက် chein-so-chat *(n.)* **appointment**
ချိန်းဆိုခြင်းမရှိဘဲ လာရောက်သော chain-so-chin-ma-shi-bal-lar-yauk-taw *(adj.)* **drop-in**
ချိန်းတွေ့ခြင်း chane-twaechinn *(n.)* **rendezvous**
ချိန်ဆခြင်း chain-sa-chin *(n.)* **contemplation**
ချိန်ဆသည် chain-sa-the *(v.)* **contemplate**
ချိန်ညှိမှုကို ဖယ်ရှားသည် chein-nyi-mu-ko-phal-shar-the *(v.)* **decalibrate**
ချိန်သည်၊ ချိန်တွယ်သည် chane sai , chanetwalsai *(v.)* **weigh**
ချိန်သီး chane-see *(n.)* **pendulum**
ချိပ်တံဆိပ်၊ ပင်လယ်ဖျံ chain tanseik, pinlaal hpyaan *(n.)* **seal**
ချိပ်ပိတ်နိုင်စွမ်း hkyaiutpateninehcwm *(n.)* **sealability**
ချိပ်ပိတ်သည် chainpatesai *(v.)* **seal**
ချိပ်ပိတ်သော hkyaiutpatesaw *(adj.)* **sealed**
ချို့တဲ့သည် choe-tae-the *(v.)* **lack**
ချို့ယွင်းချက် မရှိသော choe-ywin-chat-ma-shi-taw *(adj.)* **flawless**
ချိုးငှက် cho-nget *(n.)* **dove**
ချိုးဖောက်ခြင်း choehpoutchinn *(n.)* **violation**
ချိုးဖောက်မှု choe-hpauk-mu *(n.)* **infringement**
ချိုးဖောက်သည် choe-hpauk-the *(v.)* **infringe**
ချိုးဖဲ့ခြင်း choe-phae-chin *(n.)* **maul**
ချိုချဉ် cho-chin *(n.)* **candy**
ချိုခြင်း chochinn *(n.)* **sweetness**
ချိုင့်၊ တွင်း၊ ကျင်း chaint, twin, kyinn *(n.)* **pit**
ချိုင်းကြား kyaing-gyar *(n.)* **armpit**

ချိုင်းထောက်တစ်မျိုး chai-htauk-ta-myo *(n.)* **crutch**
ချိုင့်၊ တောင်ကြား youtyarr a say aaparr *(n.)* **vale**
ချိုစေသည် chosaysai *(v.)* **sweeten**
ချိုမြိန်ဖွယ် cho myaeinhpwal *(adj.)* **scrumptious**
ချိုသော chosaw *(adj.)* **sweet**
ချီးကျူးခြင်း chee-kyu-chin *(n.)* **commendation**
ချီးကျူးဂုဏ်ပြုခြင်း chee-kyu-gon-phyu-chin *(n.)* **acclamation**
ချီးကျူးဂုဏ်ပြုခြင်း chee-kyu-gon-phyu-ching *(n.)* **accolade**
ချီးကျူးဂုဏ်ပြုသည် chee-kyu-gon-phyu-the *(v.)* **acclaim**
ချီးကျူးထိုက်သော chee-kyu-htike-taw *(adj.)* **commendable**
ချီးကျူးထောမနာ သြဘာစကား chee-kyu-htaw-pa-nar-aw-bar-sa-kar *(n.)* **panegyric**
ချီးကျူးထောမနာသြဘာစကား chee-kyu-htaw-pa-nar-aw-bar-sa-gar *(int.)* **felicitations**
ချီးကျူးမှတ်တမ်းတင်ထိုက်သော chee-kyu-mat-tan-tin-htike-taw *(adj.)* **epical**
ချီးကျူးသည် chee-kyu-the *(v.)* **commend**
ချီးမြှင့်ငွေ cheemyint-ngway *(n.)* **recompense**
ချီးမြှောက်ခြင်း chee-hmyauk-chin *(n.)* **laud**
ချီးမြှောက်သည် chee-hmyauk-the *(v.)* **laud**
ချီးမွမ်းခြင်း chee-moon-chin *(n.)* **compliment**
ချီးမွမ်းထိုက်သော chee-mon-htike-taw *(adj.)* **creditable**
ချီးမွမ်းသော chee-moon-taw *(adj.)* **complimentary**
ချီတက်ခြင်း chee-tat-chin *(n.)* **march**
ချီတက်သည် chi-tat-the *(v.)* **march**
ချီတုံချတုံဖြစ်ခြင်း chae tone cha tonehpyitchinn *(n.)* **shilly-shally**
ချီတုံချတုံဖြစ်သည် chae tone cha tonehpyitsai *(v.)* **shilly-shally**
ချုံ chone *(n.)* **shrub**
ချုံခိုတိုက်ခြင်း chone-kho-tite-chin *(n.)* **ambush**
ချုံတန်းစည်းရိုး chon-tan-see-yoe *(n.)* **hedge**
ချုံတန်းဖြင့် စည်းရိုးကာသည် chon-tan-phit-see-yoe-kar-the *(v.)* **hedge**
ချုံထူသော၊ အမွှေးထူသော chone-htu-taw, a-hmway-htu-taw *(adj.)* **bushy**
ချုံပင် chone-pin *(n.)* **sagebrush**
ချုံပုတ် chone-boke *(n.)* **bush**
ချုပ်ကြိုး choke-kyo *(n.)* **whipcord**
ချုပ်ခြင်း၊ သီခြင်း chote chinn , sechinn *(n.)* **stitch**
ချုပ်စက် chotesaat *(n.)* **staple**
ချုပ်စက်ဖြင့် တွဲသည် chote saathpyint twalsai *(v.)* **staple**
ချုပ်တည်းသည် chote tae-sai *(v.)* **repress**
ချုပ်ထားသည် choke-htar-the *(v.)* **detain**
ချုပ်ထိန်းသည် chote hteinsai *(v.)* **restrain**
ချုပ်ရာမရှိသော chote rarmashisaw *(adj.)* **seamless**
ချုပ်ရိုး hkyaoteroe *(n.)* **seam**
ချုပ်သည် chate-sai *(v.)* **sew**
ချုပ်သည်၊ သီသည် chote sai , se-sai *(v.)* **stitch**
ချူချာသော chauu chaarsaw *(adj.)* **sickly**
ချူသံ chu-tan *(n.)* **jingle**
ချေးငွေ chay-ngwe *(n.)* **loan**

ချေးငှားသည် chay-ngar-the *(v.)* **borrow**

ချေပသည် chaay-pya-sai *(v.)* **refute**

ချေဖျက်ခြင်း chay-hpyet-chinn *(n.)* **obliteration**

ချေဖျက်သည် chay-hpyet-tai *(v.)* **obliterate**

ချော့မော့မြှောက်ပင့်နားချသည် chawt-mawt-hmyauk-pint-nar-cha-the *(v.)* **cajole**

ချော့သည်၊ နူးသည် chawt-the, nu-the *(v.)* **coax**

ချောကလက် chaw-ka-lat *(n.)* **chocolate**

ချောကလက်ရည် chaw-ka-lat-yay *(n.)* **drinking chocolate**

ချောက်ကမ်းပါး chauk-kan-par *(n.)* **cliff**

ချောက်ချားဖွယ် ဖြစ်စေသော chauk-char-phwal-phit-say-taw *(adj.)* **eerie**

ချောက်နက် chauk-nat *(n.)* **gorge**

ချောက်နူတ်ခမ်း chauk-note-khan *(n.)* **brink**

ချောင်းကြည့်ခြင်း chaung-kyi-chinn *(n.)* **peep**

ချောင်းကြည့်သည် chaung-kyi-sai *(v.)* **peep**

ချောင်းငယ် hkyaungggngaal *(n.)* **streamlet**

ချောင်းစွယ် chaung-swal *(n.)* **creek**

ချောင်းဆိုးရင်ကျပ်နာ chaung-soe-yin-kyat-nar *(n.)* **bronchitis**

ချောင်းဆိုးသည် chaung-sek-the *(v.)* **cough**

ချောင်းသည် chaunggsai *(v.)* **snoop**

ချောင်းသည်၊ ကြည့်သည် chaung-the, kyi-the *(v.)* **geek**

ချောင်းသည်၊ ခိုသည် chaung-the, kho-the *(v.)* **lurk**

ချောင်ကျသော chaungkyasaw *(adj.)* **secluded**

ချောင်ကြိုချောင်ကြား kyaung-kyo-kyaung-kyarr *(n.)* **nook**

ချောင်စေသည် chaung-say-the *(v.)* **loosen**

ချောင်ထိုးလိုက်သည် chaunghtoelitesai *(v.)* **shelve**

ချောင်ထိုးသည် chaunghtoesai *(v.)* **shunt**

ချောင်ပိတ်မိခြင်း chaung-pate-mi-chin *(n.)* **impasse**

ချောင်သော၊ လွတ်နေသော chaung-taw, hlut-nay-taw *(adj.)* **loose**

ချောဆွဲခြင်း chaww-swalchinn *(n.)* **requisition**

ချောဆွဲသည် chaww-swalsai-tonepyansai *(v.)* **requisition**

ချောဆီ chaw-si *(n.)* **lubricant**

ချောဆီထည့်ခြင်း chaw-si-htae-chin *(n.)* **lubrication**

ချောဆီထည့်သည် chaw-si-htae-the *(v.)* **lubricate**

ချောမွတ်တောက်ပြောင်နေသော chaww-mwat tout pyaungnaysaw *(adj.)* **sleek**

ချောမွေ့တောက်ပသော chaw-mway-taut-pa-taw *(adj.)* **glossy**

ချောမွေ့သော chawwmwaesaw *(adj.)* **smooth**

ချောသော chawwsaw *(adj.)* **slippery**

ချောသော လမ်း chawwsaw lam *(n.)* **slip road**

ချော်ရည် chaw-yay *(n.)* **lava**

ချဲ့ကားခြင်း chae-kar-chin *(n.)* **exaggeration**

ချဲ့ကားပြောသည် chae-kar-pyaw-the *(v.)* **exaggerate**

ချဲ့ခြင်း chae-chin *(n.)* **amplification**

ချဲ့သည် chae-the *(v.)* **amplify**

ချဲ့သည်၊ ဆန့်သည် chae-the, sant-the *(v.)* **extend**

ခရက်ကာမုန့်၊ ဖြောက်အိုး ka-rat-kar-hmont, byauk-oh *(n.)* **cracker**
ခရက်ဒစ်ကတ် kha-rat-dit-card *(n.)* **credit card**
ခရင်းကောင် kha-yin-kaung *(n.)* **barnacle**
ခရစ်ကက် kha-rit-kat *(n.)* **cricket**
ခရစ်စမတ် hka-rit-samaat *(n.)* **Xmas**
ခရစ်စမတ်ပွဲတော် kha-yit-sa-mat-pwe-taw *(n.)* **Christmas**
ခရစ်တော် ဖွားမြင်ခန်းရုပ်ပုံ kha-yit-taw-phwar-myin-khan-yoke-pon *(n.)* **nativity**
ခရစ်တော်၏ ပုံတော် kha-yit-taw-ei-pon-taw *(n.)* **Christ**
ခရစ်တော်ထံ မက်ဂီလာခြင်း အထိမ်းအမှတ်ပွဲ kha-yit-taw-htan-mag-gi-lar-chin-a-htain-a-mat-pwe *(n.)* **epiphany**
ခရစ်ယာန် kha-yit-yan *(adj.)* **Christian**
ခရစ်ယာန် ဘုရားရှိခိုးကျောင်း kha-yit-yan-pha-yar-shi-kho-kyaung *(n.)* **minster**
ခရစ်ယာန်ကဲ့သို့ ဝတ်ပြုသော kha-yit-yan-kae-tho-wit-pyu-taw *(adj.)* **liturgical**
ခရစ်ယာန်ဂိုဏ်းအုပ်နယ်ပယ် kha-yit-yan-gai-oak-nal-pal *(n.)* **diocese**
ခရစ်ယာန်ဓမ္မတေးသံစုံကျူးအဖွဲ့ kha-yit-yan-dhamma-tay-tan-sone-kyu-a-phwe *(n.)* **choir**
ခရစ်ယာန်ဓမ္မမင်္ဂလာအမှု hkaraityaran dhamm main g lar aamhu *(n.)* **sacrament**
ခရစ်ယာန်ဘာသာအားလုံးနှင့် ဆိုင်သော kha-yit-yan-bar-tar-ar-lone-nint-sai-taw *(adj.)* **catholic**
ခရစ်ယာန်ဘုန်းကြီး hkaraityaranbhonekyee *(n.)* **vicar**
ခရစ်ယာန်ဘုန်းတော်ကြီး kha-yit-yan-bhone-taw-gyi *(n.)* **bishop**
ခရစ်ယာန်ဘုန်းတော်ကြီး၊ သီလရှင် kha-yit-yan-hpone-taw-kyi, thi-la-shin *(n.)* **benediction**
ခရစ်ယာန်ဘုန်းတော်ကြီး၏ ရာထူးနှင့် လစာ kha-yit-yan-hpone-taw-kyi-ei-yar-htoo-nint-la-sar *(n.)* **benefice**
ခရစ်ယာန်ဘုရားကျောင်း kha-yit-yan-pha-yar-kyaung *(n.)* **church**
ခရစ်ယာန်ဘုရားကျောင်းဝန်းအတွင်း သင်္ချိုင်း kha-yit-yan-pha-yar-kyaung-win-a-twin-tin-gyaing *(n.)* **churchyard**
ခရစ်ယာန်ဘုရားရှိခိုးကျောင်း kha-yit-yan-pha-yar-shi-kho-kyaung *(n.)* **cathedral**
ခရစ်ယာန်ဘုရားရှိခိုးသူ ထိုင်ရာ နေရာ kha-yit-yan-pha-yar-shi-kho-thu-htai-yar-nay-yar *(n.)* **nave**
ခရစ်ယာန်လောက kha-yit-yan-law-ka *(n.)* **Christendom**
ခရစ်ယာန်သမ္မာကျမ်း၊ ဝေဒကျမ်း၊ ပိဋကကျမ်း hkaraityaran sammarkyam, wayd kyam , pitakakyam *(n.)* **scripture**
ခရစ်ယာန်သီလရှင်ကျောင်း kha-yit-yan-thi-la-shin-kyaung *(n.)* **convent**
ခရစ်ယာန်အယူ kha-yit-yan-a-yu *(n.)* **Christianity**
ခရစ်ယာန်အသင်းတော်ဝင်အဖြစ်မှ ကြဉ်သည် kha-yit-yan-a-tin-taw-win-a-phit-ma-kyin-the *(v.)* **excommunicate**
ခရစ်ယာန်အသင်းတော်အမျိုးမျိုးမှ အသင်းသားများပါသော kha-yit-yan-a-tin-taw-a-myo-myo-ma-a-tin-tar-myar-par-taw *(adj.)* **ecumenic**
ခရစ်ယာန်အသင်းနှင့် ဆိုင်သော kha-yit-yan-a-tin-nint-sai-taw *(adj.)* **ecclesiastical**
ခရစ်ယာန်ဧဝံဂေလိတရား kha-yit-yan-a-win-gay-li-ta-yar *(n.)* **evangel**
ခရစ်ယာန်ဧဝံဂေလိတရားနှင့် ဆိုင်သော kha-yit-yan-a-win-gay-li-ta-yar-nint-sai-taw *(adj.)* **evangelic**

ခရစ်ဝင်ကျမ်း kha-yit-win-kyan *(n.)* **gospel**

ခရမ်းချဉ်သီး hkaram chaisee *(n.)* **tomato**

ခရမ်းဖော့ရောင် kha-yan-phawt-yaung *(n.)* **lilac**

ခရမ်းရောင် hka-ram-raung *(adj./n.)* **purple**

ခရမ်းလွန် hkaramlwan *(adj.)* **ultraviolet**

ခရမ်းလွန်ရောင်ခြည် hkaram lwanraungchi *(n.)* **ultraviolet**

ခရမ်းသီး kha-yan-thee *(n.)* **aubergine**

ခရာ hka-rar *(n.)* **trumpet**

ခရိုင် kha-yai *(n.)* **district**

ခရိုမိုဆုမ်း kha-ro-mo-sone *(n.)* **chromosome**

ခရိုမီယမ်စိမ်ထားသော သတ္တုထည် kha-ro-mi-yan-sein-htar-taw-tat-thu-htal *(n.)* **chrome**

ခရီး kha-yee *(adv.)* **forth**

ခရီး၊ တိုးတက်မှု hkaree , toe-taatmhu *(n.)* **progress**

ခရီးကြမ်းနှင်သည် hkareekyam natesai *(v.)* **trek**

ခရီးစဉ် kha-yee-sin *(n.)* **itinerary**

ခရီးဆောင်အိတ် kha-yee-saung-aite *(n.)* **luggage**

ခရီးတို hkareeto *(n.)* **trip**

ခရီးပန်းတိုင် kha-yee-pan-tai *(n.)* **destination**

ခရီးမိုင်ပေါင်း kha-yee-mai-paung *(n.)* **mileage**

ခရီးရှည် hkareeshqy *(n.)* **voyage**

ခရီးရှည် ထွက်သည် hkareeshay htwatsai *(v.)* **voyage**

ခရီးလှည့်လည်သည် hka-ree hlae laisai *(v.)* **tour**

ခရီးသည် hka-ree-sai *(n.)* **passenger**

ခရီးသည်တင်လေယာဉ်ကြီး kha-yee-the-tin-lay-yin-kyi *(n.)* **airbus**

ခရီးသွား hkareeswarr *(n.)* **traveller**

ခရီးသွားချိန် hkareeswarrchane *(n.)* **traveltime**

ခရီးသွားခြင်း hkareeswarrchinn *(n.)* **travel**

ခရီးသွားမှတ်တမ်း hkareeswarrmhaattam *(n.)* **travelogue**

ခရီးသွားလုပ်ငန်း hka-ree-swarr-lote-ngan *(n.)* **tourism**

ခရီးသွားသည် hkareeswarrsai *(v.)* **travel**

ခရီးဦးကြိုပြု၍ နေရာချပေးသည် htonesanaatinehpyitsaw *(v.)* **usher**

ခရု hkaru *(n.)* **snail**

ခရုမျိုး ka-yu-myo *(n.)* **mollusc**

ခရုမျိုးနှင့် ဆိုင်သော kha-yu-myo-nint-sai-taw *(adj.)* **molluscous**

ခရုသင်း kha-yu-tin *(n.)* **conch**

ခရုအပါအဝင် ပြင်သစ်ဟင်းလျာတစ်ခွက် kha-yu-a-par-a-win-pyin-tit-hin-lyar-ta-khwat *(n.)* **escargot**

ခရူးဆိတ် စစ်ပွဲ kha-ru-sate-sit-pwe *(n.)* **crusade**

ခရူးဆိတ် စစ်ပွဲတွင် ပါဝင်တိုက်ခိုက်သူ kha-ru-sate-sit-pwe-twin-par-win-tite-khite-thu *(n.)* **crusader**

ခရေစေ့တွင်းကျ လိုက်လွန်းသော hka-ray-sae-twin-kya-lite-lwann-saw *(n.)* **pedantic**

ခရေပွင့်သင်္ကေတ kha-yay-pwint-tin-kay-ta *(n.)* **asterisk**

ခရေပွင့်သင်္ကေတအစု kha-yay-pwint-tin-kay-ta-a-su *(n.)* **asterism**

ခြ cha *(n.)* **termite**

ခြံ၊ ခြံခတ်ခြင်း chan,chan-khat-chin *(n.)* **enclosure**

ခြံစည်းရိုး chan-see-yoe *(n.)* **fence**

ခြံစည်းရိုးခတ်သည် chan-see-yoe-khat-the *(v.)* **fence**
ခြံတံခါးတိုင် chan-ta-khar-tai *(n.)* **gatepost**
ခြံတိုင် chan-tine *(n.)* **pale**
ခြံထွက်ပစ္စည်း chaan htwatpyit-saee *(n.)* **produce**
ခြံဝင်း chan-win *(n.)* **estate**
ခြံဝင်းဝ chan-win-wa *(n.)* **lodge**
ခြင် chin *(n.)* **mosquito**
ခြင်ဆီ chin-si *(n.)* **marrow**
ခြင်္သေ့ chin-tay *(n.)* **lion**
ခြင်္သေ့နှင့် တူသော chin-tay-nint-tu-taw *(adj.)* **leonine**
ခြင်္သေ့မ chin-tay-ma *(n.)* **lioness**
ခြစ်ခုံ chit-khone *(n.)* **grater**
ခြစ်ထုတ်သည် chit htotesai *(v.)* **scrape**
ခြစ်ရန် ကိရိယာ chitraan ka-ri-yar *(n.)* **scraper**
ခြစ်သံ chit-san *(n.)* **rasp**
ခြစ်သည် chit-the *(v.)* **grate**
ခြသတ်ဆေး cha-tat-say *(n.)* **termiticide**
ခြားထားသည် charrhtarrsai *(v.)* **space**
ခြားနားချက် char-nar-chat *(n.)* **difference**
ခြားနားလွန်း၍ နှိုင်းယှဉ်မရသော char-nar-lun-ywe-hnine-shin-ma-ya-taw *(adj.)* **disparate**
ခြားနားသည် char-nar-the *(v.)* **differ**
ခြားနားသော char-nar-taw *(adj.)* **different**
ခြိမ်းခြောက်၍ ငွေညှစ်ခြင်း chein-chauk-ywe-ngwe-hnyit-chin *(n.)* **extortion**
ခြိမ်းခြောက်ခြင်း chain-chauk-chin *(n.)* **intimidation**
ခြိမ်းခြောက်ငွေညှစ်သည့် လုပ်ရပ် chain-chauk-ngwe-hnyit-the-lote-yat *(n.)* **blackmail**
ခြိမ်းခြောက်ငွေညှစ်သူ chain-chauk-ngwe-hnyit-thu *(n.)* **blackmailer**
ခြိမ်းခြောက်မှု chaaimchaukmhu *(n.)* **threat**
ခြိမ်းခြောက်သည် chaaimchauksai *(v.)* **threaten**
ခြိုးခြံချွေတာသော choe chaan chway tarsaw *(adj.)* **thrifty**
ခြိုးခြံခြင်း choe chaanchinn *(n.)* **temperance**
ခြိုးခြံသော အကျင့်ရှိသူ choe-chan-taw-a-kyint-shi-thu *(n.)* **ascetic**
ခြိုးခြံသော အကျင့်ရှိသော choe-chan-taw-a-kyint-shi-thaw *(adj.)* **ascetic**
ခြုံခြင်း chon-chin *(n.)* **muffler**
ခြုံနိုက်တိုက်သည် chon-kho-tite-the *(v.)* **embush**
ခြုံထည်၊ ခေါင်းစွပ်မျက်နှာဖုံး chon-htae, gaung-sut-myat-nar-hpone *(n.)* **hood**
ခြုံလွှာ chuanlwhar *(n.)* **wrap**
ခြုံသည်၊ ထွေးသည် chone-the, htway-the *(v.)* **muffle**
ခြေကျင်ခရီးကြမ်း chay kyinhkareekyam *(n.)* **trek**
ခြေကျင်ခရီးသည် chay kyinhkareesai *(n.)* **wayfarer**
ခြေကျိုးနေသော chay-kyo-nay-taw *(adj.)* **lame**
ခြေကုန်သော khay-kone-taw *(adj.)* **footsore**
ခြေကုပ် chay-coke *(n.)* **foothold**
ခြေချင်း chay-chin *(n.)* **anklet**
ခြေချင်းဝတ် chay-chin-wut *(n.)* **ankle**
ခြေချောင်း chaychaung *(n.)* **toe**
ခြေချောင်းဖြင့် ထိသည် chay-chaung-phyint-thi-the *(v.)* **toe**
ခြေချော်ခြင်း chay chawchinn *(n.)* **slip**

ခြေချော်သည် chay chawsai *(v.)* **slip**

ခြေစုံကန်လျှောဆင်းသည် chay-sone-shaw-sin-the *(v.)* **abseil**

ခြေဆင်း chaysinn *(n.)* **prologue**

ခြေဆာနေသော သူ chay-sar-nay-thaw-thu *(n.)* **gimp**

ခြေဆောင့်နင်းသည် chay saw int nainnsai *(v.)* **stamp**

ခြေတစ်ပေါင်ကျိုးခုန်ခြင်း chay-ta-paung-kyo-khone-chin *(n.)* **hop**

ခြေတစ်ပေါင်ကျိုးခုန်သည် chay-ta-paung-kyo-khone-the *(v.)* **hop**

ခြေတစ်လှမ်း chay-ta-hlam *(n.)* **pace**

ခြေထောက် chay-htauk *(n.)* **foot**

ခြေနင်း chay-ninn *(n.)* **pedal**

ခြေနင်းကွင်း chay nainnkwin *(n.)* **stirrup**

ခြေဖနှောင့် chay-pha-naut *(n.)* **heel**

ခြေဖဝါး chayhpawarr *(n.)* **sole**

ခြေဖဝါးနာအထူးကု chay-pha-war-nar-a-htuu-ku *(n.)* **podiatrist**

ခြေဖဝါးနာအထူးကုသော chay-pha-war-nar-a-htuu-ku-taw *(adj.)* **podiatric**

ခြေဖဝါးအပြား chay-pha-war-a-pyar *(n.)* **flatfoot**

ခြေဗလာ khyay-ba-lar *(adj.)* **barefoot**

ခြေများသော သတ္တဝါ kyay-myar-taw-tat-ta-war *(n.)* **multiped**

ခြေရှစ်ချောင်းပါသတ္တဝါ chay-shit-chaung-par-tat-ta-war *(n.)* **octopede**

ခြေရှည်သူ chay shisuu *(n.)* **rover**

ခြေရာ chay-yar *(n.)* **footmark**

ခြေရာကောက်သူ chayrarkoutsuu *(n.)* **tracker**

ခြေရာခံနိုင်သော chay-yar-khan-nine-taw *(adj.)* **trackable**

ခြေရာခံသည် chay rar hkansai *(v.)* **track**

ခြေရာပြန်ကောက်သည် chay rar pyan koutsai *(v.)* **retrace**

ခြေလက် chay-lat *(n.)* **limb**

ခြေလျင်တပ် chay-lin-tat *(n.)* **infantry**

ခြေလှမ်း chayhlam *(n.)* **step**

ခြေလှမ်းကျဲ chayhlamkyaell *(n.)* **stride**

ခြေလှမ်းကျဲကျဲ လျှောက်သည် chayhlam kyaellkyaell shoutsai *(v.)* **stride**

ခြေလှမ်းကွက် chay-hlan-kwat *(n.)* **footwork**

ခြေလေးချောင်းသတ္တဝါ chay layy chaung-sattawar *(n.)* **quadruped**

ခြေသည် chay-the *(v.)* **mash**

ခြေသလုံးကြွက်သား၊ နွားငယ်ကလေး chay-ta-lone-kywat-tar, ngwar-nge-ka-lay *(n.)* **calf**

ခြေသလုံးအိမ်တိုင် သွားလာနေသူ chay-salone-aaintine swarrlar naysuu *(n.)* **tinker**

ခြေသုတ်ဖုံ chay-tote-hpon *(n.)* **doormat**

ခြေအိတ် chayaate *(n.)* **sock**

ခြေအိတ်ရှည် chay aateshay *(n.)* **stocking**

ခြောက် chauk *(n.)* **six**

ခြောက်ခုမြောက် chauk-hku-myaut *(adj.)* **sixth**

ခြောက်ဆယ် chauk-saal *(n., adj.)* **sixty**

ခြောက်ဆယ်ခုမြောက် chauk saal-ku-myaut *(adj.)* **sixtieth**

ခြောက်ပြစ်ကင်း သဲလဲစင် chauk-pyit-kinn-selllell-sin *(n.)* **perfection**

ခြောက်လှန့်ရေးသမား chyaut-hlant-yay-tha-mar (n.) **alarmist**

ခြောက်လုံးပြူးသေနတ် chauklone pyauusaynaat *(n.)* **revolver**

ခြောက်သည် chauksai *(v.)* **terrify**

ခြောက်သွေ့ညှိုးနွမ်းသည် chaukswae nyhaoenwmsai *(v.)* **wither**
ခြောက်သွေ့သည် chauk-thway-the *(v.)* **dry**
ခြောက်သွေ့သော chauk-thway-taw *(adj.)* **dry**
ခလုတ် hka-lote *(n.)* **switch**
ခလုတ်၊ မောင်း hkalote , maungg *(n.)* **trigger**
ခလုတ်ကန်သင်း hkalotekaansinn *(n.)* **snag**
ခလုတ်ခုံအငယ်စား kha-lote-khon-a-nge-sar *(n.)* **keypad**
ခလုတ်တိုက်ခြင်း hka-lote titechinn *(n.)* **stumble**
ခလုတ်တိုက်သည် hkalote titesai *(v.)* **stumble**
ခလောက်ဆန် kha-laut-san *(n.)* **clapper**
ခလောက်တံ hka louttan *(n.)* **whisk**
ခွ hkwa *(n.)* **spanner**
ခွကြား khwa-kyar *(n.)* **crotch**
ခွက် khwat *(n.)* **container**
ခွက်ခွက်လန်ရှုံးခြင်း hkwat hkwat laan shonechinn *(n.)* **rout**
ခွက်သော khwat-taw *(adj.)* **concave**
ခွင့် khwint *(n.)* **leave**
ခွင့်ကာလ hkwintkar-la *(n.)* **sabbatical**
ခွင့်ပြုချက် hkwint-pyu-chet *(n.)* **permission**
ခွင့်ပြုချက်၊ ပါမစ် hkwint-pyu-chet, par-mit *(n.)* **permit**
ခွင့်ပြုခြင်း kwint-pyu-chin *(n.)* **approbation**
ခွင့်ပြုမိန့်၊ ဖယ်ထုတ်ပစ်ခြင်း khwint-pyu-maint, phal-htoke-pyit-chin *(n.)* **clearance**
ခွင့်ပြုသည် khwint-pyu-the *(v.)* **allow**
ခွင့်မပြု khwint-ma-pyu *(v.)* **disallow**
ခွင့်မပြုသော မသင့်လျော်သော ပြင်ဆင်ချက်ပြုလုပ်ခြင်းကို ခံနိုင်ရည်ရှိသော hkwng mapyusaw m saint lyawsaw pyinsainhkyet pyulotehkyinnko hkannineraishisaw *(adj.)* **tamperproof**
ခွင့်မပြုသော မသင့်လျော်သော ပြင်ဆင်ချက်ပြုလုပ်သည် hkwng mapyusaw m saint lyawsaw pyinsainhkyet pyulotesai *(n.)* **tamper**
ခွင့်လွှတ်ခြင်းအနုပညာ khwint-hlut-chin-a-nu-pyin-nyar *(n.)* **condonation**
ခွင့်လွှတ်လွယ်သော hkwng lwhaat lwalsaw *(adj.)* **placable**
ခွင့်လွှတ်သင့်သော hkwint-lwhaat-saint-saw *(adj.)* **pardonable**
ခွင့်လွှတ်သည် hkwint-lwhaat-sai *(v.)* **pardon**
ခွင့်ပြုငွေ khwint-pyu-ngwe *(n.)* **allowance**
ခွင့်ပြုခြင်း khwint-pyu-chin *(n.)* **consent**
ခွင့်ပြုမိန့်၊ ခွင့်ပြုချက် hkwin pyu mein , hkwintpyuchet *(n.)* **sanction**
ခွင့်ပြုသည် hkwint-pyu-sai *(v.)* **permit**
ခွင့်မပြုနိုင်သော khwint-ma-pyu-nai-taw *(adj.)* **impermissible**
ခွင့်မပြုသော hkwint mapyusaw *(adj.)* **unapproved**
ခွင့်လွှတ်ခြင်း hkwint-lwhaat-chinn *(n.)* **pardon**
ခွနေသည် kwa-nay-the *(v.)* **bestride**
ခွန်းတုံ့ပြန်ခြင်း၊ ထွက်တိုက်ခြင်း hkwann tonepyanchinn, htwat titechinn *(n.)* **sally**
ခွန်အား hkwan-aarr *(n.)* **strength**
ခွန်အားကြီးမားသော khun-arr-kyi-mar-taw *(adj.)* **mighty**
ခွန်အားဗလ hkwanaarrbala *(n.)* **virility**

ခွန်အားမရှိသော khun-ar-ma-shi-taw *(adj.)* **nerveless**
ခွန်အားအပြည့်နှင့် တက်ကြွခြင်း khun-ar-a-pyae-nint-tat-kwa-chin *(n.)* **ebullience**
ခွန်အားအပြည့်နှင့် တက်ကြွသည် khun-ar-a-pyae-nint-tat-kwa-the *(v.)* **ebulliate**
ခွန်အားအပြည့်နှင့် တက်ကြွသော khun-ar-a-pyae-nint-tat-kwa-taw *(adj.)* **ebullient**
ခွလျက် khwa-lyat *(prep.& adv.)* **astride**
ခွာ khwar *(n.)* **hoof**
ခွာပြဲနေသော khwar-pyal-nay-thaw *(adj.)* **estranged**
ခွာသည်၊ ချွတ်သည် hkwar sai , chwatsai *(v.)* **strip**
ခွေး khway *(n.)* **dog**
ခွေးကလေး hkway-kalayy *(n.)* **puppy**
ခွေးခြေ၊ မစင် hkway-chay , masin *(n.)* **stool**
ခွေးတူဝက်တူ khway-tu-wat-tu *(n.)* **badger**
ခွေးနှင့်ဆိုင်သော khway-nint-sai-taw *(adj.)* **canine**
ခွေးဘီလူး khway-ba-lu *(n.)* **bulldog**
ခွေးမ khway-ma *(n.)* **bitch**
ခွေးရူးပြန်ရောဂါ hkway-ruu pyan-rawgar *(n.)* **rabies**
ခွေးသမင် khway-ta-min *(n.)* **greyhound**
ခွေးသွားစိတ် khway-twar-seik *(n.)* **cog**
ခွေးဟောင်သံ hkway haungsan *(n.)* **woof**
ခွေးအ khway-a *(n.)* **jackal**
ခွေးအိမ် khway-eain *(n.)* **doghouse**
ခွဲခြမ်း၍ မရနိုင်သော kwal-chan-ywe-ma-ya-nai-taw *(adj.)* **indivisible**
ခွဲခြား ဆက်ဆံခြင်း kwal-char-sat-san-chin *(n.)* **discrimination**
ခွဲခြား ဆက်ဆံသည် kwal-char-sat-san-the *(v.)* **discriminate**
ခွဲခြားနိုင်သော hkwalcharrninesaw *(adj.)* **separable**
ခွဲခြားမှု hkwalcharrmhu *(n.)* **segregation**
ခွဲခြားရွေးထုတ်ခြင်း၊ သက်သေခံကတ်ပြား kwal-char-yway-htoke-chin, thet-tay-khan-kat-pyar *(n.)* **identification**
ခွဲခြားသည် hkwalcharrsai *(v.)* **segregate**
ခွဲခြားသိမြင်သည် khwal-char-ti-myin-the *(v.)* **distinguish**
ခွဲခွာခါနီးနှုတ်ဆက်စကား kwal-kwar-khar-nee-note-set-sa-kar *(interj.)* **farewell**
ခွဲခွာသည် hkwahl-kwar-sai *(v.)* **part**
ခွဲစိတ်ကုသ၍ ရနိုင်သော kwal-sate-ku-ta-ywe-ya-nine-taw *(adj.)* **operable**
ခွဲစိတ်ကုသခြင်း kwal-sate-ku-ta-chinn *(n.)* **operation**
ခွဲစိတ်ဆရာဝန် hkwal-sate-sa-rar-waan *(n.)* **sawbones**
ခွဲစိတ်မှု hkwalsatemhu *(n.)* **surgery**
ခွဲစိတ်လေ့လာခြင်း khwal-seik-lay-lar-chin *(n.)* **dissection**
ခွဲစိတ်လေ့လာသည် khwal-seik-lay-lar-the *(v.)* **dissect**
ခွဲတမ်း hkwal-tam *(n.)* **ration**
ခွဲတမ်းချခြင်း khwe-tan-cha-chin *(n.)* **allocation**
ခွဲတမ်းချသည် hkwaltam chasai *(v.)* **portion**
ခွဲထွက်ခြင်း hkwaltwatchinn *(n.)* **secession**
ခွဲထွက်ရေးသမား hkwaltwatrayysamarr *(n.)* **secessionist**
ခွဲထွက်သည် hkwaltwatsai *(v.)* **secede**
ခွဲထုတ်မရသော kwal-htoke-ma-ya-taw *(adj.)* **inseparable**
ခွဲမွေးခြင်း khwal-mway-chin *(n.)* **cesarean**

ခွဲဝေပေးသည် khwe-way-pay-the *(v.)* **allot**

ခွဲသည် hkwal-sai *(v.)* **sunder**

ခါး hkarr *(n.)* **waist**

ခါးကိုင်းခြင်း hkarr kinechinn *(n.)* **stoop**

ခါးခြင်း၊ ခါးသီးခြင်း khar-chin, khar-thee-chin *(n.)* **bitterness**

ခါးခါးသီးသီးငြင်းပယ်ခြင်း hkarrhkarrseesee ngyinnpaalchinn *(n.)* **rebuff**

ခါးခါးသီးသီးငြင်းပယ်သည် hkarr-hkarr-seesee ngyinnpaalsai *(v.)* **rebuff**

ခါးစည်း hkarrsaee *(n.)* **waistband**

ခါးစည်းကြိုး khar-see-kyo *(n.)* **girdle**

ခါးပတ် khar-pat *(n.)* **belt**

ခါးပါတ်ခေါင်း khar-pat-khaung *(n.)* **buckle**

ခါးဖုဖြူ hkarr hpuhpyuu *(n.)* **turnip**

ခါးသော၊ ခါးသီးသော khar-taw, khar-thee-taw *(adj.)* **bitter**

ခါသည်၊ လှုပ်သည် hkar sai , hlotesai *(v.)* **shake**

ခါသာပိတ်သား khar-tar-pate-tar *(n.)* **muslin**

ခို hko *(n.)* **pigeon**

ခိုးကြောင်ခိုးဝှက် hkoe kyaung hkoewhaat *(adv.)* **stealthily**

ခိုးနားထောင်သည် kho-nar-htaung-the *(v.)* **eavesdrop**

ခိုးနားထောင်သူ kho-nar-htaung-thu *(n.)* **eavesdrop**

ခိုးဖမ်းသူ hkoe-hpam-suu *(n.)* **poacher**

ခိုးရာလိုက်ပြေးခြင်း kho-yar-lite-pyay-chin *(n.)* **eloquence**

ခိုးရာလိုက်ပြေးသည် kho-yar-lite-pyay-the *(v.)* **elope**

ခိုးရာလိုက်သော kho-yar-lite-taw *(adj.)* **eloquent**

ခိုးသည် hkoesai *(v.)* **steal**

ခိုကိုးရာ hkokoerar *(n.)* **resort**

ခိုကိုးရာမဲ့ဖြစ်သော kho-ko-yar-mae-phit-taw *(adj.)* **destitute**

ခိုက်ခိုက်တုန်သည် hkite hkite tonesai *(v.)* **shiver**

ခိုက်ရန်ဒေါသ hkiteraandawsa *(n.)* **strife**

ခိုက်ရန်ဖြစ်ခြင်း hkite-raan-hpyit-chinn *(n.)* **quarrel**

ခိုင်းဖတ်ဘဝ hkine hpaatbhawa *(n.)* **servitude**

ခိုင်ခံ့သော၊ တုတ်ခိုင်သော hkine hkan saw, tote hkinesaw *(adj.)* **stout**

ခိုင်မြဲတည်ကြည်မှု khai-myal-the-kyi-mu *(n.)* **firmness**

ခိုင်မာစေသော khai-mar-say-the *(adj.)* **corroborative**

ခိုင်မာတောင့်တင်းလာခြင်း khai-mar-taunt-tin-lar-chin *(n.)* **consolidation**

ခိုင်မာတောင့်တင်းလာသည် khai-mar-taunt-tin-lar-the *(v.)* **consolidate**

ခိုင်မာနူးညံ့သော အဝါနုရောင်အသားအရေ khai-mar-nu-nyant-taw-a-war-nu-yaung-a-thar-a-yay *(n.)* **buff**

ခိုင်မာနေပြီဖြစ်သော khai-mar-nay-p-phit-taw *(adj.)* **classical**

ခိုင်မာသော khai-mar-taw *(adj.)* **definitive**

ခိုင်လုံခြင်း၊ တရားဝင်ဖြစ်ခြင်း taungkyarr *(n.)* **validity**

ခိုင်လုံသော khaing-lon-taw *(adj.)* **authoritative**

ခိုင်လုံသော၊ လက်ဆုပ်လက်ကိုင်ပြနိုင်သော khai-lon-taw, lat-sote-lat-khai-pya-nai-taw *(n.)* **concrete**

ခိုင်သော hkinesaw *(adj.)* **tough**

ခိုလှုံခွင့် kho-hlon-kwint *(n.)* **asylum**

ခိုလှုံရာ hko-hlonrar *(n.)* **refuge**

ခိုးကောင် gon-kaung *(n.)* **clam**

ခုံတန်းလျား khon-tan-lyar *(n.)* **bench**

ခုံသမာဓိ khone-ta-mar-di *(n.)* **arbitrator**

ခုံသမာဓိဖြင့် စီရင်ဆုံးဖြတ်ခြင်း khone-ta-mar-di-phint-see-yin-sone-phat-chin *(n.)* **arbitration**

ခုံအဖွဲ့ hkoneaahpwal *(n.)* **tribunal**

ခုခံကာကွယ်ပေးသူ khu-khan-kar-kwal-pay-thu *(n.)* **bastion**

ခုခံကာကွယ်ရန် အသင့်ပြင်ထားသည် khu-khan-kar-kwe-yan-a-tint-pyin-htar-the *(v.)* **forearm**

ခုခံခြင်း၊ တော်လှန်ခြင်း hkuhkan chinn, tawhlaanchinn *(n.)* **resistance**

ခုခံသည် hkuhkansai *(v.)* **resist**

ခုခံသော၊ ခုခံအားရှိသော hkuhkan saw, hkuhkanaarr shisaw *(adj.)* **resistant**

ခုတစ်လော khu-ta-law *(adv.)* **lately**

ခုတ်ထစ်သည် khote-htit-the *(v.)* **hack**

ခုတ်ထွင်သည် hkote htwinsai *(v.)* **slash**

ခုတ်ပိုင်းခြင်း hkote pinechinn *(n.)* **slash**

ခုတ်ပိုင်းသည် khote-pai-the *(v.)* **cleave**

ခုတ်ဖြတ်သည် khote-phat-the *(v.)* **hew**

ခုတ်ဖြတ်သူ khote-phat-thu *(n.)* **cutter**

ခုတ်လှဲသည် kote-hlae-the *(v.)* **fell**

ခုတ်သည် khote-the *(v.)* **chop**

ခုနစ် hkunit *(n.)* **seven**

ခုနှစ် hkunit *(adj.)* **seven**

ခုနှစ်ခုမြောက် hkun-nit-khu-myaut *(adj.)* **seventh**

ခုနှစ်ဆယ် hkun-nit-saal *(n.)* **seventy**

ခုနှစ်ဆယ်ခုမြောက် hku nit-saal-ku-myaut *(adj.)* **seventieth**

ခုန်ခြင်း hkone-chinn *(n.)* **skip**

ခုန်ပေါက်ပြေးသည် hkone pout pyaysai *(v.)* **scamper**

ခုန်ပေါက်မြူးထူးခြင်း khone-pauk-my-htoo-chin *(n.)* **cavorting**

ခုန်ပေါက်မြူးထူးသည် khone-pauk-my-htoo-the *(v.)* **cavort**

ခုန်ပေါက်သွားသည် khone-pauk-twar-the *(v.)* **bound**

ခုန်လွှားခြင်း khone-hlwar-chin *(n.)* **leap**

ခုန်သည် hkone-sai *(v.)* **pulse**

ခုန်အုပ်တိုက်ခိုက်သည် kone-oak-tite-khite-the *(n.)* **pounce**

ခုန်အုပ်သည် hkone aote-sai *(v.)* **pounce**

ခုသည်၊ ခံသည် hku-sai , hkan-sai *(v.)* **pad**

ခူးဆွတ်သည် hkuu-swat-sai- *(v.)* **pluck**

ခူကောင် khu-kaung *(n.)* **caterpillar**

ခေတ္တ khit-ta *(adv.)* **awhile**

ခေတ္တစဲချိန် khit-ta-sal-chain *(n.)* **lull**

ခေတ္တနားချိန် khit-ta-nar-chein *(n.)* **breaktime**

ခေတ် khit *(n.)* **epoch**

ခေတ်ကုန်သွားပြီဖြစ်သော khit-kone-twar-p-phit-taw *(adj.)* **defunct**

ခေတ်ဆန်၍ ခေတ်ကို တက်တက်ကြွကြွ တော်လှန်သော မိန်းမပျို khit-san-ywe-khit-ko-tat-tat-kwa-kwa-taw-lan-taw-mein-ma-pyo *(n.)* **flapper**

ခေတ်ဆန်ကြော့မော့သော khit-san-kyawt-mawt-thaw *(adj.)* **chic**

ခေတ်ဆန်သော khit-san-taw *(adj.)* **fashionable**

ခေတ်ဆန်သော အသိုင်းအဝိုင်းတွင် ရေပန်းစားသူ hkayatsaansaw aasineaawinetwin raypaannsarrsuu *(n.)* **socialite**

ခေတ်ဆန်သော၊ ဖက်ရှင်ကျသော hkit saan-saw, hpaathlyinkyasaw *(adj.)* **stylish**
ခေတ်တလွဲဖော်ပြချက် khit-ta-lwal-phaw-pya-chat *(n.)* **anachronism**
ခေတ်ထခြင်း hkit htachinn *(n.)* **vogue**
ခေတ်ပျက်တွင် ဖောက်ထွင်း ပစ္စည်းယူသည် khit-pyat-twin-phauk-htwin-pyit-see-yu-the *(v.)* **loot**
ခေတ်ပြိုင် khit-pyai *(adj.)* **contemporary**
ခေတ်မမီတော့သော khit-ma-me-tot-taw *(adj.)* **outdated**
ခေတ်မီခြင်း khit-mi-chin *(n.)* **modernity**
ခေတ်မီသည် khit-mi-the *(v.)* **modernize**
ခေတ်မီသူ hkitmesuu *(n.)* **sophisticate**
ခေတ်မီသော hkitt-mesaw *(adj.)* **up-to-date**
ခေတ်မီအောင် ပြုလုပ်ခြင်း khit-mi-aung-pyu-lote-chin *(n.)* **modernization**
ခေါက်ချိုးညီ hkout-choenye *(adj.)* **symmetrical**
ခေါက်ချိုးညီခြင်း hkoutchoenyechinn *(n.)* **symmetry**
ခေါက်ခြင်း khauk-chin *(n.)* **folding**
ခေါက်ဆွဲ hkout-swal *(n.)* **noodle**
ခေါက်တုံ့ခေါက်ပြန်သွားသည် hkout tone hkout pyan-swarrsai *(v.)* **shuttle**
ခေါက်ရိုး khauk-yoe *(n.)* **crease**
ခေါက်သည် khauk-the *(v.)* **knock**
ခေါက်သည်၊ တွန့်သည် khauk-the, twunt-the *(v.)* **fold**
ခေါက်သော khauk-taw *(adj.)* **folding**
ခေါက်အမိုးကား khauk-a-moe-kar *(n.)* **convertible**
ခေါင်းကြီးသော gaung-gyi-taw *(n.)* **macrocephaly**
ခေါင်းကိုက်ခြင်း gaung-kite-chin *(n.)* **headache**
ခေါင်းကိုင်အဖ kaung-kai-a-pha *(n.)* **godfather**
ခေါင်းခြောက်စေသည် gaung-chyauk-say-the *(v.)* **baffle**
ခေါင်းစဉ် hkaunggsin *(n.)* **title**
ခေါင်းစဉ်၊ အာဘော်၊ အကြောင်းအရာအလိုက် hkaunggsin , aarbhaw , aakyaunggaararaalite *(adj.)* **thematic**
ခေါင်းစဉ်တင်သည် hkaunggsintinsai *(v.)* **title**
ခေါင်းစဉ်တပ်သည် gaung-zin-tat-the *(v.)* **entitle**
ခေါင်းစဉ်အကြမ်း hkaung-sin-a-kyan *(n.)* **rundown**
ခေါင်းစည်း gaung-see *(n.)* **headband**
ခေါင်းစည်းပဝါ gaung-see-pa-war *(n.)* **kerchief**
ခေါင်းစွပ်ဆွယ်တာ hkaungg swut swaltar *(n.)* **pullover**
ခေါင်းစီး gaung-see *(n.)* **heading**
ခေါင်းဆောင် gaung-saung *(n.)* **leader**
ခေါင်းဆောင်၊ တပ်ဦး hkaung-saung, tat u *(n.)* **spearhead**
ခေါင်းဆောင်မှု၊ ခဲသတ္တု gaung-saung-mu, khae-tat-tu *(n.)* **lead**
ခေါင်းဆောင်မှုပညာ gaung-saung-mu-pyin-nyar *(n.)* **leadership**
ခေါင်းဆောင်အဖြစ် kaung-saung-a-phit *(n.)* **captaincy**
ခေါင်းညိတ်ခြင်း hkaung-gnyate-chin *(n.)* **nod**
ခေါင်းညိတ်သည် hkaung-gnyate-te *(v.)* **nod**
ခေါင်းတစ်ခြမ်းကိုက်ရောဂါ khaung-ta-chan-kite-yaw-gar *(n.)* **migraine**

ခေါင်းထိခိုက်၍ သတိမေ့သွားခြင်း gaung-hti-khite-ywe-ta-di-mae-twar-chin *(n.)* **concussion**
ခေါင်းပုံဖြတ်အမြတ်ကြီးစား hkaung pone hpyat-aa-myat-kyee-sarr *(n.)* **predator**
ခေါင်းပုံဖြတ်အမြတ်ကြီးစားသည် hkaungg pone hpyat aa-myat-kyee-sarr-sai *(v.)* **profiteer**
ခေါင်းပေါက် kaung-pauk *(n.)* **cavity**
ခေါင်းပေါင်း hkaunggpaungg *(n.)* **turban**
ခေါင်းဖြတ်ကွပ်မျက်သည် gaung-phat-kwat-myat-the *(v.)* **behead**
ခေါင်းဖြတ်သည် gaung-phat-the *(v.)* **decapitate**
ခေါင်းမာခြင်း hkaung-mar-chinn *(n.)* **obduracy**
ခေါင်းမာသည် kaung-mar-tai *(v.)* **opinionate**
ခေါင်းမာသော gaung-mar-taw *(adj.)* **headstrong**
ခေါင်းရွက်ဗျပ်ထိုးဈေးသည် kaung-ywet-byat-htoe-zay-the *(n.)* **hawker**
ခေါင်းရှောင်သူ hkaungg shawinsuu *(n.)* **shirker**
ခေါင်းလျှော်ရည် hkaungg shawrai *(n.)* **shampoo**
ခေါင်းလျှော်သည် hkaungg shawsai *(v.)* **shampoo**
ခေါင်းလိမ်းဂျယ် kaung-lain-gyal *(n.)* **gel**
ခေါင်းလောင်း khaung-laung *(n.)* **bell**
ခေါင်းလောင်းထိုးသည် hkaungglaungghtoesai *(v.)* **toll**
ခေါင်းအုံး hkaung-aone *(n.)* **pillow**
ခေါင်းအုံးသည် hkaung-aone-sai *(v.)* **pillow**
ခေါင်မိုး hkaungmoe *(n.)* **roof**
ခေါင်မိုးတင်ရေတိုင်ကီ khaung-moe-tin-yay-tai-gi *(n.)* **cistern**
ခေါ်ခြင်း khaw-chin *(n.)* **call**
ခေါ်လာသည် khaw-lar-the *(v.)* **fetch**
ခေါ်သည် khaw-the *(v.)* **call**
ခဲခြင်း khal-chin *(n.)* **clot**
ခဲစေသည် hkell-saysai *(v.)* **solidify**
ခဲတံ hkell-tan *(n.)* **pencil**
ခဲတံဖြင့် ရေးသည် hkell-tan-hpyit-rayy-sai *(v.)* **pencil**
ခဲထိုးသည် hkell htoesai *(v.)* **retouch**
ခဲနှင့် ပေါက်သတ်သည် hkell-nint pout saatsai *(v.)* **stone**
ခဲဖျက် khae-phat *(n.)* **eraser**
ခဲသည် khae-the *(v.)* **congeal**

ဂဇဲဆိတ် ga-zae-seik *(n.)* **gazelle**
ဂဏန်း ga-nan *(n.)* **crab**
ဂဏန်းသင်္ချာ ga-nan-tin-char *(n.)* **arithmetic**
ဂဏာန်းခြေ ga-nan-chay *(n.)* **cardinal**
ဂတ်ဂတ်မြည်သံ၊ ရမ်းကု gaat gaat myi san , ram-ku *(n.)* **quack**
ဂတ်ဂတ်မြည်သည် gaat gaat myi-sai *(v.)* **quack**
ဂတ်စကက် gat-sa-kat *(n.)* **gasket**
ဂနာမငြိမ် ga-nar-ma-nyein *(v.)* **fidget**
ဂနာမငြိမ်သူ ga-nar-ma-nyein-thu *(n.)* **fidget**

ဂန္ဓာရုံ gan-dhar-rone *(adj.)* **olfactory**

ဂယက် ga-yat *(n.)* **backwash**

ဂယက်ရိုက်ခတ်မှု ga-yat-yite-khat-mu *(n.)* **implication**

ဂယက်ရိုက်မှု ga-yaat-ritemhu *(n.)* **repercussion**

ဂယက်အနက်ရှိသည် ga-yat-a-nat-shi-the *(v.)* **connote**

ဂယောင်ဂတမ်း ညည်းတွားခြင်း ga-yaung-ga-tan-nyie-twar-chin *(n.)* **delirium**

ဂယောင်ဂတမ်းဖြစ်စေသောဆေး ga-yaung-ga-tan-phit-say-taw-say *(n.)* **deliriant**

ဂျက်လေယာဉ် jat-lay-yin *(n.)* **jet**

ဂျက်အင်ဂျင် jat-in-gyin *(n.)* **jet engine**

ဂျင် gyin *(n.)* **whirligig**

ဂျင်းအင်္ကျီ gyin-in-gyi *(n.)* **jean**

ဂျင်နရေတာ၊ မီးစက် gyan-na-rat-tor, mee-sat *(n.)* **generator**

ဂျင်အရက် gyin-a-yat *(n.)* **gin**

ဂျစ်ဆောအရုပ်ဆက်ခြင်း jit-saw-a-yike-sat-chin *(n.)* **jigsaw**

ဂျယ်လီ jal-lee *(n.)* **jelly**

ဂျာကင်အင်္ကျီ jar-kin-in-gyi *(n.)* **jerkin**

ဂျာဆီနို့စားနွားမျိုး jar-si-noe-sar-nwar-ma-myo *(n.)* **jersey**

ဂျာနယ် jar-nal *(n.)* **journal**

ဂျာမင်း gyar-min *(n.)* **germin**

ဂျိုးဂျိုးဂျောက်ဂျောက် မြည်သံ gyoe gyoe gyawt gyawt myisan *(n.)* **rattle**

ဂျိုကာ jo-ker *(n.)* **joker**

ဂျိုက်ဖြင့် မသည် gyaik-phint-ma-the *(v.)* **jack**

ဂျိုက်သိုး gyaik-thoe *(n.)* **rubeola**

ဂျီဂါဘစ် gi-ga-bit *(n.)* **gigabit**

ဂျီဂါဘိုက် gi-ga-bite *(n.)* **gigabyte**

ဂျီနုန်း ge,hnone *(n.)* **genome**

ဂျီနီနတ်သမီး gi-ni-nat-ta-mee *(n.)* **genie**

ဂျုံ gyaone *(n.)* **wheat**

ဂျုံ၊ စပါး gyone, sa-par *(n.)* **grain**

ဂျုံစက်ပိုင်ရှင် gyone-sat-pai-shin *(n.)* **miller**

ဂျုံမှုန့် gyone-hmont *(n.)* **flour**

ဂျုံမှုန့်၊ ကြက်ဥ၊ နို့ရည်ရောထားသော အနှစ် gyon-mont-kyat-au-noe-yae-yaw-htar-taw-a-hnit *(n.)* **batter**

ဂျုံမှုန့်ပါးပါးဖြူးသည် gyone-hmont-par-par-phyue-the *(v.)* **flourish**

ဂျုံမုန့်ညက် gyon-mont-nyat *(n.)* **dough**

ဂျုံအစည်း jone-a-see *(n.)* **reap**

ဂျူးဓမ္မဆရာ juu-dham-ma-sarar *(n.)* **rabbi**

ဂျူးဗရှုး ju-ba-yu *(n.)* **jew**

ဂျူရာမေတာအပြင်ဘက်တွင်ရှိသော ju-ra-may-ta-a-pyin-bat-twin-shi-taw *(n.)* **epidural**

ဂျူရီလူကြီး ju-re-lu-gyi *(n.)* **juryman**

ဂျူရီလူကြီးအဖွဲ့ ju-re-lu-gyi-a-phwe *(n.)* **jury**

ဂျူရီအဖွဲ့ဝင်လူကြီး ju-re-a-phwe-win-lu-gyi *(n.)* **juror**

ဂျော်ကီ jaw-ki *(n.)* **jockey**

ဂရန့် ချပေးသည် ga-rant-cha-pay-the *(v.)* **grant**

ဂရန့်ငွေ ga-rant-ngwe *(n.)* **grant**

ဂရပ် ga-rat *(n.)* **graph**

ဂရမ် ga-ran *(n.)* **gramme**

ဂရိနှင့် ဆိုင်သော ga-ri-nint-sai-taw *(adj.)* **Greek**

ဂရိနိုင်ငံသား၊ ဂရိဘာသာစကား ga-ri-nai-ngan-tar, ga-ri-bar-tar-sa-kar *(n.)* **Greek**

ဂရုစိုက်ကြည့်သော garusite kyisaw *(adj.)* **watchful**

ဂရုစိုက်ခြင်း ga-yu-site-chin *(n.)* **heed**

ဂရုစိုက်သည် garusitesai *(v.)* **tend**

ဂရုပြုသည် ga-ru-pyu-te *(v.)* **note**

ဂရုမထားဘဲ ga-yu-ma-htar-pal *(adj.)* **irrespective**

ဂြိုလ် gyo *(n.)* **planet**

ဂြိုလ်၊ ကြယ်တိုင်းကိရိယာ gyo-kyal-tine-ka-ri-yar *(n.)* **astrolabe**

ဂြိုလ်၏ gyo-eat *(adj.)* **planetary**

ဂြိုလ်တု gyaoltu *(n.)* **satellite**

ဂြိုလ်သား gyo-tar *(adj.)* **alien**

ဂြိုလ်သိမ်ဂြိုလ်မွှား gyo-thein-gyo-mwar *(v.)* **asteroid**

ဂလင်း ga-lin *(n.)* **gland**

ဂလူးကို့စ် ga-lu-kose *(n.)* **glucose**

ဂလူတန်ကင်းသော ga-lu-tan-kin-taw *(adj.)* **gluten-free**

ဂလူတန်ကို စစ်ထုတ်ခြင်း ga-lu-tan-ko-sit-htoke-chin *(n.)* **deglutination**

ဂလောက်ဂလောက်မြည်သံ ga-laut-ga-laut-myi-tan *(n.)* **clatter**

ဂလောက်ဂလောက်မြည်သည် ga-laut-ga-laut-myi-the *(v.)* **clatter**

ဂွန်ဒိုလာလှေ goon-doo-lar-hlay *(n.)* **gondola**

ဂွမ်းဖတ်၊ သလိပ်နမူနာ gwam hpaat , sa late-na-muunar *(n.)* **swab**

ဂဟေ gahay *(n.)* **solder**

ဂဟေဆော်သည် ga hay sawsai *(v.)* **solder**

ဂဟေအဆက် ga hay aasaat *(n.)* **weld**

ဂါရဝပြုခြင်း gar-ra-wa-pyu-chin *(n.)* **homage**

ဂါလန် gar-lan *(n.)* **gallon**

ဂါဝန် gar-win *(n.)* **frock**

ဂိတ် gait *(n.)* **gate**

ဂိတ်စောင့် gait-saunt *(n.)* **gatekeeper**

ဂိတ်စောင့်တဲ gait-saunt-tae *(n.)* **gatehouse**

ဂိမ်းကစားရာ နေရာ game-ka-sar-yar-nay-yar *(n.)* **gamespace**

ဂိမ်းကစားသမား game-ka-sar-ta-mar *(n.)* **gameplayer**

ဂိမ်းခလုတ် game-kha-lote *(n.)* **gamepad**

ဂိမ်းပုံထွက်ကျစေသည့် သက်ရောက်မှု gain-pone-htwat-kya-say-the-thet-yauk-mu *(n.)* **debuff**

ဂိုးစောင့် goe-saunt *(n.)* **goalkeeper**

ဂိုးတိုင် goe-tai *(n.)* **goalpost**

ဂိုးတိုင်ဘားတန်း go-tai-bar-tan *(n.)* **crossbar**

ဂိုးရခြင်း goe-ya-chin *(n.)* **goalscoring**

ဂိုးသွင်းသည်၊ အမှတ်မှတ်သည် goeswin sai , aamhaat mhaatsai *(v.)* **score**

ဂိုဏ်းကွဲ gaikwal *(n.)* **sect**

ဂိုဏ်းကွဲမှု gonkwalmhu *(n.)* **schism**

ဂိုဏ်းချုပ် gaing-choke *(n.)* **archbishop**

ဂိုဏ်းဂဏဆိုင်ရာ gai nasinerar *(adj.)* **sectarian**

ဂိုဏ်းထောက်ဘုန်းတော်ကြီး gai-htauk-bone-taw-gyi *(n.)* **deacon**

ဂိုအန်းနားပုတ်သင် go-an-na-poke-tin *(n.)* **goanna**

ဂီတ gi-ta *(n.)* **music**

ဂီတနည်းပညာ ge-ta-naee-pa-nyar *(n.)* **technomusic**

ဂီတနှင့် ဆိုင်သော gi-ta-nint-sai-taw *(adj.)* **musical**

ဂီတပညာရှင် gi-ta-pyin-nyar-shin *(n.)* **musician**

ဂီတသေတ္တာ gi-ta-tit-tar *(n.)* **jukebox**

ဂီတာ gi-tar *(n.)* **guitar**

ဂီယာ gi-yar *(n.)* **gear**

ဂီယာဘီး gi-yar-bee *(n.)* **gearwheel**

ဂီယာအစုံလိုက် gi-yar-a-sone-lite *(n.)* **gearset**

ဂီယာအုံ gi-yar-ohn *(n.)* **gearbox**

ဂုဏ်၊ ဂုဏ်ယူခြင်း gon, gonyuu-chinn *(n.)* **pride**

ဂုဏ်ငယ်စေသော gon-nge-say-the *(adj.)* **demeaning**

ဂုဏ်ထူး၊ ကွဲပြားခြင်း gon-htoo, kwal-pyar-chin *(n.)* **distinction**

ဂုဏ်ထူးဆောင် gon-htoo-saung *(adj.)* **honorary**

ဂုဏ်ပြု ခြင်း gonpyu chinn *(v.)* **salute**

ဂုဏ်ပြုခြင်း gon-pyu-chin *(n.)* **honour**

ဂုဏ်ပြုထမင်းစားပွဲ gon-pyu-hta-min-sar-pwe *(n.)* **banquet**

ဂုဏ်ပြုသည် gon-pyu-the *(v.)* **felicitate**

ဂုဏ်ယူဝင့်ကြွားခြင်း gon-yu-wint-kywar-chin *(n.)* **jubilation**

ဂုဏ်ယူသည် gonyuu-sai *(v.)* **pride**

ဂုဏ်ယူသော၊ မာနကြီးသော gon-yuu saw , mar na-kyeesaw *(adj.)* **proud**

ဂုဏ်သတင်း gone-ta-din *(n.)* **fame**

ဂုဏ်သတင်းကျော်ကြားသော gon-ta-tin-kyaw-kyar-taw *(v.)* **repute**

ဂုဏ်သရေ ထိပါးသော စကား gon-tha-yay-hti-par-taw-sa-gar *(n.)* **aspersion**

ဂုဏ်သရေရှိသော gon-ta-ya-shi-taw *(adj.)* **honourable**

ဂုဏ်သိက္ခာ gon-taik-khar *(n.)* **dignity**

ဂုဏ်သိက္ခာမြင့်သော gon-sate-hkar myintsaw *(adj.)* **prestigious**

ဂုန်လျှော် gon-shaw *(n.)* **jute**

ဂုရုကြီး gu-yu-gyi *(n.)* **geek**

ဂုရုဝတ်အင်္ကျီ gu-yu-wit-in-gyi *(n.)* **geekwear**

ဂုရုအကျင့်အကြံရှိသော gu-yu-a-kyint-a-kyan-shi-taw *(adj.)* **geeky**

ဂူ gyu *(n.)* **cave**

ဂူဂဲတွင် ရှာဖွေသည် goo-gal-twin-shar-phway-the *(v.)* **google**

ဂူဗိမာန် gu-baik-man *(n.)* **mausoleum**

ဂေဇက် gay-zat *(n.)* **gazette**

ဂေရှားမယ် gay-shar-mal *(n.)* **geisha**

ဂေဟစနစ် gay-ha-sa-nit *(n.)* **ecosystem**

ဂေဟဗေဒ gay-ha-bay-da *(n.)* **ecology**

ဂေဟဗေဒဆိုင်ရာ အကြမ်းဖက်မှု လုပ်ဆောင်ခြင်း gay-ha-bay-da-sai-yar-a-kyan-phat-mu-lote-saung-chin *(n.)* **ecoterrorism**

ဂေဟဗေဒနှင့် ဆိုင်သော gay-ha-bay-da-nint-sai-taw *(adj.)* **ecological**

ဂေဟဗေဒပညာရှင် gay-ha-bay-da-pyin-nyar-shin *(n.)* **ecologist**

ဂေဟာ gayhar *(n.)* **residence**

ဂေါ့တစ်ဗိသုကာလက်ရာပုံစံ got-tit-bi-thu-kar-lat-yar-pon-san *(n.)* **gothic**

ဂေါ့တစ်လက်ရာ got-tit-lat-yar *(adj.)* **gothic**

ဂေါက် gauk *(n.)* **golf**

ဂေါက်ကွင်း gauk-kwin *(n.)* **golf course**

ဂေါက်တွန်းလှည်း gauk-toon-hlae *(n.)* **golf cart**

ဂေါက်နာ gauk-nar *(n.)* **gout**

ဂေါ်ပြား gawpyarr *(n.)* **shovel**

ဂေါ်ပြားနှင့် မြေကော်သည် gaw pyarrnhang myay kawsai *(v.)* **spade**

ဂေါ်ပြားဖြင့် ကော်သည် gaw pyarrhpyint kawsai *(v.)* **shovel**

ဂေါ်ဖီထုပ် gaw-phee-htoke *(n.)* **cabbage**

ဂေါ်ဖီလက်သုပ် gaw-phi-lat-toke *(n.)* **coleslaw**

ဂေါ်ရီလာမျောက်ဝံ gaw-ri-lar-myauk-win *(n.)* **gorilla**

ဂဲသြမေတြီ gae-aw-may-tree *(n.)* **geometry**

ဂဲသြမေတြီဆိုင်ရာ gae-aw-may-tree-sai-yar *(adj.)* **geometrical**

င

ငကြွား nga-kywar *(n.)* **braggart**

ငကြောက် nga-kyauk *(n.)* **coward**

ငတုံး nga-tone *(n.)* **blockhead**

ငတုံး၊ ငအ nga-tone, nga-a *(n.)* **goof**

ငတုံးဖြစ်သော nga-tone-phit-taw *(adj.)* **idiotic**

ငတ်မွတ်ခြင်း ngaattmwat-chinn *(n.)* **starvation**

ငတ်မွတ်ခြင်းဘေးကြီး ngat-mut-chin-bay-gyi *(n.)* **famine**

ငတ်မွတ်သည် ngaat mwatsai *(v.)* **starve**

ငနု၊ ငအ nga na, nga-a *(n.)* **simpleton**

ငနှာ၊ ငနဲ nga nar, nganell *(n.)* **sod**

ငန်း ngaann *(n.)* **swan**

ငန်းဖို ngan-pho *(n.)* **gander**

ငန်ငြိငြိ ngan-nyi-nyi *(adj.)* **brackish**

ငပျော့ ngapyaww *(n.)* **weakling**

ငပိန်း nga-pain *(n.)* **dumbo**

ငမိုက်သား ngamitesarr *(n.)* **sinner**

ငမ်းခြင်း ngan-chin *(n.)* **ogle**

ငမ်းငမ်းတက်စားသည် ngan-ngan-tat-sar-the *(v.)* **engorge**

ငမ်းသည် ngam-tai *(v.)* **ogle**

ငယ်ရွယ်သော ngaal-rwal-saw *(adj.)* **young**

ငယ်ရွယ်သော၊ ပျိုမျစ်သော ngaal-rwal-saw , pyo myitsaw *(adj.)* **youthful**

ငယ်သော hgal-taw *(adj.)* **junior**

ငရုတ်ကောင်း nga-rote-kaungg *(n.)* **pepper**

ငရုတ်ကောင်းဖြူးသည် nga-rote-kaungg-hpyuu-sai *(v.)* **pepper**

ငရုတ်မျိုး nga-yoke-myo *(n.)* **capsicum**

ငရုတ်သီး nga-yote-thee *(n.)* **chilli**

ငရူး nga-ruu *(n.)* **nutcase**

ငရဲ nga-rell *(n.)* **purgatory**

ငရဲတွင် ကျခံစေသည် nga-ye-twin-kya-khan-say-the *(v.)* **damn**

ငရဲသစ်ငုတ်ဘဝ nga-ye-tit-ngote-ba-wa *(n.)* **damnation**

ငြင်းခုံဆွေးနွေးနိုင်သော nyin-khone-sway-nway-naing-taw *(adj.)* **arguable**

ငြင်းခုံဆွေးနွေးသည် nyin-khone-sway-nway-the *(v.)* **argue**

ငြင်းဆန်ခြင်း ngyinn-saanchinn *(n.)* **refusal**

ငြင်းဆန်သည် ngyinn-saansai *(v.)* **refuse**

ငြင်းဆိုချက် nyin-soe-chat *(n.)* **denial**

ငြင်းဆိုခြင်း ngyinn-sochinn *(n.)* **refutation**

ငြင်းဆိုသည် nyin-so-the *(v.)* **decline**

ငြင်းပယ်ခြင်း ngyinn-paalchinn *(n.)* **repudiation**

ငြင်းပယ်သည် ngyinn-paalsai *(v.)* **repudiate**
ငြင်းပယ်သော nyin-pal-taw *(adj.)* **averse**
ငြင်းသည် nyin-the *(v.)* **deny**
ငြိမ်းသည်၊ ကွယ်ပျောက်စေသည် nyein-the, kwal-pyauk-say-the *(v.)* **extinguish**
ငြိမ်းသတ်သည် ngyeim saatsai *(v.)* **stifle**
ငြိစွန်းသည် nyi-sun-the *(v.)* **implicate**
ငြိမ်းချမ်းစွာ အတူနေထိုင်ခြင်း nyein-chan-swar-a-thu-nay-htain-chin *(n.)* **coexistence**
ငြိမ်းချမ်းရေး ngyeim-cham-rayy *(n.)* **peace**
ငြိမ်းချမ်းရေး ဆွေးနွေးခြင်း ngyeim-cham-rayy-sway-nway-chinn *(n.)* **parley**
ငြိမ်းချမ်းရေး ဆွေးနွေးသည် ngyeim-cham-rayy-sway-nway-sai *(v.)* **parley**
ငြိမ်းချမ်းရေးမြတ်နိုးသူ ngyeim-cham-rayymyat-noesuu *(n.)* **pacifist**
ငြိမ်းချမ်းသော ngyaim-cham-saw *(adj.)* **pacific**
ငြိမ်းချမ်းသော၊ ငြိမ်းချမ်းရေး လိုလားသော ngyeim-cham-saw, ngyeim-cham-rayy-lo-larr-saw *(adj.)* **peaceful**
ငြိမ်ချမ်းခြင်း ngyein cham-chinn *(n.)* **serenity**
ငြိမ်ခြင်း ngyein-chinn *(n.)* **stillness**
ငြိမ်ငြိမ်သက်သက် ngyein ngyein-saat-saat *(adv.)* **still**
ငြိမ်ဆိမ်စေသည် ngyein sin saysai *(v.)* **tranquillize**
ငြိမ်နေသော nyein-nay-taw *(adj.)* **dormant**
ငြိမ်သက်ခြင်း ngyeinsaatchinn *(n.)* **tranquility**
ငြိမ်သက်သည် ngyein-saatsai *(v.)* **quiet**
ငြိမ်သက်သာယာသော nyein-thet-tar-yar-taw *(adj.)* **clement**
ငြိမ်သက်အေးချမ်းသော ngyeinsaat aayychamsaw *(adj.)* **tranquil**
ငြိမ်သည် ngyein-sai *(v.)* **still**
ငြိမ်သော ngyein-saw *(adj.)* **still**
ငြိသည်၊ လိမ်ယှက်သည် ngyai sai , lin yhaatsai *(v.)* **tangle**
ငြီးငွေ့ပျင်းရိဖွယ်ကောင်းသော nyee-ngwe-pyint-yi-phwal-kaung-taw *(adj.)* **humdrum**
ငြီးငွေ့ဖွယ် ngyee ngwae-hpwal *(adj.)* **tedious**
ငြီးငွေ့ဖွယ် ခြောက်ကပ်သော ngyi-ngwe-phwal-chauk-kat-taw *(adj.)* **drab**
ငြီးငွေ့ဖွယ်ကောင်းသော nyee-ngway-phwal-kaung-taw *(adj.)* **monotonous**
ငြောင့် ngyount *(n.)* **spike**
ငြောင့်စူးသည် ngyawnt suusai *(v.)* **spike**
ငလျင် nga-lin *(n.)* **earthquake**
ငလျင်ဖြစ်ပွားမှုကို ပြသော ကိရိယာ ngalyin hpyitpwarrmhuko pyasaw kiriyar *(n.)* **seismoscope**
ငလျင်ဗဟိုချက် nga-lin-ba-ho-chat *(n.)* **epicentre**
ငလျင်လှုပ်ရှားမှု၊ မှတ်တမ်း ngalyin lhuutsharrmhu , mhaattam *(n.)* **seismography**
ငလျင်လှုပ်ရှားမှုမှတ်တမ်းဂရပ် ngalyin lhuutsharrmhumhaattam garaut *(n.)* **seismogram**
ငွေ ngway *(n.)* **silver**
ငွေ့ရည်ဖွဲ့ခြင်းမှ ရသော အရည် ngwe-yay-phwe-chin-ma-ya-taw-a-yay *(n.)* **condensate**
ငွေ၊ ချမ်းသာမှု၊ ကြွယ်ဝမှု ngway , chamsar mhu , kywal-wamhu *(n.)* **pelf**
ငွေကြိုတင်ထည့်ထားသည် ngwe-kyo-tin-htae-htar-the *(v.)* **escrow**

ငွေကြေး ခဝါချခြင်း ngwe-kyay-kha-war-cha-chin *(n.)* **money laundering**

ငွေကြေးစံအဖြစ်မှ ရပ်တန့်သည် ngwe-kyay-san-a-phit-ma-yat-tant-the *(v.)* **demonetize**

ငွေကြေးစနစ် ngwe-kyay-sa-nit *(n.)* **currency**

ငွေကြေးထောက်ပံ့သည် ngwe-kyay-htauk-pant-the *(v.)* **finance**

ငွေကြေးပစ္စည်း ထည့်ဝင်ခြင်း ngwe-kyay-pyit-see-htae-win-chin *(n.)* **contribution**

ငွေကြေးဖောင်းပွခြင်း ngwe-kyay-hpaung-pwa-chin *(n.)* **inflation**

ငွေကြေးအရ ngway-kyay-aa-ra *(adj.)* **pecuniary**

ငွေကိုင် ngwe-kai *(n.)* **cashier**

ငွေကိုင်တွယ်သူ၊ ပုံပြောသူ ngway kinetwal suu, pone pyawwsuu *(n.)* **teller**

ငွေချေးစာချုပ်၊ သံယောဇဉ် ngwe-chay-sar-choke, tan-yar-zin *(n.)* **bond**

ငွေချေးသည် ngwe-chay-the *(v.)* **loan**

ငွေစက္ကူ ngwe-sat-khu *(n.)* **banknote**

ငွေစာရင်း nwyay-sa-yin *(n.)* **account**

ငွေစာရင်းလုပ်ငန်းစဉ် ngwe-sar-yin-lote-ngan-sin *(n.)* **accounting**

ငွေတန်ဖိုး လျှော့ချသည် ngwe-tan-pho-shawt-cha-the *(v.)* **devalue**

ငွေတန်ဖိုးချင်းတူညီမှု ngway-taan-hpoe-chinn-tuu-nye-mhu *(n.)* **parity**

ငွေထည့်အံဆွဲ ngway htae aan-swal *(n.)* **till**

ငွေပဒေသာပင် စိုက်ထူပေးသည် ngwe-pa-day-tar-pin-seik-thu-pay-the *(v.)* **endow**

ငွေပြန်ထုတ်ပေးခြင်း ngway pyanhtotepayychinn *(n.)* **reimbursement**

ငွေပြန်ထုတ်ပေးသည် ngway pyanhtotepayysai *(v.)* **reimburse**

ငွေပြန်ပေးခြင်း ngwe-pyan-pay-chin *(n.)* **cashback**

ငွေပြန်အမ်းသည် ngway pyan aamsai *(v.)* **refund**

ငွေပေး၍ အဖမ်းခံရသူကို ပြန်ရွေးသည် ngway-payy-ywe aah-pham-hkan-ra-suuko pyan rwaysai *(v.)* **ransom**

ငွေပေးချေခြင်း ngway-payy-chaay-chinn *(n.)* **payment**

ငွေပေးဝေသည် ngwe-pay-wai-the *(v.)* **disburse**

ငွေပေါင်း ngway-paung *(n.)* **sum**

ငွေမက်သော ngway maatsaw *(adj.)* **venal**

ငွေများများစားစား ထုတ်ပေးခြင်း ngway-myarr-myarr-sarr-sarr-htote-payy-chinn *(n.)* **payout**

ငွေရှင် ngwe-shin *(n.)* **financier**

ငွေရေးကြေးရေး ngwe-yay-kyay-kya *(adj.)* **monetary**

ငွေရောင် ngwayraung *(adj.)* **silver**

ငွေရောင်တောက်သည် ngwayraung toutsai *(v.)* **silver**

ငွေလက်ကျန်ရှင်းတမ်း ngwe-lat-kyan-shin-tan *(n.)* **balance sheet**

ငွေလက်ခံသူ ngway-laat-hkan-suu *(n.)* **payee**

ငွေလဲနှုန်း ngwe-lal-hnone *(n.)* **exchange rate**

ငွေသား ngwe-tar *(n.)* **cash**

ငွေအနည်းငယ်မျှမရှိသော ngway aa-nae-ngaal mya-mashisaw *(adj.)* **penniless**

ငွေအပ်သည် ngwe-at-the *(v.)* **bank**

ငွေအလွဲသုံးစားပြုခြင်း ngwe-a-lwal-tone-sar-pyu-chin *(n.)* **misappropriation**

ငွေအလွဲသုံးစားပြုသည် ngwe-a-lwal-tone-sar-pyu-the *(v.)* **misappropriate**

ငှက် nget *(n.)* **bird**

ငှက်ကျား ngat-kyarr *(n.)* **stork**

ငှက်ကြည့်ခြင်း ngat-kyi-chin *(n.)* **ornithoscopy**

ငှက်ကုလားအုတ် nghaat-ka-lar-aote *(n.)* **ostrich**

ငှက်ခြေသည်းရှိသော nghaat hkyaysaeeshisaw *(adj.)* **taloned**

ငှက်စလုတ် nget-sa-lote *(n.)* **craw**

ငှက်နှုတ်သီး nyat-note-thee *(n.)* **beak**

ငှက်ပျော nghaat-pyaww *(n.)* **plantain**

ငှက်ပျောသီး hnyat-pyaw-thee *(n.)* **banana**

ငှက်ဖျား nget-phyar *(n.)* **malaria**

ငှက်မည်း nget-mal *(n.)* **blackbird**

ငှက်မွေး ngat-mway *(n.)* **feather**

ငှက်ရုံ ngyat-yone *(n.)* **aviary**

ငှက်ရဲ၏ လက်သည်း ngatrelleat laatsaee *(n.)* **talon**

ငှားရမ်းခ ngharramhka *(n.)* **rent**

ငှားရမ်းသည် ngharramsai *(v.)* **rent**

ငှားသည် hngar-the *(v.)* **hire**

ငှားသည်၊ ချေးသည် ngar-the, chay-the *(v.)* **lend**

ငါး ngar *(n.)* **fish**

ငါးကြင်းငါးသိုင်း ngar-gyin-ngar-thai *(n.)* **carp**

ငါးကြီးဆီထုတ် ပင်လယ်ငါးကြီး nga-gyi-see-htoke-pin-lal-ngar-gyi *(n.)* **cod**

ငါးခူမျိုး ngarrhkuumyoe *(n.)* **sheat**

ငါးဆယ် ngar-sal *(n.)* **fifty**

ငါးပြတိုက် ngar-pya-tite *(n.)* **aquarium**

ငါးပိသိပ် ငါးချဉ်သိပ် ပြည့်ကျပ်နေသော ngar-pi-tate-ngar-chin-tat-pyae-kyat-nay-taw *(adj.)* **jam-packed**

ငါးပိသိပ်ငါချဉ်သိပ် ngarrpi seik ngar chainseik *(n.)* **squash**

ငါးဖမ်းသည် ngar-phan-the *(v.)* **fish**

ငါးမန်း ngarrmaann *(n.)* **shark**

ငါးရှဉ့် ngary-shint *(n.)* **eel**

ငါးသန် ngar-tan *(n.)* **fry**

ငါးသလောက် ngar-ta-laut *(n.)* **herring**

ငါးအုပ် ngarrote *(n.)* **shoal**

ငါးဥဆားနယ် ngar-oo-sar-nal *(n.)* **caviar**

ငိုကြွေးသည် nyo-kway-the *(v.)* **cry**

ငိုက်မျဉ်းသည် nyeik-myae-the *(v.)* **doze**

ငိုမြည်တမ်းတခြင်း ngo-mye-tan-ta-chin *(n.)* **lamentation**

ငုံ့သည်၊ ကိုင်းသည် ngone sai , kinesai *(v.)* **stoop**

ငုံး ngone *(n.)* **quail**

ငုတ်တန်း ngote-taann *(n.)* **wicket**

ငေါ့သော ngae saw *(adj.)* **sarcastic**

ငေးစိုက်ကြည့်ခြင်း ngay-site-kyi-chin *(n.)* **gaze**

ငေးစိုက်ကြည့်သည် ngay-site-kyi-the *(v.)* **gaze**

ငေးစိုက်ဆင်ခြင်သော ngayy-site -sin-chin-saw *(adj.)* **pensive**

ငေးမောနေမိသော ngay-maw-nay-mi-taw *(adj.)* **agaze**

ငေါ့သော ngot taw *(adj.)* **ironical**

ငေါက်ကနဲ ပန်းထွက်သည် ngout kanell paann htwatsai *(n.)* **spurt**

စံ san *(n.)* **ideal**

စံ အထူအပါး san-a-htu-a-par *(n.)* **gauge**

စံ၊ မှတ်ကျောက် san, mat-kyauk *(n.)* **criterion**

စံကိုက်ချိန်ညှိခြင်း san-kaik-chain-hnyi-chin *(n.)* **calibration**

စံကိုက်ချိန်ညှိသည် san-kaik-chain-hnyi-the *(v.)* **calibrate**

စံညွှန်းထားရှိခြင်း san nyun htarr-shi-chinn *(n.)* **standardization**

စံနမူနာ san-na-mu-nar *(n.)* **epitome**

စံနမူနာပြ san-nu-mu-nar-pya *(adj.)* **ideal**

စံနမူနာယူထိုက်သူ sannamuunar yuu htitesuu *(n.)* **role model**

စံပယ်ပန်း sa-pal-pan *(n.)* **jasmine, jessamine**

စံပြ san-pya *(n.)* **exemplar**

စံပြုလောက်သော san pyu loutsaw *(adj.)* **quintessential**

စံပြုသည် san-pyu-the *(v.)* **idealize**

စံဖြစ်သော၊ စံပြု san hpyit-saw, sanpyu *(adj.)* **standard**

စံမံအုပ်ချုပ်ရေးနှင့် တပ်စင်တာ hcan man aotehkyaoterayynhang tauthcaintar *(n.)* **sich**

စံသတ်မှတ်သည် sansaatmhaatsai *(v.)* **standardize**

စကင်ဒီနေးဗီးယားနှင့်ဆိုင်သော sa-kan-de-nayy-bee-yarr-nint-sine-taw *(adj.)* **Nordic**

စကတ် sakaat *(n.)* **skirt**

စကန်ဖတ်စက် sa kaan hpaatsaat *(n.)* **scanner**

စကျင်ကျောက် sa-kyin-kyauk *(n.)* **marble**

စကြဝဠာနှင့်ဆိုင်သော sa-kya-wa-lar-nint-sai-taw *(adj.)* **cosmic**

စကြဝဠာ sa-kya-wa-lar *(n.)* **cosmos**

စကားချီး sa-kar-chee *(n.)* **foreword**

စကားစစ်ထိုးခြင်း sa-karr-sit-htoe-chinn *(n.)* **polemic**

စကားစပ် sa-kar-sat *(n.)* **context**

စကားစမြည် sa-karr-sa-myi *(n.)* **pleasantry**

စကားစမြည်ပြောသည် sa-kar-sa-mie-pyaw-the *(v.)* **converse**

စကားတံရှည်ခြင်း sakarr tan shichinn *(n.)* **verbosity**

စကားထစ်ခြင်း sakarr htaitchinn *(n.)* **stammer**

စကားထာ sakarrhtar *(n.)* **riddle**

စကားထောက်ကိရိယာ sakarr htoutka-ri-yar *(n.)* **teleprompter**

စကားနည်းသော sakarr-nae-saw *(adj.)* **taciturn**

စကားပြန် sa-kar-pyan *(n.)* **interpreter**

စကားပြေ Sa-karr-pyay *(n.)* **prose**

စကားပြေပြန်ခြင်း sa-karr-pyay-pyan-chinn *(n.)* **paraphrase**

စကားပြေပြန်သည် sa-karr-pyay-pyan-sai *(v.)* **paraphrase**

စကားပြောခန်း hcakarrpyawwhkaann *(n.)* **talkboard**

စကားပြောပုံပြောနည်း sa-karr-pyaww-pone-pyaww-naee *(n.)* **parlance**

စကားပြောသည် sa-kar-pyaw-the *(v.)* **chat**

စကားပြောဟန် sa-kar-pyaw-han *(n.)* **diction**

စကားပုံ sa-karr-pone *(n.)* **proverb**

စကားပုံလာ sa-karr-pone-lar *(adj.)* **proverbial**
စကားဖန် sakarr-hpaan *(n.)* **pun**
စကားဖန်သည် sakarr-hpaansai *(v.)* **pun**
စကားမပြောဘဲ ကပြသည့် ရှေးပုံစံပြဇာတ်တွင် သရုပ်ဆောင်သူ sa-kar-ma-pyaw-bae-ka-pya-the-shay-pon-san-pya-zat-twin-ta-yoke-saung-thu *(n.)* **mummer**
စကားများ sakarrmyarr *(adv.)* **talkatively**
စကားများခြင်း sakarrmyarrchinn *(n.)* **talkativeness**
စကားများသော sakarr-myarrsaw *(adj.)* **polyloquent**
စကားရည်လုပွဲ sa-kar-yay-lu-pwe *(n.)* **debate**
စကားရပ် sakarrrat *(n.)* **term**
စကားရိပ်သန်းသည် sa-kar-yeik-tan-the *(v.)* **hint**
စကားလှသော sa-kar-hla-taw *(adj.)* **euphemistic**
စကားလုံး sakarrlone *(n.)* **word**
စကားလုံးချန်လှပ်ခြင်း sa-kar-lon-chan-hlat-chin *(n.)* **eclipsis**
စကားလုံးဖောင်းပွသော sakarrlone hpaunggpwsaw *(adj.)* **wordy**
စကားလုံးရွေးချယ်သုံးနှုန်းသည် sakarrlone rwaychaal sone hnonesai *(v.)* **word**
စကားသံထုတ်မှု sa-kar-tan-htoke-mu *(n.)* **artifice**
စကားအစီအစဉ် sa-karr-aa-se-aa-sin *(n.)* **phraseology**
စကိတ်စီးသည် sa kate seesai *(v.)* **skate**
စကိတ်စီးသူ sa kate seesuu *(n.)* **skater**
စကီဇိုဖရီးနီးယားစ်ရောဂါနှင့် ဆိုင်သော hc ke jo hparee nee yarr hc rawgarnhang sinesaw *(n.)* **schizophreniac**
စကူတာဆိုင်ကယ် sa kuu tarsinekaal *(n.)* **scooter**
စကော့တလန် sakottalaan *(adj.)* **scotch**
စကော့တလန် ဆူးလေပင် sakottalaan suulaypin *(n.)* **thistle**
စကော့တလန်သား sakottalaansarr *(n.)* **Scot**
စကော့ဝီစကီ sakotwesake *(n.)* **scotch**
စကောစက sa-kaw-sa-ka *(prep.)* **betwixt**
စက္ကူခေါက်ပညာ sat-ku-khaut-pin-nyar *(n.)* **origami**
စက္ကူဖြတ်စက် sakkuu hpyatsaat *(n.)* **shredder**
စက္ခုအာရုံ sakhkuaarrone *(adj.)* **visual**
စက် sat *(n.)* **machine**
စက်ကျသည့်နေရာ sat-kya-the-nay-yar *(n.)* **haunt**
စက်ကွင်း sat-kwin *(n.)* **dartboard**
စက်ကွင်းချက်မ sat-kwin-chat-ma *(n.)* **bull's eye**
စက်ကိရိယာ sat-ka-yi-yar *(n.)* **mechanism**
စက်ဆရာ sat-sa-yar *(n.)* **fitter**
စက်ဆုပ်ဖွယ် sat-sote-phwal *(adj.)* **abominable**
စက်ဆုပ်ဖွယ်ကောင်းသော sat-sote-phwal-kaung-taw *(adj.)* **despicable**
စက်ဆုပ်ရွံရှာခြင်း sat-sote-yun-shar-chin *(n.)* **abomination**
စက်ဆုပ်ရွံရှာဖွယ် sat-sote-ywan-shar-hpwal *(adj.)* **obnoxious**
စက်ဆုပ်ရွံရှာသည် sat-sote-yun-shar-the *(v.)* **abominate**
စက်ဆုပ်သည် sat-sote-the *(v.)* **abhor**
စက်ဆုပ်သော sat-sote-taw *(adj.)* **abhorrent**
စက်တင်ဘာလ saattinbharla *(n.)* **September**

စက်တပ်ယာဉ်၊ ရထားလုံး sat-tat-yin, ya-htar-lone *(n.)* **buggy**
စက်နှင့်ဆိုင်သော sat-nint-sai-taw *(adj.)* **mechanical**
စက်နှင့်ဆိုင်သော sat-nint-sai-taw *(adj.)* **enginous**
စက်ပျက်ခြင်း၊ စိတ်ကျန်းမာရေး ချို့ယွင်းခြင်း sat-pyat-chin, seik-kyan-mar-yay-choe-ywin-chin *(n.)* **breakdown**
စက်ပြင် sat-pyin *(n.)* **mechanic**
စက်ပုန်းခုတ်ခြင်း sat-pone-khote-chin *(n.)* **machination**
စက်ပုန်းခုတ်သည် sat-pone-khote-the *(v.)* **machinate**
စက်ဖြင့် လုပ်သော sat-phint-lote-taw *(adj.)* **machine-made**
စက်ဘီး sat-bee *(n.)* **bicycle**
စက်ဘီး၊ ဆိုင်ကယ် sat-bee, sai-kal *(n.)* **bike**
စက်ဘီးစီးသမား sat-bain-see-ta-mar *(n.)* **cyclist**
စက်မှုလုပ်ငန်း sat-mu-lote-ngan *(n.)* **industry**
စက်မှုလုပ်ငန်းနှင့် ဆိုင်သော sat-mu-lote-ngan-nint-sai-taw *(adj.)* **industrial**
စက်မောင်း sat-maung *(n.)* **machinist**
စက်မဲ့လေယာဉ် sat-mae-lay-yin *(n.)* **glider**
စက်ယန္တရား sat-yan-da-yar *(n.)* **machinery**
စက်ရုံ sat-yone *(n.)* **factory**
စက်ရုံ၊ အလုပ်ရုံ hcaatrone , aaloterone *(n.)* **shopfloor**
စက်ရုပ် saatrote *(n.)* **robot**
စက်ရုပ်အင်္ဂါတုတပ်ဆင်ထားသော sat-yoke-in-gar-tu-tat-sin-htar-taw *(adj.)* **bionic**
စက်လှေ၊ ဖန်ခွက်ရှည် saathlaay , hpaanhkwatshi *(n.)* **schooner**
စက်လှေကား sat-hlay-kar *(n.)* **elevator**
စက်လုံး saatlone *(n.)* **sphere**
စက်လုံးခြမ်း sat-lone-chan *(n.)* **hemisphere**
စက်ဝန်း၊ စက်ဘီး၊ မော်တော်ဆိုင်ကယ် sat-win, sat-bain, maw-taw-sai-kal *(n.)* **cycle**
စက်ဝန်းပြတ် sat-wun-phyat *(n.)* **arc**
စက်ဝန်းမျဉ်း sat-win-myin *(n.)* **circumference**
စက်ဝိုင်း sat-wine *(n.)* **circle**
စက်ဝိုင်းခြမ်း sat-wai-chan *(n.)* **demicircle**
စက်သီး saatsee *(n.)* **pulley**
စခန်း sa-khan *(n.)* **camp**
စခန်းချရာနေရာ sa-khan-cha-yar-nay-yar *(n.)* **campsite**
စခန်းချသူ sa-khan-cha-thu *(n.)* **camper**
စခရင်ဆေဗာ hcahkarain saybar *(n.)* **screensaver**
စခရင်ပေါက် hcahkarainpout *(n.)* **screendoor**
စခရင်ပေါ်တွင် sa-kha-rin-paw-twin *(adj.)* **on-screen**
စခရင်ဖမ်းခြင်း hcahkarain hpamhkyinn *(n.)* **screenprint**
စခရင်ဖမ်းယူခြင်း hcahkarain hpamyuuhkyinn *(n.)* **screencast**
စခရင်အပြား sa-kha-rin-a-pyar *(n.)* **flat screen**
စခရင်အမည် hcahkarainaamai *(n.)* **screen name**
စနိုးကတ် hc hkoekaat *(n.)* **scorecard**
စင် sin *(n.)* **rack**
စင်းလုံးချော sin-lon-chaw *(adj.)* **impeccable**
စင်ကြယ်ခြင်း sin kyaal-chinn *(n.)* **purity**
စင်တာ cin-tar *(n.)* **center**

စင်တီဂရိတ် cin-te-ga-yeik *(adj.)* **centigrade**

စင်တီမီတာ cin-te-mi-tar *(n.)* **centimetre**

စင်မြင့် sin-myint *(n.)* **platform**

စင်မြင့်၊ ဗန်းပြရာ၊ မှန်ပတ်လည်ဗီရို sin myint , baann pya rar, mhaan paatlai bero *(n.)* **showcase**

စင်ရော် sin raw *(n.)* **seagull**

စင်ရော်မျိုး sin-yaw-myo *(n.)* **gull**

စင်္ကြံလမ်း sin-kyan-lan *(n.)* **corridor**

စစ် sit *(adj.)* **martial**

စစ်ကြောမှု sit-kyaw-mu *(n.)* **inquisition**

စစ်ခရာ sit-kha-yar *(n.)* **bugle**

စစ်စခန်း sit-sa-khan *(n.)* **cantonment**

စစ်စစ် sit-sit *(adj.)* **downright**

စစ်စည်းရုံးသည် sit-si-yone-the *(v.)* **mobilize**

စစ်ဆိုင်းကာလ sit-saing-kar-la *(n.)* **armistice**

စစ်ဆေးခြင်း sit-say-chin *(n.)* **check**

စစ်ဆေးစီရင်ခြင်း sitsayy serinchinn *(n.)* **trial**

စစ်ဆေးဆုံးဖြတ်သည် sit-say-sone-phat-the *(v.)* **adjudicate**

စစ်ဆေးရေးဂိတ် sit-say-yay-gate *(n.)* **checkpoint**

စစ်ဆေးသည် sit-say-the *(v.)* **check**

စစ်တပ် sit-tat *(n.)* **army**

စစ်တပ်ဖြင့် ဝိုင်းထားသည် sit-tat-phit-wine-htar-the *(v.)* **besiege**

စစ်တပ်အင်အားလျော့ချသော sit-tat-inn-ar-shawt-cha-taw *(adj.)* **demilitarized**

စစ်တမ်းမေးခွန်းလွှာ sait-tam-mayy-hkwannlwhar *(n.)* **questionnaire**

စစ်တိုက်သည် sit titesai *(v.)* **war**

စစ်တုရင် sit-tu-yin *(n.)* **chess**

စစ်တုရင်၊ ကျား။ sit-tu-yin, kyar *(n.)* **board game**

စစ်တုရင်ခုံ sit-tu-yin-khone *(n.)* **chessboard**

စစ်ထုတ်ကိရိယာ sit-htoke-ka-yi-yar *(n.)* **filter**

စစ်ထုတ်သည် sit-htoke-the *(v.)* **filter**

စစ်ထဲဝင်သည် sit-htae-win-the *(v.)* **enlist**

စစ်ပြန် sitpyan *(adj.)* **veteran**

စစ်မက် sitmaat *(n.)* **war**

စစ်မက်ရေးရာအရ sit-mat-yay-yar-a-ya *(adj.)* **military**

စစ်မြေပြင် sit-myay-pyin *(n.)* **battlefield**

စစ်မှန်ကြောင်းသက်သေပြခြင်း sit-man-kyaung-thet-tay-pya-chin *(n.)* **authentication**

စစ်မှန်ကြောင်းသက်သေပြသည် sit-man-kyaung-thet-tay-pya-the *(v.)* **authenticate**

စစ်မှန်သော sit-man-taw *(adj.)* **authentic**

စစ်မှုတမ်းအဖြစ်မှ ထွက်ခွင့်ပြုသည် sit-mu-htan-a-phit-ma-htwat-kwint-pyu-the *(v.)* **demobilize**

စစ်မှုထမ်းအဖြစ်မှ ထွက်ခွင့်ပြုခြင်း sit-mu-htan-a-phit-ma-htwat-kwint-pyu-chin *(n.)* **demobilization**

စစ်ရထား sit-ya-htar *(n.)* **chariot**

စစ်ရေးကျွမ်းသော sitrayy kyawmsaw *(adj.)* **warlike**

စစ်လက်နက် ပစ္စည်း sit-lat-nat-pyit-see *(n.)* **munitions**

စစ်လက်နက်ပစ္စည်း sit-lat-nat-pyit-see *(n.)* **ordnance**

စစ်ဝန်ထမ်း sit-win-htan *(n.)* **militia**

စစ်သင်္ဘောစု sit-tin-baw-su *(n.)* **armada**

စစ်သည် sitsai *(n.)* **troop**

စစ်သည်၊ စစ်ဆေးသည် sitsai , sitsayysai *(v.)* **test**
စစ်သား sitsarr *(n.)* **soldier**
စစ်သားများ တန်းစီသည် sit-tar-myar-tan-si-the *(v.)* **muster**
စစ်သားများနေထိုင်ရန်နေရာ sit-tar-myar-nay-htai-yan-nay-yar *(n.)* **casern**
စစ်သားအဖြစ် ထမ်းဆောင်သည် hcaitsarraahpyit htamsaungsai *(v.)* **soldier**
စစ်အတွင်းအဓမ္မလုယူသော ပစ္စည်း sit-a-twin-a-dhamma-lu-yu-taw-pyit-see *(n.)* **booty**
စဉ့် sint *(n.)* **glaze**
စဉ်းစားချင့်ချိန်တတ်သော sin sarr chint chane-taatsaw *(adj.)* **sensible**
စဉ်တွင် sintwin *(conj.)* **while**
စည် si *(n.)* **cask**
စည်းကမ်း see-kan *(n.)* **discipline**
စည်းကမ်းကလနားကြီးသူ see-kam ka la narr kyeesuu *(n.)* **stickler**
စည်းကမ်းချက် saeekamchet *(n.)* **proviso**
စည်းကမ်းတင်းကျပ်သည် seekam tinnkyatsai *(v.)* **regiment**
စည်းကမ်းတင်းကြပ်သူ see-kan-tin-kyat-thu *(n.)* **martinet**
စည်းကမ်းထားသည်၊ သတ်မှတ်သည် seekam htarr-sai , saatmhaatsai *(v.)* **stipulate**
စည်းကမ်းမဲ့ခြင်း see-kan-mae-chin *(n.)* **indiscipline**
စည်းကြပ်ခြင်း see-kyat-chin *(n.)* **levy**
စည်းကြပ်သည် see-kyat-the *(v.)* **levy**
စည်းချက်ကျသော see-chetkyasaw *(adj.)* **rhythmic**
စည်းချက်တူရိယာ see-chet-tuu-ri-yar *(n.)* **percussion**
စည်းစနစ် ဖျက်သည် see-sa-nit-phat-the *(v.)* **disorganize**
စည်းမျဉ်း seemyain *(n.)* **precept**
စည်းမျဉ်း၊ နိယာမ see-myin, ni-yar-ma *(n.)* **canon**
စည်းမျဉ်းချိုးဖောက်သည် si-myin-choe-hpauk-chin *(n.)* **rulebreaking**
စည်းမျဉ်းစာအုပ် see myinsaraote *(n.)* **rulebook**
စည်းမျဉ်းဖြင့် ထိန်းသည် see myin-hpyint hteinsai *(v.)* **regulate**
စည်းမျဉ်းဖြင့် ချုပ်ကိုင်သော see myinhpyint chotekinesaw *(adj.)* **rulebound**
စည်းရိုးညှပ်ကတ်ကြေး see roe nyat kaatkyay *(n.)* **shears**
စည်းလုံးခြင်း saeelonechinn *(n.)* **unity**
စည်းလုံးညီညွတ်မှု seelonenyenywatmhu *(n.)* **solidarity**
စည်းလုံးမှု see-lone-mhu *(n.)* **unanimity**
စည်းလုံးသည် seelonesai *(v.)* **unite**
စည်ပင်သာယာ si-pin-tar-yar *(adj.)* **municipal**
စည်ပင်သာယာရေးအဖွဲ့ si-pin-tar-yar-yay-a-phwe *(n.)* **municipality**
စည်ပိုင်း sai-pine *(n.)* **tub**
စည်သွတ်ဘူး si-thut-bu *(n.)* **can**
စည်သွတ်သည် si-thut-the *(v.)* **can**
စည်သွပ်သည် si swut-sai *(v.)* **tin**
စတက်တစ်ပညာ sa taat tait-panyar *(n.)* **statics**
စတင်ဆောင်ရွက်သည် sa-tin-saung-ywet-the *(v.)* **launch**
စတင်တွေ့ရှိသည် sa-tin-tway-shi-the *(v.)* **discover**
စတင်သည် satinsai *(v.)* **start**

စတစ်ကာ sataitkar *(n.)* **sticker**

စတာလင်ပေါင်၊ အလေးချိန် ပေါင် sa-tar-lin-paung , aalayychane paung *(n.)* **pound**

စတိုင်းဆိုင်ကြီး sa-toe-sai-gyi *(n.)* **megastore**

စတီးရွိုက်ဟော်မုန်း sa tee write-hawmone *(n.)* **steroid**

စတုဂံ sa tu gan *(n.)* **quadrilateral**

စတုရန်း saturaann *(n.)* **square**

စတုရန်းပုံ saturaannpone *(adj.)* **square**

စတူဒီယို satuudeyo *(n.)* **studio**

စတော်ဘယ်ရီ sa-tawbhaal-re *(n.)* **strawberry**

စနက်တံ ဖြုတ်သည် sa-nat-tan-phyoke-the *(v.)* **defuse**

စနစ် sa-nit *(n.)* **system**

စနစ်ကျစေသည် sanit kya-say-sai *(v.)* **systematize**

စနစ်ကျသော sanit-kya-saw *(adj.)* **systematic**

စနစ်တကျမရှိသော sa-nit-ta-kya-ma-shi-taw *(adj.)* **haphazard**

စနေ sa-nay *(n.)* **Saturday**

စနောက်ခြင်း sa noutchinn *(n.)* **tease**

စနောက်သည် sa noutsai *(v.)* **tease**

စန္ဒကူး san-da-kuu *(n.)* **sandalwood**

စန္ဒရား san-da-rar *(n.)* **piano**

စန္ဒရားဆရာ san-da-rar-sa-rar *(n.)* **pianist**

စန်ထရိုမဲမပါသော san-hta-yo-mal-ma-par-taw *(adj.)* **acentric**

စပျစ်ပင် sa pyitpin *(n.)* **vine**

စပျစ်ရည်ထည့်သည့် ဖလား sa-pyit-yay-htae-the-pha-lar *(n.)* **chalice**

စပျစ်သီး sa-pyit-thee *(n.)* **grape**

စပျစ်သီးခြောက် sa pyit see-chauk *(n.)* **raisin**

စပွန်ဆာပေးသူ sapwansar payysuu *(n.)* **sponsor**

စပါးကြီးမြွေ sa-par-gyi-mway *(n.)* **boa**

စပါးပင် saparrpin *(n.)* **rice**

စပါးအုံး sa-ba-aone *(n.)* **python**

စပိန် sapein *(adj.)* **Spanish**

စပိန်ဂီတာတေးသံအက sa-pain-gi-tar-tay-tan-a-ka *(n.)* **flamenco**

စပိန်နိုင်ငံသား hcapeinninenganarr *(n.)* **Spaniard**

စပိန်ဘာသာစကား sapeinbharsarsakarr *(n.)* **Spanish**

စပိန်ရွက်သင်္ဘော sa-pain-ywet-tin-baw *(n.)* **carrack**

စပိန်အက sa-pain-a-ka *(n.)* **bolero**

စပုတ်တိုင် sa pote-tine *(n.)* **spoke**

စပ်စုသည် sat-susai *(v.)* **pry**

စပ်စုသော sat-su-taw *(adj.)* **curious**

စပ်ဆိုသည် sat-so-the *(v.)* **compose**

စပ်သော၊ အမွှေးအကြိုင်ကဲသော sat saw, a hmway a kyaine kellsaw *(adj.)* **spicy**

စမုန်စပါး sa-hmone-sa-par *(n.)* **aniseed**

စမုန်နက် sa-hmone-nat *(n.)* **fennel**

စမ်း၊ ပြန်ကန်နိုင်သော သတ္တိ၊ စပရိန် sam , pyan kaanninesaw satti , sprein *(n.)* **spring**

စမ်းကြည့်ခြင်း sam-kyi-chinn *(n.)* **try**

စမ်းချောင်း samchaungg *(n.)* **stream**

စမ်းချောင်းကလေး san-chaung-ka-lay *(n.)* **beck**

စမ်းတံ၊ အာကာသ စူးစမ်းရေးယာဉ် sam tan , aarkars suusam rayyyarin *(n.)* **probe**

စမ်းတဝါးဝါး ဖြစ်နေသည် san-ta-war-war-phit-nay-the *(v.)* **fumble**
စမ်းသပ်ကြည့်ရှုခြင်း san-that-kyi-shu-chin *(n.)* **audition**
ဈာန်မဝင်သော zan mawinsaw *(adj.)* **uninspired**
ဈာပနာပို့ယဉ်တန်း zar-pa-nar-poe-yin-tan *(n.)* **cortege**
ဈေး zay *(n.)* **bazaar**
ဈေးကျအောင် လုပ်သည် zay-kya-aung-lote-the *(v.)* **cheapen**
ဈေးကြီးသော zay-kyi-taw *(adj.)* **expensive**
ဈေးကွက်၊ ဈေး zay-kwat, zay *(n.)* **market**
ဈေးကွက်ပမာဏ zay-kwat-pa-mar-na *(n.)* **market share**
ဈေးကွက်သုတေသန zay-kwat-thu-tay-ta-na *(n.)* **market research**
ဈေးဆစ်သည် zay-sit-the *(v.)* **haggle**
ဈေးနှုန်း zayy-hnone *(n.)* **price**
ဈေးနှုန်းစာရင်း syaayyhnonesarrinn *(n.)* **tariff**
ဈေးနှုန်းသတ်မှတ်သည် zayy-hnone-saatmatsai *(v.)* **price**
ဈေးပွဲ zay-pwe *(n.)* **mart**
ဈေးပေါသော zay-paw-taw *(adj.)* **cheap**
ဈေးမကြီးခြင်း zay-ma-kyi-chin *(n.)* **affordability**
ဈေးဝယ် zay-wal *(n.)* **customer**
ဈေးဝယ်ခြင်း syaayywaalchinn *(n.)* **shopping**
ဈေးဝယ်စွဲလမ်းခြင်း hcyaayywaalhcwallamhkyinn *(n.)* **shopaholism**
ဈေးဝယ်စွဲလမ်းသူ hcyaayywaal hcwal lamsuu *(n.)* **shopaholic**
ဈေးဝယ်ရန် စာရင်း syaayywaalraan sarrinn *(n.)* **shopping list**
ဈေးဝယ်လက်တွန်းလှည်း syaayywaal laat twannhlaee *(n.)* **shopping cart**
ဈေးဝယ်သည် syaayywaalsai *(v.)* **shop**
ဈေးသည် hcyaayysai *(n.)* **shopkeep**
စရိတ် sa-yeik *(n.)* **expense**
စရိုက် za-yite *(n.)* **character**
စရိုက်တူသော sa-yeik-tu-taw *(adj.)* **congenial**
စွက်ဖက်တတ်သော swat-hpat-tat-taw *(adj.)* **officious**
စွက်ဖက်သည် swat-phat-the *(v.)* **meddle**
စွန် soon *(n.)* **kite**
စွန့်စားခန်း sunt-sar-khan *(n.)* **adventure**
စွန့်စားမှု sunt-sar-khan *(n.)* **glitch**
စွန့်စားမှု ပြုသည် sunt-sar-mu-pyu-the *(v.)* **glitch**
စွန့်စားသည် sunt-sar-the *(v.)* **exploit**
စွန့်စားသော sunt-sar-taw *(adj.)* **adventurous**
စွန့်ပစ်ပစ္စည်း swunt paitpyit-saee *(n.)* **waste**
စွန့်ပစ်သည်၊ လွှင့်ပစ်သည် sunt-pyit-the, hlwint-pyit-the *(v.)* **discard**
စွန့်ပယ်သည် sunt-pal-the *(v.)* **abjure**
စွန့်ပယ်သူ sunt-pal-thu *(n.)* **abjurer**
စွန့်ရဲသော sunt-yaal-taw *(adj.)* **venturous**
စွန့်လွှတ်ကြောင်း တရားဝင်စာ swunt-lwut-kyaungg-tararrwinsar *(n.)* **waiver**
စွန့်လွှတ်ခြင်း swant lwutchinn *(n.)* **renunciation**
စွန့်လွှတ်ရသော swant lwutrasaw *(adj.)* **sacrificial**

စွန့်လွှတ်သည် sont-lut-the *(v.)* **abandon**

စွန့်သည် sunt-the *(v.)* **desist**

စွန့်ဦးတည်ထွင်လုပ်ငန်းရှင် shwunt-oo-the-htwin-lote-ngan-shin *(n.)* **entrepreneur**

စွန်းထင်းသည် soon-htin-the *(v.)* **tincture**

စွပ်ကျယ်အင်္ကျီ swut kyaal aainkyae *(n.)* **vest**

စွပ်စွဲချက် sut-swal-chat *(n.)* **accusal**

စွပ်စွဲပြစ်တင်ခြင်း sut-swal-pyit-tin-chin *(n.)* **impeachment**

စွပ်စွဲပြစ်တင်သည် sut-swal-pyit-tin-the *(v.)* **impeach**

စွပ်စွဲရှုတ်ချခြင်း sut-swal-shoke-cha-chin *(n.)* **denunciation**

စွပ်စွဲသည် sut-swal-the *(v.)* **accuse**

စွပ်စွဲသူ sut-swal-thu *(n.)* **accuser**

စွပ်စွဲသော sut-swal-taw *(n.)* **accusative**

စွပ်ပြုတ် swutpyote *(n.)* **soup**

စွမက်ခြင်း swal-mat-chin *(n.)* **enamourment**

စွမ်းဆောင်မှု swan-saung-mu *(n.)* **feat**

စွမ်းဆောင်ရည်မြင့်တင်သည် swan-saung-yay-myint-tin-the *(v.)* **empower**

စွမ်းရည် swan-yee *(n.)* **ability**

စွမ်းအင် swan-in *(n.)* **energy**

စွယ်စုံကျမ်း swal-sone-kyan *(n.)* **encyclopedia**

စွယ်စုံရသော swalsonerasaw *(adj.)* **versatile**

စွေသည်၊ စောင်းသည် sway sai, saungg-sai *(v.)* **slant**

စွဲချက်တင်ခြင်း swal-chat-tin-chin *(n.)* **indictment**

စွဲချက်တင်သည် swal-chat-tin-the *(v.)* **indict**

စွဲစေတတ်သော swal-say-tat-taw *(adj.)* **addictive**

စွဲနေသော၊ အားထားနေရသော swal-nay-taw, ar-htar-nay-ya-taw *(adj.)* **dependent**

စွဲမက်စေသည် swal-mat-say-the *(v.)* **fascinate**

စွဲမက်ဖွယ်ကောင်းသော swal maat hpwalkaunggsaw *(adj.)* **sensuous**

စွဲမက်သည် swal-mat-the *(v.)* **enamour**

စွဲမက်သော swal-mat-taw *(adj.)* **enamoured**

စွဲမြဲခြင်း swal-myae-chin *(n.)* **adherence**

စွဲမှတ်အောင် သွန်သင်သည် swal-mat-aung-toon-tin-the *(v.)* **inculcate**

စွဲလန်းမှု swal-lan-mu *(n.)* **affinity**

စွဲလမ်းခြင်း swal-lam-chinn *(n.)* **obsession**

စွဲလမ်းသည် swal-lam-tai *(v.)* **obsess**

စွဲလမ်းအောင် လုပ်သည် swal-lan-aung-lote-the *(n.)* **glam**

စသည် sa-sai *(v.)* **rag**

စအို sa-ao *(n.)* **rectum**

စာ sar *(n.)* **letter**

စား၍ ရသော sar-ywe-ya-taw *(adj.)* **eatable**

စားကျက်တွင် မြက်စားသည် sar-kyat-twin-myat-sar-the *(v.)* **graze**

စားကျက်တွင် လှန်သည် sarr-kyet-twin-hlaan-sai *(v.)* **pasture**

စားကျက်မြေ sarr-kyet-myay *(n.)* **pasture**

စားကောင်းသော sar-kaung-taw *(adj.)* **edible**

စားကောင်းသောက်ဖွယ်အလျှံပယ်ဖြစ်သော sar-kaung-thaut-phwal-a-hlyan-pal-phit-taw *(adj.)* **epicurean**

စားချင့်စဖွယ် sarr chintsahpwal *(adj.)* **toothsome**

စားချင်စိတ် sar-chin-seik *(n.)* **appetite**

စားခွက် sar-khwat *(n.)* **crib**

စားတတ်သော sar-tat-taw *(adj.)* **corrosive**

စားပွဲ sarr-pwal *(n.)* **table**

စားပွဲထိုး sa-pwe-htoe *(n.)* **barman**

စားဖွယ် sar-phwal *(n.)* **eatable**

စားဖိုမှူး sa-pho-hmu *(n.)* **chef**

စားမြုံ့ပြန်ခြင်း sarr myuanpyanchinn *(n.)* **rumination**

စားမြုံ့ပြန်တိရစ္ဆာန် sarr myuan pyantirate-san *(n.)* **ruminant**

စားမြုံ့ပြန်သည် sarr myuanpyansai *(v.)* **ruminate**

စားဝတ်နေရေး ဆင်းရဲခြင်း sarr-waatnayrayy sinn-rell-chinn *(n.)* **privation**

စားသည် sar-the *(v.)* **eat**

စားသုံးခြင်း sar-tone-chin *(n.)* **consumption**

စားသုံးသည် sar-tone-the *(v.)* **consume**

စားသုံးသူ sar-tone-thu *(n.)* **consumer**

စားသောက်ကုန် sar-taut-kone *(n.)* **grocery**

စားသောက်စရာ sarrsoutsarar *(n. pl)* **victuals**

စားသောက်ဆိုင် sarrsoutsine *(n.)* **restaurant**

စားသောက်ဆိုင်ငယ် sar-taut-sai-nge *(n.)* **bistro**

စာ၊ သဝဏ်လွှာ sar, ta-win-hlwar *(n.)* **missive**

စာကျန်၊ အကျအပေါက် sar-kyan,a-kya-pauk *(n.)* **lacuna**

စာကြည့်တိုက် sar-kyi-tite *(n.)* **library**

စာကြည့်တိုက်မှူး sar-kyi-tite-hmu *(n.)* **librarian**

စာကြွင်း sar-kywin *(n.)* **postscript**

စာကလေး sarkalayy *(n.)* **sparrow**

စာချုပ် sar-choke *(n.)* **contract**

စာချုပ်နှင့် ငှားသည် sar-choke-nint-ngar-the *(v.)* **lease**

စာခေါင်းစည်း sar-gaung-see *(n.)* **letterhead**

စာဂျပိုး sar-gya-poe *(n.)* **bookworm**

စာစစ် sar-sit *(n.)* **examiner**

စာစဉ် sarsin *(n.)* **series**

စာစီသမား sar-si-ta-mar *(n.)* **compositor**

စာစောင် sar-saung *(n.)* **booklet**

စာဆိုတော် sar-so-taw *(n.)* **laureate**

စာညွှန့် sar-nyunt *(n.)* **cameo**

စာညွှန့်ပေါင်း sar-nyunt-paung *(n.)* **anthology**

စာညှပ်၊ မှတ်ခြင်း sar-nyat, mote-chin *(n.)* **bookmark**

စာတတ်မြောက်ခြင်း sar-tat-myauk-chin *(n.)* **literacy**

စာတတ်မြောက်သော sar-tat-myauk-taw *(adj.)* **literate**

စာတန်း၊ ကတ်ပြား sar-taann , kaatpyarr *(n.)* **tag**

စာတမ်း sartam *(n.)* **thesis**

စာတမ်းထိုးသည် sar-tan-htoe-the *(v.)* **blazon**

စာတမ်းဖတ်ပွဲ sartamhpaatpwal *(n.)* **symposium**

စာတမ်းရှင် sar-tan-shin *(n.)* **essayist**

စာတွဲ၊ ဖိုလ်ဒါ sar-twe, fo-dar *(n.)* **folder**

စာတို sar-to *(n.)* **message**

စာတိုက် sartite *(n.)* **post-office**

စာတိုက်ဗိုလ် sar-tite-bo *(n.)* **postmaster**

စာထွင်းရှုံပြား hcar htwin rwanpyarr *(n.)* **scratchboard**

စာထွင်းသော hcar htwinsaw *(adj.)* **scratched**

စာနာစကားပြောသည် sar-nar-sa-kar-pyaw-the *(v.)* **commiserate**

စာနာစိတ်ကင်းမဲ့သော sar-nar-seik-kin-mae-taw *(adj.)* **insensitive**

စာနာစိတ်ကင်းသော sar-nar-seik-kin-taw *(adj.)* **callous**

စာနာတတ်သည် sar-nar-tat-the *(v.)* **humanize**

စာနာမှု sarnarmhu *(n.)* **solicitude**

စာနာသော sarnarsaw *(adj.)* **sympathetic**

စာပို့၊ စာတိုက်မှ ပေးပို့သော sarphoet, sar-tite-mha payy-phoet-saw *(adj.)* **postal**

စာပို့ခ sarphoet-hka *(n.)* **postage**

စာပို့တမန် sar-po-ta-man *(n.)* **messenger**

စာပို့သည် sar-poe-the *(v.)* **mail**

စာပို့သမား sar-phoet-samarr *(n.)* **postman**

စာပုဒ် sar-pike *(n.)* **paragraph**

စာပေ sar-pay *(n.)* **literature**

စာပေးခြင်း sarpayychinn *(n.)* **serve**

စာပေဝေဖန်ရေးသမား sar-pay-wai-phan-yay-ta-mar *(n.)* **litterateur**

စာပေအနုပညာကို မတိမ်းမယွင်း ထိန်းသိမ်းလိုသူ sar-pay-aanu-pa-nyar-ko ma taim ma-ywin hteinsaim losuu *(n.)* **purist**

စာဖတ်ဝါသနာကြီးသော sar-phat-war-ta-nar-kyi-taw *(adj.)* **bookish**

စာဖတ်သူ sarhpaatsuu *(n.)* **reader**

စာဖျက် sar-phat *(n.)* **burlesque**

စာဖြင့် sar-phit *(adv.)* **post**

စာမတတ်ခြင်း sar-ma-tat-chin *(n.)* **illiteracy**

စာမတတ်သော sar-ma-tat-taw *(adj.)* **illiterate**

စာမျက်နှာ sar-myet-nhar *(n.)* **page**

စာမေးပွဲ sar-may-pwe *(n.)* **examination**

စာမေးပွဲ၊ ဆေးစစ်ခြင်း sarmayypwal , sayysitchinn *(n.)* **test**

စာမေးပွဲကြီးကြပ်သူ sarmayypwal kyeekyautsuu *(n.)* **proctor**

စာမေးပွဲကြီးကြပ်သူအဖြစ် ဆောင်ရွက်သည် sarmayypwal kyeekyautsuu-aphit-saung-ywat-the *(v.)* **proctor**

စာမေးပွဲစောင့်ခြင်း sar-may-pwe-saunt-chin *(n.)* **invigilation**

စာမေးပွဲစောင့်သည် sar-may-pwe-saunt-the *(v.)* **invigilate**

စာမေးပွဲစောင့်သူ sar-may-pwe-saunt-thu *(n.)* **invigilator**

စာရင်း sa-yin *(n.)* **catalogue**

စာရင်း၊ တာလီ sarrinn , tarle *(n.)* **tally**

စာရင်းကိုင် sar-yin-kaing *(n.)* **accountant**

စာရင်းကိုင်ပညာ sar-yin-kaing-pyin-nyar *(n.)* **accountancy**

စာရင်းချုပ်သည် sar-rinn-chote-sai *(v.)* **total**

စာရင်းစစ် sa-yin-sit *(n.)* **audit**

စာရင်းစာရွက် sa-yin-sar-ywet *(n.)* **docket**

စာရင်းစာအုပ် sa-yin-sar-oak *(n.)* **ledger**

စာရင်းပြုစုသည် sa-yin-pyu-su-the *(v.)* **list**

စာရင်းရှင်း ဖျက်သိမ်းခြင်း sa-yin-shin-phat-thein-chin *(n.)* **liquidation**

စာရင်းရှင်း ဖျက်သိမ်းသည် sa-yin-shin-phat-thein-the *(v.)* **liquidate**

စာရင်းရှင်အပ်ငွေ sa-yin-shin-at-ngwe *(n.)* **current account**

စာရင်းသွင်းသည် sarrinn-swinsai *(v.)* **register**

စာရင်းအင်းပညာရှင် sarrinnaainnpanyar-shin *(n.)* **statistician**

စာရွက် sarr-rwat *(n.)* **paper**

စာရွက်စာတမ်း sar-ywet-sar-tan *(n.)* **document**

စာရွက်ထည့်အိတ် sarr-rwat-htaee-ate *(n.)* **paper bag**

စာရှင်းရှင်းသည်၊ အခြေချသည် sar hlyinnshinn sai, aachaychasai *(v.)* **settle**

စာရူး sar-yuu *(n.)* **bibliophile**

စာရေး sar-yay *(n.)* **clerk**

စာရေးကိရိယာ sarrayyka-ri-yar *(n.)* **stationery**

စာရေးကိရိယာဆိုင်ရှင် sarrayyka-ri-yarsine-shin *(n.)* **stationer**

စာရေးစားပွဲ sar-yay-sa-pwe *(n.)* **desk**

စာရေးစားပွဲမျက်နှာပြင် sar-yay-sa-pwe-myat-nar-pyi *(n.)* **desktop**

စာရေးစာချီနှင့်ဆိုင်သော sar-yay-sar-chi-nint-sai-taw *(adj.)* **clerical**

စာရေးဆရာ sarrayysarar *(n.)* **writer**

စာရေးသည် sar-rayy-sai *(v.)* **pen**

စာရေးသူ sar-yay-thu *(n.)* **author**

စာလုံးကြီးဖြင့် ရေးသည် sar-lone-kyi-phit-yay-the *(v.)* **capitalize**

စာလုံးစောင်း sar-lone-saung *(n.)* **italics**

စာလုံးနောက်တစ်လုံး sar-lone-naut-ta-lone *(adj.)* **adscript**

စာလုံးပေါင်း sarlonepaungg *(n.)* **spelling**

စာလုံးပေါင်းဆိုင်ရာ ပညာ sar-lone-paung-sine-yar-pin-nyar *(adj.)* **orthographic**

စာလုံးပေါင်းဆိုင်ရာ ပညာရှင် sar-lone-paung-sine-yar-pin-nyar-shin *(n.)* **orthographer**

စာလုံးပေါင်းသည် sarlonepaunggsai *(v.)* **spell**

စာလုံးရုပ်ပုံပါကတ် sar-lone-yoke-pon-par-kat *(n.)* **flashcard**

စာဝင်ပုံး sar-win-pone *(n.)* **inbox**

စာဝှက်ရေးနည်း sar-hwat-yay-nee *(n.)* **cypher**

စာဝါငှက် sar-war-ngat *(n.)* **canary**

စာဝေခြင်း၊ ပေးပို့ခြင်း၊ မီးဖွားခြင်း sar-wai-chin, pay-poe-chin, mee-phwar-chin *(n.)* **delivery**

စာသင်ခန်း sar-tin-khan *(n.)* **classroom**

စာသင်ပြခြင်း sarsinpyachinn *(n.)* **teaching**

စာသား sarsarr *(n.)* **text**

စာဟောပွဲ sar haw-pwal *(n.)* **recitation**

စာဟောသည် sar-hawsai *(v.)* **recite**

စာအဆက်အသွယ် sar-a-sat-a-twal *(n.)* **correspondence**

စာအမှားပြင်သည် sar-a-mar-pyin-the *(v.)* **emend**

စာအိတ် sar-aik *(n.)* **envelope**

စာအုပ် sar-oak *(n.)* **book**

စာအုပ်စင် sar-oak-sin *(n.)* **bookstall**

စာအုပ်ဆိုင် sar-oak-sai *(n.)* **bookshop**

စာအုပ်တစ်အုပ်တွင် အဓိကစာသားတစ်လျှောက်လို့ အစ်ကပ် hcaraotetaitaotetwin aadhik hcarsarr tait shoutlhoet aaitkaut *(n.)* **sidebox**

စာအုပ်ပုံနှိပ်သမိုင်း sar-oak-pon-nait-ta-mai *(n.)* **bibliography**

စာအုပ်ပုံနှိပ်သမိုင်းဆရာ sar-oak-pon-nait-ta-mai-sa-yar *(n.)* **bibliographer**

စာအုပ်ဖုံး sar-oak-hpone *(n.)* **binding**

စာအုပ်ရောင်းသူ sar-oak-yaung-thu *(n.)* **bookseller**

စိစစ်ခြင်း sisitchinn *(n.)* **scrutiny**

စိစစ်ခြင်း၊ စစ်မေးခြင်း si-sit-chin, sit-may-chin *(n.)* **interrogation**

စိစစ်ခြင်း၊ အတည်ပြုခြင်း sisit chinn , aataipyuchinn *(n.)* **verification**
စိစစ်သည်၊ စစ်မေးသည် si-sit-the, sit-may-the *(v.)* **interrogate**
စိစစ်သည်၊ အတည်ပြုသည် sisit sai , aataipyusai *(v.)* **verify**
စိတ် seik *(n.)* **mind**
စိတ်၊ ဝိညာဉ် sate , winyin *(n.)* **spirit**
စိတ်၊ ဝိညာဉ်ဆိုင်ရာ sate, winyarinsinerar *(adj.)* **psychic**
စိတ်ကစဉ့်ကလျားရောဂါ sate ka sink lyarrrawgar *(n.)* **schizophrenia**
စိတ်ကစဉ့်ကလျားရောဂါဖိစီးနေသော sate ka sink lyarr rawgar hpiseenaysaw *(adj.)* **schizophreniac**
စိတ်ကြိုက် sate-kyaite *(adj.)* **optional**
စိတ်ကြိုက်ဘာသာရပ် seik-kyaik-bar-tar-yat *(n.)* **hobbyhorse**
စိတ်ကြီးဝင်သော mar na htaung lwannsaw *(adj.)* **vain**
စိတ်ကို လှုပ်ရှားထိခိုက်စေနိုင်သော seik-ko-lote-shar-hti-khaik-say-nai-taw *(adj.)* **emotive**
စိတ်ကိုင်းညွတ်မှု ရှိသည် sate-kine-nyut-mhu-shi-tai *(v.)* **orient**
စိတ်ကုထုံး sate-ku-htone *(n.)* **psychotherapy**
စိတ်ကူး၊ ဖန်စီပစ္စည်း seik-ku, phan-si-pyit-see *(n.)* **fancy**
စိတ်ကူးကြည့်သည် sate-kuu-kyi-sai *(v.)* **picture**
စိတ်ကူးကောင်းသူ satekuu kaunggsuu *(n.)* **visionary**
စိတ်ကူးခြင်း၊ သန္ဓေတည်ခြင်း seik-khu-chin, ta-day-tal-chin *(n.)* **conception**
စိတ်ကူးစိတ်သန်း seik-ku-seik-tan *(n.)* **imagination**
စိတ်ကူးဉာဏ်ရှိသော seik-ku-nyan-shi-taw *(adj.)* **imaginative**
စိတ်ကူးဖြင့် ဖန်တီးသော seik-ku-phit-phan-tee-taw *(adj.)* **fictitious**
စိတ်ကူးယဉ်ခြင်း satekuu yinchinn *(n.)* **sentiment**
စိတ်ကူးယဉ်ဆန်သော htwatsai *(adj.)* **utopian**
စိတ်ကူးယဉ်တတ်သော seik-ku-yin-tat-taw *(adj.)* **fanciful**
စိတ်ကူးယဉ်ဘဝ seik-khu-yin-ba-wa *(n.)* **dreamworld**
စိတ်ကူးယဉ်လောက satekuu yinsaansaw *(n.)* **utopia**
စိတ်ကူးယဉ်ဝါဒ seik-ku-yin-wa-da *(n.)* **idealism**
စိတ်ကူးယဉ်သည် seik-ku-yin-the *(v.)* **imagine**
စိတ်ကူးယဉ်သည်၊ ဆန္ဒရှိသည် seik-ku-yin-the, san-da-shi-the *(v.)* **fancy**
စိတ်ကူးယဉ်သော satekuu yainsaw *(adj.)* **sentimental**
စိတ်ကူးယဉ်အိပ်မက် seik-ku-yin-eain-mat *(n.)* **fantasy**
စိတ်ကူးသက်သက် seik-ku-tat-tat *(adj.)* **imaginary**
စိတ်ကူးသည် satekuusai *(v.)* **theorize**
စိတ်ကောက်တတ်သော sate-kaut-taat-taw *(adj.)* **petulant**
စိတ်ကောင်းစေတနာ seik-kaung-say-ta-nar *(n.)* **goodwill**
စိတ်ခံစားမှု seik-khan-sar-mu *(n.)* **emotion**
စိတ်ချဉ်ပေါက်ခြင်း sate-chin-pout-chinn *(n.)* **petulance**
စိတ်ချမ်းသာမှု seik-chan-tar-mu *(n.)* **fulfilment**

စိတ်ချရသော သက်သေမဟုတ်သည့် တစ်ဦးချင်းစီအမြင် seik-cha-ya-taw-thet-tay-ma-hote-the-ta-oo-chin-si-a-myin *(n.)* **anecdote**

စိတ်ချလက်ချရှိစေသည် Satecha-laatcha shisaysai *(v.)* **reassure**

စိတ်ချောက်ချားမှု sate chauk charrmhu *(n.)* **shock**

စိတ်ချောက်ချားရောဂါ seik-chauk-char-yay-gar *(n.)* **hysteria**

စိတ်ငြိမ်စေသည့် အာနိသင်ရှိသော seik-nyein-say-the-ar-ni-tin-shi-taw *(adj.)* **calmative**

စိတ်ငြိမ်ဆေး sate ngyaainsayy *(n.)* **tranquillizer**

စိတ်ငြိမ်ဆေးတိုက်သည် sate ngyaain sayy titesai *(v.)* **sedate**

စိတ်ငြိမ်သော sate ngyeinsaw *(adj.)* **sedative**

စိတ်ငြိုငြင်စရာ sate-ngyo-ngyin-sa-yar *(n.)* **nuisance**

စိတ်စွမ်းအင်ဖြင့် ပစ္စည်းရွှေ့ခြင်း hcate swmaan-in-hpyint pyit-cee rwae chinn *(n.)* **telekinesis**

စိတ်စွမ်းအင်ဖြင့် ပစ္စည်းရွှေ့ခြင်းဆိုင်ရာ hcate swmaan-in-hpyint pyit-cee rwae chinn-sinerar *(adj.)* **telekinetic**

စိတ်စွဲလမ်းမှု sate swal lam-mhu *(n.)* **preoccupation**

စိတ်ဆတ်သော sate saatsaw *(adj.)* **temperamental**

စိတ်ဆန္ဒ sate-san-da *(n.)* **willingness**

စိတ်ဆန္ဒပြင်းပြသော seik san-da-pyin-pya-taw *(adj.)* **athirst**

စိတ်ဆိုးစေသည် seik-soe-say-the *(v.)* **irk**

စိတ်ဆိုးလွယ်သော seik-soe-lwal-taw *(adj.)* **choleric**

စိတ်ဆိုးသည် satesoesai *(v.)* **vex**

စိတ်ဆိုးသော seik-soe-taw *(adj.)* **cross**

စိတ်ဇော seik-zaw *(n.)* **ardour**

စိတ်ညှို့ပညာ seik-nyo-pyin-nyar *(n.)* **hypnotism**

စိတ်တိုစရာ seik-toe-sa-yar *(adj.)* **irksome**

စိတ်တိုစရာကောင်းသော seik-toe-sa-yar-kaung-taw *(adj.)* **annoying**

စိတ်တုန်လှုပ်စေသည် seik-tone-hlote-say-the *(v.)* **agitate**

စိတ်တူကိုယ်တူ လူသိုက် seik-tu-koe-tu-lu-theik *(n.)* **cohort**

စိတ်ထင် seik-htin *(n.)* **hunch**

စိတ်ထားကို ပြသည် seik-htar-ko-pya-the *(v.)* **evince**

စိတ်ထိခိုက်ခံစားမှု seik-hti-khite-khan-sar-mu *(n.)* **pang**

စိတ်ထိခိုက်လွယ်ခြင်း hcate htihkite lwalhkyinn *(n.)* **sentience**

စိတ်ထိခိုက်သည် seik-hti-keik-the *(v.)* **aggrieve**

စိတ်ထိန်းနိုင်ခြင်း sate hteinninechinn *(n.)* **self-control**

စိတ်ဒဏ်ရာ satedanrar *(n.)* **trauma**

စိတ်ဒဏ်ရာရသော satedanrarrasaw *(adj.)* **traumatic**

စိတ်ဓာတ် seik-dat *(n.)* **morale**

စိတ်ဓာတ်ကျခြင်း seik-dat-kya-chin *(n.)* **depression**

စိတ်ဓာတ်ကျဆင်းစေသည် seik-dat-kya-sin-say-the *(v.)* **demoralize**

စိတ်ဓာတ်ကျဆင်းသည် seik-dat-kya-sin-say-the *(v.)* **depress**

စိတ်ဓာတ်ကျသည် seik-dat-kya-the *(v.)* **discourage**

စိတ်ဓာတ်တက်လာခြင်း satedhrat taat-larchinn *(n.)* **uplift**

စိတ်ဓာတ်မြှင့်တင်ရေး seik-dat-hmyint-tin-yay *(n.)* **edification**
စိတ်ဓာတ်မြှင့်တင်သည် seik-dat-hmyint-tin-the *(v.)* **edify**
စိတ်ဓာတ်မြှင့်ပေးသည် satedhrat myint-payysai *(v.)* **uplift**
စိတ်နှံ့ခြင်း sate nhaanchinn *(n.)* **sanity**
စိတ်နှစ်ခွဖြစ်ခြင်း seik-na-kwa-phit-chin *(n.)* **ambivalence**
စိတ်နှစ်ခွဖြစ်သော seik-na-kwa-phit-taw *(adj.)* **ambivalent**
စိတ်နှစ်ခွမဖြစ်ခြင်း sate na hkwa ma-hpyit-chinn *(n.)* **unambivalence**
စိတ်နေစိတ်ထား seik-nay-seik-htar *(n.)* **mood**
စိတ်နေသဘောထား seik-nay-ta-bar-htar *(n.)* **mentality**
စိတ်နောက်ကျိသော seik-naut-kyi-taw *(adj.)* **distraught**
စိတ်ပညာ sate-panyar *(n.)* **psychology**
စိတ်ပညာရှင် sate-panyarshin *(n.)* **psychologist**
စိတ်ပျက်စရာ seik-pyat-sa-yar *(adj.)* **dismal**
စိတ်ပျက်ဖွယ်ကောင်းသော seik-pyat-phwal-kaung-taw *(adj.)* **lamentable**
စိတ်ပျက်ဖွယ်ရာ satepyethpwalrar *(adj.)* **tiresome**
စိတ်ပျက်ရသည် seik-pyat-ya-the *(v.)* **disappoint**
စိတ်ပျက်လက်ပျက်ဖြစ်ခြင်း seik-pyat-lat-pyat-phit-chin *(n.)* **dejection**
စိတ်ပျက်သည် seik-pyat-the *(v.)* **disenchant**
စိတ်ပျက်အားလျော့သည် seik-pyat-arr-shawt-the *(v.)* **dishearten**
စိတ်ပြောင်းလွယ်သော seik-pyaung-lwal-taw *(adj.)* **moody**
စိတ်ပါဝင်စားမှု seik-par-win-sar-mu *(n.)* **motivation**
စိတ်ပိုင်းဆိုင်ရာ sate-pinesinerar *(adj.)* **psychological**
စိတ်ပိုင်းဖြတ်ခြင်း seik-pai-phat-chin *(n.)* **determination**
စိတ်ပိုင်းသည် satepinesai *(v.)* **segment**
စိတ်ပုတီး sateputee *(n.)* **rosary**
စိတ်ပေါက်ခြင်း seik-pauk-chin *(n.)* **impulse**
စိတ်ဖြာသုံးသပ်ခြင်း seik-phyar-tone-tat-chin *(n.)* **analysis**
စိတ်ဖြာသုံးသပ်သည် seik-phyar-tone-tat-the *(v.)* **analyse**
စိတ်ဖြာသုံးသပ်သူ seik-phyar-tone-tat-thu *(n.)* **analyst**
စိတ်ဖြာသုံးသပ်သော seik-phyar-tone-tat-thaw *(adj.)* **analytical**
စိတ်ဖိစီးသည် seik-phi-see-the *(v.)* **deject**
စိတ်ဖောက်ပြန်သော seik-phaut-pyan-taw *(adj.)* **deranged**
စိတ်မကြည်လင်ဖွယ်ဖြစ်သော seik-ma-kyi-lin-phwal-phit-taw *(adj.)* **cheerless**
စိတ်မချဖွယ် sate-ma-cha-hpwal *(adj.)* **suspect**
စိတ်မချမ်းသာသော satemachamsarsaw *(adj.)* **wretched**
စိတ်မချရသော satemacharasaw *(adj.)* **unreliable**
စိတ်မနှံ့သော seik-ma-hnant-taw *(adj.)* **insane**
စိတ်မပါ့တပါ sate-ma par tapar *(adv.)* **tepidly**
စိတ်မပါခြင်း sait-ma-par-chin *(n.)* **apathy**
စိတ်မပါသော sate-ma-parsaw *(adj.)* **unappealing**

စိတ်မရှည်ခြင်း seik-ma-shay-chin *(n.)* **impatience**
စိတ်မရှည်သော seik-ma-shay-taw *(adj.)* **impatient**
စိတ်မြန်လက်မြန်လုပ်ခြင်း seik-myan-lat-myan-lote-chin *(n.)* **impetuosity**
စိတ်မြန်လက်မြန်လုပ်သော seik-myan-lat-myan-lote-taw *(adj.)* **impetuous**
စိတ်မဝင်စားခြင်း seik-ma-win-sar-chin *(n.)* **indifference**
စိတ်မှန်း sate-mhan *(n.)* **surmise**
စိတ်မှန်းသက်သက်၊ ကို ထောက်၍ sate mhan saat-saat ko htout-ywe *(n.)* **supposition**
စိတ်မှန်မှန် satemhaanmhaan *(adv.)* **sanely**
စိတ်မှန်သော satemhaansaw *(adj.)* **sane**
စိတ်မူမမှန်သည့် စိတ်ရောဂါ seik-mu-ma-hman-the-seik-yaw-gar *(n.)* **neurosis**
စိတ်ယုတ်စိတ်မာဖြင့် sate yote sate marhpyint *(adv.)* **satanically**
စိတ်ရှည်ခြင်း sate-shi-chinn *(n.)* **patience**
စိတ်ရှည်သော sate-shay-saw *(adj.)* **patient**
စိတ်ရှုပ်ခြင်း seik-shoke-chin *(n.)* **muddle**
စိတ်ရှုပ်စေသည် sate-shote-say-sai *(v.)* **perplex**
စိတ်ရှုပ်ထွေးခြင်း seik-shoke-htway-chin *(n.)* **bewilderment**
စိတ်ရှုပ်ထွေးစေသည် seik-shoke-htway-say-the *(v.)* **bewilder**
စိတ်ရှုပ်ထွေးသည် seik-shote-htway-the *(v.)* **confuse**
စိတ်ရှုပ်ဖွယ်ရာ sate-shote-hpwal-rar *(n.)* **perplexity**
စိတ်ရောဂါကုပညာ saterawgar kupanyar *(n.)* **psychiatry**
စိတ်ရောဂါအထူးကု saterawgaraahtuuku *(n.)* **psychiatrist**
စိတ်လွတ်လက်လွတ် ပြုမူခြင်း sate lwatlaatlwat pyumuuchinn *(n.)* **spree**
စိတ်လှည့်စားမှုကြောင့် နိမိတ်ထင်မြင်သော sate-hlae-sarr-mhu-kyount-ni-mate-htin-myin-saw *(adj.)* **phantasmal**
စိတ်လှုပ်ရှားစေသည် sate-hloat-shar-say-the *(v.)* **excite**
စိတ်လှုပ်ရှားစေသော seik-lote-shar-say-taw *(adj.)* **emotional**
စိတ်လှုပ်ရှားမှု seik-hlote-shar-mu *(n.)* **agitation**
စိတ်လိုက်မာန်ပါ ပြုလုပ်တတ်သော seik-lite-man-par-pyu-lote-tat-taw *(adj.)* **impulsive**
စိတ်လေးခြင်း sate layychinn *(n.)* **premonition**
စိတ်ဝင်စားဖွယ်ကောင်းသော seik-win-sar-phwal-kaung-taw *(adj.)* **interesting**
စိတ်ဝင်စားမှု မရှိသော seik-win-sar-mu-ma-shi-taw *(adj.)* **indifferent**
စိတ်ဝင်စားမှု၊ အကျိုး၊ အတိုး seik-win-sar-mu, a-kyo, a-toe *(n.)* **interest**
စိတ်ဝင်စားသည် seik-win-sar-the *(v.)* **engross**
စိတ်ဝင်စားသည်၊ ခြေပုန်းခုတ်သည် seik-win-sar-the, chay-pone-khote-the *(v.)* **intrigue**
စိတ်ဝင်စားသော seik-win-sar-taw *(adj.)* **interested**
စိတ်ဝင်တစားရှိစေသည် seik-win-ta-sar-shi-say-the *(v.)* **enliven**
စိတ်ဝိညာဉ် sate wi nyari *(n.)* **pneuma**
စိတ်ဝိညာဉ်၊ ဖြစ်စဉ်များကို လေ့လာသော ပညာ sate-wi-nyi , hpyit-sin-myarr-ko-lae-lar-saw-pa-nyar *(n.)* **pneumatology**
စိတ်ဝိညာဉ်၊ ဖြစ်စဉ်များကို လေ့လာသော ပညာနှင့် ဆိုင်သော sate-wi-nyi , hpyit-sin-myarr-ko-lae-lar-saw-pa-nyar-nint-sine-saw *(adj.)* **pneumatological**

စိတ်ဝေဒနာရှင် sate-waydanarshin *(n.)* **psychopath**
စိတ်သက်သာမှု satesaatsarmhu *(n.)* **solace**
စိတ်သက်သာမှု ပေးသည် satesaatsarmhu payysai *(v.)* **solace**
စိတ်သဘော satesabhaw *(n.)* **psyche**
စိတ်သောကရောက်သည် seik-taw-ka-yauk-the *(v.)* **distress**
စိတ်အနှောင့်အယှက် sate a naut-aa-shaat *(n.)* **vexation**
စိတ်အနှောင့်အယှက်ဖြစ်စေသည် seik-a-naut-a-shat-phit-say-the *(v.)* **madden**
စိတ်အပြောင်းအလဲမြန်သော seik-a-pyaung-a-lal-myan-taw *(adj.)* **mercurial**
စိတ်အားတက်ကြွသည် seik-arr-tat-kwa-the *(v.)* **motivate**
စိတ်အားထက်သန်ခြင်း sate-aarr htaat saan-chinn *(n.)* **zeal**
စိတ်အားထက်သန်စွာ seik-arr-htet-tan-swar *(adv.)* **avidly**
စိတ်အားထက်သန်မှု sate-ar-htaat-saan-mhu *(n.)* **passion**
စိတ်အားထက်သန်သော sate-aarr htaat saansaw *(adj.)* **zealous**
စိတ်အာရုံချောက်ချားခြင်း seik-arr-yone-chauk-char-chin *(n.)* **hallucination**
စိတ်အိုက်သော sate aitesaw *(adj.)* **tense**
စိတ်အေးချမ်းသော sate aayyhkyamsaw *(adj.)* **placative**
စိန် sein *(n.)* **diamond**
စိန်ခေါ်ချက် sein-khaw-chat *(n.)* **challenge**
စိန်ရွှေရတနာဆိုင်ရှင် sein-shwe-ya-da-nar-sine-shin *(n.)* **jeweller**
စိန်အဆိပ် sein-a-seik *(n.)* **arsenic**
စိမ့်၊ ရွှံ့ညွန် seint , shwan-nywan *(n.)* **swamp**
စိမ့်စိုအေးစက်သော seint-so-aye-sat-taw *(adj.)* **dank**
စိမ့်ပေါက် seint-pauk *(n.)* **leak**
စိမ့်မြေ saint-myay *(n.)* **everglade**
စိမ့်မြေထူသောကုန်းမြေ seint-myay-htu-taw-kone-myay *(n.)* **bogland**
စိမ့်မဝင်နိုင်သော seint ma-win-ninesaw *(adj.)* **repellent**
စိမ့်ဝင်ပျံ့နှံ့ခြင်း seint-win-pyant-nant-chinn *(n.)* **osmosis**
စိမ့်ဝင်ပျံ့နှံ့ခြင်းနည်းဖြင့် ပျံ့နှံ့စေသည် seint-win-pyant-nant-chinn-nae-phint-pyant-nant-say-the *(v.)* **osmose**
စိမ့်သည် saint-tai *(v.)* **ooze**
စိမ်းပြာရောင် sein-pyar-yaung *(n.)* **cyan**
စိမ်းလန်းစိုပြည်သန်စွမ်းသော sein-lan-so-pyay-tan-swan-taw *(adj.)* **lush**
စိမ်းလန်းသော saimlaannsaw *(adj.)* **verdant**
စိမ်းသော sein-taw *(adj.)* **green**
စိမ်ပြေနပြေ လမ်းလျှောက်ခြင်း sin pyay napyay lamshoutchinn *(n.)* **saunter**
စိမ်ပြေနပြေ လမ်းလျှောက်သည် sin pyay napyay lamshoutsai *(v.)* **saunter**
စိမ်ပြေနပြေ လမ်းလျှောက်သူ sin pyay napyay lamshoutsuu *(n.)* **saunterer**
စိမ်ပြေနပြေသွားသည် sein-pyay-na-pyay-twa-the *(v.)* **amble**
စိမ်သည် sinsai *(v.)* **soak**
စိမ်သည်၊ နှစ်မြှုပ်သည် sein-the, nit-hmyoke-the *(v.)* **immerse**
စိမ်သည်၊ သံချပ်ကာသည် sein-sai, san-chat-kar-sai *(v.)* **plate**
စိုးမိုးမှု soe-moe-mu *(n.)* **dominion**
စိုးမိုးသည် soemoesai *(v.)* **rule**
စိုးရိမ်၍ soe-yein-ywe *(conj.)* **lest**

စိုးရိမ်ခြင်း soerinchinn *(n.)* **worry**

စိုးရိမ်ပူပန်ခြင်း soe-yein-pu-pan-chin *(n.)* **dread**

စိုးရိမ်ပူပန်မှုကင်းသော soe-yein-pu-pan-mu-kin-taw *(adj.)* **carefree**

စိုးရိမ်ပူပန်သည် soe-yein-pu-pan-the *(v.)* **fret**

စိုးရိမ်ဖွယ်ရာ soe-yein-phwal-yar *(adj.)* **alarming**

စိုးရိမ်သည် soerinsai *(v.)* **worry**

စိုးရိမ်သော soe-yein-taw *(adj.)* **apprehensive**

စိုက်ကြည့်ခြင်း site kyany-chinn *(n.)* **stare**

စိုက်ကြည့်သည် site kyi-sai *(v.)* **stare**

စိုက်ပျိုးထွန်ယက်ခြင်း site-pyo-htun-yat-chin *(n.)* **cultivation**

စိုက်ပျိုးထုတ်ကုန် seik-pyo-htoke-kone *(n.)* **agriproduct**

စိုက်ပျိုးမွေးမြူရေး site-pyo-mway-my-yay *(n.)* **husbandry**

စိုက်ပျိုးမွေးမြူရေးခြံ seik-pyo-mway-my-yay-chan *(n.)* **farm**

စိုက်ပျိုးမွေးမြူရေးခြံငယ် site-pyo-mway-my-yay-chan-nge *(n.)* **croft**

စိုက်ပျိုးရေး seik-pyo-yay *(n.)* **agriculture**

စိုက်ပျိုးရေးဆေးနှင့် ဆိုင်သော seik-pyo-yay-say-nint-sai-taw *(adj.)* **farmaceutical**

စိုက်ပျိုးရေးဓာတုဗေဒနှင့်ဆိုင်သော seik-pyo-yay-dar-du-bay-da-nint-saing-taw *(n.)* **agrochemical**

စိုက်ပျိုးရေးနှင့်ဆိုင်သော seik-pyo-yay-nint-saing-taw *(adj.)* **agricultural**

စိုက်ပျိုးရေးလုပ်ငန်း seik-pyo-yay-lote-ngan *(n.)* **agro-industry**

စိုက်ပျိုးရေးလုပ်သူ seik-pyo-yay-lote-thu *(n.)* **agriculturist**

စိုက်ပျိုးသည်၊ ထွန်ယက်သည် site-pyo-the, htun-yat-the *(v.)* **cultivate**

စိုက်ပျိုးသူ site-pyo-thu *(n.)* **grower**

စိုက်သည် site-sai *(v.)* **plant**

စိုစွတ်သော so-sut-taw *(adj.)* **moist**

စိုစွပ်ခြင်း so swutchinn *(n.)* **wetness**

စိုစွပ်သည် so swutsai *(v.)* **wet**

စိုစွပ်သော so swutsaw *(adj.)* **wet**

စိုထိုင်းစ soe-htai-sa *(n.)* **humidity**

စိုထိုင်းသည် so-htai-the *(v.)* **dampen**

စိုထိုင်းသော soe-htai-taw *(adj.)* **humid**

စိုပြည်နီမြန်းသော so pyi ne myansaw *(adj.)* **ruddy**

စိုရွှဲစေသည် so shwellsaysai *(v.)* **saturate**

စိုသော၊ ထိုင်းသော so-taw, htai-taw *(adj.)* **damp**

စီးကျသည် see kyasai *(v.)* **trickle**

စီးကရက် see-ka-rat *(n.)* **cigarette**

စီးကြောင်းငယ် see kyaungngaal *(n.)* **trickle**

စီးချက်ကျ အစီအစဉ် see-chat-kya-a-si-a-sin *(n.)* **cadence**

စီးချင်းထိုးခြင်း si-chin-htoe-chin *(n.)* **duel**

စီးချင်းထိုးသည် see-chin-htoe-the *(v.)* **duel**

စီးဆင်းနိုင်သော၊ ပြေပြစ်ကြော့ရှင်းသော see-sin-nai-taw, pyay-pyit-kyawt-shin-taw *(adj.)* **fluid**

စီးဆင်းသည် see-sin-the *(v.)* **flow**

စီးဆင်းသွားသည် see-sin-twar-the *(v.)* **drain**

စီးနင်းသည် see-nin-tai *(v.)* **overwhelm**

စီးပွားစီမံချက် see-pwar-see-man-chat *(n.)* **business plan**

စီးပွားဖက်အဖြစ် see-pwarr-hpaat-aa-hpyit *(n.)* **partnership**

စီးပွားရေး see-pwar-yay *(n.)* **business**

စီးပွားရေး ပိုင်နိုင်စွာ လုပ်နိုင်သော see-pwar-yay-pai-nai-swar-lote-nai-taw *(adj.)* **canny**

စီးပွားရေး လုပ်ငန်း see-pwar-yay-lote-ngan *(n.)* **firm**

စီးပွားရေး လုပ်ငန်းရှင်ကြီး see-pwar-yay-lote-ngan-shin-gyi *(n.)* **magnate**

စီးပွားရေး၊ တွက်ခြေကိုက်သော see-pwar-yay, twat-chay-kite-taw *(adj.)* **economic**

စီးပွားရေးကျဆင်းမှု seepwarr-rayykya-sinn-mhu *(n.)* **recession**

စီးပွားရေးသမား see-pwar-yay-ta-mar *(n.)* **businessman**

စီကုံးသည် se-kone-sai *(v.)* **phrase**

စီခနဲ အော်သံ se hkanell aawsan *(n.)* **shriek**

စီးခြင်း၊ ယိုခြင်း si-chin,yo-chin *(n.)* **flow**

စီခြယ်သည် se chaalsai *(v.)* **stud**

စီစဉ်ခင်းကျင်းသည် si-sin-khin-kyin-the *(n.)* **array**

စီစဉ်တကျ၊ အမှာစာ se-zin-ta-kya, a mhar sar *(n.)* **order**

စီစဉ်ထားသည် sesinhtarrsai *(v.)* **schedule**

စီစဉ်သည် se-sin-sai *(v.)* **plan**

စီစီညံညံအသံ si-si-nyan-nyan-a-tan *(n.)* **din**

စီတင် see-tin *(n.)* **cetin**

စီတန်းလမ်းလျှောက်ခြင်း se-taann-lam-shout-chinn *(n.)* **parade**

စီတန်းလှည့်လည်သည် se-taann-hleet-lal-sai *(v.)* **parade**

စီတိုင်လစ်အရက်ပြန် see-tai-lit-a-yat-pyan *(adj.)* **cetylic**

စီမံကိန်း se-man-kein *(n.)* **project**

စီမံကိန်းရေးဆွဲသည် se-man-kein ray-swalsai *(v.)* **project**

စီမံကိန်းအကြမ်း ရေးဆွဲပေးအပ်သော သူ hcemankeinaakyam rayyswalpayyaautsaw suu *(n.)* **schematist**

စီမံခန့်ခွဲရေးနှင့် ဆိုင်သော si-man-khant-kwal-yay-nint-sai-taw *(adj.)* **managerial**

စီမံချက်၊ အကြံအစည် semanchet , aakyaanaasai *(n.)* **scheme**

စီမံခြင်း si-man-chin *(n.)* **management**

စီမံသည် si-man-the *(v.)* **administer**

စီမံအုပ်ချုပ်သူ see-man-oak-choke-thu *(adj.)* **ministrant**

စီရင်ချက်ချသည် si-yin-chat-cha-the *(v.)* **convict**

စီရင်စု se-rinsu *(n.)* **province**

စီရင်ဆုံးဖြတ်ခွင့် အာဏာရှိသော si-yin-sone-phat-khwint-ar-nar-shi-taw *(adj.)* **executive**

စီရင်ဆုံးဖြတ်သည် si-yin-sone-phat-the *(v.)* **adjudge**

စီရင်ပိုင်သူ si-yin-paing-thu *(n.)* **arbiter**

စီရင်သည် si-yin-the *(v.)* **mete**

စုံစမ်းခြင်း sone-san-chin *(n.)* **enquiry**

စုံစမ်းစစ်ဆေးခြင်း sone-san-sit-say-chin *(n.)* **investigation**

စုံစမ်းစစ်ဆေးသည် sone-san-sit-say-the *(v.)* **investigate**

စုံစမ်းမေးမြန်းသည် sone-san-may-myan-the *(n.)* **inquiry**

စုံထောက် sone-htauk *(n.)* **detective**

စုံမှန်ပြောင်း zone-man-pyaung *(n.)* **binoculars**

စုစည်းခြင်း su-see-chin *(n.)* **collection**

စုစည်းသည် su-see-the *(v.)* **collect**

စုစည်းသည်၊ စည်းရုံးသည် su-see-tai, see-rone-tai *(v.)* **organize**

စုစုပေါင်း susupaung *(adj.)* **total**

စုစုပေါင်း၊ အဘက်ဘက် tu-tu-paung, a-bhat-bhat *(adj.)* **overall**
စုဆောင်းမိခြင်း su-saung-mi-chin *(n.)* **accumulation**
စုဆောင်းမိသည် su-saung-mi-the *(v.)* **accumulate**
စုဆောင်းသည် su-saung-the *(v.)* **amass**
စုဆောင်းသူ su-paung-thu *(n.)* **collector**
စုတ်တံ sote-tan *(n.)* **paintbrush**
စုတ်ပျက်သော နေအိမ်နေရာ sote-pyat-taw-nay-eain-nay-yar *(n.)* **doghole**
စုန်းကဝေအတတ် sone-k-way aa-taat *(n.)* **witchcraft**
စုန်းပညာ sone-pyin-nyar *(n.)* **witchery**
စုန်းပူးချိန်တွင် ကူးစက်လာသော ဓာတ်တစ်မျိုး sone-pu-chain-twin-khu-sat-lar-taw-dat-ta-myo *(n.)* **ectoplasm**
စုန်းမ sone-ma *(n.)* **witch**
စုပြုံကျလာခြင်း su-pyone-kya-lar-chin *(n.)* **influx**
စုပြုံသွားသည် su pyuanswarrsai *(v.)* **throng**
စုပုံသည် su-pon-the *(v.)* **heap**
စုပေါင်းညှိနှိုင်းဆောင်ရွက်မှု အကျိုးရလဒ် supaungg nyhainateesaungrwatmhu aakyoeralad *(n.)* **synergy**
စုပေါင်းညှိနှိုင်းမှု supaunggnyhainateemhu *(n.)* **synthesis**
စုပေါင်းသည် su-aung-the *(v.)* **aggregate**
စုပေါင်းသည်၊ ရောသည် su-paung-the, yaw-the *(v.)* **lump**
စုပေါင်းသော su-paung-taw *(adj.)* **collective**
စုပ်ခြင်း sote-chinn *(n.)* **suck**
စုပ်စက် sotesaat *(n.)* **pump**
စုပ်စုသော sat-su-taw *(adj.)* **inquisitive**
စုပ်ထုတ်သည် sote htotesai *(v.)* **pump**
စုပ်ယူခြင်း sote-yu-chin *(n.)* **absorption**
စုပ်ယူနိုင်သော sote-yu-naing-taw *(adj.)* **absorbable**
စုပ်ယူသည် sote-yu-the *(v.)* **absorb**
စုပ်ယူသည်၊ ပိတ်သည် sote-yu-the, pate-the *(v.)* **occlude**
စုပ်ယူသော၊ ပိတ်သော sote-yu-taw, pate-taw *(adj.)* **occlusive**
စုပ်သည် sote-sai *(v.)* **suck**
စုဖွဲ့ခြင်းနှင့်ဆိုင်သော su-phwe-chin-nint-saing-taw *(n.)* **anabolic**
စုဘူး su-bhuu *(n.)* **piggy bank**
စုရုံးလာသည် su-yone-lar-the *(v.)* **congregate**
စုဝေးပွဲ su-way-pwe *(n.)* **assembly**
စုဝေးရန် ဖိတ်ကြားသည် su-way-yan-phite-kyar-the *(v.)* **convene**
စုဝေးသည် su-way-the *(v.)* **assemble**
စုသည် su-the *(v.)* **gather**
စူးစမ်းစိတ် sue-san-seik *(n.)* **curiosity**
စူးစမ်းရှာဖွေခြင်း su-san-shar-phway-chin *(n.)* **discovery**
စူးစမ်းရှာဖွေသည် suusam shar-hpwaysai *(v.)* **quest**
စူးစမ်းလေ့လာရေးခရီး su-san-lay-lar-yay-kha-yee *(n.)* **expedition**
စူးစမ်းသော sue-san-taw *(adj.)* **exquisitive**
စူးစိုက်ထားသော sue-site-htar-taw *(adj.)* **focusing**
စူးစိုက်နှစ်မြှုပ်ထားမှု sue-site-nit-hmyoke-htar-mu *(n.)* **dedication**
စူးစူး sue-sue *(adv.)* **due**
စူးစူးစိုက်စိုက် sue-sue-site-site *(adj.)* **intent**
စူးစူးရှရှ suu suushasha *(adj.)* **shrill**

စူးစူးဝါးဝါး အော်သံ suu suu warrwarr aawsan *(n.)* **scream**
စူးစူးဝါးဝါးအော်သံ suu suu warr war-aawsan *(n.)* **yell**
စူးရှတောက်ပသည် su-sha-taut-pa-the *(v.)* **glare**
စူးရှတောက်ပသော su-sha-taut-pa-taw *(adj.)* **aglare**
စူးရှတောက်ပသော အလင်း su-sha-taut-pa-taw-a-lin *(n.)* **glare**
စူးရှရှ အရသာရှိသော suu-sha-sha aa-rasarshi-saw *(adj)* **zesty**
စူးရှသော sue-sha-taw *(adj.)* **beady**
စူးရှသော၊ စိတ်ဝင်စားသော su-sha-taw, seik-win-sar-taw *(adj.)* **keen**
စူးသည်၊ နာကျင်စေသည် suu sai , narkyinsaysai *(v.)* **sting**
စူစမ်းမိသည် suu sam misai *(v.)* **wonder**
စူပါမင်း၊ အာဂလူ suuparminn , aar-ga-luu *(n.)* **superman**
စေ့စပ်ကြောင်းလမ်းခြင်း၊ ချိန်းဆိုချက် say-sat-kyaung-lan-chin, chain-so-chat *(n.)* **engagement**
စေ့စပ်ဆွေးနွေးခြင်း say-sat-sway-nway-chin *(n.)* **negotiation**
စေ့စပ်ဆွေးနွေးသည် say-sat-sway-nway-the *(v.)* **negotiate**
စေ့စပ်ဆွေးနွေးသူ say-sat-sway-nway-thu *(n.)* **negotiator**
စေ့စပ်ထားသော say-sat-htar-thaw *(adj.)* **betrothed**
စေ့စပ်ထားသော ယောကျ်ား say-sat-htar-taw-yauk-kyar *(n.)* **fiancé**
စေ့စပ်ပေးသည် sae-saut-payysai *(v.)* **reconcile**
စေ့စပ်သေချာသော saesatsay-chaarsaw *(adj.)* **scrupulous**
စေ့စပ်သေချာသော၊ ဂရုစိုက်သော say-sat-tay-char-taw, ga-yu-site-taw *(adj.)* **careful**
စေ့စပ်သော say-sat-taw *(adj.)* **meticulous**
စေ့စေ့စပ်စပ်ကြည့်ရှုစစ်ဆေးသည် saesaesatsat kyany shu sitsayysai *(v.)* **scrutinize**
စေ့ဆော်သည် sae sawsai *(v.)* **prompt**
စေးကပ်ကပ်အရာ say-kat-kat-a-yar *(n.)* **mucilage**
စေးကပ်ကပ်အရာဝတ္ထုဖြင့်ပြုလုပ်သော ငှက်ထောင်ချောက် say-kat-kat-a-yar-wut-htu-phit-pyu-lote-taw-nget-htaung-chauk *(n.)* **birdlime**
စေးကပ်သော sayy kautsaw *(n.)* **sticky**
စေးထန်းထန်း say-htan-htan *(adj.)* **clammy**
စေးပျစ်ပျစ် ဖြစ်သော say-pyit-pyit-phit-taw *(v.)* **gelatinize**
စေးပျစ်သည့် အရာ say-pyit-the-a-yar *(n.)* **gelatin**
စေတနာ့ဝန်ထမ်း saytanarwaanhtam *(n.)* **volunteer**
စေတနာ့ဝန်ထမ်းသည် saytanarwaanhtamsai *(v.)* **volunteer**
စေတနာ၊ သဒ္ဒါတရား say-ta-nar, ta-dar-ta-yar *(n.)* **benevolence**
စေတနာကောင်းသော say-ta-nar-kaung-taw *(adj.)* **benefic**
စေလွှတ်သည် say-hlut-the *(v.)* **dispatch**
စောင့်ကြည့်ခြင်း sawnt-kyi-chinn *(n.)* **observation**
စောင့်ဆိုင်းသည် sawnt sine-sai *(v.)* **wait**
စောင် saung *(n.)* **blanket**
စောင့်ကြည့်လေ့လာရာအဆောက်အအုံ saunt-kyi-lay-lar-rar-a-sout-a-ohn *(n.)* **observatory**
စောင့်ကြည့်သည် saunt-kyi-tai *(v.)* **observe**

စောင့်ကြည့်သူ၊ လက်ပတ်နာရီ saunt kyi suu, laat-paat-narre *(n.)* **watch**

စောင့်ကြည့်၊ မှတ်သား၊ စစ်ဆေးပေးသော ကိရိယာ saunt-kyi-mat-tar-sit-say-htar-taw-ka-yi-yar *(n.)* **monitor**

စောင့်ကြပ်ခြင်း saunt kyat-chinn *(n.)* **surveillance**

စောင့်ကြပ်သည်၊ saunt-kyat-the *(v.)* **guard**

စောင့်ဆိုင်းခြင်း saunt since-hinn *(n.)* **wait**

စောင့်မျှော်သည် saung-myaw-the *(v.)* **await**

စောင့်ရှောက်ခြင်း saunt-shout-chinn *(n.)* **nurture**

စောင့်ရှောက်မှု saunt-shaut-mu *(n.)* **care**

စောင့်ရှောက်သည် saunt-shaut-the *(v.)* **care**

စောင့်ရှောက်သည်၊ လိုက်ပို့သည် saunt-shaut-the, lite-poe-the *(v.)* **escort**

စောင်း saung *(n.)* **harp**

စောင်း၍ saung-ywe *(adv.)* **sideway**

စောင်းထောင်စေသည် saungg htaungsaysai *(v.)* **tip**

စောင်းပါးရိပ်ခြေပြောခြင်း saung-par-yeik-chay-pyaw-chin *(n.)* **insinuation**

စောင်းမြောင်းသည် saung-myaung-the *(v.)* **insinuate**

စောင်းသည်၊ ငဲ့သည်၊ ညွတ်သည် saung-the, nge-the, nyut-the *(v.)* **incline**

စောင်းသော၊ ကြမ်းတမ်းသော hcaungg saw , kyamtamsaw *(adj.)* **scragged**

စောစီးစွာ saw-see-swar *(adj.)* **early**

စောစော saw-saw *(adv.)* **early**

စောဒကတက်ခြင်း say-da-ma-tat-chin *(n.)* **disputation**

စော်ကားခြင်း saw-kar-chin *(n.)* **insult**

စော်ကားမှု saw-kar-mu *(n.)* **affront**

စော်ကားရာရောက်သည် saw-karr-rar-rout-tai *(v.)* **offend**

စော်ကားသည် saw-kar-the *(v.)* **insult**

စော်ကားသော saw-kar-taw *(adj.)* **offensive**

စဲသည်၊ လျော့ကျသွားသည် sell sai , lyaw-kya-swarr-sai *(v.)* **subside**

ဆံကျစ်အချောင်းချောင်းကျနေသည့် ဆံပင်ပုံ san-kyit-a-khyaung-khyaung-kya-nay-the-san-pin-pon *(n.)* **dreadlock**

ဆံချခြင်း san chachinn *(n.)* **tonsure**

ဆံခြည်မျှင်သွေးကြော san-chi-myin-tway-kyaw *(n.)* **capillary**

ဆံနွယ်ခွေ sannwahlkway *(n.)* **ringlet**

ဆံပင် sa-pin *(n.)* **hair**

ဆံပင်ညှပ်သမား san-pin-nyat-ta-mar *(n.)* **barber**

ဆံပင်တိပေးခြင်း sanpin tipayychinn *(n.)* **trim**

ဆံပင်တု sanpintu *(n.)* **wig**

ဆံပင်ထုံးဖွဲ့မှု san-pin-htone-phwe-mu *(n.)* **coiffure**

ဆံပင်နက်လူဖြူအမျိုးသမီး sa-pin-nat-lu-phyu-a-myo-ta-mee *(n.)* **brunette**

ဆံပင်ရှည် san-pin-shay *(n.)* **mane**

ဆံပင်အခြောက်ခံစက် san-pin-a-chauk-khan-sat *(n.)* **hairdryer**

ဆံရစ် san-yit *(n.)* **fringe**

ဆက်၍ sat-ywe *(adv.)* **on**

ဆက်ခံသူ saat-hkan-suu *(n.)* **successor**

ဆက်စပ်မှု ရှိသည် sat-sat-mu-shi-the *(v.)* **cohere**
ဆက်စပ်သည် saat-saut-sai *(v.)* **pertain**
ဆက်စပ်သည်၊ တည်မှီသည် saat-sat sai , tai mhaesai *(v.)* **relate**
ဆက်ဆံမှု sat-san-mu *(n.)* **intercourse**
ဆက်ဆံရေး sat-san-yay *(n.)* **liaison**
ဆက်ဆံရေး၊ ဆက်သွယ်မှု saat-sanrayy , saatswalmhu *(n.)* **relation**
ဆက်ဆံသည်၊ ဒကာခံသည် saatsan sai , dakar hkansai *(v.)* **treat**
ဆက်ဆိုဖုန်း saat sohpone *(n.)* **saxophone**
ဆက်ဆိုဖုန်းမှုတ်သူ saat so hpone mhuatsuu *(n.)* **saxophonist**
ဆက်တိုက် sat-tite *(adj.)* **consecutive**
ဆက်တိုက် စိတ်ဆိုးစေသည် saat-tite sate-soe-saysai *(adj.)* **plague**
ဆက်တိုက်ခေါင်းညိတ်ခြင်း sat-tite-hkaung-gnyate-chin *(v)* **noddle**
ဆက်တိုက်ဖြစ်သော sat-tite-phit-taw *(adj.)* **continuous**
ဆက်နွယ်ခြင်း sat-nwe-chin *(n.)* **correlation**
ဆက်နွယ်သည် sat-nwe-the *(v.)* **correlate**
ဆက်ဖီဆွဲခြင်း saat hpe swalhkyinn *(n.)* **selfie**
ဆက်ရှင်မရှိဘဲ saat shinmashibhell *(adj.)* **sessionless**
ဆက်လက်တည်တံ့စေသည် saat-laat-tai-tant-say-sai *(v.)* **perpetuate**
ဆက်လက်လုပ်ဆောင်ခြင်း sat-lat-lote-saung-chin *(n.)* **continuation**
ဆက်လက်လုပ်ဆောင်သည် sat-lat-lote-saung-the *(v.)* **continue**
ဆက်လုပ်သည် sat-lote-the *(v.)* **reassume**
ဆက်သွယ်ချက် လွှင့်သည့်၊ လက်ခံသည့် စက် sat-thwal-chat-lwint-the-lat-khan-the-sat *(n.)* **transceiver**
ဆက်သွယ်ချက်လွှင့်သည်၊ လက်ခံသည် sat-thwal-chat-lwint-the-lat-khan-the *(v.)* **transceive**
ဆက်သွယ်ခြင်း sat-thwal-chin *(n.)* **communication**
ဆက်သွယ်တုံ့ပြန်မှုနှေးရောဂါ sat-thwal-tont-pyan-mu-hnay-yaw-gar *(n.)* **autism**
ဆက်သွယ်တုံ့ပြန်မှုနှေးရောဂါရှိသူ sat-thwal-tont-pyan-mu-hnay-yaw-gar-shi-thu *(adj.)* **autistic**
ဆက်သွယ်သည် sat-thwal-the *(v.)* **communicate**
ဆင် sin *(n.)* **elephant**
ဆင့် sint *(n.)* **cent**
ဆင့်ကဲဖြစ်စဉ် sint-kae-phit-sin *(n.)* **evolution**
ဆင့်ကဲဖြစ်စဉ်နှင့် ဆိုင်သော sint-kae-phit-sin-nint-sai-taw *(adv.)* **evolutionary**
ဆင့်ခေါ်စာ sint-hkaw-sar *(n.)* **notification**
ဆင့်ခေါ်သည် sinthkawsai *(v.)* **summon**
ဆင့်ဆိုခြင်း sint sochinn *(n.)* **summons**
ဆင်းရဲခြင်း sinn-rell-chinn *(n.)* **poverty**
ဆင်းရဲစေသည် sin-ye-say-the *(v.)* **impoverish**
ဆင်းရဲဒုက္ခ sin-ye-doke-kha *(n.)* **distress**
ဆင်းရဲနွမ်းပါးသည် sinnrellnwmparrsai *(v.)* **straiten**
ဆင်းရဲနုံချာခြင်း sinnrell none chaarchinn *(n.)* **squalor**
ဆင်းရဲသားရပ်ကွက် sinnrellsarrratkwat *(n.)* **slum**
ဆင်းရဲသော sinn-rell-saw *(adj.)* **poor**

ဆင်းသက်နားနေသည် sinn-saat-narr-nay-sai *(v.)* **perch**
ဆင်းသက်လာသူ sin-thet-lar-thu *(n.)* **descendant**
ဆင်းသက်သည် sin-thet-the *(v.)* **alight**
ဆင်းသက်သည်၊ ကမ်းကပ်သည် sin-thet-the, kan-kat-the *(v.)* **land**
ဆင်ခန္ဓာဝက်ကိုယ်လုံး sin-khandar-wat-koe-lone *(adj.)* **elephantine**
ဆင်ခြင်တုံတရား sin-chintone-ta-rarr *(n.)* **rationality**
ဆင်ခြင်မြော်တွေးမှု sin-chin myaw twaymhu *(n.)* **prudence**
ဆင်ခြင်သည်၊ နှိုင်းချင့်သည် sinchin sai , nine chintsai *(v.)* **reason**
ဆင်ခြေ sin-chay *(n.)* **alibi**
ဆင်ခြေ၊ အခွင့်အလမ်း sin-chay, a-khwint-a-lan *(n.)* **excuse**
ဆင်ခြေဖုံး sin-chay-hpone *(n.)* **outskirts**
ဆင်စွယ်ရုပ်ထု sin-swal-yoke-htu *(n.)* **ivory**
ဆင်ဆင်တူသော sin-sin-tu-taw *(adj.)* **akin**
ဆင်ဆာဖြတ်ခြင်း sin-sar-phat-chin *(n.)* **censorship**
ဆင်ဆာလူကြီး sin-sar-lu-gyi *(n.)* **censor**
ဆင်တူယိုးမှားဖြစ်သော sintuu-yoe-mhar-hpyitsaw *(adj.)* **reminiscent**
ဆင်ထိန်း sin-htein *(n.)* **mahout**
ဆင်နွှဲသည် sinnwhaellsai *(v.)* **wage**
ဆင်မြန်းသည် sin-myan-the *(v.)* **adorn**
ဆင်မြန်းသည်၊ မွေးထားသည် sin myan sai , mway-htarrsai *(v.)* **sport**
ဆင်ယင်သည်၊ ချီးမြှင့်သည် sin-yin-the, chee-myint-the *(v.)* **grace**
ဆင်ဝင် sin-win *(n.)* **porch**
ဆင်သည် sinsai *(v.)* **resemble**
ဆင်သော sin-taw *(adj.)* **alike**
ဆစ်စကိုကွန်ရက်ပညာ sit-sa-ko-kun-yat-pyun-nyar *(n.)* **cisco**
ဆည်းကပ်သူ saee kutsuu *(n.)* **votary**
ဆည်၊ တာတမံ sai , tartaman *(n.)* **weir**
ဆည်မြောင်းသွယ်ခြင်း sal-myaung-thwe-chin *(n.)* **irrigation**
ဆည်ရေပေးသည် sal-yay-pay-the *(v.)* **irrigate**
ဆတက်ထမ်းပိုး ပြုလုပ်သည် sa taat htampoe pyu-lotesai *(v.)* **redouble**
ဆတိုးကိန်း sa-toe-kein *(n.)* **multiple**
ဆတ်ခနဲ ငုံ့၍ ပုန်းသည် sat-kha-nae-ngont-ywe-pon-the *(v.)* **duck**
ဆတ်ခနဲ ဆတ်ခနဲ လှုပ်ရှားခြင်း sat-kha-nae-sat-kha-nae-hlote-shar-chin *(n.)* **flicker**
ဆတ်ခနဲ ဆွဲယူသည် saath-kanell swalyuusai *(v.)* **snatch**
ဆတ်ခနဲ ယူငင်ခြင်း saath-kanell yuu ngainchinn *(n.)* **snatch**
ဆတ်ခနဲ လှုပ်ရှားမှု sat-kha-nae-lote-shar-mu *(n.)* **jerk**
ဆတ်ဆတ်ထိ မခံသော saat saathti ma hkansaw *(adj.)* **sensitive**
ဆတ်ဆတ်လူး စွာတေးမ sat-sat-lu-swar-tay-ma *(n.)* **minx**
ဆတ်တောက်ဆတ်တောက် သွားသော sat-taut-sat-taut-twar-taw *(adj.)* **jerky**
ဆတ်သည်၊ ထိုးသည် sat-the, htoe-the *(v.)* **jab**
ဆန္ဒ san-da *(n.)* **wish**
ဆန္ဒခံယူပွဲ san-da-hkan-yuupwal *(n.)* **referendum**
ဆန္ဒပြင်းပြသည် san-da-pyin-pya-the *(v.)* **aspire**
ဆန္ဒမရှိသော san-da-ma-shi-taw *(adj.)* **disinclined**

ဆန္ဒမဲပေးလွှာ san-da-mae-pay-hlwar *(n.)* **ballot paper**

ဆန္ဒရှိသည် sandashisai *(v.)* **wish**

ဆန္ဒရှိသော san-da-shi-saw *(adj.)* **willing**

ဆန့်ကျင်ခြင်း sant-kyin-chin *(n.)* **negation**

ဆန့်ကျင်ဘက် saant-kyin-bhaat *(n.)* **polarity**

ဆန့်ကျင်ဘက် ပြောခြင်း sant-kyin-bat-pyaw-chin *(n.)* **contradiction**

ဆန့်ကျင်ဘက် ပြောသည် sant-kyin-bat-pyaw-the *(v.)* **contradict**

ဆန့်ကျင်ဘက် ဖြစ်သော sant-kyin-bat-phit-taw *(adj.)* **contrary**

ဆန့်ကျင်ဘက်စကား sant-kyin-bat-sa-gar *(n.)* **antonym**

ဆန့်ကျင်ဘက်ဖြစ်သော sant-kyin-bat-phit-taw *(adj.)* **polarazing**

ဆန့်ကျင်လျက် sant-kyin-lyat *(prep.)* **against**

ဆန့်ကျင်သည် sant-kyin-the *(v.)* **counter**

ဆန့်ကျင်သော sant-kyin-taw *(adj.)* **adverse**

ဆန့်ကျင်သော စကား sant-kyin-taw-sa-kar *(n.)* **negative**

ဆန့်ကျင်အနက်ရှိ ရှေ့ဆက်စကားလုံး sant-kyin-a-nat-shi-shay-sat-sa-kar-lone *(pref.)* **contra**

ဆန့်နိုင်အား sant nineaarr *(adj.)* **tensile**

ဆန့်နိုင်အားရှိသော sant nine aarrshi-saw *(adj.)* **tensility**

ဆန်းကြယ်သော အနုပညာလက်ရာ san-kyal-taw-a-nu-pyin-nyar-lat-yar *(adj.)* **baroque**

ဆန်းစစ်ခြင်း saannsitchinn *(n.)* **review**

ဆန်းစစ်ဝေဖန်မှု san-sit-wai-phan-mu *(n.)* **critique**

ဆန်းစစ်ဝေဖန်သော san-sit-wai-phan-taw *(adj.)* **critical**

ဆန်းစစ်သည် saannsitsai *(v.)* **review**

ဆန်းဆန်းပြားပြား အရာ san-san-pyar-pyar-ayar *(n.)* **mystery**

ဆန်းပြားမှု saann pyarrmhu *(n.)* **sophistication**

ဆန်းသစ်တီထွင်ခြင်း san-tit-ti-htwin-chin *(n.* **innovation**

ဆန်းသစ်သော san-tit-taw *(adj.)* **novel**

ဆန်ခါ saanhkar *(n.)* **sieve**

ဆန်ခါချသည် saan hkar chasai *(v.)* **sieve**

ဆန်ခါတင်စာရင်း saanhkartinsarrinn *(v.)* **shortlist**

ဆန်ခါတင်စာရင်းဝင်သော saanhkartin sarrinnwinsaw *(adj.)* **shortlisted**

ဆန်ခါပေါက်ပေါက်သွားစေသည် saan hkar poutpout swarrsaysai *(v.)* **riddle**

ဆန်ပိုး၊ ကောက်နှံပိုး saan poe , kout nhaanpoe *(n.)* **weevil**

ဆန်ဘာအက saan bhar aak *(v.)* **samba**

ဆန်ဘူကအရက် saan bhuu ka aa-raat *(n.)* **sambuca**

ဆန်မိုနိုက်သတ္တု saan mo nite-sattu *(n.)* **samsonite**

ဆပ်ကပ်အဖွဲ့ sat-kat-a-phwe *(n.)* **circus**

ဆပ်ပြာ satpyaar *(n.)* **soap**

ဆပ်ပြာတိုက်သည် satpyaar titesai *(v.)* **soap**

ဆပ်ပြာပါသော satpyaar parsaw *(adj.)* **soapy**

ဆပ်ပြာမြှုပ် sat-pyar-hmyoke *(n.)* **lather**

ဆပ်ပြာမှုန့် sat-pyar-hmont *(n.)* **detergent**

ဆယ့်ခြောက် sae chauk *(n., adj.)* **sixteen**

ဆယ့်ခြောက်ခုမြောက် sae chauk-hku-myaut *(adj.)* **sixteenth**

ဆယ့်ငါး sae-ngar *(n.)* **fifteen**

ဆယ့်တစ် sat-tit *(n.)* **eleven**

ဆယ့်နှစ် sae-nit *(n.)* **twelve**

ဆယ့်နှစ်ခုမြောက် sae nit-hkumyawt *(n.)* **twelfth**

ဆယ့်နှစ်ရာသီခွင် sae na-rar-se-hkwin *(n.)* **zodiac**

ဆယ့်ရှစ် sat-shit *(n.)* **eighteen**

ဆယ့်လေး sal-lay *(n.)* **fourteen**

ဆယ့်သုံး sae-sone *(n.)* **thirteen**

ဆယ့်သုံးခုမြောက် sae sone-hkumyawt *(n.)* **thirteenth**

ဆယ်ကျော်သက် saalkyawsaat *(n.)* **teenager**

ဆယ်ခုမြောက် saahlkumyawt *(adj.)* **tenth**

ဆယ်စုနှစ် sal-su-nit *(n.)* **decade**

ဆယ်ဆ saal-sa *(adj.)* **tenfold**

ဆယ်တင်မှု saal tinmhu *(n.)* **salvage**

ဆယ်တင်သည် saaltinsai *(v.)* **salvage**

ဆယ်လီစိတ်ဖြစ်သော sal-li-seik-phit-taw *(adj.)* **decimal**

ဆယ်လူလာ၊ ဆဲလ်များဖြင့် ဖွဲ့စည်းထားသော sal-lu-lar, sal-myar-phyint-phwe-see-htar-taw *(adj.)* **cellular**

ဆရာ sa-rar *(n.)* **pedagogue**

ဆရာ ဗဟိုပြုသော sarar bahopyusaw *(adj.)* **teacher centric**

ဆရာ၊ တက္ကသိုလ်ဆရာ sa-yar, tat-ka-doe-sa-yar *(n.)* **instructor**

ဆရာကြီးလုပ်သော sa-yar-gyi-lote-taw *(adj.)* **bossy**

ဆရာဝန် sa-rar-waan *(n.)* **physician**

ဆလင်ဒါပုံ sa-lin-dar-pon *(n.)* **cylinder**

ဆလင်ဒါပုံ မြေအိုး s lain darpone myayaoe *(n.)* **tandoor**

ဆလင်ဒါပုံရှိသော sa-lin-dar-pon-shi-taw *(adj.)* **cylindrical**

ဆလပ်ရွက် sa-lat-ywet *(n.)* **butterhead**

ဆလွန်းကား salwannkarr *(n.)* **saloon**

ဆလိုက်မီး sa litemee *(n.)* **searchlight**

ဆွံ့အသူ sunt-a-thu *(n.)* **mute**

ဆွံ့အသော sunt-aa-taw *(adj.)* **dumb**

ဆွစ်ဇလန်ရှိ ဒေသစိတ်နယ်မြေ swit-za-lan-shi-day-ta-seik-nal-myay *(n.)* **canton**

ဆွစ်ဇာလန်နိုင်ငံ switzarlaan-nine-ngan *(adj.)* **Swiss**

ဆွစ်ဇာလန်သား switzarlaan-sarr *(n.)* **Swiss**

ဆွတ်ပျံ့ဖွယ် swat-pyaan-hpwal *(adj.)* **poignant**

ဆွတ်ပျံ့ဖွယ်ဖြစ်ခြင်း swat-pyaan-hpwal-pyit-chinn *(n.)* **poignacy**

ဆွတ်သည် sut-the *(v.)* **moisten**

ဆွပေးသည် swa-pay-the *(v.)* **nettle**

ဆွပေးသော swapayysaw *(adj.)* **provocative**

ဆွယ်တာ swaltar *(n.)* **sweater**

ဆွယ်သည် swalsai *(v.)* **tout**

ဆွယ်သည်၊ သွေးဆောင်သည် swal sai , swaysaungsai *(v.)* **tempt**

ဆွေးနွေးခြင်း swaynwaychinn *(n.)* **talk**

ဆွေးနွေးပွဲ swaynwaypwal *(n.)* **seminar**

ဆွေးနွေးသည် sway-nway-the *(v.)* **discuss**

ဆွေးသည် sway-sai *(v.)* **pine**

ဆွေးသည်၊ မြည့်သည် sway sai , myae-sai *(v.)* **rot**

ဆွေကြီးမျိုးကြီး sway-kyee-myoe-kyee *(n.)* **noble**

ဆွေမျိုး sway-myoe *(n.)* **relative**

ဆွေမျိုးကောင်းစားရေးဝါဒ sway-myo-kaung-sar-yay-war-da *(n.)* **nepotism**
ဆွေမျိုးမိတ်သင်္ဂဟ sway-myo-meik-tin-ga-har *(n.)* **kith**
ဆွေမျိုးရင်းချာ ဆုံးပါးသည် swe-myo-yin-char-sone-par-the *(adj.)* **bereaved**
ဆွဲချ swal-cha *(n.)* **prosecutor**
ဆွဲခြင်း swalchinn *(n.)* **pull**
ဆွဲငင်အား swal-ngin-arr *(n.)* **gravitation**
ဆွဲဆန့်ထားသည် swal santhtarrsai *(v.)* **tension**
ဆွဲဆန့်ထားသော swal santhtarrsaw *(adj.)* **tensioned**
ဆွဲဆန့်နိုင်သော swal s ant ninesaw *(adj.)* **tensible**
ဆွဲဆွဲငင်ငင် ငိုကြွေးသည် swal swal ngainngain ngokyawaysai *(v.)* **wail**
ဆွဲဆောင်ခြင်း swal-saung-chin *(n.)* **attraction**
ဆွဲဆောင်မှု swal-saung-mu *(n.)* **enticement**
ဆွဲဆောင်မှု ရှိသော swalsaungmhu shisaw *(adj.)* **winsome**
ဆွဲဆောင်မှုရှိသော swal-saung-mu-shi-taw *(adj.)* **attractive**
ဆွဲဆောင်သည် swal-saung-sai *(v.)* **persuade**
ဆွဲဆောင်အားကောင်းသူ swal-saung-arr-kaung-thu *(n.)* **enticer**
ဆွဲဆောင်အားကောင်းသော swal-saung-arr-kaung-taw *(adj.)* **enticing**
ဆွဲပုံး swal-pone *(n.)* **bucket**
ဆွဲယူခြင်း swal-yu-chin *(n.)* **obduction**
ဆွဲယူသည် swal-yu-the *(v.)* **obduct**
ဆွဲလုသည် swal lusai *(v.)* **wrest**
ဆွဲသင်္ဘော swal-tin-baw *(n.)* **towboat**
ဆွဲသည် swalsai *(v.)* **pull**
ဆွဲသည်၊ ဆန့်သည် swal sai , santsai *(v.)* **stretch**
ဆွဲသည်၊ သွယ်သည် swal sai , swalsai *(v.)* **string**
ဆွဲသည်၊ သုတ်သည် swal sai , sotesai *(v.)* **tug**
ဆွဲအား၊ ကုပ်အား swal aarr , koteaarr *(n.)* **traction**
ဆား sarr *(n.)* **salt**
ဆား၊ ငရုတ်ကောင်းပါသော sarr, nga-rote-kaung-par-saw *(adj.)* **pepper-and-salt**
ဆားကစ်ပေါ် ရှိကြိုးပြန်လှဲသည် sar-kit-paw-shi-kyo-pyan-lal-the *(v.)* **reconductor**
ဆားကစ်အတို sarr kait aato *(n.)* **short**
ဆားခတ်သည် sarr hkaatsai *(v.)* **salt**
ဆားငန် sarr ngan *(adj.)* **saline**
ဆားငန်သော sarr ngaansaw *(adj.)* **salty**
ဆားစိမ်သည် sarr-sin-sai *(v.)* **pickle**
ဆားစိမ်ဟင်းသီးဟင်းရွက် sarr-sein-hinn-see-hinn-rwat *(n.)* **pickle**
ဆားဓာတ်ပါဝင်မှု sarr dhrat-parwinmhu *(n.)* **salinity**
ဆားဖယ်ရှားသည် sar-phal-shar-the *(v.)* **desalt**
ဆားမပါသော sarrmaparsaw *(adj.)* **unsalted**
ဆားရည်၊ ပင်လယ်ရေ sar-yay, pin-lal-yay *(n.)* **brine**
ဆာတန်မာရ်နတ် sar taanmarrnaat *(n.)* **satan**
ဆာတန်မာရ်နတ်အလား sar taan marrnaat aalarr *(adj.)* **satanic**
ဆာဘွဲ့ ဖြင့် သူကောင်းပြုသည် sar-bwe-phint-thu-gaung-pyu-the *(v.)* **knight**
ဆာဘွဲ့ရသူရဲကောင်း sar-bwe-ya-thu-ye-gaung *(n.)* **knight**
ဆာမူရိုင်း sarmuurine *(n.)* **samurai**

ဆာလံကျမ်း sar-lankyam *(n.)* **psalm**

ဆာလောင်ခြင်း sar-laung-chin *(n.)* **hunger**

ဆာလောင်သော sar-laung-taw *(adj.)* **hungry**

ဆာလ်ဖာ sarhlpar *(n.)* **sulphur**

ဆာလ်ဖာပါသော sarl hpar parsaw *(adj.)* **sulphuric**

ဆိတ် seik *(n.)* **goat**

ဆိတ်၊ သိုး အော်သံ seik-toe-aw-tan *(v.)* **bleat**

ဆိတ်ခြင်း sate-chinn *(n.)* **pinch**

ဆိတ်ငြိမ်မှု sate ngyein-mhu *(n.)* **quiet**

ဆိတ်မွေးဖြင့် လုပ်ထားသည့် နူးညံ့သော အထည် seik-hmway-phit-lote-htar-the-nu-nyant-taw-a-htae *(n.)* **cashmere**

ဆိတ်သည် sate-sai *(v.)* **pinch**

ဆိတ်သည်၊ ပေါက်သည် sate-sai, pout-sai *(v.)* **peck**

ဆိပ်ကမ်း seik-kan *(n.)* **harbour**

ဆိပ်ကမ်းမြို့ seikkammyoe *(n.)* **port**

ဆိပ်ခံတံတား seik-hkan-ta-tarr *(n.)* **pier**

ဆိပ်ခံတံတား အသုံးပြုခ seik-khan-ta-dar-a-tone-pyu-kha *(n.)* **wharfage**

ဆိမ့်သော seint-taw *(adj.)* **nutty**

ဆိုးကျိုး soe-kyo *(n.)* **disadvantage**

ဆိုးဆေး soe-say *(n.)* **dye**

ဆိုးနိုင်သမျှ ဆိုးသော စိတ်ကူးသက်သက် နေရာ soe-nai-ta-mya-soe-taw-seik-ku-thet-thet-nay-yar *(n.)* **dystopia**

ဆိုးယုတ်ခြင်း soe-yoke-chin *(n.)* **devilry**

ဆိုးယုတ်သော soe yotesaw *(adj.)* **seamy**

ဆိုးယုတ်သောသူ soe yotesawsuu *(n.)* **rogue**

ဆိုးရွားသော soerwarrsaw *(adj.)* **untoward**

ဆိုးဝါးခြင်း၊ ကင်ဆာဖြစ်နိုင်သော soe-war-taw, kin-sar-phit-nai-taw *(n.)* **malignity**

ဆိုးဝါးစွာ soe-war-swar *(adv.)* **badly**

ဆိုးဝါးစွာ ဆက်ဆံသည် soe-war-swar-sat-san-the *(v.)* **ill-treat**

ဆိုးဝါးသော soe-war-taw *(adj.)* **clumsy**

ဆိုးဝါးသော အမှား soe-war-taw-a-mar *(n.)* **blunder**

ဆိုးသွမ်းလူငယ် soe-twan-lu-nge *(n.)* **delinquent**

ဆိုးသော soe-taw *(adj.)* **bad**

ဆိုက ဖျော်ဖြေခြင်း so-ka-phyaw-phae-chin *(n.)* **cabaret**

ဆိုက်ကပ်သည် site-kat-the *(v.)* **dock**

ဆိုက်ပရက်ပင် site-pa-ress-pin *(n.)* **cypress**

ဆိုင် sine *(n.)* **outlet**

ဆိုင်းခြင်း sine-chinn *(n.)* **suspension**

ဆိုင်းငံ့ထားခြင်း saing-ngan-htar-chin *(n.)* **abeyance**

ဆိုင်းငံ့ထားသော sine-ngant-htarr-saw *(adj.)* **pending**

ဆိုင်းထားသည် sine-htarr-sai *(v.)* **suspend**

ဆိုင်ကယ်၊ စက်ဘီး ရွယ်တူစီးသူ လူငယ် sai-kal-sat-bee-ywal-thu-see-thu-lu-ngal *(n.)* **biker**

ဆိုင်ကယ်မောင်းသမား sai-kal-maung-ta-mar *(n.)* **motorist**

ဆိုင်ကလုန်းမုန်တိုင်း sai-ka-lone-mone-tai *(n.)* **cyclone**

ဆိုင်ခန်း sinehkaann *(n.)* **shop**

ဆိုင်ခန်းငယ် sinehkaannngaal *(n.)* **stall**

ဆိုင်ဘာ sai-bar *(adj.)* **cyber**

ဆိုင်ဘာကဖေး sai-bar-ka-fay *(n.)* **cybercafé**

ဆိုင်ဘာစကားပြောခြင်း sai-bar-sa-kar-pyaw-chin *(n.)* **cyberchat**

ဆိုင်ဘာမှုခင်း sai-bar-mu-khin *(n.)* **cybercrime**

ဆိုင်ဘာအနိုင်ကျင့်ခြင်း sai-bar-a-nai-kyint-chin *(n.)* **cyberbullying**
ဆိုင်မျက်နှာစာ sinemyetnharsar *(n.)* **shopfront**
ဆိုင်များတွင် လူရမ်းကားများကို ဆွဲထုတ်ရန် ငှားထားသူ sai-myar-twin-lu-yan-kar-myar-ko-swal-htoke-yan-hngar-htar-thu *(n.)* **bouncer**
ဆိုင်ယာနိုက်အဆိပ် sai-yar-nide-a-seik *(n.)* **cyanide**
ဆိုင်ရှင် sineshin *(n.)* **shopkeeper**
ဆိုတာ sotar *(conj.)* **that**
ဆိုဖစ်အယူအဆ so hpaitaayuuaas *(n.)* **sophist**
ဆိုဖာ so-far *(n.)* **couch**
ဆိုရှယ်လစ်ဝါဒ soshallaitwar-da *(n.)* **socialism**
ဆိုရှယ်လစ်ဝါဒီ soshallaitwar-de *(n.)* **socialist**
ဆိုရိုး so-yoe *(n.)* **maxim**
ဆိုရိုးစကား so-yoe-sa-kar *(n.)* **adage**
ဆိုလာကွက် so larkwat *(n.)* **solar panel**
ဆိုလိုသည် so-lo-the *(v.)* **denote**
ဆီ se *(n.)* **oil**
ဆီး aaroeaoe *(n.)* **urine**
ဆီးချို sie-cho *(n.)* **diabetes**
ဆီးနှင့်ဆိုင်သော seeswarrsai *(adj.)* **urinary**
ဆီးနှင်းကျခြင်း see natenkyachinn *(n.)* **snowfall**
ဆီးနိတ် seenate *(n.)* **senate**
ဆီးဝမ်းသွားသည် see wamswarrsai *(v.)* **void**
ဆီးသွားခန်း see nintsinesaw *(n.)* **urinal**
ဆီးသွားခြင်း see *(n.)* **urination**
ဆီးသွားသည် seeswarrchinn *(v.)* **urinate**
ဆီးအိမ် see-eain *(n.)* **bladder**
ဆီကို ရောထည့်သည် si-koyaw-htae-the *(v.)* **terp**
ဆီကဲ့သို့သော se-kae-shoet-taw *(adj.)* **oily**
ဆီချေးစော်နံသည် se-gyee-zar-nan-the *(v.)* **rancidify**
ဆီချေးစော်နံသော se hkyaayy hcaw nansaw *(v.)* **stale**
ဆီဆေးပန်းချီ se-say-pan-chee *(n.)* **oil paint**
ဆီဇာနှင့် ဆိုင်သော si-zar-nint-sai-taw *(adj.)* **cesarean**
ဆီထည့်သည် se-htaet-tai *(v.)* **oil**
ဆီပူထိုးသည် se puu htoesai *(v.)* **saute**
ဆီပေကျံနေသော si-pay-kyan-nay-taw *(adj.)* **greasy**
ဆီဖြင့် လိမ်းသပ်သည် si-phit-lain-tat-the *(v.)* **anoint**
ဆီလျော်သော si-lyaw-taw *(adj.)* **apt**
ဆီလျော်သော၊ သက်ဆိုင်သော se lyaw saw , saat-sinesaw *(adj.)* **relevant**
ဆီလျော်အောင် ပြုပြင်ခြင်း si-lyaw-aung-pyu-pyin-chin *(n.)* **adaptation**
ဆီလီကွန်ဒြပ်စင် selekwan drat-sin *(n.)* **silicon**
ဆီလီကွန်အလွှာတစ်လွှာ selekwan aalwhar taitlwhar *(n.)* **silicene**
ဆီလီကာ se lekar *(n.)* **silica**
ဆီသယ်ကား se saalkarr *(n.)* **tanker**
ဆီသို့ sethoet *(prep.)* **towards**
ဆီသုတ်သည် si-toke-the *(v.)* **grease**
ဆု hsu *(n.)* **award**
ဆုံးဖြတ်ချက် sonehpyatchet *(n.)* **verdict**
ဆုံးဖြတ်သည် sonehpyatsai *(v.)* **resolve**

ဆုံးဖြတ်သည် sone-phat-the *(v.)* **decide**

ဆုံးရှုံးခြင်း sone-shone-chin *(n.)* **loss**

ဆုံးရှုံးခြင်းအပါအဝင် စုပ်ယူခြင်း sone-shone-chin-a-par-a-win-sote-yu-chin *(n.)* **attenuance**

ဆုံးရှုံးသည် sone-shone-the *(v.)* **lose**

ဆုံချက် sone-chet *(n.)* **pivot**

ဆုံချက်ဖြတ်ခြင်း sone-chat-phat-chin *(n.)* **focalization**

ဆုံချက်ဖြတ်သည် sone-chat-phat-the *(v.)* **focalize**

ဆုံမှတ် sone-mat *(n.)* **convergence**

ဆုချီးမြှင့်သည် su chaeemyintsai *(v.)* **reward**

ဆုငွေ su-ngway *(n.)* **prize money**

ဆုတံဆိပ် su-ta-seik *(n.)* **medal**

ဆုတံဆိပ်ရှင် su-ta-seik-shin *(n.)* **medallist**

ဆုတောင်းခြင်း su-taungg-chinn *(n.)* **prayer**

ဆုတောင်းပေးသည် su-taung-pay-the *(v.)* **bless**

ဆုတောင်းသည် su-taungg-sai *(v.)* **pray**

ဆုတ်ခွာသည် sotehkwarsai *(v.)* **retreat**

ဆုတ်ဖြဲသည် sote hpyaellsai *(v.)* **rip**

ဆုတ်ယုတ်ကုန်ခန်းစေသည် sote-yote-kone-khan-say-the *(v.)* **depauperate**

ဆုတ်ယုတ်စေသည်၊ ကုန်ခမ်းစေသည် soteyote saysai , kone hkamsaysai *(v.)* **sap**

ဆုတ်သည် sote-sai *(v.)* **recede**

ဆုပေးသည် hsu-pay-the *(v.)* **award**

ဆုပ်ကိုင်ခြင်း sote-kai-chin *(n.)* **hold**

ဆုပ်ကိုင်သည် sote-kai-the *(v.)* **grab**

ဆုပ်ကိုင်သည်၊ ကျင်းပသည် sote-kai-the, kyin-pa-the *(v.)* **hold**

ဆုပ်ခြင်း sote-chin *(n.)* **grip**

ဆုလာဘ် sularbh *(n.)* **reward**

ဆူး suu *(n.)* **thorn**

ဆူးတောင် su-taung *(n.)* **fin**

ဆူးထစ်ပါသော၊ နာကြည်းစေသော sue-htit-par-taw, nar-kyi-say-taw *(adj.)* **barbed**

ဆူးဖြင့် ထိုးခြင်း suu-hpyint htoechinn *(n.)* **prick**

ဆူးရှိသော suushisaw *(adj.)* **thorny**

ဆူဆူညံညံ မြူးထူးပျော်ရွှင်ပွဲ suu suunyannyan myuu htuu pyawshwinpwal *(n.)* **revelry**

ဆူဆူပူပူ suu suupuupuu *(adj.)* **turbulent**

ဆူညံငြင်းခုံသည် su-nyan-nyin-khon-the *(v.)* **brangle**

ဆူညံစွာ အရက်သောက်သည် su-nyan-swar-a-yat-taut-the *(v.)* **carouse**

ဆူညံသံ suu-nyan-tan *(n.)* **noise**

ဆူညံသော suu-nyan-taw *(adj.)* **noisy**

ဆူညံသောင်းကျန်းခြင်း su-nyan-taung-gyan-chin *(n.)* **commotion**

ဆူပူမှု suupuumhu *(n.)* **turbulence**

ဆူပူသည် suupuusai *(v.)* **scold**

ဆူရုံတည်သည် suu rone taisai *(v.)* **simmer**

ဆေး say *(n.)* **drug**

ဆေး၊ ကုသမှု sayy , kusamhu *(n.)* **remedy**

ဆေး၊ ဆေးဝါး sayy, sayywarr *(n.)* **pharmaceutical**

ဆေး၊ ဓာတုပစ္စည်းကြောင့် သတိမေ့ခြင်း say-dar-tu-pyit-see-kyaunt-ta-di-mae-chin *(n.)* **narcosis**

ဆေး၊ အရက် စွဲနေသူ say-a-yat-swal-nay-thu *(n.)* **addict**

ဆေးကျောင်းသား၊ ဆရာဝန် say-kyaung-tar, sa-yar-win *(n.)* **medic**

ဆေးကြိမ်လုံး sayy kyaainlone *(n.)* **wand**

ဆေးခန်း say-khan *(n.)* **clinic**

ဆေးချိန်လွန်ခြင်း say-chane-lwan-chinn *(n.)* **overdose**

ဆေးချိန်လွန်သည် say-chane-lwan-tai *(v.)* **overdose**

ဆေးခြောက် say-chauk *()* **cannabis**

ဆေးစက် say-sat *(n.)* **blob**

ဆေးစပ်ပြား say-saut-pyar *(n.)* **palette**

ဆေးစပ်သမား say-saut-sa-marr *(n.)* **pharmacist**

ဆေးစွဲခြင်း say-swal-chin *(n.)* **addiction**

ဆေးစွဲနေသော say-swal-nay-taw *(adj.)* **addicted**

ဆေးဆိုးသည် say-soe-the *(v.)* **dye**

ဆေးဆိုင် say-sine *(n.)* **pharmacy**

ဆေးညွှန်း say-hnyun *(n.)* **dosage**

ဆေးတောင့် say-taunt *(n.)* **capsule**

ဆေးပညာ say-pyin-nyar *(n.)* **medicine**

ဆေးပြင်းလိပ် say-pyin-leik *(n.)* **cigar**

ဆေးပြား say-pyarr *(n.)* **pill**

ဆေးပလတ်စတာ say-pa-lat-sa-tar *(n.)* **Band-Aid**

ဆေးပေးခန်း say-pay-khan *(n.)* **dispensary**

ဆေးပေါ့လိပ် say-pot-late *(n.)* **cheroot**

ဆေးဖက်ဝင်ဆီမွှေး say-phat-win-si-hmway *(n.)* **balm**

ဆေးဖက်ဝင်သော say-phat-win-taw *(adj.)* **medicinal**

ဆေးဖော်စပ်၊ ထုတ်လုပ်၊ ဖြန့်ချိမှုနှင့် ဆိုင်သော say-hpaw-sat, htote-lote, hpyant-chai-mhu-nint-sine-saw *(adj.)* **pharmaceutic**

ဆေးဘက်ဆိုင်ရာ say-bat-sai-yar *(adj.)* **medical**

ဆေးဘက်ဝင်အနံ့ဆိုးအစေး say-bat-win-a-nant-soe-a-say *(n.)* **asafoetida**

ဆေးများများစွာဆိုင်ရာ sayymyarr myarr-swar-sinerar *(adj.)* **polypharmacal**

ဆေးရည်ထည့်ရန် ဖန်ဘူးငယ် say-rai-htaeet-raan-hpaan-bhuu-ngaal *(n.)* **phial**

ဆေးရွက်ကြီး sayyrwatkyee *(n.)* **tobacco**

ဆေးရုံ say-yone *(n.)* **hospital**

ဆေးရုံအထွေထွေလုပ်သား say-rone-a-htway-htway-lote-tarr *(n.)* **orderly**

ဆေးရောင်းဆိုင် say-yaung-sai *(n.)* **druggist**

ဆေးလိပ်သောက်ခြင်း sayyliutsoutchinn *(n.)* **smoking**

ဆေးဝါး say-war *(n.)* **medicament**

ဆေးဝါးကျွမ်းကျင် sayywarr-kywam-kyin *(n.)* **pharmaceutist**

ဆေးဝါးဆိုင်ရာ sayy-warrsinerar *(adj.)* **pharmaceutical**

ဆေးသကြား sayy sakyarr *(n.)* **saccharin**

ဆေးသုံးထားသော say-tone-htar-thaw *(adj.)* **doped**

ဆေးသုတ်သည် say-sote-sai *(v.)* **paint**

ဆေးသုတ်သမား say-sote-sa-marr *(n.)* **painter**

ဆော့ sawt *(n.)* **ketchup**

ဆော့တတ်သော၊ မြူးသော sot-taat-saw, myuu-saw *(adj.)* **playful**

ဆော့ဝဲရေးသူ၊ ဖွံ့ဖြိုးရေး လုပ်သူ sot-wal-yay-thu, phwint-phyoe-yay-lote-thu *(n.)* **developer**

ဆော့သည် sotsai *(v.)* **toy**

ဆောက် saut *(n.)* **chisel**

ဆောက်လုပ်မှုပုံစံ saut-lote-mu-pon-san *(n.)* **make**

ဆောက်လုပ်ရေး saut-lote-yay *(n.)* **construction**

ဆောင့်ကြောင့်ထိုင်သည် saw int kyount htinesai *(v.)* **squat**

ဆောင့်ဆွဲခြင်း saunt swalchinn *(n.)* **wrench**

ဆောင့်ပိတ်ခြင်း saunt-pate-chinn *(n.)* **slam**

ဆောင့်ပိတ်သည် saunt-pate-sai *(v.)* **slam**

ဆောင်းခိုခြင်း saung-kho-chin *(n.)* **hibernation**

ဆောင်းခိုသည် saungg hkosai *(v.)* **winter**

ဆောင်းနှင့် တူသော saunggnint tuusaw *(adj.)* **wintry**

ဆောင်းပါး saung-par *(n.)* **article**

ဆောင်းရွက်ကြွေပင် saung-ywat-kyway-pin *(n.)* **alder**

ဆောင်းရာသီ saunggrarse *(n.)* **winter**

ဆောင်းဦးရာသီ saung-oo-yar-thi *(n.)* **autumn**

ဆောင်ကြာမြိုင် saung-kyar-hmyaing *(n.)* **brothel**

ဆောင်ပုဒ် saung-poke *(n.)* **motto**

ဆောင်ရွက်ချက် saung-ywet-chat *(n.)* **deed**

ဆောင်ရွက်ရန် တာဝန်ရှိသော saung-ywat-ran-tar-wan-shi-taw *(adj.)* **obligatory**

ဆော်သြသူ saw-aw-the *(n.)* **convener**

ဆဲခြင်း၊ ကျိန်စာတိုက်ခြင်း sal-chin, kyain-sar-tite-chin *(n.)* **malediction**

ဆဲရေးစကား၊ ကျိန်ဆဲစကား sal-yay-sa-gar, kyein-sal-sa-kar *(n.)* **curse**

ဆဲရေးတိုင်းထွာခြင်း sal-yay-tai-htwar-chin *(n.)* **invective**

ဆဲလ်၊ အခန်းငယ် sal, a-khan-nge *(n.)* **cell**

ဆဲလ်စီယပ် sal-see-yat *(adj.)* **Celsius**

ဆဲလ်တစ်ဘုန်းကြီး sal-tit-phone-gyi *(n.)* **druid**

ဆဲလ်ဖုန်း sal-phone *(n.)* **cell phone**

ဆဲလ်မပါသော sal-ma-par-taw *(adj.)* **acellular**

ဆဲလ်လူလိုက် sal-lu-lite *(n.)* **cellulite**

ဆဲသည်၊ ဆိုသည် sell sai , sosai *(v.)* **swear**

ဇက်ကြိုး zat-kyoe *(n.)* **rein**

ဇက်ကိုင်သည် zat kinesai *(v.)* **rein**

ဇက်ပိုးအုပ်သည် zaat poe aotesai *(v.)* **scruff**

ဇင့်ဓာတ် zint-dhrat *(n.)* **zinc**

ဇစ် zit *(n.)* **zip**

ဇစ်ပိတ်ထားသော zit-pate-htarr-saw *(adj.)* **ziplock**

ဇစ်ပိတ်သည် zit-pate-sai *(v.)* **zip**

ဇနပုဒ် za-na-poke *(n.)* **hamlet**

ဇနီး za-nee *(n.)* **missis, missus**

ဇန်နဝါရီလ zan-na-war-ree-la *(n.)* **January**

ဇယား zayarr *(adj.)* **tabular**

ဇယား ကွက်ခွဲခလုတ် zayarr kwat hkwal-kalote *(n.)* **tabulator**

ဇယားကွက် za-yar-kwat *(v.)* **chart**

ဇယားဆွဲသည် zayarr swalsai *(v.)* **tabulate**

ဇယားဖြင့် ဆွဲခြင်း zayarr-hpyint swalchinn *(n.)* **tabulation**

ဇရာ za-yar *(n.)* **ageing**

ဇလီ za-li *(n.)* **batten**

ဇလုံ za-lon *(n.)* **basin**

ဇွတ်လုပ်သည် zwut-lote-sai *(v.)* **persist**

ဇွန်း zwann *(n.)* **spoon**

ဇွန်း၊ ခက်ရင်း၊ ဓား zoon, khat-yin, dar *(n.)* **cutlery**
ဇွန်းဖြင့် ခပ်သည် zwann-hpyint hkautsai *(v.)* **spoon**
ဇွဲ zwal *(n.)* **tenacity**
ဇွဲလုံ့လ zwe lont-la *(n.)* **perseverance**
ဇွဲသတ္တိနှင့် ပြည့်စုံသော zwe-tat-ti-nint-pyae-sone-taw *(adj.)* **manful**
ဇာချဲ့ခြင်း zar-chae-chin *(n.)* **fuss**
ဇာတိ zar-ti *(n.)* **native**
ဇာတိပ္ဖိုလ်သီး zar-tip-hpol-tee *(n.)* **nutmeg**
ဇာတ်ကြောင်းပြန်ခြင်း zat-kyaung-pyan-chin *(n.)* **narration**
ဇာတ်ကြောင်းပြန်ပြောသည် zat-kyaung-pyan-pyaw-the *(v.)* **narrate**
ဇာတ်ကြောင်းပြန်ပြောသူ zat-lan-pyan-pyaw-thu *(n.)* **narrator**
ဇာတ်ကောင်၊ ဇာတ်လိုက် zat-kaung , zat-lite *(n.)* **protagonist**
ဇာတ်စင် zatsin *(n.)* **stage**
ဇာတ်စင်နောက်သို့ zat-sin-naut-tho *(adv.)* **backstage**
ဇာတ်ဆန်လွန်းခြင်း zat-san-lun-chin *(n.)* **melodrama**
ဇာတ်ဆန်လွန်းသော zat-san-lun-taw *(adj.)* **melodramatic**
ဇာတ်ညွှန်း zat-nyun *(n.)* **script**
ဇာတ်တိုက်သည် zat titesai *(v.)* **rehearse**
ဇာတ်ထွက်စကား zat htwatsakarr *(n.)* **soliloquy**
ဇာတ်မြူး zat-my *(n.)* **comedy**
ဇာတ်ရုံတွင် ပရိတ်သတ်ထိုင်ရာနေရာ zat-yone-twin-pa-yeik-thet-htaing-yar-nay-yar *(n.)* **auditorium**
ဇာတ်လမ်း zat-lan *(adj.)* **narrative**
ဇာတ်လမ်း၊ ပုံပြင် zat-lam , ponepyin *(n.)* **story**
ဇာတ်လမ်းကဗျာ zat-lan-la-byar *(n.)* **ballad**
ဇာတ်လမ်းတို zatlamto *(n.)* **skit**
ဇာတ်သိမ်းပိုင်း zat-thein-pai *(n.)* **finale**
ဇာတ်အချိတ်အဆက်စကား zat-a-chake-a-sat-sa-gar *(n.)* **cue**
ဇာပန်းထည် zar-pan-htal *(n.)* **lace**
ဇာဖြင့် ပြီးသော zar-phint-pi-taw *(adj.)* **lacy**
ဇိမ်ခံ zain-hkan *(adj.)* **plush**
ဇိမ်ခံပစ္စည်း zain-khan-pyit-see *(n.)* **luxury**
ဇိမ်ယစ်သူ zain yitsuu *(n.)* **voluptuary**
ဇိမ်ယစ်သော zain yitsaw *(adj.)* **voluptuous**
ဇိမ်ရှိသော zain-shi-taw *(adj.)* **comfy**
ဇီးကွက် zee-kwat *(n.)* **owl**
ဇီးကွက်ပုံစံရှိသော jeekwat pone-sanshisaw *(adj.)* **owly**
ဇီးကွက်အောင်းသံ jeekwat-aaw-san *(n.)* **owlery**
ဇီဇာကြောင်သော zezar kyaungsaw *(v.)* **snobbish**
ဇီဝဓာတုဗေဒနှင့် ဆိုင်သော zi-wa-dar-tu-bay-da-nint-sai-taw *(adj.)* **biochemical**
ဇီဝဓာတုဗေဒပညာ zi-wa-dar-tu-bay-da-pyin-nyar *(n.)* **biochemistry**
ဇီဝဓာတ်ငွေ့ zi-wa-dat-ngwe *(n.)* **biogas**
ဇီဝဖြစ်စဉ် zi-wa-phit-sin *(n.)* **metabolism**
ဇီဝဗေဒ zi-wa-bay-da *(n.)* **biology**
ဇီဝဗေဒဆိုင်ရာ zi-wa-bay-da-sai-yar *(adv.)* **biologically**
ဇီဝဗေဒနှင့် ဆိုင်သော zi-wa-bay-da-nint-sai-taw *(adj.)* **biological**
ဇီဝဗေဒပညာရှင် zi-wa-bay-da-pyin-nyar-shin *(n.)* **biologist**

ဇီဝလောင်စာ zi-wa-laung-zar *(n.)* **biofuel**

ဇီဝသက်ရှိမှ လွှမ်းမိုးသော ရာသီဥတု zi-wa-thet-shi-ma-hlwan-moe-taw-yar-thi-u-tu *(n.)* **bioclimate**

ဇီဝသက်ရှိအပေါ်အကျိုးသက်ရောက်သော zi-wa-thet-shi-a-paw-a-kyo-thet-yaut-taw *(n.)* **bioactivity**

ဇီဝအချက်အလက်ဆိုင်ရာ zi-wa-a-chat-a-lat-sai-yar *(adj.)* **biometric**

ဇီဝအင်ဂျင်နီယာပညာ zi-wa-in-gyin-nee-yar-pyin-nyar *(n.)* **bioengineering**

ဇီဝအန္တရာယ်ရှိသော zi-wa-an-da-yal-shi-taw *(adj.)* **biohazardous**

ဇုန် zone *(n.)* **zone**

ဇုန်နယ်အလိုက် zone naal-aa-lite *(adj.)* **zonal**

ဇောက်ထိုးစကား zaut-htoe-sa-kar *(n.)* **irony**

ဇောက်ထိုးထားသည် zaut-htoe-htar-the *(v.)* **invert**

ဇောင်းပေးထားသည် zaung-payy-htarr-sai *(v.)* **pitch**

ဉပါဒါန် au-par-dan *(adj.)* **morbid**

ဉပါယ်တံမျဉ် au-pal tan myin *(n.)* **ruse**

ဉာဉ်၊ လက္ခဏာ nyin , lakhkanar *(n.)* **trait**

ဉာဏ်၊ အမြော်အမြင် ကြီးမှု nyarn, a myawaamyin kyeemhu *(n.)* **sagacity**

ဉာဏ်၊ အမြော်အမြင် ကြီးသော nyarn, a myawaamyin kyeesaw *(adj.)* **sagacious**

ဉာဏ်ကွန့်မြူးမှု nyan-kyunt-my-mu *(n.)* **inspiration**

ဉာဏ်ကောင်းခြင်း nyan-kaung-chin *(n.)* **brilliance**

ဉာဏ်ကောင်းသော nyan-kaung-taw *(adj.)* **brilliant**

ဉာဏ်စမ်းပဟေဠိပြိုင်ပွဲ nyarn-sam pahay-li-pyaine-pwal *(n.)* **quiz**

ဉာဏ်ထိုင်းသောသူ nyan-htai-taw-thu *(n.)* **dunce**

ဉာဏ်ပညာ nyarnpanyar *(n.)* **wisdom**

ဉာဏ်ပူဇော်ခ nyan-pu-zaw-kha *(n.)* **honorarium**

ဉာဏ်များသော nyan-myar-taw *(adj.)* **artful**

ဉာဏ်ရည်ဉာဏ်စွမ်းရှိသော nyan-yay-nyan-swan-shi-taw *(adj.)* **intelligent**

ဉာဏ်သွားသော nyan-twar-taw *(adj.)* **brainy**

ဉာဏ်အလင်းရစေသည် nyan-a-lin-ya-say-the *(v.)* **enlighten**

ညံ့သော nyant-taw *(adj.)* **inferior**

ညက်ညက်နှင့် ပတ်တက်သူ nyaat nyaat-nint paat taatsuu *(n.)* **smoothie**

ညက်ညောစွာ ရွေ့လျားသည် nyat-nyaw-swar-shwe-lyar-the *(v.)* **glide**

ညင်းလေပြည် nyinn-lay-pyi *(n.)* **zephyr**

ညင်သာစွာ လှုပ်သိပ်သည် nyin-tar-swar-hlote-tate-the *(v.)* **lull**

ညင်သာစွာနှစ်သည် nyin-tar-swar-nit-the *(v.)* **dap**

ညင်သာနူးညံ့သော nyin-tar-nu-nyant-taw *(adj.)* **gentle**

ညစဉ်ညတိုင်း nya-hcain-nya-tine *(adv.)* **nightly**
ညစာ nya-sar *(n.)* **dinner**
ညစာစားသည် nya-sar-sar-the *(v.)* **dine**
ညစာရေးခြင်း nyahcarrayyhkyinn *(n.)* **sonography**
ညစ်ညမ်းခြင်း nyit-nyam-chinn *(n.)* **pollution**
ညစ်ညမ်းစေသည် nyat-nyan-say-the *(v.)* **contaminate**
ညစ်ညမ်းသည် nyit-nyam-sai *(v.)* **pollute**
ညစ်ညမ်းသော nyit-nyam-taw *(adj.)* **obscene**
ညစ်ညမ်းသော၊ ရိုင်းပျသော nyit-nyan-taw, yai-pya-taw *(adj.)* **lewd**
ညစ်ထားခြင်း၊ nyit htarrchinn *(n.)* **strangulation**
ညစ်ပတ်၍ မှောင်သော nyit-pat-ywe-hmaung-taw *(adj.)* **dingy**
ညစ်ပတ်ခြင်း nyit-pat-chin *(n.)* **mess**
ညစ်ပတ်ပေရေသော nyit-pat-pay-yay-taw *(adj.)* **filthy**
ညစ်ပတ်သော nyit-pat-taw *(adj.)* **dirty**
ညစ်ပေသော nyait paysaw *(adj.)* **scrub**
ညစ်သည်၊ ပေသည် nyit sai, paysai *(v.)* **soil**
ညည်းသံ nyee-tan *(n.)* **moan**
ညည်းသည် nyee-the *(v.)* **groan**
ညတွင်းချင်း၊ တစ်ညတာ nya-twin-chinn , ta-nya-tar *(adj.)* **overnight**
ညတေးသီငှက် nya-tayy-te-nghaat *(n.)* **nightingale**
ညနေခင်း nya-nay-khin *(n.)* **evening**
ညနေဆည်းဆာ nya-nay-see-sar *(n.)* **twilight**
ညပ်သပ်သည် nyat-tat-the *(v.)* **jam**
ညမထွက်ရ အမိန့် nya-ma-htwat-ya-a-maint *(n.)* **curfew**
ညမှ ကျက်စားသော nya-mha-kyet-sarr-taw *(adj.)* **nocturnal**
ညလယ်စာ nyalaalsar *(n.)* **supper**
ညွတ်ကျနေခြင်း nyut-kya-nay-chin *(n.)* **droop**
ညွတ်ကျနေသော nyut-kya-nay-taw *(adj.)* **droopy**
ညွတ်ကျသည် nyut-kya-the *(v.)* **droop**
ညွတ်ထောင်သည် nywut htaungsai *(v.)* **snare**
ညွှန်ကြားချက် hnyun-kyar-chat *(n.)* **directive**
ညွှန်ကြားချက်၊ သင်ကြားပို့ချမှု hnyun-kyar-chat, tin-kyar-poe-cha-mu *(n.)* **instruction**
ညွှန်ကြားသည် nyun-kyarr-sai *(v.)* **prescribe**
ညွှန်ကြားသည်၊ သင်ပေးသည် hnyun-kyar-the, tin-pay-the *(v.)* **instruct**
ညွှန်တံမရှိသော၊ နည်းပေးလမ်းပြမှု မရှိသော nyun-tan-ma-shi-saw, naee-payy-lam-pya-mhu-ma-shi-saw *(adj.)* **pointerless**
ညွှန်ပြသည် hnyun-pya-the *(v.)* **indicate**
ညွှန်ပြသူ hnyun-pya-thu *(n.)* **mentor**
ညွှန်ပြသော hnyun-pya-taw *(adj.)* **indicative**
ညသန်းခေါင် nya-tan-khaung *(n.)* **midnight**
ညှင်းပန်းနှိပ်စက်သော nyin-pan-nate-sat-taw *(adj.)* **crucified**
ညှစ်သည်၊ ဖျစ်သည် nyit-the, phit-the *(v.)* **constrict**
ညှဥ်းပန်းမှုဒဏ် nyin paann mhudan *(n.)* **torment**
ညှပ် hnyat *(n.)* **forceps**

ညှပ်၊ ပြုတ်တူ hnyat, pyoke-tu *(n.)* **clamp**
ညှပ်ပူးညှပ်ပိတ်ပစ်ခတ်ခြင်း nyat-poo-nyat-paik-pyit-khat-chin *(n.)* **crossfire**
ညှပ်သည် nyat-sai *(v.)* **shear**
ညှာတံ nyhartan *(n.)* **stalk**
ညှိ၍ မရသော hnyi-ywe-ma-ya-taw *(adj.)* **irreconcilable**
ညှိခြင်း nyi-chin *(n.)* **compromise**
ညှိနိူင်းဆောင်ရွက်ခြင်း nyi-nai-saung-ywet-chin *(n.)* **coordination**
ညှိနိူင်းနိုင်သော nyi-nai-nai-taw *(adj.)* **negotiable**
ညှိနိူင်းရေးသမား nyi-nai-yay-ta-mar *(n.)* **dealmaker**
ညှိသည် nyi-the *(v.)* **level**
ညှို့ဓာတ် hnyo-dat *(v.)* **allure**
ညှို့ဓာတ်ရှိသော hnyo-dat-shi-taw *(adj.)* **alluring**
ညှို့ဓာတ်အားကောင်းသော nyhahoet dharataarrkaunggsaw *(adj.)* **sexy**
ညှို့နည်းဖြင့် စိတ်ညှို့ထားသော အခြေအနေ nyo-ne-phint-sate-nyo-htar-taw-a-chay-nay *(n.)* **mesmerism**
ညှို့ယူဖမ်းစားသော nyhahoet yuu hpam sarrsaw *(adj.)* **seductive**
ညှို့သကျည်း nyoet sa kyee *(n.)* **shin**
ညှို့သည် hnyo-the *(v.)* **charm**
ညှိုးငယ်ခြင်း nyoe-ngal-chin *(n.)* **melancholy**
ညှိုးငယ်သော nyoe-ngal-taw *(adj.)* **melancholy**
ညှော်သော nyaw-taw *(adj.)* **acrid**
ညအိပ်ဝတ်စုံ nya-aik-wit-sone *(n.)* **nightie**
ညအိပ်ဝတ်ရုံ nya-aik-wut-yone *(n.)* **bedrobe**
ညအိပ်အဆောက်အအုံ nya-aik-a-saut-a-ohn *(n.)* **night shelter**
ညာခိုင်းသည် nyar-khai-the *(v.)* **dupe**
ညာဘက် nyarbhaat *(n.)* **right**
ညိတ်သည် nyeik-the *(v.)* **bob**
ညိုသော nyosaw *(adj.)* **swarthy**
ညီညွတ်စွာ ပူးပေါင်းဆောင်ရွက်သော nyi-nyut-swar-pu-paung-saung-ywet-taw *(adj.)* **concerted**
ညီညွတ်သည် nyu-nyut-the *(v.)* **accord**
ညီညာခြင်း nye nyarchinn *(n.)* **unison**
ညီညာသော nyi-nyar-taw *(adj.)* **even**
ညီမျှခြင်း nyi-mya-chin *(n.)* **equation**
ညီမျှစွာ nyi-mya-swar *(adv.)* **evenly**
ညီမျှသော nyi-mya-taw *(adj.)* **equivalent**
ညီမျှအောင်လုပ်သည် nyi-mya-aung-lote-the *(v.)* **even**
ညီရင်းအစ်ကို ပမာဖြစ်သော nyi-yin-a-ko-pa-mar-phit-taw *(adj.)* **fraternal**
ညီလာခံ nyi-lar-khan *(n.)* **conference**
ညီလာခံ၊ ထုံးနည်း nyi-lar-khan, htone-nee *(n.)* **convention**
ညီအစ်ကို တော်စပ်ခြင်း nyi-a-ko-taw-sat-chin *(n.)* **brotherhood**
ညီအစ်ကိုချင်းသတ်မှု nyi-a-ko-chin-tat-mu *(n.)* **fratricide**
ညီအစ်မ nyeaaitma *(n.)* **sister**
ညီအစ်မကဲ့သို့ nyeaaitmakathoet *(adj.)* **sisterly**
ညီအစ်မစိတ်ဓာတ် nyeaaitmasatedhat *(n.)* **sisterhood**
ညောင်မုတ်ဆိတ် nyaung-mote-seik *(n.)* **banyan**

ဌ

ဌာန htar-na *(n.)* **department**

ဌာနချုပ် htar-na-choke *(v.)* **headquarter**

ဌာနချုပ်စခန်း htar-na-chote-sa-khan *(n.)* **base camp**

ဌာနများ ခွဲခြင်း htar-na-myar-kwal-chin *(n.)* **departmentalization**

ဌာနေတိုင်းရင်းသား htar-nay-thaing-yin-thar *(n.)* **aborigine**

ဌာနေတိုင်းရင်းသားတို့၏ htar-nay-thaing-yin-thar-doe-ei *(adj.)* **aboriginal**

ဌာပနာသည် htar-pa-nar-the *(v.)* **enshrine**

ဍရင်ကောက်ပင်ကြီးတစ်မျိုး da-yin-kauk-pin-gyi-ta-myo *(n.)* **bracken**

တံခါး ta-khar *(n.)* **door**

တံခါးကျင် ta-khar-kyin *(n.)* **latch**

တံခါးလက်ကိုင်ဖု ta-khar-lat-khai-phu *(n.)* **doorknob**

တံခါးသော့ ta-khar-taw *(n.)* **deadbolt**

တံငါသည် tan-ngar-the *(n.)* **fisherman**

တံစက်မြိတ် ta-sat-myeik *(n.)* **eave**

တံစဉ် tansin *(n.)* **sickle**

တံဆိပ် ta-seik *(n.)* **badge**

တံဆိပ်ခေါင်း tanseikhkaungg *(n.)* **stamp**

တံတွေး tantway *(n.)* **saliva**

တံတား ta-dar *(n.)* **bridge**

တံတားခင်းသည် tantarr hkinnsai *(v.)* **span**

တံတိုင်း tantine *(n.)* **wall**

တံတိုင်းခတ်သည် tantine hkaatsai *(v.)* **wall**

တံတိုင်းခေါင် ta-dai-khaung *(n.)* **coping**

တံတောင်ဆစ် ta-daung-sit *(n.)* **elbow**

တံတောင်ဖြင့် တွတ်သည် tan-daung-hpyint-twat-te *(v.)* **nudge**

တံမြက်စည်း ta-myat-see *(n.)* **broom**

တံမြက်လှည်းခြင်း tan myaat hlaeechinn *(n.)* **sweep**

တံမြက်လှည်းသမား tan myaat hlaeesamarr *(n.)* **sweeper**

တံလျှပ် tan-hlyat *(n.)* **mirage**

တကယ့်ကို ta-khae-ko *(adv.)* **downright**

တကယ်တော့ takaaltot *(conj.)* **whereas**

တကယ်လား ta-kal-lar *(int.)* **really**

တကျည်ကျည်အသံပေးသည့် လျှပ်စစ်ကိရိယာ ta-kyi-kyi-a-tan-pay-the-lyat-sit-ka-yi-yar *(n.)* **buzzer**

တကျွတ်ကျွတ်ဝါးသည် ta-kywut-kywut-war-the *(v.)* **crunch**

တကောက်ကောက်လိုက်သည် a-kauk-kauk-lite-the *(v.)* **dog**

တက္ကစီ takkase *(n.)* **taxi**

တက္ကစီကား takkahce karr *(n.)* **taxicab**

တက္ကစီဘတ်စကား takkase bhaatsakarr *(n.)* **taxibus**

တက္ကစီယာဉ်မောင်း tat-ka-see-yin-maung *(n.)* **cabby**

တက္ကသိုလ် takkasol *(n.)* **university**

တက္ကသိုလ်၊ အသင်း၊ အဖွဲ့အစည်း tat-ka-do, a-tin, a-phwe-a-see *(n.)* **institute**

တက္ကသိုလ်ပရဝုဏ် tat-ka-tho-pa-ra-won *(n.)* **campus**

တက္ကသိုလ်ဝင်ခွင့် tat-ka-do-win-khwint *(n.)* **matriculation**

တက္ကသိုလ်ဝင်ခွင့်ရသည် tat-ka-do-win-khwint-ya-the *(v.)* **matriculate**

တက်ကြွစွာ tat-kwa-swar *(adv.)* **actively**

တက်ကြွလွန်းသူ taat-kya-lwann-suu *(n.)* **zealot**

တက်ကြွလှုပ်ရှားသူ tat-kwa-lote-shar-thu *(n.)* **activist**

တက်ကြွလာစေသည် taatkya larsaysai *(v.)* **stimulate**

တက်ကြွသော tat-kwa-taw *(adj.)* **active**

တက်ခတ်သမား tat-hkat-ta-mar *(n.)* **oarsman**

တက်ခြင်း tat-chin *(n.)* **ascent**

တက်ခြင်း၊ ဖမ်းဆီးခြင်း taatchinn, hpamseechinn *(n.)* **seizure**

တက်ခီလာအရက် taat hke lar aaraat *(n.)* **tequila**

တက်စတိုစတီရုန်းဟော်မုန်း taat sa to sa te ronehawmone *(n.)* **testosterone**

တက်တူး taattuu *(n.)* **tattoo**

တက်တူးထိုးသည် taattuu htoesai *(v.)* **tattoo**

တက်မ taat-ma *(n.)* **rudder**

တက်မရိုး tat-ma-yoe *(n.)* **rudderpost**

တက်ရောက်သည် tat-yauk-the *(v.)* **attend**

တက်ရောက်သူဦးရေ tat-yauk-thu-oo-yay *(n.)* **attendance**

တက်သည် taatsai *(v.)* **rise**

တက်သည်၊ တင်သည် tat-the, tin-the *(v.)* **mount**

တက်သွားသည် tat-twar-the *(v.)* **ascend**

တက်သော tat-taw *(adj.)* **epileptic**

တခစ်ခစ်ရယ်သည် ta-khit-khit-yal-the *(v.)* **chuckle**

တချက်ချက်မြည်သံ tachet chet myisan *(n.)* **tick**

တချက်ချက်မြည်သည် tachet chet myisai *(v.)* **tick**

တချွင်ချွင်မြည်သည် ta-chwin-chwin-myae-the *(v.)* **jingle**

တငွေ့ငွေ့လောင်ကျွမ်းသည် ta ngwae-ngwae laungkyawmsai *(v.)* **smoulder**

တင့်တယ်သော tint-the-taw *(adj.)* **graceful**

တင်းကျပ်သော tinnkyatsaw *(adj.)* **stringent**

တင်းကြပ်သော tinnkyautsaw *(adj.)* **tight**

တင်းနစ် tinnnit *(n.)* **tennis**

တင်းနစ်ဘောလုံး tinn-nit-bhawlone *(n.)* **racket**

တင်းနေသော ကြွက်သား tin-nay-taw-kywat-tar *(n.)* **tensor**

တင်းပုတ် tin-poke *(n.)* **cudgel**

တင်းမာစွာ tinnmarswar *(adv.)* **tensely**

တင်းမာသည် tinnmarsai *(v.)* **tense**

တင်းမာသော၊ ပြင်းထန်သော tinnmar saw , pyinn-htaansaw *(adj.)* **stern**

တင်းသည်၊ ကျပ်သည် tinn sai , kyatsai *(v.)* **tighten**

တင်းသော၊ တောင့်သော tinn saw , tawntsaw *(adj.)* **taut**

တင်းအား tin-naarr *(n.)* **tension**

တင်းအား နည်းခြင်း၊ ကိုယ်ကျင့် အားနည်းခြင်း tin-arr-nae-chin, ko-kyint-arr-nae-chin *(n.)* **laxity**

တင်ကျီးငှက် tin-kyi-nget *(n.)* **cormorant**

တင်ကြိုပြင်ဆင်မှု tin kyo-pyin-sin-mhu *(n.)* **preparation**

တင်ချာဆေးရည် tin chaar sayyrai *(n.)* **tincture**

တင်စားထားသော tin-sar-htar-taw *(adj.)* **figurative**

တင်စားမှု tin-sar-mu *(n.)* **metaphor**

တင်ဆက်မှု tin-saatmhu *(n.)* **repertoire**

တင်ဆက်သူ၊ သဘင်သည် tin-saat-suu, sa-bhin-sai *(n.)* **performer**

တင်ဒါသွင်းသည် tin dar swinsai *(v.)* **tender**

တင်ပြချက် tin-pya-chet *(n.)* **presentation**

တင်ပြခြင်း tinpyachinn *(n.)* **submission**

တင်ပြသည် tinpyasai *(v.)* **submit**

တင်ပါး tin-bar *(n.)* **hip**

တင်ပါးဆုံအာရုံကြောနှင့် ဆိုင်သော tin parr sone aarronekyawwnint sinesaw *(adj.)* **sciatic**

တင်ပါးဆုံအာရုံကြောနာ tin parr sone aarronekyawwnar *(n.)* **sciatica**

တင်သည် tinsai *(v.)* **stock**

တင်သည်၊ တိုင်သည် tin-the, tai-the *(v.)* **lodge**

တင်သည်၊ ထည့်သည် tin-the, htae-the *(v.)* **load**

တင်သွင်းသည် tin-twin-the *(v.)* **import**

တစိမ့်စိမ့် ချင့်ချိန်သည် ta-seint-seint-chint-chane-the *(adj.)* **ruminant**

တစ္ဆေ ta-say *(n.)* **spectre**

တစ္ဆေ၊ အာရုံ ta-say, ar-rone *(n.)* **phantom**

တစ်ကမ္ဘာလုံး ta-ka-bar-lone *(adv.)* **globally**

တစ်ကမ္ဘာလုံးကဲ့သို့ လွှမ်းခြုံသည် ta-ka-bar-lone-kae-tho-hlwan-chon-the *(v.)* **englobe**

တစ်ကျိုက် ta-kyaite *(n.)* **sup**

တစ်ကျိုက်၊ တစ်ငုံ ta-kyaik, ta-ngon *(n.)* **gulp**

တစ်ကျော့၊ တစ်ကန့် ta-kyaww , ta-kaant *(n.)* **stretch**

တစ်ကြိမ်က ta-kyain-ka *(adv.)* **once**

တစ်ကိုယ်ကောင်းဆန်သော ta-ko kaunggsaansaw *(adj.)* **selfish**

တစ်ကိုယ်တော် taitkotaw *(adv.)* **single-handedly**

တစ်ကိုယ်တော်သမား ta-kotaw-samarr *(n.)* **recluse**

တစ်ကိုယ်တော်သီဆိုဖြေဖျော်သူ ta-kotaw se-so hpyay hpyawsuu *(n.)* **soloist**

တစ်ကိုယ်ရေတစ်ကာယဖြစ်သည် taitkoray tait kar yahpyitsai *(v.)* **single**

တစ်ကိုယ်ရေတစ်ကာယဖြစ်သော taitkoray tait kar yahpyitsaw *(adj.)* **single**

တစ်ကိုယ်ရေလုံခြုံမှု ta-ko-ray-lone-chon-mhu *(n.)* **privacy**

တစ်ကိုယ်ရေသန့်ရှင်းရေး ta-koe-yay-tant-shint-yay *(n.)* **hygiene**

တစ်ချိန်ချိန် ta-chain-chain *(adv.)* **anytime**

တစ်ချိန်ချိန်တွင်၊ အမြဲ ta-chain-chain-twin, a-myae *(adv.)* **ever**

တစ်ချိန်တည်းဖြစ်သော ta-chain-tal-phit-taw *(adj.)* **cotemporal**

တစ်ချို့ ta-choet *(pron.)* **some**

တစ်ချောင်းထိုး ta-chaung-htoe *(n.)* **crochet**

တစ်ခြားကမ္ဘာမှ သက်ရှိများ ta-char-ka-bar-ma-thet-shi-myar *(n.)* **extraterrestrial**

တစ်ခြားစီ ta-charr-se *(adj.)* **unlike**

တစ်ခွက်စာလက်ဖက်ခြောက်အိတ် taithkwat sar laathpaatchauk-ate *(n.)* **teabag**

တစ်ခါတစ်ရံ ta-hkarta-ran *(adv.)* **sometimes**
တစ်ခါသောက်ဆေးပမာဏ ta-khar-taut-say-pa-mar-na *(n.)* **dose**
တစ်ခု ta-hku *(pron.)* **one**
တစ်ခု၊ တစ်ယောက် Ta-Khu, Ta-Yauk *(art.)* **a**
တစ်ခု၊ တစ်ယောက်ဖြစ်သော ta-khu, ta-yauk-phit-taw *(adj.)* **An**
တစ်ခုခု ta-khu-khu *(pron.)* **anything**
တစ်ခုခုကို နမ်းသည် ta-khu-khu-ko-nan-the *(v.)* **osculate**
တစ်ခုခုနှင့် ဖိသတ်သည် ta-hku-hku-nint hpi saatsai *(v.)* **smother**
တစ်ခုစီ ta-khu-si *(pron.)* **each**
တစ်ခုစီဖြစ်သော ta-khu-si-phit-taw *(adj.)* **each**
တစ်ခုတည်းသော ta-hkutaeesaw *(adj.)* **sole**
တစ်ခုနှင့် တစ်ခု ယှဉ်တွဲပြသည် ta-khu-nint-ta-khu-yin-twe-pya-the *(v.)* **juxtapose**
တစ်ခုနှင့် တစ်ခု ယှဉ်တွဲပြသော ta-khu-nint-ta-khu-yin-twe-pya-taw *(adj.)* **juxtaposed**
တစ်ခုပြီး တစ်ခု ta-hku-pyee ta-hku *(n.)* **succession**
တစ်ခုမဟုတ် တစ်ခု ta-khu-ma-hote-ta-khu *(adv.)* **either**
တစ်ခုလုံး ta-hkulone *(n.)* **whole**
တစ်ခေါက်ခေါက်ထားသော စက္ကူ ta-khauk-khauk-htar-taw-sat-khu *(n.)* **folio**
တစ်ငုံစာ tait ngone-sar *(n.)* **sip**
တစ်စက်တစ်စက်ကျခြင်း ta-sat-ta-sat-kya-chin *(n.)* **drip**
တစ်စက်တစ်စက်ကျသည် ta-sat-ta-sat-kya-the *(v.)* **drip**
တစ်စတစ်စ လျော့ပါးသည် ta-sa-ta-sa-yawt-par-the *(v.)* **dwindle**
တစ်စတစ်စကြီးပွားလာမှု ta-sa-ta-sa-kyi-pwar-lar-mu *(n.)* **accretion**
တစ်စိတ်တစ်ပိုင်း ကန်းသည် ta-seik-ta-pine-kan-the *(n.)* **purblind**
တစ်စိတ်တစ်ပိုင်း တရားဝင်ဖြစ်သော taithcatetaitpine tararrwainhpyitsaw *(adj.)* **semi-formal**
တစ်စိတ်တစ်ပိုင်း ရွှင်မြူးဖွယ် taithcatetaitpine shwin myauuhpwal *(adj.)* **semi-amusing**
တစ်စုံ ta-zone *(n.)* **traunch**
တစ်စုံတစ်ခု ta-sone-ta-khu *(pron.)* **everything**
တစ်စုံတစ်ခုနှင့် ဆင်တူခြင်း taithconetaithkunhang saintuuhkyinn *(n.)* **similitude**
တစ်စုံတစ်ယောက် ta-sonetaityout *(n.)* **somebody**
တစ်စုံတစ်ယောက်စိတ်ထဲဝင်ကြည့်သည် ta-sone-ta-yauk-seik-htae-win-kyi-the *(v.)* **envision**
တစ်စုံတစ်ရာ ta-soneta-rar *(adv.)* **something**
တစ်စုံတစ်ရာ စုတ်ဖြဲခြင်းဖြစ်စဉ် ta-sone-ta-yar-sote-phwal-chin-phit-sin *(n.)* **dilaceration**
တစ်စုံတစ်ရာကို နေထိုင်ရာ အဖြစ်ပြောင်းသည် ta-sone-ta-yar-ko-nay-htai-yar-a-phit-pyaung-the *(v.)* **terrace**
တစ်စုံတစ်ရာသည် မှုခင်းမဖြစ်တော့ရန် ဥပဒေပြောင်းသည် ta-sone-ta-yar-the-mu-khin-ma-phit-say-yan-oo-pa-day-pyaung-the *(v.)* **decriminalize**
တစ်ဆင့်ကမ်းသည် ta-sint-khan-the *(v.)* **forward**
တစ်ဆင့်ခံ taitsinthkan *(adj.)* **vicarious**
တစ်ဆင့်ခံ ရောင်းသူ ta-sint-khan-yaung-thu *(n.)* **middleman**
တစ်ဆင့်ငှားသည် ta-sint ngar-sai *(v.)* **sublet**

တစ်ဆင့်ပို့ပေးခြင်း bharsarpyansai *(n.)* **transmission**
တစ်ဆယ် taitsaal *(n.)* **ten**
တစ်ဆယ့်ကိုး ta-sae-koe *(n.)* **nineteen**
တစ်ဆယ့်ကိုးခုမြောက် ta-sae-koe-hku-myauk *(adj.)* **nineteenth**
တစ်ဆယ့်ခုနှစ် ta-sae-hkun-nit *(n.)* **seventeen**
တစ်ဆယ့်ခုနှစ်ခုမြောက် ta-sae-hkun-nit-hku-myaut *(adj.)* **seventeenth**
တစ်ဇွန်းစာ ta zwann-sar *(n.)* **spoonful**
တစ်တိတစ်တိစားခြင်း ta-ti-ta-ti-sar-chin *(n.)* **nibble**
တစ်တိတစ်တိစားသည် ta-ti-ta-ti-sar-the *(v.)* **nibble**
တစ်ထပ်တိုက်ကလေး ta-htat-tite-ka-lay *(n.)* **cottage**
တစ်ထွေးကြီး ta htwaykyee *(n.)* **welter**
တစ်ထောင်မြောက် ta-htaungmyawt *(adj.)* **thousandth**
တစ်နည်းနည်း ta-nee-nee *(adv.)* **anyway**
တစ်နည်းနည်းဖြင့် ta- nee-neehpyint *(adv.)* **somehow**
တစ်နည်းအားဖြင့် ta-nee-ar-hpyint *(conj.)* **otherwise**
တစ်နှစ်တစ်ကြိမ်ဖြစ်သော ta-nit-ta-kyein-phit-taw *(adj.)* **monoestrous**
တစ်နှစ်နှစ်ကြိမ် ta-nit-na-kyein *(adj.)* **biannual**
တစ်နှစ်လျှင် ta-nit-hlyin *(adv.)* **per annum**
တစ်နေရာတည်းတွင် ဆုံသော ta-nay-yar-te-twin-son-taw *(adj.)* **convergent**
တစ်နေရာမှ တစ်နေရာ ရွှေ့နေသော ta-nay-yar-ma-ta-nay-yar-yway-nay-taw *(adj.)* **ambulant**
တစ်နေရာမှ တစ်နေရာသို့ ကြားအကွာအဝေးကို ဖျောက်၍ ချက်ခြင်း ရောက်အောင် ပို့ဆောင်ခြင်း ta-nay-rarmha ta-nayrar-thoet kyarr aa-kwar-aa-wayy-ko hpyawt-ywe-chet-chinn routaaung phoetsaunghkyinn *(n.)* **teleportation**
တစ်နေရာရာ ta-nayrar-rar *(adv.)* **somewhere**
တစ်ပင်တိုင်လက်ဝတ်ရတနာ ta pintinelaatwaatratanar *(n.)* **solitaire**
တစ်ပတ် taitpaat *(n.)* **week**
တစ်ပတ်ရစ် taitpaatrit *(adj.)* **second-hand**
တစ်ပတ်ရိုက်သည် ta-pat-rite-tai *(v.)* **outwit**
တစ်ပြိုင်တည်း ဖြစ်ပေါ်သော ta-pyai-the-phit-paw-taw *(adj.)* **concurrent**
တစ်ပြိုင်နက်ဖြစ်သော taitpyainenaathpyitsaw *(adj.)* **simultaneous**
တစ်ပွင့် ta-pwint *(n.)* **ace**
တစ်ပွဲတွင် သွင်းသော ဂိုးသုံးဂိုး ta-pwe-twin-twin-taw-goe-tone-goe *(n.)* **hat-trick**
တစ်ပိုင်းတစ်စ ဖြစ်သော ta-pine-ta-sa-hpyit-saw *(adj.)* **partial**
တစ်ပိုင်းတစ်စစီ ဖြုတ်ရောင်းသည် ta-pine-ta-sase hpyuat raunggsai *(v.)* **scrap**
တစ်ပုံတစ်ခေါင်း ta-pone ta-hkaungg *(n.)* **profusion**
တစ်ပဲခြောက်ပြား ta-pell-chauk-pyarr *(n.)* **pittance**
တစ်ဖက်ကမ်းခပ်ခြင်း ta-phat-kan-khat-chin *(n.)* **mastery**
တစ်ဖက်ကမ်းခပ်သည် ta-phat-kan-khat-the *(v.)* **master**
တစ်ဖက်စာမျက်နှာတွင် ta-hpat-sar-myet-nhar-twin *(adv.)* **overleaf**
တစ်ဖက်စီ ta-phat-si *(adv.)* **apiece**

တစ်ဖက်တစ်ချက်တွင် ရံသည် ta-phat-ta-chat-twin-yan-the *(v.)* **flank**
တစ်ဖက်တည်းဖြစ်သော ta-phat-te-phit-taw *(adj.)* **monocular**
တစ်ဖက်တည်းမျက်မှန် ta-phat-te-myat-man *(n.)* **monocle**
တစ်ဖက်တည်းမှ ယူလျက် ta-phat-tae-ma-yu-lyat *(adv.)* **ex-parte**
တစ်ဖက်တည်းမှ ယူသော ta-phat-tae-ma-yu-taw *(adj.)* **ex-parte**
တစ်ဖက်တွင် ta-phat-twin *(prep.)* **athwart**
တစ်ဖက်သတ် ta-hpat-tat *(adj.)* **one-sided**
တစ်ဖန် ta-hpan *(adv.)* **again**
တစ်ဖန် တန်ဖိုးဖြတ်ခြင်း taithpaan taanhpoe hpyatchinn *(n.)* **revaluation**
တစ်ဖွဲ့လုံး ta-hpwal-lone *(adv.)* **teamwise**
တစ်ဘဝလုံး ta-ba-wa-lone *(adj.)* **lifelong**
တစ်မျိုးစီဖြစ်သော်လည်း နှစ်သက်ဖွယ်ကောင်းသော ta-myoe sehpyit-sawlaee nit-saat-hpwal-kaunggsaw *(adj.)* **whimsical**
တစ်မှေး ta-may *(n.)* **doze**
တစ်မှေးအိပ်ခြင်း ta-may-ate-chin *(n.)* **nap**
တစ်မှေးအိပ်သည် ta-may-ate-the *(v.)* **nap**
တစ်မူထူးခြင်း ta-mu-htuu-chinn *(n.)* **oddity**
တစ်မူထူးခြားသော ta-mu-htoo-char-taw *(adj.)* **anomalous**
တစ်မူထူးသော ta muu htuusaw *(adj.)* **zany**
တစ်ယူသန် ta-yu-tan *(n.)* **bigot**
တစ်ယူသန်ဖြစ်သော ta-yu-tan-phit-taw *(adj.)* **dogmatic**
တစ်ယူသန်သဘောထား ta-yu-tan-ta-baw-htar *(n.)* **bigotry**
တစ်ယောက်မျှ Ta-yout-mya *(pron.)* **none**
တစ်ရန်၊ တစ်စုံ ta-raan, ta-sone *(n.)* **pair**
တစ်ရှိန်ထိုး၊ ဥက္ကာပျံနှင့် ဆိုင်သော ta-shein-htoe, oak-kar-pyan-nint-sai-taw *(adj.)* **meteoric**
တစ်ရှူး tit-shuu *(n.)* **tissue**
တစ်ရာ ta-yar *(n.)* **hundred**
တစ်ရာဆဖြစ်သော ta-yar-sa-phit-taw *(adj.)* **centuple**
တစ်ရေးမှေးသည် ta rayy mhaayysai *(v.)* **snooze**
တစ်လင်မယားစလေ့ ta-lin-ma-yar-da-lay *(n.)* **monogamy**
တစ်လမ်းပြေးရထား ta-lan-pyay-ya-htar *(n.)* **monorail**
တစ်လမ်းမောင်း ta-lam-maung *(adj.)* **one-way**
တစ်လျှောက် ta-shaut *(prep. &adv.)* **along**
တစ်လှည့်စီဖြစ်သည် ta-lae-si-phit-the *(v.)* **alternate**
တစ်လှမ်းချင်းရှုန်းသည် ta-hlam-chinn-rone-sai *(v.)* **plod**
တစ်လုံးတစ်ခဲတည်း ta-hlone-ta-khae-tae *(n.)* **lump sum**
တစ်လုတ်စာ ta-lote-sar *(n.)* **morsel**
တစ်လော ထွက်သည် ta-law htwatsai *(v.)* **sally**
တစ်လောက ta-lawka *(adv.)* **recently**
တစ်ဝက် ta-wat *(n.)* **half**
တစ်ဝက်ပြဂီတသင်္ကေတ ta-wat-pya-gi-ta-tin-kay-ta *(n.)* **minim**
တစ်ဝက်ဝက်သည် ta-wat-wat-the *(v.)* **halve**
တစ်ဝန်းလုံး ta waannlone *(prep.)* **throughout**
တစ်ဝမ်းကွဲ ta-wan-kwal *(n.)* **cousin**

တစ်သမတ်တည်းဖြစ်ခြင်း၊ ရှေ့နောက်ညီညွတ်ခြင်း ta-ta-mat-the-phit-chin, shay-naut-nyi-nyut-chin *(n.)* **consistency**
တစ်သမတ်တည်းဖြစ်သော ta-tat-mat-the-phit-taw *(adj.)* **consistent**
တစ်သားတည်း ဖြစ်သော ta-tar-the-phit-taw *(adj.)* **integral**
တစ်သားတည်းဖြစ်ခြင်း ta-tar-tae-hpyit-chinn *(n.)* **oneness**
တစ်ဟုန်ထိုး ta-honehtoe *(adj.)* **torrential**
တစ်ဟုန်ထိုး တက်ခြင်း Ta-hone-htoe-tat-chinn *(n.)* **onrush**
တစ်ဟုန်ထိုး တိုးပွားလာခြင်း ta-hone-htoe toepwarr-larchinn *(n.)* **proliferation**
တစ်ဟုန်ထိုးပြေးခြင်း ta-hone-htoe pyaychinn *(n.)* **rush**
တစ်ဟုန်ထိုးပြေးသည် taithonehtoe pyaysai *(v.)* **rush**
တစ်ဦးချင်း၊ သီးခြား ta-oo-chin, thee-char *(adj.)* **individual**
တစ်ဦးတည်း ta u-tee *(adj.)* **solitary**
တစ်ဦးတည်း ဈေးကွက်ချုပ်ကိုင်ခွင့်ရ ကုမ္ပဏီ ta-oo-the-zay-kwat-choke-kai-khwint-ya-kon-pa-ni *(n.)* **monopolist**
တစ်ဦးတည်း ရှည်လျားစွာ ပြောသော စကား ta-oo-the-shay-lyar-swar-pyaw-taw-sakar *(n.)* **monologue**
တဆတ်ဆတ်တုန်ခြင်း ta-saat-saat-tone-chinn *(n.)* **palpitation**
တဆေး tasayy *(n.)* **yeast**
တညီတညွတ်တည်း ta-nye-ta-nywat-tee *(adj.)* **unanimous**
တည့်တည့်၊ ကောင်းကောင်း tae-tae, kaung-kaung *(adv.)* **full**
တည့်တည့်မတ်မတ် te te-maat-maat *(adv.)* **right**
တည်းခိုခန်း te-kho-khan *(n.)* **lodging**
တည်းဖြတ်သည် the-phat-the *(v.)* **edit**
တည်းဖြတ်သူ the-phat-thu *(n.)* **editor**
တည်ကြက် tae-kyat *(n.)* **decoy**
တည်ကြည်လေးနက်ခြင်း tai kyi layynaatchinn *(n.)* **sobriety**
တည်ကြည်လေးနက်မှုရှိခြင်း tai kyi layynaatmhushichinn *(n.)* **solemnity**
တည်ကြည်လေးနက်သော tai kyi layynaatsaw *(adj.)* **solemn**
တည်ငြိမ်ခြင်း tingyaainchinn *(n.)* **stabilization**
တည်ငြိမ်မှု tingyaainmhu *(n.)* **stability**
တည်ငြိမ်မှု မရှိခြင်း the-nyein-mu-ma-shi-chi *(n.)* **instability**
တည်ငြိမ်သည် tingyaainsai *(v.)* **stabilize**
တည်ငြိမ်သည်၊ ထိန်းထိန်းသိမ်းသိမ်းရှိသည် tingyaain sai , htein hteinsaim saimshisai *(v.)* **steady**
တည်ငြိမ်သော tai-ngyein-saw *(adj.)* **placid**
တည်ငြိမ်သော၊ ပုံမှန် tingyaainsaw , ponemhaan *(adj.)* **steady**
တည်ငြိမ်အေးဆေးမှု the-nyein-aye-say-mu *(n.)* **composure**
တည်ဆောက်ခြင်း၊ ဗိသုကာနှင့် သက်ဆိုင်သော taisout-chinn , bisukar-nint saat-sinesaw *(adj.)* **tectonic**
တည်ဆောက်သည် the-saut-the *(v.)* **build**
တည်ဆောက်သူ the-saut-thu *(n.)* **builder**
တည်ဆောက်သော the-saut-thaw *(adj.)* **edificant**
တည်ထောင်ခြင်း the-htaung-chin *(n.)* **establishment**
တည်ထောင်သည် the-htaung-the *(v.)* **establish**
တည်ထောင်သူ te-htaung-thu *(n.)* **founder**

တည်နေရာ the-nay-yar *(n.)* **locality**

တည်နေရာ၊ ဖြစ်ပွားရာ tinayrar, hpyitpwarrrar *(n.)* **site**

တည်မြဲမှု၊ ခိုင်ကျည်မှု tai-myaell-mhu, hkine-kyai-mhu *(n.)* **permanence**

တည်မြဲသော taimyaellsaw *(adj.)* **steadfast**

တည်ရှိခြင်း the-shi-chin *(n.)* **existence**

တည်ရှိသည် the-shi-the *(v.)* **exist**

တည်ရာ te-yar *(n.)* **locus**

တဏှာကင်းသော ta-nhar-kinn-saw *(adj.)* **platonic**

တဏှာကြီးသော ta-nar-kyi-taw *(adj.)* **lascivious**

တတွတ်တွတ်ပြောသည် ta-twat-twat-pyaww-sai *(v.)* **prattle**

တတိယ tati-ya *(n.)* **third**

တတိယဂရိအက္ခရာ ta-ti-ya-ga-yi-at-kha-yar *(n.)* **gamma**

တတိယမြောက် tati-ya-myawt *(adj.)* **third**

တတိယအဆင့် tatiyaaasint *(n.)* **tertiary**

တတိယအနေဖြင့် tati-ya a nay hpyint *(adv.)* **thirdly**

တတီတီမြည်သံ ta-ti-ti-myi-tan *(n.)* **beep**

တတောက်တောက်မြည်သံ ta-taut-taut-myi-tan *(v.)* **clack**

တတ်နိုင်သည် tat-naing-the *(v.)* **afford**

တတ်နိုင်သော tat-naing-taw *(adj.)* **abled**

တတ်မြောက်သော taat myawtsaw *(adj.)* **versed**

တတ်သိနားလည်ခြင်း taat sinarrlaichinn *(n.)* **sapience**

တတ်သိနားလည်မှု tat-ti-nar-lal-mu *(n.)* **comprehension**

တဒင်္ဂ da-din-ga *(n.)* **moment**

တဒုတ်ဒုတ် ကိုက်ခဲသည် ta dote-dote kite hkellsai *(v.)* **throb**

တဒုတ်ဒုတ်မြည်ခြင်း ta dote dote myichinn *(n.)* **pulsation**

တဒုတ်ဒုတ်မြည်သံ ta dote-dote myisan *(n.)* **throb**

တဒုတ်ဒုတ်မြည်သည် ta dote dote myisai *(v.)* **pulsate**

တဒုန်းဒုန်းထုသည် ta done done htusai *(v.)* **pound**

တဒေါက်ဒေါက်မြည်သည် ta dout-dout myi-sai *(v.)* **rattle**

တနင်္ဂနွေ ta nin ga-nway *(n.)* **Sunday**

တနင်္လာနေ့ ta-nin-lar-nay *(n.)* **Monday**

တန် taan *(n.)* **ton**

တန့်သည်၊ အိုသည် tant sai, aesai *(v.)* **stagnate**

တန်း tan *(n.)* **hurdle**

တန်းကျော်ပြေးသည် tan-kyaw-pyay-the *(v.)* **hurdle**

တန်းခိုး၏ သွင်ပြင် tan-kho-ei-twin-pyin *(n.)* **mystique**

တန်းဂျင့်မျဉ်း tan gyant-myin *(n.)* **tangent**

တန်းစီသည် taann-sesai *(v.)* **queue**

တန်းစီသွားခြင်း taann-se-swarr-chinn *(n.)* **procession**

တန်းညှိခြင်း tan-hnyi-chin *(n.)* **alignment**

တန်းညှိသည် tan-hnyi-the *(v.)* **align**

တန်းတူထားသည် tan-tu-htar-the *(v.)* **equate**

တန်းတူမှု tan-tu-mu *(n.)* **equality**

တန်ဂိုကသည် taan go kasai *(v.)* **tango**

တန်ဂိုအက taan-go aa-ka *(n.)* **tango**

တန်ဆာဆင်သည် taan-sar-sin-tai *(v.)* **ornament**

တန်ပြန်စွပ်စွဲခြင်း taanpyan swut-swalchinn *(n.)* **recrimination**
တန်ပြန်စွပ်စွဲသည် taanpyan swut-swalsai *(v.)* **recriminate**
တန်ပြန်တိုက်ခိုက်မှု tan-yina-tite-kite-mu *(n.)* **counter-attack**
တန်ပွန်ထည့်သည် taan pwan htaeetsai *(v.)* **tampon**
တန်ပွန်အတောင့် taan pawn a taunt *(n.)* **tampon**
တန်ဖိုး a thoet-shin *(n.)* **value**
တန်ဖိုးကြီး အဝတ်အထည်၊ လက်ဝတ်ရတနာ tan-phoe-kyi-a-wut-a-htal-lat-wut-ya-da-nar *(n.)* **bling**
တန်ဖိုးကြီးသော tan-phoe-kyi-taw *(adj.)* **costly**
တန်ဖိုးခန့်မှန်းသည် taan-hpoe hkaant mhaann-sai *(v.)* **rate**
တန်ဖိုးထားသည် taanhpoe *(v.)* **value**
တန်ဖိုးနည်းသော tan-pho-nae-taw *(adj.)* **inexpensive**
တန်ဖိုးဖြတ်ခြင်း taanhpoehtarrsai *(n.)* **valuation**
တန်ဖိုးဖြတ်သည် tan-phoe-phat-the *(v.)* **appraise**
တန်ဖိုးမဖြတ်နိုင်သော tan-hpoe-ma-hpyat-ninesaw *(adj.)* **priceless**
တန်ဖိုးရှိသော taanhpoe hpyatchinn *(adj.)* **valuable**
တန်ဖိုးလျော့ကျသည် tan-pho-shawt-kya-the *(v.)* **depreciate**
တန်သော taan-saw *(adj.)* **worth**
တပည့် ta-pyae *(n.)* **disciple**
တပည့် ta paeet *(n.)* **pupil**
တပည့်ရင်း ta-pae-ying *(n.)* **acolyte**
တပ်ကြပ် tat-kyat *(adj.)* **corporal**
တပ်ကြပ်ကြီး tautkyatkyee *(n.)* **sergeant**
တပ်စခန်း tat-sa-hkan *(n.)* **outpost**
တပ်စင်သည် tat sainsai *(v.)* **piece**
တပ်စု tat-su *(n.)* **platoon**
တပ်ဆင်ခြင်း tat-sin-chin *(n.)* **installation**
တပ်ဆင်သည် tat-sin-the *(v.)* **accoutre**
တပ်ဖြန့်သည် tat-phyant-the *(v.)* **deploy**
တပ်မကြီး tat-ma-gyi *(n.)* **corps**
တပ်မက်ခြင်း tat-mat-chin *(n.)* **lust**
တပ်မဟာ tat-ma-har *(n.)* **brigade**
တပ်မှ ထုတ်သည် tat-ma-htoke-the *(v.)* **disembody**
တပ်မှူး tat-mu *(n.)* **commander**
တပ်မှူးချုပ် tat-mu-gyoke *(n.)* **commandant**
တပ်ရင်း tat-yin *(n.)* **battalion**
တပ်ရင်းကြီး tat-rinn-kyee *(n.)* **regiment**
တပ်သားသစ် tautsarrsait *(n.)* **recruit**
တပ်အစောင့်အရှောက်ပါ ယာဉ်တန်း tat-a-saunt-a-shaut-par-yin-tan *(n.)* **convoy**
တဖန်ပြန်သိမ်းပိုက်ခြင်း ta-phan-pyan-thein-pike-chin *(n.)* **reannexation**
တဖန်ပြန်သိမ်းပိုက်သည် ta-phan-pyan-thein-pike-the *(v.)* **reannex**
တဖျစ်တောက်တောက်ပြောခြင်း ta hpyit tout toutpyawwchinn *(n.)* **tirade**
တဖျစ်ဖျစ်မြည်သည် ta-phit-phit-myi-the *(v.)* **crackle**
တဖျစ်ဖျစ်အသံပြုခြင်း ta-phit-phit-a-tan-pyu-chin *(n.)* **crepitation**
တဖျစ်ဖျစ်အသံပြုသည် ta-phit-phit-a-tan-pyu-the *(v.)* **crepitate**

တဖျပ်ဖျပ် ခတ်ခြင်း၊ ပျာယာခတ်ခြင်း ta-phat-phat-khat-chin, pyar-yar-khat-chin *(n.)* **flutter**
တဖျပ်ဖျပ် လှုပ်သည် ta-phat-phat-hlote-the *(v.)* **flap**
တဖျပ်ဖျပ်ပျံသည်၊ တောင်ပံခတ်သည် ta-phat-phat-khat-the, pyar-yar-khat-the *(v.)* **flutter**
တဖျပ်ဖျပ်လှုပ်ခြင်း ta-phat-phat-hlote-chin *(n.)* **flap**
တဖြတ်ဖြတ် လှုပ်ခတ်သော ta-phat-phat-hlote-khat-taw *(adj.)* **flapping**
တဖြောင်းဖြောင်း ta hpyaung-hpyaung *(adj.)* **thunderous**
တမင် လုပ်သော ta-min-lote-taw *(adj.)* **intentional**
တမင်ဖျက်ဆီးသည် ta-min hpyetseesai *(v.)* **sabotage**
တမင်မဟုတ်သော၊ ဂရုတစိုက်မဟုတ်သော ta-min-ma-hote-taw, ga-yu-ta-seik-ma-hote-taw *(adj.)* **casual**
တမင်လိမ်လည်လှည့်စားခြင်း ta-min-lain-lal-hlae-sar-chin *(n.)* **duplicity**
တမင်သက်သက် ta-min-saatsaat *(adv.)* **purposely**
တမင်သက်သက် ဖြစ်သော ta-min-thet-thet-phit-taw *(adj.)* **deliberate**
တမန် ta-man *(n.)* **emissary**
တမားရိုးကျမဟုတ်သော tha-ma-yoe-kya-ma-hote-taw *(adj.)* **alternative**
တမ်းချင်း tan-chin *(n.)* **elegy**
တမ်းတခြင်း tamtachinn *(n.)* **yearning**
တမ်းတသည် tamtasai *(v.)* **yearn**
တယုတယ ပွတ်သပ်သည် ta-yu-ta-ya-pwut-sat-sai *(v.)* **pet**
တယော ta-yaw *(n.)* **fiddle**
တယောကြီး ta-yaw-gyi *(n.)* **cello**
တယောသမား tayawsamarr *(n.)* **violinist**
တယ်ရီယာခွေး taal re yarhkway *(n.)* **terrier**
တယ်လီကွန်ပျူတင်း taalle kwan-pyuu-tinn *(n.)* **telecomputing**
တယ်လီကွန်ဖရန့် taalle kwan hpa raant *(n.)* **teleconference**
တယ်လီစကုပ်တီထွင်အသုံးပြုခြင်း taalle hca kote tehtwin-aa-sone-pyu-chinn *(n.)* **telescopy**
တယ်လီဈေးကွက် taalle-zyayy-kwat *(v.)* **telemarket**
တယ်လီဈေးရောင်းသူ taalle syaayyraunggsuu *(n.)* **teleshopper**
တယ်လီဈေးဝယ်ခြင်း taalle syaayywaalchinn *(n.)* **teleshopping**
တယ်လီစာသား taallesarsarr *(n.)* **teletext**
တယ်လီဆက်သွယ်ရေး taallesaatswalrayy *(n.)* **telecommunications**
တယ်လီဆက်သွယ်ရေးနည်းပညာ taalle-saatswalrayynaeepanyar *(adj.)* **telematic**
တယ်လီတိုင်းတာချက်ပို့စနစ် taalle tine tar chet phoetsanit *(n.)* **telemetry**
တယ်လီပရင်တာ taalle printar *(n.)* **teleprinter**
တယ်လီဖက်စ် taallehpaatit *(n.)* **telefax**
တယ်လီဖုန်း taallehpone *(n.)* **telephone**
တယ်လီဖုန်းခေါ်သူ tal-li-phone-khaw-thu *(n.)* **caller**
တယ်လီဘဏ်စနစ် taallebhansanit *(n.)* **telebanking**
တယ်လီမားကက်တင်း taalle marr kaattinn *(n.)* **telemarketing**
တယ်လီမိတ္တူကူးစက် taallemittuukuusaat *(n.)* **telecopier**
တယ်လီမောင်းနှင်သူ taalle maung-nate-suu *(n.)* **teleoperator**

တယ်လီရုပ်သံလွှင့်ခြင်း taalle rotesan lwint-chinn *(n.)* **telecast**
တယ်လီရုပ်သံလွှင့်သည် taalle rotesan lwintsai *(v.)* **telecast**
တယ်လီလမ်းညွှန် taallelamnywhaan *(n.)* **teleguide**
တယ်လီသင်တန်း taallesintaann *(n.)* **telecourse**
တယ်လီသတင်းစာပညာ taallesatinnsarpanyar *(n.)* **telejournalism**
တယ်လီအမှတ် taalle-aa-mhaat *(v.)* **telemark**
တရကြမ်းသွားခြင်း ta-ra-kyan-twar-chin *(v.)* **dash**
တရစပ်၊ ဘောလုံးမြေမကျမီ ရိုက်ခြင်း tarasat , bhawlone myay ma kyame ritechinn *(n.)* **volley**
တရစပ်ပစ်ခတ်ခြင်း၊ မေးခြင်း ta-ya-sat-pyit-khat-chin, may-chin *(n.)* **barrage**
တရစ်ဝဲဝဲနေသည် ta-yit-wal-wal-nay-the *(v.)* **linger**
တရွတ်ဆွဲသည် ta rwat swalsai *(v.)* **trail**
တရွတ်ဆွဲသွားသည် ta rwat swalswarrsai *(v.)* **shamble**
တရွတ်တိုက်ဆွဲသည် ta-yut-tite-swal-the *(v.)* **drag**
တရွေ့ရွေ့ချဉ်းကပ်သည် tarwaerwae chain kautsai *(v.)* **stalk**
တရှဲရှဲ မြည်သည် ta shellshell myisai *(v.)* **rustle**
တရားကျသော၊ လမ်းကျသော tararr kyasaw, lamkyasaw *(adj.)* **righteous**
တရားခံ ta-ya-khan *(n.)* **defendant**
တရားခံပြေး ta-ya-khan-pyay *(n.)* **fugitive**
တရားစွဲခြင်း tararr swalchinn *(n.)* **prosecution**
တရားစွဲဆိုသည် ta-yar-swal-so-the *(v.)* **litigate**
တရားစွဲသည် ta-rarr-swalsai *(v.)* **prosecute**
တရားစီရင်ပိုင်ခွင့် ta-yar-si-yin-pai-khwint *(n.)* **jurisdiction**
တရားစီရင်မှု ta-yar-si-yin-mu *(n.)* **judicature**
တရားစီရင်ရေး ta-yar-si-yin-yay *(n.)* **judiciary**
တရားထိုင်ခြင်း ta-yar-htai-chin *(n.)* **meditation**
တရားထိုင်သည် ta-yar-htai-the *(v.)* **meditate**
တရားထိုင်သော ta-yar-htai-taw *(adj.)* **meditative**
တရားမျှတမှု ta-yar-mya-ta-mu *(n.)* **justice**
တရားမျှတမှု မရှိခြင်း ta-yar-mya-ta-mu-ma-shi-chin *(n.)* **injustice**
တရားမျှတသော ta-yar-mya-ta-taw *(adj.)* **fair**
တရားမဝင် ပို့ကုန်၊ သွင်းကုန် ta-yar-ma-win-poe-kone-twin-kone *(n.)* **contraband**
တရားမဝင်ချစ်သူ ta-rarr-ma-win-chitsuu *(n.)* **paramour**
တရားမဝင်ခြင်း၏ လက္ခဏာ ta-yar-ma-win-chin-ei-lat-kah-nar *(n.)* **illegibility**
တရားမဝင်သော tararrmawinsaw *(adj.)* **unofficial**
တရားရုံး ta-yar-yone *(n.)* **court**
တရားရုံးတွင် လျှောက်လဲသူ ta-rarrronetwin shout lellsuu *(n.)* **pleader**
တရားရုံးပစ္စည်းထိန်းစာရေး ta-yar-yone-pyit-see-htein-sar-yay *(n.)* **bailiff**
တရားရုံးရှေ့နေ tararrroneshaenay *(n.)* **solicitor**

တရားရုံးအာဏာပြင်ပတွင် ရှိသော ta-yar-yone-ar-nar-pyin-pa-twin-shi-taw *(adj.)* **extrajudicial**
တရားရေး ta-yar-yay *(adj.)* **judicial**
တရားလို ta-rarr-lo *(n.)* **plaintiff**
တရားဝင် ta-rar-win *(adj.)* **official**
တရားဝင် ကြေညာချက် ta-yar-win-kyay-nyar-chat *(n.)* **communique**
တရားဝင် ထုတ်ပြန်ကြေညာချက် ta-yar-win-htoke-pyan-kyay-nyar-chat *(n.)* **bulletin**
တရားဝင် အတည်တကျ နေထိုင်ရာ နိုင်ငံ၊ မြို့ ရွာ ta-yar-win-a-the-ta-kya-nay-htai-yar-nai-ngan-myo-ywar *(n.)* **domicile**
တရားဝင်စေ့စပ်သည် ta-yar-win-say-sat-the *(v.)* **betroth**
တရားဝင်ဖြစ်ခြင်း ta-yar-win-phit-chin *(n.)* **legitimacy**
တရားဝင်ဖြစ်စေသည် ta-yar-win-phit-say-the *(v.)* **legalize**
တရားဝင်ဖြစ်သော ta-yar-win-phit-taw *(adj.)* **lawful**
တရားဝင်လုပ်ပိုင်ခွင့် tararrwin lote pinehkwint *(n.)* **remit**
တရားဝင်အမိန့် ta-yar-win-a-meint *(n.)* **injunction**
တရားဝန်ကြီးချုပ်ရုံး ta-yar-win-gyi-choke-yone *(n.)* **chancery**
တရားသဖြင့် ဖြစ်စေသည် tararr sa-hpyint hpyitsaysai *(v.)* **redress**
တရားသူကြီး ta-yar-thu-gyi *(n.)* **judge**
တရားသေလက်ခံထားသော ဝါဒ ta-yar-tay-lat-khan-htar-taw-war-da *(n.)* **dogma**
တရားသေလွှတ်သည် ta-yar-tay-hlut-the *(v.)* **acquit**
တရားသော ta-yar-taw *(adj.)* **just**
တရားဟော စင်မြင့် tararrhaw sinmyint *(n.)* **rostrum**
တရားဟောစင် ta-yar-haw-sin *(n.)* **dais**
တရားဟောစင်မြင့် tararrhaw sin-myint *(adj.)* **pulpit**
တရားဟောဆရာ ta-rarr-haw-sarar *(n.)* **preacher**
တရားဥပဒေနှင့် ညီညွတ်ခြင်း ta-yar-au-pa-day-nint-nyi-nyut-chin *(n.)* **legality**
တရုတ်နံနံ ta-rote-nan-nan *(n.)* **parsley**
တရုတ်နံနံကြီး ta-yoke-nan-nan-gyi *(n.)* **celery**
တရုတ်အပ်စိုက်ဆရာ ta-yoke-at-seik-sa-yar *(n.)* **acupuncturist**
တရောင်ထဲပါသော ta-yaung-htae-par-taw *(adj.)* **monochromatic**
တြိဂံ tyai gan *(n.)* **triangle**
တလက်လက် တောက်ပသည် ta laatlaat toutpa-sai *(v.)* **sparkle**
တလက်လက်တောက်ပသည် t laat laat toutpasai *(v.)* **scintillate**
တလင်းနယ်သည် ta linn naalsai *(v.)* **thresh**
တလွဲ အယုံအကြည် ta-lwal-a-yone-a-kyi *(n.)* **misbelief**
တလွဲပို့သည် ta-lwal-poe-the *(v.)* **misdirect**
တလွဲလမ်းညွှန်ခြင်း ta-lwal-lan-hnyun-chin *(n.)* **misdirection**
တလွဲသုံးခြင်း ta-lwal-tone-chin *(n.)* **misuse**
တလွဲသုံးသည် ta-lwal-tone-the *(v.)* **misuse**
တလိပ်လိပ်တက်ခြင်း ta late late-taat-chinn *(n.)* **surge**
တလိပ်လိပ်တက်သည် ta late late taat-sai *(v.)* **surge**
တလိမ့်ခေါက်ကွေးကျခြင်း ta lint hkout kwaykyachinn *(n.)* **tumble**
တလိမ့်တုံး t lintone *(n.)* **roller**
တလူလူလွင့်သည် taluuluu lwint sai *(v.)* **wave**

တဝတပြဲစားသည် ta-wa-ta-pyae-sar-the *(v.)* **gorge**

တဝီဝီမြည်သံ a-wi-wi-myae-tan *(n.)* **hum**

တဝီဝီလည်သံ ta wewe laisan *(n.)* **whir**

တွက်ချက် ခန့်မှန်းခြင်း twat-chat-khant-man-chin *(n.)* **extrapolation**

တွက်ချက် ခန့်မှန်းသည် twat-chat-khant-man-the *(v.)* **extrapolate**

တွက်ချက်ခြင်း twat-chat-chin *(n.)* **calculation**

တွက်ချက်သည် twat-chat-the *(v.)* **calculate**

တွက်ခြေကိုက်သော twat-chay-kite-taw *(adj.)* **economical**

တွက်စက် twat-sat *(n.)* **calculator**

တွက်ဖက်ပစ္စည်း twe-phat-pyit-see *(n.)* **accessory**

တွင်းကြီး၊ ချိုင့်ကြီး twin-kyi, gyaint-kyi *(n.)* **hollow**

တွင်းထွက်ဓာတ်သတ္တုပညာ twin-htwat-dat-tat-tu-pyin-nyar *(n.)* **mineralogy**

တွင်းထွက်ဓာတ်သတ္တုပညာရှင် twin-htwat-dat-tat-tu-pyin-nyar-shin *(n.)* **mineralogist**

တွင်းထွက်ပစ္စည်း twin-htwat-pyit-see *(n.)* **mineral**

တွင်းထွက်ပစ္စည်းနှင့် ဆိုင်သော twin-htwat-pyit-see-nint-sai-taw *(adj.)* **mineral**

တွင်တွင်ငြင်းသော twin-twin-nyin-taw *(adj.)* **adamant**

တွစ်တာလူမှုကွန်ရက်၊ စိုးစီစိုးစီမြည်သံ twittar luumhukwanraat , soe se soe se myisan *(n.)* **twitter**

တွတ်ထိုးသည် twat htoesai *(v.)* **twitter**

တွန့်ကျေသည်၊ ရှုံ့တွသည်၊ ကောက်သည် twunt-kyay-the, shont-twa-the, kauk-the *(v.)* **crimple**

တွန့်ကြေသည် twunt-kyay-the *(v.)* **crumple**

တွန့်ခေါက်ထားသော အင်္ကျီလက်နား twant hkouthtarrsaw aain kyae laatnarr *(n.)* **ruffle**

တွန့်ဆုတ်သည် twant sotesai *(v.)* **recoil**

တွန့်တိုသည် twant-toe-the *(v.)* **begrudge**

တွန့်တိုသော၊ ကုတ်ကတ်သော tunt-to-taw, kote-kat-taw *(adj.)* **mean**

တွန့်လိပ်တက်သည် twant late taatsai *(v.)* **ruck**

တွန့်လိပ်သည် twunt-laik-the *(v.)* **crankle**

တွန့်လိမ်ခြင်း twunt lainchinn *(n.)* **wriggle**

တွန့်လိမ်သည် twunt linsai *(v.)* **wriggle**

တွန့်သော twunt-taw *(adj.)* **curly**

တွန်းခြင်း twann-chinn *(n.)* **push**

တွန်းထုတ်သည် tun-htoke-the *(v.)* **hustle**

တွန်းမိတိုက်မိခြင်း tun-mi-tite-mi-chin *(n.)* **jostle**

တွန်းမိတိုက်မိသည် tun-mi-tite-mi-the *(v.)* **jostle**

တွန်းလှန်ခြင်း twann hlaans-chin *(n.)* **repulse**

တွန်းလှန်သည် twann hlaansai *(v.)* **repel**

တွန်းသည် twann-sai *(v.)* **push**

တွန်းသည်၊ လှုပ်သည် tun-the, hlote-the *(v.)* **jolt**

တွန်းအားပေးမှု၊ ကားမောင်းခြင်း tun-ar-pya-mu, kar-maung-chin *(n.)* **drive**

တွန်မြည်သီကျူးသည် twan myi se kyauusai *(v.)* **warble**

တွန်မြည်သီကျူးသော အသံ twan myi se kyauusaw aasan *(n.)* **warble**

တွယ်ကပ်သည် thwe-kat-the *(v.)* **accrete**

တွယ်ဖက်ထားသည် twal-phat-htar-the *(v.)* **cling**

တွယ်ဖက်ထားသော twal-phat-htar-thaw *(adj.)* **clingy**

တွားသွားသည် twar-twar-the *(v.)* **crawl**

တွားသွားသတ္တဝါ twarr swarr-sattawar *(n.)* **reptile**

တွေ့ဆုံခြင်း tway-sone-chin *(n.)* **encounter**

တွေ့ဆုံသည် tway-sone-the *(v.)* **meet**

တွေ့ရှိသည်၊ သတိပြုမိသည် tway-shi-the, ta-di-pyu-mi-the *(v.)* **detect**

တွေ့သည်၊ မြင်သည် twae sai , myinsai *(v.)* **sight**

တွေးကြည့်သည်၊ မြင်ယောင်သည် tway kyany sai , myinyaungsai *(v.)* **visualize**

တွေးခေါ်မှုအလေ့အထ tway-khaw-mu-a-lay-a-hta *(n.)* **mindset**

တွေးဆသည် tway sa-sai *(v.)* **ponder**

တွေးသည် twaysai *(v.)* **think**

တွေဝေသော tway-wai-taw *(adj.)* **dazed**

တွဲကား သို့မဟုတ် စကင်နာပါရှိသော twe-kar-toe-ma-hoke-sa-kan-nar--par-shi-taw *(adj.)* **flatbed**

တွဲစောင့်၊ ဘတ်စ်လက်မှတ်ရောင်း၊ လျှပ်ကူးပစ္စည်း twal-saunt, bat-lat-mat-yaung, lyat-ku-pyit-see *(n.)* **conductor**

တွဲလဲကျသည် twal-lae-kya-the *(v.)* **loll**

တွဲလဲဆွဲထားခြင်း twal-lal-swal-htar-chin *(adj.)* **dangling**

တွဲလဲဆွဲထားသည် twal-lal-swal-htar-the *(v.)* **dangle**

တွဲသည် twal-sai *(v.)* **pair**

တသွင်သွင်စီးဆင်းခြင်း ta-twin-twin-see-sin-chin *(n.)* **drift**

တသသ အလှပြင်သည် ta-ta-ta-a-hla-pyin-the *(v.)* **preen**

တသီးတခြား ဖြစ်ခြင်း ta-thee-ta-char-phit-chin *(n.)* **insularity**

တသီးတခြားနေသော a-thee-ta-char-nay-taw *(adv.)* **aloof**

တဟုန်ထိုးသွားသည် tahonehtoeswarrsai *(v.)* **zoom**

တအစ်အစ် မြည်သည် ta-it-it-myee-tan *(v.)* **grunt**

တအားဆွဲဖြုတ်သည် ta aarr swal hpyuatsai *(v.)* **wrench**

တအားလွှဲရိုက်သည် ta aarr lwhaell ritesai *(v.)* **swipe**

တအိအိလှုပ်သည် ta-ai-ai hlotesai *(v.)* **undulate**

တားဆီးကာကွယ်သည် tarrsee karkwalsai *(v.)* **ward**

တားဆီးခြင်း tarr-seechinn *(n.)* **prohibition**

တားဆီးသည် tarr-seesai *(v.)* **prohibit**

တားဆီးသည်၊ ကာကွယ်သည် tar-see-the, kar-kwal-the *(v.)* **insulate**

တားမြစ်ထားသော tar-myit-htar-taw *(adj.)* **forbidden**

တားမြစ်သည် tar-myit-the *(v.)* **forbid**

တာတိုပြေးပွဲ tar topyaypwal *(n.)* **sprint**

တာတိုပြေးသည် tar to pyaysai *(v.)* **sprint**

တာပင်တိုင်ဆီ tapintine-se *(n.)* **turpentine**

တာဘိုင် tarbhine *(n.)* **turbine**

တာယာ taryar *(n.)* **tire**

တာရှည်ခံ tar shay hkan *(adj.)* **preservative**

တာရှည်ခံစေသော အရာ tar shay hkansaysaw aa-rar *(n.)* **preserve**

တာရှည်ခံဆေး tar shay hkan-sayy *(n.)* **preservative**

တာရှန်အဖျား tar-shan-a-phyarr *(n.)* **tertian**

တာရာ tar-yar *(n.)* **constellation**

တာရာဂျူး tar-yar-jole *(n.)* **terajoule**

တာရာပန်းပြန်ထွင်းသည် tayar-pan-pyan-htwin-the *(v.)* **retread**

တာရာဘစ် tar-yar-bit *(n.)* **terabit**

တာရာဘိုက် tar-yar-bite *(n.)* **terabyte**

တာရာမိုက်သတ္တု tar rar mitesattu *(n.)* **taramite**

တာရိုးလမ်း tar-yoe-lan *(n.)* **causeway**

တာဝန် tar-wan *(n.)* **obligation**

တာဝန်၊ ကတိကဝတ်ဆိုင်ရာ ကျင့်ဝတ်ပညာရပ်ခွဲ tar-win-ka-ti-ka-wut-sai-yar-kyint-wut-pyin-nyar-yat-kwal *(n.)* **deontology**

တာဝန်ကျေသော tar-win-kyay-taw *(adj.)* **dutiful**

တာဝန်ခံ tar-win-khan *(n.)* **incharge**

တာဝန်ခံခြင်း tar-win-khan-chin *(n.)* **accountability**

တာဝန်ခံသော tar-win-khan-taw *(adj.)* **accountable**

တာဝန်ခွဲဝေခြင်းအနုပညာ tar-win-kwal-wai-chin-a-nu-pyin-nyar *(n.)* **delegacy**

တာဝန်ခွဲဝေသူ tar-win-kwal-wai-thu *(n.)* **delegator**

တာဝန်ထမ်းဆောင်ဆဲပုဂ္ဂိုလ် tar-winn-htan-saung-sal-poke-ko *(n.)* **incumbent**

တာဝန်ပေးခံရသူ tar-win-pay-khan-ya-thu *(n.)* **assignee**

တာဝန်ပေးခြင်း tar-win-pay-chin *(n.)* **assignment**

တာဝန်ပေးသည် tar-win-pay-the *(v.)* **assign**

တာဝန်ပေးအပ်သည် tarwaanpayyatsai *(v.)* **task**

တာဝန်မဲ့သော tar-win-mae-taw *(adj.)* **irresponsible**

တာဝန်ယူခြင်း tarwaanyuuchinn *(n.)* **responsibility**

တာဝန်ယူသည် tarwaanyuusai *(v.)* **undertake**

တာဝန်ရှိခြင်း tar-win-shi-chin *(n.)* **liability**

တာဝန်ရှိသည် tar-win-shi-the *(adj.)* **culpable**

တာဝန်ရှိသော tarwaanshisaw *(adj.)* **responsible**

တိကျစွာ ti-kya-swar *(adv.)* **accurately**

တိကျပြတ်သားစွာ ti-kya-pyat-tar-swar *(adv.)* **decidedly**

တိကျပြတ်သားသော ti-kya-pyat-tar-taw *(adj.)* **decided**

တိကျမှု ti-kya-mu *(n.)* **accuracy**

တိကျသော ti-kya-saw *(adj.)* **precise**

တိကျသော စိတ်ညွတ်ကိုင်းမှု ရှိသော ti-kya-taw-seik-kine-nyut-mu-shi-taw *(adj.)* **oriented**

တိတိ titi *(adv.)* **sharp**

တိတိကျကျ ti-ti-kya-kya *(adv.)* **exactly**

တိတ် tate *(n.)* **duct tape**

တိတ်ဆိတ်ခြင်း tatesatechinn *(n.)* **silence**

တိတ်ဆိတ်သော tate-satesaw *(adj.)* **quiet**

တိတ်တဆိတ် သွယ်ဝိုက် ဖိနှိပ်ခြင်း tate-ta-seik-thwal-wide-phi-neikchin *(v.)* **burke**

တိတ်တိတ်ဆိတ်ဆိတ် tate-tate-sate-sate *(adv.)* **silently**

တိတ်တိတ်ပုံး tate-tate-pone *(adj.)* **covert**

တိတ်ဖွင့်စက် tate hpw ng hcaat *(n.)* **tape player**

တိတ်မပါသော tatemaparsaw *(adj.)* **tapeless**

တိတ်အတိုင်းအတာ tateaatineaatar *(n.)* **tapeline**

တိတ်အောင် လုပ်သည် tate-aung lotesai *(v.)* **stem**

တိပ် tate *(n.)* **tape**

တိပ်ဖြင့် ကပ်သည် tate-hpyint kautsai *(v.)* **tape**

တိဗက်နွား ti-baat-nwarr *(n.)* **yak**

တိမ် tain *(n.)* **cloud**

တိမ်းခြင်း၊ စောင်းခြင်း taim chinn , saungchinn *(n.)* **tilt**

တိမ်းရှောင်ခြင်း tain-shaung-chin *(n.)* **elusion**

တိမ်းရှောင်သည် tain-shaung-the *(v.)* **abscond**

တိမ်းသည်၊ ယိမ်းသည် taim sai , yaimsai *(v.)* **tilt**

တိမ်ထူသော tain-htoo-taw *(adj.)* **cloudy**

တိမ်ဖုံးသော tain-hpone-taw *(adj.)* **overcast**

တိမ်မျှင် tein-hmyin *(n.)* **cirrus**

တိမ်သော tain-saw *(adj.)* **shallow**

တိရစ္ဆာန် ta-yeik-san *(n.)* **animal**

တိရစ္ဆာန်ချေး ta-yeik-san-chay *(n.)* **dung**

တိရစ္ဆာန်ဆေးကု tirassaransayyku *(adj.)* **veterinary**

တိရစ္ဆာန်မွေးမြူရေး ta-yeik-san-mway-myu-yay *(n.)* **animal husbandry**

တိရိစ္ဆာန်ရုံ ta-rate-san-rone *(n.)* **zoo**

တိရိစ္ဆာန်၏ အတိုင်တစ်ခုခု မပါသော ti rihc taraneat a tinetaithkuhku maparsaw *(adj.)* **scapeless**

တိရိစ္ဆာန်အရေပြားထိန်းသိမ်းစောင့်ရှောက်ခြင်းဆိုင်ရာ ta rate ran aaraypyarr hteinsaim hcaung shout hkyinnsinerar *(adj.)* **taxidermic**

တိသည်၊ ညှိသည် ti sai , nyhaisai *(v.)* **trim**

တို့ကာပင့်ကာ စားသည် thoet kar pint-kar sarr-sai *(v.)* **sup**

တို့သည်၊ မှတ်သည် toe-the, mat-the *(v.)* **jot**

တိုးချဲ့သည် toe-chae-the *(v.)* **enlarge**

တိုးစီခုံး toe-si-khone *(n.)* **corbel**

တိုးတက်ကောင်းမွန်ခြင်း toe-tat-kaung-mon-chin *(n.)* **betterment**

တိုးတက်ခြင်း toe-tat-chin *(n.)* **improvement**

တိုးတက်ပွားများသည် toe-taat pwarr-myarr-sai *(v.)* **proliferate**

တိုးတက်မှု toetaatmhu *(n.)* **rise**

တိုးတက်မှု ဆိတ်သုဉ်းခြင်း toetaatmhu sate suinchinn *(n.)* **stagnation**

တိုးတက်မှု တန်းသွားခြင်း၊ ကုန်းပြင်မြင့် toe-taat-mhu-taan-swarr-chinn, kone-pyin-myint *(n.)* **plateau**

တိုးတက်သည် toe-taatsai *(v.)* **progress**

တိုးတက်သော toe-taatsaw *(adj.)* **progressive**

တိုးတက်အောင် ကြိုးစားသည် toetaataaung kyaoesarrsai *(v.)* **shape up**

တိုးတိုးပြောသည် toe-toe-pyaw-the *(v.)* **hush**

တိုးတိုက် ဆောင့်မိသည် toe-tite-saunt-mi-the *(n.)* **bump**

တိုးပွားစေခြင်း toe-pwar-say-chin *(n.)* **augmentation**

တိုးပွားစေသည် toe-pwar-say-the *(v.)* **augment**

တိုးပွားလာသည် toe-pwar-lar-the *(v.)* **accrue**

တိုးမြှင့်ခြင်း toe-myint-chin *(n.)* **enhancement**

တိုးမြှင့်သည် toe-myint-the *(v.)* **enhance**

တိုးရစ် toe-rit *(n.)* **tourist**

တိုးဝှေ့ခြင်း toe whaaechinn *(n.)* **shove**

တိုးသည် toesai *(v.)* **shove**

တို၍ ထိပ်လန်နေသော to hteik laannaysaw *(adj.)* **snub**

တိုကင် tokin *(n.)* **token**

တိုက် tite *(n.)* **continent**

တိုက်ခန်း cha saatsayy *(n.)* **terrace**

တိုက်ချွတ်ခြင်း tite chwutchinn *(n.)* **scrub**

တိုက်ချွတ်ဆေးကြောသည် tite chyut sayy kyawwsai *(v.)* **scrub**

တိုက်ခိုက်ခြင်း tite-khite-chin *(n.)* **fight**

တိုက်ခိုက်ရန် အသင့်ရှိသော tite-khite-yan-a-tint-shi-taw *(adj.)* **combative**

တိုက်ခိုက်သည် tite-khaik-the *(v.)* **attack**

တိုက်ခိုက်သိမ်းယူခြင်း tite-kheik-thein-yu-chin *(n.)* **annexation**

တိုက်ခိုက်သိမ်းယူသည် tite-kheik-thein-yu-the *(v.)* **annex**

တိုက်စစ် tite-sit *(n.)* **offensive**

တိုက်စားခြင်း tite-sar-chin *(n.)* **erosion**

တိုက်စားသည် tite-sar-the *(v.)* **erode**

တိုက်စားသော tite-sar-taw *(adj.)* **erosive**

တိုက်ဆိုင်စိစစ်ခြင်း tite-sai-si-sit-chin *(n.)* **deconstruction**

တိုက်ဆိုင်စိစစ်သည် tite-sai-si-sit-the *(v.)* **deconstruct**

တိုက်ဆိုင်မှု tite-sai-mu *(n.)* **coincidence**

တိုက်ဆိုင်သည် tite-sai-the *(v.)* **coincide**

တိုက်တွန်းသည် pyinnpyinn pya paysan-da *(v.)* **urge**

တိုက်ပွဲ tite-pwe *(n.)* **battle**

တိုက်ပွဲစဉ်၊ လှုံ့ဆော်ခြင်း tite-pwe-zin, lont-sar-chin *(n.)* **campaign**

တိုက်ပွဲဝင်စစ်သည် tite-pwe-win-sit-the *(n.)* **combatant**

တိုက်ဖတ်ရောဂါ tite hpaatrawgar *(n.)* **typhus**

တိုက်ဖျက်သည် tite-phat-the *(v.)* **counteract**

တိုက်မိခြင်း tite-mi-chin *(n.)* **collision**

တိုက်မိသည် tite-mi-the *(v.)* **collide**

တိုက်ရိုက် tite-yite *(adj.)* **direct**

တိုက်ရိုက်ကိုးကားသည် tite-yite-koe-kar-the *(v.)* **cite**

တိုက်ရိုက်မဟုတ်သော tite-rite-ma-hote-taw *(adj.)* **oblique**

တိုက်အုပ်ဆရာ tite-oak-sa-rar *(n.)* **prioress**

တိုင်း၊ ခွဲဝေခြင်း tai, kwal-wai-chin *(n.)* **division**

တိုင်းတစ်ပါးမှ လာသော tai-ta-par-ma-lar-taw *(adj.)* **exotic**

တိုင်းတာ၍ ရသော tine-tar-ywe-ya-taw *(adj.)* **measurable**

တိုင်းတာသည် tine-tar-the *(v.)* **measure**

တိုင်းပြည် tai-pyi *(n.)* **country**

တိုင်၊ ပန်းတိုင် tine, paann-tine *(n.)* **post**

တိုင်၊ လောင်းကြေး tine , launggkyay *(n.)* **stake**

တိုင်ကပ်နွယ်ပင် tai-kat-nwe-pin *(n.)* **ivy**

တိုင်ကြားချက် tai-kyar-chat *(n.)* **complaint**

တိုင်ကြားသည် tai-kyar-the *(v.)* **complain**

တိုင်ကီ tineke *(n.)* **tank**

တိုင်ချက်ဖွင့်သည်၊ ဖိုင်ဖွင့်သည် tine-chat-phwint-the, fai-phwint-the *(v.)* **file**

တိုင်ခုံ tine-hkone *(n.)* **pedestal**

တိုင်ပင်ခြင်း tai-pin-chin *(n.)* **consultation**

တိုင်ပင်သည် tai-pin-the *(v.)* **consult**

တိုင်ပတ်ကချေသယ် tine-pat-ka-chay-sai *(n.)* **pole dancer**

တိုင်ဖွန်းမုန်တိုင်း tinehpwannmonetine *(n.)* **typhoon**

တိုင်လုံးပုံ tine-lone-pone *(n.)* **pillar**

တိုင်အောင် tineaaung *(conj.)* **till**

တိုတိုတောင်းတောင်း to to taunggtaungg *(adj.)* **terse**

တိုတိုနှင့် ပြည့်စုံပြီး အရေးကြီးသော အချက်များ အားလုံးပါဝင်သော toe-toe-nint-pyae-zone-p-a-yay-kyi-taw-a-chat-myar-arr-lone-par-win-taw *(adj.)* **compendious**

တိုသော to-saw *(adj.)* **short**

တိုအောင် လုပ်သည် toaaung lotesai *(v.)* **shorten**

တီးကိတ်မုန့် tee kate mone *(n.)* **teacake**

တီးခေါက်ရန် တုတ်နှစ်ချောင်း tee-khaut-yan-doke-na-khyaung *(n.)* **clave**

တီးတိုးစကား ti-toe-sa-kar *(v.)* **murmur**

တီးတိုးပြောသည် ti-toe-pyaw-the *(n.)* **murmur**

တီးတိုးရေရွတ်သည် ti-toe-yay-yut-the *(v.)* **mouth**

တီးတိုးလေသံ teetoe laysan *(n.)* **undertone**

တီးတိုးသံ teetoesan *(n.)* **whisper**

တီးမှုတ်ဖျော်ဖြေမှု tee-moke-phyaw-phyay-mu *(n.)* **gig**

တီးလုံး teelone *(n.)* **tune**

တီးဝိုင်း၊ သိုင်းကြိုး၊ အကွင်း tee-wine, taing-kyo, a-kwin *(n.)* **band**

တီကောင် te-kaung *(n.)* **worm**

တီထွင်ဉာဏ်ရှိသော ti-htwin-nyan-shi-taw *(adj.)* **creative**

တီထွင်တတ်သော ti-htwin-tat-taw *(adj.)* **inventive**

တီထွင်မှု ti-htwin-mu *(n.)* **creation**

တီထွင်သည် te-htwin-sai *(v.)* **pioneer**

တီထွင်သူ te-htwin-suu *(n.)* **pioneer**

တီထွင်သူ၊ ဖန်တီးရှင် ti-htwin-thu, phan-ti-shin *(n.)* **creator**

တီဗီတွင် လူသိများသူတို့နှင့် ပရိသတ် ရင်းရင်းနှီးနှီး တွေ့ဆုံခန်း TV-twin-lu-ti-myar-thu-doe-nint-pa-yeik-tat-yin-yin-nee-nee-tway-sone-khan *(n.)* **chat show**

တုံ့ဆိုင်းခြင်း tont-sai-chin *(n.)* **hesitation**

တုံ့ဆိုင်းတုံ့ဆိုင်းဖြစ်သော tont-sai-tont-sai-phit-taw *(adj.)* **hesitant**

တုံ့ဆိုင်းသည် tont-sai-the *(n.)* **baulk**

တုံ့ပြန်ချက် tone-pyanchet *(n.)* **reaction**

တုံ့ပြန်သည် tone-pyansai *(v.)* **react**

တုံ့ပြန်သော tonepyansaw *(adj.)* **reactive**

တုံးတိ tone-ti *(adj.)* **brusque**

တုံးလုံး၊ ဗလာ tone-lone, ba-lar *(adj.)* **bare**

တုံးသော tone-taw *(adj.)* **blunt**

တုတ်ကွေး toke-kway *(n.)* **dengue**

တုတ်ချောင်း totechaungg *(n.)* **stick**

တုတ်ခိုင်သန်မာသော tote-khaing-tan-mar-taw *(adj.)* **beefy**

တုတ်ထောက်ခုန်သည် a-moepaunggkuu *(v.)* **vault**

တုတ်နှောင်သည် tote nhaawinsai *(v.)* **strap**

တုန်ခြင်း tone-chin *(n.)* **ague**

တုန်ခါခြင်း tone hkarchinn *(n.)* **vibration**

တုန်ခါသည် tone hkarsai *(v.)* **vibrate**

တုန်တုန်ယင်ယင် ဖြစ်နေသော tone tone yin yin hpyitnaysaw *(adj.)* **shaky**

တုန်တုန်ယင်ယင်ဖြစ်ခြင်း tone tone yin yinhpyitchinn *(n.)* **tremor**

တုန်လှုပ်ချောက်ချားစေသည် tone-hlote-chauk-char-say-the *(v.)* **appal**

တုန်လှုပ်ချောက်ချားမှု ton-hloke-chauk-char-mu *(n.)* **dismay**

တုန်လှုပ်ခြင်း၊ မြားကျည်တောက် tone hlote chinn , myarr kyi-tout *(n.)* **quiver**
တုန်လှုပ်သည် tone-hlote-sai *(v.)* **perturb**
တုန်သည် tone-sai *(v.)* **palpitate**
တုန်သော၊ ခါသော၊ ရှေ့နောက်ခါသည် tone-taw, khar-taw, shay-naut-khar-the *(adj.)* **rocking**
တုပရှ် ဖြေဖျော်မှုအတတ် tu-pa-ywe-pyaw-phyay-mu-a-tat *(n.)* **mimicry**
တုပြခြင်း tu-pya-chin *(n.)* **impersonation**
တုသည် tu-the *(v.)* **mimic**
တူ thu *(n.)* **chopstick**
တူးဖော်မှု tu-phaw-mu *(n.)* **excavation**
တူးဖော်ရရှိသည် tuuhpawrashisai *(v.)* **unearth**
တူးဖော်သည် tu-phaw-the *(v.)* **excavate**
တူးမြောင်း tu-myaung *(n.)* **canal**
တူးသည် tu-the *(v.)* **dig**
တူခြင်း tu-chin *(n.)* **likeness**
တူခြင်း၊ ဆင်ခြင်း tuu chinn , sinchinn *(n.)* **resemblance**
တူညီချက် thu-nyi-chat *(n.)* **analogy**
တူညီခြင်း tu-nyi-chin *(n.)* **equal**
တူညီစွာ tuunyeswar *(adv.)* **samely**
တူညီသည် thu-nyi-the *(v.)* **correspond**
တူညီသော tu-nyi-taw *(adj.)* **equal**
တူညီသော အက်တမ်ကို ဖော်ပြသော tu-nyi-taw-at-tam-ko-phaw-pya-taw *(adj.)* **geminal**
တူညီသောအရာ ရှစ်ခု tu-nyi-taw-a-yar-shit-khu *(n.)* **octuplicate**
တူညီအောင် လုပ်သည် tu-nyu-aung-lote-the *(v.)* **equalize**
တူနှင့် ထုသည် tu-nint-htu-the *(v.)* **hammer**
တူမ tu-ma *(n.)* **niece**
တူသော tu-taw *(adj.)* **like**
တူအောင် တုသည် tu-aung-tu-the *(v.)* **impersonate**
တေ့၊ ပြတ်ပြတ် tae, pyat-pyat *(adv.)* **point blank**
တေ့တေ့ဆိုင်ဆိုင် ညှိနှိုင်းသည် tae taesinesine nyhainateesai *(v.)* **transact**
တေးဂီတဖြေဖျော်ပွဲ tay-gi-ta-phit-phyay-phyaw-pwe *(n.)* **concert**
တေးဂီတအဖွဲ့ tay-gi-ta-a-phwe *(n.)* **ensemble**
တေးဆိုငှက် tayysonghaat *(n.)* **warbler**
တေးရေး tay-yay *(n.)* **lyricist**
တေးသွား tay-twar *(n.)* **melody**
တောကြက်လိုက်သူ taw-kyat-lite-thu *(n.)* **fowler**
တောကောင်ကြီး taw-kaung-gyi *(n.)* **beast**
တောက်ပခြင်း taut-pa-chin *(n.)* **brightness**
တောက်ပစွာ taut-pa-swar *(adv.)* **aglow**
တောက်ပမှု toutpamhu *(n.)* **shine**
တောက်ပသည် taut-pa-ta *(v.)* **brighten**
တောက်ပသော taut-pa-ta *(adj.)* **bright**
တောက်ပသော၊ ပွဲတိုးသော taut-pa-taw, pwe-toe-taw *(adj.)* **festive**
တောက်လျှောက် toutshout *(adj.)* **through**
တောက်လောင်သည် taut-laung-the *(v.)* **flame**
တောက်လောင်သော taut-laung-taw *(adv.)* **ablaze**
တောက်သည် taut-the *(v.)* **glow**
တောခေါင်း၊ ရိန်ဂျားတပ်ဖွဲ့ taw hkaungg , rein gyarr-taut-hpwal *(n.)* **ranger**
တောင့်သော taunt saw *(adj.)* **rigid**

တောင့်တခြင်း taunt-ta-chin *(n.)* **longing**

တောင့်တင်းအောင် ပိုးထားသည့် တန်း taunt-tin-aung-poe-htar-the-tan *(n.)* **cleat**

တောင့်တသည် taunt-ta-the *(v.)* **hanker**

တောင့်သည်၊ မာသည် taunt sai , marsai *(v.)* **stiffen**

တောင့်သော၊ သန်သော tawnt saw , saansaw *(adj.)* **sturdy**

တောင်း taung *(n.)* **basket**

တောင်းခံခြင်း taungghkanchinn *(n.)* **request**

တောင်းခံသည် taungghkansai *(v.)* **request**

တောင်းဆိုချက်၊ လိုအပ်ချက် taung-so-chat, ko-at-chat *(n.)* **demand**

တောင်းဆိုသူ taung-so-thu *(n.)* **claimant**

တောင်းပန်ခြင်း taung-pan-chin *(n.)* **apology**

တောင်းပန်မှု taung-pan-mhu *(n.)* **plea**

တောင်းပန်သည် taung-pan-the *(v.)* **apologize**

တောင်ကြား rell swmsatti *(n.)* **valley**

တောင်ကြော taungkyaww *(n.)* **ridge**

တောင်ကုန်း၊ တောင်တန်း taung-kone, taung-tan *(n.)* **hill**

တောင်ကုန်းထိပ် taung-kone-hteik *(n.)* **brow**

တောင်ခြစ်မြောက်ခြစ်လုပ်သည် taung-chit-myauk-chit-lote-the *(v.)* **doodle**

တောင်တက်သမား taung-tat-ta-mar *(n.)* **climber**

တောင်တန်း taung-tan *(n.)* **mountain**

တောင်ထူထပ်သော taung-htu-htet-taw *(adj.)* **mountainous**

တောင်နှင့် တောင်ဖြစ်ပေါ်မှုဆိုင်ရာ ပညာရှင် taung-nint-taung-phit-paw-mu-sine-yar-pin-nyar-shin *(n.)* **orologist**

တောင်ပံရှိသော taung-pan-shi-taw *(adj.)* **aliferous**

တောင်ပြိုခြင်း taung-pyo-chin *(n.)* **rockfall**

တောင်ပို့ taung-po *(n.)* **mound**

တောင်ပိုင်း taungpine *(adj.)* **south**

တောင်ပူစာ taung-pu-zar *(n.)* **hillock**

တောင်ပေါ်သစ်သားအိမ် taung-paw-tit-tar-eain *(n.)* **chalet**

တောင်ဘက်သို့ taungbhaatthoet *(adj.)* **southerly**

တောင်မှ taung-ma *(adv.)* **even**

တောင်ဝန်ရိုးစွန်းဒေသနှင့်ပတ်သက်သော taung-win-yoe-sune-day-ta-nint-pat-thet-taw *(adj.)* **antarctic**

တောင်ဝှေး taungwhaayy *(n.)* **sceptre**

တောင်သူလယ်သမားထု taung-suu-laal-sa-marr-htu *(n.)* **peasantry**

တောင်အရပ် taung-aa-rat *(n.)* **south**

တောဆိတ်မျိုး taw-seik-myo *(n.)* **antelope**

တောတွင်းလဟာ taw-twin-la-har *(n.)* **glade**

တောပုန်းဓားပြ taw-pon-dar-pya *(n.)* **brigand**

တောမီး taw-mee *(n.)* **wildfire**

တောယုန် taw-yone *(n.)* **hare**

တောလမ်း၊ တောင်လမ်း taw lam , taunglam *(n.)* **trail**

တောလိုက်သည် taw-lite-the *(v.)* **hunt**

တောဝက်ထီး taw-wat-htee *(n.)* **boar**

တောသားလူနုံ taw-dar-lu-hnon *(n.)* **bumpkin**

တောအုပ် taw-oak *(n.)* **forester**

တော်တော် taw-taw *(adv.)* **rather**

တော်ပီဒို taw pe do *(n.)* **torpedo**

တော်ပီဒိုဖြင့် တိုက်ခိုက်သည် taw pe do-hpyint titehkitesai *(v.)* **torpedo**
တော်ဖီ tawhpe *(n.)* **toffee**
တော်လှန်ရေး tawhlaanrayy *(n.)* **revolution**
တော်လှန်ရေးပြောက်ကျား taw-hlaan-rayy-pyaut-kyarr *(n.)* **partisan**
တော်လှန်ရေးသမား tawhlaanrayysamarr *(n.)* **revolutionary**
တော်လှန်သော tawhlaansaw *(adj.)* **revolutionary**
တော်ဝင် tawwin *(adj.)* **royal**
တော်ဝင်သော taw-winsaw *(adj.)* **regal**
တော်သော taw-thaw *(adj.)* **clever**
တဲ tae *(n.)* **hut**
တဲကုပ် tell kote *(n.)* **shack**

ထက် ပိုနေရသည် htaat-po-nay-ra-tai *(v.)* **outlive**
ထက်မြက်၍ ဟာသဉာဏ်ရှင်သောပြန်ကြားချက် htet-myat-ywe-har-ta-nyan-shwin-taw-pyan-kyar-chat *(n.)* **retort**
ထက်မြက်ခြင်း၊ ပြင်းပြခြင်း htet-myat-cin, pyin-pya-chin *(n.)* **keenness**
ထက်မြက်သော ရုတ်ခြည်းခွန်းတုံ့လှယ်မှု htaat-myaatsaw rote chi hkwann tone hlaalmhu *(n.)* **repartee**
ထက်ဝက်ပိုင်းသည် htet-wat-pai-the *(v.)* **bisect**
ထက်သန်သော htet-tan-taw *(adj.)* **fervent**
ထက်သော၊ ချွန်သော htaat saw, chwansaw *(adj.)* **sharp**
ထက်အောက် ပြောင်းပြန် htaataout pyaunggpyan *(adj.)* **topsy turvy**
ထင်းခနဲမြင်သာသော htin-kha-nae-myin-tar-taw *(adj.)* **eye-catching**
ထင်းစည်း htin-see *(n.)* **faggot**
ထင်းနေစေသည် htin-nay-say-the *(v.)* **accentuate**
ထင်းရှူးပင် htinn-shuu-pin *(n.)* **pine**
ထင်ကြေးပေးသည် htin-jay-pay-the *(n. & v.)* **conjecture**
ထင်ပေါ်ကျော်ကြားမှု htin-paw-kyaw-kyar-mu *(n.)* **glory**
ထင်ပေါ်ကျော်စောခြင်း htinpaw kyaw sawchinn *(n.)* **prominence**
ထင်ပေါ်ခြင်း htin-paw-chin *(n.)* **eminence**
ထင်ပေါ်သော htinpawsaw *(adj.)* **popular**
ထင်မြင်ချက်၊ ခံစားချက် htin-myin-chat, khan-sar-chat *(n.)* **impression**
ထင်မြင်ယူဆချက် htin-myin-yu-sa-chat *(n.)* **estimation**
ထင်မြင်ယူဆချက် လွဲသည် htin-myin-yu-sa-chat-lwal-the *(v.)* **misjudge**
ထင်မြင်ယူဆချက်ထုတ်ပြောသည် htin-myin-yu-sa-chet-htoke-pyaw-the *(v.)* **opine**
ထင်မြင်ယူဆချက်မရှိသော htin-myin-yu-sa-chet-ma-shi-taw *(adj.)* **opinionless**
ထင်မြင်ယူဆချက်မေးခွန်းလွှာ htin-myin-chat-maykhun-lwar *(n.)* **opinionnaire**
ထင်ယောင်ထင်မှားဖြစ်ခြင်း htin-yaung-htin-mar-phit-chin *(n.)* **delusion**
ထင်ယောင်ထင်မှားဖြစ်သော htin-yaung-htin-mar-phit-taw *(adj.)* **delusional**
ထင်ရသည် htinrasai *(v.)* **seem**
ထင်ရသည်၊ အချက်ပေးသည် htin rasai, aachetpayysai *(v.)* **sound**

ထင်ရှားကျော်ကြားမှု htin-shar-kyaw-kyar-mu *(n.)* **limelight**
ထင်ရှားပေါ်လွင်သော htain-shar-paw-lwin-taw *(adj.)* **obvious**
ထင်ရှားသော htinsharrsaw *(adj.)* **prominent**
ထင်ရှားသော ပုဂ္ဂိုလ် htin-shar-taw-poke-ko *(n.)* **notability**
ထင်ရှားသော သဲလွန်စ htin-hsar-taw-tae-lun-sa *(v.)* **tip-off**
ထည့်သွင်းခြင်း htae-twin-chin *(n.)* **insertion**
ထည့်သွင်းစဉ်းစားသည် htae-twin-sin-sar-the *(v.)* **accommodate**
ထည့်သွင်းမစဉ်းစားသော htae swin ma sin sarrsaw *(adj.)* **unaccommodating**
ထည့်ခွက် htaeethkwat *(n.)* **scuttle**
ထည့်ဝင်ထားသော ငွေ htae-win-htar-taw-ngwe *(n.)* **escrow**
ထည့်ဝင်သည် htae-win-the *(v.)* **dob**
ထည့်သည်၊ နှန်းတင်သည် htae-the, hnone-tin-the *(n.)* **deposit**
ထည့်သွင်းသည် htae-twin-the *(v.)* **insert**
ထည်ထိုးသည်၊ ထွန်ယက်သည် htae-htoe-the, htun-yat-the *(v.)* **fallow**
ထပ်ကျော့ပုဒ်၊ သံပြိုင်ကောက်ခြင်း htat kyaww pote , san-pyaine koutchinn *(n.)* **refrain**
ထပ်ကိန်း ၁၂ ခု htet-kein-12-khu- *(n.)* **terabase**
ထပ်ကူးခြင်း htet-ku-pon *(n.)* **rubbing**
ထပ်ခိုး htet-kho *(n.)* **mezzanine**
ထပ်ဆင့် လက်မှတ်ထိုးသည် htet-sint-lat-mat-htoe-the *(v.)* **countersign**
ထပ်ဆင့်ထောက်ခံသူ htaut sainthtouthkansuu *(n.)* **seconder**
ထပ်ဆင့်ပိုင်းခြားသည် htat sint pinecharrsai *(v.)* **subdivide**
ထပ်တစ်ရာပန်း htet-ta-yar-pan *(n.)* **marigold**
ထပ်တလဲလဲဖြစ်သော htet-ta-lal-lal-phit-taw *(adj.)* **continual**
ထပ်တူညီသော htet-thu-nyi-taw *(adj.)* **congruent**
ထပ်တူဖြစ်သော htet-tu-phit-taw *(adj.)* **identical**
ထပ်နေသည့်ပမာဏ htat-nay-teet-pa-mar-na *(n.)* **overlap**
ထပ်ပြောသည် htatpyawwsai *(v.)* **repeat**
ထပ်ဖြည့်သည် htat hpyae sai *(v.)* **replenish**
ထပ်မံခြေလက်ဖြတ်တောက်သည် htet-man-chay-lat-phat-taut-the *(n.)* **reamputation**
ထပ်မံရိုက်နှိပ်သည် htatman rite natesai *(v.)* **reprint**
ထပ်ရန်အထစ်ပါသော သစ်သားပြား htaut raan a htait parsaw saitsarrpyarr *(n.)* **shiplap**
ထပ်လောင်းပြောဆိုသည် htat-laungg-pyawwsosai *(v.)* **reiterate**
ထပ်လောင်းဖွင့်ဟချက် that-laungg hpwint ha-chet *(n.)* **reiteration**
ထပ်အုပ်ထားသော အဖုံး၊ အကာ htet-oak-htar-taw-a-hpone-a-kar *(n.)* **cladding**
ထမင်းချက် hta-min-chat *(n.)* **cook**
ထမင်းပေါင်းအိုး hta-min-paung-oh *(n.)* **cooker**
ထမ်းစင် htamsin *(n.)* **sedan**
ထမ်းပိုးတပ်သည် htam poe tat-sai *(v.)* **yoke**
ထယ် htaal *(n.)* **plough**
ထယ်ကြောင်း htal-kyaung *(n.)* **furrow**
ထယ်ထိုးသည် htaal-htoe-sai *(v.)* **plough**
ထယ်ထိုးသူ htaal-htoe-suu *(n.)* **ploughman**

ထယ်သွား htaalswarr *(n.)* **sharebeam**

ထွက်ခွာခြင်း htwat-khwar-chin *(n.)* **departure**

ထွက်ခွာခွင့်ပြုသည်၊ ထွက်ခွင့်ပြုသည် htwat-khwar-khwint-pyu-the, htwat-khwint-pyu-the *(v.)* **discharge**

ထွက်ခွာသည် htwat-khwar-the *(v.)* **depart**

ထွက်ပြေးတိမ်းရှောင်နေသော htwat-pyay-tain-shaung-nay-taw *(adj.)* **fugitive**

ထွက်ပြေးသည် htwat-pyay-the *(v.)* **flee**

ထွက်ရှိသည့်ပမာဏ htwat-shi saeet-pa-mar-na *(n.)* **yield**

ထွက်သည် aakywin-mae *(v.)* **utter**

ထွင်းထုသည် htwin-htu-the *(v.)* **engrave**

ထွင်းဖောက်သည် htwin-hpaut-the *(v.)* **bore**

ထွင်လုံး htwin-lone *(n.)* **gimmickry**

ထွင်လုံး လုပ်သည် htwin-lone-lote-the *(v.)* **gimmick**

ထွင်လုံး၊ စတန့် htwin lone , sa tant *(n.)* **stunt**

ထွန့်ထွန့်လူးသည် htwunt htwunt luusai *(v.)* **writhe**

ထွန်းညှိသည် tun-hnyi-the *(v.)* **accend**

ထွန်းလင်းဝင်းပခြင်း htwann-linn winn pachinn *(n.)* **radiance**

ထွန်စက် htwansaat *(n.)* **tractor**

ထွန်ယက်သည် htwan yaatsai *(v.)* **till**

ထွားကျိုင်းသန်မာသော htwar-kyaing-tan-mar-taw *(adj.)* **hefty**

ထွေးခံ htway-hkan *(n.)* **spittoon**

ထွေးထုတ်သည် htway htotesai *(v.)* **spit**

ထွေးပိုက်သည် htway-pike-the *(v.)* **nestle**

ထွေးရောယှက်တင်ပြုသည် htway-yaw-yat-tin-pyu-the *(v.)* **intermingle**

ထွေနေသော htwaynaysaw *(adj.)* **tipsy**

ထွေပြားသော htway-pyar-taw *(adj.)* **diverse**

ထသည်၊ ထောင်သည်၊ တက်သည် hta sai , htaung sai , taatsai *(prep.)* **up**

ထားခြင်း htarr-chinn *(n.)* **placement**

ထားသည် htarr-sai *(v.)* **place**

ထာဝရ htar-wa-ra *(adj.)* **ageless**

ထာဝရဖြစ်အောင် လုပ်သည် htar-wa-ya-phit-aung-lote-the *(v.)* **eternalize**

ထာဝရဘုရားနှင့် ဆိုင်သော htar-wa-ya-pha-yar-nint-sai-taw *(adj.)* **holy**

ထာဝရဘုရားသခင်တွင် သက်ဝင်ယုံကြည်ခြင်း htarwar bhurarrsahkaintwin saatwinyonekyichinn *(n.)* **theism**

ထာဝရဘုရားသခင်တွင် သက်ဝင်ယုံကြည်သူ htarwar phararrsahkaintwin saatwin yonekyisuu *(n.)* **theist**

ထာဝရဘုရားသခင်လေ့လာမှုပညာ htarwar phararrsahkain laelarmhupanyar *(n.)* **theology**

ထာဝရရှင်သန်ခြင်း htar-wa-ya-shin-tan-chin *(n.)* **immortality**

ထာဝရရှင်သန်သော htar-wa-ya-shin-tan-taw *(adj.)* **immortal**

ထာဝရဥစ္စာ htarwa-ra-oak-sar *(n.)* **realty**

ထိခြင်း hti-chinn *(n.)* **touch**

ထိခိုက်ခြင်း hti-khaik-chin *(n.)* **damage**

ထိခိုက်ခြင်း၊ အကြမ်းဖက်ခြင်းမှ ကာကွယ်သောသူ hti-khaik-chin-a-kyan-phat-chin-ma-kar-kwal-taw-thu *(n.)* **conservator**

ထိခိုက်ခြင်းမရှိ htihkite chinnmashi *(adj.)* **unaffected**

ထိခိုက်စေသော hti-khaik-say-taw *(adj.)* **injurious**

ထိခိုက်ဒဏ်ရာ htihkitedanrar *(n.)* **wound**

ထိခိုက်နစ်နာစေသည် hti-khite-nit-nar-say-the *(v.)* **harm**
ထိခိုက်နစ်နာစေသော hti-khaik-nit-nar-say-taw *(adj.)* **damaging**
ထိခိုက်ပျက်စီးမှု hti-khite-pyat-see-mu *(v.)* **depredate**
ထိခိုက်မှုကြောင့် ရုပ်ပိုင်းစိတ်ပိုင်း ဒဏ်ရာရခြင်း hti-khait-mu-kyaunt-yoke-pine-seik-pine-dan-yar-ya-chin *(n.)* **traumatism**
ထိခိုက်မှုကို ထိန်းချုပ်ခြင်း hti-khaik-chin-ko-htein-choke-chin *(n.)* **damage control**
ထိခိုက်မှုကို လေ့လာသည့် ပညာ hti-khait-mu-ko-lae-lar-the-pin-nyar *(n.)* **traumatology**
ထိခိုက်သည် hti-khaik-the *(v.)* **affect**
ထိစပ်မှု hti sat-mhu *(n.)* **proximity**
ထိစပ်သည် hti-sat-the *(v.)* **abut**
ထိတွေ့ကိုင်တွယ်မရသော hti-tway-kai-twal-ma-ya-taw *(adj.)* **intangible**
ထိတွေ့ခြင်း၊ ပစ်ခတ်မှု ဖြစ်ပွားခြင်း hti-twaechinn, pyit-hkaatmhu hpyitpwarrchinn *(n.)* **skirmish**
ထိတွေ့မှု ရှိသော hti-tway-mu-shi-taw *(adj.)* **engaging**
ထိတွေ့သည်၊ အပြန်အလှန်တိုက်ခိုက်သည် hti-twae sai, aapyanaahlaan titehkitesai *(v.)* **skirmish**
ထိတ်တန်းကျွမ်းကျင်သူ htate-tan-kywan-kyin-thu *(n.)* **ubergeek**
ထိတ်လန့်ကြောက်ရွံ့ခြင်း htate l antkyawwatrwanchinn *(n.)* **terror**
ထိတ်လန့်သည် htaik-lant-the *(v.)* **horrify**
ထိထိရောက်ရောက် လုပ်နိုင်စွမ်း hti-hti-yauk-yauk-lote-nai-swan *(n.)* **efficiency**
ထိနေသော hti-nay-taw *(adj.)* **contiguous**
ထိန်းကျောင်းသည် htain-kyaung-the *(v.)* **marshal**
ထိန်းချုပ်ခြင်း htain-choke-chin *(n.)* **control**
ထိန်းချုပ်မှု မဲ့သည် thain-choke-mu-mae-the *(v.)* **decontrol**
ထိန်းချုပ်ရသော ကြွက်သားစွမ်းရည် ပျက်စီးခြင်း htein-choke-ya-taw-kywat-tar-swan-yay-pyat-see-chin *(n.)* **akinesia**
ထိန်းညှိကိရိယာ htein nyi-ka-ri-yar *(n.)* **regulator**
ထိန်းနိုင်သည် htein-nine-tai *(v.)* **overpower**
ထိန်းမနိုင်သိမ်းမရသော htein ma nine saimmarasaw *(adj.)* **unruly**
ထိန်းမရ သိမ်းမရ ဖြစ်သွားသည် htein ma-ra saim ma-ra hpyitswarrsai *(v.)* **rail**
ထိန်းသိမ်းကြပ်မတ်သည် htein-saim-kyat-maat-sai *(v.)* **police**
ထိန်းသိမ်းကြီးကြပ်သူ thain-thein-kyi-kyat-thu *(n.)* **controller**
ထိန်းသိမ်းစရိတ် hteinsaimsarate *(n.)* **upkeep**
ထိန်းသိမ်းစောင့်ရှောက်ခြင်း htain-tain-saunt-shaut-chin *(n.)* **conservation**
ထိန်းသိမ်းစောင့်ရှောက်မှု htain-tain-saunt-shaut-mu *(n.)* **custody**
ထိန်းသိမ်းစောင့်ရှောက်သည် htain-tain-saunt-shaut-the *(v.)* **conserve**
ထိန်းသိမ်းစောင့်ရှောက်သူ htain-tain-saunt-shaut-thu *(n.)* **custodian**
ထိန်းသိမ်းထားခြင်း hteinsaimhtarrchinn *(n.)* **retention**
ထိန်းသိမ်းထားရှိခြင်း htein-saim-htarr-shichinn *(n.)* **preservation**
ထိန်းသိမ်းထားသည် hteinsaimhtarrsai *(v.)* **retain**
ထိန်းသိမ်းမှု htein-tain-mu *(n.)* **maintenance**
ထိန်းသိမ်းသည် htein-tain-the *(v.)* **maintain**
ထိပ် hteik *(n.)* **apex**

ထိပ်ဆုံးသုံးနေရာ အဆင့်ဝင်သည် hteik-sone-tone-nay-yar-a-sint-win-the *(v.)* **podium**
ထိပ်တန်း htaik-taann *(adj.)* **paramount**
ထိပ်တန်းအရာရှိ၊ ပွဲထိန်း hteik-tan-a-yar-shi, pwe-htein *(n.)* **marshal**
ထိပ်ပြောင်သော hteik-pyaung-taw *(adj.)* **bald**
ထိပ်ပိုင်း hteikpine *(n.)* **top**
ထိပ်ဖျားတွင်ဖြစ်သော hteik-phyar-twin-phit-taw *(adj.)* **atopic**
ထိပ်သီးတွေ့ဆုံပွဲ hteikseetwaesonepwal *(n.)* **summit**
ထိမှန်ခြင်း hti-hman-chin *(n.)* **hit**
ထိမ်းမြားလက်ထပ်ခြင်း htaim myarrlaathtatchinn *(n.)* **wedlock**
ထိရောက်သော htiroutsaw *(adj.)* **telling**
ထိလွယ်ရှလွယ်သော hti lwal sh lwalsaw *(adj.)* **vulnerable**
ထိသည် htisai *(v.)* **touch**
ထိသိနိုင်သော hti-si-nine-saw *(adj.)* **palpable**
ထိအောင် htiaaung *(prep.)* **till**
ထို hto *(dem. pron.)* **that**
ထို့ကြောင့် hthoetkyount *(conj.)* **so**
ထို့နောက် hthoetnout *(adv.)* **thereafter**
ထိုပြင် htoe-pyin *(adv.)* **anyhow**
ထို့အပြင် htoe-a-pyin *(adv.)* **moreover**
ထိုးကျသွားခြင်း htoe-kya-swarr-chinn *(n.)* **plunge**
ထိုးချက်၊ ထိုးသွင်းခြင်း htoe chet , htoe swinchinn *(n.)* **thrust**
ထိုးခြင်း htoe-chinn *(n.)* **poke**
ထိုးဆင်းသည် htoe sinnsai *(v.)* **swoop**
ထိုးဆေး၊ ထိုးခြင်း htoe-say, htoe-chin *(n.)* **injection**
ထိုးထွက်ခြင်း htoe-htwat-chin *(n.)* **reak**
ထိုးထွက်သော htoe-htwat-taw *(adj.)* **projectile**
ထိုးထွင်းသိမြင်စွမ်းသော ဉာဏ် htoe-htwin-ti-myin-swan-taw-nyan *(n.)* **insight**
ထိုးနှက်သည်၊ ထိသည် htoe-nat-the, hti-the *(v.)* **hit**
ထိုးဖောက်ခြင်း htoehpout-chinn *(n.)* **piercing**
ထိုးဖောက်ဝင်ရောက်ခြင်း htoe-hpauk-win-yauk-chin *(n.)* **irruption**
ထိုးဖောက်ဝင်ရောက်သည် htoe-hpauk-win-yauk-the *(v.)* **trench**
ထိုးဖောက်သည် htoe-hpout-sai *(v.)* **penetrate**
ထိုးဝါး၊ တိုင်၊ ဝင်ရိုးစွန်း htoe-warr, tine, win-roe-swann *(n.)* **pole**
ထိုးဝါးထိုးသည် htoe-warr-htoe-sai *(v.)* **pole**
ထိုးသည် htoe-sai *(v.)* **poke**
ထိုးသည်၊ စိုက်သည် htoe sai , sitesai *(v.)* **stick**
ထိုးသည်၊ ရိုက်သည် htoe sai , ritesai *(v.)* **wallop**
ထိုးသွင်းသည် htoe-swin-sai *(v.)* **plunge**
ထိုးသုတ်ခြင်း htoe sote-chinn *(n.)* **swoop**
ထိုက်တန်သည် htike-tan-the *(v.)* **deserve**
ထိုက်တန်သော htitetaansaw *(adj.)* **worthy**
ထိုင်းနိုင်ငံနှင့် ဆိုင်သော htine-nine-ngannint sinesaw *(adj.)* **siamese**
ထိုင်းမှိုင်းခြင်း htai-mai-chin *(n.)* **lethargy**
ထိုင်းမှိုင်းသော htai-mai-taw *(adj.)* **lacklustre**
ထိုင်ခုံ htinehkone *(n.)* **seat**

ထိုင်ခုံနှစ်ခုံ၊ ခြေနင်းနှစ်စုံပါ စက်ဘီးရှည် htine-hkone na hkone , chay ninn na sonepar saatbheeshay *(n.)* **tandem**

ထိုင်လုပ်ရသော အလုပ် htine loterasaw aalote *(adj.)* **sedentary**

ထိုင်သည် htinesai *(v.)* **seat**

ထိုစဉ် htosin *(adv.)* **then**

ထိုထက် hto-htet *(adv.)* **further**

ထိုနေရာ htonayrar *(adv.)* **there**

ထိုနေရာတွင် htoe nay-yar-twin *(conj.)* **whereat**

ထို့မျှမက hto-mya-ma-ka *(adv.)* **nay**

ထိုမျှလောက် hto myahalout *(adv.)* **that**

ထိုမှ htomha *(adv.)* **thence**

ထိုသို့ဖြင့် htothoethpyint *(adv.)* **thereby**

ထိုအချိန်တွင်ဖြစ်သော htoe-a-chain-twin-phit-taw *(adj.)* **then**

ထိုအရပ်သို့ hto aarat-thoet *(adv.)* **thither**

ထီ hti *(n.)* **lottery**

ထီး htee *(n.)* **umbrella**

ထီးနန်း hteenaann *(n.)* **throne**

ထီးနန်းတက် htee-nan-tat *(n.)* **accession**

ထုံ့ပိုင်းထုံ့ပိုင်း htont-pai-htont-pai *(adj.)* **fitful**

ထုံး htone *(n.)* **lime**

ထုံးစံအတိုင်း a toe kyeehpyint ngway toe chasuu *(adv.)* **usually**

ထုံးစံအတိုင်းဖြစ်သော htonesanaatine *(adj.)* **usual**

ထုံးတမ်းစဉ်လာနောက်လိုက်သည် hton-tan-sin-lar-naut-lite-the *(v.)* **conform**

ထုံးတမ်းနှင့် ကိုက်ညီမှု hton-tan-nint-kite-nyi-mu *(n.)* **conformity**

ထုံးတမ်းနှင့်ညီအောင် ပြုလုပ်သည် htonetam nint nyeaaung pyulotesai *(v.)* **solemnize**

ထုံးဖြူမှုန့် htone hpyauu hmonet *(n.)* **whitewash**

ထုံးမြေစေးကျောက် htone-myay-say-kyauk *(n.)* **marl**

ထုံးသည် htone-the *(v.)* **knot**

ထုံးသည်၊ လိမ်သည် htone-the, lain-the *(v.)* **gnarl**

ထုံးသုတ်သည် htone sotesai *(v.)* **whitewash**

ထုံထိုင်းနေသော hton-htai-nay-taw *(adj.)* **dopey**

ထုံထိုင်းသော၊ ညံ့ဖျင်းသော htone htine saw , nyan hpyinnsaw *(adj.)* **stupid**

ထုံသော htone-taw *(adj.)* **numb**

ထုံအအ htone-a-a *(adj.)* **oafish**

ထုဆစ်သည် htu sitsai *(v.)* **sculpt**

ထုတ်ကုန် htote-kone *(n.)* **product**

ထုတ်ခြင်း htoke-chin *(n.)* **dismissal**

ထုတ်နိုင်သော htoke-nai-taw *(adj.)* **generable**

ထုတ်ပစ်ခြင်း htotepyitchinn *(n)* **takeout**

ထုတ်ပစ်သည် htoke-pyit-the *(v.)* **empty**

ထုတ်ပစ်သော htote pyitsaw *(adj.)* **takeout**

ထုတ်ပယ်သည် htoke-pal-the *(v.)* **expel**

ထုတ်ပယ်သည်၊ တားမြစ်သည်၊ htoke-pal-the, tar-myit-the *(v.)* **debar**

ထုတ်ပြန်ချက် htotepyanchet *(n.)* **statement**

ထုတ်ပြန်သည် htoke-pyan-the *(v.)* **issue**

ထုတ်ပြီး အမိန့်ကို အမိန့်သစ်ဖြင့် ပယ်ဖျက်အစားထိုးသည် htoke-pi-a-maint-ko-a-maint-tit-phint-pal-phat-a-sar-htoe-the *(v.)* **countermand**

ထုတ်ပေးသည် htotepayysai *(v.)* **secrete**

ထုတ်ဖော်ပြောသည် htotehpawpyawwsai *(v.)* **reveal**

ထုတ်ဖော်မပြောခြင်း htoke-hpaw-ma-pyaw-chin *(n.)* **non-disclosure**

ထုတ်ဖော်သည် htotehpawsai *(v.)* **voice**

ထုတ်မပေးဘဲ ထားသည် htotemapayybhell htarrsai *(v.)* **withhold**

ထုတ်ယူ ဆင်ခြင်ခြင်း htoke-yu-sin-chin-chin *(n.)* **deduction**

ထုတ်လွှတ်ခြင်း htoke-hlut-chin *(n.)* **emittance**

ထုတ်လွှတ်သည် htoke-hlut-the *(v.)* **emit**

ထုတ်လုပ်ခြင်း htoke-lote-chin *(n.)* **emission**

ထုတ်လုပ်ပေးသည့် ပမာဏ htote-lote-pay-teet-pa-mar-na *(n.)* **output**

ထုတ်လုပ်သည် htoke-lote-the *(v.)* **generate**

ထုတ်လုပ်သူ htoke-lote-thu *(n.)* **manufacturer**

ထုတ်လုပ်သောနှစ် htotelotesawnit *(n.)* **vintage**

ထုတ်ဝေခြင်း၊ စာအုပ်၊ စာနယ်ဇင်း htoteway chinn , saraote , sarnaaljainn *(n.)* **publication**

ထုတ်ဝေသည် htote-waysai *(v.)* **publish**

ထုတ်ဝေသူ htote-waysuu *(n.)* **publisher**

ထုတ်သည် htote-tai *(v.)* **oust**

ထုတ်သည်၊ မောင်းထုတ်သည် htoke-the, muang-htoke-the *(v.)* **eject**

ထုထည် htu-htae *(n.)* **mass**

ထုနှက်ချက် htu-hnat-chat *(n.)* **bash**

ထုနှက်သည် htu-nhaatsai *(v.)* **thump**

ထုပ်ပိုးပစ္စည်း htote poepyit-saee *(n.)* **wrapper**

ထုပ်ပိုးသည် htote-poe-sai *(v.)* **pack**

ထူးကွင်း htoo-kwin *(n.)* **fetter**

ထူးကဲကောင်းမွန်သော htoo-kae-kaung-mon-taw *(adj.)* **extraspecial**

ထူးကဲသာလွန်လျက် htuu kell sarlwansaw *(adv.)* **transcendentally**

ထူးကဲသာလွန်သော အထွတ်အထိပ် htu-kae-tar-lun-thaw-a-htut-ahteik *(adj.)* **transcendent**

ထူးကဲသော htuu-kell-saw *(adj.)* **phenomenal**

ထူးကဲသော၊ ပြင်းထန်သော htoo-kae-taw, pyin-htan-taw *(adj.)* **extreme**

ထူးခတ်သည် htoo-khat-the *(v.)* **fetter**

ထူးချွန်ပြောင်မြောက်စွာ htoo-chon-pyaung-myauk-swar *(adv.)* **dazzlingly**

ထူးချွန်ပြောင်မြောက်သော htoo-chon-pyaung-myauk-taw *(adj.)* **dazzling**

ထူးချွန်သည် htoo-chon-the *(v.)* **excel**

ထူးချွန်သော htuu-chun-taw *(adj.)* **outstanding**

ထူးခြားကွဲပြားမှု htuu-charr-kwal-pyarr-mhu *(n.)* **peculiarity**

ထူးခြားဆန်းကျယ်ခြင်း htoo-char-san-kyal-chin *(n.)* **antic**

ထူးခြားဆန်းကြယ်သော thoo-char-san-kyal-taw *(adj.)* **bizarre**

ထူးခြားဆန်းပြားသော htoo-char-san-pyar-taw *(adj.)* **mystic**

ထူးခြားမှု htuucharrmhu *(n.)* **sublimity**

ထူးခြားသော htoo-char-taw *(adj.)* **exceptional**

ထူးခြားသော ဉာဏ်အမြင်ကို ယုံကြည်သက်ဝင်မှု htoo-char-taw-nyan-a-myin-ko-yone-kyi-tat-win-mu *(n.)* **mysticism**

ထူးခြားသော လက္ခဏာ htuucharrsaw lakhkanar *(n.)* **singularity**

ထူးခြားသော၊ မှတ်သားဖွယ် htuucharrsaw , mhaat-sarrhpwal *(adj.)* **remarkable**
ထူးဆန်းပုံစံ htoo-san-pon-san *(n.)* **xenomorph**
ထူးဆန်းသော htoo-san-taw *(adj.)* **fancy**
ထူးထူးကဲကဲ htoo-htoo-kae-kae *(adv.)* **abnormally**
ထူးထူးကဲကဲ ကောင်းမွန်သော htoo-htoo-kae-kae-kaung-mon-taw *(adj.)* **gorge**
ထူးထူးကဲကဲ အောင်မြင်သော htuuhtuukellkell aaungmyinsaw *(adj.)* **triumphant**
ထူးထူးခြားခြားချွန်သည် htuu-htuu-charr-charr-chun-tai *(v.)* **outshine**
ထူးထူးဆန်းဆန်း ထိတ်လန့်ဖွယ်ကောင်းသော htuuhtuusaannsaann htate l ant hpwalkaunggsaw *(adj.)* **weird**
ထူခြင်း htuuchinn *(n.)* **thick**
ထူထပ်စွာ htuuhtatswar *(adv.)* **thick**
ထူထပ်သော htu-htat-taw *(adj.)* **dense**
ထူထပ်သောတော htu-htat-taw-taw *(n.)* **jungle**
ထူထဲခြင်း htu-htae-chin *(n.)* **luxuriance**
ထူထဲစွာ သုတ်လိမ်းသည် htuu htellhcwar sote laimsai *(v.)* **slather**
ထူထဲရှည်လျားသော ဆံပင် htoo-htae-shay-lyar-taw-san-pin *(n.)* **manes**
ထူထဲသော htu-htae-taw *(adj.)* **luxuriant**
ထူပိန်းလာသည် htuu peinlarsai *(v.)* **thicken**
ထူသော htuusaw *(adj.)* **thick**
ထေ့လုံး၊ ငေါ့လုံး htae lone, ngotlone *(n.)* **sarcasm**
ထေးဆေး htayysayy *(n.)* **sealant**
ထေသည် htay-tai *(v.)* **offset**
ထော့နင်းထော့နင်းသွားသည် htawt-nin-htawt-nin-twar-the *(v.)* **gimp**

ထောက်ခံချက် htauk-khan-chat *(n.)* **endorsement**
ထောက်ခံစာ htouthkansar *(n.)* **testimonial**
ထောက်ခံမှု htauk-khan-mu *(n.)* **favour**
ထောက်ခံမှု။ htaut-khan-mu *(n.)* **advocacy**
ထောက်ခံသည် htauk-khan-the *(v.)* **espouse**
ထောက်ခံသော၊ အလေးပေးသော htauk-khan-taw, a-lay-pay-taw *(adj.)* **favourable**
ထောက်ခံအားပေးသူ htauk-khan-arr-pay-thu *(n.)* **apostle**
ထောက်ခနဲ မြည်လျက် ပြတ်သည် htout hkanell myilyet pyatsai *(v.)* **snap**
ထောက်ခနဲ မြည်သံ htout hkanell myisan *(n.)* **snap**
ထောက်စမ်းသည်၊ ထိုးရှာသည် htout sam sai , htoe sharsai *(v.)* **probe**
ထောက်ထားညှာတာသော htauk-htar-nyar-tar-taw *(adj.)* **considerate**
ထောက်ထားသည် htout-htarr-sai *(v.)* **prop**
ထောက်ပံ့ htoutpan *(n.)* **supplier**
ထောက်ပံ့ကြေးငွေ htout-pankyay-ngway *(n.)* **stipend**
ထောက်ပံ့ကြေးပေးသည် htoutpankyaypayysai *(v.)* **subsidize**
ထောက်ပံ့ခြင်း htout-panchinn *(n.)* **provision**
ထောက်ပံ့ငွေ htoutpanngway *(n.)* **subsidy**
ထောက်ပံ့လှူဒါန်းခြင်း htauk-pant-hlu-dan-chin *(n.)* **endowment**
ထောက်ပံ့လှူဒါန်းသည် htout-pan hlauudarannsai *(v.)* **sponsor**
ထောက်ပံ့လှူဒါန်းသော htauk-pant-hlu-dan-taw *(adj.)* **endowed**
ထောက်ပံ့သည် htout-pan-sai *(v.)* **provide**

ထောက်ပံ့သည်၊ ထည့်ဝင်သည် htauk-pant-the, htae-win-the *(v.)* **contribute**
ထောက်ပေးသူ htout payysuu *(n.)* **prompter**
ထောက်လှမ်းသည် htauk-hlan-the *(v.)* **monitor**
ထောက်လှမ်းသော htauk-hlan-taw *(adj.)* **monitory**
ထောင် htaung *(n.)* **jail**
ထောင့် htaung *(n.)* **angle**
ထောင့်နှစ်ခုဖြစ်သော Htaung-na-khu-phit-taw *(adj.)* **biangular**
ထောင့်ဖြတ် ခွာကျရွရွပြေးသည် htaunt-hpyat hkwar kya rwa rwa pyaysai *(v.)* **trot**
ထောင့်ဖြတ်မျဉ်း htaunt-phat-myin *(adj.)* **diagonal**
ထောင့်မှန်ကျသော htaunt-mhaan-kya-saw *(adj.)* **perpendicular**
ထောင့်မှန်စတုဂံ htaunt mhaan sa tu gan *(n.)* **rectangle**
ထောင့်မှန်ပုံရှည် htaunt -mhan-pone-shay *(adj.)* **oblong**
ထောင့်မှန်မျဉ်း htaunt-mhaan-myin *(n.)* **perpendicular**
ထောင့်လေးထောင့်ပါသော htaunt-lay-htaunt-par-taw *(adj.)* **quadrangular**
ထောင့်သန်းရောဂါ htaung-tan-yaw-gar *(n.)* **anthrax**
ထောင်ကျသည် htaung-kya-the *(v.)* **jail**
ထောင်ကြပ် htaungkyaut *(n.)* **warder**
ထောင်ကဲ့သို့ နေရာတွင် အတူနေသူ htaung-kae-thoe-nay-yar-twin-a-tu-nay-tu *(n.)* **inmate**
ထောင်ချသည် htaung-cha-the *(v.)* **imprison**
ထောင်ချောက် htaungchauk *(n. pl.)* **toils**
ထောင်ချောက်ဆင်ဖမ်းခြင်း htaung-chauk-sin-phan-chin *(n.)* **entrapment**
ထောင်ချောက်လိုင်း htaung-chauk-line *(n.)* **trapline**
ထောင်စုနှစ် htaung-su-nit *(n.)* **millennium**
ထောင်ပြေး htaung-pyay *(n.)* **escapee**
ထောင်ဖောက်ပြေးခြင်း htaung-phaut-pyay-chin *(n.)* **breakout**
ထောင်မတ်ခြင်း htaung-mat-chin *(n.)* **erection**
ထောင်မတ်နိုင်သော htaung-mat-naing-taw *(adj.)* **erectile**
ထောင်မတ်သည် htaung-mat-the *(v.)* **erect**
ထောင်မတ်သော htaung-mat-taw *(adj.)* **erect**
ထောင်မှူး htaung-hmu *(n.)* **jailer**
ထောင်လျက်ရှိသော၊ တည့်မတ်သော htaung lyetshisaw , tae maat-saw *(adj.)* **upright**
ထောင်သည်၊ ပင့်သည်၊ တင်ပြသည် htaung sai , pint-sai , tinpyasai *(v.)* **raise**
ထောပတ် htaw-pat *(n.)* **butter**
ထောပတ်ထုတ်ပြီး နို့ရည် htaw-pat-htoke-p-noe-yee *(n.)* **buttermilk**
ထောပတ်သီး htaw-pat-thi *(n.)* **avocado**
ထောပနာပြုသည် htaw-pa-nar-pyu-the *(v.)* **extol**
ထဲ၊ အထဲ htae, a-htae *(prep.)* **into**

ဒ

ဒကာခံခြင်း dakar hkanchinn *(n.)* **treat**

ဒက်ဆီဘယ် dat-si-bal *(n.)* **decibel**

ဒက်ရှဘုတ် dat-sh-bote *(n.)* **dashboard**

ဒင်္ဂါးသွန်းခြင်း din-gar-thoon-chin *(n.)* **coinage**

ဒင်္ဂါးသွန်းလုပ်သည် din-gar-thoon-lote-the *(v.)* **mint**

ဒစ္စကိုကပွဲ dit-sa-ko-ka-pwe *(n.)* **discotheque**

ဒစ်ဂျစ်တယ်၊ ဂဏန်းခြေစနစ်ကို သုံးသော dit-gyit-tal, ga-nan-chay-sa-nit-ko-tone-taw *(adj.)* **digital**

ဒစ်ဂျစ်တယ်စနစ် ပြောင်းသည် dit-gyit-tal-sa-nit-ko-pyaung-the *(v.)* **digitalize**

ဒစ်ပြား dit-pyar *(n.)* **disc**

ဒစ်ပလိုမာ dit-pa-lo-mar *(n.)* **diploma**

ဒဏ္ဍာရီ dan-tar-yi *(n.)* **myth**

ဒဏ္ဍာရီပုံပြင် dan-dar-yi-pone-pyin *(n.)* **fable**

ဒဏ္ဍာရီလာ dan-tar-yi-lar *(adj.)* **mythical**

ဒဏ္ဍာရီလာ ဥစ္စာစောင့်လူပုလေး dan-tar-yee-lar-oak-sar-saunt-lu-pu-lay *(n.)* **gnome**

ဒဏ်ကြေး dan-kyay *(n.)* **forfeit**

ဒဏ်ခတ်မခံရခြင်း dan-khat-ma-khan-ya-chin *(n.)* **impunity**

ဒဏ်ခတ်သည် dan-khat-the *(v.)* **avenge**

ဒဏ်ခတ်သော dan-hkaat-saw *(adj.)* **punitive**

ဒဏ်ငွေ dan-ngwe *(n.)* **fine**

ဒဏ်ငွေဆောင်သတိပေးစာ dann-gway-saung-sa-ti-payy-sar *(n.)* **parking ticket**

ဒဏ်တပ်သည် dan-tat-the *(v.)* **fine**

ဒဏ်ရာ dan-yar *(n.)* **injury**

ဒဏ်ရာရသည် danrarrasai *(v.)* **wound**

ဒတ်ချ်ဒိန်ခဲ dat-dain-khae *(n.)* **gouda**

ဒန်းတလက် dan-ta-lat *(n.)* **balsam**

ဒမ်ဘယ် dan-ble *(n.)* **dum-bell**

ဒယီးဒယိုင်ဖြစ်သည် da yee da yine-hpyitsai *(v.)* **reel**

ဒယီးဒယိုင်ရွေ့လျားခြင်း d yee d yine rwaelyarrhkyinn *(n.)* **stagger**

ဒယ်စောက် dal-saut *(n.)* **cauldron**

ဒရမ် da-ran *(n.)* **drum**

ဒရမ်ငါး da-ran-ngar *(n.)* **drumfish**

ဒရမ်တီးချက် da-ran-tee-chat *(n.)* **drumbeat**

ဒရမ်တီးသည် da-ran-tee-the *(v.)* **drum**

ဒရမ်ပစ္စည်း da-ran-pyit-see *(n.)* **drum kit**

ဒရယ်ဖို da-raahpo *(n.)* **stag**

ဒြပ်စင်၊ လိုအပ်ချက် drat-sin, lo-at-chat *(n.)* **element**

ဒြပ်ရှိအရာဝတ္ထု drat-shi-a-yar-wut-htu *(n.)* **object**

ဒဿနသင်ကြားနည်း dဿnasainkyarrnaee *(n.)* **sophism**

ဒဿနိက dat-ta-ni-ka *(adj.)* **philosophical**

ဒဿနိကပညာရှင် dat-ta-ni-ka-pa-nyar-shin *(n.)* **philosopher**

ဒဿနိကဗေဒ dat-ta-ni-ka-bay-da *(n.)* **philosophy**

ဒသမကိန်းကို ဖော်ပြသော အစက်ငယ် dat-ta-ma-kain-ko-phaw-pya-taw-a-sat-nge *(n.)* **decimal point**

ဒါဇင် dar-zin *(n.)* **dozen**

ဒါန dar-na *(n.)* **charity**

ဒါပေမယ့် dar-pay-mae *(conj.)* **only**

ဒါပေမယ့် dar-pay-mae *(adv.)* **however**

ဒါရိုက်တာ dar-yite-tar *(n.)* **director**

ဒါလင်၊ အချစ် da-lin, a-chit *(n.)* **darling**

ဒိဋ္ဌိ di-hti *(n.)* **pagan**

ဒိန် dain *(n.)* **curd**

ဒိန်ချဉ် dein-chin *(n.)* **yoghurt**

ဒိန်ချဉ်ဖောက်သည် dain-chin-hpauk-the *(v.)* **curdle**

ဒိန်ခဲ dain-khae *(n.)* **cheese**

ဒိန်ခဲကိတ် dain-khae-kate *(n.)* **cheesecake**

ဒိန်ခဲကဲ့သို့ အနံ့အရသာရှိသော dain-khae-kae-tho-a-nant-a-ya-tar-shi-taw *(adj.)* **cheesy**

ဒိုးနတ် doe-nat *(n.)* **doughnut**

ဒိုင် dai *(n.)* **bookie**

ဒိုင်း၊ အကာအကွယ် dine , aakaraakwal *(n.)* **shield**

ဒိုင်းနမစ်ပညာ dai-na-mit-pyin-nyar *(n.)* **dynamics**

ဒိုင်းနမိုက် dai-na-mite *(n.)* **dynamite**

ဒိုင်နမို dai-na-mo *(n.)* **dynamo**

ဒိုင်နမိုပတ်ကြေးကြိုးခွေ dai-na-mo-pat-kyay-kyoe-khway *(n.)* **armature**

ဒိုင်ဗင်ထိုးခြင်း dai-bin-htoe-chin *(n.)* **dive**

ဒိုင်ဗင်ထိုးသည် dai-bin-htoe-the *(v.)* **dive**

ဒိုင်လူကြီး dineluukyee *(n.)* **umpire**

ဒိုင်လူကြီးအဖြစ် ဆောင်ရွက်သည် dineluukyeeaahpyit saungrwatsai *(v.)* **umpire**

ဒိုင်အောက်ဆိုက် dai-aut-cide *(n.)* **dioxide**

ဒိုဒိုငှက် do-do-nget *(n.)* **dodo**

ဒိုဘီဆိုင် do-be-sai *(n.)* **laundry**

ဒိုဘီသည် do-be-sal *(n.)* **laundress**

ဒိုလ်မန်ဂျာကင် do-man-gyar-kin *(n.)* **dolman**

ဒီ de *(adj.)* **tidal**

ဒီဂရီ di-ga-ree *(n.)* **degree**

ဒီဇင်ဘာလ de-zin-bar-la *(n.)* **december**

ဒီဇယ် di-sal *(n.)* **diesel**

ဒီဇိုင်း၊ ပုံစံ de-zine, pon-san *(n.)* **design**

ဒီဇိုင်နာ၊ ပုံစံထုတ်သူ de-zai-nar, pon-zan-htoke-thu *(n.)* **designer**

ဒီဘင်ချာ ငွေချေးလက်မှတ် de-bin-char-ngway-chee-lat-mat *(n.)* **debenture**

ဒီဘစ်ကတ် de-bit-kat *(n.)* **debit card**

ဒီမှာ di-mar *(adv.)* **here**

ဒီမိုကရက်၊ ဒီမိုကရေစီဝါဒီ de-mo-ka-rat, de-mo-ka-yay-see-war-di *(n.)* **democrat**

ဒီမိုကရေစီစနစ် de-mo-ka-yay-see-sa-nit *(n.)* **democracy**

ဒီမိုကရေစီဝါဒအခြေခံသော de-mo-ka-yay-see-wa-da-a-kyay-khan-taw *(adj.)* **democratic**

ဒီရေကျချိန် di-yay-kya-chain *(n.)* **ebb**

ဒီရေကျသည် di-yay-kya-the *(v.)* **ebb**

ဒီလှိုင်း dehline *(n.)* **tide**

ဒုံး၊ ကျည်စသည့် ပစ်လွှတ်ရသည်တို့ကို လေ့လာသည့် ပညာ doon-kyi-sa-the-pyit-hlut-ya-the-doe-ko-lay-lar-the-pyin-nyar *(n.)* **ballistics**

ဒုံးကျည်၊ ရှူးဒိုင်း donekyai , shuudine *(n.)* **rocket**

ဒုံးကျည်ပညာရှင် donekyaipanyar-shin *(n.)* **rocket scientist**

ဒုံးလက်နက် dote-lat-nat *(n.)* **missile**

ဒုံရင်းအခြေအနေ ပြန်ဆိုက်သည် done-rinnaachayaanay pyan sitesai *(v.)* **revert**

ဒုက္ခ duk-hka *(n.)* **trouble**

ဒုက္ခပင်လယ်ဝေသည် dote-kha-pin-lal-wai-the *(v.)* **bedevil**
ဒုက္ခပေးခြင်း doke-kha-pay-chin *(n.)* **mischief**
ဒုက္ခပေးသည် doke-kha-pay-the *(v.)* **inflict**
ဒုက္ခပေးသော doke-kha-pay-taw *(adj.)* **conniving**
ဒုက္ခရောက်နေသူများကို ကူညီသော အဖွဲ့ dukhkaroutnaysuumyarrko kuunyesaw aahpwal *(n.)* **samaritan**
ဒုက္ခသည် duk-hkasai *(n.)* **refugee**
ဒုက္ခသုက္ခ duk-hka -tuk-hka *(n.)* **ordeal**
ဒုက္ခမပေးသော dote-kha-ma-pay-taw *(adj.)* **benign**
ဒုတိယ dutiya *(adj.)* **second**
ဒုတိယအဆင့်ဘွဲ့၊ စက္ကန့် dutiya aa-sint bhwal, sakkaant *(n.)* **second**
ဒူး du *(n.)* **knee**
ဒူးဆစ်ရောက် ရိုးရာ ခါးဝတ် du-sit-yauk-yoe-yar-khar-wit *(n.)* **kilt**
ဒူးဆစ်ရောက် ရိုးရာ ခါးဝတ် ဝတ်သည် du-sit-yauk-yoe-yar-khar-wit-wit-the *(v.)* **kilt**
ဒူးထောက်သည် du-htauk-the *(v.)* **kneel**
ဒေစီပန်း dai-si-pan *(n.)* **daisy**
ဒေတာဘဏ်တိုက် da-tar-ban-tide *(n.)* **databank**
ဒေဝါလီခံရခြင်း day-war-li-khan-ya-chin *(n.)* **bankruptcy**
ဒေသ day-sa *(adj.)* **regional**
ဒေသ၊ နယ်မြေ day-sa , naal-myay *(n.)* **region**
ဒေသခံ day-ta-khan *(adj.)* **indigenous**
ဒေသစွဲ day-saswal *(n.)* **provincialism**
ဒေသတစ်ခုတွင် ငလျင်ဖြစ်နိုင်သော အတိုင်းအတာ ဒီဂရီ daysataithkutwin ngalyinhpyitninesaw aatineaatar degare *(n.)* **seismicity**
ဒေသတွင်း day-ta-twin *(adj.)* **local**
ဒေသတွင်း အခွန် daysatwin aahkwan *(n.)* **scot**
ဒေသန္တရတိုင်း daysantaratine *(adj.)* **vernacular**
ဒေသရင်း တိရစ္ဆာန် day-ta-yin-ta-yeik-san *(n.)* **fauna**
ဒေသရင်း အပင်များ day-da-yin-a-pin-myar *(n.)* **flora**
ဒေသဝေါဟာရ daysawawharr *(n.)* **vernacular**
ဒေသအာဏာပိုင်မှ ထုတ်ပြန်သည့် ဥပဒေစည်းမျဉ်း day-da-arr-nar-pai-ma-htoke-pyan-the-oo-pa-day-see-myin *(n.)* **bylaw, bye-law**
ဒေသိယစကား day-ti-ya-sa-kar *(n.)* **dialect**
ဒေါက်၊ ဝိုက်ကွင်း daut, wite-kwin *(n.)* **bracket**
ဒေါက်ခွ douth-kwa *(n.)* **spinach**
ဒေါက်တာ daut-tar *(n.)* **doc**
ဒေါက်တိုင် dout-tine *(n.)* **prop**
ဒေါင်းဖို daungg-hpo *(n.)* **peacock**
ဒေါင်းမ daungg-ma *(n.)* **peahen**
ဒေါင်းမြီးရှိ မျက်လုံးကဲ့သို့ အမှတ် daung-myi-shi-myat-lone-kae-tho-a-mat *(n.)* **eyespot**
ဒေါင်လိုက် ပြတင်းတိုင် daung-lite-pya-tin-tai *(n.)* **mullion**
ဒေါသ daw-ta *(n.)* **anger**
ဒေါသ၊ စိတ် daw-sa , sate *(n.)* **temper**
ဒေါသတကြီး daw-tha-da-kyi *(adv.)* **amuck**
ဒေါသထွက်စေသည် daw-da-htwat-say-the *(v.)* **incense**
ဒေါသထွက်သည် daw-ta-htwat-the *(v.)* **irritate**

ဒေါသထွက်သော daw-ta-htwat-taw *(adj.)* **angry**
ဒေါသဖြင့် ဝေဖန်သည် daw-tha-phit-wai-phan-the *(v.)* **berate**
ဒေါသူပုန်ထခြင်း daw sa-ponehtachinn *(n.)* **rage**
ဒေါသူပုန်ထသည် daw sa-ponehtasai *(v.)* **rage**
ဒေါ်လာ daw-lar *(n.)* **dollar**

ဓနသြဇာကြီးသူ dha-na-aw-zar-kyee-suu *(adj.)* **plutocrat**
ဓနသဟာယနိုင်ငံများ da-na-tha-har-ya-nai-ngan-myar *(n.)* **commonwealth**
ဓမ္မဆရာ dhamma-sa-yar *(n.)* **ecclesiast**
ဓမ္မတာနှင့် ဆန့်ကျင်၍ ကာမဆက်ဆံခြင်း dhammatarnint s ant kyin kar masaatsanchinn *(n.)* **sodomy**
ဓမ္မတာနှင့် ဆန့်ကျင်၍ ကာမဆက်ဆံသူ dhammatarnint s ant kyin kar m saatsansuu *(n.)* **sodomite**
ဓမ္မတေး da-ma-tay *(n.)* **hymn**
ဓမ္မဓိဋ္ဌာန်ကျသော dham-ma-date-htan-kya-taw *(adj.)* **objective**
ဓမ္မသီချင်း dham-ma-ta-chin *(n.)* **anthem**
ဓလေ့ da-lay *(n.)* **custom**
ဓလေ့၊ ရိုးရာ dhalae , roerar *(n.)* **tradition**
ဓလေ့ထုံးတမ်းနှင့်ညီသော da-lay-htone-tan-nint-nyi-taw *(adj.)* **customary**
ဓလေ့ထုံးတမ်းအားဖြင့် da-lae-hton-tan-arr-phint *(adj.)* **wonted**
ဓလေ့ထူး dha-lae-htuu *(adj.)* **quirky**

ဓလေ့သုံးစကား da-lay-tone-sa-kar *(n.)* **idiom**
ဓလေ့သုံးဆန်သော da-lay-tone-san-taw *(adj.)* **idiomatic**
ဓား dar *(n.)* **knife**
ဓားစာခံ da-sar-khan *(n.)* **hostage**
ဓားထိုးမှု dharr htoemhu *(n.)* **stab**
ဓားပြ dar-pya *(n.)* **bandit**
ဓားပြတိုက်ခြင်း da-mya-tite-chin *(n.)* **dacoity**
ဓားပြအဖွဲ့ဝင် da-mya-a-phwe-win *(n.)* **dacoit**
ဓားမြှောင် da-hmyaung *(n.)* **dagger**
ဓားရှည် dharr-shay *(n.)* **rapier**
ဓားရှည်နှင့် ခုတ်သည် da-shay-nint-khote-sai *(v.)* **sabre**
ဓားရေးပြိုင်သည် dar-yay-pyine-the *(n.)* **fencer**
ဓားရေးယှဉ်ပြိုင်ကစားနည်း dar-yay-shin-pyine-ka-sar-nee *(n.)* **fencing**
ဓားအိမ် dharraain *(n.)* **scabbard**
ဓားအိမ်၊ အစွပ်၊ ကွန်ဒုံး dharr aain, a swut, kwandone *(n.)* **sheath**
ဓားအိမ်တွင်း ထိုးသွင်းသည် dharr-ain-twin htoe swin-sai *(v.)* **sheathe**
ဓားအိမ်ထဲထည့်သည် dharr aain htell htaeetsai *(v.)* **sheath**
ဓားအိမ်မှ ထုတ်သည် dar-eain-ma-htoke-the *(v.)* **unsheathe**
ဓာတုဗေဒ da-tu-bay-da *(n.)* **chemical**
ဓာတုဗေဒနှင့်ဆိုင်သော da-tu-bay-da-nint-sai-taw *(adj.)* **chemical**
ဓာတုဗေဒပညာရှင် da-tu-bay-da-pyin-nyar-shin *(n.)* **chemist**
ဓာတ်ကြမ်းကုဆရာ dat-kyan-ku-sa-yar *(n.)* **homeopath**

ဓာတ်ကြမ်းကုသနည်း dat-kyan-ku-ta-nee *(n.)* **homeopathy**
ဓာတ်ကူပစ္စည်း dat-khu-pyit-see *(n.)* **catalyst**
ဓာတ်ကူသည် dat-khu-the *(v.)* **catalyse**
ဓာတ်ခွဲခန်း dat-kwal-khan *(n.)* **laboratory**
ဓာတ်ခွဲခန်းသုံးထည့်စရာအကြည် dat-khwal-khan-tone-htae-sa-yar-a-kyi *(n.)* **cuvette**
ဓာတ်ငွေ့ dat-ngwe *(n.)* **gas**
ဓာတ်ငွေ့ကာ dat-ngwe-kar *(n.)* **gasmask**
ဓာတ်ငွေ့နှင့် တူသော dat-ngwe-nint-tu-taw *(adj.)* **gasesous**
ဓာတ်ငွေ့ပြောင်းခြင်း dat-ngwe-pyaung-chin *(n.)* **gasification**
ဓာတ်ငွေ့ပြောင်းသည် dat-ngwe-pyaung-the *(v.)* **gasify**
ဓာတ်ငွေ့ပြောင်းသော dat-ngwe-pyaung-taw *(adj.)* **gasified**
ဓာတ်ငွေ့ပါသော dat-ngwe-par-taw *(adj.)* **gassy**
ဓာတ်စာ၊ ကိုယ်အလေးချိန်လျှော့အောင် ချင့်ချိန်စားခြင်း dat-sar, ko-a-lay-chein-yawt-aung-chint-chein-sar-chin *(n.)* **diet**
ဓာတ်ဆီ dat-see *(n.)* **gasoline**
ဓာတ်ဆီထည့်သည် dhatse htaeetsai *(v.)* **refuel**
ဓာတ်တိုးခြင်း Dhat-toe-chinn *(n.)* **oxidation**
ဓာတ်တိုးဆန့်ကျင်ပစ္စည်း dat-toe-sant-kyin-pyit-see *(n.)* **antioxidant**
ဓာတ်တိုးသည် dhat toesai *(v.)* **oxidate**
ဓာတ်တိုးအေးဂျင့် dhat toe aayy gyint *(n.)* **oxidant**
ဓာတ်ပုံ dhrat-pone *(n.)* **photo**
ဓာတ်ပုံစားသော dhrat-pone-sarr-saw *(adj.)* **photogenic**
ဓာတ်ပုံဆရာ dhrat-pone-sa-rar *(n.)* **photographer**
ဓာတ်ပုံပညာ dhrat-pone-pa-nyar *(n.)* **photography**
ဓာတ်ပုံမိတ္တူကူး dhrat-pone meit-tuu-kuu *(n.)* **xerox**
ဓာတ်ပုံမိတ္တူကူးသည် dhratpone meittuu kuusai *(v.)* **xerox**
ဓာတ်ပုံရိုက်ရာတွင် သုံးသော dhrat-pone-rite-rar-twin-sone-saw *(adj.)* **photographic**
ဓာတ်ပုံရိုက်ရုံ တောလည်ခရီး dhratponeriterone taw laihkaree *(n.)* **safari**
ဓာတ်ပုံရိုက်သည် dhrat-pone-rite-sai *(v.)* **photograph**
ဓာတ်ဘူး dhratbhuu *(n.)* **thermos (flask)**
ဓာတ်မတည့်ပစ္စည်း စမ်းသပ်နည်း dhat ma tae-pyit-see samsat-naee *(n.)* **patch test**
ဓာတ်မတဲ့ခြင်း dat-ma-tae-chin *(n.)* **allergy**
ဓာတ်မတဲ့သော dat-ma-tae-taw *(adj.)* **allergic**
ဓာတ်မပြုသော dat-ma-pyu-taw *(adj.)* **inert**
ဓာတ်မှန် dhrat-mhaan *(n.)* **x-ray**
ဓာတ်မှန်ရိုက်ခြင်း dhat mhaan rite-chinn *(n.)* **radiography**
ဓာတ်မှန်ရိုက်သည် dhrat mhaan ritesai *(v.)* **x-ray**
ဓာတ်မီး dat-mee *(n.)* **flashlight**
ဓာတ်ရထား dhrat-ra-htarr *(n.)* **tram**
ဓာတ်ရောင်ခြည်ပညာ dhat-raung-chi-pin-nyar *(n.)* **radiology**
ဓာတ်လှေကား dat-lay-kar *(n.)* **lift**
ဓာတ်လိုက်သေခြင်း dat-lite-tay-chin *(n.)* **electrocution**
ဓာတ်လိုက်သေသည် dat-lite-tay-the *(v.)* **electrocute**

နံနံပင် nan-nan-pin *(n.)* **coriander**

နံပါး nan-par *(adj.)* **flank**

နံပါတ် *()*

နံပါတ်တပ်သည် nan-pat-tat-tai *(v.)* **number**

နံရံကပ်အိပ်စင် nan-yan-kat-aik-sin *(n.)* **bunk**

နံရံကလိုင်ပေါက် nan-yan-ka-hlai-pauk *(n.)* **niche**

နံရံဆေးရေး nan-yan-say-yay *(adj.)* **mural**

နံရံဆေးရေးပန်းချီ nan-yan-say-yay-pan-chee *(n.)* **mural**

နံရံတည်ဆောက်ရာတွင် ပါဝင်ပစ္စည်း nanrantaisoutrartwin parwainpahchcaee *(n.)* **shearwall**

နံရံတွင်း လိုဏ်ကဲ့သို့ အခန်းငယ် nan-yan-twin-hlaing-kae-tho-a-khan-nge *(n.)* **alcove**

နံရံပေါ်တွင် ဆွဲသောပုံ nan-yan-paw-twin-swal-taw-pon *(v.)* **graffiti**

နံရိုး nanroe *(n.)* **rib**

နံရိုးနှင့်ဆိုင်သော nan-yoe-nint-sai-taw *(adj.)* **costal**

နကျယ်ကောင် na kyaalkaung *(n.)* **wasp**

နက္ခတ္တဗေဒ nat-khat-ta-bay-da *(n.)* **astronomy**

နက္ခတ္တဗေဒပညာရှင် nat-khat-ta-pyin-nyar-shin *(n.)* **astronomer**

နက္ခဗေဒင် nat-khat-bay-din *(n.)* **astrology**

နက္ခဗေဒင်ဆရာ nat-khat-bay-din-sa-yar *(n.)* **astrologer**

နက်နက်ရှိုင်းရှိုင်း nat-nat-shine-shine *(adv.)* **deeply**

နက်နဲ သိမ်မွေ့မှု naatnell sin-mwae-mhu *(n.)* **profundity**

နက်နဲ့သော nat-nae-taw *(adj.)* **abstruse**

နက်နဲသော nat-nae-taw *(adj.)* **esoteric**

နက်ပကျွန်းဂြိုလ် nat-pa-kyun-gyo *(n.)* **Neptune**

နက်ဗျူလာဓာတ်ငွေ့ထု nat-byu-lar-dat-ngwe-htu *(n.)* **nebula**

နက်ရှိုင်းသော ချောက်ကြီး nat-shine-taw-chauk-gyi *(n.)* **canyon**

နက်လူ့အဖွဲ့အစည်း net-lu-a-phwe-a-see *(n.)* **netizen**

နက်သည် nat-taw *(v.)* **deepen**

နက်သော nat-taw *(adj.)* **deep**

နဂါး na-gar *(n.)* **dragon**

နဂါးနှင့်ဆိုင်သော na-gar-nint-sai-taw *(adj.)* **draconic**

နဂိုပုံစံ na-go-pon-san *(n.)* **default**

နဂိုရှိရင်း မဟုတ်သော na-go-shi-yin-ma-hoke-taw *(adj.)* **extrinsic**

နဂိုအခြေအနေ na-go-a-chay-a-nay *(n.)* **normalcy**

နဂိုအတိုင်း ပြန်လည် မွမ်းမံခြင်း nagoaatine pyanlai mwmmanchinn *(n.)* **restoration**

နဂိုအတိုင်း ပြန်လည် မွမ်းမံသည် nagoaatine pyanlai mwmmansai *(v.)* **restore**

နင်းကြမ်းတံတား nin-kyan-ta-tar *(n.)* **drawbridge**

နင်းခြေသည် ninn-chay-sai *(v.)* **trample**

နင်းသည် ninn-sai *(v.)* **pedal**

နင်းသည်၊ လျှောက်သည် ninn sai , shoutsai *(v.)* **tread**

နင်းသူ nin-thu *(n.)* **treader**

နှစ်ခြင်း၊ တို့ခြင်း nit-chin, toe-chin *(n.)* **dunk**

နစ်နာကြေး၊ ချီးမြှင့်ငွေပေးသည် nitnar-kyay, cheemyint ngway-payysai *(v.)* **recompense**

နစ်နာကြေး၊ အလျော် nit-narkyay , aalyaw *(n.)* **redress**

နစ်နာချက် nit-nar-chat *(n.)* **grievance**

နစ်နာစေခြင်း nit-nar-say-chin *(v.)* **abase**

နစ်နာစေသည် nit-nar-say-the *(adj.)* **abandoned**

နည်းစနစ် ne-sa-nit *(n.)* **means**

နည်းစနစ်ကျနသော nee-sa-nit-kya-na-taw *(adj.)* **methodical**

နည်းနည်း nae-nae *(adj.)* **less**

နည်းနည်းချင်းစီ စုပ်သောက်သည် neenee-chinnse sotesoutsai *(v.)* **sip**

နည်းပညာ naee pin-nyar *(adj.)* **technical**

နည်းပညာကျွမ်းကျင်သူ nee-pin-nyar-kywam-kyin-suu *(n.)* **techy**

နည်းပညာကို ကြောက်ရွံ့သူ naee-pa-nyarko kyawwatrwansuu *(n.)* **technophobe**

နည်းပညာကို ချစ်မြတ်နိုးသူ naee-pa-nyarko chitmyatnoesuu *(n.)* **technophile**

နည်းပညာဆိုင်ရာ naeepanyarsinerar *(adj.)* **technological**

နည်းပညာနှင့် ဆိုင်သော nee-pin-nyar-nint-sine-saw *(adj.)* **tect**

နည်းပညာမျိုးစုံ naee-pin-nyarmyoe-sone *(adj.)* **polytechnic**

နည်းပညာရှင် naeepanyarshin *(n.)* **technician**

နည်းပညာရှူးသွပ်သူ nee-pin-nyar-ruu-swutsuu *(n.)* **technomad**

နည်းပြဆရာ naeepyasarar *(n.)* **tutor**

နည်းပါးစွာ nae-par-swar *(adv.)* **decreasingly**

နည်းပါးမှု nae-par-mu *(n.)* **dearth**

နည်းပါးသော nae-par-taw *(adj.)* **meagre**

နည်းဗျူဟာ neebyauuhar *(n.)* **tactics**

နည်းဗျူဟာပညာရှင် nee-byuuharpanyarshin *(n.)* **tactician**

နည်းလမ်း naeelam *(n.)* **way**

နည်းသည် nae-the *(v.)* **decrease**

နည်းအောင် လုပ်သည် nae-aung-lote-the *(v.)* **minimize**

နတ္ထိ nat-hti *(adv.)* **nothing**

နတ် nat *(n.)* **angel**

နတ်ဆရာ naatsarar *(n.)* **shaman**

နတ်ဘုရား nat-pha-yar *(n.)* **god**

နတ်ဘုရားတစ်ပါးမက ကိုးကွယ်သော naat pha-rarr ta-parr mak koe-kwal-saw *(adj.)* **polytheistic**

နတ်ဘုရားမ nat-pha-yar-ma *(n.)* **goddess**

နတ်သမီး nat-ta-mee *(n.)* **deity**

နတ်သုဓာ၊ မန်နာ nat-tode-dar, man-nar *(n.)* **manna**

နတ်သူငယ် nat-thu-ngal *(n.)* **elf**

နတ်အဖြစ် ကိုးကွယ်သည် nat-a-phit-koe-kwal-the *(v.)* **deify**

နနွင်း na-nwam *(n.)* **turmeric**

နန့်တန့်တန့် မိန်းမ nant-tant-tant-main-ma *(n.)* **coquette**

နန့်သည် nant-the *(v.)* **jiggle**

နန်းကြိုး naannkyaoe *(n.)* **wire**

နန်းချခြင်း nan-cha-chin *(n.)* **deposition**

နန်းချသည် nan-cha-chin *(v.)* **dethrone**

နန်းတက်ပွဲ nan-tat-pwe *(n.)* **coronation**

နန်းတက်သည် nan-tat-the *(v.)* **accede**

နန်းတင်သည် nan-tin-the *(v.)* **enthrone**

နန်းတွင်းသူ နန်းတွင်းသား nan-twin-thu-nan-twin-tar *(n.)* **courtier**

နန်းတော် naan-taw *(n.)* **palace**

နန်းတော်အလား naann-taw-aa-larr *(adj.)* **palatial**

နန်းမျှင်၊ အမျှင် nan-hmyin, a-hmyin *(n.)* **filament**

နပန်းပွဲ na paannpwal *(n.)* **tussle**

နပန်းလုံးခြင်း na paann lonechinn *(n.)* **wrestler**

နပန်းလုံးသည် na pan lonesai *(v.)* **wrestle**

နပန်းသတ်သည် na paann saatsai *(v.)* **tussle**

နပုလ္လိင် na-pone-lain *(adj.)* **neuter**

နဖားပေါက် na-phar-pauk *(n.)* **eyelet**

နဖူး na-phoo *(n.)* **forehead**

နဖူးစည်းစာတန်း na-hpoo-see-sar-tan *(n.)* **banner**

နဖူးပေါ် ဝဲကျနေသော ဦးစွန်းဖုတ် na-phoo-paw-wal-kya-nay-taw-oo-sun-hpoke *(n.)* **forelock**

နဘေထပ်ဆရာ na-bay-htet-sa-yar *(n.)* **rhymester**

နဘေထပ်သည် na bhay htatsai *(v.)* **rhyme**

နမူနာ namuunar *(n.)* **sample**

နမူနာ ရွေးချယ်ခြင်းဖြစ်စဉ် na-muunar rway-hkyaal-chinn-hpyit-hcain *(n.)* **sampling**

နမူနာကောက်သည် namuunar koutsai *(v.)* **sample**

နမူနာယူသည် na-mu-nar-yu-the *(v.)* **model**

နမူနာအားဖြင့် namuunar aarrhpyint *(adj.)* **typical**

နမော်နမဲ့ကောင် na-mawnamaekaung *(n.)* **scatterbrain**

နမော်နမဲ့နိုင်သော namawnamaeninesaw *(adj.)* **scatterbrained**

နမ်းသည် nan-the *(v.)* **kiss**

နမ်းသော nan-taw *(adj.)* **osculant**

နယူကလိယများစွာ n yuu k li yamyarr-swar *(adj.)* **polynucleate**

နယ်ချဲ့ဝါဒ nal-chae-wa-da *(n.)* **imperialism**

နယ်ခြား၊ နယ်စပ် nal-char, nal-sat *(n.)* **frontier**

နယ်နိမိတ် nal-ni-meik *(n.)* **border**

နယ်နိမိတ်မျဉ်း nal-ni-meik-myin *(n.)* **boundary**

နယ်မြေ naalmyay *(n.)* **sheading**

နယ်သစ်တွင် အခြေချသူ naal sittwin aachaychasuu *(n.)* **settler**

နယ်သည်၊ နှိပ်နယ်ပေးသည် nal-the, nate-nal-pay-the *(v.)* **knead**

နျူကလိယ nyuu-ka-li-ya *(n.)* **nucleus**

နျူကလီးယား nyuu-ka-lee-yarr *(adj.)* **nuclear**

နျူထရွန် nyu-hta-ron *(n.)* **neutron**

နရီစည်းဝါး na-yee-see-war *(adj.)* **iambic**

နရီသွား na-yee-twar *(adj.)* **metrical**

နွံနစ်နေသည် non-nit-nay-the *(v.)* **mire**

နွမ်းပါးသူကို စွန့်ကြဲသည့် ငွေ၊ အဝတ်၊ စားဖွယ် nwan-par-thu-ko-sunt-kyae-the-ngwe-a-wit-sar-phwal *(n.)* **alms**

နွမ်းပါးသော nwam parrsaw *(adj.)* **underpriviledged**

နွမ်းရိပါးလိုက်နေသော nwam ri parr litenaysaw *(adj.)* **threadbare**

နွမ်းလျခြင်း nwan-hlya-chin *(n.)* **languor**

နွယ်ပင် nwe-pin *(n.)* **creeper**

နွယ်ပင်နှာမောင်း nwalpin nharmaungg *(n.)* **tendril**

နွေးသည် nwhaayysai *(v.)* **warm**

နွား nwar *(n.)* **cow**

နွားကို ရည်ညွှန်းသော nwar-ko-yee-nyun-taw *(adj.)* **milch**

နွားကဲ့သို့ အော်ခြင်း nwar-kae-tho-aw-chin *(n.)* **bellowing**

နွားကဲ့သို့ အော်သည် nwar-kae-tho-aw-the *(v.)* **bellow**

နွားတင်းကုပ် nwar-tin-gote *(n.)* **byre**

နွားထီး ngwar-htee *(n.)* **bull**

နွားမ၏ နို့အုံ nwarr-ma-eat nhoet-aone *(n.)* **udder**

နွားရိုင်းသတ်သူ nwar-yine-tat-thu *(n.)* **matador**

နွားအော်သံ nwar-aw-than *(n.)* **low**

နွေးထွေးခြင်း nwayhtwaychinn *(n.)* **warmth**

နွေးရုံမျှရှိသော nway rone myahashisaw *(adj.)* **tepid**

နွေရာသီ nway-rar-se *(n.)* **summer**

နွေလယ်ကာလ nway-lal-kar-a *(n.)* **midsummer**

နွေဦး nway u *(adj.)* **vernal**

နှံ့နှံ့စပ်စပ် ရွေးချယ်တတ်ခြင်း nant-nant-sat-sat-ywe-chal-tat-chin *(n.)* **eclectic**

နှံ့နှံ့စပ်စပ် ရွေးချယ်တတ်သော nant-nant-sat-sat-ywe-chal-tat-taw *(adj.)* **eclectic**

နှံစားပင် nan-sar-pin *(n.)* **cereal**

နှံပြီစုတ်ငှက် nhaan pye sotenghaat *(n.)* **wren**

နှင့် nint *(conj.)* **and**

နှင့်ပတ်သက်၍ nint-pat-thet-ywe *(prep.)* **concerning**

နှင့်အတူ nint-aa-tuu *(prep.)* **with**

နှင်း naten *(n.)* **snow**

နှင်းကျသည် naten kyasai *(v.)* **snow**

နှင်းခူနာ hnin-khu-nar *(n.)* **eczema**

နှင်းခဲ hnin-khae *(n.)* **frost**

နှင်းဆီးဘွတ်ဖိနပ် naten see bhwathpinaut *(n.)* **snow boot**

နှင်းဆီပန်း natensepaann *(n.)* **rose**

နှင်းပျော်ဝင်နေသော nhinn pyaw winnaysaw *(adj.)* **slushy**

နှင်းပျော်ဝင်နေသော ရွှံ့ nhinn pyaw winnaysaw shwan *(n.)* **slush**

နှင်းပေါက်၊ နှင်းစက် hnin-pauk, hnin-sat *(n.)* **dew**

နှင်းဖုံးနေသော naten hponenaysaw *(adj.)* **snowy**

နှင်းမုန်တိုင်း hnin-hmone-tai *(n.)* **blizzard**

နှင်းအပ်သည် hnin-at-the *(v.)* **bestow**

နှင်တံ hnin-tan *(n.)* **goad**

နှင်ထုတ်ခြင်း hnin-htoke-chin *(n.)* **eviction**

နှင်ထုတ်သည် hnin-htoke-the *(v.)* **evict**

နှင်ထုတ်သူ hnin-htoke-thu *(n.)* **evictor**

နှစ် nhit *(n.)* **year**

နှစ် ၂၀၀ ပြည့်ပွဲ nit 200 pyae-pwe *(adj.)* **bicentenary**

နှစ်ကန့် အနွေးလက်အိတ် not-khant-a-nway-lat-aik *(n.)* **mitten**

နှစ်ကြိမ် nit-kyain *(adv.)* **twice**

နှစ်ကာလအလိုက် စီစဉ်ထားသော nit-kar-la-a-lite-si-sin-htar-taw *(adj.)* **chronological**

နှစ်ချုပ်စာအုပ် nit-choke-sar-oak *(n.)* **almanac**

နှစ်ခြမ်းကွဲသည် na-cham-kwal-sai *(v.)* **polarize**

နှစ်ခြိုက်သာယာခြင်း nit-chite sar-yar-chinn *(n.)* **zest**

နှစ်ခွ ဖြစ်သွားခြင်း na-khwa-phit-twar-chin *(n.)* **bifurcation**

နှစ်ခွ ဖြစ်သွားသည် na-khwa-phit-twar-the *(v.)* **bifurcate**

နှစ်ခု na-hku *(n.)* **two**

နှစ်ခုဖြစ်သော na-khu-phit-taw *(adj.)* **bi**

နှစ်ခုလုံး na-khu-lone *(adj & pron.)* **both**

နှစ်ခုအစုံ na-khu-a-sone *(adj.)* **binary**

နှစ်ခုအနက် တစ်ခု na-khu-a-net-ta-khu *(pron.)* **either**

နှစ်စဉ် nhit-sin *(adj.)* **yearly**

နှစ်စဉ်ထုတ်ပေးငွေ nit-sin-htoke-pay-ngwe *(n.)* **annuity**

နှစ်ဆ na-sa *(adj.)* **double**

နှစ်ဆတက်သည် ma-sa-tat-the *(v.)* **double**

နှစ်ဆယ် nit-saal *(n.)* **twenty**

နှစ်ဆယ်ခုမြောက် nit-saahl-kumyawt *(n.)* **twentieth**

နှစ်တစ်ရာမှ တစ်ခါဖြစ်သော nit-ta-yar-ma-ta-khar-phit-taw *(n.)* **centennial**

နှစ်တိုးလစာ nit-toe-la-sar *(n.)* **increment**

နှစ်ထပ်အိပ်စင် na-htat-aik-sin *(n.)* **bunk bed**

နှစ်ထောင်းအားရရှိခြင်း nit htaungg aarr-ra-shi-chinn *(n.)* **rapture**

နှစ်နှစ်တစ်ကြိမ် na-nit-ta-kyein *(adj)* **biennial**

နှစ်ပတ်တစ်ကြိမ်၊ တစ်ပတ်နှစ်ကြိမ် na-pat-ta-kyein, ta-pat-na-kyein *(adj.)* **bi-weekly**

နှစ်ပတ်လည် nit-pat-lal *(n.)* **anniversary**

နှစ်ပါတီ na-par-ti *(adj.)* **bipartisan**

နှစ်ဖက်ချွန် na-phat-choon *(adj.)* **bisexual**

နှစ်ဖက်လှ ပိုးထည်ချည်ထည် na-phat-hla-poe-htae-chi-htae *(n.)* **damask**

နှစ်ဖက်သန်သူ na-phat-tan-thu *(n.)* **ambidexter**

နှစ်ဘာသာ na-bar-tar *(adj.)* **bilingual**

နှစ်ဘာသာနှောစကား nit-bar-tar-naw-sa-kar *(n.)* **creole**

နှစ်မျိုးသုံး na-myo-tone *(adj.)* **dual-purpose**

နှစ်မြှုပ်ခြင်း nit-hmyoke-chin *(n.)* **immersion**

နှစ်မြှုပ်ထားသည် nit-hmyoke-htar-the *(v.)* **dedicate**

နှစ်ယောက်ဝိုင်း na-yauk-wine *(n.)* **duet**

နှစ်ယောက်ဝိုင်းလုပ်သည် na-yauk-wine-lote-the *(v.)* **duet**

နှစ်လတစ်ကြိမ် na-la-ta-kyein' *(adj.)* **bimonthly**

နှစ်လိုဖွယ်အလွန်ကောင်းသော nit-lo-phwal-a-lun-kaung-taw *(adj.)* **charming**

နှစ်လိုဖွယ်၊ သာယာသော nit-lo-hpwal, sar-yar-saw *(adj.)* **pleasant**

နှစ်လိုဖွယ်ကောင်းသော nit-lo-phwal-kaung-taw *(adj.)* **dashing**

နှစ်လုံးတွဲ na-lone-twe *(n.)* **duplex**

နှစ်ဝက်စာသင်ကာလ nit waat sarsinkarla *(n.)* **semester**

နှစ်သက်ကြည်နူးစေသည် nit-thet-kyi-ku-say-the *(v.)* **enchant**

နှစ်သက်ဖွယ်ဖြစ်သော nit-thet-phwal-phit-taw *(adj.)* **admirable**

နှစ်သက်သည် nit-thet-the *(v.)* **like**

နှစ်သက်သည်၊ ကြည်နူးသည် nit-thet-the, kyi-nu-the *(v.)* **enjoy**

နှစ်သက်သော nit-the-taw *(adj.)* **fond**

နှစ်သိမ့်မှု nit-theint-mu *(n.)* **consolation**

နှစ်သိမ့်သည် hnit-theint-the *(v.)* **appease**

နှစ်သိမ့်သည်၊ ချွေးသိပ်သည် nhait-seimt-sai, chway-siut-sai *(v.)* **pacify**

နှစ်အလိုက်သမိုင်း nit-a-lite-tha-mine *(n.pl.)* **annals**
နှစ်အလိုက်သမိုင်းပြုစုသူ nit-a-lite-tha-mine-pyu-su-thu *(n.)* **annalist**
နှစ်ဦးနှစ်ဖက် na-oo-na-phat *(adj.)* **multilateral**
နှစ်ဦးနှစ်ဖက်ပါဝင်သော na-oo-na-phat-par-win-taw *(adj.)* **bilateral**
နှစ်ဦးသဘောတူချက်ကို အခြေပြုသော na-oo-ta-baw-tu-chat-ko-a-chay-pyu-taw *(adj.)* **consensual**
နှပ်သည် nhautsai *(v.)* **tenderize**
နှမြောတွန့်တိုခြင်း na-myaw-tunt-to-chin *(n.)* **niggard**
နှမြောတွန့်တိုသော na-myaw-tunt-to-chin *(adj.)* **niggardly**
နှမြောသည် hna-myaw-the *(v.)* **grudge**
နှမ်း nham *(n.)* **sesame**
နှမ်းကြတ် hnan-kyat *(n.)* **linseed**
နှမ်းမှ အဆီထုတ်ခြင်း nhammha a se htotehkyinn *(n.)* **sesamin**
နှလုံးခုန်သံ na-lone-khone-tan *(n.)* **heartbeat**
နှလုံးစက် na-lone-sat *(n.)* **cardiograph**
နှလုံးနှင့်ဆိုင်သော na-hlone-nint-sai-taw *(adj.)* **cardiac**
နှလုံးရပ်ခြင်း na-hlone-yat-chin *(n.)* **cardiac arrest**
နှလုံးရောဂါပညာ na-lone-yaw-gar-pyin-nyar *(n.)* **cardiology**
နှလုံးသား na-lone-tar *(n.)* **heart**
နှလုံးအက်ကိုးရိုက်စက် na-lone-at-kho-yite-sat *(n.)* **echocardiogram**
နှာ nhar *(n.)* **snuff**
နှာချေခြင်း nhar chaaychinn *(n.)* **sneeze**
နှာချေသည် nhar chaaysai *(v.)* **sneeze**
နှာခေါင်း hnar-khaung *(n.)* **nasal**
နှာခေါင်းနှင့် ဆိုင်သော hnar-khaung-nint-sai-taw *(adj.)* **nasal**
နှာခေါင်းရှုံ့သည် nhar-hkaungg shone sai *(v.)* **wrinkle**
နှာပေါက် nhar-pout *(n.)* **nostril**
နှာမှုတ်ခြင်း nhar mhuatchinn *(n.)* **snort**
နှာရှုပ်ခြင်း nhar shotechinn *(n.)* **sniff**
နှာရှုပ်သည် nhar shotesai *(v.)* **sniff**
နှိပ်ကွပ်သည် nate-kwut-sai *(v.)* **persecute**
နှိပ်စက်ခြင်း nate-saat-chinn *(n.)* **torture**
နှိပ်စက်သည် nate-saat-sai *(v.)* **torment**
နှိပ်နယ်ပေးခြင်း nate-nal-pay-chin *(n.)* **massage**
နှိပ်နယ်ပေးသည် nate-nal-pay-the *(v.)* **massage**
နှိမ့်ချခြင်း naint-cha-chin *(n.)* **humility**
နှိမ့်ချမှုရှိသော naint-cha-mu-shi-taw *(adj.)* **humble**
နှိမ့်ချသော naimt chasaw *(adj.)* **submissive**
နှိမ်နင်းသည် aangwaepyansai *(v.)* **vanquish**
နှိမ်နင်းသည်၊ ချေမှုန်းသည် nhain-ninn sai , chaay-hmone-sai *(v.)* **quell**
နှိုးကြွစေသည် hnoe-kywa-say-the *(v.)* **arouse**
နှိုးသည် nhoe-sai *(v.)* **rouse**
နှိုက်၍ ရှာသည် nite-ywe-shar-the *(v.)* **delve**
နှိုက်ယူသည်၊ ကောက်နုတ်ဖော်ပြသည် hnike-yu-the, kauk-note-phaw-pya-the *(v.)* **extract**
နှိုင်းချင့်မျှော်ခေါ်သော nhai chint myaw-hkaw-saw *(adj.)* **prudent**
နှိုင်းဆချင့်ချိန်သော nai-sa-chint-chane-taw *(adj.)* **prudential**

နှိုင်းယှဉ်ချက်အရ nhaine yhainchetaar *(adj.)* **relative**
နှိုင်းယှဉ်ခြင်း hnai-shin-chin *(n.)* **comparison**
နှိုင်းယှဉ်လေ့လာသော hnai-shin-lay-lar-taw *(adj.)* **comparative**
နှိုင်းယှဉ်သည် hnai-shin-the *(v.)* **compare**
နှိုင်းရ ကြီးမားသော အလုံး nai-ya-kyi-mar-taw-a-lone *(n.)* **macrosphere**
နှုတ်ခမ်း hnote-khan *(n.)* **lip**
နှုတ်ခမ်းကို စုဝိုင်းထားသည် note-hkam-ko su wine-htarrsai *(v.)* **purse**
နှုတ်ခမ်းဆိုင်ရာ note-khan-sai-yar *(adj.)* **labial**
နှုတ်ခမ်းပိတ်လျက် တေးညည်းသည် hnpte-khan-pite-lyat-tay-nyee-the *(v.)* **hum**
နှုတ်ခမ်းမွေး hnote-khan-mway *(n.)* **moustache**
နှုတ်စွပ်စွပ်သည်၊ နှုတ်ပိတ်သည် note-sut-sut-the, note-pate-the *(v.)* **muzzle**
နှုတ်ဆက်ခြင်း note-sat-chin *(n.)* **farewell**
နှုတ်ဆက်ပါတယ် hnote-sat-par-the *(interj.)* **good-bye**
နှုတ်ဆက်ပါသည် note-set-par-the *(exclam.)* **adieu**
နှုတ်ဆိတ်စေသည် note satesaysai *(v.)* **silence**
နှုတ်ဆိတ်သော note-seik-taw *(adj.)* **mum**
နှုတ်နည်းခြင်း nhuat naeechinn *(n.)* **reticence**
နှုတ်နည်းသော note-nae-taw *(adj.)* **laconic**
နှုတ်ဖြင့် nhuat-hpyint *(adv.)* **verbally**
နှုတ်ဖြင့် လိင်စိတ်နိုးဆွကျမ်းကျင်သူ hnote-phyint-lain-seik-noe-swa-kyan-kyin-thu *(n.)* **mack**
နှုတ်ဖြေ note-hpyay *(adj.)* **viva voce**
နှုတ်ဖြေစာမေးပွဲ note-hpyay-sar-may-pwal *(n.)* **oral**
နှုတ်မစောင့်ခြင်း hnote-ma-saunt-chin *(n.)* **indiscretion**
နှုတ်မစောင့်သော၊ အဆင်ခြင်မဲ့သော hnote-ma-saunt-taw, a-sin-chin-mae-taw *(adj.)* **indiscreet**
နှုတ်မြိန်စာ note-myine-sar *(n.)* **appetizer**
နှုတ်သီး nhuatsee *(n.)* **snout**
နှုတ်သီး၊ ရေပန်း note see, ray-paann *(n.)* **spout**
နှုတ်သီးစွပ်၊ သေနတ်ပြောင်းဝ note-thee-sut, tay-nat-pyaung-wa *(n.)* **muzzle**
နှုတ်သီးပါဖန်ခွက် note-thee-par-hpan-khwat *(n.)* **beaker**
နှုန်း၊ အချိုးအစား hnone , aachoe-aa-sarr *(n.)* **rate**
နှုန်းလွန်အသံ hnone lawn-aa-san *(adj.)* **ultrasonic**
နှုန်းလွန်အသံလှိုင်း hnone lawn-aa-san-hline *(n.)* **ultrasonics**
နှေးကွေးခြင်း nhaayykwaychinn *(n.)* **slowness**
နှေးကွေးစွာ nhaayykwayswar *(adv.)* **slowly**
နှေးကွေးလေးကန်သော nhaayykway layy kaansaw *(adj.)* **sluggish**
နှေးသော nhaayysaw *(adj.)* **slow**
နှောင့်နှေးခြင်း naunt-nay-chin *(n.)* **delay**
နှောင့်နှေးစေသည် nhaaw int nhaayysaysai *(v.)* **retard**
နှောင့်နှေးသည် naunt-nay-the *(v.)* **delay**
နှောင့်ယှက်သည် naut-shat-the *(v.)* **annoy**
နှောင်းရက်စွဲတပ်သည် nhaung raat-swal taut-sai *(v.)* **post-date**
နား nar *(n.)* **ear**

နားကပ်၊ နိုပ်ကြယ်သီး narr kat , nate-kyaal-see *(n.)* **stud**

နားကြပ် narr-kyaut *(n.)* **stethoscope**

နားကြပ်၊ နားဆို့ nar-kyat, nar-soe *(n.)* **earbud**

နားကြပ်တံကဲ့သို့တုတ်ချောင်းငယ် *(n.)* **maulstick**

နားကဲ့သို့ပုံတူသော nar-kae-tho-pone-thu-taw *(adj.)* **auriform**

နားချိန် nar-chain *(n.)* **interlude**

နားငြီးစရာ၊ ကြားပြင်းကတ်စရာကောင်းသော narr ngyee sarar , kyarr pyinn kaat sararkaunggsaw *(adj.)* **strident**

နားစွန်နားဖျားကြားသည် narr-swan-narr-hpyar-kyar-tai *(v.)* **overhear**

နားတွင်း မှန်ပြောင်းနှင့် ကြည့်ရှုစစ်ဆေးခြင်း narrtwin mhaan pyaunggnhang kyi shu-sitsayy-chinn *(n.)* **otoscopy**

နားတွင်းကြည့်မှန်ပြောင်း narr twin kyany mhaanpyaungg *(n.)* **otoscope**

နားတွင်းကြည့်မှန်ပြောင်းနှင့် ဆိုင်သော narr twin kyany mhaan pyaungg-nint sinesaw *(adj.)* **otoscopis**

နားထောင်သည် nar-htaung-the *(v.)* **listen**

နားထောင်သူ nar-htaung-thu *(n.)* **listener**

နားနားနေနေ နေသည် nar-nar-nay-nay-nay-the *(v.)* **laze**

နားနေအဆောက်အအုံ narr-nay-aa-sout-aa-ohn *(n.)* **pavilion**

နားပင်းစေသည် nar-pin-say-the *(v.)* **deafen**

နားပင်းသော nar-pin-taw *(adj.)* **deaf**

နားပူနားဆာလုပ်ခြင်း na-pu-na-sar-lote-chin *(n.)* **nagging**

နားပူနားဆာလုပ်သည် na-pu-na-sar-lote-the *(v.)* **nag**

နားဖာကလော် na-phar-ka-lar *(n.)* **aurilave**

နားမလည်နိုင်သော nar-ma-lal-nai-taw *(adj.)* **bemused**

နားရွက်ဖားး ခွေးစုတ်ဖွား nar-ywet-phar-khway-sote-phwar *(v.)* **cocker**

နားလည်နိုင်သော nar-lal-nai-taw *(adj.)* **intelligible**

နားလည်မှု လွဲခြင်း nar-lal-mu-lwal-chin *(n.)* **misconception**

နားလည်မှု လွဲသည် nar-lal-mu-lwal-the *(v.)* **misconceive**

နားလည်ရခက်သော nar-lal-ya-khat-taw *(adj.)* **inexplicable**

နားလည်ရန် ခက်သော nar-lal-yan-khat-taw *(adj.)* **enigmatic**

နားလည်လွယ်သော nar-lal-lwal-taw *(adj.)* **lucid**

နားလည်သည် nar-lal-the *(v.)* **comprehend**

နားလည်သဘောပေါက်သည် nar-lal-ta-baw-pauk-the *(v.)* **fathom**

နားဝင်မချိုသော narr win machaosaw *(adj.)* **waspish**

နားသယ်မွေး narr saalmway *(n.)* **sideburn**

နာကျင်ခြင်း nar-kyin-chin *(n.)* **hurt**

နာကျင်မှု nar-kyin-mhu *(n.)* **pain**

နာကျင်မှု သက်သာခြင်း nar-kyin-mhu-saat-sar-chinn *(n.)* **pain relief**

နာကျင်မှုကို ဖော်ပြသံ narkyinmhuko hpawpyasan *(n.)* **ouch**

နာကျင်သည် nar-kyin-sai *(v.)* **pain**

နာကျင်သော nar-kyin-saw *(adj.)* **painful**

နာကြည်းမှု၊ ရက်စက်ရမ်းကားမှု nar-kyi-mhu, rat-sat-ram-kar-mhu *(n.)* **outrage**

နာကြည်းသည် nar-kyi-tai *(v.)* **outrage**

နာကာမုတ်ကောင် na-kar-mote-kaung *(n.)* **nacre**

နာခံခြင်း nar-hkan-chinn *(n.)* **obedience**

နာခံခြင်း၊ လိုက်နာခြင်း nar hkan chinn , litenarchinn *(n.)* **subordination**
နာခံတတ်သော nar-hkan-tat-taw *(adj.)* **obedient**
နာခံသည် nar-hkan-tai *(v.)* **obey**
နာတာရှည် nar-tar-shay *(adj.)* **chronic**
နာတာရှည်ဆေးကုဌာန nartarshi sayykuhtarna *(n.)* **sanatorium**
နာတာလူးသီချင်း nar-tar-lu-tha-chin *(n.)* **carol**
နာနတ်သီး nar-naat-see *(n.)* **pineapple**
နာနိုကွန်ပျူတာ na-no-kun-pyu-tar *(n.)* **nanocomputer**
နာနိုစက်ရုပ် na-no-sat-yoke *(n.)* **nanite**
နာနိုဆားကစ်ပြား na-no-sar-kit-pyar *(n.)* **nanochip**
နာနိုဇီဝဗေဒ na-no-zi-wa-bay-da *(n.)* **nanobiology**
နာနိုထရန်စစ္စတာ na-no-hta-ran-sis-sa-tar *(n.)* **nanotransistor**
နာနိုနည်းပညာ na-no-nee-pyin-nyar *(n.)* **nano**
နာနိုမက္ကင်းနစ်ပညာ na-no-ma-kin-nit-pin-nyar *(n.)* **nanomechanics**
နာနိုလျှပ်စစ်ပတ်လမ်းစနစ် na-no-hlyat-sit-pat-lan-sa-nit *(n.)* **nanocircuitry**
နာနိုသွေးရည်ကြည် na-no-thway-yay-kyi *(n.)* **nanoplasma**
နာနိုဟတ် na-no-hat *(n.)* **nanohertz**
နာနိုအင်ဂျင်နီယာ na-no-in-gyin-na-yar *(n.)* **nanoengineer**
နာနိုအစိတ်အပိုင်း na-no-a-seit-a-pai *(n.)* **nanocomponent**
နာနိုအမှုန် na-no-a-hmone *(n.)* **nanoparticle**
နာဖျားမကျန်းဖြစ်ခြင်း nar hpyarr ma kyannhpyitchinn *(n.)* **sickness**
နာဖာချေး na-phar-chee *(n.)* **cerumen**
နာမကျန်းသော nar-ma-kyan-taw *(adj.)* **indisposed**
နာမည် na-mal *(n.)* **name**
နာမည်၊ ဂုဏ်သတင်း narmai , gonsatinn *(n.)* **reputation**
နာမည်၊ သတင်း narmai , satinn *(n.)* **repute**
နာမည်ကြီးအောင် လုပ်သည် narmai-kyee-aaung lote-sai *(v.)* **popularize**
နာမည်ဆိုးဖြင့် ကျော်ကြားခြင်း na-mal-soe-hpyint-kyaw-kyar-chinn *(n.)* **notoriety**
နာမည်ဆိုးဖြင့် ကျော်ကြားသော na-mai-soe-hpyint-kyaw-kyarr-taw *(adj.)* **notorious**
နာမည်တံဆိပ်ပြား na-mal-ta-seik-pyar *(n.)* **nameplate**
နာမည်တု nan-mal-thu *(adv.)* **alias**
နာမည်တူ na-mal-thu *(n.)* **namesake**
နာမည်ပျက်ခြင်း nan-mal-pyat-chin *(n.)* **disrepute**
နာမည်ပြောင် nar-mal-pyaung *(n.)* **nickname**
နာမည်ပြောင်ခေါ်သည် na-mal-pyaung-khaw-the *(v.)* **nickname**
နာမည်ဖျက်သည် nan-mal-phat-the *(v.)* **besmirch**
နာမည်အပြည့်အစုံ na-mal-a-pyae-a-son *(n.)* **full name**
နာမဝိသေသန nar-ma-wi-tay-ta-na *(n.)* **adjective**
နာမ် narm *(n.)* **noun**
နာမ်စား narm-sarr *(n.)* **pronoun**
နာရီ nar-yee *(n.)* **clock**
နာရီဒိုင်ခွက်၊ ဖုန်းခလုတ် nar-yi-dai-khwat, phone-ka-lote *(n.)* **dial**

နာရေးကြော်ငြာ nar-ray-kyay-nyar *(adj.)* **obituary**

နာလန်ထ na-lan-hta *(adj.)* **convalescent**

နာလန်ထကာလ na-lan-hta-kar-la *(n.)* **convalescence**

နာလန်ထသည် na-lan-hta-the *(v.)* **convalesce**

နာလန်ထူခြင်း narlaan htuu-chinn *(n.)* **recovery**

နာသော narsaw *(adj.)* **sore**

နိဂုံး ni-gon *(n.)* **conclusion**

နိဂုံးချုပ်သည် ni-gon-choke-the *(v.)* **conclude**

နိဒါန်း ni-dan *(adj.)* **introductory**

နိဗ္ဗာန် nib-ban *(n.)* **paradise**

နိမိတ် na-mate *(n.)* **omen**

နိမိတ်စကား na-mate-sa-karr *(n.)* **oracle**

နိမိတ်ပြသည် na-matepya-sai *(v.)* **portend**

နိမိတ်ပုံ na-meik-pon *(n.)* **imagery**

နိမိတ်ဖတ်သော na-mate hpaat-saw *(adj.)* **prophetic**

နိမ့်ကျသော naint-kya-taw *(adj.)* **derogatory**

နိမ့်ဆင်းသော naint-sin-taw *(adj.)* **downward**

နိမ့်နိမ့် naint-naint *(adv.)* **low**

နိမ့်ရာသို့ naint-yar-tho *(adv.)* **downward**

နိမ့်သည် naint-the *(v.)* **low**

နိမ့်သွားသည်၊ တို့သည်၊ နှိုက်သည် naint-twar-the, toe-the, hnaik-the *(v.)* **dip**

နိမ့်သော naint saw *(adj.)* **subordinate**

နိမ်နှင်းခြင်း nain-nhinn-chinn *(n.)* **suppression**

နို့ noe *(adj.)* **mammary**

နို့၊ နို့ရည် noe, noe-yay *(n.)* **milk**

နို့စို့ကလေး no-so-ka-lay *(n.)* **infant**

နို့တက်သည် noe-thet-the *(v.)* **milk**

နို့တွင် ခရင်ပါနှုန်းတိုင်း ကိရိယာ noe-twin-kha-rin-par-hnone-tai-ka-ri-ya *(n.)* **lactometer**

နို့တိုက်ခြင်း noe tite-chinn *(n.)* **suckling**

နို့တိုက်သည် noe tite-sai *(v.)* **suckle**

နို့တိုက်သတ္တဝါ noe-tite-tat-ta-war *(n.)* **mammal**

နို့ထွက်ပစ္စည်း no-htwat-pyit-see *(n.)* **dairy product**

နို့ထွက်ပစ္စည်း ချက်ရာနေရာ၊ အရောင်းဆိုင် no-htwat-pyit-see-chat-yar-nay-yar, a-yaung-sai *(n.)* **dairy**

နို့ထုတ်သည် noe-nae-taw *(v.)* **lactate**

နို့နှင့် သက်ဆိုင်သော noe-nint-thet-sai-taw *(adj.)* **lactic**

နို့ပါသော noe-par-taw *(adj.)* **milky**

နို့ပုံး noe-pone *(v.)* **churn**

နို့ဖြတ်ခြင်း noe-phat-chin *(n.)* **ablactation**

နို့ဖြတ်သည် nhoet hpyatsai *(v.)* **wean**

နို့မှုန့် noe-hmont *(n.)* **milk powder**

နို့သီး nhoe-tee *(n.)* **nipple**

နို့သီးခေါင်း nhoet seehkaungg *(n.)* **teat**

နိုးကြားခြင်း noe-kyar-chin *(n.)* **alertness**

နိုးကြားလာသော noe kyarrlarsaw *(adj.)* **resurgent**

နိုးကြားသော noe-kyar-taw *(adj.)* **alert**

နိုးထခြင်း noe-hta-chin *(n.)* **wake**

နိုးထလာခြင်း noehtalarchinn *(n.)* **resurgence**

နိုးနိုးကြားကြားရှိခြင်း noenoe kyarr kyarrshichinn *(n.)* **vigilance**

နိုးနိုးကြားကြားရှိသော noenoe kyarr kyarrshisaw *(adj.)* **vigilant**
နိုးသည် noe-the *(v.)* **awake**
နိုက်ထရိုဂျင်ဓာတ်ငွေ့ nite-hta-ro-gyin-dhat-ngwae *(n.)* **nitrogen**
နိုင်ငံ nai-ngan *(n.)* **nation**
နိုင်ငံ၊ အစိုးရ nine-ngan , aa-soe-ra *(n.)* **state**
နိုင်ငံကူးလက်မှတ် nine-ngan-kuu-laat-mhaat *(n.)* **passport**
နိုင်ငံချစ်စိတ်ဓာတ် nai-ngan-chit-seik-dat *(n.)* **nationalism**
နိုင်ငံခြား nai-ngan-char *(adj.)* **foreign**
နိုင်ငံခြားသား nai-ngan-char-thar *(n.)* **foreigner**
နိုင်ငံခြားသားနှင့် ယဉ်ကျေးမှုကို ကြောက်သူ nine-ngan-char-tar-nint-yin-kyay-mu-ko-kyauk-suu *(n.)* **xenophobe**
နိုင်ငံခြားသားနှင့် ယဉ်ကျေးမှုကို ချစ်သူ nine-ngan-char-tar-nint-yin-kyay-mu-ko-chitsuu *(n.)* **xenophile**
နိုင်ငံဆိုင်ရာ nai-ngan-sai-yar *(adj.)* **national**
နိုင်ငံတော်၏ ထောက်ပံ့ကြေး nai-ngan-taw-ei-htauk-pant-kyay *(n.)* **dole**
နိုင်ငံတော်သစ္စာဖောက်မှု nine-ngantaw sit-sarhpoutmhu *(n.)* **treason**
နိုင်ငံတော်အား အကြည်ညိုပျက်အောင် ပြုခြင်း ninengantawaarr aakyinyopyetaaung pyuchinn *(n.)* **sedition**
နိုင်ငံတော်အား အကြည်ညိုပျက်အောင် ပြုသော ninengantawaarr aakyinyopyetaaung pyusaw *(adj.)* **seditious**
နိုင်ငံပိုင်ပြုခြင်း nai-ngan-pai-pyu-chin *(n.)* **nationalization**
နိုင်ငံပိုင်ပြုသည် nai-ngan-pai-pyu-the *(v.)* **nationalize**
နိုင်ငံပိုင်အဖြစ်မှ ပုဂ္ဂလိကပိုင်အဖြစ် ပြောင်းသည် nai-ngan-pai-a-phit-ma-poke-ga-li-ka-a-phit-pyaung-the *(v.)* **denationalize**
နိုင်ငံပေါင်းစုံတွင် ပြန့်ကျဲနေထိုင်သော လူမျိုး nai-ngan-paung-sone-twin-pyant-kyal-nay-htai-taw-lu-myo *(n.)* **diaspora**
နိုင်ငံရပ်ခြား naing-ngan-yat-char *(adv.)* **abroad**
နိုင်ငံရေး nine-ngan-rayy *(adj.)* **political**
နိုင်ငံရေးမဲဆွယ်သည် nai-ngan-yay-mae-swal-the *(v.)* **canvass**
နိုင်ငံရေးသမား nine-ngan-rayy-sa-marr *(n.)* **politician**
နိုင်ငံရေးအဟောအပြောနည်းပရိယာယ် nai-ngan-yay-a-haw-a-pyaw-nee-pa-yee-yal *(n.)* **demagogy**
နိုင်ငံသား nai-ngan-tar *(n.)* **nationality**
နိုင်ငံသားနှင့် ဆိုင်သော nai-ngan-tar-nint-sai-taw *(adj.)* **civic**
နိုင်ငံသားအဖြစ် nai-ngan-thar-a-phit *(n.)* **citizenship**
နိုင်ငံသားအဖြစ် ခံယူသည် nai-ngan-tar-a-phit-khan-yu-the *(v.)* **naturalize**
နိုင်ငံအချင်းချင်း သဘောတူစာအုပ် ninenganaachinnchinn sabhawtuusaraote *(n.)* **treaty**
နိုင်ငံဦးသျှောင် ninengan u shawn *(n.)* **sovereign**
နိုင်နိုင်နင်းနင်း ကိုင်တွယ်ဖြေရှင်းသည် nai-nai-ning-ning-kai-twal-phyay-shin-the *(v.)* **cope**
နိုင်ဖဲ၊ ဝှက်ဖဲ nine hpell , whaat-hpell *(n.)* **trump**
နိုင်မှတ် nai-mat *(n.)* **game point**
နိုင်လွန် nine-lwan *(n.)* **nylon**
နိုင်သည် naing-the *(v.)* **could**
နိုထရီ no-hta-re *(n.)* **notary**

နိုဝင်ဘာလ no-win-bhar-la *(n.)* **November**

နီးကပ်သော nee-kat-taw *(adj.)* **close**

နီးပြီ nee-pye *(adv.)* **nigh**

နီးပါး nee-parr *(prep.)* **nigh**

နီးသည် nee-the *(v.)* **near**

နီးသော nee-taw *(adj.)* **near**

နီကယ်ဒြပ်စင် nee-kal-drat-sin *(n.)* **nickel**

နီကြင်ကြင် ne kyin-kyin *(adj.)* **reddish**

နီကိုတင်းဓာတ် ni-ko-tin-dat *(n.)* **nicotine**

နီဂရိုး ne-ga-ro *(n.)* **negro**

နီဂရိုးမ ne-ga-ro-ma *(n.)* **negress**

နီညိုရင့်ရောင် ni-nyo-yint-yaung *(n.)* **maroon**

နီညိုရောင် myay nehtai nenyoraung *(adj.)* **terracotta**

နီတျာတျာ ne tyaar tyaar *(adj.)* **rosy**

နီမြန်းသည် ne myan-sai *(v.)* **redden**

နီယွန်ဓာတ်ငွေ့ ni-yoon-dat-ngwe *(n.)* **neon**

နီလာ nelar *(n.)* **sapphire**

နီလာပန်း၊ ခရမ်းရောင် nelar paann , hkaramraung *(n.)* **violet**

နီလာသည် ni-lar-the *(v.)* **rubify**

နီသော ne-saw *(adj.)* **red**

နုံးချည့်သော hnone-chee-taw *(adj.)* **listless**

နုံအခြင်း hnon-a-chin *(n.)* **naivete**

နုတ်ထွက်ခြင်း notehtwatchinn *(n.)* **resignation**

နုတ်ထွက်သည် notehtwatsai *(v.)* **resign**

နုတ်သည် notesai *(v.)* **subtract**

နုနုလှလှ nu-nu-hla-hla *(adj.)* **dainty**

နုန်း none *(n.)* **silt**

နုန်းဖြင့် ပိတ်နေသည် nonehpyint patenaysai *(v.)* **silt**

နုပျိုစေသည် nu pyosaysai *(v.)* **rejuvenate**

နုပ်နုပ်စင်းသည် note note sinnsai *(v.)* **shred**

နုသော၊ ချည့်နဲ့သော nu-taw, chae-nae-taw *(adj.)* **frail**

နူးညံ့ချောမွေ့သော nuunyan chawwmwaesaw *(adj.)* **silken**

နူးညံ့ပျော့ပျောင်းသော ဆံသား nu-nyant-pawt-pyaung-taw-san-tar *(n.)* **lanugo**

နူးညံ့သိမ်မွေ့စေသည် nuunyant sinmwaesaysai *(v.)* **sublimate**

နူးညံ့သော nu-nyant-taw *(adj.)* **delicate**

နူးနူးညံ့ညံ့ nuu nuunyannyan *(adv.)* **tenderly**

နူးအိသော nuu aisaw *(adj.)* **soggy**

နေ nay *(n.)* **sun**

နေ့၊ ရက် nae, yat *(n.)* **day**

နေ့စဉ် nay-sin *(adj. & adv.)* **daily**

နေ့စဉ်မှတ်တမ်း nay-zin-mat-tan *(n.)* **diary**

နေ့စွဲ nae-swal *(n.)* **date**

နေ့စွဲတပ်ထားသော nae-swal-tat-htar-taw *(adj.)* **dated**

နေ့စွဲတပ်သည် nae-swal-tat-the *(v.)* **date**

နေ့တစ်ဝက် nay-ta-wat *(n.)* **half-day**

နေ့တာနှင့် ညတာ ညီမျှသော ကာလ nay-tar-nint-nya-tar-nyi-mya-taw-mar-la *(n.)* **equinox**

နေ့တိုင်း nay-tine *(adj.)* **everyday**

နေ့ပွဲ nae-pwe *(n.)* **matinee**

နေ့လည် nae-lal *(n.)* **midday**

နေ့လည်စာ nae-lal-sar *(n.)* **lunch**

နေ့လည်စာစားသည် nae-lal-sar-sar-the *(v.)* **lunch**

နေ့အလင်းရောင် nae-a-lin-yaung *(n.)* **daylight**

နေကျက်ရွှံ့ nay-kyat-hswont *(n.)* **adobe**

နေကာအလွှာပါး nay-kar-aa-lwhar-parr *(n.)* **polaroid**

နေခြင်း၊ သီတင်းသုံးခြင်း naychinn , setinnsonechinn *(n.)* **sojourn**

နေဆဲ nay-sell *(adj.)* **ongoing**

နေထွက်ချိန် nay-htwat-chane *(n.)* **sunrise**

နေထားတကျ nay htarr takya *(adj.)* **shipshape**

နေထိုင်စရာအခန်း nay-htaing-sa-yar-a-khan *(n.)* **accommodation**

နေထိုင်မကောင်းသော nayhtinemakaunggsaw *(adj.)* **unwell**

နေထိုင်မှု nay-htai-mu *(n.)* **habitation**

နေထိုင်ရန် သင့်လျော်သော nay-htai-yan-tint-yaw-taw *(adj.)* **habitable**

နေထိုင်ရာနေရာ nay-htai-yar-nay-yar *(n.)* **habitat**

နေထိုင်လျက်ရှိသည် nay-htine-lyet-shi-sai *(v.)* **people**

နေထိုင်သည် nay-htai-the *(v.)* **dwell**

နေထိုင်သူ nay-htai-thu *(n.)* **inhabitant**

နေပူဆာလှုံသည် nay puu sar hlone-sai *(v.)* **sun**

နေမကောင်းသော nay-ma-kaung-taw *(adj.)* **ill**

နေရာ nay-rar *(n.)* **place**

နေရာ၊ ရာထူး nayrar, rar-htuu *(n.)* **position**

နေရာချထားသည် nayrarchahtarrsai *(v.)* **station**

နေရာတစ်ခုတွင် အတွေ့များသည့် မျိုးစိတ် nay-yar-ta-khu-twin-a-tway-myar-the-myo-seik *(n.)* **endemic**

နေရာတိုင်းမှာ nay-rar-tine-mhar *(adj.)* **omnipresent**

နေရာမှားထားသည် nay-yar-mar-htar-the *(v.)* **misplace**

နေရာယူသည်၊ ထားသည် nay-rar-yuu sai, htarrsai *(v.)* **position**

နေရာဟောင်းသို့ အလည်တစ်ပတ် ပြန်ရောက်သည် nayrar-haunggthoet aalai-ta-paat-pyan-routsai *(v.)* **revisit**

နေရာအနှံ့ရှိခြင်း nay-raraanhaanshichinn *(n.)* **ubiquity**

နေရောင် nay-raung *(n.)* **sunlight**

နေရောင်ခြည် nayraungchi *(adj.)* **solar**

နေလောင်ခြင်း nay-laungchinn *(n.)* **sunburn**

နေဝင်ချိန် nay-win-chane *(n.)* **sunset**

နေဝင်ဆည်းဆာ nay-win-see-sar *(n.)* **dusk**

နေသည် naysai *(v.)* **stay**

နေသည်၊ သီတင်းသုံးသည် naysai , setinnsonesai *(v.)* **sojourn**

နေသားကျသည် nay-tar-kya-the *(v.)* **acclimatise**

နေသားတကျ ပြန်ဖြစ်သည် nay-sarrtakya pyan-hpyitsai *(v.)* **readjust**

နေသားတကျ ဟန်ထားသည် nay-sarr-ta-kya-haan-htarr-sai *(v.)* **poise**

နေသားမကျဖြစ်စေသည် nay sarr m kyahpyitsaysai *(v.)* **unsettle**

နေသာသော nay-sar-saw *(adj.)* **sunny**

နေအိမ် nay-ain *(n.)* **abode**

နောက် naut *(adv.)* **next**

နောက်ကျ ကျန်ရစ်သည် naut-kya-kyan-yit-the *(v.)* **lag**

နောက်ကျခြင်း noutkyachinn *(n.)* **tardiness**

နောက်ကျန်ရစ်သူ noutkyaanraitsuu *(n.)* **straggler**
နောက်ကျသော naut-kya-taw *(adj.)* **late**
နောက်ကျော naut-kyaw *(n.)* **back**
နောက်ကြောင်းပြန် ပြကွက် naut-kyaung-pyan-pya-kwat *(n.)* **flashback**
နောက်ကြောင်းပြန်ရက်စွဲတပ်သည် naut-kyaung-pyan-yat-swal-tat-the *(n.)* **antedate**
နောက်ခံ သီချင်းသံ nouthkan sehkyinnsan *(n.)* **soundtrack**
နောက်ခံဖြစ်ရပ် naut-khan-phit-yat *(v.)* **backdrop**
နောက်ခံအကြောင်း naut-khan-a-kyaung *(n.)* **background**
နောက်စေ့ nout-sae *(adj.)* **occipital**
နောက်ဆက် noutsaat *(n.)* **suffix**
နောက်ဆက်တွဲ naut-sat-twe *(n.)* **follow-up**
နောက်ဆက်တွဲစောင့်ရှောက်မှု naut-set-twe-saunt-shaut-mu *(n.)* **aftercare**
နောက်ဆက်တွဲပါတီ naut-set-twe-par-ty *(n.)* **after-party**
နောက်ဆက်တွဲဖြစ်သော noutsaattwahlpyitsaw *(adj.)* **subsequent**
နောက်ဆက်တွဲအကျိုးသက်ရောက်မှု naut-set-twe-a-kyo-thet-yaut-mu *(n.)* **after-effect**
နောက်ဆက်တွဲအတွေး naut-set-twe-a-thway *(n.)* **afterthought**
နောက်ဆုံး naut-sone *(adj.)* **final**
နောက်ဆုံးဆန္ဒစာရင်း naut-sone-san-da-sa-yin *(n.)* **bucket list**
နောက်ဆုံးတွင် noutsonetwin *(adv.)* **ultimately**
နောက်ဆုံးပိတ် naut-sone-pait *(adv.)* **last**
နောက်ဆုံးဖြစ်သော၊ တိကျပြတ်သားသော naut-sone-phit-taw, ti-kya-pyat-tar-taw *(adj.)* **decisive**
နောက်ဆုံးမှာ naut-sone-mar *(adv.)* **eventually**
နောက်ဆုံးဗိုလ်လုပွဲ naut-sone-bo-lu-pwe *(n.)* **grand finale**
နောက်ဆုတ်သည် noutsotesai *(v.)* **reverse**
နောက်တွဲယာဉ် nout twal-yin *(n.)* **trailer**
နောက်တွဲလူနေယာဉ် naut-twal-lu-nay-yin *(n.)* **caravan**
နောက်တော်ပါအဖွဲ့ nouttaw paraahpwal *(n.)* **retinue**
နောက်ထပ် naut-htet *(adj.)* **additional**
နောက်ပြန် naut-pyan *(adj.)* **backward**
နောက်ပြန်ကန်ခြင်း noutpyan kaanchinn *(n.)* **recoil**
နောက်ပြောင်ကျီစယ်မှု nout pyaung kyae saal-mhu *(n.)* **prank**
နောက်ပြောင်လိမ်လည်သည် naut-pyaung-lain-lal-the *(v.)* **hoax**
နောက်ပိတ်ဆုံး naut-pate-sone *(n.)* **cut-off**
နောက်ပိုင်း naut-pai *(adj.)* **latter**
နောက်ဖေး၊ နောက်ကျော nout hpayy , noutkyaww *(n.)* **rear**
နောက်မှ naut-hma *(adv.)* **afterwards**
နောက်မှ ဆက်သည် noutmha saatsai *(v.)* **suffix**
နောက်မှ ပေါ်သည့် ရွှေကြာပင် noutmha paw-seet shway kyaarpin *(n.)* **upstart**
နောက်မှ မီးထိုးခြင်း naut-ma-mee-htoe-chin *(n.)* **backlight**
နောက်မှာ naut-mar *(prep.& adv.)* **behind**
နောက်ယောင်ခံလိုက်သည် nout yaung hkanlitesai *(v.)* **shadow**
နောက်လှည့် naut-hlae *(n.)* **about-turn**

နောက်လိုက် naut-lite *(n.)* **adherent**

နောက်လိုက်သည် naut-lite-the *(v.)* **follow**

နောက်သို့ naut-tho *(adv.)* **backward**

နောက်အမိုးပွင့်ကုန်တင်တွဲကား၊ စကန်နာ naut-a-moe-pwint-kon-tin-twe-car, sa-kan-nar *(n.)* **flatbed**

နောင်တ naung ta *(n.)* **repentance**

နောင်တရပုံ naung-ta rapone *(adj.)* **repentant**

နောင်တရသည် naungtarasai *(v.)* **rue**

နောင်ဖြစ်လာမည့် naung hpyitlarmaeet *(adj.)* **would-be**

နောင်ရေးအတွက် ဂရုတစိုက်ကြိုတင်စီမံထားသော naung-rayy-aa-twat garu-tasite kyo-tin seman-htarr-saw *(adj.)* **provident**

နောင်လာနောက်သား naung lar nout-sarr *(n.)* **posterity**

နော်ဇယ် naw-zal *(n.)* **nozzle**

ပကတိ pakati *(adj.)* **virgin**

ပကတိအခြေအနေ pakatiaachayaanay *(n.)* **tenor**

ပကတိအတိုင်း pa-ka-ti-a-tai *(adj.)* **intact**

ပက်ပင်းကြုံသည် pat-pin-kyone-the *(v.)* **encounter**

ပက်လက်တွဲ paatlaattwal *(n.)* **wagon**

ပက်သည်၊ ဖျန်းသည် paat sai, hpyannsai *(v.)* **splash**

ပခုံးကြွက်သား pa-khone-kyat-tar *(n.)* **deltoid**

ပခုံးတွန့်ခြင်း pahkone twantchinn *(n.)* **shrug**

ပခုံးတွန့်သည် pahkone twantsai *(v.)* **shrug**

ပခုံးရိုးဝတ်ရုံ pahkone ronewaatrone *(n.)* **scapular**

ပင် pin *(n.)* **preen**

ပင့်ကူ pintkuu *(n.)* **spider**

ပင့်ကူအိမ် pint kuuaain *(n.)* **web**

ပင့်မစက် p int ma-saat *(n.)* **teagle**

ပင့်မသည် pint-ma-the *(v.)* **heave**

ပင့်သက်ရှိုက်ခြင်း pint-thet-shite-chin *(n.)* **gasp**

ပင့်သက်ရှိုက်သည် pint-thet-shite-the *(v.)* **gasp**

ပင်ကိုစရိုက် pin kosarite *(n.)* **temperament**

ပင်ကိုစရိုက်ကို ထိခိုက်စေသည့် စိတ်ဝေဒနာ pin ko sa-riteko htihkite saysaeet sate-waydanar *(n.)* **psychosis**

ပင်ကိုစွမ်းရည် pin-ko-swan-yay *(n.)* **aptitude**

ပင်ကိုစွမ်းရည်စစ်ဆေးခြင်း pin-ko-swan-yay-sit-say-chin *(n.)* **aptitude test**

ပင်ကိုစိတ်ကူးဉာဏ် pin-ko-seik-ku-nyan *(n.)* **brainchild**

ပင်ကိုလက္ခဏာ pin-ko-lat-kha-nar *(n.)* **individuality**

ပင်စင်စား pin-sin-sarr *(n.)* **pensioner**

ပင်စင်ယူသည် pin-sin-yuu-sai *(v.)* **pension**

ပင်စင်လစာ pin-sin-la-sar *(n.)* **pension**

ပင်စည် pin-sai *(n.)* **trunk**

ပင်စည်၊ ရိုးတံ pin se , roetan *(n.)* **stem**

ပင်စိမ်း pin-sein *(n.)* **basil**

ပင်တိုင်ဆောင်းပါးရှင် pin-tai-saung-par-shin *(n.)* **columnist**

ပင်ပင်ပန်းပန်း မနားမနေ လုပ်သည် pinpinpaannpaann ma narr manay lotesai *(v.)* **slave**
ပင်ပင်ပန်းပန်း လုပ်သည် pinpinpaannpaann lotesai *(v.)* **toil**
ပင်ပန်းစေသည် pinpaannsaysai *(v.)* **weary**
ပင်ပန်းနွမ်းနယ်မှု pin-pan-nwan-nal-mu *(n.)* **fatigue**
ပင်ပန်းနွမ်းနယ်သည် pin-pan-nwan-nal-the *(v.)* **exhaust**
ပင်ပန်းမှုဒဏ်၊ ဝန်ပိခြင်း၊ အားအင်ကုန်ခမ်းခြင်း pinpaann mhu dan , waan pi chinn , aarr in kone hkamchinn *(n.)* **strain**
ပင်ပန်းရသော pinpaannrasaw *(adj.)* **strenuous**
ပင်ပန်းသော pinpaannsaw *(adj.)* **weary**
ပင်ပျို pinpyo *(n.)* **sapling**
ပင်မ pinma *(adj.)* **staple**
ပင်ရင်းဒေသ pin-yin-day-ta *(n.)* **locale**
ပင်လယ် pinlaal *(n.)* **sea**
ပင်လယ်ကကတစ်ငါး painlaal k k taitngarr *(n.)* **sea bass**
ပင်လယ်ကမ်းခြေ painlaalkamhkyay *(n.)* **shorefront**
ပင်လယ်ကမ်းခြေဒေသ pin-lal-kan-chay-tay-ta *(adj.)* **littoral**
ပင်လယ်ကမ်းဘေးကျောက်ဆောင် painlaal kam bhayykyawwatsaung *(n.)* **seacliff**
ပင်လယ်ကြမ်းပြင် painlaalkyampyin *(n.)* **seafloor**
ပင်လယ်ကွေ့ pin-lal-kway *(n.)* **gulf**
ပင်လယ်ကွေ့ငယ် pin-lal-kway-nge *(n.)* **cove**
ပင်လယ်စင်ရော်ကြီး pin-lal-zin-yar-gyi *(n.)* **albatross**
ပင်လယ်စာ pinlaalsar *(n.)* **seafood**
ပင်လယ်တွင်း သင်္ဘောကောင်းစွာ မောင်းနှင်ခြင်း painlaaltwin sainbhawkaungghcwar maunggnhainhkyinn *(n.)* **seakeeping**
ပင်လယ်ထုံးအိုင် pin-lal-htone-ai *(n.)* **lagoon**
ပင်လယ်ဓားပြ painlaaldharrpya *(n.)* **sea dog**
ပင်လယ်ဓားပြ၊ မူပိုင်ခွင့်ကို ထိပါးခိုးချသူ pin-laal-dharr-pya, muu-pine-hkwint-ko-hti-parr-hkoe-cha-suu *(n.)* **pirate**
ပင်လယ်ဓားပြမှု pin-laal-dharr-pya-mhu *(n.)* **piracy**
ပင်လယ်နှင့် ဆိုင်သော pin-lal-nint-sai-taw *(adj.)* **marine**
ပင်လယ်ပျော်ငှက် pinlaalpyawnghaat *(n.)* **seabird**
ပင်လယ်ပိုင်း pin-lal-pai *(adj.)* **maritime**
ပင်လယ်ဖျံကြီးမျိုး pinlaal hpyaan kyeemyoe *(n.)* **walrus**
ပင်လယ်ဖျံရေမှ လုပ်သော အထည် painlaal hpyaan raymha lotesaw aahtai *(n.)* **sealskin**
ပင်လယ်ရေညှိ painlaalraynyhai *(n.)* **shoreweed**
ပင်လယ်ရေမျက်နှာပြင်အထက် အမြင့် pin-la-yay-myat-nar-pyin-a-htet-a-myint *(n.)* **altitude**
ပင်လယ်ရေမျက်နှာပြင်အောက် pinlaalray myetnharpyinawt *(adj.)* **submarine**
ပင်လယ်ရေမြုပ် painlaalraymyuut *(n.)* **seafoam**
ပင်လယ်ရေအောက်ဓာတ်ခွဲခန်း painlaalrayaoutdharathkwalhkaann *(n.)* **sealab**
ပင်လယ်လှိုင်းစီးလှေ pinlaal hline see-hlaay *(n.)* **sailboard**
ပင်လယ်လှိုင်းစီးလှေဖြင့် လှိုင်းစီးသူ pinlaal hline see hlaayhpyint hline seesuu *(n.)* **sailboarder**

ပင်လယ်လှေ painlaallhaay *(n.)* **sea boat**

ပင်လယ်အော် pin-lal-aw *(n.)* **bay**

ပင်အပ် pin-at *(n.)* **pin**

ပင်အပ်ဖြင့် တွဲသည် pin-at-hpyint-twal-sai *(v.)* **pin**

ပစ္စည်း pyit-see *(n.)* **material**

ပစ္စည်း၊ အရာ၊ အစွမ်းအစ pyit-see , a rar , aaswm aa-sa *(n.)* **stuff**

ပစ္စည်းကိရိယာ pyit-see-ka-ri-yar *(n.)* **kit**

ပစ္စည်းခေတ္တအပ်နှံရာနေရာ pyit-see-khit-ta-at-nan-yar-nay-yar *(n.)* **left**

ပစ္စည်းပစ္စယ pyit-see-pyit-sa-ya *(n. pl)* **paraphernalia**

ပစ္စည်းသိုလှောင်ထားရာ နေရာ pyit-see-tho-hlaung-htar-yar-nay-yar *(n.)* **depository**

ပစ္စတင် pyit-sa-tin *(n.)* **piston**

ပစ္စတို pyit-sa-to *(n.)* **pistol**

ပစ္စုပ္ပန် pyit-sote-pan *(adj.)* **modern**

ပစ်ခတ်သည်၊ ဓာတ်ပုံရိုက်သည် paithkaat sai , dharatponeritesai *(v.)* **shoot**

ပစ်ခြင်း paitchinn *(n.)* **shot**

ပစ်ဂမီလူမျိုး pit ga meluumyoe *(n.)* **pygmy**

ပစ်စတေးတံ တစ်ခုတည်းပါသော pit-sa-til-tan-ta-khu-tae-par-taw *(adj.)* **monogynous**

ပစ်ထားခြင်း pyit-htar-chin *(n.)* **neglect**

ပစ်ထားသည် pyit-htar-the *(v.)* **lurch**

ပစ်ထိုင်သည် pyit htinesai *(v.)* **slump**

ပစ်ပစ်ခါခါငြင်းသည် pyit-pyit hkar hkar ngyinn-sai *(v.)* **spurn**

ပစ်ပယ်သည် pyit paalsai *(v.)* **snub**

ပစ်ပေးသည် pit-payy-sai *(v.)* **toss**

ပစ်ပေါက်ခြင်း pyit poutchinn *(n.)* **throw**

ပစ်ပေါက်သည် pyit poutsai *(v.)* **throw**

ပစ်မှောက်ခြင်း၊ ခေါင်းပန်းလှန်ခြင်း pyit-hmauk-chin, kaung-pan-hlan-chin *(n.)* **flip**

ပစ်သည် pyit-the *(v.)* **hurl**

ပစ်သည်၊ ပေါက်သည်၊ pait sai , pout sai *(v.)* **shy**

ပဉ္စဂံ pin-sa-gan *(n.)* **pentagon**

ပညတ်တော် ဆယ်ပါးအနက် တစ်ပါးပါး pyit-nyat-taw-sal-par-a-nat-ta-par-par *(n.)* **commandment**

ပညာတစ်ပိုင်းတစ်စနှင့် ကျောင်းထွက်သူ pyin-nyar-ta-pai-ta-sa-nint-kyaung-htwat-thu *(n.)* **dropout**

ပညာတတ်လူတန်းစား pyin-nyar-tat-lu-tan-sar *(n.)* **intelligentsia**

ပညာပေး pyin-nyar-pay *(adj.)* **didactic**

ပညာပေးသည် pyin-nyar-pay-the *(v.)* **educate**

ပညာမတတ်သော pa-nyar mataatsaw *(adj.)* **uneducated**

ပညာမဲ့သော pyin-nyar-mae-taw *(adj.)* **ignorant**

ပညာရှင် pyin-nyar-shin *(n.)* **academician**

ပညာရှင်ဆန်ဆန် pyin-nyar-shin-san-san *(adv.)* **academically**

ပညာရှင်ဆန်သော panyarshinsaansaw *(adj.)* **scholarly**

ပညာရှိ pyin-nyar-shi *(n.)* **savant**

ပညာရှိသော panyarshisaw *(adj.)* **sapient**

ပညာရေး pyin-nyar-yay *(n.)* **education**

ပညာရေးနှင့်ဆိုင်သော pyin-nyar-yay-nint-saing-taw *(adj.)* **academic**

ပညာသင်ဆု panyarsinsu *(n.)* **scholarship**

ပညာသင်ဆုရကျောင်းသား၊ ပညာရှင် panyarsinsu r kyaunggsarr , panyarshin *(n.)* **scholar**

ပဋိဇီဝဆေး pa-di-zi-wa-say *(n.)* **antibiotic**

ပဋိညာဉ် pa-dain-nyin *(n.)* **covenant**

ပဋိညာဉ်စာတမ်း pa-dain-nyin-sar-tan *(n.)* **charter**

ပဋိပက္ခ pa-ni-at-kha *(n.)* **conflict**

ပဋိပစ္စည်း pa-di-phit-see *(n.)* **antibody**

ပဋိသန္ထာရပြုခြင်း pati san dhar rapyuchinn *(n.)* **salutation**

ပဏာမခြေလှမ်း pa-nar-ma-chay-lan *(n.)* **initiative**

ပဏာမတေး pa-nar-ma-tayy *(n.)* **overture**

ပတ္တမြား pat-tamyarr *(n.)* **ruby**

ပတ္တလား pat talarr *(n.)* **xylophone**

ပတ္တလားကြီး pat-ta-lar-kyi *(n.)* **balafon**

ပတ်တီး pat-thee *(n.)* **bandage**

ပတ်တီး၊ အဝတ်အစားဝတ်ဆင်ခြင်း pat-thee, a-wit-a-sar-wit-sin-chin *(n.)* **dressing**

ပတ်ရံသည်၊ ရုံသည် pat-yan-the, yone-the *(v.)* **envelop**

ပတ်လည် pat-lal *(adv.&prep.)* **around**

ပတ်လည် အတွဲစဉ် paat-lai-aa-twal-sin *(n.)* **permutation**

ပတ်လမ်း pat-lam *(n.)* **orbit**

ပတ်ဝန်းကျင် paat-waannkyin *(n.)* **surroundings**

ပတ်ဝန်းကျင်၊ အသိုင်းအဝိုင်း pat-win-kyin, a-tine-a-wine *(n.)* **milieu**

ပတ်ဝန်းကျင်နှင့် အံချော်ခြင်း pat-win-kyin-nint-an-chaw-chin *(n.)* **maladjustment**

ပတ်ဝန်းကျင်အသားကျအောင် လုပ်သော pat-wan-kyin-a-tar-kya-aung-lote-taw *(adj.)* **orientational**

ပတ်သွားသည် paat-swarr-sai *(v.)* **skirt**

ပထမ pa-hta-ma *(adj.)* **first**

ပထမတန်းစား pa-hta-ma-taann-sarr *(adj.)* **premier**

ပထမအကြိမ်လုပ်ဆောင်ရာတွင် ရှိသော စွမ်းရည် pa-hta-ma-a-kyein-lote-saung-yar-twin-shi-taw-swan-yay *(n.)* **debut**

ပထဝီဝင် pa-hta-wi-win *(adj.)* **geographical**

ပထဝီဝင် နိုင်ငံရေးပညာ pa-hta-wi-win-nai-ngan-yay-pyin-nyar *(adj.)* **geopolitical**

ပထဝီဝင်ပညာရှင် pa-hta-wi-win-pyin-nyar-shin *(n.)* **geographer**

ပထုတ်သည် pa htotesai *(v.)* **rid**

ပန်း pan *(n.)* **flower**

ပန်း၏ အမမျိုးပွားအင်္ဂါ pan-ei-a-ma-myo-pwar-in-gar *(n.)* **carpel**

ပန်းကန် pa-gan *(n.)* **dish**

ပန်းကန်ခွက်ယောက် pan-kan-khwat-yauk *(n.)* **crockery**

ပန်းကန်ဆေးကန် paannkaan sayykaan *(n.)* **sink**

ပန်းကန်နှုတ်ခမ်း pan-kan-note-khan *(n.)* **brim**

ပန်းကန်ပြား pan-kaan-pyarr *(n.)* **plate**

ပန်းကန်လုံး pan-kan-lone *(n.)* **bowl**

ပန်းကုံး pan-kone *(n.)* **garland**

ပန်းကုံး၊ ပန်းဆိုင်း pan-kone, pan-sai *(n.)* **festoon**

ပန်းကုံးစွပ်သည် pan-kone-sut-the *(v.)* **garland**

ပန်းချီ၊ ဆေးသုတ်ခြင်း paann-chae, say-sote-chinn *(n.)* **painting**

ပန်းချီကား pan-chae-karr *(n.)* **picture**

ပန်းချီကားအသေးစား pan-chi-kar-a-tay-sar *(n.)* **miniature**

ပန်းခြံ paann-chaan *(n.)* **park**

ပန်းခွေ paannhkway *(n.)* **wreath**

ပန်းဂေါ်ဖီ pan-gaw-phi *(n.)* **cauliflower**

ပန်းဂေါ် ဖီစိမ်း pan-gaw-phi-sein *(n.)* **broccoli**

ပန်းစည်း pann-saee *(n.)* **nosegay**

ပန်းတိုင် pantine *(n.)* **target**

ပန်းတိုင်၊ ဂိုးပေါက် pan-tai, goe-pauk *(n.)* **goal**

ပန်းထွက်သည် paann htwatsai *(v.)* **spurt**

ပန်းထိုးအတတ် pan-htoe-a-tat *(n.)* **embroidery**

ပန်းနာ pan-nar *(n.)* **asthma**

ပန်းနုရောင် paan-nu-raung *(adj.)* **pinkish**

ပန်းပြန်တင်ထားသော တာယာ paann pyantinhtarrsaw taryar *(v.)* **remould**

ပန်းပွင့်သည် pan-pwint-the *(v.)* **bloom**

ပန်းပု၊ ပန်းတမော့ဆိုင်ရာ paannpu , paann t motsinerar *(adj.)* **sculptural**

ပန်းပုဆရာ paannpusarar *(n.)* **sculpturist**

ပန်းပုထုသည် pan-pu-htu-the *(v.)* **carve**

ပန်းပုရုပ် pan-pu-yoke *(n.)* **carving**

ပန်းပဲဖို pan-pae-pho *(n.)* **forge**

ပန်းပဲသမား paann pellsamarr *(n.)* **smith**

ပန်းဖောက်ပြား paann hpoutpyarr *(n.)* **stencil**

ပန်းများ ဝေဆာနေသော pan-myar-wai-sar-nay-taw *(adj.)* **flowery**

ပန်းရန်ဆရာ pa-yan-sa-yar *(n.)* **mason**

ပန်းရောင် paan-raung *(adj.)* **pink**

ပန်းရောင်ရင့် paannraung rint *(adj.)* **roseate**

ပန်းသည် pan-the *(n.)* **florist**

ပန်းသီး pan-thee *(n.)* **apple**

ပန်းသီးအရက် pan-thee-a-yat *(n.)* **cider**

ပန်းသေခြင်း pan-tay-chin *(n.)* **impotence**

ပန်းသေသော pan-tay-taw *(adj.)* **impotent**

ပန်းအိုး youtyarr sarr kyaww hpyatchinn *(n.)* **vase**

ပန်းဦးပန်သည် pan-oo-pan-the *(v.)* **deflower**

ပန်ကြားသည် pan-kyar-the *(v.)* **implore**

ပန်ကာ pan-kar *(n.)* **fan**

ပမာဏ pa-mar-na *(n.)* **amount**

ပမာဏ၊ အတိုင်းအတာ pa-mar-na, a-tine-a-tar *(n.)* **extent**

ပမာဏကို တိုင်းဆသည် pamarnako tine sasai *(v.)* **size**

ပမာဏအနည်းငယ် pa-mar-na-a-nae-ngal *(n.)* **dob**

ပမာမခန့်ပြုခြင်း pa mar ma hkaantpyuchinn *(n.)* **snub**

ပယင်း pa-yin *(n.)* **amber**

ပယ်ချခြင်း paal-chachinn *(n.)* **rejection**

ပယ်ချသည် paal-chasai *(v.)* **reject**

ပယ်ပယ်နယ်နယ် ဝေဖန်ရှုတ်ချသည် pal-pal-ne-ne-wai-hpan-shoke-cha-the *(v.)* **lambaste**

ပယ်ဖျက်ခြင်း pal-hpyet-chinn *(n.)* **nullification**

ပယ်ဖျက်သည် pal-hpyet-te *(v.)* **nullify**

ပျံ့နှံ့ pyant nant *(adj.)* **prevalent**

ပျံ့နှံ့နေသော pyant-hnant-nay-saw *(adj.)* **widespread**

ပျံ့နှံ့မှု pyant-nant-mhu *(n.)* **prevalence**

ပျံ့နှံ့သည် pyant-nant-the *(v.)* **diffuse**

ပျံကျဈေးသည် pyaan kyasyaayysai *(n.)* **vendor**

ပျံတက်ခြင်း pyaantaatchinn *(n.)* **take-off**

ပျံတက်သည် pyaan taatsai *(v.)* **soar**

ပျံသန်းခြင်း pyan-tan-chin *(n.)* **fly**
ပျံသန်းရန် လေကို ထိန်းနိုင်သော လေယာဉ်တောင်ပံကဲ့သို့ အထူးဒီဇိုင်း pyan-tan-yan-lay-ko-htain-naing-taw-lay-yin-taung-pan-kae-tho-a-htoo-de-zine *(n)* **aerofoil**
ပျံသန်းရေး၊ လေယာဉ်ခရီး pyan-tan-yay, lay-yin-kha-yee *(n.)* **flight**
ပျံသန်းသည် pyan-tan-the *(v.)* **fly**
ပျက်ကွက်ခြင်း pyat-kwat-chin *(n.)* **absence**
ပျက်ကွက်သည် pyat-kwat-the *(adj.)* **absent**
ပျက်ကွက်သူ pyat-kwat-thu *(n.)* **absentee**
ပျက်ခြင်း၊ ပြိုကွဲခြင်း pyat-chin, pyo-kwal-chin *(n.)* **breakup**
ပျက်စီးခြင်း pyetseechinn *(n.)* **ruin**
ပျက်စီးစေသည် pyetseesaysai *(v.)* **ruin**
ပျက်စီးရာ ပျက်စီးကြောင်း စေတနာပါသော pyet-see-rar-pyet-see-kyaungg-say-ta-nar-par-saw *(adj.)* **pernicious**
ပျက်စီးလွယ်သော pyet-see-lwal-saw *(adj.)* **perishable**
ပျက်စီးသည် pyet-see-sai *(v.)* **perish**
ပျက်ပြယ်စေသည် pyat-pyal-say-the *(v.)* **invalidate**
ပျက်သုဉ်းလုနီးပါး pyat-tone-lu-ni-par *(adj.)* **moribund**
ပျင်းစရာကောင်းသော pyin-sa-yar-kaung-taw *(adj.)* **dull**
ပျင်းရိခြင်း pyinn richinn *(n.)* **sloth**
ပျင်းရိလေ့တွဲ့သောသူ pyinn ri lae twalsawsuu *(n.)* **sluggard**
ပျင်းရိသော pyinn risaw *(n.)* **slothful**
ပျစ်ပျစ်နှစ်နှစ်ရှိခြင်း pyit pyit nit-nit-shi-chinn *(n.)* **pungency**
ပျစ်ပျစ်နှစ်နှစ်ရှိသော pyit pyit nit-nit-shi-saw *(adj.)* **pungent**
ပျစ်အောင် ကျိုသည် pyit-aung-kyo-the *(v.)* **condense**
ပျဉ်ချပ် pyin-chat *(n.)* **board**
ပျဉ်ချပ်ပါး pyin-chat-par *(n.)* **lath**
ပျဉ်ပြား၊ လမ်းစဉ်ရပ်တည်ချက် pyin-pyarr, lam-sin-rat-tai-chet *(n.)* **plank**
ပျမ်းမျှ pyin-mya *(n.)* **average**
ပျမ်းမျှဖြစ်သော pyan-mya-phit-taw *(adj.)* **median**
ပျား pyar *(n.)* **bee**
ပျားတူ pyaw-tu *(n.)* **hornet**
ပျားပန်းခပ်မျှဖြစ်သော pyar-pan-khat-mya-phit-taw *(adj.)* **febrile**
ပျားဖယောင်း pyarrhpayaungg *(n.)* **wax**
ပျားမွေးမြူရာဌာန pyar-mway-my-yay-htar-na *(n.)* **apiary**
ပျားမွေးမြူရေး pyar-mway-my-yay *(n.)* **apiculture**
ပျားမွေးမြူသူ pyar-mway-myu-thu *(n.)* **beekeeper**
ပျားရည်၊ အချစ် pyar-yay, a-chit *(n.)* **honey**
ပျားရည်စမ်းခရီး pyar-yay-san-kha-yee *(n.)* **honeymoon**
ပျားရည်အရက် pyar-yay-a-yat *(n.)* **mead**
ပျားလပို့ pyar-la-poe *(n.)* **honeycomb**
ပျားအုံ pyae-ohn *(n.)* **hive**
ပျာယာခတ်သည် pyar-yar-khat-the *(v.)* **bustle**
ပျို့ခြင်း pyoe-chin *(n.)* **nausea**
ပျိုးသည်၊ မျိုးကြဲသည် pyoe sai, myoe kyaellsai *(v.)* **sow**
ပျူရီတန်ခရစ်ယာန်ဂိုဏ်း pyuu re taan hka-rit-yan-gai *(n.)* **puritan**
ပျော့စိပျော့နဲ pyaww si pyaww-nell *(adj.)* **pulpy**

ပျော့စိပျော့နဲ အခြေအနေ pyaww si pyawwnell aa-chay-aanay *(n.)* **pulp**
ပျော့စေသည် pyawt-saysai *(v.)* **soften**
ပျော့ပျောင်းလာသည့် အခြေအနေ pyaww pyaungg larsaeet aachayaanay *(n.)* **thaw**
ပျော့ပျောင်းသော pyawt-pyaung-taw *(adj.)* **mild**
ပျော့ပြီး သွယ်သော အကိုင်း pyawt-pee-twal-taw-a-kai *(n.)* **withe**
ပျော့ပြဲသော အရာ pyawt-pyae-taw-a-yar *(n.)* **mush**
ပျော့ဖတ်အောင် နယ်သည် pyaww hpaa-taaung naalsai *(v.)* **pulp**
ပျော့အိအိ သကြားလျှောပေါ် ဝဲ pyaw-ei-ei-tha-kyar-shar-paw-wae *(n.)* **fondant**
ပျောက်ကွယ်သည် pyauk-kwal-the *(v.)* **disappear**
ပျောက်ကွယ်သွားသည် wint warchinn *(v.)* **vanish**
ပျောက်နိုင်ခဲသည် pyauk-nai-khae-the *(n.)* **diehard**
ပျောက်နေခြင်း pyauk-nay-chin *(n.)* **disappearance**
ပျောက်နေသော pyauk-nay-taw *(adj.)* **missing**
ပျောက်သည် pyauk-the *(v.)* **lost**
ပျောက်သွားခြင်း pyauk-twar-chin *(n.)* **dematerialisation**
ပျောက်သွားသည် pyauk-twar-the *(v.)* **dematerialize**
ပျော်စရာ pyaw-sa-yar *(adj.)* **joyful**
ပျော်စရာရွှင်စရာ pyaw-sa-yar-shwin-sa-yar *(n.)* **joyous**
ပျော်ပျော်ရွှင်ရွှင် pyaw-pyaw-shwin-shwin *(adj.)* **jovial**
ပျော်ပွဲ pyaw-pwe *(n.)* **gaiety**
ပျော်ပွဲစား pyaw-pwal-sarr *(n.)* **picnic**
ပျော်ပွဲစားထွက်သည် pyaw-pwal-sar-htwat-sai *(v.)* **picnic**
ပျော်ပွဲစားသည် pyaw-pwe-sar-the *(v.)* **feast**
ပျော်ပွဲရွှင်ပွဲ pyawpwalshwinpwal *(n.)* **revel**
ပျော်ရည်၊ ဖြေရှင်းနည်း pyaw rai, hpyayhlyinnnaee *(n.)* **solution**
ပျော်ရည်ဖယ်ရှားသည် pyaw-yay-phal-shar-the *(v.)* **desolvate**
ပျော်ရွှင်ကြည်နူးနိုင်စွမ်း pyaw-shwin-kyi-nu-nai-swan *(n.)* **enjoyability**
ပျော်ရွှင်ကြည်နူးဖွယ်ကောင်းသော pyaw-shwin-kyi-nu-phwal-kaung-taw *(adj.)* **enjoyable**
ပျော်ရွှင်ခြင်း pyaw-shwin-chin *(n.)* **jollity**
ပျော်ရွှင်စေသည် pyaw-shwin-say-the *(v.)* **beguile**
ပျော်ရွှင်ဖွယ်ကောင်းသော pyaw-shwin-phwal-kaung-taw *(adj.)* **delectable**
ပျော်ရွှင်မြူးတူးသည် pyaw-shwin-my-tu-the *(v.)* **exult**
ပျော်ရွှင်မှု pyaw-shwin-mhu *(n.)* **pleasure**
ပျော်ရွှင်သော pyaw-shwin-taw *(adj.)* **gleeful**
ပျော်ဝင်နိုင်သော pyaw winninesaw *(adj.)* **soluble**
ပျော်ဝင်ပါသွားသည် pyaw-win-par-twar-the *(v.)* **leach**
ပျော်ဝင်သတ္တိ pyaw winsatti *(n.)* **solubility**
ပျော်ဝင်အောက်ဆိုဒ်မှ အောက်ဆီဂျင် ထုတ်ယူခြင်း pyaw-win-awt-cide-ma-awt-see-gyin-htoke-yu-chin *(n.)* **deoxidation**
ပရင်တာစက်၊ ပုံနှိပ်စက် pa rin tar saat , pone-nate-saat *(n.)* **printer**
ပရင်တာမှ ပုံနှိပ်သော စာရွက် pa rin tar-mha pone-nate-saw sarrwat *(n.)* **printout**

ပရမ်းပတာဖြစ်ခြင်း ba-yan-ba-tar-phit-chin (n.) **chaos**
ပရမ်းပတာဖြစ်သော ba-yan-ba-tar-phit-taw (adv.) **chaotic**
ပရဟိတဝါဒ pa-ya-hi-ta-wa-da (n.) **altruism**
ပရဟိတဝါဒီ pa-ya-hi-ta-wa-di (n.) **altruist**
ပရဟိတအလုပ် pa-ra-hi-ta-aa-lote (n.) **philanthropy**
ပရိဘောဂ pa-yi-baw-ga (n.) **furniture**
ပရိဘောဂ ခင်းကျင်းသည် pa-yi-baw-ga-khin-kyin-the (v.) **furnish**
ပရိဘောဂအောက်ရှိ ဘီးငယ် pa-yi-baw-ga-awt-shi-bi-nge (n.) **caster**
ပရိယာယ် pa-ri-yal (n.) **stratagem**
ပရိယာယ်၊ မာယာ pa-yi-yal, mar-yar (n.) **guile**
ပရိသတ် pa-rait-sat (n.) **on-looker**
ပရိသတ်ကျအောင် နှိုးဆွလှုံ့ဆော်နိုင်သော နိုင်ငံရေးသမားခေါင်းဆောင် pa-yeik-tat-kya-aung-noe-swa-lont-saw-naing-taw-nai-ngan-yay-ta-mar-gaung-saung (n.) **demagogue**
ပရိုဂျက်တာ pa-rogyet-tar (n.) **projector**
ပရိုတိန်းဓာတ်များစွာ paro tein dhat myarr-swar (n.) **polyprotein**
ပရီမီယမ်ကြေး pa re me yamkyay (n.) **premium**
ပရုတ် pa-yoke (n.) **camphor**
ပရုပ်လုံး pa-yoke-lone (n.) **naphthalene**
ပရောပရည် လုပ်သည် pa-yaw-pa-yee-lote-the (v.) **flirt**
ပြကွက်တစ်ကွက်အဖြစ် ပြသည် pyakwat tait kwataahpyit pyasai (v.) **scene**
ပြကွက်သရုပ်ဖော်ပြသခြင်း pyakwat sarotehpawpyasachinn (n.) **tableau**
ပြက္ခဒိန် pyat-kha-dain (n.) **calendar**
ပြက်ရယ်ပြုခြင်း pyat-yal-pyu-chin (n.) **levity**
ပြက်ရယ်ပြုမှု pyat-yal-pyu-mu (adj.) **derivative**
ပြက်ရယ်ပြုသည် pyat-yal-pyu-the (v.) **deride**
ပြက်လုံး pyat-lone (n.) **jest**
ပြက်လုံးထုတ်သည် pyat-lone-htoke-the (v.) **jest**
ပြက်သည်၊ လက်သည် pyat-the-, let-the (v.) **flash**
ပြခန်း pyahkan (n.) **showroom**
ပြင်းထန်ကြမ်းတမ်းသော pyin-htan-kyan-tan-taw (adj.) **elemental**
ပြင်းထန်ခြင်း pyinnhtaanchinn (n.) **vehemence**
ပြင်းထန်စွာ ထုရိုက်သည် pyin-htan-swar-htu-yite-the (n.) **welt**
ပြင်းထန်စွာ ပေါက်ကွဲသည် pyin-htan-swar-pauk-kwal-the (v.) **detonate**
ပြင်းထန်စွာ ဝေဖန်သည် pyin-than-swar-wai-hpan-the (v.) **censure**
ပြင်းထန်မှု pyinnhtaanmhu (n.) **rigour**
ပြင်းထန်သော pyin-htan-taw (n.) **drastic**
ပြင်းထန်သော ရေစီး pyinn-htaansaw raysee (n.) **torrent**
ပြင်းထန်သော၊ ထက်သန်သော pyin-htan-taw, htet-tan-taw (adj.) **intense**
ပြင်းထန်သော၊ ပုံမမှန်သော အရေးတကြီး စိတ်ဆန္ဒ pyan-htan-taw-pon-ma-man-taw-a-yay-ta-kyi-seik-san-da (n.) **craving**
ပြင်းထန်သော၊ အာနိသင်ရှိသော pyinnhtaansaw , aar-ni-sin-shi-saw (adj.) **potent**

ပြင်းပြင်းထန်ထန် အကြိမ်ကြိမ် ရန်ပြုသည် pyin-pyin-htan-htan-a-kyein-kyein-yan-pyu-the *(v.)* **assail**

ပြင်းပြင်းထန်ထန်၊ ခါးခါးသီးသီး pyinnpyinnhtaanhtaan , hkarrhkarrseesee *(n.)* **virulence**

ပြင်းပြင်းပြုပြုဆန္ဒ aarayytakyee *(n.)* **urge**

ပြင်းပြသော ဆန္ဒ pyin-pya-taw-san-da *(n.)* **aspiration**

ပြင်းပြသော၊ ချစ်စိတ်ပြင်းပြသော pyinn-pya-saw, chit-sate-pyinn-pya-saw *(adj.)* **passionate**

ပြင်းအား pyin-arr *(n.)* **intensity**

ပြင်ခြင်း pyin-chin *(n.)* **correction**

ပြင်ဆင်ချက် pyin-sin-chat *(n.)* **amendment**

ပြင်ဆင်ခြင်း pyinsinchinn *(n.)* **repair**

ပြင်ဆင်မွမ်းမံသည် pyinsin mwam-mansai *(v.)* **refurbish**

ပြင်ဆင်ရန်လိုသည့် ပိုင်ဆိုင်မှုများ pyin-sin-yan-lo-the-pai-sai-mu-myar *(n.)* **fixer-upper**

ပြင်ဆင်သည် pyin-sin-the *(v.)* **amend**

ပြင်ညီ pyin-nye *(adj.)* **plane**

ပြင်ပကမ္ဘာ pyinpa-kambhar *(n.)* **outworld**

ပြင်ပနှင့် ဆိုင်သော pyin-pa-nint-sai-taw *(adj.)* **external**

ပြင်ပရင်းမြစ် pyin-pa-yin-myit *(n.)* **xenogenesis**

ပြင်ပလူနာ pyin-pa-luu-nar *(n.)* **outpatient**

ပြင်ပေးသည် pyin-pay-the *(v.)* **correct**

ပြင်သစ် pyin-thit *(adj.)* **French**

ပြင်သစ်အိမ်၊ ရဲတိုက် pyin-thit-eain, ye-tite *(n.)* **chateau**

ပြင်သည် pyinsai *(v.)* **repair**

ပြစားသော pya-sar-taw *(adj.)* **ostentatious**

ပြစ်တင် မောင်းမဲသည် pyit-tin maungg mellsai *(n.)* **rebuke**

ပြစ်တင် ဝေဖန်ရှုတ်ချခြင်း pyit-tin-wai-phan-shote-cha-chin *(n.)* **condemnation**

ပြစ်တင်ကန့်ကွက်ခြင်း pyittin kaantkwatchinn *(n.)* **reproof**

ပြစ်တင်မောင်းမဲသည် pyit-tin maungg mellsai *(v.)* **rebuke**

ပြစ်တင်ရှုတ်ချခြင်း pyittin shotechachinn *(n.)* **stricture**

ပြစ်ဒဏ် pyit-dan *(n.)* **foul**

ပြစ်ဒဏ်ကျူးလွန်သည် pyit-dan-kyu-lun-the *(n.)* **foul play**

ပြစ်ဒဏ်ချမှတ်သည် pyitdan chamhaatsai *(v.)* **sentence**

ပြစ်ဒဏ်လျှော့ပေါ့သည် pyit-dan-shawt-pawt-the *(v.)* **commute**

ပြစ်ဒဏ်အဖြစ် အသိမ်းသော pyit-dan-a-phit-thein-taw *(n.)* **forfeiture**

ပြစ်မျိုးမှဲ့မထင်သူ pyit-myoe-mhaae-ma-htin-suu *(n.)* **paragon**

ပြစ်မှု pyit-mhu *(n.)* **offence**

ပြစ်မှုကျူးလွန်သော pyit-mu-kyu-loon-taw *(n.)* **criminal**

ပြစ်မှုကြောင့် တစ်စုံတစ်ယောက် ဒဏ်ခတ်ခံရသည် pyitmhukyount taithconetaityout danhkaathkanrasai *(v.)* **scapegoat**

ပြစ်မှုငယ်များကျူးလွန်သော pyit-mu-nge-myar-kyu-lun-thaw *(adj.)* **delinquent**

ပြစ်မှုဆိုင်ရာ pyit-mhu-sine-rar *(adj.)* **penal**

ပြစ်မှုထင်ရှား စီရင်ခြင်း pyit-mu-htin-shar-si-yin-chin *(n.)* **conviction**

ပြဇာတ် pya-zat *(n.)* **drama**

ပြဇာတ်၊ ကစားခြင်း pya-zat, ka-sarr-chinn *(n.)* **play**

ပြဇာတ်ဆရာ pya-zat-sa-yar *(n.)* **dramatist**

ပြဇာတ်တင်ဆက်သည် pyajarattinsaatsai *(v.)* **stage**

ပြဇာတ်နှင့် ဆိုင်သော pya-zat-nint-sai-taw *(adj.)* **dramatic**

ပြဇာတ်ရုံ pya-zat-rone *(n.)* **playhouse**

ပြည့်ကျပ်နေသည် pyae kyatnaysai *(v.)* **stuff**

ပြည့်ခြင်း pyae-chin *(n.)* **fullness**

ပြည့်စုံခြင်း pyae sonechinn *(n.)* **sufficiency**

ပြည့်တန်ဆာ pyae-taansar *(n.)* **prostitute**

ပြည့်တန်ဆာနှင့် ဆက်ဆံသည် pyae-ta-zar-nint-sat-san-the *(v.)* **drab**

ပြည့်တန်ဆာမှု pyae taan-sar-mhu *(n.)* **prostitution**

ပြည့်နှက်နေသော pyae nhaat-naysaw *(adj.)* **replete**

ပြည့်ဝခြင်း pyae-wachinn *(n.)* **saturation**

ပြည့်အင့်ခြင်း pyae aint-chinn *(n.)* **satiety**

ပြည် pyi *(n.)* **pus**

ပြည့်ကျပ်နေသော pyae-kyat-nay-taw *(adj.)* **congested**

ပြည့်စုံခိုင်လုံသော pyae-sone-khai-lon-taw *(adj.)* **conclusive**

ပြည့်စုံသော pyae-zone-taw *(adj.)* **complete**

ပြည့်တန်ဆာမ pyi taansarma *(n.)* **strumpet**

ပြည့်နှက်သည် pyi-nhaat-sai *(v.)* **pervade**

ပြည့်ဝမှု pyae-wa-mu *(n.)* **adequacy**

ပြည့်သိပ်သည် pyi-tate-tai *(v.)* **overcrowd**

ပြည့်သော pyae-taw *(adj.)* **full**

ပြည်ကြီးဒါလီ pyi-gyi-dar-li *(n.)* **courtesan**

ပြည်ဆင်သည် pyi sinsai *(v.)* **revise**

ပြည်တည်နာ pyi-tae-nar *(n.)* **abscess**

ပြည်တည်သည် pyi-te-the *(v.)* **fester**

ပြည်ထွက်ခြင်း pyi-htwat-chin *(n.)* **pyorrhoea**

ပြည်ထောင်စု pyi-htaung-su *(n.)* **union**

ပြည်နယ်တစ်ခုလုံးကို သက်ရောက်သော pyinaaltaithkuloneko saatroutsaw *(adj.)* **statewide**

ပြည်နှင်ဒဏ်ခံရခြင်း pyi-hnin-dan-khan-ya-chin *(n.)* **exile**

ပြည်နှင်ဒဏ်ပေးခြင်း pyi-hnin-dan-pay-chin *(n.)* **banishment**

ပြည်နှင်ဒဏ်ပေးသည် pyi-hnin-dan-pay-the *(v.)* **banish**

ပြည်ပပို့ကုန် pyi-pa-poe-kone *(n.)* **export**

ပြည်ပသို့ ကုန်တင်ပို့သည် pyi-pa-poe-kone-tin-poe-the *(v.)* **export**

ပြည်သူ့နီတိ pyi-thu-ni-ti *(n.)* **civics**

ပြဋ္ဌာန်းချက်၊ သတ်မှတ်ချက် pya-htarannchet , saatmhaatchet *(n.)* **stipulation**

ပြဋ္ဌာန်းစာအုပ် pyahtarannsar-aote *(n.)* **textbook**

ပြဋ္ဌာန်းဥပဒေအရ pyahtann u-paday aa-ra *(adj.)* **statutory**

ပြတင်းကာ pya tinnkar *(n.)* **shutter**

ပြတင်းထုပ် pya-tin-htoke *(n.)* **lintel**

ပြတင်းပေါက် pya-tinn-pout *(n.)* **window**

ပြတင်းမှန်တစ်ချပ် pya-tin-man-ta-chat *(n.)* **pane**

ပြတိုက် pya-tite *(n.)* **museum**

ပြတိုက်ပစ္စည်း pya-tite-pyit-see *(n.)* **exhibit**

ပြတိုက်မှူး pya-tite-hmyu *(n.)* **curator**

ပြတ်ချက် pyatchet *(n.)* **stew**

ပြတ်ခြင်း၊ လဲခြင်း pyat hkyinn , lellhkyinn *(n.)* **tala**

ပြတ်တောင်းပြတ်တောင်း pyat taungg pyattaungg *(adj.)* **spasmodic**
ပြတ်တောင်းပြတ်တောင်း ရွာသောမိုး pyat taungg pyattaungg rwar sawmoe *(adj.)* **showery**
ပြတ်ရှခြင်း၊ ဖြတ်ခြင်း pyat-sha-chin, phat-chin *(n.)* **cut**
ပြတ်သည် pyatsai *(v.)* **sever**
ပြတ်သားတိကျသော pyat-tar-ti-kya-taw *(adj.)* **categorical**
ပြတ်သားသော pyatsarrsaw *(adj.)* **resolute**
ပြဒါး pya-dar *(n.)* **mercury**
ပြန့်ကျဲနေသည် pyant-kyae-nay-the *(v.)* **litter**
ပြန့်ကျဲနေသည်၊ ဖြန့်သည် pyant kyaell naysai, hpyantsai *(v.)* **strew**
ပြန့်ကျဲလျက် pya ant kyaelllyet *(adv.)* **scatteringly**
ပြန့်ကျဲသည် pyant kyaell-sai *(v.)* **scatter**
ပြန့်ပြူးသော pyant-pyu-taw *(adj.)* **level**
ပြန်ကစားသည် pyan kasarr-sai *(v.)* **replay**
ပြန်ကန်ထွက်သည် pyan-kan-htwat-the *(v.)* **bounce**
ပြန်ကျော့ခြင်း pyan kyawt-chinn *(n.)* **repetition**
ပြန်ကျဲလိုသော pyan kyaelllosaw *(adj.)* **scattery**
ပြန်ကြားသည် pyankyarrsai *(v.)* **reply**
ပြန်ကောက်သည် pyan koutsai *(v.)* **resume**
ပြန်ကောင်းသည်၊ နလန်ထူသည် pyan kaunggsai , n laan htuu-sai *(v.)* **recover**
ပြန်ချဲ့သည် pyan-chae-the *(v.)* **reamplify**
ပြန်စခြင်း pyan sachinn *(n.)* **resumption**
ပြန်စသည် pyan sasai *(v.)* **renew**
ပြန်စုပ်ခြင်း pyan-sote-chin *(n.)* **reabsorption**
ပြန်စုပ်သည် pyan-sote-the *(v.)* **reabsorb**
ပြန်တည့်မတ်သည် pyan te maat-sai *(v.)* **right**
ပြန်တွေးကြည့်ခြင်း pyantway kyanychinn *(n.)* **retrospection**
ပြန်တောင်းယူသည် pyan taungg yuu-sai *(v.)* **reclaim**
ပြန်ထခြင်း pyanhta-chinn *(n.)* **relapse**
ပြန်ထေမိသည် pyan htay misai *(v.)* **recoup**
ပြန်နေရာချခြင်း pyan-nay-yar-cha-chin *(n.)* **reallocation**
ပြန်နေရာချသည် pyan-nay-yar-cha-the *(v.)* **reallocate**
ပြန်ပက်ခြင်း pyan paatchinn *(n.)* **talkback**
ပြန်ပစ်အောင်ကျိုခြင်း pyan-pyit-aung-kyo-the *(v.)* **recondense**
ပြန်ပစ်အောင်ကျိုသည် pyan-pyit-aung-kyo-chin *(n.)* **recondensation**
ပြန်ပြောင်း မြော်ရှုလိုက်သောအခါ pyanpyaungg myaw shu litesawaahkar *(n.)* **retrospect**
ပြန်ပြောသည် pyanpyawwsai *(v.)* **retort**
ပြန်ပေးဆွဲခံရသူ pyan-pay-swal-thu *(n.)* **abductee**
ပြန်ပေးဆွဲခြင်း pyan-pay-swal-chin *(n.)* **abduction**
ပြန်ပေးဆွဲသည် pyan-pay-swal-the *(v.)* **abduct**
ပြန်ပေးဆွဲသူ pyan-pay-swal-thu *(n.)* **abductor**
ပြန်ပေါင်းသည် pyan paunggsai *(v.)* **rejoin**
ပြန်ပေါ်လာခြင်း pyan-pawlarchinn *(n.)* **reappearance**

ပြန်ပေါ်လာသည် pyan-pawlarsai *(v.)* **reappear**

ပြန်ဖြစ်သည် pyan-hpyitsai *(v.)* **recur**

ပြန်ဖွင့်ပြခြင်း pyan-hpwint-pya-chinn *(n.)* **playback**

ပြန်မရနိုင်သော pyan-ma-ya-nai-taw *(adj.)* **irrecoverable**

ပြန်ရေးသည် pyan-yay-the *(v.)* **rewrite**

ပြန်လက်ခံသည် pyan laathkansai *(v.)* **reaccept**

ပြန်လည် ကျင့်သုံးသည် pyan-lai kyint-sonesai *(v.)* **reapply**

ပြန်လည် ခန့်အပ်သည် pyan-lai hkaant at-sai *(v.)* **reappoint**

ပြန်လည် ထူထောင်ခြင်း pyanlai htuu-htaungchinn *(n.)* **rehabilitation**

ပြန်လည် ထူထောင်ပေးသည် pyanlai htuu-htaungpayysai *(v.)* **rehabilitate**

ပြန်လည် ရှင်သန်ခြင်း pyan-lai hlyinsaanchinn *(n.)* **rebirth**

ပြန်လည် ရှင်သန်စေသည် hpout-pyan-rayy warde *(v.)* **reactivate**

ပြန်လည် ရုပ်သိမ်းခြင်း pyanlai rotesaimchinn *(n.)* **revocation**

ပြန်လည် ရုပ်သိမ်းနိုင်စွမ်း pyan-lal-yoke-thein-nine-swan *(adj.)* **revocable**

ပြန်လည် ရုပ်သိမ်းသည် pyanlai rotesaimsai *(v.)* **revoke**

ပြန်လည် သတိရသည် pyan-lai sa-ti-rasai *(v.)* **recollect**

ပြန်လည် အစီရင်ခံစေသည် pyan-lal-a-si-yin-khan-say-the *(v.)* **debrief**

ပြန်လည် အမှတ်ရစေခြင်း pyan-lal-a-mat-ya-say-chin *(n.)* **evocation**

ပြန်လည် အမှတ်ရစေသည် pyan-lal-a-mat-ya-say-the *(v.)* **evocate**

ပြန်လည် အမှတ်ရစေသော pyan-lal-a-mat-ya-say-taw *(adj.)* **evocative**

ပြန်လည် အသက်သွင်းခြင်း pyanlai aasaat swinchinn *(n.)* **reactivation**

ပြန်လည်ကျင့်သုံးခြင်း pyan-lai kyint sonechinn *(n.)* **reapplication**

ပြန်လည်ချဉ်းကပ်သည် pyan-lai chee kautsai *(v.)* **reapproach**

ပြန်လည်ခေါ်ယူခြင်း pyan-lai-hkawyuuchinn *(n.)* **recall**

ပြန်လည်ခေါ်ယူသည် pyan-lai hkawyuusai *(v.)* **recall**

ပြန်လည်စီစဉ်ခြင်း pyan-lal-si-sin-chin *(n.)* **reconfiguration**

ပြန်လည်စီစဉ်သည် pyan-lai se-sinsai *(v.)* **rearrange**

ပြန်လည်စုစည်းသည် pyan-lal-su-see-the *(v.)* **reconsolidate**

ပြန်လည်စေ့စပ်ညှိနှိုင်းခြင်း pyanlai saesat nyi-nine-chinn *(n.)* **reconciliation**

ပြန်လည်တည်ဆောက်ခြင်း pyanlaitaisoutchinn *(v.)* **rebuild**

ပြန်လည်တာဝန်ချသည် pyanlai tarwaan chasai *(v.)* **reassign**

ပြန်လည်ပြောဆိုသည် pyanlai-pyaww-so-sai *(v.)* **rearticulate**

ပြန်လည်ပူးတွဲသည် pyan-lal-pu-twe-the *(v.)* **reattach**

ပြန်လည်သက်ဝင်လှုပ်ရှားခြင်း pyan-lal-thet-win-lote-shar-chin *(n.)* **reanimation**

ပြန်လည်သက်ဝင်လှုပ်ရှားသည် pyan-lal-thet-win-lote-shar-the *(v.)* **reanimate**

ပြန်လည်သက်ဝင်လှုပ်ရှားသော pyan-lal-thet-win-lote-shar-taw *(adj.)* **reanimate**

ပြန်လည်သင့်လျော်စေသည် pyan-lai sang lyawsaysai *(v.)* **reappropriate**

ပြန်လည်သတိရခံစားမှု pyanlai satira-hkansarrmhu *(n.)* **reminiscence**

ပြန်လည်သန်စွမ်းတိုးပွားလာစေခြင်း pyanlai saan swm toepwarrlar saychinn *(n.)* **regeneration**

ပြန်လည်သန်စွမ်းတိုးပွားလာစေသည် pyanlai saan swam toepwarrlarsaysai *(v.)* **regenerate**

ပြန်လည်သုံးသပ်ခြင်း pyan-lai-sone-sautchinn *(n.)* **reappraisal**

ပြန်လည်သုံးသပ်သည် pyan-laisone-satsai *(v.)* **reconsider**

ပြန်လည်အတည်ပြုခြင်း pyan-lai aatai-pyuchinn *(n.)* **reapproval**

ပြန်လည်အောင်နိုင်သည် pyan-lal-aung-naing-the *(v.)* **reconquer**

ပြန်လှန်ပြောဆိုချက် pyan-hlaan-pyawwsochet *(n.)* **rejoinder**

ပြန်သွားသည် pyanswarrsai *(v.)* **return**

ပြန်သိမ်းယူသည် pyan saimyuusai *(v.)* **retrieve**

ပြန်သုံးသည် pyansonesai *(v.)* **reuse**

ပြန်အပ်စာအုပ် လက်ခံရာ နေရာ pyan-at-sar-oak-lat-khan-yar-nay-yar *(n.)* **drop box**

ပြန်အမ်းငွေ pyan aam-ngway *(n.)* **refund**

ပြပွဲ၊ ဖျော်ဖြေမှု pyapwal, hpyawhpyaymhu *(n.)* **show**

ပြယုဂ် pya-yoke *(n.)* **embodiment**

ပြွတ်၊ ဆေးထိုးပြွန် pywat, sayy htoe pywan *(n.)* **syringe**

ပြွတ်ဖြင့် ဆေးကြောသည် pywat-hpyint sayy kyawwsai *(v.)* **syringe**

ပြွန် pyun *(n.)* **duct**

ပြွန်၊ သေနတ်ပြောင်းအချင်း pyun-ta-nat-pyaung-a-chin *(n.)* **calibre**

ပြွန်ပုံ pywanpone *(adj.)* **tubular**

ပြွန်သွယ်သည် pyun-thwe-the *(v.)* **duct**

ပြသခြင်း၊ ဆန္ဒထုတ်ဖော်ခြင်း pyasahkyinn , sandahtotehpawchinn *(n.)* **ostension**

ပြဿနာ pyat-ta-nar *(n.)* **bane**

ပြဿနာဖြေရှင်းနည်းစနစ် pyat-tha-nar-hpyay-shin-nee-sa-nit *(n.)* **algorithm**

ပြသနိုင်စွမ်း pya sanine-swam *(n.)* **ostensibility**

ပြသသည် pya-ta-the *(v.)* **exhibit**

ပြသသည်၊ ထင်ရှားစေသည် pya sa sai, htinsharrsaysai *(v.)* **show**

ပြာ pyar *(n.)* **ash**

ပြားနေအောင် ထုရိုက်ခြင်း pyar-nay-aung-htu-yike-chin *(n.)* **foliation**

ပြားနေအောင် ထုရိုက်သည် pyar-nay-aung-htu-yike-the *(v.)* **foliate**

ပြားသော pyar-taw *(adj.)* **flat**

ပြာဓာတ် pyaar-dhrat *(n.)* **potash**

ပြာပြာသလဲဖြစ်ခြင်း pyar-pyar-tha-lae-phit-chin *(n.)* **alacrity**

ပြာသွားသည် pyar-twar-the *(v.)* **dazzle**

ပြိုးပြိုးပြက်ပြက်လက်ခြင်း pyo-pyo-pyat-pyat-lat-chin *(n.)* **glitter**

ပြိုကျသည် pyokyasai *(v.)* **topple**

ပြိုင်စံရှား pyaine-san-sharr *(n.)* **nonpareil**

ပြိုင်ဆိုင်မှု pyainesinemhu *(n.)* **rivalry**

ပြိုင်ဆိုင်သည် pyai-sai-the *(v.)* **compete**

ပြိုင်တန်းလျက်ရှိသော pyaine-taann-lyet-shi-saw *(adj.)* **parallel**

ပြိုင်ပွဲ pyaine-pwal *(n.)* **tournament**

ပြိုင်ပွဲ၊ ပျော်ပွဲရွှင်ပွဲ pyai-pwe, pyaw-pwe-shwin-pwe *(n.)* **gala**

ပြိုင်ပွဲဝင် pyai-pwe-win *(n.)* **contender**

ပြိုင်ဘက် pyai-bat *(n.)* **competitor**

ပြိုင်ဘက်ကင်းသော pyai-bat-kin-taw *(adj.)* **incomparable**

ပြိုင်သည် pyaine-sai *(v.)* **vie**

ပြိုလဲသည် pyo-lae-the *(v.)* **collapse**

ပြီးခဲ့သော pyee-hkae-saw *(adj.)* **past**

ပြီးစလွယ် pyi-sa-lwal *(adj.)* **cursory**

ပြီးစီးရန်သတ်မှတ်ချိန် pi-see-yan-tat-mat-chain *(n.)* **deadline**

ပြီးဆုံးခြင်း pyi-sone-chin *(n.)* **finish**

ပြီးဆုံးသည် pyi-sone-the *(v.)* **finish**

ပြီးတော့ pyeetot *(adv.)* **secondly**

ပြီးနှင့်ပြီ pyi-nint-pyi *(adv.)* **already**

ပြီးနောက် pe-naut *(prep.)* **after**

ပြီးမြောက်အောင်မြင်သည် pi-myauk-aung-myin-the *(v.)* **accomplish**

ပြုံးသည် pyuansai *(v.)* **smile**

ပြုံသည် pyone-sai *(v.)* **troop**

ပြုစားသည် pyu-sar-the *(v.)* **bewitch**

ပြုစုပျိုးထောင်သည် pyu-su-pyoe-htaung-tai *(v.)* **nurture**

ပြုစုသည် pyu-su-the *(v.)* **minister**

ပြုတ်ချက်ချက်သည် pyuat chet chetsai *(v.)* **stew**

ပြုတ်ခြင်းမှရသော အနှစ် pyoke-chin-ma-ya-taw-a-nit *(n.)* **decoction**

ပြုတ်သည် pyoke-the *(v.)* **boil**

ပြုတ်သည်၊ မီးမျှဉ်းမျှဉ်းဖြင့် ချက်သည် pyoke-sai, mee-myin-myin-hpyint-chet-sai *(v.)* **poach**

ပြုတ်သော pyoke-taw *(adj.)* **poached**

ပြုတ်အောင် ဖြုတ်သည် pyoke-aung-pyoke-the *(v.)* **disengage**

ပြုန်းတီးမှု pyone-tee-mu *(v.)* **decimation**

ပြုပြင်ခြင်း pyupyinchinn *(n.)* **rectification**

ပြုပြင်ထားသည့် ချိုမြသော ဝိုင် pyu-pyin-htar-the-cho-mya-taw-win *(n.)* **malmsey**

ပြုပြင်နိုင်သည့် အခြေအနေ ရှိသော pyupyin nine-seet aachay-aanay shisaw *(adj.)* **repairable**

ပြုပြင်ပြောင်းလဲမှု pyu-pyin-pyaungg-lel-mhu *(n.)* **reform**

ပြုပြင်ပြောင်းလဲမှုနှင့်ဆိုင်သော pyu-pyin-pyaung-lal-mu-nint-sai-taw *(adj.)* **reformatory**

ပြုပြင်ပြောင်းလဲရေးသမား pyupyin-pyaungg-lellrayy-samarr *(n.)* **reformer**

ပြုပြင်ပြောင်းလဲသည် pyu-pyin-pyaungg-lel-sai *(v.)* **reform**

ပြုပြင်မရသော pyu-pyin-ma-ya-taw *(adj.)* **incorrigible**

ပြုပြင်မွမ်းမံခြင်း pyu-pyin-moon-man-chin *(n.)* **modification**

ပြုပြင်မွမ်းမံသည် pyu-pyin mwam-man sai *(v.)* **recondition**

ပြုပြင်သည် pyupyinsai *(v.)* **rectify**

ပြုမူသည် pyu-mu-the *(v.)* **behave**

ပြုလုပ်နိုင်သော pyu-lote-nai-taw *(adj.)* **doable**

ပြုလုပ်သည် pyu-lote-the *(v.)* **do**

ပြုလုပ်သူ pyu-lote-thu *(n.)* **maker**

ပြုလုပ်သော ပြစ်ဒဏ် pyu-lote-taw-pyit-dan *(n.)* **deturpation**

ပြုသမျှနုသော pyu-sa-mya-nu-saw *(adj.)* **passive**

ပြေးခြင်း pyaychinn *(n.)* **run**

ပြေးစက် pyay-sat *(n.)* **treadwheel**

ပြေးသည် pyaysai *(v.)* **run**

ပြေးသူ pyay-thu *(n.)* **runner**

ပြေငြိမ်းခြင်း၊ ကြွေးဆပ်ခြင်း၊ အခြေချခြင်း pyay ngyaaim chinn , kyaway sat chinn , aachaychachinn *(n.)* **settlement**
ပြေစာတွင် ပိုတောင်းခြင်း pyay-sar-twin-po-taung-chinn *(n.)* **overcharge**
ပြေစာတွင် ပိုတောင်းသည် pyay-sar-twin-po-taung-tai *(v.)* **overcharge**
ပြောက်ကျား pyauk-kyar *(n.)* **guerilla**
ပြောခြင်း pyawwchinn *(n.)* **telling**
ပြောင်းချောသေနတ် pyaung-chaw-ta-nat *(n.)* **musket**
ပြောင်းချောသေနတ်ကိုင်စစ်သား pyaung-chaw-ta-nat-kai-sit-tar *(n.)* **musketeer**
ပြောင်းတိုသေတန် pyaungg to saytaan *(n.)* **shottie**
ပြောင်းပြန် pyaunggpyan *(adj.)* **reverse**
ပြောင်းပြန်ဖြစ်ခြင်း pyaunggpyanhpyitchinn *(n.)* **reverse**
ပြောင်းပြန်လှန်နိုင်သော pyaung pyanhlaanninesaw *(adj.)* **reversible**
ပြောင်းဖူး pyaung-hpoo *(n.)* **corn**
ပြောင်းရွှေ့နေထိုင်ခြင်း pyaung-shway-nay-htai-chin *(n.)* **migration**
ပြောင်းရွှေ့နေထိုင်သည် pyaung-shway-nay-htai-the *(v.)* **migrate**
ပြောင်းရွှေ့နေထိုင်သူ pyaung-shwe-nay-htai-thu *(n.)* **immigrant**
ပြောင်းလွယ်ပြင်လွယ်ရှိသော pyaung-lwal-pyin-lwal-shi-taw *(adj.)* **flexible**
ပြောင်းလဲ ဖြစ်ပေါ်လာသည် pyaung-lal-phit-paw-lar-the *(v.)* **evolve**
ပြောင်းလဲခြင်း pyaung-lal-chin *(n.)* **conversion**
ပြောင်းလဲခြင်းဖြစ်စဉ် pyaung-lal-chin-phit-sin *(n.)* **alteration**
ပြောင်းလဲတတ်ခြင်း mwaylamkyaungg *(n.)* **vagary**
ပြောင်းလဲနိုင်သော pyaung-lal-nai-taw *(adj.)* **convertible**
ပြောင်းလဲမှု၊ အဆိုင်း pyaungglellmhu , aa-sine *(n.)* **shift**
ပြောင်းလဲလွယ်သော pyaung-lal-lwal-taw *(adj.)* **fickle**
ပြောင်းလဲသည် pyaung-lal-the *(v.)* **change**
ပြောင်းလဲသွားခြင်း pyaungsai *(n.)* **transfiguration**
ပြောင်းလဲသွားသည် lwhaellchinn *(v.)* **transfigure**
ပြောင်းလဲသော kwallwalchet *(adj.)* **variable**
ပြောင်းလဲသော၊ လိမ်လည်သော pyaung-lal-taw, lain-lal-taw *(adj.)* **doctored**
ပြောင်းသည် kuupyaunggpayysai *(v.)* **transfer**
ပြောင်းအသေး pyaung-a-thay *(n.)* **baby corn**
ပြောင်စရာ၊ နောက်စရာ pyaung-sa-yar, naut-sa-yar *(n.)* **fair game**
ပြောင်ပြောင်တင်းတင်း ကျူးလွန်သော pyaung-pyaung-tin-tin-kyue-loon-taw *(adj.)* **flagrant**
ပြောင်မြောက်သော pyaung-myauk-taw *(adj.)* **accomplished**
ပြောင်လက်သော pyaung laatsaw *(adj.)* **shiny**
ပြောစကားဖြင့် pyaw-sa-kar-hpyint *(adv.)* **orally**
ပြောနည်းဆိုနည်း pyaw-nee-so-nee *(n.)* **locution**
ပြောမပြနိုင်လောက်အောင် pyan-ma-pyaw-nai-laut-taw *(adj.)* **indescribable**
ပြောရေးဆိုခွင့် pyawwrayysohkwint *(n.)* **say**
ပြောရေးဆိုခွင့်ရှိသူ pyaww-rayysohkwinshisuu *(n.)* **spokesman**

ပြောသည် pyawwsai (v.) **say**

ပြောသူ၊ လွှတ်တော်ဥက္ကဋ္ဌ pyaww suu, hlut-taw-u-kkaht (n.) **speaker**

ပြဲနေသော အင်္ကျီ pyaellnaysaw aainkyae (n.) **tatter**

ပြဲသည် pyae-the (v.) **lacerate**

ပလက်တီနမ် pa-laat-te-nam (n.) **platinum**

ပလက်ဖောင်း palaathpaung (n.) **sidewalk**

ပလက်ဖောင်း၊ လူသွားစင်္ကြံ pa-laat-hpaung, luu-swarr-sin-kyaan (n.) **pavement**

ပလတ်ခေါင်း pa-laat-hkaungg (n.) **plug**

ပလတ်ခေါင်းထိုးသည်၊ ပိတ်သည် pa-laat-hkaungg-htoe-sai, pate-sai (v.) **plug**

ပလတ်စတစ် pa-laat-sa-tit (n.) **plastic**

ပလတ်ပေါက် pa laatpout (n.) **socket**

ပလွေ pa-lway (n.) **flute**

ပလွေမှုတ်သည် pa-lway-hmote-the (v.) **flute**

ပလာယာ pa laryar (n.) **plyer**

ပလုတ်ကျင်းသည် pa-hlote-kyin-the (v.) **gargle**

ပလူတိုနီယမ်ဓာတ် pa-luu-to-ne-yam-dhrat (n.) **plutonium**

ပလူတိုနီယမ်ဓာတ်ပါဝင်သော pa luu to ne yam dhatpar-winsaw (adj.) **plutonic**

ပဝါ pawar (n.) **towel**

ပဝါဖြင့် သုတ်သည် pa warhpyint sotesai (v.) **towel**

ပွက်ပွက်ညံသံ pwat-pwat-nyan-nyan (n.) **clamour**

ပွက်လောရိုက်သံ pwat-law-yite-tan (n.) **hubbub**

ပွင့်ချပ်လွှာကွာကျသော pwint-chat-hlwar-kwar-kya-taw (adj.) **flaking**

ပွင့်ချပ် pwint-chaut (n.) **petal**

ပွင့်ပွင့်လင်းလင်း pwint-pwint-lin-lin (adv.) **frankly**

ပွင့်လင်းသော pwint-lin-taw (adj.) **candid**

ပွတ်ခုံ put-khone (n.) **lathe**

ပွတ်တိုက်ခြင်းဖြင့် ပျက်စီးနေသော အသားအရည်ကို ပြုပြင်ခြင်း put-tite-chin-phit-pyat-see-nay-taw-a-tar-a-yay-ko-pyu-pyin-chin (n.) **dermabrasion**

ပွတ်တိုက်အား put-tite-arr (n.) **friction**

ပွတ်သည် pwatsai (v.) **rub**

ပွတ်သပ်ပေးသည်၊ ရိုက်သည် pwat sat payysai, ritesai (v.) **stroke**

ပွတ်သီးပွတ်သပ်လုပ်သည် put-tee-put-tat-lote-tai (v.) **nuzzle**

ပွန်းပဲ့ဒဏ်ရာ pun-pae-dan-yar (n.) **abrasion**

ပွန်းပဲဒဏ်ရာ pon-pae-dan-yar (n.) **bruise**

ပွန်းရှတတ်သော pun-sha-tat-taw (adj.) **abrasive**

ပွန်းသည့် ဒဏ်ရာ poon-the-dan-yar (n.) **graze**

ပွပွရောင်းရောင်း pwa pwa raunggraungg (adj.) **voluminous**

ပွပေါက် pwa-pauk (n.) **bonanza**

ပွယောင်းသော pwa-yaung-taw (adj.) **saggy**

ပွသည်၊ ဖောင်းသည် pwa sai , hpaunggsai (v.) **swell**

ပွေ့ဖက်ခြင်း pway-phat-chin (n.) **embrace**

ပွေ့ဖက်သည် pway-phat-the (v.) **cuddle**

ပွေး pway (n.) **ringworm**

ပွဲကြည့်ပရိသတ် pwal kyanyparisaat (n.) **spectator**

ပွဲခင်း pwe-khin (n.) **fairground**

ပွဲဈေး pwal-zay (n.) **fair**

ပွဲစား pwe-sar *(n.)* **broker**

ပွဲတက်ဂါဝန် pwe-tat-gar-win *(n.)* **gown**

ပွဲတော် pwal-taw *(n.)* **festival**

ပွဲတော်ကြီးနှင့် တိုးချိန် pwe-taw-gyi-nint-toe-chein *(n.)* **binge**

ပွဲမြောင် pwal myaung *(n.)* **sideshow**

ပွဲလမ်းသဘင် pwal-lan-ta-bin *(n.)* **festivity**

ပွဲလမ်းအခမ်းအနား pwal lamaahkamaanarr *(n.)* **spectacle**

ပွဲဦးထွက် pwe-oo-htwat *(adj.)* **maiden**

ပသာဒဖြစ်သော pa-sar-da-hpyit-saw *(adj.)* **picturesque**

ပဟေဠိ pa hay li *(n.)* **teaser**

ပဟေဠိဆန်ဆန် pa-hay-li-san-san *(adv.)* **enigmatically**

ပဟေဠိဆန်သော pa-hay-li-san-taw *(adj.)* **enigmatical**

ပါး par *(n.)* **cheek**

ပါးချိတ်ရောင်နာ par-chate-yaung-nar *(n.)* **mumps**

ပါးစပ် par-sat *(n.)* **mouth**

ပါးစပ်ကို ဆို့သည်၊ စည်းသည် pa-sat-ko-soe-the, see-the *(v.)* **gag**

ပါးစပ်ဆို့သည့် အရာ pa-sat-soe-the-a-yar *(n.)* **gag**

ပါးစပ်နှင့်ဆိုင်သော pa-sat-nint-sine-taw *(adj.)* **oscular**

ပါးစပ်အပြည့် par-sat-a-pyae *(n.)* **mouthful**

ပါးစပ်အဟောင်းသား ငေးကြည့်သည် pa-sat-a-haung-tar-ngay-kyi-the *(v.)* **gape**

ပါးနပ်သော parr nautsaw *(adj.)* **tactful**

ပါးနီ par-ni *(n.)* **blusher**

ပါးလျပေါ့ပါးသော par-lya-pawt-par-taw *(adj.)* **flimsy**

ပါးလွှာသောပိုးထည် par-lwar-taw-poe-htal *(n.)* **organza**

ပါးသွားသည် parrswarrsai *(v.)* **thin**

ပါကင်၊ ထုပ်ပိုးပြင်ဆင်ခြင်း par-kin, htote-poe-pyin-sin-chinn *(n.)* **packing**

ပါဆယ် parsaal *(n.)* **takeaway**

ပါဆယ်ထုပ် par-saahl-tote *(n.)* **parcel**

ပါဆယ်ထုပ်သည် par-saal-htote-sai *(v.)* **parcel**

ပါဆယ်သယ်နိုင်သော par saal saalninesaw *(adj.)* **takeaway**

ပါတီပွဲ၊ ပါတီ par-te pwal, par-te *(n.)* **party**

ပါတ်သည် pat-the *(v.)* **gird**

ပါမောက္ခ par-mawk-hka *(n.)* **professor**

ပါရဂူဘွဲ့ par-ya-gu-bwe *(n.)* **doctorate**

ပါရမီ၊ အထောက်အပံ့ပစ္စည်း pa-ra-mi, a-htauk-a-pnat-pyit-see *(n.)* **facility**

ပါရမီရှင် pa-ra-mi-shin *(n.)* **genius**

ပါရမီရှင်ကလေး par-rame-shin-kalayy *(n.)* **prodigy**

ပါရှိသော par-shi-taw *(adj.)* **borne**

ပါလျက် par-lyet *(prep.)* **notwithstanding**

ပါလီမန် par-le-maan *(n.)* **parliament**

ပါလီမန်နှင့် ဆိုင်သော par-le-maan-nint-sine-saw *(adj.)* **parliamentary**

ပါလီမန်အဖွဲ့ဝင် par-le-maan-aa-hpwal-win *(n.)* **parliamentarian**

ပါလီမန်အမတ် par-li-man-a-mat *(n.)* **backbencher**

ပါဝင်ခြင်း par-win-chin *(n.)* **inclusion**

ပါဝင်ပစ္စည်း par-win-pyit-see *(n.)* **ingredient**

ပါဝင်သည် par-win-sai *(v.)* **participate**

ပါဝင်သည်၊ ထည့်သည် par-win-the, htae-the *(v.)* **figure**

ပါဝင်သော par-win-taw *(adj.)* **inclusive**

ပါဝါ၊ အင်အား parwar , aain-aarr *(n.)* **power**

ပါသည်၊ တာဝန်ယူသည်၊ ခေါင်းခံသည်၊ မွေးသည် par-the, tar-win yu-the, gaung-khan-the, mway-the *(v.)* **bear**

ပိတ် pate *(n.)* **linen**

ပိတ်ခြင်း pait-chin *(n.)* **closure**

ပိတ်ဆို့ခြင်း pait-soe-chin *(n.)* **blockage**

ပိတ်ဆို့မှုကို လျော့ချသည် pate-so-mu-ko-shawt-cha-the *(v.)* **decongest**

ပိတ်ဆို့သည် pate-shoet-tai *(v.)* **obstruct**

ပိတ်ဆို့သော pate-shoet-taw *(adj.)* **obstructive**

ပိတ်ဆီးနေသော pate-see-nay-taw *(adj.)* **impenetrable**

ပိတ်ထိုးသည် pait-htoe-the *(v.)* **biff**

ပိတ်ထုခြင်း pate htuchinn *(n.)* **thump**

ပိတ်ပင်ခံရခြင်း pate-pin-khan-ya-chin *(n.)* **disqualification**

ပိတ်ပင်ခံရသည် pate-pin-khan-ya-the *(v.)* **disqualify**

ပိတ်ပင်ထားသည် pate-pin-htar-the *(v.)* **deprive**

ပိတ်ပင်ရန် လုပ်ဆောင်သော pate-pin-yan-lote-saung-taw *(adj.)* **prohibitory**

ပိတ်ပင်သည် pait-pin-the *(v.)* **ban**

ပိတ်ပင်ဟန့်တားရာရောက်သော pate-pin hant tarr rar-routsaw *(adj.)* **prohibitive**

ပိတ်မိသည်၊ ငြိနေသည် saalyuuphoetsaungrayy *(v.)* **trap**

ပိတ်လှောင်ကြောက်လွန်စိတ်ရောဂါ pait-laung-kyauk-loon-seik-yaw-gar *(n.)* **claustrophobia**

ပိတ်လှောင်သည် pait-hlaung-the *(v.)* **entrap**

ပိတ်သည် patesai *(v.)* **shut**

ပိတ်သည့်အရာ pate-the-a-yar *(n.)* **deactivator**

ပိန်ချုံးချည့်နဲ့သည် pain-chone-chae-nae-the *(v.)* **emaciate**

ပိန်ချုံးချည့်နဲ့သော pain-chone-chae-nae-taw *(adj.)* **emaciated**

ပိန်တာရိုး pein tarroe *(adj.)* **scraggy**

ပိန်လှီသော pain-hlee-taw *(adj.)* **gaunt**

ပိန်သော၊ ပါးသော pein saw , parrsaw *(adj.)* **thin**

ပိရမစ် pi ramit *(n.)* **pyramid**

ပို့ကုန် poe-kone *(n.)* **consignment**

ပို့ချခြင်း poe-cha-chin *(n.)* **lecture**

ပို့ချသည် poe-cha-the *(v.)* **lecture**

ပို့ငွေ၊ လွှဲပြောင်းပေးငွေ phoet ngway , lwhaellpyaungg payyngway *(n.)* **remittance**

ပို့ပေးသည် phoetpayysai *(v.)* **remit**

ပို့သည် phoet-sai *(v.)* **send**

ပိုး poe *(n.)* **silk**

ပိုးကြိုးမျှင်သုံး၍ သွားသန့်စင်သည် moe-kyo-hmyin-tone-ywe-twar-tant-sin-the *(v.)* **floss**

ပိုးကောင်ကလေး poe-kaung-ka-lay *(n.)* **bug**

ပိုးစာပင် poe-sar-pin *(n.)* **mulberry**

ပိုးတွန့် poe-twunt *(n.)* **crepe**

ပိုးတောင့်မာ poe-taunt-mar *(n.)* **beetle**

ပိုးထောင့်မာ poe htaw intmar *(n.)* **scarab**

ပိုးနားသန် poe-na-tan *(n.)* **millipede**

ပိုးမွှားကင်းသော poe-mwar-kin-thaw *(adj.)* **aseptic**

ပိုးမွှားဗေဒ poe-hmywar-bay-da *(n.)* **entomology**
ပိုးရုပ်ဖုံး poe-yoke-phone *(n.)* **chrysalis**
ပိုးသည်၊ စုံတွဲခုတ်သည် poe-the, zone-twal-khote-the *(v.)* **court**
ပိုးသတ်ဆေး poe-saat-sayy *(n.)* **pesticide**
ပိုးသတ်သည် poe-tat-the *(v.)* **disinfect**
ပိုးသားကဲ့သို့ poe sarrkaethoet *(adj.)* **silky**
ပိုးဟပ် poe-hat *(n.)* **cockroach**
ပိုးအမျိုးပေါင်းများစွာနှင့် ဆိုင်သော poe aamyoe paunggmyarr-swar-nint sinesaw *(adj.)* **polymicrobial**
ပိုးအိမ် poe-eain *(n.)* **cocoon**
ပို၍ စူးရှရှဖြစ်အောင် လုပ်သည် po-ywe suu-sha sha-hpyit-aaung lotesai *(v.)* **zest**
ပိုကာ ဖဲကစားနည်း pokar hpellkasarrnaee *(n.)* **rummy**
ပိုကောင်းသော po-kaung-taw *(adj.)* **better**
ပိုကောင်းအောင်လုပ်သည် po-kaung-aung-lote-the *(v.)* **meliorate**
ပိုကဲသော po kellsaw *(adj.)* **undue**
ပိုက် pite *(n.)* **pipe**
ပိုက်၊ ပိုက်ကွန် pike, pike-kun *(n.)* **net**
ပိုက်စိတ်ဖြင့် ငါးဖမ်းသော လှေ pike-seit-pyint-ngar-phan-taw-hlay *(n.)* **trawlboat**
ပိုက်စိပ်တိုက်လိုက်ခြင်း pite seik titelitechinn *(n.)* **trawl**
ပိုက်စိပ်တိုက်လိုက်သည် pite seik titelitesai *(v.)* **trawl**
ပိုက်ဆံလျှော်ပင် pike-san-shaw-pin *(n.)* **hemp**
ပိုက်ဆံအိတ် pite-sanaate *(n.)* **purse**
ပိုက်ပြင်ဆရာ pite-pyin-sa-yar *(n.)* **plumber**
ပိုက်လုံး pike-lone *(n.)* **hose**
ပိုက်သွယ်သည် pite-swal-sai *(v.)* **pipe**
ပိုခြင်း၊ သာခြင်း po chinn , sarchinn *(n.)* **superiority**
ပိုခိုင်မြဲအောင်လုပ်သည် po-khaing-myae-aung-lote-the *(v.)* **tone**
ပိုင်းခြင်းသတ်မှတ်ခြင်း pai-char-tat-mat-chin *(n.)* **demarcation**
ပိုင်းခြားခြင်း pine-charr-chinn *(n.)* **partition**
ပိုင်းခြားသတ်မှတ်သည် pai-char-tat-mat-the *(v.)* **demarcate**
ပိုင်းဝေ pine-way *(n.)* **numerator**
ပိုင်ဆိုင်ပစ္စည်း pai-sai-pyit-see *(n.)* **belongings**
ပိုင်ဆိုင်မှု pine-sinemhu *(n.)* **property**
ပိုင်ဆိုင်မှုနှင့် ပတ်သက်သော pine-sine-mhu-nint paat-saat-saw *(adj.)* **proprietary**
ပိုင်ဆိုင်မှုပြ သင်္ကေတ paing-saing-mu-pya-tin-kay-ta *(n.)* **apostrophe**
ပိုင်ဆိုင်သည် pai-sai-the *(v.)* **belong**
ပိုင်ဆိုင်သော pine-sine-taw *(adj.)* **own**
ပိုင်နက် pai-nat *(n.)* **domain**
ပိုင်နိုင်စွာ paing-naing-swar *(adv.)* **ably**
ပိုင်နိုင်သော pai-nai-taw *(adj.)* **masterly**
ပိုင်နိုင်သော၊ စီမံနိုင်သော pai-nai-taw, si-man-nai-taw *(adj.)* **manageable**
ပိုင်ရှင် pine-shin *(n.)* **owner**
ပိုစတာ po-sa-tar *(n.)* **poster**
ပိုဆိုးလာသည် posoelarsai *(v.)* **worsen**
ပိုတက်စီယမ်ဓာတ် po taat se yam-dhrat *(n.)* **potassium**
ပိုနှစ်သက်သည် po-nit-saat-sai *(v.)* **prefer**
ပိုများသည် po-myar-tai *(v.)* **outnumber**

ပိုမှောင်လာသည် po-hmaung-lar-the *(v.)* **darkle**
ပိုမိုကောင်းမွန်စေခြင်း po-mo-kaung-mon-say-chin *(n.)* **amelioration**
ပိုမိုကောင်းမွန်စေသည် po-mo-kaung-mon-say-the *(v.)* **ameliorate**
ပိုမိုဆိုးရွားစေခြင်း po-mo-soe-ywar-say-chin *(n.)* **aggravation**
ပိုမိုဆိုးရွားစေသည် po-mo-soe-ywar-say-the *(v.)* **aggravate**
ပိုမိုရှုပ်ထွေးသော အရာ po-mo-shote-htway-taw-a-yar *(n.)* **complication**
ပိုလန်တာအနှစ် polaan tar aanit *(n.)* **polenta**
ပိုလျှံခြင်း po-lyan-chin *(n.)* **redundance**
ပိုလျှံသော po shan-saw *(adj.)* **redundant**
ပိုလွန်းသည် po-lwan-tai *(v.)* **overdo**
ပိုလွန်မှု po lwan-mhu *(n.)* **preponderance**
ပိုလွန်သည် poe-lun-the *(v.)* **exceed**
ပိုလို po-lo *(n.)* **polo**
ပိုလီကာဘွန်နိတ်ဓာတ် po-le-kar-bhwan nate-dhrat *(n.)* **polycarbonate**
ပိုလီခရုန်းဓာတ် po-le hka ronedhat *(adj.)* **polychrome**
ပိုလီဂွန်ချိတ်ဆက်ခြင်းဖြင့် တည်ဆောက်ထားသော အခဲ po-le gwan chaate-saat-chinn-hpyint tai-sout-htarrsaw aahkell *(n.)* **polyform**
ပိုလီပရိုပိုင်လင်း Po-le paro pine lin *(n.)* **polypropylene**
ပိုလီဗြူတင်းဓာတ် po-le-byuu-tinn-dhrat *(n.)* **polybutene**
ပိုလီဗြူတိုင်လင်းဓာတ် po-le-byuu-tine-linn-dhrat *(n.)* **polybutylene**
ပိုလီမာ po-le-mar *(n.)* **polymer**
ပိုလီမီတင်းဒြပ်ပေါင်း po-le me tinn dyat-paungg *(n.)* **polymethine**
ပိုလီမီတိုင်လင်းဓာတ် po-le me tine linn-dhrat *(n.)* **polymethylene**
ပိုလီအက်ဆီတိုင်လင်းဓာတ် po-le-at-se-tine-linn-dhrat *(n.)* **polyacetylene**
ပိုလီအင်းဒြပ်ပေါင်း pole aainn dyatpaungg *(n.)* **polyene**
ပိုလီအန်ဒရီမျိုးနွယ် po-le aaan d re myoenwal *(n.)* **polyandrianism**
ပိုလီအန်ဒရီမျိုးနွယ်ဝင် အပင် po-le aaan d re myoe nwalwain aapin *(n.)* **polyander**
ပိုသော po-taw *(adj.)* **excess**
ပီဇာ pe-zar *(n.)* **pizza**
ပီဇာမုန့် pe jar mone *(n.)* **pizzeria**
ပီတိ pi-ti *(n.)* **beatitude**
ပီတိတဖွားဖွားဖြစ်ခြင်း pi-ti-ta-phwar-phwar-phit-chin *(n.)* **gloat**
ပီတိတဖွားဖွားဖြစ်သည် pi-ti-ta-phwar-phwar-phit-the *(v.)* **gloat**
ပီတိဖြစ်စေသည် pi-ti-phit-say-the *(v.)* **enrapture**
ပီတိဖြစ်သည် pi-ti-phit-the *(v.)* **enthral**
ပီတိဖြာသော pi-ti-pyar-taw *(adj.)* **ecstatic**
ပီတိလျှမ်းသော pi-ti-hlyan-taw *(adj.)* **beatific**
ပီပီသသ pi-pi-ta-ta *(adv.)* **legibly**
ပီယွန်ပင် pe ywan-pin *(n.)* **peon**
ပီသစွာ ရွတ်သည် pi-ta-swar-yut-the *(v.)* **enunciate**
ပုံ pon *(n.)* **image**
ပုံး pon *(n.)* **bin**
ပုံ၊ ကားချပ်ဖြင့် သရုပ်ဖော်ထားသော pone , karr chauthpyint sarotehpawhtarrsaw *(adj.)* **schematic**
ပုံ၊ သဏ္ဌာန် pon, ta-htan *(n.)* **figure**

ပုံ၊ အနေအထား pone , aanayaahtarr *(n.)* **shape**

ပုံကြမ်း ponekyam *(n.)* **sketch**

ပုံကြမ်း၊ ပုံစံ pon-kyan, pon-san *(n.)* **diagram**

ပုံကြမ်းဆွဲသည် pone-kyaa swalsai *(v.)* **sketch**

ပုံကြီးချဲ့သည် pon-gyi-chae-the *(v.)* **magnify**

ပုံကို ပစ်ဇယ်အဖြစ်ခွဲသည် poneko pait jaal aahpyit hkwalsai *(v.)* **pixelate**

ပုံခိုင်းလေ့ရှိသည် pon-khai-lay-shi-the *(v.)* **liken**

ပုံစံ pone-san *(n.)* **pattern**

ပုံစံခွက် pon-san-khwat *(n.)* **mould**

ပုံစံခွက်ထဲ လောင်းခြင်း၊ သရုပ်ဆောင်အားလုံး pon-san-khwat-htae-laung-chin, tha-yoke-saung-arr-lon *(n.)* **cast**

ပုံစံငယ် pon-san-nge *(n.)* **model**

ပုံစံတကျပုံထားသော ကောက်လှိုင်းပုံ ponesan ta kya ponehtarrsaw kout hlinepone *(n.)* **rick**

ပုံစံတစ်ခုပေးသည် ponehcan ta-hkupayysai *(v.)* **template**

ပုံစံထုတ်ခြင်း၊ ဒီဇိုင်းဆွဲခြင်းပညာ pon-zan-htoke-chin, de-zai-swal-chin-pyin-nyar *(adj.)* **designing**

ပုံစံနှစ်ခုရှိခြင်း pon-san-na-khu-shi-chin *(n.)* **biformity**

ပုံစံပြောင်းသည် ponehcanpyaunggsai *(v.)* **shapeshift**

ပုံစံများစွာ ponehcanmyarrhcwar *(n.)* **polymorph**

ပုံစံများစွာ ဆက်လက်ယူနိုင်စွမ်း pone-sanmyarrhcwar saatlaat yuu-nine-swam *(n.)* **polymorphism**

ပုံစံများစွာ ဆက်လက်ယူနိုင်စွမ်းရှိခြင်း pone-sanmyarr-swar saatlaat yuu ninehcwmshihkyinn *(n.)* **polymorphosis**

ပုံစံမျိုးစုံဖြစ်ခြင်း pon-san-myo-sone-phit-chin *(n.)* **omniformity**

ပုံစံမျိုးစုံဖြစ်သော pon-san-myo-sone-phit-taw *(adj.)* **omniform**

ပုံစံအမျိုးမျိုး pon-san-a-myo-myo *(n.)* **multiform**

ပုံဆွဲဆရာ pon-swal-sa-yar *(adj.)* **draftsman**

ပုံဆွဲပညာ pon-swal-pyin-nyar *(n.)* **drawing**

ပုံဆွဲသည် pon-swal-the *(v.)* **draw**

ပုံဆောင်မဲ့ pone-saung-mae *(adj.)* **amorphous**

ပုံဆောင်ဝတ္ထု pone-saung-wat-htu *(n.)* **parable**

ပုံဆောင်သည် pon-saung-the *(v.)* **illustrate**

ပုံတူ pone-tuu *(n.)* **portrait**

ပုံတူခိုးချသော ponetuu hkoe chasaw *(adj.)* **slavish**

ပုံတူရေးပညာ pone-tuu rayypa-nyar *(n.)* **portraiture**

ပုံတောင်း pon-taung *(n.)* **hub**

ပုံနှိပ်ခြင်း pon-neik-chin *(n.)* **edition**

ပုံနှိပ်စာလုံး pone-nate-sarlone *(n.)* **print**

ပုံနှိပ်မှားသည် pon-nate-hmar-the *(v.)* **misprint**

ပုံနှိပ်သည်၊ ပရင့်ထုတ်သည် pone-nate sai, pa rint htote-sai *(v.)* **print**

ပုံနှိပ်အမှား pon-nate-a-hmar *(n.)* **misprint**

ပုံပစ်ဇယ် pone-pit-zal *(n.)* **pixel**

ပုံပန်းပျက်စေသည် pon-pan-pyat-say-the *(v.)* **deform**

ပုံပန်းလက္ခဏာမထူးခြားသော pon-pan-lat-kha-nar-ma-htoo-char-taw *(adj.)* **bland**

ပုံပျက်ပန်းပျက် pone pyet paannpyet *(adj.)* **shapeless**

ပုံပျက်ပန်းပျက် ဝသော၊ ရိုင်းစိုင်းသော pon-pyat-pan-pyat-wa-taw, yai-sai-taw *(adj.)* **gross**

ပုံပျက်အောင် ဖျက်ဆီးသည် pon-pyat-aung-phat-see-the *(v.)* **mutilate**

ပုံပျက်အောင် လုပ်သည် pon-pyat-aung-lote-the *(v.)* **disfigure**

ပုံပြင် ponepyin *(n.)* **tale**

ပုံပြင်စာအုပ် ponepyinsar-aote *(n.)* **talebook**

ပုံပေါ်လာသည် pon-paw-lar-the *(v.)* **crystalize**

ပုံဖျက်ခြင်း pon-phat-chin *(n.)* **camouflage**

ပုံဖော်သည် ponehpawsai *(v.)* **shape**

ပုံမမှန် ဆက်တိုက်ဖြစ်နေသော အစာအငမ်းမရဖြစ်ခြင်း pon-ma-man-sat-tite-phit-nay-taw-a-sar-a-nyan-ma-ya-phit-chin *(n.)* **bulimia**

ပုံမမှန် မြန်ဆန်စွာ ရွေ့လျားသည် pon-ma-hman-myan-san-swar-ywe-lyar-the *(v.)* **fibrillate**

ပုံမမှန်စွာ သေးငယ်ခြင်း pon-ma-man-tay-nge-taw *(n.)* **nanism**

ပုံမမှန်လမ်းကြောင်း pon-ma-hman-lan-kyaung *(n.)* **fistula**

ပုံမမှန်သော pon-ma-hman-taw *(adj.)* **irregular**

ပုံများပါသော pone-myarr-par-saw *(adj.)* **pictorial**

ပုံမှန် pone-man *(adv.)* **ordinarily**

ပုံမှန်ခရီးတစ်ပတ်၊ အလှည့် ponemhaan hkaree ta-paat , a hlae *(n.)* **round**

ပုံမှန်ထက်စောသော pone-mhaan-htaat-saw-saw *(adj.)* **premature**

ပုံမှန်ပြန်ဖြစ်အောင်လုပ်ခြင်း pone-maan-pyan-hpyit-aung-lote-chinn *(n.)* **normalization**

ပုံမှန်ပြန်ဖြစ်အောင်လုပ်သည် pone-maan-pyan-hpyit-aung-lote-tai *(v.)* **normalize**

ပုံမှန်ဖြစ်ပေါ်မှု ponemhaan hpyitpawmhu *(n.)* **regularity**

ပုံမှန်မဟုတ်ခြင်း pone-man-ma-hote-chin *(n.)* **abnormality**

ပုံမှန်မဟုတ်သော pone-man-ma-hote-taw *(adj.)* **atypic**

ပုံမှန်လမ်းပေါ်တွင် ကားမောင်းရန် ရပ်ရန် လမ်း pone-man-lan-paw-twin-kar-maung-yan-kar-yat-yan-lan *(adj.)* **on-road**

ပုံမှန်လမ်းမခင်းထားသော ကားမောင်းရန်၊ ရပ်ရန် လမ်း pone-man-lan-ma-khin-htar-taw-kar-maung-yan-kar-yat-yan-lan *(adj.)* **off-road**

ပုံမှန်လုပ်ခ pone-mhaan-lote-hka *(n.)* **pay**

ပုံမှန်၊ သမားရိုးကျ pone mone , samarrroekya *(adj.)* **routine**

ပုံရိပ်၊ အရိပ် pone-rate , aa-yate *(n.)* **reflection**

ပုံရိပ်ထင်သည် pon-yeik-htin-the *(v.)* **mirror**

ပုံရိပ်ထင်သည်၊ ရောင်ပြန်ဟပ်သည် pone-rate htinsai , raungpyan hatsai *(v.)* **reflect**

ပုံရိပ်မည်း poneriutmaee *(n.)* **silhouette**

ပုံရိပ်ယောင် poneriutyaung *(adj.)* **virtual**

ပုံရေးခြင်းဆိုင်ရာ pon-yay-chin-sai-yar *(adj.)* **graphic**

ပုံရေးဆွဲပြခြင်း pon-yay-swal-pya-chin *(n.)* **depiction**

ပုံရေးဆွဲပြသည် pon-yay-swal-pya-the *(v.)* **depict**

ပုံသည် pone-sai *(v.)* **pile**

ပုံသွင်းသည် pon-twin-the *(v.)* **mould**

ပုံသွင်းသည်၊ ပုံဖော်သည် pon-twin-the, pon-phaw-the *(v.)* **form**

ပုံသေကားကျ ပုံသွင်းထားသော pone-say karrkya pone swin-htarrsaw *(adj.)* **stereotyped**
ပုံသေကားကျပုံစံ pone say karr kya *(n.)* **stereotype**
ပုံသေသတ်မှတ် မြင်သည် pone saysaatmhaat myinsai *(v.)* **stereotype**
ပုံသေအလုပ်၊ စက်ခါးပတ် pone say aa-lote , saat hkarrpaat *(n.)* **treadmill**
ပုခုံး၊ အင်္ကျီပုခုံး pu hkone , aain kyee puhkone *(n.)* **shoulder**
ပုဂ္ဂလိက လေယာဉ်သုံး လေယာဉ်ကွင်း poke-ga-li-ka-lay-yin-tone-lay-yin-kwin *(n.)* **aerodrome**
ပုစဉ်း pa-zin *(n.)* **dragonfly**
ပုစဉ်းရင်ကွဲ pa-zin-yin-kwe *(n.)* **cicada**
ပုစွန်ဆိတ်ငယ် pa-sun-seik-ngal *(n.)* **krill**
ပုစွန်တုတ်စွပ်ပြုတ် pa-zoon-htoke-sut-pyoke *(n.)* **bisque**
ပုစွန်တုပ်ကြီး pa-sun-htoke-gyi *(n.)* **lobster**
ပုစ္ဆာ poke-sar *(n.)* **enigma**
ပုဆိန် pa-sein *(n.)* **axe**
ပုဆိန်တို၊ ရဟတ်ယာဉ် pa-sein-toe, ya-hat-yin *(n.)* **chopper**
ပုဇွန် pa-zon *(n.)* **crevet**
ပုတီးစေ့ pa-tee-say *(n.)* **bead**
ပုတ်သည် pote-sai *(v.)* **pat**
ပုဒ်စု pud-su *(n.)* **phrase**
ပုဒ်ဖြတ်ပုဒ်ရပ် poke hpyat poke-raut *(n.)* **punctuation**
ပုဒ်ရပ်သင်္ကေတ poke-yat-tin-kay-ta *(n.)* **comma**
ပုန်းကွယ်သည် pone-kwal-the *(v.)* **hide**
ပုန်းလျှိုးကွယ်လျှိုး pon-shyo-kwal-sho *(adj.)* **clandestine**
ပုန်ကန်ခြင်း ponekaanchinn *(n.)* **revolt**
ပုန်ကန်မှု pon-kan-mu *(n.)* **mutiny**
ပုန်ကန်မှု၊ ဆူပူအုံကြွမှု pon-kan-mu, su-pu-ohn-kwa-mu *(n.)* **insurrection**
ပုန်ကန်လိုသော pone-kaan-losaw *(adj.)* **rebellious**
ပုန်ကန်သည် ponekaansai *(v.)* **revolt**
ပုပ်စော်နံသည် pote-saw nan-sai *(v.)* **stink**
ပုပ်ရဟန်းမင်းကြီး poterahaannmainnkyee *(n.)* **pope**
ပုပ်ရဟန်းမင်းကြီးတစ်ဦး၏ လက်ထက် pote-ra-haan-minn-kyee-ta-u-eat-laat-htaat *(n.)* **papacy**
ပုပ်ရဟန်းမင်းကြီးနှင့် အတူ လုပ်ရန် ရှိသော pote-rahaann-minn-kyee-nint aatuu lote-raan shisaw *(adj.)* **papal**
ပုပ်သိုးခြင်း poke-thoe-chin *(n.)* **decomposition**
ပုပ်သိုးသည် poke-thoe-the *(v.)* **decompose**
ပုပ်သိုးသည်၊ စွန်းထင်းသည် pote soe sai , swann htinnsai *(v.)* **taint**
ပုပ်သော၊ ဆိုးရွားသော pote saw , soerwarrsaw *(adj.)* **rotten**
ပုရွက်ဆိတ် pa-ywet-seik *(n.)* **ant**
ပုရွတ်ဆိတ် pa-ywat-seik *(n.)* **emmet**
ပုရိသဘာဝအသွင်ရှိသော pu-ri-sa-bhar-wa-aa-swin-shi-saw *(adj.)* **phallic**
ပုလင်း pa-lin *(n.)* **bottle**
ပုလုကွေးလေး pu-lu-kway-lay *(n.)* **mite**
ပုလဲ pu-lell *(n.)* **pearl**
ပူးတွဲ pu-twal *(adj.)* **joint**
ပူးတွဲထည့်သည် pu-twe-htae-the *(v.)* **enclose**
ပူးတွဲနေသည် pu-twal-nay-the *(v.)* **couple**

ပူးတွဲပေးလိုက်သည် pu-twe-pay-lite-the *(v.)* **append**
ပူးတွဲသည် pu-twal-the *(v.)* **attach**
ပူးတွဲသော pu-twal-taw *(adj.)* **conjunct**
ပူးတွဲအားထုတ်ခြင်း pu-twal-arr-htoke-chin *(n.)* **joint effort**
ပူးပေါင်းကြံစည်သူ pu-paung-kyan-see-thu *(n.)* **conspirator**
ပူးပေါင်းခြင်း poe-paung-chin *(n.)* **collaboration**
ပူးပေါင်းဆောင်ရွက်ခြင်း pu-paung-saung-ywet-chin *(n.)* **cooperation**
ပူးပေါင်းဆောင်ရွက်မှု puupaunggsaung-rwatmhu *(n.)* **teamwork**
ပူးပေါင်းဆောင်ရွက်သည် pu-paung-saung-ywet-the *(v.)* **cooperate**
ပူးပေါင်းလိမ်လည်ရန် ညှိထားခြင်း pu-paung-lain-lal-yan-nyi-htar-chin *(n.)* **collusion**
ပူးပေါင်းသည် poe-paung-the *(v.)* **collaborate**
ပူခြင်း၊ စူခြင်း puu chinn , suuchinn *(n.)* **swell**
ပူဆွေးမှု pu-sway-mu *(n.)* **grief**
ပူဆွေးသောက puusway sawka *(n.)* **woe**
ပူဆွေးသောက ရောက်ခြင်း pu-sway-thaw-ka-yauk-chin *(n.)* **bereavement**
ပူတင်း puu-tinn *(n.)* **pudding**
ပူဒီနာ pu-di-nar *(n.)* **mint**
ပူနွေးသော puu nwaysaw *(adj.)* **warm**
ပူပန်စွာ pu-pan-swar *(adv.)* **anxiously**
ပူပန်မှု pu-pan-mu *(n.)* **anxiety**
ပူပန်မှု၊ အခက်အခဲ၊ စိတ်အနှောင့်အယှက် pu-pan-mu, a-khat-a-khae, seik-a-naut-a-shat *(n.)* **botheration**
ပူပန်သော pu-pan-taw *(adj.)* **anxious**
ပူပြင်းခြောက်သွေ့သော puu pyinn chaukswaesaw *(adj.)* **torrid**
ပူဖောင်း buu-hpaung *(n.)* **balloon**
ပူဖောင်းပလပ်စတစ် pu-hpaung-pa-lat-sa-tit *(n.)* **bubble wrap**
ပူသည် pu-the *(v.)* **heat**
ပူသော pu-taw *(adj.)* **hot**
ပေ pay *(n.)* **anvil**
ပေ့ါဆမှု pot-sa-mu *(n.)* **negligence**
ပေ့ါဆသော pot-sa-taw *(adj.)* **negligent**
ပေ့ါပါးသွက်လက်စွာ pot-par-thwat-lat-swar *(adv.)* **lightly**
ပေ့ါပါးသေ ာ ကားငယ် pot parrsaw karrngaal *(n.)* **runabout**
ပေ့ါပေ့ါပါးပါး မြန်မြန် ပြေးခြင်း paear paearparrparr myanmyan pyayhkyinn *(n.)* **scamper**
ပေးချေနိုင်သော payy-chaay-nine-saw *(adj.)* **payable**
ပေးငွေ pay-ngwe *(n.)* **debit**
ပေးဆပ်ခြင်း payysatchinn *(n.)* **repayment**
ပေးဆပ်ခြင်း၊ အဖတ်ဆယ်ခြင်း payy-satchinn , a hpaat saalchinn *(n.)* **redemption**
ပေးရန် တန်ဖိုးပေါ် ပြန်အမ်းငွေ payy-raan taan-hpoe paw pyan an-ngway *(n.)* **rebate**
ပေးသည် pay-the *(v.)* **give**
ပေးသည်၊ ဝေသည် pay-the, wai-the *(v.)* **hand**
ပေးသွင်းခြင်း payyswinchinn *(n.)* **supply**
ပေးသွင်းသည်၊ မှာယူသည် payyswin sai , mhar yuusai *(v.)* **subscribe**
ပေးအပ်လိုက်ရသည် pay-at-lite-ya-the *(v.)* **cede**
ပေကတ်ကတ် pay-kaat-kaat *(n.)* **perversity**

ပေဂျာဖြင့် ဆက်သွယ်သည် pay-gyaar-hpyint-saat-swal-sai *(v.)* **page**
ပေရစုတ်ချာသော pay ra sote chaarsaw *(adj.)* **squalid**
ပေါ့တန်သောစကား pot taan sawsakarr *(n.)* **prattle**
ပေါ့ပြက်ခြင်း pot pyaat-chinn *(n.)* **superficiality**
ပေါ့ပလာပင် pot pa lar-pin *(n.)* **poplar**
ပေါ့ပါးဖျတ်လတ်နိုင်စွမ်း pot-par-phat-lat-naing-swan *(n.)* **agility**
ပေါ့ပါးဖျတ်လတ်သော pot-par-phat-lat-taw *(adj.)* **agile**
ပေါ့ပေါ့ဆဆ pot-pot-sa-sa *(adj.)* **slipshod**
ပေါ့ရှတ်ရှတ်နိုင်ခြင်း pot-shyut-shyut-nai-chin *(n.)* **insipidity**
ပေါကြွယ်သည် paw-kywe-the *(v.& prep.)* **abound**
ပေါကြောင်ကြောင်နိုင်သော paw-kyaung-kyaung-nai-taw *(adj.)* **daft**
ပေါက်ကရစိတ်ကူး pauk-ka-ya-seik-khu *(n.)* **chimera**
ပေါက်ကြားစေသည် pauk-kyar-say-the *(v.)* **divulge**
ပေါက်ကွဲခြင်း pauk-kwal-chin *(n.)* **eruption**
ပေါက်ကွဲတတ်သော pauk-kwal-tat-taw *(adj.)* **explosive**
ပေါက်ကွဲတတ်သော ပစ္စည်း pauk-kwal-tat-taw-pyit-see *(n.)* **explosive**
ပေါက်ကွဲမှု pauk-kwal-mu *(n.)* **blast**
ပေါက်ကွဲသည် pauk-kwal-the *(v.)* **burst**
ပေါက်ခြင်း၊ ဆိတ်ခြင်း pout-chinn, sate-chinn *(n.)* **peck**
ပေါက်တတ်ကရစကား pauk-tat-ka-ya-sa-kar *(n.)* **eyewash**
ပေါက်တူး pauk-tu *(n.)* **mattock**
ပေါက်ပေါက်ရှာရှာစိတ်ကူး poutpoutsharsharsatekuu *(n.)* **whim**
ပေါက်ဖွားဖြစ်စေသည် pauk-phwar-say-the *(v.)* **gig**
ပေါက်သည် pout-sai *(v.)* **puncture**
ပေါက်သည်၊ ဖြောင်းဆန်သည် pauk-the, byaung-san-the *(n.)* **freak-out**
ပေါင် paung *(n.)* **sterling**
ပေါင်းခံချွေးထုတ်ခန်းသုံးသည် paungg hkan hkyaway htote hkaann-sonesai *(v.)* **sauna**
ပေါင်းခံချွေးထုတ်ခြင်း paungg hkan chaway htotechinn *(n.)* **sauna**
ပေါင်းခံခြင်းအလယ်ဆင့်မှ ရရှိသော အရည်စီးကြောင်း paungg hkan hkyinn aalaal saintmha rashisaw aarai hceekyaungg *(n.)* **side-stream**
ပေါင်းခံသည် paung-khan-the *(v.)* **distil**
ပေါင်းချုပ် paung-chote *(n.)* **omnibus**
ပေါင်းခြင်း paung-chin *(n.)* **amalgamation**
ပေါင်းစည်းသည် paung-see-the *(v.)* **affiliate**
ပေါင်းစပ်ခြင်း paung-sat-chin *(n.)* **combination**
ပေါင်းစပ်သည် paung-sat-the *(v.)* **combine**
ပေါင်းစီးခြင်း paung-see-chin *(n.)* **unification**
ပေါင်းစုံ paung-sone *(adj.)* **multiple**
ပေါင်းစုံသော paung-sone-taw *(adj.)* **confluent**
ပေါင်းထည့်ခြင်း paung-htae-chin *(n.)* **addition**
ပေါင်းထည့်ဆော့ဝဲလ် သို့မဟုတ် ပစ္စည်း paung-htae-soft-ware-tho-ma-hote-pyit-see *(n.)* **add-in**
ပေါင်းထည့်သည် paung-htae-the *(v.)* **add**
ပေါင်းပင် paunggpin *(n.)* **weed**

ပေါင်းသင်သည် paungg sinsai *(v.)* **weed**

ပေါင်းသည် paung-the *(v.)* **amalgamate**

ပေါင်၊ ပေါင်တံ paung , paungtan *(n.)* **thigh**

ပေါင်ခွင်၊ ပေါင် paung-kwin, paung *(n.)* **lap**

ပေါင်ဒါ၊ အမှုန့် paung dar , a hmont *(n.)* **powder**

ပေါင်ဒါရိုက်သည် paung dar-ritesai *(v.)* **powder**

ပေါင်မုန့် paung-hmont *(n.)* **bread**

ပေါင်မုန့် အကာသား paung-hmont-a-kar-tar *(n.)* **crust**

ပေါင်မုန့်ချပ် paung mu anthkyaut *(n.)* **shive**

ပေါင်မုန့်ဖုတ်သူ paung-mont-hpoke-thu *(n.)* **baker**

ပေါင်မုန့်မီးကင် paung mont meekin *(n.)* **toast**

ပေါင်မုန့်ရှည် paung-hmont-shay *(n.)* **baguette**

ပေါင်မုန့်လုံး paung-hmont-lone *(n.)* **loaf**

ပေါင်မုန့်သားအပဲ့ paung-hmont-tar-a-pae *(n.)* **breadcrumb**

ပေါင်မုန့်သားအပဲ့ဖြင့် အုပ်သော paung-hmont-tar-a-pae-phyint-oak-taw *(adj.)* **breaded**

ပေါင်မုန့်အကွင်း paung-mont-a-kwin *(n.)* **bagel**

ပေါင်ရင်းသား paung-yin-tar *(n.)* **loin**

ပေါင်ရိုး paung-yoe *(n.)* **femur**

ပေါများစွာ paw-myar-swar *(adv.)* **galore**

ပေါများသော၊ ရက်ရောသော paw-myar-taw, yat-yaw-taw *(adj.)* **bountiful**

ပေါလောပေါ်ခြင်း၊ ရေကူးခြင်း paw-law-paw-chin, yay-ku-chin *(adj.)* **natant**

ပေါလောပေါ်သည် paw-law-paw-the *(v.)* **float**

ပေါလောပေါ်သော paw-law-paw-taw *(adv.)* **afloat**

ပေါ်တင် paw-tin *(adj.)* **blatant**

ပေါ်ထွက်ခြင်း paw-htwat-chin *(n.)* **emanation**

ပေါ်ထွက်လာသည် paw-htwat-lar-the *(v.)* **emerge**

ပေါ်ထွက်သည် paw-htwat-the *(v.)* **emanate**

ပေါ်ထွန်းမှု paw-htun-mu *(n.)* **advent**

ပေါ်ပင် paw-pin *(adj.)* **ephemeral**

ပေါ်ပင်ပစ္စည်း paw-pin-pyit-see *(n.)* **ephemera**

ပေါ်ပင်လိုက်၍ အရူးထခြင်း paw-pin-lite-ywe-a-yu-hta-chin *(n.)* **craze**

ပေါ်ပလင်ပိတ် paw pa lin-pate *(n.)* **poplin**

ပေါ်ပေါက်ခြင်း paw-pout-chinn *(n.)* **outbreak**

ပေါ်ပေါက်လာသည် paw-pauk-lar-the *(v.)* **materialize**

ပေါ်ပေါက်လာသည်၊ တီထွင်သည် paw-pout-lar-tai, te-htwin-tai *(v.)* **originate**

ပေါ်ပေါက်သည် paw-paut-the *(v.)* **befall**

ပေါ်မှာ paw-mhar *(prep.)* **on**

ပေါ်လစ်တင်ခြင်း paw-lit-tin-chinn *(n.)* **polish**

ပေါ်လစ်တင်သည် paw-lit-tin-sai *(v.)* **polish**

ပေါ်လွင်သည် paw-lwin-the *(v.)* **manifest**

ပေါ်လွင်သော paw-lwin-taw *(adj.)* **evident**

ပေါ်လာခြင်း pay-lar-chin *(n.)* **appearance**

ပေါ်လာသည် paw-lar-the *(v.)* **appear**

ပေါ်သို့ paw-tho *(adv.)* **aboard**

ပဲ့ pae *(n.)* **stern**

ပဲ့တင်ထပ်ခြင်း pae-tin-htet-chin *(n.)* **echo**

ပဲ့တင်ထပ်သည် pae tin htatsai *(v.)* **resound**

ပွဲထင်ထပ်သည် pae-tin-htet-the *(v.)* **echo**

ပွဲထွက်သော အစ paehtwatsaw aa-sa *(n.)* **splinter**

ပွဲထိန်းလက်ကိုင်ဘီး pae-htain-lat-kai-bee *(n.)* **helm**

ပွဲပိုင်း pae-paing *(n.)* **aft**

ပဲစေ့ pell-sae *(n.)* **pea**

ပဲတောင့်ပင်၊ ပဲသီးတောင့် pal-taunt-pin, pal-thee-taunt *(n.)* **bean**

ပဲနီ pell-ni *(n.)* **penny**

ပဲနီကလေး pae-ni-ka-lay *(n.)* **lentil**

ပဲပိုးတီ pae-poe-ti *(n.)* **artichoke**

ဖ

ဖက်စပ် phat-sat *(adj.)* **cooperative**

ဖက်စ် phat *(n.)* **fax**

ဖက်စ်ပို့သည် phat-poe-the *(v.)* **fax**

ဖက်တက်သည် phat-tat-the *(v.)* **clamber**

ဖက်ဒရယ်နှင့် ဆိုင်သော fat-da-ral-nint-sai-taw *(adj.)* **federal**

ဖက်ပြိုင်သည် phat-pyai-the *(v.)* **contend**

ဖက်ယားပင် phat-yar-pin *(n.)* **nettle**

ဖက်ရှင် fas-shin *(n.)* **fashion**

ဖက်ရှင်စတိုး phat-shin-sa-toe *(n.)* **boutique**

ဖက်ရှင်လျှောက်လမ်း phat-shin-shauk-lan *(n.)* **catwalk**

ဖခင်၏ hpah-kin-eat *(adj.)* **paternal**

ဖခင်ကို သတ်မှု hpa-hkin-ko-saat-mhu *(n.)* **patricide**

ဖခင်ဖြစ်သည် pha-khin-phit-the *(v.)* **beget**

ဖင့်နွဲလေးကန်သူ phint-nwe-kan-the *(n.)* **laggard**

ဖတ်၍ ရနိုင်သော phat-ywe-ya-nai-taw *(adj.)* **legible**

ဖတ်ဖတ်မော၊ ဖန်တစ်ရာတေအောင် သုံးထား၍ စုတ်ချာနေသော hpant-hpaat maw , hpaan taitrar tayaaung sonehtarr sote chaarnaysaw *(adj.)* **worn**

ဖတ်မရသော phat-ma-ya-taw *(adj.)* **illegible**

ဖတ်ရှုခြင်း hpaat-shu-chinn *(n.)* **perusal**

ဖတ်ရှုသည် hpaat-shu-sai *(v.)* **peruse**

ဖတ်သည် hpaatsai *(v.)* **read**

ဖနောင့်သံဆူး hpa naut sansuu *(v.)* **spur**

ဖနောင့်သံဆူး၊ တွန်းအား hpa naut san suu, twann-aarr *(n.)* **spur**

ဖန် phan *(n.)* **glass**

ဖန်းပင် hpan-pin *(n.)* **fern**

ဖန်ချက်သူ phan-chat-thu *(n.)* **glassmaker**

ဖန်တစ်ရာတေနေသော စကားလုံး phan-ta-yar-tay-nay-taw-sa-kar-lone *(n.)* **cliché**

ဖန်တီးသည် phan-tee-the *(v.)* **contrive**

ဖန်ဘူးငယ် hpaan bhuungaal *(n.)* **vial**

ဖန်မျှင်ထည် phan-hmyin-htae *(n.)* **fibreglass**

ဖန်မျှင်နန်းကြိုး phan-hmyin-nan-kyo *(adj.)* **fibre-optic**

ဖန်လုံအိမ် phan-lon-eain *(n.)* **glasshouse**

ဖန်ဝါရောင် သလင်းကျောက် phan-war-yaung-tha-lin-kyauk *(n.)* **citrine**

ဖန်အဖြစ် ပြောင်းလဲသည် hpan-aphit-pyaung-lal-the *(v.)* **glassify**

ဖမ်းကိုင်သည် hpam kinesai *(v.)* **seize**

ဖမ်းခြင်း hpan-chin *(n.)* **capture**

ဖမ်းစီးသည် hpan-see-the *(v.)* **arrest**

ဖမ်းဆီးထားသူကို ပြန်ရွေးရာ၌ ပေးရသည့်ငွေ hpamsee-htarr suuko pyan rwayrar-nite payyr saeetngway *(n.)* **ransom**

ဖမ်းဆီးသည် phan-see-the *(v.)* **nail**

ဖမ်းဆုပ်ခြင်း phan-sote-chin *(n.)* **grasp**

ဖမ်းထားသော phan-htar-taw *(adj.)* **captive**

ဖမ်းမိခြင်း hpan-mi-chin *(n.)* **apprehension**

ဖမ်းမိသည် hpan-mi-the *(v.)* **apprehend**

ဖမ်းယူသည် hpan-yu-the *(v.)* **capture**

ဖမ်းသည် phan-the *(v.)* **catch**

ဖယောင်းတိုင် pha-yaung-tai *(n.)* **candle**

ဖယောင်းတိုင်မီး pha-yaung-tai-mee *(n.)* **candlelight**

ဖယောင်းဖြင့် ဖုံးထားသော pha-yaung-phit-hpone-htar-taw *(adj.)* **cerated**

ဖယောင်းဖြင့် အရောင်တင်သည် hpayaungghpyint aaraungtinsai *(v.)* **wax**

ဖယ်ကြဉ်ခြင်း phal-kyin-chin *(n.)* **abnegation**

ဖယ်ကြဉ်သည် phal-kyin-the *(v.)* **abnegate**

ဖယ်ထုတ်ခြင်း phal-htoke-chin *(n.)* **ablation**

ဖယ်ထုတ်ထားသော phal-htoke-htar-taw *(adj.)* **ablative**

ဖယ်ထုတ်မှု hpaal-htote-mhu *(n.)* **parry**

ဖယ်ထုတ်သည် phal-htoke-the *(v.)* **ablate**

ဖယ်ပစ်သည် phal-pyit-the *(v.)* **dismiss**

ဖယ်ရှားခြင်း၊ ချွတ်ခြင်း hpaalsharr chinn , chyut-chinn *(n.)* **removal**

ဖယ်ရှားပစ်ခြင်း phal-shar-pyit-chin *(n.)* **disposal**

ဖယ်ရှားသည် hpaal-sharrsai *(v.)* **remove**

ဖယ်ရီ phal-re *(n.)* **ferry**

ဖယ်ရီလှေ phal-re-lay *(n.)* **ferryboat**

ဖျံ hpyaan *(n.)* **otter**

ဖျံကြီးတစ်မျိုး hpyan-gyi-ta-myo *(n.)* **beaver**

ဖျံအရေပြား hpyan-a-yay-pyar *(n.)* **beaverskin**

ဖျက်၍ ရသော pyat-ywe-ya-taw *(adj.)* **deletable**

ဖျက်ကောင် hpyet-kaung *(n.)* **pest**

ဖျက်ခနဲ ကြည့်သည် phat-kha-nae-kyae-the *(v.)* **glance**

ဖျက်ခြင်း phat-chin *(n.)* **cancellation**

ဖျက်ဆီးခြင်း phat-see-chin *(n.)* **destruction**

ဖျက်ဆီးမရနိုင်သော phat-see-ma-ya-nai-taw *(adj.)* **incorruptible**

ဖျက်ဆီးမှုဒဏ် hpyet-see mhu-dan *(n.)* **ravage**

ဖျက်ဆီးသည် hpyet-seesai *(v.)* **ravage**

ဖျက်ဆီးသည့် စိတ်ထားဖြင့် pyat-see-the-seik-htar-phyint *(adv.)* **deconstructively**

ဖျက်ဆီးသည်၊ သိမ်ဖျင်းစေသည် hpyetsee sai , sin hpyinnsaysai *(v.)* **vitiate**

ဖျက်ဆီးသူ hpyetseesuu *(n.)* **wrecker**

ဖျက်လိုဖျက်ဆီး လုပ်သည်၊ နှောင့်ယှက်သည် phat-lo-phat-see-lote-the, naut-shat-the *(v.)* **foil**

ဖျက်သည် phat-the *(v.)* **cancel**

ဖျက်သည်၊ တန်ဖိုးလျှော့စေသည် phat-the, tan-phoe-shawt-say-the *(v.)* **debase**

ဖျက်သိမ်းခြင်း phat-thein-ching *(n.)* **abolition**

ဖျက်သိမ်းသည် phat-tain-the *(v.)* **disband**

ဖျစ်သည် hpyit-te *(v.)* **nip**

ဖျစ်သည်၊ ညစ်သည် hpyit sai , nyaitsai *(v.)* **squeeze**
ဖျန်းသည်၊ ဖြူးသည် hpyann sai, hpyuu-sai *(v.)* **sprinkle**
ဖျန်ဖြေခြင်း phyan-phyay-chin *(n.)* **mediation**
ဖျန်ဖြေသည် phyan-phyay-the *(v.)* **mediate**
ဖျန်ဖြေသူ phyan-phyay-thu *(n.)* **mediator**
ဖျာ pyar *(n.)* **mat**
ဖျားနာခန်း hpyarr narhkaann *(n.)* **sickbay**
ဖျားနာခြင်း phyar-nar-chin *(n.)* **ailment**
ဖျားနာသူ၏ အိပ်ရာ hpyarr narsuueat ait-rar *(n.)* **sickbed**
ဖျားနာသော hpyarr narsaw *(adj.)* **sick**
ဖျူးကြိုး phyue-kyo *(n.)* **fuse**
ဖျူးကြိုး ပြတ်သည် phyue-kyo-pyat-the *(v.)* **fuse**
ဖျောက်သည်၊ လွန်မြောက်သည် hpyaut-tai, lwan-myaut-tai *(v.)* **outgrow**
ဖျောင်းဖျသည် hpyaung-hpya-sai *(v.)* **placate**
ဖျော်ဖြေပွဲ phyaw-phyay-pwe *(n.)* **entertainment**
ဖျော်ဖြေမှု phyaw-phyay-mu *(n.)* **amusement**
ဖျော်ဖြေရေး၊ စွမ်းဆောင်မှု hpyaw-hpyay-rayy, swam-saung-mhu *(n.)* **performance**
ဖျော်ဖြေသည် phyaw-phyay-the *(v.)* **entertain**
ဖျော်ရည် hpyawrai *(n.)* **solvent**
ဖရိုဖရဲ hparohparell *(adj.)* **shambolic**
ဖရိုဖရဲ ပြန့်ကျဲနေသည် hparohparell pyant kyaellnaysai *(v.)* **straggle**
ဖရိုဖရဲ ဖြစ်ခြင်း pha-yo-pha-ye-phit-chin *(n.)* **misrule**
ဖရိုဖရဲဖြစ်ခြင်း pha-yo-pha-ye-phit-chin *(n.)* **disarray**
ဖရိုဖရဲဖြစ်စေသည် pha-yo-pha-ye-phit-say-the *(v.)* **disarrange**
ဖရီးရိုက်သည် pha-ree-rite-the *(v.)* **freewheel**
ဖရဲသီး hparellsee *(n.)* **water-melon**
ဖြစ်ကတတ်ဆန်း၊ ပေါက်လွှတ်ပဲစား hpyit k taat saann , pout lwut pellsarr *(adj.)* **slovenly**
ဖြစ်ကတတ်ဆန်းလုပ်သည် phit-ka-tat-san-lote-the *(v.)* **botch**
ဖြစ်ကြောင်းကုန်စင် ပြန်ပြောပြခြင်း hpyit-kyaung-konesin pyan-pyaww-pyachinn *(n.)* **recital**
ဖြစ်ကောင်းဖြစ်နိုင်စွာ hpyit-kaungg hpyit-nine-swar *(adv.)* **probably**
ဖြစ်ကောင်းဖြစ်နိုင်သည် hpyit-kaung-hpyit-nine-sai *(adv.)* **perhaps**
ဖြစ်ချင်သော hpyitchinsaw *(adj.)* **wishful**
ဖြစ်စဉ် hpyit-sin *(n.)* **phenomenon**
ဖြစ်စေသည် hpyitsaysai *(v.)* **render**
ဖြစ်တည်ခြင်း phit-the-chin *(n.)* **being**
ဖြစ်ထွန်းစည်ပင်သော hpyit-htwann sai-pin-saw *(adj.)* **prosperous**
ဖြစ်ထွန်းမှု hpyit-htwann-mhu *(n.)* **realization**
ဖြစ်ထွန်းသည် hpyit-htwann-sai *(v.)* **yield**
ဖြစ်ထွန်းသော hpyit-htwann-saw *(adj.)* **productive**
ဖြစ်နိုင်ချေမရှိခြင်း phit-nai-chay-ma-shi-chin *(n.)* **impossibility**
ဖြစ်နိုင်ခြေ hpyitnine-chay *(n.)* **possibility**
ဖြစ်နိုင်ခြေမရှိသော phit-naing-chay-ma-shi-taw *(adj.)* **absurd**
ဖြစ်နိုင်သော hpyitninesaw *(adj.)* **probable**
ဖြစ်ပျက်သည် phit-pyat-the *(v.)* **betide**

ဖြစ်ပြီးသွားသော phit-pi-twar-taw *(adj.)* **bygone**

ဖြစ်ပွားမှုပမာဏ phit-pwar-mu-pa-mar-na *(n.)* **incident**

ဖြစ်ပွားလေ့ရှိသော phit-pwar-lay-shi-taw *(adj.)* **endemic**

ဖြစ်ပွားသည် hpyit-pwar-tai *(v.)* **occur**

ဖြစ်ပေါ်စေသည် hpyitpawsay-sai *(v.)* **pose**

ဖြစ်ရပ်၊ အပိုင်း phit-yat, a-pai *(n.)* **episode**

ဖြစ်လွယ်သော hpyit lwalsaw *(adj.)* **prone**

ဖြစ်လာသည် phit-lar-the *(v.)* **become**

ဖြစ်သည်၊ ရှိသည် phit-the, shi-the *(abbr.)* **am**

ဖြစ်အံ့ဆဲဆဲ phit-ant-sal-sal *(adj.)* **imminent**

ဖြည့်စွက်ချက် hpya ny swatchet *(n.)* **supplement**

ဖြည့်သွင်းခြင်း phyae-twin-chin *(n.)* **infusion**

ဖြည့်သွင်းသည် pyae-twin-the *(v.)* **incorporate**

ဖြည့်သွင်းသော pyae-twin-taw *(adj.)* **incorporate**

ဖြည့်သွင်းသော အချက်အလက်၊ ဖြည့်သွင်းခြင်း phyae-twin-taw-a-chat-a-let, phyae-twin-chin *(n.)* **input**

ဖြည့်စွက်ချက် phyae-swat-chat *(n.)* **addendum**

ဖြည့်စွမ်းသည် phyae-swan-the *(v.)* **fulfil**

ဖြည့်သည် pyae-the *(v.)* **lade**

ဖြည်းညင်းသော phyae-nyin-taw *(adj.)* **gradual**

ဖြည်ခြင်း phyay-chin *(n.)* **decrypt**

ဖြည်သည် phyay-the *(v.)* **decrypt**

ဖြတ်၍ hpyat-ywe *(adv.)* **through**

ဖြတ်ကျော်နိုင်သော phat-kyaw-nine-taw *(adj.)* **traversable**

ဖြတ်ကျော်သည် hpyat-kyaw-sai *(n.)* **pass**

ဖြတ်ခြင်း၊ ပြတ်ခြင်း hpyat chinn , pyatchinn *(n.)* **severance**

ဖြတ်စ phat-sa *(n.)* **cutting**

ဖြတ်စ၊ ညှပ်စ phat-sa, nyat-sa *(n.)* **clipping**

ဖြတ်ညှပ်ကပ်ရန် ဗလာစာအုပ် hpyat-nyhaut-kat-raan balar-saraote *(n.)* **scrapbook**

ဖြတ်တိုက်ခြင်း hpyat titehkyinn *(n.)* **T-bone**

ဖြတ်တိုက်သည် hpyat titesai *(v.)* **T-bone**

ဖြတ်တောက်ကုသခြင်း phat-taut-ku-ta-chin *(n.)* **amputation**

ဖြတ်တောက်ကုသသည် phat-taut-ku-ta-the *(v.)* **amputate**

ဖြတ်တောက်ခံရသူ phat-taut-khan-ya-thu *(n.)* **amputee**

ဖြတ်တောက်သည် Hpyat-toutsai *(v.)* **prune**

ဖြတ်ပိုင်း phat-pai *(n.)* **coupon**

ဖြတ်ယူခြင်း phat-yu-chin *(n.)* **interception**

ဖြတ်လမ်း hpyat-lam *(n.)* **shortcut**

ဖြတ်လျက် phat-lyat *(prep.)* **across**

ဖြတ်သည် phat-the *(v.)* **intersect**

ဖြတ်သည်၊ ကျော်သည် hpyat sai , kyawsai *(v.)* **traverse**

ဖြတ်သန်းခ၊ ဖုန်းပြောခ hpyatsaann hka , hpone pyawwhka *(n.)* **toll**

ဖြတ်သန်းသွားလာရန် မဖြစ်နိုင်သော phat-tan-twar-lar-yan-ma-phit-nai-taw *(adj.)* **impassable**

ဖြန့်ကားနိုင်သော အတိုင်းအတာ hpya ant karrninesaw aatineaatar *(n.)* **spread**

ဖြန့်ဖြူးရောင်းချခြင်း phyant-phyu-yaung-cha-chin *(n.)* **distribution**

ဖြန့်ဖြူးရောင်းချသည် phyant-phyu-yaung-cha-the *(v.)* **distribute**

ဖြန့်သည် hpyant-sai *(v.)* **unfold**

ဖြန့်သည်၊ မျိုးပွားသည် hpya ant sai , myoe pwarr-sai *(v.)* **propagate**

ဖြားယောင်းမှု hpyarryaunggmhu *(n.)* **temptation**

ဖြားယောင်းသွေးဆောင်မှု hpyarryaungg swaysaungmhu *(n.)* **seduction**

ဖြားယောင်းသွေးဆောင်သူ hpyarryaungg swaysaungsuu *(n.)* **tempter**

ဖြာထွက်သည် hpyaar htwat-sai *(v.)* **radiate**

ဖြိုချခြင်း phyo-cha-chin *(n.)* **demolition**

ဖြိုချသည် phyo-cha-the *(v.)* **demolish**

ဖြိုခွင်းသည် phyo-kwin-the *(n.)* **crackdown**

ဖြိုဖျက်သည် hpyo-hpyet-sai *(v.)* **subvert**

ဖြီးသည်၊ ဖြန်းသည် phee-the, phyan-the *(v.)* **bluff**

ဖြုတ်ချခြင်း hpyoke-cha-chinn *(n.)* **overthrow**

ဖြုတ်ချသည် hpyoket-cha-tai *(v.)* **overthrow**

ဖြုတ်သည် hpyote-sai *(adj.)* **uninstall**

ဖြုန်းတီးခြင်း hpyuann tee-chinn *(n.)* **profligacy**

ဖြုန်းတီးမှု hpyone-tee-mu *(n.)* **extravagance**

ဖြုန်းတီးသည် hpyone tee-sai *(v.)* **squander**

ဖြုန်းတီးသော hpyone tee-saw *(adj.)* **profligate**

ဖြူးစရာ phyue-sa-yar *(n.)* **garnish**

ဖြူးသည် phyue-the *(v.)* **garnish**

ဖြူတူတူ hpyauutuutuu *(adj.)* **whitish**

ဖြူဖပ်ဖြူရော် phyu-phat-phyu-yaw *(adj.)* **ashen**

ဖြူဖပ်ဖြူရော်နှင့် ပိန်သော phyu-phat-phyu-yar-nint-pai-taw *(adj.)* **cadaverous**

ဖြူဖပ်ဖြူရော်ဖြစ်ခြင်း hpyu-hpaut-hpyu-raw-hpyit-chinn *(n.)* **paleness**

ဖြူရော်သော hpyu-raw-saw *(adj.)* **pale**

ဖြူလာသည် hpyuularsai *(v.)* **whiten**

ဖြူသော hpyuusaw *(adj.)* **white**

ဖြေကြားချက် hpyaykyarrchet *(n.)* **response**

ဖြေကြားသူ hpyay kyarrsuu *(n.)* **respondent**

ဖြေစက် phyay-set *(n.)* **answering machine**

ဖြေဆိုသူ phyay-soe-thu *(n.)* **examinee**

ဖြေဆေး phyay-say *(n.)* **antidote**

ဖြေနိုင်သော phyay-naing-taw *(adj.)* **answerable**

မြေဖြူဖြင့် ရေးသည် myay-phyu-phyint-yay-the *(v.)* **chalk**

ဖြေသိမ့်ပေးသည် Hpay-theint-pay-the *(v.)* **allay**

ဖြောင့်တန်းသော hpyaunt taannsaw *(adj.)* **straight**

ဖြောင့်ချက်ပေးခြင်း pyaunt-chat-pay-chin *(n.)* **confession**

ဖြောင့်ချက်ပေးသည် pyaunt-chat-pay-the *(v.)* **confess**

ဖြောင့်ဖြောင့်တန်းတန်း hpyaunt hpyunt taanntaann *(adv.)* **straight**

ဖြောင့်မတ်သော hpyaunt maatsaw *(adj.)* **straightforward**

ဖြောင့်သည် hpyauntsai *(v.)* **straighten**

ဖလံ pah-lan *(n.)* **moth**

ဖလန်နယ်စ pha-lan-nal-sa *(n.)* **flannel**

ဖလှယ်ခြင်း pha-lal-chin *(n.)* **interchange**

ဖလားဆု hpalarrsu *(n.)* **trophy**

ဖဝါး hpa-warr *(n.)* **paw**

ဖွံ့ဖြိုးစ phwint-phyo-sa *(adj.)* **nascent**

ဖွံ့ဖြိုးမှုနည်းခြင်း hpwan-hpyoemhu neechinn *(n.)* **retardation**

ဖွံ့ဖြိုးရေး phwint-phoe-yay *(n.)* **development**

ဖွံ့ဖြိုးသည် phwint-phoe-the *(v.)* **develop**

ဖွခြင်း hpwa-chinn *(n.)* **rummage**

ဖွင့်သည် hpwint-tai *(v.)* **open**

ဖွင့်သော hpwint-taw *(adj.)* **open**

ဖွင့်ဟခြင်း lonelonelyarrlyarr *(n.)* **utterance**

ဖွင့်ဟပြောဆိုသည် phwint-ha-pyaw-soe-the *(v.)* **disclose**

ဖွင့်ဟသည် hpwint ha-sai *(v.)* **profess**

ဖွင့်သည် phwint-the *(v.)* **dup**

ဖွတ်မြီးကြိုး phut-myee-kyo *(n.)* **braid**

ဖွဖွပုတ်ခြင်း hpwa-hpwa-pote-chinn *(n.)* **pat**

ဖွယ်ရှိသော hpwalshisaw *(adj.)* **subject**

ဖွသည် hpwsai *(v.)* **ruffle**

ဖွဲ့စည်းခြင်း phwe-see-chin *(n.)* **formation**

ဖွဲ့စည်းတည်ဆောက်ပုံနှင့်ဆိုင်သော hpwal-see taisout pone nintsinesaw *(adj.)* **structural**

ဖွဲ့စည်းပုံ၊ အဆောက်အအုံ hpwal-see-pone , aa-sout-aa-ohn *(n.)* **structure**

ဖွဲ့စည်းပုံဇယား hpwalsaeeponezayarr *(n.)* **schematic**

ဖွဲ့စည်းပုံဇယားကျကျ hpwalhcaeepone jayarrkyakya *(adv.)* **schematically**

ဖွဲ့စည်းပုံအခြေခံဥပဒေ phwe-see-pon-a-chay-khan-au-pa-day *(n.)* **constitution**

ဖွဲ့စပ်ပုံ၊ အနေအထား hpwal sat pone , aanayaahtarr *(n.)* **texture**

ဖွဲနု phwe-nu *(n.)* **bran**

ဖား phar *(n.)* **frog**

ဖား၊ မှို hpar, hmoe *(n.)* **mildew**

ဖားပြုပ် hparr pyote *(n.)* **toad**

ဖားဖို phar-pho *(n.)* **bellows**

ဖားမြည်သံကဲ့သို့ အသံ phar-myi-tan-kae-tho-a-tan *(n.)* **croak**

ဖာထေးသည် hpar-htayy-sai *(v.)* **patch**

ဖာရင်ဟိုက် phar-yin-hike *(adj.)* **Fahrenheit**

ဖာလာစေ့ pha-lar-say *(n.)* **cardamom**

ဖာလုံ phar-lon *(n.)* **furlong**

ဖိခြေသည် hpi chaysai *(v.)* **squash**

ဖိစက် phi-sat *(n.)* **compressor**

ဖိစီးနှိပ်စက်မှု hpi-see-nate-saat-mhu *(n.)* **persecution**

ဖိစီးနှိပ်စက်လျက် ရှိသည် hpi see nhate-saatlyet shisai *(v.)* **rack**

ဖိစီးမှု hpi see-mhu *(n.)* **stress**

ဖိစီးမှု လျော့ချသည် phi-see-mu-shawt-cha-the *(v.)* **destress**

ဖိစီးသည် hpi see-sai *(v.)* **preoccupy**

ဖိစီးသော phi-see-taw *(adj.)* **burdensome**

ဖိတ်ကြားခြင်း phate-kyar-chin *(n.)* **invitation**

ဖိတ်ကြားသည် phate-kyar-the *(v.)* **invite**

ဖိတ်ဖိတ်တောက်သည် phate-phate-taut-the *(v.)* **glitter**

ဖိတ်သည် hpate-sai *(v.)* **spill**

ဖိနပ် pha-nat- *(n.)* **footwear**

ဖိနပ်ချုပ်သမား phi-nat-choke-ta-mar *(n.)* **cobbler**

ဖိနပ်ခုံလဲတပ်သည် hpinaut hkone lell tautsai *(v.)* **sole**
ဖိနှိပ်ချုပ်ချယ်ခြင်း hpinate chotechaalchinn *(n.)* **subjugation**
ဖိနှိပ်ခြင်း hpi-nate-chinn *(n.)* **oppression**
ဖိနှိပ်မှု hpi-natemhu *(n.)* **repression**
ဖိနှိပ်သည် hpi-nate-tai *(v.)* **oppress**
ဖိနှိပ်သူ hpi-nate-tuu *(n.)* **oppressor**
ဖိနှိပ်သော hpi-nate-taw *(adj.)* **oppressive**
ဖိနှိပ်သည် hpi nate-sai *(v.)* **press**
ဖိရွတ်ခြင်း၊ အလေးပေးခြင်း phi-yut-chin, a-lay-pay-chin *(n.)* **emphasis**
ဖိရာ phi-yar *(n.)* **imprint**
ဖိရာ ထင်ကျန်သည် phi-yar-htin-kyan-the *(v.)* **imprint**
ဖိသည် phi-the *(v.)* **compress**
ဖိသည်၊ ထုသည်၊ ခြေသည် hpi-the, htu-the, chay-the *(v.)* **crush**
ဖိအား၊ လေထုဖိအား hpi-aarr , lay-htu-hpi-aarr *(n.)* **pressure**
ဖိအားတဖြည်းဖြည်း လျှော့ပေးခြင်း phi-arr-ta-phyae-phyae-shawt-pay-chin *(n.)* **decompression**
ဖိအားတဖြည်းဖြည်း လျှော့ပေးသည် phi-arr-ta-phyae-phyae-shawt-pay-the *(v.)* **decompress**
ဖိအားတူမျဉ်း phi-arr-tu-myin *(n.)* **isobar**
ဖိအားပေးသည် hpi-aarr-payy-sai *(v.)* **pressurize**
ဖိအားပေးအမှတ် phi-arr-pay-a-mat *(n.)* **acupressure**
ဖို hpo *(n.)* **oven**
ဖိုကြီး pho-gyi *(n.)* **kiln**
ဖိုက်ဘရွိုက် phite-ba-roid *(adj.)* **fibroid**
ဖိုင်၊ ဖိုင်တွဲ၊ စာတွဲ fai, fai-twe, sar-twe *(n.)* **file**
ဖိုင်ကွဲခြင်းကို လျှော့ချခြင်း phai-kwal-chin-ko-shawt-cha-chin *(n.)* **defragmentation**
ဖိုင်ကွဲခြင်းကို လျှော့ချသည် phai-kwal-chin-ko-shawt-cha-the *(v.)* **defragment**
ဖိုင်ဘာ၊ အမျှင် phi-bar, a-myin *(n.)* **fibre**
ဖိုရမ်၊ ဆွေးနွေးပွဲ pho-ran, swe-nwe-pwe *(n.)* **forum**
ဖုံးကွယ်ထားသော hpone-kwahltarrsaw *(adj.)* **ulterior**
ဖုံးကွယ်သည် hpone-kwal-the *(v.)* **conceal**
ဖုံးကွယ်သော hpone-kwal-taw *(adj.)* **encrypted**
ဖုံးထားသည် hpone-htar-the *(v.)* **encase**
ဖုံးထားသော hpone-htar-taw *(adj.)* **encrusted**
ဖုံးလွှမ်းသည် hpone lwhamsai *(v.)* **wreathe**
ဖုံးသည် hpone-the *(v.)* **cap**
ဖုံးအုပ်သည် hpone aote-sai *(v.)* **veil**
ဖုံကွပ်သေတ္တာ hpone-kwut-tayt-tar *(n.)* **ottoman**
ဖုတ်ကောင် phoke-kaung *(n.)* **ghoul**
ဖုတ်ကောင်ဆန်သော phoke-kaung-san-taw *(adj.)* **ghoulish**
ဖုတ်ခနဲ ကျသည် hpoke-kha-nae-kya-the *(v.)* **flop**
ဖုတ်ပူမီးတိုက်အချိန် phoke-pu-mee-tite-a-chein *(n.)* **bout**
ဖုတ်သည် hpoke-the *(v.)* **bake**
ဖုန် hpone *(n.)* **dust**
ဖုန်း hpone *(n.)* **phone**
ဖုန်းခေါ်စင်တာ phone-khaw-cen-tar *(n.)* **call centre**
ဖုန်းပြောသည် hponepyawwsai *(v.)* **telephone**
ဖုန်းရွှေ hpone-shway *(n.)* **fengshui**

ဖုန်ခါသည် hpone-khar-the *(v.)* **dust**

ဖုန်စုပ်စက်ဖြင့် စုပ်သည် lay lwint saw *(v.)* **vacuum**

ဖုန်သုတ်အဝတ် hpone-tote-a-wit *(n.)* **duster**

ဖူးစကက် phoo-sa-khat *(n.)* **foolscap**

ဖူးစာရေးနတ် phoo-sar-yay-nat *(n.)* **cupid**

ဖူးသစ်စ phoo-tit-sa *(adj.)* **budding**

ဖေဖော်ဝါရီလ hpay-pha-war-yee-la *(n.)* **February**

ဖော့ phort *(n.)* **cork**

ဖော့စဖရပ်ဓာတ် hpot-sa-hpa-rat-dhrat *(n.)* **phosphorus**

ဖော့စဖိတ်ဓာတ် hpot-sa-hpate-dhrat *(n.)* **phosphate**

ဖောက်ခနဲမြည်သံ hpout hka nell myi-san *(n.)* **pop**

ဖောက်ခနဲမြည်သည် hpout hka nell myi-sai *(v.)* **pop**

ဖောက်ထွင်းမြင်နိုင်သော ta-sint phoetpayychinn *(adj.)* **transparent**

ဖောက်ထွင်းမှု phaut-htwin-mu *(n.)* **burglary**

ဖောက်ထွင်းသူခိုး hpaut-htwin-tha-khoe *(n.)* **burglar**

ဖောက်ထားသော၊ ကုန်ခန်းသွားသော hpout htarrsaw , kone hkaannswarrsaw *(adj.)* **shot**

ဖောက်ပြန်ခြင်း၊ မူမမှန်ခြင်း phaut-pyan-chin, mu-ma-man-chin *(n.)* **aberration**

ဖောက်ပြန်ရေး ဝါဒီ hpaut-pyan-yay-war-de *(adj.)* **reactionary**

ဖောက်ပြန်သော hpauk-pyan-taw *(adj.)* **extramarital**

ဖောက်မြင်နိုင်သော၊ မတ်စောက်သော hpout myinnine saw , maat soutsaw *(adj.)* **sheer**

ဖောက်သည် hpout-sai *(v.)* **pierce**

ဖောက်သည်၊ ခွဲသည် hpaut-the, khwal-the *(v.)* **lance**

ဖောက်သည်၊ ထုတ်သည် hpoutsai , htotesai *(v.)* **tap**

ဖောင်းကားနေသည့် အရာ၊ အဖု၊ အဖောင်း hpaung-kar-nay-the-a-yar-a-phu-a-hpaung *(n.)* **bulge**

ဖောင်၊ ပုံစံ phaung, pon-san *(n.)* **form**

ဖောင်တော် hpaung-taw *(n.)* **barge**

ဖောင်ဒေးရှင်း၊ တည်ထောင်ခြင်း၊ အုတ်မြစ် phaung-day-shin, the-htaung-chin, oak-myit *(n.)* **foundation**

ဖောဖောသီသီ သုံးစွဲသော phaw-phaw-ti-ti-tone-swal-taw *(adj.)* **lavish**

ဖော်ကောင် hpawkaung *(n.)* **telltale**

ဖော်ဆောင်သည် phaw-saung-the *(v.)* **incarnate**

ဖော်ညွှန်းမှု hpaw nywhaannmhu *(n.)* **signification**

ဖော်ထုတ်တင်ပြသည် hpaw-htote-tin-pya-sai *(v.)* **propound**

ဖော်ထုတ်သည် phaw-htoke-the *(v.)* **formulate**

ဖော်ထုတ်သည်၊ ရွေးထုတ်သည်၊ ခွဲခြားနိုင်သည် phaw-htoke-the, yway-htoke-the, kwal-char-nai-the *(v.)* **identify**

ဖော်ပြချက် phaw-pya-chat *(n.)* **description**

ဖော်ပြခြင်း phaw-pya-chin *(n.)* **inscription**

ဖော်ပြနိုင်သော phaw-pya-naing-taw *(adj.)* **effable**

ဖော်ပြနိုင်သော နည်းလမ်းဖြင့် phaw-pya-naing-taw-nee-lan-phit *(adv.)* **effably**

ဖော်ပြသည် phaw-pya-the *(v.)* **describe**

ဖော်ပြသော phaw-pya-taw *(adj.)* **descriptive**

ဖော်မြူလာ phaw-myu-lar *(n.)* **formula**

ဖော်ယူခြင်း၊ ဆယ်တင်ခြင်း hpaw yuu-chinn , saal-tin-chinn *(n.)* **reclamation**

ဖော်ရွေစွာ ဆက်ဆံခြင်း၊ သုတေသန ထောက်ပံ့ကြေး hpaw-yway-swar-sat-san-chin, thu-tay-ta-na-htauk-pant-kyay *(n.)* **fellowship**

ဖော်ရွေနိုင်စွမ်း hpaw-yway-naing-swan *(n.)* **amiability**

ဖော်ရွေသော hpaw rwaysaw *(adj.)* **sociable**

ဖော်လံဖားသည် phaw-lan-phar-the *(v.)* **beslaver**

ဖဲ hpell *(n.)* **playcard**

ဖဲ့ထုတ်သည် phae-htoke-the *(v.)* **dislodge**

ဖဲ့သည်၊ ပဲ့သည် phae-the, pae-the *(v.)* **crumble**

ဖဲတံဆိပ် phal-ta-seik *(n.)* **cockade**

ဖဲပြား hpellpyarr *(n.)* **ribbon**

ဖဲဝေသည် phal-wai-the *(v.)* **deal**

ဗက်ဆလင် kyaal-pyawwsaw *(n.)* **vaseline**

ဗက်တာ၊ ညွှန်ရပ်၊ ရောဂါသယ်ဆောင်သော တိရစ္ဆာန် *(n.)* **vector**

ဗက်တာနှင့်ဆိုင်သော vat-tar-nint-sine-taw *(adj.)* **vectorial**

ဗက်တာသို့ဦးတည်ရာပြောင်းပေးသည် vat-tar-tho-u-the-yar-pyaung-pay-the *(v.)* **vector**

ဗက်တီးရီးယားပိုး bat-tee-yee-yar-poe *(n.)* **bacteria**

ဗက်တီးရီးယားပိုးဖြင့် ဆွေးမြည့်နိုင်ခြင်း bat-te-ri-yar-poe-phit-sway-myae-naing-chin *(n.)* **biodegradation**

ဗန်းစကား baannsakarr *(n.)* **slang**

ဗန်းထဲ ထည့်သည် ban-htae-htae-the *(v.)* **tray**

ဗန်းပြထားသည့် ထွင်လုံး ban-pya-htar-the-htwin-lone *(n.)* **gimmick**

ဗန်ကား laat saram hpyet-seesai *(n.)* **van**

ဗျစ်ဖြင့် လုပ်သော ရှာလကာရည် byit-phit-lote-taw-sha-la-kar-yay *(n.)* **alegar**

ဗျည်းသံ pyi-tan *(n.)* **consonant**

ဗျပ်စောင်းတူရိယာ byat-saung-tu-ri-yar *(n.)* **lute**

ဗျာများနေသော byaw-myar-nay-taw *(adj.)* **frantic**

ဗျူရိုကရက်အရာရှိ byu-ro-ka-yat-a-yar-shi *(n.)* **bureaucrat**

ဗျူရိုကရေစီစနစ် byu-ro-ka-yay-si-sa-nit *(n.)* **bureacuracy**

ဗရုပ္ပ ba-ra-pwa *(n.)* **jumble**

ဗရုတ် barote *(adj.)* **rowdy**

ဗရုတ်သုတ်ခ ဟာသဖြစ်ရပ် Ba-rote-sote-hka-har-sa-hpyit-rat *(n.)* **pantomime**

ဗြဟ္မစရိယကျင့်ခြင်း bwa-ma-sa-yi-yar-kyint-chin *(n.)* **celibacy**

ဗြိတိသျှ byi-ti-sha *(adj.)* **british**

ဗြုတ်စဗျင်းတောင်း byoke-sa-byin-taung *(n.)* **junk**

ဗြုပ်စဗျင်းတောင်းဖယ်ရှားသည် byoke-sa-byin-taung-phal-shar-the *(v.)* **declutter**

ဗြောင်းဆန်ခြင်း byaung-san-chin *(n.)* **havoc**

ဗြောင်၊ ပေါ်ပေါ်ထင်ထင် byaung, paw-paw-htin-htin *(adj.)* **plain**

ဗြောင်ကျသော byaung-kya-taw *(adj.)* **overt**

ဗလက္ကာရ ba-lat-kar-ya *(n.)* **molestation**

ဗလာ ba-lar *(adj.)* **empty**

ဗလာကျင်းခြင်း balar kyinn-chinn *(n.)* **strip**

ဗလီ ba-li *(n.)* **mosque**

ဗလီမျှော်စင် ba-li-myaw-sin *(n.)* **minaret**

ဗလုံးဗထွေး မပီမသ ပြောဆိုသည် ba-lone-ba-htway-ma-pi-ma-ta-pyaw-so-the *(v.)* **bumble**

ဗလုံးဗထွေးစကားသံ Ba-lone-ba-htway-sa-kar-tan *(n.)* **babble**

ဗလုံးဗထွေးပြောခြင်း ba-lone-ba-htway-pyaw-chin *(n.)* **gibber**

ဗလုံးဗထွေးပြောသည် ba-lon-ba-htway-pyaw-the *(v.)* **jabber**

ဗလုံးဗထွေးပြောသော ba-lone-ba-htway-pyaw-thaw *(adj.)* **incoherent**

ဗွက်ပေါက်သော bwat-pauk-taw *(adj.)* **marshy**

ဗွက်အိုင် bwat-ai *(n.)* **podge**

ဗွက်အိုင်ဖြစ်လာသည် bwat-ine phit-lar-the *(v.)* **puddle**

ဗွတ်ကုလား bwat-ka-lar *(n.)* **jay**

ဗွမ်းခနဲ bwam-hka-nell *(adv.)* **overboard**

ဗွမ်းခနဲ မြည်သံ bwam hka-nell myisan *(n.)* **splash**

ဗဟို၊ အချက်အချာ၊ ဆုံချက် ba-ho, a-chat-a-char, sone-chat *(n.)* **focus**

ဗဟိုက ချုပ်ကိုင်သည် ba-ho-ga-choke-kai-the *(v.)* **centralize**

ဗဟိုချက်ပျောက်သည် ba-ho-chat-pyauk-the *(v.)* **decentre**

ဗဟိုချက်များစွာရှိသော နိုင်ငံရေး၊ ယဉ်ကျေးမှုစနစ် baho hkyet myarrswarshisaw ninenganrayy , yinkyaayy-mhu-sanit *(n.)* **polycentrism**

ဗဟိုတူသော ba-ho-tu-taw *(adj.)* **concentric**

ဗဟိုများစွာ ရှိသော bahomyarrswar shisaw *(adj.)* **polycentric**

ဗဟိုမှ ခွာသော ba-ho-ma-khwar-taw *(adj.)* **centrifugal**

ဗဟိုသော့စနစ် ba-ho-taw-sa-nit *(n.)* **central locking**

ဗဟုနာထဝါဒ bahu nar hta-war-da *(n.)* **polytheism**

ဗဟုနာထဝါဒီ bahu nar hta-war-de *(n.)* **polytheist**

ဗဟုဝါဒကိုးကွယ်သော bahu warda-koekwalsaw *(adj.)* **paganistic**

ဗဟုဝုစ် ba-hu-wit *(adj.)* **plural**

ဗဟုသုတနှံ့စပ်သူ bahusut nhaan sautsuu *(n.)* **polymath**

ဗဟုသုတပေးသော ba-hu-tu-ta-pay-taw *(adj.)* **informative**

ဗဟုသုတရှိသော ba-hu-thu-ta-shi-taw *(adj.)* **conversant**

ဗားရှင်း barrhlyinn *(n.)* **version**

ဗာဟီရဝါဒ bar-he-ra-war-da *(n.)* **paganism**

ဗာဟီရဝါဒီတို့၏ bar-he-ra-war-de-thoet-eat *(adj.)* **pagan**

ဗိမာန် baik-man *(n.)* **edifice**

ဗိသုကာ bi-thu-kar *(n.)* **architect**

ဗိသုကာပညာ bi-thu-kar-pyin-nyar *(n.)* **architecture**

ဗို့ bhoet *(n.)* **volt**

ဗို့အား bhoetaarr *(n.)* **voltage**

ဗိုက်စထွက်လာခြင်း bite-sa-htwat-lar-chin *(n.)* **baby bump**

ဗိုက်သား bite-tar *(n.)* **belly**

ဗိုင်းကောင်းကျောက်ဖိ bai-kaung-kyauk-phi *(n.)* **decorum**

ဗိုင်းရပ်စ် binerat *(n.)* **virus**

ဗိုင်းရပ်စ်နှင့်ဆိုင်သော bineratit nintsinesaw *(adj.)* **viral**

ဗိုင်းလိပ်တံ bine late-tan *(n.)* **spindle**

ဗိုလ်ကြီး bo-gyi *(n.)* **lieutenant**

ဗိုလ်ထိုင် bo-htai *(n.)* **commode**

ဗိုလ်မှူးကြီး bo-mu-gyi *(n.)* **colonel**

ဗိုလ်မှူးချုပ် bo-hmu-gyoke *(n.)* **brigadier**

ဗိုလ်လောင်း bo-laung *(n.)* **cadet**

ဗီဇ bi-za *(n.)* **instinct**

ဗီတာမင်အားဆေး betarmain aarrsayy *(n.)* **vitamin**

ဗီတိုအာဏာ betoaarnar *(n.)* **veto**

ဗီတိုအာဏာသုံး၍ ပယ်ချသည် betoaarnarsone paalchasai *(v.)* **veto**

ဗီဒီယို bedeyo *(n.)* **video**

ဗီဒီယိုကက်ဆက် bedeyo kaatsaat *(n.)* **videocassette**

ဗီဒီယိုဂိမ်း bedeyogaim *(n.)* **videogaming**

ဗီဒီယိုစာအုပ် bedeyosaraote *(n.)* **videobook**

ဗီဒီယိုတိတ်ခွေ bedeyotatehkway *(n.)* **videotape**

ဗီဒီယိုဖုန်းခေါ်ခြင်း bedeyo hponehkawchin *(n.)* **videotelephone**

ဗီဒီယိုဘလော့ဂါ bedeyobhalotkar *(n.)* **videoblogger**

ဗီဒီယိုရိုက်သည် bedeyo ritesai *(v.)* **video**

ဗီရို bero *(n.)* **sideboard**

ဗီရို၊ စင် be-ro, sin *(n.)* **pantry**

ဗီရို၊ စတိုခန်းငယ် bi-yo, sa-to-khan-nge *(n.)* **closet**

ဗီလိန် belein *(n.)* **villain**

ဗုံး bone *(n.)* **bomb**

ဗုံးကြဲတိုက်ခိုက်သည် bone-kywal-tite-khaik-the *(v.)* **bombard**

ဗုံးကြဲလေယာဉ် bone-kywal-lay-yin *(n.)* **bomber**

ဗုံးဆန် bonesan *(n.)* **shrapnel**

ဗုဒ္ဓဟူး buddhahuu *(n.)* **Wednesday**

ဗုန်းခနဲ ရိုက်သည် bone hkanell ritesai *(v.)* **whack**

ဗေရီယမ်ဒြပ်စင် bay-yee-yan-drat-sin *(n.)* **barium**

ဗောက် bauk *(n.)* **dandruff**

ဘက်စုံတော်ခြင်း bat-sone-taw-chin *(n.)* **omnicompetence**

ဘက်စုံတော်သော bat-sone-taw-taw *(adj.)* **omnicompetent**

ဘက်တံဖြင့် ရိုက်ရသည့် အလှည့် bat-tan-phit-yite-ya-the-a-hlae *(n.)* **innings**

ဘက်တီးယီးယားပိုးသတ်သော bat-tee-yee-yar-poe-tat-taw *(adj.)* **antibacterial**

ဘက်တီးယီးရားကို တွယ်ကပ်သော ဗိုင်းရပ်စ်ဆိုင်ရာ bhaat tee yee rarrko twel katsaw bine-rat sinerar *(adj.)* **phagic**

ဘက်ထရီ bat-hta-yee *(n.)* **battery**

ဘက်ပေါင်းစုံဦးတည်ခြင်း bat-paung-sone-u-te-chin *(n.)* **omnidirectionality**

ဘက်ပေါင်းစုံဦးတည်သော bat-paung-sone-u-te-taw *(adj.)* **omnidirectional**

ဘက်မလိုက် bat-ma-lite *(adj.)* **neutral**

ဘက်မလိုက်ခြင်း bat-ma-lite-chin *(n.)* **impartiality**

ဘက်မလိုက်ရေးဝါဒ bhat-ma-lite-ray-war-da *(n.)* **non-alignment**

ဘက်မလိုက်သော bat-ma-lite-taw *(adj.)* **impartial**

ဘက်လိုက်ခြင်း bat-lite-chin *(n.)* **bias**

ဘက်လိုက်မှု bhaat-lite-mhu *(n.)* **partiality**

ဘက်လိုက်သော bat-lite-taw *(adj.)* **biased**

ဘင်ဂျို bin-gyo *(n.)* **banjo**

ဘင်ဂိုလောင်းကစား bin-go-laung-ka-sar *(n.)* **bingo**

ဘင်္ဂလားဆီးသီး bin-ga-lar-zee-thee *(n.)* **apricot**

ဘစ်ကွိုင်ဒစ်ဂျစ်တယ်ငွေစနစ် bit-coi-dit-git-tal-ngwe-sa-nit *(n.)* **bitcoin**

ဘဇူကာဒုံးလောင်ချာ ba-zu-kar-don-laung-char *(n.)* **bazooka**

ဘဏ္ဍာစိုး ban-nar-soe *(n.)* **butler**

ဘဏ္ဍာတိုက် bhandartite *(n.)* **treasury**

ဘဏ္ဍာရေး ban-nar-yay *(n.)* **finance**

ဘဏ္ဍာရေးမှူး bhandarrayymhauu *(n.)* **treasurer**

ဘဏ္ဍာသေတ္တာ ban-dar-tit-tar *(n.)* **coffer**

ဘဏ် bhan *(n.)* **repository**

ဘဏ်ပိတ်ရက် ban-pait-yat *(n.)* **bank holiday**

ဘဏ်လုပ်ငန်းရှင် ban-lote-ngan-shin *(n.)* **banker**

ဘတ်ကတ်နှင့် သက်ဆိုင်သော bat-kat-nint-tat-sai-taw *(adj.)* **bacchanal**

ဘတ်စကက်ဘော bat-sa-kat-baw *(n.)* **basketball**

ဘတ်စကား bat-sa-kar *(n.)* **bus**

ဘတ်စကားမှတ်တိုင် bat-sa-kar-mat-tai *(n.)* **bus stop**

ဘတ်တံ bat-tan *(n.)* **bat**

ဘန်းမုန့် banp-hmont *(n.)* **bun**

ဘန်ဂလို ban-ga-lo *(n.)* **bungalow**

ဘန်ဂီခုန်ခြင်း ban-gee-khone-chin *(n.)* **bungee jumping**

ဘန်ဇင်းဓာတ်ဆေးရည် ban-zin-dat-say-yae *(n.)* **benzene**

ဘယ် bhaal *(adj.)* **which**

ဘယ်ဆီသို့ bhaalsethoet *(adv.)* **whither**

ဘယ်တော့မှ bal-taw-ma *(adv.)* **never**

ဘယ်နား bhaalnarr *(adv.)* **whereabout**

ဘယ်နေရာမဆို bhaalnayrarmaso *(adv.)* **wherever**

ဘယ်မှာ bhaal-mhar *(adv.)* **where**

ဘယ်မှာမှ bal-mar-mha *(adv.)* **nowhere**

ဘယ်လို bal-lo *(adv.)* **how**

ဘယ်သူ bhaalsuu *(pron.)* **who**

ဘယ်သူမျှ၊ တစ်ခုမျှ bal-thu-mya, ta-khu-mya *(conj.)* **neither**

ဘယ်ဟာ bhaahlar *(pron.)* **which**

ဘယ်အချိန်မဆို bhal-aa-chane maso *(conj.)* **whenever**

ဘယ်အခါမှမျှား bhaalaahkarmhamyarr *(adv.)* **whenever**

ဘယ်အရာ bhaalaarar *(pron.)* **what**

ဘရင်ဂျီဘာသာ ba-yin-gyi-bar-tar *(n.)* **catholicism**

ဘရင်ဂျီဘုရားစာအုပ် ba-yin-gyi-pha-yar-sar-oak *(n.)* **breviary**

ဘရင်ဂျီဝါဝင်ပွဲ ba-yin-gyi-wa-win-pwe *(n.)* **carnival**

ဘရန်ဒီလောင်း၍ မီးရှို့လောင်မြိုက်စေပြီးမှ စားရသော ba-yan-di-laung-ywe-mee-sho-laung-hmyike-pay-pyi-ma-sar-ya-taw *(adj.)* **flambé**

ဘရန်ဒီလောင်း၍ မီးရှို့လောင်မြိုက်စေပြီးမှ စားရသော စားဖွယ် ba-yan-di-laung-ywe-

mee-sho-laung-hmyike-pay-pyi-ma-sar-ya-taw-sar-phwal *(n.)* **flambé**
ဘရန်ဒီလောင်း၍ မီးရှို့လောင်မြိုက်စေပြီးမှ စားရသော စားဖွယ်ကို စားသည် ba-yan-di-laung-ywe-mee-sho-laung-hmyike-pay-pyi-ma-sar-ya-taw-sar-phwal-ko-sar-the *(v.)* **flambé**
ဘရန်ဒီအရက် ba-yan-di-a-yat *(n.)* **brandy**
ဘရိတ် ba-rake *(n.)* **brake**
ဘရိတ်အုပ်သည် ba-rake-oak-the *(v.)* **brake**
ဘရိုကိတ်စ ba-ro-kaik-sa *(n.)* **brocade**
ဘရိုမိုက်ဒြပ်ပေါင်း ba-ro-mite-drat-paung *(n.)* **bromide**
ဘရောက်ဇာ ba-yaut-zar *(n.)* **browser**
ဘလိတ်ဓား ba-lade-dar *(n.)* **blade**
ဘလူးတု ba-lu-tut *(n.)* **bluetooth**
ဘလေဇာကုတ် ba-lay-zar-cote *(n.)* **blazer**
ဘလော့ ba-lot *(n.)* **blog**
ဘလော့ဂါ ba-lot-gar *(n.)* **blogger**
ဘလော့ရေးခြင်း ba-lot-yay-chin *(v.)* **blogging**
ဘလောက်အင်္ကျီ ba-laut-inn-gyi *(n.)* **blouse**
ဘဝ ba-wa *(n.)* **life**
ဘဝင်ကိုင်ခြင်း bha win kinechinn *(n.)* **snobbery**
ဘဝင်ခိုက်နေသော ba-win-khaik-nay-taw *(adj.)* **elate**
ဘဝင်ခိုက်သည် ba-win-khaik-the *(v.)* **elate**
ဘဝင်စိတ်ကျခြင်း bhawin-sate-kyachinn *(n.)* **trance**
ဘဝင်မြင့်ခြင်း ba-win-myint-chin *(n.)* **conceit**
ဘဝင်မြင့်သူ ba-win-myint-thu *(n.)* **bighead**
ဘဝလူနေမှုပုံစံ ba-wa-lu-nay-mu-pon-san *(n.)* **lifestyle**
ဘွင်းဘွင်း၊ တဲ့တိုး bwin-bwin, tae-doe *(adv.)* **bluntly**
ဘွင်းဘွင်းပျော်ပျော်သမား bwin-bwin-pyaw-pyaw-ta-mar *(n.)* **extrovert**
ဘွင်းဘွင်းရှင်းရှင်း bhwin bhwinhlyinnhlyinn *(adv.)* **outright**
ဘွတ်ဖိနပ် boot-pha-nat *(n.)* **boot**
ဘွတ်ဖိနပ်ရှည် bhwat hpinautshay *(n.)* **wellington**
ဘွတ်အဲဟု အော်သည် boot-ae-hu-aw-the *(v.)* **moo**
ဘွားခနဲပေါ်လာသည် bwar-kha-nae-paw-lar-the *(v.)* **loom**
ဘွိုင်လာအိုး boi-lar-oh *(n.)* **boiler**
ဘွဲ့နှင်းသဘင် bwe-hnin-ta-bin *(n.)* **graduation ceremony**
ဘွဲ့ရသည် bwe-ya-the *(v.)* **graduate**
ဘွဲ့ရသူ bwe-ya-thu *(n.)* **graduate**
ဘွဲ့လွန် bhwal-lwan *(adj.)* **postgraduate**
ဘွဲ့နှင်းသဘင် bwe-hnin-tha-bin *(n.)* **convocation**
ဘာ bhar *(adj.)* **what**
ဘားကုတ် bar-cote *(n.)* **barcode**
ဘားဒေါ့ပင် bar-dot-pin *(n.)* **clive**
ဘာကြောင့် bharkyount *(adv.)* **why**
ဘာဂါ bar-gar *(n.)* **burger**
ဘာပြောတယ် bharpyawwtaal *(interj.)* **what**
ဘာပဲဖြစ်ဖြစ် bharpelhlpyithpyit *(pron.)* **whatever**
ဘာဘွန်းမျောက် bar-boon-myaut *(n.)* **baboon**
ဘာမျှ ထူးပြီး Bhar-mya-htuu-pyee *(adv.)* **none**
ဘာမဟုတ်တာကို ငြင်းခံသည် bar-ma-hote-tar-ko-nyin-khan-the *(v.)* **bicker**

ဘာရာဇီယာ ba-yar-zi-yar *(n.)* **bra**

ဘာသာ bar-tar *(n.)* **creed**

ဘာသာခြားစကား bar-tar-char-sa-gar *(n.)* **lingo**

ဘာသာစကား bar-tar-sa-kar *(n.)* **language**

ဘာသာစကားနှင့် ဆိုင်သော bar-tar-sa-kar-nint-sai-taw *(adj.)* **lingual**

ဘာသာစကားပေါင်းစုံ ပြောသော bar-tar-sa-kar-paung-sone-pyaw-taw *(adj.)* **multilingual**

ဘာသာစကားပေါင်းစုံပြောခြင်း bar-tar-sa-kar-paung-sone-pyaw-chin *(n.)* **omnilingual**

ဘာသာစကားပေါင်းစုံပြောသော bar-tar-sa-kar-paung-sone-pyaw-taw *(adj.)* **omnilingual**

ဘာသာစကားအမျိုးမျိုးပြောနိုင်သော bhar-sar-sa-karr-aa-myoe-myoe-pyaw-nine-saw *(adj.)* **polyglot**

ဘာသာစကားအမျိုးမျိုးပြောနိုင်သောသူ bhar-sar-sa-karr-aa-myoe-myoe-pyaw-nine-saw-suu *(n.)* **polyglot**

ဘာသာတရားကိုင်းရှိုင်းမှု bhar-sar-ta-rarr-kine-shine-mhu *(n.)* **piety**

ဘာသာတရားကိုင်းရှိုင်းသော bhar-sar-ta-rarr-kine-shine-saw *(adj.)* **pious**

ဘာသာပြန် bar-tar-pyan *(n.)* **terp**

ဘာသာပြန်ခြင်း kanshi *(n.)* **translation**

ဘာသာပြန်သည် a kuu aapyaungg *(v.)* **translate**

ဘာသာပြန်သည်၊ အဓိပ္ပါယ်ကောက်သည် bar-tar-pyan-the, a-dait-pal-kauk-the *(v.)* **interpret**

ဘာသာဗေဒ bar-tar-bay-da *(n.)* **linguistics**

ဘာသာဗေဒပညာရှင် bar-tar-bay-da-pyin-nyar-shin *(n.)* **linguist**

ဘာသာရပ်တစ်ခုတွင် လူသိမများလှသည့် နယ်ပယ် bar-tar-yat-ta-khu-twin-lu-thi-ma-myar-hla-the-nal-pal *(n.)* **byway**

ဘာသာရပ်ပေါင်းစုံမှ ပါဝင်သော bar-tar-yat-paung-sone-ma-par-win-taw *(adj.)* **mutidisciplinary**

ဘာသာရေး bhar-sar-rayy *(adj.)* **religious**

ဘာသာရေး ကျွမ်းကျင်သူ bharsarrayy - kyawmkyinsuu *(n.)* **theologian**

ဘာသာရေး၊ ယဥ်ကျေးမှုအရ ခွင့်မပြုထားသည့်အရာ bharsarrayy , yainkyaayymhu aar hkwng m pyuhtarr saeet aarar *(v.)* **taboo**

ဘာသာရေး၊ ရိုးရာထုံးတမ်းဓလေ့ bharsarrayy , roerar htonetamdhalae *(n.)* **rite**

ဘာသာရေးခေါင်းဆောင် bhar-sar-rayy-hkaunggsaung *(n.)* **priestess**

ဘာသာရေးဂိုဏ်း bar-tar-yay-gai *(n.)* **denomination**

ဘာသာရေးနှင့်ဆိုင်သော bharsarrayy nintsinesaw *(adj.)* **theological**

ဘာသာအယူဝါဒ bharsar-aa-yuuwarda *(n.)* **religion**

ဘာသိဘာသာနေတတ်ခြင်း bar-ti-bar-tar-nay-tat-chin *(n.)* **introvert**

ဘိချ်သစ်ပင် bi-thit-pin *(n.)* **beech**

ဘိန်း bhein *(n.)* **opium**

ဘိန်းပါသော bane-par-taw *(adj.)* **opiate**

ဘိန်းပါသော ဆေးဝါး bane-par-taw-say-war *(n.)* **opiate**

ဘိန်းဖြင့်ကုသသည် bane-phit-ku-ta-the *(v.)* **opiate**

ဘိန်းဖြူ bain-phyu *(n.)* **heroine**

ဘိလပ်မြေ bi-lat-myay *(n.)* **cement**

ဘိလိယက် bi-li-yat *(n.)* **billiards**

ဘိလိယက်ခုံ bi-li-yat-khon *(n.)* **billiard table**
ဘိုး၊ ဘေး၊ ဘီ၊ ဘင် bo, bay, bi, bin *(n.)* **forefather**
ဘိုးတော်ဘုရား လက်ထက်က boe-taw-pha-yar-lat-htet-ka *(adj.)* **antiquated**
ဘိုးဘွားပိုင် boe-bwar-paing *(adj.)* **ancestral**
ဘိုးဘအမွေ bhoe-bha-aa-mway *(n.)* **patrimony**
ဘိုးဘေးဘီဘင် boe-bay-bi-bing *(n.)* **ancestor**
ဘိုက် bite *(n.)* **byte**
ဘိုင်ကျသော bai-kya-taw *(adj.)* **broke**
ဘီး bee *(n.)* **comb**
ဘီးချော်ခြင်း bhee chawchinn *(n.)* **skid**
ဘီးချော်သည် bhee chawsai *(v.)* **skid**
ဘီးပေါက်ခြင်း bhee pout-chinn *(n.)* **puncture**
ဘီးရာ အပြိုင်းအရိုင်းမွနေသော bheerar a pyaine aa-rine mwa-nay-saw *(adj.)* **rut**
ဘီးရာချိုင့် bhee rar chaine *(n.)* **rut**
ဘီးလှည့်သည် bhee hlae sai *(v.)* **wheel**
ဘီကီနီ bi-ki-ni *(n.)* **bikini**
ဘီစကစ် bee-sa-kit *(n.)* **biscuit**
ဘီစကွတ် bi-sa-kut *(n.)* **macaroon**
ဘီစကွတ်မွမွ bi-sa-kwut-mwa-mwa *(n.)* **flatbread**
ဘီစကွတ်ရွရွ bhe sa kwat rwa-rwa *(n.)* **shortbread**
ဘီတာ be-ta *(adj.)* **beta**
ဘီယာ bee-yar *(n.)* **beer**
ဘီယာ၊ ဗျစ်။ beer, byit *(n.)* **ale**
ဘီယာချက်စက်ရုံ be-yar-chat-sat-yone *(n.)* **brewery**
ဘီယာချက်စက်ရုံငယ် bee-yar-chat-sat-yone-ngal *(n.)* **microbrewery**
ဘီယာချက်သည် be-yar-chat-the *(v.)* **brew**
ဘီယာဆိုင် bi-yar-sai *(n.)* **brasserie**
ဘီလုံးငှက် bi-lone-nget *(n.)* **lark**
ဘီလူး ba-lu *(n.)* **brute**
ဘီလူးမ ba-lu-ma *(n.)* **giantess**
ဘုံပိုင်ခေါင်း bon-bai-gaung *(n.)* **faucet**
ဘုံဘိုင်ခေါင်း bhone bhinehkaungg *(n.)* **tap**
ဘုံအဖွဲ့ bon-a-phwe *(n.)* **commune**
ဘုဇပတ်ပင် bu-za-pat-pin *(n.)* **birch**
ဘုတ်ခနဲ မြည်သံ bhote hkanell myisan *(n.)* **thud**
ဘုတ်ခနဲကျသည် bhote hk nell kyasai *(v.)* **thud**
ဘုတ်ပြား bhotepyarr *(n.)* **shide**
ဘုန်းကြီး phone-gyi *(n.)* **monk**
ဘုန်းကြီးကျောင်း hpone-gyi-kyaung *(n.)* **monastery**
ဘုန်းတော်ကြီးမြတ်သော bhone-taw-kyi-myat-taw *(adj.)* **almighty**
ဘုရင် ba-yin *(n.)* **king**
ဘုရင့်နိုင်ငံတော် ba-yin-nai-ngan-taw *(n.)* **kingdom**
ဘုရင့်ဘုန်းတန်ခိုး ba-yint-hpone-ta-kho *(n.)* **majesty**
ဘုရင့်အိမ်တော်ဝန် ba-yint-eain-taw-win *(n.)* **chamberlain**
ဘုရင်၊ ဘုရင်မကို သတ်မှု ba-rin , ba-rinmako saatmhu *(n.)* **regicide**
ဘုရင်ခံ ba-yin-khan *(n.)* **governor**
ဘုရင်စနစ်ကို ထောက်ခံသူ bhurinsanitko htouthkansuu *(n.)* **royalist**
ဘုရင်မ ba-rin-ma *(n.)* **queen**

ဘုရား pha-rarr *(n.)* **pagoda**

ဘုရားကျောင်း pha-rarrkyaungg *(n.)* **temple**

ဘုရားကျောင်းတွင် သီးသန့် ဝတ်ပြုရာ နေရာ pha-ya-kyaung-twin-thee-tant-wut-pyu-yar-nay-yar *(n.)* **chapel**

ဘုရားကျောင်းဝန်ကြီးဌာနသို့ ဝင်ခွင့်ပေးသော pha-rar-kyaung-win-gyi-htar-na-tho-win-khwint-pay-taw *(adj.)* **ordained**

ဘုရားကျောင်းအရာရှိ hpa-ya-kyaung-a-yar-shi *(n.)* **beadle**

ဘုရားစင် pha-rar-sin *(n.)* **oratory**

ဘုရားတစ်ဆူတည်း ကိုးကွယ်သော ဝါဒ pha-yar-ta-su-the-ko-kwal-taw-war-da *(n.)* **monotheism**

ဘုရားတစ်ဆူတည်း ကိုးကွယ်သော သူ pha-yar-ta-su-the-ko-kwal-taw-thu *(n.)* **monotheist**

ဘုရားတစ်ပါးတည်းကိုးကွယ်ခြင်း phayar-ta-bar-tae-koe-kwal-chin *(n.)* **monolatry**

ဘုရားတရားကို စော်ကားသည် pha-rarr ta-rarr-ko saw-karrsai *(v.)* **profane**

ဘုရားတရားကို စော်ကားသော pha-rarr ta-rarrko sawkarrsaw *(adj.)* **profane**

ဘုရားတရားကိုင်းရှိုင်းသော pha-yar-ta-yar-kai-shai-taw *(adj.)* **godly**

ဘုရားဖြစ်မည့် အုတ်ခဲ pha-yar-phit-mae-oak-nee-khae *(n.)* **moralist**

ဘုရားဖူး pha-rarr-hpuu *(n.)* **pilgrim**

ဘုရားမခြင်း pha-yar-ma-chin *(n.)* **godsend**

ဘုရားမှ အုပ်ချုပ်ခြင်း pa-yar-ma-oak-choke-chin *(n.)* **theocracy**

ဘုရားမဲ့ဝါဒ phar-yar-mae-wa-da *(n.)* **atheism**

ဘုရားမဲ့ဝါဒီ phar-yar-mae-wa-di *(n.)* **atheist**

ဘုရားရှိခိုးကျောင်းမျှော်စင် pha-rarrshihkoekyaungg-myaw-sin *(n.)* **steeple**

ဘုရားရှိမှုကို သံသရရှိသူ pha-yar-shi-mu-ko-tan-ta-ya-shi-thu *(n.)* **agnostic**

ဘုရားရှိမှုကို သံသရရှိသော ဝါဒ pha-yar-shi-mu-ko-tan-ta-ya-shi-taw-wa-da *(n.)* **agnosticsm**

ဘုရားရေ pha-rar-ray *(n.)* **sake**

ဘုရားသခင် pha-yar-ta-khin *(adj.)* **divine**

ဘုရားသခင်၏ ကောင်းချီးမင်္ဂလာ pha-yar-tha-khin-ei-kaung-chee-min-ga-lar *(n.)* **blessing**

ဘုရားသခင်၏ ဂုဏ်တော်ကျေးဇူး pha-yar-ta-khin-ei-gon-taw-kyay-zu *(n.)* **divinity**

ဘုရားသခင်၏ တမန်တော် pha-rarr-sa-hkin-eat ta-maan-taw *(n.)* **prophet**

ဘုရားသခင်က သတ္တဝါအပေါင်းကို ကြည့်ရှုစောင့်ရှောက်ပုံ pha-rarr-sa-hkin-ka-sat-ta-war-aa-paungg-ko kyi shu saunt shout-pone *(n.)* **providence**

ဘုရားသခင်မှ ကြိုတင်ပြဌာန်းသည့်အတိုင်း ဖြစ်သည်ဟူသော ဝါဒ pha-rarrsahkinmha kyotin pyahtann seet-aa-tine hpyit-sai-huu-saw war-da *(n.)* **predestination**

ဘုရားသခင်ရှိမှုကို ထိန်းသိမ်းသော အယူအဆ pha-rar-ta-khin-shi-mu-ko-htein-tain-taw-a-yu-a-sa *(n.)* **ontologism**

ဘူးသီး bu-thee *(n.)* **gourd**

ဘူတာ၊ ကားဂိတ် bhuutar , karrgate *(n.)* **station**

ဘူတာရုံ၊ ဂိတ် bhuutarrone , gate *(n.)* **terminal**

ဘူဖေး bu-phae *(n.)* **buffet**

ဘူမိဗေဒ bu-mi-bay-da *(n.)* **geology**

ဘူမိဗေဒနှင့် ဆိုင်သော bu-mi-bay-da-nint-sai-taw *(adj.)* **geological**

ဘူမိဗေဒပညာရှင် bu-mi-bay-da-pyin-nyar-shin *(n.)* **geologist**

ဘေ့စ်သံ bae-tan *(n.)* **bass**

ဘေး၊ အန္တရာယ် bay, an-da-yal *(n.)* **hazard**

ဘေးကင်းရာသို့ ပြောင်းရွှေ့ပေးခြင်း bay-kin-yar-tho-shway-pyaung-pay-chin *(n.)* **evacuation**

ဘေးကင်းရာသို့ ပြောင်းရွှေ့ပေးသည် bay-kin-yar-tho-shway-pyaung-pay-the *(v.)* **evacuate**

ဘေးကျပ်နံကျပ်ကာလ bay-kyat-nan-kyat-kar-la *(n.)* **crisis**

ဘေးဆီးရန်ကာ bhayy see raankar *(n.)* **safeguard**

ဘေးတစ်ဖက်ယိမ်းသည် bhayy taithpaat yaimsai *(v.)* **side**

ဘေးတွဲကား bhayy twalkarr *(n.)* **sidecar**

ဘေးတိုက် bhayytite *(n.)* **sideway**

ဘေးတိုက်ပုံ၊ တစ်စေ့တစ်စောင်း၊ ကိုယ်ရေးအကျဉ်း bhayy-tite pone, ta-sae-ta-saung , ko-rayy-aa-kyin *(n.)* **profile**

ဘေးထွက်နေရသည် bhayyhtwatnayrasai *(v.)* **sideline**

ဘေးထွက်ပစ္စည်း bay-htwat-pyit-see *(n.)* **by-product**

ဘေးဒဏ်၏ နောက်ဆက်တွဲ bay-dan-ei-naut-set-twe *(n.)* **aftermath**

ဘေးနံရံ bhayynanran *(n.)* **sidewall**

ဘေးပန်း bhayypaann *(n.)* **sideline**

ဘေးဘက်၊ အစွန်း၊ အမြင်၊ ရှုထောင့် bhayy bhaat , aaswann , aamyin , shu htaung *(n.)* **side**

ဘေးဘက်တွင် bay-bat-twin *(adv.)* **aside**

ဘေးဘက်ရွှေ့သည် bhayy bhaat rwaesai *(n.)* **sidewind**

ဘေးဘား bhayybharr *(n.)* **sidebar**

ဘေးမျဉ်း၊ မာဂျင်၊ အနားသတ်မျဉ်း bay-myin, mar-gyin, a-nar-tat-myin *(n.)* **margin**

ဘေးမှာ bay-mar *(prep.)* **beside**

ဘေးသင့်မှု bhayy-sint-mhu *(n.)* **peril**

ဘေးသင့်သည် bhayy-sint-sai *(v.)* **peril**

ဘေးအန္တရာယ် bay-an-da-yal *(n.)* **disaster**

ဘေးအန္တရာယ်လွတ်မြောက်ခြင်း bhay-yaantararallwatmyautchinn *(n.)* **survival**

ဘေထုပ် bay-htoke *(n.)* **bale**

ဘောဂဗေဒ baw-ga-bay-da *(n.)* **economics**

ဘောင် baung *(n.)* **frame**

ဘောင်းဘီ bhaung-bhe *(n. pl.)* **trousers**

ဘောင်းဘီတို၊ အောက်ခံဘောင်းဘီ bhaunggbhe to, aout-hkan-bhaung-bhe *(n. pl.)* **shorts**

ဘောင်းဘီပုံစံအမျိုးမျိုး bhaung-bhe-pone-san-aa-myoe-myoe *(n.)* **pantaloon**

ဘောင်းဘီရှည် bhaung-bhe-shay *(n.)* **slacks**

ဘောင်းဘီသိုင်းကြိုး baung-bi-thai-kyo *(n.)* **braces**

ဘောင်ခတ်သည် baung-khat-the *(v.)* **frame**

ဘောင်ခတ်သည်၊ ကျဉ်းမြောင်းစေသည် baung-khat-the, kyin-myaung-say-the *(v.)* **constrain**

ဘောဘယ်ယာရင် baw-bal-yar-yin *(n.)* **ball bearing**

ဘောလုံး baw-lone *(n.)* **ball**

ဘောလုံး မြေမကျမီ ရိုက်သည် bhawlone myay ma kyame ritesai *(v.)* **volley**

ဘောလုံး ဝင်လုခြင်း၊ ဖျက်ခြင်း bhawlone win lu chinn , hpyetchinn *(n.)* **tackle**

ဘောလုံးနောက်ပြန်လိုက်သည် baw-lone-naut-pyan-lite-the *(n.)* **runback**

ဘောလုံးပစ်သူ baw-lone-pyit-thu *(n.)* **bowler**

ဘောလုံးပွဲ baw-lone-pwe *(n.)* **football**

ဘော်ဒါဆောင် baw-dar-saung *(n.)* **hostel**

ဘော်ဒါဖြတ်သော baw-dar-phat-taw *(adj.)* **transborder**

ဘော်လီအင်္ကျီ baw-li-inn-gyi *(n.)* **bodice**

ဘဲငန်း bae-ngan *(n.)* **goose**

ဘဲလေးကချေသည် bal-lay-ka-chay-the *(n.)* **ballerina**

ဘဲလေးအက bal-lay-a-ka *(n.)* **ballet**

ဘဲသွားသွားသည် bhell swarrswarrsai *(v.)* **waddle**

ဘဲဥပုံ bae-oo-pon *(n.)* **ellipse**

ဘဲဥပုံရှိသည် bae-oo-pon-shi-the *(v.)* **ellipse**

ဘဲဥပုံရှိသော bae-oo-pon-shi-taw *(adj.)* **elliptic**

မံသည်၊ ကျံသည် man sai , kyaansai *(v.)* **surface**

မကပ်သော ma-kat-taw *(adj.)* **non-stick**

မကျန်းမာခြင်း ma-kyan-mar-chin *(n.)* **illness**

မကျန်းမာမှု ma-kyan-mar-mu *(n.)* **morbidity**

မကျန်းမာသော ma kyannmarsaw *(adj.)* **unhealthy**

မကျွမ်းကျင်သော ma-kyun-kyin-taw *(adj.)* **incompetent**

မကျေနချမ်းနိုင်ဖြစ်သည် ma kyaay ma cham ninehpyitsai *(v.)* **resent**

မကျေနပ်ခြင်း ma-kyay-nat-chin *(n.)* **discontent**

မကျေနပ်သူ ma-kyay-nat-thu *(n.)* **malcontent**

မကျေနပ်သော ma-kyay-nat-taw *(adj.)* **malcontent**

မကျေမချမ်းမှု ma kyaay ma chammhu *(n.)* **resentment**

မကျေမနပ်ဖြစ်ခြင်း ma-kyay-nat-phit-chin *(n.)* **displeasure**

မကျော်လွှားနိုင်သော ma-kyaw-hlwar-nai-taw *(adj.)* **insurmountable**

မကရရာသီဖွား ma-ka-ya-yar-thi-phwar *(n.)* **capricorn**

မကြားရသော ma-kyaw-ya-taw *(adj.)* **inaudible**

မကြာခဏ ma-kyar-hka-na *(adv.)* **oft**

မကြာခဏ ပေါ်ပေါက်သော makyaar-hkan paw-poutsaw *(adj.)* **recurrent**

မကြာမီ makyaarme *(adv.)* **soon**

မကြာမီ၊ လောလောဆယ် makyaarme, law-lawsaal *(adv.)* **presently**

မကြာသေးမီကဖြစ်သော ma-kyaar-sayyme-kahpyitsaw *(adj.)* **recent**

မကွယ်မဝှက်သော ma-kwal-ma-what-taw *(adj.)* **outspoken**

မကာကွယ်နိုင်သော ma-kar-kwal-nai-taw *(adj.)* **indefensible**

မကိုးကားသော ma-koe-kar-taw *(adj.)* **unquote**

မကောင်းဆိုးဝါး ma-kaung-soe-war *(n.)* **demon**

မကောင်းပြောသည် ma-kaung-pyaw-the *(v.)* **malign**

မကောင်းမြင်ဝါဒ ma-kaungg-myin-war-da *(n.)* **pessimism**

မကောင်းမှု makaunggmhu *(n.)* **sin**

မကောင်းမှုပြုသည် makaunggmhupyusai *(v.)* **sin**

မကောင်းသတင်း makaunggsatinn *(n.)* **scandal**

မကောင်းသော ma-kaung-taw *(adj.)* **ominous**

မက္ကင်းနစ်ပညာ ma-kan-nit-pyin-nyar *(n.)* **mechanics**

မက္ကဆီကို ချာပါတီ ma-si-ko-char-par-tee *(n.)* **nacho**
မက်စဖွယ် mat-sa-hpwal *(adj.)* **nubile**
မက်ထရစ်စနစ် mat-hta-rit-sa-nit *(adj.)* **metric**
မက်ထရစ်တန် maat hta rittaan *(n.)* **tonne**
မက်မွန်သီး maat-mwan-see *(n.)* **peach**
မက်မောဖွယ်ရာ mat-maw-phal-yar *(n.)* **glamour**
မက်လုံး mat-lone *(n.)* **incentive**
မခံချင်အောင် ထိကပါးရိကပါး အမူအရာဖြင့် ma hkan chinaaung hti k parr ri kaparr aamuuaararhpyint *(adv.)* **tauntingly**
မခံချင်အောင် ပြောသည် ma hkan chinaaung pyawwsai *(v.)* **taunt**
မခံချင်အောင် ပြောသူ ma hkan chinaaung pyawwsuu *(n.)* **taunter**
မခံချင်အောင် ပြောသော ma hkan chinaaung pyawwsaw *(adj.)* **taunting**
မခံချင်အောင် ပြောသောစကား ma hkan chinaaung pyawwsawsakarr *(n.)* **taunt**
မခံချိမခံသာစကား၊ ဆူးထစ် a-khan-chi-ma-khan-tar-sa-kar, sue-htit *(n.)* **barb**
မခံမရပ်နိုင်ဖြစ်ခြင်း ma-khan-ma-yat-nai-phit-chin *(n.)* **indignation**
မခံမရပ်နိုင်ဖြစ်သော ma-khan-ma-yat-nai-phit-taw *(adj.)* **indignant**
မချင့်မရဲဖြစ်စေသည် ma chint ma relhlpyitsaysai *(v.)* **tantalize**
မချစ်ခင်သော ma chit-hkin-saw *(adj.)* **unaffectionate**
မချိတင်ကဲ အခြေအနေ ma-chi tinkell aachayaanay *(n.)* **throe**
မချိတင်ကဲဝေဒနာ ma-chi-tin-kae-way-da-nar *(n.)* **agony**
မချိတရိပူပန်သည် ma-chi-ta-yi-pu-pan-the *(v.)* **agonize**
မချိသော machaisaw *(adj.)* **rueful**
မချိုးဖောက်အပ်သော ma-choe-hpauk-at-taw *(adj.)* **inviolable**
မခိုင်မာစွာ mahkinemarswar *(adv.)* **tenuously**
မခိုင်မာသော ma-hkine-marsaw *(adj.)* **tenuous**
မခိုင်မာသော၊ ဝမ်းပျဉ်းကျသော ma-khaing-mar-taw, wan-pyin-kya-taw *(adj.)* **flabby**
မဂ္ဂဇင်း ma-ga-zin *(n.)* **magazine**
မငြင်းနိုင်သော ma-nyin-nai-taw *(adj.)* **indisputable**
မင် min *(n.)* **ink**
မင်း မိဖုရားနှင့် မင်းမျိုးမင်းနွယ် min mihpurarrnint min myoeminnwal *(n.)* **royalty**
မင်းဆက် min-sat *(n.)* **dynasty**
မင်းဆိုးမင်းညစ်၏ အုပ်ချုပ်မှု၊ ကြီးစိုးဖိစီးမှု min soe min nyaiteat aotechotemhu , kyeesoe hpi seemhu *(n.)* **tyranny**
မင်းညီမင်းသားသုံး စကားလုံး min-nyi-min-tar-tone-sa-kar-lone *(n.)* **Highness**
မင်းတုပ် min-htoke *(n.)* **bolt**
မင်းပြုသည် min-pyusai *(v.)* **reign**
မင်းမျိုးစိုးနွယ် min-myo-soe-nwe *(n.)* **aristocracy**
မင်းမဲ့စိုးရိက် min-mae-sa-yite *(n.)* **anarchy**
မင်းမဲ့ဝါဒ min-mae-wa-da *(n.)* **anarchism**
မင်းမဲ့ဝါဒီ min-mae-wa-di *(n.)* **anarchist**
မင်းလမ်းမကြီး min-lan-ma-kyi *(n.)* **aisle**
မင်းသမီး min-sa-mee *(n.)* **princess**
မင်းသား minn sarr *(n.)* **prince**
မင်းသား ကြီးကဲအုပ်စိုးသော minn sarr kyee kell aote-soesaw *(adj.)* **princely**

မင်ခံမိတ္တူ min-khan-mait-thu *(n.)* **carbon copy**
မင်နီ သို့မဟုတ် ကျန်စာသားနှင့် ကွဲအောင် ရိုက်နှိပ်ထားသော ခေါင်းစီး၊ ညွှန်ကြားချက်၊ ကျင့်စဉ် mine thoetmahote kyaan sarsarrnint kwalaaung rite natehtarrsaw hkaungg see , nywhaankyarrchet , kyint-sin *(n.)* **rubric**
မင်္ဂလာစကားပြောသည် min-ga-lar-sa-gar-pyaw-the *(v.)* **auspicate**
မင်္ဂလာဆောင်ခြင်း main-ga-lar-saung-chinn *(n.)* **nuptials**
မင်္ဂလာမရှိသော min-ga-lar-ma-shi-taw *(adj.)* **inauspicious**
မင်္ဂလာရှိသော min-ga-lar-shi-taw *(adj.)* **auspicious**
မစင် ma-sin *(n.)* **feces**
မစင်စွန့်သည် ma-sin-sunt-the *(v.)* **defecate**
မစင်နှင့် ဆိုင်သော ma-sin-nint-sai-taw *(adj.)* **fecal**
မစွမ်းဆောင်နိုင်ခြင်း ma-swan-saung-nai-chin *(n.)* **incapacity**
မစာနာသော ma-sar-nar-taw *(adj.)* **inconsiderate**
မစေ့စပ်မသေချာသော၊ ဂရုမစိုက်သော ma-say-sat-ma-tay-char-taw, ga-yu-ma-site-taw *(adj.)* **careless**
မစ်စတာ၊ အမျိုးသားကို ရည်ညွှန်းပြောသော စကား mit-sa-tar-a-myo-tar-ko-yay-hnyum-pyaw-taw-sa-kar *(n.)* **mister**
မစ်ရှင် mit-shin *(n.)* **mission**
မဆင်မခြင် ma-sin-ma-chin *(adj.)* **reckless**
မဆင်မခြင်ပြုလုပ်သော ma sin m chin-pyulotesaw *(adj.)* **rash**
မဆီမဆိုင်ဖြစ်သော ma-si-ma-sai-phit-taw *(adj.)* **inapplicable**
မဆီလျော်သည့် အမည် ma-si-hlyaw-the-a-mee *(n.)* **misnomer**
မဆီလျော်သော ma-se-lyaw-taw *(adj.)* **irrelevant**
မဆုံးနိုင်သော ma-sone-nai-taw *(adj.)* **interminable**
မဆုံးဖြတ်နိုင်သော ma sonehpyatninesaw *(adj.)* **undecided**
မဆုတ်မနစ် ကြိုးပမ်းမှု ma-sote-ma-nit -kyoe-pam-mhu *(n.)* **persistence**
မဆုတ်မနစ်သော ma-sote-ma-nit-taw *(adj.)* **grim**
မဆုတ်သာ မတိုးသာ အခြေအနေ ma-sote-tar-ma-toe-tar-a-chay-a-nay *(n.)* **deadlock**
မဇီလာရိုး ma-zi-lar-yoe *(n.)* **maxilla**
မညာတာသော ma-hnyar-tar-taw *(adj.)* **astringent**
မညီညာသော ma nye nyarsaw *(adj.)* **uneven**
မညီမျှခြင်း ma-nyi-mya-chin *(n.)* **imbalance**
မည်းစေသည် mal-say-the *(v.)* **blacken**
မည်ကာမတ္တ mai kar mat-ta *(adj.)* **titular**
မည်သည့်အရာ mai saeet aarar *(pron.)* **whichever**
မည်သည့်အရာမဆို me-the-a-yar-ma-so *(n.)* **aught**
မည်သို့ပင်ဖြစ်စေ me-tho-pin-phit-say *(conj.)* **nevertheless**
မည်သူ maisuu *(pron.)* **whom**
မည်သူ၏ maisuueat *(pron.)* **whose**
မည်သူကမျှ အသိအမှတ်မပြုသော maisuukamyaha aasiaamhaatmapyusaw *(adj.)* **thankless**
မည်သူဖြစ်စေ mai suuhpyitsay *(pron.)* **whoever**

မည်သူမှ me-tuu-mha *(pron.)* **nobody**

မတင်းတိမ်သော ma-tin-tain-taw *(adj.)* **insatiable**

မတင်းသော ma tinn-saw *(adj.)* **slack**

မတည်ကြည်သော ma tai kyisaw *(adj.)* **shifty**

မတည်ငြိမ်သော ma-te-nyein-taw *(adj.)* **astatic**

မတည်တံ့သော a-the-tant-taw *(adj.)* **capricious**

မတည်မငြိမ်ဖြစ်စေခြင်း ma-the-ma-nyein-phit-say-chin *(n.)* **destabilization**

မတည်မငြိမ်ဖြစ်စေသည် ma-the-ma-nyein-phit-say-the *(v.)* **destabilize**

မတတ်နိုင်ခြင်း ma-tat-nai-chin *(n.)* **inability**

မတတ်နိုင်သော ma-tat-nai-taw *(adj.)* **incapable**

မတတ်သာ၍ ma-taat-sar-ywe *(adv.)* **perforce**

မတတ်သာသည့်အဆုံး ကျင့်သုံးရသည် mataat sar saeet aasone kyint sonerasai *(v.)* **resort**

မတန်တဆပမာဏ ma-tan-ta-sa-pa-mar-na *(n.)* **overload**

မတန်တဆဝန်တင်သည် ma-taan-ta-sa-wan-tin-tai *(v.)* **overload**

မတရား matararr *(adj.)* **wrongful**

မတရားဖိနှိပ်ခံရသည် matararr hpinatehkanrasai *(v.)* **victimize**

မတရားသဖြင့် ခံရသည် ma-ta-rarr sa-hpyint hkan-ra-sai *(v.)* **wrong**

မတရားသိမ်းယူခြင်း a toe kyeesarr ngway toe chachinn *(n.)* **usurpation**

မတရားသော matararrsaw *(adj.)* **unfair**

မတွန့်မဆုတ်သော a-twunt-ma-sote-taw *(adj.)* **dauntless**

မတိကျသော ma ti-kya-saw *(adj.)* **unaccurate**

မတိုးသာမဆုတ်သာ အခြေအနေ ma toe sar masotesar aachayaanay *(n.)* **stalemate**

မတိုင်မှီ အတော်အတွင်း ma-tine-mha-aa-taw-aa-twin *(prep.)* **pending**

မတိုင်မီ me-tine-mee *(prep. &adv.)* **before**

မတိုင်မီက ma-tine-me-ka *(n.)* **prior**

မတုပနိုင်သော ma-tu-pa-nai-taw *(adj.)* **inimitable**

မတူ ma-tuu *(prep.)* **unlike**

မတူညီခြင်း၊ ဂရုမစိုက်ခြင်း ma-tu-nyi-chin, ga-yu-ma-site-chin *(n.)* **nonchalance**

မတူညီသော၊ ဂရုမစိုက်သော ma-tu-nyi-taw, ga-yu-ma-site-taw *(adj.)* **nonchalant**

မတူသော ma-tu-taw *(adj.)* **dissimilar**

မတော်တဆ ma-taw-ta-sa *(adv.)* **accidentally**

မတော်တဆ ထိခိုက်ပျက်စီးပျောက်ဆုံးသော အရာ ma-taw-ta-sa-hti-kheik-pyat-see-pyauk-sone-taw-a-yar *(n.)* **casualty**

မတော်တဆဖြစ်သော ma-taw-ta-sa-mu-phit-taw *(adj.)* **accidental**

မတော်တဆမှု ma-taw-ta-sa-mu *(n.)* **accidence**

မတော်တရော် matawtaraw *(adv.)* **scandalously**

မတော်တရော် လိင်တံ လှစ်ပြသူ ma-taw-ta-yaw-lain-tan-hlit-pya-thu *(n.)* **flasher**

မတော်တရော်ပြုမူခြင်း ma-taw-ta-yaw-pyu-mu-chin *(n.)* **indecency**

မတော်တရော်ဖြစ်သော ma-taw-ta-yaw-phit-taw *(adj.)* **grotesque**

မတော်မတရား ma-taw-ma-tayar *(adv.)* **absurdly**

မတော်လောဘ ma-taw-law-ba *(n.)* **avarice**

မတ်ခွက် mat-khwat *(n.)* **mug**

မတ်ခွက်ကြီး maat hkwatkyee *(n.)* **tankard**

မတ်စောက်သော maat soutsaw *(adj.)* **vertical**

မတ်ရပ်ဗီရို maat rat bero *(n.)* **wardrobe**

မတ်လ mat-la *(n.)* **March**

မထင်ပေါ်ခြင်း ma-htain-paw-chinn *(n.)* **obscurity**

မထင်မရှားဖြစ်သည် ma-htin-ma-shar-phit-the *(v.)* **fuzz**

မထမ်းနိုင်သော၊ မခံနိုင်သော ma-htan-nai-taw, ma-khan-nai-taw *(adj.)* **insupportable**

မထိခလုတ် ထိခလုတ် ma-hti-kha-lote-hti-kha-lote *(adj.)* **allusive**

မထိခိုက်မနစ်နာစေဘဲ ma-hti-khaik-ma-nit-nar-say-bal *(n.)* **detriment**

မထိန်းမသိမ်းနိုင်ကြမ်းတမ်းစွာ ကားမောင်းခြင်း ma-htein-ma-thein-ning-kyan-tan-swar-kar-maung-chin *(n.)* **road rage**

မထိရောက်သော ma-hti-yauk-taw *(adj.)* **ineffective**

မထီတရီ ma-thi-ta-yee *(adj.)* **brash**

မဒမ် ma-dan *(n.)* **madam**

မနက်ခင်း ma-nat-khin *(n.)* **forenoon**

မနက်စာ ma-nat-sar *(n.)* **breakfast**

မနက်နေ့လည်စာ ma-nat-nae-lal-sar *(n.)* **brunch**

မနက်ဖြန် ma-naathpyan *(adv.)* **tomorrow**

မနွသ၊ မြားသမား ma-nwat-ta, myar-ta-mar *(n.)* **sagittary**

မနှစ်မြို့ ma nit myoet *(adj.)* **repugnant**

မနှစ်မြို့ခြင်း ma-nit-myo-chin *(n.)* **disgust**

မနှစ်မြို့ခြင်းကို ဖော်ပြသံ ma-nit-myo-chin-ko-phaw-pya-tan *(interj.)* **fie**

မနှစ်မြို့ဖွယ် ma-nit-myo-phwal *(adj.)* **deplorable**

မနှစ်မြို့သော m nhait myahoetsaw *(adj.)* **sickened**

မနှစ်သက်ခြင်း ma-hnit-thet-chin *(n.)* **aversion**

မနှစ်သက်စရာဖြစ်သော ma-nit-thet-sa-yar-phit-taw *(adj.)* **disagreeable**

မနာခံဘဲနေသည် ma-nar-khan-bae-nay-the *(v.)* **disobey**

မနာလိုစရာကောင်းသော ma-nar-lo-sa-yar-kaung-taw *(adj.)* **enviable**

မနာလိုဖြစ်သော ma-nar-lo-phit-taw *(adj.)* **envious**

မနာလိုမှု ma-nar-lo-mu *(n.)* **jealousy**

မနာလိုသော ma-nar-lo-taw *(adj.)* **jealous**

မနိုင်သော ma-nine-saw *(adj.)* **unable**

မနုဿဗေဒ ma-note-ta-bay-da *(n.)* **anthropology**

မနေ့က ma-nae-ka *(n.)* **yesterday**

မနောနှင့် ဆက်သွယ်ခြင်း manaw-nint saatswalchinn *(n.)* **telepathy**

မနောနှင့် ဆက်သွယ်သူ manaw-nint saatswalsuu *(n.)* **telepathist**

မနောနှင့် ဆက်သွယ်သော manaw-nint saatswalsaw *(adj.)* **telepathic**

မန္တန် mantaan *(n.)* **spell**

မန်ကျည်းသီး maan kyaeesee *(n.)* **tamarind**

မန်ဂနိ man-ga-ni *(n.)* **manganese**

မန်နေဂျာ man-nay-gyar *(n.)* **manager**

မပျံနိုင်သေးသော ငှက်ပေါက်စ ma-pyan-nai-tay-taw-ngat-pauk-sa *(n.)* **nestling**

မပျက်စီးနိုင်သော ma-pyat-see-nai-taw *(adj.)* **imperishable**

မပျော်ရွှင်ခြင်း ma-pyaw-shwinchinn *(adj.)*
unamused
မပျော်ရွှင်သော mapyawshwinsaw *(adj.)*
unhappy
မပျော်ရွှင်သော၊ တုန်လှုပ်သော ma-pyaw-shwin-taw, ton-hloke-taw *(adj.)*
disgruntled
မပျော်ဝင်နိုင်သော ma-pyaw-win-nai-taw *(n.)*
insoluble
မပြည့်စုံသော ma-pyae-sone-taw *(adj.)*
incomplete
မပြည့်စုံသော ma-pyae-sone-taw *(adj.)*
imperfect
မပြည့်ဝသော ma-pyae-wa-taw *(adj.)*
deficient
မပြတ်မသားဖြစ်သည် layharnaal *(v.)*
vacillate
မပြတ်မသားမရေမရာ ma-phat-ma-tar-ma-yay-ma-yar *(adj.)* **equivocal**
မပြီးနိုင် မဆုံးနိုင်သော ma-pi-nai-ma-sone-nai-taw *(adj.)* **never-ending**
မပြေမလည်ဖြစ်သော ma-pyay-ma-lal-phit-taw *(adj.)* **acrimonious**
မပြေလည်မှု ma-pyay-lal-mu *(n.)* **acrimony**
မပြောင်းလဲသော ma-pyaung-lal-taw *(adj.)*
constant
မပြောပလောက်သော ma-pyaw-pa-laut-taw *(adj.)* **negligible**
မပြောမဆို ma pyaw maso *(adj.)*
unannounced
မပြောအပ်၊ မလုပ်အပ်ဟု တားမြစ်ထားသော ma pyaww at, ma-lote at-hu tarr-myit-htarr-saw *(adj.)* **taboo**
မပြောအပ်၊ မလုပ်အပ်ဟု တားမြစ်ထားသော အမှု ma pyaww at, malote athu tarrmyithtarrsaw aamhu *(n.)* **taboo**
မပွင့်တပွင့် ပြောသည် ma-pwint-ta-pwint-pyaw-the *(v.)* **mumble**
မပွင့်လင်းသော ma-pwint-lin-taw *(adj.)*
evasive
မပါဘဲ maparbhell *(adv.)* **without**
မပိမရိ အလွမ်းသယ်သော ma-pi-ma-yi-a-lwan-tal-thaw *(adj.)* **mawkish**
မပီကလာ ပီကလာ ပြောခြင်း ma-pi-ka-lar-pi-ka-lar-pyaw-chin *(n.)* **lisp**
မပီကလာ ပီကလာ ပြောသည် ma-pi-ka-lar-pi-ka-lar-pyaw-the *(v.)* **lisp**
မဖတ်ရသေးသော mahpaatrasayysaw *(adj.)*
unread
မဖြစ်ခဲ့လျှင် ma hpyithkaehlyin *(conj.)*
unless
မဖြစ်စလောက် mahpyitsalout *(adj.)* **scanty**
မဖြစ်နိုင်သော ma-phit-nai-taw *(adj.)*
impossible
မဖြစ်မနေ လုပ်ရမည့် အရာ ma-phit-ma-nay-lote-ya-me-a-yar *(n.)* **must**
မဖွယ်မရာ ma-hpwal-ma-rar *(n.)*
obscenity
မဖော်ရွေသော ma-phaw-yway-taw *(adj.)*
inhospitable
မမြင်ရသော ma-myin-ya-taw *(adj.)*
invisible
မမှန်ကန်သော ma-hman-kan-taw *(adj.)*
erroneous
မမှန်မကန် ma-hman-ma-kan *(adv.)* **ill**
မမှန်မကန် ပြုလုပ်ထားမှု ma-hman-ma-kan-pyu-lote-htar-mu *(n.)* **falsification**
မမှန်မကန်သော ma-hman-ma-kan-taw *(adj.)*
fraudulent
မမှန်သည်ကို ဖွင့်ချသည် ma-man-the-ko-phwint-cha-the *(v.)* **debunk**
မမှန်သော၊ မသင့်လျော်သော ma-man-taw, ma-tint-lyaw-taw *(adj.)* **improper**
မယဉ်ကျေးသော ma yin kyaayysaw *(adj.)*
uncivilized

မယားခိုးမှု ကျူးလွန်သူ ma-yar-khoe-mu-kyu-lun-thu *(n.)* **adulterer**
မယားစရိတ် ma-yar-sa-yeik *(n.)* **alimony**
မယားပြိုင် ma-yarr-pyaine *(adj.)* **polygamous**
မယားပြိုင်ယူစလေ့ ma-yarr-pyaine-yuu-dha-lae *(n.)* **polygamy**
မယုံကြည် ma-yone-kyi *(v.)* **disbelieve**
မယုံကြည်နိုင်လောက်သော ma-yone-kyi-nai-laut-taw *(adj.)* **incredible**
မယုံကြည်မှု ma-yone-kyi-mu *(n.)* **distrust**
မယုံနိုင်ခြင်း ma-yone-nai-chin *(n.)* **disbelief**
မျက်ကပ်မှန် myat-kat-man *(n.)* **contact lens**
မျက်ကြည်လွှာ myat-kyi-hlwar *(n.)* **cornea**
မျက်ခွံ myat-khun *(n.)* **eyelid**
မျက်ခုံး myat-khone *(n.)* **eyebrow**
မျက်စိ myet-si *(adj.)* **optic**
မျက်စိကြည့်မှန်ပြောင်း myet-si-kyi-mhan-pyaung *(n.)* **ophtalmoscope**
မျက်စိကို အဝတ်ဖြင့် ပိတ်စည်းသည် myat-si-ko-a-wut-phit-pait-see-the *(n.)* **blindfold**
မျက်စိကုပညာ myet-si-ku-pyin-nyar *(n.)* **ophtalmology**
မျက်စိကုပညာရှင် myet-si-ku-pyin-nyar-shin *(n.)* **ophtalmologist**
မျက်စိစွန်ခြင်း myetsi-swanchinn *(n.)* **sty**
မျက်စိစွေခြင်း myetsi swaychinn *(n.)* **squint**
မျက်စိဆိုင်ရာ myet-si-sine-rar *(adj.)* **ophtalmic**
မျက်စိဆုံချက်မညီခြင်း myat-si-sone-chat-ma-nyi-chin *(n.)* **astigmatism**
မျက်စိတစ်ဖက်မှိတ်ပြခြင်း myetsi taithpaat mhaate pyachinn *(n.)* **wink**
မျက်စိတစ်ဖက်မှိတ်ပြသည် myet-si ta-hpaat-mhaate-pyasai *(v.)* **wink**
မျက်စိနာ myit-si-hnar *(n.)* **conjunctivitis**
မျက်စိပညာနှင့် ဆိုင်သော myet-si-pyin-nyar-nint-sine-taw *(adj.)* **ophtalmologic**
မျက်စိပသာဒရှိသော myetsi pyit-ardashisaw *(adj.)* **tasteful**
မျက်စိဖွင့်ပေးသော myat-si-phwint-pay-taw *(adj.)* **docent**
မျက်စိမှတ် ဘက်လိုက်ခြင်း myet-si-mate bhaat-lite-chinn *(n.)* **prejudice**
မျက်စိမှေး၍ ကြည့်သည် myetsi mhaayy kyanysai *(v.)* **squint**
မျက်စိရှက်စရာ myetsishatsarar *(adj.)* **scandalous**
မျက်စိရှက်စရာ လုပ်ပြသည် myetsishatsarar lotepyasai *(v.)* **scandalize**
မျက်စိရှင်သော myet-si-shin-taw *(adj.)* **observant**
မျက်စိလျှမ်းသည် myet-si-shan-tai *(v.)* **overlook**
မျက်စိအထူးကု myet-si-a-htu-ku *(n.)* **oculist**
မျက်ဆန် myat-san *(n.)* **eyeball**
မျက်တွင်းကျသော myat-twin-kya-taw *(adj.)* **haggard**
မျက်တောင် myat-taung *(n.)* **eyelash**
မျက်တောင်ခတ်သည် myat-taung-khat-the *(v.)* **blink**
မျက်နှာ myat-nar *(n.)* **face**
မျက်နှာ နုပျိုအောင် ခွဲစိတ်ကုသမှု myat-nar-nu-pyo-aung-khwal-seik-ku-ta-mu *(n.)* **facelift**
မျက်နှာ နုပျိုအောင် ခွဲစိတ်ကုသသည် myat-nar-nu-pyo-aung-khwal-seik-ku-ta-the *(v.)* **facelift**

မျက်နှာ သွေးရောင်ဖြန်းခြင်း၊ ရေဆွဲခြင်း myat-nar-thway-yaung-phyan-chin, yay-swal-chin *(n.)* **flush**

မျက်နှာကြက် myat-nar-kyat *(n.)* **ceiling**

မျက်နှာချင်းဆိုင်သည်၊ ရင်ဆိုင်သည် myat-nar-chin-sai-the, yin-sai-the *(v.)* **face**

မျက်နှာချိုသွေးသည် myat-nar-cho-thway-the *(v.)* **flatter**

မျက်နှာစာ myat-nar-sar *(n.)* **forecourt**

မျက်နှာထား myat-na-htar *(n.)* **countenance**

မျက်နှာထား၊ ဖော်ပြခြင်း myat-nar-htar, phaw-pya-chin *(n.)* **expression**

မျက်နှာနှင့် ဆိုင်သော myat-nar-nint-sai-taw *(adj.)* **facial**

မျက်နှာနှစ်ခု ရှိသော myat-nar-na-khu-shi-taw *(adj.)* **bifacial**

မျက်နှာနီမြန်းသွားသည် myat-nar-ne-myan-thwar-the *(v.)* **blush**

မျက်နှာနီရဲသွားသည်၊ ရေဆွဲသည် myat-nar-nee-ye-twar-the, yay-swal-the *(v.)* **flush**

မျက်နှာပျက်ရခြင်း myat-nar-pyat-ya-chin *(n.)* **humiliation**

မျက်နှာပြင် myet-nharpyin *(n.)* **surface**

မျက်နှာပြင် ကြမ်းတမ်းသော myetnharpyin kyamtamsaw *(adj.)* **rugged**

မျက်နှာပြင်ညီဖြတ်သည် myat-nar-pyin-nyi-phat-the *(v.)* **facet**

မျက်နှာပြင်အပူ myetnharpyinaapuu *(n.)* **scorch**

မျက်နှာပြုသည် myat-nar-pyu-the *(v.)* **front**

မျက်နှာဖုံး myat-nar-hpone *(n.)* **mask**

မျက်နှာဖုံး တပ်သည် myat-nar-hpone-tat-the *(v.)* **mask**

မျက်နှာဖုံးသတင်း myat-hnar-phone-ta-din *(n.)* **front page**

မျက်နှာများသူ myat-nar-myar-thu *(n.)* **flirt**

မျက်နှာလွှားဇာ myetnhar lwharjar *(n.)* **veil**

မျက်နှာလွှဲသည် myat-nar-hlwal-the *(v.)* **avert**

မျက်နှာအကာ myat-nar-a-kar *(n.)* **face mask**

မျက်မမြင် myat-ma-myin *(adj.)* **blind**

မျက်မမြင်စာ myat-ma-myin-sar *(n.)* **braille**

မျက်မြင် myet-myin *(adj.)* **ocular**

မျက်မြင်တွေ့သည် myet myintwaesai *(v.)* **witness**

မျက်မှန် myat-man *(n.)* **eyeglass**

မျက်မှန်ကျွမ်းကျင်သူ myet-mhan-kyam-kyin-tuu *(n.)* **optician**

မျက်မှန်တပ်ထားသော myat-hman-tat-htar-taw *(adj.)* **bespectacled**

မျက်မှောက်၊ ယခု myat-mawk, ya-khu *(adj.)* **current**

မျက်မှောက်ခေတ် အိုလံပစ်ပွဲတော် myet-maut-hkit-ao-lan-pit-pwal-taw *(n.)* **olympiad**

မျက်မှောက်ရေးရာ လေ့လာသုံးသပ်သူ myat-mauk-yay-yar-lay-lar-tone-tat-thu *(n.)* **commentator**

မျက်မှောင်ကြုတ်သည် myat-hmaung-kyoke-the *(v.)* **frown**

မျက်ရက်စက် myetraatsaat *(n.)* **teardrop**

မျက်ရည် myetrai *(n.)* **tear**

မျက်ရည်ကျသည် myetrai kyasai *(v.)* **weep**

မျက်ရည်ယိုဓာတ်ငွေ့ myet-rai yodhrat-ngwae *(n.)* **tear gas**

မျက်ရည်လည်သော myetrai laisaw *(adj.)* **tearful**

မျက်လှည့်ပညာရှင်၊ မှော်ပညာရှင် myat-hlae-pyin-nyar-shin, maw-pyin-nyar-shin *(n.)* **magician**

မျက်လှည့်ပြသည် myat-hlae-pya-the *(v.)* **conjure**
မျက်လုံး myat-lone *(n.)* **eye**
မျက်လုံးကြွက်သားကျုံ့ခြင်း myat-lone-kwyat-tar-kyont-chin *(n.)* **myosis**
မျက်လုံးနားတဝိုက် ဘက်တီးရီးယားပိုးဝင်ခြင်း myetlone narrtawite bhaatteereeyarrpoewainhkyinn *(n.)* **stye**
မျက်လုံးပြူးသွားသည် myat-lone-pyu-twar-the *(v.)* **freak**
မျဉ်းခုံး myin-khon *(n.)* **curve**
မျဉ်းတားထားသည် myin-tar-htar-the *(v.)* **line**
မျဉ်းပြိုင် myin-pyaine *(v.)* **parallel**
မျှတစွာ mya-ta-swar *(adv.)* **fairly**
မျှတသော hmya-ta-taw *(adj.)* **balanced**
မျှတသော ကုန်သွယ်မှု mya-ta-taw-kone-twal-mu *(n.)* **fair trade**
မျှတသော၊ လက်တွေ့ကျသော myata-saw , laat-twaekyasaw *(adj.)* **reasonable**
မျှဝေခံစားခြင်း mya-wai-khan-sar-chin *(n.)* **empathy**
မျှဝေခံစားသူ mya-wai-khan-sar-thu *(n.)* **empath**
မျှဝေခံစားသော mya-wai-khan-sar-taw *(adj.)* **empathic**
မျှသာ mya-tar *(adj.)* **mere**
မျှော့၊ ပိုင်းလုံး myawt, pine-lone *(n.)* **leech**
မျှော်စင် myaw-sin *(n.)* **tower**
မျှော်မြင်တွေးခေါ်မှုရှိခြင်း myaw-myin-tway-khaw-mu-shi-chin *(n.)* **sageness**
မျှော်မှန်းချက် myaw-mhaannchet *(n.)* **vision**
မျှော်လင့်ချက် hmyaw-lint-chat *(n.)* **expectation**
မျှော်လင့်ချက်ကုန်နေသော myaw-lint-chat-kone-nay-taw *(adj.)* **despondent**
မျှော်လင့်ချက်ထားသော myahaaw lint chethtarrsaw *(adj.)* **sanguine**
မျှော်လင့်ချက်ပျက်သုဉ်းခြင်း hmyaw-lint-chat-pyat-tone-chin *(n.)* **despair**
မျှော်လင့်ချက်မရှိသော myaw-lint-chat-ma-shi-taw *(adj.)* **hopeless**
မျှော်လင့်ထားသော၊ ရက်ချိန်းစေ့သော myaw-lint-htar-taw, yat-chain-say-taw *(adj.)* **due**
မျှော်လင့်သည် hmyaw-lint-the *(v.)* **expect**
မျှော်လင့်သော myaw-lint-taw *(adj.)* **hopeful**
များစွာ myar-swar *(adj.)* **many**
များပြားစွာ myar-pyar-swar *(adv.)* **abundantly**
များပြားမှု myarr-pyarr-mhu *(n.)* **plurality**
များပြားသော myar-pyar-taw *(adj.)* **abundant**
များများ myar-myar *(adv.)* **much**
များလာသော myar-lar-taw *(adj.)* **cumulative**
မျိုးကန်းခြင်း myoe kaannchinn *(n.)* **sterility**
မျိုးချစ်စိတ် myoe-chit-sate *(n.)* **patriotism**
မျိုးချစ်ပုဂ္ဂိုလ် myoe-chit-poke-gol *(n.)* **patriot**
မျိုးချစ်သော myoe-chit-saw *(adj.)* **patriotic**
မျိုးစပ်သည် myo-sat-the *(v.)* **fertilize**
မျိုးစပ်သော myo-sat-taw *(adj.)* **hybrid**
မျိုးစိတ် myoe-sate *(n.)* **species**
မျိုးစုံ moe-sone *(n.)* **multiplicity**
မျိုးဆက် myo-sat *(n.)* **generation**
မျိုးတူစုသည် myoe tuu susai *(v.)* **sort**

မျိုးတူပစ္စည်းကို ဖြုတ်ယူသုံးစွဲသည် myo-thu-pyit-see-ko-phoke-yu-tone-swal-the *(v.)* **cannibalise**

မျိုးတူဖြစ်သော myo-tu-phit-taw *(adj.)* **homogeneous**

မျိုးနွယ်စု myoenwalsu *(n.)* **tribe**

မျိုးနွယ်စုငယ်အကြောင်းလေ့လာမှုပညာ myo-nwe-su-ngal-a-kyaung-lay-lar-mu-pyin-nyar *(n.)* **micrology**

မျိုးနွယ်စုအကြီးအကဲ myo-nwe-su-a-kyi-a-kal *(n.)* **chieftain**

မျိုးပွားခြင်း myoe pwarr-chinn *(n.)* **propagation**

မျိုးပွားနိုင်ခြင်း myo-pwar-nai-chin *(n.)* **fecundation**

မျိုးပွားနိုင်သော myo-pwar-nai-taw *(adj.)* **fecund**

မျိုးပွားမှု myoe pwarr-mhu *(adj.)* **reproductive**

မျိုးပွားသည်၊ ပြန်လည်ဖော်ထုတ်သည် myoe pwarr sai , pyanlai-hpaw-htotesai *(v.)* **reproduce**

မျိုးပွားအင်္ဂါ myo-pyaw-inn-gar *(n.)* **gonads**

မျိုးရိုး myo-yoe *(n.)* **ancestry**

မျိုးရိုးစဉ်ဆက်ပြမှတ်တမ်း myoe-roe-sin-saat-pya-mhaat-tam *(n.)* **pedigree**

မျိုးရိုးဆက်ခံနိုင်သော myo-yoe-sat-khan-nai-taw *(adj.)* **heritable**

မျိုးရိုးထက် တောင်းဆိုမှုကြောင့်ရသော ပိုင်ဆိုင်မှု myo-yoe-htet-taung-so-mu-kyaunt-ya-taw-paing-saing-mu *(n.)* **acquest**

မျိုးရိုးဗီဇ myo-yoe-bi-za *(n.)* **gene**

မျိုးရိုးဗီဇဆိုင်ရာ myo-yoe-bi-za-sai-yar *(adj.)* **genealogical**

မျိုးရိုးဗီဇနှင့်ဆိုင်သော myo-yoe-bi-za-nint-sai-taw *(adj.)* **genetic**

မျိုးရိုးဗီဇပညာ myo-yoe-bi-za-pyin-nyar *(n.)* **genealogy**

မျိုးရိုးဗီဇပညာရှင် myo-yoe-bi-za-pyin-nyar-shin *(n.)* **geneticist**

မျိုးရိုးလိုက်သော myo-yoe-lite-taw *(adj.)* **hereditary**

မျိုးသုဉ်းသွားသော myo-tone-twar-taw *(adj.)* **extinct**

မျိုးအောင်ခြင်း myo-aung-chin *(n.)* **fertility**

မျိုးအောင်သော myo-aung-taw *(adj.)* **fertile**

မျောက် myauk *(n.)* **monkey**

မျောက်မထားသော မိန်းမ၏ လင်ယောကျ်ား myauk-ma-htar-taw-mein-ma-ei-lin-yauk-kyar *(n.)* **cuckold**

မျောက်လွှဲကျော် myauk-hlwal-kyaw *(n.)* **gibbon**

မျောက်ဝံ myauk-wun *(n.)* **ape**

မျောပါသည် myaw-par-the *(v.)* **drift**

မရင်းနှီးသော ma-rinn-nee-saw *(adj.)* **unacquainted**

မရပ်မနားဖြစ်သော ma ratmanarr-hpyitsaw *(adj.)* **relentless**

မရပ်မနားသော ma-rat-ma-narr-saw *(adj.)* **perpetual**

မရမကတောင်းဆိုခြင်း ma-ya-ma-ka-taung-so-chin *(n.)* **insistence**

မရမကတောင်းဆိုသော ma-ya-ma-ka-taung-so-taw *(adj.)* **insistent**

မရမနေ ဇွဲကောင်းသော ma-ra-ma-nay-zwal-kaungg-saw *(adj.)* **persistent**

မရမနေခိုင်းတတ်သော ma-ya-ma-nay-khai-tat-taw *(adj.)* **demanding**

မရွှင်ပျသော ma shwin pyasaw *(adj.)* **woebegone**

မရွှေ့ရှားနိုင်သော ma-shway-shar-nai-taw *(adj.)* **immovable**

မရှက်မကြောက် ma shatmakyawt *(adv.)* **unabashedly**

မရှက်သော ma shat-saw *(adj.)* **unabashed**

မရှင်းလင်းသော ma-shinnlinnsaw *(adj.)* **unclear**

မရှင်းလင်းသော၊ မပြတ်သားသော ma-shin-lin-taw, ma-pyat-tar-taw *(adj.)* **indistinct**

မရှိ ma-shi *(n.)* **nil**

မရှိမဖြစ် ရှိထားရမည့် mashimahpyit shihtarr ra-meet *(adj.)* **prerequisite**

မရှိမဖြစ် ရှိထားရမည့် အချက် mashimahpyit shihtarr ra-meet aa-chet *(n.)* **prerequisite**

မရှိမဖြစ် အရေးပါသော ma-shi-ma-phit-a-yay-par-taw *(adj.)* **essential**

မရှိမဖြစ်လိုအပ်သော mashimahpyitloatsaw *(adj.)* **vital**

မရှိမဖြစ်သော ma-shi-ma-phit-taw *(adj.)* **indispensable**

မရှိမှု ma-shi-mu *(n.)* **lack**

မရှုံးနိမ့်နိုင်သော ma shone-nint-ninesaw *(adj.)* **undefeated**

မရှုမလှုရှုံးခြင်း ma-shu-ma-hla-shone-chin *(n.)* **checkmate**

မရှောင်နိုင်သော ma shaung-ninesaw *(adj.)* **unavoidable**

မရိုးသားမှု ma-yoe-tar-mu *(n.)* **dishonesty**

မရိုးသားသော ma-yoe-tar-taw *(adj.)* **dishonest**

မရိုးသော ma roesaw *(adj.)* **sly**

မရေတွက်နိုင်သော ma-yay-twat-nai-taw *(adj.)* **countless**

မရေမတွက်နိုင်သော ma-yay-ma-twat-nai-taw *(adj.)* **infinite**

မရောင်းသော ma raunggsaw *(adj.)* **unsold**

မြ mya *(n.)* **emerald**

မြက် myat *(n.)* **grass**

မြက်ခင်း myat-khin *(n.)* **lawn**

မြက်ခင်းပြင် myat-khin-pyin *(n.)* **grassland**

မြက်ခင်းလွင်ပြင် myaat hkinnlwinpyin *(n.)* **steppe**

မြက်ခြောက် myat-chauk *(n.)* **hay**

မြက်မြက်စက်စက်ရှိသော myaat-myaat-saat-saat-shi-saw *(adj.)* **piquant**

မြက်ယမ်းဓား myaat yamdharr *(n.)* **scythe**

မြက်လွှာ myaatlwhar *(n.)* **turf**

မြင့်မြတ်ခြင်း myint-myat-chin *(n.)* **nobility**

မြင့်မြတ်စွာ myint-myat-swar *(adv.)* **nobly**

မြင့်မြတ်သည့် အရာ myint myatsaeet aarar *(n.)* **sublime**

မြင့်မြတ်သော myint-myat-taw *(adj.)* **noble**

မြင့်မားစွာ myint-mar-swar *(adv.)* **highly**

မြင့်မားစိုးမိုးခြင်း myint-mar-soe-moe-chin *(n.)* **domination**

မြင့်မားသော တောင် myint-mar-taw-taung *(n.)* **alp**

မြင့်မားသော တောင်ပေါ်ဒေသရှိ myint-mar-taw-taung-paw-day-ta-shi *(adj.)* **alpine**

မြင့်သော myint-taw *(adj.)* **high**

မြင်း myin *(n.)* **horse**

မြင်းကျား myinn-kyarr *(n.)* **zebra**

မြင်းကို ပြုစုစောင့်ရှောက်သည် myin-ko-pyu-su-saunt-shaut-the *(v.)* **groom**

မြင်းကုန်းနှီး myinn konenhaee *(n.)* **side-saddle**

မြင်းကုန်းနှီးပေါ် myinn kone nhaeepaw *(adv.)* **side-saddle**

မြင်းစားဂျုံ myin-sar-gyone *(n.)* **oat**

မြင်းစာ၊ ကျွဲနွားစာ myin-sar, kywe-sar *(n.)* **forage**

မြင်းစီးတတ်သူ၊ နောက်ဆက်တွဲ မှတ်ချက် myinnsee taat suu , noutsaattwal mhaatchet *(n.)* **rider**

မြင်းစီးသေနတ် myin-see-tay-nat *(n.)* **carabine**

မြင်းဇက်ကြိုး myin-zat-kyo *(n.)* **bridle**

မြင်းဇောင်း myinn-zaungg *(n.)* **stable**

မြင်းတပ်၊ သံချပ်ကာယန္တရားတပ် myin-tat, tan-chat-kar-yan-da-yar-tat *(n.)* **cavalry**

မြင်းထိန်း myin-htein *(n.)* **groom**

မြင်းပု myinn-pu *(n.)* **pony**

မြင်းပေါက်စ myin-pauk-sa *(n.)* **foal**

မြင်းမ myin-ma *(n.)* **mare**

မြင်းမောင်းရန် တောက်ခေါက်သံ myinn maunggraan tout-hkoutsan *(n.)* **tchick**

မြင်းမောင်းရန် တောက်ခေါက်သည် myinn maungg-raan tout hkoutsai *(v.)* **tchick**

မြင်းလှည်း myin-hlae *(n.)* **barouche**

မြင်းလား myinnlarr *(n.)* **stallion**

မြင်းသံခွာ myin-tan-kwar *(n.)* **horseshoe**

မြင်းအပျော်စီးသည် myinn aapyawseesai *(v.)* **ride**

မြင်းအသားကျပြေးခြင်း myin-a-tar-kya-pyay-chin *(n.)* **canter**

မြင်းအိုမြင်းနာ myin-oh-myin-nar *(n.)* **nag**

မြင်ကွင်း myinkwin *(n.)* **visibility**

မြင်ကွင်း၊ ရှုခင်း myinkwin , shuhkinn *(n.)* **view**

မြင်ကွင်းကျယ် myin-kwin-kyaal *(n.)* **panorama**

မြင်ကွင်းပိတ်သည် myin-kwin-pate-the *(v.)* **occult**

မြင်နိုင်သော myin-nine-saw *(adj.)* **visible**

မြင်ရုံမျှဖြင့် myin rone mya-hpyint *(adv.)* **prima facie**

မြင်လွှာ myinlwhar *(n.)* **retina**

မြင်သည် myinsai *(v.)* **see**

မြင်သာအောင် လုပ်ခြင်း myin-tar-aung-lote-chin *(n.)* **highlight**

မြစ် myit *(n.)* **river**

မြစ်စောင့်နတ်သမီး myit-saunt-nat-ta-mee *(n.)* **nymph**

မြစ်ဆုံ၊ ပေါင်းဆုံခြင်း myit-sone, paung-sone-chin *(n.)* **confluence**

မြစ်ဝ myit-wa *(n.)* **estuary**

မြစ်ဝကျွန်းပေါ်ဒေသ myit-wa-kyun-paw-day-ta *(n.)* **delta**

မြည်း myae *(n.)* **donkey**

မြည်းစမ်းသည်၊ ရှာဖွေလေ့လာသည် pyie-san-the, shar-phway-lay-lar-the *(v.)* **browse**

မြည်းဟီသံ myie-hee-tan *(n.)* **bray**

မြည်ကြွေးခြင်း myi kywaychinn *(n.)* **ululation**

မြည်ခြင်း myichinn *(n.)* **rung**

မြည်တမ်းသည် myi tamsai *(v.)* **ululate**

မြည်ဟိန်းသည် myi-hein-the *(n.)* **boom**

မြတ်နှာချင်းဆိုင် အစည်းအဝေး myat-na-chin-sine-a-see-a-way *(n.)* **tete-a-tete**

မြတ်နိုးသည် myat-noe-the *(v.)* **adore**

မြတ်သော myat-taw *(adj.)* **blessed**

မြန်ဆန်သည် myan-san-the *(v.)* **fast**

မြန်ဆန်သော myan-saansaw *(adj.)* **rapid**

မြန်နှုန်းမြင့်ကွန်ရက် myanm-hnone-myint-kun-yat *(n.)* **broadband**

မြန်မြန် myan-myan *(adv.)* **fast**

မြန်မြန်ဆန်ဆန် myan-myan-san-san *(adv.)* **apace**

မြန်သော myansaw *(adj.)* **speedy**

မြွေ myway *(n.)* **snake**

မြွေကြီး myawaykyee *(n.)* **serpent**

မြွေပါ mway-par *(n.)* **mink**

မြွေပါကတိုးဖြူ mway-par-ka-toe-phyu *(n.)* **ferret**

မြွေလိမ်မြွေကောက် myway lain myway-kout *(n.)* **zigzag**

မြွေလိမ်မြွေကောက်၊ ဝင်္ကပါ myway lin myaway kout , win kapar *(n.)* **serpentine**

မြွေလိမ်မြွေကောက်ပုံစံဖြင့် myway lain myway kout ponesanhpyint *(adv.)* **zigzag**

မြွေလိမ်မြွေကောက်ဖြစ်သော myway lain myway kout-hpyit-saw *(adj.)* **zigzag**

မြွေလိမ်မြွေကောက်သွားသည် myway lain myway kout-swarrsai *(v.)* **zigzag**

မြွေဟောက် mway-hauk *(n.)* **cobra**

မြှင့်တင်ခြင်း hmyint-tin-chin *(n.)* **boost**

မြှင့်တင်ပေးသောအရာ hmyint-tin-pay-taw-a-yar *(n.)* **booster**

မြှင့်တင်သည် hmyint-tin-the *(v.)* **boost**

မြှင့်သည် hmyint-the *(v.)* **heighten**

မြှုပ်သည် myahuutsai *(v.)* **submerge**

မြှောက်ခြင်း myaut-chinn *(n.)* **toss**

မြှောက်ခြင်း၊ ဆတိုးခြင်း hmauk-chin, sa-toe-chin *(n.)* **multiplication**

မြှောက်ပင့်သည် hmyaut-pint-the *(v.)* **hoist**

မြှောက်ဖော်ကိန်း hmyaut-phaw-kein *(n.)* **coefficient**

မြှောက်လုံးပင့်လုံး hmyauk-lone-pint-lon *(n.)* **flattery**

မြှောက်သည်၊ တိုးပွားသည် hmyauk-the, toe-pwar-the *(v.)* **multiply**

မြား myar *(n.)* **arrow**

မြားသမား myar-ta-mar *(n.)* **archer**

မြိန်မြိန်ရှက်ရှက် myein myein shatshat *(n.)* **relish**

မြိန်သည် myein-sai *(v.)* **relish**

မြို့ myo *(n.)* **city**

မြို့ကြီး myo-kyi *(n.)* **metropolis**

မြို့စားကတော် myo-sar-ka-taw *(n.)* **countess**

မြို့စားကြီး myo-sar-gyi *(n.)* **duke**

မြို့ဆိုး myo-soe *(n.)* **ghost town**

မြို့တော် myo-taw *(n.)* **capital**

မြို့တော်ဝန် myo-taw-win *(n.)* **mayor**

မြို့နယ် myoet-naal *(n.)* **shire**

မြို့ပတ်လမ်း myoe-pat-lam *(n.)* **orbital**

မြို့ပြ myoe-pya rai-mwansaw *(adj.)* **urban**

မြို့ပြင် အိမ်ကြီးရခိုင် myoet-pyin aainkyeerahkine *(n.)* **villa**

မြို့လယ် myo-lal *(adj.)* **centrical**

မြိုချခြင်း myo chachinn *(n.)* **swallow**

မြိုချသည် myo chasai *(v.)* **swallow**

မြီစား myie-sar *(n.)* **debtor**

မြုံ့သည် myone-the *(v.)* **munch**

မြုံသော myone-saw *(adj.)* **sterile**

မြုပ်သည် myuutsai *(v.)* **sink**

မြုပ်သည့် အခြေအနေ myoke-the-a-chay-a-nay *(n.)* **sag**

မြုပ်သည်၊ ကာသည် myoke-the, kar-the *(v.)* **whelm**

မြူးကြွခြင်း myuu kywachinn *(n.)* **vivacity**

မြူးကြွသည့် အက myuu kywa-seet-aa-ka *(n.)* **samba**

မြူးကြွသော my-kwa-taw *(adj.)* **chirpy**

မြူးခြင်း myu-chin *(n.)* **frolic**

မြူးတူးခုန်ပေါက် ဆော့ကစားခြင်း myauu tuu hkonepout sotkasarrchinn *(n.)* **romp**

မြူးတူးခုန်ပေါက် ဆော့ကစားသည် myauu tuu hkonepout sot kasarrsai *(v.)* **romp**

မြူးတူးပျော်ရွှင်ခြင်း my-tu-pyaw-shwin-chin *(n.)* **hilarity**
မြူးတူးပျော်ရွှင်နေသော my-tu-pyaw-shin-nay-taw *(adj.)* **exultant**
မြူးတူးပျော်ရွှင်သော myu-tu-pyaw-shwin-pwe *(n.)* **wassail**
မြူးတူးသောင်းကျန်းသော my-tu-taung-kyan-taw *(adj.)* **boisterous**
မြူးထူးဆော့ကစားသည် myu-tu-saw-ka-sar-the *(v.)* **frolic**
မြူ၊ မြူခိုး myu, my-khoe *(n.)* **mist**
မြူဆိုင်းသော myu-sai-taw *(adj.)* **hazy**
မြူထူ myu-htu *(n.)* **fog**
မြူထူထပ်ခြင်း myu-htu-htet-chin *(n.)* **fogbank**
မြူပိတ်သော myu-htu-taw *(adj.)* **foggy**
မြူဖြင့်ဖုံးလွှမ်းထားသော my-phint-hpone-hlwan-htar-taw *(adj.)* **misty**
မြူမှုန် myu-hmone *(n.)* **mote**
မြေကတုတ် myay-ka-htoke *(n.)* **bulwark**
မြေကမ္ဘာနှင့် အပူဆိုင်ရာ myay-ka-bar-nint-a-pu-sai-yar *(adj.)* **geothermal**
မြေကျွန် myaykywan *(n.)* **serf**
မြေကြွက် myay-kywat *(n.)* **rat**
မြေကြီး myay-gyi *(n.)* **ground**
မြေကြီးဆိုင်ရာ သိပ္ပံပညာခွဲ myay kyee-sinerar sippan-pin-nyarhkwal *(n.)* **paedology**
မြေကြီးနှင့် လုပ်သော myay-gyi-nint-lote-taw *(adj.)* **earthen**
မြေကွက် myay-kwat *(n.)* **plot**
မြေခွေး myay-khway *(n.)* **fox**
မြေခွေးမ myayhkwayma *(n.)* **vixen**
မြေခဲရှံ့ခဲ myay-khae-shwunt-khae *(n.)* **clod**
မြေငလျင် myayngalyin *(adj.)* **seismic**
မြေငလျင်ပညာ myayngalyinpanyar *(n.)* **seismology**
မြေငလျင်ပညာရှင် myayngalyinpanyarshin *(n.)* **seismologist**
မြေငလျင်မှတ်စက် myayngalyin mhaatsaat *(n.)* **seismograph**
မြေတွန့်ခေါက်ခြင်းနှင့် ဆိုင်သော myay-twunt-khaut-chin-nint-sai-taw *(adj.)* **orogenic**
မြေတွန့်ခေါက်ခြင်းဖြင့် ပုံပန်းပျက်သွားသော ကျောက် myay-twunt-khaut-chin-phyint-pone-pan-pyat-twar-taw-kyauk *(n.)* **orogen**
မြေထည် myay-htai *(n.)* **pottery**
မြေထည်ပစ္စည်း myay-htae-pyit-see *(n.)* **earthenware**
မြေထိုးစက် myay-htoe-sat *(n.)* **bulldozer**
မြေနီထည် titehkaann *(n.)* **terracotta**
မြေပြင် ရှင်းလင်းခြင်း myay-pyin-shin-lin-chin *(n.)* **ground clearance**
မြေပြင်တိုက်ခိုက်ခြင်း myay-pyin-tite-khite-chin *(n.)* **ground attack**
မြေပြင်သို့ ဆင်းသက်ခြင်း myay-pyin-toe-sin-thet-chin *(n.)* **landing**
မြေပြန့် myay-pyant *(n.)* **flatland**
မြေပြန့်လွင်ပြင် myay-pyant-lwin-pyin *(n.)* **plain**
မြေပိုင်ရှင် myay-pai-shin *(n.)* **landlord**
မြေပုံ myay-pon *(n.)* **map**
မြေပုံ၊ ဗိသုကာတွင် သုံးသော အစွန်းများ myay-pon-bi-tu-kar-twin-tone-taw-a-sune-myar *(n.)* **orthograph**
မြေပုံစာအုပ် myay-bone-sar-oak *(n.)* **atlas**
မြေပုံဆွဲသူ myay-pon-swal-thu *(n.)* **cartographer**
မြေပုံထုတ်သည် myay-pon-htoke-the *(v.)* **map**

မြေဖြူ myay-phyu *(n.)* **chalk**

မြေဖြူမှုန့် myay-phyu-hmont *(n.)* **chalkdust**

မြေမျက်နှာသွင်ပြင် myay myetnharswinpyin *(n.)* **topography**

မြေမျက်နှာသွင်ပြင်နှင့်ဆိုင်သော myay myetnhar swinpyin nintsinesaw *(adj.)* **topographical**

မြေမျက်နှာသွင်ပြင်ပညာရှင် myay myetnhar swinpyinpanyarshin *(n.)* **topographer**

မြေမြှုပ်သည် myay-hmyoke-the *(v.)* **entomb**

မြေမြှုပ်သင်္ဂြိုလ်ခြင်း myay-myoke-tha-gyo-chin *(n.)* **burial**

မြေမြှုပ်သင်္ဂြိုလ်သည် myay-myoke-tha-gyo-the *(v.)* **bury**

မြေမှရသော သတ္တုအတုံးအခဲ myay-mha-ya-taw-tat-tu-a-tone-a-hkae *(n.)* **nugget**

မြေရှင်ပဒေသရာဇ်စနစ်နှင့် ဆိုင်သော myay-shin-pa-day-ta-yit-sa-nit-nint-sai-taw *(adj.)* **feudal**

မြေရိုးတံတိုင်း myay roetantine *(n.)* **rampart**

မြေရိုင်း myay-yai *(n.)* **fallow**

မြေရိုင်းကွင်း myay-yai-kwin *(n.)* **moor**

မြေလတ်ပိုင်း myay-lat-pai *(n.)* **midland**

မြေဩဇာ myay-aw-zar *(n.)* **fertilizer**

မြေဩဇာကျွေးသည် myay-aw-zar-kway-the *(v.)* **manure**

မြေအနေအထား myayaanayaahtarr *(n.)* **terrain**

မြေအောက် myay-out *(adj.)* **subterranean**

မြေအောက်ကမ္ဘာ myay-aoutkambhar *(n.)* **underworld**

မြေအောက်ခန်း myay-aut-khan *(n.)* **basement**

မြေအောက်မြောင်း myay-awt-myaung *(n.)* **culvert**

မြေအောက်ရထားစနစ် myay-awt-ya-htar-sa-nit *(n.)* **metro**

မြေအောက်အကျဉ်းတိုက် myay-aut-a-kyin-tite *(n.)* **dungeon**

မြောက်ဘက် myauk-bhaat *(adj.)* **northern**

မြောက်ဘက်သွား myauk-bhaat-twarr *(adj.)* **northerly**

မြောက်ဘက်သို့ myauk-bhaat-thoet *(adv.)* **northerly**

မြောက်အရပ် myauk-a-yat *(n.)* **north**

မြောင်း myaung *(n.)* **ditch**

မြောင်းတူးသည် myaung-tu-the *(v.)* **groove**

မြော်မြင်မှု myaw-myin-mu *(n.)* **foresight**

မြဲစွဲစွာ အားကိုးထိုက်သော myaell swalswar aarrkoehtitesaw *(adj.)* **staunch**

မလွန်ဆန်နိုင် ma-lwansaannine *(v.)* **succumb**

မလွယ်ကူသော ma-lwal-kuusaw *(adj.)* **uneasy**

မလွှမ်းမိုးနိုင်သော ma-hlwan-moe-nai-taw *(adj.)* **invincible**

မလွှဲသာဖြစ်သည် ma-lwal-tar-hpyit-tai *(v.)* **oblige**

မလှုပ်ရှားသော၊ သေသော ma-hlote-shar-taw, tay-taw *(adj.)* **inactive**

မလိမ္မာခြင်း ma-lain-mar-chin *(n.)* **imprudence**

မလိမ္မာသော ma-lain-mar-taw *(adj.)* **imprudent**

မလိုက်လျောသော ma-lite-lyaw-taw *(adj.)* **inflexible**

မလိုချင်သော malochinsaw *(adj.)* **unwanted**

မလိုင်၊ ခရင် ma-hlai, kha-yin *(n.)* **cream**

မလိုမုန်းထားစိတ် ma lo mone htarrsate *(n.)* **spite**
မလိုမုန်းထားမှု ma-lo-hmone-htar-mu *(n.)* **animus**
မလိုလားသော ma-lo-lar-taw *(adj.)* **inimical**
မလိုလားသော အရာတစ်ခုကို ကြော်ငြာသည် ma-lo-lar-taw-a-yar-ta-khu-ko-kyaw-nyar-the *(n.)* **monger**
မလိုလားအပ်သော malolarratsaw *(adj.)* **superfluous**
မလိုအပ်ပဲ ကြေးများသည် ma-lo-at-pal-kyay-myar-the *(v.)* **cavil**
မလိုအပ်သော maloatsaw *(adj.)* **unnecessary**
မလုံခြုံမှု ma-hlone-chone-mu *(n.)* **insecurity**
မလုံခြုံသော ma-hlone-chone-taw *(adj.)* **insecure**
မလုံမလဲ ma lonemalell *(adj.)* **sheepish**
မလုံလောက်သော ma-lon-laut-taw *(adj.)* **inadequate**
မလုပ်ပါ malotepar *(v.)* **undo**
မလုပ်မနေ လုပ်ရခြင်း ma-lote-ma-nay-lote-ya-chin *(n.)* **compulsion**
မလုပ်မနေ လုပ်ရသော ma-lote-ma-nay-lote-ya-taw *(adj.)* **compulsory**
မလုပ်မဖြစ်သော ma-lote-ma-phit-taw *(adj.)* **mandatory**
မလုပ်မီ စဉ်းစားရန် သတိပေးခြင်း ma-lote-mu-sin-sar-yan-ta-di-pay-chin *(n.)* **caveat**
မလုပ်ရန် တားမြစ်သည် ma-lote-yan-tar-myit-the *(v.)* **dehort**
မလုပ်ရန် ဖျောင်းဖျသည် ma-lote-yan-hpaung-pya-the *(v.)* **dissuade**
မလေးမခန့်ပြုခြင်း ma layy m hkaantpyuchinn *(n.)* **sacrilege**
မလေးမခန့်ပြုသော ma layy m hkaantpyusaw *(adj.)* **sacrilegious**
မဝံ့မရဲ ma-want-ma-rell *(n.)* **timidity**
မဝံ့မရဲဖြစ်သော ma-wint-ma-ye-phit-taw *(adj.)* **diffident**
မဝတ်ခေါင်းစွပ် ma-waat-hkaung-swut *(n.)* **wimble**
မွတ်စလင် ဘာသာရေးခေါင်းဆောင် mu-sa-lin-bar-tar-yay-gaung-saung *(n.)* **mullah**
မွန်းခြင်း moon-chin *(n.)* **asphyxia**
မွန်းစေသည် moon-say-the *(v.)* **asphyxiate**
မွန်းတည့် mwann-tae *(n.)* **noon**
မွန်းလွဲပိုင်း mun-lwe-paing *(n.)* **afternoon**
မွန်းသည် hmune-the *(v.)* **choke**
မွန်မြတ်သန့်စင်မှု mwanmyat saant sinmhu *(n.)* **sanctity**
မွန်မြတ်သော mon-myat-taw *(adj.)* **glorious**
မွမ်းကျပ်ခြင်း mwam kyat-chinn *(n.)* **suffocation**
မွမ်းကျပ်သည် mwam kyatsai *(v.)* **suffocate**
မွမ်းမံမှု၊ ချက်လုပ်ခြင်း mwam-man mhu , chet-lotechinn *(n.)* **refinement**
မွှေးကြိုင်သည် hmway-kyaine-sai *(v.)* **perfume**
မွှေးသော၊ ကြိုင်သော hmway-taw, kyaing-taw *(adj.)* **fragrant**
မွှေစက် hmway-sat *(n.)* **blender**
မွှေနှောက်ဖျက်ဆီးသည် hmway-naut-phat-see-the *(v.)* **devastate**
မွှေနှောက်ရှာဖွေသည် hmway-naut-shar-phway-the *(v.)* **ferret**
မွှေနှောက်လှန်လှောသည် mwhaay nhaout hlaan hlaawsai *(v.)* **rifle**
မွှေသည် mwhaaysai *(v.)* **stir**
မွေ့ရာ mway-yar *(n.)* **mattress**

မွေ့ရာနှင့် အိပ်ရာခင်း mwaay-yar-hnint-aik-yar-khin *(n.)* **bedding**
မွေးကင်းစ mway-kin-sa *(adj.)* **newborn**
မွေးကင်းစ၊ အစပျိုးစ mway-kin-sa, a-sa-pyo-sa *(n.)* **infancy**
မွေးကင်းစများ myay-kin-sa-myar *(adj.)* **infantile**
မွေးစား mway-sar *(adj.)* **adoptive**
မွေးစားခြင်း mway-sar-chin *(n.)* **adoption**
မွေးစားသည် mway-sar-the *(v.)* **adopt**
မွေးစားသားသမီးစောင့်ရှောက်ခြင်း mway-sar-tar-ta-mee-saunt-shaut-chin *(n.)* **foster care**
မွေးနေ့ mway-nae *(n.)* **birthdate**
မွေးဖွားခြင်း mway-phwar-chin *(n.)* **birth**
မွေးဖွားခြင်းနှင့်ဆိုင်သော mway-phwar-chin-nint-sai-taw *(adj.)* **natal**
မွေးမြူရေးခြံကြီး mway-myuu-rayy chaan-kyee *(n.)* **ranch**
မွေးမြူရေးခြံလုပ်ငန်းလုပ်ဆောင်သည် mway-myuu-rayy chaan-lote-ngan-lote-saung-the *(v.)* **ranch**
မွေးရာပါ mway-yar-par *(adj.)* **born**
မွေးရာပါ အမှတ်အသား mway-yar-par-a-mat-a-tar *(n.)* **birthmark**
မွေးရာပါ အသား၊ ဆံပင်ဖြူပြီး မျက်ဆန် ပန်းရောင်ရှိသော လူ၊ တိရစ္ဆာန် mway-yar-par-a-tar-sin-pin-phyu-pee-myat-san-pan-yaung-shi-taw-lu-ta-yeik-san *(n.)* **albino**
မွေးရာပါ၊ ဝမ်းတွင်းပါ mway-yar-par, wan-twin-par *(adj.)* **inherent**
မွေးရာပါတာဝန်ဟု ခံယူချက် mwayrarpar tarwaanhu hkanyuuchet *(n.)* **vocation**
မွေးလမ်းကြောင်း ma sell kwalsaw *(n.)* **vagina**
မသံမထွက်သော ma-tan-ma-htwat-taw *(adj.)* **noiseless**
မသက်ဆိုင်ကြောင်း ငြင်းဆိုသည် ma-thet-sai-kyaung-nyin-soe-the *(v.)* **disclaim**
မသက်မသာ ဖြစ်သော ma-thet-ma-tar-phit-taw *(adj.)* **miserable**
မသက်မသာဖြစ်ခြင်း ma-thet-ma-tar-phit-chin *(n.)* **discomfort**
မသင့်မတင့် ma-tint-ma-tint *(adj.)* **injudicious**
မသင့်လျော်သော၊ ချစားသော အပြုအမူ ma-tint-lyaw-taw-cha-sar-taw-a-pyu-a-mu *(n.)* **jobbery**
မသင်္ကာဖွယ်ဖြစ်သူ ma sin kar hpwal-pyit-suu *(n.)* **suspect**
မသင်္ကာမှု ma-sin karmhu *(n.)* **suspicion**
မသတီစရာ ma sa te-sa-rar *(adj.)* **vile**
မသနားတတ်သော ma-ta-nar-tat-taw *(adj.)* **merciless**
မသန့်စင်ခြင်း ma-tant-sin-chin *(n.)* **impurity**
မသန့်စင်သော ma-tant-sin-taw *(adj.)* **impure**
မသန့်မပြန့် ဖိုသီဖတ်သီ ma saant ma pyant hpo se hpaatse *(adj.)* **slatternly**
မသန့်မပြန့် ဖိုသီဖတ်သီ မိန်းမ ma saant ma pyant hpo se hpaatse meinm ma *(n.)* **slattern**
မသန်စွမ်းဖြစ်သည် ma-tan-swan-phit-the *(v.)* **disable**
မသန်စွမ်းမှု ma-tan-swan-mu *(n.)* **disability**
မသန်စွမ်းသော ma-tan-swan-taw *(adj.)* **disabled**
မသန်မစွမ်းသူ ma-tan-ma-swan-thu *(n.)* **cripple**
မသပ်မရပ်ပုံစံနှင့်သူ m saut m raut ponehcan nhangsuu *(n.)* **scruff**

မသိကျိုးကျွန်ပြုခြင်း a-ti-kyoe-kyun-pyu-chin *(n.)* **connivance**

မသိခြင်း ma-thi-chin *(n.)* **ignorance**

မသိမသာ ma-ti-ma-thar *(adj.)* **discreet**

မသိမသာကွဲပြားချက် ma-ti-ma-tar-kwal-pyar-chet *(n.)* **nuance**

မသိသော masisaw *(adj.)* **unknown**

မသိုးမသန့်ဖြစ်သော ma soe ma saanthpyitsaw *(adj.)* **uncanny**

မသေချာသော masaychaarsaw *(adj.)* **uncertain**

မသဲကွဲသော ma sell makwal *(adj.)* **vague**

မသဲမကွဲ sate kyeewinsaw *(n.)* **vagueness**

မဟာဌာန ma-har-htar-na *(n.)* **faculty**

မဟာဌာနမှူး ma-har-htar-na-hmu *(n.)* **dean**

မဟာဗျူဟာ maharbyauuhar *(n.)* **strategy**

မဟာဗျူဟာမြောက် တွေးခေါ်သူ maharbyauuharmyawt tway hkawsuu *(n.)* **strategist**

မဟာမိတ်ပြုခြင်း ma-har-meik-pyu-chin *(n.)* **alliance**

မဟာမိတ်ဖြစ်သော ma-har-meik-phit-taw (adj.) **allied**

မဟာမိတ်ဖွဲ့သည် ma-har-meik-phwe-the *(n.)* **ally**

မဟုတ် ma-hote *(n.)* **no**

မဟုတ်မတရား စွပ်စွဲ ပြောဆိုချက် mahotematararr swutswal pyawwsochet *(n.)* **slur**

မဟုတ်မမှန်ကြောင်း ထင်ရှားစေသည် ma-hote-ma-man-kyaung-htin-shar-say-the *(v.)* **disprove**

မဟူရာဖလား ma-huu-ra-pha-lar *(n.)* **opal**

မဟော်ဂနီသစ်၊ နီညိုရောင် ma-haw-ga-ni-tit, ni-nyo-yaung *(n.)* **mahogany**

မှ hma *(prep.)* **from**

မှ၊ က mha, ka *(prep.)* **off**

မှက်၊ ထိုးနှက် ဝေဖန်သူ hmat, htoe-nat-wai-phan-thu *(n.)* **gadfly**

မှင်တက်မိလျက် hmin-thet-mi-lyat *(adj.)* **aghast**

မှင်တက်မိသည် hmin-thet-mi-the *(v.)* **astound**

မှင်သက်မိစေသည် hmin-tat-mi-say-the *(v.)* **mystify**

မှင်သက်မိသည် hmin-tat-mi-te *(v.)* **nonplus**

မှင်သက်မိသော hmin-thet-mi-thaw *(adj.)* **dumbfounded**

မှည့်လာသည် mha ny larsai *(v.)* **ripen**

မှည့်သော mhae saw *(adj.)* **ripe**

မှတစ်ဆင့်ဖြင့် mha-ta-sint-hpyint *(prep.)* **via**

မှတစ်ပါး hma-ta-par *(prep.)* **barring**

မှတ်ချက်ချသည် mhaatchetchasai *(v.)* **remark**

မှတ်ချက်ပြုသည် mat-chat-pyu-the *(v.)* **annotate**

မှတ်ချက်ပေးသည် mat-chat-pay-the *(n.)* **comment**

မှတ်စု mhat-su *(n.)* **note**

မှတ်စု၊ မှတ်တမ်း mat-su, mat-tan *(n.)* **memorandum**

မှတ်စုစာအုပ် mhaatsusaraote *(n.)* **scratchpad**

မှတ်ဉာဏ် mat-nyan *(n.)* **memory**

မှတ်ဉာဏ်ကူ mat-nyan-ku *(adj.)* **mnemonic**

မှတ်ဉာဏ်ကူ အတိုမှတ်ခြင်း mat-nyan-ku-a-to-mat-chin *(n.)* **mnemonization**

မှတ်ဉာဏ်ကူ အတိုမှတ်နည်း mat-nyan-ku-a-to-mat-nee *(n.)* **mnemonic**

မှတ်ဉာဏ်ပျောက်သွားခြင်း mat-nyan-pyauk-twar-chin *(n.)* **blackout**

မှတ်တမ်း mhaat-tam *(n.)* **record**

မှတ်တမ်း၊ မှတ်ပုံတင်စာရင်း mhaat-tam , mhaatpone-tinsarrainn *(n.)* **register**

မှတ်တမ်းထားသည် mhaat-tamhtarrsai *(v.)* **record**

မှတ်တမ်းထုတ်ပြန်ချက်၊ အစီအစဉ် mhaat-tam htote-pyan-chet , aa-sea-a-sin *(n.)* **proceeding**

မှတ်တမ်းရုပ်ရှင် mat-tan-yoke-shin *(n.)* **documentary**

မှတ်တိုင်၊ ရပ်တန့်ခြင်း mhaattine , rat-tantchinn *(n.)* **stop**

မှတ်တိုင်တွင် ခရီးသည်များ နားခိုရာ mat-tai-twin-kha-yee-the-myar-nar-kho-yar *(n.)* **bus shelter**

မှတ်ပုံတင်ခြင်း mhaatpone-tinchinn *(n.)* **registration**

မှတ်ပုံတင်မူပိုင် mhaat-pone-tin-muu-pine *(n.)* **patent**

မှတ်ပုံတင်အရာရှိ mhaatpone-tin-aarar-shi *(n.)* **registrar**

မှတ်မိသည် mhaat-misai *(v.)* **remember**

မှတ်ယူခြင်း mhaat-yuu-chinn *(n.)* **presumption**

မှတ်ယူသည် mat-yu-the *(v.)* **attribute**

မှတ်ယူသည်၊ မှန်းဆသည် mhaat yuu sai, mann-sa-sai *(v.)* **presume**

မှန်းကြည့်သည် man-kyi-the *(v.)* **envisage**

မှန်းဆချက် man-hsa-chat *(n.)* **guess**

မှန်းဆခြင်း mhaannsachinn *(n.)* **speculation**

မှန်းဆသည် man-hsa-the *(v.)* **guess**

မှန်ကန်ကြောင်း တရားဝင်ဖော်ပြသည် man-kan-kyaung-ta-yar-win-phaw-pya-the *(v.)* **certify**

မှန်ကန်ကြောင်း သက်သေထူခြင်း mhaankaankyaungg saatsay htuuchinn *(n.)* **sanctification**

မှန်ကန်ကြောင်း သက်သေထူသည် mhaankaankyaungg saatsay htuusai *(v.)* **sanctify**

မှန်ကန်ခြင်း mhaankaanchinn *(n.)* **veracity**

မှန်ကန်စွာ man-kan-swar *(adv.)* **aright**

မှန်ကန်မှု mhaankaanmhu *(n.)* **sincerity**

မှန်ကန်သော man-kan-taw *(adj.)* **correct**

မှန်ကြည်စက္ကူ man-kyi-sat-kyu *(n.)* **cellophane**

မှန်စီရွှေချ man-si-shway-cha *(n.)* **mosaic**

မှန်တင်ခုံ man-tin-khone *(n.)* **dressing table**

မှန်တပ်သည် man-tat-the *(v.)* **glaze**

မှန်တပ်သမား mam-tat-ta-mar *(n.)* **glazier**

မှန်ပြောင်း man-pyaung *(adj.)* **binocular**

မှန်ပုံကွက်၊ ဘောင်ကွက်၊ ဦးဆောင်ဆွေးနွေးသူအဖွဲ့ hman-pon-kwat, baung-kwat, u-saung-sway-nway-thu-a-phwe *(n.)* **panel**

မှန်ဘီလူး hman-ba-lu *(n.)* **lens**

မှန်မှန် mhaanmhaan *(n.)* **steadiness**

မှန်မှန်ကန်ကန် man-man-kan-kan *(adv.)* **justly**

မှန်မှန်ကန်ကန် man-man-kan-kan *(adv.)* **duly**

မှန်သော man-taw *(adj.)* **dim**

မှလွဲ၍ hma-lwal-ywe *(prep.)* **except**

မှအပ mha a-pa *(prep.)* **save**

မှာ hmar *(prep.)* **in**

မှားကြောင်း သက်သေပြသည် mar-kyaung-thet-tay-pya-the *(v.)* **confute**

မှားခေါ်သည် mar-khaw-the *(v.)* **miscall**

မှားတွက်ခြင်း mar-twat-chin *(n.)* **miscalculation**

မှားတွက်သည် mar-twat-the *(v.)* **miscalculate**

မှားယွင်းစွာ တင်ပြခြင်း hmar-ywin-swar-tin-pya-chin *(n.)* **misrepsentation**

မှားယွင်းစွာ တင်ပြသည် hmar-ywin-swar-tin-pya-the *(v.)* **misrepresent**

မှားယွင်းစွာ ပြုကျင့်ခြင်း mar-ywin-swar-pyu-kyint-chin *(n.)* **mal-treatment**

မှားယွင်းစွာ ယူဆခြင်း mar-ywin-swar-yu-sa-chin *(n.)* **misapprehension**

မှားယွင်းစွာ ယူဆသည် mar-ywin-swar-yu-sa-the *(v.)* **misapprehend**

မှားယွင်းပြီး ဂုဏ်သိက္ခာကျစေသော ထုတ်ပြန်ချက် ပြုလုပ်သည် hmar-ywin-pi-gon-tate-khar-kya-say-taw-htoke-pyan-chat-pyu-lote-the *(v.)* **calumniate**

မှားယွင်းသည် hmar-ywin-the *(v.)* **mistake**

မှားယွင်းသော mhar-ywin-saw *(adj.)* **wrong**

မှားသည် hmar-the *(v.)* **err**

မှားသော hmar-taw *(adj.)* **amiss**

မှာ၊ တွင် mar, twin *(prep.)* **at**

မှိတ်တုတ်မှိတ်တုတ်လင်းသည် maik-toke-maik-toke-lin-the *(v.)* **flicker**

မှိတ်တုတ်မှိတ်တုတ်အလင်းရောင် mate-tote matetoteaalinnraung *(n.)* **twinkle**

မှိန်သွားသည် လျော့စေသည် main-twar-the-shawt-say-the *(v.)* **dull**

မှို hmo-tat-taw *(n.)* **mushroom**

မှိုင်းသော mhainesaw *(adj.)* **sombre**

မှိုင်တွေရောဂါ hmai-tway-yaw-gar *(n.)* **melancholia**

မှိုင်တွေသည် hmai-tway-the *(v.)* **mope**

မှိုင်တွေသော hmai-tway-taw *(adj.)* **melancholic**

မှိုတက်ခြင်း hmo-tat-the *(n.)* **fungus**

မှိုတက်သော hmo-tat-taw *(adj.)* **mouldy**

မှီခိုနေရခြင်း mi-kho-nay-ya-chin *(n.)* **dependence**

မှီခိုသည် mi-kho-the *(v.)* **depend**

မှီခိုသူ mi-kho-thu *(n.)* **dependant**

မှီသည် hmi-the *(v.)* **lean**

မှုံဝါးအောင် လုပ်သည် hmone-war-aung-lote-the *(v.)* **maculate**

မှုခင်း mu-khin *(n.)* **crime**

မှုခင်းဆေးပညာဆိုင်ရာ mu-khin-say-pyin-nyar-sai-yar *(adj.)* **forensic**

မှုတ်ထုတ်သည် mote htote-sai *(v.)* **puff**

မှုတ်သည်၊ ဖျန်းသည် mote sai, hpyann-sai *(v.)* **spray**

မှုတ်သည်၊ လေတိုက်သည် hmot-the, lay-tite-the *(v.)* **blow**

မှုန်ကုပ်ကုပ်မျက်နှာ hmon-kote-kote-myit-nar *(n.)* **frown**

မှုန်ဆန်သော hmone-san-taw *(adj.)* **dour**

မှုန်မွှားသော hmone-hmwar-taw *(adj.)* **minuscule**

မှုန်မှိုင်းနေခြင်း hmone-hmine-nay-chin *(n.)* **gloom**

မှုန်မှိုင်းနေသော hmone-hmine-nay-taw *(adj.)* **gloomy**

မှုန်မှိုင်းမဲ့မှောင်ခြင်း mhone mhaine mhaell mhaung-chinn *(n.)* **tenebrosity**

မှုန်မှိုင်းမဲ့မှောင်သော mhone mhaine mhaell mhaung-saw *(adj.)* **tenebrose**

မှုန်မှုန်မွှားမွှား hmone-hmone-hmwar-hmwar *(adv.)* **dimly**

မှုန်ဝါးဝါးဖြစ်ခြင်း hmone-war-war-phit-chin *(n.)* **haze**

မှုန်ဝါးဝါးအလင်းရောင် hmone-war-war-a-lin-yaung *(n.)* **glimmer**
မှုန်ဝါးသည် hmone-war-the *(v.)* **blur**
မှူးမတ် hmue-mat *(n.)* **baron**
မှူးမတ်ကတော် hmue-mat-ka-taw *(n.)* **baroness**
မှေးမှိန်ကွယ်ပျောက်စေသည် may-maing-kwal-pyauk-say-the *(v.)* **efface**
မှေးမှိန်သော mhay-mhein-taw *(adj.)* **obscure**
မှောက်လျက် နေသည် mout-lyet nay-sai *(v.)* **prostrate**
မှောက်လျက်၊ ဝမ်းလျားမှောက် mout lyet , wam lyarr-mout *(adj.)* **prostrate**
မှောက်လျက်သားနေခြင်း mout lyet sarr-naychinn *(n.)* **prostration**
မှောက်သည် maut-the *(v.)* **capsize**
မှောင်ခိုသမား mhaawinhkosamarr *(n.)* **smuggler**
မှောင်ခိုသွင်း၊ ထုတ်သည် mhaawinhko swin , htotesai *(v.)* **smuggle**
မှောင်သည် hmaung-the *(v.)* **darken**
မှောင်သော hmaung-taw *(adj.)* **dark**
မှော်၊ မျက်လှည့် maw, myat-hlae *(n.)* **magic**
မှော်ဆန်သော၊ မျက်လှည့်ဆန်သော maw-san-taw, myat-hlae-san-taw *(adj.)* **magical**
မှော်ဆရာ maw-sa-yar *(n.)* **mage**
မှော်အတတ် mhaaw aataat *(n.)* **sorcery**
မှဲ့ mae *(n.)* **mole**
မအီမသာဖြစ်ခြင်း ma-ei-ma-tar-phit-chin *(n.)* **malaise**
မအောင့်အည်းနိုင်သော ma-aung-ae-nai-taw *(adj.)* **irresistible**
မအောင်မြင်နိုင်သော ma-aung-myin ninesaw *(adj.)* **unachievable**
မအောင်မြင်ဖြစ်သည် ma-aung-myin-phit-the *(v.)* **bungle**
မအောင်မြင်သော ma-aung-myin-taw *(adv.)* **abortive**
မအောင်မြင်သော၊ ကံဆိုးသော ma-aung-myin-taw, kan-soe-taw *(adj.)* **luckless**
မာကျူရီ mar-kyuu-re *(n.)* **quicksilver**
မာကြမ်းသော အမွေးတို mar-kyan-taw-a-mway-tho *(n.)* **bristle**
မာကြမ်းသော အမွေးတိုပါရှိသည် mar-kyan-taw-a-mway-tho-par-shi-taw *(v.)* **brustle**
မာကာဒားမီးယားအသီး ma-kar-dar-mee-yar-a-thee *(n.)* **macadamia**
မာဂျင်ထဲတွင် ရေးထားသော၊ မဖြစ်စလောက် mar-gyin-htae-twin-yay-htar-taw, ma-phit-sa-laut *(adj.)* **marginal**
မာဂျရင်း mar-gya-yin *(n.)* **margarine**
မာစတာ၊ အုပ်ချုပ်သူ mar-sa-tar, oak-choke-thu *(n.)* **master**
မာနကြီးသော ma-na-kyi-taw *(adj.)* **haughty**
မာနထောင်လွှန်းခြင်း a chaeenhaee *(n.)* **vainglory**
မာနထောင်လွှန်းသော mar na htaung lwannchinn *(adj.)* **vainglorious**
မာန်ပါခြင်း man parchinn *(n.)* **verve**
မာန်ပါသော man parsaw *(adj.)* **spirited**
မာန်ဖီခြင်း man hpe-chinn *(n.)* **snarl**
မာန်ဖီသည် man-phi-the *(v.)* **growl**
မာဖီးယား mar-phee-yar *(n.)* **mafia**
မာယာ mar-yar *(n.)* **wile**
မာရသွန် mar-ra-thon *(n.)* **marathon**
မာရေကျောရည်နိုင်သော mar-yay-kyaw-yay-naing-taw *(adj.)* **acerbic**
မာရ်နတ်၊ နတ်ဆိုး man-nat, nat-soe *(n.)* **devil**
မာလကာသီး ma-la-kar-thee *(n.)* **guava**

မာလိန်မှူး mar lein-mhauu *(n.)* **skipper**

မိကျောင်း mi-kyaung *(n.)* **crocodile**

မိကျောင်းခေါင်းတို mi-kyaung-khaung-to *(n.)* **alligator**

မိခင် mi-khin *(n.)* **mother**

မိခင်ကဲ့သို့ mi-khin-kae-tho *(adj.)* **motherlike**

မိခင်ကဲ့သို့ ဂရုစိုက်သည် mi-khin-kae-tho-ga-yu-site-the *(v.)* **mother**

မိခင်ကဲ့သို့သော mi-khin-kae-tho-taw *(adj.)* **motherly**

မိခင်နှင့်ဆိုင်သော mi-khin-nint-sai-taw *(adj.)* **maternal**

မိခင်နိုင်ငံသားပြန်ဖြစ်ခြင်း mi-khin-nine-ngan-tar-pyan-phit-chin *(n.)* **repatriate**

မိခင်နိုင်ငံသားပြန်ဖြစ်သည် mi-khin-nine-ngan-tar-pyan-phit-the *(v.)* **repatriate**

မိခင်ဘဝ mi-khin-ba-wa *(n.)* **maternity**

မိစ္ဆာအဖြစ် ပြောင်းသွားသည် meik-sar-a-phit-pyaung-twar-the *(v.)* **demonize**

မိတ္တူ meik-thu *(adj.)* **duplicate**

မိတ္တူ၊ ပုံတူ meik-tu, pon-tu *(n.)* **facsimile**

မိတ္တူကူးစက် meik-thu-ku-sat *(n.)* **copier**

မိတ္တူကူးသည် meik-tu-ku-the *(v.)* **copy**

မိတ္တူပွားသည် meik-thu-pwar-the *(v.)* **duplicate**

မိတ္တူသုံးစောင် meittuu sonesaung *(n.)* **triplicate**

မိတ္တူသုံးစောင်ကူးခြင်း meittuu sone saung kuuchinn *(n.)* **triplication**

မိတ္တူသုံးစောင်ကူးသည် meittuu sone saung kuusai *(v.)* **triplicate**

မိတ္တူသုံးစောင်ကူးသော meittuu sone saung kuusaw *(adj.)* **triplicate**

မိတ်ကပ် meik-kat *(n.)* **make-up**

မိတ်ဆက် meik-sat *(n.)* **introduction**

မိတ်ဆက်သည် meik-sat-the *(v.)* **introduce**

မိတ်ဆွေ mate-sway *(n.)* **pal**

မိတ်ဆွေဖြစ်လာသည် meit-swe-phit-lar-the *(v.)* **befriend**

မိတ်ဖက်အဖွဲ့ meik-phat-a-phwe *(n.)* **affiliation**

မိတ်လိုက်သည် meik-lite-the *(v.)* **copulate**

မိနစ် mi-nit *(n.)* **minute**

မိန့်ခွန်း meint-hkwan *(n.)* **oration**

မိန့်ခွန်း၊ စကား mein hkwan, sakarr *(n.)* **speech**

မိန့်ခွန်းပြောသူ maint-khun-pyaw-thu *(n.)* **addresser**

မိန်းကြိုး၊ mein-kyo *(n.)* **main**

မိန်းကလေး mein-ka-lay *(n.)* **girl**

မိန်းမ mein-ma *(n.)* **wife**

မိန်းမခြင်း ရန်ဖြစ်ခြင်း main-ma-chin-yan-phit-chin *(n.)* **catfight**

မိန်းမစိုး mein-ma-soe *(n.)* **eunuch**

မိန်းမဆန်သော mein-ma-saan-saw *(adj.)* **womanish**

မိန်းမပျက် mein-ma-pyet *(n.)* **slut**

မိန်းမပျို main-ma-pyo *(n.)* **damsel**

မိန်းမဖော် main-ma-phaw *(n.)* **chaperone**

မိန်းမဘဝ mein-ma-bha-wa *(n.)* **womanhood**

မိန်းမလိုက်စားခြင်း mein-ma-lite-sarr-chinn *(n.)* **philander**

မိန်းမလိုက်စားသည် mein-ma lite-sarr-sai *(v.)* **womanise**

မိန်းမလိုက်စားသူ mein-ma lite-sarr-suu *(n.)* **womaniser**

မိန်းမအနိုင်ခံရသည် mein-ma-a-nai-khan-ya-the *(v.)* **henpeck**
မိဘ mi-bha *(n.)* **parent**
မိဘ၏ mi-bha-eat *(adj.)* **parental**
မိဘနှစ်ပါးနှင့် သားသမီးများသာပါသော မိသားစု mi-bha-na-par-nint-tar-ta-mee-myar-tar-par-taw mi-tarr-su *(n.)* **nuclear family**
မိဘမျိုးရိုး mi-bha-myoe-roe *(n.)* **parentage**
မိဘမဲ့ mi-bha-mae *(n.)* **orphan**
မိဘမဲ့ ကလေးဂေဟာ mi-bha-mae-ka-layy-gay-har *(n.)* **orphanage**
မိဘမဲ့ဖြစ်သွားသည် mi-bha-mae-hpyit-twar-tai *(v.)* **orphan**
မိဘအပြင်သွားခိုက်ကလေးကြည့်ပေးခြင်း mi-ba-a-pyin-twar-khite-ka-lay-kyi-pay-chin *(n.)* **babysitting**
မိဘအပြင်သွားခိုက်ကလေးကြည့်ပေးသည် mi-ba-a-pyin-twar-khite-ka-lay-kyi-pay-the *(v.)* **babysit**
မိမိ မိသားစုနှင့် ဆွေမျိုးသားချင်း mi-mi-mi-tar-su-nint-swe-myo-tar-chin *(n.)* **kin**
မိမိကိုယ်ကို တန်ဖိုးထားခြင်း mimikoko taanhpoehtarrchinn *(n.)* **self-esteem**
မိမိကိုယ်ကို ထိခိုက်စေခြင်း mimikoko htihkite hcayhkyinn *(n.)* **self-abuse**
မိမိကိုယ်ကို ပြန်လည် ဆန်းစစ်ခြင်း mi-mi-ko-ko-pyan-lal-san-sit-chin *(n.)* **introspection**
မိမိကိုယ်ကို ပြန်လည် ဆန်းစစ်သည် mi-mi-ko-ko-pyan-lal-san-sit-the *(v.)* **introspect**
မိမိကိုယ်ကို ဖျက်စီးခြင်း mimikoko hpyethceehkyinn *(v.)* **self-destruct**
မိမိကိုယ်ကို ယုံကြည်လွန်းသော mi-mi-ko-ko-yone-kyi-loon-taw *(adj.)* **assertive**
မိမိကိုယ်ကို သံသယရှိခြင်း mimikoko sansayashihkyinn *(n.)* **self-doubt**
မိမိကိုယ်ကို အဆုံးစီရင်ခြင်း mimikoko aasoneserinchinn *(n.)* **suicide**
မိမိကိုယ်ကို အဆုံးစီရင်လိုသည့် သဘောရှိသော mimikoko aasoneserin losaeet sabhawshisaw *(adj.)* **suicidal**
မိမိကိုယ်ကိုယ် ယုံကြည်သော mimikoko yonekyisaw *(adj.)* **self-confident**
မိမိကိုယ်ကိုယ် အကျပ်ကိုင်သော mimikoko a kyat kinesaw *(adj.)* **self-imposed**
မိမိတစ်ဦးတည်း ကြေညာချက်ထုတ်သော mimi tait utaee kyaynyarhkyet htotesaw *(adj.)* **self-proclaimed**
မိမိဘဏ်စာရင်းရှိငွေထက် ပိုထုတ်ခြင်း mi-mi-bhan-sar-rin-shi-ngway-htat-po-htote-chinn *(n.)* **overdraft**
မိမိဘဏ်စာရင်းရှိငွေထက် ပိုထုတ်သည် mi-mi-bhan-sar-rin-shi-ngway-htat-po-htote-tai *(v.)* **overdraw**
မိမိဘာသာ ခန့်အပ်သော mi-mi-bhar-sar hkaantatsaw *(adj.)* **self-appointed**
မိမိဘာသာ အားရကျေနပ်သော mi-mi-bar-tar-arr-ya-kyay-nat-taw *(adj.)* **complacent**
မိမိလက်ဖြင့် အာသာဖြေခြင်း mi-mi-lat-phint-ar-tar-phyay-chin *(v.)* **masturbate**
မိမိသဘောဆန္ဒဖြင့် mimi sabhaw sandahpyint *(adv.)* **voluntarily**
မိမိသဘောဆန္ဒအရဖြစ်သော mimi sabhaw sandaaarahpyitsaw *(adj.)* **voluntary**
မိမိအသံကို တစ်ခြားမှ ထွက်ပေါ်လာဟန် ဖန်တီးဖျော်ဖြေမှု mimiaasanko taitcharrmha htwatpawlarhaan hpaanteehpyawhpyaymhu *(n.)* **ventriloquism**
မိမိအသံကို တစ်ခြားမှ ထွက်ပေါ်လာဟန် ဖန်တီးဖျော်ဖြေသည် mimiaasanko taitcharrmha htwatpawlarhaan hpaantee hpyawhpyaysai *(v.)* **ventriloquize**

မိမိအသံကို တစ်ခြားမှ ထွက်ပေါ်လာဟန် ဖန်တီးဖျော်ဖြေသူ mimiaasanko taitcharrmha htwatpawlarhaan hpaantee hpyawhpyaysuu *(n.)* **ventriloquist**

မိမိအသံကို တစ်ခြားမှ ထွက်ပေါ်လာဟန် ဖန်တီးဖျော်ဖြေသော mimiaasanko taitcharrmha htwatpawlarhaan hpaantee hpyawhpyaysaw *(adj.)* **ventriloquistic**

မိလ္လာသိမ်းစနစ် main lar saim-sa-nit *(n.)* **sewerage**

မိဿရာသီဖွား meik-ta-yar-the-phwar *(n.)* **aries**

မိသားစု mi-tar-su *(n.)* **family**

မိသားစုနှင့် သက်ဆိုင်သော mi-tar-su-nint-thet-sai-taw *(adj.)* **domestic**

မိသားစုအမည် misarrsuaamai *(n.)* **surname**

မိုး moe *(n.)* **rain**

မိုးကုပ်စက်ဝိုင်း moe-kote-sat-wine *(n.)* **horizon**

မိုးကောင်းကင် moe-kaung-kin *(n.)* **firmament**

မိုးချုန်းသည် moe chonesai *(v.)* **thunder**

မိုးခြိမ်းသံ moe chaimsan *(n.)* **thunder**

မိုးခေါင်ခြင်း moe-khaung-chin *(n.)* **drought**

မိုးတဖွဲဖွဲရွာသည် moe-ta-phwe-phwe-ywar-the *(v.)* **drizzle**

မိုးထိတိုက်ခန်း moe-hti-tite-hkaann *(n.)* **penthouse**

မိုးထိအောင် မြှောက်သည် moe-htiaaung myaut-sai *(v.)* **sky**

မိုးဒဏ်လေဒဏ်ကြောင့် လွင့်ပြယ်သည် moe dan laydankyount lwint pyaalsai *(v.)* **weather**

မိုးနှင့် သက်ဆိုင်သော moe-nint sat-sinesaw *(adj.)* **pluvial**

မိုးနေသည် moenaysai *(v.)* **tower**

မိုးပြာရောင် moe-pyar-yaung *(n.)* **azure**

မိုးပွင့် moe-pwint *(n.)* **Face cream**

မိုးပုဆိန် moe-pa-sein *(n.)* **cloudburst**

မိုးဖွဲ moe-phwe *(n.)* **drizzle**

မိုးမခပင် moe-ma-hka-pin *(n.)* **willow**

မိုးမည်းတိမ်တောင် moe-mae-tain-taung *(n.)* **nimbus**

မိုးမျှော်တိုက် moe-myaw-tite *(n.)* **skyscraper**

မိုးရွာသည် moe rwar-sai *(v.)* **rain**

မိုးရွာသော moe rwar-saw *(adj.)* **rainy**

မိုးရွာသော ကာလ moe rwarsaw karl *(n.)* **pluvial**

မိုးရေခံ moe rayhkan *(adj.)* **showerproof**

မိုးရေချိန်တိုင်းကိရိယာ moerayhkyane tinekiriyar *(n.)* **pluviometer**

မိုးလေကာအပေါ်အင်္ကျီ moe-lay-kar-a-paw-inn-gyi *(n.)* **anorak**

မိုးလေဝသပညာ moe-lay-wa-ta-pyin-nyar *(n.)* **meteorology**

မိုးလေဝသပညာရှင် moe-lay-wa-ta-pyin-nyar-shin *(n.)* **meteorologist**

မိုးသက်မုန်တိုင်း moe saatmonetine *(n.)* **tempest**

မိုးသည်းထန်သည် moesaeehtaansai *(v.)* **teem**

မိုးသီး moe-thee *(n.)* **hail**

မိုးသီးကြွေသည် moe-thee-kyway-the *(v.)* **hail**

မိုးသီးမုန်တိုင်း moe-thee-mon-tine *(n.)* **hailstorm**

မိုးသောက်ပန်း moe-taut-pan *(n.)* **aurora**

မိုက်ကန်းသော mite-kan-taw *(adj.)* **lunatic**

မိုက်ခရိုပရော်ဆက်ဆာ mite-kha-ro-pa-yaw-sat-sar *(n.)* **microprocessor**

မိုက်ခရိုဖလင် mite-kha-ro-pha-lin *(n.)* **microfilm**
မိုက်ခရိုမီတာ mite-ka-ro-me-ter *(n.)* **micrometer**
မိုက်ခရိုဝေ့ဖ် mite-kha-ro-wave *(n.)* **microwave**
မိုက်ခွက် mite-khwat *(n.)* **microphone**
မိုက်မှားသောဟောပြောချက် mite-mar-taw-haw-pyaw-chat *(n.)* **onology**
မိုက်မိုက်မဲမဲ တုံးအသော mite-mite-mae-mae-ton-aa-taw *(adj.)* **dorky**
မိုက်မဲမှု mite-mae-mu *(n.)* **folly**
မိုက်မဲမှု၊ ဆင်ခြင်ဉာဏ်မရှိမှု mite mell mhu , sinchin nyan mashimhu *(n.)* **stupidity**
မိုက်မဲမှုများ mike-mae-mu-myar *(n.)* **follies**
မိုက်မဲသော mite mellsaw *(adj.)* **silly**
မိုက်ရူးရဲ mite-yu-ye *(n.)* **daredevil**
မိုက်ရိုင်းမှု mite-yai-mu *(n.)* **insolence**
မိုက်ရိုင်းသော mite-yai-taw *(adj.)* **insolent**
မိုင် mai *(n.)* **mile**
မိုင်းအလုပ်သမား mai-a-lote-ta-mar *(n.)* **miner**
မိုင်တိုင်းကိရိယာ mine-tine-ka-ri-yar *(n.)* **odometer**
မိုတယ် mi-the *(n.)* **motel**
မိုနိုမာကို ပိုလီမာပြောင်းသည် mo no marko polemar pyaunggsai *(v.)* **polymerize**
မီး mee *(n.)* **fire**
မီးကြီး mee-kyi *(n.)* **blaze**
မီးကဲ့သို့သော mee-kae-tho-taw *(adj.)* **fiery**
မီးခံ mee-khan *(adj.)* **fireproof**
မီးခံသံဘောင် mee-khan-tan-baung *(n.)* **grate**
မီးခံသည် mee-khan-the *(v.)* **fireproof**
မီးခံသေတ္တာ mee-khan-tit-tar *(n.)* **safebox**
မီးခံသေတ္တာဖောက်သူ mee-khan-tit-tar-phaut-thu *(n.)* **safecracker**
မီးခြစ် mee-chit *(n.)* **lighter**
မီးခိုး meehkoe *(n.)* **smoke**
မီးခိုးခေါင်းတိုင် mee-kho-khaung-tai *(n.)* **chimney**
မီးခိုးငွေ့လွှမ်းသည် meehkoe ngway lwmsai *(v.)* **soot**
မီးခိုးထွက်သည် meehkoe htwatsai *(v.)* **smoke**
မီးခိုးမြူ meehkoemyauu *(n.)* **smog**
မီးခိုးရောင် me-kho-yaung *(adj.)* **grey**
မီးခိုးအူသော meehkoe auusaw *(adj.)* **smoky**
မီးစဉ်ကြည့်ကတတ်သော mi-sin-kyi-ka-tat-taw *(adj.)* **adaptable**
မီးစွမ်းအားရှင် mee-swan-arr-shin *(n.)* **pyromantic**
မီးစာ mee-sar *(n.)* **wick**
မီးဆွတံ၊ ပိုကာဖဲကစားနည်း mee-swa-tan, po-kar-hpell-ka-sarr-nee *(n.)* **poker**
မီးဆေးသည်၊ ဖေးမသည် mee sayy sai , hpayymasai *(v.)* **temper**
မီးညှိသည်၊ မီးစွဲသည် mee-nyi-the, mee-swal-the *(v.)* **light**
မီးတောက် mee-taut *(n.)* **flame**
မီးတောက်၊ ပြိုးပြိုးပြက်ပြက် အလင်းရောင် mee-taut, pyo-pyo-pyat-pyat-a-lin-yaung *(n.)* **flash**
မီးတောက်ထွက်ရာ အပိုင်း mee-taut-htwat-yar-a-pai *(n.)* **burner**
မီးတောင် mee-taung *(adj.)* **volcanic**
မီးတောင်ဝ mee-taung-wa *(n.)* **crater**
မီးထိုးသည် mee htoesai *(v.)* **stoke**

မီးထိုးသမား mee htoesamarr *(n.)* **stoker**

မီးဒဏ်ခံ mee-dan-khan *(adj.)* **fire-resistant**

မီးဒဏ်ခံဝတ်စုံ mee-dan-khan-wit-sone *(n.)* **firesuit**

မီးပန်းဆိုင်း mee-pan-sai *(n.)* **chandelier**

မီးပွား meepwarr *(n.)* **spark**

မီးပွားထွက်သည် mee pwarr htwatsai *(v.)* **spark**

မီးပုံ mee-pon *(n.)* **bonfire**

မီးပုံပွဲ mee-pon-pwe *(n.)* **campfire**

မီးပူတိုက်သည် mee-pu-tite-the *(v.)* **iron**

မီးပေးရသော အပိုင်း mee-pay-ya-taw-a-pai *(n.)* **ignition**

မီးဖွားခြင်း mee-phwar-chin *(n.)* **childbirth**

မီးဖို mee-hpo *(n.)* **stove**

မီးဖိုချောင် mee-pho-chaung *(n.)* **kitchen**

မီးမဖွားမီ mee-ma-phwar-mi *(adj.)* **antenatal**

မီးမြှိုက်ခြင်း mee myahaitechinn *(n.)* **singe**

မီးမြှိုက်သည် mee myahaitesai *(v.)* **singe**

မီးမွှေးသည်၊ နှိုးဆွသည် mee-hmway-the, noe-swa-the *(v.)* **kindle**

မီးမောင်း mee-maung *(n.)* **floodlight**

မီးမောင်းထိုးသည် mee-maung-htoe-the *(v.)* **floodlight**

မီးရထားသံလမ်း၊ ရထားလမ်း mee-ra-htarr sanlam , ra-htarrlam *(n.)* **railway**

မီးရှို့စင် mee-shoet-sin *(n.)* **pyre**

မီးရှူးမီးပန်း mee-shu-mee-pan *(n.)* **fireworks**

မီးလင်းဖို mee-lin-pho *(n.)* **hearth**

မီးလုံး mee-lone *(n.)* **fireball**

မီးလောင်လျှင် ထွက်ပေါက် mee-laung-lyin-htwat-pauk *(n.)* **fire exit**

မီးလောင်လွယ်သော mee-laung-lwal-taw *(adj.)* **combustible**

မီးလောင်သည်၊ ပစ်သည် mee-hlaung-the, pyit-the *(v.)* **fire**

မီးလောင်သည်၊ မီးရှို့သည် mee-laung-the, mee-shoe-the *(v.)* **burn**

မီးလောင်သော meelaungsaw *(adj.)* **seared**

မီးသင့်သည်၊ ညှိုးရော်သည်၊ တစ်ရှိန်ထိုးမောင်းသည် mee sint sai , nyhaoe raw sai , tait shein htoe maunggsai *(v.)* **scorch**

မီးသဂြိုလ်ခြင်း mee-tha-gyo-chin *(n.)* **cremation**

မီးသဂြိုလ်ရုံ mee-tha-gyo-yone *(n.)* **crematorium**

မီးသဂြိုလ်သည် mee-tha-gyo-the *(v.)* **cremate**

မီးသင်္ဘော၊ ပေါင်းအိုး mee sinbhaw , paungg-oe *(n.)* **steamer**

မီးသတ်ကား mee-tat-kar *(n.)* **fire engine**

မီးသတ်ခြင်း mee-tat-chin *(n.)* **firefight**

မီးသတ်စခန်း mee-tat-sa-khan *(n.)* **fire station**

မီးသတ်ပိုက် mee-tat-pike *(n.)* **firehose**

မီးသတ်ဘူး mee-tat-bu *(n.)* **fire extinguisher**

မီးသတ်သမား mee-tat-ta-mar *(n.)* **firefighter**

မီးသွေး mee-thway *(n.)* **charcoal**

မီးသီး၊ ဥ mee-thee, oo *(n.)* **bulb**

မီးအိမ် mee-eain *(n.)* **lamp**

မီတာ mi-tar *(n.)* **meter**

မီနူး mee-nu *(n.)* **menu**

မုချ mote-cha *(adv.)* **certainly**

မုခ်ဝ mote-wa *(n.)* **portal**

မုဆိုး mote-soe *(n.)* **hunter**

မုဆိုးဖို musoe-hpo *(n.)* **widower**

မုဆိုးမ musoe-ma *(n.)* **widow**

မုဆိုးမ၊ မုဆိုးဖိုဖြစ်သည် musoe-ma , mu-soe hpohpyitsai *(v.)* **widow**

မုတ်ကောင် mote-kaung *(n.)* **oyster**

မုတ်ဆိတ် mote-seik *(n.)* **beard**

မုတ်ဆိတ်ပျားစွဲတတ်သော ပါရမီ motesate pyarr swaltaatsaw parrame *(n.)* **serendipity**

မုတ်ဆိတ်ရိတ်ပယ်ပြီး သုံးသောရေမွှေး mote-sate-yeik-pal-pi-tone-taw-yay-hmwe *(n.)* **aftershave**

မုတ်သုံလေ mote-thon-lay *(n.)* **monsoon**

မုဒိန်းကျင့်သည် mu-dein kyint-sai *(v.)* **rape**

မုဒိန်းမှု mu-deinmhu *(n.)* **rape**

မုန့်တိုက် hmont-tite *(n.)* **confectionery**

မုန်းခြင်းကို ဖော်ပြသော mone-chin-ko-phaw-pya-taw *(adj.)* **despiteful**

မုန်းတီးမှု hmone-tee-mu *(n.)* **animosity**

မုန်းသည် hmone-the *(v.)* **hate**

မုန်တိုင်း monetine *(n.)* **storm**

မုန်တိုင်းထန်သော monetine htaansaw *(adj.)* **stormy**

မုန်လာဥဝါ hmone-lar-u-war *(n.)* **carrot**

မုန်လာဥ mone-lar-u *(n.)* **radish**

မုန်လာဥနီ hmone-lar-u-nee *(n.)* **beet**

မုယော mu-yaw *(n.)* **malt**

မုယောစပါး mu-yaw-sa-par *(n.)* **barley**

မုရန်စေး mu-yan-say *(n.)* **myrrh**

မုသား၊ အမှား mu-tar, a-mar *(n.)* **falsehood**

မုသားသက်သေခံခြင်း mu-sarr-saat-say-hkan-chinn *(n.)* **perjury**

မုသားသက်သေခံသည် mu-sarr-saat-say-hkan-sai *(v.)* **perjure**

မူး၍ တငိုငိုတရီရီ ဖြစ်နေသော mu-ywe-a-ngo-ngo-ta-ye-ye-phit-nay-taw *(adj.)* **maudlin**

မူးမေ့သတိလစ်သွားစေသည် muu mae satilait swarrsaysai *(v.)* **stun**

မူးမော်ခြင်း muu-maw-chinn *(n.)* **swoon**

မူးယစ်ခြင်း mu-yit-chin *(n.)* **intoxication**

မူးယစ်စေတတ်သော အရာ mu-yit-say-tat-taw-a-yar *(n.)* **intoxicant**

မူးယစ်ဆေးဝါး mu-yit-say-war *(n.)* **dope**

မူးယစ်ပြီး ဗရမ်းဗတာ အောင်ပွဲခံခြင်း mu-yit-pyi-ba-yan-ba-taw-aung-pwe-khan-chin *(n.)* **bacchanal**

မူးယစ်သည် mu-yit-the *(v.)* **intoxicate**

မူးယစ်သောက်စားသည် mu-yit-taut-sar-the *(v.)* **booze**

မူးဝေသည် mu-wai-the *(v.)* **daze**

မူးဝေသော mu-wai-taw *(adj.)* **giddy**

မူးဝေသော အခြေအနေ mu-wai-taw-a-chay-a-nay *(n.)* **daziness**

မူကြမ်း mu-kyan *(n.)* **draft**

မူကြမ်းရေးသည် mu-kyan-yay-the *(v.)* **draft**

မူစလင်ဘာသာဝင် mu-sa-lin-bar-tar-win *(adj.)* **muslim**

မူပိုင်ခွင့်မှတ်ပုံတင်ပြီးသော muu-pine-hkwint-mhaat-pone-tin-pyee-saw *(adj.)* **patent**

မူပိုင်ခွင့်မှတ်ပုံတင်သည် muu-pine-hkwint-mhaat-pone-tin-sai *(v.)* **patent**

မူပိုင်ခွင့် mu-pai-kwint *(n.)* **copyright**

မူပိုင်ခွင့်ကို ထိပါး၍ ခိုးချသည် muu-pine-hkwint-ko-hti-parr-hkoe-cha-sai *(v.)* **pirate**

မူမမှန်ချက် mu-ma-hman-chat *(n.)* **anomaly**

မူမရှိသော muumashisaw *(adj.)* **unprincipled**

မူရင်း mu-yin *(n.)* **master copy**

မူရင်းအတိုင်းဖြစ်သော muurinnaatinehpyitsaw *(adj.)* **unabridged**

မူလ၊ ပင်ရင်း mu-la , pin-rinn *(n.)* **original**

မူလ၊ အစ mu-la, a-sa *(n.)* **origin**

မူလဘာသာစကားအစား အခြားဘာသာစကားဖြင့် အသံသွင်းသည် mu-la-bar-tar-sa-kar-a-sar-a-char-bar-tar-sa-kar-phyint-a-tan-twin-the *(n.)* **dub**

မူလရာထူး၌ ပြန်လည်ခန့်အပ်သည် mu-la rar-htuu pyanlai hkaant atsai *(v.)* **reinstate**

မူလအကြောင်းမှ ဘေးချော်သွားခြင်း mu-la-a-kyaung-ma-bay-chaw-twar-chin *(n.)* **digression**

မူလအကြောင်းမှ ဘေးချော်သွားသည် mu-la-a-kyaung-ma-bay-chaw-twar-the *(v.)* **digress**

မူလအတိုင်း ထိန်းသိမ်းထားသည် muu-la-aa-tine hteinsaim-htarrsai *(v.)* **preserve**

မူလအတိုင်းမဟုတ်သော ပုံစံဖြင့် mu-la-a-tine-ma-hoke-taw-pon-san-phint *(adv.)* **extrinsically**

မူဝါဒ muu-war-da *(n.)* **policy**

မူဝါဒ ကြေညာစာတမ်း mu-war-da-kyay-nyar-sar-tan *(n.)* **manifesto**

မေ့ဆေး mae-say *(n.)* **anaesthesia**

မေ့မြောခြင်း mae-myaw-chin *(n.)* **coma**

မေ့လျော့သည် mae-lyaw-the *(v.)* **forget**

မေ့လျော့သော mae-lyaw-thaw *(adj.)* **forgetful**

မေးခွန်း may-hkwann *(n.)* **query**

မေးစေ့ may-sae *(n.)* **chin**

မေးမြန်းစုံစမ်းသည် may-myan sonesamsai *(v.)* **quiz**

မေးမြန်းသည် may-myansai *(v.)* **query**

မေးမြန်းသော may-myan-taw *(adj.)* **interrogative**

မေးရိုး mae-yoe *(n.)* **jaw**

မေတ္တာရပ်သည် myit-tar-yat-the *(v.)* **appeal**

မေထုန်ရာသီဖွား may-htone-yar-ti-phwar *(n.)* **Gemini**

မေမေ may-may *(n.)* **mamma**

မေလ may-la *(n.)* **May**

မော့၍ ကြည့်သော mot-ywe kyi-saw *(adj.)* **upward**

မော့၍ ထောင်၍ mot-ywe htaung-ywe *(adv.)* **upwards**

မော့တေးလ်အရက် mot-tay-a-yat *(n.)* **mocktail**

မောင်း maung *(n.)* **gong**

မောင်းနှင်သည် maunggnhinsai *(v.)* **taxi**

မောင်းနှင်သည်၊ တွန်းပို့သည် maung-nhin sai , twann phoetsai *(v.)* **propel**

မောင်းနှင်သည်၊ တွန်းအားပေးသည် maung-hnin-the-, tun-arr-pay-the *(v.)* **drive**

မောင်းနှင်သွားလာခြင်း maung-hnin-twar-lar-chin *(n.)* **navigation**

မောင်းသည် maung-sai *(v.)* **pilot**

မောင်းသူမဲ့လေယာဉ် maung-thu-mae-lay-yin *(n.)* **drone**

မောင်နှမအရင်း maung-nha-maa-a-rinn *(n.)* **sibling**

မောပန်းကြီး၍ ပါးစပ်ဖြင့် ရှူရှိုက်သည် maw-paann-kyee-parr-sat-hpyint-shuu-shite-sai *(v.)* **pant**

မောပန်းကြီး၍ ပါးစပ်ဖြင့် ရှူရှိုက်သောအသက် maw-paann-kyee-ywe-parr-saut-hpyint-shuu-shite-saw-a-saat *(n.)* **pant**

မောပန်းသော maw paannsaw *(adj.)* **tired**

မော်ကွန်းတင်အပ်သည် maw-kun-tin-at-taw *(v.)* **immortalize**

မော်ကွန်းတိုက် maw-khun-tite *(n.)* **archive**

မော်ကွန်းထိန်းဌာန mawkwann htein-htarna *(n.)* **registry**

မော်ဂျူး maw-ju *(n.)* **module**

မော်ဂျူးပုံစံ maw-ju-pon-san *(adj.)* **modular**

မော်တာစက် maw-tar-sat *(n.)* **motor**

မော်တော်ကား maw-taw-kar *(n.)* **automobile**

မော်ဖင်း maw-phine *(n.)* **morphine**

မော်ဖိန်း maw-fane *(n.)* **morphia**

မော်လီကျူး maw-li-kyu *(n.)* **molecule**

မော်လီကျူးဆိုင်ရာ maw-li-kyu-sai-yar *(adj.)* **molecular**

မော်လီကျူးများစွာ maw le kyauumyarr-swar *(adj.)* **polymolecular**

မဲ mell *(n.)* **vote**

မဲဆန္ဒနယ် ma-san-da-nal *(n.)* **constituency**

မဲဆန္ဒပေးပိုင်ခွင့်၊ လုပ်ပိုင်ခွင့် mae-san-da-pay-pai-khwint, lote-pai-khwint *(n.)* **franchise**

မဲဆန္ဒပေးပိုင်ခွင့်ရသည် mae-sanda-pay-pai-khwint-ya-the *(v.)* **enfranchise**

မဲဆန္ဒရရှိသည် mell-san-da-ra-shi-sai *(v.)* **poll**

မဲဆန္ဒရှင်များ mae-sanda-shin-myar *(n.)* **electorate**

မဲနယ်ရောင် mae-nal-yaung *(n.)* **indigo**

မဲနှိုက်ခြင်း mae-hnite-chin *(n.)* **draw**

မဲပေးပိုင်ခွင့် mell-payy pinehkwint *(n.)* **suffrage**

မဲပေးသည် mellpayysai *(v.)* **vote**

မဲပေးသူ mellpayysuu *(n.)* **voter**

မဲအရေအတွက် mell-aa-ray-aa-twat *(n.)* **poll**

ယခင် ya-hkin *(adj.)* **previous**

ယခင်က ya-khin-ka *(adv.)* **formerly**

ယခုတိုင် ya-hku-tine *(adv.)* **yet**

ယခုအချိန် ya-hku-a-chane *(adv.)* **now**

ယစ်မျိုးခွန် yit-myo-khun *(n.)* **excise**

ယဇ်ပလ္လင် yit-pa-ling *(n.)* **altar**

ယဉ်ကျေးဖွယ်ရာရှိသော yain kyaayy hpwalrarshisaw *(adj.)* **seemly**

ယဉ်ကျေးမှု yin-kyay-mu *(n.)* **culture**

ယဉ်ကျေးမှု ဖွံ့ဖြိုးလာခြင်း yin-kyay-mu-phwint-phyo-lar-chin *(n.)* **civilization**

ယဉ်ကျေးမှု ဖွံ့ဖြိုးလာသည် yin-kyay-mu-phwint-phyo-lar-the *(v.)* **civilize**

ယဉ်ကျေးမှုနှင့် ဆိုင်သော yan-kyay-mu-nint-sai-taw *(adj.)* **cultural**

ယဉ်ကျေးသည် yin-kyay-the *(adj.)* **courteous**

ယဉ်ကျေးသိမ်မွေ့မှု yin-kyaayy-sin-mwae-mhu *(n.)* **politeness**

ယဉ်ကျေးသိမ်မွေ့သော yin-kyay-tint-mway-taw *(adj.)* **gracious**

ယဉ်ကျေးသော yin-kyaayy-saw *(adj.)* **polite**

ယဉ်စွန်းတန်း yin swanntaann *(n.)* **tropic**

ယဉ်ပါးစေသည် yin parrsaysai *(v.)* **tame**

ယဉ်ပါးသော yin parrsaw *(adj.)* **tame**

ယထာဘူတဝါဒီ yahtar bhuu ta-warde *(n.)* **realist**

ယနေ့ yanae *(n.)* **today**

ယနေ့ည yanaenya *(adv.)* **tonight**

ယန်းငွေ yaann-ngway *(n.)* **Yen**

ယန်ဗော်ပင် yan-baw-pin *(n.)* **orl**

ယမန်နေ့က ya-maan-nae-ka *(adv.)* **yesterday**

ယမ်းသည် yamsai *(v.)* **wag**

ယှဉ်ကြည့်သည် yin-kyi-the *(n.)* **contrast**

ယှဉ်တွဲ ခိုင်းနှိုင်းခြင်း shin-twe-khai-nai-chin *(n.)* **juxtaposition**

ယှဉ်နိုင်သည် yhainninesai *(v.)* **rival**

ယှဉ်ပြိုင်မှု yin-pyai-mu *(n.)* **contention**

ယှဉ်ပြိုင်သည် yin-pyai-the *(v.)* **match**

ယှဉ်ပြေးသည် shin pyaysai *(v.)* **race**

ယှဉ်လျက် shin-lyat *(prep.)* **alongside**

ယားကျိကျိရှိသော yarr kyai kyaishisaw *(adj.)* **scratchy**

ယားခြင်း yar-chin *(n.)* **itch**

ယားလွယ်သော yarr lwalsaw *(adj.)* **ticklish**

ယားသည် yar-the *(v.)* **itch**

ယာဉ် yin *(n.)* **vehicle**

ယာဉ်စီးခ yin-see-kha *(n.)* **fare**

ယာဉ်စီးနင်းခြင်း yin seenainnchinn *(n.)* **ride**

ယာဉ်တိုက်ခြင်း yin-tite-chin *(v.)* **crash**

ယာဉ်မောင်း yin-maung *(n.)* **driver**

ယာဉ်မောင်းထိုင်ရာ နေရာ yin-maung-htai-yar-nay-yar *(n.)* **cab**

ယာဉ်အသွားအလာ yinaaswarraalar *(n.)* **traffic**

ယာယီ yarye *(adj.)* **provisional**

ယာယီညွန့်ပေါင်းအဖွဲ့ yar-yee-nyunt-paung-a-phwe *(n.)* **coalition**

ယိမ်းထိုးလှျောက်သည် yaim htoe shoutsai *(v.)* **stagger**

ယိမ်းထိုးသည် yaim htoesai *(v.)* **sway**

ယိမ်းယိုင်ခြင်း yein-yine-chin *(n.)* **lurch**

ယိမ်းယိုင်မှု yaimyinemhu *(n.)* **tendency**

ယိမ်းယိုင်သည် yaimyinesai *(v.)* **waver**

ယို yo *(n.)* **jam**

ယိုးမယ်ဖွဲ့ခြင်း yoe maal hpwalchinn *(n.)* **pretext**

ယိုစိမ့်သည် yoe-seint-the *(v.)* **leak**

ယိုယွင်းပျက်စီးခြင်း yo-ywin-pyat-see-chin *(n.)* **decay**

ယိုယွင်းပျက်စီးသည် yo-ywin-pyat-see-the *(v.)* **decay**

ယိုယွင်းသည် yo-ywin-the *(v.)* **degenerate**

ယိုယွင်းသော yo-ywin-taw *(adj.)* **decadent**

ယိုသည်၊ စိမ့်သည် yo sai , seint-sai *(v.)* **seep**

ယီးတီးယားတားလုပ်သည် yee tee yarr tarrlotesai *(v.)* **trifle**

ယုံကြည်ချက် yone-kyi-chat *(n.)* **belief**

ယုံကြည်ခြင်း yonekyi-chinn *(n.)* **trust**

ယုံကြည်စိတ်ချမှု yone-kyi-seik-cha-mu *(n.)* **assurance**

ယုံကြည်စိတ်ချရသော yone-kyi-sate-cha-ra-saw *(adj.)* **trustworthy**

ယုံကြည်မှု yone-kyi-mu *(n.)* **confidence**

ယုံကြည်မှု ကင်းသည် yone-kyi-mu-kin-the *(v.)* **mistrust**

ယုံကြည်မှု ကင်းသော yone-kyi-mu-kin-taw *(v.)* **distrust**

ယုံကြည်မှု၊ ဘာသာတရား၏ အတွင်းပုံစံ yone-kyi-mu, bar-tar-ta-yar-ei-a-twin-pon-san *(n.)* **esoterism**

ယုံကြည်မှုကင်းမဲ့ခြင်း yonekyimhukinnmaechinn *(n.)* **scepticism**

ယုံကြည်မှုကင်းမဲ့သော yonekyimhu kinnmaesaw *(adj.)* **sceptical**

ယုံကြည်မှုဆိုင်ရာ ကျင့်ထုံး yone-kyi-mu-sai-yar-kyint-htone *(n.)* **cult**

ယုံကြည်မှုမရှိသော yonekyimhumashisaw *(adj.)* **unbelievable**

ယုံကြည်မှုရေးရာ ရေသောက်မြစ် yonekyimhurayyrar ray soutmyit *(n.)* **tenent**

ယုံကြည်ရသော yone-kyi-ya-taw *(adj.)* **trustful**

ယုံကြည်သက်ဝင်မှု yonekyi saatwinmhu *(n.)* **spirituality**

ယုံကြည်သည် yone-kyisai *(v.)* **trust**

ယုံကြည်သော yone-kyi-taw *(adj.)* **confident**

ယုံကြည်အားထားရသော yonekyi-aarrhtarr-rasaw *(adj.)* **reliable**

ယုံစားလွယ်ခြင်း yone-sar-lwal-chin *(n.)* **credulity**

ယုံလွယ်လွန်းသော yone-lwal-loon-taw *(adj.)* **credulous**

ယုတ္တိတန်သော yote-ti taan-saw *(adj.)* **rational**

ယုတ္တိဗေဒ yoke-ti-bay-da *(n.)* **logic**

ယုတ္တိဗေဒပညာရှင် yoke-ti-bay-da-pyin-nyar-shin *(n.)* **logician**

ယုတ္တိမရှိခြင်း yote-ti-ma-shi-chin *(adj.)* **irrational**

ယုတ္တိမရှိသော yoke-ti-ma-shi-taw *(adj.)* **illogical**

ယုတ္တိရှိသော yoke-ti-shi-taw *(adj.)* **logical**

ယုတ်ညံ့သော yoke-nyant-taw *(adj.)* **ignoble**

ယုတ်မာမှု yote-mar-mu *(n.)* **infamy**

ယုတ်မာသော yoke-mar-taw *(adj.)* **evil**

ယုတ်မာသော လုပ်ရပ် yote-mar-taw-lote-yatt *(n.)* **atrocity**

ယုန် yone *(n.)* **rabbit**

ယုန်တွင်း စနစ် yone-twin-sa-nit *(n.)* **warren**

ယုန်သားရေ yone-ta-yay *(n.)* **doeskin**

ယုယုယယ ပွတ်သပ်ခြင်း yu-yu-ya-ya-put-tat-chin *(n.)* **fondling**

ယုယုယယ ပွတ်သပ်သည် yu-yu-ya-ya-put-tat-the *(v.)* **fondle**

ယုယုယယ ပွတ်သပ်သူ yu-yu-ya-ya-put-tat-thu *(n.)* **fondler**

ယူကျူ yuu-kyu *(v.)* **You Tube**

ယူကလစ်ပင် u-ka-lit-pin *(n.)* **eucalypt**

ယူဆချက် yu-sa-chat *(n.)* **assumption**

ယူဆလျက် yuusalyet *(adv.)* **say**

ယူဆသည် yu-sa-the *(v.)* **assume**

ယူဆသည်၊ သဘောထားသည် yuusasai , sabhawhtarrsai *(v.)* **view**

ယူဆောင်နိုင်သော yuusaung-nine-saw *(adj.)* **takeable**

ယူနစ် yuunit *(n.)* **unit**

ယူလာသည် yu-lar-the *(v.)* **bring**

ယူသည်၊ ဆွဲသည် yuu sai , swalsai *(v.)* **take**

ယေဘုယျအားဖြင့် yay-buu-ya-arr-phit *(adv.)* **generally**

ယောကျာ်း yauk-kyar *(n.)* **man**

ယောကျာ်းဆန်ခြင်း yauk-kyar-san-chin *(n.)* **manliness**

ယောကျာ်းဆန်သော yauk-kyar-san-taw *(adj.)* **manly**

ယောကျ်ားဘဝ yauk-kyar-ba-wa *(n.)* **manhood**
ယောကျ်ားကို သဘောကျသူ yauk-kyaarrko sa-bhawkyasuu *(n.)* **philandry**
ယောကျ်ားကဲ့သို့ yaut-kyar-kae-tho *(adj.)* **manlike**
ယောကျ်ားများ ပစ်ကျရသည့် ချာတိတ်မ yauk-kyar-myar-pyit-kya-ya-taeet-char-tate-ma *(n.)* **nymphet**
ယောကျ်ားရုပ်သွင် ရှိသော yauk-kyar-yoke-twin-shi-taw *(adj.)* **masculine**
ယောကျ်ားလျာ yawkyaarrlyaar *(n.)* **tomboy**
ယောကျ်ားလိင်တံ yaut-kyaarr-lain-tan *(n.)* **phallus**
ယောက်ချို yauk-cho *(n.)* **ladle**
ယောကျ်ားသားကြောဖြတ်ခြင်း baat salin *(n.)* **vasectomy**
ယောကျ်ားအစေအပါး rell swam sattishisaw *(n.)* **valet**
ယောဂဒဿန yaw-ga-dattana *(n.)* **yoga**
ယောဂနည်းပြဆရာ yaw-ga naee-pya-sarar *(n.)* **yogi**
ယောင်ပေပေ လုပ်သည် yaung-pay-pay-lote-the *(v.)* **loiter**

ရံဖန်ရံခါ ran-hpan-ran-hkar *(adv.)* **occasionally**
ရံသည်၊ ပတ်သည် ran sai , paatsai *(v.)* **surround**
ရက်ကန်းသမား raatkaannsamarr *(n.)* **weaver**
ရက်ကမ်းစင် yat-kan-sin *(n.)* **loom**
ရက်ချိန်း yat-chain *(n.)* **fixture**
ရက်စက်ကြမ်းကြုတ်မှု raatsaat kyam kyuatmhu *(n.)* **savagery**
ရက်စက်ခြင်း yat-sat-chin *(n.)* **cruelty**
ရက်စက်ခြင်း၌ သာယာမှု raatsaat chinn-nite saryarmhu *(n.)* **sadism**
ရက်စက်ခြင်း၌ သာယာသူ raatsaat chinn-nite saryarsuu *(n.)* **sadist**
ရက်စက်မှု yat-sat-hmu *(n.)* **barbarity**
ရက်စက်သော raatsaatsaw *(adj.)* **vicious**
ရက်ဘီ ဘောလုံးပွဲအစတွင် ရှေ့တန်းလူများ ခပ်ကျဲကျဲ နေရာယူခြင်း raatbhe bhawlonepwal a satwin shaetaannluumyarr hkaut kyaellkyaell nayraryuuchinn *(n.)* **ruck**
ရက်မ yat-ma *(n.)* **girder**
ရက်ရက်စက်စက် raatraatsaatsaat *(adv.)* **savagely**
ရက်ရက်စက်စက် ကိုက်ဖဲ့သည် raatraatsaatsaat kite hpaesai *(v.)* **savage**
ရက်ရောမှု yat-yaw-mu *(n.)* **generosity**
ရက်ရောသည် yat-yaw-the *(v.)* **lavish**
ရက်ရောသော yat-yaw-taw *(adj.)* **generous**
ရက်လုပ်သည် raatlotesai *(v.)* **weave**
ရက်သတ္တနှစ်ပတ် yat-tat-ta-na-pat *(n.)* **fortnight**
ရင် yin *(n.)* **breast**
ရင့်ကျက်ခြင်း yint-kyat-chin *(n.)* **maturity**
ရင့်ကျက်ခြင်းမရှိသော yint-kyat-chin-ma-shi-taw *(adj.)* **callow**
ရင့်ကျက်မှုမရှိခြင်း yint-kyat-mu-ma-shi-chin *(n.)* **immaturity**
ရင့်ကျက်မှုမရှိသော yint-kyat-mu-ma-shi-taw *(adj.)* **immature**
ရင့်ကျက်သော yint-kyat-taw *(adj.)* **mature**

ရင့်မှည့်သော yint-mae-taw *(adj.)* **mellow**

ရင့်သီးစွာ yint-thee-swar *(adv.)* **abusively**

ရင့်သီးသော yint-thee-taw *(adj.)* **abusive**

ရင့်သီးသော၊ ပက်စက်သော yint-the-taw, pat-sat-taw *(adj.)* **biting**

ရင်းနှီးဖော်ရွေသော၊ ရိုးရိုး yin-hnee-hpaw-yway-taw, yoe-yoe *(adj.)* **informal**

ရင်းနှီးမြှုပ်နှံခြင်း yin-nee-hmyoke-nan-chin *(n.)* **investment**

ရင်းနှီးမြှုပ်နှံသည် yin-nee-hmyoke-nan-the *(v.)* **invest**

ရင်းနှီးမှု yin-nee-mu *(n.)* **intimacy**

ရင်းနှီးသော yin-hnee-taw *(adj.)* **familiar**

ရင်းမြစ်တူသော yit-myit-thu-taw *(adj.)* **cognate**

ရင်းမြစ်ဗေဒ yin-myit-bay-da *(n.)* **etymology**

ရင်းမြစ်များဖြင့် ထောက်ကူပေးသည် yin-myit-myar-phint-htaut-ku-pay-the *(v.)* **flapping**

ရင့်ကျက်သည် yint-kyat-the *(v.)* **mature**

ရင်ကြားစေ့သည် yin-gyar-say-the *(v.)* **conciliate**

ရင်ကွဲသိုးမွေးအင်္ကျီ yin-kwal-tho-mway-inn-gyi *(n.)* **cardigan**

ရင်ခွဲရုံ yin-khwal-yone *(n.)* **morgue**

ရင်ဆိုင်တွေ့သည် yin-sai-tway-the *(v.)* **confront**

ရင်ဆိုင်တိုက်ခိုက်သည် yin-sai-tite-khite-the *(v.)* **clash**

ရင်ထိုး yin-htoe *(n.)* **brooch**

ရင်ပေါင်တန်း yin-baung-tan *(adv.)* **abreast**

ရင်ဖွင့်သည် rin-hpwint sai *(v.)* **unburden**

ရင်ဖိုခြင်း rin hpochinn *(n.)* **thrill**

ရင်ဖိုစေသည် rin hposaysai *(v.)* **thrill**

ရင်ဘတ် rin-bhaat *(n.)* **thorax**

ရင်ဘတ်နှင့် ထိသည် yin-bat-nint-hti-the *(v.)* **breast**

ရင်ဘတ်အောင့်ခြင်း yin-bat-aung-chin *(n.)* **angina**

ရင်သပ်ရှုမော အံ့သြခြင်း rinsatshumaw aan syachinn *(n.)* **wonder**

ရင်သပ်ရှုမောဖွယ် yin-thet-shu-maw-phwal *(adj.)* **breathtaking**

ရင်သပ်ရှုမောဖွယ်ရာ rinsat shumawhpwalrar *(adj.)* **sublime**

ရစ်ပတ်နွယ်တက်သော rit-paat nwal taatsaw *(adj.)* **spiral**

ရစ်ပတ်နေသည် yit-pat-nay-the *(v.)* **entangle**

ရစ်ပတ်ပြေးသည့် မျဉ်း rit paat pyaysaeet myin *(n.)* **spiral**

ရစ်ပတ်သည် yit-pat-the *(v.)* **convolve**

ရစ်လုံး ritlone *(n.)* **reel**

ရစ်လုံးငယ် yit-lone-nge *(n.)* **bobbin**

ရစ်သည် ritsai *(v.)* **twist**

ရစ်သမ် rit-sam *(n.)* **rhythm**

ရည်ကြည်ဖု yay-kyi-phu *(n.)* **blister**

ရည်ညွှန်းချက် yee-hnyun-chat *(n.)* **mention**

ရည်ညွှန်းပြောဆိုခြင်း rai-nyunn-pyaww-sochinn *(n.)* **reference**

ရည်ညွှန်းသည် ray-nyunn-sai *(v.)* **refer**

ရည်မွန်ခြင်း yi-mon-chin *(n.)* **gentility**

ရည်မွန်မှု lay lwintsuungaal *(n.)* **urbanity**

ရည်မွန်မှု၊ မှန်ကန်မှု rai-mwan mhu , mhaan-kaan-mhu *(n.)* **propriety**

ရည်မွန်သော raimwanmhu *(adj.)* **urbane**

ရည်မှန်းချက် rai-mhan-chet *(n.)* **objective**

ရည်မှန်းချက်ကြီးသော yee-man-chat-kyi-taw *(adj.)* **ambitious**
ရည်ရွယ်ချက် rai-rwal-chet *(n.)* **purport**
ရည်ရွယ်ချက်မဲ့သော yee-ywal-chat-mae-taw *(adj.)* **aimless**
ရည်ရွယ်သည် rai-rwalsai *(v.)* **purpose**
ရတနာ ratanar *(n.)* **treasure**
ရတနာစီချယ်သည် ya-da-nar-si-chal-the *(v.)* **jewel**
ရတုကဗျာ ra-tu-ka-byar *(n.)* **ode**
ရတ်စဘယ်ရီသီး raat sa bhaal re-see *(n.)* **raspberry**
ရတ်စဘယ်ရီသီးကောက်သည် raat sa bhaal re-see kauk the *(adj.)* **raspberry**
ရထား rahtarr *(n.)* **train**
ရထားကို လမ်းချော်စေခြင်း ya-htar-ko-lan-chaw-say-chin *(n.)* **derailment**
ရထားကို လမ်းချော်စေသည် ya-htar-ko-lan-chaw-say-the *(v.)* **derail**
ရထားစားသောက်တွဲ ya-htar-sar-taut-twe *(n.)* **diner**
ရထားလုံး ya-thar-lon *(n.)* **coach**
ရထိုက်သော အရာ ya-htike-taw-a-yar *(n.)* **due**
ရနံ့ ra-nant *(n.)* **scent**
ရနံ့၊ ရေမွှေး ya-nant, yay-mway *(n.)* **fragrance**
ရနံ့ကုထုံး ya-nant-khu-htone *(n.)* **aromatherapy**
ရနံ့သင်းသော ra-nant-tin-taw *(adj.)* **odorous**
ရနံ့အိတ်ငယ် ranan aatengaal *(n.)* **sachet**
ရနံဗေဒ ya-nant-bay-da *(n.)* **olfactics**
ရနိုင်သော ra-nine-taw *(adj.)* **obtainable**
ရန်စ yan-sa *(v.)* **feud**
ရန်စခြင်း raan-sachinn *(n.)* **provocation**
ရန်စသည် raan sasai *(v.)* **provoke**
ရန်ညိုး yan-nyo *(n.)* **antagonism**
ရန်ပွဲ yan-pwe *(n.)* **brawl**
ရန်ပုံငွေ yan-pon-ngwe *(n.)* **fund**
ရန်ပုံငွေတိုးအောင်လုပ်သည် yan-pon-ngwe-toe-aung-lote-the *(v.)* **fundraise**
ရန်ဖြစ်သည်၊ စကားများသည် raan hpyit-sai , sakarr-myarrsai *(v.)* **quarrel**
ရန်ဘက် yan-bat *(n.)* **antagonist**
ရန်လိုစိတ် yan-lo-seik *(n.)* **hostility**
ရန်လိုမှု yan-lo-mu *(n.)* **aggression**
ရန်လိုသူ yan-lo-thu *(n.)* **militant**
ရန်လိုသော raan-lo-saw *(adj.)* **quarrelsome**
ရန်လိုသော၊ အပြင်းအထန်ဆန့်ကျင်သော yan-lo-taw, a-pyin-a-htan-sant-kyin-taw *(adj.)* **hostile**
ရန်လုပ်သည် yan-lote-the *(v.)* **antagonize**
ရန်သူ yan-thu *(n.)* **enemy**
ရန်သူကို မထိပဲ ဂိမ်းနိုင်ရန် နောက်ထပ် စိန်ခေါ်မှု raansuuko ma htipell gaim-nineraan nout-htaut sein-hkaw-mhu *(n.)* **pacifism**
ရန်သူအဝိုင်းခံရသော yan-thu-a-wine-khan-ya-taw *(adj.)* **beleaguered**
ရပိုင်ခွင့် စွန့်လွှတ်သည် rapinehkwint swant lwutsai *(v.)* **renounce**
ရပ်ကွက် yat-kwat *(n.)* **neighbourhood**
ရပ်ကွက်အဖြစ် သတ်မှတ်ခြင်း rat-kwataahpyit saatmhaatchinn *(n.)* **wardship**
ရပ်ခြင်း၊ ဖြတ်ခြင်း yat-chin, phat-chin *(n.)* **cessation**
ရပ်စတာဘာသာဝင် art-sa-tar-bar-tar-win *(n.)* **rasta**

ရပ်စဲခြင်းမရှိသော yat-sal-chin-ma-shi-taw (*adj.*) **ceaseless**

ရပ်စဲသည် yat-sal-the (*v.*) **cease**

ရပ်ဆိုင်းသည် yat-sai-the (*v.*) **discontinue**

ရပ်တည်ချက်၊ စင် rattaichet, sin (*n.*) **stand**

ရပ်တန့်ခြင်း rat-tant-chinn (*n.*) **pause**

ရပ်တန့်သည် rat-tant-sai (*v.*) **pause**

ရပ်နားချိန် ratnarr-chane (*n.*) **recess**

ရပ်နေသော၊ ပုံသေ rat naysaw , ponesay (*adj.*) **stationary**

ရပ်သည်၊ ထောင်သည်၊ မူတည်သည် rat sai, htaung sai , muu-tai-sai (*v.*) **stand**

ရပ်သူရွာသား rat suu rwarsarr (*n.*) **resident**

ရမည် ya-me (*v.*) **must**

ရမန်၊ ချုပ်မိန့် ra maan , chote-meint (*n.*) **remand**

ရမန်ပေးသည်၊ ချုပ်မိန့်ပေးသည် ra maan payysai , chote meinpayysai (*v.*) **remand**

ရမ္မက်နှိုးဆွမှု yan-mat-hnoe-swa-mu (*n.*) **eroticism**

ရမ္မက်နှိုးဆွသည် yan-mat-hnoe-swa-the (*v.*) **eroticize**

ရမ္မက်လျှမ်းသော ya-mat-hlyan-taw (*adj.*) **amorous**

ရမ်းကားကြမ်းတမ်းသော yan-kar-kyan-tan-taw (*adj.*) **desperate**

ရမ်းကားဖျက်ဆီးသော ramkarr hpyetseesaw (*adj.*) **trashed**

ရမ်းကုခြင်း ram ku-chinn (*n.*) **quackery**

ရမ်းကုဆေး yan-ku-say (*n.*) **nostrum**

ရမ်းဆသည် ram sasai (*v.*) **surmise**

ရမ်းရမ်းကားကားပျော်ပွဲ ram-ram-kar-kar-pyaw-pwal (*n.*) **orgy**

ရမ်အရက် ram aaraat (*n.*) **rum**

ရယူခြင်း rayuu-chinn (*n.*) **procurement**

ရယူနိုင်ခဲ့သည် ra-yuuninehkaesai (*v.*) **secure**

ရယူပေးသည် rayuu-payysai (*v.*) **procure**

ရယ်စရာ၊ ဟာသ yal-sa-yar, har-ta (*n.*) **joke**

ရယ်စရာကောင်းသော yal-sa-yar-kaung-taw (*adj.*) **comical**

ရယ်စရာပြောသည် yal-sa-yar-pyaw-the (*v.*) **joke**

ရယ်ဖွယ်ကောင်းမှု yal-phwal-kaung-mu (*n.*) **absurdity**

ရယ်ဖွယ်ဖြစ်သော yal-phwal-phit-taw (*adj.*) **laughable**

ရယ်ဖွယ်ရာ၊ မဖြစ်နိုင်တာ raal hpwalrar , mahpyitninetar (*adj.*) **ridiculous**

ရယ်မှောလှောင်ပြောင်မှု raal mhaaw lhaawinpyaungmhu (*n.*) **scoff**

ရယ်မောခြင်း၊ ရယ်သံ yal-maw-chin, yal-tan (*n.*) **laugh**

ရယ်မောသည် yal-maw-the (*v.*) **laugh**

ရယ်သွေးလွှမ်းသည် ywal-thway-lwan-the (*v.*) **mock**

ရရှိသည် ra-shi-tai (*v.*) **obtain**

ရရာစုပေါင်းစပ်ပေါင်း ra rarsu paunggsatpaungg (*adj.*) **scratch**

ရလဒ် ralad (*n.*) **upshot**

ရလဒ်၊ အကျိုးဆက် ralad , aakyoesaat (*n.*) **result**

ရလဒ်ပေါ်ထွက်သည် ya-lat-par-htwat-the (*v.*) **ensue**

ရွှံ့ shwunt (*n.*) **argil**

ရွှံ့ကျောက် rwankyawwat (*n.*) **talc**

ရွှံ့စေး shwunt-say (*n.*) **clay**

ရွံစရာကောင်းသော yon-sa-yar-kaung-taw (*adj.*) **loathsome**

ရွံမုန်းမှု yount-hmone-mu *(n.)* **antipathy**

ရွံရှာခြင်း rwan shar-chinn *(n.)* **repugnance**

ရွံရှာဖွယ် rwan sharhpwal *(adj.)* **repulsive**

ရွံရှာဖွယ်ရာ rwan sharhpwalrar *(n.)* **repellent**

ရွံရှာမှု rwan sharmhu *(n.)* **repulsion**

ရွံရှာသည် yon-shar-the *(v.)* **loathe**

ရွက် rwat *(n.)* **sail**

ရွက်တစ်ခုထက် ပိုပါသော လှေ ywet ta-khu-htet-po-par-taw-hlae *(n.)* **sailcraft**

ရွက်တိုင် ywet-tai *(n.)* **mast**

ရွက်ဖျင်တဲ rwat hpyintell *(n.)* **tent**

ရွက်ဖျင်တဲ့ ထောင်သော တုတ် ywet-phyin-tae-htaung-taw-dote *(n.)* **tentpole**

ရွက်ဖျင်တဲထုတ်လုပ်သူ ywet-phyin-tae-htoke-lote-thu *(n.)* **tentmaker**

ရွက်လွှင့်ခြင်း rwat lwint chinn *(n.)* **sailing**

ရွက်လွှင့်သည် rwat lwint sai *(v.)* **sail**

ရွက်လွှင့်သည် ywet-lwint-the *(v.)* **yacht**

ရွက်လွှင့်သော rwat lwint-saw *(adj.)* **sailing**

ရွက်လှေ rwathlaay *(n.)* **sailboat**

ရွက်လှေစီးခြင်း rwathlaayseechinn *(n.)* **sailboating**

ရွက်လှေစီးသူ rwathlaay seesuu *(n.)* **sailboater**

ရွက်သင်္ဘော၊ ကတ်ကြေး၊ လက်သည်းညှပ် ywet-tin-baw, kat-kyay, lat-the-nyat *(n.)* **clipper**

ရွရွ ပြေးသည် ywa-ywa-pyay-the *(v.)* **jog**

ရွှံ့ shwunt *(n.)* **mud**

ရွှံ့တော ဗွက်တော shwantaw bwattaw *(n.)* **slough**

ရွှံ့နှစ် shwan-nit *(n.)* **ooze**

ရွှံ့လူးသည် shwan luusai *(v.)* **wallow**

ရွှင်ပျသော shwin-pya-taw *(adj.)* **cheerful**

ရွှင်မြူး၍ တမူထူးသူ shwin-myu-ywe-ta-mu-htoo-thu *(adj.)* **wacko**

ရွှင်မြူးကြည်နူးဖွယ် shwin-myi-kyi-nu-phwal *(n.)* **merriment**

ရွှင်မြူးသော လူကြောင် shwin-myu-taw-lu-kyaung *(n.)* **wacko**

ရွှတ်နောက်နောက် shwat noutnout *(adj.)* **saucy**

ရွှန်းရွှန်းစားစား shwann shwann sarrsarr *(adj.)* **rapt**

ရွှန်းလဲ့တောက်ပခြင်း shun-lae-taut-pa-chin *(n.)* **gloss**

ရှိခနဲ အသံပြုသည် shwe hkanell aasanpyusai *(v.)* **whistle**

ရွှေ shwe *(n.)* **gold**

ရွှေ့ဆိုင်းခြင်း shwae-sinechinn *(n.)* **postponement**

ရွှေ့ဆိုင်းထားနိုင်ရန် အစီအစဉ် ပြန်လည်ရေးဆွဲသည် shwaesine htarr-nineraan aaseaasin pyanlai rayyswalsai *(v.)* **reschedule**

ရွှေ့ဆိုင်းသည် shwae-sine-sai *(v.)* **postpone**

ရွှေ့ပြောင်းခြင်း shway-pyaung-chin *(n.)* **move**

ရွှေ့ပြောင်းနိုင်သော shway-pyaung-nai-taw *(adj.)* **mobile**

ရွှေ့ပြောင်းနိုင်သော ပစ္စည်းများ shway-pyaung-nai-taw-pyit-see *(n.)* **movables**

ရွှေ့ပြောင်းသည် shway-pyaung-the *(v.)* **move**

ရွှေချည်ထိုး ပိုးထည်စ shway hkyaihtoe poe htaih-ca *(n.)* **samite**

ရွှေချသည် shwe-cha-the *(v.)* **gild**

ရွှေချောင်း၊ ငွေချောင်း shwe-chaung, ngwe-chaung *(n.)* **bullion**

ရွှေငါး shwe-ngar *(n.)* **koi**

ရွှေပန်းထိမ် shwe-pan-htein *(n.)* **goldsmith**

ရွှေဖရုံ shway hparone *(n.)* **pumpkin**

ရွှေရည်စိမ်သော shwe-ch-sein-taw *(adj.)* **gilt**

ရွှေသား၊ ရွှေရောင် shwe-tar, shwe-yaung *(adj.)* **golden**

ရွှဲရွှဲစိုသည် shwe-shwe-so-the *(v.)* **drench**

ရွာ rwar *(n.)* **village**

ရွာသား rwar-sarr *(n.)* **villager**

ရွှေ့ဆိုင်းခြင်း shway-saing-chin *(n.)* **adjournment**

ရွှေ့ဆိုင်းသည် shway-saing-the *(v.)* **adjourn**

ရွှေ့ပြောင်း shway-pyaung *(n.)* **migrant**

ရွှေ့ပြောင်းသည် rwaepyaunggsai *(v.)* **shift**

ရွှေ့လျားနိုင်မှု shway-lyar-nai-mu *(n.)* **mobility**

ရွှေ့လျားမှု shway-lyar-mu *(n.)* **motion**

ရွှေ့လျားမှု မရှိသော shway-lyar-mu-ma-shi-taw *(adj.)* **motionless**

ရွေးကောက်ပွဲ yway-kauk-pwe *(n.)* **election**

ရွေးကောက်သည် yway-kauk-the *(v.)* **elect**

ရွေးချယ်ခြင်း၊ လက်ရွေးစင် rwaychaalchinn , laatrwaysin *(n.)* **selection**

ရွေးချယ်မှု yway-chal-mu *(n.)* **choice**

ရွေးချယ်သည် rwaychaalsai *(v.)* **select**

ရွေးစရာ rway-sa-rar *(n.)* **option**

ရွေးထားသော rwayhtarrsaw *(adj.)* **select**

ရွေပေါ်စာ rway pawsar *(n.)* **shavings**

ရွေပေါ်ထိုးသည် rway-paw-htoe-sai *(v.)* **plane**

ရွေသည် rwaysai *(v.)* **whittle**

ရွဲ့စောင်းသည် ywe-saung-the *(v.)* **distort**

ရွဲ့သော ywe-taw *(adj.)* **ironic**

ရသကို ခံစားတတ်သော ya-ta-ko-khan-sar-tat-taw *(adj.)* **artistic**

ရသခံစားနိုင်စွမ်း ra sa hkansarrnineswam *(n.)* **sensibility**

ရသုံးမှန်းခြေစာရင်း ya-tone-man-chay-sa-yin *(n.)* **budget**

ရသေ့ ya-thae *(n.)* **hermit**

ရသေ့သင်္ခမ်းကျောင်း ya-thae-tin-khan-kyaung *(n.)* **hermitage**

ရဟန်းဘဝ ya-han-ba-wa *(n.)* **monasticism**

ရှက်ကိုးရှက်ကန်း ဖြစ်ခြင်း shat-koe-shat-kan-phit-chin *(n.)* **embarrassment**

ရှက်ကိုးရှက်ကန်း ဖြစ်သည် shat-koe-shat-kan-phit-the *(v.)* **embarrass**

ရှက်ကိုးရှက်ကန်း ဖြစ်သော shat-koe-shat-kan-phit-taw *(adj.)* **embarrassing**

ရှက်ချင်ဟန်ဆောင်ခြင်း shat chin-haan-saung-chinn *(n.)* **prude**

ရှက်စိတ် shatsate *(n.)* **shame**

ရှက်ဖွယ် shathpwal *(adj.)* **shameful**

ရှက်သည် shatsai *(v.)* **shame**

ရှက်သော shat-taw *(adj.)* **ashamed**

ရှက်ဟန်ဆောင်သော shat-han-saung-taw *(adj.)* **coy**

ရှင်းချက်ထုတ်သည် shin-chat-htoke-the *(v.)* **justify**

ရှင်းပြချက် shin-pya-chat *(n.)* **explanation**

ရှင်းပြသည် shin-pya-the *(v.)* **elucidate**

ရှင်းမပြနိုင်သော shinn ma pya-ninesaw *(adj.)* **unaccountable**

ရှင်းရှင်းလင်းလင်း ဖြစ်စေသည် shin-shin-bwin-bwin-phit-say-the *(v.)* **demystify**

ရှင်းလင်းချက်မှတ်စု shin-lin-chat-mat-su *(n.)* **commentary**

ရှင်းလင်းခြင်း shin-lin-chin *(n.)* **clarification**
ရှင်းလင်းစွာ ဖော်ထုတ်ခြင်း shin-lin-swar-phaw-htoke-chin *(n.)* **enunciation**
ရှင်းလင်းစွာ ဖော်ထုတ်သော shin-lin-swar-phaw-htoke-taw *(adj.)* **enunciatory**
ရှင်းလင်းစွာပြောဆိုနိုင်သော shin-lin-swar-pyaw-so-naing-taw *(adj.)* **articulate**
ရှင်းလင်းထိရောက်စွာ ပြောဆိုနိုင်ခြင်း shin-lin-hti-yauk-swar-pyaw-soe-nai-chin *(n.)* **elocution**
ရှင်းလင်းပြတ်သားမှု shin-lin-pyat-tar-mu *(n.)* **lucidity**
ရှင်းလင်းသည် shin-lin-the *(v.)* **clarify**
ရှင်းလင်းသုတ်သင်ခြင်း shin-lin-toke-tin-chin *(n.)* **elimination**
ရှင်းလင်းသုတ်သင်သူ shin-lin-toke-tin-thu *(n.)* **eliminator**
ရှင်းလင်းသုတ်သင်သော shin-lin-toke-tin-taw *(adj.)* **eliminatory**
ရှင်းလင်းသော shin-lin-taw *(adj.)* **manifest**
ရှင်ဘုရင်၊ သူကောင်းမျိုး shin-ba-yin, thu-kaung-myo *(n.)* **lord**
ရှင်မီးအင်္ကျီ shin-mee-inn-gyi *(n.)* **chemise**
ရှင်သန်သည် shin-saansai *(v.)* **thrive**
ရှစ် shit *(n.)* **eight**
ရှစ်ခုထိတိုးသည် shit-khu-hti-toe-the *(v.)* **octuple**
ရှစ်ခုပမာဏ shit-khu-pa-mar-na *(n.)* **octuple**
ရှစ်ခုပါ shit-khu-par *(adj.)* **octuple**
ရှစ်ဆယ် shit-sal *(n.)* **eighty**
ရှစ်သံတွဲ shit-tan-twal *(n.)* **octave**
ရှဉ့် shint *(n.)* **squirrel**
ရှည်စေသည် shaysaysai *(v.)* **prolong**
ရှည်ရှည်လျားလျား shay-shay-lyar-lyar *(adj.)* **lengthy**
ရှည်လျား ရှုပ်ထွေးသော အငြင်းအခုံ shilyarr shotehtway-saw aangyinn-aahkone *(n.)* **wrangle**
ရှည်လျားစူးရှသော အသံ shay-lyarr suushsaw aasan *(n.)* **whine**
ရှည်လျားစူးရှသော အသံ ပြုသည် shay-lyarr suushsaw aasan pyusai *(v.)* **whine**
ရှည်လာသည် shay-lar-the *(v.)* **lengthen**
ရှည်သော shaysaw *(adj.)* **tall**
ရှန်ပိန်ဝိုင် shan-pain-wine *(n.)* **champagne**
ရှပ်တိုက်ခြင်း shut titechinn *(n.)* **shuffle**
ရှပ်တိုက်လျှောက်သည် shut tite shoutsai *(v.)* **shuffle**
ရှယ်ယာဈေးကွက် shal rarsyaayykwat *(n.)* **share market**
ရှယ်ယာရှင် shal rarshin *(n.)* **shareholder**
ရှလကာရည် sha la karrai *(n.)* **vinegar**
ရှလကာရည်ဆန်သော sha-la-kar-yay-san-taw *(adj.)* **acetic**
ရှသံပါခြင်း sh san parhkyinn *(n.)* **sibilating**
ရှသံပါသော sh san parsaw *(adj.)* **sibilant**
ရှသံပြုသည် sh sonepyusai *(v.)* **sibilate**
ရှားစောင်းပင် shar-saung-pin *(n.)* **cactus**
ရှားစောင်းလက်ပတ် shar-saung-lat-pat *(n.)* **aloe**
ရှားပါးခြင်း sharr-parrchinn *(n.)* **rarity**
ရှားပါးစွာ shar-par-swar *(adv.)* **rarely**
ရှားပါးမှု shar-par-mu *(n.)* **rareness**
ရှားပါးသော sharr-parrsaw *(adj.)* **rare**
ရှားပါးအောင် လုပ်သည် shar-par-aung-lote-the *(v.)* **rarefy**

ရှားရှားပါးပါး sharrsharrparrpar *(adv.)* **scarcely**
ရှာကျွေးသူ shar-kway-thu *(n.)* **breadwinner**
ရှာတွေ့သည်၊ ရိပ်စားမိသည် shar twae sai , rate sarr mi-sai *(v.)* **spot**
ရှာဖွေခြင်း shar-hpwaychinn *(n.)* **quest**
ရှာဖွေမှု shar-hpwaymhu *(n.)* **pursuit**
ရှာဖွေဝရမ်း sharhpwaywaram *(n.)* **search warrant**
ရှာဖွေသည် sharhpwaysai *(v.)* **search**
ရှာမှီးရရှိသော ဥစ္စာ shar-mi-ya-shi-taw-oat-sar *(n.)* **acquisition**
ရှာသည် shar-the *(v.)* **locate**
ရှိနေခြင်း shi-naychinn *(n.)* **presence**
ရှိနေသော shi-naysaw *(adj.)* **present**
ရှိန်သွားသည် shein-swar-tai *(v.)* **overawe**
ရှိမှုပညာ shi-mhu-pyin-nyar *(n.)* **ontology**
ရှိမှုပညာနှင့် ဆိုင်သော shi-mhu-pyin-nyar-nint-sine-taw *(adj.)* **ontologic**
ရှိမှုပညာရှင် shi-mhu-pyin-nyar-shin *(n.)* **ontologist**
ရှိသည် shi-the *(v.)* **have**
ရှိသည်၊ ဖြစ်သည် shi-the, phit-the *(v.)* **be**
ရှို့မီး shooet-mee *(n.)* **arson**
ရှိုက်ငိုသည် shite ngosai *(v.)* **sob**
ရှိုက်သံ shitesan *(n.)* **sob**
ရှုံးထွက်ပြိုင်ပွဲ shone-htwat-pyai-pwe *(n.)* **knockout**
ရှုံးနိမ့်သည် shone-naint-the *(v.)* **fail**
ရှုံးပွဲမရှိသော shone pwalmashisaw *(adj.)* **unbeaten**
ရှုံးသည်၊ အရေးနိမ့်သည် shone sai , aa-rayy naint-sai *(v.)* **worst**
ရှုံ့မဲ့မဲ့ဖြစ်သည် shone-mae-mae-hpyit-sai *(v.)* **wince**
ရှုခင်း shuhkinn *(n.)* **vista**
ရှုခင်းကြည့် အဆောက်အအုံငယ် shyu-khin-kyi-a-saut-a-ohn-nge *(n.)* **belvedere**
ရှုတ်ချပြောသည် shoke-cha-pyaw-the *(v.)* **detract**
ရှုတ်ချပုတ်ခတ်သူ shoke-cha-poke-khat-thu *(n.)* **detractor**
ရှုတ်ချသည်၊ ပြစ်တင်ဝေဖန်သည် shote-cha-the, pyit-tin-wai-phan-the *(v.)* **condemn**
ရှုထောင့် shu htaung *(n.)* **standpoint**
ရှုထောင့်၊ အမြင် shu htawnt, aamyin *(n.)* **slant**
ရှုထောင့်နှစ်ခု shu-htaunt-na-khu *(adj.)* **bidimensional**
ရှုပ်ထွေးသော shoke-htway-taw *(adj.)* **intricate**
ရှုပ်ပွနေသည် shote-pwa-nay-the *(v.)* **clutter**
ရှုမြင်သည် shu-myin-the *(v.)* **behold**
ရှုမောဖွယ်ရာ shumawhpwalrar *(adj.)* **splendid**
ရှူးရှူးမြည်သံ shu-shu-myee-tan *(n.)* **hiss**
ရှူးဟု အသံပြုသည် shu-hu-a-tan-pyu-the *(v.)* **hiss**
ရှူသည်၊ နှာမှုတ်သည် shuu sai, nhar mhuatsai *(v.)* **snort**
ရှူသွင်းသည် shu-twin-the *(v.)* **inhale**
ရှေ့ shay *(adj.)* **forward**
ရှေ့ကတည်းက တည်ရှိခဲ့သော အခြေအနေ shae-ka-tae-ka-the-shi-khae-taw-a-chay-a-nae *(n.)* **preexistence**
ရှေ့ကို ကြို၍ မြင်နိုင်ခြင်း shae-ko kyo myin-ninechinn *(n.)* **prescience**
ရှေ့ခြေ၊ လက် shay-chay, lat *(n.)* **foreleg**

ရှေ့ဆက်ခြင်းအတွက် အတားအဆီး shaesaat hkyinnaatwat aatarraasee *(n.)* **showstopper**
ရှေ့ဆက်ပုဒ် shae-saat-pote *(n.)* **prefix**
ရှေ့ဆက်သည် shae-saatsai *(v.)* **proceed**
ရှေ့တန်းစစ်မြေပြင် shay-tan-sit-myay-pyin *(n.)* **battlefront**
ရှေ့တန်းတင်လွန်းသူ shae-taann-tin-lwann-suu *(n.)* **pedant**
ရှေ့တိုးသည် shay-toe-the *(v.)* **advance**
ရှေ့တော်ပြေး shay-taw-pyay *(n.)* **forerunner**
ရှေ့နေ shay-nay *(n.)* **attorney**
ရှေ့နောက် ရွှေ့သည် shay-naut-shae-sai *(v.)* **wabble**
ရှေ့နောက်မစဉ်းစားဘဲ ပြောချသည် shay-naut-ma-sin-sar-bae-pyaw-cha-the *(v.)* **blurt**
ရှေ့နောက်ရွှေ့လိုသော shay-naut-shae-lo-taw *(adj.)* **wabbly**
ရှေ့ပြေး၊ အတိတ်နိမိတ် shae-pyay, aa-tate-na-mate *(n.)* **prelude**
ရှေ့ပြေးနိမိတ် shae-pyayna-mate *(n.)* **precursor**
ရှေ့ပြေးပုံစံ Shae-pyay-pone-san *(n.)* **prototype**
ရှေ့ပြေးအဖြစ် မိတ်ဆက်ထားသည် shae-pyay-a-phit-mate-sat-htar-the *(v.)* **prelude**
ရှေ့ပိုင်းကျသော shay-paing-kya-taw *(adj.)* **anterior**
ရှေ့ဖြစ်ဟောသူ shaehpyit haw suu *(n.)* **seer**
ရှေ့ဖုံးခါးစည်း shay-hpone-khar-see *(n.)* **apron**
ရှေ့ဘက် shay-bat *(adj.)* **frontside**
ရှေ့မှ မြင်ရသော shay-ma-myin-ya-taw *(adj.)* **rearview**
ရှေ့မီး shay-mee *(n.)* **headlight**
ရှေ့ရောက်နှင့်နေသော shay-yaut-nint-nay-taw *(adj.)* **advanced**
ရှေ့ရောက်နှင့်သည် shay-yaut-nint-the *(v.)* **antecede**
ရှေ့ရောက်သည် shae-rout-sai *(v.)* **precede**
ရှေ့လာမည့်၊ မျှော်မှန်းရသော shae lar-meet, myaw mhaann-rasaw *(adj.)* **prospective**
ရှေ့သို့ shae-thoet *(adj.)* **onward**
ရှေ့သို့ ဆတ်ခနဲ လှမ်းခြင်း shay-tho-sat-kha-nae-hlan-chin *(v.)* **lunge**
ရှေးကျ၍ တန်ဖိုးကြီးသော shay-kya-ywe-tan-phoe-kyi-taw *(adj.)* **antique**
ရှေးခေတ်စောင်း shay-khit-saung *(n.)* **lyre**
ရှေးခေတ်မိတ္တူပွားစက် shay-khit-meik-thu-pwar-sat *(n.)* **cyclostyle**
ရှေးခေတ်သင်္ချိုင်းမှတ်တိုင် shay-khit-tin-gyai-mat-tai *(n.)* **dolmen**
ရှေးဂျာမန်အက္ခရာ shayy gyaarmaanaakhkarar *(n.)* **rune**
ရှေးပဝေသဏီ shay-pa-way-tha-ni *(n.)* **antiquity**
ရှေးရိုးစဉ်လာ၊ ပုံပြင်၊ ဓလေ့ လေ့လာမှု shay-yoe-sin-lar, pon-pyin, da-lay-lay-lar-mu *(n.)* **folklore**
ရှေးရိုးစဉ်လာ၊ ပုံပြင်၊ ဓလေ့ လေ့လာမှုနှင့်ဆိုင်သော shar-yoe-sin-lar, pon-pyin, da-lay-lay-lar-mu-nint-sai-taw *(adj.)* **folkloric**
ရှေးရိုးစွဲ shay-yoe-swal *(adj.)* **conservative**
ရှေးရိုးအလွန်ဆန်သူ shayy roe aalwan saansuu *(n.)* **ultraconservative**
ရှေးလူ့အသုံးအဆောင်ပစ္စည်း shay-lu-a-tone-a-saung-pyit-see *(n.)* **artefact**
ရှေးသင်္ချိုင်းကြီး shay-tin-gyai-gyi *(n.)* **necropolis**
ရှေးဟောင်း shay-haung *(adj.)* **ancient**

ရှေးဟောင်းဂရိမြို့၏ ရဲတိုက် shay-haung-ga-yeh-myo-ei-yae-tite *(n.)* **acropolis**
ရှေးဟောင်းဂေဟဗေဒ shayyhaungg gay habayda *(n.)* **paleoecology**
ရှေးဟောင်းဂေဟဗေဒပညာရှင် shayyhaungg gay ha bayda-pin-nyarshin *(n.)* **paleoecologist**
ရှေးဟောင်းရှားပါးပစ္စည်း shay-haung-shar-par-pyit-see *(adj.)* **antiquarian**
ရှေးဟောင်းရှားပါးပစ္စည်းစုဆောင်းသူ shay-haung-shar-par-pyit-see-su-saung-thu *(n.)* **antiquary**
ရှေးဟောင်းသုသေတနပညာ shay-haung-thu-tay-ta-na-pyin-nyar *(n.)* **archaeology**
ရှေးဟောင်းသုသေတနပညာရှင် shay-haung-thu-tay-ta-na-pyin-nyar-shin *(n.)* **archaeologist**
ရှေးအတီတေ shay-a-te-tay *(adj.)* **immemorial**
ရှေးဦး shayy u *(adj.)* **primitive**
ရှေးဦးသာဓက shay-oo-thar-da-ka *(n.)* **antecedent**
ရှေးဦးသူနာပြုစုခြင်း shay-oo-thu-nar-pyu-su-chin *(n.)* **first aid**
ရေညှိ yay-hnyi *(n.)* **algae**
ရှောက်၊ သံပရာမျိုးဝင် အသီးများ shaut-tan-pa-yar-myo-win-a-thee-myar *(n.)* **citrus**
ရှောင်ကြဉ်ခြင်း shaung-kyin-chin *(n.)* **abstinence**
ရှောင်ကြဉ်သည် shaung-kyin-the *(v.)* **abstain**
ရှောင်ခြင်း shaung-chin *(n.)* **avoidance**
ရှောင်တခင် shawintahkin *(adj.)* **snap**
ရှောင်တိမ်းနိုင်သော အခြေအနေ shaung-tain-nai-taw-a-chay-a-nay *(n.)* **evitability**
ရှောင်တိမ်းမှု shaung-tein-mu *(n.)* **evasion**
ရှောင်တိမ်းသည် shaung-tein-the *(v.)* **evade**
ရှောင်ဖယ်သည် shawng hpaalsai *(v.)* **shun**
ရှောင်ရှားခြင်း shaung-shar-chin *(n.)* **eschewment**
ရှောင်ရှားသည် shaung-shar-the *(v.)* **eschew**
ရှောင်လွှဲမရသော shaung-hlwal-ma-ya-taw *(adj.)* **inexorable**
ရှောင်သည် shaung-the *(v.)* **avoid**
ရှောင်သည်၊ အချောင်ခိုသည် shawin sai , a chaung hkosai *(v.)* **shirk**
ရှောစောင် shawsaung *(n.)* **shawl**
ရှဲဒိုးရေးသူ shal-doe-yay-thu *(n.)* **ghostwriter**
ရှဲရှဲမြည်သံ shell shell myisan *(n.)* **sizzle**
ရှဲရှဲမြည်သည် shell shell myisai *(v.)* **sizzle**
ရာကျော်ဘိုးဘွား yar-kyaw-boe-bwar *(n.)* **centenarian**
ရာဂလွန်ကဲသော yar-ga-lwan-kell-taw *(adj.)* **nymphomaniac**
ရာဂလွန်ကဲသော အမျိုးသမီး yar-ga-lwan-kell-taw-a-myoe-ta-mee *(n.)* **nymphomaniac**
ရာစု yar-su *(n.)* **century**
ရာဇမတ်ကွက် ya-za-mat-hwat *(n.)* **lattice**
ရာဇသံ rar-za-san *(n.)* **ultimatum**
ရာထူးကြီးသော ဘုန်းတော်ကြီး rar-htuu-kyee-saw bhone-taw-kyee *(n.)* **prelate**
ရာထူးချသည် yar-htoo-cha-the *(v.)* **demote**
ရာထူးဂုဏ်သိမ်အဆင့်ဆင့် yar-htoo-gon-tein-a-sint-sint *(n.)* **hierarchy**
ရာထူးတက်ခြင်း၊ အရောင်းမြှင့်တင်ခြင်း rarhtuu taatchinn , aaraungg myint-tinchinn *(n.)* **promotion**
ရာထူးပေးသည် yar-thoo-pay-the *(v.)* **tenure**
ရာထူးမြင့်သော ra htuu myintsaw *(adj.)* **senior**

ရာထူးသက်တမ်း rarhtuusaattam *(n.)* **tenure**

ရာထူးအပ်နှင်းသည် yar-htoo-at-hnin-the *(v.)* **induct**

ရာနှုန်း rar-hnone *(n.)* **percentage**

ရာနှုန်းအားဖြင့် rar-hnone-ar-hpyint *(adv.)* **per cent**

ရာပြည့်ပွဲ yar-pyae-pwe *(n.)* **centenary**

ရာဘာ yar-bar-bal-yoke *(n.)* **rubber duck**

ရာသီနှင့် ဆိုင်သော yar-thi-nint-sai-taw *(adj.)* **menstrual**

ရာသီပေါ် rarsepaw *(adj.)* **seasonable**

ရာသီလာခြင်း yar-thi-lar-chin *(n.)* **menstruation**

ရာသီသွေး yar-thi-tway *(n.)* **menses**

ရာသီအလိုက် rarseaalite *(adj.)* **seasonal**

ရာသီဥတု rarseutu *(n.)* **weather**

ရာသီဥတုထိန်းသိမ်းခြင်း yar-thi-oo-tu-htein-tain-chin *(n.)* **climate control**

ရာသီဥတုပြောင်းလဲခြင်း yar-thi-oo-tu-pyaung-lal-chin *(n.)* **climate change**

ရိတ်ခြင်း ratechinn *(n.)* **shaving**

ရိတ်ထားသော ratehtarrsaw *(adj.)* **shaven**

ရိတ်သည် ratesai *(v.)* **rook**

ရိတ်သည်၊ ဖြတ်သည် yeik-the, phat-the *(v.)* **mow**

ရိတ်သိမ်းသည် rate sai-sai *(v.)* **reap**

ရိပ်ခနဲမြင်ခြင်း yeik-kha-nae-myin-chin *(n.)* **glimpse**

ရိပ်သာလမ်း yeik-tar-lan *(n.)* **avenue**

ရိုးတိုးရွတဖြစ်သော yoe-toe-ywa-ta-phit-taw *(adj.)* **agog**

ရိုးနေပြီဖြစ်သော yoe-nay-pi-phit-taw *(adj.)* **commonplace**

ရိုးပြတ် roepyat *(n.)* **stubble**

ရိုးရှင်းသော roeshinn-saw *(adj.)* **simple**

ရိုးရှင်းသော အဖြေ yoe-shin-taw-a-phyay *(n.)* **quick fix**

ရိုးရာ roerar *(adj.)* **ritual**

ရိုးရာဓလေ့ roerardhalae *(n.)* **ritual**

ရိုးရာပုံပြင်၊ အကျော်ဇေယျ yoe-yar-pon-pyin, a-kyaw-zay-ya *(n.)* **legend**

ရိုးသားဖြူစင်သော yoe-tar-phyu-sin-taw *(adj.)* **devout**

ရိုးသားမှု yoe-tar-mu *(n.)* **honesty**

ရိုးသားသော yoe-tar-taw *(adj.)* **honest**

ရိုးသော yoe-taw *(adj.)* **banal**

ရိုးအီနေခြင်း yoe-e-nay-chin *(n.)* **monotony**

ရိုက်ချက်၊ ပွတ်သပ်ခြင်း၊ ritechet , pwat sat chinn *(n.)* **stroke**

ရိုက်ချိုးခြင်း ritechoechinn *(n.)* **smash**

ရိုက်ခြင်း၊ စကန်ဖတ်ခြင်း rite chinn , sa kaan hpaatchinn *(n.)* **scan**

ရိုက်ခြင်း၊ ပုတ်ခြင်း rite chinn , pote-chinn *(n.)* **slap**

ရိုက်ခွဲသည် rite hkwalsai *(v.)* **smash**

ရိုက်နှက်သည် ritenhaatsai *(v.)* **thrash**

ရိုက်နှိပ်ခြင်း rite natechinn *(n.)* **reprint**

ရိုက်လှည့်ကျသူ yite-hlae-mya-thu *(n.)* **batsman**

ရိုက်သည် yite-the *(v.)* **beat**

ရိုက်သည်၊ ပုတ်သည် rite sai, pote-sai *(v.)* **slap**

ရိုင်းခြင်း rine-chinn *(n.)* **wilderness**

ရိုင်းဂျုံ rine-gyaone *(n.)* **rye**

ရိုင်းစိုင်းကြမ်းကြုတ်သော rinesine kyam kyuatsaw *(adj.)* **savage**

ရိုင်းစိုင်းမှု yai-sai-mu *(n.)* **impertinence**

ရိုင်းစိုင်းသော rinesinesaw *(adj.)* **rude**

ရိုင်းပင်းကူညီခြင်း rine-pinn-kuu-nyechinn *(n.)* **succour**

ရိုင်းပင်းကူညီသည် rine-pinn-kuu-nye-sai *(v.)* **succour**

ရိုင်းပင်းခင်မင်တတ်သော yin-pin-khin-min-tat-taw *(adj.)* **neighbourly**

ရိုင်းပင်းသည် rine pinn-sai *(v.)* **rally**

ရိုင်းပျခြင်း yai-pya-chin *(n.)* **disrespect**

ရိုင်းပျသော yaing-pya-taw *(adj.)* **barbarous**

ရိုင်းသော rinesaw *(adj.)* **unmannerly**

ရိုင်ဖယ် rinehpaal *(n.)* **rifle**

ရိုသေလေးစားသော ro saylayysarrsaw *(adj.)* **reverential**

ရီနေဆန်းခေတ် re nay saannh-khit *(n.)* **renaissance**

ရီပါဗလီကန်ပါတီ re par bale kaanparte *(n.)* **republican**

ရီဝေသော yee-wai-taw *(adj.)* **bleary**

ရုံ rone *(n.)* **shed**

ရုံး yone *(n.)* **office**

ရုံးတင်သည် yone-tin-the *(v.)* **arraign**

ရုံးပတီ rone-pa-te *(n.)* **okra**

ရုံးသုံးလက်ဆွဲအိတ် yone-tone-lat-swal-aik *(n.)* **briefcase**

ရုံးအိတ်၊ အချက်အလက်အစုစု rone aate, aa-chet-aa-laat-aa-susu *(n.)* **portfolio**

ရုံငယ် yone-nge *(n.)* **booth**

ရုံမတင်မှီ အထူးပွဲ၊ ကြိုတင်အသိပေးချက် rone ma tin-mhae aahtuu pwal , kyo-tin-aa-si-payy-chet *(v.)* **preview**

ရုံမျှသာ yone-mya-tar *(adv.)* **barely**

ရုက္ခကွန်းသာ yoke-kha-kun-thar *(n.)* **arbour**

ရုက္ခဗေဒ yoke-kha-bay-da *(n.)* **botany**

ရုက္ခဗေဒဆိုင်ရာ yoke-kha-bay-da-sai-yar *(adj.)* **botanical**

ရုတ်ခြည်းကျလာခြင်း rote chi kyalarchinn *(n.)* **spate**

ရုတ်ခြည်းသယ်ယူသွားသည် rote chi saalyuuswarrsai *(v.)* **whisk**

ရုတ်တရက် rote-ta-raat *(n.)* **sudden**

ရုတ်တရက် ထတောက်၍ လင်းဖြာသည် yoke-ta-yat-hta-tauk-ywe-lin-phar-the *(v.)* **flare**

ရုတ်တရက် သေသည် rotetaraat saysai *(v.)* **stall**

ရုတ်တရက်၊ အကျဉ်းချုပ် rotetaraat , aakyainhkyaote *(adv.)* **short**

ရုတ်တရက်ကျရောက်သော ကပ်ဆိုး yote-ta-yat-kya-yauk-taw-kat-soe *(n.)* **cataclysm**

ရုတ်တရက်ကြီးလာသော yote-ta-yat-kyi-lar-taw *(adj.)* **cephaloid**

ရုတ်တရက်ချက်ခြင်းဖြစ်သော yote-ta-yat-chat-chin-phit-taw *(adj.)* **acute**

ရုတ်တရက်ပစ်ခြင်း yote-ta-yat-pyit-chin *(n.)* **darting**

ရုတ်တရက်ဖြစ်ပွားသော ကပ်ဘေး yote-ta-yat-phyit-pwar-taw-kat-bay *(n.)* **catastrophe**

ရုတ်တရက်ဖြစ်သော yote-ta-yat-phit-taw *(adj.)* **abrupt**

ရုတ်ရုတ်ရုတ်ရုတ် rote rote roterote *(n.)* **ruckus**

ရုန့်ကြမ်းကျယ်လောင်သော ront kyam kyaal-laungsaw *(adj.)* **raucous**

ရုန်းကန်ခြင်း ronekaanchinn *(n.)* **struggle**

ရုန်းကန်သည် ronekaansai *(v.)* **struggle**

ရုပ်၊ အသံ ဖမ်းစက် rote , aa-san hpamsaat *(n.)* **recorder**

ရုပ်ကြွင်းလေ့လာမှုပညာ rotekyawin laelar-mhupin-nyar *(n.)* **paleontology**

ရုပ်ကြွင်းလေ့လာမှုပညာရှင် rotekyawin laelar-mhupin-nyarshin *(n.)* **paleontologist**
ရုပ်ငြိမ် rote-ngyein *(n.)* **still**
ရုပ်စုံမှန်ပြောင်း yoke-sone-man-pyaung *(n.)* **kaleidoscope**
ရုပ်ဆိုးအောင်လုပ်သည် yoke-soe-aung-lote-sai *(v.)* **uglify**
ရုပ်တု yoke-htu *(n.)* **effigy**
ရုပ်တု ကိုးကွယ်သူ yoke-htu-koe-kwal-thu *(n.)* **idolater**
ရုပ်ထု rotehtu *(n.)* **statue**
ရုပ်ပျက်ဆင်းပျက် ဖြစ်သည် yoke-pyat-sin-pyat-phit-the *(v.)* **mangle**
ရုပ်ပိုင်း၊ စိတ်ပိုင်း စည်းဝါးကျကျ ဖြစ်ပေါ်ခြင်း yoke-pai-seik-pai-see-war-kya-kya-phit-paw-chin *(n.)* **biorhythm**
ရုပ်ပုံ မိတ္တူ rotepone meittuu *(n.)* **tracing**
ရုပ်ပုံကြည်သော ဆုံချက်၊ ဆုံချက်ဆိုင်ရာ yoke-pon-kyi-taw-sone-chat, sone-chat-sai-yar *(adj.)* **focal**
ရုပ်ဖျက်သည် yoke-phat-the *(v.)* **disguise**
ရုပ်ဖြောင့်သော yauk-phaunt-taw *(adj.)* **handsome**
ရုပ်မြင်သံကြား rotemyinsankyarr *(n.)* **television**
ရုပ်မြင်သံကြားမှ ထုတ်လွှင့်သည် rotemyinsankyarrmha htote lwintsai *(v.)* **televise**
ရုပ်ရှင် yoke-shin *(n.)* **film**
ရုပ်ရှင်ကား yoke-shin-kar *(n.)* **footage**
ရုပ်ရှင်ဇာတ်ညွှန်းဆရာ roteshinjaratnywhaannsarar *(n.)* **scenarist**
ရုပ်ရှင်နှင့် ပတ်သက်သော yoke-shin-nint-pat-tat-taw *(adj.)* **cinematic**
ရုပ်ရှင်ဖလင် yoke-shin-pha-lin *(n.)* **celluloid**
ရုပ်ရှင်ရိုက်ကူးရေးပညာ yoke-shin-yite-khu-yay-pyin-nyar *(n.)* **cinematography**
ရုပ်ရှင်ရိုက်ကူးသူ yoke-shin-yite-ku-thu *(n.)* **filmmaker**
ရုပ်ရှင်ရိုက်သည် yoke-shin-yite-the *(v.)* **film**
ရုပ်ရှင်ရုံ yoke-shin-yone *(n.)* **bioscope**
ရုပ်ရှင်ရုံကြီး yoke-shin-yone-gyi *(n.)* **cineplex**
ရုပ်ရှင်အတွက် အလုပ်ပြီးမြောက်ခြင်း roteshinaatwat a lotepyee myawwathkyinn *(n.)* **screenwork**
ရုပ်လက္ခဏာ rote-lak-hka-nar *(n.)* **physiognomy**
ရုပ်လွန်ပညာ yoke-lun-pyin-nyar *(n.)* **metaphysics**
ရုပ်လွန်ပညာနှင့်ဆိုင်သော yoke-lun-pyin-nyar-nint-sai-taw *(adj.)* **metaphysical**
ရုပ်လုံးသွင်းပညာ rote lone swinpanyar *(n.)* **taxidermy**
ရုပ်လုံးသွင်းသူ rote lone swinsuu *(n.)* **taxidermist**
ရုပ်ဝတ္ထုရှိသော yoke-wit-htu-shi-taw *(adj.)* **material**
ရုပ်ဝါဒ yoke-war-da *(n.)* **materialism**
ရုပ်သံဆိုင်ရာ yoke-than-saing-yar *(adj.)* **audiovisual**
ရုပ်သွင်ပညာ yoke-twin-pyi-nyar *(n.)* **morphology**
ရုပ်သွင်အဆင့်အမျိုးမျိုးကူးပြောင်းဖြစ်ပေါ်သော rote swin aa-sint aa-myoe-myoe kuu-pyaung-hpyit-paw-saw *(adj.)* **polymorphic**
ရုပ်သိမ်းခြင်း rotesaimchinn *(n.)* **repeal**
ရုပ်သိမ်းသည် rotesaimsai *(v.)* **repeal**
ရုပ်သေးရုပ် rotesayyrote *(n.)* **puppet**

ရုရှားတော်လှန်ရေးခေါင်းဆောင် ထရော့စကီး၏ နောက်လိုက် rusharr tawhlaanrayyhkaunggsaung hta rot sa kee-eat nout-lite *(n.)* **trot**

ရုရှားနိုင်ငံသုံးငွေ ရူဘယ် rusharrninengansonengway ruubhaal *(n.)* **rouble**

ရူးကြောင်ကြောင်၊ လက်လွှတ်စပယ်စကား yuu-kyaung-kyaung-lat-lut-sa-pal-sa-kar *(n.)* **blabber**

ရူးကြောင်ကြောင်ဖြစ်သော ruukyaungkyaunghpyitsaw *(adj.)* **scatty**

ရူးခြင်း yuu-chin *(n.)* **insanity**

ရူးသွပ်ခြင်း yu-tut-chin *(n.)* **lunacy**

ရူးသွပ်သော yu-thwut-taw *(adj.)* **crazy**

ရူးသော yu-taw *(adj.)* **demented**

ရူပက အလင်္ကာတွဲ yu-pa-ka-a-link-kar-twe *(n.)* **allegory**

ရူပဗေဒ ruu-pa-bay-da *(n.)* **physics**

ရူပဗေဒပညာရှင် ruu-pa-bay-da-pa-nyar-shin *(n.)* **physicist**

ရူပီးငွေ ruupeengway *(n.)* **rupee**

ရူဘီအန်ဓာတ် ru-bi-an-dat *(n.)* **rubian**

ရေ ray *(n.)* **water**

ရေးကြီးခွင်ကျယ်လုပ်သည် yay-kyi-khwin-kyal-lote-the *(v.)* **fuss**

ရေးစပ်သီကုံးခြင်း၊ ပါဝင်ပစ္စည်းများ yay-sat-thi-kone-chin, par-win-pyit-see-myar *(n.)* **composition**

ရေးမှတ်သည် ray-mhaat-sai *(v.)* **plot**

ရေးသည်၊ စီကုံးသည် rayysai , se konesai *(v.)* **write**

ရေ၊ လေတိုက်စားခံ ကျောက်တုံးကြီး yay-lay-tite-sar-khan-kyauk-tone-gyi *(n.)* **boulder**

ရေကန် yay-kan *(n.)* **lake**

ရေကန်ငယ် ray kaan-ngaal *(n.)* **pond**

ရေကျောက် raykyaut *(n.)* **smallpox**

ရေကြက်ဒုံ yay-kyat-don *(n.)* **coot**

ရေကြည်ရာမြက်နုရာ လှည့်လည်နေထိုင်သူ yay-kyi-yar-myat-nu-yar-hlae-lal-nay-htine-tuu *(n.)* **nomad**

ရေကြည်ရာမြက်နုရာ လှည့်လည်နေထိုင်သော yay-kyi-yar-myat-nu-yar-hlae-lal-nay-htine-taw *(adj.)* **nomadic**

ရေကြီးခြင်း yay-kyi-chin *(n.)* **flood**

ရေကြောင်းပြဖော်ယာ yay-kyaung-pya-baw-yar *(n.)* **buoy**

ရေကာတာ yay-kar-tar *(n.)* **embankment**

ရေကာတာ၊ ဆည် yay-kar-tar, sal *(n.)* **dam**

ရေကူးခြင်း ray kuuchinn *(n.)* **swim**

ရေကူးလေဖြတ်ခြင်း ray kuu layhpyathkyinn *(n.)* **sidestroke**

ရေကူးသည် ray kuusai *(v.)* **swim**

ရေကူးသမား ray kuusamarr *(n.)* **swimmer**

ရေကဲ့သို့သော raykaethoetsaw *(adj.)* **watery**

ရေချိုးခြင်း yay-choe-chin *(n.)* **bath**

ရေချိုးသည် yay-choe-the *(v.)* **bathe**

ရေချိုင့် yay-chaint *(n.)* **jug**

ရေခြင်္သေ့ ray hkyinsae *(n.)* **sealion**

ရေခဲ yay-khae *(n.)* **ice**

ရေခဲစိမ် yay-khae-sein *(adj.)* **iced**

ရေခဲစိုင်ကြီး yay-khae-sai-gyi *(n.)* **iceberg**

ရေခဲတမျှ အေးသော yay-khae-ta-hmya-aye-taw *(adj.)* **ice-cold**

ရေခဲတုံး yay-khae-tone *(n.)* **iceblock**

ရေခဲထာဝစဉ် ဖုံးလွှမ်းခြင်း yay-khae-htar-wa-zin-phone-hlwan-chin *(n.)* **icecap**

ရေခဲပန်းဆွဲ yay-khae-pan-swal *(n.)* **icicle**

ရေခဲပြင်ခွဲသင်္ဘော yay-khae-pyin-khwal-tin-baw *(n.)* **icebreaker**

ရေခဲပြင်စီးစကိတ် rayhkellpyin see sakate *(n.)* **skate**
ရေခဲပုံး yay-khae-pone *(n.)* **ice bucket**
ရေခဲမြစ် yay-khae-myit *(n.)* **glacier**
ရေခဲမုန့် yay-khae-hmont *(n.)* **ice cream**
ရေခဲရိုက်ခြင်း ray hkell ritechinn *(n.)* **refrigeration**
ရေခဲရိုက်သည် ray hkell ritesai *(v.)* **refrigerate**
ရေခဲလျှောစီး ray hkell shawsee *(n.)* **slide**
ရေခဲသည် yay-khae-the *(v.)* **ice**
ရေခဲသေတ္တာ rayhkellsit-tar *(n.)* **refrigerator**
ရေခဲသေတ္တာမှ ရေခဲကို ဖယ်ရှင်းသည် yay-khae-tit-tar-ma-yay-khae-ko-phal-shar-the *(v.)* **defrost**
ရေငတ်ပြေစေသည် ray ngaat pyay-saysai *(v.)* **quench**
ရေငုပ်သင်္ဘော ray ngotesinbhaw *(n.)* **submarine**
ရေစိမ်ခံ raysinhkan *(n.)* **waterproof**
ရေစိမ်ခြင်း ray sinchinn *(n.)* **soak**
ရေစုန်မျောနေသော yay-sone-myaw-nay-taw *(adj.)* **adrift**
ရေစေးချွတ်ဆေး ray sayy chyutsayy *(n.)* **softener**
ရေဆင်းပိုက် yay-sin-pipe *(n.)* **drainpipe**
ရေဆာခြင်း ray sarchinn *(n.)* **thirst**
ရေဆာသည် ray sarsai *(v.)* **thirst**
ရေဆာသော ray sarsaw *(adj.)* **thirsty**
ရေဆိုးပိုက် ray soepite *(n.)* **sewer**
ရေဆေးခြင်း ray say-chinn *(n.)* **wash**
ရေဆေးဆွဲရန် ကူညီပေးသော အရာ yay-say-swal-yan-ku-nyi-pay-taw-a-yar *(n.)* **emulsifier**
ရေဆေးဖြင့် ပြုလုပ်သည် yay-say-phint-pyu-loat-the *(v.)* **emulsify**
ရေဆေးသည် ray sayysai *(v.)* **rinse**
ရေညှိ yay-nyi *(n.)* **moss**
ရေညှိမှ ထုတ်သော ကျောက်ကျောပုံအဆီအနှစ် yay-nyi-hma-htoke-taw-kyauk-kyaw-pone-a-si-a-hnit *(n.)* **agar**
ရေတံခွန် raytanhkwan *(n.)* **waterfall**
ရေတံခါး yay-ta-khar *(n.)* **flood gate**
ရေတံလျှောက် yay-ta-shaut *(n.)* **gutter**
ရေတပ် yay-tat *(n.)* **navy**
ရေတပ်နှင့် ဆိုင်သော yay-tat-nint-sai-taw *(adj.)* **naval**
ရေတပ်ဗိုလ်ချုပ်ကြီး yay-tat-bo-gyoke-gyi *(n.)* **admiral**
ရေတပ်မတော်ဆိုင်ရာဦးစီးဌာန yay-tat-ma-taw=saing-yar-au-see-htar-na *(n.)* **admiralty**
ရေတပ်သင်္ဘောစု yay-tat-tin-baw-su *(n.)* **fleet**
ရေတွက်ခြင်းနှင့် သက်ဆိုင်သော yay-thwat-chin-nint-thet-sai-taw *(adj.)* **enumerative**
ရေတွက်တိုင်းတာသော ray-twat tine tarsaw *(adj.)* **quantitative**
ရေတွက်နိုင်သော yay-thwat-nai-taw *(adj.)* **enumerable**
ရေတွက်သည် yay-thwat-the *(v.)* **enumerate**
ရေတွင်း raytwin *(n.)* **well**
ရေတိမ် yay-tein *(n.)* **glaucoma**
ရေတို rayto *(adj.)* **short-term**
ရေတိုက်စားခြင်း yay-tite-sar-chin *(n.)* **aggradation**
ရေဒါဖန်သားပြင်ပေါ်မှ အလင်းပြောက် yay-dar-phan-tar-pyin-paw-ma-a-lin-pyauk *(n.)* **blip**

ရေဒီယမ်ဒြပ်စင် ray de yam dyatsin *(n.)* **radium**
ရေဒီယို ray-deyo *(n.)* **radio**
ရေဒီယိုကြေးနန်း ray-deyo-kyay-nan *(n.)* **radiotelegraphy**
ရေဒီယိုစကန် ray-deyo-sa-kan *(n.)* **radioscan**
ရေဒီယိုဓာတ်သတ္တိကြွအမှုန်များ ra-di-yo-dat-tat-ti-kwa-a-hmone-myar *(n.)* **fallout**
ရေဒီယိုမာကျူရီ ray-deyo-mar-cu-ry *(n.)* **radiomercury**
ရေဒီယိုရောဂါပြီးပညာ ray-deyo-yaw-gar-pi-pin-nyar *(n.)* **radiommunology**
ရေဒီယိုလှိုင်းနှုန်း yay-di-yo-line-hnone *(n.)* **airband**
ရေဒီယိုလှိုင်းမှ ပေးပို့သော စာတို ray-deyo-hlaing-ma-pay-poe-taw-sar-to *(n.)* **radiogram**
ရေဒီယိုလှိုင်းမှ ပေးပို့သော တည်နေရာ ray-deyo-hlaing-ma-pay-poe-taw-te-nay-yar *(n.)* **radiolocation**
ရေဒီယိုလှိုင်းသုံးဖုန်း ray-deyo-hline-tone-phone *(n.)* **radiophone**
ရေဒီယိုသတ္တိကြွသော ray deyo satti kyawsaw *(adj.)* **radioactive**
ရေနံ ray-nan *(n.)* **petroleum**
ရေနံဆီ ray-nan-se *(n.)* **paraffin**
ရေနံတူးစင် ray-nan-tuu-sin *(n.)* **oil rig**
ရေနဂါး raynagarr *(n.)* **seahorse**
ရေနစ်သည် yay-nit-the *(v.)* **drown**
ရေနွေးကရား yay-nway-ka-yar *(n.)* **kettle**
ရေနွေးငွေ့ raynwayngwae *(n.)* **steam**
ရေနွေးအိုး raynwayoe *(n.)* **samovar**
ရေနှစ်သည် yay-nit-the *(v.)* **douse**
ရေနုတ်မြောင်း yay-note-myaung *(n.)* **drainage**

ရေနေ၊ ရေပျော် yay-nay, yay-pyaw *(adj.)* **aquatic**
ရေပန်း ray-pan *(n.)* **shower**
ရေပန်းခေါင်း ray paannhkaungg *(n.)* **showerhead**
ရေပန်းစားနေသော အလုပ် yay-pan-sar-nay-taw-a-lote *(n.)* **bandwagon**
ရေပန်းစားမှု ray-paann-sarr-mhu *(n.)* **popularity**
ရေပန်းစားသော raypaannsarrsaw *(adj.)* **topical**
ရေပန်းဖြင့် ချိုးသည် ray pan-hpyint choesai *(v.)* **shower**
ရေပွက်သကဲ့သို့ မြည်သည် yay-pwat-tha-kae-tho-myae-the *(v.)* **burble**
ရေပုတ်သင် raypotesin *(n.)* **salamander**
ရေပူစမ်း yay-pu-san *(n.)* **geyser**
ရေပေါ်ပေါ်နိုင်သော yay-paw-paw-nai-taw *(adj.)* **buoyant**
ရေဖတ်တိုက်သည် ray hpaat titesai *(v.)* **sponge**
ရေဖျန်းခြင်းမင်္ဂလာ yay-phyan-min-ga-lar *(n.)* **baptism**
ရေဖျန်းခြင်းမင်္ဂလာပြု၍ ခရစ်ယာန်ဖြစ်စေသည် yay-phyan-min-ga-lar-ywe-kha-yit-yan-phit-say-the *(v.)* **baptize**
ရေဘဝဲ ray-bha-well *(n.)* **octopus**
ရေဘဲ raybhell *(n.)* **sawbill**
ရေမချိုးပဲ ray m hkyoepell *(adj.)* **showerless**
ရေမခဲဆေး yay-ma-khae-say *(n.)* **antifreeze**
ရေမျက်နှာပြင် အညစ်အကြေး raymyetnharpyin aanyaitaakyay *(v.)* **scum**
ရေမြှုပ် ray myote *(n.)* **sponge**
ရေမြောင်း yay-myaung *(n.)* **drain**

ရေမွှေး ray-hmway *(n.)* **perfume**

ရေယဉ်ကို တရားမဝင် ထိန်းချုပ်ခြင်း ray yainko tararrmawain hteinhkyaotehkyinn *(n.)* **seajack**

ရေယဉ်ကို တရားမဝင် ထိန်းချုပ်သည် ray yainko tararrmawain hteinhkyaotesai *(v.)* **seajack**

ရေယဉ်ကို တရားမဝင် ထိန်းချုပ်သူ ray yainko tararrmawain hteinhkyaotesuu *(n.)* **seajacker**

ရေရွတ်သည် yay-yut-the *(v.)* **mutter**

ရေရှည် yay-shay *(adj.)* **long-term**

ရေရောသည် yay-yaw-the *(v.)* **dilute**

ရေလက်ကြား raylaatkyarr *(n.)* **strait**

ရေလက်ကြား၊ လမ်းကြောင်း၊ ဦးတည်ရာ yay-lat-kyar, lan-kyaung, oo-the-yar *(n.)* **channel**

ရေလမ်းဖြင့် ကုန်ပစ္စည်းပို့သည် raylamhpyint konepahchcaee phoetsai *(v.)* **ship**

ရေလွှမ်းမိုးခြင်း yay-hlwan-moe-chin *(n.)* **deluge**

ရေလွှမ်းမိုးသည် yay-hlwan-moe-the *(v.)* **flood**

ရေလွှမ်းသည် raylwhamsai *(v.)* **swamp**

ရေလွှာလှိုင်းစီးကစားသည် ray lwhar hline see-kasarrsai *(v.)* **surf**

ရေလွှဲပေါက် ray lwhaellpout *(n.)* **sluice**

ရေလှောင်ကန် ray hlaawinkaan *(n.)* **reservoir**

ရေလုံသော ray lonesaw *(adj.)* **waterproof**

ရေလုံအောင် လုပ်သည် ray loneaaung lotesai *(v.)* **waterproof**

ရေလောင်းသည် ray launggsai *(v.)* **water**

ရေလဲဝတ်ရုံ ray lellwaatrone *(n.)* **robe**

ရေသွယ်တံတား yay-thwe-ta-dar *(n.)* **aqueduct**

ရေသုတ်ကုတ်အင်္ကျီ yay-tote-coat-inn-gyi *(n.)* **bathrobe**

ရေသူထီး yay-thu-htee *(n.)* **merman**

ရေသူမ yay-thu-ma *(n.)* **mermaid**

ရေသေ raysay *(adj.)* **stagnant**

ရေသောက်မြစ် ray soutmyit *(n.)* **tenet**

ရေအနက်တစ်လံ yay-a-net-ta-lan *(n.)* **fathom**

ရော့ကက်ဒီဇိုင်းလုပ်သည်၊ ပစ်သည်၊ ဒုံးစီးနင်းသည် yot-kat-da-zine-lote-the, pyit-the, done-si-nin-the *(n.)* **rocketman**

ရော့ကက်ဒီဇိုင်းလုပ်သူ၊ ပစ်သူ၊ ဒုံးစီးနင်းသူ yot-kat-da-zine-lote-thu, pyit-th, done-si-nin-thu *(n.)* **rocketeer**

ရော့ခ်ကာသမား rothk karsamarr *(n.)* **rocker**

ရောကျော်ခွေး yaw-kyaw-khway *(n.)* **mongrel**

ရောက်တတ်ရာရာ ပြောသည် yauttat-yar-yar-pyaw-the *(v.)* **yak**

ရောက်တတ်ရာရာပြောသည် yauk-tat-yar-yar-pyaw-the *(v.)* **chatter**

ရောက်ရှိခြင်း yauk-shi-chin *(n.)* **arrival**

ရောက်ရှိသည် yauk-shi-the *(v.)* **arrive**

ရောက်သည်၊ လှမ်းယူသည် routsai , hlam yuusai *(v.)* **reach**

ရောခြင်း yaw-chin *(n.)* **adulteration**

ရောဂါ yaw-gar *(n.)* **disease**

ရောဂါကြောင့် အိပ်ရာမှ မထနိုင်သော yaw-gar-kyaunt-aik-yar-hma-ma-hta-nai-taw *(adj.)* **bedridden**

ရောဂါကုထုံး rawgarkuhtone *(n.)* **therapy**

ရောဂါကူးစက်ခြင်း yaw-gar-ku-sat-chin *(n.)* **contagion**

ရောဂါပြန်ထခြင်း rawgar pyan-htachinn *(v.)* **relapse**

ရောဂါပိုး yaw-gar-poe *(n.)* **germ**

ရောဂါပိုးဝင်ခြင်း yaw-gar-poe-win-chin *(n.)* **infection**

ရောဂါပိုးဝင်သည် yaw-gar-poe-win-the *(v.)* **infect**

ရောဂါဗေဒ raw-gar-bay-da *(n.)* **pathology**

ရောဂါအမည်တပ်ခြင်း yaw-gar-a-me-tat-chin *(n.)* **diagnosis**

ရောဂါအမည်တပ်သည် yaw-gar-a-me-tat-the *(v.)* **diagnose**

ရောဂါအမည်မှားတပ်သည် yaw-gar-a-me-mar-tat-the *(v.)* **misdiagnose**

ရောင့်ရဲခြင်း yaunt-ye-chin *(n.)* **contentment**

ရောင့်ရဲသော yaunt-ye-taw *(adj.)* **content**

ရောင်းကုန်ခြင်း raunggkonechinn *(n.)* **sell-out**

ရောင်းချခြင်း raunggchachinn *(n.)* **sale**

ရောင်းချသည် raunggchasai *(v.)* **sell**

ရောင်းစားသည်၊ ပြည့်တန်ဆာ လုပ်သည် raungg-sarr sai , pyae-taansar lotesai *(v.)* **prostitute**

ရောင်းနိုင်သော yaung-nai-taw *(adj.)* **salable**

ရောင်းပန်းလှသော yaung-pan-hla-taw *(adj.)* **marketable**

ရောင်းပြီးနောက် ဖြစ်သော yaung-pi-naut-phit-taw *(adj.)* **aftersales**

ရောင်းသည် raunggsai *(v.)* **retail**

ရောင်းသူ raunggsuu *(n.)* **seller**

ရောင်းအားအကောင်းဆုံး yaung-arr-a-kaung-sone *(n.)* **bestseller**

ရောင်ခြည် raung-chi *(n.)* **ray**

ရောင်ခြည်တစ်ခုခုပေးသည် yaung-che-ta-khu-khu-pay-the *(v.)* **irradiate**

ရောင်ခြည်တန်း yaung-chee-tan *(n.)* **beam**

ရောင်ခြည်ဖြာခြင်း raung-chi hpyaar-chinn *(n.)* **radiation**

ရောင်စဉ် raungsin *(n.)* **spectrum**

ရောင်စုံချည်ဖြင့် ပုံဖော် ထိုးထားသော အထည် raungsone chaihpyint ponehpaw htoehtarrsaw aahtai *(n.)* **tapestry**

ရောင်စုံချယ်ပန်းချီကား raung-sone-chaal-pa-chae-karr *(n.)* **pastel**

ရောင်စုံခဲတံ yaung-zon-khae-tan *(n.)* **crayon**

ရောင်ပြန်ပြား raung-pyanpyarr *(n.)* **reflector**

ရောင်ရမ်းခြင်း yaung-yan-chin *(n.)* **edema**

ရောင်ရမ်းသော yaung-yan-taw *(adj.)* **inflammatory**

ရောင်ဝါလက္ခဏာ yaung-war-lat-kha-nar *(n.)* **aura**

ရောစပ်မှု yaw-set-mu *(n.)* **amalgam**

ရောစပ်သည် yaw-sat-the *(v.)* **blend**

ရောနှောသည် yaw-hnaw-the *(v.)* **mix**

ရောနှောသော rawnhaawsaw *(adj.)* **scrambled**

ရောပုံထားသည် yaw-pon-htar-the *(v.)* **jumble**

ရောမခေတ် တိရစ္ဆာန်နှင့် သတ်ပုတ် ဖျော်ဖြေရသူ yaw-ma-khit-ta-yeik-san-nint-tat-poke-phyaw-phyay-ya-thu *(n.)* **gladiator**

ရောမခေတ် တိရစ္ဆာန်နှင့် သတ်ပုတ် ဖျော်ဖြေရသော yaw-ma-khit-ta-yeik-san-nint-tat-poke-phyaw-phyay-ya-taw *(adj.)* **gladiatorial**

ရောမွှေ၍ ပစ်ခဲအောင် လုပ်သည် yaw-mway-ywe-pyit-khae-aung-lote-the *(v.)* **ream**

ရောသည် yaw-the *(v.)* **adulterate**

ရောသည်၊ နှောသည် yaw-the, naw-the *(v.)* **mingle**

ရော်ဘာ rawbhar *(n.)* **rubber**

ရော်ဘာကျည် rawbharkyai *(n.)* **rubber bullet**

ရော်ဘာပင် rawbharpin *(n.)* **rubber tree**

ရော်ဘာဘွတ်ဖိနပ်ရှည် yaw-bar-boot-phi-nat-shay *(n.)* **gumboot**

ရဲ rell *(n.)* **police**

ရဲဝံ့သော ye-wint-taw *(adj.)* **courageous**

ရဲကင်းစခန်း rell kinnsahkaann *(n.)* **police beat**

ရဲစခန်းပိုင်နက်၊ အိမ်ကြီးရခိုင် ye-sa-khan-pai-net, eain-kyi-ya-khine *(n.)* **manor**

ရဲစွမ်းသတ္တိ taanhpoeshisaw *(n.)* **valour**

ရဲစွမ်းသတ္တိရှိသော aasaatwinsaw *(adj.)* **valiant**

ရဲစသည့် အပိတ်အဆို့ ya-sa-the-a-pait-a-soe *(n.)* **cordon**

ရဲဆေးတင်သည် ye-say-tin-the *(v.)* **embolden**

ရဲတင်းမှု ye-tin-mu *(n.)* **audacity**

ရဲတင်းသော ye-tin-taw *(adj.)* **audacious**

ရဲတပ်ဖွဲ့ ye-tat-phwe *(n.)* **constable**

ရဲတိုက် yae-tite *(n.)* **castle**

ရဲတိုက်အုပ်ချုပ်ရေးမှူး yae-tite-oak-choke-yay-hmue *(n.)* **castellan**

ရဲဘော်ရဲဘက် ye-baw-ye-bat *(n.)* **comrade**

ရဲမရှိသော rellmashisaw *(adj.)* **policeless**

ရဲရင့်သော ye-yint-taw *(adj.)* **bold**

ရဲရင့်ခြင်း ye-yint-chin *(n.)* **courage**

ရဲရင့်စွာ ye-yint-swar *(adv.)* **boldly**

ရဲရင့်မှု ye-yint-mu *(n.)* **boldness**

ရဲရင့်သော ye-yint-taw *(adj.)* **brave**

ရဲလှေ relllhaay *(n.)* **policeboat**

ရဲဝံ့ခြင်း rellwanchinn *(n.)* **temerity**

ရဲဝံ့သော rellwansaw *(adj.)* **temeritous**

ရဲသား rell-sarr *(n.)* **policeman**

ရဲအုပ် ye-oak *(n.)* **inspector**

လံကြိုး lankyoe *(n.)* **tether**

လံထားသည် lanhtarrsai *(v.)* **tether**

လက္ခဏာ lakhkanar *(n.)* **symptom**

လက္ခဏာဆရာ lakh-ka-nar-sa-rar *(n.)* **palmist**

လက္ခဏာနှစ်ရပ် ဒွန်တွဲနေမှု lat-kha-nar-na-yat-dun-twe-nay-mu *(n.)* **duality**

လက္ခဏာဗေဒင် lakh-ka-nar-bay-din *(n.)* **palmistry**

လက် lat *(n.)* **hand**

လက်ကမ်းကြော်ငြာ lat-khan-kyaw-nyar *(n.)* **handbill**

လက်ကမ်းစာစောင် lat-kan-sar-saung *(n.)* **brochure**

လက်ကမ်းစာစောင်ရေးသူ lat-khan-sar-saung-yay-thu *(n.)* **pamphleteer**

လက်ကျန်ငွေ၊ နှစ်ဖက်ညီမျှမှု lat-kyan-ngwe, na-phat-nyi-hmya-hmu *(n.)* **balance**

လက်ကား laatkarr *(n.)* **wholesale**

လက်ကားဈေးဖြင့် laat karrsyaayyhpyint *(adv.)* **wholesale**

လက်ကားရောင်းသူ laat karrraunggsuu *(n.)* **wholesaler**

လက်ကိုင် lat-kai *(n.)* **handle**

လက်ကိုင်ပဝါ lat-kai-pa-war *(n.)* **handkerchief**

လက်ကိုင်ပိုစတာ lat-kine-po-sa-tar *(n.)* **placard**

လက်ကောက် lat-kauk *(n.)* **bracelet**

လက်ကောက်၊ ခြေချင်း lat-kauk, chay-chin *(n.)* **bangle**

လက်ကောက်ဝတ် laatkoutwaat *(n.)* **wrist**

လက်ခံခြင်း laat-hkan-chinn *(n.)* **reception**

လက်ခံထားသည် laat-hkan-htarrsai *(v.)* **reckon**

လက်ခံထားသော lat-khan-htar-taw *(adj.)* **accepted**

လက်ခံနိုင်စွမ်း lat-khan-naing-swan *(n.)* **acceptability**

လက်ခံနိုင်သော lat-khan-naing-taw *(adj.)* **acceptable**

လက်ခံဖြတ်ပိုင်း lat-khan-phat-pai *(n.)* **counterfoil**

လက်ခံယုံကြည်စေသည် lat-khan-yone-kyi-say-the *(v.)* **convince**

လက်ခံရရှိခြင်း laat-hkan-rashichinn *(n.)* **receipt**

လက်ခံရရှိသည် laat-hkan-rashisai *(v.)* **receive**

လက်ခံရရှိသူ laat-hkan-rashisuu *(n.)* **recipient**

လက်ခံသည် lat-khan-the *(v.)* **accept**

လက်ခံသူ laathkansuu *(n.)* **taker**

လက်ခံသော lat-khan-taw *(adj.)* **acceptant**

လက်ခနဲ ထွက်သော အလင်းရောင် lat-kha-nae-htwat-taw-a-lin-yaung *(n.)* **flare**

လက်ချာရိုက်သည် laatchaar ritesai *(v.)* **sermonize**

လက်ချောင်း lat-chaung *(n.)* **finger**

လက်ချောင်းရိုး laat-chaungg-roe *(n.)* **phalange**

လက်ခုပ်တီးသည် lat-khote-tee-the *(v.)* **clap**

လက်ခုပ်ဩဘာပေးသည် lat-khote-aw-bar-pay-the *(v.)* **applaud**

လက်ခုပ်ဩဘာသံ lat-khote-aw-bar-tan *(n.)* **applause**

လက်စည်း၊ နက်ကတိုင် laat saee , naat katine *(n.)* **tie**

လက်စလက်န laat sa laatna *(n.)* **vestige**

လက်စွပ် laatswut *(n.)* **ring**

လက်စွဲ lat-swal *(n.)* **handbook**

လက်စသတ်စရာ lat-sa-tat-sa-yar *(n.)* **loose end**

လက်စားချေခြင်း laat sarr chaaychinn *(n.)* **revenge**

လက်စားချေလိုစိတ် ပြင်းပြသော laat sarr chaay losate pyinnpyasaw *(adj.)* **revengeful**

လက်စားချေသည် laat sarr chaaysai *(v.)* **revenge**

လက်ဆင့်ကမ်းပြိုင်ပွဲ laat sint kam-pyainepwal *(n.)* **relay**

လက်ဆင့်ကမ်းပေးသည် laat sint kampayysai *(v.)* **relay**

လက်ဆစ် lat-sit *(n.)* **knuckle**

လက်ဆစ်ချိုးသည် lat-sit-choe-the *(v.)* **knuckle**

လက်ဆွဲကွန်ပျူတာ lat-swal-kun-pyu-tar *(n.)* **laptop**

လက်ဆွဲပုံး laat-swal-pone *(n.)* **pail**

လက်ဆွဲဘရိတ် lat-swal-ba-rate *(n.)* **handbrake**

လက်ဆွဲမီးအိမ် lat-swal-mee-eain *(n.)* **lantern**

လက်ဆွဲအိတ် lat-swal-aik *(n.)* **duffel bag**

လက်ဆောင် lat-saung *(n.)* **gift**

လက်ဆောင်၊ ပစ္စုပ္ပန် laatsaung , pyit-sote-paan *(n.)* **present**

လက်ဆောင်၊ လှူဖွယ်ပစ္စည်း lat-saung, hlu-hpwal-pyit-see *(n.)* **offering**
လက်ဆောင်ပစ္စည်း လှလှပပ ထုပ်ပေးသည် lat-saung-pyit-see-hla-hla-pa-pa-htoke-pay-the *(v.)* **giftwrap**
လက်ဆောင်ပေးသည် laat-saung-payy-sai *(v.)* **present**
လက်ဆောင်အဖြစ်ပေးသည် lat-saung-a-phit-pay-the *(v.)* **gift**
လက်ညှိုး lat-hnyo *(n.)* **forefinger**
လက်ညှိုးထိုးသည်၊ ညွှန်ပြသည် laat-nyoe-htoe-sai, nyun-pya-sai *(v.)* **point**
လက်ညှိုးပန်းချီ lat-nyo-pan-chi *(n.)* **fingerpaint**
လက်တက် laattaat *(n.)* **tributary**
လက်တက်ဖြစ်သော laat taathpyitsaw *(adj.)* **tributary**
လက်တင်ကုလားထိုင် lat-tin-ka-la-htaing *(n.)* **armchair**
လက်တင်အဖုံး lat-tin-a-hpone *(n.)* **armrest**
လက်တစ်ဆုပ်စာ lat-ta-soke-sar *(n.)* **handful**
လက်တွန်းလှည်း lat-ton-lal *(n.)* **bartender**
လက်တွေ့ laat-twae *(adj.)* **practical**
လက်တွေ့ကျကျ laat-twaekyakya *(adv.)* **practically**
လက်တွေ့ကျမှု laat-twae kyamhu *(n.)* **practicability**
လက်တွေ့ကျသော laat-twaekyasaw *(adj.)* **practicable**
လက်တွေ့ဆန်သော laat-twaesaansaw *(adj.)* **pragmatic**
လက်တွေ့ဘဝနှင့် သက်ဆိုင်သော lat-tway-ba-wa-nint-thet-sai-taw *(adj.)* **earthly**
လက်တွေ့မကျခြင်း lat-tway-ma-kya-chin *(n.)* **impracticability**
လက်တွေ့မကျသော laat-twaema-kyasaw *(adj.)* **quixotic**
လက်တွေ့မျက်မြင်ကို အခြေခံသော lat-tway-myat-myin-ko-a-chay-khan-taw *(adj.)* **empirical**
လက်တွေ့လုပ်သည် laat-twaelotesai *(v.)* **practise**
လက်တွေ့လုပ်သူ lat-thway-lote-tu *(n.)* **doer**
လက်တွေ့သုတေသန lat-thway-thu-tay-ta-na *(n.)* **experiment**
လက်တွေ့အကျိုးမျှော်ဝါဒ laat-twae aakyoe myahaawward *(n.)* **pragmatism**
လက်တွေ့အသုံးချ lat-tway-a-tone-cha *(adj.)* **applied**
လက်တို့သကြား lat-toe-ta-kyar *(n.)* **lactose**
လက်တိုလက်တောင်း lat-to-lat-taung *(n.)* **errand**
လက်တုံ့ပြန်မှု laattonepyanmhu *(n.)* **retaliation**
လက်တုံ့ပြန်သည် laattonepyansai *(v.)* **retaliate**
လက်ထက် laat-htaat *(n.)* **reign**
လက်ထပ်၊ ခြေထိပ် laat-htaik , chay-hteik *(n.)* **quick**
လက်ထပ်ခြင်း laathtatchinn *(n.)* **wedding**
လက်ထပ်ခြင်းကို ဒီဇိုင်းလုပ်သော lat-htet-chin-ko-ta-zai-lote-taw *(adj.)* **morganatic**
လက်ထပ်ခြင်းနှင့် ဆိုင်သော laathtauthkyinnnhang sinesaw *(adj.)* **spousal**
လက်ထပ်ထိမ်းမြားခြင်း lat-htet-htein-myar-chin *(n.)* **matrimony**
လက်ထပ်နိုင်သော lat-htet-nai-taw *(adj.)* **marriageable**
လက်ထပ်ရန် သဘောတူမှု lat-htet-yan-ta-baw-thu-mu *(n.)* **betrothal**
လက်ထပ်သည် laathtatsai *(v.)* **wed**

လက်ထိတ် laat htate *(n.)* **shackle**

လက်ထိတ်ခတ်သည် laat htate hkaatsai *(v.)* **shackle**

လက်ထိပ် lat-htaik *(n.)* **handcuff**

လက်ထိပ်ခတ်သည် lat-htaik-khat-the *(v.)* **handcuff**

လက်ထိပ်ဖောက်ခြင်း lat-htike-phauk-chin *(n.)* **fingerstick**

လက်ထောက် lat-htauk *(n.)* **aide**

လက်ထဲတွင် lat-htae-twin *(adv.)* **aloft**

လက်ထဲတွင် ဝှက်သည် laat-htell-twin-whaat-sai *(v.)* **palm**

လက်နက် laatnaat *(n.)* **sidearm**

လက်နက်ကြီးများ lat-nat-kyi-myar *(n.)* **armament**

လက်နက်တိုက် lat-nat-tite *(n.)* **armoury**

လက်နက်မဲ့တိုက်ခိုက်ခြင်း lat-nat-mae-tite-khite-chin *(n.)* **melee**

လက်နက်မဲ့သော laat-naatmaesaw *(adj.)* **unarmed**

လက်နက်သိမ်းခြင်း lat-nat-thein-chin *(n.)* **disarmament**

လက်နက်သိမ်းသည် lat-nat-thein-the *(v.)* **disarm**

လက်နက်အသုံးပြုသော lat-nat-kyi-a-tone-pyu-taw *(adj.)* **armed**

လက်နှင့်ပါ ကုတ်ကတ်တက်သည် laat nintpar kote kaat taatsai *(v.)* **scramble**

လက်နှိပ်စက်ရိုက်သူ laat natesaat ritesuu *(n.)* **typist**

လက်ပတ် lat-pat *(adj.)* **armlet**

လက်ပတ်ကြိုး laatpaatkyoe *(n.)* **strap**

လက်ပြင်ရိုး laat pyinroe *(n.)* **scapula**

လက်ပြင်ရိုးနှင့် ဆိုင်သော laat pyin roenhang sinesaw *(adj.)* **scapular**

လက်ပြန် lat-pyan *(n.)* **backhand**

လက်ပါးစေ lat-par-say *(n.)* **lackey**

လက်ဖက်ပင်၊ လက်ဖက်ရည် laathpaat pin , laathpaatrai *(n.)* **tea**

လက်ဖက်ရည်ဆိုင် laathpaatraisine *(n.)* **teahouse**

လက်ဖက်ရည်ပန်းကန်လုံး laathpaatrai paannkaanlone *(n.)* **teacup**

လက်ဖက်ရည်ဖျော်ဆရာ laathpaat-rai hpyawsarar *(n.)* **tea maker**

လက်ဖက်ရည်ဘူး la-phat-yay-bu *(n.)* **canister**

လက်ဖက်ရည်သယ်ရန် ထည့်ရန် သေတ္တာ laathpaatrai saalraan htaeet-raan sayttar *(n.)* **teabox**

လက်ဖက်ရည်သောက်သည် laathpaat-rai-soutsai *(v.)* **tea**

လက်ဖက်ရည်အိုး laathpaatrai-aoe *(n.)* **teapot**

လက်ဖျံ lat-phyan *(n.)* **forearm**

လက်ဖျားခါလောက်သော lat-pyar-khar-laut-taw *(adj.)* **mind-blowing**

လက်ဖျားခါသည် lat-phyar-khar-the *(v.)* **marvel**

လက်ဖြင့်ပေါင်းသင်သည် lat-phint-paung-tin-the *(n.)* **runcation**

လက်ဖြောင့် laat hpyount *(n.)* **sniper**

လက်ဖြောင့်သူ lat-phaunt-thu *(n.)* **marksman**

လက်ဖဝါး laat-hpa-war *(n.)* **palm**

လက်ဖွာသူ laat hpwarsuu *(n.)* **spendthrift**

လက်ဗလာ lat-ba-lar *(adj.)* **empty-handed**

လက်ဗွေ lat-bway *(n.)* **fingerprint**

လက်မ laat-ma *(n.)* **thumb**

လက်မခံနိုင်သော laat-mahkanninesaw *(adj.)* **unacceptable**

လက်မထက်ရသေးသော မိန်းမငယ် lat-ma-htet-ya-tay-taw-mein-ma-nge *(n.)* **bachelorette**
လက်မထပ်ဘဲ အတူနေသည် laat-ma htatbhell aatuunaysai *(v.)* **shack**
လက်မထပ်မီ laat-ma-htat-me *(adj.)* **premarital**
လက်မဖြင့်ထိသည် lat-ma-phint-hti-the *(v.)* **thumb**
လက်မဗွေရာ laat-ma bwayrar *(n.)* **thumbprint**
လက်မှတ် laatmhaat *(n.)* **signature**
လက်မှတ်တိုထိုးသည် lat-mat-toe-htoe-the *(v.)* **initial**
လက်မှတ်ထိုးသည် laatmhaathtoesai *(v.)* **sign**
လက်မှတ်ပါဝင်ရေးထိုးသူ laatmhaat parwin rayyhtoesuu *(n.)* **signatory**
လက်မှတ်ရေးထိုးခြင်း laatmhaatrayyhtoechinn *(n.)* **signing**
လက်မှိုင်ချသည်၊ ကြမ်းခင်းသည် lat-hmai-cha-the, kyan-khin-the *(v.)* **floor**
လက်မှုပညာ lat-mu-pyin-nyar *(n.)* **artisan**
လက်မှုပညာသည် lat-mu-pyin-nyar-the *(n.)* **craftsman**
လက်မောင်း lat-maung *(n.)* **arm**
လက်မောင်းတစ်ဖက်ဖြင့် ဘောလုံးပစ်သည် laat maungg taithpaathpyint bhawlone paitsai *(v.)* **sidearm**
လက်မောင်းအရှည်ကို မူတည်သော ရှေးဟောင်းအရှည်တိုင်းတာမှု lat-maung-a-shay-ko-mu-the-taw-shay-haung-a-shay-tine-tar-mu *(n.)* **cubit**
လက်ယပ်ခေါ်သည် lat-yat-khaw-the *(v.)* **beckon**
လက်ယာရစ် lat-yar-yit *(adv.)* **clockwise**
လက်ရန်း laat raann *(n.)* **rail**
လက်ရွေးစင် laat-rway-sin *(n.)* **pick**
လက်ရွေးစင်သင်ခန်းစာ lat-yway-sin-tin-khan-sar *(n.)* **master class**
လက်ရှည်အင်္ကျီ လက်အနားခေါက် lat-shay-inn-gyi, lat-a-nar-khauk *(n.)* **cuff**
လက်ရှိမြင့်မားသော အခွန်နှုန်း laatshi myint marrsaw aahkwannhuann *(n.)* **supertax**
လက်ရာ lat-yar *(n.)* **handiwork**
လက်ရိပ်ပြသည် lat-yeik-pya-the *(v.)* **motion**
လက်ရုံးကြွက်သား lat-yone-kwat-tar *(n.)* **biceps**
လက်ရေးစာမူ lat-yay-sar-mu *(n.)* **manuscript**
လက်ရေးဆက် lat-yay-sat *(adj.)* **cursive**
လက်ရေးတို laatrayyto *(n.)* **shorthand**
လက်ရေးတိုလက်နှိပ်စက် laat-rayy to laatnatesaat *(n.)* **stenographer**
လက်ရေးအတတ် lat-yay-a-tat *(n.)* **calligraphy**
လက်လွှတ်ရသည် lat-hlut-ya-the *(v.)* **forfeit**
လက်လှည့်၊ မျက်လှည့် laat hlae, myet hlae *(n.)* **sleight**
လက်လှည့်ဆရာ lat-hlae-sa-yar *(n.)* **juggler**
လက်လှည့်အစွမ်းပြသည် lat-hlae-a-swan-pya-the *(v.)* **juggle**
လက်လှမ်း laath-lam *(n.)* **reach**
လက်လိမ်းလိုးရှင်း lat-lain-lo-shin *(n.)* **hand lotion**
လက်လီဖြန့်ချိသူ laatle hpyant chisuu *(n.)* **retailer**
လက်လီရောင်းခြင်း laatle raunggchinn *(n.)* **retail**
လက်ဝင်သော lat-win-taw *(adj.)* **laborious**
လက်ဝတ်လက်စား lat-wit-lat-sar *(n.)* **jewellery**

လက်ဝှေ့ lat-hwai *(n.)* **boxing**

လက်ဝှေ့သမား lat-hwai-ta-mar *(n)* **boxer**

လက်ဝါးကပ်တိုင် တင်ထားသော ခရစ်တော်ပုံ lat-war-kat-tai-tin-htar-taw-kha-yit-taw-pon *(n.)* **crucifix**

လက်ဝါးကပ်တိုင်ကြီး laatwarrkauttinekyee *(n.)* **rood**

လက်ဝါးကြီး အုပ်သည် lat-war-gyi-oak-the *(v.)* **monopolize**

လက်ဝါးကြီးအုပ် ချုပ်ကိုင်မှုစနစ် lat-war-gyi-oak-choke-kai-mu-sa-nit *(n.)* **monopoly**

လက်ဝါးဖြင့် ရိုက်ခြင်း laatwarrhpyint ritechinn *(n.)* **smack**

လက်ဝါးဖြင့် ရိုက်သည် laatwarrhpyint ritesai *(v.)* **smack**

လက်ဝဲရစ် lat-wal-yit *(adv.)* **anticlockwise**

လက်ဝဲဝါဒီ lat-wal-wa-di *(n.)* **leftist**

လက်သင့်ခံနိုင်သော laat-sint-hkan-nine-saw *(adj.)* **permissible**

လက်သင့်ခံသည် lat-tint-khan-the *(v.)* **harbour**

လက်သင် lat-tin *(n.)* **beginner**

လက်သည်း lat-the *(n.)* **claw**

လက်သည်း၊ သံ lat-the, tan *(n.)* **nail**

လက်သည်းထိုးခြင်း lat-thae-htoe-chin *(n.)* **manicure**

လက်သမား lat-ta-mar *(n.)* **carpenter**

လက်သမားအတတ် lat-ta-mar-a-tat *(n.)* **carpentry**

လက်သရမ်း ဖျက်ဆီးသည် pyawt-kwalswarrsai *(v.)* **vandalize**

လက်သီး lat-thee *(n.)* **fist**

လက်သီးနှင့် ထိုးသည် laatsee-nint htoesai *(v.)* **punch**

လက်သီးပြင်းပြင်း lat-thee-pyin-pyin *(n.)* **biff**

လက်သီးပုန်းထိုးသော laat-see pone htoesaw *(adj.)* **underhand**

လက်သီးဖြင့်ထိုးသည် lat-thee-phit-htoe-the *(v.)* **fist**

လက်ဟန်ခြေဟန် lat-han-chay-han *(n.)* **gesture**

လက်ဟွန်းကြက် lat-hone-kyat *(n.)* **leghorn**

လက်အား၊ ကာယဖြင့် လုပ်သော lat-arr-kar-ya-phint-lote-taw *(adj.)* **manual**

လက်အိတ် lat-aik *(n.)* **glove**

လက်အိတ်ဘူး lat-aik-bu *(n.)* **glovebox**

လက်အောက်ခံ laataouthkan *(n.)* **subordinate**

လက်အောက်ခံအဖြစ်သွတ်သွင်းသည် laataouthkan aahpyit swat swinsai *(v.)* **subjugate**

လက်ဦးမှု ရယူသော lat-oo-mu-ya-yu-taw *(adj.)* **preemptive**

လချေး la-chay *(n.)* **mica**

လခြမ်းကွေး la-chan-kway *(n.)* **crescent**

လခြမ်းကွေးပေါင်မုန့် la-chan-kway-paung-hmont *(n.)* **croissant**

လင် သို့မဟုတ် မယား lin thoetmahote mayarr *(n.)* **spouse**

လင်းတငှက် linntanghaat *(n.)* **vulture**

လင်းတအကြီးစား lon-ta-a-kyi-sar *(n.)* **condor**

လင်းထိန်ခြင်း linn hteinchinn *(n.)* **refulgence**

လင်းထိန်သော linn hteinsaw *(adj.)* **refulgent**

လင်းပိုင် lin-pai *(n.)* **dolphin**

လင်းယုန်ငှက် lin-yone-nget *(n.)* **eagle**

လင်းလက်ခြင်း linnlaatchinn *(n.)* **sparkle**

လင်းလက်ပြိုးပြက်သော linnlaat pyoe pyaatsaw *(n.)* **scintillation**

လင်းသော lin-taw *(adj.)* **light**

လင်ပန်း lin-paann *(n.)* **tray**

လင်ပြိုင်ယူခြင်း lin-pyaine-yuu-dha-lae *(n.)* **polyandry**

လင်မနစ် lin-ma-nit *(n.)* **lemonade**

လစဉ် la-sin *(adv.)* **monthly**

လစာ lasar *(n.)* **salary**

လစ်ဘရယ်၊ အစွန်းမရောက်သော lit-ba-ral, a-sun-ma-yauk-taw *(adj.)* **liberal**

လစ်ဘရယ်ဆန်ဆန် lit-ba-ral-san-san *(n.)* **liberality**

လစ်ဘရယ်ဝါဒ lit-ba-ral-war-da *(n.)* **liberalism**

လစ်သည်၊ ကျော်သည် lit sai , kyaw-sai *(v.)* **skip**

လစ်သွားသည် lat-twar-the *(v.)* **decamp**

လဆုတ် lasote *(n.)* **wane**

လဆုတ်သည် la sotesai *(v.)* **wane**

လည်းပဲ laeepell *(adv.)* **too**

လည်ချောင်း lai-chaung *(n.)* **throat**

လည်ချောင်းသံ lal-chaung-tan *(adj.)* **guttural**

လည်ခြင်း laichinn *(n.)* **rotation**

လည်စည်း lai-see *(n.)* **scarf**

လည်ဆွဲ lal-swal *(n.)* **necklace**

လည်ညှစ်သတ်သည်၊ လည်ပင်းအစ်သည် lai nyit saat sai , laipinn aaitsai *(v.)* **strangle**

လည်ပင်း lal-pin *(n.)* **neck**

လည်ပင်းကို ကြိုးဖြင့် ညှစ်သတ်သူ lal-pin-ko-kyo-phyint-nyit-tat-thu *(n.)* **garrotter**

လည်ပင်းညှစ်သည် laipinn nyhaitsai *(v.)* **throttle**

လည်ပင်းညှစ်သတ်စရာ ကြိုး lal-pin-nyit-tat-sa-yar-kyo *(n.)* **garrotte**

လည်ပတ်ခြင်း laipaatchinn *(n.)* **visit**

လည်ပတ်သည် laipaatsai *(v.)* **revolve**

လည်ပတ်သော laipaatsaw *(adj.)* **rotary**

လည်သည်၊ အလှည့်ကျဖြစ်သည် lai sai , a hla ny kyahpyitsai *(v.)* **rotate**

လည်သိုင်း အရောင်တောက် လက်ကိုင်ပဝါ lal-thaing-a-yaung-taut-lat-kaing-pa-war *(n.)* **bandana**

လည်သိုင်းပတ်တီး lai-sine paattee *(n.)* **sling**

လည်သော lal-taw *(adj.)* **crafty**

လတ္တီတွဒ် lat-ti-tut *(n.)* **latitude**

လတ်လျားလတ်လျားနေသည် lat-lyar-lat-lyar-nay-the *(v.)* **lounge**

လနှင့်ဆိုင်သော la-nint-sai-taw *(adj.)* **lunar**

လန့်စရာကောင်းသော lant-sa-yar-kaung-taw *(adj.)* **daunting**

လန့်စေသည်၊ လှန့်သည် lant saysai , hlant-sai *(v.)* **startle**

လန့်ပြီး ဆတ်ခနဲ တွန့်သည် lant-pyi-sat-kha-nae-twant-the *(v.)* **blench**

လန့်ဖျပ်ခြင်း lant-phat-chin *(n.)* **fright**

လန့်သည် lant-the *(v.)* **daunt**

လန့်သွားသည် lantswarrsai *(v.)* **scare**

လန်ချား laan charr *(n.)* **rickshaw**

လပြည့် la-pyae *(n.)* **full moon**

လမ်း lam *(n.)* **road**

လမ်းက ဆီး၍ စောင့်သည် lamk see saungsai *(v.)* **waylay**

လမ်းကြောင်း lamkyaungg *(n.)* **route**

လမ်းကြောင်း၊ စင်္ကြံ၊ ဖြတ်သန်းခြင်း lam-kyaung, sin-kyaan, hpyat-sann-chinn *(n.)* **passage**

လမ်းကြောင်း၊ ပြေးလမ်း lamkyaungg , pyaylam *(n.)* **track**

လမ်းကြောင်း၊ လူသွားလမ်း lam-kyaung, luu-swarr-lam *(n.)* **path**
လမ်းကောင်းစွာ မလျှောက်နိုင်ခြင်း lan-kaung-swar-ma-shaut-nai-taw *(v.)* **lame**
လမ်းခင်းကျောက်ဆန်ကွဲ lan-khin-kyauk-san-kwe *(n.)* **chipping**
လမ်းခင်းကျောက်လုံး lan-khin-kyauk-lone *(n.)* **cobble**
လမ်းခရီးတွင် lan-kha-yee-twin *(adv.)* **en route**
လမ်းခွဲ lamhkwal *(n.)* **turn-off**
လမ်းဆို့ lamshoet *(n.)* **roadblock**
လမ်းဆို့သည် lam shoetsai *(v.)* **roadblock**
လမ်းဆုံ lan-son *(n.)* **crossing**
လမ်းညွှန် lan-hnyun *(n.)* **directory**
လမ်းညွှန်ချက် lan-hnyun-chat *(n.)* **guidance**
လမ်းညွှန်စာအုပ် lam-nyun-sar-aote *(n.)* **prospectus**
လမ်းညွှန်သည် lin-hnyun-the *(v.)* **guide**
လမ်းညွှန်အတိုင်း သွားသည် lan-nyun-a-tai-twar-the *(v.)* **navigate**
လမ်းတား၊ lam tarr , *(n.)* **sawbuck**
လမ်းပခုံး lampahkone *(n.)* **verge**
လမ်းပြ lan-pya *(n.)* **guide**
လမ်းပြကြယ် lan-pya-kyal *(n.)* **loadstar**
လမ်းပြသင်္ကေတ lampya sin kay-ta *(n.)* **traffic sign**
လမ်းပိတ်ငုတ်တိုင် lan-pait-ngote-tai *(n.)* **bollard**
လမ်းပေါ်ကားပြိုင်ပွဲ lan-paw-kar-pyaing-pwe *(n.)* **road race**
လမ်းပေါ်တွင် တရိစ္ဆာန်ကားတိုက်သေခြင်း lan-paw-twin-ta-yeik-san-kar-tite-tay-chin *(n.)* **roadkill**
လမ်းဘေးကြော်ငြာဆိုင်းဘုတ် lan-bay-kyar-nyar-sai-board *(n.)* **billboard**
လမ်းဘေးဖျော်ဖြေပွဲ lan-bay-phyaw-phyay-pwe *(n.)* **roadshow**
လမ်းမ lam-ma *(n.)* **thoroughfare**
လမ်းမကျယ် lan-ma-kyal *(n.)* **boulevard**
လမ်းရိုးသမား lan-yoe-ta-mar *(n.)* **conformist**
လမ်းလျှောက်ခြင်း lamshoutchinn *(n.)* **walk**
လမ်းလျှောက်သည် lamshoutsai *(v.)* **walk**
လမ်းလျှောက်ဟန် lamshouthaan *(n.)* **tread**
လမ်းလွှဲ lan-hlwal *(n.)* **bypass**
လမ်းလွှဲခြင်း lam lwhaellchinn *(n.)* **sidetrack**
လမ်းလွှဲသည် lam lwhaellsai *(v.)* **sidetrack**
လမ်းလွဲခြင်း lan-hlwal-chin *(n.)* **deviation**
လမ်းလွဲသွားသည် lan-hlwal-twar-the *(v.)* **deviate**
လမ်းသရဲ lan-ta-ye *(n.)* **hooligan**
လမ်းသွားလမ်းလာ lam-swarr-lam-lar *(n.)* **pedestrian**
လမ်းအတည့် lam a taeet *(adv.)* **straightway**
လယ်ကွက် laal-kwat *(n.)* **paddy**
လယ်ယာဥယျာဉ်ခြံမြေဆိုင်ရာ lal-yar-au-yin-chan-myay-saing-yar *(adj.)* **agrarian**
လယ်သမား laal-sa-marr *(n.)* **peasant**
လယ်သမားနေအိမ် lal-ta-mar-nay-eain *(n.)* **farmhouse**
လျက်ခြင်း lyat-chin *(n.)* **lick**
လျက်သည် lyat-the *(v.)* **lick**
လျင်မြန်ခြင်း lyin-myan-chinn *(n.)* **speed**

လျင်မြန်စွာ ကြီးထွားဖွံ့ဖြိုးလာသည် lyin-myan-swar-kyi-htwar-phwint-phoe-lar-the *(v.)* **burgeon**
လျင်မြန်စွာ ပေါက်ပွားသော lyin-myanswar pout pwarr-saw *(adj.)* **prolific**
လျင်မြန်သော lyin-myansaw *(adj.)* **quick**
လျင်မြန်သော အဟုန် lyinmyan-saw a hone *(n.)* **rapidity**
လျစ်လျူရှုသည် hlyit-lyu-shu-the *(v.)* **neglect**
လျှံထွက်သည် shan htwatsai *(v.)* **well**
လျှင် hlyin *(prep.)* **per**
လျှပ်ကူးခြင်း lyat-ku-chin *(n.)* **conduction**
လျှပ်ငြိမ် shutngyein *(n.)* **static**
လျှပ်စစ်၊ အပူကာ ပစ္စည်း lyat-sit, a-pyu-kar-pyit-see *(n.)* **insulator**
လျှပ်စစ်ကြိုးသွယ်တန်းတပ်ဆင်မှု shutsit kyaoe swaltaann tautsinmhu *(n.)* **wiring**
လျှပ်စစ်ဓာတ်အား lyat-sit-dat-ar *(n.)* **electricity**
လျှပ်စစ်ဓာတ်အားပြတ်တောက်သော ကာလ lyat-sit-dhat-ar-pyat-tout-taw-kar-la *(n.)* **outage**
လျှပ်စစ်ဓာတ်အားလွှတ်ထားသည် lyat-sit-dat-ar-hlut-htar-the *(v.)* **electrify**
လျှပ်စစ်ဓာတ်အားသုံး lyat-sit-dat-ar-tone *(adj.)* **electric**
လျှပ်စစ်လှိုင်းတိုင်း ကိရိယာ lyat-sis-hline-tine-ka-yi-yar *(n.)* **oscillograph**
လျှပ်စီး၊ စီးကြောင်း hlyat-see, see-kyaung *(n.)* **current**
လျှပ်စီးစမ်းကိရိယာ hlyat-see-san-ka-yi-yar *(n.)* **galvanoscope**
လျှပ်စီးတိုင်းကိရိယာ hlyat-see-tai-ka-yi-yar *(n.)* **galvanometer**
လျှပ်စီးပတ်လမ်း hlyat-see-pat-lan *(n.)* **circuit**
လျှပ်တစ်ပြက် မီးသီး hlyat-ta-pyat-meet-thee *(n.)* **flashbulb**
လျှပ်တစ်ပြက်ဖြစ်ရပ် shuttaitpyaathpyitrat *(n.)* **spasm**
လျှပ်လိုက်ရည် lyat-lite-yay *(n.)* **electrolyte**
လျှာ shar *(n.)* **tongue**
လျှို့ဝှက်ကြံစည်ခြင်း၊ ကျိတ်ကြံခြင်း sho-hwat-kyan-see-chin, kyaik-kyan-chin *(n.)* **intrigue**
လျှို့ဝှက်ကြံစည်သည် shhoetwhaat kyaansaisai *(v.)* **scheme**
လျှို့ဝှက်ချက် shoetwhaatchet *(n.)* **secret**
လျှို့ဝှက်ခြင်း shoetwhaatchinn *(n.)* **secrecy**
လျှို့ဝှက်ဆန်းကြယ်သော shoet-what-san-kyal-taw *(adj.)* **occult**
လျှို့ဝှက်သည်းဖိုဇာတ်လမ်း shoetwhaat saee hpo-zatlam *(n.)* **thriller**
လျှို့ဝှက်သော shhoetwhaatsaw *(adj.)* **secret**
လျှို့ဝှက်အဆင့်အတန်း လျှော့ချသတ်မှတ်သည် sho-hwat-a-sint-a-tan-shawt-cha-tat-mat-the *(v.)* **declassify**
လျှို၊ မြောင် sho , myaung *(n.)* **ravine**
လျှိုထားသော shohtarrsaw *(adj.)* **reticent**
လျှော့ချခြင်း shotchachinn *(n.)* **retrenchment**
လျှော့ခြင်း shawt-chin *(n.)* **deflation**
လျှော့ဈေး shawt-zay *(n.)* **discount**
လျှော့ပေးသည်၊ ဖျော့လိုက်သည် shot payy-sai, hpyaw-litesai *(v.)* **slacken**
လျှော့ပေါ့ခြင်း shot potchinn *(n.)* **remission**
လျှော့သည် hlyawt-the *(v.)* **curtail**
လျှောက်ထားသူ shaut-htar-thu *(n.)* **applicant**

လျှောက်လွှာတင်ခြင်း shaut-lwar-tin-chin *(n.)* **application**

လျှောက်လှမ်းသည် shout-hlam-sai *(v.)* **pace**

လျှောက်သည် shaut-the *(v.)* **apply**

လျှောခနဲသွားခြင်း shaw-kha-nae-twar-chin *(n.)* **glide**

လျှောဆင်းသည် shaw sinnsai *(v.)* **slide**

လျှောမွေးနှင့် ဗာရာဏသီချဲ့သည် shaw-mway-nint-bar-yar-na-the-chae-the *(v.)* **maunder**

လျှောသည်၊ စောင်းသည် shaw sai, saung-sai *(v.)* **slope**

လျှော်နိုင်သော shawninesaw *(adj.)* **washable**

လျှော်ဖွပ်သည် shaw-hput-the *(v.)* **launder**

လျှော်သည် shawsai *(v.)* **wash**

လျာထားငွေ lyar-htar-ngwe *(n.)* **appropriation**

လျို့ဝှက် sho-hwat *(adj.)* **confidential**

လျို့ဝှက်ဆန်းကြယ်သော shoe-wat-san-kyal-taw *(adj.)* **arcane**

လျို့ဝှက်နေရာ sho-hwat-nay-yar *(n.)* **hide**

လျို့ဝှက်ပူးပေါင်းကြံစည်ချက် sho-hwat-pu-paung-kyan-see-chat *(n.)* **conspiracy**

လျို့ဝှက်ပူးပေါင်းကြံစည်သည် sho-hwat-pu-paung-kyan-see-the *(v.)* **conspire**

လျို့ဝှက်မဲပေးစနစ် Hlyoe-hwat-mae-pay-sa-nit *(n.)* **ballot**

လျော့၍ yawt-ywe *(prep.)* **less**

လျော့ခြင်း၊ စဲခြင်း shot-chin, sal-chin *(n.)* **abatement**

လျော့စေသည် shaw-zay-the *(v.)* **moderate**

လျော့နည်းခြင်း shawt-nae-chin *(n.)* **deficiency**

လျော့နည်းလာခြင်း yawt-nae-lar-chin *(n.)* **diminution**

လျော့နည်းသော yawt-ne-taw *(adj.)* **lesser**

လျော့ပါးသည် yawt-par-the *(v.)* **lessen**

လျော့ရဲသော yawt-ye-thaw *(adj.)* **lax**

လျော့လာသည်၊ နည်းလာသည် yawt-lar-the, nae-lar-the *(v.)* **diminish**

လျော့သည်၊ စဲသည် shot-the, sal-the *(v.)* **abate**

လျော်ကန်သော lyaw-kan-taw *(adj.)* **justifiable**

လျော်ကြေး yaw-kyay *(n.)* **compensation**

လျော်ကြေးငွေ lyaw-kyay-ngwe *(n.)* **indemnity**

လျော်ညီစွာ lyaw-nyi-swar *(adv.)* **accordingly**

လရောင် la-yaung *(n.)* **moonlight**

လွင့်စဉ်ခြင်း lwint sinchinn *(n.)* **spill**

လွတ်ငြိမ်းချမ်းသာခွင့် lut-nyein-chan-tar-khwint *(n.)* **amnesty**

လွတ်ငြိမ်းခွင့်ပြုသည် lut-ngyeim hkwint-pyusai *(v.)* **release**

လွတ်ငြိမ်းခွင့်ရသည် lut-nyein-khwint-ya-the *(v.)* **exempt**

လွတ်ငြိမ်းခွင့်ရသော lut-nyein-khwint-ya-taw *(adj.)* **exempt**

လွတ်မြောက်ခြင်း hlut-myauk-chin *(n.)* **deliverance**

လွတ်မြောက်စေခြင်း hlut-myauk-say-chin *(n.)* **emancipation**

လွတ်မြောက်စေမှု lut-myauk-say-mu *(n.)* **liberation**

လွတ်မြောက်စေသည် hlut-myauk-say-the *(v.)* **emancipate**

လွတ်မြောက်စေသူ lut-myauk-say-thu *(n.)* **liberator**

လွတ်မြောက်နိုင်စွမ်း lut-myauk-naing-swan *(n.)* **escapability**

လွတ်မြောက်နိုင်သော lut-myauk-naing-taw *(adj.)* **escapable**
လွတ်မြောက်မှုနည်းပညာ lut-myauk-mu-nee-pyin-nyar *(n.)* **escapology**
လွတ်မြောက်ရောက်ရှိခြင်း lut-myauk-yauk-shi-chin *(n.)* **escapism**
လွတ်မြောက်ရောက်ရှိသူ lut-myauk-yauk-shi-thu *(n.)* **escapist**
လွတ်မြောက်သည် lwatmyawwatsai *(v.)* **scape**
လွတ်လပ်ခွင့်မပေးခြင်း lut-lat-khwint-ma-pay-chin *(n.)* **intolerance**
လွတ်လပ်မှု lut-lat-mu *(n.)* **freedom**
လွတ်လပ်ရေး lut-lat-yay *(n.)* **independence**
လွတ်လပ်သော lut-lat-taw *(adj.)* **free**
လွတ်လပ်သော အချုပ်အခြာအာဏာ lwatlautsaw aachoteaachaaraarnar *(n.)* **sovereignty**
လွတ်လွတ်ကျွတ်ကျွတ်၊ မထိမရှ lwatlwat kyawatkyawat , m hti mash *(adj.)* **scot-free**
လွန် lun *(n.)* **drill**
လွန်း lwann *(n.)* **shuttle**
လွန်းပြန်ပြေးဆွဲသည် lwann-pyan-pyay-swal-sai *(v.)* **ply**
လွန်၍ lun-ywe *(prep.& adj.)* **beyond**
လွန်ကဲစွာ မြှောက်စားခြင်း lun-kae-swar-hmyaut-sar-chin *(n.)* **adulation**
လွန်ကဲစွာ မြှောက်စားသည် lun-kae-swar-hmyaut-sar-the *(v.)* **adulate**
လွန်ကဲသော lun-kae-taw *(adj.)* **excessive**
လွန်ခြင်း၊ ကြူးခြင်း၊ အလျှံပယ်ဖြစ်ခြင်း lwan chinn , kyuu chinn , a shan paal hpyit-chinn *(n.)* **surfeit**
လွန်ခဲ့သော နှစ်နှစ်သန်းခွဲကာလ lwanhkaesaw nit-nha saann hkwal-karla *(n.)* **paleolithic**
လွန်စူး lun-sue *(n.)* **auger**
လွန်ဖြင့် ဖောက်သည် lun-phit-phaut-the *(v.)* **drill**
လွယ်ကူချောမောစေခြင်း lwal-khu-chaw-maw-say-chin *(n.)* **facilitation**
လွယ်ကူချောမောစေသည် lwal-khu-chaw-maw-say-the *(v.)* **facilitate**
လွယ်ကူခြင်း lwal-ku-chin *(n.)* **ease**
လွယ်ကူစွာ အောင်ပွဲခံသည် lwal-khu-swar-aung-pwe-khan-the *(v.)* **cakewalk**
လွယ်ကူစေသည်၊ လျော့လာသည် lwal-ku-say-the, shawt-lar-the *(v.)* **ease**
လွယ်ကူသော lwal-ku-taw *(adj.)* **easy**
လွယ်ခြင်း၊ ရိုးခြင်း lwal chinn, roe-chinn *(n.)* **simplicity**
လွယ်သည်၊ ပိုးသည် lwal sai , poe-sai *(v.)* **shoulder**
လွယ်အောင် ပြုလုပ်ခြင်း lwal-au pyulotechinn *(n.)* **simplification**
လွယ်အောင် ပြုလုပ်သည် lwalaaung pyulotesai *(v.)* **simplify**
လွှ lwa *(n.)* **saw**
လွှငါး lwhangarr *(n.)* **sawfish**
လွှင့်သည် bharsarpyanchinn *(v.)* **transmit**
လွှစာ lwhasar *(n.)* **sawdust**
လွှတိုက်သည် lwa titesai *(v.)* **saw**
လွှတ်ခနဲ ထွက်သွားသည် hlut-kha-nal-htwat-twar-the *(v.)* **blab**
လွှတ်တော်ကိုယ်စားလှယ်ရှိသော မြို့ ခရိုင် hlut-taw-ko-sa-lal-shi-taw-myo-kha-yai *(n.)* **borough**
လွှတ်တော်အမတ် hluttaw-aa-mat *(n.)* **senator**
လွှတ်တော်အမတ်နှင့် ပတ်သက်၍ lwhaattawaamaatnhang paatsaat *(adj.)* **senatorial**

လွှတ်ပေးခြင်း၊ လွှတ်ငြိမ်းစေခြင်း၊ ထုတ်ပြန်ချက် lwut-payychinn , lwut-ngyeim say chinn , htote-pyanchet *(n.)* **release**

လွှတ်သည်၊ ဖယ်ရှားသည် hlut-the, phal-shar-the *(v.)* **free**

လွှဖြင့် ဖြတ်လုပ်ထားသော ခုံ lwha-hpyint hpyat lote-htarr-saw hkone *(n.)* **sawbench**

လွှဖြင့် သစ်ကို အလယ်ကြားမှ ဖြတ်သည် lwha-hpyint saitko aa-laal-kyarr-mha hpyat-sai *(n.)* **saw pit**

လွှဖြတ်သမား lwha hpyatsamarr *(n.)* **sawyer**

လွှမြက် lwhamyaat *(n.)* **sawgrass**

လွှမ်းခြုံသည် hlwan-chon-the *(v.)* **drape**

လွှမ်းဖုံ hlwan-hpone *(n.)* **duvet**

လွှမ်းမိုးမှု lwam-moemhu *(n.)* **predominance**

လွှမ်းမိုးသည် hlwan-moe-the *(v.)* **engulf**

လွှမ်းမိုးသော lwam-moesaw *(adj.)* **predominant**

လွှသွားပုံ လှိုင်း lwha swarrpone lhaine *(n.)* **sawtooth**

လွှားခနဲ ခုန်သည် lwhar hkanell hkonesai *(v.)* **spring**

လွှဲခြင်း aasanko saraahpyit narrhtaung pyaunggpayysuu *(n.)* **transfer**

လွှဲပြောင်းပေးနိုင်သော aasanko saraahpyit narrhtaung pyaunggpayychinn *(adj.)* **transferable**

လွှဲယူခြင်း lwhaellyuuchinn *(n.)* **takeover**

လွှဲသည် lwhaellsai *(v.)* **rock**

လွှဲသည်၊ ယမ်းသည် lwhaell sai , yamsai *(v.)* **swing**

လွှဲအပ်သည် hlwal-at-the *(v.)* **consign**

လွှဲချော်မှု တိမ်းစောင်းမှု ပမာဏ lwal-chaw-mu-tain-saung-mu-pa-mar-na *(n.)* **deflection**

လွဲမှားစွာ စီမံခန့်ခွဲခြင်း lwal-mar-swar-si-man-khant-khwal-chin *(n.)* **mismanagement**

လွဲမှားစွာ ဆုံးဖြတ်သည် lwal-mar-swar-sone-phat-the *(v.)* **misguide**

လွဲမှားစွာ ပြုမူခြင်း lwal-mar-swar-pyu-mu-chin *(n.)* **misbehaviour**

လွဲမှားစွာ ပြုမူသည် lwal-mar-swar-pyu-mu-the *(v.)* **misbehave**

လွဲမှားစွာ အသုံးချခြင်း lwal-mar-swar-a-tone-cha-chin *(n.)* **misapplication**

လွဲမှားစွာသိမြင်ခြင်း lwal-mar-swar-ti-myin-chin *(n.)* **misperception**

လွဲမှားသော lwalmharsaw *(adj.)* **sinful**

လသဏ္ဌာန်အဆင့်ဆင့် la-san-htan-aa-sint-sint *(n.)* **phase**

လသာဆောင် la-thar-saung *(n.)* **balcony**

လဟာပြင်ဈေး la-har-pyin-zay *(n.)* **flea market**

လှံ၊ လှံတံ hlaan, hlaantan *(n.)* **spear**

လှံချွန်လက်နက် hlaan hkyawan-laatnaat *(n.)* **polearm**

လှံစွပ် hlan-sut *(n.)* **bayonet**

လှံတံ hlan-tan *(n.)* **javelin**

လှံတို၊ မြားငယ် lan-to, myar-nge *(n.)* **dart**

လှံသမား lan-ta-mar *(n.)* **lancer**

လှစ်ဟ၍ သိမြင်စေခြင်း hlit ha simyin saychinn *(n.)* **revelation**

လှည့်စက် lha ny hcaat *(n.)* **spinner**

လှည့်စားမှု hlae sarrmhu *(n.)* **trick**

လှည့်စားသည် hlae-sar-the *(v.)* **delude**

လှည့်စားသည်၊ ကလိသည် hlae-sar-the, ka-li-the *(v.)* **fool**

လှည့်ဖြားတတ်သော hlae-phyar-tat-taw *(adj.)* **deceptive**

လှည့်လည်သွားလာသည် hla ny lai swarrlarsai *(v.)* **rove**

လှည့်လည်သောင်းကျန်းသူ hlae-lal-taung-kyan-thu *(n.)* **marauder**

လှည့်သည် hlae sai *(v.)* **spin**

လှည့်သည်၊ ပြောင်းသည် hlae sai , pyaungsai *(v.)* **switch**

လှည့်ခြင်း hlae-chinn *(n.)* **turn**

လှည့်ပတ်ထုတ်သွားသည် hlae-pat-htoke-twar-the *(v.)* **decoy**

လှည့်ပတ်သည် hlae-pat-the *(v.)* **circulate**

လှည့်လည်သောင်းကျန်းသည် hlae-lal-taung-kyan-the *(v.)* **maraud**

လှည့်သူ hlae-thu *(n.)* **turner**

လှည်း hlal *(n.)* **cart**

လှည်းကျင်းသည် hlaee kyinnsai *(v.)* **sweep**

လှည်းဖြင့် တိုက်ခြင်း ဖြစ်စဉ်၊ ကုန်ကျစရိတ် hlal-phit-tite-chin-phit-sin, kone-kya-sa-yeik *(n.)* **cartage**

လှည်းယဉ် hlaee-yain *(n.)* **oxcart**

လှန့်သည် hlantsai *(v.)* **stampede**

လှန်လှောမွှေနှောက် ရှာဖွေသည် hlaan hlaaw mwhaaynhaout sharhpwaysai *(v.)* **rummage**

လှန်သည်၊ ဒေါသအိုး ပေါက်ကွဲသည် hlan-the, daw-ta-oh-pauk-kwe-the *(v.)* **flip**

လှပစေသော hla-pa-say-taw *(adj.)* **decorative**

လှပတင့်တယ်သော hla-pa-tint-tal-taw *(adj.)* **comely**

လှပသော hla-pa-taw *(adj.)* **beautiful**

လှမ်းယူနိုင်သော hlam yuu-ninesaw *(adj.)* **reachable**

လှမ်းသည် hlamsai *(v.)* **step**

လှိမ့်လုံး hlaint-lone *(n.)* **hoax**

လှိုက်လှဲစွာ hlite-lal-swar *(adv.)* **heartily**

လှိုက်လှိုက်လှဲလှဲ hlite-hlite-hlae-hlae *(adj.)* **whole-hearted**

လှိုက်လှဲသော lite-hlae-taw *(adj.)* **cordial**

လှိုင်းခေါင်းဖြူ hline hkaungghpyauu *(n.)* **surf**

လှိုင်းစီးလေစီးခြင်းအားကစားလှေကျင့်ခြင်း hlaing-see-lay-see-chin-arr-ka-sar-lae-kyint-chin *(v.)* **sailboard**

လှိုင်းတံပိုး hlaing-ta-poe *(v.)* **billow**

လှိုင်းတွန့် hline twant *(n.)* **ripple**

လှိုင်းထသည် hline htasai *(v.)* **ripple**

လှိုင်းပုံကြည့်ကိရိယာ hlaine-pone-kyi-ka-ri-yar *(n.)* **oscilloscope**

လှိုင်းလုံး hlinelone *(n.)* **wave**

လှီးသည်၊ ခွဲသည် hlee sai, hkwal sai *(v.)* **slit**

လှီးသည်၊ ရိတ်သည် hlee-the, yate-the *(v.)* **fleece**

လှီသော၊ ညှက်သော hlae saw , nyat-saw *(adj.)* **puny**

လှုံ့ဆော်ချက် hlont-saw-chat *(n.)* **instigation**

လှုံ့ဆော်ပေးသည့်အရာ hlont saw payy seet aarar *(n.)* **stimulus**

လှုံ့ဆော်သည် hlont-saw-the *(v.)* **inflame**

လှုပ်ခြင်း hlotechinn *(n.)* **shake**

လှုပ်ယမ်းခြင်း hlote yamchinn *(n.)* **sway**

လှုပ်ရှားဆောင်ရွက်ခြင်း lote-shar-saung-ywet-chin *(n.)* **manoeuvre**

လှုပ်ရှားမှု lote-shar-mu *(n.)* **movement**

လှုပ်လှုပ်ရွရွဖြစ်ခြင်း hloke-hloke-ywa-ywa-phit-chin *(n.)* **ferment**

လှုပ်လှုပ်ရွရွဖြစ်သော hlotehlote rw rwhpyitsaw *(adj.)* **restive**

လှုပ်သည် hlote-sai *(v.)* **quake**

လှုပ်သည်၊ နဲ့သည် hlote sai , naesai *(v.)* **wobble**

လှုပ်သည်ဆိုရုံမျှ လှုပ်သည် hloke-the-so-yone-mya-hloke-the *(v.)* **budge**

လှူဒါန်းခြင်း hlu-dan-chin *(n.)* **donation**

လှူသည် hlu-the *(v.)* **consecrate**

လှေ hlay *(n.)* **boat**

လှေ့သည် hlaaesai *(v.)* **winnow**

လှေး hlae *(n.)* **flea**

လှေ၊ သင်္ဘောများ သွားလာနိုင်သော hlay-tin-baw-myar-twar-lar-nai-taw *(adj.)* **navigable**

လှေကား hlaaykarr *(n.)* **stair**

လှေကားလက်ရန်း hlay-kar-lat-yan *(n.)* **bannister**

လှေကားအုံ hlaaykarraone *(n.)* **staircase**

လှေရုံ hlay-yone *(n.)* **boathouse**

လှောင်ပြောင်သည် hlaung-paung-the *(v.)* **jeer**

လှောင်ပြောင်သရော်မှု hlaawinpyaung sarawmhu *(n.)* **ridicule**

လှောင်လုံး၊ ပြောင်လုံး htaung-lone, pyaung-lone *(n.)* **gibe**

လှောင်သည် hlaawinsai *(v.)* **ridicule**

လှောင်သည်၊ တုတ်သည်၊ တွယ်သည် hlaung sai, tote sai , twalsai *(v.)* **scoff**

လှောင်သည်၊ သရော်သည် hlawng sai, sa-rawsai *(v.)* **sneer**

လှောင်သော၊ မွန်းသော hlaung saw , mwann-saw *(adj.)* **stuffy**

လှောင်သော၊ သရော်သော hling saw, sa-rawsaw *(adj.)* **sardonic**

လှောင်အိမ် laung-ain *(n.)* **cage**

လှော်ခတ်သည် hlaaw hkaatsai *(v.)* **row**

လှော်တက် hlaaw-taat *(n.)* **paddle**

လှော်သည် hlaaw-sai *(v.)* **paddle**

လား lar *(n.)* **mule**

လား လား larr larr *(conj.)* **whether**

လားမားဘုန်းတော်ကြီး lar-ma-phone-taw-gyi *(n.)* **lama**

လာဆုံသည်၊ အလားတူ ဖြစ်သည် lar-sone-the, a-lar-tu-phit-the *(v.)* **converge**

လာဗင်ဒါပန်း la-vin-dar-pan *(n.)* **lavender**

လာဘ်ကောင် lat-kaung *(n.)* **mascot**

လာဘ်ထိုးသည် lat-htoe-the *(v.)* **bribe**

လာဘ်မြင်သော lat-myin-taw *(adj.)* **astute**

လာမည့် lar-mae *(adj.)* **forthcoming**

လာလမ်းအတိုင်းပြန်သည် lar-lan-a-tine-pyan-the *(v.)* **backtrack**

လာသည် lar-the *(v.)* **come**

လိင် lain *(n.)* **gender**

လိင်၊ လိင်ဆက်ဆံခြင်း lain, lainsaatsanchinn *(n.)* **sex**

လိင်ကွဲစိတ်ဝင်စားသူ ဖြစ်သော lain-kwal-seik-win-sar-thu-phit-taw *(n.)* **ubersexual**

လိင်ကိစ္စကို ခိုးကြည့်ရသည်ကို မွေ့လျော်ခြင်း linkissako hkoe kyi rasaiko mwae lyawchinn *(n.)* **voyeurism**

လိင်ကိစ္စကို ခိုးကြည့်ရသည်ကို မွေ့လျော်သူ linkissako hkoe kyi rasaiko mwae lyawsuu *(n.)* **voyeur**

လိင်ကိစ္စများတွင် ကိုယ်ကျင့်သိက္ခာ ကင်းမဲ့သော lain-kait-sa-myar-twin-koe-kyint-theik-khar-kin-mae-taw *(adj.)* **licentious**

လိင်ခွဲခြားသည် liin hkwalhkyarrsai *(v.)* **sex**

လိင်စိတ်ချစ်ခြင်းနှင့် ဆိုင်သော lain-seik-chit-chin-nint-thet-saing-taw *(adj.)* **amatory**

လိင်စိတ်ဖြင့် linsatehpyint *(adv.)* **sexily**

လိင်စိတ်အလိုကို ဖြည့်ဆည်းပေးသည် lain-sate-a-lo-ko-pyae-see-pay-the *(v.)* **mack**

လိင်ဆက်ဆံဖက် lain-sat-san-phat *(n.)* **lay**

လိင်တံ lain-tan *(n.)* **penis**

လိင်တံကို စုပ်၍ နိုးကြွစေသည် lain-tan-ko-sote-ywe-noe-kwa-say-the *(n.)* **fellatio**

လိင်တံကို အဓိကထားသော laintanko aadhikahtarrsaw *(adj.)* **phallocentric**

လိင်တံထိပ်အရေပြားဖြတ်သည် lain-tan-hteik-a-yay-pyar-phat-the *(v.)* **circumcise**

လိင်တူချင်း ဆက်ဆံသူ lain-tu-chin-sat-san-thu *(n.)* **gay**

လိင်တူချင်း ဆက်ဆံသော lain-tu-chin-sat-san-taw *(adj.)* **gay**

လိင်တူချင်းဆက်ဆံသော ယောက်ျား lain-tuuchinn saat-sansaw yout-yarr *(n.)* **queer**

လိင်တူချင်းဆက်ဆံသော၊ ထူးခြားသော lain-tuuchinn saat-san saw , htuu-charrsaw *(adj.)* **queer**

လိင်နှစ်မျိုးလုံး လက္ခဏာရှိသော lain-na-myo-lone-lat-kha-nar-shi-taw *(adj.)* **epicene**

လိင်ပိုင်းဆိုင်ရာ အနှောင့်အယှက်ပေးခြင်း lain-pai-sai-yar-a-naut-a-shat-pay-chin *(n.)* **eve-teasing**

လိင်မှုဆိုင်ရာ linmhu-sine-rar *(adj.)* **sexual**

လိင်မဲ့ lain-mae *(adj.)* **asexual**

လိင်အင်္ဂါ lain-in-gar *(n.)* **genitalia**

လိင်အင်္ဂါနှင့်ဆိုင်သော lain-in-gar-nint-sai-taw *(adj.)* **genital**

လိင်အထွတ်အထိပ် lain-a-htwat-a-hteik *(n.)* **orgasm**

လိင်အထွတ်အထိပ်ရောက်သော lain-a-htwat-a-hteik-yauk-taw *(adj.)* **orgasmic**

လိပ် late *(n.)* **tortoise**

လိပ်ခေါင်း leit-hkaung *(n.)* **piles**

လိပ်စာ leik-sar *(n.)* **address**

လိပ်စာကတ် leik-sar-kat *(n.)* **business card**

လိပ်စာရှင် leik-sar-shin *(n.)* **addressee**

လိပ်ပြာ leik-pyar *(n.)* **butterfly**

လိပ်ပြာခေါ်ခြင်း late-pyaar hkawchinn *(n.)* **spiritualism**

လိပ်ပြာမလုံခြင်း lake-pyar-ma-lon-chin *(n.)* **compunction**

လိပ်သည် lait-the *(v.)* **furl**

လိမ္မာပါးနပ်မှု laimmar parr nautmhu *(n.)* **tact**

လိမ္မာပါးနပ်သော laimmar parr natsaw *(adj.)* **shrewd**

လိမ္မာသိုသိပ်မှု lain-mar-tho-tate-mu *(n.)* **discretion**

လိမ္မော်ရောင် laim-maw-raung *(adj.)* **orange**

လိမ္မော်သီး lain-maw-thee *(n.)* **clementine**

လိမ့်မည် lin-mai *(v.)* **will**

လိမ့်သည်၊ လိပ်သည် lint sai , lattsai *(v.)* **roll**

လိမ်းဆေး laim-say *(n.)* **ointment**

လိမ်းဆေး၊ လိုးရှင်း lane-say, lo-shin *(n.)* **lotion**

လိမ်းသည် lain-the *(n.)* **daub**

လိမ်ခြင်း၊ လှည့်ခြင်း lin chinn , hlae chinn *(n.)* **twist**

လိမ်ညာခြင်း lain-nyar-chin *(n.)* **lie**

လိမ်ညာမှု lain-nyar-mu *(n.)* **deceit**

လိမ်ညာလှည့်ဖျားမှု lain-nyar-lae-hpyar-mu *(n.)* **knavery**

လိမ်ညာသည် lain-nyar-the *(v.)* **lie**

လိမ်နည်း lain-nee *(n.)* **cheat**

လိမ်ဖည်သော lain-phal-taw *(adj.)* **crooked**

လိမ်လည် လှည့်ဖျားရန် ပေါင်းကြံသည် lain-lal-lae-pyar-yan-paung-kyan-the *(v.)* **collude**

လိမ်လည်မှု lain-lal-mu *(n.)* **fraud**

လိမ်လည်လှည့်စားမှု linlai hlae sarrmhu *(n.)* **trickery**

လိမ်လည်လှည့်ဖြားခြင်း lain-lal-hlae-phyar-chin *(n.)* **deception**
လိမ်လည်လှည့်ဖြားသော lain-lal-hlae-phyar-taw *(adj.)* **deceitful**
လိမ်လည်သည် lain-lae-the *(v.)* **hoodwink**
လိမ်လည်အတုပြုမှု lain-lae-a-tu-pyu-mu *(n.)* **forgery**
လိမ်သည် lain-the *(v.)* **cheat**
လိမ်သည်၊ လှည့်ဖြားသည် lain-the, hlae-phyar-the *(v.)* **deceive**
လိမ်သော lain-taw *(adj.)* **mendacious**
လို့မို့ loet-mhoet *(conj.)* **now**
လိုက်ကာ lite-kar *(n.)* **curtain**
လိုက်စမ်းသည် lite-san-the *(v.)* **grope**
လိုက်နာခြင်း lite-narchinn *(n.)* **pursuance**
လိုက်နာသည် lite-nar-the *(v.)* **comply**
လိုက်ပါစောင့်ရှောက်သော lite-par-saunt-shaut-taw *(adj.)* **escorted**
လိုက်ပါသည် lite-par-the *(v.)* **accompany**
လိုက်ပေးသူ lite-pay-thu *(n.)* **accompanist**
လိုက်ဖက်မညီ lite-phat-ma-nyi *(v.)* **mismatch**
လိုက်ဖက်သော lite-phat-taw *(adj.)* **complementary**
လိုက်ဖက်အောင် ပြင်ဆင်သည် lite-phat-aung-pyin-sin-the *(v.)* **adapt**
လိုက်ရှာခြင်း lite-shar-chin *(n.)* **foraging**
လိုက်ရှာသည် litesharsai *(v.)* **trace**
လိုက်ရှာသူ lite-shar-thu *(n.)* **forager**
လိုက်လျောချက် lite-lyaw-chat *(n.)* **concession**
လိုက်လျောလွန်းသော lite-lyaw-loon-taw *(adj.)* **compliant**
လိုက်လျောသည် lite-lyaw-the *(v.)* **acquiesce**
လိုက်လျောသော lite-lyaw-taw *(adj.)* **accommodating**
လိုက်သည် lite-sai *(v.)* **pursue**
လိုချင်ဆန္ဒကြီးသော lo-chin-san-da-kyi-taw *(adj.)* **acquisitive**
လိုချင်ဖွယ်ရာဖြစ်သော lo-chin-phwal-yar-phit-taw *(adj.)* **desirable**
လိုချင်သည် lo-chin-the *(v.)* **desire**
လိုငွေ lo-ngwe *(n.)* **deficit**
လိုငွေ၊ အလိုပြခြင်း lo ngway, a lo pyachinn *(n.)* **shortfall**
လိုင်း၊ မျဉ်း line, myin *(n.)* **line**
လိုင်စင် hlai-sin *(n.)* **licence**
လိုင်စင်ထုတ်ပေးသည် hlai-sin-htoke-pay-the *(v.)* **license**
လိုင်စင်မရှိသော အရက်ဆိုင် linehcainmashisaw aaraatsine *(adj.)* **shanty**
လိုင်စင်ရသူ hlai-sin-ya-thu *(n.)* **licensee**
လိုင်နာတောင့် lai-nar-taunt *(n.)* **eyeliner**
လိုဏ်ခေါင်း hlaing-khaung *(n.)* **burrow**
လိုဏ်ခေါင်းဖောက်သည် lonhkaungghpoutsai *(v.)* **tunnel**
လိုဏ်ဂူကြီး hlaing-gu-gyi *(n.)* **cavern**
လိုရင်းမရောက် lo-yin-ma-yauk *(v.)* **misfire**
လိုရင်းအချုပ်ဖော်ပြသည် lo-rinn-a-chaote-hpaw-pya-tai *(v.)* **outline**
လိုလားမှု lolarr-mhu *(n.)* **preference**
လိုလိုလားလားလက်ခံတတ်သော lo-lo-lar-lar-lat-khan-tat-taw *(adj.)* **amenable**
လိုလီပေါ့ lo-li-pot *(n.)* **lollipop**
လိုအင်၊ တပ်မက်မှု lo-inn, tat-mat-mu *(n.)* **desire**

လိုအင်ဆန္ဒ lon-inn-san-da *(n.)* **inclination**

လိုအပ်ချက် lo-at-chat *(n.)* **need**

လိုအပ်ချက်များ lo-at-chat-myar *(adv.)* **needs**

လိုအပ်ခြင်း lo-at-chin *(n.)* **necessity**

လိုအပ်လာသည် lo-at-lar-the *(v.)* **necessitate**

လိုအပ်သည် lo-atsai *(v.)* **require**

လိုအပ်သည်ကို ဖြည့်တင်းပေးသည် lo-at-the-ko-pyae-tin-pay-the *(v.)* **cater**

လိုအပ်သော lo-at-taw *(adj.)* **necessary**

လိုအပ်သော အရာများ lo-at-taw-a-yar-myar *(n.)* **necessary**

လီတာ li-tar *(n.)* **litre**

လီဗာ lebar *(n.)* **throttle**

လီမွန်သီး၊ ရှောက်သီး li-mon-thee, shaut-thee *(n.)* **lemon**

လီလီပန်း li-li-pan *(n.)* **lily**

လုံ့လဝီရိယ lont-la-wi-ri-ra *(n.)* **diligence**

လုံ့လဝီရိယရှိသော lont-la-wi-ri-ra-shi-taw *(adj.)* **diligent**

လုံးကောက် ပန်းစာလုံး lone-kauk-pan-sar-lone *(n.)* **monogram**

လုံးချင်း lonechinn *(adj.)* **verbatim**

လုံးထွေးသတ်ပုတ်ခြင်း lone htway saatpotechinn *(n.)* **scuffle**

လုံးထွေးသတ်ပုတ်သည် lone htway saatpotesai *(v.)* **scuffle**

လုံးလုံးလျားလျား aalote laitlautmhu *(adv.)* **utterly**

လုံးလုံးလျားလျားဖြိုပစ်သည် lonelone-lyarrlyarr hpyo pyitsai *(v.)* **raze**

လုံးဝ lone-wa *(adj.)* **alacrious**

လုံးဝဥဿုံ lonewa oak-tone *(adv.)* **scrupulously**

လုံးဝအကြွမ်းထည်နီးပါး lone-wa-a-kyan-thae-nee-par *(adj.)* **rear**

လုံးဝဥဿုံရပ်ခြင်း lonew oak-tone ratchinn *(n.)* **standstill**

လုံးသော lonesaw *(adj.)* **spherical**

လုံခြုံစွာ lonechuanswar *(adv.)* **safely**

လုံခြုံစွာ ခိုင်အောင်းနိုင်သော အိမ် lonechuanswar hkine aaunggninesaw aain *(n.)* **safehouse**

လုံခြုံစွာ သိမ်းဆည်းထားသည် lone-chone-swar-thein-see-htar-the *(n.)* **safekeeping**

လုံခြုံမှု lonechuanmhu *(n.)* **safety**

လုံခြုံရေး lonechuanrayy *(n.)* **security**

လုံခြုံရေးလေအိတ် lone-chone-yay-lay-aik *(n.)* **airbag**

လုံခြုံသော lonechuansaw *(adj.)* **safe**

လုံခြုံသော ကွန်းခိုရာ lone-shone-taw-kun-kho-yar *(n.)* **safe harbour**

လုံလောက်စွာ lone-laut-swar *(adv.)* **adequately**

လုံလောက်စေသည် loneloutsaysai *(v.)* **warrant**

လုံလောက်သည် loneloutsai *(v.)* **suffice**

လုံလောက်သော lone-laut-taw *(adj.)* **adequate**

လုနီးပါး lu-nee-par *(adv.)* **nearly**

လုပ်၍ ဖြစ်နိုင်သော lote-ywe hpyitninesaw *(adj.)* **workable**

လုပ်ကြံ၍ အသရေဖျက်သည် lote-kyaan-ywe-a-sa-ray hpyetsai *(v.)* **slander**

လုပ်ကြံခြင်း lote-kyan-chin *(n.)* **assassination**

လုပ်ကြံစွပ်စွဲခြင်း lote-kyan-sut-swal-chin *(n.)* **fabrication**

လုပ်ကြံပြောဆိုသည် lote-kyan-pyaw-so-the *(v.)* **fabricate**

လုပ်ကြံသည် lote-kyan-the *(v.)* **assassinate**

လုပ်ကြံသူ lote-kyan-thu *(n.)* **assassin**

လုပ်ခ၊ ဝန်ဆောင်ခ ရှင်းပေးသည် lotehka , waansaunghka shinnpayysai *(v.)* **remunerate**

လုပ်ခငွေ lote-kha-ngwe *(n.)* **emolument**

လုပ်ငန်း lotengaann *(n.)* **venture**

လုပ်ငန်း၊ ကိစ္စ၊ အရောင်းအဝယ် lotengan , kait-sa , aaraunggaawaal *(n.)* **transaction**

လုပ်ငန်းကျွမ်းကျင်၊ နိုင်နင်းမှု lote-ngan kywam-kyin , nine ninn-mhu *(n.)* **workmanship**

လုပ်ငန်းစဉ် lote-ngaann-sin *(n.)* **process**

လုပ်ငန်းစဉ်အဆင့်ဆင့်ပြကားချပ် lote-ngan-sin-a-sint-sint-pya-kar-chat *(n.)* **flow chart**

လုပ်ငန်းဆောင်တာ lote-ngan-saung-tar *(n.)* **function**

လုပ်ငန်းဆောင်ရွက်သည့် စက် lote-ngaann saungrwat seet saat *(n.)* **processor**

လုပ်ငန်းတစ်ခု အစပျိုးခြင်း lote-ngan-ta-khu-a-sa-pyo-chin *(n.)* **launch**

လုပ်ငန်းတာဝန် lotengaanntarwaan *(n.)* **task**

လုပ်ငန်းပူးပေါင်းလုပ်ဆောင်သူများ lote-ngan-pu-baung-lote-saung-thu-myar *(n.)* **cartel**

လုပ်ငန်းအသေးစိတ် ရှင်းပြခြင်း lote-ngan-a-thay-seik-shin-pya-chin *(n.)* **briefing**

လုပ်ဆောင်ချက် lote-saung-chat *(n.)* **action**

လုပ်ဆောင်ချက်ချွတ်ယွင်းသည် lote-saung-chat-chut-ywin-the *(v.)* **malfunction**

လုပ်ဆောင်နိုင်စွမ်း loat-saung-nine-swan *(n.)* **operability**

လုပ်ဆောင်မှု lote-saung-mu *(n.)* **activity**

လုပ်ဆောင်သည် lote-saung-sai *(v.)* **perform**

လုပ်ဆောင်သည်၊ လည်ပတ်သည် lote-saung-the, lal-pat-the *(v.)* **function**

လုပ်ဇာတ် lote-zat *(n.)* **concoction**

လုပ်ထုံးလုပ်နည်း lote-htone-lote-naee *(n.)* **technicality**

လုပ်ထုံးလုပ်နည်း၊ ကျင့်ထုံး lotehtone-lote-nee, kyint-htone *(n.)* **procedure**

လုပ်နိုင်စွမ်း lote-nai-swan *(n.)* **capability**

လုပ်နိုင်သော lote-nai-taw *(adj.)* **capable**

လုပ်ပိုင်ခွင့် lote-pai-khwint *(n.)* **mandate**

လုပ်ပိုင်ခွင့်လွှဲအပ်သည် lote-paing-kwint-hlwal-at-the *(v.)* **authorize**

လုပ်ဖော်ကိုင်ဖက် lote-hpaw-kine-hpaat *(n.)* **partner**

လုပ်ဖော်ကိုင်ဘက် lote-phaw-kai-phat *(n.)* **co-worker**

လုပ်ရည်ကိုင်ရည် lote-yay-kai-yay *(n.)* **competence**

လုပ်ရည်ကိုင်ရည်ရှိသော lote rai kine raishisaw *(adj.)* **resourceful**

လုပ်ရိုးလုပ်စဉ် lote-yoe-lote-sin *(n.)* **formality**

လုပ်သက်ဆု lote-thet-su *(n.)* **gratuity**

လုပ်သင့်သော lote sangsaw *(adj.)* **well-to-do**

လုပ်အားခ loteaarrhka *(n.)* **wage**

လုယက်တိုက်ခိုက်သည် lu-yat-tite-khite *(v.)* **foray**

လုယက်မှု luyaatmhu *(n.)* **robbery**

လုယက်ယူခြင်း lu-yaat-yuu-chinn *(n.)* **plunder**

လုယက်ယူသည် lu-yaat-yuu-sai *(v.)* **plunder**

လုယက်သည် luyaatsai *(v.)* **rob**

လုယူသည် matararrsaimyuuchinn *(v.)* **usurp**

လူ lu *(n.)* **mortal**

လူခွစာ lu-khwa-sar *(n.)* **misfit**

လူ့ထုံးတမ်း လိုက်နာခြင်း hluhtonetam litenarchinn *(n.)* **sociability**

လူ့ဘဝနှင့် ဆိုင်သော lu-ba-wa-nint-sai-taw *(adj.)* **existential**

လူ့အဖွဲ့အစည်း hluaahpwalaasaee *(n.)* **society**

လူ့အဖွဲ့အစည်းတွင် ဝင်ရောက်သော လူချမ်းသာ မိန်းမပျို lu-a-phwe-a-see-twin-win-yauk-taw-lu-chan-tar-mein-ka-lay *(n.)* **debutante**

လူးလာဆန်ခတ်လှုပ်ရှားသည် luu-lar-san-hkaat-lote-shar-tai *(v.)* **oscillate**

လူးသည်၊ လိမ်းသည်၊ ပေကျံသည် luu sai , laim sai , pay kyaansai *(v.)* **smear**

လူက ထိန်းရန် မလိုသော luuk hteinraan malosaw *(adj.)* **unmanned**

လူကြမ်းလူရိုင်း lu-kyan-lu-yai *(n.)* **boor**

လူကြီး lu-gyi *(n.)* **dignitary**

လူကြီး၏ ယာဉ်မောင်း lu-gyi-ei-yin-maung *(n.)* **chauffeur**

လူကြီးလူကောင်း lu-gyi-lu-gaung *(n.)* **gentleman**

လူကြီးသူမမှန်း မသိသော မိန်းကလေး lu-kyi-thu-ma-man-ma-thi-taw-main-ka-lay *(n.)* **chit**

လူကြောင်၊ လူထူးလူဆန်း lu-kyaung, lu-htoo-lu-san *(n.)* **freak**

လူကို မပုတ်သိုးအောင် ဆေးရည်စိမ်ခြင်း lu-ko-ma-poke-tho-aung-say-yay-sein-chin *(n.)* **embalming**

လူကို မပုတ်သိုးအောင် ဆေးရည်စိမ်သည် lu-ko-ma-poke-tho-aung-say-yay-sein-the *(v.)* **embalm**

လူကို မုန်း၍ လူ့အသိုင်းအဝိုင်းကို ရှောင်ကြဉ်သော သူ lu-ko-hmone-ywe-lu-a-tine-a-win-ko-shaung-kyin-taw *(n.)* **misanthrope**

လူကုံထံ luu konehtan *(n.)* **squire**

လူကူးမျဉ်းကျား luu-kuu-myin-kyarr *(n.)* **zebra crossing**

လူချမ်းသာ luuchamsar *(n.)* **riches**

လူခွန် lu-khun *(n.)* **capitation**

လူခေါင်းနှင့် မြင်းကိုယ် lu-gaung-nint-myin-ko *(n.)* **centaur**

လူခေါ်ခေါင်းလောင်း lu-khaw-khaung-laung *(n.)* **doorbell**

လူငယ် lu-ngal *(n.)* **lad**

လူငယ်ပြုပြင်ရေးကျောင်း luungaal pyu-pyin-rayy-kyaungg *(n.)* **reformatory**

လူငယ်များ ကျူးလွန်သော ပြစ်မှုများ lu-ngal-myar-kyu-lun-taw-pyit-mu *(n.)* **delinquency**

လူငယ်လူရွယ် lu-ngal-lu-ywe *(adj.)* **juvenile**

လူစစ်ဆေးခြင်း luusitsayychinn *(n.)* **roll-call**

လူစိမ်း luu-saim *(n.)* **stranger**

လူစီးတွဲ lu-see-twe *(n.)* **carriage**

လူစီးယဉ် luu seeyin *(n.)* **pneumatic**

လူစု lu-su *(n.)* **concourse**

လူစု၊ ရပ်ကွက် lu-su, yat-kwat *(n.)* **community**

လူစု၊ လူထု lu-su, lu-htu *(n.)* **folk**

လူစုခြင်း lu-su-chin *(n.)* **muster**

လူစုလူဝေး lu-su-lu-way *(n.)* **horde**

လူဆင်းပေါက် lu-sin-pauk *(n.)* **manhole**

လူဆန်ပဲပင် lu-san-pae-pin *(n.)* **lucerne**

လူဆန်သော lu-san-thaw *(adj.)* **humane**

လူဆိုးဂိုဏ်း lu-soe-gai *(n.)* **gang**

လူဆိုးဂိုဏ်းဝင် lu-soe-gai-win *(n.)* **gangster**

လူတန်း၊ ယာဉ်တန်း luu-taann , yintaann *(n.)* **queue**

လူတန်းစားနိမ့်သော သူများ နေထိုင်ရာ ရပ်ကွက် lu-tan-sar-naint-taw-thu-myar-nay-htai-yar-yat-kwat *(n.)* **ghetto**

လူတွေ့မေးမြန်းခြင်း၊ အင်တာဗျူး lu-tway-may-myan-chin, in-ter-byu *(n.)* **interview**

လူတွေ့မေးမြန်းသည်၊ အင်တာဗျူးသည် lu-tway-may-myan-the, in-ter-byu-the *(v.)* **interview**

လူတိုင်း lu-tine *(pron.)* **everybody**

လူထု luu-htu *(n.)* **populace**

လူထု၊ ပြည်သူ luu-htu , pyisuu *(adj.)* **public**

လူထုစည်းဝေးပွဲ luu-htu-see-wayypwal *(n.)* **rally**

လူထုဆန္ဒ ခံယူပွဲ luu-htu-san-da-hkan-yuu-pwal *(n.)* **plebiscite**

လူထုအသည်းစွဲ luu-htu-aa-see-swal *(n.)* **stardom**

လူထူး၊ လူကြောင် lu-htoo, lu-kyaung *(n.)* **wack**

လူနည်းစုကို ကိုယ်စားပြုနိုင်ငံသား lu-nae-su-ko-sar-pyu-nine-ngan-tar *(n.)* **oligarch**

လူနည်းစုကို ကိုယ်စားပြုသော အစိုးရ lu-nae-su-ko-ko-sar-pyu-taw-a-soe-ra *(n.)* **oligarchy**

လူနည်းစုကို ကိုယ်စားပြုအစိုးရနှင့် ဆိုင်သော lu-nae-su-ko-sar-pyu-a-soe-ya-nint-sine-taw *(adj.)* **oligarchal**

လူနှင့်ဆင်သော lu-nint-sin-taw *(adj.)* **anthropoid**

လူနာ luu-nar *(n.)* **patient**

လူနာစောင့် lu-nar-saunt *(n.)* **carer**

လူနာဆောင် luunarsaung *(n.)* **ward**

လူနာတင်ကား lu-nar-tin-car *(n.)* **ambulance**

လူနာတင်ထမ်းစင် luu nar tin htamsin *(n.)* **stretcher**

လူနုံ lu-hnon *(n.)* **ass**

လူနုံ၊ လူအ lu-hnon, lu-a *(n.)* **fool**

လူပျင်း lu-pyin *(n.)* **idler**

လူပျို၊ တက္ကသိုလ် ပထမဘွဲ့ lu-pyo, tat-ka-do-pa-hta-ma-bwe *(n.)* **bachelor**

လူပျိုချွတ်ပါတီ lu-pyo-chut-par-ti *(n.)* **bachelor party**

လူပျိုလှည့်ခြင်း lu-byo-lae-chin *(n.)* **courtship**

လူပြက် lu-byat *(n.)* **clown**

လူပြည့်ကျပ်သည် lu-pyae-kyat-the *(adj.)* **crowded**

လူပြိန်းကြိုက်သတင်းစာ luupyaeinkyaitesatinnsar *(n.)* **tabloid**

လူပု lu-pu *(n.)* **dwarf**

လူပုံစံရုပ် lu-pon-san-yoke *(n.)* **mannequin**

လူပုဂ္ဂိုလ်အဖြစ် တင်စားသုံးနှုန်းမှု luu-poke-gol-aa-hpyit-tin-sarr-sone-hnone-mhu *(n.)* **personification**

လူပုဂ္ဂိုလ်အဖြစ် တင်စားသုံးနှုန်းသည် luu-poke-gol-aa-hpyit-tin-sarr-sone-hnone-sai *(v.)* **personify**

လူဖျင်း၊ ဆန်ကုန်မြေလေး luu hpyinn , saan kone myaylayy *(n.)* **scum**

လူဖြူလူမည်းကပြား lu-phyu-lu-mae-ka-pyar *(n.)* **mulatto**

လူမဆန်သော lu-ma-san-taw *(adj.)* **beastly**

လူမည်း lu-me *(n.)* **kaffir**

လူမမာ၊ ဒုက္ခိတ lu-ma-mar, dote-khi-ta *(n.)* **invalid**

လူမမာရုပ်ပေါက်နေသော luu m mar rote poutnaysaw *(adj.)* **wan**

လူမျိုးကြီးဝါဒ lu-myo-gyi-wa-da *(n.)* **chauvinism**
လူမျိုးကြီးဝါဒီ lu-myo-gyi-wa-di *(adj.& n.)* **chauvinist**
လူမျိုးစု lu-myo-su *(n.)* **ethnicity**
လူမျိုးစုနှင့် ဆိုင်သော lu-myo-su-nint-sai-taw *(adj.)* **ethnic**
လူမျိုးတုံးသတ်ဖြတ်ခြင်း lu-myo-tone-tat-phat-chin *(n.)* **genocide**
လူမျိုးနွယ်စု luumyoenwalsu *(adj.)* **tribal**
လူမျိုးနှစ်ခုပါဝင်သော အဖွဲ့ဝင်များဆိုင်ရာ lu-myo-na-khu-par-win-taw-a-phwe-win-myar-saing-yar *(adj.)* **biracial**
လူမျိုးပေါင်းစုံရှိသော lu-myo-paung-sone-shi-taw *(adj.)* **cosmopolitan**
လူမျိုးရေး luumyoe-rayy *(adj.)* **racial**
လူမျိုးရေးခွဲခြားမှု lu-myo-yay-kwal-char-mu *(n.)* **apartheid**
လူမျိုးရေးဝါဒီ luumyoe-rayywarde *(adj.)* **racist**
လူမွဲစာခံခြင်း lu-mwe-sar-khan-chin *(n.)* **insolvency**
လူမှုဗေဒ luumhubay-da *(n.)* **sociology**
လူမှုရေး luumhurayy *(n.)* **social**
လူမှုရေး ခေါင်းပါးသော lu-mu-yay-khaung-par-taw *(adj.)* **antisocial**
လူမှုရေး၊ နိုင်ငံရေးကိစ္စရပ်များအပေါ် လူအများ၏ တုံ့ပြန်ချက် lu-mu-yay, nai-ngan-yay-kait-sa-yat-myar-a-paw-lu-a-myar-ei-tont-pyan-chat *(n.)* **backlash**
လူမှုလောကမှ ဖယ်ရှားခြင်း ဖြစ်စဉ် lu-mu-law-ka-ma-phal-shar-chin-phit-sin *(n.)* **desocialization**
လူမှုအဆင့်မြင့်သော lu-mu-a-sint-myint-taw *(adj.)* **elite**
လူမိုက် luumite *(n.)* **thug**
လူယုံ lu-yone *(n.)* **confidant**
လူယုံတော် lu-yone-taw *(n.)* **henchman**
လူယုတ်မာ luuyotemar *(n.)* **swine**
လူယောင်ဆောင်သော lu-yaung-saung-taw *(adj.)* **incarnate**
လူရတတ် lu-ya-hat *(n.)* **gentry**
လူရမ်းကား luuramkarr *(n.)* **ruffian**
လူရွှင်တော် lu-shwin-taw *(n.)* **comedian**
လူရှုပ်ကလေး luu shotekalayy *(n.)* **rascal**
လူရိုင်း luurine *(n.)* **savage**
လူလွတ်ဖြစ်သော lu-lut-phit-taw *(adj.)* **footloose**
လူလိမ် lu-lain *(n.)* **cheater**
လူလိမ်၊ လူညာ lu-lain, lu-nyar *(n.)* **liar**
လူလိမ်လူညစ် lu-lain-lu-nyit *(n.)* **crook**
လူလုပ်ဂြိုလ်တု luu lote gyaoltu *(n.)* **sputnik**
လူလေလူလွင့် lu-lay-lu-lwint *(n.)* **loafer**
လူဝင်မှု lu-win-mu *(n.)* **immigration**
လူသံဆူညံနေသော နေရာ lu-tan-su-nyan-nay-taw-nay-yar *(n.)* **babel**
လူသစ်စုဆောင်းသည် luu sit susaunggsai *(v.)* **recruit**
လူသတ်ပွဲ luu-saatpwal *(n.)* **slaughter**
လူသတ်မှု lu-tat-mu *(n.)* **homicide**
လူသတ်ရန် ဝန်မလေးသော lu-tat-yan-win-ma-lay-taw *(adj.)* **murderous**
လူသတ်သည် lu-tat-the *(v.)* **murder**
လူသတ်သမား lu-tat-ta-mar *(n.)* **murderer**
လူသန်ကြီး lu-than-gyi *(n.)* **cyclops**
လူသွားလမ်း lu-twar-lan *(n.)* **alley**
လူသား lu-tar *(adj.)* **human**

လူသားချင်းစာနာသော lu-tar-chin-sar-nar-taw *(adj.)* **humanitarian**
လူသားစားသူ lu-tar-sar-thu *(n.)* **cannibal**
လူသာမန် lu-tar-man *(adj.)* **lay**
လူသိများသူ lu-thi-myar-thu *(n.)* **celebrity**
လူသိများသော luusimyarrsaw *(adj.)* **well-known**
လူသိရှင်ကြား စွပ်စွဲ ရှုတ်ချသည် lu-thi-shin-kyar-sut-swal-shoke-cha-the *(v.)* **denounce**
လူသုံးကုန် lu-tone-kone *(n.)* **commodity**
လူသုံးများသော စကားလုံး lu-tone-myar-taw-sa-kar-lone *(n.)* **byword**
လူသူကင်းမဲ့သော lu-thu-kin-mae-taw *(adj.)* **desolate**
လူသူလေးပါးမနေသော luu suu lay-parr manaysaw *(adj.)* **waste**
လူသူဝေးရာ luu suuwayyrar *(n.)* **seclusion**
လူသေ lu-thay *(n.)* **dead**
လူသေကောင် luu saykaung *(n.)* **stiff**
လူသေမြှုပ်မြေအောက်လိုဏ်ခေါင်း lu-tay-myoke-myay-awt-hlaing-khaung *(n.)* **catacomb**
လူသေအလောင်း lu-tay-a-laung *(n.)* **cadaver**
လူအ lu-aa *(n.)* **gooney**
လူအစားစက်ကို အစားထိုးသုံးသည် lu-a-sar-sat-ko-a-sar-htoe-tone-the *(v.)* **automate**
လူအဖြစ်ဝင်စားခြင်း lu-a-phit-win-sar-chin *(n.)* **incarnation**
လူအားဖြင့် ရွှေ့သည် lu-arr-phint-shwae-the *(v.)* **manhandle**
လူအုပ် lu-oak *(n.)* **crowd**
လူအုပ်၊ ငှက်အုပ် lu-oak, hnget-oak *(n.)* **flock**
လူဦးရေ luu uray *(n.)* **population**
လူဦးရေလေ့လာခြင်းနှင့် ဆိုင်သော lu-oo-yay-lay-lar-chin-nint-sai-taw *(adj.)* **demographic**
လူဦးရေသိပ်သည်းသော luu u ray seik saee-saw *(adj.)* **populous**
လေ lay *(n.)* **air**
လေ မမြင်ရဘဲ တည်ရှိခြင်း lay mamyinrabhell taishihkyinn *(n.)* **sylph**
လေ့ကျင့်ခန်း lay-kyint-khan *(n.)* **exercise**
လေ့ကျင့်ခန်းပြုလုပ်သည် lay-kyint-khan-pyu-lote-the *(v.)* **exercise**
လေ့ကျင့်ပေးသည် lae kyintpayysai *(v.)* **train**
လေ့လာချက်၊ လေ့လာခြင်း laelarchet , laelarchinn *(n.)* **study**
လေ့လာသင်ယူခြင်း lay-lar-tin-yu-chin *(n.)* **learning**
လေ့လာသင်ယူသူ lay-lar-tin-yu-thu *(n.)* **learner**
လေ့လာသည် laelarsai *(v.)* **regard**
လေ့လာသည်၊ သင်ယူသည် laelar sai , sinyuusai *(v.)* **study**
လေ့လာသော lay-lat-taw *(adj.)* **learned**
လေး lay *(n.)* **bow**
လေးကြိုးတပ်ဂစ်တာ lay-kyo-tat-gittar *(n.)* **ukelele**
လေးကြိုးတပ်ဂစ်တာပညာရှင် lay-kyo-tat-gittar-pyin-nyar-shin *(n.)* **ukeleleist**
လေးချောင်းထောက်ခုံ layy hkyaungg htouthkone *(n.)* **sawhorse**
လေးခု layyhku *(n.)* **tetra**
လေးစားခြင်း lay-sar-chin *(n.)* **cachet**
လေးစားမှု lay-sar-mu *(n.)* **admiration**
လေးစားမှု၊ ကြွေးရှင်စာရင်း lay-sar-mu, kyway-shin-sa-yin *(n.)* **credit**
လေးစားလိုက်နာခြင်း lay-sar-lite-nar-chin *(n.)* **compliance**

လေးစားသည် lay-sar-the *(v.)* **admire**

လေးဆ lay-sa *(adj.)* **quadruple**

လေးဆ၊ လေးစီး layy sa, layysee *(v.)* **quadruple**

လေးဆယ် lay-sal *(n.)* **forty**

လေးညှင်းပွင့် lay-nyin-pwint *(n.)* **clove**

လေးထောင့်ပုံမြေကွက်လပ် layy htaunt pone myay-kwatlaut *(n.)* **quadrangle**

လေးနက်သော lay-nat-taw *(adj.)* **grave**

လေးပိုင်းပိုင်းသည် layy pine pine sai *(v.)* **quarter**

လေးပုံတစ်ပုံ layypone-ta-pone *(n.)* **quarter**

လေးဘီးလှည်း lay-bi-lal *(n.)* **wain**

လေးလံစွာ lay-lan-swar *(adv.)* **heavily**

လေးလံသော lay-lan-taw *(adj.)* **massy**

လေးလက်တွန်းလှည်း lay-laat-twann-hlaee *(n.)* **perambulator**

လေးလေးနက်နက် တွေးတတ်သော layylayy-naatnaat tway-taatsaw *(adj.)* **reflective**

လေးအတတ် lay-a-tat *(n.)* **archery**

လေ၊ အရည်ကြောင့် ဝမ်းရောင်ခြင်း lay-a-yay-kyaunt-wan-yaung-chin *(v.)* **bloat**

လေကြောင်း၊ လေထုဆိုင်ရာ နည်းပညာ lay-kyaung, lay-htu-saing-yar-nee-pyin-nyar *(n.)* **aerospace**

လေကြောင်းပြ၊ လမ်းညွှန် lay-kyaung-pya, lan-hnyun *(n.)* **navigator**

လေကြောင်းဖြင့်ပို့သော ကုန်ပစ္စည်း lay-kyaung-phit-po-taw-kone-pyit-see *(n.)* **air freight**

လေကြောင်းမှ အလုံးအရင်း ရုတ်တရက် စစ်ဆင်ခြင်း lay-kyaung-ma-a-lone-a-yin-yote-ta-yat-sit-sin-chin *(n.)* **blitz**

လေကွယ် lay-kwal *(n.)* **lee**

လေကာမှန် lay kar-mhaan *(n.)* **windscreen**

လေကာရေကာမျက်မှန် lay-kar-yay-kar-myat-man *(n.)* **goggles**

လေကူရှင်ခံ လူဝင်နိုင်သော ဘောလုံး lay kuu hlyinhkan luu win-nine-saw bhaw-lone *(n.)* **Zorb**

လေကောင်းလေသန့်ရပြီး ကျယ်ဝန်းသော lay-kaung-lay-thant-ya-pi-kyal-wun-taw *(adj.)* **airy**

လေငြိမ်၍ မရွေ့နိုင်သော လှေကို စွန့်ခွာသည် lay-nyien-ywe-ma-ywe-nai-taw-hlay-ko-sount-khwar-the *(v.)* **becalm**

လေစိမ်း lay-sein *(n.)* **draught**

လေစိမ်းတိုက်သော lay-sein-tite-taw *(adj.)* **drafty**

လေဆင်နှာမောင်း laysinnharmaungg *(n.)* **tornado**

လေဆိပ်ရှိ ပစ္စည်းတင် တွန်းလှည်း lay-seik-shi-pyit-see-tin-toon-lal *(n.)* **carousel**

လေညင်း lay-nyin *(n.)* **breeze**

လေတက်သည် lay-tat-the *(v.)* **belch**

လေတပ်စခန်း lay-tat-sa-khan *(n.)* **airbase**

လေတိုက်သော lay-tite-saw *(adj.)* **windy**

လေထိုးရသော lay htoe-ra-saw *(adj.)* **pneumatic**

လေထိုးလေအောင့်နာ lay-htoe-lay-aunt-nar *(n.)* **colic**

လေထီး lay-htee *(n.)* **parachute**

လေထီးခုန်သူ lay-htee-hkone-suu *(n.)* **parachutist**

လေထု lay-htu *(n.)* **atmosphere**

လေထုဆိုင်ရာ စတက်တစ်ပညာခွဲ lay-htu-saing-yar-sa-tat-tic-pyin-nyar-khwal *(n.)* **aerostatics**

လေထုနှင့်ဆိုင်သော lay-htu-nint-saing-taw *(adj.)* **atmospheric**

လေနှင့်ပါလာသည် lay nint parlarsai *(v.)* **waft**
လေနှင့်ပါလာသော အနံ့ lay nintparlarsaw aanant *(n.)* **waft**
လေပြင်း lay-pyin *(n.)* **gust**
လေပြင်းမုန်တိုင်း lay-pyin-hmone-tai *(n.)* **gale**
လေပြွန် lay pywan *(n.)* **trachea**
လေပြွန်ကြည့်မှန်ပြောင်း lay pywan kyi mhaanpyaung *(n.)* **tracheoscopy**
လေပြွန်နှင့် ဆိုင်သော lay pywan-nint sinesaw *(adj.)* **tracheal**
လေပွခြင်း lay-pwa-chin *(n.)* **flatulence**
လေပွသော lay-pwa-taw *(adj.)* **flatulent**
လေပွေ laypway *(n.)* **whirlwind**
လေပေါ lay-paw *(n.)* **windbag**
လေဖြတ်ခြင်း lay-hpyat-chinn *(n.)* **palsy**
လေဖိအားတိုင်းကိရိယာ lay-hpi-arr-taing-ka-yi-yar *(n.)* **barometer**
လေဖိအားသုံး လေမှုတ်ဘူး lay-phi-arr-tone-lay-mote-bu *(n.)* **aerosol**
လေဖိအားသုံးဘရိတ် lay-phi-arr-tone-lay-ba-rake *(n.)* **airbrake**
လေဘယ်လ်ကတ် lay-bal-kat *(n.)* **label**
လေဘယ်လ်ထိုးသည် lay-bal-htoe-the *(v.)* **label**
လေမှတစ်ဆင့်ကူးစက်သော lay-ma-ta-sint-ku-set-taw *(n.)* **airborne**
လေမှုတ်စက် lay-mote-sat *(n.)* **winder**
လေယာဉ် lay-rin *(n.)* **plane**
လေယာဉ်ကွင်း lay-yin-kwin *(n.)* **airfield**
လေယာဉ်ကို ခက်ခဲစွာ အလှပြပျံသန်းခြင်း lay-yin-ko-khat-khae-swar-a-hla-pya-pyan-tan-chin *(n.)* **aerobatics**
လေယာဉ်ခ lay-yin-kha *(n.)* **airfare**
လေယာဉ်ချင်း အနီးကပ်တိုက်ပွဲ lay-yin-chin-a-nee-kat-tite-pwe *(n.)* **dogfight**
လေယာဉ်ချင်း အနီးကပ်တိုက်ပွဲ ဆင်နွှဲသည် lay-yin-chin-a-nee-kat-tite-pwe-sin-nwe-the *(v.)* **dogfight**
လေယာဉ်ပစ် lay-yin-phit *(adj.)* **anti-aircraft**
လေယာဉ်ပညာ lay-yin-pyin-nyar *(n.)* **aeronautics**
လေယာဉ်ပေါ်သို့ တက်သည် lay-yin-paw-tho-tat-the *(v.)* **embark**
လေယာဉ်ဖြင့်သယ်ပို့ခြင်း lay-yin-phyit-tal-poe-chin *(n.)* **airlift**
လေယာဉ်မယ် lay-yin-mal *(n.)* **air hostess**
လေယာဉ်မှချသော ပစ္စည်းများ lay-yin-hma-cha-taw-pyit-see-myar *(n.)* **airdrop**
လေယာဉ်မှူး lay-rin-mhau *(n.)* **pilot**
လေယာဉ်မှူး၊ လက်ကမ်းကြော်ငြာစာ lay-yin-hmue, lat-kan-kyaw-nyar-sar *(n.)* **flyer**
လေယာဉ်မှူးအခန်း lay-yin-muu-a-khan *(n.)* **cockpit**
လေယာဉ်မောင်းအတတ် lay-yin-maung-a-tat *(n.)* **aviation**
လေယာဉ်မောင်မယ် lay-yin-maung-mal *(n.)* **aircrew**
လေယာဉ်အုပ် lay yin-ote *(n.)* **squadron**
လေရှူကုထုံး lay-shu-ku-htone *(n.)* **pneumotherapy**
လေရဟတ် lay-ra-haat *(n.)* **windmill**
လေရှည်သော lay shisaw *(adj.)* **verbose**
လေလံဆွဲသည် lay-lan-swal-the *(v.)* **bid**
လေလံဆွဲသူ lay-lan-swal-thu *(n.)* **bidder**
လေလံပွဲ lay-lan-pwe *(n.)* **auction**
လေလံပေးသည့် ဈေး lay-lan-pay-the-zay *(n.)* **bid**

လေလံအရ ဆွဲသွားသည် lay-lan-a-ra-swal-twar-tai *(v.)* **outbid**
လေလျှော့သည် lay-shawt-the *(v.)* **deflate**
လေလွင့်ဆုံးရှုံးမှု lay lwint soneshonemhu *(n.)* **wastage**
လေလွင့်သော luu lay luu lwint *(adj.)* **vagabond**
လေလွင့်နေသော lay lw intnaysaw *(adj.)* **stray**
လေလွင့်သည်၊ လမ်းလွဲသည်၊ စိတ်ကစားသည် lay-lwint sai , lam lwal sai , sate kasarrsai *(v.)* **stray**
လေလွင့်သူငယ် titetwannsai *(n.)* **urchin**
လေလုံးထွားသည် lay-lone-htwar-the *(v.)* **brag**
လေလုံးထွားသော lay lone htwarr-saw *(adj.)* **pretentious**
လေဝင်ပေါက် laywinpout *(n.)* **ventilator**
လေဝင်လေထွက် laywinlayhtwat *(n.)* **ventilation**
လေဝင်လေထွက်ကောင်းသည် laywinlayhtwat kaunggsai *(v.)* **ventilate**
လေဝင်လေထွက်အပေါက် laywinlayhtwat aapout *(n.)* **vent**
လေသန့်စက် lay-thant-set *(n.)* **air freshner**
လေသလပ်ပေးသည် lay-tha-lat-pay-the *(v.)* **aerate**
လေသေနတ် lay-tha-nat *(n.)* **airgun**
လေဟာနယ် hpone sote saathpyint sotesai *(n.)* **vacuum**
လေအရှိန်၊ ဦးတည်ချက်၊ ရေရွေ့လျားမှုတိုင်းကိရိယာ lay-a-shein-oo-the-chat-yay-shwe-lyar-mu-taing-ka-yi-yar *(n.)* **anemometer**
လေအိတ်မွေ့ရာ lay-aik-mway-yar *(n.)* **airbed**
လေအေးပေးခြင်း lay-aye-pay-chin *(n.)* **air conditioning**
လော့ကက်သီး lot-kat-thee *(n.)* **locket**
လော့ဒ်ဘွဲ့ရ lot-bwe-ya *(n.)* **lordship**
လောက law-ka *(n.)* **realm**
လောကကို စိတ်ပျက်မှု law-ka-ko-seik-pyat-mu *(n.)* **angst**
လောကဓံတရား lawkadhantararr *(n.)* **vicissitude**
လောကဓံတရားကို ကြံ့ကြံ့ခံနိုင်သူ law-ka-dhan-ta-rarr-ko kyan-kyaanhkan ninesuu *(n.)* **stoic**
လောကသဘာဝနှင့် သာမန်လူတို့ မမီနိုင်သော law-ka-ta-barwanint-tar-man-lu-thoe-ma-minine-taw *(adj.)* **transcendental**
လောကီရေးရာ lawkerayyrar *(adj.)* **secure**
လောကီသီးသန့်ဝါဒ law-ke-see saantwarda *(n.)* **secularism**
လောက် laut *(n.)* **maggot**
လောက်လေးခွ၊ ကျောက်တုံးပစ်ကိရိယာ laut-lay-kwa, kyauk-tone-pyit-ka-yi-yar *(n.)* **catapult**
လောင်းကစား laung-ka-sar *(n.)* **gamble**
လောင်းကစားခြင်း laung-ka-sar-chin *(adj.)* **betting**
လောင်းကစားသည် laung-ka-sar-the *(v.)* **bet**
လောင်းကစားသည်၊ ဂိမ်းကစားသည် laung-ka-sar-the, game-ka-sar-the *(v.)* **game**
လောင်းကစားသမား laung-ka-sar-ta-mar *(n.)* **bettor**
လောင်းကြေးထပ်သည်၊ တိုင်၊ ငုတ်ဖြင့်ထောက်မပေးသည် launggkyay htat sai, tine, ngotehpyint htout mapayysai *(v.)* **stake**
လောင်းရိပ်မိသည် laung-yeik-mi-tai *(v.)* **overshadow**
လောင်းသည် launggsai *(v.)* **wager**

လောင်ကျွမ်းခြင်း laung-kywan-chin *(n.)* **combustion**

လောင်ကျွမ်းစေသည် laungkyamsaysai *(v.)* **parch**

လောင်ကျွမ်းသည် laung-kywan-the *(v.)* **combust**

လောင်ဂျီတွဒ် laung-gi-tut *(n.)* **longitude**

လောင်ဂျီတွဒ်မျဉ်း laung-gyi-tut-myin *(n.)* **meridian**

လောင်စာဆီ laung-sar-si *(n.)* **fuel**

လောင်တတ်သော၊ ငေါ့သော laung-tat-taw, ngawt-taw *(adj.)* **caustic**

လောင်မြိုက်သည်၊ မီးဟပ်သည် laung myaite sai, mee hatsai *(v.)* **sear**

လောင်သည် laung-the *(v.)* **ignite**

လောဘ law-ba *(n.)* **cupidity**

လောဘကြီးသော law-ba-kyi-taw *(adj.)* **greedy**

လောဘဇော lawbhazaw *(n.)* **venality**

လောသည် law-the *(v.)* **hurry**

လော်ဂရစ်သမ် law-ga-rit-tan *(n.)* **logarithm**

လော်ရယ်ပင် law-yal-pin *(n.)* **laurel**

လော်ရီကား lor-yi-kar *(n.)* **lorry**

လဲပြို့လုလုကုမ္ပဏီကို ငွေကြေးအကူအညီပေးခြင်း lal-pyo-lu-lu-com-pa-nee-ko-ngwe-kyay-a-khu-a-nyi-pay-chin *(n.)* **bailout**

လဲလျောင်းသည် lell lyaungg-sai *(v.)* **repose**

လဲလှယ်ခြင်း lae-lal-chin *(n.)* **exchange**

လဲလှယ်သည် lae-lal-the *(v.)* **exchange**

လဲသည်၊ ခွာသည် lell sai, hkwarsai *(v.)* **slough**

ဝံ့သည် wint-the *(v.)* **dare**

ဝံပုလွေ wanpulway *(n.)* **wolf**

ဝက် waat *(n.)* **pig**

ဝက်ခြံ waat-chaan *(n.)* **pimple**

ဝက်ဆားနယ်ခြောက် wat-sar-nal-chyauk *(n.)* **bacon**

ဝက်ဆီ wat-si *(n.)* **lard**

ဝက်မ waat-ma *(n.)* **sow**

ဝက်ဝံ wat-win *(n.)* **bear**

ဝက်သက် wat-that *(n.)* **measles**

ဝက်သစ်ချပင် wat-tit-cha-pin *(n.)* **oak**

ဝက်သစ်ချသီး wat-thit-cha-thee *(n.)* **acorn**

ဝက်သစ်ချအခေါက် waat sait hkyaaahkout *(n.)* **tanbark**

ဝက်သား waatsarr *(n.)* **pork**

ဝက်သိုက် waatsite *(n.)* **shambles**

ဝက်အူ၊ လိင်ဆက်ဆံခြင်း၊ လိင်ဆက်ဆံဖော် waat auu , linsaatsanchinn , linsaatsanhpaw *(n.)* **screw**

ဝက်အူချောင်း waatauuchaungg *(n.)* **sausage**

ဝက်အူစုပ်သည် waat auu sotesai *(v.)* **screw**

ဝင့်ကြွား ဝမ်းမြောက်သော wint-kywar-wan-myauk-taw *(adj.)* **jubilant**

ဝင့်ကြွားခြင်း wint-kyar-chinn *(n.)* **ostentation**

ဝင့်ကြွားစွာ wint-kywar-swar *(adv.)* **gloatingly**

ဝင့်ကြွားမှု wint-kywar-mu *(n.)* **flamboyance**

ဝင့်ဝါခြင်း nhaainnainnsai *(n.)* **vanity**
ဝင့်ဝါလွန်းခြင်း wint-war-lun-chin *(n.)* **flamboyant**
ဝင့်ဝါလွန်းသော wint-war-lun-taw *(adj.)* **flamboyant**
ဝင်း win *(n.)* **courtyard**
ဝင်းခြံ winnchaan *(n.)* **yard**
ဝင်းလက်သည် win-latt-the *(v.)* **gleam**
ဝင်းလက်သော win-lat-taw *(adj.)* **gleaming**
ဝင်ခွင့် win-khwint *(n.)* **admission**
ဝင်ခွင့်ပုံစံ win-khwint-pon-san *(n.)* **entry form**
ဝင်ခွင့်မရသော win hkwintmarasaw *(adj.)* **unaccessible**
ဝင်ခွင့်လက်မှတ် win-khwint-lat-mat *(n.)* **ducat**
ဝင်ငွေ win-ngwe *(n.)* **income**
ဝင်ငွေ လစာကောင်းသော winngway lasar-kaunggsaw *(adj.)* **remunerative**
ဝင်ငွေရှာသည် win-ngwe-shar-the *(v.)* **earn**
ဝင်ဆောင့်သည် win saunt-sai *(v.)* **ram**
ဝင်ပေါက်၊ ဝင်ခွင့် win-pauk, win-khwint *(n.)* **entrance**
ဝင်ရိုး win-yoe *(n.)* **axis**
ဝင်ရိုးစွန်း win-roe-swann *(adj.)* **polar**
ဝင်ရိုးစွန်းတစ်ဘက်သို့ သွားသော win-roe-swann-ta-bat-thoe-twar-taw *(adj.)* **polary**
ဝင်ရိုးအလယ်မှတ် win-yoe-a-lal-mat *(n.)* **coaxial**
ဝင်ရောက်ခြင်း win-yauk-chin *(n.)* **induction**
ဝင်ရောက်စွက်ဖက်ခြင်း win-yauk-swat-phat-chin *(n.)* **interference**
ဝင်လမ်း win-lan *(n.)* **access**

ဝင်သည် win-the *(v.)* **enter**
ဝင်သုံးခွင့်ရခြင်း win-tone-kwint-ya-chin *(n.)* **accessibility**
ဝင်သုံးခွင့်ရသော win-tone-kwint-ya-taw *(adj.)* **accessible**
ဝင်္ကပါ win-ka-bar *(n.)* **labyrinth**
ဝဏ္ဏ wan-na *(n.)* **syllable**
ဝဏ္ဏပါဝင်သော wannaparwainsaw *(adj.)* **syllabic**
ဝတိုသော wa-to-saw *(adj.)* **podgy**
ဝတ္ထု wut-htu *(n.)* **fiction**
ဝတ္ထုစွဲကာမစိတ် wut-htu-swal-kar-ma-seik *(n.)* **fetishism**
ဝတ္ထုဆန်သော wut-htu-san-taw *(adj.)* **fictional**
ဝတ္ထုရှည် wathtushay *(n.)* **saga**
ဝတ္ထုရေးဆရာ wit-htu-yay-sa-yar *(n.)* **novelist**
ဝတ္ထုလတ် wut-htu-lat *(n.)* **novelette**
ဝတ်ကောင်းစားလှဖြင့် ရှိုးထုတ်လွန်းသူ wut-kaung-sar-hla-phint-sho-htoke-lun-thu *(n.)* **dandy**
ဝတ်စုံ waat-sone *(v.)* **outfit**
ဝတ်ဆင်ထားသော wit-sin-htar-taw *(adj.)* **clad**
ဝတ်ဆင်သည် waatsinsai *(v.)* **wear**
ဝတ်မှုန် waat-hmone *(n.)* **pollen**
ဝတ်ရည် wit-yay *(n.)* **nectar**
ဝတ်ရုံ waatrone *(n.)* **vestment**
ဝတ်ရုံ၊ ခြုံထည် wit-yone, chone-htal *(n.)* **cloak**
ဝတ်ရုံခြုံသည် wut-yone-chone-taw *(adj.)* **vested**
ဝတ်ရုံလွှာ waatronelwhar *(n.)* **toga**

ဝတ်လှုံ၊ ရာထူး wit-hline, yar-htoo *(n.)* **mantle**

ဝတ်လုံတော်ရ ရှေ့နေ waat lone tawra shaenay *(n.)* **templar**

ဝတ်လုံဝတ်ထားသည် waat lone waathtarrsai *(v.)* **robe**

ဝတ်သည် wit-the *(v.)* **clothe**

ဝန် win *(n.)* **load**

ဝန်းကျင် win-kyin *(adj.)* **ambient**

ဝန်းကျင်ထိန်းသိမ်းရေးဝါဒ win-kyin-htain-thein-yay-wa-da *(n.)* **environmentalism**

ဝန်းကျင်ထိန်းသိမ်းရေးဝါဒီ win-kyin-htain-thein-yay-wa-di *(n.)* **environmentalist**

ဝန်းကျင်ဓလေ့စရိုက် win-kyin-da-lay-sa-yite *(n.)* **ambience**

ဝန်းပတ်သည် win-pat-the *(v.)* **girdle**

ဝန်းရံလုပ်ကြံခြင်း waann-ran lotekyaanchinn *(n.)* **siege**

ဝန်းရံလုပ်ကြံသည် waannran lotekyaansai *(v.)* **siege**

ဝန်းရံသည်၊ ဝိုင်းထားသည် win-yan-the, wine-htar-the *(v.)* **encircle**

ဝန်းရံသည်၊ အနားသတ်သည် win-yan-the, a-nar-tat-the *(v.)* **fringe**

ဝန်ကျယ်သော wun-kyal-taw *(adj.)* **bulky**

ဝန်ကြီး win-gyi *(n.)* **minister**

ဝန်ကြီးချုပ် win-kyee-chote *(n.)* **premier**

ဝန်ကြီးဌာန win-gyi-htar-na *(n.)* **ministry**

ဝန်ခံရမည်မှာ win-khan-ya-me-mar *(adv.)* **admittedly**

ဝန်ခံသည် win-khan-the *(v.)* **admit**

ဝန်ချတောင်းပန် win-cha-taung-pan *(adj.)* **aplogetic**

ဝန်ချီဂျိုက် win-chi-gyaik *(n.)* **jack**

ဝန်ချီစက် waan chaesaat *(n.)* **windlass**

ဝန်ဆောင်ခ win-saung-kha *(n.)* **fee**

ဝန်ဆောင်မှု waansaungmhu *(n.)* **service**

ဝန်ဆောင်မှုပေးသည် waansaungmhupayysai *(v.)* **service**

ဝန်ထမ်း waanhtam *(n.)* **staff**

ဝန်ထုတ်ဝန်ပိုး wun-htoke-wun-poe *(n.)* **burden**

ဝန်ပိသည် wan-pi-tai *(v.)* **overburden**

ဝန်ပို win-po *(n.)* **excess baggage**

ဝန်ရိုးကျသော wun-yoe-kya-taw *(adj.)* **axial**

ဝန်ရိုးနှစ်ခုပါသော win-yoe-na-khu *(adj.)* **biaxial**

ဝန်လျော့ခြင်း၊ ပေါ့ပါးသွားခြင်း win-yawt-chin, pot-par-twar-chin *(n.)* **lightening**

ဝန်လျော့သည်၊ ပေါ့ပါးသွားသည် win-yawt-the, pot-par-twar-the *(v.)* **lighten**

ဝပ် waut *(n.)* **watt**

ဝပ်သည် wit-the *(v.)* **incubate**

ဝဘ်ကင်မရာ wabhkinmarar *(n.)* **webcam**

ဝဘ်စတိုး wabh satoe *(n.)* **web store**

ဝဘ်စာမျက်နှာ wabhsarmyetnhar *(n.)* **web page**

ဝဘ်ဆွေးနွေးပွဲ wabhswaynwaypwal *(n.)* **webinar**

ဝဘ်ဆိုက်တစ်ခုရှိသော web-site-ta-khu-shi-taw *(adj.)* **webby**

ဝဘ်မာစတာ wabhmarsatar *(n.)* **webmaster**

ဝဘ်အပိုင်းတွဲ wabh aapinetwal *(n.)* **webisode**

ဝမည်စိုး၍ ဖြစ်သော အစားအသောက်ပျက်ရောဂါ wa-me-soe-ywe-phit-taw-a-sar-a-taut-phat-yaw-gar *(n.)* **anorexia**

ဝမည်စိုး၍ ဖြစ်သော အစားအသောက်ပျက်ရောဂါ ရှိသော wa-me-soe-ywe-phit-taw-a-sar-a-taut-phat-yaw-gar-shi-taw *(adj.)* **anorexic**
ဝမ်းကိုက်ရောဂါ wan-kite-yaw-gar *(n.)* **dysentery**
ဝမ်းချုပ်ခြင်း wan-choke-chin *(n.)* **constipation**
ဝမ်းတွင်းပါ wan-twin-par *(adj.)* **innate**
ဝမ်းနည်းကြေကွဲခြင်း wan-nae-kyay-kwe-chin *(n.)* **mourning**
ဝမ်းနည်းကြေကွဲဖွယ်ရာ wan-nae-kyay-kwal-phwal-yar *(adj.)* **grievous**
ဝမ်းနည်းကြေကွဲသည် wan-nae-kyay-kwal-the *(v.)* **grieve**
ဝမ်းနည်းကြေကွဲသော wan-nae-kyay-kwe-taw *(n.)* **mournful**
ဝမ်းနည်းကြောင်းပြောသည် wan-nae-kyaung-pyaw-the *(v.)* **bemoan**
ဝမ်းနည်းခြင်း wam-naeechinn *(n.)* **regret**
ဝမ်းနည်းခြင်း၊ ပူဆွေးခြင်း wamnaeechinn , puuswaychinn *(n.)* **sorrow**
ဝမ်းနည်းစကား wan-nae-sa-kar *(n.)* **condolence**
ဝမ်းနည်းစရာ wamnaeesarar *(adj.)* **tragic**
ဝမ်းနည်းစေသည် wamnaeesaysai *(v.)* **sadden**
ဝမ်းနည်းပက်လက်ပြောသည် wan-nae-pat-lat-pyaw-the *(v.)* **bewail**
ဝမ်းနည်းပူဆွေးသော wam-naee puuswaysaw *(n.)* **woeful**
ဝမ်းနည်းမှု wamnaeemhu *(n.)* **sadness**
ဝမ်းနည်းသည် wamnaeesai *(v.)* **upset**
ဝမ်းနည်းသည်၊ ပူဆွေးသည် wamnaee sai , puuswaysai *(v.)* **sorrow**
ဝမ်းနည်းသော wamnaeesaw *(adj.)* **sad**
ဝမ်းနုတ်ခြင်း wan-note-chin *(n.)* **purgation**
ဝမ်းနုတ်ဆေး wam notesayy *(n.)* **purgative**
ဝမ်းပျော့ဆေး wam pyawt-sayy *(n.)* **physic**
ဝမ်းဗိုက် one-bike *(n.)* **abdomen**
ဝမ်းဗိုက်နှင့် ဆိုင်သော one-bike-nint-saing-taw *(adj.)* **abdominal**
ဝမ်းဘဲ wan-bae *(n.)* **duck**
ဝမ်းမြောက်ကြောင်းပြောခြင်း wan-myauk-kyaung-pyaw-chin *(n.)* **congratulation**
ဝမ်းမြောက်ကြောင်းပြောသည် wan-myauk-kyaung-pyaw-the *(v.)* **congratulate**
ဝမ်းမြောက်ခြင်း wan-myauk-chin *(n.)* **gratification**
ဝမ်းမြောက်စွာ wan-myauk-swar *(adv.)* **gladly**
ဝမ်းမြောက်ဝမ်းသာဖြစ်စေသည် wan-myauk-wan-tar-phit-say-the *(v.)* **gladden**
ဝမ်းမြောက်ဝမ်းသာဖြစ်သည် wam-myaut wamsar-hpyitsai *(v.)* **rejoice**
ဝမ်းမြောက်သော wan-myauk-taw *(adj.)* **glad**
ဝမ်းလျှောသည် wan-shaw-the *(n.)* **runs**
ဝမ်းလျှောခြင်း wan-shaw-chin *(n.)* **diarrhea**
ဝမ်းသွားစေသော wan-twar-say-the *(adj.)* **laxative**
ဝမ်းသာခြင်း wan-tar-chin *(n.)* **joy**
ဝမ်းသာပီတိ wan-tar-pi-ti *(n.)* **euphoria**
ဝယ်ယူခြင်း waal-yuuchinn *(n.)* **purchase**
ဝယ်ယူသည် waal-yuusai *(v.)* **purchase**
ဝယ်သည် wal-the *(v.)* **buy**
ဝယ်သူ wal-thu *(n.)* **buyer**
ဝယ်သူထံတိုက်ရိုက်ကုန်စည်နှင့် ဝန်ဆောင်မှုရောင်းဝယ်ခြင်းဆိုင်ရာ wal-thu-htan-tite-yite-kone-see-nint-win-saung-muu-yaung-wal-chin-sine-yar *(adj.)* **retail**

ဝယ်သူထံတိုက်ရိုက်နည်းဖြင့် wal-thu-htan-tite-yite-nae-phyit *(adv.)* **retail**
ဝရန်တာ waraantar *(n.)* **veranda**
ဝရမ်းထုတ်ခံရသူ waram htotehkanrasuu *(n.)* **warrantee**
ဝရမ်းထုတ်သူ waram htotesuu *(n.)* **warrantor**
ဝရမ်းပြေး wa-ram-pyay *(n.)* **outlaw**
ဝရမ်းပြေးကြော်ညာသည် wa-ram-pyay-kyaw-nyar-tai *(v.)* **outlaw**
ဝရုန်းသုန်းကား wa-rone-sonekarr *(n.)* **rabble**
ဝရုန်းသုန်းကား ပြေးလွှားသောင်းကျန်းခြင်း wa-ronesone-karr pyay-lwar saungg-kyannchinn *(v.)* **rampage**
ဝရုန်းသုန်းကား ပြေးလွှားသောင်းကျန်းသည် wa-ronesone-karr pyay-lwar saungg-kyannsai *(n.)* **rampage**
ဝရုန်းသုန်းကား ဖြစ်ခြင်း wa-yone-tone-gar-phit-chin *(n.)* **pandemonium**
ဝရုန်းသုန်းကားနိုင်သော နေရာ wa-yone-tone-kar-nai-taw-nay-yar *(n.)* **madhouse**
ဝရုန်းသုန်းကားအခြေအနေ waronesonekarraachayaanay *(n.)* **turmoil**
ဝလွန်းသော၊ ဝန်ပိုသော wa-lwan-taw, wan-po-taw *(adj.)* **overweight**
ဝဝကစ်ကစ် wa-wa-kit-kit *(adj.)* **chubby**
ဝဝလုံးလုံး၊ အဖုပုံစံရှိသော wa-wa-lone-lone, a-phu-pone-san-shi-taw *(adj.)* **bulbous**
ဝသော wa-taw *(adj.)* **fat**
ဝှက်စာဖော်နည်း၊ ရေးနည်း hwat-sar-phaw-nee, yay-nee *(n.)* **cryptography**
ဝှက်စာဖော်သည် hwat-sar-phaw-the *(v.)* **decipher**
ဝှက်စာဖော်သူ hwat-sar-phaw-thu *(n.)* **decoder**
ဝှက်ထားသော လက်နက်၊ အစားအစာ၊ ငွေ hwat-htar-taw-lat-nat-a-sar-a-sar-ngwe *(n.)* **cache**
ဝှီးခနဲ မြည်၍ သွားသည် whaee hkanell myi swarrsai *(v.)* **whiz**
ဝှေ့ရမ်းသည် hwai-yan-the *(v.)* **brandish**
ဝှေ့သည်၊ ခတ်သည် hwai-the, khat-the *(v.)* **butt**
ဝှေးစေ့ wai-say *(n.)* **bollocks**
ဝှေးစေ့ဖယ်ရှားသည် wai-say-phal-shar-the *(n.)* **demasculinization**
ဝါး war *(n.)* **bamboo**
ဝါးလုံးကွဲ war-lone-kwal *(n.)* **outburst**
ဝါးသည် war-the *(v.)* **chew**
ဝါကျ၊ စီရင်ချက် warkya , serinchet *(n.)* **sentence**
ဝါကျဖွဲ့ထုံး warkya hpwahltone *(n.)* **syntax**
ဝါကြင့်ကြင့် war kyint kyint *(adj.)* **yellowish**
ဝါစက war sa-ka *(n.)* **predicate**
ဝါဒဖြန့်ချိရေးသမား war-da hpyant chae rayysamarr *(n.)* **propagandist**
ဝါဒဖြန့်ခြင်းလက္ခဏာရှိသော ward hpya ant hkyinn lakhkanar-shisaw *(adj.)* **polemic**
ဝါဒဖြန့်မှု war-da hpyant-mhu *(n.)* **propaganda**
ဝါရင့်ခြင်း၊ ရာထူး၊ အသက်အားဖြင့် မြင့်သူ warrint chinn , rarhtuu , aasaat aarrhpyint myintsuu *(n.)* **seniority**
ဝါရှာ warshar *(n.)* **washer**
ဝါရော်သည် war raw sai *(v.)* **yellow**
ဝါသနာ war-ta-nar *(n.)* **hobby**
ဝါသနာပါ၍ လုပ်သော အလုပ် war-sa-nar-par-ywe-lote-saw-aa-lote *(n.)* **pastime**
ဝါသနာအိုး wa-ta-nar-oh *(n.)* **devotee**

ဝါသော war-saw *(adj.)* **yellow**

ဝိညာဉ်၊ လိပ်ပြာ၊ စိတ်ထား wit-nyin, late-pyaar, satehtarr *(n.)* **soul**

ဝိဘတ် wi-bhaat *(n.)* **preposition**

ဝိရယနဗုဒ္ဓဘာသာကို ဖော်ပြသော wi r y nabuddhabharsarko hpawpyasaw *(adj.)* **tantric**

ဝိရောဓိ wi-raw-dhi *(n.)* **paradox**

ဝိရောဓိဖြစ်သော wi-raw-dhi-hpyit-saw *(adj.)* **paradoxical**

ဝိသေသလက္ခဏာ wi-tay-ta-lat-kha-nar *(n.)* **hallmark**

ဝိုက်ကွင်း wite-kwin *(n.)* **parenthesis**

ဝိုင်းထားသည် winehtarrsai *(v.)* **ring**

ဝိုင်းပတ်လျက် wine paatlyet *(adv.)* **round**

ဝိုင်းပယ်သည် wine-pal-tai *(v.)* **ostracize**

ဝိုင်းဝန်းကူညီမှု winewaannkuunyemhu *(n.)* **support**

ဝိုင်းသည်၊ လုံးသည် wine sai , lone-sai *(v.)* **round**

ဝိုင်းသော wine-taw *(adj.)* **circular**

ဝိုင်းသော၊ ဝကစ်သော wine saw , w kaitsaw *(adj.)* **round**

ဝိုင်ကလပ်ခွက် wai-ka-lat-khwat *(n.)* **goblet**

ဝိုင်ယာနှင့် ပူးချည်သည် wine yarnint puu chaisai *(v.)* **wire**

ဝိုင်ယာလက် wine yarlaat *(adj.)* **wireless**

ဝိုင်အရက် wine aa-raat *(n.)* **wine**

ဝီစကီအနည်းငယ် wi-sa-ki-a-nae-ngal *(n.)* **dram**

ဝီစကီအရက် we-sa-ke aa-raat *(n.)* **whisky**

ဝီစီ wese *(n.)* **whistle**

ဝေ့ခနဲ ရသော အနံ့ wae hkanell rasaw aanan *(n.)* **whiff**

ဝေ့စကုတ်အင်္ကျီ waist-kote aainkyae *(n.)* **waistcoat**

ဝေ့သည်၊ လည်သည် wae sai , laisai *(v.)* **swirl**

ဝေးကွာလျက် way-kwar-lyat *(adv.)* **apart**

ဝေးကွာသော way-kwar-taw *(adj.)* **distant**

ဝေးလံသော wayy lansaw *(adj.)* **remote**

ဝေးဝေး way-way *(adv.)* **afield**

ဝေးသော way-taw *(adj.)* **far**

ဝေခွဲမရခြင်း way hkwal ma-ra-chinn *(n.)* **quandary**

ဝေခွဲမရဖြစ်သည် wai-kwal-ma-ya-phit-taw *(v.)* **confound**

ဝေစု way-su *(n.)* **allotment**

ဝေစု၊ ရှယ်ယာ way su, shalyar *(n.)* **share**

ဝေဒနာ wai-da-nar *(n.)* **misery**

ဝေဒနာခံစားနေရသည် way-da-nar-khan-sar-nay-ya-the *(v.)* **ail**

ဝေဒနာခံစားရသည် waydanarhkansarrrasai *(v.)* **suffer**

ဝေပုံကျသည် wai-pon-kya-sai *(v.)* **proportion**

ဝေပေးသည်၊ ထုတ်ပေးသည် sai-pay-the, htoke-pay-the *(v.)* **dispense**

ဝေဖန်ချက် wai-phan-chat *(n.)* **criticism**

ဝေဖန်ချက်၊ မှတ်ချက် wayhpaanchet , mhaatchet *(n.)* **remark**

ဝေဖန်ပြစ်တင်သည် wai-phan-pyit-tin-the *(v.)* **chastise**

ဝေဖန်ပိုင်းခြားနိုင်စွမ်း wai-phan-pai-char-nai-swan *(n.)* **judgement**

ဝေဖန်သည် wai-phan-the *(v.)* **criticize**

ဝေဖန်သည်၊ ရှုတ်ချသည် wai-phan-the, shoke-cha-the *(v.)* **decry**

ဝေဖန်သူ wai-phan-thu *(n.)* **critic**

ဝေလငါး way-la-ngar *(n.)* **orca**

ဝေလငါး၏ အထက်မေးရိုးမှ ရသော အရိုးကဲ့သို့ အမျှင် way-la-ngar-ei-a-htet-may-yoe-ma-ya-taw-a-yoe-kae-doe-a-hmyin *(n.)* **baleen**

ဝေသည်၊ မျှသည် way sai, mya-sai *(v.)* **share**

ဝေါခနဲ မြည်၍ ဖြတ်သွားသံ waw hka-nell myi-ywe hpyat-swarrsan *(n.)* **zoom**

ဝေါယဉ် waw-yin *(n.)* **palanquin**

ဝေါဟာရ waw-har-ra *(n.)* **vocabulary**

ဝေါဟာရစာရင်း wor-har-ya-sa-yin *(n.)* **lexicon**

ဝေါဟာရဗေဒ waw-har-ra-bay-da *(n.)* **philology**

ဝေါဟာရဗေဒနှင့် သက်ဆိုင်သော waw-har-ra-bay-da-nint-saat-sine-saw *(adj.)* **philological**

ဝေါဟာရဗေဒပညာရှင် waw-har-ra-bay-da-pa-nyar-shin *(n.)* **philologist**

ဝေါဟာရစာရင်း wor-ha-ya-sa-yin *(n.)* **concordance**

ဝဲ wal *(adj.)* **left**

ဝဲ၊ ဝဲကတော့ well , well-ka-tot *(n.)* **whirlpool**

ဝဲသံ wal-than *(n.)* **accent**

ဝဲသံပါသည် wal-than-par-the *(v.)* **accent**

သံ tan *(n.)* **iron**

သံကြိုး၊ နှောင်ကြိုး tan-kyo, naung-kyo *(n.pl.)* **bonds**

သံကြိုးစာ sankyaoesar *(n.)* **telegram**

သံခင်းတမန်ခင်း tan-khin-ta-man-khin *(n.)* **diplomacy**

သံခမောက်ပုံအိမ်ငယ် tan-kha-mauk-pon-eain-nge *(n.)* **igloo**

သံချပ်ကာတပ် sanchautkartat *(n.)* **trooper**

သံချေးတက်ခြင်း san-chay-taat-chinn *(n.)* **oxidization**

သံချေးတက်သည် sanchaayytaatsai *(v.)* **rust**

သံချေးတက်သော sanchaayytaatsaw *(adj.)* **rusty**

သံချေးရောင် san chaayyraung *(n.)* **rust**

သံခွာရိုက်သည် san hkwar ritesai *(v.)* **shoe**

သံစုံခေါင်းလောင်းသံ tan-sone-khaung-laung-than *(n.)* **chime**

သံစုံတီးဝိုင်း tan-sone-tee-wine *(n.)* **orchestra**

သံစုံတီးဝိုင်းအတွက် တေးသွား san sone teewineaatwat tayyswarr *(n.)* **symphony**

သံစုံသီးဝိုင်းဆိုင်ရာ tan-sone-tee-wine-sine-rar *(adj.)* **orchestral**

သံဆူးကြိုး tan-sue-kyo *(n.)* **barbed wire**

သံတမန် tan-ta-man *(n.)* **diplomat**

သံတမန်ရေးရာ tan-ta-man-yay-yar *(adj.)* **diplomatic**

သံတူးရွင်း tan-ta-ywin *(n.)* **crowbar**

သံပြိုင်အပိုဒ် tan-pyaing-a-pite *(n.)* **chorus**

သံပိုင်းမော်ကွန်း tan-pai-maw-gun *(n.)* **epic**

သံဖြူဒြပ်စင် san hpyuu dyatsin *(n.)* **tin**

သံမဏိ sanmani *(n.)* **steel**

သံမှိုစွဲသည် san mhao swalsai *(v.)* **tack**

သံမှိုနှက်သည် san mhao nhaatsai *(v.)* **rivet**

သံမှူး tan-muu *(n.)* **attache**

သံယောဇဉ် tan-yaw-zin *(n.)* **attachment**

သံရုံး tan-yone *(n.)* **embassy**

သံလက် san-laat *(n.)* **trowel**

သံလွင်သီး tan-lwin-tee *(n.)* **olive**

သံလိုက် tan-lite *(n.)* **magnet**

သံလိုက်ကျောက် tan-lite-kyauk *(n.)* **loadstone**

သံလိုက်ဓာတ် tan-lite-dat *(n.)* **magnetism**

သံလိုက်ဓာတ်ဖယ်ရှားသည် tan-lite-dat-phal-shar-the *(v.)* **demagnetize**

သံလိုက်သတ္တိ tan-lite-tat-ti *(adj.)* **magnetic**

သံလိုက်အိမ်မြှောင် tan-lite-ain-hmyaung *(n.)* **compass**

သံသယ tan-da-ya *(n.)* **doubt**

သံသယဖြစ်ဖွယ် sansayahpyithpwal *(adj.)* **suspicious**

သံသယဖြစ်သည် tan-da-ya-phit-the *(v.)* **doubt**

သံသယဖြစ်သည်၊ မှားယွင်းပေးသည် tan-ta-ya-phit-the, mar-ywin-pay-the *(v.)* **misgive**

သံသယရှိသော tan-ta-ya-shi-taw *(adj.)* **dubious**

သံသရဖြစ်ဖွယ်ရာ san sa ra hpyit-hpwalrar *(adj.)* **questionable**

သံသရာလည်နေသော tan-ta-yar-lal-nay-taw *(adj.)* **cyclic**

သံအမတ် tan-a-mat *(n.)* **ambassador**

သံအမတ်ကြီးခင်ဗျား tan-a-mat-kyi-khin-myar *(n.)* **excellency**

သကြား sa-kyarr *(n.)* **sugar**

သကြားထည့်သည် sa kyarr htae-sai *(v.)* **sugar**

သကြားရည် sa kyar-rai *(n.)* **syrup**

သကြားလွှာ tha-kyar-hlwar *(n.)* **frosting**

သကြားလုံးအမာ ta-gyar-lone-a-mar *(n.)* **caramel**

သကာ ta-kar *(n.)* **molasses**

သကုဏဗေဒပညာ ta-ku-na-bay-da-pyin-nyar *(n.)* **ornithology**

သကုဏဗေဒပညာရှင် ta-ku-na-bay-da-pyin-nyar-shin *(n.)* **ornithologist**

သက္ကလတ်အကြမ်းစား sak ka laat aakyamsarr *(n.)* **serge**

သက်ကြီး thet-kyi *(adj.)* **elderly**

သက်ကြီးပု thet-kyi-pyu *(n.)* **midget**

သက်ကြီးရွယ်အို tat-kyee-rwal-ao *(n.)* **old**

သက်ငယ်ဖြင့် မိုးသည် saat ngaahlpyang moesai *(v.)* **thatch**

သက်ငယ်အမိုး saat ngaal aamoe *(n.)* **thatch**

သက်စောင့်ဆေး tat-saunt-say *(n.)* **elixir**

သက်ဆိုင်မှု saat-sinemhu *(n.)* **relevance**

သက်ဆိုင်သည်၊ စိုးရိမ်သည် thet-sai-the, soe-yein-the *(v.)* **concern**

သက်ဆိုင်သော thet-saing-taw *(adj.)* **applicable**

သက်ဆိုင်သော saat-sine-saw *(adj.)* **pertinent**

သက်ညှာခြင်း tat-nyar-chin *(n.)* **clemency**

သက်ညှာခွင့်ပေးသည် saatnyhar hkwintpayysai *(v.)* **waive**

သက်ညှာမှု tat-nyar-mu *(n.)* **leniency**

သက်ညှာသော tat-nyar-taw *(adj.)* **lenient**

သက်တံ့ saat-tan *(n.)* **rainbow**

သက်တမ်းကုန်ဆုံးခြင်း thet-tan-kone-sone-chin *(n.)* **expiry**

သက်တမ်းကုန်ဆုံးသည် thet-tan-kone-sone-the *(v.)* **expire**

သက်တမ်းလွန်သွားသည် thet-tan-lun-twar-the *(v.)* **lapse**

သက်တူ saat-tuu *(n.)* **peer**

သက်တောင့်သက်သာ thet-taunt-thet-tar *(adj.)* **effortless**

သက်တောင့်သက်သာ ရှိသော tat-taunt-tat-tar-shi-taw *(adj.)* **hospitable**
သက်ပြင်း saatpyinn *(n.)* **sigh**
သက်ပြင်းချသည် saatpyinn chasai *(v.)* **sigh**
သက်မွေးလုပ်ငန်း thet-mway-lote-ngan *(n.)* **career**
သက်မဲ့ thet-mae *(adj.)* **inanimate**
သက်ရှိ tat-shi *(n.)* **organism**
သက်ရှိကင်းမဲ့သော thet-shi-kin-mae-taw *(adj.)* **abiotic**
သက်ရှိနှင့်ဆိုင်သော ဒြပ်ပေါင်းတစ်မျိုး thet-shi-nint-saing-taw-drat-paung-ta-myo *(n.)* **acene**
သက်ရှိနေထိုင်သော အရည်ပျစ်လာပြီးမှ အစပြုသော သက်ရှိ စုဖွဲ့ဖြစ်ပေါ်ခြင်း thet-shi-nay-htine-taw-a-yay-pyit-lar-pi-ma-a-sa-pyu-taw-thet-shi-su-phwe-phit-paw-chin *(n.)* **osmobiosis**
သက်ရှိနေထိုင်သော အရည်ပျစ်လာပြီးမှ အစပြုသော သက်ရှိ စုဖွဲ့ဖြစ်ပေါ်ခြင်းဆိုင်ရာ thet-shi-nay-htine-taw-a-yay-pyit-lar-pi-ma-a-sa-pyu-taw-thet-shi-su-phwe-phit-paw-chin-sine-yar *(adj.)* **osmobiotic**
သက်ရှိမျိုးဆက်နှင့် ဖွံ့ဖြိုးခြင်း thet-shi-myo-sat-nint-phwint-phyoe-chin *(n.)* **ontogeny**
သက်ရှိမျိုးဆက်နှင့် ဖွံ့ဖြိုးခြင်းနှင့် ဆိုင်သော thet-shi-myo-sat-nint-phwint-phyoe-chin-nint-sai-taw *(adj.)* **ontogenic**
သက်ရှိအင်္ဂါ၏ သိပ္ပံနည်းကျဖွဲ့စည်းပုံနှင့် လုပ်ငန်းဆောင်တာ thet-shi-inn-gar-ei-tate-pan-nee-kya-phwe-see-pone-nint-lote-ngan-saung-tar-phaw-pya-chat *(n.)* **organography**
သက်လွှတ်သော toke-hlut-taw *(adj.)* **ejaculatory**
သက်ဝင်လှုပ်ရှားနည်းပညာ thet-win-lote-shar-nee-pyin-nyar *(n.)* **animation**
သက်ဝင်လှုပ်ရှားသည် thet-win-lote-shar-the *(v.)* **animate**
သက်သက် saat-saat *(adj.)* **rank**
သက်သာခြင်း thet-tar-chin *(n.)* **alleviation**
သက်သာစေခြင်း thet-tar-say-chin *(n.)* **mitigation**
သက်သာစေသည် thet-tar-say-the *(v.)* **alleviate**
သက်သာရာရခြင်း saatsar-rar-rachinn *(n.)* **relief**
သက်သာရာရစေသည် saatsar-rar rasaysai *(v.)* **relieve**
သက်သေ saat-say *(n.)* **proof**
သက်သေခံကတ်ပြား tat-tay-khan-kat-pyar *(n.)* **identity card**
သက်သေခံချက် saatsayhkanchet *(n.)* **testimony**
သက်သေခံသည် saatsayhkansai *(v.)* **testify**
သက်သေထူခြင်း saatsay htuuchinn *(n.)* **vindication**
သက်သေပြခြင်း saatsay pyachinn *(n.)* **substantiation**
သက်သေပြသည် saat-say-pya-sai *(v.)* **prove**
သက်သေပြုသည် thet-tay-pyu-the *(v.)* **attest**
သက်သေပေးသူ thet-tay-pay-thu *(n.)* **deponent**
သက်သေဖြစ်သည်၊ ညွှန်ပြသည်၊ အမိန့်ပေးသည် thet-tay-phit-the, nyun-pya-the, a-maint-pay-the *(v.)* **bespeak**
သက်သောင့်သက်သာ သေဆုံးခွင့်ပေးသည် tat-taunt-tat-tar-tay-sone-khwint-pay-the *(v.)* **euthanize**
သက်သောင့်သက်သာ မရှိသော saat saunt-saat-sar mashisaw *(adj.)* **uncomfortable**
သက်သောင့်သက်သာ ရှိခြင်း tat-taunt-tat-tar-shi-chin *(n.)* **comfort**

သက်သောင့်သက်သာ ရှိသော tat-taunt-tat-tar-shi-taw *(adj.)* **comfortable**
သက်ဦးဆံပိုင်စနစ် thet-oo-san-paing-sa-nit *(n.)* **autocracy**
သက်ဦးဆံပိုင်ဘုရင် thet-oo-san-pai-ba-yin *(n.)* **despot**
သက်ဦးဆံပိုင်မင်း thet-oo-san-paing-sa-min *(n.)* **autocrat**
သက်ဦးဆံပိုင်အုပ်ချုပ်သော thet-oo-san-paing-oat-choke-taw *(adj.)* **autocratic**
သခွားသီး ta-kwar-thee *(n.)* **cucumber**
သင့်လျော်သည်၊ မှန်ကန်သည် tint-lyaw-the, hman-kan-the *(v.)* **fit**
သင့်တင့်လျောက်ပတ်ယဉ်ကျေးဖွယ်ရာ ရှိခြင်း tint-tint-shaut-pat-yin-kyay-phwal-yar-shi-chin *(n.)* **decency**
သင့်တော်ခြင်း tint-taw-chin *(n.)* **advisability**
သင့်တော်လျော်ကန်သော tint-taw-lyaw-kan-taw *(adj.)* **expedient**
သင့်တော်သော tint-taw-taw *(adj.)* **advisable**
သင့်တော်သော အရည်အချင်း tint-taw-thaw-a-yay-a-chin *(n.)* **credential**
သင့်မြတ်ခြင်း tint-myat-chin *(n.)* **concord**
သင့်မြတ်စွာ saint-myat-swar *(adv.)* **pat**
သင့်ရုံမျှ tint-yone-mya *(n.)* **modesty**
သင့်လျော်စွာ sint lyawswar *(adv.)* **properly**
သင့်လျော်မှု sint lyawmhu *(n.)* **suitability**
သင့်လျော်သည် sint lyawsai *(v.)* **suit**
သင့်လျော်သော sint lyawsaw *(adj.)* **proper**
သင့်သည် sintsai *(v.)* **should**
သင်းကွပ်ခြင်း thin-kwut-chin *(n.)* **gelding**
သင်းကွပ်သော thin-kwut-taw *(adj.)* **gelded**
သင်းပြီးနွား tin-pi-nwar *(n.)* **bullock**
သင်းသည် thin-the *(v.)* **geld**
သင်းအုပ်ဆရာ sin-aote-sa-rar *(n.)* **parson**
သင်ကြားနည်းပညာ sin-kyarr-nee-pa-nyar *(n.)* **pedagogy**
သင်ကိုယ်တိုင် sin-ko-tine *(pr.)* **yourself**
သင်ခန်းစာ tin-khan-sar *(n.)* **lesson**
သင်တန်း sintaann *(n.)* **training**
သင်တန်းသား sintaannsarr *(n.)* **trainee**
သင်တိုင်း sintine *(n.)* **smock**
သင်တုန်းဓား sin tone dharr *(n.)* **razor**
သင်တုန်းဓားဖြင့် ရိတ်ခြင်း sintone dharrhpyint ratechinn *(n.)* **shave**
သင်တုန်းဓားဖြင့် ရိတ်သည် sintone dharrhpyint ratesai *(v.)* **shave**
သင်ပြနိုင်သော sin pyaninesaw *(adj.)* **teacheable**
သင်ပုန်းကျောက် sin ponekyawt *(n.)* **slate**
သင်ပုန်းကြီး sin-pone-kyee *(n.)* **primer**
သင်ပေးသည် sinpayysai *(v.)* **teach**
သင်ရိုးညွှန်းတမ်း tin-yoe-nyoon-tan *(n.)* **curriculum**
သင်ရိုးမာတိကာ sin-roemar[tikar *(n.)* **syllabus**
သင်သည်၊ လေ့ကျင့်သည် sinsai, lae kyintsai *(v.)* **school**
သင်္ကန်းထောင့်ချိုးဆက် tin-khan-htaunt-choe-sat *(n.)* **mitre**
သကြိန်အမြောက်ပစ်ခြင်း tha-gyan-a-myauk-phaut-chin *(n.)* **bravado**
သကြိန်အမြောက်ဖောက်သည် tha-gyan-a-myauk-phaut-the *(v.)* **bluster**
သင်္ကာမကင်း sin kar ma-kinn *(v.)* **suspect**
သင်္ကာရှင်းသည် sin kar shinn-sai *(v.)* **vindicate**

သင်္ကေတ sin kay-ta *(n.)* **symbol**

သင်္ကေတစနစ် tin-kay-ta-sa-nit *(n.)* **notation**

သင်္ကေတဖြစ်သော sin kay tahpyitsaw *(adj.)* **symbolic**

သင်္ကေတဝှက်စာ၊ ကိုဒဥပဒေ၊ ကျင့်ဝတ်စည်းကမ်း tin-kay-ta-hwat-sar, ko-da-oo-pa-day, kyint-wit-see-kan *(n.)* **code**

သင်္ချာ tin-char *(adj.)* **mathematical**

သင်္ချာပညာ tin-char-pyin-nyar *(n.)* **mathematics**

သင်္ချာပညာရှင် tin-char-pyin-nyar-shin *(n.)* **mathematician**

သင်္ချိုင်း tin-gyai *(n.)* **cemetery**

သင်္ချိုင်းဂူ sain hkyaineguu *(n.)* **sepulture**

သင်္ချိုင်းစာ thin-gyai-sar *(n.)* **epitaph**

သင်္ဘော sinbhaw *(n.)* **ship**

သင်္ဘော တည်ဆောက်သူ sinbhaw tai-soutsuu *(n.)* **shipbuilder**

သင်္ဘော ရေကြောင်းနှင့် ဆိုင်သော tin-baw-yay-kyaung-nint-sai-taw *(adj.)* **nautic(al)**

သင်္ဘော၊ လေယာဉ်ဖြင့် ပို့သော ကုန်ပစ္စည်း tin-baw-lay-yin-phit-poe-taw-kone-pyit-see *(n.)* **cargo**

သင်္ဘောကပ္ပတိန် sainbhawkappatein *(n.)* **shipmaster**

သင်္ဘောကျင်း sinbhawkyinn *(n.)* **shipyard**

သင်္ဘောကျင်းကြီးကြပ် tin-baw-kyin-kyi-kyat *(n.)* **dockmaster**

သင်္ဘောကျင်းအလုပ်သမား tin-baw-kyin-a-lote-ta-mar *(n.)* **dockworker**

သင်္ဘောကုန်းပတ် tin-baw-kone-pat *(n.)* **deck**

သင်္ဘောခွေး sinbhawhkway *(n.)* **spaniel**

သင်္ဘောစားပွဲထိုး၊ ပစ္စည်းထိန်း၊ ကြီးကြပ်သူ၊ ရိက္ခာမှူး sinbhaw sarrpwahltoe , pyit-saee htein , kyeekyaut suu , rikhkarmhauu *(n.)* **steward**

သင်္ဘောတစ်စီးစာ အပြည့် sinbhaw taitseesar aapyi *(n.)* **shipload**

သင်္ဘောတွင် အတူ လုပ်ဖော်ကိုင်ဖက် sinbhawtwin aatuu lotehpawkinehpaat *(n.)* **shipmate**

သင်္ဘောနှင့် ထောက်ပံ့ပေးသည် sainbhawnhang htoutpanpayysai *(adj.)* **shipped**

သင်္ဘောနောက်ကျခြင်း tin-baw-naut-kya-chin *(n.)* **demurrage**

သင်္ဘောပျက် sinbhawpyet *(n.)* **wreck**

သင်္ဘောပျက်ခြင်း sinbhawpyetchinn *(n.)* **shipwreck**

သင်္ဘောပျက်ရာတွင် ပါသည် sinbhaw pyetrartwin parsai *(v.)* **shipwreck**

သင်္ဘောပျက်သည် sinbhawpyetsai *(v.)* **wreck**

သင်္ဘောပိုင်ရှင် sinbhawpineshin *(n.)* **shipowner**

သင်္ဘောပေါ်၌ ကျင့်သုံးသော sinbhawpaw kyintsonesaw *(adj.)* **shipboard**

သင်္ဘောပေါ်တင်သော sainbhaw pawtainsaw *(adj.)* **shipborne**

သင်္ဘောပေါ်တွင် ရှိနေသော sainbhawpawtwin shinaysaw *(n.)* **shipboard**

သင်္ဘောများဖြင့် သယ်ဆောင်သော sinbhaw-myarrhpyint saalsaungsaw *(adj.)* **seaborne**

သင်္ဘောမဟူရာ thin-baw-ma-hu-yar *(n.)* **agate**

သင်္ဘောသား sinbhawsarr *(n.)* **sailor**

သစ္စာခံ tit-sar-khan *(n.)* **loyalist**

သစ္စာခံခြင်း thit-sar-khan-chin *(n.)* **allegiance**

သစ္စာခံယူခြင်း tit-sar-khan-yu-chin *(n.)* **loyalty**

သစ္စာစောင့်သိခြင်း tit-sar-saunt-ti-chin *(n.)* **fealty**
သစ္စာဖောက် sit-sar-hpout *(n.)* **traitor**
သစ္စာဖောက်ခြင်း tit-sar-phaut-chin *(n.)* **betrayal**
သစ္စာဖောက်မှု sit-sarhpoutmhu *(n.)* **treachery**
သစ္စာဖောက်သည် tit-sar-phaut-the *(v.)* **betray**
သစ္စာဖောက်သော sit-sar-hpout-saw *(adj.)* **treacherous**
သစ္စာမရှိခြင်း tit-sar-ma-shi-chin *(n.)* **insincerity**
သစ္စာမရှိသော tit-sar-ma-shi-taw *(adj.)* **disloyal**
သစ္စာမဲ့မှု sit-sar-mae-mhu *(n.)* **perfidy**
သစ္စာရှိခြင်း tit-sar-shi-chin *(n.)* **fidelity**
သစ္စာရှိသော tit-sar-shi-taw *(adj.)* **faithful**
သစ် sit *(n.)* **timber**
သစ်ကတိုး tit-ka-toe *(n.)* **cedar**
သစ်ကျုတ် tite-kyoke *(n.)* **cheetah**
သစ်ကြံပိုးခေါက် tit-kyan-poe-khaut *(n.)* **cinnamon**
သစ်ကြားသီး sit kyarrsee *(n.)* **walnut**
သစ်ကုလားအုပ် tit-ka-lar-oak *(n.)* **giraffe**
သစ်ခက် sit-hkat *(n.)* **twig**
သစ်ခေါက်၊ ဟောင်းသံ tit-khaut, haung-tan *(n.)* **bark**
သစ်ငုတ်တို sit ngote-to *(n.)* **stump**
သစ်စက် sitsaat *(n.)* **sawmill**
သစ်တော sittaw *(n.)* **woods**
သစ်တော ဖုံးလွှမ်းနေသော နယ်မြေ sittaw hpone lwhamnaysaw naalmyay *(n.)* **woodland**

သစ်တောပညာ tit-taw-pyin-nyar *(n.)* **forestry**
သစ်တောပျိုးထောင်သည် tit-taw-pyo-htaung-the *(v.)* **afforest**
သစ်တောပြုန်းစေသည် tit-taw-pyone-say-the *(v.)* **deforest**
သစ်တောပြုန်းတီးခြင်း tit-taw-pyone-tee-chin *(n.)* **deforestation**
သစ်တောသစ်ပင်များကို စိုက်ပျိုးသူ saittaw saitpainmyarrko hcitepyoesuu *(n.)* **sylviculturist**
သစ်တော်သီး sit-tawtsee *(n.)* **pear**
သစ်နံကိုင်းပင် sit-nan-kine-pin *(n.)* **wormwood**
သစ်နက် sait-naat *(n.)* **panther**
သစ်ပင် sit-pin *(n.)* **plant**
သစ်ပင်ချိုင်သည် tit-pin-chai-the *(v.)* **lop**
သစ်ပင်ချုံနွယ်ထူသော နေရာ tit-pin-chon-nwe-htu-taw-nay-yar *(n.)* **coppice**
သစ်ပင်ခုတ်လှဲသည် tit-pin-khote-hlae-the *(v.)* **log**
သစ်ပင်မှ အရွက်ခြွေသည် thit-pin-ma-a-ywet-chway-the *(v.)* **exfoliate**
သစ်ရည်၊ ပင်ရည်၊ အစေး sit rai , pin rai , aasayy *(n.)* **sap**
သစ်ရွက် thit-ywet *(n.)* **foliage**
သစ်ရွက်ခြွေဓာတုပစ္စည်း tit-ywet-chway-dar-tu-pyit-see *(n.)* **defoliant**
သစ်ရွက်ဆွေးမြေဩဇာ tat-ywet-sway-myay-aw-zar *(n.)* **compost**
သစ်ရွက်နှင့် ဆိုင်သော thit-ywet-nint-sai-taw *(adj.)* **foliate**
သစ်ရွက်များကို ကြွေစေသည် tit-ywet-myar-ko-kyway-say-the *(v.)* **defoliate**
သစ်လုံး tit-lone *(n.)* **log**
သစ်သား sit-sarr *(n.)* **wood**

သစ်သားနှင့် လုပ်သော sit-sarr-nint lotesaw *(adj.)* **wooden**

သစ်သားပြားဖြင့် ကာရံသည် saitsarr pyarr-hpyint kar-ransai *(v.)* **plank**

သစ်သားပေါ်တွင် ရှိသော tit-tar-paw-twin-shi-taw *(adj.)* **xylophilous**

သစ်သားအဖု tit-tar-a-phu *(n.)* **gnarl**

သစ်သီး tit-thee *(n.)* **fruit**

သစ်သီးခြံ tit-tee-chan *(n.)* **orchard**

သစ်သီးရည် tit-tee-yay *(n.)* **juice**

သစ်အယ်ပင် tit-al-pin *(n.)* **chestnut**

သညာထားသည် sanyarhtarrsai *(v.)* **symbolize**

သည့်နေရာတွင် saeetnayrartwin *(adv.)* **wherein**

သည့်အရပ် seet-aa-rat *(conj.)* **where**

သည်းခံခြင်း saeehkanchinn *(n.)* **toleration**

သည်းခံနိုင်သော saeehkanninesaw *(adj.)* **tolerant**

သည်းခံရခက်သော saee-hkan-ra-hkaatsaw *(adj.)* **trying**

သည်းခံသည် saeehkansai *(v.)* **tolerate**

သည်းခံသည်၊ အောင့်အည်းသည် the-khan-the, aung-ae-the *(v.)* **forbear**

သည်းခြေရည် tae-chay-yay *(n.)* **bile**

သည်းညည်းခံသည်၊ စိတ်ရှည်သည် see nyee hkan sai , sateshi sai *(v.)* **stomach**

သည်းထိတ်ခြင်း sae htate-chinn *(n.)* **suspense**

သည်းမခံနိုင်သော see ma hkan-ninesaw *(adj.)* **unbearable**

သည်းမခံသော tee-ma-khan-taw *(adj.)* **intolerant**

သည်ကစ၍ the-ka-sa-ywe *(adv.)* **since**

သည်နှင့် sinint *(conj.)* **whereupon**

သဏ္ဍာန်လုပ် ta-dan-lote *(adj.)* **mock**

သဏ္ဍာန်လုပ်သရုပ်တူခြင်း san daran lote sarote tuuchinn *(n.)* **verisimilitude**

သတင်း ta-din *(n.)* **news**

သတင်းစကား satinnsakarr *(n. pl.)* **tidings**

သတင်းစာ ta-din-sar *(n.)* **newspaper**

သတင်းစာပညာ ta-din-sar-pyin-nyar *(n.)* **journalism**

သတင်းဆိုးဖြင့် ကျော်ကြားသော ta-tin-soe-phyint-kyaw-kyar-taw *(adj.)* **infamous**

သတင်းဆောင်းပါးတိုရေးသည် sa-tinn-saungg-parr to-rayy-sai *(v.)* **profile**

သတင်းထောက် sa-tinn-htout *(n.)* **reporter**

သတင်းပေး ta-din-pay *(n.)* **informer**

သတင်းပေါက်ကြားမှု၊ ယိုစိမ့်မှု ta-din-pauk-kyar-mu, yoe-seint-mu *(n.)* **leakage**

သတင်းဝေဖန်ချက် sa-tinn-way-hpaanchet *(n.)* **press**

သတင်းအချက်အလက် ta-din-a-chat-a-lat *(n.)* **information**

သတိ tha-di *(n.)* **caution**

သတိကင်းမဲ့သော ta-di-kin-mae-taw *(adj.)* **insensible**

သတိကင်းမဲ့သော အခြေအနေ ta-di-kin-mae-taw-a-chay-a-nay *(n.)* **insensibility**

သတိထားသည် ta-di-htar-the *(v.)* **beware**

သတိပြန်လည်လာသည် sati pyanlailarsai *(v.)* **revive**

သတိပြုဖွယ် ta-ti-pyu-hpwal *(adj.)* **noteworthy**

သတိပြုမိခြင်း tha-di-pyu-mi-chin *(n.)* **awakening**

သတိပြုမိသည် ta-ti-pyu-mi-te *(v.)* **notice**

သတိပြုမိသော tha-di-pyu-mi-taw *(adj.)* **aware**

သတိပေးချက် satipayychet *(n.)* **warning**

သတိပေးချက်၊ တပ်လှန့်ခြင်း tha-di-pay-chat, tat-hlant-chin *(n.)* **alarm**

သတိပေးသည် satipayysai *(v.)* **warn**

သတိပေးသော tha-di-pay-taw *(adj.)* **cautionary**

သတိမပြုမိသော sa-ti-mapyumisaw *(adj.)* **unaware**

သတိမမူမိခြင်း ta-ti-ma-mu-mi-chinn *(n.)* **oversight**

သတိမမူသော ta-ti-ma-mu-taw *(adj.)* **oblivious**

သတိမူမိသည် sa-ti-muu-mi-sai *(v.)* **perceive**

သတိမေ့မြောနေသော ta-di-mae-myaw-nay-taw *(adj.)* **comatose**

သတိမဲ့သော ta-di-mae-taw *(adj.)* **mindless**

သတိရခြင်း၊ အမှတ်တရပစ္စည်း sati-rachinn , aamhaat-tarapyit-saee *(n.)* **remembrance**

သတိရသည် ta-di-ya-the *(v.)* **miss**

သတိရှိသော sati-shi-saw *(adj.)* **wary**

သတိလစ်သည် ta-di-lit-the *(v.)* **faint**

သတိလစ်ဟင်းမှု ta-di-lit-hin-mu *(n.)* **lapse**

သတိလွတ်ခြင်း ta-ti-lwat-chinn *(n.)* **oblivion**

သတို့သမီး tha-doe-tha-mee *(adj.)* **bridal**

သတို့သမီးက သတို့သားဘက်ပေးရသော အတွင်းပစ္စည်း ta-do-ta-mee-ka-ta-do-tar-bat-pay-ya-taw-a-twin-pyit-see *(n.)* **dowery**

သတို့သား the-doe-tar *(n.)* **bridegroom**

သတ္တဗေဒ sat-ta-bay-da *(n.)* **zoology**

သတ္တဗေဒနှင့် ဆိုင်သော sat-ta-bay-da-nint sinesaw *(adj.)* **zoological**

သတ္တဗေဒပညာရှင် sat-ta-bay-da-pa-nyar-shin *(n.)* **zoologist**

သတ္တဝါအခြားတစ်မျိုးမှ နောက်တစ်မျိုးသို့ ဆင့်ကဲပေါ်ထွန်းလာခြင်း tat-ta-war-ta-myo-hma-naut-ta-myo-tho-sint-kae-pay-htun-chin *(adj.)* **anamorphosis**

သတ္တိ sat-ti *(n.)* **pluck**

သတ္တိကြောင်သည့် ကလိမ်ကကျစ် satti kyaungsaeet kalinkakyit *(n.)* **sneak**

သတ္တိပြောင်ခြင်း tat-ti-pyaung-chin *(n.)* **intrepidity**

သတ္တိပြောင်သော tat-ti-pyaung-taw *(adj.)* **intrepid**

သတ္တိသွေး tat-ti-thway *(n.)* **mettle**

သတ္တိသွေးကောင်းသော tat-ti-thway-kaung-taw *(adj.)* **mettlesome**

သတ္တု tat-tu *(n.)* **metal**

သတ္တုကြမ်းခင်း tat-tu-kyan-khin *(n.)* **treadplate**

သတ္တုစပ် tat-thu-sat *(n.)* **alloy**

သတ္တုတွင်း၊ မိုင်း tat-tu-twin, mai *(n.)* **mine**

သတ္တုဓာတ်များစွာပါဝင်သော sattu dhat myarr-swarparwinsaw *(adj.)* **polymetallic**

သတ္တုနှင့်တူသော tat-tu-nint-tu-taw *(adj.)* **metallic**

သတ္တုပြား tat-tu-pyar *(n.)* **flashing**

သတ္တုပြားပေါ်တွင် ငရဲမီးဖြင့် စား၍ ပုံဖော်သည် tat-tu-pyar-paw-twin-nga-ye-mee-phit-sar-ywe-pon-phaw-the *(v.)* **etch**

သတ္တုပြားပေါ်တွင် ငရဲမီးဖြင့် စား၍ ပုံဖော်သော tat-tu-pyar-paw-twin-nga-ye-mee-phit-sar-ywe-pon-phaw-taw *(adj.)* **etched**

သတ္တုပြားပေါ်တွင် ငရဲမီးဖြင့် စား၍ ပုံဖော်သော အတတ်ပညာ tat-tu-pyar-paw-twin-nga-ye-mee-phit-sar-ywe-pon-phaw-taw-a-tat-pyin-nyar *(adj.)* **etching**

သတ္တုပုံလောင်းစက်ရုံ tat-tu-pon-laung-sat-yone *(n.)* **foundry**
သတ္တုဗေဒ tat-tu-bay-da *(n.)* **metallurgy**
သတ္တုရိုင်း tat-tu-rine *(n.)* **ore**
သတ္တုရိုင်းကို အရည်ကျိုသည် sattu rineko aaraikyaosai *(v.)* **smelt**
သတ္တုလက်အိတ် tat-tu-lat-aik *(n.)* **gauntlet**
သတ်ခြင်း tat-chin *(n.)* **kill**
သတ်ပွဲကျင်းပသည် saat pwalkyinnpa-sai *(v.)* **slaughter**
သတ်ပုံခေါ်ခြင်း tat-pon-khaw-chin *(n.)* **dictation**
သတ်ပုံခေါ်သည် tat-pon-khaw-the *(v.)* **dictate**
သတ်ပုတ်နှောင့်ယှက်မှု tat-poke-naunt-shat-mu *(n.)* **affray**
သတ်ဖြတ်သည် saat-hpyat-sai *(v.)* **slay**
သတ်မှတ် ဝတ်စုံ tat-mat-wit-sone *(n.)* **garb**
သတ်မှတ် ဝတ်စုံ ဝတ်သည် tat-mat-wit-sone-wit-the *(v.)* **garb**
သတ်မှတ်ချက် saatmhaatchet *(n.)* **set**
သတ်မှတ်ချိန် သုညထား၍ တစက္ကန့်စီ နောက်ပြန်ရေတွက်ခြင်း tat-mat-chain-ton-nyay-htar-ywe-ta-sat-kant-si-naut-pyan-yay-twat-chin *(n.)* **countdown**
သတ်မှတ်ခြင်း tat-mat-chin *(n.)* **imposition**
သတ်မှတ်ထားသော saat-mhaathtarrsaw *(adj.)* **requisite**
သတ်မှတ်ထုထည်အတွင်း သက်ရှိအရေအတွက် tat-mat-htu-htal-a-twin-thet-shi-a-yay-a-thwat *(n.)* **biomass**
သတ်မှတ်ရိုက်ချက် saat-mhaat-rite-chet *(n.)* **par**
သတ်မှတ်သည် saatmhaatsai *(v.)* **set**
သတ်မှတ်သည်၊ စည်းကြပ်သည် tat-mat-the, see-kyat-the *(v.)* **impose**
သတ်မှတ်သော tat-mat-taw *(adj.)* **designated**
သတ်သည် tat-the *(v.)* **kill**
သတ်သတ်လွတ်စားသူ saatsaatlwat sarrsuu *(n.)* **vegetarian**
သတ်သတ်လွတ်စားသော saatsaatlwat sarrsaw *(adj.)* **vegan**
သတ်သတ်လွတ်သမား saatsaatlwatsamarr *(n.)* **vegan**
သဒ္ဒဗေဒ sad-da-bay-da *(adj.)* **phonetic**
သဒ္ဒါ ta-dar *(n.)* **grammar**
သဒ္ဒါပညာရှင် ta-dar-pyin-nyar-shin *(n.)* **grammarian**
သဒ္ဓါတော်မူသည် saddhar taw muusai *(v.)* **vouchsafe**
သနပ်ခါးလိမ်းသည် sanauthkarr laimsai *(v.)* **revamp**
သနားကရုဏာသက်စရာ sa-narr-ka-ru-nar-saat-sa-rar *(adj.)* **pitiable**
သနားချင့်စဖွယ် sa-narr-chint-sa-hpwal *(adj.)* **pitiful**
သနားခြင်း sa-narr-chinn *(n.)* **pity**
သနားစဖွယ် sa-narr-sa-hpwal *(adj.)* **pathetic**
သနားစရာ sa-narr-sa-rar *(adj.)* **piteous**
သနားသည် sa-narr-sai *(v.)* **pity**
သန္တာ tan-dar *(n.)* **coral**
သန္တာကျောက်ကျွန်း tan-dar-kyauk-kyun *(n.)* **atoll**
သန္ဓေပြောင်းခြင်း ta-day-pyaung-chin *(n.)* **mutation**
သန္ဓေပြောင်းသော ta-day-pyaung-taw *(adj.)* **mutative**
သန္ဓေသား ta-day-tar *(n.)* **embryo**
သန့်စင်ခန်း tant-sin-khan *(n.)* **cloakroom**

သန့်စင်ခြင်း saant sin-chinn *(n.)* **purification**
သန့်စင်သည် saant sin-sai *(v.)* **purify**
သန့်စင်သော saant sinsaw *(adj.)* **pure**
သန့်စန်သည်၊ ချက်သည် saant saan sai , chet-sai *(v.)* **refine**
သန့်ရှင်းစင်ကြယ်စေသည် tant-shin-sin-kyal-say-the *(v.)* **hallow**
သန့်ရှင်းစေသည် tant-shin-say-the *(v.)* **cleanse**
သန့်ရှင်းပြီး ရောဂါမဖြစ်စေနိုင်သော tant-shin-pi-yaw-gar-ma-phit-say-nai-taw *(adj.)* **hygienic**
သန့်ရှင်းမှု tant-shin-mu *(n.)* **cleanliness**
သန့်ရှင်းရေး၊ ကျန်းမာရေးနှင့် ညီညွတ်သော saant hlyinn rayy , kyannmarrayynint nyenywatsaw *(adj.)* **sanitary**
သန့်ရှင်းရေးသမား၊ သန့်စင်ဆေး၊ tant-shin-yay-ta-mar, tant-sin-say *(n.)* **cleaner**
သန့်ရှင်းသည် tant-shin-the *(v.)* **clean**
သန်း tan *(n.)* **louse**
သန်းကြွယ်သူဌေး tan-kywe-ta-htay *(n.)* **millionaire**
သန်းခြင်း၊ စွက်ခြင်း saann chinn , swatchinn *(n.)* **tinge**
သန်းခေါင်စာရင်း ta-khaung-sar-yin *(n.)* **census**
သန်းတစ်ထောင် tan-ta-htaung *(n.)* **billion**
သန်းပေါင်းထောင်ချီချမ်းသာသူ tan-paung-htaungchi-chan-tar thu *(n.)* **billionaire**
သန်းသည်၊ စွက်သည် saann sai , swatsai *(v.)* **tinge**
သန်မြင်သော saan myinsaw *(adj.)* **sprightly**
သန်မြန်သော saan myansaw *(adj.)* **robust**
သန်မာသော saan marsaw *(adj.)* **strong**
သန်သည့်ကိစ္စ tan-the-kait-sa *(n.)* **forte**
သန်သော၊ သန်မာသော saan saw , saan marsaw *(adj.)* **virile**
သပြေမှည့်ရောင် sa-pyay-mhae-raung *(n.)* **plum**
သပိတ်တားသည် sa-pate-tarr-sai *(v.)* **picket**
သပိတ်တားသူ sa-pate-tarr-suu *(n.)* **picket**
သပိတ်မှောက်ခြင်း sapatemhaoutchinn *(n.)* **stoppage**
သပိတ်မှောက်သည် sapatemhaoutsai *(v.)* **strike**
သပိတ်မှောက်သူ sapatemhaoutsuu *(n.)* **striker**
သပ္ပာယရှိခြင်း sap par yashichinn *(n.)* **versatility**
သပ် sat *(n.)* **wedge**
သပ်ရပ်ကြော့မော့ခြင်း sat rat kyaww motchinn *(n.)* **smart**
သပ်ရပ်ကြော့မော့စွာ sat rat kyaww motswar *(adv.)* **smartly**
သပ်ရပ်ကြော့မော့သည် sat rat kyawt mot-sai *(v.)* **smart**
သပ်ရပ်ကြော့မော့သော sat rat kyaww motsaw *(adj.)* **smart**
သပ်ရပ်သန့်ရှင်းသော sat rat saant shinn-saw *(adj.)* **spotless**
သပ်ရပ်သော tat-yat-taw *(adj.)* **neat**
သပ်ရပ်သော၊ ရှပ်ဖြောင့်သော tat-yat-taw-yoke-pyaunt-taw *(adj.)* **gimp**
သပ်လျှိုသည် satshosai *(v.)* **wedge**
သပ်သပ်ရပ်ရပ် tat-tat-yat-yat *(adv.)* **nicely**
သဖန်းပိုးစာ sa hpan-poesar *(n.)* **sycamore**
သဖန်းသီး၊ ကတွတ်သီး ta-phan-tee, ka-tut-tee *(n.)* **fig**
သဖွယ်ဖြစ်သော sahpwahlpyitsaw *(adj.)* **veritable**

သဗ္ဗညုတ tab-ba-nyu-ta *(adj.)* **omniscient**
သဗ္ဗညုတဉာဏ် tab-ba-nyu-ta-nyarn *(n.)* **omniscience**
သဘင်အတတ် ta-bin-a-tat *(n.)* **mime**
သဘာဝ ta-bar-wa *(adj.)* **natural**
သဘာဝဆီမှ ရသော ဒြပ်ပေါင်း ta-bar-wa-see-ma-ya-tawdat-paung *(n.)* **oleochemical**
သဘာဝပတ်ဝန်းကျင် ta-bar-wa-pat-win-kyin *(adj.)* **environmental**
သဘာဝပသာဒ sabharwapata-da *(adj.)* **scenic**
သဘာဝပေါက်ပင် sabharwapoutpin *(n.)* **vegetation**
သဘာဝရှုခင်း sabharwashuhkinn *(n.)* **scenery**
သဘာဝလွန်ဖြစ်ရပ် ta-bar-wa-lun-phit-yat *(n.)* **occult**
သဘာဝလွန်ဖြစ်သော sabharwalwanhpyitsaw *(adj.)* **supernatural**
သဘာဝလွန်မီးစွမ်းအားနှင့် ဆိုင်သော ta-bar-wa-lun-mee-swan-arr-nint-sai-taw *(adj.)* **pyromantic**
သဘာဝလောကပညာရှင် ta-bar-wa-law-ka-pyin-nyar-shin *(n.)* **naturalist**
သဘာဝအကျိုးဆက် ta-bar-wa-a-kyo-sat *(n.)* **corollary**
သဘာဝအတိုင်း ဖြတ်ခနဲ ဓာတ်ပုံ ရိုက်ခြင်း sabharwaaatine hpyathkanell dhratpone ritechinn *(n.)* **snapshot**
သဘာဝအားဖြင့် ta-bar-wa-ar-phint *(adv.)* **naturally**
သဘော sabhaw *(n.)* **volition**
သဘောကျလောက်အောင် သွက်လက်သော sabhawkyaloutaaung swat laatsaw *(adj.)* **slick**
သဘောကျသည် ta-baw-kya-the *(v.)* **amuse**
သဘောကွဲလွဲသည် ta-baw-kwe-lwal-the *(v.)* **disagree**
သဘောဆောင်သည် sabhaw saungsai *(v.)* **signify**
သဘောတိုက်ဆိုင်သည် ta-baw-tite-sai-the *(v.)* **concur**
သဘောတူညီချက် ta-baw-thu-nyi-chat *(n.)* **agreement**
သဘောတူညီမှု ta-baw-thu-nyi-mu *(n.)* **assent**
သဘောတူသည် sabhawtuusai *(v.)* **sanction**
သဘောတူသော ta-baw-thu-taw *(adj.)* **agreeable**
သဘောထား ta-baw-htar *(n.)* **attitude**
သဘောထား ကွဲလွဲမှု sabhawhtarr kwallwalmhu *(n.)* **rupture**
သဘောထားကြီးခြင်း ta-baw-htar-kyi-chin *(n.)* **magnanimity**
သဘောထားကြီးသော ta-baw-htar-kyi-taw *(adj.)* **bighearted**
သဘောထားကွဲလွဲခြင်း ta-baw-htar-kwal-lwalchin *(n.)* **discord**
သဘောထားကို ထင်ဟပ်သော sabhaw-htarrko htinhautsaw *(adj.)* **representative**
သဘောထားအမြင် ta-bhaw-htar-a-myin *(n.)* **outlook**
သဘောပေါက်လက်ခံလွယ်သော sa-bhawpout laat-hkan lwalsaw *(adj.)* **receptive**
သဘောမကျဖြစ်စေသည် ta-baw-ma-kya-phit-say-the *(v.)* **displease**
သဘောမတူ ta-baw-ma-tu *(v.)* **disapprove**
သဘောမတူခြင်း sabhaw-matuuchinn *(n.)* **reluctance**
သဘောသက်ရောက်သော sabhaw saatroute-saw *(adj.)* **tantamount**
သမင် ta-min *(n.)* **deer**

သမင်ကြီး ta-min-gyi *(n.)* **elk**

သမင်ချို ta-min-gyo *(n.)* **antler**

သမင်ဖို tha-min-pho *(n.)* **buck**

သမင်မ ta-min-ma *(n.)* **doe**

သမားရိုးကျ ta-mar-roe-kya *(adj.)* **orthodox**

သမားရိုးကျ အတွေးအကျင့် sa-mar-roe-kya-a-tway-a-kyint *(n.)* **orthodoxy**

သမားရိုးကျဆန်သော ta-ma-yoe-kya-san-taw *(adj.)* **formal**

သမိုင်း ta-mai *(n.)* **history**

သမိုင်းနှင့်ဆိုင်သော ta-mai-nint-sai-taw *(adj.)* **historical**

သမိုင်းပညာရှင် ta-mai-pyin-nyar-shin *(n.)* **historian**

သမိုင်းဖြစ်ရပ်ကို ခေတ်ကာလအလိုက် သတ်မှတ်သည့် ပညာရပ် tha-mai-phit-yat-ko-khit-kar-la-a-lite-tat-mat-the-pyin-nyar *(n.)* **chronology**

သမိုင်းမတင်မီ sa-mine ma tin-me *(adj.)* **prehistoric**

သမိုင်းမှတ်တမ်း tha-mai-mat-than *(n.)* **chronicle**

သမိုင်းမှတ်တိုင် ta-mai-mat-tai *(n.)* **milestone**

သမိုင်းဝင် ta-mai-win *(adj.)* **historic**

သမီး ta-mee *(n.)* **daughter**

သမုဒ္ဒရာ ta-mode-ta-rar *(n.)* **ocean**

သမုဒ္ဒရာရှေ့ရှိ ပိုင်ဆိုင်မှု ta-mode-ta-rar-shae-shi-pai-sai-mu *(n.)* **oceanfront**

သမုဒ္ဒရာရှေ့ရှိ ပိုင်ဆိုင်မှု၏ ta-mode-ta-rar-shae-shi-pai-sai-mu-ei *(adj.)* **oceanfront**

သမ္ဗန္ဓ tan-ban-da *(n.)* **conjunction**

သမ္မတ sam-ma-ta *(n.)* **president**

သမ္မတနိုင်ငံ sam-mata-sanit *(n.)* **republic**

သမ္မတစနစ်လိုလားသော sam-mata sanit-lolarrsaw *(adj.)* **republican**

သမ္မာကျမ်းစာ ta-mar-kyan-sar *(n.)* **bible**

သမ္မာကျမ်းစာပါ လှေကြီး than-mar-kyan-sar-par-hlay-gyi *(n.)* **ark**

သမ်းဝေခြင်း sam waychinn *(n.)* **yawn**

သမ်းသည် samsai *(v.)* **yawn**

သယ်ခဲ့သော saal-kaesaw *(adj.)* **taken**

သယ်ဆောင်ခြင်း tal-saung-chin *(n.)* **portage**

သယ်ဆောင်ပေးသူ tal-saung-pay-thu *(n.)* **carrier**

သယ်ဆောင်သည် tal-saung-the *(v.)* **carry**

သယ်ပို့ပေးသည့် အရာ tal-poe-pay-the-a-yar *(n.)* **conveyor**

သယ်ယူပို့ဆောင်မှု tal-yu-poe-saung-mu *(n.)* **conveyance**

သယ်ယူပို့ဆောင်ရေး aa-sarrhtoe kusachet *(n.)* **transport**

သယ်ယူပို့ဆောင်သည် aasarrhtoekusachinn *(v.)* **transport**

သယ်ရလွယ်သော saal ra lwalsaw *(adj.)* **portable**

သရက်ရွက် sa raatrwat *(n.)* **spleen**

သရက်သီး ta-yat-thee *(n.)* **mango**

သရဖူ ta-ya-phu *(n.)* **crown**

သရဖူငယ် ta-ya-phu-nge *(n.)* **coronet**

သရဖူဆောင်းသော ta-ya-phoo-saung-taw *(adj.)* **laureate**

သရွတ်၊ အင်္ဂတေ sa-rwat, eain-ga-tay *(n.)* **plaster**

သရွတ်ကိုင်သည် sa-rwat-kine-sai *(v.)* **plaster**

သရအက္ခရာ sa raaakhkarar *(n.)* **vowel**

သရုပ်ဆောင် နှစ်ယောက်တွဲ ta-yoke-saung-na-yauk-twe *(n.)* **duo**
သရုပ်ဆောင်ခြင်း ta-yoke-saung-chin *(n.)* **acting**
သရုပ်ဆောင်စေခြင်း tha-yoke-saung-say-chin *(n.)* **casting**
သရုပ်ဆောင်စေသည်၊ ကြည့်သည်၊ ပစ်သည် tha-yoke-saung-say-the, kyi-the, pyit-the *(v.)* **cast**
သရုပ်ဆောင်မှု sa-rotesaung-mhu *(n.)* **portrayal**
သရုပ်ဆောင်ရာတွင် ပိုလွန်းသည် tar-yote-saung-rar-twin-polwan-tai *(v.)* **overact**
သရုပ်ဆောင်သည် ta-yoke-saung-the *(v.)* **enact**
သရုပ်ဆောင်သည်၊ ဖော်ပြသည် sa-rotesaung sai, hpawpya-sai *(v.)* **portray**
သရုပ်ပြခြင်း ta-yoke-pya-chin *(n.)* **demonstration**
သရုပ်ပြသည် ta-yoke-pya-the *(v.)* **demonstrate**
သရုပ်ဖော်ကစားပွဲ ကျင်းပသည် ta-yoke-phaw-ka-sar-pwe-kyin-pa-the *(v.)* **gamemaster**
သရုပ်သကန် ta-yoke-ta-kan *(n.)* **manifestation**
သရေစာ sa ray-sar *(n.)* **snack**
သရောခြင်း၊ သရော်စာ sa raw chinn , sarawsar *(n.)* **satire**
သရောစာရေးသည် s raw sar-rayysai *(v.)* **satirize**
သရော်၊ အထေ့အခေ့ါ saraw , a htae a hkaear *(adj.)* **satirical**
သရော်ခြင်း sa-raw-chinn *(n.)* **parody**
သရော်စာ ta-yaw-sar *(n.)* **lampoon**
သရော်မှုပညာရှင် saraw mhupanyarshin *(n.)* **satirist**
သရော်သည် sa-raw-sai *(v.)* **parody**
သရဲ ta-ye *(n.)* **ghost**
သြဂုတ်လ aw-gote-la *(n.)* **August**
သြဇာ လွှမ်းမိုးသော aw-zar-hlwan-moe-taw *(adj.)* **influential**
သြဇာတိက္ကမနှင့် ပြည့်စုံခြင်း aw-zar-taik-ka-ma-nint-pyae-zone-chin *(n.)* **charisma**
သြဇာတိက္ကမနှင့် ပြည့်စုံသော aw-zar-taik-ka-ma-nint-pyae-zone-taw *(adj.)* **charismatic**
သြဇာဖြန့်ကျက်သည် aw-zar-phant-kyat-the *(v.)* **aggrandize**
သြဇာလွှမ်းမိုးသည် aw-zar-hlwan-moe-the *(v.)* **influence**
သြဇာအာဏာရှိသော aw-zar-ar-nar-shi-taw *(adj.)* **magisterial**
သြဘာ aw-bhar *(n.)* **telling-off**
သြဘာပေးခြင်း aw-bhar-pay-chinn *(n.)* **ovation**
သြဘာပေးသည် aw-bar-pay-the *(v.)* **cheer**
သြဝါဒ aw-war-da *(n.)* **doctrine**
သလင်းကျောက် tha-lin-kyauk *(n.)* **crystal**
သလင်းနယ်စက် ta-lin-nal-sat *(n.)* **thresher**
သလိပ် salate *(n.)* **sputum**
သဝေထိုးသည် sawayhtoesai *(v.)* **roam**
သွက်ချာပါဒ swat-chaar-par-da *(adj.)* **paralytic**
သွက်လက်ကျွမ်းကျင်သော twat-lat-kyan-kyin-taw *(adj.)* **nimble**
သွက်လက်ဖျတ်လတ်သော thwat-lat-phat-lat-taw *(adj.)* **brisk**
သွက်လက်မြူးကြွသော swat laat myauu kyawsaw *(adj.)* **rollicking**
သွက်လက်သော swat laatsaw *(adj.)* **vivacious**
သွင်းကုန် twin-kone *(n.)* **import**
သွင်းပေးသည် twin-pay-the *(v.)* **infuse**

သွတ်သွင်းပေးသည် twat-twin-pay-the *(v.)* **instil**
သွပ်ရည်စိမ်သည် tut-yay-sein-the *(v.)* **galvanize**
သွယ်လျသော၊ ကြော့ရှင်းသော swal lya saw , kyaww hlyinnsaw *(adj.)* **trim**
သွယ်လျသော၊ ပေါ့တန်သော swal lya saw, pot taansaw *(adj.)* **slight**
သွယ်ဝိုက် twal-wite *(adj.)* **indirect**
သွယ်ဝိုက်ညွှန်းဆိုသည် twal-wite-hnyun-soe-the *(v.)* **imply**
သွယ်ဝိုက်ပြောသည် twal-wite-pyaw-so-the *(v.)* **allude**
သွယ်ဝိုက်သော twal-wite-taw *(adj.)* **implicit**
သွယ်သည်၊ လျော့သည် swal sai , lyawwsai *(v.)* **taper**
သွား swarr *(n.)* **tooth**
သွားဆရာဝန် twar-sa-yar-win *(n.)* **dentist**
သွားနာခြင်း swarr narchinn *(n.)* **toothache**
သွားပွတ်တံ၊ ဝက်မှင်ဘီး twar-put-tan, wat-hmin-bee *(n.)* **brush**
သွားပိုးစားသော twar-poe-sar-taw *(adj.)* **carious**
သွားပေါက်သည် swarr poutsai *(v.)* **teethe**
သွားဖုံး twar-hpone *(n.)* **gum**
သွားရည် twar-yay *(n)* **drool**
သွားရည်ခံ twar-yee-khan *(n.)* **bib**
သွားရည်ယိုသည် twar-yay-yo-the *(v.)* **drool**
သွားရေယိုစေသည် swarr ray yosaysai *(v.)* **whet**
သွားလာလှုပ်ရှားတတ်သူ twar-lar-lote-shar-tat-thu *(n.)* **mover**
သွားလေ့လာမှုပညာ twar-lae-lar-mu-pin-nyar *(n.)* **odontology**
သွားသည် twar-the *(v.)* **go**
သွားသည်၊ ပြောသည်၊ စွန့်သည် swarrsai , pyawwsai , swunt-sai *(v.)* **venture**
သွေး thway *(n.)* **blood**
သွေးကြီး မွေးကြီး နိုင်ခြင်း swaykyee mwaykyee ninechinn *(n.)* **snoot**
သွေးကြော sway-kyaww *(n.)* **vessel**
သွေးကြောကဲ့သို့ ပုံစံ thway-kyaw-kae-tho-pon-san *(v.)* **vein**
သွေးကြောဓာတ်မှန် tway-kyaw-dat-man *(n.)* **angiogram**
သွေးကြောမကြီး tway-kyaw-ma-kyi *(n.)* **aorta**
သွေးခုန်ခြင်း sway hkone-chinn *(n.)* **pulse**
သွေးဆိပ်သင့်ခြင်း sway siut sainthkyinn *(n.)* **sepsis**
သွေးဆုံးခြင်း tway-sone-chin *(n.)* **menopause**
သွေးဆုတ်သွားသည် sway-sote-swarr-sai *(v.)* **pale**
သွေးဆောင်ဖြားယောင်းသည် swaysaung hpyarryaunggsai *(v.)* **seduce**
သွေးဆောင်သည် tway-saung-the *(v.)* **lure**
သွေးဆောင်သည့်အရာ tway-saung-the-a-yar *(n.)* **lure**
သွေးထွက်နေသော thway-thwat-nay-taw *(adj.)* **bloody**
သွေးထွက်သံယို thway-htwat-tan-yo *(n.)* **gore**
သွေးထွက်သံယိုမှု thway-htwat-tan-yo-mu *(n.)* **bloodshed**
သွေးထွက်သည် thway-htwat-the *(v.)* **bleed**
သွေးပြန်ကြော sway pyankyaww *(n.)* **vein**
သွေးမလျှောက်၍ ခြေထောက် ပုပ်ပွပျက်စီးခြင်း tway-ma-shaut-ywe-chay-htaut-poke-pwa-pyat-see-chin *(n.)* **gangrene**

သွေးရူးသွေးတန်းဖြစ်ခြင်း tway-yu-tway-tan-phit-chin *(n.)* **frenzy**
သွေးလွှတ်ကြော thway-hlut-kyaw *(n.)* **artery**
သွေးလွှတ်ခန်း thway-hlut-khan *(n.)* **atrium**
သွေးလှည့်ပတ်ခြင်း thway-hlae-pat-chin *(n.)* **circulation**
သွေးသားချင်း သတ်ဖြတ်ခြင်း sway-sarr-chinn-saat-hpyat-chinn *(n.)* **parricide**
သွေးသားဆန္ဒနှင့် ဆိုင်သော thway-tar-san-da-nint-sai-taw *(adj.)* **carnal**
သွေးသားတော်စပ်မှု tway-tar-taw-sat-mu *(n.)* **kinship**
သွေးအားနည်း thwe-arr-nae *(n.)* **anaemia**
သွေဖည်မှု sway-hpai-mhu *(n.)* **perversion**
သွေဖည်လျက် thway-phal-lyat *(adv.)* **astray**
သွေလှန်သည် sway-hlaan-sai *(v.)* **pervert**
သသမေဓအခွန် sat ta may dhaaahkwan *(n.* **tithe**
သဟဇာတဖြစ်သော ta-ha-zar-ta-phit-taw *(adj.)* **compatible**
သဟဇာတဖြစ်သော၊ သင့်မြတ်သော ta-ha-zar-ta-phit-taw, tint-myat-taw *(adj.)* **harmonious**
သဟဇီဝ sa-ha-zee wa *(n.)* **symbiosis**
သား sarr *(n.)* **son**
သား၊ ဥ tarr, u *(n.)* **ovum**
သားကြောဖြတ်ခြင်း၊ ပိုးသတ်ခြင်း sarr kyaww hpyat chinn , poe saatchinn *(n.)* **sterilization**
သားကြောဖြတ်သည်၊ ပိုးသတ်သည် sarr kyaww hpyat sai , poe saatsai *(v.)* **sterilize**
သားကောင် sarr-kaung *(n.)* **prey**
သားကောင်ဖြစ်သွားသည် sarr-kaung-hpyit-swarrsai *(v.)* **prey**
သားစားတိရိစ္ဆာန် tar-sar-ta-yeik-san *(n.)* **carnivore**
သားနားမှု၊ ထည်ဝါမှု sarr narr mhu , htai warmhu *(n.)* **splendour**
သားပိုက်ကောင် tar-bike-kaung *(n.)* **kangaroo**
သားပေါက် sarrpout *(n.)* **whelp**
သားပေါက်သည် tar-pauk-the *(v.)* **breed**
သားဖွား tar-phwar *(n.)* **midwife**
သားဖွားဆရာဝန် tar-hpwar-sa-rar-wan *(n.)* **obstetrician**
သားဖွားပညာ tar-hpwar-pyin-nyar *(adj.)* **obstetric**
သားရေ sarrray *(n.)* **satchel**
သားရေကွင်း၊ မျှော့ကွင်း ta-yay-kwin, myawt-kwin *(n.)* **garter**
သားရေဆေးဆိုးသူ sarr ray sayy soesuu *(n.)* **tawer**
သားရဲတွင်း tar-ye-twin *(n.)* **den**
သားသတ်သမား tar-tat-ta-mar *(n.)* **butcher**
သားသမီး sarr-sa-mee *(n.)* **progeny**
သားသမီးတစ်အုပ် tar-ta-mee-ta-oak *(n.)* **brood**
သားအိမ် kaungkyoepyumhu shayyshusaw *(n.)* **uterus**
သားအိမ်ခေါင်းနှင့် ဆိုင်သော tar-eain-kaung-nint-sai-taw *(adj.)* **cervical**
သားဥနှင့် ဆိုင်သော sarr u-nint sine-saw *(adj.)* **ovular**
သာတူညီမျှဖြစ်သော tar-tu-nyi-mya-phit-taw *(adj.)* **equitable**
သာဓက tar-da-ka *(n.)* **onomatopoeia**
သာဓက၊ အစဉ်အလာ sar-dha-ka, a sin aalar *(n.)* **precedent**
သာဓကပြခြင်း၊ ပုံဆောင်ခြင်း tar-da-ka-pyu-chin, pon-saung-chin *(n.)* **illustration**

သာဓကေဖြစ် ဖွဲ့စည်းသောစကားလုံး tar-da-ka-phint-phwal-see-taw-sa-kar-lone *(n.)* **onomatope**
သာမည sarmanya *(adj.)* **secondary**
သာမညောင်ညာ tar-ma-nyaung-nya *(n.)* **mediocrity**
သာမန် sar-maan *(adj.)* **workaday**
သာမန်ကာလျှံကာ sarmaan kar shankar *(adj.)* **scant**
သာမန်ထက် လွန်ကဲသော tar-man-htet-lun-kae-taw *(adj.)* **extraordinary**
သာမန်ထက်ကြီးသော sar-man-htat-kyee-taw *(adj.)* **outsize**
သာမန်မျှ tar-man-mya *(adj.)* **mediocre**
သာယာကြည်နူးခြင်း tar-yar-kyi-nu-chin *(v.)* **delight**
သာယာကြည်နူးဖွယ် taw-yar-kyi-nu-phwal *(adj.)* **melodious**
သာယာမှုကို စွဲလမ်းသောသူ tar-yar-mu-ko-swal-lan-taw-thu *(n.)* **epicurean**
သာယာအဆင်ပြေခြင်း tar-yar-a-sin-pyay-chin *(n.)* **amenity**
သာလျှင် tar-lyin *(adv.)* **only**
သာလွန်မှု sarlwanmhu *(n.)* **supremacy**
သာလွန်သည် sarlwansai *(v.)* **surpass**
သာလွန်သော sarlwansaw *(adj.)* **superior**
သာသည် sar-sai *(v.)* **out-balance**
သာသနာ့ဘောင် sarsa-narbhaung *(n.)* **priesthood**
သာသနာပြုအဖွဲ့ tar-ta-nar-pyu-a-phwe *(n.)* **missionary**
သိက္ခာ sate-hkar *(n.)* **prestige**
သိက္ခာချသည် taik-khar-cha-the *(v.)* **demean**
သိက္ခာစောင့်စည်းမှု sikhkar sawng saeemhu *(n.)* **scruple**
သိက္ခာစောင့်စည်းသည် sikhkar sawng saeesai *(v.)* **scruple**
သိက္ခာစောင့်စည်းမှု မရှိသော sikhkar hcaung hcaeemhu mashisaw *(adj.)* **scrupleless**
သိက္ခာတော်ဘွဲ့အပ်နှင်းသည်၊ ပဉ္စင်းတက်ပေးသည် hteik-hkar-taw-bhwal-at-hnin-tai, pa-zin-tat-pay-tai *(v.)* **ordain**
သိက္ခာတော်ရ sikhkar tawra *(adj.)* **reverend**
သိတတ်ခြင်း ti-tat-chin *(n.)* **complaisance**
သိတတ်သော ti-tat-taw *(adj.)* **complaisant**
သိန်း thein-the *(n.)* **lac, lakh**
သိပ္ပံခန်းသုံး ပုလင်း tate-pan-khan-tone-pa-lin *(n.)* **flask**
သိပ္ပံနည်းကျသော sippannaeekyasaw *(adj.)* **scientific**
သိပ္ပံနှင့် နည်းပညာကောလိပ် seik-pan-nint naeepanyarkawliut *(n.)* **polytechnic**
သိပ္ပံပညာ sippanpanyar *(n.)* **science**
သိပ္ပံပညာရှင် sippanpanyarshin *(n.)* **scientist**
သိပ်ထည့်သည် tate-htae-the *(v.)* **cram**
သိပ်သည်းခြင်း tate-tae-chin *(n.)* **density**
သိပ်သည်းသော taik-the-taw *(adj.)* **compact**
သိမြင်ခြင်း ti-myin-chin *(n.)* **cognition**
သိမြင်တတ်သော ti-myin-tat-taw *(adj.)* **cognitive**
သိမြင်နားလည်ခြင်း si-myin-narr-lai-chinn *(n.)* **perception**
သိမှုပျောက်ဆုံးသည် ti-mu-pyauk-sone-the *(v.)* **disorient**
သိမ့်သိမ့်တုန်သည် theint-theint-tone-the *(v.)* **convulse**
သိမ်းငှက် thein-hnget *(n.)* **falcon**

သိမ်းပိုက်သည်၊ နေသည် taim-pite-tai, nay-tai *(v.)* **occupy**
သိမ်းယူခြင်း thein-yu-chin *(n.)* **confiscation**
သိမ်းယူထားသည် saimyuuhtarrsai *(v.)* **sequester**
သိမ်းယူသည် thein-yu-the *(v.)* **confiscate**
သိမ်းသည် thein-the *(v.)* **keep**
သိမ်းသွင်းခြင်း tain-twin-chin *(n.)* **incorporation**
သိမ်ငယ်ခြင်း thein-nge-chin *(n.)* **inferiority**
သိမ်မွေ့ခြင်း sinmwaechinn *(n.)* **tenderness**
သိမ်မွေ့နက်နဲခြင်း sinmwae naat nellchinn *(n.)* **subtlety**
သိမ်မွေ့နူးညံ့ခြင်း tein-mway-nu-nyant-chin *(n.)* **delicacy**
သိမ်မွေ့သော sinmwaesaw *(adj.)* **tricky**
သိမ်မွေ့သော ကိုယ်အမူအရာဖြင့် thein-mway-taw-koe-a-mu-a-yar-phint *(adj.)* **mannerly**
သိမ်သွားခြင်း thein-twar-chin *(v.)* **atrophy**
သိသည် ti-the *(v.)* **know**
သိသာသော si-sar-saw *(adj.)* **perceptible**
သိသိသာသာ si-si-sar-sar *(adv.)* **stark**
သိဟ်ရာသီဖွား theik-yar-thee-phwar *(n.)* **Leo**
သို့မဟုတ် ထိုအနီးဝန်းကျင် thoetmahote hto aaneewaannkyin *(adv.)* **thereabouts**
သို့မဟုတ်လျှင် thoet-ma-hote-hlyin *(adv.)* **otherwise**
သို့လော သို့လော ဖြစ်ခြင်း tho-law-tho-law-phit-chin *(n.)* **misgiving**
သို့သော် tho-thaw *(conj.)* **but**
သို့သော်ငြားလည်း thoe-taw-nyar-lal *(conj.)* **albeit**
သို့သော်လည်း thoetsawlaee *(adv.)* **though**
သိုး soe *(n.)* **sheep**
သိုးငယ် thoe-ngal *(n.)* **lambkin**
သိုးထိန်း soehtein *(n.)* **shepherd**
သိုးထီး soehtee *(n.)* **ram**
သိုးမ thoe-ma *(n.)* **ewe**
သိုးမွေးခေါင်းစွပ် thoe-hmway-gaung-sut *(n.)* **balaclava**
သိုးမွေး soemway *(n.)* **wool**
သိုးမွေး ပန်းဖွားလုံး toe-mway-pan-phwar-lone *(n.)* **bobble**
သိုးမွေးထိုးသည် toe-mway-htoe-the *(v.)* **knit**
သိုးမွေးနှင့် လုပ်သော soe mway-nint lotesaw *(n.)* **woollen**
သိုးမွေးအထည်စ thoe mway aa-htai-sa *(n.)* **worsted**
သိုးသား toe-dar *(n.)* **mutton**
သိုးသားညှပ်မုန့် soe sarr nyhaut mone *(n.)* **shawarma**
သိုက် tite *(adj.)* **oracular**
သိုလှောင်ထားသည့် အရာ so-hlaung-htarr-seet aarar *(n.)* **store**
သိုလှောင်မှု so-hlaungmhu *(n.)* **storage**
သိုလှောင်သည် so-hlaungsai *(v.)* **store**
သိုဝှက်သော so whaatsaw *(adj.)* **secretive**
သီးခြား seecharr *(adj.)* **separate**
သီးခြားစရိုက်လူ့အဖွဲ့အစည်း see charr sa rite-hlu-aa-hpwal-aa-sae *(n.)* **subculture**
သီးခြားထားသည်၊ ခွဲထားသည် thee-char-htar-the, kwal-htar-the *(v.)* **isolate**
သီးစားလုပ်ခြင်း see sarrlotechinn *(n.)* **tenancy**

သီးစုံရေခဲမုန့် see sone ray hkell mone *(n.)* **sundae**
သီးနှံကြိတ်ခွဲစက် thee-nan-kyaik-kwal-sat *(n.)* **mill**
သီးနှံစိုက်ပျိုးမြေနှင့်ဆိုင်သော စိုက်ပျိုးရေးပညာခွဲ thee-nan-seik-pyo-myay-nint-saing-taw-seik-pyo-yay-pyin-nyar-kwe *(n.)* **agrology**
သီးနှံစိုက်ပျိုးရေးပညာ thee-nan-seik-pyo-yay-pyin-nyar *(n.)* **agronomy**
သီးနှံဖြစ်ထွန်းသော thee-nan-phit-htun-taw *(adj.)* **arable**
သီးနှံရိတ်သိမ်းခြင်း thee-nan-yeik-thein-chin *(n.)* **harvest**
သီးနှံရိတ်သိမ်းသည် thee-nan-yeik-thein-the *(v.)* **harvest**
သီးနှံရိတ်သိမ်းသူ thee-nan-yeik-thein-thu *(n.)* **harvester**
သီးသန့်၊ ကိုယ်ပိုင် see sant , ko-pine *(adj.)* **private**
သီးသန့်၊ စိစိစစ်စစ်ရှိသော see saant , si-si-sit sitshisaw *(adj.)* **selective**
သီးသန့်စီစဉ်ထားရှိသည် thee-tant-si-sin-htar-shi-the *(v.)* **configure**
သီးသန့်ထားခြင်း tee-tant-htar-chin *(n.)* **isolation**
သီးသန့်ထားသည် see saanthtarrsai *(v.)* **reserve**
သီးသန့်ဖြစ်သော the-tant-phit-taw *(adj.)* **exclusive**
သီချင်း se-chinn *(n.)* **song**
သီချင်းကို အသံ အဆုံးထိမြှင့်တင်၍ ပြန်ချဆိုသည် se-chinnko aa-san aasonehti myaha inttin pyan cha-sosai *(v.)* **yodel**
သီချင်းစာရင်း sehkyinnhcarrainn *(n.)* **setlist**
သီချင်းဆိုရာတွင် အလွန်မြင့်သော အသံ thi-chin-so-yar-twin-a-lun-myint-taw-a-tan *(n.)* **falsetto**
သီချင်းညည်းသည် tha-chin-nyee-the *(v.)* **croon**
သီဆိုခြင်း၊ တီးခတ်ခြင်း၊ ရွတ်ဆိုခြင်း thi-so-chin, tee-khat-chin, yut-so-chin *(n.)* **antiphony**
သီဆိုသည် se-so-sai *(v.)* **sing**
သီလရှင် te-la-shin *(n.)* **nun**
သီလရှင်ကျောင်း te-la-shin-kyaung *(n.)* **nunnery**
သီဟိုဠ်သရက်ပင် thi-ho-tha-yat-pin *(n.)* **cashew**
သီအိုရမ် se aoram *(n.)* **theorem**
သီအိုရီ sea-o-re *(n.)* **theory**
သီအိုရီပညာရှင် seaorepanyarshin *(n.)* **theorist**
သုံး sone *(n.)* **three**
သုံးကြိမ် sonekyain *(adv.)* **thrice**
သုံးချောင်းထောက် sone chaungghtout *(n.)* **tripod**
သုံးစွဲနေသော tone-swal-nay-taw *(adj.)* **occupied**
သုံးစွဲသည် tone-swal-the *(v.)* **expend**
သုံးဆတိုးသည် sone-sa toesai *(v.)* **triple**
သုံးဆယ် sone-saal *(n.)* **thirty**
သုံးဆယ်ခုမြောက် sone-saahl-kumyawt *(n.)* **thirtieth**
သုံးဆောင်သည် sone-saung-sai *(v.)* **partake**
သုံးနားညီ tone-nar-nyi *(adj.)* **equilateral**
သုံးပွင့်ဆိုင် sone pwintsine *(adj.)* **triangular**
သုံးပိုင်းရှိသော sone pineshisaw *(adj.)* **tripartite**
သုံးဖက်မြင်ဓာတ်ပုံ tone-phat-myn-dat-pon *(n.)* **holograph**

သုံးဘီးစက်ဘီး sonebheesaatbhee *(n.)* **tricycle**
သုံးမရသော sonemarasaw *(adj.)* **worthless**
သုံးယောက်တွဲ အဆိုအတီး soneyouttwal a so aatee *(n.)* **trio**
သုံးယောက်အစု soneyout aasu *(n.)* **trinity**
သုံးရောင်ခြယ်သော soneraungchaalsaw *(adj.)* **tricolour**
သုံးရောင်ခြယ်အလံ soneraungchaalaalan *(n.)* **tricolour**
သုံးလတစ်ကြိမ် sone lata-kyaain *(adj.)* **quarterly**
သုံးလအပိုင်းအခြား sone laaapineaacharr *(n.)* **trimester**
သုံးလေးမျိုး စသည် ခွဲလုပ်သည် tone-lay-myo-sa-the-khwal-lote-the *(v.)* **diversify**
သုံးသပ်ခြင်း tone-tat-chin *(n.)* **consideration**
သုံးသပ်သည် tone-tat-the *(v.)* **consider**
သုံးဦးသုံးဖလှယ်ပါသော sone u sone hpahlaal parsaw *(adj.)* **triple**
သုံ့မှို sonemhao *(n.)* **rivet**
သုက် sote *(n.)* **semen**
သုက်နှင့်ဆိုင်သော sote nintsinesaw *(adj.)* **seminal**
သုက်လွှတ်ခြင်း toke-hlut-chin *(n.)* **ejaculation**
သုက်လွှတ်ခြင်း toke-hlut-chin *(n.)* **ejaculate**
သုက်လွှတ်သည် toke-hlut-the *(v.)* **ejaculate**
သုည su-nya *(n.)* **zero**
သုတေသန sutaysan *(n.)* **research**
သုတေသနပြုသည် sutay-sana-pyusai *(v.)* **research**
သုတ်ခြင်း sotechinn *(n.)* **wipe**
သုတ်သင်သည်၊ သန့်စင်သည် sote-sin sai , saant sinsai *(v.)* **purge**
သုတ်သည် sotesai *(v.)* **wipe**
သုတ်သည်၊ ခင်းသည် sote sai , hkinnsai *(v.)* **spread**
သုတ်သီးသုတ်ပျာပြေးသည် sote see sote pyaar pyaysai *(v.)* **scuttle**
သုတ်သုတ်ပျာပျာပြေးသည် sote sote pyaar pyaar pyaysai *(v.)* **scurry**
သုန်မှုန်နေသော sone-hmone-nay-saw *(adj.)* **sullen**
သုန်မှုန်သော ton-hmone-taw *(adj.)* **morose**
သုန်သုန်မှုန်မှုန် ကြည့်သည် sone sone hmonehmone kyanysai *(v.)* **scowl**
သုန်သုန်မှုန်မှုန် အကြည့် sone sone hmonehmone aakyany *(n.)* **scowl**
သူ thu *(pron.)* **he**
သူ၏ thu-ae *(pron.)* **his**
သူကောင်းပြုသည် thu-kaung-pyu-the *(v.)* **ennoble**
သူကောင်းဘွဲ့ thu-kaung-bwe *(n.)* **dame**
သူခိုး suuhkoe *(n.)* **theft**
သူခိုးဓားပြ suuhkoedharrpya *(n.)* **robber**
သူခိုးလှန့် ခေါင်းလောင်း tha-khoe-hlant-khaung-laung *(n.)* **burglar alarm**
သူငယ်ချင်း tha-ngal-chin *(n.)* **mate**
သူငယ်တန်း thu-ngal-tan *(n.)* **kindergarten**
သူငယ်ပြန်ခြင်း suungaalpyanchinn *(n.)* **senility**
သူငယ်ပြန်နေသော suu-ngaal-pyannaysaw *(adj.)* **senile**
သူစိမ်းကြောက်ခြင်း sasaim kyawwatchinn *(n.)* **xenophobia**

သူစိမ်းနှင့် ပတ်သက်၍ စိတ်စွဲလမ်းခြင်း ta-zein-nint- pat-thet-ywe-seik-swal-lan-chin *(n.)* **xenomania**

သူဆင်းရဲ suu-sinn-rell *(n.)* **pauper**

သူဌေး၊ လူကြီး tha-htay, lu-gyi *(n.)* **boss**

သူတစ်ပါး သားပျိုသမီးပျိုကို ဖျက်ဆီးသည် thu-ta-par-tar-pyo-ta-mee-pyo-ko-phat-see-the *(v.)* **debauch**

သူတစ်ပါးအတွက် ကြားက ဒဏ်ခံရသူ suutaitparraatwat kyarrk danhkanrasuu *(n.)* **scapegoat**

သူတို့၏ suuthoeteat *(adj.)* **their**

သူတို့၏ ဟာ suuthoeteat har *(pron.)* **theirs**

သူတို့ကို suuthoetko *(pron.)* **them**

သူတောင်းစား thu-taung-sar *(n.)* **beggar**

သူတော်ကောင်းတရား suutawkaunggtararr *(n.)* **virtue**

သူတော်ကောင်းဟန်ဆောင်ခြင်း thu-taw-kaung-han-saung-chin *(n.)* **hypocrisy**

သူတော်စင် suutawsin *(n.)* **saint**

သူတော်စင်ကဲ့သို့ suutawsinkaethoet *(adj.)* **saintly**

သူနာပြု tu-nar-pyu *(n.)* **nurse**

သူနာပြုစုသည် tu-nar-pyu-su-tai *(v.)* **nurse**

သူနာပြုအုပ် thu-nar-pyu-oak *(n.)* **matron**

သူပုန် suu-pone *(n.)* **rebel**

သူပုန်ထခြင်း suuponehtachinn *(n.)* **uprising**

သူပုန်ထသည် sa-pone-htasai *(v.)* **rebel**

သူမ suu-ma *(pron.)* **she**

သူမ၏ thu-ma-ei *(adj.)* **her**

သူများထက် သာအောင် လုပ်သည် tuu-myar-htat-ta-aung-lote-tai *(v.)* **outdo**

သူရသတ္တိ thu-ra-that-ti *(n.)* **gallantry**

သူရဲကောင်း thu-ye-gaung *(n.)* **hero**

သူရဲကောင်းကိုးကွယ်ဝါဒ thu-ye-gaung-koe-kwal-war-da *(n.)* **heroism**

သူရဲဘောနည်းခြင်း ta-ye-baw-nae-chin *(n.)* **cowardice**

သူလျှို suusho *(n.)* **spy**

သူလျှိုလုပ်သည် suusholotesai *(v.)* **spy**

သူလိုငါလို thu-lo-ngar-lo *(adj.)* **mundane**

သေးခံ tay-khan *(n.)* **diaper**

သေးငယ်ခြင်း sayy ngaalchinn *(adv.)* **smallness**

သေးငယ်မှုန်မွှားသော tay-nge-hmone-hmwar-taw *(adj.)* **microscopic**

သေးငယ်သော sayyngaalsaw *(adj.)* **tiny**

သေးငယ်သော စိမ့်မြေကွက် tay-nge-taw-seint-myay-kwat *(n.)* **boglet**

သေးငယ်သော မီးလောင်ဖု tay-ngwe-taw-mee-laung-phu *(n.)* **bleb**

သေးနုပ်စေသည် tay-note-say-the *(v.)* **dwarf**

သေးနုပ်သော say-note-saw *(adj.)* **paltry**

သေးသွယ်ကျစ်လျစ်သော say-swal-kyit -lyit-saw *(adj.)* **petite**

သေးသွယ်သော ဖယောင်းတိုင်လေး sayy swalsaw hpayaunggtinelayy *(n.)* **taper**

သေးသိမ်စေသည် tay-tain-say-the *(v.)* **belittle**

သေးသော၊ နည်းသော၊ ငယ်ရွယ်သော say-saw , naee saw , ngaalrwalsaw *(adj.)* **small**

သေချာခြင်း tay-char-chin *(n.)* **certitude**

သေချာစွာ say-chaar-swar *(adv.)* **surely**

သေချာစေသည် tay-char-say-the *(v.)* **ensure**

သေချာသလောက် tay-char-ta-laut *(adj.)* **doubtless**

သေချာသော say-chaar-saw *(adj.)* **sure**

သေချာအောင် လေ့လာစိစစ်သည် tay-char-aung-lay-lar-si-sit-the *(v.)* **ascertain**
သေခြင်း tay-chin *(n.)* **demise**
သေစေနိုင်သော tay-say-nai-taw *(adj.)* **fatal**
သေစေသော tay-say-taw *(adj.)* **lethal**
သေဆုံးခြင်း tay-sone-chin *(n.)* **death**
သေဆုံးပြီးနောက်ဘဝ saysonepyeenoutbhaw *(n.)* **otherworld**
သေဆုံးသူသည် သူတော်စဉ်ဖြစ်ကြောင်း တရားဝင် ပြောကြားသည် tay-sone-thu-the-thu-taw-zin-phit-kyaung-ta-yar-wiin-pyaw-kyar-the *(v.)* **canonize**
သေတမ်းစာ၊ စိတ်စွမ်းအား၊ စိတ်သဘော say-tam-sar , sateswmaarr , satesabhaw *(n.)* **will**
သေတမ်းစာဖြင့် ပေးခဲ့သည် tay-tan-sar-phyit-pay-khae-the *(v.)* **bequeath**
သေတမ်းစာဖြင့် ပေးသည့် အမွေ tay-tan-sar-phyit-pay-the-amway *(n.)* **bequest**
သေတ္တာ tit-tar *(n.)* **boist**
သေဒဏ်စီရင်ခြင်း tay-dan-si-yin-chin *(n.)* **execution**
သေဒဏ်ပေးသည် tay-dan-pay-the *(v.)* **lynch**
သေနတ် saynaat *(n.)* **scattergun**
သေနတ်ပစ်ခတ်မှု၊ saynaat paithkaatmhu *(n.)* **shooting**
သေနတ်ပြောင်းရင်း ta-nat-pyaung-yin *(n.)* **breech**
သေနတ်ဖြင့် တော့၍ ta-nat-phint-tay-ywe *(n.)* **gunpoint**
သေနှုန်း tay-hnone *(n.)* **mortality**
သေနိုင်လောက်အောင် ပြင်းထန်သော say nineloutaaung pyinnhtaansaw *(adj.)* **virulent**
သေနိုင်သော tay-naing-taw *(adj.)* **fetal**
သေပြီးနောက် စစ်ဆေးခြင်း say-pi-naut-sis-say-chinn *(n.)* **post-mortem**
သေပြီးနောက်ဖြစ်သော say-pi-naut-phit-saw *(adj.)* **post-mortem**
သေမျိုးဖြစ်သော tay-myo-phit-taw *(adj.)* **mortal**
သေမှုသေခင်း စုံစမ်းစစ်ဆေးခြင်း tay-mu-tay-khin-sone-san-sit-say-chin *(n.)* **inquest**
သေရည်သေရက် ရှောင်ကြဉ်သူ say rai sayraat shawin kyinsuu *(n.)* **teetotaller**
သေရည်သေရက် ရှောင်ကြဉ်သော say rai sayraat shaung kyinsaw *(adj.)* **teetotal**
သေလုနီးသော tay-lu-nee-taw *(adj.)* **deadly**
သေသည် tay-the *(v.)* **die**
သေသပ်ခြင်း say satchinn *(n.)* **tidiness**
သေသပ်သည် say satsai *(v.)* **tidy**
သေသပ်သော say satsaw *(adj.)* **tidy**
သေသော tay-thaw *(adj.)* **dead**
သော့၊ သော့ချက် tot, tot-chat *(n.)* **key**
သော့ခတ်သည် tot-kha-the *(v.)* **lock**
သော့ခလောက် tot-kha-laut *(n.)* **lock**
သော့ပေါက် tot-pauk *(n.)* **keyhole**
သော့ဖျက်သူ taw-phat-thu *(n.)* **keysmith**
သော့ရေးသည် sotrayysai *(v.)* **scrawl**
သော့ရေးသော လက်ရေး sotrayysaw laatrayy *(n.)* **scrawl**
သောကရောက်စေသည် saw ka routsaysai *(v.)* **trouble**
သောကြာနေ့ taut-kyar-nae *(n.)* **Friday**
သောကြောင့် thaw-kyaunt *(conj.)* **because**
သောက်စားမြူးထူးနေသူ soutsarr myauu htuu naysuu *(n.)* **reveller**
သောက်စားမြူးထူးသည် soutsarr myauu htuusai *(v.)* **revel**

သောက်ဖွယ် taut-phwal *(n.)* **drink**

သောက်ရည် taut-yay *(n.)* **drinking water**

သောက်သည် taut-the *(v.)* **drink**

သောင်းကျန်းသည် saung-kyan-tai *(v.)* **overrun**

သောင်းကျန်းသူ taung-kyan-thu *(n.)* **insurgent**

သောင်းကျန်းသော saung-kyannsaw *(adj.)* **rampant**

သောင်းပြောင်း taung-pyaung *(n.)* **hotchpotch**

သောင်းပြောင်းထွေလာ taung-pyaung-htway-lar *(n.)* **miscellany**

သောင်းသောင်းသဲသဲ saunggsaunggsellsell *(adj.)* **uproarious**

သောင်ခုံ saunghkone *(n.)* **sandbank**

သောင်တင်သည် saungtinsai *(v.)* **strand**

သောအခါ sawaahkar *(conj.)* **when**

သော်ငြားလည်း daw-nyar-lal *(conj.)* **however**

သော်လည်း saw-laee *(conj.)* **yet**

သော်လည်းကောင်း taw-lae-kaung *(conj.)* **nor**

သဲ sell *(n.)* **sand**

သဲ့သဲ့ပြောသံ sae sae pyawwsan *(n.)* **purr**

သဲ့သဲ့ပြောသည် sae sae pyawwsai *(v.)* **purr**

သဲကန္တာရ the-kan-dar-ya *(n.)* **desert**

သဲကျောက် sell-kyaut *(n.)* **sandstone**

သဲငါး sell-ngarr *(n.)* **sandfish**

သဲဆန်သော sell-saansaw *(adj.)* **sand**

သဲတောင်ပူစာ sell taung puu-hcar *(n.)* **sandhill**

သဲထူသော sell htuusaw *(adj.)* **sandy**

သဲနာရီ sell-nar-re *(n.)* **sandglass**

သဲဖြည့်ကျင်း sell hpyay kyinn *(n.)* **sandbox**

သဲဖြည့်ကျင်း sell hpyay kyin *(n.)* **sandpit**

သဲဗွက် sell bwat *(n.)* **quicksand**

သဲမုန်တိုင်း sell-monetine *(n.)* **sandstorm**

သဲရဲတိုက် sell rell-tite *(n.)* **sandcastle**

သဲလျှောစီးဘုတ်စီးသည် sell shaw hcee bhote hcee-sai *(v.)* **sandboard**

သဲလျောစီးဘုတ် sell lyaww hcee-bhote *(n.)* **sandboard**

သဲလွန်စ selllwansa *(n.)* **trace**

သဲလွန်စ၊ ခြေရာ selllwans , chayrar *(adj.)* **telltale**

သဲလွန်စမရှိသော the-lun-sa-ma-shi-taw *(adj.)* **clueless**

သဲလွန်စလိုက်နိုင်သော selllwansa liteninesaw *(adj.)* **traceable**

သဲသုံး ရှုခင်း sellsone shu-hkinn *(n.)* **sandscape**

ဟက်ကာ hat-kar *(n.)* **hacker**

ဟက်တက်ကွဲ ဒဏ်ရာ hat-tat-kwal-dan-yar *(n.)* **gash**

ဟက်တက်ကွဲသည် hat-tat-kwal-the *(v.)* **gash**

ဟက်တက်ကွဲသော hat-tat-kwal-taw *(adj.)* **gashing**

ဟက်တက်ရာ၊ အကွဲ haat taat rar, aakwal *(n.)* **slit**

ဟင်းခတ်အမွှေးအကြိုင် hinn hkaat a hmway a kyaine *(n.)* **spice**

ဟင်းလင်းပြင်၊ ဟာကွက် hinnlinnpyin , harkwat *(n.)* **void**
ဟင်းလင်းပြင်အကြောက်လွန်ခြင်း hin-lin-pyin-a-kyauk-lun-chin *(n.)* **agoraphobia**
ဟင်းလိုက်သည် hin-lite-the *(v.)* **ladle**
ဟသ်ပဒါး hin sa pa darr *(adj.)* **vermillion**
ဟစ်ရယ်သံ hit-yal-tan *(n.)* **hoot**
ဟစ်အော်ရယ်မောသည် hit-aw-yal-maw-the *(v.)* **hoot**
ဟစ်အော်သည် hit aawsai *(v.)* **shriek**
ဟန့်တားသည် hant tarr-sai *(v.)* **preclude**
ဟန်၊ အမူအယာ han, a-mu-a-yar *(n.)* **bearing**
ဟန်ချက်ညီအောင်ထားသည် han-chat-nyi-aung-htar-the *(v.)* **balance**
ဟန်ဆောင်ခြင်း han-saung-chin *(n.)* **masquerade**
ဟန်ဆောင်မှု haan-saung-mhu *(n.)* **pretence**
ဟန်ဆောင်မှု ကင်းသော han-saung-mu-kin-taw *(adj.)* **artless**
ဟန်ဆောင်သည် haan-saungsai *(v.)* **purport**
ဟန်ဆောင်သော၊ အတု haan-saung saw, aatu *(adj.)* **sham**
ဟန်ပြင်လျက်ရှိသော han-pyin-lyat-shi-taw *(adv.)* **afoot**
ဟန်ပြသရုပ်ဆောင်သည်၊ ဆိုဟန်ဆောင်သည် han-pya-ta-yoke-saung-the, so-han-saung-the *(v.)* **mime**
ဟန်ပါပါ လျှောက်သည် haan parpar shoutsai *(v.)* **strut**
ဟန်မူရာ ကြော့မော့ခြင်း haan-muu-rar-kyaww-mot-chinn *(n.)* **poise**
ဟန်အမူအရာ han-a-mu-a-yar *(n.)* **mannerism**
ဟလျက်ရှိသော ha-lyat-shi-taw *(adv.)* **ajar**
ဟာမိုနီ၊ သဟဇာတဖြစ်ခြင်း har-mo-ni, ta-ha-zar-ta-phit-chin *(n.)* **harmony**
ဟာရီကိန်းမုန်တိုင်း har-yee-kain-mone-tine *(n.)* **hurricane**
ဟာသ har-ta *(adj.)* **comic**
ဟာသစာတိုစာစ har-ta-sar-toe-sar-sa *(n.)* **epigram**
ဟာသဉာဏ် harsanyarn *(n.)* **wit**
ဟာသဉာဏ်ရွှင်သူ har-ta-nyan-shwin-thu *(n.)* **humorist**
ဟာသဉာဏ်ရွှင်သော har-sa nyarn shwin-saw *(adj.)* **witty**
ဟာသဉာဏ်ရှိသော har-ta-nyan-shwin-taw *(adj.)* **humorous**
ဟာသဖြစ်သော har-ta-phit-taw *(adj.)* **mirthful**
ဟာသမြောက်သော စကား har-sa myawt-saw sa-karr *(n.)* **witticism**
ဟာသသက်သက် har-tat-thet-thet *(n.)* **farce**
ဟာသော harsaw *(adj.)* **void**
ဟိတ်ဟန် hate-haan *(n.)* **pomposity**
ဟိတ်ဟန်ပါသော heik-han-par-taw *(adj.)* **ceremonious**
ဟိတ်ဟန်များသော hate haan-myarr-saw *(adj.)* **pompous**
ဟိန္ဒူ hinduu *(n.)* **tantra**
ဟိန်းသံ heinsan *(n.)* **roar**
ဟိန်းသည် heinsai *(v.)* **roar**
ဟိန်းသော heinsaw *(adj.)* **resonant**
ဟိုက်ဒရိုဂျင်ဒြပ် hai-da-ro-gyin-drat *(n.)* **hydrogen**
ဟိုင်းဝေးလမ်းမကြီး hai-way-lan-ma-gyi *(n.)* **highway**
ဟိုင်အီးနားတိရစ္ဆာန် hai-ei-nar-ta-yeik-san *(n.)* **hyaena, hyena**

ဟိုစပ်စပ် ဒီစပ်စပ် လုပ်သည် ho-sat-sat-di-sat-sat-lote-the *(v.)* **dabble**
ဟိုတယ် ho-tal *(n.)* **hotel**

ဟိုနား honarr *(adj.)* **yonder**

ဟီဘရူး ၂၃ လုံးမြောက်စာလုံး he bharuu 2 3 lone myawwathcarlone *(n.)* **taw**
ဟီမိုဂလိုဗင်သွေးဆဲလ် hae-mo-ga-lo-bin-tway-sal *(n.)* **haemoglobin**
ဟီသံ hi-tan *(n.)* **neigh**

ဟီသည် hi-the *(v.)* **neigh**

ဟုတ်ပါ့၊ တကယ်ပါပဲ hoke-pa, ta-kal-par-pal *(adv.)* **indeed**
ဟုတ်မှန်ကြောင်း ပြသသည့် hote-man-kyaung-pya-tha-the *(adj.)* **affirmative**
ဟုတ်သည် hote-sai *(adv.)* **yes**

ဟူးရေ hoo-yay *(interj.)* **hurrah**

ဟူးရေး huu-yay *(int.)* **eureka**

ဟေး hey *(interj.)* **ahoy**

ဟော့သွန်းဆူးပင် hot-toon-su-pin *(n.)* **hawthorn**
ဟောကြားသော တရား hawkyarrsaw tararr *(n.)* **sermon**
ဟောကိန်း hawkein *(n.)* **prediction**

ဟောကိန်းထုတ်သည် haw-kain-htoke-the *(v.)* **foretell**
ဟောက်သံ houtsan *(n.)* **snore**

ဟောက်သည် houtsai *(v.)* **snore**

ဟောက်သည်၊ အာခြစ်သံဖြင့် ပြောသည် hout sai, aar chit san-hpyint pyaww-sai *(v.)* **rasp**
ဟောင်းနွမ်းစုတ်ပြတ်သော haunggnwm sotepyatsaw *(adj.)* **shabby**
ဟောင်သည် haung-the *(v.)* **bark**

ဟောပြောသည် haw-pyaww-sai *(v.)* **preach**

ဟောပြောသည်၊ ပေးအပ်သည် haw-pyaw-the, pay-at-the *(v.)* **deliver**
ဟောဟဲဟိုက်သူ၏ အပြုအမူ haw hell hite-suueat aapyu-aamuu *(n.)* **panting**
ဟော်ကီ hor-ky *(n.)* **hockey**

ဟော်တယ်အစောင့် ho-tal-a-saunt *(n.)* **bellboy**
ဟဲလ်မတ်ဦးထုပ် hel-mat-oo-htoke *(n.)* **helmet**

အံ့ဖွယ်တစ်ပါး ant-phwal-ta-par *(n.)* **marvel**

အံ့ဖွယ်သရဲ ant-phwe-ta-ye *(n.)* **miracle**

အံ့သြတုန်လှုပ်သည် ant-aw-ton-lote-the *(v.)* **deplore**
အံ့သြတုန်လှုပ်သည်၊ ထုံထိုင်းတွေဝေသွားသည် ant aw tonehlote sai , htone htine twaywayswarrsai *(v.)* **stupefy**
အံ့သြဖွယ် aan aw-hpwal- *(adj.)* **wondrous**

အံ့သြဖွယ်ကောင်းသော aan aw hpwal-kaung-saw *(adj.)* **wonderful**
အံ့သြဖွယ်ကောင်းသော သူ ant-aw-phwal-kaung-taw-thu *(adj.)* **marvellous**
အံ့သြသည် ant aw-sai *(v.)* **surprise**

အံ့သြသော၊ ရုပ်ပိုင်းညီမျှမှုမရှိသော ant-aw-taw, yoke-pai-nyi-mya-mu-ma-shitaw *(adj.)* **off balance**
အံ့အားသင့်ခြင်း ant-aarr-sint-chinn *(n.)* **surprise**
အံ့အားသင့်ခြင်း၊ ဆောင့်ခြင်း ant-arr-tint-chin, saunt-chin *(n.)* **jolt**
အံ့အားသင့်စွာ ပြောသည် ant-arr-tint-swar-pyaw-the *(v.)* **exclaim**

အံ့အားသင့်စေခြင်း ant-arr-tint-say-chin *(n.)* **amazement**
အံ့အားသင့်စေသည် ant-arr-tint-say-the *(v.)* **amaze**
အံ့အားသင့်သွားခြင်း ant-arr-tint-twar-chin *(n.)* **flabbergast**
အံ့အားသင့်သွားသည် ant-arr-tint-twar-the *(adv.)* **aback**
အံ့အားသင့်သွားသော ant-arr-tint-twar-taw *(adj.)* **flabbergasted**
အံဆွဲ an-swal *(n.)* **drawer**
အံဆွဲ၊ ဗီရိုငယ် an-swal, bi-yo-ngwe *(n.)* **locker**
အံဆုံး aansone *(n.)* **wisdom-tooth**
အံဝင်ခွင်ကျ စီမံထားပေးသည် aan-winhkwinkya seman htarrpayysai *(v.)* **tailor**
အံဝှက်တံခါး saalyuuphoetsaungrayy *(n.)* **trapdoor**
အံသွား an-twar *(n.)* **molar**
အံသွားနှင့်ဆိုင်သော an-twar-nint-sai-taw *(adj.)* **molar**
အကတိလိုက်စားခြင်း a-ka-ti-lite-sar-chin *(n.)* **corruption**
အကန့်တစ်ကန့်၏ လေးစိတ်တစ်စိတ် တန်ဖိုးရှိသော နရီချိန်သင်္ကေတ a-kant-ta-kant-ei-lay-seik-ta-seik-tan-phoe-shi-taw-na-yee-chain-tin-kay-ta *(n.)* **crotchet**
အကန့်အသတ် a-kant-a-thet *(n.)* **limitation**
အကန့်အသတ်၊ ဖိအား a-kant-a-tat, phi-arr *(n.)* **constraint**
အကန့်အသတ်ဖယ်ရှားခြင်း a-kant-a-thet-phal-shar-chin *(n.)* **delimitation**
အကန့်အသတ်ဖယ်ရှားသည် a-kant-a-thet-phal-shar-the *(v.)* **delimitate**
အကန့်အသတ်မဲ့သော a-kant-a-thet-mae-taw *(adj.)* **limitless**
အကဗေဒ a-ka-bay-da *(n.)* **choreography**
အကယ်၍ a-kal-ywe *(conj.)* **if**
အကျင့် aa-kyint *(n.)* **wont**
အကျင့်စာရိတ္တဆိုင်ရာ a-kyint-sar-yeik-ta-sai-yar *(n.)* **morality**
အကျင့်စာရိတ္တပျက်ပြားစေသည် a-kyint-sar-yeik-ta-pyat-pyar-say-the *(v.)* **deprave**
အကျင့်ပျက်ချစားခြင်း a-kyint-pyat-cha-sar-chin *(n.)* **depravation**
အကျင့်ပျက်ချစားသော နေရာ a-kyint-pyat-cha-sar-taw-nay-yar *(n.)* **cesspool**
အကျင့်ပျက်ခြင်း၊ မကောင်းမှု a-kyint-pyat-chin, ma-kaung-mu *(n.)* **immorality**
အကျင့်ပျက်သည် a-kyint-phat-the *(adj.)* **corrupt**
အကျင့်ပျက်သော a-kyint-pyat-taw *(adj.)* **immoral**
အကျင့်မှား a-kyint-hmar *(n.)* **malpractice**
အကျင့်သိက္ခာစောင့်စည်းမှု တင်းကျပ်လွန်းသော a kyint sate-hkar saunt see-mhu, tinnkyat lwann-saw *(adj.)* **puritanical**
အကျင့်သိက္ခာနှင့် ပတ်သက်၍ ဟောပြော ရေးသားသည် a-kyint-take-khar-nint-pat-tat-ywe-haw-pyaw-yay-tar-the *(v.)* **moralize**
အကျင့်သိက္ခာရှိသော a-kyiint-taik-khar-shi-taw *(adj.)* **moral**
အကျင့်သီလမဲ့သူ a-kyint-thi-la-mae-thu *(n.)* **libertine**
အကျင့် a-kyint *(n.)* **habit**
အကျင့်ခြိုးခြံသော a-kyint-choe-chan-taw *(adj.)* **austere**
အကျင့်ရှိသော a-kyintshisaw *(adj.)* **wont**
အကျဉ်းကျခြင်း a-kyin-kya-chin *(n.)* **confinement**

အကျဉ်းချခံရခြင်း a-kyin-cha-khan-ya-chin *(n.)* **captivity**

အကျဉ်းချသည် a-kyin-cha-the *(v.)* **encage**

အကျဉ်းချုံးသည် a-kyin-chone-the *(v.)* **abridge**

အကျဉ်းချုပ် aa-kyin-chote *(adj.)* **summary**

အကျဉ်းချုပ်၊ သံခိပ် aa-kyin chote, san hkate *(n.)* **precis**

အကျဉ်းချုပ်သည် aa-kyin chote-sai *(v.)* **summarize**

အကျဉ်းချုပ်အားဖြင့် aa-kyin chote aarr-hpyint *(adv.)* **summarily**

အကျဉ်းရုံးသည် aa-kyin ronesai *(v.)* **sum**

အကျဉ်းသား aa-kyin-sarr *(n.)* **prisoner**

အကျဉ်းသားဘဝ a-kyin-tar-ba-wa *(n.)* **bondage**

အကျဉ်းအကျပ် aa-kyin-aa-kyat *(n.)* **plight**

အကျန် a-kyan *(adj.)* **residual**

အကျပ်ကိုင်သည် a-kyat-kai-the *(v.)* **coerce**

အကျပ်ရိုက်ခြင်း a-kyat-yite-chin *(n.)* **dilemma**

အကျပ်အတည်း aa-kyat-aa-tee *(n.)* **predicament**

အကျယ် aakyaal *(adv.)* **wide**

အကျွမ်းတဝင်ပြုသည် a-kyuwn-ta-wiwn-pyu-the *(v.)* **hobnob**

အကျွေးအမွေးတာဝန်ယူရသူ a-kyay-a-mway-tar-win-yu-ya-thu *(n.)* **caterer**

အကျိအချွဲ aakyi a chwal *(n.)* **slime**

အကျိအချွဲဖြစ်သော a-kyi-a-chwe-phit-taw *(adj.)* **mucous**

အကျိုး a-kyo *(n.)* **advantage**

အကျိုးကျေးဇူးပြုသော a-kyo-kyay-zu-pyu-taw *(adj.)* **advantageous**

အကျိုးခံစားခွင့် aa-kyoe-hkan-sarr-hkwint *(v.)* **perk**

အကျိုးခံစားသူ a-kyo-khan-sar-thu *(n.)* **beneficiary**

အကျိုးဆက် aa-kyoesaat *(n.)* **sequel**

အကျိုးဆက် ဖြစ်ပေါ်သည် aakyoesaat hpyitpawsai *(v.)* **result**

အကျိုးဆက်ဖြစ်သော a-kyo-sat-phyit-taw *(adj.)* **consequent**

အကျိုးဆောင်ခ a-kyo-saung-kha *(n.)* **brokerage**

အကျိုးတရား a-kyo-ta-yar *(n.)* **effect**

အကျိုးတရားကို ဖြစ်စေခြင်း a-kyo-ta-yar-ko-phit-say-chin *(n.)* **causation**

အကျိုးပြုသည် aakyoepyusai *(v.)* **sustain**

အကျိုးပြုသော aakyoepyusaw *(adj.)* **salutary**

အကျိုးများသော a-kyo-myar-taw *(adj.)* **uberous**

အကျိုးမရှိ aa-kyoe-ma-shi *(adj.)* **pointless**

အကျိုးရှိသော a-kyo-shi-taw *(adj.)* **beneficial**

အကျိုးသက်ရောက်မှု a-kyo-tat-yauk-mu *(n.)* **impact**

အကျိုးသက်ရောက်မှု ညီမျှသော aakyoesaatroutmhu nyemyahasaw *(v.)* **tantamount**

အကျိုးသက်ရောက်မှုရှိသည် a-kyo-tat-yauk-mu-shi-the *(v.)* **effect**

အကျိုးအမြတ် aa-kyoe-aa-myat *(n.)* **profit**

အကျိုးအမြတ်မပါသော a-kyoe-a-myat-ma-par-taw *(adj.)* **non-profit**

အကျုံးဝင်စေသည် a-kyone-win-say-the *(v.)* **encompass**

အကျုံးဝင်မှု၊ လွှမ်းချုံနိုင်မှု a-kyone-win-mu, hlwan-chon-nai-mu *(n.)* **coverage**

အကျောနှင့် ဆက်ဆံသည် a-kyaw-nint-saat-san-sai *(v.)* **patronize**
အကျော်အမော်ပုဂ္ဂိုလ်များ aa-kyaw-aa-maw-poke-gol-myarr *(n.)* **personage**
အကြံဉာဏ် a-kyan-nyan *(n.)* **advice**
အကြံပြုခြင်း aakyaanpyuchinn *(n.)* **suggestion**
အကြံပြုထောက်ခံသည် aa-kyaan-pyu htout-hkansai *(v.)* **recommend**
အကြံပြုသည် aakyaanpyusai *(v.)* **suggest**
အကြံပေးသော a-kyan-pay-taw *(adj.)* **advisory**
အကြံရသည်၊ ကိုယ်ဝန်ဆောင်သည် a-kyan-ya-the, ko-win-saung-the *(v.)* **conceive**
အကြံသမား aakyaansamarr *(n.)* **schemer**
အကြံအိုက်စေသည် aa-kyaan aite-saysai *(v.)* **puzzle**
အကြင်နာမဲ့စေသည် a-kyin-nar-mae-say-the *(v.)* **brutalize**
အကြင်နာမဲ့သော aa-kyinnar maesaw *(adj.)* **ruthless**
အကြည့် a-kyi *(n.)* **glance**
အကြည့် a-kyi *(n.)* **look**
အကြမ်းခံနိုင်စေသည် aa-kyam hkan ninesaysai *(v.)* **toughen**
အကြမ်းဖက်မှု aakyamhpaatmhu *(n.)* **violence**
အကြမ်းဖက်ဝါဒ aakyamhpaatwarda *(n.)* **terrorism**
အကြမ်းဖက်သမား aakyamhpaatsamarr *(n.)* **terrorist**
အကြမ်းဖျင်းခန့်မှန်းဖြစ်သော a-kyan-phin-khant-man-phit-taw *(adj.)* **estimative**
အကြမ်းဖော်ပြချက် a-kyan-phaw-pya-chat *(n.)* **conspectus**
အကြွင်းမဲ့ a-kywin-mae *(adv.)* **absolutely**
အကြွင်းမဲ့ အာဏာပိုင်စိုးခြင်း a-kywin-mae-ar-nar-paing-soe-chin *(n.)* **absolutism**
အကြွင်းမဲ့ အာဏာရှင်စနစ် aa-kywin-mae aar-narhlyinsanit *(adj.)* **totalitarian**
အကြွင်းမဲ့ဖြစ်သော a-kywin-mae-phit-taw *(adj.)* **absolute**
အကြွင်းအကျန် aakywin aakyaan *(n.)* **residue**
အကြွေး a-kyway *(n.)* **debt**
အကြွေးဆပ်သည် aakyaway satsai *(v.)* **repay**
အကြွေးတင်ရှိသော a-kyay-tin-shi-taw *(adj.)* **indebted**
အကြွေးတင်သည် a-kyay-tin-tai *(v.)* **owe**
အကြွေးမဆပ်နိုင်၍ ပိုင်ဆိုင်ပစ္စည်းကို လက်ဝယ်ထားခွင့် a-kyay-a-sat-nai-ywe-pai-sai-pyit-see-ko-lat-wal-htar-khwint *(n.)* **lien**
အကြွေးမဆပ်နိုင်သော a-kyay-ma-sat-nai-taw *(adj.)* **insolvent**
အကြွေစေ့ a-kyway-say *(n.)* **coin**
အကြား a-kyar *(prep.)* **between**
အကြား၊ ကြားကာလ a-kyar, kyar-kar-la *(n.)* **interval**
အကြား၊ အဟ a kyarr , aah *(n.)* **rift**
အကြားစွမ်းရည်အဓိကဖြင့် သင်ယူနိုင်သော သူ a-kyar-swan-yay-a-di-ka-phint-tin-yu-naing-taw-thu *(adj.)* **auditive**
အကြားတွင် a-kyar-twin *(prep.)* **among**
အကြားသက်သေ a-kyaw-thet-tay *(n.)* **hearsay**
အကြို၊ ပဏာမ aa-kyo , pa-nar-ma *(adj.)* **preliminary**
အကြိုက် a-kyaik *(n.)* **like**
အကြိုက်ဆုံး a-kyaik-sone *(adj.)* **favourite**
အကြိုပြုလုပ်သော aakyo-pyulotesaw *(adj.)* **preparatory**

အကြိုဗိုလ်လုပွဲတက်သူ aakyao bollupwal taatsuu *(n.)* **semi-finalist**
အကြီး a-kyi *(n.)* **macro**
အကြီးဖြစ်သူ a-kyi-phit-thu *(n.)* **elder**
အကြီးဖြစ်သော a-kyi-phit-taw *(adj.)* **elder**
အကြီးအကျယ် aa-kyee-aa-kyaal *(adj.)* **profound**
အကြီးအကျယ် ပူပန်သည် a-kyi-a-kyal-pu-pan-the *(v.)* **dread**
အကြေးထိုးသည် a kyay htoesai *(v.)* **scale**
အကြောက်ကြီးသော a-kyauk-kyi-taw *(adj.)* **craven**
အကြောင်းကြားသည် a-kyaung-kyar-te *(v.)* **notify**
အကြောင်းခံ a-kyaung-khan *(n.)* **factor**
အကြောင်းခံသည် a-kyaung-khan-the *(v.)* **cause**
အကြောင်းတရား a-kyaung-ta-yar *(n.)* **cause**
အကြောင်းတရားအဖြစ် မှတ်ယူသည် a-kyaung-ta-yar-a-phit-mat-yu-the *(v.)* **ascribe**
အကြောင်းပြချက် aa-kyaunggpya-chet *(n.)* **reason**
အကြောင်းပြချက် ပိတ်ပင်သည် a-kyaung-pya-chat-pate-pin-the *(v.)* **dement**
အကြောင်းပြချက်၊ သဘောတရား aa-kyaungg-pyachet, sa-bhaw-tararr *(n.)* **rationale**
အကြောင်းပြသော a-kyaung-pya-taw *(adj.)* **ostensible**
အကြောင်းမဲ့ aa-kyaunggmae *(adj.)* **wanton**
အကြောင်းရင်း a-kyaung-yin *(n.)* **motive**
အကြောင်းရှာသည် aakyaungg sharsai *(v.)* **rationalize**
အကြောင်းအကျိုးအယူအဆ aakyaunggaakyoeaayuuaas *(n.)* **teleology**
အကြောင်းအကျိုးအယူအဆရှိသူ aakyaunggaakyoe aayuuaasashisuu *(n.)* **teleologist**
အကြောင်းအကျိုးအယူအဆရှိသော aakyaunggaakyoe aayuuaasashisaw *(adj.)* **teleologic**
အကြောင်းအချက် aa-kyaung-aa-chet *(n.)* **particular**
အကြောင်းအရာ အကျဉ်းချုပ် a-kyaung-a-yar-a-kyin-choke *(n.)* **blurb**
အကြောင်းအရာ၊ ဘာသာရပ် aakyaunggaarar , bharsarrat *(n.)* **subject**
အကြောင်းအရာတစ်ရပ်ကို ပြုစုထားသော စာတမ်း a-kyung-a-yar-ta-yat-ko-pyu-su-htar-taw-sar-tan *(n.)* **monograph**
အကြောလျှော့ လေ့ကျင့်ခန်း a-kyaw-shawt-lay-kyint-khan *(n.)* **limber**
အကြောလျှော့ လေ့ကျင့်ခန်း လုပ်သည် a-kyaw-shawt-lay-kyint-khan-lote-the *(v.)* **limber**
အကြောသေခြင်း aa-kyaww-say-chinn *(n.)* **paralysis**
အကြောသေသည် aa-kyaww-say-sai *(v.)* **paralyse**
အကွက်စေ့စေ့ aakwat saesae *(adv.)* **tautly**
အကွက်ဆင်ခြင်း a-kwat-sin-chin *(n.)* **gambit**
အကွက်ဖော်သည် a-kwat-phaw-the *(v.)* **panel**
အကွာအဝေး aakwaraawayy *(adj.)* **spatial**
အကွေ့အဝိုက်များသော aakwae a witemyarrsaw *(adj.)* **sinuous**
အကွေး a-kway *(n.)* **curvature**
အကွဲ a-lwal *(n.)* **cleavage**
အကွဲကြောင်း a-kwal-kyaung *(n.)* **fissure**
အကာ a-kar *(n.)* **envelopment**
အကာအကွယ် aa-kar-aakwal *(n.)* **protection**

အကာအကွယ်၊ လိုက်ကာ aakaraakwal , litekar *(n.)* **screen**
အကာအကွယ်ပေးသော aa-kar-aa-kwalpayysaw *(adj.)* **protective**
အကာအကွယ်မဲ့သော a-kar-a-kwal-mae-taw *(adj.)* **defenceless**
အကိုက်အခဲ a-keik-a-khae *(n.)* **ache**
အကိုက်အခဲပျောက်ဆေး a-kite-a-khae-pyauk-say *(n.)* **analgestic**
အကိုင်း၊ ဘေးဖြာနေသည့် အရာ a-kai, bay-phyar-nay-the-a-yar *(n.)* **lop**
အကိုင်း၊ အဖွဲ့ ခွဲ a-kai, a-phwe-khwal *(n.)* **branch**
အကိုင်ကြမ်းသည် a-kai-kyan-the *(v.)* **mistreat**
အကုသိုလ် a-ku-do *(n.)* **misdeed**
အကုသိုလ် ဝိပါက် a-ku-tho-wi-pat *(n.)* **nemesis**
အကူ a-khu *(adj.)* **auxiliary**
အကူးအပြောင်း aaswinpyaunggchinn *(n.)* **transit**
အကူအညီ a-ku-a-nyi *(n.)* **assistance**
အကူအညီ။ ကူညီသည် a-khu-a-nyi, khu-nyi-the *(n.& v.)* **aid**
အကူအညီတောင်းသည် a-ku-a-nyi-taung-the *(v.)* **help**
အကူအညီမပါဘဲဖြစ်သော aa-kuu-aa-nye ma-parbhelhlpyitsaw *(adj.)* **unaided**
အကူအညီမဲ့သော a-ku-a-nyi-mae-taw *(adj.)* **helpless**
အကူအပံ့သဘောမျှသာဖြစ်သော aakuu-a-pant sabhaw myahasarhpyitsaw *(adj.)* **subsidiary**
အကေရှားပင် a-kay-shar-pin *(n.)* **acacia**
အကောက်မဲ့ a-kauk-mae *(adj.)* **duty-free**
အကောက်အခွန်လွတ် aakoutaahkwanlwat *(adj.)* **tax-free**
အကောင်း a-kaung *(n.)* **good**
အကောင်းဆုံး a-kaung-sone *(adj.)* **best**
အကောင်းဆုံးဖြစ်သော a-kaung-sone-phit-taw *(adj.)* **dope**
အကောင်းဆုံးဖြစ်အောင် လုပ်ဆောင်သည် aa-kaung-sone-hpyit-aung-lote-saung-sai *(v.)* **perfect**
အကောင်းဆုံးအသုံးချသည် a-kaung-sone-a-tone-cha-the *(v.)* **maximize**
အကောင်းပကတိ a kaunggpakati *(adj.)* **sound**
အကောင်းမြင်ခြင်း a-kaung-myin-chinn *(n.)* **optimism**
အကောင်းမြင်ဝါဒီ a-kaung-myin-war-de *(n.)* **optimist**
အကောင်းမြင်သော a-kaung-myin-taw *(adj.)* **optimistic**
အကောင်အထည်ဖော်သည် a-kaung-a-htae-phaw-the *(v.)* **implement**
အကဲဖြတ်ခြင်း a-kae-phat-chin *(n.)* **assessment**
အကဲဖြတ်သည် a-kae-phat-the *(v.)* **assess**
အက္ခရာ at-kha-yar- *(n.)* **alphabet**
အက္ခရာသင်္ချာ at-kha-yar-thin-char *(n.)* **algebra**
အက္ခရာအစဉ်အတိုင်းဖြစ်သော at-kha-yar-a-sin-a-taing-phit-taw *(adj.)* **alphabetical**
အက်ကြောင်း at-kyaung *(n.)* **chink**
အက်ကွဲကြောင်း at-kwal-kyaung *(n.)* **cleft**
အက်ကွဲသည် at-kwal-the *(v.)* **crack**
အက်ကွဲသော at-kwal-taw *(adj.)* **husky**
အက်ခရိုင်လိတ်ဒြပ်ပေါင်း at-kha-ri-late-drat-paung *(n.)* **acrylate**
အက်ဆစ် at-cit *(n.)* **acid**

အက်ဆစ် စမ်းသပ်ချက် at-cit-san-tat-chat *(n.)* **acid test**
အက်ဆစ်တစ် အက်ဆစ် at-cit-tit-at-cit *(n.)* **acetic acid**
အက်ဆစ်ဓာတ်များသော at-cit-dat-myar-taw *(adj.)* **acidic**
အက်ဆစ်မိုး at-cit-moe *(n.)* **acid rain**
အက်ဆာပန်း at-sar-pan *(n.)* **acer**
အက်ဆီတိတ် ဓာတုဒြပ်ပေါင်း at-se-tate-dar-du-drat-paung *(n.)* **acetate**
အက်ဆီတိုင်လင်း ဓာတ်ငွေ့ at-se-ti-lin-drat-ngwe *(n.)* **acetylene**
အက်ဆီတုန်း ဒြပ်ပေါင်း at-se-tone-drat-paung *(n.)* **acetone**
အက်ဆေး၊ စာတမ်းတို၊ စာစီစာကုံး at-say, sar-tan-toe, sar-si-sar-kone *(n.)* **essay**
အက်တမ် at-tan *(n.)* **atom**
အက်ဒါမြွေပွေး at-dar-mway-pway *(n.)* **adder**
အက်ပ် ap *(n.)* **app**
အခက် aahkaat *(n.)* **sprig**
အခက်၊ ရေမှုန်ရေမွှား aah-kaat, ray hmone ray mwhar *(n.)* **spray**
အခက်တွေ့သည်၊ သစ်ငုတ်တို aa-hkaat-twae sai , sit ngote-to *(v.)* **stump**
အခက်အခဲ a-hat-a-khae *(n.)* **hitch**
အခက်အခဲရင်ဆိုင်နိုင်စွမ်း a-khet-a-khae-yin-sai-nai-swan *(n.)* **flapping**
အခင်း aa-hkainn *(n.)* **plantation**
အခင်းဖြစ်ရာ၊ ရှုခင်း၊ ပြကွက် a hkinn hpyitrar, shuhkinn , pyakwat *(n.)* **scene**
အခင်းအကျင်းပုံစံ a-khin-a-kyin-pon-san *(n.)* **layout**
အခန်း aahkaann *(n.)* **room**
အခန်းငယ် a-khan-nge *(n.)* **cubicle**
အခန်းငယ်၊ တဲ a-khan-nge, the *(n.)* **cabin**
အခန်းဆက်ဝတ္ထု aahkansaatwathtu *(n.)* **serial**
အခန်းဖော် aahkaannhpaw *(n.)* **room-mate**
အခမဲ့ a-kha-mae *(adv.)* **gratis**
အခမ်းအနား a-khan-a-nar *(adj.)* **ceremonial**
အခမ်းအနား၊ သဘင်၊ ဟိတ်ဟန် a-khan-a-nar, ta-bin, heik-han *(n.)* **ceremony**
အခမ်းအနားကျင်းပသည် a-khan-a-nar-kyin-pa-the *(v.)* **celebrate**
အခမ်းအနားဝတ်စုံ a-khan-a-nar-wut-sone *(n.)* **costume**
အချက်၊ ပစ္စည်း၊ သတင်းတစ်ပုဒ် a-chat, pyit-see, ta-din-ta-poke *(n.)* **item**
အချက်ပြခြင်း aachet pyachinn *(n.)* **signal**
အချက်ပြတုတ်တံ a-chat-pya-dote-tan *(n.)* **baton**
အချက်ပြမီး၊ မီးပြတိုက် a-chat-pya-mee, mee-pya-tite *(n.)* **beacon**
အချက်ပြသည် aachetpyasai *(v.)* **signal**
အချက်ပြသော aachetpyasaw *(adj.)* **signal**
အချက်ပေးဥသြ aachetpayy oak-aw *(n.)* **siren**
အချက်အချာ၊ သော့ချက် a-chat-a-char, tot-chat *(n.)* **keystone**
အချက်အပြုတ်ဆိုင်ရာ a-chat-a-pyoke-sai-yar *(adj.)* **culinary**
အချက်အလက် a-chat-a-lat *(n.)* **data**
အချက်အလက် ရိုက်သွင်းသည် a-chat-a-lat-yite-twin-the *(v.)* **key**
အချက်အလက် လွှဲပြောင်းသည် a-chat-a-lat-hlwal-pyaung-the *(v.)* **download**
အချက်အလက်စာရင်း a-chat-a-lat-sa-yin *(n.)* **database**
အချင်း aa-chinn *(n.)* **placenta**

အချင်းများခြင်း aachinnmyarrchinn *(n.)* **warfare**

အချင်းဝက် a chinn-waat *(n.)* **radius**

အချစ် a-chit *(n.)* **love**

အချစ်ကြီးမှု a-chit-kyi-mu *(n.)* **devotion**

အချစ်ကိစ္စ a-chit-keik-sa *(n.)* **amour**

အချစ်ဆုံး a-chit-sone *(adj.)* **dearest**

အချစ်အကြင်နာစကား a-chit-a-kyin-nar-sa-kar *(n.)* **endearment**

အချဉ်ပေါက်သည် a chin poutsai *(v.)* **sour**

အချဉ်ဖောက်ခြင်း a-chin-phauk-chin *(n.)* **fermentation**

အချဉ်ဖောက်သည် a-chin-phauk-the *(v.)* **ferment**

အချည်းနှီး chaine , taungkyarr *(adv.)* **vainly**

အချည်းနှီးဖြစ်ခြင်း a-chee-nee-phit-chin *(n.)* **futility**

အချည်းနှီးဖြစ်စေသည် a-chee-nee-phit-say-the *(v.)* **negate**

အချည်းနှီးဖြစ်သော a-chee-nee-phit-taw *(adj.)* **futile**

အချပ်၊ အပြား a chat, aa-pyarr *(n.)* **slab**

အချပ်၊ အယှက် a chat, aa-shaat *(n.)* **slice**

အချပ်လိုက် အလွှာလိုက် လှီးသည် a chat-lite aa-lwhar-lite hlee-sai *(v.)* **slice**

အချိန် aachane *(n.)* **time**

အချိန်ကန့်သတ်ချက် aachane kant saatchet *(n.)* **time limit**

အချိန်ကိုက်သည် aachanekitesai *(v.)* **time**

အချိန်ကုန်စေသည် aachanekonesaysai *(v.)* **while**

အချိန်ဆွဲခြင်း aa-chane-swalchinn *(n.)* **procrastination**

အချိန်ဆွဲသည် aa-chane-swalsai *(v.)* **procrastinate**

အချိန်ဆွဲသူ a-chain-swal-thu *(n.)* **dawdler**

အချိန်တခဏသာလျှင်ကြာသော aahkyane tahkan sarshin kyaarsaw *(adj.)* **temporal**

အချိန်တိုအတွင်း ပြင်းပြင်းထန်ထန်ကြိုးပမ်းရသော a-chain-to-a-twin-pyin-pyin-htan-htan-kyoe-pan-ya-taw *(adj.)* **intensive**

အချိန်နှင့်အမျှ တန်ဖိုးကျသော a-chein-nint-a-mya-tan-pho-kya-taw *(adj.)* **depreciating**

အချိန်နှောင်းသော a-chain-hnaung-taw *(adj.)* **belated**

အချိန်ပို a-chane-po *(n.)* **overtime**

အချိန်ပိုင်းမျှသာခံသော kuupyaunggsai *(adj.)* **transitory**

အချိန်ဖြုန်းသည် a-chain-hpyone-the *(v.)* **loaf**

အချိန်မဆိုင်း a-chain-ma-sai *(adj.)* **instantaneous**

အချိန်မှန်ခြင်း aa-chane-mhaanchinn *(n.)* **punctuality**

အချိန်မှန်သော aa-chane-mhaansaw *(adj.)* **punctual**

အချိန်မှီ aachanemhae *(adj.)* **timely**

အချိန်ယူစဉ်းစားခြင်း a-chain-yu-sin-sar-chin *(n.)* **mull**

အချိန်ယူစဉ်းစားသည် a-chain-yu-sin-sar-the *(v.)* **mull**

အချိန်လွန်မှ a-chain-lun-hma *(adv.)* **late**

အချိန်သင့် a-chane-tint *(adj.)* **opportune**

အချိန်သင့်သော၊ မှန်ကန်စွာဖြစ်သော a-chane-tint-taw-man-kan-swar-phit-taw *(adj.)* **well-timed**

အချိန်အကန့်အသတ်မရှိသော a-chain-a-kant-a-tat-ma-shi-taw *(adj.)* **indefinite**

အချိန်အတောအတွင်း a-chain-a-taw-a-twin *(adv.)* **meanwhile**
အချိန်အလိုက် အဖြစ်အပျက်များ aachaneaalite aahpyitaapyetmyarr *(n.)* **timeline**
အချို aacho *(n.)* **sweet**
အချိုး aa-choe *(n.)* **ratio**
အချိုးကျ aa-choe-kya *(adj.)* **proportionate**
အချိုးကျဖြစ်သော aa-choe-kya-hpyit-saw *(adj.)* **proportional**
အချိုးကျသော aa-choekyasaw *(adj.)* **shapely**
အချိုးမကျခြင်း a-choe-ma-kya-chin *(n.)* **disproportion**
အချိုးမကျသော a-choe-ma-kya-taw *(adj.)* **awkward**
အချိုးမညီခြင်း a-choe-ma-nyi-chin *(n.)* **asymmetry**
အချိုးမညီသော a-choe-ma-nyi-taw *(adj.)* **asymmetrical**
အချိုးမပြေသူ a-choe-ma-pyay-tuu *(n.)* **oaf**
အချိုခဲဖွယ် a hkyao hkellhpwal *(n.)* **sweetmeat**
အချိုင့် ဖြစ်ပေါ်စေသည် a-chaine-hpyit-paw-say-sai *(v.)* **pit**
အချိုတည်းစရာ a-cho-te-sa-yar *(n.)* **dessert**
အချိုရည်တစ်ခုတည်းကို ပုံမှန်သောက်သူ a-cho-yay-ta-khu-tae-ko-pon-man-taut-thu *(n.)* **bibber**
အချုပ်ကို ထုတ်ပြသည် a-choke-ko-htoke-pya-the *(v.)* **encapsulate**
အချုပ်အခြာ aa-chote-aa-chaar *(adj.)* **sovereign**
အချောင်းအတံ a chaungg aatan *(n.)* **rod**
အချောင်သမားဝါဒ a-chaung-ta-mar-war-da *(n.)* **opportunism**
အချောသတ်သည် a chaww saatsai *(v.)* **smooth**
အချောအလှ a-chaw-a-hla *(n.)* **belle**
အခရိုင်လစ်ပန်းချီဆေး a-kha-ri-lit-pa-chi-say *(adj.)* **acrylic**
အခြား a-char *(adj.)* **another**
အခြားကမ္ဘာဂြိုလ်နှင့် ဆိုင်သော a-char-ka-bar-gyo-nint-sai-taw *(adj.)* **extraterrestrial**
အခြားဂဏန်းနှင့် မြောက်ခံရသော ဂဏန်း a-char-ga-nan-nint-myaut-khan-ya-taw-ga-nan *(n.)* **multiplicand**
အခြားနိုင်ငံတွင် ပြောင်းရွှေ့နေထိုင်ခြင်း a-char-nai-ngan-twin-pyaung-shway-nay-htai-chin *(n.)* **emigration**
အခြားနိုင်ငံတွင် ပြောင်းရွှေ့နေထိုင်သည် a-char-nai-ngan-twin-pyaung-shway-nay-htai-the *(v.)* **emigrate**
အခြားဘဝကူးပြောင်းနိုင်စွမ်း aahkyarr bhaw kuu-pyaungg-nineswam *(n.)* **otherworldliness**
အခြားသူများထက် သာလွန်ခြင်း a-char-thu-myar-htet-tar-lun-chin *(adj.)* **pre-eminent**
အခြားသူအတွက် ယုံကြည်မှုနှင့် ပူပန်မှုကို ပြသောလိမ်ကွဲစိတ်ဝင်စားသူ အမျိုးသား a-char-thu-a-twat-yone-kyi-mu-nint-pu-pan-mu-ko-pya-taw-lain-kwal-seik-win-sar-thu-amyo-tar *(adj.)* **ubersexual**
အခြားသူအား ပြင်းထန်စွာ ဝေဖန်သော a-char-thu-arr-pyin-htan-swar-wai-phan-taw *(adj.)* **censorious**
အခြားသော acharr-taw *(adj.)* **other**
အခြေခံ aa-chay-hkan *(adj.)* **primary**
အခြေခံကျသော a-chay-khan-kya-taw *(adj.)* **fundamental**
အခြေခံပညာအဆင့် နောက်ဆုံးစာမေးပွဲ a-chay-khan-pyin-nyar-a-sint-naut-sone-sar-may-pwe *(n.)* **baccalaureate**

အခြေခံမျှသာ ဖြစ်သော aachayhkanmya-sar hpyitsaw *(adj.)* **rudimentary**
အခြေခံသဘောတရား aachayhkansabhawtararr *(n.)* **rudiment**
အခြေခံအကြောင်းရင်း a-chay-khan-a-kyaung-yin *(n.)* **basis**
အခြေခံအားဖြင့် a-chay-khan-arr-phyit *(adv.)* **basically**
အခြေချနေထိုင်နိုင်သော a-chay-cha-nay-htai-nai-taw *(adj.)* **inhabitable**
အခြေအနေ aachayaanay *(n.)* **situation**
အခြေအနေကောင်းလာပြီးမှ ဒုံရင်းအတိုင်း ပြန်ဖြစ်ခြင်း a-chay-a-nay-kaung-lar-pee-ma-don-yin-a-tine-pyan-phyit-chin *(v.)* **backslide**
အခြေအနေယိုင်သည် a-chay-a-nay-yai-the *(v.)* **falter**
အခြေအနေအရဖြစ်သော a-chay-a-nay-a-ya-phit-taw *(adj.)* **conditional**
အခြေအမြစ်မရှိသော a-chay-a-myit-ma-shi-taw *(adj.)* **baseless**
အခြောက်ခံစက် a-chauk-khan-sat *(n.)* **dryer**
အခြောက်ခံနည်းဖြင့် ဆေးဆိုးသည် a hkyawwat hkan naeehpyint sayy soesai *(v.)* **taw**
အခြောက်လျှော်သည် a-chauk-shaw-the *(v.)* **dry-clean**
အခွံ aa-hkwan *(n.)* **peel**
အခွံ၊ အဖုံး a-khoon, a-hpone *(n.)* **casing**
အခွံခွာသည် a hkwan hkwarsai *(v.)* **shell**
အခွံနွှာသည် a-hkwan-nwhar-sai *(v.)* **peel**
အခွံမာ a hkwanmar *(n.)* **shell**
အခွံမာသီး a-hkwan-mar-tee *(n.)* **nut**
အခွက်တွင် ထည့်ထားသော ညွှန်ပြအလုံး a-khwat-twin-htae-htar-taw-nyun-pya-a-lone *(n.)* **trackball**

အခွင့်အရေး a-kwint-a-ray *(n.)* **opportunity**
အခွင့်အလမ်း၊ နယ်ပယ် a-hkwint a lam , naalpaal *(n.)* **scope**
အခွင့်အာဏာ a hkwint-aar-nar *(n.)* **prerogative**
အခွင့်ကောင်းစောင့်သည် a-khwint-kaung-saunt-the *(v.)* **bide**
အခွင့်အရေး a-khwint-a-yay *(n.)* **chance**
အခွန် aahkwan *(n.)* **tax**
အခွန်စည်းကြပ်ခြင်း aahkwan saeekyautchinn *(n.)* **taxation**
အခွန်စည်းကြပ်ရန် ဝင်ငွေစာရင်း aahkwan saeekyautraan win-ngway-sarrinn *(n.)* **tax return**
အခွန်စည်းကြပ်သည် aahkwan saeekyautsai *(v.)* **tax**
အခွန်တော် ဆောင်ရန် aahkwantaw saungraan *(adj.)* **taxable**
အခွန်ထမ်း aahkwanhtam *(n.)* **taxpayer**
အခွန်ဘဏ္ဍာ aahkwanbhandar *(n.)* **revenue**
အခွေ a-khway *(n.)* **coil**
အခွေ၊ အလိပ်ပုံ အပြောက်အမွမ်း aahkway , a liutpone a pyaut a mwm *(n.)* **scroll**
အခွေအလိပ် a-khway-a-ote *(v.)* **curl**
အခါ၊ အခိုက် a-hkar, a-hkite *(n.)* **occasion**
အခါက a-kha-ka *(adv.)* **ago**
အခါအားလျော်စွာ a-hkar-ar-lyaw-swar *(adj.)* **occasional**
အခိုင်အမာဆိုသည် a-khaing-a-mar-so-the *(v.)* **assert**
အခိုင်အမာဆိုသည်၊ တောင်းဆိုသည် a-khai-a-mar-so-the, taung-so-the *(v.)* **claim**
အခိုင်အမာပြောသည် a-khaing-a-mar-pyaw-the *(v.)* **affirm**

အခုံး a-khone *(n.)* **arch**

အခု၊ အခံ a-hku, a-hkan *(n.)* **pad**

အခုအခံ a-hku a-hkan *(n.)* **padding**

အခေါက်၊ ခေါက်ရာ၊ ခေါက်ရိုး၊ အတွန့် a-khauk, khauk-yar, khauk-yoe, a-twunt *(n.)* **fold**

အခေါင်း a-khaung *(n.)* **coffin**

အခေါင်းပေါက်ရှိသော a-khaung-paut-par-taw *(adj.)* **hollow**

အခဲ aahkell *(n.)* **solid**

အခဲ၊ အတုံး a-khae, a-tone *(n.)* **lump**

အဂ္ဂိရတ် at-gi-yat *(n.)* **alchemy**

အဂ္ဂိရတ်ဆရာ at-gi-yat-sa-yar *(n.)* **alchemist**

အငမ်းမရ မျိုချသည် a-ngan-ma-ya-myo-cha=the *(n.)* **gobble**

အငမ်းမရစားသည် a-ngan-ma-ya-sar-the *(v.)* **devour**

အငမ်းမရဖြစ်သည် a-ngan-ma-ya-phit-the *(v.)* **covet**

အငယ်ဆုံးအဖွဲ့၊ တပ်ဖွဲ့ငယ် aangaalsone aahpwal , tauthpwalngaal *(n.)* **squad**

အငယ်တန်း a-nge-tan *(n.)* **junior**

အငြင်းပွားဖွယ် a-nyin-pwar-phwal *(adj.)* **controversial**

အငြင်းပွားမှု a-nyin-pwar-mu *(n.)* **controversy**

အငြင်းအခုံ a-nyin-a-khone *(n.)* **argument**

အငြိမ်းစားယူခြင်း aangyeim-sarryuuchinn *(n.)* **retirement**

အငြိမ်းစားယူသည် aangyeim-sarr yuusai *(v.)* **retire**

အငြိုး a-nyoe *(n.)* **malice**

အငြိုးထားသော၊ အန္တရာယ်ရှိသော a-nyoe-htar-taw, an-da-yal-shi-taw *(adj.)* **malicious**

အငွေ့ pyaungglellsaw *(n.)* **vapour**

အငွေ၊ အရည်နှစ်ခုလုံးဖြစ်သော ငွေ့ရည်သိပ္ပံပညာ aangwae , aarai nhaithku lonehpyitsaw ngwaerai sippanpanyar *(n.)* **pneudraulics**

အငွေ့ပြန်သည် aangwae pyansaw *(v.)* **vaporize**

အငွေ့ပြန်သော aangwae *(adj.)* **vaporous**

အငွေ့ပြသည် a-ngae-pya-the *(v.)* **evaporate**

အငှား a-hngar *(n.)* **hire**

အငှားပရိသတ် a-nyar-pa-yeik-tat *(n.)* **claque**

အငှားလိုက်သူ a-hngar-lite-thu *(n.)* **hireling**

အငိုက်ဖမ်းတိုက်ခိုက်ခြင်း a ngite hpam tite-hkitechinn *(n.)* **raid**

အငိုက်ဖမ်းတိုက်ခိုက်သည် a ngite hpam tite-hkitesai *(v.)* **raid**

အငိုလွယ်သော a-nyo-lwal-the *(adj.)* **lachrymose**

အငုတ်၊ ငုတ်တို a ngote , ngote-to *(n.)* **stub**

အငူ a-ngu *(n.)* **cape**

အင်းဆက်ပိုး in-set-poe *(n.)* **insect**

အင်းဆက်သတ်ဆေး in-set-tat-say *(n.)* **insecticide**

အင်ဂျင်စက် in-gyin-sat *(n.)* **engine**

အင်ဂျင်နီယာ in-gyin-na-yar *(n.)* **engineer**

အင်ဂျင်နီယာပညာ in-gyin-na-yar-pyin-nyar *(n.)* **engineering**

အင်ဇိုင်း in-zai *(n.)* **enzyme**

အင်ဇိုင်းနှင့်ဆိုင်သော in-zai-nint-sai-taw *(adj.)* **enzymic**

အင်တင်တင် ဖြစ်နေသော in tintin hpyit-naysaw *(adj.)* **reluctant**

အင်တာနက် inn-tar-net *(n.)* **extranet**

အင်တာနက်ပေါ်တွင် အသံလွှင့်ခြင်း in-ter-net-paw-twin a-tan-lwint-chin *(n.)* **webcasting**

အင်တာနာတိုင် in-ta-nar-taing *(n.)* **antenna**

အင်တိုက်အားတိုက်ဖြစ်သော inn-tite-arr-tite-phit-taw *(adj.)* **dynamic**

အင်တီဂျင် an-ti-gen *(n.)* **antigen**

အင်တုံ inn-ton *(n.)* **bidet**

အင်ထရိုပီ en-ta-ro-pi *(n.)* **entropy**

အင်ထရိုပီနှင့်ဆိုင်သော en-ta-ro-pi-nint-sai-taw *(adj.)* **entropic**

အင်ပါယာ in-par-yar *(n.)* **empire**

အင်ပါယာနှင့် ဆိုင်သော in-par-yar-nint-sai-taw *(adj.)* **imperial**

အင်အားကြီးမားသော in-arr-kyi-mar-taw *(adj.)* **herculean**

အင်္ကျီ aainkyae *(n.)* **shirt**

အင်္ကျီ၊ အခြားအရာတစ်ခုခုနှင့် ခြုံသည် aain kyae , aahkyarr a rar taithkuhkunhang hkyuansai *(v.)* **sheet**

အင်္ကျီလက် ain kye-laat *(n.)* **sleeve**

အင်္ကျီလက်ပေါက် inn-gyi-lat-pauk *(n.)* **armhole**

အင်္ဂတေ in-ga-day *(n.)* **masonry**

အင်္ဂလိပ် in-ga-late *(n.)* **English**

အင်္ဂါ in-gar *(n.)* **organ**

အင်္ဂါချွတ်ယွင်းခြင်း in-gar-chyut-ywin-chin *(n.)* **mutilation**

အင်္ဂါဂြိုလ် in-gar-gyo *(n.)* **Mars**

အင်္ဂါတစ်ခုတွင် အမျှင်တစ်ရှူးဖြစ်ပေါ်ခြင်း in-gar-ta-khu-twin-a-hmyin-tit-shu-phit-paw-chin *(n.)* **fibrosis**

အင်္ဂါရပ် in-gar-yat *(n.)* **feature**

အစ a-sa *(n.)* **beginning**

အစ၊ စတင်ခြင်း a sa , sa-tin-chinn *(n.)* **start**

အစ၊ ဇာတိ၊ မြစ်ဖျားခံရာ၊ ရင်းမြစ် a sa, zarti , myithpyarrhkanrar , rinn-myit *(n.)* **source**

အစက် aasaat *(n.)* **speck**

အစက်ချသည် a-sat-cha-the *(v.)* **dribble**

အစက်ဖြင့် မှတ်သားသည် a-sat-phit-mat-tar-the *(v.)* **dot**

အစက်များဖြင့် မှတ်သားသည် a-sat-myar-phint-mat-tar-the *(v.)* **dapple**

အစက်အပြောက် a saat aapyaut *(n.)* **speckle**

အစက်အပြောက်ဖြင့် ပုံဖော်ပန်းချီဆရာ a-saat-a-pyatt-hpyint-pone-hpaw-pan-chae-sa-rar *(n.)* **pointillist**

အစက်အပြောက်ဖြင့် ပုံဖော်ပန်းချီရေးနည်း a-saat-a-pyaut-hpyint-pone-hpaw-pan-chae-rayy-nee *(n.)* **pointillism**

အစက်အပေါက် a-sat-a-paut *(n.)* **drop**

အစချီထားသည် aa-sa-chee-htarr-sai *(v.)* **preface**

အစင်း၊ အရေးအကြောင်း a sinn , aa-rayy-aa-kyaung *(n.)* **stripe**

အစစာလုံး အသံတူအောင်ပြု၍ ရေးခြင်း a-sa-sar-lone-a-tan-thu-aung-pyu-ywe-yay-chin *(n.)* **alliteration**

အစစာလုံး အသံတူအောင်ပြု၍ ရေးသည် a-sa-sar-lone-a-tan-thu-aung-pyu-ywe-yay-the *(v.)* **alliterate**

အစစ်၊ တရားဝင် a-sit, ta-yar-win *(adj.)* **bonafide**

အစစ်အမှန် aasait-aamhaan *(n.)* **reality**

အစစ်အမှန်ကမ္ဘာကို စာပေထဲရှိ

အတုကိုယ်စားပြုမှု a-sit-a-man-ka-bar-ko-sar-pay-htae-shi-a-tu-a-yaung-koe-sar-pyu-mu *(n.)* **mimesis**

အစဉ်ချစ်ခင်၍ သစ္စာရှိသော a-sin-chit-khin-ywe-tit-sar-shi-taw *(v.)* **devote**

အစဉ်လိုက်ဖြစ်သော a sin litehpyitsaw *(adj.)* **serial**

အစဉ်အလာ a sin aalar *(adj.)* **traditional**

အစဉ်အလာစကား a-sin-a-lar-sa-kar *(n.)* **lore**

အစဉ်အလာမှ လမ်းခွဲ၍ ခေတ်ဆန်လွန်းသော a-sin-a-lar-ma-lan-kwal-ywe-khit-san-lun-taw *(adj.)* **futuristic**

အစည်း၊ အတွဲ၊ အခိုင်၊ အဖီး a-see, a-twal, a-khai, a-phee *(n.)* **bunch**

အစည်း၊ အထုပ် a-see, a-htoke *(n.)* **bundle**

အစည်းအရုံး a-see-a-yone *(n.)* **guild**

အစည်းအဝေး a-see-a-way *(n.)* **meeting**

အစည်းအဝေးဖိတ်သည် a-see-a-way-phate-the *(v.)* **convoke**

အစည်းအဝေးအစီအစဉ် a-see-a-way-a-si-a-sin *(n.)* **agenda**

အစည်းအဝေးအထမြောက်ရန် အနည်းဆုံးလိုသည့် ဦးရေ aa-see-aa-wayy a hta-myawt-raan aa-nae-sone lo-seet u-ray *(n.)* **quorum**

အစန်တာငှက် a-san-tar-nyat *(n.)* **accentor**

အစပျိုးပေးသည် aasapyoepayysai *(v.)* **trigger**

အစပြုခြင်း၊ ဘွဲ့နှင်းသဘင် a-sa-pyu-chin, bwe-hnin-ta-bin *(n.)* **commencement**

အစပြုသည် a sapyusai *(v.)* **prefix**

အစပ်အချဉ်ရည် a-sat-a-chin-yay *(adj.)* **arrabbiata**

အစမှ a-sa-mha *(n.)* **outset**

အစမ်း aasam *(adj.)* **tentative**

အစမ်းခန့်ကာလ၊ ခံဝန်ချုပ်ဖြင့် လွှတ်ခြင်း a sam hkaant karla , hkan waan-chote-hpyint lwut-chinn *(n.)* **probation**

အစမ်းခန့်ကာလတွင် ရှိသူ၊ ခံဝန်ချုပ်ဖြင့် လွှတ်ခံရသူ a sam hkaant karla twin shi-thu , hkan waan-chote-hpyint lwut-khan-ya-thu *(n.)* **probationer**

အစမ်းလေ့ကျင့်ခြင်း a sam lae kyintchinn *(n.)* **rehearsal**

အစရှိသဖြင့် a-sa-shi-ta-phit *(adv.)* **etcetera**

အစွန်း a-sun *(n.)* **edge**

အစွန်း၊ အစက် a-soon-a-sat *(n.)* **blot**

အစွန်းခံ aaswannhkan *(adj.)* **stainless**

အစွန်းချင်းထပ်သည် a-swan-chinn-htaut-tai *(v.)* **overlap**

အစွန်းနှစ်ဖက်ရောက်ခြင်းဆိုင်ရာ a-soon-na-phat-yaut-chin-saing-yar *(adj.)* **bipolar**

အစွန်းပိုင်း၊ အဖျားအနား aa-swann-pine, aa-hpyarr-aa-narr *(n.)* **periphery**

အစွန်းမရောက်ခြင်း a-sun-ma-yauk-chin *(n.)* **moderation**

အစွန်းရောက်မှု a-sun-yauk-mu *(n.)* **extreme**

အစွန်းရောက်ဝါဒီ a-sun-yauk-war-di *(n.)* **extremist**

အစွန်းအထင်း aaswann aahtinn *(n.)* **smear**

အစွန်းအထင်း၊ အမည်းစက် aaswann a htinn , aamaeesaat *(n.)* **taint**

အစွန်အဖျား a-sun-a-pyar *(n.)* **extremity**

အစွမ်းကုန် satekuu yinlawk *(n.)* **utmost**

အစွမ်းထက်မှု a-swan-htet-mu *(n.)* **efficacy**

အစွမ်းသတ္တိ aa-swam-satti *(n.)* **potentiality**

အစွယ် aaswal *(n.)* **tusk**

အစွယ်ပြပြီး မာန်ဖီသည် aa-swal pyapyee man hpesai *(v.)* **snarl**

အစွဲကင်းခြင်း၊ ဘက်မလိုက်ခြင်း၊ လျစ်လျူရှုခြင်း a-swal-kin-chin, bat-ma-lite-chin, lyit-lyu-shu-chin *(n.)* **detachment**

အစွဲအလမ်းကြီးခြင်း a-swal-a-lan-kyi-chin *(n.)* **fetish**

အစွဲအလမ်းကြီးလွန်းသော a-swal-a-lam-kyee-lwan-taw *(adj.)* **obsessive**

အစအန aa-sa-aa-na *(n)* **shard**

အစား a-sar *(n.)* **lieu**

အစားကြီးသူ a-sar-kyi-thu *(n.)* **glutton**

အစားကြီးသော aasarrkyeesaw *(adj.)* **voracious**

အစားကြူးခြင်း a-sar-kyu-chin *(n.)* **gluttony**

အစားကောင်းကြိုက်သူ a-sar-kaung-kyaik-taw *(n.)* **epicure**

အစားထိုးကုသချက် aa-san hlwint-saat *(n.)* **transplant**

အစားထိုးကုသခြင်း hpouth-twin-myin-nine-saw *(n.)* **transplantation**

အစားထိုးကုသည် hlwintsai *(v.)* **transplant**

အစားထိုးကုသမှု ခံယူသူ aa-sarr-htoe ku-sai *(n.)* **transplantee**

အစားထိုးခြင်း aasarrhtoechinn *(n.)* **substitution**

အစားထိုးသည် aasarrhtoesai *(v.)* **substitute**

အစားထိုးသူ aasarrhtoesuu *(n.)* **substitute**

အစားလောဘကြီးမှု a-sar-law-ba-kyi-mu *(n.)* **greed**

အစားဝင်၍ နေရာယူသည် a-sar-win-ywe-nay-yar-yu-the *(v.)* **displace**

အစားအစာ a-sar-a-sar *(n.)* **food**

အစားအစာ၊ အာဟာရ a-sar-a-sar, a-har-ya *(n.)* **aliment**

အစားအစာနှင့် တူသော a-sar-a-sar-nint-tu-taw *(adj.)* **mealy**

အစားအသောက် aasarr-aasout *(n.)* **refreshment**

အစားအသောက်ကောင်းရွေးနည်း၊ ချက်ပြုတ်နည်း၊ စားခြင်း a-sar-a-taut-kaung-ywe-nee, chat-pyoke-nee, sar-chin *(n.)* **gastronomy**

အစားအသောက်ပေါင်းစုံကို မြည်းစမ်းခြင်း a-sar-a-thaut-paung-sone-ko-myae-san-chin *(n.)* **degustation**

အစာခြေခြင်း a-sar-chay-chin *(n.)* **digestion**

အစာခြေသည် a-sar-chay-the *(v.)* **digest**

အစာမကျေခြင်း a-sar-ma-kyay-chin *(n.)* **indigestion**

အစာမကျေသော a-sar-ma-kyay-taw *(adj.)* **indigestible**

အစာရေမြိုပြွန်နှင့် ဆိုင်သော a-sar-yay-myo-pyun-nint-sai-taw *(adj.)* **esophageal**

အစာအိမ်၊ ဗိုက် aa-saraain , bite *(n.)* **stomach**

အစာအိမ်နှင့် သက်ဆိုင်သော a-sar-eain-nint-thet-sai-taw *(adj.)* **gastric**

အစာအိမ်အက်ဆစ်ဓာတ်ချိန်ညှိဆေး a-sar-eain-at-sit-dat-chain-nyi-say *(adj.)* **antacid**

အစာအိမ်အချိုင့်နေရာ a-sar-eain-a-chyaint-nay-yar *(n.)* **antecardium**

အစိတ်၊ အပိုင်း a sate , aapine *(n.)* **segment**

အစိတ်စိတ်အမြှာမြှာ ကွဲသည် a sate sate aa-mwar mwar kwalsai *(v.)* **shatter**

အစိတ်အပိုင်း a-seik-a-pai *(n.)* **fraction**

အစိတ်အပိုင်းခွဲသည် a-seik-a-pine-kwal-the *(v.)* **traunch**

အစိတ်အပိုင်းခွဲသော a-seik-a-pine-kwal-taw *(adj.)* **traunch**

အစိတ်အပိုင်းတစ်ရပ် aa-sate-aa-pine-ta-rat *(n.)* **proportion**

အစိတ်အပိုင်းတစ်ရပ်အဖြစ် ပါဝင်သော a-seik-a-pai-ta-yat-a-phit-par-win-taw *(adj.)* **constituent**

အစိတ်အပိုင်းပေါင်းစုခြင်း a-seik-a-pai-paung-su-chin *(n.)* **crasis**

အစိတ်အပိုင်းဖြစ်သော a-seik-a-pai-phit-taw *(adj.)* **component**

အစိမ်း a-sein *(n.)* **green**

အစိမ်း၊ အရိုင်း၊ အကြမ်းထည် aasaim , aarine , aakyam-htai *(adj.)* **raw**
အစိမ်းညို့ရောင် a-sein-nyoe-yaung *(n.)* **sage-green**
အစို့၊ အတက်၊ အမဲပစ်ပွဲ၊ ဓာတ်ပုံရိုက်ခြင်း a shoet, a taat, a mell pait pwal , dharatponeritechinn *(n.)* **shoot**
အစို့၊ အဖူး a-soe, a-phoo *(n.)* **bud**
အစို့အညှောက် a shoet a nyaut *(n.)* **sprout**
အစို့အညှောက်ထွက်သည် a shoet a nyaut htwatsai *(v.)* **sprout**
အစိုးရ a-soe-ya *(n.)* **government**
အစိုးရစနစ် aa-soe-rasanit *(n.)* **regime**
အစိုးရဆန့်ကျင်သော a-soe-ya-sant-kyin-taw *(adj.)* **insurgent**
အစိုးရဌာန၊ ဗီရိုစားပွဲ a-soe-ya-htar-na, bi-ro-sa-pwe *(n.)* **bureau**
အစိုးရပုံစံနှင့် လုပ်ငန်းစဉ် aa-soe-ra-pone-san-nint-lote-ngaann-sin *(n.)* **polity**
အစိုးရဝန်ကြီးအဖွဲ့၊ ဗီရို a-soe-ya-win-gyi-a-phwe, bi-ro *(n.)* **cabinet**
အစိုဓာတ် a-so-dat *(n.)* **moisture**
အစိုဓာတ်ကို ဖယ်ရှားသည် a-soe-dat-ko-phal-shar-the *(v.)* **dehumidify**
အစီတကျဖြစ်သော a-se-ta-kya-hpyit-taw *(adj.)* **orderly**
အစီရင်ခံစာ aase-rinhkansar *(n.)* **report**
အစီရင်ခံသည် aase-rinhkansai *(v.)* **report**
အစီအစဉ် aa-se-aa-sin *(n.)* **plan**
အစီအစဉ်၊ ဇာတ်ကွက် aaseaasin, zatkwat *(n.)* **sequence**
အစီအစဉ်စနစ် a-si-a-sin-sa-nit *(n.)* **configuration**
အစီအစဉ်မရှိ aaseaasinmashi *(adj.)* **unplanned**
အစီအစဉ်ရှိသည် aa-se-aa-sinshisai *(v.)* **programme**
အစု ရှယ်ယာများကို တရားဝင် ထုတ်မပေးမီ ရောင်းချခြင်း a-su-shal-yar-myar-ko-ta-yar-win-htoke-ma-pay-mi-yaung-cha-chin *(n.)* **grey market**
အစုံစားသတ္တဝါ a-sone-sar-tat-ta-war *(n.)* **omnivore**
အစုံစားသော a-sone-sar-taw *(adj.)* **omnivorous**
အစုံအစေ့ aa-sone-aa-sae *(adj.)* **thorough**
အစု၊ အသိုက် a-su, a-tite *(n.)* **bevy**
အစု၊ အအုံ a su , aa-aone *(n.)* **swarm**
အစုတ်အပြတ် a sotea-pyat *(n.)* **shred**
အစုပေါ်အမြတ် a-su-paw-a-myat *(n.)* **dividend**
အစုရှယ်ယာပမာဏ aasushalyarpamarna *(n.)* **shareholding**
အစုရှယ်ယာပမာဏဖြစ်သော aahcushalyar pamarnahpyitsaw *(adj.)* **shareholding**
အစုလိုက်အပြုံလိုက် aa-su-liteaa-pyone-lite *(adj.)* **wholesale**
အစုလိုက်အပြုံလိုက်သတ်ဖြတ်ခြင်း a-su-lite-a-pyone-lite-tat-phat-chin *(n.)* **massacre**
အစုလိုက်အပြုံလိုက်သတ်ဖြတ်သည် a-su-lite-a-pyone-lite-tat-phat-the *(v.)* **massacre**
အစုအတွဲ a-su-a-twe *(n.)* **batch**
အစုအပြုံလိုက် လူသတ်ခြင်း a-su-a-pyone-lite-lu-tat-chin *(n.)* **carnage**
အစုအပုံ a-su-a-pon *(n.)* **heap**
အစုအပေါင်း a-su-a-paung *(n.)* **conglomerate**
အစေ့ aasae *(n.)* **seed**
အစေ့ကျသည်၊ မျိုးပွားသည် aasae kya sai , myoe pwarrsai *(v.)* **seed**
အစေခံ a sayhkan *(n.)* **servant**

အစေအပါး a-say-a-par *(n.)* **menial**

အစေအပါးအလုပ် a-say-a-par-a-lote *(adj.)* **menial**

အစောင့်အရှောက် a-saunt-a-shaut *(n.)* **escort**

အစောင့် a-saunt *(n.)* **attendant**

အစောင့်အကြပ် a-saunt-a-kyat *(n.)* **guard**

အစောင်း a-saung *(adj.)* **italic**

အစ်ကို၊ ညီ a-ko, nyi *(n.)* **brother**

အစ်ထုတ်သည် it-htoke-the *(v.)* **elicitate**

အစ်အစ် မြည်သံ it-it-tan-myee-tan *(n.)* **grunt**

အဆက် a-sat *(n.)* **joint**

အဆက်မပြတ်စီးဆင်းသည် aa-saatmapyat seesinnsai *(v.)* **stream**

အဆက်အစပ် a-sat-a-sat *(n.)* **cohesion**

အဆက်အသွယ် a-sat-a-twal *(n.)* **contact**

အဆက်အသွယ်၊ ကွင်းဆက် a-sat-a-thwe, kwin-sat *(n.)* **link**

အဆင့် a-sint *(n.)* **level**

အဆင့်ဆင့် a-sint-sint *(n.)* **gradation**

အဆင့်တူ ပုဂ္ဂိုလ် a-sint-thu-poke-ko *(n.)* **counterpart**

အဆင့်မြင့်တန်း a-sint-myint-tan *(n.)* **business class**

အဆင့်မြင့်ပညာရေး a-sint-myint-pyin-nyar-yay *(n.)* **higher education**

အဆင့်မြှင့်သည် aasintmyahaintsai *(v.)* **upgrade**

အဆင့်အတန်း aasint-aataann *(n.)* **rank**

အဆင့်အတန်း သတ်မှတ်သည် aasint-aataann saat-mhaat-sai *(v.)* **rank**

အဆင့်အတန်း၊ စံချိန် aa-sint aa-taann, san-chane *(n.)* **standard**

အဆင့်အတန်း၊ သက်တမ်း aasint aataann , saattam *(n.)* **standing**

အဆင်း a-sin *(n.)* **descent**

အဆင်းလှသော a-sin-hla-taw *(adj.)* **aesthetic**

အဆင်တန်ဆာ a saintaansar *(n.)* **ornamentation**

အဆင်ပြေမှု a-sin-pyay-mu *(n.)* **convenience**

အဆင်ပြေသည် a-sin-pyay-tai *(v.)* **okay**

အဆင်ပြေသော a-sin-pyay-taw *(adj.)* **convenient**

အဆင်မပြေသော a-sin-ma-pyay-taw *(adj.)* **inconvenient**

အဆင်ရှိသော a sinshisaw *(adj.)* **venomous**

အဆင်သင့် a sinsint *(adv.)* **readily**

အဆင်သင့်ဝတ်ရန် ချုပ်လုပ်ထားသော a sin tint wit-raan chote lote-htarrsaw *(adj.)* **ready-made**

အဆစ်ရောင်နာ a-sit-yaung-nar *(n.)* **arthritis**

အဆစ်ရောင်ရောဂါ aasitraungrawgar *(n.)* **rheumatism**

အဆစ်ရောင်သော aasit raungsaw *(adj.)* **rheumatic**

အဆစ်လွဲခြင်း aa-sit-lwal-chinn *(n.)* **sprain**

အဆစ်လွဲသည် aa-sote-lwal-sai *(v.)* **sprain**

အဆန်၊ အစေ့ a-san, a-say *(n.)* **kernel**

အဆွေး aasway *(n.)* **rot**

အဆာသွတ်မုန့် a-sar-swat-mone *(n.)* **pastry**

အဆိပ် aa-seik *(n.)* **poison**

အဆိပ်၊ အငြိုး aaseik, aangyaoe *(n.)* **venom**

အဆိပ်ခပ်သည် aa-seik-hkat-sai *(v.)* **poison**

အဆိပ်ဆူး၊ စပ်ဖျဉ်းဖျဉ်းဖြစ်ခြင်း၊ နာခြင်း aaseik suu , sat hpyain hpyain hpyitchinn , narchinn *(n.)* **sting**
အဆိပ်ပညာ aa-seik-pa-nyar *(n.)* **toxicology**
အဆိပ်ပညာရှင် aa-seik-pa-nyarshin *(n.)* **toxicologist**
အဆိပ်ဖယ်ရှားခြင်း a-seik-phal-shar-chin *(n.)* **detoxication**
အဆိပ်ဖြစ်ခြင်း a-seik-phit-chin *(n.)* **toxification**
အဆိပ်ဖြစ်စေသော a satehpyitsaysaw *(adj.)* **toxic**
အဆိပ်ရှိသော aa-seik-shi-saw *(adj.)* **poisonous**
အဆိပ်အလုံးစုံဖြေဆေး a-seik-a-lone-sone-hpyay-say *(n.)* **mithridate**
အဆိပ်အာနိသင် aa-seik-aar-ni-sin *(n.)* **toxicity**
အဆို့ရှင် baankarr *(n.)* **valve**
အဆိုးဆုံး aasoesone *(n.)* **worst**
အဆိုးဆုံးအပိုင်း a-soe-sone-a-pai *(n.)* **brunt**
အဆိုးဘက်မှ အကောင်းဘက်သို့ ပြန်ဆိုက်လာခြင်း aa-soebhaat-mha a kaungg-bhaat-thoet pyan site-larchinn *(n.)* **rebound**
အဆိုးမြင်ဝါဒီ aa-soe-myin-war-de *(n.)* **pessimist**
အဆိုးမြင်သော a-soe-myin-taw *(adj.)* **cynical**
အဆိုတော် aasotaw *(n.)* **singer**
အဆိုပြုခံရသူ a-so-pyu-hkan-ya-tuu *(n.)* **nominee**
အဆိုပြုချက် aa-so-pyu-chet *(n.)* **proposition**
အဆိုပြုချက်၊ ချစ်ရေးဆိုခြင်း aa-so-pyu-chet, chit rayy so-chinn *(n.)* **proposal**
အဆိုပြုခြင်း a-so-pyu-chin *(n.)* **nomination**
အဆိုပြုသည် a so-pyu-sai *(v.)* **propose**
အဆိုရှိသည် a soshisai *(v.)* **state**
အဆိုလွှာတင်ခြင်း a so lwhartainhkyinn *(n.)* **solicitation**
အဆိုအမိန့် a-so-a-maint *(n.)* **dictum**
အဆီ a-si *(n.)* **fat**
အဆီ၊ အနှစ်၊ ကောက်နုတ်ချက် a-si, a-nit, kauk-note-chat *(n.)* **extract**
အဆီခဲထုတ်အတံ a-si-khar-htoke-a-tan *(n.)* **cornicle**
အဆီနည်းသော a-see-nae-taw *(adj.)* **low-fat**
အဆီနှင့်ဆိုင်သော a-se-nint-saing-taw *(adj.)* **adipose**
အဆီဖယ်ရှားခြင်း a-si-phal-shar-chin *(n.)* **delipidation**
အဆီဖယ်ရှားသည် a-si-phal-shar-the *(v.)* **delipidate**
အဆီဖယ်ရှားသော a-si-phal-shar-taw *(adj.)* **delipidate**
အဆီအငေါ်တည့်သော a-si-a-ngaw-tae-taw *(adj.)* **coherent**
အဆုံ a-sone *(n.)* **juncture**
အဆုံး a-sone *(n.)* **close**
အဆုံးကာရန်တူ နှစ်ကြောင်းကဗျာ a-sone-kar-yan-thu-nit-kyaung-ka-byar *(n.)* **couplet**
အဆုံးပြ သင်္ကေတ a-sone-pya-tin-kay-ta *(n.)* **full stop**
အဆုံးမဲ့ a-sone-mae *(adj.)* **endless**
အဆုံးရှိသော a-sone-shi-taw *(adj.)* **terminable**
အဆုံးသတ်ခြင်း aasonesaatchinn *(n.)* **termination**
အဆုံးသတ်သည် aasonesaatsai *(v.)* **terminate**

အဆုံးအစမရှိ a-sone-a-sa-ma-shi *(adj.)* **eternal**
အဆုံးအဖြတ်ပေးသည် a-sone-a-phat-pay-the *(v.)* **determine**
အဆုတ် a-sote *(n.)* **lung**
အဆုတ်၊ အစာအိမ်နှင့် ဆိုင်သော a-sote-a-sar-eain-nint-sine-taw *(adj.)* **pneumogastric**
အဆုတ်တီဘီရောဂါ aasotetebherawgar *(n.)* **tuberculosis**
အဆုတ်နှင့် ဆိုင်သော a-sote-nint-sai-taw *(adj.)* **pneumonic**
အဆုတ်ရောင်ရောဂါ aa-sote-raung-raw-gar *(n.)* **pneumonia**
အဆုတ်ရောင်ရောဂါရှိသူ aa-sote-raung-raw-gar-shi-thu *(n.)* **pneumoniac**
အဆောက်အအုံ၊ အစုအဖွဲ့ a-saut-a-ohn, a-su-a-phwe *(n.)* **entity**
အဆောက်အအုံမျက်နှာစာ a-saut-a-ohn-myat-nar-sar *(n.)* **facade**
အဆောက်အဦး a-saut-a-oo *(n.)* **building**
အဆောင် aa-saung *(n.)* **talisman**
အဆောင်အယောင် a-saung-a-yaung *(n.)* **accoutrement**
အဇုဓာတ်ငွေ့ a-zu-dat-ngwe *(n.)* **azote**
အညံ့စား a nyantsarr *(n.)* **trash**
အညစ်အကြေး aanyaitaakyay *(n.)* **sewage**
အညတြ a-nya-ta-ya *(n.)* **nonentity**
အညွှန်း a-hnyun *(n.)* **index**
အညှီအဟောက် a-hnyi-a-haut *(n.)* **erotica**
အညှောက်ပေါက်ခြင်း a-hnyauk-pauk-chin *(n.)* **germination**
အညှောက်ပေါက်သည် a-hnyauk-pauk-the *(v.)* **germinate**
အညို a-nyo *(adj.)* **brown**
အညိုမှိုင်းမှိုင်းအထည်၊ ပြည့်တန်ဆာ a-you-hmai-hmai-a-htaw, pyae-ta-zar *(n.)* **drab**
အညိုရောင် aa-nyoraung *(n.)* **tan**
အဋ္ဌဂံ a-hta-gan *(n.)* **octagon**
အဏုကြည့်မှန်ပြောင်း a-nu-kyi-man-pyaung *(n.)* **microscope**
အဏုမြူ a-nu-my *(adj.)* **atomic**
အဏုမြူဓာတ်ပေါင်းဖို aanumyauudharatpaungghpo *(n.)* **reactor**
အဏ္ဏဝါ an-na-war *(adj.)* **oceanic**
အဏ္ဏဝါဗေဒ an-na-war-bay-da *(n.)* **oceanology**
အဏ္ဏဝါဗေဒနှင့် ဆိုင်သော an-na-war-bay-da-nint-sine-taw *(adj.)* **oceanographic**
အဏ္ဏဝါဗေဒပညာရှင် an-na-war-bay-da-pyin-nyar-shin *(n.)* **oceanographer**
အတက် a-tat *(n.)* **offshoot**
အတက်ရောဂါ a-tat-yaw-gar *(n.)* **epilepsy**
အတက်ရောဂါရှိသူ a-tat-yaw-gar-shi-thu *(n.)* **epileptic**
အတက်အကျ ရှိသည် a-tat-a-kya-shi-the *(v.)* **fluctuate**
အတက်အကျတိုင်း ကိရိယာ a-tat-a-kya-tine-ka-yi-yar *(adj.)* **oscillometric**
အတက်အကျဖြစ်ပေါ် ခြင်း a-tat-a-kya-hpyit-paw-chin *(n.)* **oscillation**
အတင်း လုပ်ခိုင်းသည် a-tin-lote-khai-the *(v.)* **force**
အတင်းချခြင်း a-tin-cha-chin *(n.)* **backbiting**
အတင်းအကျပ်ခိုင်းသည် a-tin-a-kyat-khai-the *(v.)* **compel**
အတင်းအဓမ္မ a-tin-a-da-ma *(adj.)* **forcible**
အတင်းအဖျင်းစကား a-tin-a-phyin-sa-kar *(n.)* **gossip**

အတင်းအဖျင်းစကားပြောသည် a-tin-a-phyin-sa-kar-pyaw-the *(v.)* **gossip**
အတည်တကျ နေထိုင်သော a-the-ta-kya-nay-htai-taw *(adj.)* **domiciled**
အတည်ပြုချက် a-the-pyu-chat *(n.)* **affirmation**
အတည်ပြုချက်ပေးသည် a-tin-pyu-chat-pay-the *(v.)* **endorse**
အတည်ပြုချက်ပေးသူ a-the-pyu-chat-pay-thu *(n.)* **endorser**
အတည်ပြုသည် aataipyusai *(v.)* **ratify**
အတတ်ပညာဆိုင်ရာ aa-taat-pa-nyar-sine-rar *(adj.)* **professional**
အတန်း aataann *(n.)* **row**
အတန်းဖော် a-tan-phaw *(n.)* **classmate**
အတန်းလိုက် နေရာယူသည် aataann-lite nayraryuusai *(v.)* **range**
အတန်များသော a-tan-myar-taw *(adj.)* **considerable**
အတွက် a-twat *(prep.)* **for**
အတွင်း aatwin *(prep.)* **within**
အတွင်းကျကျ a-twin-kya-kya *(adj.)* **inside**
အတွင်းကြေ a-twin-kyay *(n.)* **contusion**
အတွင်းခံစကတ် aa-twin-hkan-sa-kaat *(n.)* **petticoat**
အတွင်းခံဘောင်းဘီ aatwin hkanbhaunggbhe *(n.)* **underwear**
အတွင်းစကားပြောပြသည် a-twin-sa-kar-pyaw-pya-the *(v.)* **confide**
အတွင်းတိမ် a-twin-tain *(n.)* **cataract**
အတွင်းဒဏ်ထိသည် a-twin-dan-hti-the *(v.)* **contuse**
အတွင်းပိုင်း a-twin-pai *(n.)* **inside**
အတွင်းဘက် a-twin-bat *(adj.)* **inner**
အတွင်းဘက်ဆုံး a-twin-bat-sone *(adj.)* **innermost**
အတွင်းဘက်လှည့်သော၊ ဝင်လာသော a-twin-bat-hlae-taw, win-lar-taw *(adj.)* **inbound**
အတွင်းမှ aatwinmha *(adv.)* **within**
အတွင်းရေးမှူး aatwinrayymhauu *(n.)* **secretary**
အတွင်းရေးအကျဆုံး a-twin-yay-a-kya-sone *(adj.)* **inmost**
အတွင်းဝန်များရုံး aatwinwaan myarrrone *(n.)* **secretariat**
အတွင်းသို့ a-twin-thoe *(adv.)* **inwards**
အတွင်းဟိုက်ကမ်းရိုးကွေ့ a-twin-hite-kan-yoe-kway *(n.)* **bight**
အတွင်းအောင်း aa-twinaaungg *(n.)* **undercurrent**
အတွန့်ကြောင်း a twunt-kyaung *(n.)* **wrinkle**
အတွန့်အလိပ် a-twunt-a-laik *(v.)* **crinkle**
အတွေ့အကြုံ a-tway-a-kyone *(n.)* **experience**
အတွေ့အကြုံနည်းသော သူ aa-twae-aa-kyon nee-saw suu *(n.)* **tenderfoot**
အတွေ့အကြုံများသော aatwaeaakyuanmyarrsaw *(adj.)* **sophisticated**
အတွေ့အကြုံမရှိခြင်း a-tway-a-kyone-ma-shi-chin *(n.)* **inexperience**
အတွေ့အကြုံမရှိသော a-tway-a-kyone-ma-shi-taw *(adj.)* **naive**
အတွေ့အကြုံရသည် a-tway-a-kyone-ya-the *(v.)* **experience**
အတွေ့အထိ a twaeaahti *(n.)* **sensation**
အတွေး aatway *(n.)* **thought**
အတွေးနယ်ချဲ့ခြင်း aatway naalchaaechinn *(n.)* **reverie**

အတွေးနယ်ချဲ့သော aatway naalchaaesaw (*adj.*) **thoughtful**
အတွေးမှား a-tway-hmar (*n.*) **illusion**
အတွေးမှားခြင်း a-tway-mar-chin (*n.*) **fallacy**
အတွေးအခေါ်ပညာရှင် aatwayaahkawpanyarshin (*n.*) **thinker**
အတွေးအမြင် ပဓာနဖြစ်သော a-tway-a-myin-pa-dar-na-phit-taw (*adj.*) **idealistic**
အတွေးအမြင် ပဓာနဝါဒီ a-tway-a-myin-pa-dar-na-wa-di (*n.*) **idealist**
အတွဲ aatwal (*n.*) **volume**
အတွဲဖြင့် စီသည် a-twe-phit-see-the (*v.*) **geminate**
အတွဲဖြစ်သော a-twe-phit-taw (*adj.*) **geminate**
အတွဲအဖက် a-twe-a-phat (*n.*) **accompaniment**
အတားအဆီး aatarraasee (*n.*) **setback**
အတားအဆီးကျော်ပြေးပွဲတွင် စီးသော မြင်း a-tar-a-see-kyaw-pyay-pwe-twin-see-taw-myin (*n.*) **chaser**
အတိတ်ကာလ aa-tate-kar-la (*n.*) **past**
အတိတ်ကို တသလွမ်းဆွတ်ခြင်း a-tate-ko-ta-ta-lwan-sut-chinn (*n.*) **nostalgia**
အတိတ်ကို ပြန်ဖော်နိုင်ခြင်း a-tate-ko-pyan-phaw-naing-chin (*n.*) **anamnesis**
အတိတ်ခြေရာကောက် aatatechayrarkout (*adj.*) **retrospective**
အတိတ်မေ့ရောဂါ a-tate-may-yaw-gar (*n.*) **amnesia**
အတိဒုက္ခ aatidukhka (*n.*) **tribulation**
အတိပြီးသော a-ti-pi-taw (*adj.*) **fraught**
အတိဝုတ္တိ a-ti-woke-ti (*n.*) **hyperbole**
အတိအကျ aa-ti-aakya (*n.*) **precision**
အတိအကျပြောရသော် a-ti-a-kya-pyaw-ya-taw (*adv.*) **namely**
အတိအလင်းဝန်ခံသည် a-ti-a-lin-win-khan-the (*v.*) **avow**
အတို့အထောင်လုပ်သည် a thoet a htaunglotesai (*v.*) **sneak**
အတိုးကြီးစား၍ ငွေတိုးချခြင်း aasoneaasaung (*n.*) **usury**
အတိုးကြီးဖြင့် ငွေတိုးချသူ lu yuusai (*n.*) **usurer**
အတိုကောက် a-to-kaut- (*n.*) **acronym**
အတိုက်အခံပြုခြင်း a-tite-a-hkan-pyu-chinn (*n.*) **opposition**
အတိုက်အခိုက်ခံရခြင်း aa-tite-aa-hkite-hkan-ra-chinn (*n.*) **subjection**
အတိုက်အခိုက်ရပ်စဲခြင်း aa-titeaahkite ratsellchinn (*n.*) **truce**
အတိုချုံးခြင်း a-to-chone-chin (*n.*) **abbreviation**
အတိုချုံးသည် a-to-chone-the (*v.*) **abbreviate**
အတိုင်း a-tine (*n.*) **fit**
အတိုင်းမသိ a-tine-ma-ti (*adj.*) **immeasurable**
အတိုင်းအတာ a-tai-a-tar (*n.*) **dimension**
အတိုင်းအတာ၊ aatineaatar (*n.*) **scale**
အတိုင်းအတာ၊ ပမာဏ aa-tine-aatar , pa-marna (*n.*) **quotient**
အတိုင်းအတာမဲ့သော a-tai-a-tar-mae-taw (*adj.*) **measureless**
အတိုင်းအတာရှစ်ခုဆိုင်ရာ အသုံးချသင်္ချာပညာ a-tine-a-tar-shit-khu-sai-yar-a-tone-cha-tin-cha-pyin-nyar (*n.*) **octonionics**
အတိုင်ပင်ခံ a-thai-pin-khan (*n.*) **consultant**
အတိုင်ပင်ခံပုဂ္ဂိုလ် a-tine-pin-khan-poke-ko (*n.*) **counsellor**
အတိုင်အဖောက်ညီညီ a tine a hpoutnyenye (*adv.*) **tandem**

အတီးသက်သက်ဖြစ်သော၊ အရေးပါသော a-tee-tat-tat-phit-taw, a-yay-par-taw *(adj.)* **instrumental**
အတီးအမှုတ်သမား a-tee-a-hmoke-ta-mar *(n.)* **instrumentalist**
အတု aatu *(n.)* **synthetic**
အတုံ့အပြန် ရှိသော a-tont-a-pyan-shi-taw *(adj.)* **interactive**
အတုံးအတစ် a-tone-a-tit *(n.)* **chunk**
အတုခိုးခြင်း a-tu-khoe-chin *(n.)* **imitation**
အတုခိုးသည် a-tu-khoe-the *(v.)* **imitate**
အတုခိုးသူ a-tu-khoe-thu *(n.)* **imitator**
အတုဖြစ်သော aa-tu-hpyit-saw *(adj.)* **prosthetic**
အတုယူခြင်း a-tu-yu-chin *(n.)* **emulation**
အတုယူသည် a-tu-yu-the *(v.)* **emulate**
အတုလုပ်ပြသူ a-tu-lote-pya-thu *(n.)* **mimic**
အတုလုပ်သည် a-tu-lote-the *(v.)* **fake**
အတုလုပ်သူ a-tu-lote-thu *(n.)* **counterfeiter**
အတုအယောင် aa-tu-aa-yaung *(adj.)* **spurious**
အတူခံစားခြင်း a-thu-khan-sar-chin *(n.)* **communion**
အတူတကွ aatuutakwa *(adv.)* **together**
အတူတကွ ခရီးသွားသူ လူစု a-thu-ta-gwa-kha-yee-twar-thu-lu-su *(n.)* **carpool**
အတူနေထိုင်သည် a-thu-nay-htain-the *(v.)* **coexist**
အတောင့်ဖြစ်သည် a taw inthpyitsai *(v.)* **tablet**
အတောင့်ဖြစ်သော a-taunt-phit-taw *(adj.)* **capsular**
အတောင်ပံ aa-taung-pan *(n.)* **wing**
အတောအတွင်း a-taw-a-twin *(prep.)* **during**
အတော်အတန် aataw-aataan *(adv.)* **pretty**
အတော်အတန်ကြီးမားသော aatawaataankyeemarrsaw *(adj.)* **sizable**
အတော်အတန်တိုသော aatawaataan tosaw *(adj.)* **shortish**
အတ္တ at-ta *(n.)* **ego**
အတ္တကင်းသော a-ta-kinnsaw *(adj.)* **selfless**
အတ္တကြီးသော at-ta-kyi-taw *(adj.)* **egocentric**
အတ္တပေမဝါဒ at-ta-pay-ma-war-da *(n.)* **narcissism**
အတ္တဗဟိုပြုသော at ta-bahopyusaw *(adj.)* **self-centered**
အတ္တဘဝအမှန်ဝါဒ at-ta-ba-wa-a-man-wa-da *(n.)* **existentialism**
အတ္ထုပ္ပတ္တိ at-htoke-pat-ti *(n.)* **biography**
အတ္ထုပ္ပတ္တိရုပ်ရှင်ကား at-htoke-pat-ti-yoke-shin-kar *(n.)* **biopic**
အတ္ထုပ္ပတ္တိရေးသူ at-htoke-pat-ti-yay-thu *(n.)* **biographer**
အထက် aa-htaat *(adj.)* **plus**
အထက်စီးဆန်ခြင်း a-htet-see-san-chin *(n.)* **arrogance**
အထက်စီးဆန်သော a-htet-see-san-taw *(adj.)* **arrogant**
အထက်စီးရခြင်း a-htet-see-ya-chin *(n.)* **ascendancy**
အထက်တွင် a-htat-twin *(prep.)* **over**
အထက်ဖား အောက်ဖိ aahtaathparr athpi *(n.)* **snob**
အထင်ကရ a-htin-ka-ya *(adj.)* **foremost**
အထင်ကရနေရာ a-htin-ka-ya-nay-nar *(n.)* **landmark**
အထင်ကရဖြစ်သော a-htin-ka-ya-phit-taw *(adj.)* **legendary**
အထင်ကြီးခြင်း a-htin-kyi-chin *(n.)* **esteem**

အထင်ကြီးစေသည် a-htin-kyi-say-the *(v.)* **impress**
အထင်ကြီးလွန်းသည် a-htin-kyee-lwan-tai *(v.)* **overrate**
အထင်ကြီးသည် a-htin-kyi-the *(v.)* **esteem**
အထင်သေးကြောင်းကို ပြသည့် ပုံစံ a htin sayykyaunggko pyasaeet ponesan *(n.)* **sneer**
အထင်သေးခြင်း a htin sayychinn *(n.)* **scorn**
အထင်သေးသည် a-htin-tay-the *(v.)* **disdain**
အထင်သေးသော a-htin-tay-taw *(adj.)* **contemptuous**
အထင်အမြင်ကြီးလောက်သော a-htin-a-myin-kyi-laut-taw *(adj.)* **impressive**
အထင်အမြင်သေးသည် aa-htinaamyinsayysai *(v.)* **scorn**
အထင်အရ a-htin-a-ya *(adj.)* **notional**
အထစ် a-htait *(n.)* **notch**
အထစ်အထစ်နှင့် ပြောသည် a htait a htait-nint pyawwsai *(v.)* **stammer**
အထည် a-htal *(n.)* **cloth**
အထည်စအလွှာ aa-htai-saa-a-lwhar *(n.)* **ply**
အထည်သည် a-htae-the *(n.)* **draper**
အထည်သား a-htal-tar *(n.)* **fabric**
အထည်အလိပ် aahtai-aalate *(n.)* **textile**
အထပ်၊ အဆင့် a htat , aasint *(n.)* **tier**
အထပ်သား a-htat-sarr *(n.)* **plywood**
အထမ်းသမား aa-htamsa-marr *(n.)* **porter**
အထွက်၊ အပြင်ပန်း a-htwat, a-pyin-pan *(adj.)* **outward**
အထွက်သီးနှံအပေါ်တွင် ငွေကြေးစီမံခွင့်ရရှိသည် a htwat seenhaanaapawtwin ngwaykyay hceman hkwngrashisai *(n.)* **sharecrop**
အထွတ်၊ လှိုင်းခေါင်းဖြူ a-htwut, hlaing-gaung-phyu *(n.)* **crest**
အထွတ်အထပ်ပုဂ္ဂိုလ်ရှိကြောင်း ယုံကြည်သူ a-htut-a-htaik-poke-ko-shi-kyaung-yone-kyi-thu *(n.)* **deist**
အထွတ်အထိပ် aa-htwat-aa-hteik *(n.)* **pinnacle**
အထွတ်အထိပ်ပုဂ္ဂိုလ်ရှိကြောင်း ယုံကြည်ခြင်း a-htut-a-htaik-poke-ko-shi-kyaung-yone-kyi-chin *(n.)* **deism**
အထွတ်အမြတ်ထားရာ ဗိမာန် aahtwat aamyat htarrrar biman *(n.)* **shrine**
အထွေထွေ၊ အားလုံး၊ ယေဘုယျ a-htway-htway, arr-lone, yay-buu-ya *(adj.)* **general**
အထိ aahti *(prep.)* **until**
အထိတ်တလန့် ဖြစ်စေသည် a-htate-ta-laant-hpyit-say-sai *(v.)* **panic**
အထိတ်တလန့်ဖြစ်စေသည် a-hteik-ta-lant-phit-say-the *(v.)* **frighten**
အထိန်း a-htein *(n.)* **brace**
အထိန်းအချုပ် a-htain-a-choke *(v.)* **curb**
အထိမခံနိုင်ခြင်း aahti ma hkanninechinn *(n.)* **sensitivity**
အထိမခံသော aa-hti m hkansaw *(adj.)* **sacrosanct**
အထိမ်းအမှတ် a-htein-a-mat *(n.)* **memorial**
အထိမ်းအမှတ် အဆောက်အအုံ a-htein-a-mat-a-saut-a-ohn *(n.)* **monument**
အထိမ်းအမှတ် အဆောက်အအုံနှင့် ဆိုင်သော a-htein-a-mat-a-saut-a-ohn-nint-sai-taw *(adj.)* **monumental**
အထိမ်းအမှတ်ပွဲ a-htain-a-mat-pwe *(n.)* **commemoration**
အထိမ်းအမှတ်ဖြစ်သော a-htein-a-mat-phit-taw *(adj.)* **memorial**
အထိမ်းအမှတ်အဖြစ် အမှတ်တရ ကျင်းပသည် a-htain-a-mat-a-phit-a-mat-ta-ya-kyin-pa-the *(v.)* **commemorate**

အထိအတွေ့ဖြင့် သိသော aa-hti a twaehpyint si-saw *(adj.)* **tactile**
အထိုင်ဖုန်း a-htai-phone *(n.)* **landline**
အထီး a-htee *(adj.)* **male**
အထီးကျန်ခြင်း aa-hteekyaanchinn *(n.)* **solitude**
အထီးကျန်ဖြစ်သော a-htee-kyan-phit-taw *(adj.)* **forlorn**
အထီးကျန်သော a-htee-kyan-taw *(adj.)* **lonely**
အထီးကျန်သော၊ တစ်ခုတည်း a-htee-kyan-taw, ta-khu-tae *(adj.)* **lone**
အထုံး a-htone *(n.)* **knot**
အထုံပါမှု aa-htone par-mhu *(n.)* **proclivity**
အထုံပါရမီ a-hton-pa-ra-mi *(n.)* **bent**
အထုံပါရမီရှိသော a-htone-pa-ra-mi-shi-taw *(adj.)* **gifted**
အထုတ်အပိုး a-htoke-a-poe *(n.)* **baggage**
အထုပ် a-htote *(n.)* **package**
အထူး aa-htuu *(adj.)* **particular**
အထူးကျွမ်းကျင်သူ aa-htuukywamkyinsuu *(n.)* **specialist**
အထူးခြားဆုံး၊ ဖြစ်ရိုးဖြစ်စဉ် a-htoo-char-sone, phit-yoe-phit-sin *(adj.)* **classic**
အထူးတန်ဖိုးထားသည် aa-htuu taan-hpoe-htarr-sai *(v.)* **prize**
အထူးထူး အပြားပြားဖြစ်သော a-htoo-htoo-a-pyar-pyar-phit-taw *(adj.)* **multifarious**
အထူးပညာသင်ကျောင်း a-htoo-pyin-nyar-tin-kyaung *(n.)* **academy**
အထူးပြုခြင်း aa-htuu-pyu-chinn *(n.)* **specialization**
အထူးပြုသည် aa-htuu-pyu-sai *(v.)* **specialize**
အထူးလုပ်ငန်း aahtuulotengan *(n.)* **speciality**
အထူးဝတ်စုံ a-htu-wat-sone *(n.)* **outfit**
အထူးသဖြင့် aa-htuu-sa-hpyint *(adv.)* **particularly**
အထူးအခွင့်အရေး aa-htuu-aa-hkwin-aa-rayy *(n.)* **privilege**
အထောက်အကူ a-htauk-a-khu *(adj.)* **ancillary**
အထောက်အထားပြသည် aahtoutaahtarrpyasai *(v.)* **shore**
အထောက်အထားပါသော a-htaut-a-htar-par-taw *(adj.)* **documentary**
အထောက်အပံ့ a-htaut-a-pant *(n.)* **backing**
အဒရီနယ် a-da-ree-nal *(adj.)* **adrenal**
အဓိက aa-dhi-ka *(adj.)* **principal**
အဓိက စကားလုံး a-di-ka-sa-kar-lone *(n.)* **keyword**
အဓိက ဖြစ်သော a-di-ka-phit-taw *(adj.)* **dominant**
အဓိက အပြောင်းအလဲ a-di-ka-a-pyaung-a-hlae *(n.)* **makeover**
အဓိကကျသော a-di-ka-kya-taw *(adj.)* **key**
အဓိကဆိုလိုရင်း aadhikasolorinn *(n.)* **theme**
အဓိကပံ့ပိုးမှု a-di-ka-pant-poe-mu *(n.)* **mainstay**
အဓိကရုဏ်း aadhikarun *(n.)* **riot**
အဓိကရုဏ်းတွင် ပါဝင်သည် aadhikaruntwin parwinsai *(v.)* **riot**
အဓိကအားဖြင့် aa-dhi-ka-aarr-hpyint *(adv.)* **primarily**
အဓိဋ္ဌာန် aadhihtaran *(n.)* **vow**
အဓိဋ္ဌာန်ပြုသည် aadhihtaranpyusai *(v.)* **vow**
အဓိပတိ a-di-pa-ti *(n.)* **chancellor**
အဓိပတိလမ်း a-di-pa-ti-lan *(n.)* **broadway**

အဓိပ္ပါယ်ကောက်လွဲသည် a-dait-pal-kauk-lwal-the *(v.)* **misconstrue**
အဓိပ္ပါယ်ဖွင့်ဆိုချက် a-date-pal-phwint-so-chat *(n.)* **definition**
အဓိပ္ပါယ်များစွာ ဖြစ်နိုင်သော စကားလုံး၊ လက္ခဏာ၊ သင်္ကေတဂုဏ်သတ္တိ aa-dhate-palmyarr-swar hpyit-ninesaw sa-karrlone , lakhkanar , sin-k-tay gonsatti *(n.)* **polysemia**
အဓိပ္ပါယ်မဲ့စကား a-date-pal-mae-sa-karr *(n.)* **nonsense**
အဓိပ္ပါယ်မဲ့သော a-dait-pal-mae-taw *(adj.)* **meaningless**
အဓိပ္ပါယ်ရသည်၊ ဆိုလိုသည် a-dait-pal-ya-the, so-lo-the *(v.)* **mean**
အဓိပ္ပါယ်ရှိသော a-dait-pal-shi-taw *(adj.)* **meaningful**
အနံ a-nan *(n.)* **breadth**
အနံ့ aanan *(n.)* **smell**
အနံ့ခံသည် aanan hkansai *(v.)* **scent**
အနံ့စူးစူး aanant suu-suu *(n.)* **tang**
အနံ့စူးသည် aa-nant suusai *(v.)* **tang**
အနံ့စူးသော aanant suu-saw *(adj.)* **tanged**
အနံ့ဆိုး aanansoe *(n.)* **stench**
အနံ့ရသည် aananrasai *(v.)* **smell**
အနံ့အရသာ a-nant-a-ya-tar *(n.)* **flavour**
အနံ့အရသာရှိသော a-nant-a-ya-tar-shi-taw *(adj.)* **luscious**
အနံ့အာရုံနှင့် ဆိုင်သော a-nant-arr-yone-nint-sine-taw *(adj.)* **olfactic**
အနက် a-nat *(n.)* **depth**
အနက်တူ aa-naattuu *(adj.)* **synonymous**
အနက်ထွေပြားခြင်း a-nat-htway-pyar-chin *(n.)* **ambiguity**
အနက်မပြတ်သားခြင်း a-nat-ma-phat-tar-chin *(adj.)* **ambiguous**
အနည်းငယ် aa-nee-ngaal *(adv.)* **somewhat**
အနည်းငယ်စီ ဝေငှပေးသည် a-nae-ngal-si-wai-nga-pay-the *(v.)* **dole**
အနည်းငယ်ဖြတ်ညှပ်ခြင်း a-nae-ngal-phyat-nyat-chin *(n.)* **nick**
အနည်းငယ်သော aanaeengaalsaw *(adj.)* **sightly**
အနည်းစု a-nae-su *(n.)* **minority**
အနည်းဆုံး a-nae-sone *(adj.)* **minimal**
အနည်းဆုံး ဖြစ်သော a-ne-sone-phit-taw *(adj.)* **least**
အနည်အနှစ် a nai aa-nhit *(n.)* **sediment**
အနန္တ a-nan-da *(n.)* **infinity**
အနန္တစကြဝဠာ aanantasakyawalar *(n.)* **universe**
အနမ်း a-nan *(n.)* **kiss**
အနှံ့ကြည့်သည်၊ စေ့စေ့ကြည့်သည် a-nhaan kyi sai , sae sae kyi-sai *(v.)* **scan**
အနှံ့အစပ် a-nant-a-sat *(n.)* **omnipresence**
အနှင်ခံရသည် a-hnin-khan-ya-the *(v.)* **exile**
အနှစ် aa-nit *(n.)* **yolk**
အနှစ်ချုပ် aanitchote *(n.)* **synopsis**
အနှစ်သာရ aa-nit-sarra *(n.)* **quintessence**
အနှပ်ခံရသူ a-nat-khan-ya-thu *(n.)* **dupe**
အနှိပ်သည် a-nate-the *(n.)* **masseur**
အနှိမ်ခံလူတန်းစား aa-nain-hkan-luu-taan-sarr *(n.)* **underdog**
အနှေးရိုက်ချက် a nhaayyritechet *(n.)* **slow motion**
အနှောင့်အယှက် a-naut-a-shat *(n.)* **annoyance**

အနှောင့်အယှက်ကင်းသော a naut a-shat kinnsaw *(adj.)* **uninterrupted**
အနှောင့်အယှက်ပေးသည် a-naut-a-shat-pay-the *(v.)* **harass**
အနှောင့်အယှက်မဲ့ သွားပိုင်ခွင့် a nhaut aa-shaatmae swarr pinehkwint *(n.)* **safe-conduct**
အနာ aanar *(n.)* **sore**
အနားကွပ် a-nar-kut *(n.)* **lining**
အနားတွန့် a-nar-tunt *(n.)* **frill**
အနားပြိုင်စတုဂံ aa-narr-pyaine-sa-tu-gan *(n.)* **parallelogram**
အနားမပြိုင်စတုဂံ kaunggkainbharr *(n.)* **trapezoid**
အနားယူခြင်း၊ အိပ်စက်ခြင်း anarr-yuuchinn, ait-saatchinn *(n.)* **rest**
အနားယူသည် aanarryuu-sai *(v.)* **rest**
အနားရှစ်ထောင့်ရှိသော a-narr-shit-htaunt-shi-taw *(adj.)* **octangular**
အနားဝန်း aanarrwaann *(n.)* **rim**
အနားသတ်သည် a-nar-tat-the *(v.)* **delimit**
အနာကြီးရောဂါ a-nar-gyi-yaw-gar *(n.)* **leprosy**
အနာကြီးရောဂါရှိသော a-nar-gyi-yaw-gar-shi-taw *(adj.)* **leprous**
အနာကြီးရောဂါသည် a-nar-gyi-yaw-gar-the *(n.)* **leper**
အနာဂတ်ကာလတွင် a-nar-gat-kar-la-twin *(n.)* **hereafter**
အနာဂတ်ဖြစ်နိုင်ခြေ၊ ဇာတ်ညွှန်း aanargaat hpyitninechay , zatnyun *(n.)* **scenario**
အနာဂါတ် a-nar-gat *(adj.)* **future**
အနာဂါတ်လေ့လာမှုပညာ a-nar-gat-lay-lar-mu-pyin-nyar *(n.)* **futurology**
အနာနှင့်ဆိုင်သော a-nar-nint-sine-taw *(adj.)* **ulcerous**

အနာဖေး aanar hpayy *(n.)* **scab**
အနာဖေးတက်လာသည် aanar hpayy taatlarsai *(v.)* **scab**
အနာရင်းသော aanar rinnsaw *(adj.)* **septic**
အနိမ့်ဆုံး a ni msone *(v.)* **rock-bottom**
အနိုင်ကျင့်ကာလ a-nai-kyint-kar-la *(n.)* **dogbreath**
အနိုင်ကျင့်သူ a-nai-kyint-thu *(n.)* **bully**
အနိုင်မခံ အရှုံးမပေးသော a-nai-ma-khan-a-shone-ma-pay-taw *(adj.)* **indomitable**
အနိုင်ယူသည် a-nai-yu-the *(v.)* **defeat**
အနိုင်ရခြင်း a-nine-ra-chinn *(n.)* **win**
အနိုင်ရသည် aa-nine-ra-sai *(v.)* **win**
အနိုင်ရသူ aaninerasuu *(n.)* **winner**
အနီ aa-ne *(n.)* **red**
အနီး aanee *(n.)* **vicinity**
အနီးကပ်ဆုံး aaneekautsone *(adj.)* **proximate**
အနီးမှာ a-nee-ar *(prep.)* **near**
အနီးအနားတွင် a-nee-a-nar-twin *(adv.)* **hereabouts**
အနီကွက်ထခြင်း a ne kwat hta-chinn *(n.)* **rash**
အနီဖြင့် မှတ်သားသည် a-ni-phint-mat-tar-the *(v.)* **rubricate**
အနုစိတ် a-nu-seik *(adv.)* **minutely**
အနုတ် aa-note *(n.)* **subtraction**
အနုပညာ a-nu-pyin-nyar *(n.)* **art**
အနုပညာကို ခံစားနားလည်သူ a-nu-pyin-nyar-ko-khan-sar-nar-lal-thu *(n.)* **connoisseur**
အနုပညာစျာန်ဝင်စားခြင်း a-nu-pyin-nyar-zan-win-sar-chin *(n.)* **muse**
အနုပညာစျာန်ဝင်စားသည် a-nu-pyin-nyar-zan-win-sar-the *(v.)* **muse**

အနုပညာရပ် a-nu-pyin-nyar-yat *(n.)* **art form**
အနုပညာရှင် a-nu-pyin-nyar-shin *(n.)* **artist**
အနုပညာသည် a-nu-pyin-nyar-the *(adj.)* **bohemian**
အနုပညာအမျိုးအစား a-nu-pyin-nyar-a-myo-a-sar *(n.)* **genre**
အနုပညာဦးတည်ချက် a-nu-pyin-nyar-oo-tee-chat *(n.)* **art direction**
အနုမာန အယူအဆ a-nu-mar-na-a-yu-a-sa *(n.)* **hypothesis**
အနုမာန အယူအဆကို အခြေခံသော a-nu-mar-na-a-yu-a-sa-ko-a-chay-khan-taw *(adj.)* **hypothetical**
အနူးအညွတ်တောင်းပန်သည် a-nu-a-nyut-taung-pan-the *(v.)* **entreat**
အနေခက်စေသည် a-nay-khat-say-the *(adj.)* **abashed**
အနေအထားမပြုပြင်နိုင်သော a-nay-a-htarr ma pyu-pyin-ninesaw *(adj.)* **unadjusted**
အနေအထားမမှန်မှု a-nay-a-htar-ma-man-mu *(n.)* **deformity**
အနေအထိုင် ကျဉ်းကျပ်သော aanayaahtine kyain kyautsaw *(adj.)* **restrictive**
အနေအထိုင်ပိပြားသော a-nay-a-htai-pi-pyar-taw *(adj.)* **demure**
အနောက်တိုင်း aanouttine *(adj.)* **western**
အနောက်ဘက် aanoutbhaat *(adj.)* **west**
အနောက်မှ တိုက်သော aanoutmha titesaw *(adv.)* **westerly**
အန္တရာယ် aantararal *(n.)* **risk**
အန္တရာယ် မရှိသော an-da-yal-ma-shi-taw *(adj.)* **harmless**
အန္တရာယ်ပြုမည့် လက္ခဏာရှိသော aanta-ral pyumaeet lakhkanarshisaw *(adj.)* **sinister**
အန္တရာယ်ပေးသည် an-da-yal-pay-the *(v.)* **imperil**
အန္တရာယ်ဖြစ်စေသည် an-ta-yal-phit-say-the *(v.)* **endanger**
အန္တရာယ်ဖြစ်စေသော an-ta-yal-phit-say-taw *(adj.)* **endangered**
အန္တရာယ်များသော aan-ta-ral-myarr-saw *(adj.)* **perilous**
အန္တရာယ်များသော အပြုအမူ an-da-yal-myar-taw-a-pyu-a-mu *(n.)* **roguery**
အန္တရာယ်ရှိသော an-da-yal-shi-taw *(adj.)* **harmful**
အန္တရာယ်ရှိသော ဇီဝအေးဂျင့် an-ta-yal-shi-taw-zi-wa-aye-gent *(n.)* **bioagent**
အန်းဒရိုက် an-da-yite *(n.)* **android**
အန်စာတုံး an-sar-tone *(n.)* **dice**
အန်တီ an-ti *(n.)* **aunt**
အန်တီပိုဒီဒေသ an-ti-po-de-day-ta *(n.)* **antipodes**
အန်ဖတ် aaanhpaat *(n.)* **vomit**
အန်ရန် အိတ် aaanraan aate *(n.)* **sickbag**
အန်သည် aaansai *(v.)* **vomit**
အပင်၊ သတ္တဝါရုပ်ကြွင်းလေ့လာမှုပညာ a pain , sattawar rotekywin laelarmhupin-nyar *(n.)* **paleobiology**
အပင်၊ သတ္တဝါရုပ်ကြွင်းလေ့လာမှုပညာနှင့်ဆိုင်သော a pin , sattawar rote-kywin laelarmhu pinnyar-nint sinesaw *(adj.)* **paleobiological**
အပင်၊ သတ္တဝါရုပ်ကြွင်းလေ့လာမှုပညာရှင် a pain , sattawar rotekywin laelarmhupin-nyarshin *(n.)* **paleobiologist**
အပင်စိုက်ရန် ကျွမ်းတူးဆူး a-pin-seik-yan-kyun-tu-sue *(n.)* **dibble**
အပင်စိုက်ရန် မှန်လုံဆောင် a-pin-site-yan-man-hlone-saung *(n.)* **conservatory**
အပင်ပန်းခံသော a-pin-pan-hkan-saw *(adj.)* **painstaking**

အပင်ပျော့ a-pin-pawt *(n.)* **herb**

အပင်ရောဂါ a-pin-yaw-gar *(n.)* **blight**

အပစ်အခတ်ရပ်စဲခြင်း a-pyit-a-khat-yat-sal-chin *(n.)* **ceasefire**

အပတ်စဉ် aapaatsin *(adv.)* **weekly**

အပတ်စဉ် စာစောင် aa-paat-sin-sar-saung *(n.)* **periodical**

အပတ်စဉ်ထုတ် သတင်းစာ၊ စာစောင် aapaat sinhtote satinnsar , sarsaung *(n.)* **weekly**

အပတ်စဉ်ဖြစ်သော aapaat sinhpyitsaw *(adj.)* **weekly**

အပတ်တကုတ်ကြိုးစားသည် aa-paat-ta-kote-kyoe-sarr-sai *(v.)* **persevere**

အပန်းဖြေ aapaan-hpyay *(adj.)* **recreational**

အပန်းဖြေခြင်း aapaann-hpyaychinn *(n.)* **relaxation**

အပန်းဖြေမှု aapaan-hpyay-mhu *(n.)* **recreation**

အပန်းဖြေလမ်းလျှောက်ခြင်း aa-paannhpyay lamshoutchinn *(n.)* **stroll**

အပန်းဖြေသည် aapaann-hpyaysai *(v.)* **relax**

အပယ်ခံ a-paal-hkan *(n.)* **outcast**

အပယ်ခံဖြစ်သော a-paal-hkan-hpyit-taw *(adj.)* **outcast**

အပျက်သဘောဆန်ဆန် အသိအမှတ်ပြုသည် a-pyat-ta-baw-san-san-ta-ti-a-mat-pyu-the *(v.)* **nack**

အပျက်အစီး aapyetaasee *(n.)* **wreckage**

အပျင်းပြေလမ်းလျှောက်ခြင်း aa-pyinn-pyay lam-shoutchinn *(n.)* **ramble**

အပျင်းပြေလမ်းလျှောက်သည် aa-pyinn-pyay lam-shoutsai *(v.)* **ramble**

အပျိုစင် aapyosin *(n.)* **virgin**

အပျိုစစ်စစ်ဖြစ်ခြင်း aapyo sitsithpyitchinn *(n.)* **virginity**

အပျိုပေါက် a-pyo-pauk *(n.)* **maiden**

အပျိုဖော်၊ လူပျိုဖော်ဝင်ခြင်း aa-pyao hpaw , luupyao hpaw wainchinn *(n.)* **puberty**

အပျိုရံ a-pyo-yan *(n.)* **bridesmaid**

အပျိုဟိုင်း aa-pyohine *(n.)* **spinster**

အပျော် a-pyaw *(n.)* **fun**

အပျော်ခရီး a-pyaw-kha-yee *(n.)* **excursion**

အပျော်ခရီးတို a-pyaw-hka-ree-to *(n.)* **outing**

အပျော်တမ်း a-pyaw-tan *(n.)* **amateur**

အပျော်အပါး ကျူးသူ a-pyaw-a-par-kyu-thu *(n.)* **debauchee**

အပြင် a-pyin *(prep.)* **outside**

အပြင်းအထန်တိုက်ခိုက်ခြင်း a-pyin-a-htan-tite-hkite-chinn *(n.)* **onslaught**

အပြင်းအထန်တောင်းဆိုသည် a-pyin-a-htan-taung-so-the *(v.)* **insist**

အပြင်ပန်း a-pyin-pan *(adj.)* **outside**

အပြင်ပန်းအားဖြင့် a-pyin-pan-ar-hpyint *(adv.)* **ostensibly**

အပြင်ဘက် aapyin-bhaat *(prep.)* **out**

အပြင်ဘက်ဆုံးနံရံ a-pyin-bat-sone-nan-yan *(n.)* **bailey**

အပြင်ဘက်တွင် a-pyin-bhat-twin *(adv.)* **outside**

အပြင်ဘက်ရွှေ့သည် a-pyin-bat-shway-the *(v.)* **evert**

အပြင်ဘက်သို့ a-pyin-bhat-thoet *(adv.)* **outward**

အပြင်လူ a-pyin-luu *(n.)* **outsider**

အပြင်သွားသော aapyin-swarrsaw *(adj.)* **out**

အပြင်သို့ a-pyin-thoet *(adv.)* **out**

အပြစ် a-pyit *(n.)* **demerit**

အပြစ်၊ အနာ a-phit, a-nar *(n.)* **flaw**

အပြစ်ကင်းခြင်း a-pyit-kin-chin *(n.)* **innocence**
အပြစ်ကင်းသော a-pyit-kin-taw *(adj.)* **guilt-free**
အပြစ်ကျူးလွန်သူဖြစ်ကြောင်း ထွက်ဆိုသည် a-pyit-kyu-lun-thu-phit-kyaung-htwat-soe-the *(v.)* **incriminate**
အပြစ်ဆိုသည် a-pyit-soe-the *(v.)* **deprecate**
အပြစ်တင်ခြင်း aapyit-tinchinn *(n.)* **reproach**
အပြစ်တင်သည် aapyit-tinsai *(v.)* **reproach**
အပြစ်ပြေအောင်ပြုလုပ်သည် a-pyit-pyay-aung-pyu-lot-the *(v.)* **atone**
အပြစ်ပြေအောင်ပြုလုပ်ခြင်း a-pyit-pyay-aung-pyu-lot-chin *(n.)* **atonement**
အပြစ်ပေးသည် aapyit-payysai *(v.)* **punish**
အပြစ်ဖြေပေးခြင်း a-phit-phyay-pay-chin *(n.)* **absolution**
အပြစ်ဖော်ဆုံးမခြင်း aapyit hpaw-sonemachinn *(n.)* **reprimand**
အပြစ်ဖော်ဆုံးမသည် aapyit hpaw sone masai *(v.)* **reprimand**
အပြစ်မရှိကြောင်း စီရင်ချက် a-pyit-ma-shi-kyaung-si-yin-chat *(n.)* **acquittal**
အပြစ်ရှိခြင်း a-pyit-shi-chin *(n.)* **guilt**
အပြစ်ရှိသော a-pyit-shi-taw *(adj.)* **guilty**
အပြစ်အနာအဆာ a-pyit-a-nar-a-sar *(n.)* **imperfection**
အပြည့်အဝ a pyi aawa *(adv.)* **wholly**
အပြည်ပြည်ဆိုင်ရာ a-pyi-pyi-sai-yar *(adj.)* **international**
အပြန် aapyan *(n.)* **return**
အပြန်အလှန် aapyanaahlaan *(adv.)* **vice-versa**
အပြန်အလှန် ဆွေးနွေးခြင်း a-pyan-a-lan-sway-nway-chin *(n.)* **dialogue**
အပြန်အလှန် မှီခိုသည် a-pyan-a-hlyan-mi-kho-the *(n.)* **interdependence**
အပြန်အလှန် မှီခိုသော a-pyan-a-hlyan-mi-kho-taw *(adj.)* **interdependent**
အပြန်အလှန် သက်ရောက်မှု a-pyan-a-lan-thet-yauk-mu *(n.)* **interplay**
အပြန်အလှန်နားလည်မှုဖြင့် သိသာသော aa-pyan-aa-hlaan narr-lai-mhuhpyint si-sarsaw *(adj.)* **tacit**
အပြန်အလှန်ပြုလုပ်သည် aapyan-aahlaan-pyu-lotesai *(v.)* **reciprocate**
အပြန်အလှန်အကျိုးစီးပွားအတွက် ပူးပေါင်းထားသော နိုင်ငံအဖွဲ့အစည်း a-pyan-a-lan-a-lyo-see-pwar-a-twat-pu-paung-thar-taw-nai-ngan-a-phwe-a-see *(n.)* **confederation**
အပြန်အလှန်အကျိုးပြုခြင်း aapyanaalhaan aakyoepyuhkyinn *(n.)* **symbiote**
အပြွတ်၊ အခိုင်၊ အစုအပြုံ a-phywut, a-khai, a-su-a-pyon *(n.)* **cluster**
အပြားခတ်သည် a-pyar-khat-the *(v.)* **laminate**
အပြာရောင် a-pyar-yaung *(n.)* **blue**
အပြီးစွန့်ခွာသည် a-pyi-sunt-khwar-the *(v.)* **desert**
အပြီးသတ်ခြင်း a-pi-tat-chin *(n.)* **completion**
အပြီးအပိုင် ချေမှုန်းသည် aapyeeaapine chaayhmonensai *(v.)* **rout**
အပြီးအပိုင် စွန့်သည် a-pee-a-pai-sunt-the *(v.)* **forswear**
အပြုံး aapyuan *(n.)* **smile**
အပြုမှား၊ အပြောမှား a-pyu-hmar, a-pyaw-hmar *(n.)* **gaffe**
အပြုသဘောဆောင်သော aa-pyu-sa-bhaw-saung-saw *(adj.)* **positive**
အပြုအမူ a-pyu-a-mu *(n.)* **conduct**

အပြုအမူ a-pyu-a-mu *(n.)* **behaviour**

အပြေးပြိုင်ပွဲ a pyay-pyaine-pwal *(n.)* **race**

အပြော aa-pyaww *(adj.)* **verbal**

အပြောက် aapyawt *(n.)* **spot**

အပြောင်းအလဲ a-pyaung-a-lal *(n.)* **change**

အပြောင်းအလဲလွယ်ခြင်း a-pyaung-a-lal-lwal-chin *(n.)* **caprice**

အပြောင်းအလဲလုပ်သည် aa-pyaungg-aa-lell-lote-sai *(v.)* **zig**

အပြောင်မြောက်ဆုံးလက်ရာ a-pyuang-myauk-sone-lat-yar *(n.)* **masterpiece**

အပြောင်အပြက် a-pyaung-a-pyat *(adj.)* **jocular**

အပြောအဆိုပွင့်လင်းခြင်း a-pyaw-a-so-pwint-lin-chin *(n.)* **candour**

အပွင့်အဖတ် a-pwint-a-phat *(n.)* **flake**

အပို aapo *(n.)* **spare**

အပို၊ ပိုကဲခြင်း a-po, po-kae-chin *(n.)* **excess**

အပို၊ အရန် a po, aaraan *(adj.)* **spare**

အပိုကြေး aa-po-kyay *(n.)* **surcharge**

အပိုကြေးယူသည် aa-po-kyay-yuu-sai *(v.)* **surcharge**

အပိုချဲ့ပြောသည် a-po-chae-pyaw-the *(v.)* **belabour**

အပိုခွန် a pohkwan *(n.)* **surtax**

အပိုင်း aapine *(n.)* **section**

အပိုင်း၊ ဆက်ရှင် aapine , saatshin *(n.)* **session**

အပိုင်း၊ အခန်း aa-pine, aa-hkaann *(n.)* **part**

အပိုင်း၊ အစိတ်အပိုင်း aa-pine , aa-sate-aa-pine *(n.)* **portion**

အပိုင်းပိုင်းအစစ ကွဲသည် aapine pine a sa-sa-kwalsai *(v.)* **splinter**

အပိုင်းအခြား aapine-aa-charr *(n.)* **range**

အပိုင်းအခြားကာလ aapineaahkyarrkarl *(adj.)* **sessional**

အပိုင်းအစ aa-pine-aa-sa *(n.)* **piece**

အပိုင်းအစဖြစ်အောင် ကွဲသွားသည် aapineaahcahpyitaaung kwalswarrsai *(v.)* **shard**

အပိုဆု a-po-su *(n.)* **bonus**

အပိုဆောင်းသည် a po saunggsai *(v.)* **supplement**

အပိုထောက်ပံ့ကြေး a-po-htaut-pant-jay *(n.)* **weightage**

အပိုဒ်ငယ် a-pike-ngal *(n.)* **clause**

အပိုအလျှံ a po aashan *(n.)* **surplus**

အပုံ aa-pone *(n.)* **pile**

အပုပ်ကောင်စား သားငှက် a pote kaungsarr sarrnghaat *(n.)* **scavenger**

အပုပ်နံ့ a pote-nan *(n.)* **stink**

အပူ a-pu *(n.)* **heat**

အပူကြောင့် လေဖြတ်ခြင်း a-pu-kyaunt-lay-phat-chin *(n.)* **heatstroke**

အပူချိန် aapuuchane *(n.)* **temperature**

အပူချိန်တိုင်းကိရိယာ aapuuchane tineka-ri-yar *(n.)* **thermometer**

အပူစီးကူးခြင်း a-pu-see-kyu-chin *(n.)* **convection**

အပူဒဏ်ခံနိုင်သော a-pu-dan-khan-nai-taw *(adj.)* **heat-resistant**

အပူဓာတ်ပေးသော a-pu-dat-pay-taw *(adj.)* **calorific**

အပူဓာတ်ရှိသော aapuu dharatshisaw *(adj.)* **thermal**

အပူပိုင်းဒေသ aapuupineday-sa *(adj.)* **tropical**

အပူအပင်မရှိသော a-pu-a-pin-ma-shi-taw *(adj.)* **blithe**

အပူအအေးမျှတသည် aapuu aaaayy myahatasai *(v.)* **temperate**
အပူအအေးမျှတသော aapuu aaaayymyahatasaw *(adj.)* **temperate**
အပေးအကမ်းရက်ရောမှု a-pay-a-kan-yat-yaw-mu *(n.)* **largesse**
အပေးအယူ a-pay-a-yu *(n.)* **bargain**
အပေခံ အပေါ် ရုံကုတ် a-pay-hkan-a-paw-rone-kote *(n.)* **overall**
အပေါက် aapout *(n.)* **slot**
အပေါက်၊ ကွက်လပ်၊ ကွာဟချက်၊ လိုအပ်ချက် a-pauk, kwat-lat, kwar-ha-chat, lo-at-chat *(n.)* **gap**
အပေါက်ဖောက်သည် a-pauk-hpauk-the *(v.)* **hollow**
အပေါက်လုပ်သည် a-pauk-lote-the *(v.)* **gap**
အပေါက်အပြဲ a-pout a-pyaell *(n.)* **tear**
အပေါက်အလမ်းတည့်ခြင်း a pout a lam teet-chinn *(n.)* **rapport**
အပေါင်းလက္ခဏာ aa-paungg-lak-hka-nar *(n.)* **plus**
အပေါင်းအသင်း a-paung-a-tin *(n.)* **buddy**
အပေါင်းအသင်းမင်သော a-paung-a-thin-min-taw *(adj.)* **convivial**
အပေါင်ခံသူ a-paung-khan-thu *(n.)* **mortgagee**
အပေါင်စာချုပ် a-puang-sar-choke *(n.)* **mortgage**
အပေါင်ထားသည် a-paung-htar-the *(v.)* **mortgage**
အပေါင်ထားသူ a-paung-htar-thu *(n.)* **mortgagor**
အပေါင်ပစ္စည်း a-paung-pyit-see *(n.)* **collateral**
အပေါ် aa-paw *(adj.)* **upper**
အပေါ်တွင် ဖြစ်သော a-paw-twin-hpyit-taw *(adj.)* **on**
အပေါ်မှာ aapaw-mhar *(prep.)* **upon**
အပေါ်ယံ aapawyan *(adj.)* **sketchy**
အပေါ် ရုံ ကုတ်အင်္ကျီရှည် a-paw-rone-kote-ain-kyae-shay *(n.)* **overcoat**
အပေါ်သို့ aapawthoet *(adv.)* **up**
အပေါ်အင်္ကျီ a-paw-in-gyi *(n.)* **jacket**
အပဲ့၊ ပဲ့ရာ a-pae, pae-yar *(n.)* **chip**
အပ် at *(adj.)* **lancet**
အပ်ချည် atchai *(n.)* **thread**
အပ်ချုပ်သမား at-chote-samarr *(n.)* **tailor**
အပ်စိုက်ကုထုံး at-seik-ku-htone *(n.)* **acupuncture**
အပ်ထောက် at-htout *(n.)* **thimble**
အပ်နှံသည် at-nan-the *(v.)* **entrust**
အပ်နှင်းသည် at-hnin-the *(v.)* **confer**
အပ်ပေါက်ထိုးသည် at pout htoesai *(v.)* **thread**
အဖတ်ဆယ်သည် a hpaat saal-sai *(v.)* **redeem**
အဖန်တလဲလဲ ဖြစ်ခြင်း a hpaan ta lell-lell hpyit-chinn *(n.)* **recurrence**
အဖျက်အမှောင့် a hpyet a mhaunt *(adj.)* **subversive**
အဖျက်အမှောင့်လုပ်ငန်း a hpyet a mhaunt lote-ngan *(n.)* **sabotage**
အဖျား a-phyar *(n.)* **fever**
အဖျား၊ အစက်၊ အမှတ် aa-hpyarr, a-saat, aa-mhaat *(n.)* **point**
အဖျား၊ အစွန်း၊ ထိပ် aa-hpyarr , aa-swann , hteik *(n.)* **tip**
အဖျားချွန်း a-phar-chun *(n.)* **cusp**

အဖျားမော့ဓားရှည် aahpyarr mot dharrshay *(n.)* **sabre**

အဖျားရှိနေသော a-phyar-shi-nay-taw *(adj.)* **feverish**

အဖျားရှိသော a-phyarshi-taw *(adj.)* **tertian**

အဖျားရှူးခြင်း a-phyar-shue-chin *(n.)* **anticlimax**

အဖျော်ယမကာ a-phaw-ya-ma-kar *(n.)* **beverage**

အဖျော်ယမကာကောင်တာ a-phyaw-ya-ma-kar-kaung-tar *(n.)* **bar**

အဖြစ်များရောဂါလေ့လာသောပညာ a-phit-myar-yaw-gar-lay-lar-thaw-pyin-nyar *(n.)* **endemiology**

အဖြစ်အပျက် a-hpyit-a-pyet *(n.)* **occurrence**

အဖြည့်ခံ a-phyae-khan *(n.)* **appendage**

အဖြည့် a-phyae *(n.)* **adjunct**

အဖြည့်ပစ္စည်း a-phyae-pyit-see *(n.)* **additive**

အဖြိုက်ကျောက် a-phyike kyauk *(n.)* **muscovite**

အဖြူ aahpyuu *(n.)* **white**

အဖြေ aahpyay *(n.)* **reply**

အဖြေထုတ်သည် a-phyay-htoke-the *(v.)* **deduce**

အဖြေရှာသည် aahpyaysharsai *(v.)* **solve**

အဖွင့် a-phwint *(adj.)* **inaugural**

အဖွင့် a-phwint *(n.)* **inauguration**

အဖွဲ့ aahpwal *(n.)* **team**

အဖွဲ့ချုပ် a-phwe-choke *(n.)* **federation**

အဖွဲ့ဖွဲ့ခြင်း aahpwal hpwalchinn *(n.)* **team building**

အဖွဲ့ဖွဲ့သည် aahpwal hpwalsai *(v.)* **team**

အဖွဲ့ဝင် aa-hpwal-win *(n.)* **participant**

အဖွဲ့ဝင်ဖြစ်ခြင်း a-phwe-win-phit-chin *(n.)* **membership**

အဖွဲ့ဝင်ရန် တစ်နေရာရာ ရောက်ရှိသည် aahpwalwainraan taitnayrarrar routshisai *(n.)* **showup**

အဖွဲ့သား aahpwalsarr *(n.)* **teammate**

အဖွဲ့အစည်း a-hpw-a-see *(n.)* **organization**

အဖွဲ့အစည်း၊ အထင်ကရ ပုဂ္ဂိုလ်၊ အလေ့အထ a-phwe-a-see, a-htin-ka-ya-poke-ko, a-lay-a-hta *(n.)* **institution**

အဖာ၊ မျက်စိကာ a-hpar, myet-si-kar *(n.)* **patch**

အဖိုးငွေပမာဏ aahpoengwaypamarn *(n.)* **worth**

အဖိုးအခ a-phoe-a-kha *(n.)* **charge**

အဖုံး a-hpone *(n.)* **lid**

အဖုံး၊ အကာ a-hpone, a-kar *(n.)* **cover**

အဖုံးပါအိုးစောက် a-hpone-par-oh-saut *(n.)* **casserole**

အဖုငယ် a-hpu-ngaal *(n.)* **node**

အဖေ a-hpay *(n.)* **dad (or daddy)**

အဖော် a-phaw *(n.)* **companion**

အဖော်၊ အပေါင်းအသင်း a-hpaw, a-paung-a-tin *(n.)* **fellow**

အဖော်မဲ့ စိတ်အားငယ်သော a-phaw-mae-seik-arr-ngal-taw *(adj.)* **lonesome**

အဖော်အချွတ် a-hpaw-a-chyaut *(n.)* **nudity**

အဘိဓာန် a-bi-dan *(n.)* **dictionary**

အဘိဓာန်ပြုစုမှု a-bi-dan-pyu-su-mu *(n.)* **lexicography**

အမ a-ma *(n.)* **female**

အမည်းစက် aa-maeesaat *(n.)* **stigma**

အမည်၏ သမိုင်း၊ မူလအစလေ့လာချက်ဆိုင်ရာ a-mee-ei-ta-mine-mu-la-a-sa-lae-lar-chat-sine-yar *(adj.)* **onomastic**

အမည်ခံ a-me-hkan *(adj.)* **nominal**

အမည်စာတန်း ချိတ်ဆွဲသည် aa-mai-sartaann chaateswalsai *(v.)* **tag**

အမည်စာရင်းသွင်းသည် a-me-sa-yin-thwin-the *(n.)* **check-in**

အမည်တစ်မျိုးပေးခေါ်သည် a-me-ta-myo-pay-khaw-the *(v.)* **dub**

အမည်တပ်သည် a-mal-tat-the *(v.)* **name**

အမည်တူအမျိုးစုံ a-me-tu-a-myo-sone *(adj.)* **assorted**

အမည်ပျက်စာရင်းသွင်းသည် a-me-pyat-sa-yin-thwin-the *(n.)* **blacklist**

အမည်ပါစာလုံးဖြင့်အနာဂတ်ဟောခြင်း a-mee-par-sar-lone-phint-a-nar-gat-haw-chin *(n.)* **onomancy**

အမည်ပေးစနစ် a-me-pay-sa-nit *(n.)* **nomenclature**

အမည်ပေးသည် aamaipayysai *(v.)* **term**

အမည်ဗေဒပညာ a-mee-bay-da-pin-nyar *(n.)* **onomatology**

အမည်ဗေဒပညာရှင် a-mee-bay-da-pin-nyar-shin *(n)* **onomast**

အမည်မသိယာဉ်ပျံ aa-mai-ma-si yinpyaan *(n.)* **ufo**

အမည်မသိယာဉ်ပျံ လေ့လာမှု aa-mai-ma-si yinpyaan laelarmhu *(n.)* **ufology**

အမည်မသိယာဉ်ပျံဆိုင်ရာ ပညာရှင် aa-mai-ma-si yin pyaansinerar panyarshin *(n.)* **ufologist**

အမည်မသိသော a-me-ma-thi-taw *(adj.)* **anonymous**

အမည်ဝှက် aamaiwhaat *(n.)* **pseudonym**

အမည်ဝှက်ထားခြင်း a-me-wat-htar-chin *(n.)* **anonymity**

အမည်သမိုင်းကျွမ်းကျင်သူ a-mee-ta-mine-kyun-kyin-thu *(n.)* **onomatologist**

အမည်အစ a-me-a-sa *(n.)* **initial**

အမနာပ ပြောသည် aamanarp pyawwsai *(v.)* **vilify**

အမဖြစ်သော a-ma-phit-taw *(adj.)* **female**

အမျက် a-myat *(n.)* **ire**

အမျက်ဒေါသ a myetdawsa *(n.)* **wrath**

အမျက်သည်းခြင်း a-myat-thae-chin *(n.)* **fury**

အမျက်သိုခြင်း a myet so-chinn *(n.)* **rancour**

အမျှင်ကြီး a-myin-gyi *(n.)* **macrofibre**

အမျှင်ကြီးထွားလာခြင်း a-hmyin-kyi-htwar-lar-chin *(n.)* **filamentation**

အမျှင်စု aa-myin-su *(n.)* **wisp**

အမျှင်နှင့်ဆိုင်သော a-hmyin-nint-sai-taw *(adj.)* **fibrous**

အမျှင်အရည်အသွေး a-hmyin-a-yay-a-thway *(n.)* **fibrosity**

အများစု a-myar-su *(n.)* **bulk**

အများဆုံး a-myar-son *(adj.)* **most**

အများနှင့် ဆိုင်သော a-myar-nint-sai-taw *(adj.)* **common**

အများနှင့် မတူ တစ်မူထူးသော a-myar-nint-ma-tu-ta-mu-htoo-taw *(adj.)* **eccentric**

အများနှင့် ယှဉ်ပြိုင်ရသော a-myar-nint-yin-pyai-ya-taw *(adj.)* **competitive**

အများပြည်သူ aa-myarr-pyi-suu *(n.)* **public**

အများပြည်သူနှင့် ဆိုင်သော a-myar-pyi-thu-nint-sai-taw *(adj.)* **civil**

အများလက်ခံထားသော ဓလေ့များကို ပုတ်ခတ်ပြောဆိုသော a-myaw-lat-khan-htar-taw-da-lay-myar-ko-poke-khat-pyaw-soe-taw *(adj.)* **iconoclastic**

အများသဘော a-myar-ta-baw *(n.)* **consensus**

အများသုံး a-myar-tone *(adj.)* **communal**

အများသုံး တယ်လီဖုန်းရုံ၊ ဆိုင်ငယ် a-myar-tone-tal-le-phone-yone, sai-ngal *(n.)* **kiosk**
အများသုံးသယ်ယူပို့ဆောင်ရေး aa-myarr-sonesaalyuuphoetsaungrayy *(n.)* **public transport**
အများအပြား aa-myarr-aa-pyarr *(n.)* **plenty**
အများအပြား သေကျေပြုန်းတီးသည် a-myar-a-pyar-tay-kyay-pyone-tee-the *(v.)* **decimate**
အများအားဖြင့် a-myar-arr-phint *(adv.)* **mostly**
အမျိုး၊ အစား aamyoe, aasarr *(n.)* **sort**
အမျိုးစုံသော a-myo-sone-taw *(adj.)* **manifold**
အမျိုးဇာတ် a-myo-zat *(n.)* **caste**
အမျိုးတူစုသည် a-myo-thu-su-the *(v.)* **assort**
အမျိုးမျိုး aa-myoe-myoe *(adj.)* **sundry**
အမျိုးမျိုး ရောနှော ဖော်စပ်သည် a-myo-myo-yaw-naw-phaw-sat-the *(v.)* **concoct**
အမျိုးမျိုးပါဝင်သော a-myo-myo-par-win-taw *(adj.)* **composite**
အမျိုးမျိုးသော aaraungtinsai *(adj.)* **various**
အမျိုးမျိုးသော ပစ္စည်းစု a-myo-myo-taw-pyit-see-su *(n.)* **assortment**
အမျိုးသမီး a-myo-ta-mee *(n.)* **lady**
အမျိုးသမီး ရောင်းသူ a-myo-ta-mee-yaung-thu *(n.)* **milliner**
အမျိုးသမီး ဦးထုပ်လုပ်ငန်း a-myo-ta-mee-oo-htoke-lote-ngan *(n.)* **millinery**
အမျိုးသမီးခေါင်းဆောင် a-myo-ta-mee-kaung-saung *(n.)* **matriarch**
အမျိုးသမီးဝတ်စုံချုပ်သူ a-myo-ta-mee-wit-sone-choke-thu *(n.)* **dressmaker**
အမျိုးသမီးဝါဒ a-myo-ta-mee-wa-da *(n.)* **feminism**
အမျိုးသမီးဝါဒကို ထောက်ခံသော a-myo-ta-mee-wa-da-ko-htauk-khan-taw *(adj.)* **feminist**
အမျိုးသမီးဝါဒီ a-myo-ta-mee-wa-di *(n.)* **feminist**
အမျိုးသမီးအပေါ် ညှာတာထောက်ထားခြင်း a-myo-ta-mi-a-paw-nyar-tar-htauk-htar-chin *(n.)* **chivalry**
အမျိုးသမီးအပေါ် ညှာတာထောက်ထားသော a-myo-ta-mi-a-paw-nyar-tar-htauk-htar-taw *(adj.)* **chivalrous**
အမျိုးသမီးဦးစားပေးသူ လူငယ် a-myo-ta-mee-oo-sar-pay-thu-lu-ngal *(n.)* **gallant**
အမျိုးသား သားဖွား a-myo-tar-tar-phwar *(n.)* **accoucheur**
အမျိုးသားရေး a-myo-tar-yay *(n.)* **nationalist**
အမျိုးအစား aamyoeaasarr *(n.)* **type**
အမျိုးအစားခွဲခြင်း a-myo-a-sar-khwal-chin *(n.)* **classification**
အမျိုးအစားစုံလင်ခြင်း aamyoemyoesaw *(n.)* **variety**
အမြင့် a-myint *(n.)* **height**
အမြင့်ကြောက်သော a-myint-kyauk-taw *(n.)* **acrophobia**
အမြင့်ဆုံး aa-swamkone *(adj.)* **utmost**
အမြင့်ဆုံး ယောက်ျားသီချင်းဆိုသံ a-myint-sone-yauk-kyar-tha-chin-so-than *(n.)* **alto**
အမြင့်ဆုံးအသံအထိ သံစဉ်ပါသော a myint sone aasanaahti san sin parsaw *(adj.)* **tenor**
အမြင့်တွင် ရှိသော နေရာ a-myint-twin-shi-saw-nay-rar *(n.)* **perch**
အမြင့်ပြကိရိယာ a-myint-pya-ka-yi-yar *(n.)* **altimeter**
အမြင့်မှ အနိမ့်သို့ a-myint-ma-a-naint-tho *(prep.)* **down**
အမြင့်မှန်းသူ a-myint-hman-thu *(n.)* **aspirant**

အမြင်ကျယ်စေသော အတွေ့အကြုံ a-myin-kyal-say-taw-a-tway-a-kyone *(n.)* **eye-opener**
အမြင်တွင် ဆွဲဆောင်မှု ရှိသော သူ၊ အရာဝတ္ထု a-myin-twin-swal-saung-mu-shi-taw-thu-a-yar-wut-htu *(n.)* **eyecatcher**
အမြင်ထက်မြက်မှု a-myin-htet-myat-mu *(n.)* **acumen**
အမြင်လှအောင် ခွဲစိတ်ပြုပြင်သော a-myin-hla-aung-kwal-seik-pyu-pyin-taw *(adj.)* **cosmetic**
အမြင်အားဖြင့် a-myin-ar-hpyint *(adv.)* **outwardly**
အမြင်အာရုံ aamyinaarrone *(n.)* **sight**
အမြစ် aamyit *(n.)* **root**
အမြစ်တွယ်ခြင်း a-myit-twal-chin *(n.)* **entrenchment**
အမြစ်တွယ်နေသည် a-myit-twal-nay-the *(v.)* **entrench**
အမြစ်တွယ်သည် aamyit twalsai *(v.)* **root**
အမြစ်ပြုတ်သည် aamyit pyote-sai *(v.)* **uproot**
အမြစ်ဖြတ်ခြင်း a-myit-phat-chin *(n.)* **annihilation**
အမြစ်ဖြတ်သည် a-myit-phat-the *(v.)* **annihilate**
အမြစ်ဖြတ်သူ a-myit-phat-thu *(n.)* **eradicator**
အမြစ်မှ တိုက်ရိုက်ထွက်လာသော အရွက်မဲ့ရိုးတံ aamyitmha titeritehtwatlarsaw a rwat mae roetan *(n.)* **scape**
အမြတ်ထွက်သည် aa-myat htwat-sai *(v.)* **profit**
အမြတ်ထွက်သော a-myat-htwat-taw *(adj.)* **gainful**
အမြတ်ထွက်သော၊ အကျိုးရှိသော aa-myat htwat-saw, aa-kyoe-shi-saw *(adj.)* **profitable**

အမြတ်အစွန်း aa-myat-aa-swann *(n.)* **spoil**
အမြန် a-myan *(adj.)* **express**
အမြန်ပြီးစေသည် a-myan-pi-say-the *(v.)* **hasten**
အမြန်ရထား a-myan-ya-htar *(n.)* **express**
အမြန်လမ်းမဘေးတွင် ဖွင့်ထားသော စားသောက်ဆိုင် aamyan lam mabhayytwin hpwint htarrsaw sarrsoutsine *(n.)* **roadhouse**
အမြန်လုပ်ဆောင်ခြင်း a-myan-lote-saung-chin *(n.)* **haste**
အမြွာ aa-mywar *(adj.)* **twin**
အမြှုပ် a-hmyoke *(n.)* **foam**
အမြှုပ်တက်သော a-hmyoke-tat-taw *(adj.)* **fizzy**
အမြှုပ်တစီစီ ထွက်ခြင်း a-hmyoke-ta-si-si-htwat-chin *(n.)* **fizz**
အမြှုပ်တစီစီ ထွက်သည် a-hmyoke-ta-si-si-htwat-the *(v.)* **fizz**
အမြှုပ်တစီစီထနေသော a-hmyoke-ta-se-se-hta-nay-taw *(adj.)* **foamy**
အမြှုပ်ထသည် a-hmyoke-hta-the *(v.)* **foam**
အမြေးပါး a-myay-par *(n.)* **membrane**
အမြှောင်းပုံ ဖော်ထားသော a-hmyaung-pon-phaw-htar-taw *(adj.)* **corrugated**
အမြီး aamyee *(n.)* **tail**
အမြီးပိုင်း a-myi-pai *(adj.)* **caudal**
အမြှုပ်တစီစီထသည် a myoke ta se-se htasai *(v.)* **seethe**
အမြောက် a-myauk *(n.)* **artillery**
အမြောက်၊ ဗုံး၊ ဒုံးဖြင့် ဆက်တိုက် တိုက်ခိုက်ခြင်း a-myauk-bone-doon-phit-sat-tite-tite-khaik-chin *(n.)* **bombardment**
အမြောက်ကြီးအဆက်မပြတ်ပစ်ခတ်ခြင်း a-myauk-kyi-a-sat-ma-pyat-pyit-khat-chin *(v.)* **cannonade**

အမြောက်တပ်သား a-myauk-tat-tar *(n.)* **bombardier**
အမြောက်အများ a-myauk-a-myar *(n.)* **multitude**
အမြော်အမြင် a-myaw-a-myin *(n.)* **forethought**
အမြော်အမြင်ကြီးသော a myaw aamyinkyeesaw *(adj.)* **sage**
အမြော်အမြင်ရှိ၊ တီထွင်ဉာဏ်ကောင်းသော သူ a-myaw-a-myin-shi-ti-htwin-nyan-kaung-taw-thu *(n.)* **game changer**
အမြော်အမြင်ရှိသော a myaw aamyinshisaw *(adj.)* **visionary**
အမြဲ အဆင်သင့် a-myae-a-sin-tint *(adj.)* **ever-ready**
အမြဲစိမ်း a-myae-sein *(adj.)* **evergreen**
အမြဲစိမ်းပင် a-myae-sein-pin *(n.)* **evergreen**
အမြဲတမ်း aa-myaell-tam *(adj.)* **permanent**
အမြဲပေါ်ပေါက်သော aa-myaell-paw-pout-saw *(adj.)* **perennial**
အမွန်အမြတ်ထားသည် a mwan aamyathtarrsai *(v.)* **venerate**
အမွှမ်းတင်ခြင်း a-hmun-tin-chin *(n.)* **glorification**
အမွှမ်းတင်သည် a-hmun-tin-the *(v.)* **glorify**
အမွှေး a-hmway *(n.)* **fur**
အမွှေးနံ့သာ a-hmway-nant-taw *(n.)* **incense**
အမွှေးအကြိုင်ကဲသော a hmway a kyaine kellsaw *(adj.)* **savoury**
အမွှေးအကြိုင်ခတ်သည် a hmway a kyaine-hkaatsai *(v.)* **spice**
အမွေး a-mway *(n.)* **fleece**
အမွေးချွတ်သော a-mway-chyut-taw *(adj.)* **depilatory**
အမွေးချသည် a-mway-cha-he *(v.)* **moult**
အမွေးတိုင်ထွန်းခွက် a-mway-tai-htun-khwat *(n.)* **censer**
အမွေးထူ aa-mwayhtuu *(adj.)* **woollen**
အမွေးနံ့သာ လောင်ကျွမ်းသည် a-mway-nant-tar-laung-kywan-the *(v.)* **cense**
အမွေးနု a-mway-nu *(n.)* **fuzz**
အမွေးပွပိုး aa-mway-pwa-poe *(n.)* **plush**
အမွေးပွသော a-mway-pwa-taw *(adj.)* **fuzzy**
အမွေးရှည်ဆင် a-mway-shay-sin *(n.)* **mammoth**
အမွေခံ a-mway-khan *(n.)* **heir**
အမွေခံအမျိုးသမီး a-mway-khan-a-myo-ta-mee *(n.)* **heiress**
အမွေဆက်ခံခြင်း a-myay-sat-khan-chin *(n.)* **inheritance**
အမွေဆက်ခံသည် a-myay-sat-khan-the *(v.)* **inherit**
အမွေအနှစ် a-mway-a-nit *(n.)* **legacy**
အမွေအနှစ် aamway-aanit *(n.)* **relic**
အမှတ် aamhaat *(n.)* **score**
အမှတ်စာအုပ် aamhaatsaraote *(n.)* **scorebook**
အမှတ်တံဆိပ် a-mat-ta-seik *(n.)* **emblem**
အမှတ်တရ လက်ဆောင် a-mat-ta-ya-lat-saung *(n.)* **keepsake**
အမှတ်တရ လက်ဆောင်ပစ္စည်း aa-mhaattara laatsaungpyit-see *(n.)* **souvenir**
အမှတ်တရပစ္စည်း a-mat-ta-ya-pyit-see *(n.)* **memento**
အမှတ်တရဖြစ်သော a-mat-ta-ya-pyit-taw *(adj.)* **memorable**
အမှတ်တရလက်မှတ် a-mat-ta-ya-lat-mat *(n.)* **autograph**
အမှတ်ပေးသည် a-hmat-pay-the *(v.)* **mark**

အမှတ်ပေးသူ ထိုင်ရာ နေရာ aamhaatpayysuu htinerar nayrar *(n.)* **scorebox**
အမှတ်မှတ် စာရွက် aamhaatmhaat hcarrwat *(n.)* **scorepad**
အမှတ်မှတ်ခြင်း aamhaat mhaathkyinn *(n.)* **scorekeeping**
အမှတ်မှတ်သူ aamhaat mhaatsuu *(n.)* **scorekeeper**
အမှတ်မဲ့ တုံ့ပြန်မှု aamhaat-mae tont-pyanmhu *(n.)* **reflex**
အမှတ်မဲ့ တုံ့ပြန်သော aamhaat-mae tont-pyansaw *(adj.)* **reflex**
အမှတ်ရခြင်း aa-mhaat-ra-chinn *(n.)* **recollection**
အမှတ်သင်ပုန်း aamhaat sinpone *(n.)* **scoreboard**
အမှတ်သညာဖြင့် သရုပ်ဖော်မှု aa-mhaat sa-nyar-hpyint sarotehpawmhu *(n.)* **symbolism**
အမှတ်အစု a-mat-a-su *(n.)* **pointwork**
အမှတ်အသား၊ လက္ခဏာ a-mat-a-tar, lat-kha-nar *(n.)* **indication**
အမှန်ကို ဖုံးကွယ် လှည့်စားသည် a-man-ko-hpone-kwal-hlae-sar-the *(v.)* **belie**
အမှန်တကယ် aa-mhaan-takaal *(adv.)* **really**
အမှန်တကယ်ဖြစ်သော a-man-ta-kal-phit-taw *(adj.)* **actual**
အမှန်တကယ်ရှိသော aa-mhaan-takaalshisaw *(adj.)* **tangible**
အမှန်တကယ်အားဖြင့် a-man-ta-kal-arr-phit *(adv.)* **actually**
အမှန်တရား aa-mhaan-ta-rarr *(n.)* **truth**
အမှန်တရားမြတ်နိုးသူ aa-mhaan-ta-rarr-myatnoesuu *(n.)* **philalethist**
အမှန်အတိုင်း မြင်သိစေသည် a-man-a-tai-myin-ti-say-the *(v.)* **disillusion**
အမှား a-hmar *(n.)* **error**
အမှားကင်းသော a-hmar-kin-taw *(adj.)* **infallible**
အမှားပြုလုပ်သူ a-hmar-pyu-lote-thu *(n.)* **malefactor**
အမှားမှားအယွင်းယွင်း aamhar mhar a ywin-ywin *(adv.)* **wrong**
အမှားအယွင်း a-hmar-a-ywin *(n.)* **mistake**
အမှိုက်ပုံ a-mite-pon *(n.)* **dump**
အမှိုက်ပုံး၊ ပေါက်ကရစကား a-hmite-pone, pauk-ka-ya-sa-kar *(n.)* **garbage**
အမှိုက်ပုံးကြီး a-mite-pone-gyi *(n.)* **dumpster**
အမှိုက်ပုံသည် a-mite-pon-the *(v.)* **dump**
အမှိုက်သရိုက် aamhaite sarite *(n.)* **rubbish**
အမှီပြုသည်၊ အားထားသည် aamhae pyusai , aarr-htarrsai *(v.)* **rely**
အမှုထမ်း aa-mhu-htam *(n.)* **personnel**
အမှုထမ်းခန့်အပ်သည် aamhuhtam hkaant atsai *(v.)* **staff**
အမှုန် aa-hmone *(n.)* **particle**
အမှုန့်ကို ဆန်ခါချသည် a mhu antko saan hkar chasai *(v.)* **sift**
အမှုသည် a-mu-the *(n.)* **litigant**
အမှောင် a-hmaung *(n.)* **dark**
အမှောင်ထု a-hmaung-htu *(n.)* **darkness**
အမာခံနယ်မြေ aa-marhkannaalmyay *(n.)* **stronghold**
အမာရွတ် aamarrwat *(n.)* **sear**
အမာရွတ်ထင်သည် aamarrwathtinsai *(v.)* **scar**
အမိကိုသတ်ခြင်း a-mi-ko-tat-chin *(n.)* **matricide**
အမိကိုသတ်သော a-mi-ko-tat-taw *(adj.)* **matricidal**

အမိန့်၊ စည်းမျဉ်း၊ စည်းကမ်း၊ ဥပဒေ a-meint, see-myain, see-kam, u-pa-day *(n.)* **ordinance**
အမိန့်၊ ဥပဒေ a-maint, oo-pa-day *(n.)* **decree**
အမိန့်ချမှတ်သည် a-maint-cha-mat-the *(v.)* **decree**
အမိန့်စာ a meinsar *(n.)* **warrant**
အမိန့်စာ၊ စာချွန်တော်၊ ရုံးထုတ်မိန့် a-maint-sar, sar-chun-taw, yone-htoke-maint *(n.)* **habeas corpus**
အမိန့်စာချွန် a mein sarchwan *(n.)* **writ**
အမိန့်ပြန်တမ်း a-maint-pyan-tan *(n.)* **edict**
အမိန့်ပေးသည် a-maint-pay-the *(v.)* **adjure**
အမိန့်ပေးသည်၊ အော်ဒါမှာသည် a-meint-pay-tai, aw-dar-mhar-tai *(v.)* **order**
အမိန့်ပေးသော a-meint-pay-taw *(adj.)* **imperative**
အမိန့်ဖြင့် ဖွဲ့စည်းထားသော အဖွဲ့အစည်း၏ သတ်မှတ်ချက် ပြည့်မှီသော a-maint-phit-phwe-see-htar-taw-a-phwe-a-see-ei-tat-mat-chat-pyae-mi-taw *(adj.)* **chartered**
အမိန့်မနာခံခြင်း a-meint-ma-nar-khan-chin *(n.)* **insubordination**
အမိန့်မနာခံသော a-meint-ma-nar-khan-chin *(adj.)* **insubordinate**
အမိန့်အရ a-maint-a-ya *(n.)* **behest**
အမိုးခုံး a-moe-khone *(n.)* **dome**
အမိုးခုံးပါရုံ a-moe-khone-par-yone *(n.)* **arcade**
အမိုးနီးယားဓာတ်ငွေ့ a-moe-ni-yar-dat-ngwe *(n.)* **ammonia**
အမိုးပါစင်္ကြံ a-moe-par-sin-gyan *(n.)* **cloister**
အမိုးပေါင်းကူး baat tar , nyun rat , rawgar saalsaungsaw tirassaran *(n.)* **vault**
အမိုးပေါ် a moepaw *(n.)* **rooftop**
အမိုးမိုးသည် a moemoesai *(v.)* **roof**
အမိုးမဲ့ပွဲကြည့်စင် a-moe-mae-pwe-kyi-sin *(n.)* **amphitheatre**
အမိုးအောက် a-moe-aut *(adv.)* **indoors**
အမိုးအောက် ထပ်ခိုး a-moe-awt-htet-kho *(n.)* **loft**
အမိုးအောက်ထပ်ခိုး a-moe-aut-htet-kho *(n.)* **attic**
အမုန်း a-hmone *(n.)* **hate**
အမူအရာ၊ စတိုင် aamuuaarar , satine *(n.)* **style**
အမေးပုဒ် a-may-poke *(n.)* **interrogative**
အမေရိကန် မြင်းရိုင်း a-may-ri-kan-myine-yai *(n.)* **mustang**
အမေရိကန်ပြောင် a-may-ri-kan-pyaung *(n.)* **bison**
အမဲ a-mal *(adj.)* **black**
အမဲကင် a mellkin *(n.)* **roast**
အမဲဆီ a mellse *(n.)* **tallow**
အမဲဆီ၊ ချောဆီ a-mae-si, chaw-si *(n.)* **grease**
အမဲလိုက်ခြင်း a-me-lite-chin *(n.)* **hunt**
အမဲလိုက်ခွေး a mell litehkway *(n.)* **talbot**
အမဲသား a-mae-tar *(n.)* **beef**
အမ်းဘာရိုက်အမှုန့် am-bar-yite-a-hmont *(n.)* **amberite**
အမ်ပီယာ am-pi-yar *(n.)* **ampere**
အယုံအကြည်ကင်းမဲ့သူ aayoneaakyi kinnmaesuu *(n.)* **sceptic**
အယုတ်တမာကောင် a-yote-ta-mar-kaung *(n.)* **bastard**
အယူခံဝင်သည် a-yu-khan-win-the *(n.)* **appellant**

အယူသီးခြင်း a yuu seechinn *(n.)* **superstition**
အယူသီးသော a yuu seesaw *(adj.)* **superstitious**
အယူအဆ a-yu-a-sa *(n.)* **concept**
အယူအဆစုပ်ကိုင်ထားသူ a-yu-a-sa-sote-kine-htar-thu *(n.)* **opinator**
အယူအဆဆိုင်ရာ aayuuaasasinerar *(adj.)* **theoretical**
အယူအဆနှစ်ခု ဆန့်ကျင်ခြင်း a-yu-a-sa-nit-khu-sant-kyin-chin *(n.)* **antinomy**
အယောင်ဆောင် aayaungsaung *(n.)* **sham**
အယောင်ဆောင်၍ လိမ်လည်ခြင်း a-yaung-saung-ywe-lain-lal-chin *(n.)* **imposture**
အယောင်ဆောင်ခြင်း aa-yaung-saung-chinn *(n.)* **pretension**
အယောင်ဆောင်ထားသော အသွင် a-yaung-saung-htar-taw-a-twin *(n.)* **guise**
အယောင်ပြသည် a-yaung-pya-the *(v.)* **dummy**
အယ်ဇိုင်းမားရောဂါ al-zaing-mar-yaw-gar *(n.)* **Alzheimer's disease**
အယ်ဒီတာနှင့် ဆိုင်သော al-di-tar-nint-sai-taw *(adj.)* **editorial**
အယ်ဒီတာအာဘော် al-di-tar-ar-baw *(n.)* **editorial**
အယ်ဘန်ပါ သီချင်းစာရင်း al-ban-par-thi-chin-sa-yin *(n.)* **tracklist**
အယ်လကာလီသဘာဝရှိသော al-kar-li-tha-bar-wa-shi-taw *(adj.)* **alkaline**
အယ်လဖာ al-far *(n.)* **alfa**
အယ်လဘန် al-ban *(n.)* **album**
အယ်လမွန်သီး al-mon-thee *(n.)* **almond**
အယ်လ်ကာလီ al-kar-li *(n.)* **alkali**
အရ a-ya *(adv.)* **according**
အရက် a-yat *(n.)* **alcohol**
အရက်၊ ဆေး စွဲသည် a-yat-say-swal-the *(v.)* **addict**
အရက်ချက်စက်ရုံ a-yat-chat-sat-yone *(n.)* **distillery**
အရက်စွဲခြင်း a-yat-swal-chin *(n.)* **alcoholism**
အရက်ဆိုင် aaraatsine *(n.)* **tavern**
အရက်ဆိုင်ရှိ သီးသန့်ထိုင်ရန် နေရာ aaraatsineshi see saant htineraan nayrar *(n.)* **snug**
အရက်ပြင်း a-yat-pyin *(n.)* **liquor**
အရက်ပါဝင်သော a-yat-par-win-taw *(n.)* **alcoholic**
အရက်မပါသော a-yat-ma-par-taw *(adj.)* **non-alcoholic**
အရက်မသောက်သော a raat ma soutsaw *(adj.)* **sober**
အရက်မူးသမား a-yat-mu-ta-mar *(n.)* **drunkard**
အရက်မူးသော a-yat-mu-taw *(adj.)* **drunk**
အရင်းရှင် a-yin-shin *(n.)* **capitalist**
အရင်းရှင်လူတန်းစား a-yin-shin-lu-tan-sar *(n.)* **bourgeoise**
အရင်းရှင်ဝါဒ a-yin-shin-wa-da *(n.)* **capitalism**
အရင်းရှင်ဝါဒီ၊ လူလတ်တန်းစား a-yin-shin-war-di, lu-lat-tan-sar *(adj.)* **bourgeois**
အရင်းအနှီး aarinnaanhaee *(n.)* **resource**
အရင်းအမြစ်ဖြစ်သော၊ အခြေခံကျသော aa-rinn-aa-myit hpyit-saw , aa-chayhkankyasaw *(adj.)* **radical**
အရင်ဟာ a-yin-har *(pron.)* **former**
အရစ်ကျ ငွေပေးချေခြင်း a-yit-kya-ngwe-pay-chay-chin *(n.)* **instalment**
အရစ်ဖော်စက် a-yit-phaw-sat *(n.)* **reamer**
အရည် a-yay *(n.)* **fluid**

အရည်ကျိုထားသော a-yay-kyo-htar-taw *(adj.)* **molten**
အရည်စုပ်ယူသော a-yay-sote-yu-taw *(adj.)* **absorbent**
အရည်ညှစ်သည် aarai nyit-sai *(v.)* **wring**
အရည်တွင် နှစ်သည်၊ တို့သည် a-yay-twin-nit-the-toe-the *(v.)* **dunk**
အရည်ထုတ်ပေးခြင်း aarai htotepayychinn *(n.)* **secretion**
အရည်ဓာတ် ခန်းခြောက်ခြင်း a-yay-dat-khan-kyauk-say-chin *(n.)* **dehydration**
အရည်ဓာတ် ခန်းခြောက်စေသည် a-yay-dat-khan-kyauk-say-the *(v.)* **dehydrate**
အရည်ပျော်စေသည် a-yay-pyaw-say-the *(v.)* **dissolve**
အရည်ပျော်သည် aarai pyawsai *(v.)* **thaw**
အရည်ဖြစ်သော a-yay-phit-taw *(adj.)* **liquid**
အရည်ဖြစ်အောင် လုပ်သည် a-yay-phit-aung-lote-the *(v.)* **liquefy**
အရည်ရွှမ်းသော a-yay-shwan-taw *(adj.)* **juicy**
အရည်ရောခြင်း a-yay-yaw-chin *(n.)* **dilution**
အရည်အချင်း aa-rai-aa-chinn *(n.)* **qualification**
အရည်အချင်းရှိသော a-yay-a-chin-shi-taw *(adj.)* **competent**
အရည်အချင်းအရ aa-rai-aa-chinn aa-ra *(adj.)* **qualitative**
အရည်အတွက် နည်းသည် aaraiaatwat naeesai *(v.)* **scant**
အရည်အသွေး aa-rai-aa-sway *(n.)* **quality**
အရည်အသွေးပြည့်မှီသော a-yay-a-thway-pyae-mi-taw *(adj.)* **eligible**
အရည်အသွေးမဲ့သော a-yay-a-thway-mae-thaw *(adj.)* **bereft**
အရည်အသွေးသတ်မှတ်ချက် a-yay-a-thway-tat-mat-chat *(n.)* **eligibility**
အရည်အိတ် a-yay-aik *(n.)* **cyst**
အရန်၊ အကူအညီ a-yan, a-khu-a-nyi *(n.)* **backup**
အရပ်တစ်ပါး a-rat-ta-par *(adj.)* **outbound**
အရပ်သား a-yat-tar *(n.)* **civilian**
အရပ်သုံး a-yat-tone *(adj.)* **colloquial**
အရပ်သုံးစကား a-yat-tone-sa-kar *(n.)* **colloquialism**
အရပ်အမောင်း aa-rat-aa-maung *(n.)* **stature**
အရမ်းကာရော ပြုမူသော a-yan-kar-yaw-pyu-mu-taw *(adj.)* **indiscriminate**
အရမ်းချစ်သော a-yan-chit-taw *(adj.)* **doating**
အရွက် (၅၀၀) ပါသော စက္ကူထုပ် aa-rwat (500) parsaw sak-kuuhtote *(n.)* **ream**
အရွက်ဝေဆာသော a-ywet-wai-sar-taw *(adj.)* **leafy**
အရွတ် aa-rwat *(n.)* **tendon**
အရွတ်ရောင်ရမ်းခြင်း a -rwat raung ram-chinn *(n.)* **tendinitis**
အရွယ် aarwal *(n.)* **size**
အရွယ်ကောင်း aar-walkaungg *(n.)* **prime**
အရွယ်ရောက်သူ a-ywal-yaut-thu *(n.)* **adult**
အရွေ့ a-shway *(adj.)* **kinetic**
အရသာ aa-ra-sar *(n.)* **savour**
အရသာ ခံနိုင်စွမ်း aarasar hkannineswam *(n.)* **taste**
အရသာကို ခံသည် aarasarko hkansai *(v.)* **taste**
အရသာခံသည် aa-ra-sar hkansai *(v.)* **savour**

အရသာဂုဏ်သတ္တိ aarasar gon-satti *(n.)* **sapidity**
အရသာတွေ့သည် a-ya-tar-tway-the *(v.)* **indulge**
အရသာမရှိသော a-ya-tar-ma-shi-taw *(adj.)* **insipid**
အရသာရှိသော aa-ra-sar-shi-saw *(adj.)* **palatable**
အရှက်ခွဲသည် aashat hkwalsai *(v.)* **slight**
အရှက်မဲ့သော aa-shat maesaw *(adj.)* **shameless**
အရှက်ရခြင်း a-shat-ya-chin *(n.)* **dishonour**
အရှက်ရစေသည် a-shat-ya-say-the *(v.)* **mortify**
အရှက်ရစေသော a-shat-ya-say-taw *(adj.)* **degrading**
အရှက်အကြောက်၊ ချုပ်ချယ်ခြင်း a-shat-a-kyauk, choke-chal-chin *(n.)* **inhibition**
အရှင် aashin *(adj.)* **removable**
အရှည် a-shay *(n.)* **length**
အရှာရခက်သော a-shar-ya-khat-taw *(adj.)* **elusive**
အရှိကို အရှိအတိုင်းလက်ခံခြင်း a shiko aashi-aatine-laath-kanchinn *(n.)* **realism**
အရှိန် aa-shein *(n.)* **velocity**
အရှိန်နှုန်းမှန်မှန် မောင်းနှင်သည် a-shein-hnone-man-man-maung-hnin-the *(v.)* **cruise**
အရှိန်မြှင့်ကိရိယာ a-shain-hmyint-ka-yi-yar *(n.)* **accelerator**
အရှိန်မြှင့်ခြင်း a-shain-hmyint-chin *(n.)* **acceleration**
အရှိန်မြှင့်သည် a-shain-myint-the *(v.)* **accelerate**
အရှိန်မြှင့်သည်၊ မြင့်တက်သည် a-shain-hmyint-the, myint-tat-the *(v.)* **escalate**
အရှိန်လျှော့ချသည် aashein shotchasai *(v.)* **slow**
အရှိန်လျှော့ခြင်း a-shein-shawt-chin *(n.)* **deceleration**
အရှိန်လျှော့သည် a-shein-shawt-the *(v.)* **decelerate**
အရှိန်အဝါ၊ ဩဇာ a-shein-a-war, aw-zar *(n.)* **influence**
အရှိအရှိအတိုင်းဖြစ်သော a shi aa-shi-aa-tine-hpyitsaw *(adj.)* **stark**
အရှိုး aashoe *(n.)* **weal**
အရှုံး a-shone *(n.)* **failure**
အရှုံးကြီး ရှုံးခြင်း a-shone-gyi-shone-chin *(n.)* **fiasco**
အရှုံးကြီးရှုံးခြင်း a-shone-gyi-shone-chin *(n.)* **debacle**
အရှုံးပေးခြင်း aa-shone-payy-chinn *(n.)* **surrender**
အရှုံးပေးသည် aa-shone-payy-sai *(v.)* **surrender**
အရှုံးပေးသော a-shone-pay-taw *(adj.)* **foldup**
အရှုပ်အထွေး aa-shote aa-htway *(n.)* **tangle**
အရှေ့ a-shay *(n.)* **east**
အရှေ့တိုင်း a-shae-tine *(n.)* **orient**
အရှေ့တိုင်းသား a-shae-tine-tarr *(n.)* **oriental**
အရှေ့ဘက် a-shay-bat *(adv.)* **east**
အရှောင်အတိမ်း a-shaung-a-thein *(n.)* **dodge**
အရာ aa-rar *(n.)* **thing**
အရာ၊ ဟာ၊ အခြေအမြစ် a rar , har , aachayaamyit *(n.)* **substance**
အရာခပ်သိမ်းကို ဘုရားအဖြစ် ကိုးကွယ်မှု ဝါဒ a-rar-khat-saim-ko-pha-rar-aa-hpyit-koe-kwal-mhu-war-da *(n.)* **pantheism**

အရာခပ်သိမ်းကို ဘုရားအဖြစ် ကိုးကွယ်မှု ဝါဒီ a-rar-hkat-saim-ko-pha-rar-aa-hpyit-koe-kwal-mhu-war-de *(n.)* **pantheist**
အရာထမ်း a-yar-htan *(n.)* **functionary**
အရာမရောက် a-yar-ma-yauk *(v.)* **emasculate**
အရာမရောက်ခြင်း a-yar-ma-yauk-chin *(n.)* **emasculation**
အရာရှိ a-rar-shi *(n.)* **officer**
အရာရာ စွမ်းခြင်း a-rar-rar-swam-chinn *(n.)* **omnipotence**
အရာရာ စွမ်းသော a-rar-rar-swam-taw *(adj.)* **omnipotent**
အရိပ် aa-rate *(n.)* **shadow**
အရိပ်ကောင်းသော နေရာ a-yeik-kaung-taw-nay-yar *(n.)* **bower**
အရိပ်ရသော a rate-ra-saw *(adj.)* **shadowy**
အရိပ်လက္ခဏာ a riutlakhkanar *(adj.)* **symptomatic**
အရိပ်အခြည် a-yeik-a-chay *(n.)* **inkling**
အရိပ်အမြွက် a-yeik-a-mywat *(n.)* **allusion**
အရိပ်အမြွက်ပြသော aa-rate-aa-myawt-pya-saw *(adj.)* **suggestive**
အရိပ်အာဝါသ a riutaarwarsa *(n.)* **shade**
အရိုး aa-roe *(n.)* **skeleton**
အရိုး အဆစ်လွဲသည် a-yoe-a-sit-lwal-the *(v.)* **dislocate**
အရိုး၊ အတံ aaroe, aatan *(n.)* **shaft**
အရိုးငေါငေါနှင့် ဖြစ်သော a-yoe-ngaw-ngaw-nint-phit-taw *(adj.)* **angular**
အရိုးစွဲသော a-yoe-swal-taw *(adj.)* **ingrained**
အရိုးထွင်ပြီးသား ငါး၊ အသား a-yoe-htwin-pi-tar-ngar-a-tar *(n.)* **fillet**
အရိုးထွင်ပြီးသား ငါး၊ အသားကို တုံးတစ်သည် a-yoe-htwin-pi-tar-ngar-a-tar-ko-tone-tit-the *(v.)* **fillet**
အရိုးနှစ်ခုကြားအဆက် a-yoe-na-khu-kyar-a-sat *(n.)* **commissure**
အရိုးနု a-yoe-nu *(n.)* **cartilage**
အရိုးပျော့နာ aaroe pyaw-nar *(n.)* **rickets**
အရိုးဖြစ်သွားသည် a-roe-hpyit-twar-tai *(v.)* **ossify**
အရိုးမဲ့သော a-yoe-mae-taw *(adj.)* **boneless**
အရိုးရောဂါကုပညာ a-roe-raw-gar-ku-pyin-nyar *(n.)* **orthopaedia**
အရိုးရောဂါနှင့် ဆိုင်သော a-roe-raw-gar-nint-sine-taw *(adj.)* **orthopaedical**
အရိုးအိုး aasonepyuninesaw *(n.)* **urn**
အရိုင်း a-yai *(adj.)* **crude**
အရိုင်းအစိုင်း a-yai-a-sai *(n.)* **barbarian**
အရိုင်းအစိုင်းကဲ့သို့သော a-yai-a-sai-kae-tho-taw *(adj.)* **brutish**
အရိုင်းအစိုင်းဘဝ a-yai-a-sai-ba-wa *(n.)* **barbarism**
အရိုအသေ a-yo-a-tay *(n.)* **obeisance**
အရိုအသေတန်စေသည် a-yo-a-tay-tan-say-the *(v.)* **degrade**
အရုဏ်ကျင်းသည် ar-yone-kyin-the *(v.)* **dawn**
အရုဏ်ကျင်းအလင်းရောင် ar-yone-kyin-a-lin-yaung *(n.)* **dawnlight**
အရုဏ်တက် ar-yone-tat *(n.)* **dawn**
အရုဏ်ဦး ar-yone-oo *(n.)* **daybreak**
အရုပ်စတိုး a rote satoe *(n.)* **toystore**
အရုပ်ဆိုးခြင်း a rote-soechinn *(n.)* **ugliness**
အရုပ်ဆိုးဆိုး အဖွားကြီး a-yoke-soe-soe-a-phwar-gyi *(n.)* **crone**
အရုပ်ဆိုးသော a rotesoesaw *(adj.)* **ugly**

အရုပ်ရောင်းသူ a roteraunggsuu *(n.)* **toyseller**
အရုပ်လုပ်သူ a-yoke-lote-thu *(n.)* **toymaker**
အရုပ်အိမ် a-yoke-eain *(n.)* **toyhouse**
အရူး aa-ruu *(n.)* **zany**
အရူးထောင် a-ruu-htaung *(n.)* **nuthouse**
အရူးလို a-yu-lo *(adv.)* **mad**
အရူးအမူးစွဲလမ်းမှု a-yu-a-mu-swal-lan-mu *(n.)* **infatuation**
အရူးအမူးစွဲလမ်းသော a-yu-a-mu-swal-lan-taw *(v.)* **infatuate**
အရူးအမူးဖြစ်နေသည် aa-ruu-aa-muu-hpyit-nay-sai *(v.)* **swoon**
အရူးအမူးဖြစ်သူ a-yu-a-mu-phit-thu *(n.)* **fanatic**
အရူးအမူးဖြစ်သော a-yu-a-mu-phit-taw *(adj.)* **fanatic**
အရေးကြီးခြင်း a-yay-kyi-chin *(n.)* **importance**
အရေးကြီးဆုံး aa-rayy-kyeesone *(adj.)* **prime**
အရေးကြီးမဟုတ်သော a-yay-ma-kyi-ma-hote-taw *(adj.)* **acritical**
အရေးကြီးသည် a-yay-kyi-the *(v.)* **matter**
အရေးကြီးသော a-yay-kyi-taw *(adj.)* **important**
အရေးစိုက်သည် a-yay-site-the *(v.)* **mind**
အရေးစိုက်သည်၊ ဖိရွတ်သည် aa-rayy site sai , hpi rwat-sai *(v.)* **stress**
အရေးတကြီး aarayytakyee *(n.)* **urgency**
အရေးတကြီး တောင်းခံသည် a-yay-ta-gyi-taung-khan-the *(v.)* **beseech**
အရေးတယူရှိသော aarayytayuushisaw *(adj.)* **solicitous**
အရေးတယူလုပ်သည် a-yay-ta-yu-lote-the *(v.)* **deign**
အရေးပါမှု aarayyparmhu *(n.)* **significance**
အရေးပါလှသော a-yay-par-hla-taw *(adj.)* **crucial**
အရေးပါသော aarayyparsaw *(adj.)* **significant**
အရေးပေါ် a-yay-paw *(n.)* **contingency**
အရေးမကြီးသော၊ ဒြပ်မရှိသော a-yay-ma-kyi-taw, drat-ma-shi-taw *(adj.)* **immaterial**
အရေးမပါခြင်း a-yay-ma-par-chin *(n.)* **insignificance**
အရေးမပါလှသော aarayy ma parhlasaw *(adj.* **trivial**
အရေးမပါသော a-yay-ma-par-taw *(adj.)* **insignificant**
အရေးမယူလောက်သော aarayymayuu loutsaw *(adj.)* **venial**
အရေးယူရန် ပျက်ကွက်မှု a-yay-yu-yan-pyat-kwat-mu *(n.)* **inaction**
အရေခွံခွာသည် a ray hkwan hkwarsai *(v.)* **skin**
အရေထူ သတ္တဝါ a-ray-htuu-sat-ta-war *(n.)* **pachyderm**
အရေထူသည်၊ မာကျောစေသည် a-yay-htu-the, mar-kyaw-say-the *(v.)* **harden**
အရေထူသော a ray htuusaw *(adj.)* **pachidermatous**
အရေပြား၊ အခွံ aaraypyarr, aahkwan *(n.)* **skin**
အရေပြားရောဂါဗေဒ a-yay-pyar-yaw-gar-bay-da *(n.)* **dermatology**
အရေပြားအရေအိတ် a-yay-pyar-a-yay-ate *(n.* **wen**
အရေလဲသည် a ray lellsai *(v.)* **shed**
အရေအတွက် aa-ray-aatwat *(n.)* **quantity**

အရေအတွက်၊ အရည်အသွေး တဖြည်းဖြည်းကျဆင်းခြင်း a-yay-a-twat-a-yay-a-thway-ta-phyae-phyae-kya-sin-chin *(n.)* **decrement**
အရောင် a-yaung *(n.)* **colour**
အရောင်းစာရင်းစာအုပ် aaraungg hcarrainnhcaraote *(n.)* **shopbook**
အရောင်းစာရေး aaraunggsarrayy *(n.)* **salesman**
အရောင်းမြှင့်တင်သည်၊ အားပေးသည် aaraungg myaha int tinsai , aarrpayysai *(v.)* **promote**
အရောင်းအင်အားစု a-yaung-inn-arr-su *(n.)* **salesforce**
အရောင်းအဝယ် a-yaung-a-wal *(n.)* **dealings**
အရောင်ကန်းသော a-yaung-kan-taw *(adj.)* **colour-blind**
အရောင်ကျွတ်သည် a-yaung-kyut-the *(v.)* **bleach**
အရောင်ကွက်ကျား a-yaung-kwat-kyar *(n.)* **mottle**
အရောင်စိုခြင်း a-yaung-so-chin *(n.)* **lustre**
အရောင်စိုသော a-yaung-so-taw *(adj.)* **lustrous**
အရောင်စုံသော a-yaung-sone-taw *(adj.)* **colourful**
အရောင်တင်ဆီ charrnarrsai *(n.)* **varnish**
အရောင်တင်သည် aaraung tinse *(v.)* **varnish**
အရောင်တစ်ခု၏ ရှည်လျားသော အပိုင်း aaraungtaithkueat shilyarrsaw aapine *(v.)* **stripe**
အရောင်နု aa-raung-nu *(adj.)* **pastel**
အရောင်ပစ္စည်း aa-raung-pyit-see *(n.)* **pigment**
အရောင်ပါရေ a-yaung-par-yay *(n.)* **aquatint**
အရောင်မှေးမှိန်သွားသည် aa-raung mhaayy mhaeinswarrsai *(v.)* **tarnish**
အရောင်မဲ့ မှန်ဘီလူး a-yaung-mae-man-bi-lu *(n.)* **achromat**
အရောင်မဲ့သော a-yaung-mae-taw *(adj.)* **achromatic**
အရောင်လွင့်သည်၊ မှိန်သွားသည် a-yaung-lwint-the, mein-twar-the *(v.)* **fade**
အရောင်သန်းခြင်း aaraung saannchinn *(n.)* **tint**
အရောင်သန်းထားသည် aaraung saannhtarrsai *(v.)* **tint**
အရောင်အဝါ တောက်ပ ခံ့ညားသော aaraung aawar toutp hkan nyarrsaw *(adj.)* **resplendent**
အရောအနှော a-yaw-a-hnaw *(n.)* **mixture**
အရဲစွန့်ပြောသည် a-ye-sunt-pyaw-the *(v.)* **hazard**
အလံ a-lan *(n.)* **flag**
အလင်း၊ အပူဓာတ် ဖြာထွက်သော aa-lainn , aa-puu-dhrat hpyaar-htwat-saw *(adj.)* **radiant**
အလင်းကာသည် a-linn karsai *(v.)* **shade**
အလင်းထွက်သော a-linn-htwat-thaw *(adj.)* **fluorescent**
အလင်းထုတ်သော a-lin-htoke-taw *(adj.)* **lucent**
အလင်းပိတ်မှု a-lin-pate-mhu *(n.)* **opacity**
အလင်းပိတ်သော a-lin-pate-taw *(adj.)* **opaque**
အလင်းပေးသည် a-lin-pay-the *(v.)* **aluminate**
အလင်းမှိန်ခြင်း a-lin-main-chin *(n.)* **dimness**

အလင်းရောင် a-lin-yaung *(n.)* **illumination**
အလင်းရောင်ပေးသည် aalinnraungpayysai *(v.)* **shine**
အလင်းရောင်မှိန်မှိန် a-lin-yaung-mein-mein *(n.)* **gleam**
အလင်းဝင်ပေါက် a-linn-win-pauk *(n.)* **aperture**
အလင်္ကာ aa-linkar *(adj.)* **rhetorical**
အလစ် aa-lit *(adv.)* **unawares**
အလစ်သုတ်သည် a lait sotesai *(v.)* **shoplift**
အလစ်သုတ်သမား a lait sotesamarr *(n.)* **shoplifter**
အလည်ခရီး aa-lai-hka-ree *(n.)* **tour**
အလည်အပတ်၊ ညအိပ်ခြင်း aalaiaapaat , nyaainchinn *(n.)* **stay**
အလည်အပတ်သွားသည် aalai-aapaatswarrsai *(v.)* **visit**
အလန့်တကြား a lant takyarr *(n.)* **scare**
အလယ် a-lal *(adj.)* **central**
အလယ်၊ အုပ်ချုပ်ရေးဗဟို a-lal, oak-choke-yay-ba-ho *(n.)* **centre**
အလယ်ခေတ် a-lal-khit *(adj.)* **medieval**
အလယ်တွင် a-lal-twin *(prep.)* **amid**
အလယ်ပုံ a-lal-pon *(n.)* **jackpot**
အလယ်အတွင်းဘက် a-lal-a-twin-bat *(n.)* **mid-on**
အလယ်အပြင်ဘက် a-lal-a-pyin-bat *(n.)* **mid-off**
အလယ်အလတ် a-lal-a-lat *(adj.)* **middling**
အလယ်အလတ်၊ ပျမ်းမျှ a-lal-a-lat, pyin-mya *(n.)* **mean**
အလယ်အလတ်ဖြစ်သော a-lal-a-lat-phit-taw *(adj.)* **intermediate**
အလျင်စလိုမျိုချသည် a-lyin-sa-lo-myo-cha-the *(v.)* **gulp**
အလျင်လူ a lyin-luu *(n.)* **predecessor**
အလျှံပယ် a-shan-paal *(n.)* **superabundance**
အလျှံပယ်ပေါခြင်း a-hlyan-pal-paw-chin *(n.)* **glut**
အလျှံပယ်ဖြစ်သည် a-hlyan-pal-phit-the *(v.)* **glut**
အလျှော့ပေးသည် a shot-payysai *(v.)* **relent**
အလျူမီနီယံ a-lyu-mi-ni-yan *(n.)* **aluminium**
အလျော်ပေးသည် a-yaw-pay-the *(v.)* **compensate**
အလွတ် a-hlut *(adj.)* **blank**
အလွတ်ကျက်ခြင်း a lwat kyetchinn *(n.)* **rote**
အလွတ်တန်းပညာရှင် a-lut-tan-pyin-nyar-shin *(n.)* **freelancer**
အလွတ်ပုံစံ ခရိုရှေးအပိုင်းအစ a lwatponehcan hk ro shayyaapineaahc *(n.)* **scrumble**
အလွန် aa-lwan *(adj.)* **very**
အလွန် စိတ်ကျေနပ်ခြင်း a-lun-seik-kyay-nat-chin *(n.)* **delectability**
အလွန် ဝမ်းသာသော a-lwan-wam-tar-taw *(adj.)* **overjoyed**
အလွန့်အလွန် a-lunt-a-lun *(adv.)* **most**
အလွန့်အလွန် ဆိုးဝါးသော a-lwunt-a-lun-soe-war-thaw *(adj.)* **damnable**
အလွန်ကျယ်လောင်သော a-lun-kyal-laung-taw *(adj.)* **deafening**
အလွန်ကြမ်းကြုတ်သော a-lun-kyan-kyoke-taw *(adj.)* **atrocious**
အလွန်ကြီးကြီးမားမား aalwankyeekyeemarrmarr *(adj.)* **titanic**
အလွန်ကြီးမားသော a-lun-kyi-mar-taw *(adj.)* **gigantic**

အလွန်ကြီးမားသော ပမာဏ a-lun-kyi-mar-taw-pa-mar-na *(n.)* **immensity**
အလွန်ကောင်းသော a-lun-kaung-taw *(adj.)* **deluxe**
အလွန်ချစ်ရသော a-lun-chit-ya-taw *(adj.)* **darling**
အလွန်ချမ်းသာသူ a-lun-chan-tar-thu *(n.)* **nabob**
အလွန်စိတ်ဆိုးသော a-lun-seik-soe-taw *(adj.)* **irate**
အလွန်ဆန္ဒ ပြင်းပျသည် a lun-san-da-pyin-pya-taw *(v.)* **yen**
အလွန်ဆိုးဝါးသော a-lun-soe-war-taw *(adj.)* **dreadful**
အလွန်ဆိုးသော အရာ a-lun-soe-taw-a-yar *(n.)* **dreadful**
အလွန်တက်ကြွသော a-lun-tat-kwa-taw *(adj.)* **ardent**
အလွန်နူးညံ့ချောမွတ်သော aa-lwan-nuu-nyan-chaw-mwat-saw *(adj.)* **superfine**
အလွန်ပြင်းပြသော a-loon-pyin-pya-taw *(adj.)* **burning**
အလွန်မြင့်သော a-lun-myint-taw *(adj.)* **lofty**
အလွန်မုန်းတီးသည် a-lun-hmon-tee-the *(v.)* **detest**
အလွန်ယုတ်မာသော a-lun-yoke-mar-taw *(adj.)* **heinous**
အလွန်ရက်ရောသော a-lun-yat-yaw-thaw *(adj.)* **munificent**
အလွန်ရယ်ဖွယ်ကောင်းသည် a-lun-ye-phwal-kaung-the *(adj.)* **hilarious**
အလွန်ရှေးဆန်သော a-lun-shay-san-taw *(adj.)* **archaic**
အလွန်ရှေးရိုးဆန်သော aalwan shayy roesaansaw *(adj.)* **ultraconservative**
အလွန်လှပ သိမ်မွေ့သော a-lun-hla-pa-thein-mway-taw *(adj.)* **exquisite**
အလွန်လုံခြုံသော aalwan lonechon-saw *(adj.)* **ultrasecure**
အလွန်လူကြိုက်များသည့် ရုပ်ရှင်၊ ဝတ္ထု a-lun-lu-kyaik-myar-the-yoke-shin-wut-htu *(n.)* **blockbuster**
အလွန်ဝခြင်း a-lwan-wa-chinn *(n.)* **obesity**
အလွန်ဝသော a-lwan-wa-taw *(adj.)* **obese**
အလွန်သိပ်သည်းသော aa-lwan seik saeesaw *(adj.)* **ultracompact**
အလွန်သေးငယ်စာ ပုံနှိပ်ခြင်း a-lun-tay-ngal-swar-pon-nate-chin *(n.)* **microprint**
အလွန်သေးငယ်သော a-lun-tay-nge-taw *(adj.)* **diminutive**
အလွန်အံ့အားသင့်စေသည် a-lun-ant-arr-tint-say-the *(v.)* **astonish**
အလွန်အကျွံ aa-lwan-aa-kywan *(n.)* **ultra**
အလွန်အမင်း aalwan-aa-minn *(adj.)* **profuse**
အလွန်အမင်းခက်ခဲမှုကို ခံနိုင်စွမ်း a-lun-a-min-khat-khae-mu-ko-lat-khan-nai-swan *(n.)* **hardihood**
အလွန်အမင်းခေတ်နောက်ကျခြင်း aalwan-aa-minn hkit nout-kyahkyinn *(adj.)* **paleolithic**
အလွန်အမင်းဆိုးရွားသော a-lun-a-min-soe-ywar-taw *(adj.)* **awful**
အလွန်အမှတ်မထင်ဖြစ်သော aa-lwan-aa-mhaatmahtinhpyitsaw *(adj.)* **ultracasual**
အလွန်အရေးကြီးခြင်း a-lun-a-yay-kyi-chin *(n.)* **pre-eminence**
အလွန်အရေးပါသော a-lun-a-yay-par-taw *(adj.)* **momentous**
အလွန်အလေးအနက်ထားသော a-lun-a-lay-a-nat-htar-taw *(adj.)* **earnest**
အလွန်အံ့သြခြင်း a-lun-aunt-aw-chin *(n.)* **astonishment**
အလွန်အေးရှ် ဆိုးဝါးသော a-lun-aye-ywe-soe-war-taw *(adj.)* **bleak**

အလွန်အေးသော a-lun-aye-taw *(adj.)* **frozen**

အလွမ်းဇာတ်သဘင် aalwmjaratsabhain *(n.)* **tragedy**

အလွမ်းပြဇာတ်ရေးဆရာ aalwm pyajarat rayysarar *(n.)* **tragedian**

အလွယ်တကူပုံသွင်း၍ ရသော a-lwal-ta-ku-pon-twin-ywe-ya-taw *(adj.)* **malleable**

အလွှာ aalwhar *(n.)* **stratum**

အလွှာအလွှာ ကွာကျစေသည် a-hlwar-a-hlwar-kwar-kya-say-the *(v.)* **flake**

အလွဲလွဲအချော်ချော် လုပ်တတ်သူ a-lwal-lwal-a-chaw-chaw-lote-tat-thu *(n.)* **bungle**

အလွဲသုံးစားပြုသည် a-lwe-tone-sar-pyu-the *(v.)* **abuse**

အလှ aa-hla *(n.)* **prettiness**

အလှစိုက် စိမ်းလန်းသော သစ်ပင်၊ ခြုံနွယ် a-hla-site-sein-lan-taw-tit-pin-chon-nwe *(n.)* **greenery**

အလှဆင်ခြင်း a-hla-sin-chin *(n.)* **decoration**

အလှဆင်သည် a-hla-sin-the *(v.)* **decorate**

အလှဆီ a-hla-se *(n.)* **glycerine**

အလှည့်၊ အမွှေ့ a hlae, aa-mwae *(n.)* **spin**

အလှတန်ဆာ a-hla-taan-sar *(adj.)* **ornamental**

အလှပျက်စေသည် a-hla-pyat-say-the *(v.)* **deface**

အလှပြင်ဆိုင် aahlapyinsine *(n.)* **Salon**

အလှပြင်ပစ္စည်း a-hla-pyin-pyit-see *(n.)* **cosmetic**

အလှပြင်သည် a-hla-pyin-the *(v.)* **beautify**

အလှမယ်ပွဲ၊ ကောင်မလေး၊ ကလေးမ၊ သူငယ်မကို ရည်ညွှန်းသော စကား a-hla-mal-bwe, kaung-ma-lay, ka-lay-ma, thu-nge-ma-ko-yay-hnyun-taw-sa-gar *(n.)* **miss**

အလှရသခံစားတတ်သူ a-hla-ya-th-khan-sar-tat-thu *(n.)* **aesthete**

အလှအပ a-hla-a-pa *(n.)* **beauty**

အလှအယက် တိုးဝှေ့ကြိုးပမ်းရခြင်း a hla aayaat toe whaae kyaoepamrachinn *(n.)* **scramble**

အလှူ a-hlyu *(n.)* **benefaction**

အလှူခံသည် a-hlyu-khan-the *(v.)* **beg**

အလှူရှင် a-hlu-shin *(n.)* **donor**

အလားတူ a-lar-tu *(adv.)* **likewise**

အလားတူမှု aa-larr-tuu-mhu *(n.)* **parallelism**

အလားတူသော a-lar-thu-taw *(adj.)* **analogous**

အလားအလာ aa-larr-aalar *(n.)* **potential**

အလားအလာ၊ မျှော်လင့်ချက် aa-larr-aalar, myaw lint-chet *(n.)* **prospect**

အလားအလာကောင်းသော aalarr-aalar-kaunggsaw *(adj.)* **promising**

အလားအလာမရှိ aalarraalarmashi *(adj.)* **unlikely**

အလားအလာရှိသည် a-lar-a-lar-shi-tai *(n.)* **offing**

အလားအလာရှိသော aalarr-aalar-shisaw *(adj.)* **potential**

အလိပ်၊ ပေါင်မုန့်အလုံး a late, paung mont aalone *(n.)* **roll**

အလိုက်သင့် ပြုမူနေထိုင်ခြင်း a-lite-tint-pyu-mu-nay-htaing-chin *(n.)* **adjustment**

အလိုက်သင့် ပြုမူနေထိုင်သည် a-lite-tint-pyu-mu-nay-htaing-the *(v.)* **adjust**

အလိုက်သင့် သွင်းသည် aa-lite-sint swinsai *(v.)* **slot.**

အလိုဆန္ဒ a losanda *(n.)* **want**

အလိုလိုက်ခံရခြင်း a-lo-lite-khan-ya-chin *(n.)* **indulgence**

အလိုလိုက်ခံရသော a-lo-lite-khan-ya-taw *(adj.)* **indulgent**
အလိုလိုက်သည် a-lo-lite-the *(v.)* **pamper**
အလိုလိုသိခြင်း a-lo-lo-ti-chin *(n.)* **intuition**
အလိုလိုသိသော a-lo-lo-ti-taw *(adj.)* **intuitive**
အလိုလေး a-lo-lay *(interj.)* **alas**
အလိုအလျောက်အသိပေးချက် a-lo-a-lyauk-a-thi-pay-chat *(n.)* **trackback**
အလိုအလျောက် a-lo-a-lyaut *(adj.)* **automatic**
အလိုအလျောက် ဆုံချက်ချိန်ညှိခြင်း a-lo-a-lyaut-sone-chat-chein-nyi-chin *(n.)* **autofocus**
အလိုအလျောက် ပြင်ဆင်ခြင်း a-lo-a-lyaut-pyin-sin-chin *(n.)* **autocorrect**
အလိုအလျောက်ဖြစ်သော aaloaalyawwathpyitsaw *(adj.)* **spontaneous**
အလိုအလျောက်လုပ် စက်ကိရိယာသုံးခြင်း a-lo-a-lyaut-lote-sat-ka-yi-yar-tone-chin *(n.)* **automation**
အလိုအလျောက်လေယာဉ်မောင်းခြင်း a-lo-a-lyaut-lay-yin-maung-chin *(n.)* **autopilot**
အလိုအလျောက်သဘောသက်ဝင်ခြင်း aaloaalyawwat sabhaw saatwinchinn *(n.)* **spontaneity**
အလုံးစုံ a-lone-sone *(n.)* **over**
အလုံးစုံ စစ်ဆေးခြင်း a-lone-sone-sit-say-chinn *(n.)* **overhaul**
အလုံးစုံ စစ်ဆေးသည် a-lone-sone-sit-say-tai *(v.)* **overhaul**
အလုံးစုံကောင်းမွန်နှစ်သက်ဖွယ်ဖြစ်ခြင်း a-lone-sone-kaung-mon-nit-tat-phwal-phit-chin *(n.)* **omnibenevolence**
အလုံးစုံကောင်းမွန်နှစ်သက်ဖွယ်ဖြစ်သော a-lone-sone-kaung-mon-nit-tat-phwal-phit-taw *(adj.)* **omnibenevolent**
အလုံးဖြစ်အောင်လုံးခြင်း a-lone-phit-aung-lone-chin *(n.)* **agglomerate**
အလုံးဖြစ်အောင်လုံးသည် a-lone-phit-aung-lone-the *(v.)* **agglomerate**
အလုပ် aa-lote *(n.)* **work**
အလုပ်၊ ငွေ၊ နေစရာ မဲ့သော a-lote-ngwe-nay-sa-yar-mae-taw *(adj.)* **down and out**
အလုပ်ကြပ် a-lote-kyat *(n.)* **foreman**
အလုပ်ကြမ်း aalotekyam *(n.)* **toil**
အလုပ်ကြမ်းသမား a-lote-kyan-ta-mar *(n.)* **labourer**
အလုပ်ကြွေး a-lote-kyway *(n.)* **backlog**
အလုပ်ကြိုးစားသည် a-lote-kyo-sar-the *(v.)* **moil**
အလုပ်ကြိုးစားသော a-lote-kyo-sar-taw *(adj.)* **hard-working**
အလုပ်ခန့်ခြင်း a-lote-khant-chin *(n.)* **employment**
အလုပ်ခန့်သည် a-lote-khant-the *(v.)* **employ**
အလုပ်ခန့်သောသူ a-lote-khant-taw-thu *(n.)* **jobber**
အလုပ်တွင်စေသည် a-lote-twin-say-the *(v.)* **expedite**
အလုပ်တာဝန်ခွဲဝေပေးသည် a-lote-tar-win-kwal-wai-pay-the *(v.)* **delegate**
အလုပ်ပြုတ်သူ a-lote-pyoke-thu *(n.)* **lay-off**
အလုပ်ပိခြင်း a-lote-pi-chinn *(n.)* **overwork**
အလုပ်ပိသည် a-lote-pi-tai *(v.)* **overwork**
အလုပ်များသော a-lote-myar-taw *(adj.)* **busy**
အလုပ်မှ ထုတ်ပစ်သည် aalotemha htote paitsai *(v.)* **sack**
အလုပ်ရှင် a-lote-shin *(n.)* **employer**
အလုပ်ရုံ၊ ဝပ်ရှော့ aa-lote-rone , wautshot *(n.)* **workshop**
အလုပ်လက်မဲ့ a-lote-lat-mae *(adj.)* **jobless**

အလုပ်လက်မဲ့ဖြစ်ခြင်း a-lote-lat-mae-phit-chin *(n.)* **idleness**
အလုပ်လစ်လပ်မှု aalote laitlautsaw *(n.)* **vacancy**
အလုပ်လစ်လပ်သော htwatsai *(adj.)* **vacant**
အလုပ်လုပ်သည် aa-lote-lote-sai *(v.)* **work**
အလုပ်လုပ်သည်၊ မောင်းသည် a-lote-lote-tai, maung-tai *(v.)* **operate**
အလုပ်သင် a-lote-tin *(n.)* **apprentice**
အလုပ်သမား aa-lote-sa-marr *(n.)* **worker**
အလုပ်သမားသမဂ္ဂဝင် aa-lote-samarrsamaggawin *(n.)* **unionist**
အလုပ်အကျွေးပြုသည်၊ အမှုထမ်းသည် aalote a kyaway pyusai , aamhuhtamsai *(v.)* **serve**
အလုပ်အကိုင် a-lote-a-kine *(n.)* **occupation**
အလုပ်အကိုင် မကောင်းသည့် အချိန် aaloteaakine makaunggsaeet aachane *(n.)* **slump**
အလုပ်အကိုင်၊ အတတ်ပညာရှင် aa-lote-aakine, aa-taat-pa-nyar-shin *(n.)* **profession**
အလုပ်အမှုဆောင် a-lote-a-hmu-saung *(n.)* **executive**
အလေ့ပါအောင် ကျင့်ယူသည် a-lay-par-aung-kyint-yu-the *(v.)* **habituate**
အလေးချိန် aa-layychane *(n.)* **weight**
အလေးထားမှု aalayy-htarrmhu *(n.)* **regard**
အလေးထားသော aalayyhtarrsaw *(adj.)* **respectful**
အလေးပေးသည် a-lay-pay-the *(v.)* **emphasize**
အလေးမထားခြင်း a-lay-ma-htar-chin *(n.)* **flippancy**
အလေးသာသည် a-lay-tar-tai *(v.)* **outweigh**
အလေးအနက် မရှိသော a-lay-a-net-ma-shi-taw *(adj.)* **facile**
အလေးအနက် အကျယ်တဝင့် ပြောဟောချက် a-lay-a-nat-a-kyal-ta-wint-haw-pyaw-chat *(n.)* **discourse**
အလေးအနက်တိုက်တွန်းခြင်း a-lay-a-net-tite-tune-chin *(n.)* **adjuration**
အလေးအနက်ပြုသည် aalayy-aa-naatpyusai *(v.)* **punctuate**
အလေးအနက်ပြောခြင်း aa-layy-aa-naatpyaww-chinn *(n.)* **protestation**
အလေးအနက်ပြောသော a-lay-a-nat-pyaw-taw *(adj.)* **emphatic**
အလေးအနက်မထားသော a-lay-a-nat-ma-htar-taw *(adj.)* **frivolous**
အလေးအမြတ်ထားသော a layy aamyathtarrsaw *(adj.)* **sacred**
အလေအလွင့် a lay a-lwint *(n.)* **stray**
အလောင်း a-laung *(n.)* **corpse**
အလောင်းကို ခွဲစိတ်စစ်ဆေးခြင်း a-laung-ko-kwal-seik-sit-say-chin *(n.)* **autopsy**
အလောင်းစင် a-laung-sin *(n.)* **bier**
အလောင်းအစား aalaunggaasarr *(n.)* **wager**
အလောတကြီး a-law-ta-gyee *(n.)* **hurry**
အလောတကြီး ပြောဆို၊ ပြုမူသည် a-law-ta-gyi-pyaw-se-pyu-mu-the *(adj.)* **hasty**
အလောတကြီးဖြစ်သော အစားအစာ a law t kyeehpyitsaw aahcarraahcar *(n.)* **scambling**
အဝင် a-win *(n.)* **entry**
အဝင်ဝတံခါး a-win-wa-ta-khar *(n.)* **gateway**
အဝင်အဆင့် a-win-a-sint *(adj.)* **entry-level**
အဝတ် a-wit *(n.)* **garment**
အဝတ်စ aawaat-sa *(n.)* **shroud**
အဝတ်စုတ် aa-wit-sote *(n.)* **rag**
အဝတ်ညှပ် aa-waat-nyat *(n.)* **peg**
အဝတ်ညှပ်သည် aa-waat-nyat-sai *(v.)* **peg**

အဝတ်ဗလာအနုပညာ a-wut-ba-lar-a-nu-pyin-nyar *(n.)* **nude**
အဝတ်မဆင်သော a-wut-ma-sin-taw *(adj.)* **nude**
အဝတ်လဲခန်း a-wut-lae-khan *(n.)* **fitting room**
အဝတ်လဲတဲ a-wut-lal-tae *(n.)* **cabana**
အဝတ်ဝတ်သည် a-wit-wit-the *(v.)* **dress**
အဝတ်အစား a-wit-a-sar *(n.)* **clothes**
အဝတ်အစား ဖက်ရှင်ဒီဇိုင်းထွင်ခြင်း a-wit-a-sar-phat-shin-de-zine-htwin-chin *(n.)* **couture**
အဝတ်အစား၊ အသုံးအဆောင် a-wit-a-sar, a-tone-a-saung *(n.)* **clobber**
အဝတ်အစားစွဲလမ်းခြင်း a-wit-a-sar-swal-lan-thu *(adj.)* **textile**
အဝတ်အထည် a-wit-a-htal *(n.)* **clothing**
အငွေ့ aa-whaae *(n.)* **puff**
အဝါ a-war *(n.)* **yellow**
အဝါဖျော့ရောင် a-war-phaw-yaung *(n.)* **mustard**
အဝါရောင် aa-warraung *(adj.)* **saffron**
အဝါရောင် ဒိန်ခဲမာတစ်မျိုး a-war-yaung-dain-khae-mar-ta-myo *(n.)* **cheddar**
အဝါရောင်ပန်း a-war-yaung-pan *(n.)* **daffodil**
အဝါရောင်ပြောင်းလဲသည် a-war-yaung-paung-htae-sai *(n.)* **saffron**
အဝါရောင်အလေ့ကျပန်း a-war-yaung-a-lay-kya-pan *(n.)* **dandelion**
အစီစီ a-wi-si *(adj.)* **artesian**
အဝေး a-way *(adv.)* **afar**
အဝေးကြည့်မှန်ပြောင်း aa-wayy kyi mhaanpyaungg *(adj.)* **telescopic**
အဝေးကြည့်အနီးကြည့် ပါဝါမျက်မှန် a-way-kyi-a-nee-kyi-pa-war-myat-man *(adj.)* **bifocal**
အဝေးပို့ aawayy-phoet *(n.)* **teleport**
အဝေးပို့သည် aawayy phoet-sai *(v.)* **teleport**
အဝေးမှ ပရင့်ထုတ်ခြင်း aa-wayymha print htotechinn *(v.)* **teleprint**
အဝေးမှုန်ခြင်း a-way-hmone-chin *(n.)* **myopia**
အဝေးမှုန်သော a-way-hmone-taw *(adj.)* **myopic**
အွန့် awnt *(n.)* **oink**
အွန့်ခနဲ မြည်သည် awnt-hka-nell-myi-tai *(v.)* **oink**
အွန့်ခနဲ့ မြည်သူ ommt-kha-nae-myae-thu *(n.)* **oinker**
အွန်လိုင်းဖြစ်သော on-line-hpyit-taw *(adj.)* **online**
အွန်လိုင်းလူ့အဖွဲ့အစည်းမှ စုပေါင်းလှူဒါန်းခြင်း on-line-lu-a-phwe-a-see-ma-su-paung-hlu-dan-chin *(n.)* **crowdfunding**
အသံ aasan *(n.)* **sound**
အသံကို စာအဖြစ် နားထောင်ပြောင်းပေးခြင်း kyawlwanlyet *(n.)* **transcription**
အသံကို စာအဖြစ် နားထောင်ပြောင်းပေးသူ htuu kell sarlwanlyet *(n.)* **transcriber**
အသံကို အဆုံးထိမြှင့်တင်၍ ပြန်ချဆိုသော သီချင်း aa-san-ko aa-sone-hti myint-tin pyan-ywe cha-sosaw sechinn *(n.)* **yodel**
အသံချဲ့စက် a-tan-chae-set *(n.)* **amplifier**
အသံငါးခုကို အခြေခံသော aa-san ngarr-hkuko aa-chyay-hkansaw *(adj.)* **pentatonic**
အသံစနစ် aasansanit *(n.)* **sound system**
အသံစူးစူးဖြင့် ဟောင်သံ aa-san suu-suu-hpyint haungsan *(n.)* **yap**

အသံစူးစူးဖြင့် ဟောင်သည် aasan suu suuhpyint haungsai *(v.)* **yap**
အသံတအိအိ ပြုသည် aasantaaiai pyusai *(v.)* **whimper**
အသံတိတ်ကိရိယာ aasantateka-ri-yar *(n.)* **silencer**
အသံထက်မြန်သော aa-san-htat myansaw *(adj.)* **supersonic**
အသံထွက် aa-san-htwat *(n.)* **pronunciation**
အသံထွက်၍ a-than-htwat-ywe *(adv.)* **aloud**
အသံထွက်သည် aa-sanht-watsai *(v.)* **pronounce**
အသံနှင့်ဆိုင်သော a-tan-nint-saing-taw *(adj.)* **acoustic**
အသံပညာ a-tan-pyin-nyar *(n.)* **acoustics**
အသံပြာသော a-tan-pyar-taw *(adj.)* **hoarse**
အသံဖမ်းစက် a-tan-phan-sat *(n.)* **gramophone**
အသံဖျောက်ဆိုခြင်း a-than-phyauk-so-chin *(n.)* **elision**
အသံမစဲ တလိမ့်လိမ့်သွားသည် aasan masell ta lint lint-swarr-sai *(v.)* **rumble**
အသံမထွက်နိုင်ခြင်း a-tan-ma-htwat-naing-chin *(n.)* **aphasia**
အသံမထွက်သော a-tan-ma-htwat-taw *(adj.)* **mute**
အသံရှည်ဆုံးဖြင့် အသံထွက်သည် a-tan-shay-sone-phint-a-tan-htwat-the *(v.)* **assibilate**
အသံရှိသော aasanshisaw *(adj.)* **toned**
အသံလွှင့်ချက်ပို့သည် aa-san lwint chet phoetsai *(v.)* **radio**
အသံလွှင့်စက် hkandhar sitko winyin kuupyaungg mhae twalchinn *(n.)* **transmitter**
အသံလွှင့်သည် a-tan-hlwint-the *(v.)* **broadcast**
အသံလှိုင်း aa-sanhline *(adj.)* **sonic**
အသံလုံသော aasan lonesaw *(adj.)* **soundproof**
အသံသြဇာ၊ ဟိန်းသံ aasan sya zar, heinsan *(n.)* **resonance**
အသံအစီအစဉ် a-san-a-si-a-sin *(n.)* **podcast**
အသံအစီအစဉ်လွှင့်သည် a-san-a-si-a-sin-hlwint-sai *(v.)* **podcast**
အသံအစီအစဉ်လွှင့်သူ a-san-a-si-a-sin-hlwint-suu *(n.)* **podcaster**
အသံအနေအထား aasanaanayaahtarr *(n.)* **tone**
အသံအိုးဖုံး a-tan-o-phone *(n.)* **epiglottis**
အသံအော a-tan-aw *(n.)* **baritone**
အသံအောင်ခြင်း aa-sanaaungchinn *(n.)* **sonority**
အသံအောသော aa-san aaw-saw *(adj.)* **throaty**
အသက် a-thet- *(n.)* **age**
အသက် ၈၀ ကျော် ၉၀ အောက် a-tat-80-kyaw-90-out *(n.)* **octogenarian**
အသက် ၈၀ ကျော် ၉၀ အောက်ဖြစ်သော a-tat-80-kyaw-90-out-hpyit-taw *(adj.)* **octogenarian**
အသက်ကယ်အင်္ကျီ a-thet-kal-in-gyi *(n.)* **life jacket**
အသက်ကို ပဓာနမထားဘဲ တဇောက်ကန်း လုပ်ဆောင်သော a-tat-ko-pa-dar-na-ma-htar-bae-ta-zaut-kan-lote-saung-taw *(n.)* **kamikaze**
အသက်ပါခြင်း aasaat parchinn *(n.)* **vitality**
အသက်ပါသည် aasaatparsai *(v.)* **vitalize**
အသက်ပါသော a-thet-par-taw *(adj.)* **expressive**
အသက်မရှူနိုင်ဖြစ်သည် aa-saat ma shuu ninehpyitsai *(v.)* **wind**

အသက်မွေးပညာ a-thet-mway-pyin-nyar *(n.)* **calling**
အသက်မွေးမှု a-thet-mway-mu *(n.)* **living**
အသက်မွေးဝမ်းကျောင်း a-thet-mway-wan-kyaung *(n.)* **livelihood**
အသက်မွေးသူ aa-saat-mway-suu *(n.)* **practitioner**
အသက်မဲ့သော a-thet-mae-taw *(adj.)* **lifeless**
အသက်ရှင်ကျန်ရစ်သည် aa-saat-shin-kyaan-rit-sai *(v.)* **survive**
အသက်ရှင်နေနိုင်မှု aa-saat-shin nayninemhu *(n.)* **subsistence**
အသက်ရှင်နေသည် aa-saat-shin-naysai *(v.)* **subsist**
အသက်ရှင်သော a-thet-shin-taw *(adj.)* **alive**
အသက်ရှည်ခြင်း a-thet-shay-chin *(n.)* **longevity**
အသက်ရှိသော a-thet-shi-taw *(adj.)* **live**
အသက်ရှူခြင်း aasaatshuuchinn *(n.)* **respiration**
အသက်ရှူပြွန်နှင့် ဆိုင်သော a-thet-shu-pywun-nint-sai-taw *(adj.)* **bronchial**
အသက်ရှူလမ်းကြောင်းနှင့် အင်္ဂါလေ့လာသော ပညာရပ် a-thet-shu-lan-kyaung-nint-inn-gar-lae-lar-taw-pa-nyar-yat *(n.)* **pneumology**
အသက်ရှူသည် aasaatshuusai *(v.)* **respire**
အသက်ဝင်ခြင်း a-thet-win-chin *(n.)* **activation**
အသက်ဝင်သည် a-thet-win-the *(v.)* **activate**
အသက်ဝင်သော aasaatwinaaung lotesai *(adj.)* **valid**
အသက်ဝင်သော၊ အကျိုးသက်ရောက်သော a-tat-win-taw, a-kyoe-tat-rout-taw *(adj.)* **operative**
အသက်ဝင်အောင် လုပ်သည် hkine lone chinn , tararrwinhpyitchinn *(v.)* **validate**
အသက်အထောက်အကူ a-thet-a-htauk-a-ku *(n.)* **life support**
အသက်အရွယ်ကြီးရင့်ခြင်းကို ဆန့်ကျင်သော a-the-a-ywe-kyi-yint-chin-ko-sant-kyin-taw *(adj.)* **anti-ageing**
အသက်အရွယ်ရှိသော a-thet-a-ywal-shi-taw *(adj.)* **aged**
အသင့်စားဖွယ် a-tint-sar-phwal *(n.)* **delicatessen**
အသင့်စားအစားအစာ a-tint-sar-a-sar-a-sar *(n.)* **fast food**
အသင့်ဆုံး a-tint-sone *(n.)* **optimum**
အသင့်ဆုံးဖြစ်သော a-tint-sone-hpyit-taw *(adj.)* **optimum**
အသင့်ပြင်သည် a sint pyinsai *(v.)* **prime**
အသင့်လျော်သော မဟာမိတ် ma-tint-lyaw-thaw-ma-har-mate *(n.)* **misalliance**
အသင့်အတင့် ဖြစ်သော a-tint-a-tint-phyit-taw *(adj.)* **modest**
အသင်း၊ အဖွဲ့ချုပ် a-tin, a-phwe-chike *(n.)* **league**
အသင်းတော်နယ်ပယ် aa-sainn-taw-naal-paal *(n.)* **parish**
အသင်းဝင်ကြေး၊ ပုံမှန် အလှူထည့်ဝင်ငွေ aasinnwin kyay , ponemhaan aahluu htaee-win-ngway *(n.)* **subscription**
အသင်းအဖွဲ့ဖြစ်သော aasinnaahpwal hpyitsaw *(adj.)* **teamed**
အသချေ a-tin-chay *(adj.)* **innumerable**
အသစ် a-thit *(adj.)* **new**
အသစ်၊ လတ်လတ်ဆတ်ဆတ် a-thit, lat-lat-sat-sat *(adj.)* **fresh**
အသစ်တစ်ဖန် a-thit-ta-hpan *(adv.)* **afresh**
အသစ်ထွင်သည် a-thit-htwin-the *(v.)* **innovate**

အသစ်ပြုပြင် ဆောက်လုပ်ခြင်း aasitpyupyin soutlotechinn *(n.)* **renovation**
အသစ်ပြုပြင်သည် aasit pyupyinsai *(v.)* **renovate**
အသစ်လဲလှယ်ခြင်း aasit lell-hlaalchinn *(n.)* **renewal**
အသစ်အဆန်း a-tit-a-san *(n.)* **novelty**
အသည်း a-tae *(n.)* **liver**
အသည်းကျော် a-the-kyaw *(n.)* **favourite**
အသည်းကွဲခြင်း a-tal-kwe-chin *(n.)* **heartbreak**
အသည်းခြောက်ရောဂါ a-the-chauk-yaw-gar *(n.)* **cirrhosis**
အသည်းငယ်သော aa-saee ngaalsaw *(adj.)* **timorous**
အသည်းစွဲ a-the-swal *(n.)* **idol**
အသည်းမာစေသည် a-the-mar-say-the *(v.)* **brutify**
အသနားခံခြင်း a-ta-nar-khan-chin *(n.)* **entreaty**
အသနားခံစာ aa-sa-narr-hkan-sarr *(n.)* **petition**
အသနားခံသည် aa-sa-narr-hkan-sai *(v.)* **petition**
အသနားခံသူ aa-sa-narr-hkan-suu *(n.)* **petitioner**
အသနားခံသော a-ta-nar-khan-taw *(n.)* **beseeching**
အသရေပျက်ခြင်း a-tha-yay-pyat-chin *(n.)* **disgrace**
အသရေပျက်စေသော a-tha-yay-pyat-say-taw *(adj.)* **defamatory**
အသရေဖျက်မှု a sa ray-hpyet-mhu *(n.)* **slander**
အသရေဖျက်သည် a-ta-yay-phat-the *(v.)* **libel**
အသရေဖျက်သည့်စာ a-ta-yay-phat-the-sar *(n.)* **libel**
အသရေဖျက်သော a sa ray hpyetsaw *(adj.)* **slanderous**
အသွင်၊ ပုံပန်း aaswin , ponepaann *(n.)* **semblance**
အသွင်ပြောင်းခြင်း pyaunglellswarrchinn *(n.)* **transformation**
အသွင်ပြောင်းလဲခြင်း a-twin-pyaung-lal-chin *(n.)* **metamorphosis**
အသွင်ပြောင်းသည် lwhaellpyaungpayyninesaw *(v.)* **transform**
အသွားလက်မှတ် a swarrlaatmhaat *(n.)* **single**
အသား a-tar *(n.)* **flesh**
အသားကင် a-tar-kin *(n.)* **barbecue**
အသားကို ဖယ်ရှားသည် a-tar-ko-phal-shar-the *(v.)* **deflesh**
အသားငါးရွက်ပြုတ်ဟင်းချို a-tar-ngar-ywat-pyoke-hin-cho *(n.)* **broth**
အသားစ ဓာတ်ခွဲစစ်ဆေးခြင်း a-tar-sa-dat-khwal-sit-say-chin *(n.)* **biopsy**
အသားစားကောင် a-tar-sar-kaung *(n.)* **marten**
အသားစိမ်းစားခြင်း a-tar-sein-sar-chin *(n.)* **omophagia**
အသားညှပ်ပေါင်မုန့် a sarr nyat paung mone *(v.)* **sandwich**
အသားညိုသည် a sarr nyosai *(v.)* **tan**
အသားတင် a-tan-tin *(adj.)* **net**
အသားဓာတ် a sarr-dhrat *(n.)* **protein**
အသားနူးအောင်မချက်ခင်ထည့်ရသော အရာ a sarr nuu aaung ma-chet-hkin hteet-rasaw aarar *(n.)* **tenderizer**
အသားပို a sarrpo *(n.)* **tumour**

အသားပေးသည် a-tar-pay-the *(v.)* **feature**

အသားမည်းနက်မာကျောသော ရင်းတိုက်ပင် a-tar-mae-nat-mar-kyaw-taw-yin-tite-pin *(n.)* **ebony**

အသားလှန်ခြင်း a-thar-hlan-chin *(n.)* **avulsion**

အသားဝါခြင်း a-tar-war-chin *(n.)* **jaundice**

အသားဝါသည် a-tar-war-the *(v.)* **jaundice**

အသားအရေ a-tar-a-yay *(n.)* **complexion**

အသာလွန်ဆုံး a sarlwan-sone *(adj.)* **superlative**

အသာလွန်ဆုံးအဆင့် နာမဝိသေသန၊ ကြိယာဝိသေသန a sarlwan sone-aa-sint narmawisaysa-na , kyaiyarwisaysa-na *(n.)* **superlative**

အသိ၊ သတိရှိမှု a-thi, ta-di-shi-mu *(n.)* **cognizance**

အသိခက်သော a-ti-khat-taw *(adj.)* **cryptic**

အသိဉာဏ် a-ti-nyan *(n.)* **intellect**

အသိဉာဏ်၊ ကျင့်ဝတ်၊ လူမှု အမှောင်ထု လွှမ်းခြုံသည် a-thi-nyan-kyint-wut-lu-mu-a-hmaung-htu-hlwan-chon-the *(v.)* **benight**

အသိဉာဏ်ထူးကို ရသော ပုဂ္ဂိုလ် a-ti-nyan-htoo-ko-ya-taw-poke-ko *(n.)* **mystic**

အသိဉာဏ်အတု a-ti-nyan-a-tu *(n.)* **artificial intelligence**

အသိတရားရသည်၊ သဘောပေါက်မိသည် aasitararr rasai , sabhawpout misai *(v.)* **realize**

အသိပညာ a-ti-pyin-nyar *(n.)* **knowledge**

အသိပညာကြွယ်သော a-ti-pyin-nyar-kywe-taw *(adj.)* **knowledgeable**

အသိပညာနည်းခြင်း a-ti-pin-nyar-nae-chin *(n.)* **nescience**

အသိပေးသည် a-thi-pay-the *(v.)* **acquaint**

အသိရှိခြင်း a-thi-shi-chin *(n.)* **awareness**

အသိရှိသော aa-si-shi-saw *(adj.)* **sentient**

အသိအကျွမ်း a-thi-a-kywan *(n.)* **acquaintance**

အသိအမှတ်ပြုခြင်း a-ti-a-mat-pyu-chin *(n.)* **appreciation**

အသိအမှတ်ပြုသည် a-ti-a-mat-pyu-the *(v.)* **appreciate**

အသိအမှတ်ပြုခံရသည် aa-si-aa-mhaat-pyu-hkan-rasai *(v.)* **qualify**

အသိအမှတ်ပြုခြင်း aa-si-aa-mhaat-pyu-chinn *(n.)* **recognition**

အသိအမှတ်ပြုလက်မှတ် a-ti-a-mat-pyu-lat-mat *(n.)* **certificate**

အသိအမှတ်ပြုသည် a-thi-a-mat-pyu-the *(v.)* **acknowledge**

အသိအမှတ်ပြုသော a-thi-a-mat-pyu-taw *(adj.)* **accredited**

အသိုက် a-thaik *(n.)* **nest**

အသိုက်ဖွဲ့သည် a-thaik-phwe-the *(v.)* **nest**

အသိုင်းအဝိုင်း a-thai-a-wai *(n.)* **ethos**

အသိုင်းအဝိုင်း၊ အသင်း၊ ကလပ်၊ သဟာယစိတ်ဓာတ် a-thai-a-wai, a-tin, ka-lat, ta-har-ya-seik-dat *(n.)* **fraternity**

အသီးခိုးသည် a see hkoesai *(v.)* **scrump**

အသီးတောင့် a-see-taung *(n.)* **pod**

အသီးတောင့် သီးသည် a-tee-taung-see-sai *(v.)* **pod**

အသီးသီး aaseesee *(adj.)* **respective**

အသီးအပွင့်ဖြစ်ထွန်းသော၊ အကျိုးများသော၊ လှိုင်လှိုင်သီးသော a-thee-a-pwint-phit-htun-taw, a-kyo-myar-taw, hlaing-hkaing-thee-taw *(adj.)* **fruitful**

အသီးအရွက် aaseeaarwat *(adj.)* **vegetable**

အသုံးကြီးသော aa-sone-kyeesaw *(adj.)* **prodigal**

အသုံးချသည် a-tone-cha-the *(v.)* **avail**

အသုံးစရိတ် a-tone-sa-yeik *(n.)* **expenditure**

အသုံးပြုခြင်း aasonepyasai *(n.)* **utilization**

အသုံးပြုနိုင်သော aasoneaahnone *(adj.)* **usable**

အသုံးပြုရန်လွယ်ကူသော a-ton-pyu-yan-lwal-khu-taw *(adj.)* **easy-to-use**

အသုံးပြုသည် a myintsone *(v.)* **utilize**

အသုံးပြုသော aasonewinsaw *(adj.)* **used**

အသုံးမကျသော a-tone-ma-kya-taw *(adj.)* **idle**

အသုံးမဝင်တော့သော a-tone-ma-win-tot-taw *(adj.)* **obsolete**

အသုံးဝင်ခြင်း၊ အသုံးဝန်ဆောင်မှုလုပ်ငန်း aasonepyuchinn *(n.)* **utility**

အသုံးဝင်သော a-tone-win-taw *(adj.)* **handy**

အသုံးအဆောင် sarraain *(n.)* **utensil**

အသုံးအဆောင် ပရိဘောဂ aasoneaasaung paribhawg *(n.)* **wicker**

အသုံးအနှုန်း aasoneaahnone *(adj.)* **terminological**

အသုံးအဖြုန်း aa-sone a hpyone *(n.)* **prodigality**

အသုံးအဖြုန်းကြီးသော a-tone-a-hpyone-kyi-taw *(adj.)* **extravagant**

အသုပ် aa-sote *(n.)* **salad**

အသုဘ a-thu-ba *(n.)* **funeral**

အသုဘပို့လိုက်သူ a-tu-ba-boe-lite-thu *(n.)* **mourner**

အသူတစ်ရာနက်သောချောက် a-thu-tayar-nat-taw-chauk *(n.)* **abyss**

အသေးစား a-tay-zar *(adj.)* **miniature**

အသေးစားဟိုတယ် a-tay-sar-ho-tal *(n.)* **inn**

အသေးစားဟိုတယ်စောင့် aasayyhcarr hotaalhcaung *(n.)* **tavernkeeper**

အသေးစားဟိုတယ်ပိုင်ရှင် aasayyhcarr hotaalpineshin *(n.)* **taverner**

အသေးစိတ် a-tay-seik *(n.)* **detail**

အသေးစိတ် စီစဉ် ပြင်ဆင်ထားသော a-tay-seik-si-sin-pyin-sin-htar-taw *(adj.)* **elaborate**

အသေးစိတ် ဖော်ပြရှင်းလင်းသည် a-tay-seik-phaw-pya-shin-lin-the *(v.)* **elaborate**

အသေးစိတ်ချပြသည် a-tay-seik-cha-pya-the *(v.)* **delineate**

အသေးစိတ်ပြန်ပြောပြသည် aasayy-sate pyanpyaw-pyasai *(v.)* **recount**

အသေးစိတ်ဖော်ပြချက် aa-sayy-sate-hpawpyachet *(n.)* **specification**

အသေးစိတ်ဖော်ပြသော a-tay-seik-phaw-pya-taw *(adj.)* **circumstantial**

အသေးအဖွဲ a sayyaahpwal *(n.)* **trifle**

အသေးအဖွဲကို ဇာချဲ့ခြင်း a-sayy-aa-hpwal-ko-jar-chaae-chinn *(n.)* **pedantry**

အသေးအဖွဲအမှား a-tay-a-phwe-a-hmar *(n.)* **misdemeanour**

အသေကောင်ရှာစားသည် a say kaung shar sarrsai *(v.)* **scavenge**

အသေကောင်လို၊ သုသာန်တစပြင်ပမာ a-tay-kaung-lo, tote-tan-ta-sa-pyin-pa-mar *(adj.)* **deathly**

အသေအကျေတိုက်ပွဲ a say a kyaay-tite-pwal *(n.)* **showdown**

အသေအပျောက် a-tay-a-pyauk *(n.)* **fatality**

အသောက်အစား အပျော်အပါးကြူးခြင်း a-taut-a-sar-a-pyaw-a-par-kyu-chin *(n.)* **debauch**

အဟန့်ကောင်းသော a-hant-kaung-taw *(adj.)* **imposing**

အဟန့်အတား a-hant-a-tar *(n.)* **hindrance**

အဟန့်အတားဖြစ်သည် a-hant-a-tar-phit-the *(v.)* **handicap**

အဟုန် a-hon *(n.)* **momentum**

အဟုန်မြင့်သည် a hone myint sai *(v.)* **speed**

အဟောအပြော a-haw-a-pyaw *(adj.)* **oratorical**

အဟောအပြောကောင်းသူ a-haw-a-pyaw-kaung-tuu *(n.)* **orator**

အအိပ်လွန်သည် a-ait-lwan-tai *(v.)* **oversleep**

အအေးခံဘူး a-aye-khan-bu *(n.)* **cooler**

အအေးပေးရာတွင် သုံးသော အရည် a-aye-pay-yar-twin-tone-a-yae *(n.)* **coolant**

အအေးလွန် a-aye-lun *(n.)* **cryogenics**

အားကစား aarrkasarr *(n.)* **sport**

အားကစားကွင်း ar-ka-sar-kwin *(n.)* **arena**

အားကစားစိတ်ဝင်စားသော aarrkahcarr hcatewainhcarrsaw *(adj.)* **sportive**

အားကစားပြိုင်ပွဲတွင် ဆေးသုံးသည် arr-ka-sar-pyai-pwe-twin-say-tone-the *(v.)* **dope**

အားကစားရုံ aarrkasarrrone *(n.)* **stadium**

အားကစားဝတ်စုံ aarrkasarrwaatsone *(n.)* **tracksuit**

အားကစားသမား aarrkasarrsamarr *(n.)* **sportsman**

အားကျသည် arr-kya-the *(v.)* **envy**

အားကိုးအားထား aarr-koe aarr-htarr *(n.)* **recourse**

အားကုန်စေသည် arr-kone-say-the *(v.)* **enervate**

အားကုန်စေသော arr-kone-say-taw *(adj.)* **enervated**

အားကောင်းလာသည် aarrkaungglarsai *(v.)* **strengthen**

အားကောင်းသော၊ အစွမ်းထက်သော၊ ပါဝါရှိသော aarr kaunggsaw , aa-swam-htaat saw , parwarshisaw *(adj.)* **powerful**

အားစိုက်လုပ်ရသော၊ တက်ကြွသော arr-site-lote-ya-taw, tat-kwa-taw *(adj.)* **energetic**

အားစိုက်သည်၊ တင်းမာစေသည် aarr site sai , tinnmarsaysai *(v.)* **strain**

အားဆေး aarrsayy *(n.)* **tonic**

အားတက်စေသော အရာ aarr-taatsaysaw aarar *(n.)* **stimulant**

အားတက်အောင် ဦးဆောင်အားပေးသူ arr-tat-aung-oo-saung-arr-pay-thu *(n.)* **cheerleader**

အားထားနေရသော ar-htar-nay-ya-taw *(n.)* **contingent**

အားထားမှု၊ မှီခိုခြင်း aarr htarr mhu , mhae-hkochinn *(n.)* **reliance**

အားထားရသူ aarr htarr rasuu *(n.)* **stalwart**

အားထားရသော aarrhtarrrasaw *(adj.)* **stalwart**

အားထုတ်မှု arr-htoke-mu *(n.)* **effort**

အားထုတ်သည် arr-htoke-the *(v.)* **energize**

အားနည်းချက် aarrnaeechet *(n.)* **shortcoming**

အားနည်းခြင်း aarrnaeechinn *(n.)* **weakness**

အားနည်းသည် aarrnaeesai *(v.)* **weaken**

အားနည်းသော aarrnaeesaw *(adj.)* **weak**

အားနည်းသော၊ ချည့်နဲ့သော arr-nae-taw, chi-nae-taw *(adj.)* **feeble**

အားနည်းသော၊ မူးမေ့မလိုဖြစ်သော arr-nae-taw, mu-mae-ma-lo-phit-taw *(adj.)* **faint**

အားပျော့သူ arr-pyawt-thu *(n.)* **debilitant**

အားပျော့သော arr-pyawt-taw *(adj.)* **debile**

အားပြန်ကောင်းလာခြင်း aarrpyankaungglarchinn *(n.)* **revival**

အားပေးကူညီခြင်း ar-pay-khu-nyi-chin *(n.)* **abettor**

အားပေးကူညီသည် ar-pay-khu-nyi-the *(v.)* **abet**

အားပေးခြင်း arr-pay-chin *(n.)* **encouragement**

အားပေးခြင်း၊ ထောက်ခံခြင်း aarr-payychinn , htout-hkanchinn *(n.)* **reinforcement**

အားပေးမှု ar-payy-mhu *(n.)* **patronage**

အားပေးသည် arr-pay-the *(v.)* **encourage**

အားပေးသည်၊ ချီးမြှင့်သည် aarr payysai , chaeemyintsai *(v.)* **support**

အားပေးသည်၊ မွေးစားသည် arr-pay-the, mway-sar-the *(v.)* **foster**

အားပေးသည်၊ အားပေးထောက်ခံသည် aarr payysai , aarrpayy htout-hkansai *(v.)* **reinforce**

အားပေးသူ၊ ဖောက်သည် ar-payy-suu, hpout-sai *(n.)* **patron**

အားဖြင့် arr-phyint *(prep.)* **by**

အားမလိုအားမရဖြစ်ခြင်း arr-am-lo-arr-ma-ya-phit-chin *(n.)* **frustration**

အားမာန်ပါသော aarrmarn parsaw *(adj.)* **vigorous**

အားရစရာ မရှိသော ar-ra-sa-rar-ma-shi-saw *(adj.)* **pessimistic**

အားရဝမ်းသာ arr-ya-wan-tar *(adv.)* **gleefully**

အားလပ်ချိန် arr-lat-chain *(n.)* **leisure**

အားလပ်ရက် arr-lat-yat *(n.)* **holiday**

အားလျော့စေခြင်း arr-shawt-say-chin *(n.)* **debilitation**

အားလျော့စေသည် arr-shawt-say-the *(v.)* **debilitate**

အားလျော့စေသော arr-shawt-say-taw *(adj.)* **debilitating**

အားလုံး arr-lone *(adj.)* **all**

အားလုံး၊ တိုင်း arr-lone, tine *(adj.)* **every**

အားလုံး၊ များစွာ arr-lone, myar-swar *(n.)* **lot**

အားလုံးထည့်သွင်းစဉ်းစား arr-lone-thae-twin-sin-sar *(adv.)* **withal**

အားလုံးနှင့်ဆိုင်သော aarrlone nintsinesaw *(adj.)* **universal**

အားလုံးပေါင်း aarr-lone-paung *(n.)* **totality**

အားသစ်လောင်းပေးခြင်း aarr-sitlaungg-payychinn *(n.)* **rejuvenation**

အားသစ်လောင်းသည် aarrsit-launggsai *(v.)* **refresh**

အားသွင်းတုံး arr-twin-tone *(n.)* **charger**

အားအင်ကုန်ခန်းသည် aarr aain kone hkaannsai *(v.)* **tire**

အားအင်လျော့လာသည် arr-inn-shawt-lar-the *(v.)* **languish**

အာကာသ ar-kar-tha *(adj.)* **celestial**

အာကာသယဉ်မှူး arr-kar-ta-yin-hmu *(n.)* **astronaut**

အာကာသယာဉ် aarkarsayin *(n.)* **spacecraft**

အာခံခြင်း ar-khan-chin *(n.)* **defiance**

အာခံသည် ar-khan-the *(v.)* **defy**

အာခံသော ar-khan-taw *(adj.)* **defiant**

အာခေါင် aar-hkaung *(n.)* **palate**

အာခေါင်နှင့် ဆိုင်သော aar-hkaung-nint-sine-saw *(adj.)* **palatal**

အာဂ aar-ga *(adj.)* **superhuman**

အာဃာတ arr-gar-ta *(n.)* **grudge**

အာစလျှာစ aar sa shar-sa *(n.)* **rhetoric**

အာဇာနည် ar-zar-ne *(n.)* **martyr**

အာဇာနည်အဖြစ် ar-zar-ne-a-phit *(n.)* **martyrdom**

အာဏာကို ဒေသအစိုးရသို့ ခွဲဝေပေးသည် arr-nar-ko-day-tha-a-soe-ya-tho-khwal-wai-pay-the *(v.)* **decentralize**

အာဏာကို ဖယ်ရှားသည် ar-nar-ko-phal-shar-the *(v.)* **delegalize**
အာဏာတည်စေသည် ar-nar-the-say-the *(v.)* **enforce**
အာဏာပါးကွက်သား ar-nar-par-kwat-tar *(n.)* **executioner**
အာဏာဖီဆန်သော ar-nar-phi-san-taw *(adj.)* **mutinous**
အာဏာရှင် aarnarshin *(n.)* **tyrant**
အာဏာသိမ်းမှု ar-nar-tain-mu *(n.)* **coup**
အာတိတ်ဒေသ ar-tate-day-ta *(adj.)* **Arctic**
အာဒါလွှတ် ar-dar-hlut *(n.)* **arrowroot**
အာနိသင်၊ ထိရောက်မှု aarnisin, hti-rout-mhu *(n.)* **potency**
အာနိသင်မရှိသောဆေး aar-ni-sin-ma-shi-saw-sayy *(n.)* **placebo**
အာနိသင်မဲ့ဆေးကဲ့သို့ အလုပ်လုပ်သော aarnisin mae sayy-kaeshoet aalotelotesaw *(adj.)* **placebic**
အာနိသင်လျော့ပါးစေသည် arr-ni-tin-shawt-par-say-the *(v.)* **neutralize**
အာမခံ aarmahkan *(n.)* **warranty**
အာမခံချက် arr-ma-khan-chat *(n.)* **guarantee**
အာမခံငွေ ar-ma-khan-ngwe *(n.)* **bail**
အာမခံငွေထုတ်ရန် သတ်မှတ်ချက်ပြည့်မှီသော ar-ma-khan-ngwe-htoke-yan-tat-mat-chat-pyae-mi-taw *(adj.)* **bailable**
အာမခံသည် aarmahkansai *(v.)* **vouch**
အာမခံသူ aarmahkansuu *(n.)* **voucher**
အာမခံသေတ္တာ aarmahkansayttar *(n.)* **safe**
အာမခံသေတ္တာများထားရာ အဆောက်အအုံ aarmahkan sayttar myarr htarrrar aasoutaaaone *(n.)* **safe-deposit**
အာမင် arr-min *(interj.)* **amen**
အာမေဍိတ် arr-may-daik *(n.)* **exclamation**
အာယုဗေဒဆေးပညာ ar-yu-bay-da-say-pyin=nyar *(n.)* **Ayurveda**
အာရပ် ar-yat *(n.)* **Arab**
အာရာဂွမ်ပင် ar-yar-gwin-pin *(n.)* **estragon**
အာရိုက်သည် aar ritesai *(v.)* **trumpet**
အာရုံ၊ ခံစားတတ်မှု aar-rone , hkan-sarr taat-mhu *(n.)* **sense**
အာရုံကြော ar-yone-gyaw *(n.)* **nerve**
အာရုံကြောဆိုင်ရာ ဆေးပညာ arr-yone-kyaw-sai-yar-say-pyin-nyar *(n.)* **neurology**
အာရုံခံ အဖု aarronehkan aahpu *(n.)* **taste bud**
အာရုံစိုက်ခြင်း ar-yone-seik-chin *(n.)* **attention**
အာရုံစိုက်သည်၊ စူးစိုက်သည် arr-yone-site-the, sue-site-the *(v.)* **focus**
အာရုံစိုက်သော ar-yone-seik-taw *(adj.)* **attentive**
အာရုံစူးစိုက်ခြင်း arr-yone-sue-site-chin *(n.)* **concentration**
အာရုံစူးစိုက်သည် arr-yone-sue-site-the *(v.)* **concentrate**
အာရုံစူးစိုက်သော arr-yone-sue-site-the *(adj.)* **focused**
အာရုံတစ်ပါးပါး arr-yone-ta-par-par *(n.)* **modality**
အာရုံအနှောင့်အယှက် arr-yone-a-naut-a-shat *(n.)* **distraction**
အာလုပ်စကား ar-lote-sa-kar *(n.)* **Messrs**
အာလူး aarluu *(n.)* **potato**
အာလူးပြုတ်ထောင်း arr-lu-pyoke-htaung *(n.)* **mash**
အာသီး aarsee *(n.)* **tonsil**
အာဟာရ aarhar-ra *(n.)* **sustenance**
အာဟာရ ဖြစ်စေသည် a-har-hpyit-say-te *(v.)* **nourish**

အာဟာရချို့တဲ့ခြင်း a-har-ya-choe-tae-chin *(n.)* **malnutrition**
အာဟာရချို့တဲ့သော a-har-ya-choe-tae-taw *(adj.)* **malnourished**
အာဟာရဓာတ် a-har-a-dat *(n.)* **nutrient**
အာဟာရပြည့်ဝသော aarharr pyany wasaw *(adj.)* **wholesome**
အာဟာရဖြစ်သော a-har-ra-hpyit-taw *(adj.)* **nutritious**
အာဟာရဗေဒပညာရှင် a-har-ra-pyin-nyar-shin *(n.)* **dietician**
အာဟာရသိပ္ပံ a-har-ya-tait-pan *(adj.)* **macrobiotic**
အိကျသည်၊ လျော့ကျသည် ai kya sai , lyawwkyasai *(v.)* **sag**
အိတ် aate *(n.)* **pouch**
အိတ်ကပ် ate-kat *(n.)* **pocket**
အိတ်ကပ်ထဲ ထည့်လိုက်သည် ate-kat-htel-htae-lite-sai *(v.)* **pocket**
အိတ်ဇောပေါက်သည် ait-zaw-paut-the *(v.)* **backfire**
အိတ်ထဲ ထည့်သည် aik-htae-htae-teh *(v.)* **bag**
အိတ်ပလွေမှုတ်သမား aik-pa-lway-hmote-ta-mar *(n.)* **bagpiper**
အိတ်ဖြင့် သားငယ်ကို သယ်သော သားပိုက်ကောင်ကဲ့သို့ နို့တိုက်သတ္တဝါ aik-phint-tar-nge-ko-tal-taw-tar-pike-kaung-kae-tho-noe-tite-tat-ta-war *(n.)* **marsupial**
အိတ်သွန်ဖာမှောက် ရှာသည် ate swan hpar-mhaout sharsai *(v.)* **ransack**
အိန္ဒိယ eain-di-ya *(adj.)* **Indian**
အိပ်ခန်း aik-khan *(n.)* **bedroom**
အိပ်ချင်မူးတူး aik-chin-mu-tu *(adj.)* **dreamy**
အိပ်ငိုက်ခြင်း ait ngitechinn *(n.)* **somnolence**
အိပ်ငိုက်သော ait ngitesaw *(adj.)* **sleepy**
အိပ်စက်ခြင်း ait-saat-chinn *(n.)* **repose**
အိပ်စက်ခြင်း မပြုဘဲ နေခြင်း aitsaatchinn mapyubhell naychinn *(n.)* **vigil**
အိပ်စက်ခြင်း၊ အိပ်ရေး ait-saat-chinn, ait-rayy *(n.)* **slumber**
အိပ်စက်သည်၊ အိပ်မောကျသည် aitsaat sai , ait-maw-kyasai *(v.)* **slumber**
အိပ်ဆောင် aik-saung *(n.)* **dormitory**
အိပ်တန်း aintaann *(n.)* **roost**
အိပ်တန်းတက်သည် ain taann taatsai *(v.)* **roost**
အိပ်နေစဉ် ရုတ်တရက် အသက်ရှူခထာရပ်ခြင်း aik-pyaw-nay-zin-yote-ta-yat-a-tet-shu-ka-na-yat-chin *(n.)* **apnoea**
အိပ်နေသူ ait naysuu *(n.)* **sleeper**
အိပ်ပျော်နေသော aik-pyaw-nay-taw *(adv.)* **asleep**
အိပ်ပျော်လျက် လမ်းလျှောက်ခြင်း aitpyawlyet lamshoutchinn *(n.)* **somnambulism**
အိပ်ပျော်လျက် လမ်းလျှောက်တတ်သူ aitpyawlyet lamshout taatsuu *(n.)* **somnambulist**
အိပ်ပျော်သည် aitpyawsai *(v.)* **sleep**
အိပ်မက် aik-mat *(n.)* **dream**
အိပ်မက်ဆန်ဆန် aik-mat-san-san *(adv.)* **dreamily**
အိပ်မက်ဆိုး ain-mat-soe *(n.)* **nightmare**
အိပ်မက်ဖမ်းပစ္စည်း aik-mat-phan-pyit-see *(n.)* **dreamcatcher**
အိပ်မက်မက်သည် aik-mat-mat-the *(v.)* **dream**
အိပ်မက်မက်သူ aik-mat-mat-thu *(n.)* **dreamer**

အိပ်မက်သဖွယ် လှုပ်ရှားမှုမြင်ကွင်း ain-maat-sa-hpwal-hlote-sharr-mhu-myin-kwin *(n.)* **phantasmagoria**

အိပ်မရသော aitmarasaw *(adj.)* **wakeful**

အိပ်ရာ aik-yar *(n.)* **bed**

အိပ်ရာခင်း aik-yar-khin *(n.)* **bed sheet**

အိပ်ရာထဲတွင် aik-yar-htal-twin *(adj.)* **aberrant**

အိပ်ရာနာ aik-yar-nar *(n.)* **bedsore**

အိပ်ရာဖုံး aik-yar-hpone *(n.)* **bedcover**

အိပ်ရာမှ ထသည် ait-rar-mha htasai *(v.)* **wake**

အိပ်ရာလွှမ်း ait-rar-lwam *(n.)* **quilt**

အိမ် eain *(n.)* **home**

အိမ်ကြီးရခိုင် eain-gyi-ra-khine *(n.)* **mansion**

အိမ်ကြီးရခိုင်နှင့် ဆိုင်သော eain-gyi-ra-khine-nint-sai-taw *(adj.)* **manorial**

အိမ်ခြံမြေအကျိုးဆောင် ain-chan-myay-a-kyo-saung *(n.)* **estate agent**

အိမ်ငှား aainnghar *(n.)* **tenant**

အိမ်ငှား၊ မြေငှားစာချုပ် eain-ngar, yay-ngar-sar-choke *(n.)* **lease**

အိမ်စီစဉ်ပေးသည် eain-see-sin-pay-the *(v.)* **house**

အိမ်စေ eain-say *(n.)* **domestic**

အိမ်တွင်း eain-twin *(adj.)* **indoor**

အိမ်တွင်းပုံစံ eain-twin-pon-san *(n.)* **decor**

အိမ်တွင်းမှုကိစ္စစိတ်ဝင်စားသူ eain-twin-mu-kaik-sa-seik-pay-win-sar-thu *(n.)* **domesticator**

အိမ်တွင်းမှုကိစ္စများကို စိတ်ပါဝင်စားစေသည် eain-twin-mu-kaik-sa-myar-ko-seik-pay-win-sar-say-the *(v.)* **domesticate**

အိမ်တွင်းလုပ် eain-twin-lote *(adj.)* **home-made**

အိမ်တိုင်ရာရောက်သွားသော eain-tai-yar-yauk-twar-taw *(adj.)* **domiciliary**

အိမ်ထောင်စု eain-htaung-su *(n.)* **household**

အိမ်ထောင်နှင့်ဆိုင်သော eain-htaung-nint-sai-taw *(adj.)* **marital**

အိမ်ထောင်ပြုခြင်းနှင့် ဆိုင်သော ain-htaung-pyu-chin-hnint-sine-taw *(adj.)* **nuptial**

အိမ်ထောင်ဖက်၊ အကူအညီပေးသူ ain-htaung-phat, a-ku-a-nyi-pay-thu *(n.)* **helpmate**

အိမ်ထောင်ဖက်၏ မိသားစုဝင်များ eain-htaung-phat-ei-mi-tar-su-win-myar *(n.)* **in-laws**

အိမ်ထောင်မပြုသော eain-htaung-ma-pyu-taw *(adj.)* **celibate**

အိမ်ထောင်ရှိလျက် နောက်တစ်ယောက်နှင့် လက်ထပ်ခြင်းအပြစ် eain-htaung-shi-lyat-naut-ta-yaut-nint-lat-htet-chin-a-pyit *(n.)* **bigamy**

အိမ်ထောင်ရှိလျက် နောက်တစ်ယောက်နှင့် လက်ထပ်ခြင်းအပြစ်ရှိသော eain-htaung-shi-lyat-naut-ta-yaut-nint-lat-htet-chin-a-pyit-shi-taw *(adj.)* **bigamous**

အိမ်ထောင်ရှိလျက် နောက်တစ်ယောက်နှင့် လက်ထပ်သူ eain-htaung-shi-lyat-naut-ta-yaut-nint-lat-htet-thu *(n.)* **bigamist**

အိမ်ထောင်ရေး eain-htaung-yay *(adj.)* **conjugal**

အိမ်ထောင်ရေးဖောက်ပြန်ခြင်း ain-htaung-yay-phaut-pyan-chin *(n.)* **adultery**

အိမ်နီးချင်း eain-nee-chin *(n.)* **neighbour**

အိမ်နောက်ဘက် လှေကား eain-naut-bat-hlay-kar *(n.)* **backstairs**

အိမ်ပြေး aainpyay *(n.)* **runaway**

အိမ်ဖော် eain-phaw *(n.)* **maid**

အိမ်မမှ ခွဲထုတ်ထားသော အိမ်သာ ain-ma-mha-hkwal-htote-htar-taw-ain-tar *(n.)* **outhouse**
အိမ်မြှောင် eain-hmyaung *(n.)* **lizard**
အိမ်မွေးတိရစ္ဆာန် eain-mway-ti-rait-san *(n.)* **pet**
အိမ်ရှင်၊ တစ်ပြုံတစ်ခေါင်း eain-shin, ta-pyone-ta-khaung *(n.)* **host**
အိမ်ရှင်မ eain-shin-ma *(n.)* **mistress**
အိမ်ရာမြေအကျိုးဆောင် ain rar myay-aa-kyoesaung *(n.)* **realtor**
အိမ်လွမ်းသော eain-luan-taw *(adj.)* **homesick**
အိမ်သာ aain-sar *(n.)* **toilet**
အိမ်သူအိမ်သား ain-tuu-ain-tar *(n.)* **occupant**
အိမ်အပြင်ဘက် ain-a-pyin-bhat *(adj.)* **outdoor**
အိမ်ဦးခန်း၊ ခန်းမကြီး eain-oo-khan, khan-ma-gyi *(n.)* **hall**
အိသော၊ ညက်ညောသော ai saw , nyaat nyawsaw *(adj.)* **satin**
အိုး aoe *(n.)* **pot**
အိုးတွင် ထည့်စိုက်သည် aoetwin htae site-sai *(v.)* **pot**
အိုးထိန်းသည် aoehteinsai *(n.)* **potter**
အိုးနင်းခွက်နင်း ဖြစ်သည် oh-nin-khwat-nin-phit-the *(v.)* **goof**
အိုးလုံပိတ်၍ နှပ်သည် oh-lon-pait-ywe-nat-the *(v.)* **braise**
အိုးလုပ်ငန်း aoe-lotengaann *(n.)* **ware**
အိုကေ o-kay *(n.)* **okay**
အိုကေသော ok taw *(adj.)* **okayish**
အိုက်စပ်စပ်ဖြစ်သော aik-sat-sat-phit-taw *(adj.)* **muggy**
အိုက်စပ်သော aite sat-saw *(adj.)* **sultry**
အိုင်ကွန် ai-kon *(n.)* **icon**
အိုင်ကွန်ဖြစ်သော၊ အထိန်းအမှတ်ဖြစ်သော ai-kon-phit-taw, a-htein-a-mat-phit-taw *(adj.)* **iconic**
အိုင်ဒီယာ၊ အယူအဆ ai-de-ya, a-yu-a-sa *(n.)* **idea**
အိုင်ဒီယာထုတ်သည် i-de-ya-htoke-the *(v.)* **ideate**
အိုင်ယာလန်နိုင်ငံနှင့် ဆိုင်သော i-ra-land-nai-ngan-nint-sai-taw *(adj.)* **Irish**
အိုင်ယာလန်လူမျိုး၊ အိုင်ယာလန်နိုင်ငံသား i-ra-land-lu-myo, i-ra-land-nai-ngan-tar *(n.)* **Irish**
အိုဇုန်းဓာတ်ငွေ့ ao -zone-dhat-ngwae *(n.)* **ozone**
အိုဇုန်းဓာတ်ပေါင်း ao jone dhatpaungg *(n.)* **ozonate**
အိုဇုန်းဖြတ်ထားခြင်း ao jone hpyat-htarrhkyinn *(n.)* **ozonation**
အိုဇုန်းဖြတ်ထားသည် ao jone hpyat-htarrsai *(v.)* **ozonate**
အိုဇုန်းလွှာ ao-zone-lwhar *(n.)* **ozone layer**
အိုပယ်ဝါဒီ o-pal-war-di *(n.)* **ageism**
အိုမင်းမစွမ်းခြင်း oh-min-ma-swan-chin *(n.)* **infirmity**
အိုမင်းမစွမ်းသော oh-min-ma-swan-taw *(adj.)* **infirm**
အိုမင်းသော ao-min-taw *(adj.)* **old**
အိုမီဂါ ao-me-gar *(n.)* **omega**
အိုလေးရှားမျိုးနှင့် ဆိုင်သော o-le-shar-myo-nint-sine-taw *(adj.)* **oleaceous**
အိုအေစစ် o-a-sit *(n.)* **oasis**
အီးမေးလ် e-male *(n.)* **email**
အီကွေတာ e-quay-tar *(n.)* **equator**
အီချီးနစ်ပင် e-chee-nit-pin *(n.)* **echinid**
အီစတာပွဲတော် e-sa-tar-pwe-taw *(n.)* **easter**

အီစတိုဂျင်ဟော်မုန်း e-sa-to-gyin-haw-hmone (n.) **estrogen**
အီတလီနှင့်ဆိုင်သော ae-ta-li-nint-sai-taw (adj.) **Italian**
အီတလီနိုင်ငံသား ae-ta-li-nai-ngan-tar (n.) **Italian**
အီနားရှားဂုဏ်သတ္တိ e-nar-shar-gon-tat-ti (n.) **inertia**
အီပေါက်စီအစေး e-pauk-si-a-say (n.) **epoxy**
အီလက်ထရွန် e-lat-hta-ron (n.) **electron**
အီလက်ထရွန်နစ် e-lat-hta-yaw-nit (adj.) **electronic**
အီလက်ထရောနစ်စာအုပ် e-lat-hta-yaw-nit-sar-oak (n.) **e-book**
အီလက်ထရောနစ်စီးပွားရေး e-lat-hta-yaw-nit-see-pwar-yay (n.) **e-commerce**
အီလိုက်ဝါဒ e-lite-war-da (n.) **elitism**
အီလိုက်ဝါဒီ e-lite-war-di (n.) **elitist**
အီလိုက်အုပ်စု e-lite-oak-su (n.) **elite**
အီသည်၊ အင့်သည် ae sai , a intsai (v.) **satiate**
အီသာ e-thar (n.) **ether**
အုံကြွမှု၊ ဆူပူမှု aonekyawmhu , suupuumhu (n.) **unrest**
အံ့ဖွယ် ant-phwal (adj.) **fabulous**
အုံသည်၊ စွဲသည် ant-sai , swalsai (v.) **swarm**
အုံသည်၊ အအုပ်အသင်းဖွဲ့သည် ohn-the, a-oak-a-tin-phwe-the (v.) **flock**
အံ့သြတုန်လှုပ်ခြင်း ant-aw-ton-lote-chin (n.) **consternation**
အံ့သြဖွယ် aunt-aw-phwal (adj.) **awesome**
အုချ် auch (int.) **ouch**
အုတ် oak (n.) **brick**
အုတ်ကျိုးအုတ်ပဲ့ aote kyoe aote pae (n.) **rubble**
အုတ်ကျိုးအုတ်ပဲ့စီထားသော အင်္ဂတေ oak-kyoe-oak-pae-si-htar-taw-in-ga-day (n.) **rubblework**
အုတ်ကြွပ်ပြား aote kywutpyarr (n.) **tile**
အုတ်ဂျုံမုန့် ote-gyone-mone (n.) **oatmeal**
အုတ်ဂျုံမုန့်ဖြင့် လုပ်သော အစားအစာ ote-gyone-mone-phyint-lote-taw-a-sar-a-sar (adj.) **oatmeal**
အုတ်ဂျုံယာဂု aote gyaone-yar-gu (n.) **porridge**
အုတ်ဂူ aoteguu (n.) **tomb**
အုတ်အသေး oak-a-thay (n.) **briquet**
အုတ်အုတ်ကျက်ကျက်ဖြစ်ခြင်း aote aote kyet kyethpyitchinn (n.) **uproar**
အုတ်အုတ်ကျက်ကျက်အသံ aote aote kyet kyet-aa-san (n.) **tumult**
အုတ်အော်သောင်းတင်း aote aaw saunggtinn (adj.) **sensational**
အုတ်အော်သောင်းသဲဆဲသံ aote-aw-taung-tell-sell-tan (adj.) **outcry**
အုန်းခနဲ မြည်အောင် ထုရိုက်သည် ohn-kha-nal-me-aung-htu-yite-the (n.) **bang**
အုန်းဆံမျှင် ohn-san-hmyin (n.) **coir**
အုန်းသီး ohn-thee (n.) **coconut**
အုပ် aote (n.) **throng**
အုပ်ကို ထိန်းကျောင်းသူ oak-ko-htain-kyaung-thu (n.) **herdsman**
အုပ်ချုပ်ခြင်း aote-chotechinn (n.) **ruling**
အုပ်ချုပ်ပုံ oak-choke-pon (n.) **governance**
အုပ်ချုပ်မှုဆိုင်ရာ oat-choke-mu-saing-yar (adj.) **administrative**
အုပ်ချုပ်မှုညံ့ခြင်း oak-choke-mu-nyant-chin (n.) **maladministration**

အုပ်ချုပ်ရေး oat-choke-yay *(n.)* **administration**

အုပ်ချုပ်ရေး ညံ့ဖျင်းမှု oak-choke-yay-nyant-pyin-mu *(n.)* **misconduct**

အုပ်ချုပ်သည် oak-choke-the *(v.)* **govern**

အုပ်ချုပ်သူ aote-chotesuu *(n.)* **ruler**

အုပ်ချုပ်သူများစွာဖြင့် အုပ်ချုပ်သည် aotehkyote-suu myarr-swar-hpyang aotehkyotesai *(n.)* **polycracy**

အုပ်စု oak-su *(n.)* **faction**

အုပ်စုကြောင့်ဖြစ်သော oak-su-kyaunt-phit-taw *(adj.)* **factious**

အုပ်စုခွဲသည် aotesuhkwalsai *(v.)* **split**

အုပ်စုအလိုက် ခွဲထားသော oak-su-a-lite-kwal-htar-taw *(adj.)* **classified**

အုပ်ထားသည်၊ ဖွဲ့စည်းသည် oak-htar-the, phwe-see-the *(v.)* **encrust**

အုပ်ထိန်းသူ aote thein-suu *(n.)* **trustee**

အုပ်လိုက်သင်းလိုက် ဝိုင်းသည် oak-lite-tin-lite-wine-the *(v.)* **mob**

အူ au *(n.)* **intestine**

အူကျွံနာ oo-kywun-nar *(n.)* **hernia**

အူကြောင်ကြောင်ခေါင်းကို လှည့်ကြည့်သည် au-kyuang-kyaung-kaung-ko-hlae-kyi-the *(n.)* **rubberneck**

အူကြောင်ကြောင်ခေါင်းကို လှည့်ကြည့်သူ au-kyuang-kyaung-kaung-ko-hlae-kyi-thu *(v.)* **rubberneck**

အူဇိုအရက်ပြင်း auu-zo-a-rat-pyinn *(n.)* **ouzo**

အူတွင်းဖြစ်သော au-twin-phit-taw *(adj.)* **intestinal**

အူတိုင် au-thai *(n.)* **core**

အူမ aw-ma *(n.)* **colon**

အူမြူးခြင်း au-myue-chin *(n.)* **glee**

အူရောင်ငန်းဖျား auu raung ngaannhpyarr *(n.)* **typhoid**

အူသံ၊ အော်သံ au-tan, aw-tan *(n.)* **howl**

အူသည်၊ အော်သည် au-the, aw-the *(v.)* **howl**

အူသိမ်အူမ au-tain-au-ma *(n.)* **bowel**

အူအတက် au-a-tat *(n.)* **appendix**

အူအတက်ရောင်ခြင်း au-a-tat-yaung-chin *(n.)* **appendicitis**

အေးချမ်းစွာ နေလိုသော aye-cham-swar-nay-lo-saw *(adj.)* **peaceable**

အေးခဲသည် aye-khae-the *(v.)* **freeze**

အေးဂျင့် a-gent *(n.)* **agent**

အေးစိမ့်ခြင်း aye-saint-chin *(n.)* **chill**

အေးစိမ့်သော aye-saint-taw *(adj.)* **chilly**

အေးတိအေးစက်နိုင်သော aye-ti-aye-sat-nai-taw *(adj.)* **impersonal**

အေးမြလတ်ဆတ်သော aye-mya-lat-sat-taw *(adj.)* **bracing**

အေးသော aye-taw *(adj.)* **cold**

အေးအေးဆေးဆေး aye-aye-say-say *(adj.)* **leisurely**

အေးအေးလူလူ aye-aye-lu-lu *(adj.)* **laid-back**

အေးအေးလူလူ လမ်းလျှောက်သည် aye-aayy-luuluu lamshoutsai *(v.)* **stroll**

အေဂျင်စီ a-gen-cy *(n.)* **agency**

အေရိုးဗစ်အားကစား a-yoe-bit-arr-ka-sar *(n.)* **aerobics**

အေရိုဒိုင်းနမစ်ပညာ a-ro-dy-na-mic-pyin-nyar *(n.)* **aerodynamics**

အော့ဖ်ဆက်စက် off-sat-sat *(n.)* **offset**

အော့ဖ်လိုင်းဖြစ်သော aot-pha-line-hpyit-taw *(adj.)* **offline**

အောက် aout *(adj.)* **under**

အောက်ကျို့တတ်သော awt-kyo-tat-taw *(adj.)* **meek**

အောက်ခံ aut-khan *(n.)* **base**

အောက်ခံတုံး awt-khan-tone *(n.)* **block**

အောက်ခံပန်းကန်ပြား aout-hkanpaannkaanpyarr *(n.)* **saucer**

အောက်ခံဘောင်၊ အဆောက်အအုံ၊ ဘောင်ကန့်သတ်ချက် aut-khan-baung, a-saut-a-ohn, baung-kant-tat-chat *(n.)* **framework**

အောက်ချသည်၊ awt-cha-the *(v.)* **lower**

အောက်ခြေ aut-chay *(adj.)* **basal**

အောက်ခြေက လှိုက်စားသည် aout-chay-ka hlite sarrsai *(v.)* **undermine**

အောက်ခြေမှတ်ချက် aut-chay-mat-chat *(n.)* **footnote**

အောက်ခြေမှတ်ချက်ချသည် aut-chay-mat-chat-cha-the *(v.)* **footnote**

အောက်ဆိုက် aout-site *(n.)* **oxidate**

အောက်ဆီဂျင် aout-se-gyin *(n.)* **oxygen**

အောက်ဆီဂျင်ထည့်ခြင်း aout-segyin htaeethkyinn *(n.)* **oxygenation**

အောက်ဆီဂျင်ထည့်သည် aout-segyin htaeetsai *(v.)* **oxygenate**

အောက်ဆီဂျင်ပါသော aout-segyin parsaw *(adj.)* **oxygenated**

အောက်ဆီဂျင်ပါသော အက်ဆစ် aout-segyin parsaw at-sait *(n.)* **oxyacid**

အောက်ဆုံး awt-sone *(n.)* **nadir**

အောက်တန်းကျခြင်း aout taannkyachinn *(n.)* **vulgarity**

အောက်တန်းကျသော aout taannkyasaw *(adj.)* **vulgar**

အောက်တွင် aout-twin *(adv.)* **underneath**

အောက်တိန်းဆီ out-tein-se *(n.)* **octane**

အောက်တိုဘာလ out-to-bhar-la *(n.)* **October**

အောက်ထပ်မှာဖြစ်သော aut-htet-mar-phit-taw *(adj.)* **downstairs**

အောက်ပိုင်း awt-pai *(adj.)* **nether**

အောက်မျဉ်းသားသည် aout myin sarr-sai *(v.)* **underline**

အောက်မှာ aout-mhar *(prep.)* **under**

အောက်ရုံး awt-yone *(n.)* **magistracy**

အောက်ရုံးတရားသူကြီး awt-yone-ta-yar-thu-gyi *(n.)* **magistrate**

အောက်လမ်းဆရာ awt-lan-sa-yar *(n.)* **necromancer**

အောက်သို့ aout-thoet *(adv.)* **over**

အောက်သို့တိမ်းစောင်းခြင်း awt-tho-tain-saung-chin *(n.)* **declivity**

အောက်သော၊ သိုးသော awt-taw, toe-taw *(adj.)* **musty**

အောင့်အည်းထားသည် awnt aaee-htarrsai *(v.)* **refrain**

အောင်းနေသော၊ ငုပ်နေသော aung-nay-taw, ngoke-nay-thaw *(adj.)* **latent**

အောင်စ aung-sa *(n.)* **ounce**

အောင်နိုင်ခြင်း aung-nai-chin *(n.)* **conquest**

အောင်နိုင်သည် aaungninesai *(v.)* **triumph**

အောင်နိုင်သည်၊ ပျံ့နှံ့သည် aaung nine-sai , pyant-nant-sai *(v.)* **prevail**

အောင်နိုင်သူ aaungninesuu *(n.)* **victor**

အောင်ပွဲ aaungpwal *(n.)* **triumph**

အောင်ပွဲခံ aaungpwahlkan *(adj.)* **triumphal**

အောင်ပွဲခံခြင်း aung-pwe-khan-chin *(n.)* **celebration**

အောင်မြင် ရရှိသည် aung-myin-ya-shi-the *(v.)* **attaint**

အောင်မြင်စွာ ရယူနိုင်ခြင်း aung-myin-swar-ra-yu-naing-chin *(n.)* **attainment**

အောင်မြင်မှု aaungmyinmhu *(n.)* **victory**

အောင်မြင်သည် aung-myin-sai *(v.)* **succeed**

အောင်မြင်သူ aung-myin-thu *(n.)* **achiever**

အောင်မြင်သော aaungmyinsaw *(adj.)* **victorious**

အောင်မြင်သော အဆိုတော် aung-myin-taw-a-so-taw *(n.)* **chartbuster**

အောင်သွယ် aung-twal *(n.)* **matchmaker**

အော်ကြီးဟစ်ကျယ်ငြင်းခုံသည် aaw kyee hait kyaal ngyinn hkonesai *(v.)* **wrangle**

အော်ဂင် aw-gan *(n.)* **harmonium**

အော်ဂလီဆန်စေသည် aaw g le saansaysai *(v.)* **sicken**

အော်ငိုခြင်း aaw ngochinn *(n.)* **wail**

အော်ဒီကလုန်းရေမွှေး aw-di-ka-lone-yay-mywe *(n.)* **cologne**

အော်ပရာ aw-pa-rar *(n.)* **opera**

အော်ပရေတာ၊ လုပ်ငန်းရှင် aw-pa-ray-tar, lote-ngan-shin *(n.)* **operator**

အော်လန် aww-lan *(n.)* **megaphone**

အော်သံ aawsan *(n.)* **shout**

အော်သည် aawsai *(v.)* **shout**

အော်ဟစ် ငြင်းခုံခြင်း aw-hit-nyin-khone-chin *(n.)* **altercation**

အော်ဟစ်သည် aawhaitsai *(v.)* **scream**

အဲမောင်း၊ လှံရှည် ae-maung, lan-shay *(n.)* **lance**

ဣန္ဒြေတင်းလွန်းသော eain dyay tinn lwannsaw *(adj.)* **staid**

ဣန္ဒြေမဲ့ခြင်း ain-dray-mae-chin *(n.)* **immodesty**

ဣန္ဒြေမဲ့သော ain-dray-mae-taw *(adj.)* **immodest**

ဤနေရာသို့ e-nay-yar-tho *(adv.)* **hither**

ဤမျှ imya *(adv.)* **so**

ဤမှ နောက် e-ma-naut *(adv.)* **hereafter**

ဤသို့ပင် i-thoet-pin *(pron.)* **such**

ဤအကြောင်းကြောင်းကြောင့် e-a-kyaung-kyaung-kyaunt *(adv.)* **hence**

ဤအချိန်မှစ၍ နောင်တွင် e-a-chain-ma-sa-ywe-naung-twin *(adv.)* **henceforth**

ဤအချိန်အထိ e-a-chain-a-hti *(adv.)* **hitherto**

ဥ u *(n.)* **spawn**

ဥ ဥသည် u u-sai *(v.)* **spawn**

ဥက္ကဋ္ဌ oak-ka-hta *(n.)* **chairman**

ဥက္ကာပျံ oak-kar-pyan *(n.)* **meteor**

ဥစား၊ အသားစား ကြက်၊ ဘဲ u sarr , aa-sarr-sarr kyaat , bhell *(n.)* **poultry**

ဥစ္စာဓန oak-sar-da-na *(n.)* **loot**

ဥစ္စာဓန၏ ဆိုးကျိုး oak-sar-da-na-ei-soe-kyo *(n.)* **mammon**

ဥတည်သည် u-tai-tai *(v.)* **ovulate**

ဥတု u-tu *(n.)* **season**

ဥပဒေ au-pa-day *(n.)* **law**

ဥပဒေက ခွင့်မပြုသော au-pa-day-ka-khwint-ma-pyu-taw *(adj.)* **illicit**

ဥပဒေချိုးဖောက်သည် u-pa-day-choe-hpout-tai *(n.)* **offender**

ဥပဒေဆိုင်ရာ au-pa-day-sai-yar *(adj.)* **legal**

ဥပဒေနှင့် ငြိစွန်းသော au-pa-day-nint-nyi-sune-taw *(adj.)* **actionable**

ဥပဒေနှင့်အညီ အရေးယူခြင်း au-pa-day-nint-a-nyi-a-yay-yu-chin *(n.)* **legal action**

ဥပဒေပညာရှင် au-pa-day-pyin-nyar-shin *(n.)* **jurist**

ဥပဒေပြု au-pa-day-pyu *(adj.)* **legislative**

ဥပဒေပြု လွှတ်တော် au-pa-day-pyu-hlut-taw (n.) **legislature**
ဥပဒေပြု လွှတ်တော်အမတ် au-pa-day-pyu-hlut-taw-a-mat (n.) **legislator**
ဥပဒေပြုသည် au-pa-day-pyu-the (v.) **legislate**
ဥပဒေပြောင်းလိုက်သောကြောင့် တစ်စုံတစ်ရာသည် မှုခင်းမဖြစ်တော့ခြင်း oo-pa-day-pyaung-lite-taw-kyaunt-ta-sone-ta-yar-the-mu-khin-ma-phit-taw-chin (n.) **decriminalization**
ဥပဒေမဲ့ au-pa-day-mae (adj.) **lawless**
ဥပဒေသိပ္ပံပညာ au-pa-day-tate-pan-pyin-nyar (n.) **jurisprudence**
ဥပမာ oo-pa-mar (n.) **example**
ဥပုသ်စောင့်နိုင်သော oo-boke-nint-sine-taw (adj.) **sabbatical**
ဥပုသ်နေ့ upusnae (n.) **sabbath**
ဥပေက္ခာပြုခြင်း oo-phyit-khar-phyu-chin (n.) **abdication**
ဥပေက္ခာပြုသည် oo-phyit-khar-phyu-the (v.) **abdicate**
ဥပေါက်အပင် au-pauk-a-pin (n.) **narcissus**
ဥမှ သားပေါက်သည် oo-ma-tar-pauk-the (v.) **hatch**
ဥယျာဉ်စိုက်ခြင်းအတတ် oo-yin-site-chin-a-tat (n.) **horticulture**
ဥယျာဉ်မှူး au-yin-hmue (n.) **gardener**
ဥရောပ ရေချိုငါးငယ် urawp ray cho ngarrngaal (n.) **roach**
ဥဿဖရားကျောက် oak ta hpararrkyawt (n.) **topaz**
ဥသြငှက် oat-aw-nget (n.) **cuckoo**
ဥသြမိသားစုဝင်ငှက်မျိုး oat-aw-mi-tar-su-win-ngat-myo (n.) **roadrunner**
ဥဥသော u u-saw (adj.) **oviferous**
ဦးဟု ရွတ်သည် ohn-hu-yut-the (v.) **orn**
ဦးကျိုးစေသည် oo-kyo-say-the (v.) **chasten**
ဦးချို oo-cho (n.) **horn**
ဦးချို၊ အစွယ်ဖြင့် ထိုးသည် oo-cho-a-swal-phint-htoe-the (v.) **gore**
ဦးခွံ u-hkwan (n.) **skull**
ဦးခေါင်း oo-kaung (n.) **head**
ဦးစားပေး u sarrpayy (adj.) **preferential**
ဦးစားပေးမှု u sarr-payy-mhu (n.) **precedence**
ဦးစားမပေး u sarr mapayy (v.) **subordinate**
ဦးစောက်ကျွမ်းပြန် oo-saut-kyun-pyan (adv.) **headlong**
ဦးဆုံးပွဲ u sone-pwal (n.) **premiere**
ဦးဆောက်ပန်း u soutpaann (n.) **tiara**
ဦးဆောင်ရှေ oo-saung-ywe (n.) **auspice**
ဦးဆောင်ပြေးသူ၊ နှလုံးခုန်နှုန်းမှန်ကိရိယာ u-saung-pyay -suu, nha-lone-hkone-hnone-mhaan-ka-ri-yar (n.) **pacemaker**
ဦးဆောင်သည် au-saung-the (v.) **lead**
ဦးတည်ချက် oo-the-chat (n.) **direction**
ဦးတည်ချက် ရုတ်တရက်ပြောင်းခြင်း u-taichet rotetaraatpyaunggchinn (n.) **zig**
ဦးတည်ချက်မှ သွေဖည်စေသည် oo-the-chat-ma-thway-phal-say-the (v.) **deflect**
ဦးတည်ရာ u tairar (n.) **trend**
ဦးတည်သည် oo-the-the (v.) **gravitate**
ဦးတည်သွားသည် u taiswarrsai (v.) **steer**
ဦးထုတ် oo-htoke (n.) **hat**
ဦးထုတ်မြင့် u htotemyint (n.) **topper**
ဦးနှောက် oo-naut (n.) **brain**
ဦးနှောက်ငယ် oo-naut-nge (n.) **cerebellum**

ဦးနှောက်ထိခိုက်ဒဏ်ရာရမှု oo-naut-hti-khaik-dan-yar-ya-mu *(n.)* **dementia**
ဦးနှောက်နှင့် အာရုံကြောပါရဂူ oo-naut-nint-arr-yone-kyaw-pa-ra-gu *(n.)* **neurologist**
ဦးနှောက်နှင့် ဆိုင်သော oo-naut-nint-sai-taw *(adj.)* **cerebral**
ဦးနှောက်အမြှေးရောင်ရောဂါ oo-naut-a-myay-yaung-yaw-gar *(n.)* **meningitis**
ဦးမှင်နှစ်ခုပါသော u-min-na-khu-par-taw *(adj.)* **biantennary**
ဦးရေ u-ray *(n.)* **scalp**
ဦးလေး ulayy *(n.)* **uncle**
ဧက a-ca *(n.)* **acre**
ဧကန်ဖြစ်သော aye-kan-phit-taw *(adj.)* **inevitable**
ဧကန်ဖြစ်သောအရာ a-kan-phit-taw-a-yar *(n.)* **certainty**
ဧကပမာဏ a-ca-pa-mar-na *(n.)* **acreage**
ဧကရာဇ် a-ka-rit *(n.)* **emperor**
ဧကရီဘုရင်မ a-ka-ri-ba-yin-ma *(n.)* **empress**
ဧကဝဏ္ဏ a-ka-wunna *(adj.)* **monosyllabic**
ဧကဝဏ္ဏ စကားလုံး a-ka-wunna-sa-kar-lone *(n.)* **monosyllable**
ဧကဝုစ် eka wote *(adj.)* **singular**
ဧည့်ကြို ae-kyo *(n.)* **footman**
ဧည့်ခန်း ae-khan *(n.)* **drawing-room**
ဧည့်ခန်းပါဟိုတယ်ခန်း et hkan par hotaahlkaann *(n.)* **suite**
ဧည့်လမ်းညွှန် ae-lan-hnyun *(n.)* **courier**
ဧည့်ဝတ်ကျေပွန်မှု ae-wit-kyay-pon-mu *(n.)* **hospitality**
ဧည့်သည် ae-the *(n.)* **guest**
ဧည့်သည် အိပ်ခန်း ae-the-aik-khan *(n.)* **guest room**
ဧည့်သည်စာရင်း ae-the-sa-yin *(n.)* **guest list**
ဧပြီလ a-pri-la *(n.)* **April**
ဧရာမ a-yar-ma *(adj.)* **colossal**
ဧရာမကျောက်တုံးကြီး a-yar-ma-kyauk-tone-kyi *(n.)* **megalith**
ဧရာမကျောက်တုံးကြီးဖြင့် တည်ဆောက်ထားသော a-yar-ma-kyauk-tone-kyi-phint- te-saut-htar-taw *(adj.)* **megalithic**
ဧရိယာ aye-ri-yar *(n.)* **area**